WILDLIFE
IN TRUST

*To be ignorant of what occurred before
you were born is to remain always a child.
For what is the worth of human life, unless
woven into the life of our ancestors by the
records of history?*

From Cicero, *Orator ad M Brutum, XXXIV (120)*

WILDLIFE IN TRUST

A hundred years of nature conservation

TIM SANDS

First published in 2012, to commemorate the centenary of
The Wildlife Trusts. This first edition was issued as a limited edition
hardback and a soft cover print run

The Wildlife Trusts
The Kiln, Mather Road, Newark, Nottinghamshire NG24 1WT
wildlifetrusts.org

Design, typesetting and origination by FDA Design Limited
Hathersage, Derbyshire S32 1BB
fdadesign.co.uk

First published 2012 by Elliott and Thompson Limited
27 John Street, London WC1N 2BX
eandtbooks.com

ISBN 978 1 9087394 9 0

Front cover: *Cranes* by Vadim Gorbatov (reproduced with the permission
of the Artists for Nature Foundation)
Back cover: Young volunteers at an Urban Wildlife Group event,
Birmingham, early 1980s (courtesy of the Wildlife Trust for Birmingham
and Black Country)

Contents

Foreword

In its centenary year, Tim Sands has produced a masterly account of The Wildlife Trusts' leading role in the conservation of Britain's wildlife heritage and the remarkable changes of character and fortune that it has undergone in the process. Charles Rothschild's reason for founding the Society for the Promotion of Nature Reserves in 1912 was to ensure the protection of places for nature at a time of rapidly growing human demands on land and natural resources. In spite of the preparation of a countrywide list of places 'worthy of preservation', Rothschild's visionary plans went largely unheeded in a country exhausted by four years of devastating war. It was the devotion of its long-serving Honorary Secretary Dr Herbert Smith that kept the Society alive through the bleak interwar years, and so enabled it to play a vital role in the planning for conservation and nature reserves after the Second World War.

With the creation of the Nature Conservancy and provisions for government action on nature reserves one of Rothschild's principal aims had been achieved, but the future of the Society, hampered by an archaic constitution and meagre resources, was once again uncertain. At that point in the late 1950s, the rapidly growing grassroots movement of county and regional Wildlife Trusts adopted the Society as their national association, providing 'old premises for a new movement' and giving it new life and purpose.

In 1975, at a critical time in the Society's history, the author becomes involved in the action and for the next 30 years fills a succession of senior posts. This ideally qualifies him to compile this history, but as a good historian he makes a dispassionate assessment of developments, seeking the recollections and views of others involved. The Society's first task, as he describes, was to help Trusts strengthen their local base, disseminate experience and attract funding from national sources to enable them to acquire nature reserves and employ staff. Devising a structure and system of governance which reconciles the essential independence of the individual Trusts with their need to act together to achieve shared objectives was not always a smooth process, as his account reveals. But a determination to succeed has produced a strong and influential organisation to serve the interests of the Trusts and promote the environmental and social purposes of wildlife conservation so that 'Space for Nature' is no longer confined to isolated bastions – vital though those have been for the last hundred years – but becomes an integral element in the management of land and natural resources.

The breadth and variety of the Wildlife Trusts movement is conveyed by accounts of all the 47 associated Trusts and by a Reference Section which describes the events and principal characters which have shaped the development of the Society and the Trusts. Outstanding among those is Tim Sands, the author of this timely and remarkable book, who for more than 40 years with quiet modesty but firm and dedicated purpose has played a vitally important role across the whole of the environmental movement.

Arthur Edward 'Ted' Smith *January 2012*

Preface

Wildlife in Trust is a history, not *the* history of The Wildlife Trusts. It is not a book about British wildlife *per se*. Instead it takes a wider look at the threats that have faced the country's wildlife and wild places over the past 100 years, and The Wildlife Trusts' responses to these challenges. It also provides the organisation with a comprehensive record of its history for the first time.

Part I describes a selection of the most significant moments in the organisation's history, from its formation as the Society for the Promotion of Nature Reserves in 1912, through an inter-war lull, to its resurgence during and after the Second World War. It tells the story of how the Society was adopted by the young Trust movement as its national organisation in the 1950s and 60s, and then describes the remarkable expansion of the Trusts and the evolution of their national body.

Part II is a series of essays on the history of the 47 Wildlife Trusts, written by people intimately associated with them. Every Trust has a rich history of its own people and places that is difficult to do justice to in a single essay. Nevertheless, these contributions ensure that the story of local nature conservation is still writ large across the pages of this book.

Part III is a reference section containing additional information about personalities and office holders, campaigns and events, organisations and statistics.

This book is designed to be used as a 'handbook'. Entries in Part II (individual Trust names) and Part III (names of people, places,

documents and subject areas such as 'otter conservation') appear throughout in uppercase lettering, generally where they are first mentioned on each page. In this way the entries in Part II and Part III are clearly signposted for those wanting to find out more. This entails a certain amount of repetition but in this way it has been possible for Part I, in particular, to keep to the 'main path' of the story.

I use 'the Society' throughout for the central organisation and, latterly, the collective movement of Trusts. For simplicity, I refer to each of the Trusts using their city, county or country prefix, for example, the Cornwall Trust.

Much of the story in Part I reflects the activities and decisions of the key players and committees and it is their names that dominate the pages of this book. But the dedication and determination of thousands of other people have made the many achievements of The Wildlife Trusts possible. Although their names may not appear, the following pages are testament to their contribution.

As well as living and working through many of the events described in *Wildlife in Trust* I have researched the Society's archives and met with many of the key figures involved. I hope readers of *Wildlife in Trust* will enjoy exploring its pages and will be inspired by what has gone before, and what it can teach us about rising to future challenges. After all, one of the best things about history is creating it.

Tim Sands *May 2012*

PART I

A HISTORY OF
THE ROYAL SOCIETY OF
WILDLIFE TRUSTS

CHAPTER 1

Beginning and belief 1912–1939

*Here and there in these islands are to be found bits of 'wilderness' where some of the
ancient life – now so rapidly being destroyed – still flourishes.*

From *Diversions of a Naturalist* by Sir Ray Lankester, 1915

**It is Thursday 16th May 1912, 30 years since the death of Charles Darwin, a few weeks since Captain
Robert Scott perished on his heroic polar expedition and two years before the start of the First World
War. *The Times* carries a full report of the latest evidence in the 15 day-old inquiry into the sinking of
the Titanic. On this sunny but blustery May day, CHARLES ROTHSCHILD* has arranged to get together
with three others – CHARLES EDWARD FAGAN, Assistant Secretary at the Natural History Museum in
London; WILLIAM ROBERT OGILVIE-GRANT, its Assistant Keeper of Zoology and the HONORABLE FRANCIS
ROBERT HENLEY, a fellow Northamptonshire landowner and close friend. He wants to discuss with them
his ideas for a new society, ideas that he has been pondering for a dozen or more years. Rothschild plans
to call the new society – the Society for the Promotion of Nature Reserves (SPNR). Its main aim will be
"to urge by means of the press, by personal efforts, and by correspondence with local societies and
individuals the desirability of preserving in perpetuity sites suitable for nature reserves".[1]**

The four men who met that day could never
have imagined the huge changes that would
befall society and the British countryside in the
decades to come; nor the central role their new
Society would play in the nation's response to
those changes.

PROTECTING PLACES FOR WILDLIFE
The idea of protecting wildlife habitats rather
than individual species of wildlife was not at
the forefront of thinking at the time. During the
previous century, studying the natural world
had remained popular and, although the threats
to plants and animals had been recognised,
the main focus had been on legislation to stop
cruelty and over-collecting. The emphasis was
not on safeguarding sites nor, still less, on
changing land-use policy. The Royal Society

Opposite: Charles Rothschild by Hubert von Herkomer, 1908
*Words in upper case denote entries in Reference Section

for the Prevention of Cruelty to Animals
(RSPCA), founded in 1824 to reduce cruelty to
domestic animals, such as cows and horses,
had widened its brief first to stop bear-baiting
and cockfighting and later in the century to bird
protection. The Royal Society for the Protection
of Birds (RSPB) had been formed in 1889 to stop
the killing of thousands of birds, such as egrets,
herons and birds of paradise, for their feathers
as fashion accessories.

What Rothschild was now proposing was
a society to develop a broader-based, more
coherent policy towards the protection of
wildlife. His plan was twofold: first, to identify
wildlife areas in the country 'worthy of
preservation' and second, to encourage others
to acquire the sites and to look after them. In
the first place, the proposal was to hand over
sites to The National Trust for protection under
special conditions.

The Natural History Museum in London and the Society's first home – viewed in 1905 from an unsurfaced Cromwell Road

ROTHSCHILD's ideas were not widely accepted or understood. Indeed, for many, establishing sanctuaries for wildlife was considered a very expensive solution and one likely to attract the attention of collectors. The historian, John Sheail, writes, "during the first twenty or thirty years of its existence the SPNR and its concept of nature reserves were outside the mainstream of the nature preservation movement, which was primarily concerned with crushing cruelty towards animals and such practices as bird-catching and egg-collecting".[2]

Undaunted, the Society held its first formal meeting on 26th July 1912 in the Board Room of the Natural History Museum in London when the nature and objects of the Society were outlined by Rothschild from the chair. They were to:

"collect and collate information as to areas of land in the United Kingdom which retain primitive conditions and contain rare and local species liable to extinction owing to building, drainage and disafforestation, or in consequence of the cupidity of collectors;

prepare a scheme showing which areas should be secured;

obtain these areas and hand them over to The National Trust under such conditions as may be necessary;

preserve for posterity as a national possession some part at least of our native land, its fauna, flora and geological features;

encourage the love of nature, and to educate public opinion to a better knowledge of the value of nature study".[3]

It was agreed to publicise these through a circular to members, the many existing independent local natural history societies and the press. It was also agreed to invite the Speaker of the House of Commons, James Lowther MP,

James Lowther MP, Speaker of the House of Commons, the Society's first President

(see ULLSWATER, VISCOUNT) to become the Society's first PRESIDENT.

SHAPING THE ORGANISATION

It would be a year before the Society decided to proceed with incorporating itself as a limited company. However, an 'unexpected delay' in its Memorandum and Articles being approved by the Board of Trade meant that by February 1914 it was considering becoming incorporated by Royal Charter instead. Things moved slowly and almost two years passed before the Society finally went ahead and petitioned the Privy Council for a Charter of incorporation – a Royal Charter. This was soon granted and was duly signed by King George V on 20th September 1916. The Society adopted a RED KITE, drawn by the naturalist and accomplished wildlife artist GEORGE EDWARD LODGE, as its first LOGO three years later.

There was no intention that the Society should be an open or democratic organisation. There were places for up to 50 members of Council and an unlimited number of Associates. All members of Council were elected for life or until they resigned, so there was little opportunity for replacing inactive members or bringing in new blood. Candidates for election as Associates had to be recommended from 'personal knowledge' by two members of the Society. Decisions were taken by a few individuals on the Society's Executive Committee and to a lesser extent on its Council and relied heavily on ROTHSCHILD himself.

At the fourth meeting of the Executive in June 1913, Sir Robert Hunter "deprecated the proposals"[4] to incorporate the Society as a limited company and the rights this might give to Associate members was questioned. It was not until 1923 that the Society felt any compunction to communicate with its Associates and began to publish a HANDBOOK containing brief accounts of the Society's activities, a short annual report and a list of members. The first edition of the Handbook acknowledged that the Associates "might justifiably suppose that it (the Society) is inert or even moribund".[5] The editorial tried, rather unconvincingly, to blame the previous lack of communication on the fact that the Society, as a rule, had had to "act quietly and unobtrusively lest by directing public attention to a particular area it should bring about the destruction of what it desired to preserve".[6] It would be 1943 before the Society held its first General Meeting in the apartments of the Linnean Society of London at Burlington House.

The Society's first logo

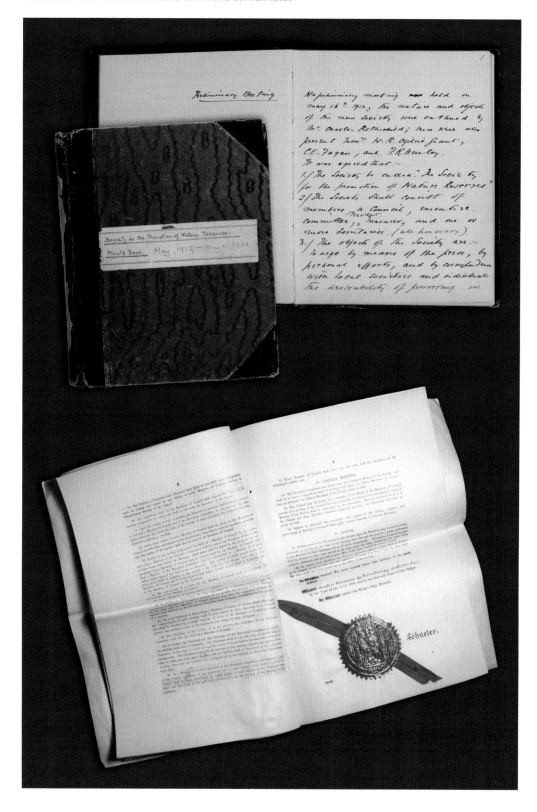

FOUNDING FATHERS AND EARLY ACTIVITY

In addition to his three co-founders, ROTHSCHILD gathered around him a formidable group of people. Among them was a future Prime Minister, Neville Chamberlain, and a high-ranking civil servant, Sir Sydney Olivier – the Permanent Secretary at the Board of Agriculture and Fisheries. On the Council were his friend and neighbour, the 'king of plants', GEORGE CLARIDGE DRUCE, and the eminent plant ecologist, Arthur George Tansley. Sir Robert Hunter, one of the three founding figures of The National Trust, attended the first few meetings but was replaced as The National Trust's representative on his death in 1913 by Francis Wall Oliver, Professor of Botany at University College London. There were also four Members of Parliament – the Foreign Secretary, Sir Edward Grey; the Secretary of State for the Colonies, the Right Honourable Lewis Harcourt; Liberal MP for Chesterton and later Secretary of State for India, Edwin Samuel Montagu; and the Liberal MP for Walworth (later for Southwark South East), James Arthur Dawes, who was appointed as the Society's Honorary Solicitor in June 1913. Across the membership there were no less than 50 Fellows of the Royal Society. By April 1914, at the time of the first Council meeting, there were 33 Council members and 173 Associates, all potential helpers in the task of compiling Rothschild's proposed list of nature reserves (ROTHSCHILD'S LIST).

With Rothschild's enthusiasm, influential friends and money the Society's first few years were very productive. It concentrated on preparing its schedule of areas of wildlife importance in England, Wales, Scotland and Ireland.

In December 1912, *The Times* had published an article, drafted in part by Rothschild, and a special leader publicising the launch of the Society. Reflecting views that would become all too familiar later in the century, the article quoted a recent address to a meeting of the British Association for the Advancement of Science held in Dundee by Dr Chalmers Mitchell, Secretary of the Zoological Society of London. He had reminded his audience that "each generation is the guardian of the existing resources of the world; it has come into a great inheritance, but only as a trustee".[7] The article continued, "to carry out the objects of the Society prompt action must be taken, for year by year suitable areas become fewer; and local plants and insects are found to have been extirpated when acquisition of a few acres of land would have saved them. Such land is often unsuitable for other purpose; an isolated spot on Government property, a piece of marshland, a bird-haunted cliff, or a stretch of wood and copse where the undergrowth has been allowed to follow its own devices are admirable subjects for nature reserves".[8] The leading article refers to "an urban as well as a rural exodus; and the sum of these movements threaten to destroy both the old densely-packed city areas and the old 'unspoilt' country and to substitute a sort of universal suburbanism".[9] However, the article ends on an optimistic note. "The new Society bids fair to provide an admirable organisation for arousing and giving effect to the interest of the public in this cause, and it deserves active support in every county".[10]

Opposite: Minutes of the inaugural meeting and the Society's first Royal Charter, signed in 1916
Right: Press cuttings about the launch of the Society from *The Times* (left) and the *Sydney Evening News* (right)

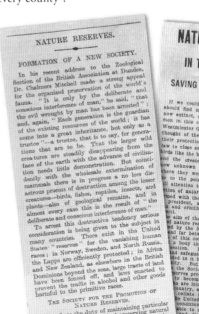

There were at least 50 other press articles over the coming months, largely stimulated by the original publicity in *The Times*. In the *Daily Telegraph* the zoologist, Sir Ray Lankester, for example, wrote, "there are some coast-side marshes, there are East Anglian fens, some open heath-land, and some bits of forest which are yet unspoilt, un-ravaged by blighting, reckless humanity. . . under these circumstances a society has been founded for the formation of 'nature-reserves' in the British Islands. . . all who sympathise with the objects of the society should write to the secretary".[11]

To keep things moving, in April 1913 the Society also sent out the planned letter, circular and questionnaire to the many independent local natural history clubs and societies, signed by the Society's joint HONORARY SECRETARIES, asking them to supply information about potential sites.

ROTHSCHILD was at the centre of this activity, coordinating the whole exercise, talking at meetings – for example at a Penzance Chamber of Commerce banquet in February 1914 (see ROTHSCHILD'S LIST) – and visiting and negotiating over sites that he knew about or were brought to his attention. But he also marshalled support, despatching others, mainly friends and members, to all corners of the kingdom.

DRUCE, for example, was "a most willing helper".[12] He travelled to County Kerry, Ireland, in 1914 to check out "an estate at Clooney, on Kenmare Bay, belonging to the Marquis of Lansdowne".[13] The Society's PRESIDENT, James Lowther (see ULLSWATER, VISCOUNT), had been in communication with Lord Lansdowne who "seemed very willing that the Society should 'acquire' the area of land in question".[14] After careful consideration it was decided to refuse the offer. Druce relates how he also examined the "Saltings at Kirby-le-Soken. . . Ray Island, Monk's Wood. . . Clova and Caenlochan".[15]

In December 1913, Sir Edward Grey informed the Honorary Secretary, OGILVIE-GRANT, that the businessman Andrew Carnegie "had offered to hand over part of his Skibo Castle property in Sutherland, to the west of the Shin, should such ground be suitable for the purposes of forming a nature reserve".[16] The Honorary Secretary and the ornithologist EDMUND GUSTAVUS BLOOMFIELD MEADE-WALDO were asked to visit the area the following summer "to see what possibilities the ground offered".[17] Meade-Waldo was a founder member of the Committee set up in 1903 to protect the RED KITE in Wales and had become famous for his sighting in 1905 of a so-called 'great sea-serpent'[18] at the mouth of the Parahiba River in Brazil! Druce also visited Skibo, but once again the offer was turned down.

The Society's Executive meeting in February 1914, once again chaired by Rothschild, was the most important to date. He came armed with a large number of detailed proposals to take things forward. For example, Rothschild was well aware that if the Society's ideas were to make headway it needed the backing of key players outside the Society, not least backing from the Government. There was no doubting that it already had impressive contacts with the Government at the highest level, but it needed more formal recognition. It was agreed at the meeting to communicate with the Board of Agriculture and Fisheries and the Board of Education to "ascertain whether they were willing to support the Society, and if so, in what way".[19] Among other things, the Society wanted the Boards represented on the Council of the Society. Thomas Fair Husband, a member of the Government's Board of Agriculture and Fisheries (The Ministry of Agriculture from December 1919), did indeed attend the first Council meeting two months later together with the Board's young and recently appointed entomologist, John Claud Fortescue Fryer (see also WOODWALTON FEN).

It was Husband, probably encouraged by Fryer, who alerted Rothschild to a plan for the Government's Development Commission to reclaim extensive areas of 'wasteland' to grow more food – exactly the sorts of places the Society wanted to see as nature reserves. The 'tip-off' was taken as a signal that the Society should complete its survey and make a list of sites available to Government as quickly as possible. At the February meeting it was also suggested that, "in the event of any area scheduled by the SPNR being acquired by the Development Commissioners they be asked to consider if a small portion of the same could not be retained as a nature reserve".[20]

ROTHSCHILD's ambitions for nature reserves went beyond these shores. At the February meeting he also proposed that the Society "ask the Governments of India, the Crown Colonies and the self-governing Colonies and Dominions to consider the advisability of making reserves, and to offer to furnish those Governments with a scheme suitable for each country. A tract of virgin forest land ought to be secured in the Solomon Islands, also reserves in the Fanning Islands and Seychelles".[21] It was partly as a result of the Society's advice to the New Zealand Government, for example, that the New Zealand Forest and Bird Protection Society was established in 1914.

By April 1914, a list of 98 sites had been compiled and "preliminary negotiations with the owners respecting their acquisition or purchase"[22] were in hand. These negotiations involved many sites familiar to us today – Box Hill in Surrey, the coombs and cliffs of Cornwall between Bude and Boscastle, Dovedale in Derbyshire, Puffin Island off Anglesey and the archipelago of St Kilda – the latter destined to become Scotland's first World Heritage Site in 1986.

The task of analysing the many suggestions for sites, and who owned them, took place during 1914 and 1915 and it was finally possible to submit a provisional typewritten schedule of areas 'worthy of preservation' (ROTHSCHILD's LIST) to the Board of Agriculture. A bound version, containing 284 sites in Britain and Ireland, was lodged with the Board in the summer of 1915, and a final revised list was submitted a year later.

Documentation for each of the Rothschild sites, stored in Rothschild Bank blue linen envelopes

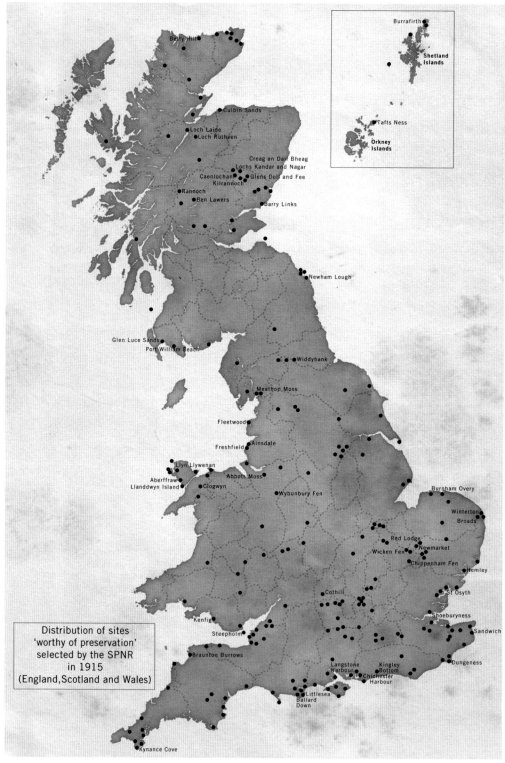

Burrafirth

Shetland
Islands

Tafts Ness

Orkney
Islands

Berry Hill

Culbin Sands

Loch Laide
Loch Ruthven

Creag an Dail Bheag
Lochs Kandar and Nagar
Caenlochan Glens Doll and Fee
Kilrannoch
Rannoch
Ben Lawers
Barry Links

Newham Lough

Glen Luce Sands
Port William Beach

Widdybank

Meathop Moss

Fleetwood

Freshfield Ainsdale

Llyn Llywenan
Aberffraw
Llanddwyn Island Clogwyn
Abbots Moss
Wybunbury Fen

Burnham Overy

Winterton
Broads

Red Lodge
Newmarket
Wicken Fen
Chippenham Fen
Hemley

Cothill
St Osyth
Shoeburyness
Kenfig
Steepholm
Sandwich

Braunton Burrows
Langstone Kingley
Harbour Bottom Dungeness
Chichester
Harbour

Littlesea
Ballard
Down

Kynance Cove

Distribution of sites
'worthy of preservation'
selected by the SPNR
in 1915
(England, Scotland and Wales)

After Sheail *Nature in Trust*, 1976

PARTNERSHIP WITH THE NATIONAL TRUST?

The original objective of the Society was the 'promotion' of nature reserves, the idea being to identify areas of importance and to ask others to look after them. ROTHSCHILD hoped that The National Trust would be the Society's main partner. Founded in 1895, it was already the subject of an Act of Parliament – the National Trust Act 1907 – which gave it the power to preserve 'land and tenements (including buildings) of beauty or historic interest' for the benefit of the nation and introduced the concept that the Trust's properties would be inalienable. There was initial enthusiasm from The National Trust for Rothschild's approach. For example, there was close cooperation between the two organisations over the future of Blakeney Point in Norfolk. Rothschild had been impressed with a report on Blakeney by members of the International Society of Phyto-geographers and, when it came onto the market as a potential building site, he was determined to acquire it to stop the development. The site was acquired by Rothschild through public appeal and private donation, largely organised by Professor Francis Oliver (The National Trust's representative on the Society's Council) and was handed over to The National Trust in 1912. Blakeney Point was Norfolk's first nature reserve and for seven years from 1920 the Society helped fund 'watchers' to observe the visitors as well as the birds!

There were many cases too of the Society supporting The National Trust's appeals. For example, parcels of land at one of Britain's oldest and most famous reserves, Wicken Fen (NATURE RESERVES) in Cambridgeshire, were purchased by The National Trust in 1915, 1916, 1919, 1921 and 1926 with the help of donations from the Society (DONATIONS BY THE SOCIETY BEFORE THE SECOND WORLD WAR). The Society followed this up with further donations towards the management of the reserve on at least ten occasions between 1927 and 1947.

But the close partnership with The National Trust, envisaged by Rothschild, failed to materialise.

Above: Box Hill, Surrey in 1906. One of the 284 sites identified by the Society as 'worthy of preservation'
Opposite: Distribution of the sites 'worthy of preservation' selected by the SPNR in 1915 (England, Scotland and Wales only)

Millers Dale, Derbyshire in 1914 – one of the sites selected by the SPNR for its 'mountains and cliffs'

After 1918, Peter Marren reports, The National Trust "showed itself cool about acquiring more properties 'of interest only to the naturalist'"[23] and Adrian Phillips comments, "in general… the Trust saw nature reserves as a less important aspect of its work than saving threatened landscapes from encroachment".[24]

So in 1919, with The National Trust a reluctant player, ROTHSCHILD decided to transfer, 'free of cost', 340 acres of WOODWALTON FEN to the Society, including a stilted bungalow built in 1911. Woodwalton Fen, a relic of the once extensive Huntingdonshire Fens, had been acquired by Rothschild in 1910 as a private reserve. The Society's decision to accept the gift was made all the easier when Rothschild backed it up with a large donation of just over £2,000 of five per cent War Loan stock as an endowment. Rothschild also continued to dip into his own pocket to support the management of the site after this initial gift. The following year, for example, he offered to transfer the lease of 20 acres of additional fen at £10 a year rent

and at the same time gave £130 for payment of the rent for 12 years. This was gratefully accepted by the Society. Indeed, after Rothschild's death, a further 154 acres of land adjoining Woodwalton Fen, purchased by Rothschild at this same time, were also gifted to the Society by his widow.

THE FIRST WORLD WAR YEARS

The country had gone to war with Germany only two years after the formation of the Society. The period that followed had been, not surprisingly, both stressful and disruptive for those left at home. In his Preface to *Diversions of a Naturalist*, published in September 1915, the zoologist Sir Ray Lankester reflected the country's anxiety and recommended an interest in nature as a valuable distraction in difficult times. "At this time of stress and anxiety we all, however steadfast in giving our service to the great task in which our country is engaged, must, from time to time, seek intervals of release from the torrent of thoughts which is set going by the tremendous fact that we are fighting for our existence".[25]

Woodwalton Fen, Main Drove in 1935 with the keeper of the fen, George Mason

For the Society too, the war was debilitating. We have seen already, for example, how long it took the Society to complete the process leading up to the Royal Charter. By the sixth anniversary of the inaugural meeting there had only been two Council meetings. The Society's third Council meeting – the first since the granting of the Royal Charter – should legally have taken place by December 1916 but "owing to the preoccupation of almost every person connected with the Society in matters arising out of the war it has been impossible to comply with the strict letter of the law of the Charter".[26] The meeting was finally convened in June 1918. It received a formal, written report from the Executive Committee for the first time. This spelt out in more detail how the Society's activities had been hit, not just by the war, but by the ill health of one of its Honorary Secretaries and, more significantly, the ill health of ROTHSCHILD himself.

"The war has. . . necessarily interrupted the work of the Society, whose activities have been largely in abeyance not only in consequence of the outbreak of hostilities but also owing to the regrettable absence of MR WR OGILVIE GRANT, one of the Honorary Secretaries, who has unfortunately been in such bad health. . . while the HONORARY FR HENLEY, the other Honorary Secretary, and Mr JA Dawes MP, the Honorary Solicitor, have been on service with the Forces. To make matters worse the Honorary N Charles Rothschild, to whose keen and enthusiastic interest the Society owes its inception and development, has owing to ill health been compelled temporarily to give up work and go abroad".[27]

Sadly, from 1917 onwards Rothschild was absent from all but one of the Society's Council and Executive meetings. From time to time during his life he had suffered from mental

Personalised metal bank box used by Rothschild for storing Society papers at the Natural History Museum in London

health problems and at the age of 40 he also "fell victim to the epidemic of encephalitis associated with the so-called Spanish influenza which swept across Europe towards the end of the war".[28] Thereafter, ROTHSCHILD experienced further bouts of deep depression that were to end tragically in his taking his own life at his home at ASHTON WOLD on 12th October 1923. His death was "severely felt by the Society"[29] and his obituary in *Nature* stated that by his death "nature in a literal sense, entomology, and it may be added, tropical medicine, have each sustained a formidable blow".[30] The Society had not only lost a "generous and real friend"[31] but also its main driving force.

THE LOST YEARS

In May 1919, six months after the end of the war, the Executive presented its second formal report to Council and tried hard to sound more optimistic. "Since the cessation of hostilities a recrudescence of the activities of the Society has been marked, and several important questions are at present under the consideration of the Committee".[32] An updated membership list and a revamped leaflet about the Society were published in 1921 and the Society's annual HANDBOOK appeared for the first time in 1923. But, in practice, new initiatives were few and far between and, when they did occur, were seldom followed through.

In 1922, for example, the President, VISCOUNT ULLSWATER, and Council member, Viscount Grey of Falloden (James Lowther and Sir Edward Grey had both been elevated to the peerage), wrote a letter to all owners and occupiers of deer forests in Scotland pointing out the "desirability of affording such protection as was possible to the wild cat and pine marten, the two rarest British mammals".[33] When favourable replies were received they were taken at face value and little further action was taken.

When in 1923 "a considerable amount of correspondence"[34] was received about plans to construct a 'motor road' between Bournemouth

and Studland, the Society tried to negotiate with local owners to "secure some part of the district as a reserve before it is too late".[35] But the Handbook again betrays the Society's accepting stance. "It is doubtful whether anything can be done to save even a portion of this land in its natural and unspoilt state".[36]

Two further examples can be cited from the year 1927. In October, the Society was represented by Sir David Prain, MEADE-WALDO and HERBERT SMITH on a deputation of several organisations to the Secretary of State for War. They were protesting against a Government bill to enable the War Office to acquire the manorial rights on certain Surrey commons so it could use them for military manoeuvres and training. The Society, however, appears to have played little part in resolving the issue. The bill was eventually withdrawn when the 'lords of the manor' granted the War Office reasonable use of the commons for such purposes without the need for legislation.

In November 1927, the opportunity arose to buy 'the islands on the edge of the world', the St Kilda group, as a nature reserve for £3,000. However, "after some discussion the Committee decided to take no action as the scheme was so large and it did not appear that the fauna there was in serious danger".[37]

The Society not only lacked motivation, it also lacked funds. Rothschild had hoped that Andrew Carnegie, the Scottish-American businessman and philanthropist who had established a Trust yielding an annual income of £2 million, would support the Society's objectives. The Society believed that if a quarter of this figure was invested on behalf of the Society, it would be able "to purchase and maintain all the nature reserves it (they) desired to acquire in the British Isles for all time".[38] Despite approaches by Grey and others, Carnegie had declined to help.

Opposite: Pine marten by Archibald Thorburn, 1919. In 1922 the Society wrote to Scottish landowners about protection for the pine marten in Scottish deer forests

Although the Society received a bequest of £5,000 under ROTHSCHILD's will this had to be used exclusively for the management of WOODWALTON FEN. Rothschild also left Ray Island in Essex (NATURE RESERVES OWNED BY THE SOCIETY) to either the Society or The National Trust. When The National Trust turned down the bequest, it was Rothschild's wife, Roszika, who wrote to the Society advising that it be "sold, and the proceeds handed over to the Society and devoted to the expense of the upkeep of Woodwalton Fen".[39] The Society felt it was left with no other option but to agree.

Precluded by its Royal Charter from demanding subscriptions, the Society did use the HANDBOOK to appeal, in the most gentle of ways, for funds. The appeal fell on deaf ears. In 1927 six members responded and the next year, much to the consternation of the Handbook's author, this had fallen to three. There appeared to be no thought of changing the Royal Charter or of fundraising more widely. The best the Society could come up with two years later was a further appeal in the Handbook for each member to donate ten shillings – again there was little response.

With many of the Society's day-to-day expenses almost certainly being absorbed by the Natural History Museum in London (the Trustees were kindly providing the Society with office accommodation in the Museum) (OFFICES OF THE SOCIETY), and most of its income tied up in managing Woodwalton Fen, the opportunity to branch out into new activities was severely limited. It did acquire further nature reserves, such as MEATHOP MOSS in Cumbria in 1920, Sharpham Moor Plot in Somerset in 1924 and later Mickfield Meadow in Suffolk in 1938 (NATURE RESERVES OWNED BY THE SOCIETY). In 1930, the Handbook rather fatalistically noted "with an annual income, which even with donations does not exceed £500... the Society has little chance of launching out into large and spectacular schemes".[40] Over the next few years, the Society also experienced the cold blast of the country's deep recession. "As with the

Above: The botanist Professor Arthur Tansley at Sharpham Moor Plot nature reserve in Somerset, June 1923
Opposite: Promotional poster for the Society. Reproduced in French for the International Congress for the Protection of Nature in 1923

SOCIETY FOR THE PROMOTION OF NATURE RESERVES.

President: The Right Hon. J. W. LOWTHER, M.P., *Speaker of the House of Commons.*

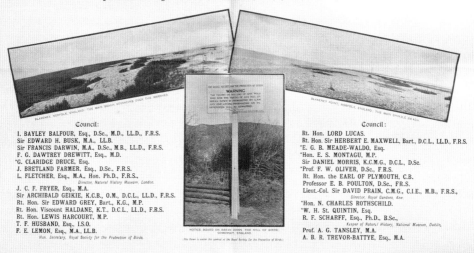

BLAKENEY, NORFOLK, ENGLAND : THE MAIN BEACH ADVANCING OVER THE MARSHES.

BLAKENEY POINT, NORFOLK, ENGLAND : THE MAIN SHINGLE BEACH.

NOTICE BOARD ON BREAN DOWN : THE HILL OF BIRDS.
SOMERSET, ENGLAND.

(The Down is under the control of the Royal Society for the Protection of Birds.)

Council:

I. BAYLEY BALFOUR, Esq., D.Sc., M.D., LL.D., F.R.S.
Sir EDWARD H. BUSK, M.A., LL.B.
Sir FRANCIS DARWIN, M.A., D.Sc., M.B., LL.D., F.R.S.
F. G. DAWTREY DREWITT, Esq., M.D.
*G. CLARIDGE DRUCE, Esq.
J. BRETLAND FARMER, Esq., D.Sc., F.R.S.
L. FLETCHER, Esq., M.A., Hon. Ph.D., F.R.S.,
  Director, Natural History Museum, London.
J. C. F. FRYER, Esq., M.A.
Sir ARCHIBALD GEIKIE, K.C.B., O.M., D.C.L., LL.D., F.R.S.
Rt. Hon. Sir EDWARD GREY, Bart., K.G., M.P.
Rt. Hon. Viscount HALDANE, K.T., D.C.L., LL.D., F.R.S.
Rt. Hon. LEWIS HARCOURT, M.P.
T. F. HUSBAND, Esq., I.S.O.
F. E. LEMON, Esq., M.A., LL.B.
  Hon. Secretary, Royal Society for the Protection of Birds.

Council:

Rt. Hon. LORD LUCAS.
Rt. Hon. Sir HERBERT E. MAXWELL, Bart., D.C.L., LL.D., F.R.S.
*E. G. B. MEADE-WALDO, Esq.
*Hon. E. S. MONTAGU, M.P.
Sir DANIEL MORRIS, K.C.M.G., D.C.L., D.Sc.
*Prof. F. W. OLIVER, D.Sc., F.R.S.
Rt. Hon. the EARL OF PLYMOUTH, C.B.
Professor E. B. POULTON, D.Sc., F.R.S.
Lieut.-Col. Sir DAVID PRAIN, C.M.G., C.I.E., M.B., F.R.S.,
  Director, Royal Gardens, Kew.
*Hon. N. CHARLES ROTHSCHILD, Esq.
*W. H. ST. QUINTIN, Esq.
R. F. SCHARFF, Esq., Ph.D., B.Sc.,
  Keeper of Natural History, National Museum, Dublin.
Prof. A. G. TANSLEY, M.A.
A. B. R. TREVOR-BATTYE, Esq., M.A.

Hon. Secretaries { *W. R. OGILVIE-GRANT, Esq. | *Hon. F. R. HENLEY, M.A. } *Ex-officio.*

Hon. Treasurer—*C. E. FAGAN, Esq., I.S.O. *(Ex-officio)*

Hon. Solicitor—J. ARTHUR DAWES, Esq., M.A., B.C.L., M.P.

* Members of the Executive Committee.

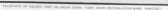

TELEPHOTO OF DISUSED FORT ON BREAN DOWN, TAKEN FROM WESTON-SUPER-MARE, SOMERSET.

BREAN DOWN FROM THE WESTON-SUPER-MARE SANATORIUM.

BLAKENEY POINT, NORFOLK, ENGLAND : THE BEACON SAND HILLS WHERE THE TERNS BREED.

This Society has been formed with the object of preserving for posterity as a national possession some part at least of the native fauna, flora, and geological features of the British Isles.

It is hoped to do this by acquiring, under such conditions as may be necessary, areas of land in the United Kingdom that retain their primitive state, and that contain rare and local species liable to extinction either owing to building, drainage and disafforestation or in consequence of the cupidity of collectors.

There is no subscription: Members are elected by invitation of the Executive Committee.

Persons interested are requested to communicate with The Secretaries, Society for the Promotion of Nature Reserves, Natural History Museum, Cromwell Road, London, S.W.

LONDON : PRINTED BY WILLIAM CLOWES AND SONS, LIMITED

rest of the world the Society has not escaped the chilly effects of the economic blizzard, and securities which aforetime were regarded as steady as a rock have shown unexpected shakiness with a consequential drying up of the stream of dividends. It is some, though possibly cold, comfort to reflect that the Society's income has stood the assault better than the majority of organisations, and may be expected to be restored to its former figure as soon as trade begins to improve".[41] However, there were two notable new initiatives.

WILDFLOWERS AND THE INTERNATIONAL SCENE
First, in 1925, the Society became involved in an energetic and extensive campaign for improved bye-law protection for wildflowers, which lasted for more than ten years. The countryside was becoming more accessible, partly because of an increase in both public and private transport. In some places large quantities of wildflowers were being gathered for 'pleasure' as well as for educational and small-scale commercial use. In addition, "great deforestation during the war, road widening and destruction of verges, a passion for cleaning up the country roads, drainage schemes, and other concomitants of civilisation, all tend to the destruction of the native flora".[42]

The Society's commitment to the wildflower campaign undoubtedly helped raise public awareness of the damage being done, particularly to attractive and collectable species, and increased the number of local authorities taking up bye-law powers. In 1931, the various bodies interested in better wildflower protection formed the Wild Plant Conservation Board under the auspices of the Council for the Protection of Rural England (CPRE) to coordinate their activities. The Society's Joint Honorary Secretary, HERBERT SMITH, became the Chairman and for a time it went purposefully, if unobtrusively, in pursuit of its cause. With the onset of the Second World War, however, the Board achieved very little and afterwards it was gradually eclipsed by the activities of other bodies. Nevertheless, this work during the 1930s lit a campaigning flame for wildflower protection

that was never entirely extinguished by the Second World War, a flame that with the Society's help burnt brightly once again 40 years later (WILDFLOWERS – BYE-LAW PROTECTION).

The second initiative was the Society's active and in general sustained support, both before and after the Second World War, for the establishment of an international organisation for nature conservation. The Society's support would eventually contribute to the establishment of the organisation known today as the International Union for the Conservation of Nature (IUCN). As early as November 1913, CHARLES ROTHSCHILD had attended a conference in Berne to discuss a proposal by the Swiss League for the Protection of Nature to establish an Advisory Commission for the International Protection of Nature, but the outbreak of the First World War brought the initiative to a standstill. In May 1923, an abortive attempt to revive the idea was made at the first International Congress for the Protection of Nature in Paris where the Society was represented by its President,

The Society's wildflower handbill widely distributed to County Councils, schools, Women's Institutes and Holiday Associations

VISCOUNT ULLSWATER, MEADE-WALDO and Dr Percy Roycroft Lowe, Curator of Birds at the Natural History Museum in London. Viscount Ullswater spoke on the Society's activities and the delegation took with them a poster translated into French. But the British position on a potential new international organisation was at odds with the views of many of the other delegations. "The proper course was to establish in each country a committee representative of all interests concerned and for these committees to be represented on the central international committee".[43] The Society convened a meeting of interested British societies in January the following year and a Central (later British) Correlating Committee was formed in 1924. However, after an initial flurry of activity (five meetings in 1924–25) and as its example had not been followed in other countries, the Committee was dissolved after a few years. The Society's involvement in international conservation is discussed in more detail in Part III under TOWARDS IUCN.

In both these early endeavours – wildflower protection and international conservation – the Society has tended, over the years, to receive less recognition than it deserves.

THE CALM BEFORE THE STORM

Despite these initiatives and its early successes, after CHARLES ROTHSCHILD's death the Society for the most part failed to set the world alight. Rothschild's enthusiasm and energy was sorely missed and the importance he had attached to the establishment of nature reserves had not been picked up by either The National Trust or, indeed, the Government at that point. The impact of the First World War and the Society's unwillingness to interest and involve a wider public had all militated against the development of the organisation and its ideas. Its leaders were idealistic and, it could be argued, largely impractical. They not only missed the opportunity to broaden the Society's appeal but, perhaps more significantly, to acquire or safeguard more land for conservation. In contrast, between 1920 and

1940, The National Trust's "membership increased from 713 to 6,800 and. . . the total acreage held by the Trust rose from 13,200 to 68,544".[44]

Sheail writes, "in view of this lack of enthusiasm for nature reserves between the wars, the SPNR was even more heavily dependent on dynamic leadership, strong regional and local support, and large financial resources. . . the Society lacked all three assets, and consequently languished throughout the inter-war period".[45]

Better times were, however, around the corner. In its Honorary Secretary, HERBERT SMITH, the Society had someone of "unusual administrative ability and organising skill".[46] After his retirement from the Natural History Museum in London in 1937, he was able to devote a great deal more of his time to the affairs of the Society.

In addition, in 1932, the Society received some unexpected news. Charles Rothschild's friend, the botanist, GEORGE CLARIDGE DRUCE, who had been a member of the Society from the beginning, died and left half his estate to the Society. Although it took some time for certain legal matters to be ironed out, when the Society finally received its share of his legacy in 1939 it was worth £13,000, equivalent to £620,000 in today's money. Overnight, the Society's income had been trebled to £1,500. As Sheail puts it, "from 1939 onwards, Herbert Smith was able to reap the rewards of keeping the Society alive during the critical years of the 1930s. The Society was for the first time 'pretty well off', and looked forward to playing a more positive role in the future. At first, the outbreak of war threatened to end this renaissance, but by 1942 Herbert Smith remarked that 'the Society is surprisingly busy, not only in spite of the war but possibly also because of it'".[47]

CHAPTER 2

The war and its aftermath 1940–1949

*The hum of the engines continues without a break; it is a canopy of death over the world,
a strange and appalling fact which seems hardly linked with the lower strata in which remains
the familiar world, the passing curlew's high-pitched doubled note, the owls and the sparrows.*

From *The Leaves Return* by EL Grant Watson, 1947

At the outbreak of war with Germany in 1939, the Society's initial response to the "emergency"[48] and the "rapidly increasing tension in the international position"[49] reflected the sombre mood of the nation and the uncertain future. The Honorary Secretary, HERBERT SMITH, made arrangements for correspondence to be diverted to his home address, as a temporary measure, and for records and papers to be safely stored either in the basement of the Natural History Museum in London or in the strong rooms of the Society's bank and solicitors.

In September 1940, the importance of these precautions was demonstrated. London experienced the largest aerial attack since the beginning of the war and the RSPB's London office in Victoria Street "received a direct hit".[50] Fortunately, it was a Sunday and the office was empty.

Other measures were put in place. The size of the HANDBOOK was reduced to a minimum due to likely paper shortages and holding or attending meetings was avoided, if at all possible. For example, at the end of August 1939, just before the outbreak of war, Herbert Smith had decided against travelling to Dundee to the British Association for the Advancement of Science's annual meeting; in October the CPRE's conference in Tunbridge Wells, which he would also have attended, was cancelled; and in November the Society's Annual Dinner (DINNERS AND LUNCHEONS)

Opposite: Victoria Street, London in 1940 – a few doors down from the RSPB's offices at No 82

was "indefinitely postponed without, however, any compensation being demanded".[51] Within the year, the Society had also unanimously agreed that the interest on its £1,000 three per cent Defence Bonds should be foregone to help the war effort.

In the circumstances the Society and other voluntary bodies resigned themselves to a period of relative inactivity, attending to their day-to-day business and seeing no likelihood of making progress on issues that had begun to preoccupy them before the war, such as land-use planning, national parks and access to the countryside and the protection of wildlife. This state of affairs was reinforced by the announcement that no legislation was to be introduced to Parliament unless directly relevant to the war.

PLANNING AHEAD

As with the war itself, however, this was the calm before the storm. Surprisingly, as early as the end of 1940, the Government realised it needed to think about planning for life after the war, not simply for the more obvious reason that blitzed cities would require reconstruction but also for the boost that a vision of a brighter post-war Britain – the 'new Jerusalem' – could bring to a battered, yet defiant, public.

In addition, subjects that politicians and public alike had been grappling with before the war – changes in industrial patterns, the consequent drift of the population towards the south-east and the early mechanisation of farming and loss of agricultural land – had not gone away.

Lord Onslow, President of the Society (1936–42)

Quite unexpectedly, within a few months of the outbreak of war, the Government's interest in post-war land-use planning issues created the circumstances in which the Society, and other voluntary organisations, could once again advance their arguments for nature reserves, national parks and the protection of the countryside. The Society found itself caught up in this process with an enormously increased workload so that its "business in 1942 easily surpassed that of any previous year, but was itself equalled in 1943 within the first six months".[52]

Despite these encouraging developments, early in 1941, "many naturalists were concerned lest efforts to preserve the native flora and fauna for the benefit of posterity should be neglected".[53] HERBERT SMITH raised the issue with the Society's Executive and noted that the businessman and all-round field naturalist, Geoffrey Dent, had "called attention to the need for safeguarding natural history interests".[54] Dent, a Council member of the RSPB and Chairman of its

Watchers' Committee, had already persuaded RSPB "in view of the probability of Government action for the utilisation of land after the war... to formulate a plan for the definitive reservation of suitable sanctuaries for the preservation of the fauna and flora of Great Britain".[55] He also urged the RSPB to convene meetings to coordinate proposals on post-war nature protection policy and to feed these into the Government.

Initially, there was little progress on this latter front but it was Herbert Smith who, after discussing the idea with the RSPB's hard-pressed Secretary, Robert Preston Donaldson, enthusiastically took up the baton. He was supported by LORD ONSLOW, who had succeeded the founder's brother, LORD WALTER ROTHSCHILD, as the Society's PRESIDENT. Onslow believed that separate action by interested societies and associations must be avoided and that the Society should drive things forward by convening, chairing and financing a standing Conference on NATURE PRESERVATION IN POST-WAR RECONSTRUCTION.

The process now moved quickly. Three meetings, chaired by Onslow, were organised in the Moses Room of the House of Lords within a five-month period. The first, in June 1941, was attended by 16 societies and other organisations. Herbert Smith acted as Secretary and drafted the first memorandum setting out "the principles that in the opinion of the Conference should be adopted by the Government when planning the use of the land after the war".[56] It was published in November 1941 and such was the interest generated by the report that it had to be reprinted within the year.

Three distinct needs were recognised – first, the preservation of rural amenities, including fauna and flora, natural scenic beauty, places of interest and antiquities; second, the preservation of forest areas; and third, a need that had been "almost entirely neglected by Government",[57] the preservation of natural fauna and flora for the advancement of scientific knowledge and education. What was needed were national parks for the recreation and enjoyment of the public; the possible extension and better use of forest and wildlife reserves; areas where development would be prohibited or drastically restricted; and the acquisition or preservation of areas as nature reserves. The public would be generally excluded from nature reserves, except by permit. The Conference wanted the principle of statutory nature reserves accepted and recommended the appointment of an official body, representative of scientific interests, to draw up detailed proposals. The management of these reserves should be placed in the hands of those able to handle the "highly technical problems included in the maintenance of the balance of life"[58] and their "general control should be vested in a central authority representative of the different interests concerned".[59] The Conference made it clear that it was willing at a later stage, if the principles were accepted, to submit a detailed memorandum on site selection.

There was disagreement, however, between representatives of CPRE and the Standing Committee on National Parks on the one hand,

and the local authority associations on the other. The dispute concerned the respective powers of a proposed National Parks Authority. While a compromise was reached, the two sides remained hostile to one another. Sheail describes how "the clash led to an even greater concentration on the 'scientific aspects of nature preservation'. A yearning to break free from the amenity and recreational elements can be discerned, especially following the appointment of CYRIL DIVER as 'scientific' secretary to the drafting Committee"[60] of the Conference.

The Conference's report was sent to the Prime Minister and other Government Ministers. In January 1942, the Society accepted an invitation from CPRE's Standing Committee on National Parks for a joint deputation to present the Conference's findings to Lord Reith, former manager of the British Broadcasting Corporation. Reith had been Minister of Works and Buildings since 1940 and had been given responsibility

The Moses Room, House of Lords in 1905 – venue for the Society's Conference on Nature Preservation in Post-War Reconstruction in 1941, attended by 16 societies and other organisations

for the planning of the physical environment in post-war Britain. He responded positively to the deputation and proposed a small group to consider the findings in more detail. A Government re-shuffle, however, meant the group never met.

It was Sir William Jowitt, newly-appointed Paymaster General, who took on the role of Chairman of the Government's war-time Reconstruction Committee. It was therefore to Jowitt in early 1942 that first the Standing Committee on National Parks and then the Conference's drafting committee turned to press their case for national parks and nature reserves respectively. Jowitt had had a lifelong interest in wildlife and, like Reith, was very supportive.

But, knowing there was little prospect of the Government itself pushing the nature agenda, he challenged the delegation from the Conference drafting committee to take things forward and to advise the Government on "proposals for the establishment of nature reserves as part of any general scheme of national planning".[61]

If it seized this moment, here was the vehicle through which the Society could realise its founding dream. It had the track record and, with HERBERT SMITH at the helm, someone with the ability and standing to drive through such an inquiry. Here too was the chance to see informed, evidence-based arguments for nature reserves embedded within Government for the first time.

The moment was not allowed to pass. Herbert Smith once again took on the all-important secretarial role and orchestrated the huge amount of work that it soon became clear would be required. Within two months the Conference published its second memorandum with the terms of reference for a Nature Reserves Investigation Committee (NRIC) (NATURE PRESERVATION IN POST-WAR RECONSTRUCTION CONFERENCE). The Committee would be under the Chairmanship of Sir Lawrence Chubb (General Secretary of the National Playing Fields Association) and would examine the proposals for nature reserves in more detail and report back.

Herbert Smith, the Society's 'stage manager' and longest serving Honorary Secretary (1921–53)

This it did the following February in a more comprehensive and forceful document, *Nature Conservation in Great Britain* (Memorandum 3). The document provided a classification of reserve types and detailed notes on their acquisition, protection and management. It argued that establishing a few national parks would be insufficient to meet the needs of Britain's 'wild life' (wildlife was not yet one word). "In a densely populated country like Great Britain the primary purpose of a National Park would be more to provide the public with opportunities for open-air recreation amidst natural scenery than to preserve particular plants and animals, though… the preservation of the characteristic vegetation is inseparably interwoven with the enjoyment of the scene".[62] The role of a National Parks Authority would be to

Nature Conservation in Great Britain – 'a comprehensive and forceful document'

manage the Park more generally in the interest of wildlife, with nature reserves established both inside and *outside* Parks in their own right for their habitat or species interest, for education and research and for their national or local importance. It also proposed conservation areas where development would be controlled. The Government should take formal responsibility not only for the establishment of these nature reserves but also for the conservation of native wildlife more generally under a special department of the Ministry of Town and Country Planning. The cost, it argued, would be "negligible when compared with the direct and indirect values received".[63]

The report was widely circulated in early 1943 and, like its earlier sister report, had to be reprinted within the year. It attracted much attention even as far afield as South Africa and the USA. In the States, for example, the National Park Service circulated a synopsis to their field staff and some of the leaders in American conservation with the following foreword:

"Imagine – Great Britain in March 1943, with bombs still dropping sporadically on London and environs; the country pushed to the utmost in manpower and domestic economy; and no certainty, whatever the hope, that it can survive the impact of war; and yet these sturdy, un-panicked people initiate and go ahead with plans for the amenities of future Britons; for the protection of natural resources; for the preservation of plant and animal species with relations to their habitat. . . what imagination is this, which sees that, if Britain is worth dying for, these things are worth dying for, because they are intrinsic to the enjoyment of freedom itself! And they feel that future generations would not forgive them if they preserve the husk, after letting the kernel be destroyed. Surely there is a lesson here for us, who encounter not one per cent of the difficulties in the way of Great Britain".[64]

While working on its report, the NRIC was asked by the Ministry of Town and Country Planning to fast-track information about sites of wildlife interest in four potential National Park areas – the Lake District, Peak District, Dartmoor

and Snowdonia. Four sub-committees identified more than 30 tracts of land for preservation and special management and more than 20 more sites of outstanding scientific importance. In providing the information, the Committee once again took the opportunity to draw distinctions between the amenity and scientific camps and correct, as it saw it, a misconception. "There appears to be some prejudice against measures for nature conservation because of a widespread, but wholly fallacious, idea that for the adequate protection of plants and animals it is necessary to fence particular tracts, and to exclude the public from them, except by permit. The view which the Committee have expressed. . . is quite different. In their opinion the public should be allowed as free access as possible to parts of the National Parks of natural history interest, though in a few special reserves entry would need to be controlled at certain times of year, namely the flowering season of particular plants and the nesting season of rare birds".[65]

This was a welcome departure from the approach to public access adopted in Memorandum 1 drafted by HERBERT SMITH. Although the policy of excluding the public from reserves would die hard, the more enlightened view now put forward in *Nature Conservation in Great Britain* would soon be picked up elsewhere. The strictly confidential report on the natural history interest of the four potential National Parks was provided to the Ministry (Memorandum 4) on 23rd August 1943 and the same day the Committee was asked to extend its survey to even more areas and, subsequently, to a complete survey of England and Wales.

The task facing the NRIC, its Secretary Herbert Smith, a growing band of experts and more than 200 volunteers was now immense. LORD MACMILLAN, who had taken over in April 1942 as PRESIDENT of the Society after ONSLOW had retired due to ill health, described in the Committee's final report how the workload was "embarrassing both in its extent and in its character. . . rendered difficult by war-time restrictions on transport".[66] Twenty-two sub-committees for various counties, or groups of counties, had been established and asked to 'collate and sift areas of natural history interest in their counties'. They had supplied data on numerous sites of wildlife, as well as geological, importance. The "highly invidious duty of making the final selection"[67] fell to the central committee.

The British Ecological Society (BES), founded a year after the Society in 1913, had set up its own inquiry in April 1943 under the chairmanship of Arthur Tansley. Despite an initially cool relationship with the NRIC, the two parties developed a good working relationship and the BES sent a list of vegetation types and areas to the NRIC later in the year. The NRIC also used the list drawn up by CHARLES ROTHSCHILD (ROTHSCHILD'S LIST) and lists from the British Correlating Committee for the Protection of Nature, the Royal Entomological Society of London, the Geological Society of London and the RSPB.

In April 1944, with London still experiencing German bombing, the NRIC broadened its scope still further. In an unprecedented move, it established a sub-committee to "advise on

Horseback at Skrinkle Haven, Pembrokeshire – one of the 48 geological monuments proposed by the NRIC

questions relating to Geological Parks and Geological Monuments, and to draw up a list of such reserves for England and Wales on the basis of the proposals received from the Regional Committees".[68] The sub-committee "imperturbably held their meetings during the savage attack on the London area by robot planes, and did an immense amount of work in a very short time".[69] In its report, published in September 1945 (Memorandum 5), it recommended 48 geological monuments, 198 controlled sections, 73 'registered' sections and 70 geological conservation areas. No other country was giving geological sites a second thought and without this far-sighted work Britain would have been no different.

The most extensive survey of areas of both natural history and geological importance in England and Wales was now complete and *National Nature Reserves and Conservation Areas* (Memorandum 6) was published in December 1945. The Committee had been asked to grade the sites selected. Of the 47 proposed national nature reserves, 26 were in category A – sites of outstanding merit that must be safeguarded; 14 in category B – sites of special importance the destruction of which would be a serious loss to science; and seven in category C – sites that should find a place in any complete national scheme. A further eight sites were not thought to be at risk (see NATURE PRESERVATION IN POST-WAR RECONSTRUCTION CONFERENCE for more details of the six memoranda and the membership of the drafting committees).

Significantly, 24 of the sites selected by Rothschild 30 years earlier were omitted – 12, while undamaged, were no longer thought to qualify but 12, or about seven per cent, had been completely destroyed. Nor was this the whole picture. The NRIC had re-selected most of the areas chosen by Charles Rothschild. But, as an article written anonymously by his daughter, MIRIAM ROTHSCHILD, in the weekly journal *Nature* observed, "a large proportion have been greatly changed and partially spoiled in the intervening period. Thus we find that areas which headed county lists in 1915 have now fallen to the bottom of such compilations. . . the situation,

Roudsea Wood, Cumbria in the mid-1950s – a reserve proposed by the NRIC, which later became a National Nature Reserve

far from being satisfactory, is extremely serious. If the Government procrastinates further, and 'pigeon-holes' the present report for another thirty years, it is safe to say that any third list will have little, if anything, in common with its two predecessors".[70]

LORD MACMILLAN reflected in his foreword to the final report that "it was fortunate that the unexpectedly early termination of the World War has not found the Committee with their task uncompleted. . . the report will provide the Government with the information which it is essential they possess, and which they cannot disregard".[71] The timing was indeed perfect. A committee, chaired by Sir Arthur Hobhouse, had just been appointed to take forward a report by John Dower on National Parks, including its proposals on nature conservation.

PIONEERING WORK BEARS FRUIT
There was, however, a somewhat naïve expectation by the Society that the Government would turn to the NRIC as the logical source of advice on wildlife matters. After all, it argued, it was the Ministry that had asked the NRIC for help previously. But it was not to be. The Ministry preferred the idea of the Hobhouse Committee appointing its own nature reserves sub-committee. Dower rejected the idea favouring a special committee with wider terms of reference and greater status and, in the event, it was a Wild Life Conservation Special Committee that was appointed under the chairmanship of Sir Julian Huxley. The Committee's Vice Chairman, Arthur Tansley, took over the work of the Chairman from May 1946 when Huxley became the first Executive Secretary of the Preparatory Commission of UNESCO and later its Director General.

In October 1945, a meeting of the NRIC was called to consider the "awkward position which has arisen by the action taken by the Minister of Town and Country Planning in ignoring the existence of the Committee and appointing a Wild Life Special Committee with much the same objective".[72] The NRIC's nose, and probably more particularly, HERBERT SMITH's nose,

The Farne Islands – a Rothschild site proposed as a National Nature Reserve by the Huxley Committee in 1947 and 'one of the most important breeding stations for sea-birds on the north-east coast of England'

had been well and truly put out of joint. It was MACMILLAN who "lent his great influence to the dignified course which was adopted, namely to place the results of the natural history survey of England and Wales, which had just been completed, unreservedly at the disposal of the new Committee, although it was realised that (the NRIC) would not receive full recognition for their work".[73] That pessimism was, perhaps, understandable, and it is possibly why in January 1946 the Society rather short-sightedly decided to present written and oral evidence to the main Hobhouse Committee and not to the Huxley Committee because "automatically it would reach the latter in due course".[74]

The NRIC need not have been so worried. From the outset Sir Julian Huxley's Wild Life Conservation Special Committee took on board the evidence from the NRIC as well as from the Royal Society and the British Ecological Society. It also emphasised the underlying importance of science and of better understanding the "complex of interactions that makes up the natural landscape. These are the things that must be studied if the beauty of that landscape is to be preserved and enjoyed".[75] The Huxley Committee's seminal report, *Conservation of Nature in England and Wales* (Command 7122), distinguished between the "aesthetic and scientific approaches".[76] Despite its protestations that "it is wrong to suppose that there is any essential conflict between these two sets of interests",[77] it nevertheless acknowledged that "their special requirements may differ".[78] The report was clear and pulled no punches. The Government should take "general responsibility for the conservation and control of the flora and fauna of this country and for the protection of features of geological and physiographical interest".[79] It should establish a Biological Service and National Nature Reserves both within and outside National Parks – attached was an appendix of 73 potential sites. A parallel report for Scotland – *Conservation of Nature in Scotland* (Command Paper 7235) – was published in 1947. A further report listing proposed nature reserves – *Nature Reserves in Scotland: Final Report* (Command Paper 7814) – was published in 1949.

The naturalist and author, Richard Fitter, writing later, recalled that CYRIL DIVER drafted the Huxley Committee's "far seeing main report".[80] His own task, as the Committee's Secretary, was the "more mundane one of preparing the detailed appendices, almost wholly based on the NRIC report of proposed national nature reserves, conservation areas and reserves in national parks".[81] The report itself acknowledged that it could not have been drawn up without the work of the NRIC. "We may say at once that, although our recommendations may vary in detail or emphasis and may cover ground that was not completely explored by that committee, we find ourselves in the closest general agreement with the considered and carefully weighed views expressed in their third report and we would reiterate its final sentence. 'After the long years of death and destruction, these modest proposals are unhesitatingly commended as a first step to the renewed study and appreciation of life'".[82]

The pioneering work of the Society and CHARLES ROTHSCHILD in producing the first list of important wildlife sites (ROTHSCHILD'S LIST) in 1915 was also acknowledged, as was the Society's initiative in calling together the NATURE PRESERVATION IN POST-WAR RECONSTRUCTION

Conservation of Nature in England and Wales (Command 7122) set out the Government's responsibility for nature conservation for the first time

CONFERENCE. The report concludes, the Society has been responsible "directly or indirectly for work of the greatest importance to our inquiry".[83]

MAX NICHOLSON had been appointed head of the office of the Lord President, Herbert Morrison, in the new Labour Government elected immediately after the war. His position, which carried with it the rank of Under-Secretary, also included responsibility for coordinating the Government's policy on national economic planning and development. Nicholson wrote later in his book, *The New Environmental Age,* that this key position provided the Wild Life Conservation Special Committee's proposals with "a more sympathetic understanding than usual in Whitehall, being steered gently through mechanisms which would normally have quietly buried them".[84]

The recommendations of the Wild Life Conservation Special Committee and of the Hobhouse National Parks Committee, published in 1947, were soon translated into legislation, mainly in the National Parks and Access to the Countryside Act 1949. This set up a National Parks Commission covering England and Wales and spelt out the range of work for a new body, the Nature Conservancy (the Conservancy), established under a Royal Charter in March 1949 following the Huxley recommendation for a 'Biological Service'. Sheail describes how Ministers had been persuaded that responsibility for nature conservation should be placed not with the planning sector, as had been initially assumed, but within the science sector of Government. The new body would be "in all but name, a research council of comparable status to that of the Agricultural Research Council and Medical Research Council".[85]

Scotland decided against establishing National Parks, although proposals were on the table for areas in Wester Ross, Glen Affric, Glencoe and around Loch Lomond. When the Nature Conservancy was formed in 1949, Scotland was included but with a semi-autonomous Scottish Committee and an office in Edinburgh from the outset.

The Society's contribution to this, one of the most important moments in the history of nature conservation, had been considerable. Indeed, because of all its preparatory work during and immediately after the war, Lowe and Goyder were later to describe the Society as the "midwife of the Nature Conservancy".[86] They continued, "somewhat paradoxically, its slim organisation and network of connections proved well adapted to the peculiar conditions of war-time lobbying. It was able both to respond quickly and sensitively to favourable initiatives within Government, and to coordinate a staggering amount of groundwork prior to official action. HERBERT SMITH, being retired, was able to devote much of his time to the considerable amount of organisation and coordination that was required".[87]

WAR-TIME BUSINESS

Throughout the war period the Society had also had to continue the day-to-day job of running the organisation, including managing its own properties. There was no let up, for example, in correspondence. Sadly the postbag could bring unwanted news – a member missing after an operational flight and presumed killed, or another

Fly orchid at Dancer's End reserve, Buckinghamshire, acquired by the Society in 1941. The site is notable for its rare plant life
Opposite: Woodwalton Fen in 1949

fatally injured after a flying bomb hit his home. One of the more unusual telegrams received just prior to the outbreak of war was from the Subsecretario Instruccion Publica, Barcelona. Addressed to the Society's President, LORD WALTER ROTHSCHILD, it protested "against the bombing of Spanish cities by German and Italian aircraft, and asking that influence be brought to bear on the British Government to take steps to put a stop to these crimes against civilisation".[88] The telegram was passed on to the Foreign Office.

In 1941, a letter from the Chief Inspector of Taxes queried the Society's entitlement to charity relief under the War Damage Act 1941. "I cannot, on the face of it, see from the Society's objects that its proprietary interests are held solely for the objects in 39(2)(d). The main objects seem to be the preservation of Nature Reserves, doubtless a purpose beneficial to the community, but not in itself directly for the advancement of education, science or research".[89] A lengthy reply from the Society followed three days later. In October the Chief Inspector wrote, "the matter has been fully considered, and it is agreed that the proprietary interests held by the Society in the various properties occupied and used by the Society are held and used for charitable purposes. . . and that the Society is therefore entitled to two-thirds relief of the payment of the War Damage contributions".[90]

The Society had largely managed its own properties at arm's length with the help of local committees before the war but during hostilities closer involvement was necessary. At WOODWALTON FEN, for example, the local War Agricultural Committee was keen to reduce flooding in the area to increase war-time food production. The Society therefore entered into negotiations with the Committee over its proposed drain clearance to protect the reserve from further drying out. At the Society's MEATHOP MOSS reserve, gulls' eggs were proving a useful addition to war-time food supplies. They were described soon after the war as having been "sold for cake-making".[91] Although the Society felt a ban on collecting was necessary for a period after the middle of May to 'allow the birds to reproduce in sufficient numbers',

for the rest of the time collecting was tolerated. A bombing range using practice smoke bombs was proposed by the Admiralty on Marbury Mere at the Society's COWARD MEMORIAL RESERVES in Cheshire. And at DANCER'S END in the Chilterns, the Society was asked to eradicate large numbers of rabbits as Bittams Wood was scheduled for ploughing. At Mickfield Meadow in Suffolk (NATURE RESERVES OWNED BY THE SOCIETY), a hedge was laid bare when, without the requisite notice to the Society, Italian prisoners of war were employed to ensure a clear flying approach to a new aerodrome at RAF Mendlesham.

Towards the end of the war, however, life began to get back to some degree of normality. In 1943, for the first time in its history, the Society had experimented by arranging a General Meeting at the Linnean Society's apartments with a guest speaker, William Sheperd Morrison, the Minister of Town and Country Planning. Attendance, however, had been disappointing. With the cessation of hostilities, the Society felt confident enough to try again. So in 1946 it replaced the pre-war annual dinners with the first in a series of five annual luncheons (DINNERS AND LUNCHEONS) linked to its annual meeting. The first two luncheons were hosted on behalf of the Society by its President, LORD MACMILLAN. They were addressed on the first occasion by the Right Honorable Lewis Silkin, the Minister of Town and Country Planning, who spoke about post-war planning, the countryside and the Society's contribution. On the second occasion the speaker was the Lord High Chancellor, the Right Honorable Viscount Jowitt, who was piloting the Town and Country Planning Bill through the House of Lords.

In 1946, Lord Macmillan announced that he would not be seeking re-election as President when his five-year term finished the following year. The Society looked around for a successor. Among those in the frame were Viscount Jowitt

Marbury Mere, Cheshire, proposed as a bombing range during the Second World War

Lord Macmillan addresses the Society's 1946 Luncheon at the Connaught Rooms in London with Lewis Silkin, Sir Lawrence Chubb and Earl Lucan on the top table

and Field Marshall Alan Brooke (recently ennobled as Viscount Alanbrooke) who had been one of the chief architects of the Allies' victory in Europe. Alanbrooke was known to a member of the Society's Council at the time, David Armitage Bannerman, a fellow ornithologist. Bannerman later recalled a visit during the war with Alanbrooke to the studio of another member, the eminent artist-naturalist and creator of the Society's logo, GEORGE LODGE. Alanbrooke had taken "an afternoon off to refresh his mind".[92] Alanbrooke initially accepted the invitation to become the Society's President, provided he was not expected to be concerned with the question of military training areas, but eventually declined due to other heavy commitments. In the end, it was the DUKE OF DEVONSHIRE who was elected the Society's fifth President and he chaired his first meeting in November 1947.

With restrictions on travel lifted and with international cooperation encouraged, the Society now had its attention drawn, once again, to the international arena.

INTERNATIONAL COOPERATION

In 1945, in his capacity as Chairman of the Government's Wild Life Conservation Special Committee, Sir Julian Huxley visited the Swiss National Park and was so impressed with what he saw that he recommended a return visit by British conservationists. The Swiss League for the Protection of Nature took up the idea and the following year organised a tour for representatives from half a dozen European countries. The British delegation was surprised when the visit was used by the League, not just to show off its country's nature conservation achievements, but also to try to get agreement on establishing a new international nature conservation body. Somewhat reluctantly, the British delegation agreed a post-tour statement that recognised the need for better international cooperation over nature conservation *and* for a new international body.

The League convened a further meeting in Brunnen the following year to take matters forward. However, getting final agreement on establishing the new organisation would prove to be far from straightforward. It was a rocky path, fraught with disagreement between the various international players involved. The majority of British bodies were keen to see any new international organisation under the aegis of the United Nations Educational, Scientific and Cultural Organisation (UNESCO), rather than reviving the Advisory Commission for the International Protection of Nature active in Switzerland before the war. The Society, and particularly its Secretary, HERBERT SMITH, were closely involved throughout with these 'comings-and-goings'. He corresponded over the nature and financing of the new organisation; acted as Secretary at three meetings in February and April 1947 to coordinate the British response to the 1946 'conference'; and even chaired a group of the main British nature conservation organisations that came up with a possible alternative Constitution. In the end, the International Union for the Protection of Nature (IUPN) finally came into being as a part of UNESCO at a 1948 meeting at Fontainebleau near Paris.

IUPN's first objective was to encourage and facilitate cooperation between Governments and national and international organisations concerned with, and persons interested in, the protection of nature. Its membership was to be drawn from Governments, public services and international (inter-governmental and non-governmental) organisations, institutions and associations concerned with the protection of nature. This meant the organisation was unique as the first Governmental and Non-Governmental Organisation or GONGO. Martin Holdgate describes it as having "no parallel at the time (and very few afterwards)".[93] At the IUPN's second General Assembly in 1950 in Brussels, Herbert Smith was made a Vice President. In 1956, at its General Assembly in Edinburgh, the IUPN adopted the name by which we know the organisation today – the International Union for the Conservation of Nature and Natural Resources or, more popularly, IUCN for short (TOWARDS IUCN).

In 1949, the Society agreed to establish, as one of its own committees, the British Coordinating Committee for Nature Conservation to coordinate and act as a conduit for British policy on matters raised at the IUPN and for financial contributions. The new Committee's Chairman was the Society's President of two years' standing, the DUKE OF DEVONSHIRE, and HERBERT SMITH became its Secretary.

The time for the idea of national committees feeding into an international organisation uniting worldwide effort for nature conservation – that the Society had supported so enthusiastically 20 or so years earlier – had arrived. In the shadow of a bloody global war and in the wake of new international institutions, such as the United Nations and its agencies, people were now ready to embrace closer international cooperation.

In the Society's 1949 HANDBOOK, Herbert Smith was able to write, "by the establishment of the Nature Conservancy at home and of the International Union for the Protection of Nature in the world at large, the past twelve months have seen remarkable progress towards the goal which was set before the Society at the time of its inception, now thirty-seven years ago".[94]

COLLECTIVE ACTION

The dark days of the first half of the decade had demonstrated that the country could be mobilised for war and that collective action could triumph. People now recognised that collective effort could also be mobilised for peace. The shock defeat of war-time leader, Winston Churchill, at the 1945 general election had heralded a post-war Labour Government with a mandate to introduce national town and country planning, to nationalise coal and steel and, with the Beveridge Report in 1947, to prepare for a welfare state and the National Health Service.

The value of the collective effort for nature conservation had also been there for all to see in the legacy of the NATURE PRESERVATION IN POST-WAR RECONSTRUCTION CONFERENCE and the Nature Reserves Investigation Committee (NRIC) – convened, coordinated and largely financed by the Society. For the first time the voluntary countryside sector had cooperated at both the international and national level, not only to produce the most comprehensive natural history survey of Britain, but also national policy proposals to safeguard its nature conservation value, natural beauty and amenity interest. There were also two new institutions – the Conservancy and IUCN – to take forward nature conservation on an unprecedented scale.

The collective national nature conservation effort had in turn stimulated local action, particularly through the NRIC's Regional Committees. At the Society's second post-war luncheon in 1947, the daughter of the Society's founder, MIRIAM ROTHSCHILD, spoke with passion about how her local NRIC Regional Committee had identified her home, ASHTON WOLD in Northamptonshire, as warranting permanent preservation – no doubt at her request! She described her role as the local naturalist and as a "sort of one-man management

Above: Arthur Tansley's plea for nature conservation

Ashton Wold, soon after it was built – the Northamptonshire home of Charles Rothschild and his daughter, Miriam

committee",[95] successfully caring for the site despite the many and varied obstacles put in her way. Here, in this example, can be seen some of the legacies of the war years. The way in which individuals and, with the loss of a large proportion of the male population, women in particular, could make a difference. There were signs of a changing social order.

In 1945, Arthur Tansley wrote about this new order and about a new concept – the "positive policy of nature conservation"[96] – in a groundbreaking treatise, *Our Heritage of Wild Nature – A Plea for Organised Nature Conservation*. "In the past very large parts of rural Britain have been safeguarded by the private ownership of large tracts of beautiful country, estates of which their proprietors were proud and which they desired to keep intact even when they could have profited substantially by leasing or selling their land. Heavy taxation and death duties have already greatly weakened the position of land-owners, and many large estates

have been broken up. In the future it is probable that this safeguard will disappear altogether, and some kind of public action will then be the only means by which rural beauty can be preserved".[97]

The NRIC's final report had emphasised the importance of local action and a reviewer at the time observed that its Regional Committees were ideally placed "to carry out the task of promoting local interest and preservation. Every effort should be made to turn them into permanent organisations".[98] The Regional Committees had prepared the ground for a local nature conservation movement – the sort of 'public action' to which Tansley had referred. The seed had been planted and was ready to take root. Indeed, the young green shoots of this movement were already beginning to emerge.

CHAPTER 3

Crossroads 1950–1959

Only too often one finds naturalists strangely unaware of the need for conservation or indifferent to it.

From a lecture to the Society by Ted Smith, 1954

In 1951, after a remarkable period of social reform under the post-war Labour Government, the Conservatives were once again returned to power and with Winston Churchill as Prime Minister they pledged to make a bonfire of regulation.

On the land there were still 500,000 working horses and, with continued petrol rationing, travel was totally dominated by public transport. Only 14 per cent of British households had the regular use of a private car. But, despite post-war austerity, the country was beginning to emerge from the shadows of the war. The inspirational Festival of Britain exhibition in 1951 and the coronation in 1953 of a new monarch, Queen Elizabeth II, heralded a new 'Elizabethan age'. The public felt a new sense of optimism and more empowered than they had for decades.

With the formation under Royal Charter of a Government agency – the Nature Conservancy – to create and manage statutory nature reserves and the enactment of the National Parks and Access to the Countryside Act 1949, there were those in the Society who thought that its work was done. Nothing could have been further from the truth. Speaking at the Society's fourth post-war official luncheon in June 1949 (DINNERS AND LUNCHEONS), Lewis Silkin, the Minister in charge of taking the new legislation through

Parliament, hoped the Society would not "wind up and sit back"[99] on its achievements. Silkin supported a watchdog role for the Society to keep the new agency, local authorities and Government on their toes, to educate the general public and to champion science in the face of the "material side of life".[100]

The Society was proud to be seen as a science-based organisation. Knowledge of nature, where it was and how it worked, was a subject with which it felt comfortable and one that needed a champion. But away from the Society there were those who felt it should be doing more. The changes befalling the natural world were becoming increasingly serious and could no longer be ignored. The conservation of nature – as well as the science of nature – needed a champion, one that could take up these concerns, as Silkin had suggested, by protecting important sites, keeping an eye on Government and above all publicising the issues to a wider and more diverse audience.

A NEW ROLE?

Despite a lively period, actively and successfully promoting the cause of wildlife internationally and as part of Britain's post-war reconstruction, there was a real danger that the Society would now fail to pick up on the country's mood and would revert to

Opposite: Gibraltar Point nature reserve, Lincolnshire
Right: Festival of Britain Science Exhibition Programme sporting the Festival's iconic logo

its inter-war torpor. The main symbol of its war-time activity – the Nature Reserves Investigation Committee (NRIC) – was still nominally in existence but with the completion of its survey of reserves and the publication of its reports, the Society took the view that its work was complete. The NRIC's few remaining financial assets were absorbed into the Society's General Fund and it was finally wound-up in December 1953.

The Society remained active in international affairs, in particular the work of the IUPN and the British Coordinating Committee for Nature Conservation (TOWARDS IUCN). For example, it jointly sponsored, with the Conservancy, the IUPN's fifth General Assembly in Edinburgh in 1956. But at the beginning of the decade the management of WOODWALTON FEN was still placing a heavy financial burden on the Society. This was only lifted in 1954 when the Society agreed a 99-year lease of the reserve to the Government's new agency, the Nature Conservancy.

In 1950, the Society's PRESIDENT, the DUKE OF DEVONSHIRE, died, and with a lack of clarity over the procedure for filling a mid-term vacancy, it was more than six months before his successor, LORD HURCOMB, took up his office. In addition, in April 1953, after more than 30 years service and at the age of 80, its hard-working and efficient HONORARY SECRETARY, HERBERT SMITH, also died. It was only in the last few weeks of his life that he had taken 'time off' from the Society's affairs and, although at the end he had become more set in his ways, the Society was to sorely miss his "role of stage manager"[101] and "his tireless devotion to its affairs".[102] It said something about his contribution to the Society that after his death it decided to appoint three joint Secretaries in his place. The first, NORMAN RILEY, would be responsible for policy and education work, the second, PHYLLIS BARCLAY-SMITH, would be responsible for international affairs and the third would be responsible for nature reserves. This third position was, however, not filled and the "office was left in abeyance".[103]

The Society's wake-up call, when it came around 1954, had its origins in an event six years earlier. The Lincolnshire Naturalists' Union had established a committee to continue and develop the work of the county's NRIC Regional Committee. However, it was soon evident that it was inadequate in both "status and resources for the tasks which it had been set"[104] and a larger body, with the ability to own and manage land, was required. In 1948, the decision had been taken to establish a new organisation to be known as the LINCOLNSHIRE NATURALISTS' TRUST.

LOCAL STIRRINGS

In fact three other bodies of a similar nature had already been formed elsewhere in the country. First, in Norfolk, back in 1926, a Naturalists' Trust had been established to acquire Cley Marshes when The National Trust declined to take on the land itself as a nature reserve. By 1941, the NORFOLK TRUST had acquired eight reserves. A second body, the WEST WALES FIELD SOCIETY, was also actively engaged in nature conservation work, for example, with the conservation of the RED KITE and the purchase of Dale Fort in Pembrokeshire as a field centre. From 1947 onwards, the centre was run by the newly-formed Council for the Promotion of Field Studies (later the Field Studies Council). Founded in 1945, MAX NICHOLSON was later to describe the West Wales Field Society as "in effect the second Trust to be founded in Britain".[105] Finally, the Yorkshire Philosophical Society had acquired Askham Bog as a nature reserve in 1946 and, after taking advice from Norfolk, had formed the YORKSHIRE NATURALISTS' TRUST the same year.

But it was the Lincolnshire Trust, the third of the 'official' Trusts, which was now forging ahead. The Honorary Secretary

Watching birds, not bombs! German binoculars procured by the Society from the Ministry of Supply after the Second World War for £7

Reedcutting at Cley, Norfolk in 1932 – Sydney Long (founder of the Norfolk Trust) with Robert Bishop, the 'Watcher' of Cley Marshes

of this new Trust was Arthur Edward Smith (TED SMITH) who had also been an active member of the county's NRIC Regional Committee. Ted Smith had written to HERBERT SMITH in November 1948 to let the Society know about the new Trust and, in February 1950, secured a promise of its support. The Society immediately became a life member of the LINCOLNSHIRE TRUST (paying £25 rather than the normal £10 fee). In 1954, the Society agreed to a 50 per cent grant of £200 towards the Trust's purchase of 30 acres of wet heath in the north-west of the county at Scotton Common. Two years later it made another 50 per cent grant, this time of £500, towards the Trust's purchase of a further 37 acres of heath at Linwood Warren. The Society was even-handed in this respect also helping, for example, the NORFOLK TRUST in 1952 with its acquisition of Surlingham Broad in the Yare valley and the YORKSHIRE TRUST in 1959 with its acquisition of Spurn Point in the Humber Estuary.

At the meeting of the Society's Executive Committee in December 1953 when the central NRIC had been finally wound up, CYRIL DIVER had suggested that "though some of the NRIC Regional Committees had ceased to function, others were active and quite useful".[106] In 1946, for example, the Northamptonshire and Bedfordshire Regional Committee had remained in existence to keep an eye on its NRIC sites and to "obtain fore-knowledge of threatened destruction"[107] so that it was "in a position to approach owners or local authorities before the damage has actually been done".[108] But active Regional Committees were the exception rather than the

Red kite. The West Wales Field Society was involved with protecting red kite nests in Wales when the species was on the brink of extinction

rule and the Executive Committee had decided "the situation needed reviewing".[109]

In early 1954, the Society went ahead with a health check of the 24 Regional Committees that were nominally still in existence. Only three were found to be functioning in their original form while several had become committees of their local societies. All those remaining in any way functional were cooperating directly with the Nature Conservancy. Seven did not reply at all. As a result, in March 1954, the Society took the decision to formally dissolve the Regional Committee structure. Those wanting to continue were initially advised to form themselves into conservation committees of their local natural history societies rather than into new local Trusts.

In contrast, the LINCOLNSHIRE TRUST's reply to the survey had emphasised the need for more counties to start new Trusts similar to its own to fight the increasing number of harmful developments threatening the countryside. For example, it had

already been involved in a successful campaign to stop a caravan site for 120 vans being developed in the heart of the first Local Nature Reserve in England – Gibraltar Point on the Lincolnshire coast (NATURE RESERVES). Not only was the Trust acquiring nature reserves and confronting threats from development and agriculture, but it was also pioneering educational and visitor projects and collaborating closely with its local authority. The Trust hoped that the Society would champion the formation of more Trusts like its own and "perform a co-ordinating function".[110] What was needed was a strong national association that might also be of help to the Government's newly-formed Conservancy.

The Society accepted that some coordination of local effort was desirable and agreed that the view expressed in some of the replies from the NRIC Regional Committees that "everything could now be left to the Conservancy was 'a fatal attitude to adopt'".[111] SMITH was invited to speak about

Max Nicholson, Ted Smith and Lord Hurcomb at Gibraltar Point, 1960

his Trust's work to the Society's annual meeting in July 1954 and used this more public stage to repeat his message. He believed that natural history societies and naturalists in general were surprisingly indifferent to the need for conservation. What was wanted in each county was not more of the same but an "independent organisation devoted primarily to conservation, incorporated to hold property, with some financial resources and, most importantly perhaps, deriving its support from a much wider section of community than the average natural history society".[112]

Back home, SMITH was also using every opportunity to show friends, colleagues and anyone who expressed an interest, what could be achieved on the ground. Lincolnshire was leading by example and Smith's charm offensive soon sparked off a remarkable chain reaction. In Cambridgeshire, fuelled by a talk from Smith and led by a young taxonomist and ecologist, Dr Max Walters, the CAMBRIDGESHIRE AND ISLE OF ELY TRUST was launched in November 1956. At the same time in Leicestershire, another of Smith's friends, RONALD HICKLING, with strong support from other local naturalists and the museum, encouraged the still active NRIC Regional Committee to form itself into the LEICESTERSHIRE TRUST. Further Trusts followed soon afterwards in the WEST MIDLANDS in 1957, KENT in 1958, SURREY in 1959 and BERKSHIRE, BUCKINGHAMSHIRE AND OXFORDSHIRE in 1960. There were at least five more potential Trusts waiting in the wings.

FINDING A NATIONAL VOICE

By the time of the Society's annual meeting in July 1956, its President, LORD HURCOMB, was expressing his support for the fledgling Trust movement by calling for the acquisition and management of more local nature reserves by the Trusts and proposing a series of regional meetings to give a lead to their formation. He had picked up this idea from Smith who had offered to help arrange the first of these for the eastern and south-eastern counties of England. Other members of the Society's Executive, including

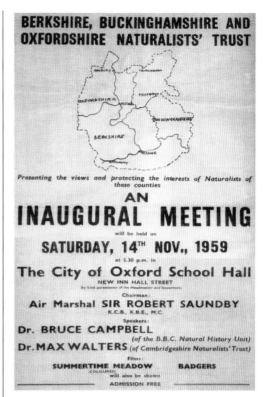

Poster for the inaugural meeting of the Berkshire, Buckinghamshire and Oxfordshire Naturalists' Trust, November 1959

DIVER, MAX NICHOLSON and Sir William Taylor, were closely involved with the Conservancy either as members or, in the case of Nicholson, as its Director General. The Conservancy was openly promoting the need for a strong voluntary sector capable of supporting its role as advisors to Government. Nicholson, at least, saw the Society as the most likely body to take up this mantle. In November 1955, however, he had circulated a memorandum in which he expressed the view that "the days of an effective amateur-guided, spare time operation in such matters on a national scale"[113] were now over. He had made it known that he was "appalled by how little the SPNR had spent, and the poor return on its investments".[114] If the Society would not provide the effective and adequate measures required for nature conservation, his view was that it should at least stand to one side. In February 1957, the Society's confidential minutes record that "a considerable and animated discussion took place on a paper submitted to the meeting by NICHOLSON on the whole range of the Society's past and present activities and future policy".[115] The paper contained proposals for a new national 'umbrella' body to support and promote conservation, a body that could support the Conservancy which could not be expected "unaided and unsupported" to "win all the necessary victories".[116] A 'policy' sub-committee was formed by the Society to take forward Nicholson's paper.

Meanwhile, SMITH in Lincolnshire, initially unaware of these developments, was also dismayed at the lack of progress and impatient to see moves towards establishing an association for the Trusts to "deal with matters of mutual interest and concern".[117] He was in touch with the other Trusts and they agreed to hold a meeting in Whiteslea Lodge at the NORFOLK TRUST's Hickling Broad nature reserve in September 1957 to try to progress matters further. Three of the Trusts – LINCOLNSHIRE, CAMBRIDGESHIRE AND LEICESTERSHIRE – met in Cambridge in June to prepare for the meeting. Smith acted as Secretary and in his memoirs recalls the wide-ranging discussion on the Trusts' needs and on ways to improve relationships with the Conservancy. What was to make this an historic occasion, however, was the group's determination to press ahead with plans for an association of Trusts and to formally approach the Society as a group to take on this task "for which it seemed. . . eminently suited".[118] There is no doubt that the Trusts' representatives, in agreeing to make this approach, were also well aware that the Society was spending less than £1,800 a year and sitting on a not inconsiderable General Fund of £50,000. Smith, reflecting on the Society's lack of activity, later described it as rather like gazing on "a very desirable mansion to which one finally gains entry only to find most of the rooms empty".[119]

The resulting document, subsequently dubbed the Cambridge Declaration by Smith, was sent to the Society with an invitation to attend the Trusts' September meeting in Norfolk. The Society welcomed the initiative, accepted the invitation and gave the first intimation to the Trusts that it was likely to back the idea of a new national body. The 'Declaration' represented the first formal statement of intent to create a national association of Trusts. It read:

"Our main purpose was to satisfy ourselves that an association of Trusts is desirable. Our discussions convinced us that it is, and we agreed unanimously to recommend that it be established. We felt that each Trust, whilst losing nothing of its independence or local status, would benefit from association with the others and that the conservation movement generally would thereby be strengthened. We considered what form an association should take and we agreed that the Society for the Promotion of Nature Reserves should first be asked if it would undertake a co-ordinating function of this kind for which it seemed to us to be eminently suited. We envisage it performing for the voluntary conservation movement a function comparable in some respects to that of CPRE".[120]

At the September meeting, HURCOMB, RILEY and NICHOLSON represented the Society and Smith presented the Cambridge Declaration on behalf of the Trusts.

A COUNCIL FOR NATURE

It soon became clear, however, that Nicholson was not entirely on the same wavelength. He was encouraging the Society to have grander ideas. He was proposing a national body but one that would represent the whole natural history and nature conservation movement. Encouraging the formation of new Trusts would be only one of the objectives of this new Council for Nature, as it was to be called. There was no specific mechanism proposed to facilitate cooperation and self-help between the Trusts. The Trust representatives were taken aback, "bewildered and in danger of being blown off course".[121] They were caught between their own new expanding breed of conservation-led local societies, working towards their own national association, and a bunch of influential players bent on forming a powerful and broadly-based national conservation body. The latter saw no reason for the Trusts to have special treatment, while some

Whiteslea Lodge on the Norfolk Trust's Hickling Broad nature reserve – venue in the 1950s and 1960s for discussions on the future organisation of the Trusts and the nature conservation movement

of the former saw the Council for Nature as a huge distraction. This tension continued over the coming months with the Trusts' representatives, led by SMITH, trying to reach a compromise but emphasising the importance of grassroots conservation. Meanwhile, NICHOLSON and others were emphasising the importance of a national body "representative of both the scientific and the widespread, but diffuse, public and popular interest in nature conservation".[122]

Smith submitted a memorandum to the Society in early November 1957 which supported the Council for Nature but which also tried to secure a more central role for the Trusts. A few days later, at the end of November, the Society met and debated the findings of its policy sub-committee set up to consider Nicholson's proposals. No mention of Smith's memorandum is made in the minutes of this meeting, even though Smith sent it to the Society in time. The Society preferred instead to minute a letter from the YORKSHIRE TRUST (also

party to Smith's memorandum) that supported the proposed Council for Nature in principle but suggested it would be wise to start gently. The Yorkshire Trust attached great importance to the Society remaining in a position to assist local Trusts to acquire new nature reserves. They were views supported by members of the Executive, including MIRIAM ROTHSCHILD, CYRIL DIVER and John Gilmour. After 'considerable discussion' the need for a Council for Nature, and its proposed aims and objectives, were agreed. But, significantly, the meeting also reached the conclusion that "instead of attempting to re-organise itself so as to assume the functions of the organisation (the proposed Council for Nature), the Society for the Promotion of Nature Reserves should, as it has so successfully done in the past, act as a catalyst in the creation of an independent organisation, leaving itself free to continue playing the part of benefactor to local organisations concerned with the acquisition and running of nature reserves".[123]

A working group created and financed by the Society, but not a committee of the Society, was now established to draft an outline scheme for a Council for Nature, chaired even-handedly by CYRIL DIVER. The working group was in effect given a deadline of 19th February 1958 when a meeting, "having as its object the definitive establishment of the Council",[124] was planned. The working group set about laying the foundation for the Council for Nature.

Meanwhile, the representatives of the Trusts agreed to meet in February 1958 in Lincoln to clarify their position ahead of the Council for Nature's inaugural meeting. They would support the Council for Nature – despite deep concerns that too little attention would be placed on conservation. However, with inadequate representation of the Trusts on the new Council they would revert to their original plan and seek approval from the various Trusts' Councils to set up a joint Trusts' Committee. They would also approach the Society again with a view to "securing representation for Trusts on the SPNR and making the Society the medium for their collaboration".[125]

The inaugural meeting of the Council for Nature served to underline the Trusts' concerns. SMITH reports that "in a brief encounter. . . before the meeting"[126] NICHOLSON pragmatically expressed his support for the Trusts' approach to the Society and urged them not to "rock the boat"[127] at the meeting. It was not the Trusts, however, that he needed to be worried about. It was the natural history interests, led by Lord 'Jock' Cranbrook. They demanded that membership should be open to all interested local or national natural history societies, not just national conservation bodies. Nicholson was strongly opposed and the plans for the Council for Nature were sent back in some disarray to the working group. When the Council for Nature was re-launched in July, under the chairmanship of the ornithologist and medical

administrator, Sir Landsborough Thomson, it did embrace all the natural history societies, as well as the national scientific and conservation organisations. It was a very different body to the one conceived of originally by Nicholson and indeed by the Trusts.

As far as the Trusts were concerned, the Council for Nature was not going to be the champion of practical nature conservation that they were looking for. Their course of action was now even clearer than before. They would go ahead and establish their own Trust Committee and, if they could persuade the Society to adopt it as one of its own, so much the better. Smith wrote again to the Society at the beginning of March 1958 outlining the Trusts' proposal.

The Society too was on the case and moved quickly. Led by Cyril Diver, it was already reorganising the way it worked. At the Executive meeting later in March, Diver "stressed the importance of making proper use of the Society's Council as a policy-forming body and suggested that representatives of the Naturalists' Trusts be elected to Council so as to provide a nucleus of members who were actively engaged in reserve management. Matters relating to the reserves which the Society held, or had direct interest in, should be dealt with by a

Opposite: Portrait of Ted Smith by Bill Bates
Right: Scotton Common, in 1959. One of the last remaining fragments of heathland in Lincolnshire and acquired by the Lincolnshire Trust in 1954

reconstituted reserves committee".[128] It was also agreed to meet with Trust representatives in April. Five Trusts were represented – LINCOLNSHIRE, CAMBRIDGESHIRE, LEICESTERSHIRE, KENT and West Midlands – and SMITH reiterated the Trusts' ideas on the functions of a Trust Committee. It should represent the Trusts' interests at a national level through the Society, enable effective networking between the Trusts and encourage the formation of new Trusts.

When DIVER returned to the Society's Executive in June, his recommendations had picked up on these ideas and included a new proposal to create a REGIONAL LIAISON COMMITTEE consisting of a member of the Executive Committee, four members of Council, two members of the Nature Reserves Committee and five representatives of the Trusts. His proposal that the Society's Council should be opened up to Trust representatives also remained. In addition, the membership of the Executive would be regularised – cut to the seven members allowed under the Royal Charter – and the Society's existing Nature Reserves Committee would be reconstituted with membership made up of three members of the Executive Committee, three representatives of the Trusts and one representative from each of the Society's reserve properties. Diver had not been enthusiastic about NICHOLSON's ambitions. His influence on behalf of the Trusts at this stage had been crucial and now his down-to-earth and realistic approach to integrating the Trusts and the Society meant that his proposals were adopted unanimously by the Executive. At the Society's Council in July 1958, the new arrangements were put in place. Smith, CHRISTOPHER CADBURY and Professor LA Harvey were elected to Council in their own right. Five representatives of Trusts were also elected on the understanding that they would be prepared to withdraw from Council should they find themselves unable to actively represent their Trusts. Cyril Diver was appointed Chairman of the new Regional Liaison Committee and Professor William Harold Pearsall Chairman of the reconstituted Nature Reserves Committee.

The new arrangements were a major step-change for the Society. Its focus had been shifted decisively onto practical nature *conservation* and the new local Trusts. As far as the Trusts were concerned, Diver's recommendations were undoubtedly a "half-way house".[129] Nevertheless, they recognised the progress that had been made and accepted the new arrangements. The Society and Trusts would still be independent of one another but a strong link had been forged between them for the first time. The first foundation stones for a national association for Trusts had been laid.

A NATIONAL COMMITTEE FOR TRUSTS

Frustratingly, for the Trusts, the first meeting of the Regional Liaison Committee was delayed until November that year by the Society's involvement with the IUPN's Edinburgh Conference. Six Trusts were represented and the minutes betray the tensions of bedding in the new arrangements. The Chairman emphasised that the new Committee was "not a meeting of delegates but a Committee of the Society"[130] with administrative support handled through the Society's office. In addition, there were the added tensions surrounding the Society's relationship with the Council for Nature. Diver, as always ready to oil the wheels, expressed the hope that the Council for Nature would "develop in the natural history field, in a position equivalent to the Council for the Protection of Rural England while the Society, Trusts and other comparable bodies would continue to fulfil their proper functions of dealing with all matters relating to the choice, acquisition, holding and management of reserves and the general conservation of specially interesting plants, animals and places".[131] It was, however, a pious hope. The meeting heard that the Council for Nature had already set up a Conservation Committee and although an urgently-called meeting between the parties patched up relationships, the underlying tensions between the Society and the Council for Nature, evident from the beginning, remained.

Nevertheless, the Society's Regional Liaison Committee was underway and it set about its

Christopher Cadbury – the Society's President (1962–88)

task with energy and enthusiasm, supporting the formation of new Trusts, providing a model Memorandum and Articles of Association and promoting the idea of a fund to purchase reserves that might become available at short notice. In June 1959, the Society got the ball rolling by transferring £100 to a new Emergency Fund account. The meetings were used to exchange information. SMITH, for example, reported that in Lincolnshire his Trust had secured a grant of £250 – a relatively large sum for the time – from a local fund resulting from "the collection and sale of herbs, rose hips etc during the war, and that. . . other Trusts might well enquire as to the existence of similar idle sums of money in other counties".[132] The Committee acted as an information clearing house for the newly-emerging Trusts and began to publish a regular newsletter.

In 1958, at the inaugural meeting of the Council for Nature, Smith had met CHRISTOPHER CADBURY for the first time and, finding themselves in agreement over many issues, struck up a working partnership and a friendship that was to last for more than 30 years. Cadbury had been closely involved with the NORFOLK TRUST since working as representative of his family's firm in East Anglia. Within four months he was appointed to the Society's Council and became a founder member of the new REGIONAL LIAISON COMMITTEE. At first, however, his views on the Council for Nature and on the Trusts struck a discordant note for many on the Regional Liaison Committee. In particular, he believed the Committee should just concentrate on land-holding and management issues, leaving all other matters to the Council for Nature. He was also concerned about the long-term viability of the Trusts. Smith refers to a letter to the Society's Honorary Secretary in November 1959 in which Cadbury comments, "unfortunately, with changing conditions it would be a brave man who

Spurn Point in 1960. It was acquired by the Yorkshire Trust a year earlier from the Ministry of Defence, who had used the 3-mile long sandy spit as a coastal defence during WWII. It is now a National Nature Reserve and home to one of the UK's Bird Observatories

could feel certain that all the Nature Trusts being formed today will be in existence in fifty years time and adequately supported by voluntary subscriptions".[133] The Society thought it a matter for the Trusts themselves but agreed to recommend that Trusts include a provision in their Memorandum and Articles that, in the event of their being wound up or dissolved, their nature reserves should, as far as possible, revert to the Society. SMITH reports that this compromise "seemed to satisfy everyone".[134] CADBURY's "misgivings soon disappeared and he threw himself wholeheartedly into the building of a strong Trusts' movement".[135]

In 1959, the Society's HANDBOOK carried news from the Trusts for the first time. Reports from the eight Trusts that had been formed so far were introduced by HURCOMB, the Society's President.

"I have constantly advocated the establishment of County or Regional Naturalists' Trusts as an effective means of preserving and protecting our surviving natural life, both plants and animals. . . fears have been expressed that such Trusts may overlap or even duplicate the work of other bodies. I do not think this need or should be so".[136] He continued, "the best answer to these fears and the positive case for the Trusts will be found, admirably illustrated, in these brief descriptions of the achievements of the older Trusts and the objectives of all of them".[137]

AT THE CROSSROADS

The Society's commitment to the new Trusts' movement and indeed to the other new bodies – the Council for Nature and the Conservancy – had been added to its traditional role as reserves' manager and, up to 1959, to its international interests. Although DIVER's reorganisation had helped, it brought with it the need to administer an increasing number of meetings. The Society's resources were also "heavily taxed in making good its promised grant of £1,000 to the Council for Nature and in meeting certain heavy and unexpected charges in respect of the Warden's Lodge at WOODWALTON FEN".[138]

The world was changing quickly and the Society was still in danger of being torn in too many directions. It was standing at the crossroads and sooner or later it would have to make a choice about the direction it wished to take. In the meantime, for the Trusts, there were no such complications. The future looked bright. Eight Trusts had been formed, four Trusts were about to be incorporated and two more were in the process of formation. Three thousand copies of the HANDBOOK article on the Trusts had been distributed and plans were well advanced for their first national conference to be held in Skegness at the invitation of the LINCOLNSHIRE TRUST in May 1960 (SKEGNESS CONFERENCE). NICHOLSON, by now Director General of the Conservancy, in an inspiring conclusion to the Skegness Conference, would reflect on the post-war period and the coming decade. "Owing largely to the war and to the heavy losses of leaders of the movement for nature conservation, a severe difficulty has been experienced in regaining and surpassing the earlier momentum which was built up mainly through the efforts of the Society for the Promotion of Nature Reserves. During the past year or two, however, concrete results have been emerging at a more encouraging rate and, above all, solid progress has been made in achieving the long overdue modernisation, reorganisation and revivification of natural history and nature conservation in Great Britain. Younger men and women are also coming forward to take their full share of responsibility and make good the gaps in the ranks".[139] He concluded, "disastrous and irreversible changes affecting wild life are being initiated all over the world with bewildering speed

Skomer Island was purchased by the West Wales Field Society, (now the Wildlife Trust for South and West Wales) in 1959, safeguarding one of the UK's finest seabird sites

and energy. Such forces as conservation has hitherto been able to muster are quite negligible in scale compared with what must now be faced. On the other hand the potential strength of conservation is also immeasurably great, if only it can be tapped and made effective in time. The race is now on and, although it is much too early to prophesy, we at least have some grounds for declining to take a pessimistic view of the outcome. Very soon, certainly within the next five years, we will be able to judge whether the response of naturalists to the challenge is or is not going to prove significant in determining the result".[140]

CHAPTER 4

Defining moments 1960–1969

Spring now comes unheralded by the return of the birds, and early mornings are strangely silent where once they were filled with the beauty of bird song.

From *Silent Spring* by Rachel Carson, 1963

Despite the activities of organisations like the Society and the emerging Trusts, at the beginning of the 1960s there were relatively few people in the wider world who fully recognised the seriousness of the threat to the natural world. There were still fewer who were doing anything about it. The UK Government had established the Nature Conservancy (the Conservancy) as its wildlife advisors and acknowledged the need to protect certain special wildlife sites. But it was under little pressure from public opinion to go further. Indeed, the optimism and enthusiasm so evident immediately after the war was beginning to fade and there was a danger that some of the advances would be lost.

From time to time, issues concerning individual species protection – the conservation of deer in Scotland and protection of wildflowers, for instance – hit the headlines. Individual site issues also attracted attention. The controversial proposal to build an atomic energy power station on a top grade wildlife site at Dungeness was a case in point. But until there was a reliable and accepted understanding of the problems and the foreseeable trends facing the natural environment, combined with an increased awareness of the issues, neither the Government nor the public at large were likely to take the matter more seriously.

Opposite: Sparrowhawk. Taken by the wildlife photographer Eric Hosking in 1961. Birds of prey were particularly affected by the toxic chemicals used in agriculture
Right: Stamp commemorating National Nature Week, 1963

This then was the challenge for the growing, but still small, band of 'nature conservationists'. It needed to develop its understanding not just of individual species but of their ecology and management. It also needed to make sense of man's past and present inter-relationship with nature. The next step would be to articulate all this in a popular way that would secure public and, ultimately, further Government support.

This challenge was taken up by both the Society and the Trusts in the next few years. For example, by the Society's active support of the Council for Nature's hugely popular NATIONAL NATURE WEEKS in 1963 and 1966.

A "natural sequel"[141] to National Nature Week was a series of three conferences on the theme of THE COUNTRYSIDE IN 1970. The initial conference spawned a set of ongoing study groups and, together with a second conference  in November 1965, these were especially important in defining the pressures facing wildlife and the environment and provided some much needed structure to conservation thinking.

CHANGES IN AGRICULTURE

As the decade unfolded, the tensions between man and nature increasingly came to the fore. Nowhere were these demonstrated more clearly than in the modernisation of British agriculture.

49

A demonstration at the Glanllyn Estate in Wales in 1954 to show how grassland productivity could be increased

In the 1940s and 1950s, the deterioration of the countryside – from war-time activity, spreading towns, new industries and a developing transport network – was largely recognised and, to a degree, was being addressed through the planning system. However, agriculture had been left outside the planning system and many post-war commentators had misjudged the likely pace of change. Even an authority like Arthur Tansley felt able to write in 1945, "it is scarcely probable that the extension of agriculture will go much further, for the limits of profitable agricultural land must have been reached in most places".[142] Likewise, the authors of the Huxley Committee's report in 1947, whilst not dismissing the impact of agriculture, commented, "competition for land between scientific and agricultural interests, though it may occur, is hardly an important factor. The land most suitable for reservation is not that which it has been thought sufficiently profitable to bring under recent cultivation".[143]

Opposite: Promotional poster for 1966 National Nature Week, using the winning entry in a children's poster competition

However, by the 1960s, Britain was fast becoming the most mechanised of farming nations. The corresponding drop in the number of horses (only one farm in ten had a working horse in 1965) brought with it a corresponding drop in the production of oats and the availability of manure to replace soil nutrients. There was a move to larger fields and larger farming units to maximise economic returns. With a generous Government subsidy system and increasing use of chemicals, farming practices were rapidly transformed, enabling hitherto 'poor' land to be brought into production and diseases and infestations to be controlled with an array of new fungicides and insecticides.

The issues surrounding TOXIC CHEMICALS AND WILDLIFE – highlighted so dramatically in one of the most influential books of the century, Rachel Carson's *Silent Spring* – came to dominate the environmental agenda throughout the decade and beyond. The publication of *Silent Spring* in Britain in 1963 was among a series of high profile events that began to force environmental issues into the public consciousness and onto the

Bird's-eye primrose – one of several rare flowers threatened by the new Cow Green reservoir

political agenda. Others included the 1964 proposal to build a reservoir on a scientifically-important upland area at COW GREEN in Upper Teesdale, Northumberland and the 1967 TORREY CANYON oil tanker disaster off the Cornish coast. It was on such issues that the young statutory and non-statutory conservation movements began, rather tentatively, to cut their campaigning teeth.

The decision to ignore the pleas of conservationists, and to go ahead with the Cow Green reservoir, was one of the factors that prompted the Conservancy to undertake a Nature Conservation Review in 1967 – "a stock-taking exercise of the nation's 'natural heritage'".[144] This would be the first such stocktake since the survey work of the Nature Reserves Investigation Committee in the

1940s in which the Society had played such a prominent part. The plan was to apply a "more rigorous and comprehensive approach"[145] to the establishment of a reserve series that would be "truly representative of the major British ecosystems and their variants".[146]

THE MOVEMENT EXPANDS

With Britain in the midst of a new agricultural revolution, Skegness in Lincolnshire was a good choice of venue for the Trusts' first national conference in May 1960 (SKEGNESS CONFERENCE). Here in the eastern counties was further proof, if further proof was necessary, of why a new local conservation movement was needed.

Introducing Lincolnshire to delegates, Dick Cornwallis (Lincolnshire farmer and Chairman of the LINCOLNSHIRE TRUST) and TED SMITH described how on the county's higher ground and peat fens, "holdings are large, and there is a trend elsewhere to even bigger farms. As a result, farming is intensive and the effects of new methods and techniques are quickly apparent. In many areas, for example, the landscape which the eighteenth and early nineteenth century landowners and farmers created after enclosure has disappeared: the hedges, trees, copses, ponds and other semi-natural features which supported a wide variety of plants and animals have been removed and the countryside is bare and windswept".[147] The Lincolnshire Trust, they reported, was on a salvage or rescue operation. Without the Trusts' intervention, five of its 13 nature reserves would have been destroyed or severely damaged and the value of several others significantly impaired.

For the Society and the 15 existing and nascent Trusts that attended the first national conference (CONFERENCES), Skegness was a significant landmark. The representatives returned to their counties with renewed confidence and enthusiasm, keen to get on with the job and to encourage the setting up of even more Trusts.

Left: Literature to support the fight to save Upper Teesdale's internationally-important wildlife
Right: Delegates at the Trusts' first national conference at Gibraltar Point, near Skegness, in 1960

THE THREAT to Upper Teesdale

AN APPEAL BY THE BOTANICAL SOCIETY OF THE BRITISH ISLES

The threatened area

Members of the Society's REGIONAL LIAISON COMMITTEE – eventually renamed the County Naturalists' Trusts' Committee – also helped to expand the movement by encouraging others around the country and advising about formation procedures, publicity, finances and conservation problems. One of the first requirements of the newly-forming Trusts was the need for a constitution that would enable them to achieve charitable status. In June 1960, the Committee agreed a model Memorandum and Articles of Association drafted by RON HICKLING and based on those adopted by the LEICESTERSHIRE TRUST. It was a more modern version of the Memorandum and Articles approved by the NORFOLK TRUST in 1926. In September, it was reported that "these were being well used by Trusts in the process of formation and... proving of value".[148]

Prominent amongst the committee's members were its new HONORARY SECRETARY (from November 1959), SMITH and its new CHAIRMAN (from January 1960), CHRISTOPHER CADBURY. Both were involved with increasing amounts of correspondence and with travelling to all corners of the country to attend inaugural events and to meet with a growing band of Trust enthusiasts. One such enthusiast was the 'master of field botany', Dr Francis Rose. Rose had helped form the KENT TRUST and was now actively promoting the formation of Trusts across all of south-east England. The Society's annual report to March 1961 records "a further most gratifying, indeed an almost spectacular, growth in the Naturalists' Trust movement".[149] In 1960, new Trusts were being established in ESSEX, BEDFORDSHIRE AND HUNTINGDONSHIRE, BERKSHIRE, BUCKINGHAMSHIRE AND OXFORDSHIRE and HAMPSHIRE AND THE ISLE OF WIGHT.

For Smith the workload was becoming critical. He was not keen to relinquish his position as Honorary Secretary at such an important time but was reluctant to give up his university career. In any case the Society did not have the resources to employ Smith on a permanent basis. There was the danger too, if he eased off, that the Council for Nature might move to fill any vacuum and so jeopardise the independent position the Trusts had struggled to secure. In December 1960, Smith wrote to NORMAN RILEY saying "this business is snowballing and we shall have to look again at our means of coping with it".[150] The time was also fast approaching when the 15 places allocated for Trusts on the County Naturalists' Trusts' Committee would be exceeded. In June 1961, the Society's Council agreed to expand the Committee to allow a representative of every Trust to be a member; for the Committee to meet annually but to have a smaller Standing Sub-Committee; and in June 1961 to appoint an Administrative Assistant – its first member of staff, John Ellis. This appointment made it possible for Smith to remain as Honorary Secretary.

Ellis had been a clerk in Lincolnshire's East Lindsey District planning office but was keen to work in conservation, even at a lower salary. The appointment was funded by a grant from the Society (£250 in the first year and £500 in each of the succeeding three years) and by a £150 donation from the LINCOLNSHIRE TRUST and a smaller amount from the University of Nottingham.

During 1961, Trusts were being formed in DORSET, SUSSEX, DEVON, DERBYSHIRE, SUFFOLK and GLOUCESTERSHIRE with many more in the pipeline. The same year a Trust was formed in GLAMORGAN, and the WEST WALES FIELD SOCIETY, which covered the old counties of Pembroke, Carmarthen, Cardigan and Merioneth, also became an incorporated Trust. On the occasion of the Society's 50th birthday (ANNIVERSARIES), at the second Naturalists' Trusts' Conference held in Norwich in May 1962, 30 Trusts were represented – twice as many as at Skegness. The conference also encouraged the NORFOLK TRUST to engage and interact more with the growing family of Trusts. By the end of 1963 there were 34 Trusts and, with the formation of Trusts in SOMERSET and SCOTLAND the following year, coverage of almost all of England, Scotland and Wales was complete.

FINDING NEW RESOURCES

It was one thing to start a Trust, it was another to maintain and widen membership and sustain educational and conservation activity. For this the Trusts needed early successes. Whilst driven by necessity, the acquisition of nature reserves was also one of the best ways to demonstrate credibility and attract support. Opening the Trusts' 1962 Norwich conference Tim Colman, President of the Norfolk Trust, entreated Trusts to never miss a chance to acquire reserves – "tomorrow it may be too late".[151] But relatively large sums of money were required, often at short notice, and young Trusts, despite several successful largely site-based appeals, were frequently stretched financially.

The Society moved decisively to help. It agreed to supplement its Reserves Fund (established in

1958) with a £5,000 revolving loan fund for the use of the Trusts. In January 1962, following negotiations by CADBURY, an interest free loan of £25,000 was secured from the Nuffield Foundation for the express purpose of financing Trusts' reserve acquisition programmes. In April the same year, the Pilgrim Trust made the first of several outright annual grants of £3,000 for the same purpose and in May, money (albeit a smaller amount than anticipated) was made available for small grants from the recently formed World Wildlife Fund (WWF) (WWF FUNDING). The County Naturalists' Trusts' Committee (REGIONAL LIAISON COMMITTEE) now took on the task of processing funding applications from the Trusts for financial aid for nature reserve acquisition and management. By 1965, the Society was advising on and processing some 20 to 25 grant and loan applications a year.

The HANDBOOK for 1965 summarised the use of the Nuffield, Pilgrim and WWF Funds. Important sites such as Hayley Wood and the Ouse Washes in Cambridgeshire; Fingringhoe Wick in Essex; Cors Goch in Anglesey (NATURE RESERVES OWNED BY THE SOCIETY); the Great and Little Fens at Redgrave and Lopham in Suffolk; and the Gower Cliffs and Whiteford Burrows in Glamorgan were acquired between 1961 and 1965. A further notable acquisition in 1962 was the KENT TRUST's first freehold property, the chalk grassland site of Downe Bank. The site was close to what had been Charles Darwin's home for the last 40 years of his life. Known by the Darwin family as Orchis Bank, observations on this 'entangled bank', particularly of the wildflowers, provided Darwin with important evidence to support his theory of evolution by natural selection.

Twenty-six properties covering nearly 2,400 acres were acquired in this period at a cost of little more than £86,500 (or just £36 per acre), and they benefited from grants of nearly £20,000 and loans of just over £39,000. The Trustees of the Nuffield Foundation were so pleased with the use of the Loan Fund that they converted the loan into an outright donation in June 1965.

Naturalists at Downe Bank, Darwin's 'entangled bank' acquired by the Kent Wildlife Trust in 1962 as its first reserve

The Society's financial support of Trusts at this critical point in their development was a great achievement. In the ten years to 1970, 500 nature reserves were acquired by the Trusts. As the Handbook put it, "it is no exaggeration to say that had it been necessary for the Trusts concerned to find unaided the means to acquire these reserves many would have been lost before adequate funds could have been raised".[152]

THE WORKLOAD INCREASES

Despite the additional secretarial support, the central administration continued to struggle to meet the Trusts' demands. A more fundamental solution was needed. Fortunately, SMITH's employer, Nottingham University, were willing to agree an 11-month secondment and permission

was secured from the Nuffield Foundation Trust to use the interest from its generous loan to employ him as Coordinating Adviser to the Trusts.

Smith resigned from the Society's Council and as Honorary Secretary to the County Naturalists' Trusts' Committee at the Council meeting in June 1962. He took up his appointment at the beginning of September. At the same time, after holding the presidential office for 11 years, LORD HURCOMB retired and CHRISTOPHER CADBURY was elected to take his place as the Society's seventh PRESIDENT. The Smith-Cadbury partnership that had proved so valuable in promoting the Trust movement and in the work of the Society's Trust Committee, was now in an even stronger position to bring about further integration of the Trusts into the life of the Society.

For SMITH, the coming 'secondment' months were hectic, not least because the period included work on two new important initiatives to improve relationships with the statutory sector.

The first of these was designed to improve relations with the Forestry Commission (FC). After negotiations, an agreement was eventually concluded in June 1964 whereby Trusts could be granted a licence in return for an annual payment to manage important FC wildlife sites.

The second initiative was aimed at improving relations between the Trusts and the Conservancy. There were already close links, with several prominent individuals in the Trusts on the Conservancy's Council and England Committee, including (not all at the same time) WALTER LANE (Lincolnshire), Charles Sinker (Shropshire), Ted Smith (Lincolnshire), David Streeter (Sussex) and Max Walters (Cambridgeshire). In addition, a liaison scheme was agreed in April 1963 to encourage closer joint working on policy, for example, on the coordination of responses to planning applications and on Sites of Special Scientific

Interest (SSSIs). Sheail writes "an obvious instance of collaboration between the Conservancy and voluntary bodies was in making surveys of SSSIs, maintaining contact with their owners and occupiers, and alerting the Conservancy to any threat".[153] Referring to the Trusts, he continues, "an obvious difficulty was that of obtaining a similar level and quality of response from each Trust. Whereas the CAMBRIDGESHIRE and LINCOLNSHIRE TRUSTS rapidly assembled files of information on their SSSIs, the NORFOLK TRUST claimed to be too preoccupied with its reserves".[154]

But the new liaison arrangement with the Conservancy was to prove valuable in other ways too. In 1965, the Government decided to incorporate the Conservancy into a new Natural Environment Research Council (NERC) designed to improve the coordination of environmental research. In its new guise the Conservancy increasingly felt that its conservation functions were being impaired. It was grateful when it received not just the practical support of its voluntary 'friends' (including the Society), but their advocacy

Hayley Wood in Cambridgeshire, acquired by the local Trust in 1962. By the 1960s, traditional woodland management (pictured here) was in rapid decline, resulting in the loss of many woodland species

Predatory Mammals in Britain, first published in 1967.
The Society contributed to this report which advised landowners
on how to manage predators with the least damage to wildlife

as well. Amid growing controversy at the beginning of the 1970s, the Council of NERC appointed a committee to recommend a solution to the problem. This was the start of a process that would lead to further reorganisation, with the loss of the Conservancy's major research function, including research stations like Monks Wood, and the passing of its conservation, advisory and education functions to a new Nature Conservancy Council in 1973.

In addition to the work with the FC and the Conservancy, SMITH was being drawn more and more into mainstream conservation issues. These included the protection of wild plants (CONSERVATION OF WILD CREATURES AND WILD PLANTS ACT 1975), the management of predatory mammals, the preservation of the coastline, the effects of toxic chemicals on wildlife (TOXIC CHEMICALS AND WILDLIFE) and the educational use of nature reserves.

But the bulk of Smith's time continued to be taken up with the emerging Trusts. He visited more than 20 during his secondment, talking at events, providing them with advice and assistance and studying the many problems and opportunities confronting them. This included assessing their individual financial and administrative needs.

A NATIONAL SECRETARIAT

When Smith returned full-time to Nottingham University in July 1963, he was able to resume a voluntary position with the Society which took the decision to 'promote' him as the Society's Joint Honorary Secretary with NORMAN RILEY. Riley concentrated on the Society's traditional core work, its daily correspondence, the Society's properties and aspects of its relationship with other national and international bodies, while Smith continued to deal with the Trusts' affairs.

Gradually the surge of activity across the country to establish new Trusts began to slow down. The Society's hands, however, were still full with networking advice, and being a dependable focal point for practical support and a safety net for the vulnerable and weaker Trusts in the early stages of their development.

In November 1963, the Duke of Edinburgh described the Trusts in a newspaper article as "the front line troops"[155] in conservation. It was increasingly true and, as a consequence, the Society's workload showed no signs of diminishing. Early in 1964, the general consensus was that it was no longer possible to cater for the needs of the Trusts on a part-time honorary basis. A properly staffed secretariat with office accommodation had to be established.

The Society turned once again to Ted Smith. Fortunately, he was able to secure a further secondment of three years from his University (eventually extended to four) to work 40 per cent of his time with the Society as Principal Advisory Officer. Smith started work on 1st October 1964. After appointing an Assistant Advisory Officer, William (Wilf) Dawson in early 1965, the day-to-day operation dealing with the Trusts' affairs moved from Smith's house to more spacious offices at the Manor House in Alford, Lincolnshire, in May 1965 (OFFICES OF THE SOCIETY).

The new national secretariat was not the only sign of a growing relationship between the Society and the Trusts. The Society began leasing its smaller reserves to the Trusts; started selling Christmas cards in 1963; and, perhaps most significantly of all, in 1964, asked Trusts for financial support towards the expanding work of the County Naturalists' Trusts' Committee (REGIONAL LIAISON COMMITTEE). The Trusts

Ted Smith (left) and Wilf Dawson outside Ted's home, 'Pyewipes', in 1968 – the Society's first office in Lincolnshire

unanimously accepted this request – with most needing little persuasion – and agreed to make a minimum contribution of £2 per 100 members for all Trusts that had completed one full financial year after inauguration. Two years later this was increased to £5 per 100 members – another sign of growing confidence in the Committee and the Society's patronage. The principle of Trusts providing some funding for their national association had been established.

The Society's move to create a national secretariat was not universally supported. SMITH relates how "there were unfortunately some who were closely involved with the Council for Nature who continued to agitate for Trusts' affairs to be dealt with by the Council. Even within the Society some of the older Honorary Officers – perhaps because understandably they shied away from extra work and responsibility – were opposed. . . WOODDISSE, the Honorary Treasurer, made this quite plain to me; RILEY's attitude was always somewhat equivocal, and HURCOMB, although he

had supported the Trusts' involvement with SPNR, would still have preferred them to go in with the Council for Nature".[156]

The move to develop a national secretariat was also seen as empire building and divisive by the Council for Nature. In November 1963, Smith was head-hunted to become the Council for Nature's Secretary, no doubt in a move to try to neutralise the Society's national position. Smith declined the offer and in the following year the relationship reached an all-time low when the Council openly accused the Society, and CADBURY and Smith in particular, of being intent on splitting the conservation movement. The row only succeeded in stiffening the resolve of the Trusts' Committee to encourage the Society to press ahead with the strengthening of its secretariat and to embark on intensive negotiations to reform the Council for Nature. This process, in cooperation with the RSPB, was progressed by a special meeting with officers of the Council for Nature in March 1965.

The future organisation of the Council for Nature remained of concern to both the Society and the RSPB. In 1968, the Council adopted a revised constitution designed to facilitate cooperation with the Society, the RSPB and other interested organisations, reverting in effect to the form of constitution originally proposed for the Council by its founder bodies.

This pre-occupation with the organisation of the conservation movement was a recurring theme throughout the decade. As we shall now discover, at times this threatened to get in the way of real progress with nature conservation on the ground.

A MERGER TOO FAR?

At the Trusts' fourth national conference in Bournemouth in 1966 the RSPB's Director, Peter Conder, proposed a merger between the RSPB and the Society. This was done with SMITH's knowledge and built on the close ties that existed between the two organisations. "There is a growing feeling amongst many of us that what is now needed is one major reserve-owning voluntary conservation organisation, concerned with the protection of birds, plants and animals and with conservation in its widest sense".[157] The proposal was welcomed at the conference by the then Deputy Director General of the Conservancy, Robert (Bob) Boote. "Rapidly-increasing pressures on the countryside demanded even more from the voluntary bodies in being the 'spearhead of ideas', pioneering new standards, acting as watchdogs… conserving sites and species and educating and informing others".[158] The merger, to include in Boote's mind, the Council for Nature, would "provide a framework for the unification of purpose throughout the conservation movement".[159] He went further, why not a move towards a grand alliance of naturalist and amenity bodies acting in concert under an umbrella title, such as the Royal Society or Council for the Conservation of Nature and Landscape?

Right: Sir Landsborough Thomson's *Plan for a Merger* and the merger proposals by a small group of RSPB staff

This was a step too far for both bodies but Conder's proposal met with a cautious, but nevertheless positive, response from the Society. Negotiations to establish a Society for the Conservation of Nature were conducted bilaterally through an existing RSPB/SPNR Liaison Committee, with the discussions over the reorganisation of the Council for Nature carrying on in parallel. There was much analysis of the two societies and in fact agreement on many issues. But behind the scenes there were those on both sides who were less than enthusiastic. In the Society there were fears of a takeover by the RSPB. In January 1967, when negotiations failed to secure parity of representation for the Trusts on the new body's Council (a core demand of the Society), the Society decided that a merger in a new body was premature. It was agreed that a full merger should remain the aim of both the Society and the RSPB but that Smith and Conder should go away and explore alternative ways of bringing about closer collaboration between the two bodies.

It was not long, however, before the issue began to rise up the agenda once again. In February 1969, no sooner had the Council for Nature been reorganised than its Chairman, Sir Landsborough Thomson, put forward his own *Plan for a Merger* (see MERGER PROPOSALS) designed to bring about a tripartite merger between the Society, the RSPB and the Council for Nature. By including the Council for Nature, Sir Landsborough was keeping the natural history societies in the mix. This move was welcomed by some naturalists who remained upset that local societies and field clubs were being squeezed out by, what they saw as, the headlong rush to establish Trusts. By May, for the Society's part, the plan was considered "impracticable and inadequate"[160] and "not a suitable basis for fruitful negotiation".[161] By December it was effectively dead in the water.

NATIONAL VOLUNTARY BODIES
FOR NATURE CONSERVATION

Plan for a Merger

Open Memorandum by
SIR LANDSBOROUGH THOMSON
Chairman, Council for Nature

Zoological Gardens,
London N.W.1.   February 1969

A PLAN FOR A
NEW ORGANISATION
TO REPLACE THE
COUNTY NATURALISTS
TRUSTS, RSPB & SPNR

As part of its response, however, the Society had drafted a broader policy statement on the future of the voluntary nature conservation movement at a two-day meeting at Whiteslea Lodge on Hickling Broad in Norfolk. The policy recognised that in the long term a new organisation would be needed as long as it properly balanced local and national interests. The thinking that had gone into this paper was to prove useful soon afterwards in preparing a new joint RSPB/SPNR document entitled, *A New Look at the Future of the Voluntary Nature Conservation Movement* (MERGER PROPOSALS). The Society considered this paper at its Executive meeting in November 1969 and endorsed a joint proposal by the RSPB/SPNR Liaison Committee to invite six 'wise men' (eventually four) to map out a way forward. The negotiations over their report, completed in 1971, went on for another two years before finally failing once again. The consultants' plan was formally rejected by the RSPB in March 1973, having been accepted by almost all the Trusts and the Society a year earlier.

SMITH, who had been at the centre of nearly eight years of negotiations, recalls how both sides at the end were "suffering from negotiation fatigue".[162] He attributed failure to the fact that "the RSPB perceived itself to be the stronger body and was therefore reluctant to accept the principle of parity on the governing body".[163] However, the 'wise men' had found no significant difference in resources between the two organisations when the vast amount of voluntary help available to the Trusts was taken into account. At the RSPB there had been a genuine desire to strengthen the nature conservation movement but there had also been mistrust of WALTER LANE, the leader of the 'wise men'. Conder had had to contend with strongly opposing views internally. David Lea, the RSPB's Conservation Director – who was closely in touch with David Streeter, a young academic and member of the Society's Executive – along with Dawson, had been keen to see a positive outcome to the negotiations. Stanley Cramp, Chairman of the RSPB's Council, was opposed and Cecil

Winnington-Ingram, the RSPB's Finance Director, had been unconvinced by the proposals of the 'wise men' and had produced his own version of the merger plan. Conder summed up his personal position. "I am clear in my own mind. . . having two sorts of autonomy or forty or fifty autonomies, however many it may be, is only going to add enormously to the existing problems. If I am committed to anything I am committed to a single body, with a single unity and a single loyalty".[164] This was never going to happen. Sir Landsborough's prediction at the time, that without mergers the movement would suffer "in its practical effectiveness and in its public image",[165] can be seen with hindsight as somewhat over-dramatic, but it is nevertheless fascinating to speculate on what might have been.

There was a final postscript to all the merger negotiations. In October 1973, a further, somewhat bureaucratic, merger plan was circulated by a small group of RSPB staff entitled, *A Plan for a New Organisation to Replace the County Naturalists Trusts, RSPB and SPNR*. There was, however, little appetite for yet another proposal and it too died a death. No serious recriminations followed as a result of the merger failure which, in the end, both sides accepted as inevitable. Conder and Smith remained on good terms and there was continuing collaboration between the Society and the RSPB on a number of issues.

DEVELOPING POLICY

There was a growing amount of business being generated for the County Naturalists' Trusts' Committee (REGIONAL LIAISON COMMITTEE), partly through two successful liaison groups – one with the RSPB and the other with the Nature Conservancy. In the case of the RSPB, while the merger discussions dominated many of the joint meetings, time was found to debate 'real' conservation matters. There was collaboration between the two organisations over the impact of various barrage schemes on wildlife, representation on Sports Councils and joint policies on oil pollution following the TORREY CANYON and other oil tanker disasters. A recurring issue raised with the Conservancy was its imposition of a limit on the number of SSSIs, contrary to the official scientific guidelines on SSSI selection. The Conservancy's desire to see improvements in the management and protection for chalk grassland was, however, strongly backed by the Society and the Trusts. The agenda of the main County Naturalists' Trusts' Committee also reflected the wide range of issues with which the conservation movement was now engaged. These ranged from the promotion of a site recording system for Trust reserves (BIOLOGICAL SITES RECORDING SCHEME) and a policy on introductions to nature reserves, to the environmental impact of straw and stubble burning, and the wildlife management of roadside verges and common land.

The Trusts' Committee was also spending more time scrutinising legislation. For example, the latest Agriculture Bill included provisions for the removal of hedgerows, and a Farm and Garden Chemicals Bill proposed better labelling for chemicals. There was a Conservation of Seals Bill and a Lea Valley Regional Park Bill to establish an authority responsible for the development, preservation and management of an area adjacent to the River Lea of interest to the HERTFORDSHIRE AND MIDDLESEX TRUST.

The most significant piece of legislation for the countryside, however, was a Countryside Bill designed to convert the existing National Parks Commission into a broader-based Countryside Commission. It also held out the prospect of a revision of Part III (Nature Conservation) of the National Parks and Access to the Countryside Act 1949 and with it, better protection for SSSIs. In 1964, the MP for Gainsborough, Marcus Kimball, had presented a Private Members Bill for the better protection of SSSIs following the drainage and ploughing of Waddingham Common SSSI in

The *Lincolnshire Times* 14th December, 1963 carries a front page story about the threat to Waddingham Common. A few months later the site was ploughed up despite its SSSI status

Lincolnshire with the help of a Government grant. The bill had failed but it had been among a number of factors that had led the Government to bring forward its Countryside Bill. The Society made representations on behalf of the Trusts and in July the Countryside Act 1968 received Royal Assent. In the circumstances, Section 15 of the Act was of particular interest. It enabled the Conservancy to give financial incentives to owners and occupiers for the preservation and appropriate management of their SSSIs. The Act also enabled local authorities to make grants for land purchase. Above all, it imposed, for the first time, a duty (Section 11) on every Minister, Government Department and public body to "have regard to the desirability of conserving the natural beauty and amenity of the countryside".[166] The 'conservation of natural beauty' was interpreted to include the 'conservation of flora, fauna and geological and physiographical features'. Just over ten years later the Government's Countryside Review Committee, reporting on this new obligation, noted considerable public scepticism about how far it was being heeded. The Committee believed that the lack of transparency in policy making and the low level of public expenditure, hardly suggested that conservation measures were taken seriously.

From March 1965, much of the work of the Society's Trusts' Committee was done through two advisory groups. The Conservation Group was chaired by David Streeter (converted to a full Committee in 1968) and the Administration and Publicity Group was chaired initially by Group Captain Montgomery of the NORFOLK TRUST and later by Captain Sir Thomas Barlow of the BERKSHIRE, BUCKINGHAMSHIRE AND OXFORDSHIRE TRUST. The latter took on the responsibility for the growing number of sales and promotional items, such as tea towels, scarves, Christmas cards, calendars, WILDLIFE FILMS and exhibitions. The Society's soon to be ubiquitous corporate tie, featuring its badger's head design, appeared in the spring of 1965. Produced by Messrs CH Munday Ltd to a specification from ANDREW RUCK of the KENT TRUST (and later the Society's Honorary Treasurer), the Society ordered an initial 1,000 ties costing twelve shillings each. They were sold on for seventeen shillings and sixpence. Such was the growth in sales over the next few years – by 1969 sales of Christmas cards were benefiting Trusts to the tune of £7,000 per year – that by the end of the decade the Society made the decision to appoint a junior officer to handle the increased sales business.

In October 1968, SMITH returned to full-time employment with Nottingham University and once again became the HONORARY SECRETARY, with NORMAN RILEY switching roles to become Honorary Treasurer. Much of the day-to-day work on policy, office structures, sales and reserve matters

Seal conservation – one of the topics on the Trusts' Committee's agenda

were now handled by Wilf Dawson. Indeed, when Smith's secondment had finished, Dawson had been joined by an Assistant Administrative Officer.

During 1968, the Society also took the step of opening up its Conservation Committee to membership by other conservation bodies. It was a sign of growing confidence. The idea was that the new committee, called the CONSERVATION LIAISON COMMITTEE, would stimulate the networking of information and ideas on practical conservation, research and management – a 'round table' for both the Government and non-government conservation community. In doing so it was setting itself up in potential competition with the Council for Nature. With the Council's reorganisation the same year, however, ruffled feathers were soon smoothed. An understanding was reached whereby the Society provided the forum that largely concentrated on practical conservation, while the Council for Nature concentrated on political lobbying and national policy issues.

The Society was fortunate to have David Streeter as the first Chairman of the new Conservation Liaison Committee. Streeter, a Lecturer in Ecology at the University of Sussex, was passionate to see some science and discipline applied to the principles of conservation and its practice on the ground, and for clearer messages to be disseminated to the public about nature conservation. He wrote, "the extent to which the aims and meaning of conservation are still either totally misunderstood or even completely unheard of today is disturbing. In spite of the activities of conservationists and the publicity given to them by press, radio and TV, the essentials still have not taken root in the minds of either the general public or a large proportion of those in authority".[167]

Leading the new Conservation Liaison Committee gave Streeter the opportunity to play a part in changing this situation and to be a means by which new thinking on natural resource conservation could be passed on and become a common currency – for example, in universities like University College London, where a new

An illustration for one of the Society's early Christmas cards

MSc course on conservation had been established in 1960. Streeter's communication skills and systematic approach were evident in his ordered and visionary speech *Countryside Conservation – the role of the County Trusts* to the Trusts' fifth national conference (CONFERENCES) in Canterbury in 1968.

In this speech Streeter felt confident enough to attempt a definition of conservation. He believed that because it is still "a relatively new, and therefore actively evolving, discipline, it appears to many to be a rather diffuse, unconnected, incoherent subject with ill-defined boundaries. This image does little to recommend it to those whom one is seeking to convert. Definitions of complex subjects are almost always inadequate, but if conservation has to be defined then something along the lines of 'the planned long term management of the countryside and its natural resources for the benefit of the community as a whole, without prejudice to its productivity or potential' includes the essential elements".[168] At around the same time, SMITH was describing conservation as a word "increasingly used and often imperfectly understood".[169] In his presidential address to the Lincolnshire Naturalists' Union in March 1969, SMITH adopted an even more succinct definition – "the wise use of those resources which constitute the major elements of our natural environment: air, land, water and wildlife".[170]

In his 'Canterbury' definition, Streeter went on to describe four important constituents to conservation. First, it involved a synthesis of three separate disciplines, namely ecology, economics and sociology; second, conservation did not exist simply to serve the interests of naturalists but, within agreed limits, should benefit as many people as possible; third, conservation involved long-term planning; and fourth, there were limits to the amount of pressure a piece of land could withstand without itself deteriorating in the process. Streeter visualised conservation operating at three overlapping and interdependent levels. First, broad policies of land utilisation (including assessing priorities of land-use) using ecological and sociological considerations, not just economic criteria; second, once an area of land had been allotted to various interests, it was necessary to ensure each minimised their impact on the environ-ment; and third, the direct administration and management of nature reserves and conservation education in field biology. Streeter identified the Trusts' role in this brave new world. They were uniquely placed to influence local government, River Authorities, Regional Sports Councils and to advise land managers, including farmers, and to create an enlightened membership in a position to influence public opinion.

FINDING THE WORKFORCE
While a few individuals in Trusts were beginning to take this message to heart, most had their heads down, preoccupied with getting their Trusts established and developing skills to manage their nature reserve portfolios. Some Trusts, for example, had initially used the Council for Nature's NATIONAL CONSERVATION CORPS for practical management when it was launched in 1959.

But Trusts soon began making their own arrangements for reserve management. In 1961, the LINCOLNSHIRE TRUST established its own conservation corps and went on to support two independent corps in Lincoln and Grimsby. The same year, along with Lincolnshire, Trusts in CAMBRIDGESHIRE, KENT, SURREY and BERKSHIRE, BUCKINGHAMSHIRE AND OXFORDSHIRE were described as having "organised their own conservation corps teams using Boy Scouts, members of youth clubs and school parties in addition to their own members".[171] The GLOUCESTERSHIRE TRUST started its own conservation corps in 1965, attracting volunteers mostly in the "thirteen to seventeen age bracket with older ones always welcome"[172] who were prepared to "devote some of their spare time to the common weal".[173]

Establishing a Trust was a roller-coaster experience – from the high of acquiring a new nature reserve to the low of a core-funding deficit. Trusts were still run by enthusiastic individuals and were firmly rooted in a voluntary culture. But the volume and technical nature of the work already undertaken, let alone the matters being proposed by Streeter, meant that Trusts had to begin to think increasingly of employing full-time paid assistance. At the very least paid help would be needed to carry out practical conservation work and to provide continuity in their Trust's day-to-day activities.

But Trusts frequently needed a kick-start in this process and in 1968 the Society seized on an opportunity provided by the Carnegie United

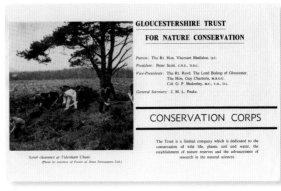

Promotional leaflet for the Gloucestershire Trust's Conservation Corps

National Conservation Corps, 1962

Kingdom Trust. The Carnegie Trust had announced that during its next funding quinquennium it would be accepting applications for grants towards countryside projects. The Society immediately applied for a grant towards Trust staff appointments and was rewarded when Carnegie agreed to make available £30,000 for five years (CARNEGIE FUNDS). Trusts were able to apply for grants to support administrative and conservation officers and nature reserve wardens, and also for educational facilities on their nature reserves and in the wider countryside.

The Trusts were quick to respond and in 1969, the first full year of the grants, 14 Trusts were successful with all but one Trust applying for grants for salaried staff. The Carnegie Trustees commented in their annual report that this was "not surprising as most Trusts have outgrown the capacity of part-time voluntary officers to cope with the increasing volume and complexity of work in such a lively movement. Paid assistance should enable more voluntary help to be recruited and used more effectively".[174]

THE SOCIETY TRANSFORMED

As the decade began to draw to a close the Society's life was now almost entirely taken up with activities and services undertaken on behalf of the 37 Trusts in England and Wales and the SCOTTISH WILDLIFE TRUST through its Trusts' Committee (REGIONAL LIAISON COMMITTEE). In the last year of the decade, the Trusts' combined membership increased by almost 16,000 and the number of nature reserves by more than 100, covering more than 3,000 hectares. In May 1969, all members of the Trusts had automatically been made Associates of the Society without further payment. The administration of the Funds established to help with the purchase of new Trust reserves and with the employment of full-time Trust staff, had become a major undertaking. In contrast, the Society's Council agenda was increasingly confined to legal issues and administrative matters concerning the Society's small number of nature reserves, and to receiving reports from the Trusts' Committee with its associated advisory and liaison groups.

In passing, it is interesting to note a decision by the Society in June 1969 that its Committee members should be entitled to six old pence (2½ new pence) per mile for *authorised* car journeys and £2.00 for "overnight absences".[175]

The Trusts had in effect taken over the Society and had turned it into "their national organisation adapting it to their needs".[176] The time was not far away when a major overhaul of the Society's Royal Charter to reflect the 'new order', together with a further expansion of its secretariat, would be needed. Most Trusts turned naturally to the Society's Trusts' Committee and to national conferences for national leadership, for the security of networking and sharing experience, and above all for the financial support that the Society had been able to marshal on their behalf. But, in the same way that the Society and the Trusts' Committee had begun to look outwards again, particularly through the CONSERVATION LIAISON COMMITTEE, so the Trusts were also beginning to gain in confidence. This meant strengthening their positions, not just as reserve managers, but also as local centres of conservation expertise and as advisors to a wider local constituency. The messages from the Canterbury conference were being heeded.

Nevertheless, most naturalists were, as yet, unused to getting involved in public issues – for example, many had to steel themselves to give evidence at planning inquiries. But the Trust movement, and indeed the conservation movement more generally, was recognising that it could no longer simply discover and define the world around it and just protect what it treasured. It was time to move on from its teenage years; it was time to grow up. It was time, in MAX NICHOLSON's words, to become 'eco-politicians'.

In 1964, the wildlife film-maker and later television executive, Aubrey Buxton, had noted that the willingness of millions of greyhound racing enthusiasts and fans of football and

The Beatles to pay for their passions, was in marked contrast to the 'ingrained stinginess' of naturalists and conservationists. "If they accepted the same obligations as other members of the community towards their interests and hobbies, the conservation movement would be buoyant".[177] As Max Walters, speaking at a Botanical Society of the British Isles' conference towards the end of the decade, put it, "many of us naturalists have learned over the past twenty years that, if we want to preserve for our children and grandchildren the range of communities and species which we ourselves have enjoyed finding and studying, we shall have to be prepared to spend time, effort and money on nature conservation... we must get out of our selfishness and think of the community... we are the first generation to have the power to consign, by indifference or by greed and insensitivity, a sizeable proportion of our native flora to extinction... how much survives is up to us, collectively, in Local Wildlife Trusts, in this Society, in the Committees of the Nature Conservancy or the Local Government Department".[178]

Opposite: Early appeal poster for the Hampshire and Isle of Wight Naturalists' Trust
Above: In 1969, a pair of breeding osprey attracted more than 30,000 visitors to the Scottish Trust's Loch of the Lowes reserve

CHAPTER 5

Taking up the challenge 1970–1979

We may not have had much direct influence on the countryside itself, but I believe we have had a direct influence on man's minds.

From the opening address by HRH The Duke of Edinburgh at *The Countryside in 1970* conference, 1970

As the decade began, preparations for the final COUNTRYSIDE IN 1970 CONFERENCE were going well. Contributors from across the statutory and voluntary sectors, including the Society, were engrossed in eight study groups. Their findings were helping to develop a greater understanding of the factors contributing to the changes in the countryside, even if working out many of the solutions was proving more elusive.

The Council of Europe had declared 1970 European Conservation Year (ECY) to "encourage all Europeans to care for, work for, and enjoy a high quality environment".[179] The Council of Europe, founded in 1949 to create greater unity between its ten (later 40) member nations, was the first European political institution of its kind. More than 20 countries from Iceland to Turkey were taking part in ECY and 10,000 events were being organised in the UK alone, including a memorable sixth biennial conference for the Trusts in Oxford.

In June, the 'environment' registered for the first time as an issue for voters at a general election. It was also mentioned for the first time in a Queen's speech at the opening of Parliament. New, more radical, groups were being formed with a broader environmental agenda; Friends of the Earth and Greenpeace were both established in the UK in 1971.

Opposite: Young naturalists at Gibraltar Point. The 1970s saw the development of the junior branch of the Trusts and environmental projects and activities for young people

The Society was quick to remind the new Conservative Government under Prime Minister Edward Heath that it "should be under no illusions about public concern for conservation which the phenomenal growth of our movement indicates. This is not a political craze which will die down now that the election is over. The voluntary movement will soon want to see action – on anti-pollution measures and on positive conservation through, for example, strengthening the Nature Conservancy and the Countryside Commission. The new Government's response to the final Countryside in 1970 conference at the end of October may tell us how seriously they take the environment".[180]

In the event, there was a robust response from the Government at the October conference. According to the Prime Minister, the protection of the countryside, the avoidance of pollution, and striking of the right balance between the needs of conservation and development were now among "the most important and the most difficult tasks of Government".[181] The functions of land-use planning, prevention of pollution, construction and transport would be brought together into a single Department of the Environment for the first time. The new Secretary of State for the Environment, Peter Walker, was charged with getting "agreement with local authorities to a series of regional strategies within which proper protection can be given to the countryside".[182] The Prime Minister concluded by stating that the protection of the countryside and the prevention of pollution would be among the highest priorities of the 1970s and "it is in that spirit that this Government will tackle the problems".[183]

At a time when politicians were viewed with less cynicism than today, the announcement of a new environment department was seen as genuine progress. But there was still healthy scepticism about how much the new Government would really be prepared to take on board the fundamental changes in policy and practice that were required. As a sign that words were perhaps speaking louder than deeds, the Society pointed to the position of the pollution over-lord – a cabinet post in the previous administration – that had been down-graded to Parliamentary Secretary level in the new Government.

The journalist, Jon Tinker, in an article in the *New Scientist*, however, expressed the view that "if politicians were beginning to show signs of wanting to jump on the conservation bandwagon, the question was now whether environmentalists were ready and capable of steering it. What were their shopping lists of administrative acts and guidelines to cope with habitat destruction and pollution?"[184] It was a fair question. Wildlife habitats across the board were being lost and damaged at an unprecedented rate and policies and action on the ground still lagged far behind the rhetoric. The voluntary sector had to articulate more precisely what action was needed and to do it soon.

The huge challenge for the Society and the Trusts was how they were going to expand their advocacy role whilst continuing to fulfil their considerable land management responsibilities. They felt impelled to maintain their fire-fighting on the ground – protecting the best wildlife (it now appeared as one word) areas by defending them by any means at their disposal. But at the same time they were increasingly aware that this was no long-term solution. They would have to reach out to those who were increasingly showing an interest

in the emerging nature conservation agenda – farmers, industrialists and educators as well as local and national Government. They had to convince all these sectors of the need for new ways of working, new guidance and new laws to conserve an increasingly beleaguered natural world. In fact, the shopping list that Tinker was demanding.

A NEW PROFESSIONALISM

Significantly, in the circumstances, the mood amongst the record-breaking attendance of 250 delegates at the Trusts' Oxford conference in April 1970 (CONFERENCES) "was one of militancy for the cause. . . with the realisation that the message must be driven home at all levels"[185] and that Trusts, "whilst strengthening their individual identity, must together realise their national potential".[186] This was coupled with a recognition that to be effective both the Society and the Trusts had to become more professional. This meant improving their governance, working practices and knowledge base and expanding their workforce to include staff and volunteers who were not only skilled at managing nature reserves but also able to teach children, run a sales business or lobby Parliament.

In fact some appointments of this nature were being made. In October 1972, for example, the Society made the decision to employ a full-time Sales Officer, Ann Rule, who had been working for Helena Rubinstein cosmetics in New York. The same year the SURREY TRUST employed a teacher/ecologist, Doug Hulyer, at its newly-acquired Nower Wood Education Centre. Of the first 21 grants made to Trusts under the Society's Carnegie scheme (CARNEGIE FUNDS), nine had been for Trust administrators or executive officers rather than conservation staff. In 1971, about 80 Trust honorary officers and administrative staff met at Monks Wood Experimental Station in Huntingdonshire to discuss the day-to-day management of the Trusts, including the use of paid staff and the skills they required.

The first Trust visitor centre opened in 1968 at Woods Mill, Sussex

However, these developments were not going to happen without increasing the overall financial resources of the movement. The Society's existing funding programmes for Trusts were already being well used. In the year ending March 1972, WWF's grant aid of £28,840 towards reserve purchase was the largest amount awarded in one year since the start of its support in the autumn of 1961 (WWF FUNDING). By March 1973, the Society's Nuffield Revolving Loan Fund had lent more than £110,000 since its establishment in 1962. Fortunately, these Funds, together with the Society's Cadbury, Carnegie and Pilgrim Funds, were about to be supplemented with additional money from Carnegie and from three new sources.

By March 1973, the Carnegie Funds for Trusts, administered by the Society, were almost exhausted. Its support for staff – a much more difficult area to raise funds for than nature reserves – had been particularly welcome and had proved very successful. It had enabled

18 Administrative Officers, ten Conservation Officers and six Field Officers and Wardens to be appointed by 32 Trusts. Since 1968, membership had grown from 30,000 to more than 80,000 and the number of nature reserves had increased from almost 400 to more than 750.

Carnegie was now prepared to top up this fund to enable all Trusts to benefit and extended its support to cover Trusts' interpretative schemes with an additional grant of £20,000. By the middle of the decade Trusts were expanding their educational and interpretative work. Major new visitor centres were opened by the ESSEX TRUST at Fingringhoe and the SOMERSET TRUST at Fyne Court; the LINCOLNSHIRE TRUST modernised their educational centre at Gibraltar Point; and others were under construction by the DURHAM TRUST at Bowlees in Upper Teesdale, the NORFOLK TRUST at Ranworth Broad and the SHROPSHIRE TRUST at Earls Hill. It would be a prelude to the fine track record of the Trust movement in this field (VISITOR CENTRES).

As well as providing support to several of these projects, Carnegie also wanted to help the Society "strengthen its central services to Trusts, particularly in the advisory field".[187] In September 1973, an award of a further £25,000 over five years enabled the Society to employ TED SMITH as its first General Secretary from January 1975 (PRINCIPAL OFFICERS). Carnegie's continuing support owed much to the personal interest of its Secretary, MICHAEL HOLTON, and his predecessor, David Lowe. Holton became a member of the Society's Council and Executive in 1976 and, after retiring from the civil service in 1988, its HONORARY SECRETARY.

The first of the new sources of money involved the Countryside Commission. When it was formed under the Countryside Act 1968, it had been given the power to grant-aid land purchase, particularly land of landscape and amenity interest, as well as countryside facilities such as hides and walkways. By 1972, the Society had successfully negotiated an agreement with the Commission over the types of Trust project that would qualify for its support under the new legislation. It was the "first general scheme for Government aid to Trusts"[188] and, as such, was particularly welcomed by the Society. In the first year, three grants were made to Trusts through the Society.

A legacy of £50,000, received by the Society in 1972 from Henry Newlin of Tunbridge Wells in Kent, formed part of the second source of new funding. Shortly before his death, Newlin had also transferred the assets of a charitable Trust worth more than £55,000 to the Society and had requested that the deed of gift, and the subsequent bequest, should be pooled to form the PAUL AYRES MEMORIAL FUND. The donor agreed that part of the sum could be made available as a revolving loan fund for nature reserve purchase and part, in the short term, for general purposes.

The third tranche of new funding came later in the decade. The Society was fortunate to secure an anonymous loan of £250,000 for an initial period of ten years, at a fixed interest rate of seven per cent per annum, for Trusts to 'invest in land

or property in the interests of conservation in the broadest sense'. The anonymous source was later disclosed as the Mary Snow Trust. The idea of this new LAND FUND, as it became known, was that loans could be made to Trusts not just for the purchase and management of nature reserves but also for capital projects, such as the development of new headquarters and retail outlets.

The Society had recognised as early as July 1970 that the growth in its grants and loans programme, the development of its trading enterprise and the consequent increase in staff numbers, made it desirable to keep closer control over expenditure and to examine its budgeting and accounting procedures. It established a finance and administration working party which was converted to a full-blown Finance and General Purposes Committee in May 1971. An example of its work was the announcement in October 1973 of a new grants and loans policy for the purchase of reserves. Loans would in future be made available from a joint Nuffield and Paul Ayres 'pot' with the Paul Ayres Memorial Fund also providing pump-priming grants for nature reserves and nationally-important sites. The Society continued to process grant applications to the WWF.

In passing, it is also worth noting that in 1973, through the generosity of its President, CHRISTOPHER CADBURY, the Society acquired several overseas island properties – nine small islands in the Falklands and the internationally-

Seychelles warbler – over 2,000 pairs breed on Aride Island

Aride Island nature reserve, Seychelles, purchased by the Society in 1973

important ARIDE ISLAND in the Seychelles (NATURE RESERVES OWNED BY THE SOCIETY). The freehold of these islands was in danger of being temporarily 'lost' by the Society in 1982 as a result of the Argentinean invasion of the Falklands and a brief period of military unrest in the Seychelles. By 1980, responsibility for the management of the islands in the Falklands had been handed over to the Falklands Island Foundation with the freehold gifted to the Foundation in 1992. The Society continued to be actively involved in the management of Aride Island in the Seychelles for more than 30 years.

THE SALES BUSINESS

In 1974, the Society moved into a new headquarters after outgrowing the Manor House in Alford. In its search for a new home the Society had considered, and then for various reasons rejected, Charnwood Lodge, Loughborough (recently bequeathed to the LEICESTERSHIRE

AND RUTLAND TRUST), the President's home at Beaconwood, near Rednal in Worcestershire, as well as the option of acquiring additional accommodation in Alford. The final choice was the Old Church Institute at Nettleham, near Lincoln which the Society purchased for £10,000 and converted to office use (OFFICES OF THE SOCIETY). The decision had been made because the new property was still in commuting distance from the homes of the Honorary Secretary and existing staff, there was better access to trunk routes and to London by rail, and the opportunities for staff recruitment were significantly improved. An adjoining cottage was purchased for £17,500 five years later.

Up to now the Society's sales business had been a comparatively low-key operation. The move to more satisfactory premises in September 1974 now gave the Society, under Dawson's guiding hand, the opportunity to make substantial improvements. These included the employment of the Society's first full-time professional Sales Officer in October

The Society's new offices in Nettleham, Lincolnshire in 1974

and the centralisation of mail order sales for both the Society and the Trusts for the 1975–76 season. Sales goods, including a range of educational items, were also promoted through a widely distributed, 24-page, full-colour gift catalogue. An opportunity to promote the Trusts and to showcase merchandise was taken in January at a camping and outdoor life exhibition at the Empire Hall, Olympia in London.

The aim of these improvements was to free up the Trusts' financial and manpower resources for the development of more profitable over-the-counter sales' outlets. One of the issues that faced this new arrangement was a legacy of old lines. Although products, such as a popular series of Curwen calendars and most Christmas cards, had been successful, other lines had not. Some items could also be unpredictable. For example, a Christmas card featuring a rather strange-looking brown hare failed to sell in its first year. Yet it was a best seller the second time around. There was every expectation that the business would take time to bed down. But as it turned out, despite high inflation in the country at large, the first-year results were promising. The Society's total income doubled during the year to more than £86,500. In addition, the Trusts made an encouraging surplus of some £18,000 on the sale of goods obtained from the Society, as well as receiving almost £9,000 in donations.

Below: Educational materials – Original layout for a Woodland Ecology Wallchart by artist Denys Ovenden, one in a series of charts produced by the Society

An early sales item – a tea towel with a coltsfoot and butterbur design,
competitively priced at 80p in today's money
Right: The first gifts catalogue for the centralised mail order sales business

A NEW NAME AND ROYAL CHARTER

Alongside negotiations over the office move to
Nettleham and the expansion of the sales business,
important decisions were being made about the
Society's governance and its developing
relationship with the Trusts. All Trusts now had
nominees serving on the Society's Council. So,
in October 1972, "after fourteen years of vigorous
and profitable activity",[189] it was decided the time
had come for the County Naturalists' Trusts'
Committee (REGIONAL LIAISON COMMITTEE) to
be wound up and its functions formally transferred
to the Society's Council. Further integration
of the Trusts and the Society between 1974 and
1976 was reflected in the Society's use of the
strapline 'ACT – the Association of County Trusts
for Nature Conservation'.

In 1976, these new arrangements were
incorporated into a new Royal Charter under
which the Trusts became Corporate Members of
the Society, each with a place on Council in its
own right. For the first time the Society was
given a specific power to encourage and support
Trusts. A new position of CHAIRMAN OF THE
EXECUTIVE COMMITTEE was created and filled
by WALTER LANE who, two years before, had
taken early retirement as Clerk of Lindsey
County Council in Lincolnshire. He had been on
the Executive, played a prominent role in the
merger negotiations with the RSPB and had been
active in THE COUNTRYSIDE IN 1970 initiative.
It was not long before the position of Chairman
of the Society's Executive Committee became
the senior Trustee position as far as the day-to-day

In 1976 the Society purchased 14,500 acres of the Ben Mor Coigach estate in the Highlands – home to raven, red deer, scottish wildcat and golden eagle. The reserve was initially jointly managed with the Scottish Wildlife Trust before it was transferred to the Trust in 1987

operation of the Society was concerned. At last, responsibility for the Society's affairs rested in a committee structure largely made up of Trust representatives. Perhaps now, the Society's claim to be the 'association of Nature Conservation Trusts' could be truly justified.

The granting of the new Royal Charter had coincided with the 50th anniversary of the founding of the first Trust – the NORFOLK TRUST – and the establishment of the movement's thousandth nature reserve. The Society used the occasion for a 'makeover'. Under the new Royal Charter the Society's name (NAMES OF THE SOCIETY) changed to the Society for the Promotion of Nature Conservation (SPNC) to reflect its broader aims and objectives. The Society adopted a new, more modern badger logo (LOGOS) and launched a new-look colour production of *Conservation Review* (see NATURAL WORLD) – its twice-yearly Trust member magazine.

The Society was also able to announce that His Royal Highness, The Prince of Wales had accepted an invitation to become the Society's first Patron. His Royal Highness formally took up this role on 1st April 1977.

Heavily committed to the Queen's Silver Jubilee celebrations, it was not until July 1978 that His Royal Highness was able to formally meet representatives of the Society for the first time. At the conclusion of the meeting, held in the grand surroundings of Buckingham Palace, His Royal Highness announced that he had requested that half the proceeds from the Royal Premiere of the film, *Watership Down*, planned for the autumn, should go to the Society.

The new Royal Charter also prompted a review of the "special position of the Scottish Wildlife Trust".[190]

The new Royal Charter

HRH The Prince of Wales at the *Watership Down* film premiere, with (left to right) Tim Sands, Gren Lucas and Christopher Cadbury

In the 1950s and early 1960s the possibility of starting local Trusts in Scotland – in the Lothians and in Perthshire for example – had been on the cards. But these moves had been pre-empted by the formation in Edinburgh of the SCOTTISH TRUST early in 1964. Its principal promoter and founder, Sir Charles Connell, wanted the new Trust to be a member of the Society's County Trusts' Committee but, as a national body, expected it to have special status. In the years since its formation, the relationship between the Society and the Trust had indeed evolved to reflect the Trust's national role in Scotland. The Scottish Trust had secured the right to appoint a member of the Society's Executive Committee whose members were otherwise elected by Council. The Trust was also exempted from paying capitation fees on its members and instead paid for the house-magazine, *Conservation Review* – distributed free to all other Trusts – and a lump sum of £100. It had also secured two places on the Council, as opposed to the one place available to all other Trusts. The constitutional elements of this package – the Scottish Trust's representation on the Executive and Council – were enshrined in the new Royal Charter granted in 1976. These were important concessions and they helped to ensure that the Scottish Trust became further integrated into the movement of Trusts.

Nevertheless, the Trust's position as a national body differed from that of a local Trust in England and it felt this was not understood by an anglo-centric Society focusing its lobbying on the Westminster Parliament. The Society, for its part, felt uncomfortable about the precedent created by the different formula applied to the SCOTTISH TRUST's financial contribution and was somewhat uncertain about its overall commitment. Discussions about the Trust's relationship with the Society and the rest of the movement continued over the autumn of 1976. Confidence was restored and by November a new agreement (or 'concordat' as it was called) had been reached as a basis for the Scottish Trust's future membership of the Society.

The discussions with Scotland, however, were also of interest to the Trusts in Wales. Just over a year earlier, they had established a liaison body – the Association of Welsh Trusts, chaired by the NORTH WALES TRUST's Chairman, Professor Bill Lacey (CHRISTOPHER CADBURY MEDAL CITATIONS). If Scotland had secured special arrangements, they wanted them too. They wanted full representation on the Executive Committee and a similar concession on the contributions levied on Trusts in Wales. New arrangements regarding membership were eventually agreed (see WELSH TRUSTS, ASSOCIATION OF).

BRINGING YOUNG PEOPLE ON BOARD

In the first half of the decade, the number of people joining the Trusts had been particularly high. Adult membership had increased by 80 per cent in the first five years. But the Society had also begun to look for ways to help Trusts encourage more involvement by young people and to build a junior membership. Wilf Dawson, now the Society's Assistant Secretary, was aware of the pioneering work of the Advisory Centre for Education (ACE) in Cambridge. Its projects were regularly promoted in *The Sunday Times* newspaper and the young people taking part could join a Watch Club and received a regular club magazine, *Watchword*. The Centre's first

Exploring nature at Gibraltar Point reserve, 1960s. The development of Watch built on local environmental education work undertaken by the Trusts

project in 1971, a national survey of water pollution, had attracted 10,000 children and families. It had followed this up a year later with a similar survey of air pollution using lichens as indicators of air quality. "Some children travelled over one hundred miles under their own steam on the survey and one girl mapped the lichens growing above ground at every station on the London Underground".[191]

More than enough had been achieved by ACE in its first five years to justify *The Sunday Times'* involvement and to convince both ACE and the Society that closer collaboration could be worthwhile. ACE was attracting large numbers of young people, but there was still a feeling in the Society that retaining their interest was going to be difficult without a strong local base. Dawson believed the Trusts could provide such a base. So he set about creating the team and administrative structure to put the Watch project on a more permanent footing as the junior wing of the Trust movement. As a result the Watch Trust for Environmental Education Ltd (WILDLIFE WATCH) was incorporated in August 1977 with the support, including financial support, of *The Sunday Times* and a Board of Management.

Above: Watch badge, sporting its original 'amoeba' logo
Opposite: Watch produced a number of wallcharts to accompany its projects. This one is for the 1985 Shoresearch project

Life in rock pools. Breadcrumb sponge **1** is an animal! Bladder wrack **2**, a brown seaweed, covers a shore crab **3**, while the hermit crab **4** lives in an old shell. Corallina **5** is a red seaweed, while Enteromorpha **6** is green and peacock's tail **7** a fan-shaped weed. Other animals are whelk **8**, prawn **9**, beadlet anemone **10**, snakelocks anemone **11** and the common goby **12**. Seals **13** bask on rocks and an oyster catcher **14** feeds on mussels. Rocks are covered with toothed wrack **15**, mussels **16** and limpets **17**. Acorn barnacles **18** close up at low tide. Common terns **19**

SOME SHORE THINGS

Your summer `Watchword` wall chart brings the smell of the salty sea air to your sitting rooms. Firm sand, warm sun and sparkling sea, a scramble over seaweed-covered rocks: for many that is what the seaside offers. But if you look carefully there is a multitude of wildlife along our shorelines

Action Stations!

Are you going to the coast this summer? Why not take part in Watch's Project Coast Guard. Best entry wins a pair of Nikon binoculars and a Raleigh bicycle. Runners-up receive copies of The National Trust's Guide to The Coast, written by Tony Soper.

The National Trust and Watch have put together a pack of reading material to help with this project. It includes information on identifying animals on the seashore, how to be a shore detective, a coastal colouring book and much much more.

Write to Watch enclosing £1.50 which includes p&p.

Edge of a dune **1** held together by marram grass **2**. Larger gulls include herring gull **3** and lesser black-backed gull **4**. Kittiwakes **5** are smaller. Caves **6** form in softer rock while water drains from the cliff **7**. Harder rock forms an arch **8** and a stack **9**. Gannets drop from the air for fish **10** while cormorants **11** duck dive from the surface.

The starfish **12** is a predator. Lurking under the sand are the rag worm **13**, razorshell **14**, lugworm **15** and cockle **16** which get food from eating sand or filtering water. Stranded above the high tide mark are whelk eggs **17**, plastic bottles **18** and nylon rope **19**. The 'mermaid's purse' **20** is an empty egg case of dog fish or skate and the

cuttlefish bone **21** is all that remains of a squid-like animal. Driftwood **22**, eaten by ship worms, lies by an oiled, dead, little tern **23**. Birds on the beach feed in different ways. The turnstone **24** hunts under rocks, while the redshank **25** with a larger bill, probes by the water line. Black-headed gulls **26** circle

Wildlife television presenters, such as Chris Packham (pictured), David Bellamy and Nick Baker raised the profile of Wildlife Watch

The Board was made up equally of representatives from the newspaper and the Society. The separate Watch Trust was considered essential in securing *The Sunday Times'* financial support.

In the next decade or so, the Watch club's national profile was enhanced by exciting, often large scale, Watch projects that were normally guaranteed exposure in *The Sunday Times*. On one occasion, the project resulted in the discovery of a species of ladybird new to the UK.

After ten years its membership had increased to more than 30,000, with more than 700 groups and more than 1,000 affiliated schools and youth groups. Almost all Trusts had a Watch organiser, coordinating a team of local leaders running groups, county-wide events and producing a local newsletter to complement *Watchword* – the house magazine. Its annual Watch Day gave members a chance for national gatherings on a grand scale. For example, in 1987, ten years after its incorporation, a Watch picnic at Coombe Park in Coventry attracted 3,000

'Watchers', drawn "partly by the helicopter arrival of President, DAVID BELLAMY"[192] (WILDLIFE WATCH).

BUILDING STAFF EXPERTISE

As might be expected, the growing confidence of the Society and the Trusts was evident too in the development of its core conservation work with increasing numbers of conservation staff, better networking and an ambitious range of activities and projects.

In 1973, in a further move to improve standards and professionalism, the Society and the LINCOLNSHIRE TRUST invited the Trusts' 11 existing conservation and field officers to a conference at Horncastle Residential College in Lincolnshire (CONFERENCES). The aim was to share their concerns, exchange ideas and develop their conservation management skills.

One outcome of the conference was a decision to prepare a CONSERVATION OFFICERS' BULLETIN (COB) to help "produce a standardisation of system and methodology over a range of common issues and

The first Conservation Officers Conference in Lincolnshire – delegates at the Trust's Moor Farm reserve, 1973

problems that will result in improved communication and efficiency and will lead to further improvement of the image of the County Trusts in the sphere of conservation".[193]

The second Conservation Officers' Conference was held in 1974 at Missenden Abbey in Buckinghamshire. By the third Conference at Dartington Hall in Devon in 1975, there were 23 Conservation Officers listed in the resulting COB. These were the first of more than 20 such annual conferences that would prove to be profoundly influential in the conservation and administrative development of the movement. The Conservation Conference was nearly always held in July and in most years seemed blessed with good weather. Days were long and productive with sleep in short supply as the world was put to rights until the early hours! They were important social occasions providing a vital support mechanism for a growing number of largely young, and sometimes inexperienced, conservation staff who frequently had a great deal of responsibility laid at their door.

The Society's staff team was growing too. Soon after SMITH took up his position as General Secretary in January 1975, Tim Sands joined Dawson as a second Assistant Secretary following four years as first Information Officer, and then Secretary, of the Council for Nature. He had played a prominent part in the voluntary bodies' campaign for The Conservation of Wild Creatures and Wild Plants Bill which finally received Royal Assent on his first day with the Society (CONSERVATION OF WILD CREATURES AND WILD

PLANTS ACT 1975). He was also the adviser to an ALL PARTY PARLIAMENTARY CONSERVATION AND WILDLIFE COMMITTEE of both Houses of Parliament. The Society's pioneering work for COMPREHENSIVE WILDLIFE LEGISLATION was gathering pace and Sands' valuable Parliamentary lobbying experience was exactly what the Society was looking for.

The CONSERVATION LIAISON COMMITTEE was continuing its busy programme. In 1969, as a result of the Committee's work, the Society had published a leaflet, *Scrub Clearance – a conservation code* and a booklet, a BIOLOGICAL SITES RECORDING SCHEME – *Technical Publication No 1*. These were followed the next year by the publication of *A Policy on Introduction to Nature Reserves – Technical Publication No 2*. The early 1970s saw the Committee pursue a wide range of activities. They included talks with the Masters of Otter Hounds Association about limiting hunting in the interest of protecting otters, backing for the formation of a new advisory committee on the conservation of reptiles and amphibians, and a conference with the Council for British Archaeology on the rapid destruction of old grasslands.

CONSERVATION AND AGRICULTURE

The Society and the movement generally remained anxious about the impact on wildlife of increasingly intensive agricultural practices. The Society had supported the groundbreaking Silsoe Conference held in 1969 at the National College of Agricultural Engineering in Bedfordshire. A small group, including Derek Barber (Ministry of Agriculture, Fisheries and Food), Norman Moore (Nature Conservancy), David Lea (RSPB) and Dick Cornwallis (LINCOLNSHIRE TRUST), had met

Above: The Conservation Liaison Committee's leaflet published for the 'Plant a Tree in '73' initiative

in late 1967 to discuss how to bring farmers and conservationists together to explore the common ground between them. The Silsoe Conference had been the key outcome and it was now spawning a raft of initiatives designed to improve the dialogue between the two sides. Among these was a speech on the relationship between farming and wildlife by the Minister of Agriculture which was "most favourably received on all sides".[194] As Moore put it, "the Silsoe experiment seemed too valuable to lose. We were determined that it should continue in some form, so we founded the Farming and Wildlife Advisory Group (FWAG)"[195] (see FARMING AND WILDLIFE). A farmer from Cambridgeshire, Jim Hall, was appointed as a national Farming and Wildlife Advisor. Initially his job was to organise national exercises similar to Silsoe "but soon we felt the way ahead lay in developing FWAGs at the county level".[196]

The Society supported FWAG and the appointment with time and money, but was concerned about the benefits for the Trusts and the possible mismatch between FWAG's executive and liaison roles. Its reservations were partly based on a view in some quarters that conservationists should spend less time seeking compromise solutions and more on fighting the core problem – the relentless drive for 'food from our own resources'. This was exemplified by the growth of agricultural production in the UK by 2.5 per cent per year, and in Europe by 'food-mountains'. There was, for example, half a million tonnes of 'unwanted' butter in Europe.

The Society's concerns were only slowly dispelled, helped by the determination and energy of the Society's Assistant Secretary, Wilf Dawson. In 1977, he became a member in his own right of a reconstituted, more independent, FWAG and became its Chairman in 1980. Throughout, Dawson was a strong proponent of local FWAGs and promoted the Trusts' involvement wherever possible. In 1983, he left the Society to become

Director of a new Farming and Wildlife Trust established by FWAG to promote the appointment of county advisors.

Agriculture was continuing to dominate the environmental agenda. In 1976, the Society was consulted in strict confidence by the Conservancy about a draft discussion paper *Nature Conservation and Agriculture.* This was rather worryingly subtitled '*an urgent new problem*'. The paper was launched by the Conservancy the following year, and coincided with another landmark document, *New Agricultural Landscapes,* from the Countryside Commission. Both emphasised the urgency of the situation with all the evidence pointing to "a serious decline in wildlife habitats on farmland in lowland Britain with no real sign as yet of an end to it".[197] The Conservancy called for a comprehensive national policy for rural land use. The Society welcomed both publications but was critical that the Conservancy could "virtually dismiss the concept of conservation zones, areas of countryside which retain more variety of wildlife habitats and landscape features".[198] Without realising it the Society was putting down an early marker for its 'larger area' concept that it would begin to promulgate more actively around the turn of the century.

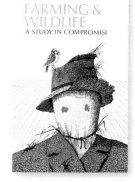

FARMING & WILDLIFE
A STUDY IN COMPROMISE

WATER, WETLANDS AND WILDLIFE

Three further important and inter-related conservation matters on the Society's radar at this time were the conservation of rivers and wildlife; the serious decline in otters; and the need for a comprehensive, rather than a piecemeal approach, to wildlife legislation. It is worth considering each of these three developments in a little more detail. They demonstrate a more concerted and outward-looking approach by the Society to its wildlife policy campaigning.

Opposite: Farmland wildlife, such as the brown hare, benefited from improved advice to farmers on wildlife management
Right: The edited version of the report of the Silsoe Conference

On the conservation of rivers and wildlife, SMITH relates how in talks on *Conservation Aspects of River Management* to the technical officers of River Authorities in 1972 and on *The Impact of Lowland River Management* to the British Trust for Ornithology's annual conference in 1974, he described the "effects of intensive land drainage and river management on birds and other wildlife".[199] Half of Britain's wetlands had been lost since 1945 and the unsympathetic management of rivers and streams was all too prevalent.

With the passage of the Water Act 1973 a series of new regional Water Authorities was being established. They had a re-stated duty 'to have regard' to the needs of nature conservation. In October 1974, the Society agreed to "take the initiative"[200] with the RSPB, initially on behalf of the Council for Nature, to arrange meetings with each of these new Authorities. By the end of the decade, formal arrangements involving regular meetings and early consultation over plans, projects and site visits, were established with eight of the ten regional authorities. The Society and the RSPB had also initiated a series of pioneering regional site-based river and wildlife exercises. These would eventually lead in 1984 to the joint publication of a much-needed comprehensive *Rivers and Wildlife Handbook* (WATER FOR WILDLIFE). It was an impressive achievement.

At the beginning of the whole exercise both the conservation interests and Water Authorities struggled to understand the complexities of each other's interests, the practical constraints and even, on occasions, each other's language. But the massive effort to bring both sides together proved worthwhile in the end. Close, often long-lasting, relationships were established between the Trusts, the RSPB and the new Water Authorities and their successors. An increasing number of the Water Authorities' capital and management schemes began to adopt alternative solutions and to integrate conservation measures at the design stage. In a few cases schemes were dropped altogether. It was an early example of conservationists moving outside their comfort zone and also an early example of the Trusts working collectively at a regional level within Water Authority boundaries.

The Society's autumn *Conservation Review* in 1976 featured articles on wetland flora in danger, dragonflies and otters. In the same year the Society's biennial conference in Newcastle adopted the future of wetlands as its theme as a contribution to the Council of Europe's European Wetlands Campaign. At the conference, Trust delegates were particularly exercised about the continuing decline in otter populations in Britain. Afterwards, Tim Sands worked closely with the Conservancy's Director of Conservation, Brian O'Connor, to encourage the formation of a Joint Otter Group, bringing together a team of ecologists and conservationists already investigating their decline. The Group, serviced by the Society, met for the first time in September 1976.

In the early 1950s, otters had been relatively abundant in Britain but it was felt that a crash in otter numbers, precisely linked to the years 1957 and 1958, had to be caused by a new environmental factor. The introduction of the organochlorine pesticide, dieldrin, for among other things sheep dipping, coincided particularly closely with this drop in numbers and was eventually identified as the key factor in the otter's decline. By 1966, most uses of organochlorine pesticides were banned and other factors assumed greater relevance and militated against the otter's recovery. What was lacking were secure breeding sites at frequent intervals with good cover and low levels of disturbance. There was a need to manage existing otter haunts and to reinstate suitable habitat elsewhere.

The Society's work with the Joint Otter Group was particularly significant in helping to hold together the different factions during these early years while the facts about the otter's biology, status and decline, and proposals for its recovery, were painstakingly worked out. The Group was also

A familiar tale. Above: The view of the River Lymn from Northorpe Bridge, 1964. Below: The same view, 1971. Rivers and wildlife across the UK were being damaged by unsympathetic management

important in securing legislative protection for the otter in January 1978. This was not the end of the Society and Trusts' involvement in otter conservation and later developments are described under OTTER CONSERVATION in Part III.

TOWARDS COMPREHENSIVE WILDLIFE LEGISLATION
The Society and the Trusts' involvement in otter conservation was the second of the three new conservation initiatives. The third was a campaign to see the introduction of COMPREHENSIVE WILDLIFE LEGISLATION. In 1970, the Society's CONSERVATION LIAISON COMMITTEE had established a working party and this had gathered examples of existing wildlife legislation from six continents, including most European countries. After gradually honing its ideas, it compiled a draft bill. By November 1972, the

Society felt confident enough to promote the idea more widely, including addressing an early meeting of the ALL-PARTY PARLIAMENTARY CONSERVATION AND WILDLIFE COMMITTEE of both Houses of Parliament. The Society's idea was to consolidate existing legislation, including existing bird legislation, and to extend this to invertebrates, vertebrates and plants. It also wanted the law to safeguard wildlife in sanctuary areas, including in nature reserves. The All-Party Parliamentary Conservation and Wildlife Committee's reaction was encouraging. It agreed that comprehensive wildlife legislation was "desirable and should be adopted"[201] and thought the Society's "proposals would form a suitable starting point".[202] After further work, the Society consulted a wide range of interested bodies and received a large measure of support. It was

sufficiently heartened by the response to keep pressing ahead and initiated high level discussions with the Conservancy and the Department of the Environment.

While the Society's proposals were generally well supported, there were also those who had reservations. For example, there was the danger that existing legislation, particularly bird legislation with its extensive case law, could just as easily be weakened as strengthened in the redrafting and Parliamentary process. In addition, on a more practical level, a Wild Plant Bill and a separate Wild Creatures Bill were going through Parliament. While they remained as separate bills and struggled for Parliamentary time, the Society's bill continued to be an attractive proposition. But when Peter Hardy, MP for the Rother Valley, secured first place in the ballot for Private Members' Bills, the situation changed. The two separate bills were withdrawn from the House of Lords and Hardy intoduced a combined CONSERVATION OF WILD CREATURES AND WILD PLANTS BILL that became law at the beginning of August 1975.

It was soon realised that, effectively, the opportunity to progress the Society's bill had gone. Nevertheless, the Society's drive for comprehensive legislation helped kick-start a move to further legislative reform. Although its bill was now mothballed, the Society's determination to see further improvements in the law, particularly better protection for wildlife habitats, was undiminished, and would lead ultimately to the Wildlife and Countryside Act 1981.

By its 1979–80 annual report, the Society considered "the decline in important wildlife habitats, and in particular the need for adequate protection of all Sites of Special Scientific Interest, to be the most urgent issue facing the nature conservation movement in Great Britain today".[203]

Something more had to be done. The Society started collecting evidence through the Trusts on the rate of loss and damage to SSSIs. It was confident that this was running at more than the

Opposite: The Society employed an Otter Project Officer in 1978, and serviced the Joint Otter Group

four per cent per year quoted by the Conservancy. During 1979, the Society's level of activity had increased dramatically. The Society had joined with the RSPB, Friends of the Earth and other voluntary bodies to launch "a coordinated campaign of unprecedented focus and ferocity"[204] to improve the legal protection afforded to wildlife, particularly through SSSIs. The campaign was to be waged through a new coalition, WILDLIFE LINK, forged for the purpose and chaired by ex-Labour minister, Lord Melchett. The Council for Nature had been languishing, ill-equipped to cope with the new wave of more radical organisations, and in financial difficulty. It was time for a leaner coalition, capable of uniting the campaigning nature conservation bodies, and responding forcefully to the increasing evidence of damage to SSSIs and a more demanding political climate. With the Society's active support, Wildlife Link held its inaugural meeting in August 1979. The Council for Nature was disbanded the same year.

This strong public campaign was reinforced by a requirement on the Government to implement a series of international agreements, notably the European Birds Directive adopted in April 1979. December 1979 saw the Society attend its first annual meeting of the European Environment Bureau (EEB) in Brussels (EUROPE AND THE SOCIETY). In June 1979, the new Conservative Government made the welcome announcement that it would introduce a comprehensive wildlife bill and in the autumn it published information about its content. The non-government organisations were, however, outraged. Not only was the Government planning to restrict additional protection to a few 'super' SSSIs, but its wildlife advisor – the Conservancy – was backing the Government's proposals.

In fact it was another year before the bill was introduced. In that time, the Society and others in the Wildlife Link 'family' engaged in intense lobbying, not just of politicians and the Conservancy but also of farming and landowning interests. In addition, the evidence from the ground, not least from the Trusts, confirmed that incidence of damage to SSSIs was far higher than the Government and the Conservancy were claiming. In some cases SSSIs were even being damaged or destroyed by operations grant-aided by the Government itself.

Just before the bill's Second Reading, Lord Melchett led a WILDLIFE LINK team at an historic meeting with the Conservancy at its Belgrave Square offices in London. The Conservancy was "on the back foot".[205] It now accepted that the proposals to protect only a selection of SSSIs did not go far enough and it agreed to ask the Government for further measures. In addition, the Conservancy now had evidence itself that SSSIs were being lost and damaged at an unacceptable rate. Its findings confirmed what the Trusts and others had been saying – that the decline was not at four per cent, but at an alarming eight per cent per year. The Government had to make concessions and give all SSSIs

increased protection. After more than 200 hours of debate and 2,000 amendments, the country's first comprehensive legislation for wildlife – the Wildlife & Countryside Act – became law in October 1981.

A NATURE REVIEW

It had been over 30 years since the Nature Reserves Investigation Committee compiled its 1945 national list of important wildlife sites. A similar time had elapsed since the publication of the Government's reports on nature conservation – *Conservation of Nature in England and Wales* (Command Paper 7122) and *Conservation of Nature in Scotland* (Command Paper 7235). The Conservancy had begun a further major scientific review of sites of special importance for nature conservation in 1967 (see Chapter 4). It needed more robust data with which to fight high profile development proposals. There were plans, for example, for a third London Airport and

Destruction of ancient woodland at Monks Park Wood, Suffolk

various water impounding schemes similar to the one that was going ahead at COW GREEN in Upper Teesdale.

After a long gestation period, the results were published in 1977. *A Nature Conservation Review* was an impressive achievement, identifying 735 sites chosen to "represent all the main types of natural and semi-natural vegetation with their characteristic communities of plants and animals".[206] The Review was published by the Nature Conservancy Council – the successor body to the Nature Conservancy (STATUTORY NATURE CONSERVATION AGENCIES).

At the end of 1976, whilst this was going on, the Society had determined that 181 reserves held by itself and the Trusts were, in whole or in part, Nature Conservation Review sites. In the circumstances, the Society considered it a good time to look again at the contribution that its nature reserves, and more particularly those owned and managed by the Trusts, could make to a national reserve network. TED SMITH observes in his memoirs that, despite the need for the Society and Trusts to adopt an ever growing set of measures to influence the treatment of the environment, "nature reserves had stood the test of time".[207] A case was put to the Conservancy who offered a contract to the Society for a two-year study (NATURE RESERVES STUDY). A young biologist, Dr Cameron Easton, was appointed as Project Officer to collect and analyse data.

The results of the study were discussed by the Society's biennial conference held in Bromsgrove, near Birmingham, in 1978. It was the first major national conference on nature reserves for 30 years. The conference had three main themes: first, the value, selection and function of sites for nature conservation; second, safeguarding and managing sites; and third, the resources needed for acquiring and managing nature reserves. The conference also considered an impressive collection of papers under these three themes. These were published with the programme ahead of the conference and its findings were incorporated into

a two-part report on the Nature Reserves Study, published in 1979.

A NEW GENERAL SECRETARY

By 1978, Smith had completed four of his five years as General Secretary. He was beginning to feel that for both the Society and himself it was time for a change. He had largely achieved what he set out to do more than 20 years before, "to help promote the formation of a country-wide network of Wildlife Trusts, and at the same time to give new life and new purpose to the near moribund SPNR to act as the Trusts' national association".[208] He decided to leave his full-time position but did not leave altogether. For three years he was a part-time Special Advisor concerned mainly with the completion of the Nature Reserves Study and a handbook to Trust reserves (NATURE RESERVE GUIDES) eventually published in 1982. After that, he remained on the Society's Executive Committee until 1995 and on its Council as an Honorary Vice President until 1998.

In 1990, the Society would award Smith the first-ever Christopher Cadbury medal for services to nature conservation. The accompanying citation summed up his many achievements for the Society and the Trusts. He "has given his all to nature conservation and has probably had more influence than anyone else on the events which have determined the important role of the voluntary nature conservation movement in the British Islands today"[209] (CHRISTOPHER CADBURY MEDAL CITATIONS).

The Society looked around for a replacement General Secretary, and soon found one. He was FRANK PERRING, a regular broadcaster, active member of the NORTHAMPTONSHIRE and the CAMBRIDGE AND ISLE OF ELY TRUSTS and Head of the Biological Records Centre at Monks Wood. He was already well known to the Society and the Trusts when he took up his position in January 1979.

Perring's term, however, did not start well, through no fault of his own. The country was

Frank Perring joined the Society as its General Secretary in 1979

experiencing massive inflation. Since 1973, prices had risen faster than at any peacetime period in the previous three centuries. The economic crisis had resulted in cuts to the Conservancy's budget. PERRING's arrival came soon after an announcement that the Conservancy would be unable to fulfil its promise to provide capacity grants for all Trusts. This was a devastating blow. SMITH had spent the last three years negotiating an agreement with the Conservancy which had culminated in a high-level Ministerial meeting. On the table had been potential funding of £40,000 over three years for the Society (£8,000 of this to the SCOTTISH TRUST). All Trusts would also receive £5,000 each for each of three years to develop their capacity "to tackle important tasks for the NCC and bring identifiable benefit to their own organisation".[210] Smith describes in his memoirs how it was a "somewhat sour note on which to end my span as General Secretary. Although it (this) was completely outside my control, I nevertheless felt a sense of responsibility for the disappointed expectations of the Trusts who had been waiting to enter the scheme".[211]

One of Perring's first tasks, therefore, was to try to salvage something from the wreckage. There were letters from the Trusts to their MPs, questions asked on two occasions in Parliament and correspondence between the Society's President and the Minister of State at the Department of Environment, Dennis Howell. By the autumn of 1979, Perring was able to write in his first opening column in *Conservation Review*, "by a supreme effort from all concerned it was possible to ensure that seventeen Trusts received three-year grants – but for the time being the rest must wait until, as we hope, this imaginative scheme begins again".[212]

CHALLENGES AND NEW OPPORTUNITIES

As the decade drew to a close, the general economic gloom and the "deep sense of injustice felt by the Trusts which did not receive capacity grants",[213] cast a shadow over the Society and the movement as a whole. Characteristically, Perring was upbeat, determined to fight the Trusts' corner and to turn the situation around. An early meeting was sought with the new Secretary of State for the Environment, Michael Heseltine, to "impress upon him the contribution the voluntary movement, and particularly the Trusts, can make to nature conservation. At a time when they (the Government) are seeking ways of reducing expenditure we shall be claiming that the last organisations to be cut are the voluntary bodies which give such good value for money".[214] Perring believed that to justify such a claim it was no time to sit back waiting for government money to flow again. "We hope it will, we know it ought to – but it may not".[215]

Despite the setback, Perring was still inheriting an organisation that had made huge strides over the past decade or so. Perring himself was to describe the Society as 'a sleeping giant'.

In 1978, the final major piece of the Trust jigsaw had been put into place at a special conference at Queens University, Belfast. It was the launch of the movement's 41st member, the ULSTER TRUST for Nature Conservation, by one of the Society's Vice Presidents, SIR DAVID ATTENBOROUGH. Speakers at the conference also included Ian Mercer of the DEVON TRUST and Bernard Gilchrist of the Scottish Trust.

Trust membership, land holdings and influence had all grown enormously over the decade. Membership and reserves had increased by

ULSTER TRUST FOR NATURE CONSERVATION
Organising Secretary: Maurice McNeely, 67A Huntley Road.
Banbridge, Co. Down, BT32 3UR

An early poster promoting the Ulster Trust, formed in 1978

Government's MSC schemes. Ironically, the country's financial malaise – which lay behind the demise of the Conservancy's capacity grant initiative – was now the very factor fuelling the increase in the Trusts' activity. Rising staffing levels and a corresponding increase in capacity enabled them to take forward a wide range of projects that only a few months before had been put on hold.

PERRING now put the finishing touches to the Society's first three-to-five-year rolling programme. It still distinguished two functions for the Society. "A dual role as the association of the Nature Conservation Trusts (NAMES OF THE TRUSTS) and as the principal voluntary body concerned nationwide with all aspects of nature conservation".[216] Rather than seeing its role as the Trusts' association as the means to achieve its second aspiration, the tendency was still to view the two roles as separate. For now, though, the trick would be to wake 'the sleeping giant' without the Trusts feeling that the Society was pursuing a separate agenda.

substantially more than 300 per cent. Many Trusts were recognising the opportunities presented by the launch in October 1975 of the Government's Job Creation Programme (JCP). Under this, the Manpower Services Commission (MSC) could finance full-time temporary jobs on projects that benefitted the community for people who would otherwise be unemployed (EMPLOYMENT SCHEMES).

One unexpected benefit of the stalled Conservancy capacity grant initiative was that many of the Trusts, who were denied Conservancy funding, found themselves with relatively sophisticated forward-looking plans in their pending trays. They were now able, in some instances, to dust these down and re-work them to use when applying for JCP projects.

By 1980, the Trusts employed 150 staff. Only three Trusts were without at least one professional administration or conservation officer. In the previous three years they had provided employment for an estimated 460 young people under the

CHAPTER 6

Widening the horizons 1980–1989

Whenever I find myself growing grim about the mouth; whenever it is a damp, drizzly November in my soul... then, I account it high time to get to sea as soon as I can.

From *Moby Dick* by Herman Melville, 1851

In 1980, conservationists were facing up to an uncomfortable truth – despite their efforts, habitat destruction was continuing at an accelerating pace. The past decade had underlined the fact that simply designating areas as nature reserves or Sites of Special Scientific Interest was not enough. It was true that the public were more aware of the threats facing wildlife, and that conservationists were taking an increasingly resourceful approach to their work. But all the designated sites and all the efforts of conservationists could not stem this tide of destruction. Those who owned and worked the land had to be convinced that they had some responsibility for conservation too. Politicians also had to see conservation as a mainstream issue – one that voters cared about. All sectors of society, including conservationists, had to appreciate that conservation, on the scale now required, would need new thinking and more money – in particular, more public money. The conservation movement, having become more politically sophisticated, was now going to have to embrace the world of economics.

The omens were not good. Despite being under pressure to meet commitments to implement European legislation, the Government, and even more worryingly the Conservancy, were having to be pushed into strengthening the proposals for new wildlife law. This pressure was coming from a

Opposite: A whole new world – kelp forest, Farne Islands. In the 1980s, the Trusts began to have a national influence on marine conservation

united voluntary movement under the WILDLIFE LINK coalition. Wildlife Link had come into existence in 1979 for this very task. Its formation and lobbying activities reflected the growing strength and political maturity of the wider voluntary conservation movement.

The resulting Wildlife and Countryside Act 1981 was the most comprehensive piece of legislation of its type to date. It brought together in one place species, habitat and wider countryside measures and established a more formal notification system for SSSIs. The political framework for discussions on countryside and wildlife issues would never be the same again. Nevertheless, it was hugely frustrating that more was not achieved. Perhaps the Act that emerged was not, as Rose and Secret were to describe it, "a wretched and dishevelled piece of legislation".[217] But for many SSSIs it would prove to be too little, too late.

The landowning lobby had won some key concessions. At its core the new legislation was dependent on a voluntary approach and many sites could still be damaged with impunity. For example, a new emergency procedure for halting SSSI destruction would only apply to certain SSSIs. If a case reached court, the punishment for damaging a site unlawfully would be a paltry £500. The payment to landowners for entering a land management agreement was in the form of compensation for 'profits foregone'. This was an invitation to landowners to threaten damaging schemes that might never have otherwise seen the light of day. Matters were compounded by the fact that in 1978, while the Ministry of Agriculture, Fisheries and Food's Improvement Grants ran at £540 million, the total budget from which the Conservancy had to fund SSSI agreements was a mere £7 million. As a result, despite the new legislation, the year 1983–84 saw no let up in the damage suffered by SSSIs. The Conservancy was reporting that 156 notified or potential SSSIs had been damaged, 67 of them seriously, and by the end of the year 46 had had to be de-notified.

The feelings of frustration over the new Wildlife and Countryside Act 1981 and the continuing destruction of SSSIs spilled over into expressions of anger across both the environmental and farming communities. In 1980, Marion Shoard had published her contentious and influential book, *The Theft of the Countryside*, describing how the English countryside was being destroyed by a 'far reaching agricultural revolution'. In 1982, a conservative MP, Richard Body, weighed in with *Agriculture: The Triumph and the Shame*. Later, in February 1983, angry farmers on West Sedgemoor in Somerset would burn effigies of leading figures in the Conservancy and the RSPB to protest at the moor's designation as an SSSI.

During the passage of the new legislation, the politicians had failed to grasp just how much agriculture was changing. Despite the destruction,

The 1980s saw continuing destruction of SSSIs. In 1986, following damage to Stubbers Green Bog SSSI, the Birmingham and Black Country Trust stepped in to successfully protect the remainder of the site

Sheail thought that Shoard's book reflected "a sense that the dominance of farming in rural affairs was beginning to slip".[218] The coming decade would be dominated by the challenges thrown up by these changes and, in particular, new European initiatives for controlling over-production and encouraging more environmentally-sustainable farming.

The Society was amongst those that took up the challenge. Encouraged by Dawson and Streeter, among others, it established a study group under the chairmanship of Lord Melchett who had led for the Opposition front bench in the House of Lords on the Wildlife and Countryside Bill. The group's remit was to look at the impact of the market economy on rural land-use policy. Its findings, published in the Society's consultative paper *Towards 2000*, argued strongly, like Shoard, for the Government to support environmentally-sensitive farming. More controversially, it also argued for planning controls to curb fundamental changes to agricultural land in order to protect its landscape and wildlife heritage. The paper went on to provide the foundation for much of the Society's future agricultural policy, although the Society never formally adopted the policy of seeking planning controls over agriculture. The Society's involvement in agricultural reform and its various agricultural campaigns are covered in FARMING AND WILDLIFE in Part III.

TRUSTS ON THE NATIONAL STAGE

The Society had spent a large amount of its time over the previous two decades assisting the development of the individual Trusts. It had successfully sought funds from a wide variety of sources to help increase both its own capacity and that of the Trusts. In particular, it had helped Trusts to increase the extent of their landholdings to an impressive 1,300 nature reserves by 1981. The Society had also helped the Trusts to take on staff to manage these sites and to continue to expand their sphere of influence beyond the confines of their nature reserves and their local communities. One new source of funds for the Society in this period (and one that would

Ebernoe Common. In 1981, the Sussex Trust acquired 177 acres of this woodland and wood pasture nature reserve, home to 14 species of bat including Bechstein's and barbastelle

continue and increase well into the future) was an annual donation of £2,000 in 1978–79, rising to £6,000 in 1984–85, from the Moorgate Fund. The Fund had been established by Sir John Ellerman, an expert in rodents and a member of the Society from 1937 until his death in 1973.

However, for the movement to realise its potential collective strength, it needed to help those Trusts still in their infancy; improve the networking of information and expertise; and raise its profile nationally and locally. While the foundations might now be in place for the construction of a more substantial nationwide Trust movement, a roller-coaster of a decade lay ahead for the Society. It would see fundamental changes in the Society's relationship with the Trusts; the Trusts growing and increasingly determined to influence the Society's national agenda; and the movement appealing to a wider audience.

FRANK PERRING believed the Society's particular task was to establish the movement as a national force – the principal voluntary body concerned nationwide with all aspects of nature conservation. Of course the Society must continue to service the Trusts' needs more directly. But the challenge, as he saw it, was to broaden the movement's influence and to reach out to a new generation of 'environmentalists'. The debate that was raging over the 'theft of the countryside', and the Government's inadequate response to calls for agricultural reform, added weight to Perring's argument that the movement had to

Towards 2000, the Society's first major report on agriculture and nature conservation

95

step outside its comfort zone to increase its reach and bring about change in national policies on land management and the environment.

Developing the Society's national footprint and representing the Trusts' interests on the national stage, would, PERRING believed, bring additional benefits to the Trusts. These were more resources at both the national and local level and a more sympathetic political environment in which to work. Over the remaining seven years of his contract, Perring instinctively and relentlessly pursued opportunities that would achieve these ends. Sometimes this was done without waiting for his colleagues to catch up with his ideas, or without much overt interest in the financial consequences of his plans. However, it was always done passionately and with the best interests of wildlife, the Society and the Trusts at heart.

Many in the Society and the Trusts went along with Perring's thinking, believing that the Society had until then punched far below its weight. In particular, they were keen to see the Society achieve a higher political and media profile on behalf of the movement. The Trusts were happy to see the Society spearhead national activity when it was straightforward and the objectives were clearly understood, as in the case of the Society's campaign to improve the Wildlife and Countryside Bill. The Society had engaged extensively with Trusts on proposals for comprehensive legislation over several years and consequently they were well aware of, and had contributed to, the case being made for Government to improve the protection of SSSIs. Many Trusts had supported the Society by supplying data, sometimes for the first time, on the damage and loss of SSSIs and by lobbying their MPs at the appropriate moments. As well as securing increased protection for wildlife, Trusts welcomed the increased media attention and influence – at both local and national levels – that the campaign brought about.

Collective action for the movement required the Society to listen to grassroots thinking and to build a broad consensus on the way forward.

But, perhaps unsurprisingly, this did not always happen. Two particular examples illustrate this.

BREAKING NEW GROUND

The first example involves Peterborough Development Corporation (PDC) and its proposals for a country park at Ferry Meadows in the Nene valley. Perring saw the park as a showcase for bringing wildlife and people closer together and as a suitable place for a new headquarters for the Society. Ferry Meadows was situated in a central location in England and in an area attracting 350,000 visitors a year. By 1981, Perring had secured an offer from the PDC to build a new national office for the Society in the country park. The idea was that the Society would then rent this from the PDC.

Difficulties arose because the PDC needed to go ahead with the development before the Society had the formal agreement and the finances ready to make such a move possible. In the event, Perring secured an alternative offer. The PDC would fund the Society to coordinate interpretative services on the Ferry Meadows site and the Society subsequently agreed to take on a three-year contract.

In the first season, "materials and guidance were given to seventy school parties. . . Ferry Meadows was also the venue for a one-day course on interpretation for Trust officers and volunteers".[219] It also paved the way in 1987 for the Society to pick up on a NORTHAMPTONSHIRE TRUST initiative to encourage communities to adopt local 'pocket parks'. This led to the Society launching a more ambitious Parish Pocket Parks (PPP) project, sponsored by Schering Agriculture.

But the decision to go ahead with the Ferry Meadows project had been made reluctantly. There were concerns that the project was diverting the Society away from its mainstream national activities and that it would have been better if it had been developed and managed locally. In 1988, the PDC transferred what had now become Nene Park to an independent Trust on which the Society and Trusts were represented. The Society then 'converged' the Northamptonshire pocket park initiative and the Society's PPP project. This prompted one member of the Executive Committee to describe the 'rescue' of the Parish Pocket Park project as a "salutary lesson for the Society – a good idea had initially not been thought through and not promoted properly".[220] However, despite these reservations the whole episode was a prelude to the movement under-taking even bigger and better community projects in the years that followed.

A second example involved a development that would have far reaching and long-lasting consequences for the whole Trust movement.

During the 1970s, attitudes to open spaces in urban areas and their value for wildlife and people had changed. The Conservancy had launched an urban programme in 1978 with a pioneering study of the natural history of Birmingham and the Black Country by the naturalist 'Bunny' Teagle, evocatively named *The Endless Village*.

Trusts had traditionally drawn their membership from a white, middle-class, middle-aged and largely rural strata of society. Now new groups were springing up that were engaging the large number of people living in cities and towns who were actively interested in environmental issues and wanted opportunities to enjoy 'green-space' on their doorstep. They were often younger and from a wide range of social and ethnic backgrounds. In Birmingham, for example, the publication of *The Endless Village* led to the establishment of just such a body – a new Urban Wildlife Group – which would later become the BIRMINGHAM AND BLACK COUNTRY TRUST (URBAN AREAS AND NATURE CONSERVATION).

PERRING, predictably, was among those keen to seize these new opportunities. He reflected that "when historians look back on the growth of our movement, they may well identify 1980 as the year in which 'nature conservation went to town'".[221]

Conservation work at Brandon Hill in Bristol, 1980s. In 1981, the reserve was acquired by the Avon Trust as one of the UK's first urban nature reserves

He encouraged a swift move by the Society to adopt this urban theme for the Trusts' 1980 biennial conference in Nottingham (CONFERENCES). In May, the movement welcomed its first predominantly urban Trust – the AVON TRUST – as a member. Summing up at the Nottingham Conference, Perring thought the climate was right for the Trusts to "become involved in a new type of conservation in towns. This does not involve buying or leasing reserves but lending their expertise and support to local action groups of all kinds whose immediate aims are a healthy environment for themselves rather than wildlife. Once involved, the Trusts can show that the two run side-by-side, thus protecting areas for wildlife and finding new recruits for conservation at the same time".[222]

In some counties such as Lancashire, Trusts were already embracing urban conservation and, in others, Trusts welcomed the new urban groups and integrated them into their own structure. There were also proposals for further new Trusts in Cleveland and London as well as in Birmingham. The Cleveland (later the TEES VALLEY) Trust was welcomed into the fold in December 1981. The LONDON TRUST and Urban Wildlife Group in Birmingham (BIRMINGHAM AND BLACK COUNTRY TRUST) became members in late 1983.

However, in other areas several existing Trusts, "nominally trying to cover. . . conurbations,

resisted change because of fears of loss of members to the new Trusts".[223] There remained those in the Society and the Trusts who were unsettled by these new developments. They saw them as unstructured and a threat to traditional values. They feared they would drain the Society's already stretched financial resources and turn the movement's attention away from the more scientific approach to nature conservation that they were accustomed to.

By 1985, there were three types of urban conservation organisation emerging – new Trusts like Avon, Cleveland, Birmingham and London; urban groups within existing Trusts, like those in Exeter, Leicester, Lincoln, Nottingham, Reading and Telford; and an increasing number of independent groups, like Leeds, Norwich and Sheffield. All had similar interests but lacked a common forum.

However, such a forum emerged in June 1985 with the formation of the Fairbrother Group at a meeting in Birmingham. The Group took its name from Nan Fairbrother's seminal 1970 book, *New Lives, New Landscapes*, and was formed to advance the cause of urban nature conservation. The meeting considered proposals which, if accepted, would have led to the formation of an Association of Urban Wildlife Groups – independent of the Society. No final decision was taken at that meeting, but the Society's hand had been forced. Until now, despite Perring's enthusiasm for the new urban movement, it had continued to procrastinate. Now, if it failed to take on the responsibility and find resources to do the job, the Fairbrother Group would set up a new association itself. It was agreed to meet again in November in Norwich and, after "considerable debate and careful negotiation, all agreed that (the Society) should be asked to become the umbrella body".[224] There is little doubt that if this agreement had not been reached "the voluntary conservation

movement would have been split between urban and countryside groups to the disadvantage of both".[225]

The Society responded positively to the challenge. An urban steering group was soon established and three-year funding of nearly £70,000 was successfully secured from the Conservancy and the Carnegie Trust. This would support the new post of an Urban Wildlife Development Officer to service the urban groups (whether directly affiliated to the Society or not) and the setting up of new groups. The post would be based initially in Birmingham.

Gradually over the next decade or so the urban groups, and the principles to which they aspired, would be assimilated into the Trust movement. The development of the urban conservation movement is described in more detail under URBAN AREAS AND NATURE CONSERVATION in Part III.

NEW PUBLISHING VENTURES

But we have moved ahead. In 1980, despite the economic gloom that still pervaded the country, the fortunes of the Society and the Trusts were surprisingly good. There is no doubt that some "Trusts were looking anxiously at their bank balances and were preparing to tighten their belts",[226] but the public's interest in, and concern for, wildlife and environmental issues was growing steadily. The Trusts were successfully widening their appeal to new audiences. In 1980, there was a net increase of 9,000 members, almost double the average annual increases of the previous three years.

The decade had begun on a high note for the Society too. It was a prominent member of WILDLIFE LINK, the consortium of environmental groups, including the RSPB and Friends of the Earth that was strongly influencing the political process surrounding the Wildlife and Countryside Act 1981. That process would lead to 1981 being dubbed the 'year when wildlife came to Westminster'. The experience of those involved in these events would mould their future careers and the camaraderie and trust built up at the time would have benefits for the movement for several years to come.

Opposite: The London Trust's Camley Street reserve was created in 1984 from an old coal yard in the shadow of King's Cross and St Pancras Stations and King's Cross Gas Works

Bishop Middleham quarry, County Durham – home to rare orchid species and one of many Trust reserves featured in the *MacMillan Guide*

In April 1981, the Society unveiled its new name, the Royal Society for Nature Conservation at a reception supported by Martini & Rossi in their suite in New Zealand House, London (NAMES OF THE SOCIETY). Her Majesty the Queen had bestowed the title 'Royal' on the Society the previous December. At the same event the Society also launched a new colour magazine, NATURAL WORLD, published by the *Illustrated London News* to replace *Conservation Review*.

By the fourth issue, 37 of the 42 Trusts at the time were taking the new

The first edition of *Natural World* in 1981

magazine and sending it to their members. At the end of the year, the Society also published its first *Nature Reserves Handbook* (NATURE RESERVE GUIDES), edited by TED SMITH, describing more than 350 of the movement's reserves. The handbook proved a valuable membership recruiting tool in the coming months and the magazine was more effective than *Conservation Review* in networking local and national news throughout the movement.

The publishers, Macmillan, were also preparing an ambitious guide to nature reserves managed by both statutory and non-statutory organisations. This would be the first ever comprehensive guide to many of Britain's finest wildlife sites. A number of Trusts were caught in the difficult position of wishing to promote the majority of their nature reserves, whilst at the same time needing to be very careful with information about a minority of very sensitive sites. Although some of these concerns were slow to be resolved, *The Macmillan Guide to Britain's Nature Reserves*, describing some 2,000 sites, was published in 1984 with the support of the Gulf Oil Corporation and 'in association' with the Society. There was also an agreement for royalties from the *Guide* to be paid into a Macmillan Fund to assist Trusts with interpretative projects (see also NATURE OF BRITAIN BOOKS for more information about a series of books published under the Society's name between 1982 and 1991).

GATHERING STORM CLOUDS

At the turn of the decade the Society's finances seemed to be holding up surprisingly well in the face of the country's financial blues. For example, it had successfully negotiated an on-pack promotion with Weetabix. The sales operation was also performing strongly, helped by a rapid increase in wholesale purchases by Trusts and a doubling of sales turnover since 1977.

On the back of this, in 1980 the Society felt emboldened to go ahead with a major reorganisation of its sales business at a total cost of £60,000. This included building a new warehouse, covering 5,000 square feet, to handle pre-Christmas trading at the end of the year. However, a steel strike interrupted construction and it was not fully operational until 1981.

The Treasurer believed that "taking a conservative view of the growth in our sales operation, this investment could be met out of profits over the next three years".[227] In the circumstances, the decision seemed reasonable, even business-like. There appeared to be every reason to feel confident about the future. After all the Society had never been in serious financial difficulties in the past, why should things be any different now?

In fact, financial storm clouds were gathering. For example, the Society knew that a grant from

the Conservancy would have to be renegotiated in 1981 with no guarantee that it would be renewed. The Society's central budget for 1980–81 was showing a significant projected deficit – perhaps not surprising with inflation in the country running at a historic high, and it faced possible cost-of-living awards to staff of more than 15 per cent. PERRING was also keen to press on with his ambitious plans. He was persuasive in his argument that good money would follow good projects. Finally, despite the Executive's "general feeling. . . that the extra investment in sales was only acceptable on the basis of the sales operation being self-financing",[228] no formal mechanism was put in place to ensure that this would be the case. If the sales operation did collapse for any reason the Society's main account would still have to pick up the bill.

Meanwhile, differences had developed between the passionate and entrepreneurial Perring and the careful and legalistic Chairman of the Executive, WALTER LANE. In some respects this reflected some of the tensions being felt as a result of the steady transition towards a more staff-dependant movement. In the Society, with notable exceptions, the view, encouraged from the top by CHRISTOPHER CADBURY and Lane, was that the honorary officers still ran the day-to-day operation with staff employed to deliver their decisions. It had only been ten years since Cadbury had spoken proudly of a "voluntary movement dependent on voluntary workers. . . not run, like so many other national organisations, from a head office manned by paid officials".[229]

Right: An on-pack promotion in 1979 saw the Society's logo on 22 million packs of Weetabix

New warehousing under construction at the Society's headquarters in Nettleham, Lincolnshire, 1980

The time when a clear distinction would be made between the honorary officers as Trustees of the charity – overseeing its governance and strategy – and a chief executive supporting this process and taking operational responsibility, was still some way off.

In the last few months of 1981 the storm arrived. Sales, particularly to mail order customers, dropped dramatically. Budgeted profits of £36,000 collapsed to a £22,000 deficit. This swing in fortunes would be the main reason why the Society's income and expenditure accounts for the end of the financial year showed an overall deficit of £59,500 on a turnover of £498,000.

When the full extent of the financial problems became clear in October and November 1981, alarm bells were set ringing. Some staff were put onto part-time working and senior staff were instructed to prepare a report on how "savings can best be made".[230] Several Trustees felt that as volunteers they were being marginalised by Perring; that he was promoting the Society's own growth at the expense of its role as the Trusts' association; and that not all of the staff's hard work "had been used to the best advantage".[231]

TO CALMER WATERS
In mid-November, CADBURY wrote to all Trusts informing them that it was the unanimous decision of the Executive to recommend to Council the adoption of the following aims and objectives:

"Purpose and role
The Society is primarily the Trusts' association, its purpose being to assist Trusts in securing their aims. This gives it a dual role to:
a) service the Trusts, and in this to be both initiatory as well as responsive;
b) give Trusts a collective identity by developing a national image.

Size of organisation
The Trusts should be the growth points. The Society should maintain a small and highly professional organisation to retain clarity of purpose and a sense of service to Trusts.

Volunteers
Volunteers should be used to the maximum, as in the Trusts, not only on essential committees but also in the creation of work and the Society should be organised to facilitate and encourage this".[232]

Almost without realising it, Cadbury was finally laying to rest the 'old Society' and re-establishing a clear, more user-friendly purpose for the movement as a whole. The relationship between the Society and the Trusts had changed fundamentally.

The "extremely serious position"[233] that now faced the organisation had to be confronted. The Society was anxious to be seen to be in an open and listening mode. The Trusts were consulted about what they wanted from their national association and what they were prepared to pay for.

Internally, there was a determination by the Executive to get a grip of the situation. A working party, chaired by the Society's HONORARY TREASURER, ANDREW RUCK, urgently reviewed the situation and made 23 recommendations, all but one of which were taken on board by Council. This process was strengthened by a further working party appointed to look at the finances, chaired by John McMeeking. In March 1983, it was agreed that "the budget for 1983–84 onwards must be balanced; Trusts should meet one-third of the costs of the services to Trusts through capitation, but should know the costs of these services, and if the costs are not acceptable should decide which services should be discontinued; Sales and Conservation accounts should be separated".[234]

During 1983, MICHAEL BENDIX took over from Andrew Ruck as the Honorary Treasurer, but by October 1983 he too was replaced by ALAN NEWTON, who was about to retire as the Senior Manager at Barclays Bank in Lincoln. Important changes were also made to the staff structure. With Wilf Dawson's move to be Director of a new Trust set up by the Farming and Wildlife Group to promote the appointment of county advisers, it was agreed that the number of senior staff should be reduced from four to three. PERRING was to remain as General Secretary, but with additional duties as Fundraising Manager; Tim Sands, one of the two remaining Assistant Secretaries, was to fill a new post of Deputy General Secretary; and

the other Assistant Secretary, Andy Wilson, was to take on major responsibility for financial management. Despite its scant resources, the Society also decided to strengthen its conservation team by appointing Andrew Heaton from Sevenoaks Wildfowl Reserve as its first Conservation Officer.

Two new Committees – a Finance Committee and an Appeal Committee – were established to improve the financial and fundraising advice available to the Society. It was also decided that the Society should raise £50,000 to match £50,000 offered by an anonymous donor (later revealed as money from the LAND FUND) and that this £100,000 should be used to restore capital reserves and run a fundraising campaign. It was agreed to set up a Fundraising Unit to assist Trusts with fundraising, to coordinate a central appeal and to build up the Society's own income.

Despite the energy invested in reorganisation, relatively little thought was given to the role and responsibilities of the Trustees. Instead, most of the solutions so far had focused on staff accountability, structure and fundraising. Nevertheless, the process led to a clearer understanding of the Society-Trust relationship and the potential for better financial management. The Society was now more aware than ever of its dependence on the Trusts for its funding, status and credibility.

By the end of the financial year to 1984, although the sales figures again showed a substantial loss, the separate conservation accounts were in the black and the Society's reserves had been restored to more than £70,000.

A NEW FUNDRAISING ERA

In the circumstances, there had been little surprise when WALTER LANE, Chairman of the Executive Committee, resigned at the end of 1981. CHRISTOPHER CADBURY had stepped in whilst the search for Lane's successor was underway. A replacement came in 1983 with the appointment of DUNSTAN ADAMS, a retired academic who had been active in the YORKSHIRE TRUST. His carefully crafted prologue to his first meeting in April 1983, while somewhat old fashioned in style, set the scene for his term of office. A stickler for procedure, precise in his use of language and determined to tackle what he saw as a need for greater control of Society business, he was a strong believer that each Trust was "autonomous and different".[235] We do a "grave disservice, if in an attempt to make life easier for ourselves we seek to impose (or even encourage) unnecessary uniformity upon our corporate members".[236] The word 'unnecessary' had been chosen carefully. The Executive, PERRING and the staff welcomed Adams' courteous and democratic approach and his recognition of the "need for friendliness and good humour".[237] The financial problems and major reviews of the previous few years had, at times, soured relations between honorary officers and staff. But Adams, with his fellow officers, was now able to secure accountability in a way that channelled Perring's energy and supported and encouraged him to fulfil his undoubted vision for the Society and the Trusts.

By 1984, plans to launch local fundraising appeals had been developed with BBOWT, CUMBRIA, DURHAM, NORTHAMPTONSHIRE and WORCESTERSHIRE TRUSTS. An Appeal Steering Committee was also undertaking the preparatory work for a proposed 'coordinated central appeal'. This was to be a genuinely large-scale national appeal aiming to raise £10 million over five years: £5 million raised nationally and £5 million through local and regional appeals. In this one major project, now called the BRITISH WILDLIFE APPEAL (BWA), Perring could see a way of raising money for conservation and also meeting some of the wider goals set for the movement at the turn of the decade: a higher profile, greater influence and more national cohesion.

There was also a practical reason why the appeal was needed. More land, particularly SSSIs, had been coming onto the market, partly as a result of the economic recession but also as a result of the passing of the Wildlife and Countryside Act in 1981. The situation was exacerbated by the

Government's instruction to the Forestry Commission to raise £82 million over four years by selling assets, including many of its woodlands. The Society conducted a survey of the Trusts' negotiations for land. It revealed that at the end of 1982, Trusts were considering the purchase of 37 sites at a cost of £1 million. A year later, despite many successful purchases (65 reserves in 1982), this had increased to more than 50 sites requiring £1.25 million.

The Society used this data and the "full weight of its implications"[238] in discussions with the Conservancy, Countryside Commission, WWF and National Heritage Memorial Fund to try to secure additional funding for land purchase. Support from this quarter, already running at £273,000 in 1982, increased to £314,000 a year later. Welcome though they were, in the circumstances, the movement could no longer rely on these funds alone. It now had to look to its BWA to supplement the money coming from these grant-giving bodies.

The BWA demanded careful planning and extensive engagement with the Trusts. There was a mixture of excitement and relief when the pieces of the jigsaw began to fall into place. A Director of the Appeal, John Guy, was appointed. Rent-free offices in Bury Street in the City of London were secured thanks to the Honorable Vincent Weir, who also became Chairman of the high-powered Appeal Steering Committee. Endorsement and offers of direct support came from celebrities, such as Monty Python star, Michael Palin, Goodies star and naturalist, Bill Oddie and television presenter, Julian Pettifer. Public affairs, advertising and fundraising companies also offered help in kind, or at favourable rates. Above all, there was the

Above left: Mass-produced badger collecting box still in use today
Opposite: Environment Minister, William Waldegrave, joins Sir David Attenborough and Watch members at the high profile launch of the British Wildlife Appeal at the Natural History Museum in London

Glaslyn in the Cambrian Mountains, mid-Wales. 1982 saw the Montgomeryshire Trust formation and this was its first reserve

reassuring news that the naturalist and television broadcaster, SIR DAVID ATTENBOROUGH, had accepted an invitation to become Appeal Chairman. Here was someone with impeccable credentials and an international reputation who could speak just as passionately about wildlife in Britain as he could about wildlife in Borneo. He would be able to attract new, influential supporters and, above all, instil genuine confidence in the whole process.

The BWA, with the strapline 'Tomorrow is Too Late', was launched by the Patron and Attenborough at the Society's birthplace, the Natural History Museum in London, in October 1985. They were supported by an impressive audio-visual presentation and a speech and pledges of money from the Duchy of Cornwall and from the Minister of Environment, William Waldegrave, on behalf of the Government. The evening featured on the BBC nine o'clock television news and was covered extensively in the media the following morning.

A NEW WORKFORCE

The demand for a growing and increasingly well-trained Trust workforce continued. At the turn of the decade there had been 150 Trust staff and an estimated 460 young people employed under the Government's job creation programmes, run by the Manpower Services Commission

(MSC) (EMPLOYMENT SCHEMES). By 1984, a sample survey of 18 Trusts revealed that these Trusts alone were employing more than 500 MSC staff. More than 80 people were employed in equal numbers on administration, education, and on interpretation and graphics. Nearly 275 were employed on site management and more than 110 on surveys, management plans and planning.

The Trusts were now a significant player in MSC schemes and for the newly-emerging urban groups, sometimes struggling for resources – particularly for non-manual labour – they were a godsend. For example, between 1980 and 1987, the number of staff in the Urban Wildlife Group in Birmingham grew to 130 and only two of these were non-MSC staff.

But there was a growing feeling that the schemes could be used more effectively to produce higher quality environmental projects. Richard Woolnough at the SUFFOLK TRUST wrote, "environmental schemes are highly favoured by MSC but who decides whether all the schemes are good for the environment? . . Why don't we tell them (the Government) what we want?"[239]

In an early (even the first) example of Trusts taking the initiative on a major collective national objective, several Trusts began to formulate a vision for the way ahead for the environmental aspects of the Government's employment schemes. Woolnough, among others, worked with other non-government organisations to keep up the pressure for a Government review. Finally, in 1985, the British Trust for Conservation Volunteers and the Dartington Trust were asked by the Government to carry out a study on the scale, nature and potential for growth of environmental work in England and Wales carried out by volunteers and under MSC schemes, and to make recommendations. The Society gave evidence passing on the Trusts' extensive experience.

In April 1986, Secretary of State for the Environment, Kenneth Baker, called the Society to a meeting in his Ministerial office with a handful of other environmental organisations. He asked all those present to commit, pretty well

MSC employees repairing a drystone wall

'there and then', to running a new scheme targeted at environmental projects. The scheme, to be known as UK2000, was launched in July 1986 by head of the Virgin business empire, Richard Branson.

The Trusts, working collectively, had managed to influence the form of the new Government initiative. PERRING was quick to claim that the new profile, gained as a result of the BWA and other initiatives, had played its part in the Secretary of State's decision to include the Society in the group to run the new UK2000 scheme. He was almost certainly right.

It was also significant that, despite the short notice and the high level of commitment being asked of the Society, it was able to reach a decision quickly. This was partly due to the more efficient decision-making process introduced by ADAMS and the greater trust that had built up between staff and Trustees. It also owed much to the fact that the origins of the new scheme lay largely with

the Trusts themselves. There had been a collective desire to see a more environmentally-focused employment scheme and a willingness to work with the Society to lobby the Government. Here was reinforcement of an important lesson. When the Trust movement put forward a strong collective case, supported with local evidence, and matched this with effective national campaigning, it created a powerful combination.

The Society agreed to join the UK2000 Board and shortly afterwards employed Richard Woolnough as UK2000 Development Officer. His immediate task was to increase the number of unemployed people on MSC Community Programmes with the Trusts and the Society from 1,000 to 1,500 in the first year.

Two of the five themes on which the extra employees were expected to work were – partly as a result of the Society's lobbying – directly relevant to the Trusts. They were 'Making More of Nature' and 'Greening the Cities'.

Not only was the new scheme a great opportunity but it also had "great potential in removing blockages at local level to Trust use of schemes and for influencing future national MSC initiatives".[240] Moreover, it was driving the movement to improve its organisation, management and governance further. All those involved needed managing; money had to be precisely accounted for; and complex bureaucratic processes had to be administered. With the Urban Development Officer in place and the UK2000 initiative also underway, Perring believed that now "the movement. . . not only has the structure but also the means to coordinate and guide urban conservation".[241]

However, the introduction of Employment Training in September 1988, signalled the beginning of the end of this particular opportunity. The shift away from a focus on the type of work completed to the training of individuals did not suit the requirements of the Trusts. Nevertheless, over the previous ten years or so the various employment schemes had left a profound legacy. They had enabled Trusts to grow and develop in terms of their size, scale and overall influence. Even after the schemes had come to an end most Trusts held on to the many advances they had made (EMPLOYMENT SCHEMES).

THE COMPUTER AGE ARRIVES

With increasing numbers of staff employed by Trusts in the mid-1980s, a recurring theme was the need to share information and to improve training.

Among the conservation priorities was the need for a register of management practices and a unified system for site recording. The former got off the ground, in a rudimentary form, in 1980. A register of 26 topics and topic 'leaders' was published in the CONSERVATION OFFICERS' BULLETIN in May 1982. But paper systems for managing information, or for harmonising site and species recording, were always going to be relatively cumbersome.

Staff at the Society's Nettleham office with an early 'Comart' computer

By 1983, there was an element of frustration amongst staff, notably the Conservation Officers, that computerisation of the various aspects of Trust life was moving too slowly and, in some quarters, was meeting resistance. The Society had acquired its first computer – a Hewlett Packard HP 250 Mini-Computer – in 1980, but this was very much the exception rather than the rule (COMPUTERS IN THE TRUSTS).

During 1983, information on the Trusts' nature reserves had been transferred onto a computer at Hatfield Polytechnic by a British Petroleum (BP) funded placement student. A pilot study, looking at the recording of habitat data for reserves and the storage of data from other sites of interest, had also been started in six Trust areas. This led to further demand from many Trusts for their own micro-computers to deal not only with site and species recording but with membership records, administration and accounts.

The Society needed to demonstrate that it was capable of fulfilling its role as the Trusts' national association by coordinating the next move. As ever, financing the initiative was going to be the challenge. A study group was established to consider the immediate and future computing needs of the Trusts. In 1984, funding was secured from the Conservancy and BP for 60 per cent of the cost of 14 micro-computer systems for the Trusts. Thirty-one systems had been funded in a similar way by 1987.

A full systems analysis of the Society's future computer requirements, including everything from wildlife recording to finance, was also undertaken in 1984. This in turn benefited from 50 per cent funding from the Conservancy. The Computers in the Trusts scheme, as it was subsequently named, was now underway. Over the next few years, an energetic in-house team at the Society's Nettleham office helped most of the Trusts with their first steps towards computerisation, providing them with their initial equipment and also with training and advice.

ACQUIRING NEW SKILLS

The installation of the first computers was just one reason why some Trust staff began to question whether they had the skills necessary for the jobs they were being asked to do. Many of them had been taken on as practical conservationists, but they were now being asked, for example, to run large and complex MSC-funded projects or to install and maintain new information technology – often without any additional training. Not surprisingly, similar issues were arising in other environmental organisations, such as the Field Studies Council (FSC) and the British Trust for Conservation Volunteers (BTCV).

Once again help came from the Conservancy. It was keen to support a more business-like approach in the voluntary sector. As with the 'Computers in the Trusts' scheme, the Conservancy, and in particular its Grants Officer Ted Hammond, were able to enlist the support of BP and WWF. Key figures in BTCV, FSC and the Society were encouraged to develop a series of BUSINESS OF CONSERVATION training courses tailored to their own needs. In 1984, these were initially identified as 'Time and Team Management' and 'Promoting Yourself and Your Organisation'. These (and other training courses) were rolled out on a regular basis over the

next few years, helping to develop a growing professionalism within the movement. In December 1986, the Society also held its first formal 'induction course'. Similar events introducing new Trust officers and staff to the Society continued to be held from time to time after this date. A regular programme of twice yearly Open Days was introduced in 2005.

THE BRITISH WILDLIFE APPEAL GAINS MOMENTUM

The Society's 1985–86 annual report was headed '1985 – The Year of Change'. There was a strong feeling that with the urban movement negotiated into the fold, the BWA impressively launched, and the Society picking up on several Trust-led initiatives to improve their 'businesses', it had successfully overcome some key hurdles. The Society and Trusts had collectively "turned to show the nation for the first time all that it had achieved and what it was capable of achieving in the future".[242] Perhaps the most immediate visible sign of this was a gruelling 14-day tour by SIR DAVID ATTENBOROUGH for the BWA in the autumn of 1985. His lectures helped promote the work of the Trusts and the challenges they faced. They were heard by more than 20,000 people, with his interviews on television and radio by thousands more.

A year later Chris Baines, one of the leading lights of the urban conservation movement, embarked on a rather different tour, this time with The Albion Band, promoting a folk-rock record, *The Wild Side of Town*, in support of the BWA.

Internally too, there was progress. Behind the scenes there was support from Trusts for a change in the way they funded the Society. The old capitation fee based on 'pence per adult member' changed to a percentage levy on Trust subscription income (initially set at 11.5 per cent). This had been discussed in 1978 and 1981 but now the Honorary

Treasurer, ALAN NEWTON, was able to get agreement for the new system to be introduced in the financial year 1987–88. There were also encouraging signs that the BWA had turned a corner. It had inevitably taken time to bed down. Initially the amount of money raised, whilst publicly 'on target', included little 'new' national money. The Society was also concerned about how soon it would see a return on the Appeal's up-front costs and about the degree of autonomy enjoyed by the Appeal Steering Committee (ASC). But the Chairman of the ASC, the Appeal Director and PERRING were all insisting on a 'light touch' and the need to let it 'get on with the job', an approach that was eventually endorsed.

The Appeal team, including Perring, spent the first few months out and about with the Trusts encouraging a new round of local appeals. As the publicity machine began to swing into action the Appeal began to gather momentum. By the end of 1987, it had reached nearly £6.5 million, with 55 per cent of this figure raised through the local and regional appeals and 45 per cent from the national appeal. By 1989, the total raised had broken the £9 million barrier.

The idea that the BWA would also act as a catalyst, particularly for non fundraising activity, was also proving to be the case. For example, in winter 1985 a special, longer issue of NATURAL WORLD reviewed the plight of the nation's wildlife habitats – woodlands, sea and coast, natural grasslands, uplands and wetlands. It described how Trusts were protecting them and involving more and more people in the process.

In another example, the BWA's Director, John Guy, and Perring had worked on the idea of raising funds through running wildlife holidays. In 1988, WILDLIFE TRAVEL was established as an independent venture to provide group holidays for naturalists in Europe and to other continents. From the outset it was concerned to promote eco-tourism, with an agreement that any profits would go to the Society and the work of the Trusts.

The Society's Wildflower Week garden, sponsored by Gales Honey, won silver medal at the RHS Chelsea Flower Show

In a return to an old theme for the Society – the loss of the country's wildflowers – the BWA also prompted a series of highly popular WILDFLOWER WEEKS over the coming five years. As part of these events, the Society secured a coveted stand each year at the Chelsea Flower Show. In 1988, it won a Silver Medal with its country garden built with the support of the Wildflower Weeks' sponsors, Gales Honey. On another occasion, the Society's Chelsea stand exhibited a series of Impressionist-style flower paintings by Fiona Millais, great grand-daughter of the 19th century, Pre-Raphaelite painter, Sir John Everett Millais.

The year 1989 saw the first British Birdwatching Fair promoted jointly by the LEICESTERSHIRE AND RUTLAND TRUST and the RSPB. This was held on the Trust's Egleton Nature Reserve on the shores of Europe's largest man-made reservoir – Rutland Water. Known colloquially as the 'Birdfair' and held each August, over the next two decades the event would develop into the 'world's most prestigious birdwatching event' with exhibitors drawn from all corners of the globe. The first Birdfair attracted 2,000 visitors. Twenty years later, the number of visitors had risen to more than 22,000 and the money raised for Birdlife International's conservation projects had reached £2.6 million, enough to safeguard half a million hectares of land for wildlife around the world with a further £16 million generated in matched funds.

It was not just SIR DAVID ATTENBOROUGH and Chris Baines who were out on the road. Julian Pettifer also embarked on an Appeal lecture tour. All were stressing not just the wonders of the natural world, but the losses and damage that it was suffering, and the part played by the Society

and Trusts in trying to reverse these declines. Indeed, the Appeal had the effect of injecting even more energy into this aspect of the Society's work. After all, if the BWA was to reach its targets it was essential for the press, the public and politicians to be constantly reminded of why the funds were so urgently needed.

As an example, the Society chose to campaign on the level of protection afforded to the badger. It would be one of its "biggest campaigns ever".[243] In the Appeal issue of NATURAL WORLD, twin threats to the badger were discussed: the issues surrounding badgers and bovine tuberculosis (bTB) in cattle, and their death and severe injury from the so-called 'sport' of badger digging and baiting.

Martin Davies and Tim Appleton at an early Birdfair

PROTECTING BADGERS

Bovine tuberculosis had been common in cattle for 40 years and in most areas had been eradicated by the Ministry of Agriculture. However, it still persisted in parts of the south-west of England. In 1971, a badger was found with the disease for the first time in an area where cattle were also affected. Further investigation by the Ministry showed evidence of a badger-cattle connection. The link was contested by many and, when the Ministry decided to gas badgers with cyanide in the areas concerned, there was a public outcry. Many farmers whose livelihoods were at risk were in favour of this decisive action. But many animal lovers were equally opposed to any intervention. The Society was prominent amongst those that questioned the wisdom of the Ministry's strategy, including the efficiency of its methods. The Ministry found itself 'between a rock and a hard place'. Even today, after more than 30 years, with many tens of thousands of badgers dead, many herds of cattle destroyed, and many Ministers come and gone, the Government still struggles to find a long-term solution (BADGERS AND BOVINE TB).

The second threat facing badgers was predominantly a cruelty issue, but had a conservation aspect too. Since the beginning of the 1980s, the Society had received numerous reports from the Trusts and elsewhere that the cruel 'sport' of badger digging and baiting was on the increase. Not only were individual animals suffering but, in certain areas, local badger populations were in severe decline. It was this latter point that persuaded the Society that there was a conservation case, as well as an animal welfare case, to be answered.

In truth, the Society was in a difficult position. It felt it could neither ignore the pleas of the most concerned Trusts, many of which either ran, or were associated with, local badger groups. Nor could it ignore what was happening to the species it had chosen as its emblem – even if the overall badger population was not endangered. Trusts were keen to provide first-hand accounts of the

problems faced by badgers on the ground, and in the end the Society was able to draw together data from 15 Trusts in an impressive *Badger Report*. The YORKSHIRE TRUST, for example, reported that in the ten years up to 1984, 836 active setts had been reduced by half. Even when cases had been taken to court they had nearly always been unsuccessful and had often been dismissed on technicalities.

The report, the media coverage and the public interest that it generated, were designed to support the MP for South Shields, David Clark. He had introduced a Private Member's Bill into Parliament to curtail the activities of the badger diggers by, in particular, closing the loophole allowing them to claim they were in pursuit of foxes rather than badgers. Despite agreeing the initial wording of the bill with the Home Office, at the eleventh hour, the Government introduced a clause which, if anything, weakened the existing badger legislation. Intensive negotiations followed. The night before a decisive joint meeting of the Home Office and Department of Environment Ministers with Clark and the NGOs, Tim Sands was telephoned in his hotel room by a Minister to secure support for a Department of Environment amendment to the Home Office clause. New satisfactory wording was agreed the next day, just in time for the report stage of the bill. The Wildlife and Countryside (Amendment) Act 1985, including stronger protection for badgers, became law soon afterwards.

KEEPING UP THE PRESSURE

Throughout the decade the Society remained focused on the continuing loss of wildlife habitats. The protection of SSSIs under the Wildlife and Countryside Act 1981 was slightly strengthened under the Wildlife and Countryside (Amendment) Act 1985. But the 1981 Act was still generally failing to prevent damage to SSSIs. Sheail thought that "more than usually, it was the Act itself that appeared to be on trial. . . the manner in which

Opposite: Badgers were under threat as a result of measures to eradicate bovine TB in cattle and from badger digging and baiting

the Wildlife and Countryside Act 1981 was interpreted and implemented within its first few years would determine the level of restriction that might ultimately be required".[244]

Indeed, the ink had hardly dried on the Act before problems began to arise. Soon after it was passed, the owner of wet grassland within the Walland Marshes SSSI in Kent threatened drainage and cultivation of the site. Unwilling to "commit resources that might later be required for more pressing cases",[245] the Government refused the Conservancy additional funds to secure a management agreement and the site was subsequently ploughed and de-scheduled as a SSSI. When the Somerset Levels were threatened with agricultural improvement and peat extraction, the RSPB, with the support of the SOMERSET TRUST, announced it would take legal action if the whole of West Sedgemoor was not scheduled as an SSSI. It was scheduled in November 1982. But in February 1983, angry local farmers challenged the decision, burning effigies of leading figures in the

Conservancy and the RSPB. This pushed the Government to go beyond the provisions of the Act and it gave an assurance to compensate, not just for profits foregone in revenue terms but for any loss of capital value.

At the Trusts' Conservation conference in Kent in 1984, Lord Melchett, in a memorable and rousing address – 'Conservationists' Shame and How to Triumph' – talked of the unwillingness of the farming community to recognise the need for a change to agricultural policies. He accused them of "defending a system of agricultural support which puts money into agricultural developments which are destructive of the countryside; lead to more production and therefore more problems with surpluses; lead to larger farms and more farm amalgamations and therefore less small farms; and which lead to greater intensification and therefore less jobs in agriculture. An agricultural support system, in short, which doesn't benefit rural communities, and which does great damage to the natural beauty and wildlife of our countryside".[246]

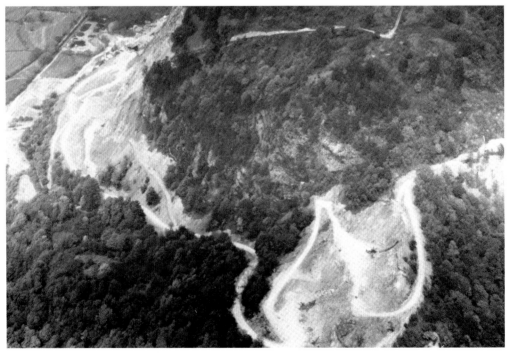

Craig Breidden SSSI, near Welshpool, c1970 – one of the damaged SSSIs highlighted in the Society's *Losing Ground* report. Quarrying for dolerite and basalt destroyed areas of the upper part of the hill, despite its status as a SSSI

Conservationists did not escape his criticism. They should feel shame for presiding over a litany of losses in the countryside since the war. His solutions resonated well with his largely young audience. The increasing number of voluntary conservation bodies should "act more like allies, not like enemies";[247] they should no longer remain neutral in the face of the catalogue of destruction; and should act more decisively, both collectively and as individuals. For some Trusts whose lives were tightly interwoven with their local farming communities, this was sometimes a difficult message to hear. Significantly, he also called on Trusts to give unequivocal support and encouragement to the Society to fight more vigorously on a few national issues, leaving local issues to the Trusts.

What Trusts and the Society also had to do was to keep up the pressure on the Conservancy and, more particularly, the Government. Otherwise the 1981 Act would remain flawed and valuable wildlife sites would continue to be lost. Relationships with the Conservancy had shown a marked improvement following the appointment of Sir William Wilkinson as its Chairman the previous May. He had encouraged it to adopt a more robust stance in support of nature conservation and earlier in the year had signed off what, in the context of the day, was a challenging document, *Nature Conservation in Great Britain*. The report was presented as a contribution to the UK's response to the United Nations Environment Programme's *World Conservation Strategy*. It was also produced to draw a line in the sand. With its authoritative habitat decline statistics and forward-looking, more confrontational strategy for nature conservation, it was designed to show the Government that the Conservancy, along with other nature conservation organisations, was prepared to fight for what it believed in. "Nature conservation has in the past sometimes conducted its business on too apologetic and timid a note. Such a tendency to submissive posture is a recipe for retaining a low peck-order position in the league of land and resource use interests. . . this is

not to advocate aggressiveness and exaggeration, but the playing of a hard yet clean game for our side".[248] On one level, Wilkinson was skilfully drawing nature conservationists together. The Society on behalf of the Trusts could say a resounding 'yes' to the sentiments being expressed. Together with 32 other organisations, it endorsed the Conservancy's bold new strategy. But later Wilkinson's 'hard, yet clean game' would ultimately prove to be a step too far in the eyes of the Government.

Administering the 1981 Act was still putting an enormous strain on the Conservancy. It had to re-notify all the existing SSSIs, designate new ones and defend them against an increasing number of threats, all with resources that were less than adequate. But, for the time being, the Conservancy and voluntary sector were more frequently 'singing from the same song sheet'. The Society and the other non-governmental organisations could concentrate their energies on supporting the Conservancy and on putting more pressure on the Government for further legal reform.

In May 1988, despite growing evidence to the contrary, Lord Caithness, the Minister of Housing, Environment and the Countryside, proclaimed the Wildlife and Countryside Act 1981 the "most far reaching legislation of its kind ever in this country. . . providing effective protection both for natural habitats and threatened species".[249] In February 1989, on BBC Radio 4's *World at One* programme, Caithness modified his line – but only very slightly. "There has been some damage to SSSIs in the past but, as I said, over the last three years the NCC hasn't been able to identify an SSSI which has been substantially damaged".[250] Four months later, however, Virginia Bottomley, Parliamentary Under-Secretary for the Environment, in an answer to a Parliamentary Question, reported that between 1st April 1984 and 31st March 1988, 687 SSSIs (about 14 per cent) had sustained damage. Caithness remained steadfast. Writing in response to a letter from the Society a month later he concluded, "I remain to be convinced that there is a better way of protecting our natural heritage".[251]

The painfully slow and worryingly small shift in the Government's position served to underline the importance of WILDLIFE LINK, supported by the Society, carrying on the fight for a further change in the law. In 1989, the Society took the decision to complement Link's efforts with its own campaign. Using the Trusts' first-hand experience of habitat and species losses on the ground, it compiled a report *Losing Ground – Habitat Destruction in the UK*. This was published in September 1989 and marked the beginning of a series of campaigns over five years using the *Losing Ground* banner.

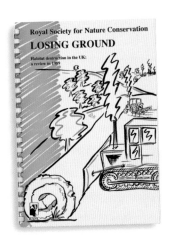

The report brought together 100 case studies from 37 Trusts and presented a damning indictment of the Government and the 1981 legislation. The report looked at the way that development, agriculture and forestry, the sheer number of people and lack of appropriate management were eroding the wider countryside. Even the special sites that the Government claimed were safe were being damaged or lost. The report called for amendments to the Act; Government support for an EU Habitats Directive; and for non-statutory LOCAL WILDLIFE SITES to be recognised in the planning process. It also argued for a national audit and incentives for heritage farming.

LOOKING TO THE WIDER COUNTRYSIDE

The reference in this first *Losing Ground* report to the losses of non-statutory sites and the call for action was perhaps surprising when the battle for SSSIs was still raging and had yet to be won.

But the Society was consciously putting down a marker to the Government. Even if SSSIs eventually received proper protection, that was not going to be the end of the story. The loss and damage to the wider countryside outside SSSIs was just as worrying. The wider countryside, and especially Local Wildlife Sites (non-statutory sites of local conservation interest designated by local authorities), held the majority of the country's wildlife wealth. As the Conservancy's Chairman, Sir William Wilkinson, said in March 1989, "the more the wider environment becomes impoverished in its wildlife the sharper is the distinction between what is 'special' and what is not. And the more that natural and semi-natural habitats decline through human impact, the more important do the remaining areas become".[252]

This was a historic moment. The Society was not about to abandon its core belief in site protection. Nevertheless, with improved protection for SSSIs in the pipeline and an inevitable slowdown in the rate of nature reserve acquisition as land prices increased, it was conscious that future wildlife would depend as much on the wider countryside as on these special sites. The Society and the Trusts already had a good track record in this field. They had introduced pioneering schemes as early as the 1960s to protect ROADSIDE VERGES, for example, and had run campaigns for the retention and better management of hedgerows. By the 1950s, these two habitats often formed the largest remaining tracts of semi-natural vegetation in many lowland counties. The Trusts had also become increasingly involved in the development of effective systems for identifying and protecting Local Wildlife Sites. The Society and the Trusts felt justified in claiming to be *the* wildlife guardians of the wider countryside. This was not yet the quantum leap in thinking that would result in the Trusts adopting a twin-track approach – not just the protection and conservation, but also the restoration and rebuilding, of wildlife habitats and species. This would emerge in the 1990s and lead to larger area projects and eventually, at the beginning of the new millennium, to the development of the

Tim Sands hands over the Society's Commons Report to Environment Minister, Virginia Bottomley

movement's Living Landscape vision (LIVING LANDSCAPES AND LIVING SEAS). But in the 1980s, there was still a fear that going that far would channel resources into 'easy' restoration projects – wetland creation and tree planting – and away from the more immediate job of protecting existing species and semi-natural habitats from neglect and damage. Nevertheless the movement had to convince key players, including the Government, that nature conservation was about more than protecting a few examples of the richest habitats, essential though that was. It had to find its way, for example, into many more corners of Government policy and of society more generally.

More immediately, the Society was concerned about the quality and extent of the Conservancy's data on the wider countryside. It set about carrying out a 'survey of surveys' to establish where information was lacking. The idea was to approach the Conservancy to encourage it to fill any gaps itself or to use Trusts to do it for them. The results of the Society's work confirmed that much more needed to be done to establish a clearer picture of sites of nature conservation value outside the statutory system (LOCAL WILDLIFE SITES).

A further opportunity to highlight the importance of the wider countryside arose in the middle of the decade. In 1984, the Countryside Commission (CC) had drawn attention to the urgent need for new legislation to regulate the management of common land, described 30 years earlier as 'the last reserve of uncommitted land'. It had established a Common Land Forum (CLF) that had published its findings in 1986. The Society agreed with most of its conclusions but wildlife interests had received scant attention. The Society successfully argued to the CC and to the Conservancy that it should carry out a 'quick and dirty' assessment of the wildlife value of common land. It should also take a more detailed look at the implications for wildlife of the CLF report. The results of its investigations were dramatic: more than half the common land in 16 counties, that had data available, was of high wildlife value. In some counties, such as Gloucestershire, the figure was as high as 87 per cent.[253]

In *A Future for Wildlife on Commons* published in 1989, the Society recommended that wildlife conservation should be a primary and routine management objective on commons identified by the Conservancy as of High Wildlife Interest. The CLF had proposed that commons should be divided into grazing and amenity commons. However, the Society thought there should simply be 'commons' with the emphasis placed on effective and appropriate management. The Management Associations, proposed by the CLF, should promote the conservation and enhancement of wildlife and publish approved management schemes. Tree planting on commons should be undertaken with 'great care'. Agricultural improvement of common land of High Wildlife Interest – particularly ploughing, re-seeding and the use of artificial fertiliser – should be discouraged and incentives found for more traditional management.

A detailed report on this was summarised into an accessible news-sheet format – *Common Sense*. The launch of this document and the presentation of the Society's findings to the Minister, Virginia Bottomley, received considerably more media coverage than most of the Society's conservation campaigns had enjoyed to date (COMMON LAND CAMPAIGN).

Perhaps the most striking example at this time of the Society looking 'beyond the boundary fence' was its recognition that marine conservation had remained for too long the 'Cinderella' of Britain's environmental movement. Up to the 1970s, neither the Society nor the Trusts had paid much attention to the marine environment beyond the coastal strip. There had been some exceptions. Trusts in the south-west of England, in west Wales and in Scotland were establishing some of

An early marine campaign poster

The Trusts' first Marine Officer, Joan Edwards, at Wembury marine reserve in Devon, in 1987

the first voluntary marine nature reserves and the Society had responded robustly at a policy level to damaging oil spills, for example. But, in general, the marine world was little understood and its management was in the hands of industries, institutions and individuals largely unknown to conservationists at the time. In 1977, the Society had supported Underwater Conservation Year and had been one of a handful of bodies backing the idea of a new Underwater Conservation Society. This was formed in 1979 and four years later it changed its name and became the Marine Conservation Society (MCS). The Wildlife and Countryside Act 1981 had enabled statutory Marine Nature Reserves to be established, but take-up of this provision was slow, not helped by a flawed designation process. By 1985, such was the level of concern at the lack of interest being shown in conserving the marine environment that the Society decided to join the MCS and WWF to run a summer-long Marine Life Campaign. In addition to putting a much-needed spotlight on the subject, it also supported a, sadly unsuccessful, move by David Clark MP to strengthen the marine reserve sections of the Wildlife and Countryside Act 1981. These were among the Society's first forays into the world of marine conservation. Together with the pioneering work of a handful of Trusts, this marked the beginning of a fight for better protection for the marine environment that would see the movement deepen its involvement and that would eventually lead to the passing of the first comprehensive marine legislation – the Marine and Coastal Access Act – in November 2009 (MARINE CONSERVATION).

Not all the Society's wider countryside work could be meticulously planned in advance. On the night of 15th October 1987, a ferocious storm ripped through the south-east of England leaving a trail of destruction in its wake (GREAT STORM).

The Trusts were soon out surveying its effects on trees and woodlands in their areas and carrying out remedial practical work. The Government acted swiftly too, allocating £2.75 million to the Countryside Commission to immediately establish a special Task Force Trees unit. A grant pot of £250,000 was established for replanting and this had to be allocated by 27th November. If the Trusts wanted to apply they had to move swiftly. They were up to the challenge, and within a week of the announcement, the Society had organised a meeting for the 11 Trusts affected, a pro forma application had been agreed and applications were submitted on time to the Commission.

Once the dust, or perhaps more fittingly the leaves, had settled, the Society went on to help coordinate the Trusts' longer-term response to the storm and to woodland management more generally. It employed a Storm Damage Coordinator, Tony Whitbread who, with his more naturalistic, less interventionist philosophy, later became a key advocate of the Trust's LIVING LANDSCAPE approach in the new millennium. His report, *When the Wind Blew*, was published by the Society in 1991. The storm had a profound immediate effect on the physical landscape of

south-east England. In many quarters there was a rush to remove the fallen timber, 'tidy up' and replant. But two years after the event Whitbread's blunt verdict was that "the reasoning behind this was almost 100% wrong".[254] In the future, he believed, "ecologically the gale will be remembered as a natural event which added variety to our woodlands and offered a unique opportunity for research, the outcome of which could well change our understanding of natural systems and have unforeseeable repercussions on our attitudes towards managing nature reserves".[255]

Ten years later the evidence supported Whitbread's view. "In some areas the damage caused by the clear-up was so great that only five in every one hundred trees planted survived. Yet a tour of Wildlife Trust reserves in Kent and Sussex showed the natural regeneration that occurs in mature woodland after a storm".[256] In the context of its wider countryside work, the Society and

Storm damage at Hayley Wood, a Trust nature reserve in Cambridgeshire

the Trusts could look back and view the 'great storm' as a blessing. It reinforced the social, economic and environmental value of the natural fabric of the wider countryside and was a vivid demonstration of the importance and force of natural processes in shaping the environment.

A NEW CHIEF EXECUTIVE

In spring 1986, the Society began the search for a new PRINCIPAL OFFICER to take over from PERRING at the end of his contract in July 1987. CADBURY's term of office as PRESIDENT also finished in September the same year. In the event, he agreed to remain as President for a further two years to provide some continuity while the former appointment was secured. The Society consulted Trusts for the first time about the nature of both posts. The title for the new principal officer post aroused debate. The word 'Director' was dismissed because it was not "the function of the chief member of staff to 'direct' the work of the Society: policy making is the function of the Council".[257] The choice was for 'Chief Executive' being "the least divisive".[258] The post was advertised in November 1986 and, after interviews, Tim Sands was offered and accepted the post. Unfortunately soon afterwards he was advised not to take the post on medical grounds. For Sands, at the time, having to turn down the post was a considerable disappointment but, in retrospect, it almost certainly led to his making a longer lasting contribution to the Society.

Meanwhile, 1987 also saw the Society celebrate its 75th anniversary. Many events and publications were tagged with the '75 years' impress. In May, on the anniversary of the Society's foundation day, MIRIAM ROTHSCHILD held a party at her home village of Ashton in Northamptonshire. It was a particularly appropriate swan-song event for Perring who lived close-by and who was two months away from his retirement.

Looking back on his term in office, what gave Perring particular satisfaction was that the Trust movement had become better known and more united than ever before. In thanking him, the Society felt able to say that the national association of Nature Conservation Trusts (as it was collectively called at the time), could "justifiably claim to be the premier voluntary organisation for all aspects of nature conservation in Britain. Founded on the base – or perhaps spring-board – largely created by his predecessor, TED SMITH, our rise to that status has been most noticeable during Frank's years as General Secretary. We gratefully recognise his enormous contribution, often in the face of considerable difficulty, but always with cheerful optimism".[259]

After re-advertising, the Chief Executive post was finally filled in November 1987 by TIM CORDY, a geographer and planner who had been working for local government, first in Leicester and then in Bolton. Unlike Smith and Perring who had gone before him, Cordy was neither a naturalist nor was he familiar with the Trust movement. His experience lay in the world of management, strategic planning and negotiation. At Bolton he had been a senior official responsible for around 400 staff and for the strategic planning of a large unitary local authority. In addition, he had managed two county-wide activities: liaison with the European Economic Community and a grants scheme for local non-governmental organisations in Greater Manchester. He would bring new skills and a new approach to the future planning of the Society and the Trusts. For Cordy it was also an opportunity to escape the bureaucratic excesses of local government. But for the Society, Trusts and for Cordy there were aspects of his appointment that would involve a steep learning curve.

With the Chief Executive in post it was possible for the Society to turn its attention to the Presidency. The first choice was SIR DAVID ATTENBOROUGH. But his many broadcasting commitments and his role with the Society's BWA meant that, for the time being at least, he felt unable to take on this appointment. In January 1988, the Society's Executive Committee proposed its Chairman, DUNSTAN ADAMS, as the Society's President-elect and he took up his position in the autumn. There was a special lunch for CADBURY on his retirement as PRESIDENT after 30 eventful years with the Society. His contribution to the local nature conservation movement had been momentous, and his generosity was reflected in a gift from the Society and many Trusts and colleagues – a cheque that Cadbury was instructed to spend "entirely selfishly on things that will make life more comfortable".[260]

On Adams' appointment the headline in NATURAL WORLD read 'RSNC Elects a Democrat'. As Chairman of the Executive Committee he had helped steer the Society

through a period of change. He was now keen to preside over a period of peace and stability. JOHN PHILLIPSON took on the role of CHAIRMAN OF THE EXECUTIVE, chairing his first meeting in November 1988. With the demise of the post of General Secretary, the Society reinstated the position of HONORARY SECRETARY which was filled by MICHAEL HOLTON.

NEW PRESSING ISSUES

While these appointments were taking place the Society was engrossed in three other pressing internal issues: the future management of fundraising after the BWA; the resolution of ongoing issues surrounding the relationship with the Urban Groups; and the relocation of the Society's offices from Nettleham.

In the 1980s, Trusts continued to acquire valuable wildlife sites. This is Pendarves Wood, purchased by the Cornwall Trust in 1988

The first of these was made the more urgent because BWA staff contracts were up for renewal in March 1988. As early as the summer of 1987, the Society had to consider how best to "retain the 'entrepreneurial abilities' of the British Wildlife Appeal structure".[261] It also needed to complete the objectives of the Appeal and, at the same time, decide how best to develop new in-house fundraising capability.

There was a view that this new structure should be a 'British Wildlife Trust', independent of the Society and the Trusts. Not everyone agreed and the minutes of a meeting in September between the key figures involved recorded that "a very frank exchange of views took place in an entirely amicable atmosphere. The discussion was based on the need to get the principles right and to avoid being entangled in either details or personalities"![262] By November, after consulting the Trusts, a compromise was agreed. It was decided to establish a Fundraising Section but to allow the BWA to be managed by an 'arm's length' Appeal Management Group for the remainder of its life. This would annually agree its financial targets, budget, broad operating objectives and policy guidelines with the Society and then 'get on with it'. As the Honorary Treasurer, ALAN NEWTON, put it, the Society had reached a "significant point in its history – the success of RSNC's internal fundraising activities over the last four to five years and of the British Wildlife Appeal needed to be built upon".[263] The new arrangements would "integrate the whole of the Society's fundraising activity".[264]

The second issue was a growing sense that arrangements for the urban wildlife groups within the Society's urban steering group were less than satisfactory. Under the guidance of its dynamic Chair, Alison Millward, the steering group had been a "steadying influence in a potentially unstable situation".[265] But there was too much distance between it and the inner workings of the Society. The solution was the establishment of a Development Committee, with equivalent status to the Society's Conservation and Education Committees, to oversee "the work of the urban and UK steering groups with special responsibility for ensuring liaison between our associated Trusts and the urban groups and assisting with the coordinated development of the movement"[266] (URBAN AREAS AND NATURE CONSERVATION).

The third issue, the relocation of the Society's offices, was becoming a matter of growing concern. By early 1986, it was clear that the Society's days at Nettleham were numbered. More room was needed and a burst pipe, following severe frost on the previous New Year's Eve, had caused serious flooding and damage to its offices in the adjoining cottage.

The search for new premises in central England would rumble on for some time. Meanwhile, the decision was taken to sell the cottage in Nettleham and use the proceeds to convert part of the Society's sales warehouse into offices as a stop-gap measure. Finally, it was agreed that the search should concentrate on Lincoln, which provided some low-cost options. ALAN NEWTON's local knowledge and contacts with the City and County Council would prove invaluable. Two properties were considered. The first was The Lawn, a former private psychiatric hospital being redeveloped by Lincoln City Council. It had been the workplace of the enlightened doctor credited with a revolutionary approach to the so-called madness experienced by George III. However, in June 1990, the go-ahead was given for a move to the second property: renovated office and factory space on the south side of the River Witham in the east of Lincoln. Newton reminded the County Council that retaining a national charity and its staff within the county was a distinct 'feather in its cap' and the Council agreed to a generous donation of £10,000 to help finance the move. The new, more spacious offices were rented and the proceeds from the sale of the Nettleham property invested.

Opposite: Environment Minister, David Trippier, opens the Society's new offices in Lincoln (left to right: Dunstan Adams, David Trippier, Tim Cordy and Sir David Attenborough)

When the Society had moved to Nettleham 16 years earlier, it would never have contemplated inviting a Minister to open its new premises. Now it was testament to the advances that had been made in the movement's standing and profile that an invitation to the Minister of Environment, David Trippier, to open the new offices was accepted and took place on 11th April 1991 (OFFICES OF THE SOCIETY).

A CHANGING WORLD

How things had changed since 1974 when the Society had moved to Nettleham. The Society and the Trusts were so much more professional and confident. The BWA had brought the Trusts and the Society closer together and for the time being the Society's finances were on a stronger footing. Although the national campaign programme was still being run *for* the Trusts, rather than *by* the Trusts, they were increasingly influencing its direction.

In late 1985 and early 1986, the Society had been exercised by two documents – *Membership: A Vital Resource* and *Is Conservation Too Parochial?* These two papers, written by Dr John Box of the SHROPSHIRE TRUST, asked how the Society could help Trusts to increase their membership and whether the movement recognised that it had an identity crisis. The papers were a "breath of fresh air",[267] and also provided encouragement to CORDY, the Development Committee and to those who wanted to keep moving the organisation forward.

By early 1989, the finishing touches were being put to a Corporate Strategy for 1989–92. Originally started by PERRING, it would be the first such document for the Society. It was based on a framework developed by a secondee from the Countryside Commission, Dick Sisman. Sisman had been taken on by Perring in 1986 to help Trusts progress their own three-year development plans.

The 'environment' was beginning to rise up the political agenda. The Government and its Ministers wanted to be seen to be supporting the green movement and, with its constituency-level focus, The Wildlife Trusts in particular. The Society was enjoying increased funding from the Government's Special Grant Programme and helping to run the Government's UK 2000 job-creation scheme. Ten years earlier the Society would have used the Conservancy as its main route into Government. It was now spending as much time at the Department of Environment in London as it was at the Conservancy's national offices in Peterborough.

The Society and the Trusts were becoming a force to be reckoned with. Trusts inevitably varied in their scale and capacity, but were operating throughout the UK in a way that had no parallel in other bodies. The public's awareness of the Society and the Trusts, and more particularly the fact that the two were linked, still needed to be improved. But such had been the progress in its relationship with Government and its standing within the environmental movement that the Society and the Trusts could now justifiably claim that they were becoming the 'national force' that Perring had set out to establish ten years earlier.

SUSTAINABILITY – THE NEW BUZZWORD

In 1983, the United Nations had convened a Commission, chaired by Gro Harlem Brundtland, Norway's first woman Prime Minister, to address growing concern about the deteriorating state of the human and natural environment worldwide and the consequences for economic and social development. Its report, *Our Common Future* (more commonly referred to as the Brundtland Report), was published in 1987 and dealt with how to achieve development that was sustainable. The report became famous for a new term 'sustainable development' and a much-cited definition of 'development that meets the needs of the present without compromising the ability of future generations to meet their own needs'.

The Brundtland Report would provide momentum for a UN Earth Summit proposed for Rio de Janeiro in 1992 and a touchstone for much new thinking about the environment in the 1990s.

Acid rain damage in the Erzeberge Mountains, Czech Republic. The 1980s saw growing concern for global environmental issues

The UK Prime Minister, Margaret Thatcher, for example, was quick to reflect the Brundtland philosophy in statements in the autumn of 1988. In their turn, environmentalists were quick to see the political value of her support for the cause. Thatcher's speech to the Conservative Party Conference in Brighton in October included the much-quoted statement, "no generation has a freehold on this earth. All we have is a life-tenancy with full repairing lease. This Government intends to meet the terms of that lease in full".[268] A month before Thatcher had addressed the Royal Society citing three changes in 'atmospheric chemistry' that had become familiar subjects of concern: increases in greenhouse gas emissions; the discovery of a large hole in the ozone layer; and acid rain. She stated her support for the concept of what had now, disturbingly, been described more frequently as 'sustainable economic development'. She believed that "stable prosperity can be achieved throughout the world provided the environment is nurtured and safeguarded. Protecting this balance of nature is therefore one of the great challenges of the late twentieth century".[269] Significantly, however, there was no talk of limiting growth. Thatcher acknowledged the costs, but stated her belief that it was money well and necessarily spent, because the health of the economy and the health of the environment were totally dependent upon each other.

In the context of growing international concern for the environment, the Government and its Ministers were anxious to display their green credentials. A year later Chris Patten, Thatcher's new Secretary of State for the Environment, promised "to bring together the Government's whole strategy on the environment in a comprehensive White Paper that will set the environmental agenda until the end of the century".[270] It was the first such White Paper by a British Government.

The White Paper and the Earth Summit in 1992 would be the curtain raisers for the coming decade which would see the term 'sustainable development' and a new term, 'biodiversity', come to dominate the environmental agenda.

CHAPTER 7

Reconstruction 1990–1994

The power and influence for nature conservation has passed into the hands of the voluntary bodies. You must take and use this power.

Sir William Wilkinson, Chairman of Nature Conservancy Council, 1990

Although great progress had been made, it would be wrong to give the impression that nature conservation was still anything other than a minority interest as far as the Government was concerned. Evans even goes so far as to observe that, "as the 1990s opened, conservation was nothing more than a minor irritation in the world of politics".[271] It was true that the conservation organisations, including the Society and the Trusts, had become much more robust and sophisticated and were not without their successes. But it was also true that overall they were still failing to effect real and lasting change in the Government's commitment, either to nature conservation or to the environment more generally.

The 1970s and 1980s had seen the emergence of more politically-orientated 'green' groups. Among these were the Socialist Environment and Resources Association formed as early as 1973; the Ecology Groups of the Liberals and Conservatives formed in 1977; and the Green Alliance formed in 1978. In 1985, the Ecology Party – which owed its origins to a much-publicised treatise, the *Blueprint for Survival* – changed its name to the Green Party. The Party enjoyed fleeting success coming third, with 15 per cent of the overall vote, in the 1989 European Parliament elections. Like their less political counterparts, these organisations

Opposite: Biodiversity decade – the 1990s saw the development of biodiversity action plans for a range of threatened plants, animals and habitats. A barn owl hovers over the Kent Trust's Oare Marshes reserve

generated greater public and political awareness of environmental issues. But they failed to radically shift Government policy and action on the environment. Government still promised much, but delivered far too little. The White Paper, *This Common Inheritance: Britain's Environmental Strategy*, unveiled by the Secretary of State for the Environment, Chris Patten, in September 1990, was a case in point. The Society's response was that it was "a good workmanlike review of the state of the environment but with very few remedies. . . Britain is standing at a green crossroads but the Government has failed to commit itself to a new route".[272]

Julian Pettifer, a Vice President of the Society, believed it showed that, "despite the new focus on 'green issues', wildlife conservation is still not treated with the seriousness it deserves in the corridors of power. Pollution, recycling and waste may have moved into Division One of the political agenda, but nature conservation is still in Division Two".[273] This view was all too graphically illustrated with the Government's announcement that it planned to reorganise – or as conservationists were saying, 'dismember' – its nature conservation watchdog, the Nature Conservancy Council.

THE BANGOR MANIFESTO

The start of each of the previous three decades had seen the Society organise groundbreaking conferences. Skegness in 1960 was a springboard for the Trust movement; Oxford in 1970 lit the

David Bellamy, the Society's President, addresses the national conference in Nottingham, 1990

fire in the movement's campaigning 'belly'; and Nottingham in 1980 brought 'nature to town' (CONFERENCES).

In April 1990, the Society's national conference – *Our Next Decade* – was again in Nottingham and, in DAVID BELLAMY's words, looked away from the "doom and destruction" of the eighties and forward to "a decade of construction".[274] It was also memorable for an inspiring speech from the Chairman of the beleaguered Conservancy, Sir William Wilkinson (see later in the chapter). But it would be the Conservation Conference in Bangor in July that would be more innovative, attempting in the space of four days to produce the Society's own alternative White Paper on the environment.

There was a positive mood amongst the 100 or so conservation staff who assembled in North Wales. They were eager to be part of a grassroots process, "leading the way on these subjects".[275] The resulting draft document, dubbed the BANGOR MANIFESTO, covered many of the major

environmental issues of the day, from energy and transport through to food, land-use planning and public access. It would provide the Society with a yardstick against which to measure the Government's document promised for the autumn.

There was great enthusiasm from those who attended the Bangor Conference to make sure that the manifesto would be approved and taken forward publicly. One Conservation Officer summed up the feeling. The manifesto "is a remarkable success – the first time it had been tried at a conference to get 100 people involved in policy making. I hope as a movement we'll be able to turn it into formal RSNC/Trust policy. Now is the time to influence Government and political parties".[276]

Despite its unorthodox roots, the Bangor Manifesto had the support of the new Chairman of the Society's Conservation and Scientific Committee, Dr John Barkham. Under his leadership it secured formal approval and went on to inform both the Society's response to the Government's Environment White Paper and a new report, *The Health of the United Kingdom – a commentary from the RSNC on the welfare of the nation's environment.*

This report was based on the tenet that a healthy environment depended on healthy wildlife. Perhaps for the first time, it showed the movement overcoming what one commentator later described as its "fear that nature conservation will drown in the new debates on global issues".[277]

The Bangor experience, the subsequent manifesto and *The Health of the UK* report were the early signs of a new confidence to promote nature conservation as part of the broader environmental and social agenda. Introducing the report, Vice President at the time, SIR DAVID ATTENBOROUGH said,

HRH The Prince of Wales during a visit to the Society's Lincoln Office in 1990 with Chief Executive, Tim Cordy (left)

"nature is our very environment and we need to ensure that its conservation is seen as a central part of all other environmental concerns".[278]

JOINING FORCES

By late 1988, the Chief Executive, TIM CORDY, had completed a nationwide tour of all the Trusts. He was therefore able to ensure that the Corporate Strategy for 1989–92, reflected what he had seen and heard on his travels. A commonly held view was that the Trusts needed a stronger public image and greater media presence. Locally the main organisational requirement was for more financial and practical support from the Society to achieve "viability for all corporate members (the Trusts)".[279]

A post-graduate study by Janet Dwyer at the time revealed the disparity between the rates of development of the Trusts. Dwyer suggested that

Left: *The Health of the UK* – the Society's commentary on the welfare of the nation's wildlife and its response to the Government's 1990 Environment White Paper

there were three general 'types' of Trusts, "each type representing a stage in a more or less common path of growth and development, albeit a path which is pursued at different rates and to different degrees by individual Trusts".[280] She estimated that there were about ten to 13 small Trusts, about 23 Trusts that were developing and campaigning, and known largely within their own county area, and a third group of about ten Trusts that had become nationally influential.

Cordy was now pressing for a further programme of 'reconstruction' rolled out on at least two fronts. On the one hand, there should be a "fight for the habitat that is left, and just as in the cities after the last war, we must be prepared to reconstruct habitat ourselves, and to use every possible opportunity to encourage others to do similarly".[281] On the other hand, work had already begun on overhauling the Society's structure, marketing and work programmes. The new Development Committee was in place, the Society had successfully relocated to Lincoln, and its *Health of the UK* report was launched in October 1990.

In a video he recorded for the launch, the Patron, HRH The Prince of Wales, welcomed the report because it made "us face up to the state of our own rather special piece of the natural world, here and now".[282] He was concerned that "we can go on nibbling away at the corners of our remaining unspoiled and valuable habitats, justifying our actions on the basis of economic necessity or even just personal convenience, but what will the overall picture be like in ten years time, twenty years time, fifty years time, or is that looking too far ahead. I don't think our children will think it is fifty years from now. History, after all, is full of cases where the younger generation have berated their parents' generation for taking the short-term view".[283]

A month later the Patron paid a flying visit to the Society's new Lincoln offices – the royal helicopter landing in the adjoining car park.

The Health of the UK report also carried a new logo – the existing badger accompanied by the words 'RSNC – The Wildlife Trusts Partnership'. This, together with a new strapline, 'Joining Forces for Nature', had been chosen to emphasise the new importance placed on applying a common image and approach across the Society, the Trusts *and* the urban wildlife groups.

A decision had been made to retain a reference to the Society in the logo for now. But the increasingly popular term 'Wildlife Trusts' was officially introduced for the first time. The unifying word 'Partnership' was chosen to send a powerful message, both to the outside world and to the movement itself. Whilst the new corporate image was a major breakthrough it was "an unwieldy label"[284] and would ultimately be replaced by a simpler solution (LOGOS).

The Society's first-ever marketing plan was also being developed in close collaboration with the Trusts to ensure it "fully reflected local needs"[285] and to encourage Trusts to support its

implementation. For the first time, guidelines on the use of a shared corporate identity were available and Trusts began to use the new Partnership logo alongside their own. A training programme was rolled-out in Bristol, Birmingham, London and Leeds to help all Trusts promote themselves and the movement as a whole.

The 1990 winter issue of NATURAL WORLD also reflected the new marketing package. Sporting the new logo, prominent personalities of the time, known for their strong views on conservation, were invited to write contributions. Broadcaster, Brian Redhead, put forward plans for a green map of the countryside; television presenter, Julian Pettifer, recommended better protection for wildlife habitats; naturalist, DAVID BELLAMY, looked for cleaner seas; Pamela Stephenson, popular comedienne at the time, demanded stronger controls on pesticides;

The Prime Minister, John Major (centre), meets the Society's Chief Executive, Tim Cordy (left), during a visit to *The Sunday Times Wildlife, Environment and Conservation Exhibition* at Olympia in London

Geoff Larminie

Dunstan Adams

John Guy

David Attenborough

Brian Goswell

The Ralph Sallon cartoon presented to Brian Goswell, Chairman of the Appeal Management Group, at the end of the British Wildlife Appeal and Goodies' star and naturalist, Bill Oddie, called for a 'u-turn' on the road building programme.

Julian Pettifer was soon helpful with another marketing opportunity. The BBC was planning to re-screen its series, *The Living Isles,* as part of a new *Safari UK* programme to be broadcast the following summer and autumn. Pettifer was joined on *Safari UK* by fellow television presenter, Jill Dando, whose tragic murder would hit the headlines eight years later. The series was launched in July 1991 with a special programme from *The Sunday Times Wildlife, Environment and Conservation Exhibition* at Olympia. The Partnership was chosen as the sole charitable beneficiary of funds raised from ticket sales for this event. During the series, 300 summer 'safari' events were organised and it ended in September with an ambitious live outside broadcast involving a number of Trust nature reserves.

LIFE AFTER THE BRITISH WILDLIFE APPEAL

In December, the Society finally wound up the BWA. Its closing act was the publication of *Tomorrow is Too Late*, an anthology of British wildlife specially compiled by some of the country's best known natural history writers and artists. The Appeal's final total reached £16.1 million, with around 60 per cent raised through local and regional appeals.

It had substantially exceeded its target and the overall impact on the number of nature reserves purchased and wildlife sites saved, as well as the strengthening of the relationship between the Trusts and the Society, had been impressive. The Appeal's costs had been slightly more than expected, but the benefits far outweighed this.

A review of 'life after BWA' concluded that it would be inappropriate to launch a BWA 'Mark II'. Instead, the Society should "regroup its fundraising activities with particular emphasis on potential new sources of funds. . . whilst maintaining a running campaign theme".[286] Moves were made to approach companies and businesses for support. In 1992, 11 companies joined a national Business Supporters Scheme and a further 20 or so companies each donated £10,000 or more.

Meanwhile, the Society's Development Committee was pursuing the possibility of setting up a subsidiary company to broker environmental consultancy work across the Trust movement under the UK2000 initiative. The principle was accepted but the legal, charitable and practical implications needed to be resolved before RSNC Environmental Services Ltd could be launched in February 1991. Not long after, an Association was established to promote quality standards amongst the Wildlife Trusts' consultancies and to provide a mechanism for working together and for sharing knowledge and training (ASSOCIATION OF WILDLIFE TRUST CONSULTANCIES).

Tomorrow Is Too Late – the final British Wildlife Appeal project. This 120-page book contained contributions from leading wildlife artists and writers

ON THE CAMPAIGN TRAIL

The Society's determination to "campaign more visibly and forcefully across the country"[287] – and to pick up on the idea of a running campaign theme –meant that it now embarked on an ambitious programme of activity to "set the agenda for the next decade".[288]

The Countryside Commission's Countryside Survey of 1990, based partly on satellite imagery, confirmed that between 1978 and 1990 there had continued to be "an overall loss of species diversity and an associated decrease in species characteristic of less intensively managed vegetation".[289] Habitats had been lost and species diversity had decreased. There was every reason, therefore, to sustain the existing *Losing Ground* campaign theme. But the time had come to make the case for bringing wildlife back to the wider countryside. A decision was made to rebrand the campaign as *Losing Ground–Gaining Ground* and, with this, the Society began a period of concerted advocacy and lobbying for wildlife.

This decision was also a further public nod by the Partnership towards a 'restoration'

agenda – one that the movement would lead over the coming decades. Five new campaigns, deliberately linked to the *Losing Ground– Gaining Ground* theme, were introduced. In addition, in March 1991, the consultancy arm of the SHROPSHIRE TRUST was a prime mover in organising a workshop for all Trusts at the Ironbridge Gorge Institute. Entitled NEW GROUND, its aim was to take forward the Partnership's wider countryside agenda. The resulting report and discussion document, *Conservation in the Wider Countryside: Best Practice and How to Achieve It,* was one more step along the road of integrating the wider countryside theme across all aspects of the movement's work.

After decades devoted to the Partnership's organisational development, the late 1980s and early 1990s was a period in which the Society and Trusts reinforced their position as a campaigning movement, unafraid to 'stand up for wildlife'. During this time work coalesced around the five overarching national campaigns.

The first campaign, on MINERALS PLANNING, sprang out of a project, the WOODLAND INITIATIVE

Lily-of-the-valley – one of several species at Coeddyd Carmel SSSI saved by a decision to overturn a historic quarrying application

Peat extraction at Thorne Moor, Yorkshire – levelling off older peat cuttings in preparation for surface milling

launched in autumn 1990. A central element of this was the Society's support of the Dyfed Trust (now the SOUTH AND WEST WALES TRUST) in its fight to save ancient Carmel Woods (Coedydd Carmel SSSI) from limestone quarrying. This led to a three-year battle to expose the serious impact mineral extraction was having on wildlife. Three reports – *Skeletons in the Cupboard, Leaving the Stone Age* and *Blast from the Past* – and the accompanying campaign, helped to secure improvements to the Government's mineral planning guidance.

Finally, in November 1995, there was a successful outcome to the Carmel Woods' case itself. This opened the door to improved understanding between The Wildlife Trusts and the aggregate industry; a relationship that would develop further in the future.

The second, and largest, campaign involved peat. Discussions about the continuing destruction of the country's peatlands had featured on the margins of the 1988 and 1989 Conservation Conferences in Belfast and Cambridge. As a result the Society's new Conservation Officer, Caroline

Steel, secured agreement to run a large-scale peatland campaign. Steel, who had been the DEVON TRUST's Conservation Officer, was the first member of the Society's conservation staff to have worked professionally in a Trust. Her appointment would go on to demonstrate the value of a Trust background to working for the movement at the national level.

Several other national conservation organisations were also concerned about peatlands and they agreed to work together as a Peatlands Consortium. A joint campaign was launched in the spring of 1990 (PEATLANDS CAMPAIGN).

The Society also immediately launched its Peatlands' Protection Charter at the Nottingham National Conference in 1990. Signatories of the Charter agreed to phase out the use of peat and promote its replacement with substitutes or composting. Support was secured from some powerful quarters. Not only did local authorities sign the Charter, but the Society's Patron, HRH The Prince of Wales, also agreed to ban the use of peat in the gardens of his home at Highgrove and on landscape projects within the Duchy of

Cornwall. The campaign attracted media interest too, contibuting a plotline in *The Archers*, BBC Radio 4's long-running soap. Jack Woolley of Grey Gables signed the Charter and spent a week of episodes encouraging the inhabitants of Ambridge to use alternatives to peat. The media interest, the success of the Charter and the Prince's forthright endorsement of the Peatlands Campaign, were particularly timely and helpful in view of the anticipated hostile reaction anticipated from the peat industry.

Later that year, the Society published *The Peat Report* on behalf of the ten organisations in the Peatlands Consortium. This was a comprehensive review of the industry, the use of the peat resource and the destruction of peatlands. The Consortium demanded the protection or rehabilitation of peatlands; a review of the planning consents for peat extraction; the development of alternative materials and practices to replace peat; and the

implementation of a UK strategy for peatlands' conservation. By March 1991, the Society was able to chart progress in a further publication of its own, *Losing Ground–Gaining Ground: Peatlands*. It reported the welcome news that the Government had been persuaded to review commercial peat extraction and had agreed to stop local authorities granting new planning consents. This campaign and its further successes are described under PEATLANDS CAMPAIGN in Part III.

A third campaign began with the appointment of a Transport Campaigner by the south-east Wildlife Trusts. The aim was to highlight the impact on the region of "the largest roadbuilding programme in British history",[290] announced by the Department of Transport in its 1989 White Paper, *Roads for Prosperity*. It sparked a robust response from environmental groups angry at the Department's assertion that it would play an important part in protecting and conserving the

Cartoon depicting the effect of road building on wildlife, used in several of the *Head on Collision* reports

environment. In 1990, a consortium, including the CPRE and the Society, published *Roads to Ruin*. Later the Trusts in the south-east of England published *Head on Collision – Road Building and Wildlife in South-East England*. The Trusts' report catalogued the impact of the Government's road programme on wildlife in the region. It proved to be the catalyst for a national 'Head on Collision' campaign involving many of the Trusts. Over the next seven years, five more regional reports were published as well as reports for Scotland and Wales. They revealed that countrywide, road schemes threatened more than 1,000 wildlife sites. Another report, *Death at Pooh Corner*, in 1991, showed that an estimated 40,000 badgers were killed by road traffic each year.

By the mid 1990s, there were several signs that the 'Head on Collision' campaign could claim some success. In 1994, more environmentally-sensitive planning guidance was issued and a

The Meadows Campaign, complete with hay bales and sheep, takes to the streets of London – Stephen Warburton of the Yorkshire Trust holds a 'health and safety compliant' scythe

number of trunk road schemes were removed from the programme. Also the Royal Commission on Environmental Pollution recommended a reduction in the road building programme and more investment in public transport. These were, however, modest successes. Transport remained a political hot potato and a priority for the Partnership into the new millennium (ROAD BUILDING AND WILDLIFE).

In June 1991, aware that the UK would assume the European Union's Presidency in a year's time, the Society's fourth campaign focused on agricultural policy. Building on the success of its annual WILDFLOWER WEEKS, the campaign would target one particularly wildflower-rich habitat, the country's vanishing meadows. The main aim was for the Government to apply its Environmentally Sensitive Areas scheme (ESAs) to all of the country's few remaining meadows. The ESA scheme offered farmers incentives for adopting agricultural practices which would safeguard and enhance parts of the country of particularly high landscape, wildlife or historic value.

The *Vanishing Meadows* report highlighted the value of meadows and the terrible losses of this habitat. In the UK in 1984, 95 per cent of lowland grasslands on neutral soils (including herb-rich hay meadows) lacked significant wildlife interest. Only three per cent remained undamaged by agricultural intensification. More than 85 Trust case studies were quoted to demonstrate this loss. Nor was it a problem confined to the UK. In France, 99 per cent of meadows on the chalk soils of the Champagne region had been lost between 1948 and 1981. Contributing factors were ploughing and reseeding, the use of inorganic fertilisers and other chemicals, drainage, a switch to silage production and overgrazing.

The campaign argued that the protection of the remaining fragments *was* possible. In particular, ESA payments should be extended to cover the whole of the UK, not just a few designated areas, and European funding should be redistributed to support environmentally-friendly farming more generally. The Society produced a

The 'human badgers' joined by supportive MP, Tony Banks, at a rally in London, September 1990

number of publications in support of the campaign – a *Focus on Meadows* leaflet in January 1991 and *CAP Reform – the Farmer, Countryside and Wildlife* in June 1992. It also published technical publications containing advice on grassland and meadow management – *The Lowland Grassland Management Handbook* in April 1994, and *Pastures New – How to Create and Care for Wildflower Meadows* in July 1994 (see also MEADOWS CAMPAIGN and FARMING AND WILDLIFE).

The Society's fifth campaign was on a familiar theme – the wetland environment. In the early 1990s, the combination of prolonged drought and an increasingly profligate use of water reinforced the view amongst the Trusts that a hard-hitting campaign was required. It should tackle not just wetland management but, more controversially, water quantity and quality issues. As with the four other campaigns it reflected *The Health of the UK*'s 'whole environment' approach and the *Losing*

Ground–Gaining Ground theme. In 1992, the Society secured sponsorship from the makers of the 'Down to Earth' range of cleaning products enabling it to launch a WATER FOR WILDLIFE campaign. It tackled the three water issues: quantity, quality and wetland management. The three-year campaign would be a factor behind a new Environment Bill for England and Wales in 1994 that would further reorganise the water industry.

In addition to the five campaigns, the Society began a successful three-year venture of running joint conferences with the RSPB for POLICE WILDLIFE LIAISON OFFICERS to encourage the development of a network of officers and with the exchange of information. By the time of the third annual conference, held at Butterly Hall in Ripley, all forces had a Wildlife Liaison Officer.

The Society continued to work on its *Losing Ground* report on habitat loss and on the management of common land for wildlife. The conservation of otters and badgers also remained high profile. In September 1990, for example, the Society had held a rally in central London featuring 48 'human badgers' – one from each Trust – travelling in an open-topped bus to lobby Parliament on better legal protection for badger setts. Further legislation to improve and consolidate existing badger law was passed in 1992.

This conservation campaigning was accompanied by a more sophisticated approach to political lobbying by the national office. There was more contact with civil servants at the earlier stages of policy development and more proactive engagement with Ministers. Within the space of a few months in 1994, the Secretary of State for the Environment and Ministers for Agriculture, Environment and Transport, as well as other MPs, were all whisked away from London on field visits to Trusts, usually within their constituencies. Confronting wildlife and conservation issues on the ground meant Ministers and MPs became more aware of what Trusts, with their local connections and expertise, could offer. Visits often made a more lasting impression than any number of letters or reports. They had the distinct advantage of face-to-face contact without most of the normal entourage of civil servants present at London meetings. There was also the added bonus that a chance encounter with a smooth snake or with the electric-blue flash of a passing kingfisher might spark further interest. At the very least it could prove a useful conversational ice-breaker at future meetings.

CORDY was also working closely with the Patron's office. Extended visits were made by His Royal Highness to several Trusts, including DEVON, KENT and LANCASHIRE. These were matched by the Patron's support for a number of national fundraising events.

EMBRACING THE EARTH SCIENCES

There was a further important development in the early 1990s – a brief but significant

A Rockwatch promotion involved collecting chocolate fossils and minerals, available from Thorntons

re-engagement with the earth sciences. Towards the end of the 1980s, the Conservancy had found the lack of a "local geological voice a real disadvantage"[291] when defending geological SSSIs at public inquiries. Geologists were equally concerned that locally important geological sites were coming under pressure. These sites had so far failed to attract the same voluntary sector support enjoyed by their wildlife site equivalents. A number of museums, geological societies, local authorities and Wildlife Trusts had taken the matter in hand and were identifying key geological and geomorphological localities in their counties. The term Regionally Important Geological and Geomorphological Sites (RIGS) was increasingly used to describe these sites and a more coordinated approach to their selection and conservation was being advocated. If this happened it would also help develop the 'local geological voice' that had so far been lacking.

Support for this movement grew slowly. From 1992, the Society took on a coordinating role with backing from the Conservancy to employ a coordinator. The same year the Society started publishing a newsletter, *RIGS Exposure*, in collaboration with the Geologists' Association. This continued to be issued on a regular basis until it was merged with the Joint Nature Conservation Committee's publication, *Earth Heritage*, in 1997. In 1999, the Society completed a handbook on "how to start up a RIGS Group and record, designate, notify, conserve, interpret, manage and promote RIGS for the public".[292]

Around the same time, the Society was also approached by the Geologists' Association (GA) who wanted to establish a club for young geologists using the Watch model. Sponsorship from British Gas was secured and Rockwatch was launched, in partnership with the GA. Members received their own magazine three times a year from spring 1992 onwards. A welcome pack was supplemented with information cards linked to the regular articles and projects featured in the magazine. As with the main Watch club, these were designed to be fun and to capture members' imaginations. One magazine article looked at the minerals used to make different coloured paints and another at how to make an 'erupting volcano'. A live Rockwatch appearance on the BBC's flagship programme, *Blue Peter*, ended when a bag containing cabbages and stones – designed to show the digestive system of dinosaurs – burst, much to the delight of the programme's resident dog.

By the time the RIGS Groups held their first UK Conference in 1998, there were more than 2,000 sites and 47 English RIGS Groups with at least two further Scottish Groups and four regional Groups in Wales. A year earlier the Society had prepared a Development Strategy for 1997–2000 in consultation with all the RIGS' stakeholders. By the second UK Conference in 1999, an independent Association of UK RIGS Groups had been formed.

MANAGING SSSIS

In May 1992, some welcome news for Trusts came in the form of financial support from the Conservancy for SSSI management.

In 1989, the Conservancy and WWF had commissioned a review of funding support for voluntary conservation organisations (VCOs). One recommendation had been "that funding should be given to VCOs to ensure that, at a minimum, each VCO can find the long-term costs of managing their land".[293] Inflation and the cessation of the Government's Community Programme employment scheme in 1988 meant the cost of managing SSSIs had risen steeply. Meanwhile, grants from Government had "remained elusive".[294]

In addition, the Conservancy was now threatening to limit money for management agreements under Section 38 of the Wildlife and Countryside Act 1981. In April 1990, the Trusts urged the Society to commission a study to determine what Trusts were actually spending and, even more importantly, what they would ideally like to spend on managing the 855 SSSIs now under their care.

The resulting study was based on a relatively small sample, but it was a sound basis for discussions. Above all, it showed that supporting the Trusts' management of SSSIs would represent good value for money.

Partly because of the break-up of the Conservancy in 1990, it was the end of 1991 before further progress could be made. Negotiations finally got underway with a series of productive meetings between a small team of Society, Trust and agency representatives.

Fencing work at Red Moor, Cornwall – one of many Trust reserves to benefit from Reserves Enhancement Scheme funding

A new scheme for Trusts in England – the RESERVES ENHANCEMENT SCHEME (RES) – was born five months later. Initially this was to be exclusively for the Wildlife Trusts. There would be grant-aid over five years for the management of SSSIs and the costs of capital items. A scheme that provided Government funding for the management of SSSIs, such as the RES, had been an ambition of the Trusts and others for years. If Trusts could deliver and make a success of the pilot then the prospects were good. The RES was successful. In the first five years the Trusts benefited by £1 million. A precedent had also been set, not only for maintaining and developing the scheme itself into the new millennium, but also for parallel initiatives elsewhere in the UK.

STRETCHED BY OUTSIDE EVENTS

It was proving a very busy time for the relatively small number of conservation staff at the Partnership's national office. The large campaigning programme, the NEW GROUND initiative, and the RES negotiations were all underway. The Society also had to find space to respond to two further events – one of national, the other of international, significance.

The first involved yet more reorganisation of the Conservancy. In July 1989, the then Secretary of State for the Environment, Nicholas Ridley, had announced that the Government proposed not only to split the Conservancy into separate organisations for England, Scotland and Wales, but also to cut its budget.

The Conservancy's Chairman, Sir William Wilkinson, said the "proposals make little sense in national, international or economic terms. I am greatly concerned that the scientific capability of NCC will be undermined".[295] The Society believed the new devolved agencies would be less effective and more expensive to run. There was also a lack of clarity over how nature conservation issues with a UK or international dimension would be handled under the new arrangements. The first reaction was that the "organisational bombsite"[296] that the Government

A *Natural World* cartoon by David Smith depicting Nicholas Ridley's splitting up of the Nature Conservancy Council

looked like creating could potentially involve "six different bodies in the United Kingdom responsible for countryside conservation to no less than four Ministers".[297]

Despite the furore that ensued, the bill to split up the Conservancy went ahead. Following discussions with the Trusts, particularly the SCOTTISH TRUST and the Trusts in Wales, the Society had moved its position. It was not now opposed to greater federalism and delegation – even devolution – so long as Government demonstrated a greater commitment to nature conservation. But concerns remained at the lack of a body to drive forward nature conservation at the Great Britain level.

As the legislation threaded its way through Parliament, the House of Lords Science and Technology Committee, chaired by Lord Carver, decided to open up an inquiry into one aspect of the proposed changes – the weakening of the agencies' science base. The Society joined with the RSPB to give oral evidence to the Carver Committee. "A new nature conservation organisation for Great Britain as a whole,"[298] they argued, "must provide a strong policy and science base; remain independent from Government; be funded separately from the agencies for each country; have a standard approach based on sound research and set a series of objectives and standards to be applied on a Great Britain basis".[299] In a bid to placate the opponents, the new

Secretary of State for the Environment, Chris Patten, had already announced a Joint Committee to link the three new agencies and to give advice on UK and international nature conservation issues. But he now went further, agreeing that the Joint Nature Conservation Committee (JNCC), as it would be called, should have an explicit scientific responsibility and an independent chair. The proposals for this Committee and to establish what would become English Nature, the Countryside Council for Wales and Scottish Natural Heritage were finally enacted by the Environmental Protection Act 1990 and, shortly afterwards, the Natural Heritage (Scotland) Act 1991 (STATUTORY NATURE CONSERVATION AGENCIES). Northern Ireland still lacked an agency of comparable stature or independence. However, although not a 'full' member, the Northern Ireland Government was invited to attend and to participate in the JNCC meetings. It was not until 2005 that JNCC's remit was formally extended to cover Northern Ireland.

In a closing speech to a 1989 Wildlife and Countryside Link (WILDLIFE LINK) conference on *Future Structures for Countryside Protection in the UK*, Stuart Housden, then Head of Conservation Planning at the RSPB and a stalwart of the Wildlife and Countryside Act 1981 campaign, summed up the views of many in the voluntary sector at the time. The break-up of the Conservancy had been a political act which was all about day-to-day control over the use of its regulatory powers. It was not motivated by a measured analysis of the problems faced by it or any other agency in delivering effective conservation. The Government had wrested the initiative "away from those who have worked with the post-war consensus on nature conservation. Once the Wildlife and Countryside Act 1981 had became law, the NCC became a serious player, it joined the big boys".[300] Its new powers were thus a mixed blessing and by using them the Conservancy had "sowed the seeds of its own destruction".[301] Housden believed it

would be wise for conservationists to learn the lessons from this experience and apply them in the future.

Wilkinson, for his part, had talked passionately and courageously in his speech to the Society's National Conference in Nottingham in April 1990 about his dislike of the Government's proposals. He was prepared to support the idea of strong independent agencies in England, Scotland and Wales provided there was a strong UK- and science-orientated centre. But the strong centre had not materialised. Wilkinson's prophetic words in closing his speech now had more than a ring of truth. "You should realise that with the split-up of NCC, the power and influence for nature conservation has passed into the hands of the voluntary bodies. You must take and use this power".[302]

The Society's second additional commitment at this time had its origins in a major international event. Almost 20 years had passed since the UN Conference on the Human Environment in Stockholm, the "first global response to the unfolding environmental crisis".[303] The 1987 UN World Commission on Environment and Development had linked the issue of environmental protection and global economic growth and development. It had "thrust the concept of 'sustainable development' into the mainstream of world debate".[304] In December 1989, the UN General Assembly had taken the unprecedented step of calling all nations together for an Earth Summit in Rio de Janeiro, Brazil in 1992.

The event was historic on two levels. It was the largest gathering to date of world leaders and governments – nearly 100 leaders and 172 nations. It was historic too in the way that, in the lead up to the Summit, it stimulated people around the world to voice their concerns about the future of the planet. "Participation ranged from gatherings of the Council of Elders on the tiny Pacific island nation of Tokelau to meetings of the Parliament of the United Kingdom; from assemblies of the Swaziland Boy Scouts

The President of the United States, George Bush Senior, addresses the Earth Summit in Rio in 1992

to conventions of business people in the upper echelons of multinational corporations".[305] Despite the euphoria of the moment and the undoubted impetus the event gave to new national initiatives worldwide, the opportunity was missed for agreement on common action at the international level.

The central agreement of the Earth Summit was Agenda 21, a blueprint for actions in all areas of human activity. It contained 40 separate sections and 120 action programmes, designed to integrate environmental concerns across a broad range of activities. It included a section on biological diversity and pressed for the adoption of a Biological Diversity Convention. Signed by 153 of the participating nations, the Biodiversity Convention (as it became known) called for each Contracting Party, as far as it was able, to:

" (a) develop national strategies, plans or programmes for the conservation and sustainable use of biological diversity or adapt for this purpose existing strategies, plans or programmes which

shall reflect, inter alia, the measures set out in this Convention relevant to the Contracting Party concerned; and

(b) Integrate, as far as possible and as appropriate, the conservation and sustainable use of biological diversity into relevant sectoral or cross-sectoral plans, programmes and policies".[306]

In December 1993, the Convention came into effect, 90 days after it was ratified by the 30th country.

Britain managed to do more than most to follow up Rio. Soon after the Summit, the Prime Minister, John Major, wrote to leaders of the European Community and G7 countries urging them to deliver on their commitments to publish plans for action on biodiversity. The British Government felt it had the moral high ground in this respect. It had made the decision to publish a UK Biodiversity Plan for the first time and to establish an internal Government steering group to prepare it.

This was an encouraging start. But the Society's fear was that the plan would end up being yet another bland review that failed to properly quantify the scale of the problem or to adequately identify targets and priorities for action. The plan needed to encourage action, not just by the statutory conservation agencies, but by *all* Government departments and *all* sections of society.

The 'biodiversity' NGOs shared the Society's fears. They also wanted to bring about a step change in the way the country tackled the conservation of its biodiversity. They realised that if this was to happen, they were the ones that collectively had to come up with the blueprint.

MAKING WAVES ON BIODIVERSITY

As a result, just six organisations – Butterfly Conservation, Friends of the Earth, Plantlife, the RSPB, The Wildlife Trusts and WWF – agreed to create a new Biodiversity Challenge Group. This would be a 'ginger group' to influence the Government and to present it with a comprehensive and detailed assessment of the approach that it believed should now be adopted. There was a strong sense of purpose amongst the six that fuelled a remarkable level of energy, commitment and camaraderie. They were keen for the Government to focus on ends, rather than means, and to adopt an ambitious, albeit realistic, approach. Above all, the six were willing and, they believed, very able to play an active part in preparing and implementing what would be the first UK strategy for biodiversity.

It was important for the Group to get these views across and, if necessary, to 'make waves'. To this end in late 1993, shortly before the publication of the Government's plan, the Group dropped its own rock into the biodiversity pond. It published *Biodiversity Challenge – an Agenda for Conservation in the UK*. Described later by Marren as "one of the milestones on the journey of the voluntary bodies from amateur natural history societies to partners in environmental policy-making",[307] material in the report had been "offered to the Government during the past

six months with a desire to help in what is undoubtedly a complex task".[308] The motive was a strong desire to influence the Government's approach and to keep it on its toes. In addition, the Group wanted to continue to be involved in the next stage of the process.

In its report, the Group called for the Government to introduce a process based on a logical and relatively simple cycle of activity. The cycle should start with an audit of the resource to establish priorities and then proceed to the production of costed species and habitat action plans with realistic but ambitious targets. Implementation and monitoring of these

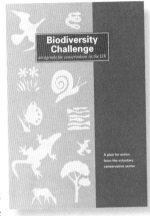

plans should follow with a final review of the process based on the successes and failures on the ground. The purpose of the monitoring was to make amendments to the plans, if necessary, and then to start the cycle once more.

As well as sharing material with the Government there had been some intensive behind the scenes discussions. When the Government's own report, *Biodiversity – The UK Action Plan*, appeared in January 1994, the Group was relieved to see that it included most of the components of its 'cycle of activity', even if they were not put in such a logical fashion. It was "a tentative though valuable step in the right direction".[309]

The third section of the Government's report proposed a forward work programme, including "mechanisms for implementation, reporting and review, and proposes a new UK Biodiversity Action Plan (BAP) Steering Group which will have responsibility for overseeing the development of targets for biodiversity, and the techniques and programmes necessary to achieve them".[310] The all-important word 'targets' was included. When the UK BAP Steering Group got

Large blue butterfly – one of several threatened species given its own Biodiversity Action Plan

down to its work in June, the voluntary conservation organisations had secured five places on the group, two of which were filled by David Erwin (from the ULSTER TRUST) and Tim Sands. The Trusts were also represented on three of four sub-groups (see BIODIVERSITY ACTION PLANNING).

NEW STRUCTURE, NEW STRATEGY

Meanwhile, by July 1990, the Society's Development Committee had brought forward its proposals on the options for the future structure of the Society and Trusts. They were radical, although its Chairman, David Bodger, recalls that "he had some problems keeping them as non-radical as he did".[311] It was not easy to reach a decision, given the large size of Council which included a representative from every Trust. Bodger described how, at the ensuing Council meeting where the proposals were presented, "chaos had ensued resulting in great upset to the Development Committee and its members".[312]

But by the beginning of November, ADAMS and PHILLIPSON had secured agreement to work up a new paper to "separate the issues clearly into matters of principle and matters of practice and procedure".[313] In January 1991, the Council agreed to review the Royal Charter and the committee structure. An independent review of the services provided by the Society to the Trusts, led by Julian Greatrix, brought new and more independent thinking to bear on the issues of the moment. Greatrix presented his proposals in April 1991 under the theme of 'Enabling Leadership' or what became known, more colloquially, as 'Letting Go'.

In July, Cordy responded to the Greatrix findings and to the Development Committee's work with an action plan to address the internal changes that were needed. It had seven tasks: developing and communicating a vision of the Partnership up to 1995; reviewing 'attitudes'; making the national office fit for purpose (including an overhaul of systems and procedures); improving systems for working with

Trusts; reviewing the committee system; developing training; and finally monitoring plans.

It was a refreshing appraisal of the need for change. More joined-up thinking and greater cooperation was required for the whole organisation to realise its true potential. A new senior staff and committee structure was put in place at the Society's Council meeting in September 1991. DUNSTAN ADAMS retired as President and Chairman of the Council and ALAN NEWTON as Honorary Treasurer. With a satisfactory conclusion to the BWA, SIR DAVID ATTENBOROUGH accepted the invitation to become President, JOHN PHILLIPSON was appointed Chairman of Council and the post of Honorary Treasurer was filled by REES JONES.

Adams, as retiring President, delivered a valedictory address pointing out the value of the Partnership and that constitutional change was not enough. "We have together come through a period of self-examination which has involved reconsideration of our methods of working. . . constitutional changes in themselves will achieve little, it is people who do the appointed things that matter. . . in the words of MAX NICHOLSON, 'conservation looks after the environment but people look after conservation'".[314]

The Trusts welcomed the determination to achieve greater delegation from the national office. This meant more work sub-contracted to Trusts and the greater use of advisory groups, expert panels and individuals from Trusts on national initiatives. It was also about acknowledging that the national office could not be expected to fight national campaigning battles on its own. In December, following a series of regional meetings between CORDY, Phillipson and the Trusts, Cordy reported progress on the action plan. The vision would be captured in a new Corporate Strategy. The Society's 1989-92 Corporate Strategy had been of "considerable value to RSNC staff and Committees".[315] It had helped "develop the spirit of partnership with the Wildlife Trusts".[316]

Sir David Attenborough became the Society's President in 1991

The purpose of the Society's national office was becoming more clearly defined. It would have a representation role (mainly at the UK level) and be a provider of services and support that could most "economically and effectively be provided centrally".[317] There were still some lingering doubts linked to "Trusts' fears of a central take-over"[318] and there would be a need for "considerable persistence"[319] if more open communication and decision-making were to prevail. There was an acceptance that in effect there was a need for an unwritten "contractual relationship"[320] between all elements of the Partnership. In fact, a Memorandum of Understanding was signed by the majority of Trusts. However, it would not be until 2010, almost two decades later, that a more formal Memorandum of Cooperation was signed by all Wildlife Trusts.

FINANCIAL CLOUDS RETURN

The programme of internal changes was in full swing. But Cordy was undoubtedly frustrated at how complex it was proving to move things forward. The Executive Committee wanted to be sure that the Society could manage such an ambitious campaigning and reform programme.

It believed the "output of the office, and its quality, had been very high but that it cannot be sustained for much longer at present levels of resources, especially in times of financial stress".[321] The country was in recession and inflation was still running at around ten per cent.

Cordy had been keen to "seize every opportunity to attract quick funds"[322] using "UK2000 to increase RSNC office capacity and... business donations to fund key national projects".[323] But, with relatively little change in the contribution from Trusts, the Society's cash flow was still precarious and overly dependent on funding from the Department of Environment under its Special Grants programme and under the UK2000 Project. Core activity was too reliant on sponsors and project funding and there was a danger of the Society taking on schemes that failed to address the Trust's most immediate day-to-day concerns. A major new sustainability initiative – ENVIRONMENT CITY – was seen by some as a case in point.

Just like PERRING ten years earlier, Cordy was struggling to get the books to balance and meet all the demands on the national office. To save costs the 1992 National Conference was cancelled and there was tacit agreement that a "higher proportion of the nationally-earned income should go to national activity if ever the Office in particular, and the Partnership as a whole, is to progress".[324] This latter point was, perhaps, an understandable reaction to the difficulties. The danger was that by adopting such a strategy, funding would skew the Society's national activities away from those favoured by the Trusts.

CELEBRATING EIGHTY YEARS

Progress was still being made and in October 1992 the Society celebrated its 80th birthday (ANNIVERSARIES) with a Royal Gala dinner at The Banqueting House in London in the presence of its Patron, HRH The Prince of Wales. The same month a special conference was convened at Framlingham in Suffolk to enable the Trusts to discuss the new Corporate Strategy. Despite a somewhat dramatic reference to its being the "last chance of getting the partnership to work effectively",[325] the new Corporate Strategy 1993–98 was unanimously agreed in June 1993 – a significant accomplishment for both Cordy and the officers. A new internal newsletter, *Conservation News*, was introduced to network information about its conservation work to Trust staff and volunteers.

The Society's marketing work shifted up a few gears. The size, format and editorial approach of NATURAL WORLD were re-modelled for the spring/summer issue. As part of a new national legacy campaign, the same issue carried a half-page advertisement promoting a booklet – *How to Make or Change Your Will*. The decision was also taken to finally drop reference to the Society from the corporate identity. A new square logo, incorporating the badger's head and just the words 'The Wildlife Trusts' with a new strapline 'Putting Wildlife on the Map', was launched at the 1994 National Conference.

A new marketing department had been created and it was not long before its new Director was developing a public relations strategy and discussing ideas with some of the key staff in the Trusts. This highlighted the innovative educational and outreach programmes run by Trusts in SCOTLAND, SUFFOLK, WARWICKSHIRE, WILTSHIRE and elsewhere.

There were philosophical debates about whether the conservation of wildlife was for the wildlife itself or primarily, if not solely, for the benefit of people. These debates sensibly coalesced around the view that it was for both. The two were inextricably linked. These discussions were the gestation for a new campaign – 'A Million for Wildlife' – which embraced an agenda for both wildlife *and* people. The aim was to achieve a million days of work by staff and volunteers; a million pledges of commitment; and a million pounds during European Nature Conservation Year (ENCY) in 1995. The theme of the Council of Europe's ENCY was action for nature outside designated areas and in the community.

'A Million for Wildlife' was launched by the Lincoln MP, Kenneth Carlisle, on the terrace of the House of Commons in October 1994. At the same event, the Society's President, SIR DAVID ATTENBOROUGH, took the opportunity to announce three other national projects: a new national Wildlife Week in June; a village nature trail competition; and a national action pack for creating wildlife habitats.

Significantly the 'Million for Wildlife' campaign was largely the brainchild of the Trusts. They considered that this was exactly the sort of proactive, high profile, public activity with which The Wildlife Trusts should be involved and exactly the sort of activity the Society should be helping to coordinate.

NATURE COMES TO TOWN

The spring of 1993 had seen further work to bring the urban movement into the 'family' of The Wildlife Trusts. The Fairbrother Group established in 1985 now transformed itself into the Urban Wildlife Partnership (UWP), and adopted the identity and logo of The Wildlife Trusts Partnership. The UWP Company formally came into being in September 1994. It would go on to campaign on urban issues, provide advice, publish guidance and information, organise meetings and conferences and help develop hundreds of local urban groups across the UK (URBAN AREAS AND NATURE CONSERVATION).

Left: The 1993–94 *Annual Review* promoted the Society's new strapline – Putting Wildlife on the Map

At the end of 1992, the Sheffield City Wildlife Trust applied to become a Corporate Member of the Society. Because the Trust operated entirely in the bailiwick of the YORKSHIRE TRUST, it was unhappy about this application. MICHAEL HOLTON, who had just stepped down as the Society's Honorary Secretary, was asked to mediate. The Yorkshire Trust believed "the interests of the Partnership would be better serviced by encouraging the SHEFFIELD TRUST to cross-affiliate with Yorkshire".[326] However, in September 1993, the application was approved by 32 votes to nil with two abstentions, and the two Trusts have had a close working relationship since.

In 1993, there was an explosion of important urban and community initiatives. The previous October the Society had published a guide for urban wildlife groups on *How to Write a Development Plan*. It was based partly on the outcomes from a Partnership conference supported by WWF and Marks and Spencer. The Society's ENVIRONMENT CITY programme now had its full quota of four designated cities in place, with Leeds and Peterborough joining Middlesbrough and Leicester as "pioneers of sustainability in the UK".[327] The spring issue of the Society's magazine for urban groups, *Urban Wildlife*, highlighted the ultimately successful battles to save Oxleas Wood in south-east London and Royate Hill in Bristol (AVON TRUST). In May, the Society published *Grassroots*, a review of community action; in September, the Urban Wildlife Partnership held its fourth national conference, 'Breaking down the Barriers', in Luton; and in October, a further conference 'Wildlife, People and Parks' was held to discuss urban green space.

CITIZEN SCIENCE

By the early 1990s, the junior branch, WILDLIFE WATCH, had grown significantly and the number of young members had risen to 30,000. A series of annual surveys reached its highpoint in 1991 with National Riverwatch – Watch's largest project yet. An extensive three-year survey was undertaken to study the state of the country's rivers, river banks and river catchments. Children, families and schools investigated the quality of river water using surveys of invertebrate diversity and simple chemical tests. One hundred and seventy thousand people took part and the Society's education team even travelled to Russia to demonstrate the project to educationalists interested in replicating it there.

In fact, Riverwatch was the latest in a long line of participative Watch surveys. The 1980s had seen a series of groundbreaking projects, such as 'Acid Drops' in 1985–86, where children measured the pH of rainfall to analyse the effects of acid rain using flat-pack rain gauges sent to them by post. Huge publicity saw the project taken up internationally. Another innovative project in 1989 saw children growing two cultivars of the tobacco plant, *Nicotiana tabacum*, as a way of measuring atmospheric pollution. The cultivars started to display spots when exposed to differing levels of ozone. Children grew the seeds and then monitored spots appearing on the leaves as they responded to low level ozone. The project was promoted on the BBC's *Blue Peter* programme and was launched by the Environment Minister in Parliament Square in London.

These were pioneering projects which engaged huge numbers of children around the UK with practical experiments and studies of nature. They were forerunners of the 'citizen science' projects that would come to characterise the next decade with the arrival of the BBC's Springwatch television programme and projects to track nature's calendar and the effects of climate change.

MORE CHANGE AHEAD

Despite the success of the 'Million for Wildlife' initiative, the Watch projects and the large national programme of conservation campaigns, behind the scenes there were still matters to resolve. A new Business Plan attempted to address this, including a new position of Director of Resources that was filled in July 1994 by Martin Gough. A financial strategy was introduced that

Children taking part in the National Riverwatch project

David Bellamy joins London Trust campaigners protesting against proposals to build a road through Oxleas Wood in London

was designed to achieve working capital equivalent to ten weeks' spending and to decrease the Society's dependence on sponsorship and Government grant-aid. But there would be no silver bullet and the financial struggles continued. A paper put before Council, called *A Parliament for the Wildlife Trusts*, highlighted the need for a more active forum through which the Trusts could help to resolve such difficulties.

Meanwhile, the Grantham National Conference in September was treated to speeches from "three great men"[328] from the world of conservation, SIR DAVID ATTENBOROUGH, Sir William Wilkinson and MAX NICHOLSON. Attenborough was later to say how he had been "truly impressed by the Trusts' absolute determination to popularise nature conservation".[329] But in the end-of-conference speech, CORDY found it difficult to be upbeat. The Society's financial difficulties were attracting criticism from the newly-emerging powerbase of Trust Directors, and he was under increasing pressure.

At the Executive meeting at the end of October 1994, Cordy presented a final financial 'rescue package', in part the result of an internal Trustee review. Sensing that the Trusts were losing confidence, the Trustees agreed that a "full and clear statement should be prepared about these matters, to counter rumours circulating".[330] Within a few days, however, Cordy felt his position was untenable and on 11th November 1994 he resigned. Three days later, the Honorary Treasurer, REES JONES, tendered his resignation and was succeeded by George Wright.

Despite some occasional turbulence, it had been an extremely productive period in the Society's history. Cordy had undoubtedly expanded and developed the organisation. He had helped it confront its need for more modern management and had led it and the Partnership a considerable way along a path of necessary growth and development.

Even before these latest events, it was clear that there was to be a contested election for CHAIRMAN

OF COUNCIL at its meeting on 17th November. In the event, it was a somewhat reluctant ROBIN CRANE (who had recently ended his Chairmanship of the Sussex Trust) who was elected. At the Society's Grantham national conference a few weeks earlier Crane had presented 'Reaching Our Full Potential'. It was a comprehensive analysis of the strengths, opportunities and weaknesses of the movement, including some of the ways he thought "the Wildlife Trusts should now be moving forward both as a partnership and individually".[331]

He believed there were two golden opportunities. The first was to develop a very high profile national role for the Trusts as auditors and monitors of the country's biological diversity. The second was for the Trusts to be "proactive leaders in the development of exciting new countryside wildlife enhancement policies".[332] Together with a paper on a future financial strategy for the Society prepared by Crane in January 1993, these were the aspirations that guided him in his forthcoming chairmanship. He believed there was a need for a strong centre with the resources and leadership to support and strengthen the individual Trusts. The Society had to tackle its large underlying deficit by cutting costs and increasing legacies, and by establishing a legacy equalisation account to build up a stronger capital base. There was also an urgent need to address the movement's national administration – not least the size of the Council. But, above all, the task ahead was to build stronger trust and lines of communication across the movement.

Even as this was unfolding, the new Director of Finance, Gough, was quick to assert his position by presenting a detailed examination of the Society's financial health. His tell-it-as-it-is and no-nonsense presentation of his findings impressed the Society and would soon prove popular with the Trusts as well.

Before he left, Cordy had proposed applying "'scalpel' rather than 'axe'",[333] but the view now was that more radical surgery was needed. As soon as Crane was appointed Chairman, he proposed a major reduction in the number of national office staff. But Gough's advice was that the Society was too dependent on its multiplicity of grants and funding and that radical cuts would be too dangerous a policy to pursue.

Crane also needed to appoint a new Executive leader but considered the role of managing the business affairs of the national office and leading the Trusts forward at this critical time was beyond the capacity of one person. He now proposed dividing the role between a Director General, who would act as a national spokesman and strengthen the relationship with the individual Wildlife Trusts, and a Managing Director who would be responsible for running the national office. When Cordy resigned, it had been with some relief that the Society found itself with Gough to 'hold the fort'. It was now agreed that Gough should be re-styled Acting Managing Director while the Society began recruiting a new Director General.

CHAPTER 8

Partition and partnership 1995–1999

It is interesting to contemplate a tangled bank, clothed with many plants of many kinds, with birds singing on the bushes, with various insects flitting about, and with worms crawling through the damp earth, and to reflect that these elaborately constructed forms, so different from each other, and dependent upon each other in so complex a manner, have all been produced by laws acting around us.

From *On the Origin of Species by Means of Natural Selection* by Charles Darwin, 1859

Halfway through the 'biodiversity decade' there was a real buzz of excitement – 1995, European Nature Conservation Year, opened with the six organisations in the Biodiversity Challenge Group (BCG), including The Wildlife Trusts, on the front foot. They were leading the thinking on planning and action to try to halt, and then reverse, the decline in UK wildlife. They were also keen to see the Government rise to the challenges of the 1992 Rio de Janeiro Earth Summit by pioneering a more systematic, objective-led approach to biodiversity conservation.

To keep up the pressure, in January 1995, the BCG launched an enlarged and revised edition of *Biodiversity Challenge – an Agenda for Conservation in the UK* at the Natural History Museum in London. The new edition identified targets for more than 600 species and 35 habitats, including detailed action plans for 44 plants and animals and six habitats. This compared to detailed action plans for just two species in the first edition. The new report also began to tackle the difficult issue of costs.

The report was offered in a spirit of collaboration to the many organisations and individuals on the Government's UK Biodiversity Action Plan (UKBAP) Steering Group who were busy preparing their own report for publication later in the year.

Opposite: Red squirrel – the 1990s saw a coordinated effort by Wildlife Trusts to bring the red squirrel 'back from the brink'

The BCG saw its work not only "as a visionary but practical contribution"[334] but also a benchmark against which to judge the Steering Group's findings.

Its own report had kept the BCG busy but it had not stopped it becoming fully engrossed in the Government's process. Indeed, through the RSPB, it was contracted to draft the majority of the official species action plans for the Steering Group's report.

Biodiversity: The UK Steering Group Report, Volume 1: Meeting the Rio Challenge was finally published in December 1995. It was accompanied by a second, larger volume containing action plans for 116 species and 14 habitats. It was a landmark publication, not least because of the consensus that had been reached amongst such a wide range of interests and institutions. The Government officially welcomed the report five months later. It endorsed its main proposals as the basis for follow-up action. In particular, it accepted the need for a further 286 species plans and 24 habitat plans within two to three years. But, above all, implicit in the Government's support was an acceptance of the Steering Group's philosophy that biodiversity conservation was about more than protecting what was left, it was also about putting back what had been lost.

The philosophy of species and habitat *protection*, that had dominated Government thinking since the Second World War, had been moved on by the biodiversity process to openly embrace species

153

recovery and habitat *restoration*. This change in approach would probably turn out to be the most important legacy of the biodiversity process. There were those who, perhaps justifiably, would criticise the process as cumbersome and bureaucratic. But it provided a means of checking progress on the conservation and restoration of species and habitats that had previously not been available. It also provided a framework for Government engagement. With the key elements of the process enshrined in the Countryside and Rights of Way (CROW) Act 2000 in England and Wales and in the Nature Conservation (Scotland) Act 2004, it was hoped that the new philosophy would be taken more seriously by governments in the future.

It was perhaps not until after the movement's Conservation Conference in Exeter in the summer of 1995, which was largely devoted to the Biodiversity Action Plan process, that Trusts fully recognised the opportunity it might provide. It was the chance to embed biodiversity conservation, not only into the national, but also into the local, environmental agenda in a new way. Trusts began to take a prominent role in many local Biodiversity Action Plan initiatives. For example, the SUSSEX TRUST published *Vision for the Wildlife of Sussex* in 1996 and the DERBYSHIRE TRUST published a *Mid Derbyshire Local Biodiversity Action Plan* in 1997.

(BIODIVERSITY ACTION PLANNING in Part III has more information about the Biodiversity Action Plan process and the work of Biodiversity Challenge).

RINGING THE CHANGES

There had been concerns about changes in the Society's structure before CORDY's resignation.

Above: The Wildlife Trusts played a leading role in the production of many local Biodiversity Action Plans published in the 1990s

Now, in the interregnum, they surfaced again. Following a meeting in Birmingham in November 1994, a technical action group was set up to canvas opinion from Trusts on the Society's structure and business model. The Trusts wanted a structure that not only gave them a formal voice in decision making but also, where appropriate, a mandate to operate at a national level on behalf of the movement.

They backed the idea of a new Director General who would provide entrepreneurial skills and leadership – and be the public voice of The Wildlife Trusts on key national policy issues. But they recognised, as ROBIN CRANE did, that this might mean the day-to-day business of the UK office could no longer be part of the Director General's role.

A clear boundary needed to be drawn between the role of the UK office as a service provider to Trusts and the Society as a charitable grant-making Trust in its own right. The UK office should not be doing what could best be done by the Trusts and any projects it did undertake should be self-financing. The day when the Trusts would fund their own UK office was still some way off, but the meeting agreed to recommend a review by independent consultants. This would not only consider potential efficiency savings across the movement but also the way Trusts funded the UK office.

In February 1995, Crane introduced improvements to the way the Executive Committee operated and set up a new group to monitor and manage the Society's finances. The decision was also taken to advertise for a Director General.

By June, ideas for a new Partnership management structure were being discussed at a meeting of Trust Chairs and Directors at Sevenoaks in Kent. Proposals were emerging for a Partnership Forum, chaired by the Chair of the Society's Council. The Forum would develop and promote consensus on the broad outlines of Partnership structure, strategy, policy and priorities. A Partnership Management Board (PMB), chaired by the Director General, would then secure agreement on the Partnership's programmes and report on their delivery. Trust regional groups would elect representatives to the PMB and to a set of six new policy advisory groups covering different specialisms.

The Society's Council would remain in place to oversee the effective delivery of the national programmes of the Forum and PMB, and to elect the Society's Executive and specialist committees. The Society's Executive would oversee the UK office and advise Council on matters of strategy and policy, and on the delivery of the Partnership's national activities. To mirror these changes the Director General would be responsible to the Chairman of Council, and the Managing Director to the Chairman of the Executive Committee.

It was an important step forward. The Trusts had moved closer to centre stage with unwieldy Council meetings now a thing of the past. Instead each region and country was represented on the PMB by a chairman and director of a Trust. This provided a much more practical structure whilst remaining democratic.

CAMPAIGNING ZEAL CONTINUES

In August 1995, collective spirits were lifted with the announcement that the movement's new Director General (PRINCIPAL OFFICERS) would take up his position at the beginning of December. He was DR SIMON LYSTER, a lawyer and an enthusiastic and committed nature conservationist who had been working for WWF on the international stage and most recently as Head of Conservation Policy at WWF-UK. He had made his name as an influencer in the drafting and implementation of international treaties. He was also a successful campaigner, notably having fought for a ban on the ivory trade. Before he started, Lyster made refreshingly confident and energetic appearances at the Society's first joint Marketing and Conservation Conference in Exeter in July and at its National Conference in York in September.

In the time between CORDY's departure and LYSTER's arrival, the Society had continued an active programme of conservation campaigning. As a result of the 1992 reforms of the European Common Agricultural Policy, the Government

Red grouse – a species that suffers from overgrazing of upland habitats

had introduced an agri-environment regulation that marked a welcome and historic move away from increasing agricultural production to more environmentally-friendly farming. In a report, *Realising our Assets*, the Society expressed its concern that the regulation remained essentially a bolt-on extra, not fully integrated with mainstream agricultural subsidies. What was needed was a more comprehensive, UK-wide, set of agri-environment schemes targeted on areas of high biodiversity value. There was also a need for a five-fold increase in the Government's planned budget for this area of activity over the next decade.

The next year, the Society continued to call for more support generally for environmentally-sensitive farming, but switched its attention to the uplands. In *Crisis in the Hills,* it reported on the adverse effect of sheep overgrazing on upland biodiversity. There was a need for Government to change livestock support in the short term, and to campaign in Europe for a move away from headage payments to an area-based scheme within three years. The Society also wanted the introduction of an integrated rural development policy that would replace production subsidies and deliver biodiversity targets in the next five years.

The Society's 1995 *Annual Review* noted the publication of its report, *New Force for Wildlife Conservation*, analysing the potential weaknesses in the UK's implementation of the EC Habitats Directive. Part I of *New Force* had been published by the Society in 1994 and was now supplemented by Part II, describing three case studies. In addition, 1995 saw the Society compile a Wildlife Sites Handbook (LOCAL WILDLIFE SITES) to encourage the development, recognition and protection of non-statutory sites of wildlife importance.

The *Annual Review* also reported on new contacts and influence in the Westminster Parliament; the Society's leading role in the UK Biodiversity planning process; and the continuation of campaigns on safeguarding sites,

WATER FOR WILDLIFE, the PEATLANDS CAMPAIGN, ROAD BUILDING AND WILDLIFE, and MINERALS' PLANNING.

In 1994, the minerals campaign had moved on to expose what it called the 'great rock robbery' – the illegal destruction of limestone pavements in Cumbria, Lancashire and Yorkshire, and in smaller areas in Scotland and Wales. The extraordinarily shaped, water-worn limestone was highly-prized by gardeners as a rockery stone. The Wildlife Trusts had been amongst those that had successfully campaigned for Limestone Pavement Orders (LPOs) under the Wildlife and Countryside Act 1981. Sadly their destruction had continued, partly because there were loopholes in the law – LPOs did not override planning consents, for example – and partly because the law was being openly flouted.

The CUMBRIA TRUST was coordinating a Limestone Pavement Action Group on behalf of the voluntary sector, publicly supported by the BBC *Gardeners' World* presenter, Geoff Hamilton. At its public launch in September 1995 at Gait Barrows National Nature Reserve in Cumbria – one of the most important examples of limestone pavement in the country – Hamilton appealed to gardeners to use man-made 'rock'. He also called for the revocation of existing planning permissions and for an end to illegal excavation. The Action Group produced a booklet, *Limestone Pavements – Our Fragile Heritage*. It was backed by the statutory agencies (including Scottish Natural Heritage), Forest Enterprise and the two National Parks most affected, as a contribution to the UK Biodiversity Action Plan for limestone pavement.

Limestone pavement had been accorded priority status under the EC Habitats Directive but this did not address the cause of the habitat destruction. In 1996, The Wildlife Trusts had returned to the Chelsea Flower Show where its stand, incorporating the great rock robbery theme, won a Certificate of Merit. By 1999, The Wildlife Trusts were calling for a Europe-wide trade ban on water-worn limestone.

Destruction of limestone pavement, Yorkshire Dales

There have been some good news stories. For example a campaign to stop limestone pavement extraction on Orton Scar in Cumbria ended successfully. Sadly, however, there is still a demand for the stone today and the need to raise public awareness through increased publicity and campaigning, aimed at both retailers and consumers, remains.

SIGNED, SEALED AND DELIVERED

By October 1995, the finishing touches had been put to the new Partnership structure. Bob Page, who had led the technical action group tasked with reviewing this, was able to write to all Trusts' chairs and directors with a final, considered proposal. The new structure was duly approved in December 1995. At the Council meeting in January 1996, PROFESSOR DAVID BELLAMY took over from SIR DAVID ATTENBOROUGH as the new PRESIDENT of the Society and The Wildlife Trusts to lead the movement into the new millennium.

A fortnight later the Partnership Management Board held its first meeting. The role of its

Chairman was now in the hands of the new Director General, rather than a Trustee of the Society or a Trust. LYSTER, chairing the first meeting, expressed the hope that everyone concerned would "work hard to become the driving force behind the Partnership".[335]

MARSHALLING FORCES FOR A NATIONAL OFFENSIVE

It was a fresh beginning and Lyster was excited by the opportunities that the new arrangements presented. He could concentrate his time on supporting the Trusts and advancing their national standing, largely unencumbered by the day-to-day management of the national office and with a degree of autonomy denied his predecessors.

Interviewed by the *Daily Telegraph's* environment editor, Charles Clover, for the winter 1995 issue of *Natural World*, Lyster spoke about the enormous potential of the Trust movement. "National profile is lacking but, if this can be changed, I see no reason why they shouldn't become the number one conservation organisation in the country. . . by the time I finish being

David Bellamy, the Society's new President in 1995

Director General I want The Wildlife Trusts to be a household name".[336]

Both PERRING and CORDY had expressed similar ambitions on their appointment. To be fair, whilst The Wildlife Trusts could not be described as a 'household name', at the local level Trusts were much better known. Even so, a MORI Business and Environment public opinion survey in June 1996 concluded that The Wildlife Trusts had some way to go before it was seen as a "top environmental organisation".[337] The recent changes, including Lyster's appointment, provided the opportunity for things to improve more quickly.

Lyster's strategy from the beginning was to interact with his constituency – the Trusts – at a personal level. He was keen to meet Trust staff and engage ambassadors, people in the Trusts prepared to champion issues and policies, spread the workload and create a sense of shared owner-ship of the Partnership. In some cases he was pressing at an open door and several directors were already keen to play a role on the national stage.

In the spring of 1996, there was a feeling that the time was right for the movement to approach the National Lottery for funds for the Trusts' nature reserves network. After a meeting between Lyster, the WILTSHIRE TRUST's Director, Gary Mantle, and the KENT TRUST's Director, Pete Raine, with Lord Jacob Rothschild, Chairman of the National Heritage Memorial Fund (NHMF), the Fund agreed to consider putting aside £25 million over the coming five years. The Fund wanted applications to come from individual Trusts but it was prepared to negotiate over a category of projects agreed at a national level.

By March 1997, 20 Trusts had received more than £5 million between them from the NHMF's HERITAGE LOTTERY FUND (HLF). Across the UK spectacular wildlife sites were saved and enhanced. Quarries were restored for bats in Dorset, 1000 hectares of upland habitat was acquired at Whitelee Moor in Northumberland and the Gwent Trust was able to purchase three ancient wildflower-rich farms. HLF funding enabled the purchase of 150 acres of unimproved grassland at Clattinger Farm in Wiltshire and management of 750 acres of ancient woodland at Lower Woods in Gloucestershire.

In the first ten years, the HLF would end up committing £72 million through no fewer than 317 separate grant awards to a variety of projects managed by the 47 Trusts. These were huge amounts and closer to the sort of money that CHARLES ROTHSCHILD had hoped would be forthcoming from the Carnegie Trust in the 1920s. It had a transformative impact on the movement, funding work on 1,250 nature reserves. Ancient woodlands were coppiced again after years of neglect, historic grasslands restored and wetlands saved as traditional reed cutting and grazing patterns were reintroduced.

LYSTER was also successful in attracting other Trust ambassadors for the Partnership. The SUSSEX TRUST Director was soon chairing a group working on the second stage of a bid to the Millennium Commission for a £22 million partnership project to establish a National Biodiversity Network –

a network of data custodians working together to give a complete picture of the status of the UK's wildlife. The bid was sadly unsuccessful, but those involved – the statutory agencies, Marine Biological Association, National Federation of Biological Recording, the Natural History Museum, the RSPB and The Wildlife Trusts – were still determined to take matters further.

The Wildlife Trusts had an early success when it secured a grant from the Esmée Fairbairn Charitable Trust to produce standards and recommendations for developing and running local record centres (LRCs). These would be informed by the experience gained over three years from the establishment of three pilot centres in north-east Scotland, Cheshire and Powys. A newsletter – *Linking LRCs* – kept LRCs and local and national data collectors up to date with the pilot centres and with the development of the National Biodiversity Network (NBN).

It would be a period of close involvement in the development of LRCs, and the necessary supporting software, and would culminate in the production of guidance on *Developing a Local Records Centre* in 1999 and on *Running a Local Records Centre as Part of the NBN* in 2001. The initial aim of the NBN was to improve the communication and sharing of biodiversity data by developing standards and tools; species dictionaries; technical data sets and access terms; accreditation schemes; and an innovative NBN Index and internet gateway to data held by custodians. A National Biodiversity Network Trust was formally established as an independent charity in 2000 with the Society hosting the secretariat until 2008.

Other ambassadorial appointments followed. The Directors of the SUFFOLK TRUST and the NOTTINGHAMSHIRE TRUST were asked to co-lead a review of NATURAL WORLD. The Director of the SHROPSHIRE TRUST was asked to lead a review of WILDLIFE WATCH and the Director of the WARWICKSHIRE TRUST a working group to consider a possible national membership scheme.

In addition, LYSTER was anxious to strengthen the senior team at the UK office and believed that headhunting from within the Trusts and other national environmental bodies could yield rich pickings. In 1996, for example, after nine years heading up the Urban Wildlife Trust in the West Midlands, Peter Shirley was seconded to run a new Urban and Community Unit at the UK office. Its aim was to progress The Wildlife Trusts' urban conservation work, including managing the Urban Wildlife Partnership (URBAN AREAS AND NATURE CONSERVATION). The secondment was successful and continued until the end of the millennium when Shirley returned to become Regional Director for the Trusts in the West Midlands. In 1998, a new role of Director of Programmes, incorporating the role of Head of Conservation, was established. This was filled for a short time by the former Director of the MONTGOMERYSHIRE TRUST, then a few months later by another of Lyster's Trust ambassadors, the Director of the Suffolk Trust.

A visit by HRH The Prince of Wales to Clattinger Farm – a new Wiltshire Trust reserve purchased with support from the Heritage Lottery Fund

INTO THE CORRIDORS OF POWER

With much of the internal housekeeping in hand, attention turned to raising the national profile of The Wildlife Trusts' work. Lyster had had a chance to go public soon after his appointment in December 1995 when the Government launched the UK Biodiversity Action Plan Steering Group's report, *Meeting the Rio Challenge*. It was a world first that, as NATURAL WORLD acknowledged, went "beyond lofty platitudes and worthy intentions".[338] Lyster talked up its welcome commitments in the media to try to hold the Government to them. He labelled it a historic moment, "never before have there been such clear targets for recovery of threatened species and habitats in the UK".[339] Everything now depended on the Government's follow-up of the report's recommendations, particularly the reaction of powerful players like the Departments of Transport and Trade and Industry. As Sara Hawkswell at the UK office put it, "it will determine whether this impressive piece of work becomes a milestone in conservation or a doorstop at the Department of Environment"[340] (BIODIVERSITY ACTION PLANNING).

Lyster was equally comfortable in front of a camera or microphone as he was in the presence of a Minister. In the first few months of 1996, opportunities to promote the movement's views more widely came thick and fast. In January 1996, The Wildlife Trusts joined a partnership of the six largest environmental NGOs to campaign, as it turned out unsuccessfully, against a proposal to build a road bypass around Newbury in Berkshire. It was, nevertheless, a high-profile development. The NGOs had written to the *The Times* and a photograph of the leaders of the six organisations crossing a bridge on the affected site was widely used in the press. CRANE, as Chairman of The Wildlife Trusts, also wrote a follow-up letter to *The Times* drawing attention to the evidence presented by the Trusts at the 1988 public inquiry and to the lack of any attempt by the planners to ameliorate the serious environmental damage to prime wildlife sites.

Clearing up after the Sea Empress disaster, Saundersfoot, South Wales

In February 1996, the oil tanker, Sea Empress, went aground spilling 72,000 tonnes of crude oil and polluting 118 miles of coast, including the Dyfed Trust's island nature reserves of Skomer and Skokholm. LYSTER drove overnight so as to be available on site for the gathering media.

In April, The Wildlife Trusts joined other environmental organisations to launch *Plants without Peat* (PEATLANDS CAMPAIGN) and that June, the Shadow Environment Secretary, Frank Dobson, visited the Society's national office in Lincoln to meet with Lyster and key staff.

In October, Lyster with the Director of the WILTSHIRE TRUST, Gary Mantle, led opposition – this time successfully – to the building of a bypass across Salisbury's medieval water-meadows, famously immortalised by the artist, Constable, in his painting *Salisbury Cathedral from the Meadows*.

A NEW PLAN

The Trust-inspired roads and limestone pavement campaigns had made some headway but now there was a feeling that a national conservation plan was needed to re-focus and be more reflective of grassroots thinking. The plan should "set out the focal areas for partnership conservation activities over the next three to five years".[341] In effect there was a call for 'ground-truthing' of the existing campaign programme.

Preparation of such a plan began in earnest in 1997. A sub-group, overseen by MARTIN SPRAY of the BERKSHIRE, BUCKINGHAMSHIRE AND OXFORDSHIRE TRUST (BBOWT), was charged with establishing the Trusts' conservation priorities based on wildlife needs and the movement's ability to influence the outcomes. There was also a desire to link the plan to the Government's emerging Biodiversity Action Plan.

Above: A Society newsletter reports on the Salisbury bypass plans and the clean-up after the Sea Empress disaster

While the plan was in development, LYSTER encouraged the group to identify some initial flagship species for the Partnership to champion and 'bring back from the brink'. The initial choices were the otter and red squirrel – two species on which The Wildlife Trusts had a strong track record. In England, red squirrel partnerships, under the banner Red Alert, continued their work of protecting and raising awareness. Red Squirrel Week alerted hundreds of people in Cumbria and Lancashire to the plight of the native squirrel. In Durham and Northumberland surveys, supplementary feeding programmes and grey squirrel trapping were carried out with the support of English Nature. Meanwhile The Wildlife Trusts' Otters and Rivers Project (OTTER CONSERVATION) provided another focus for action, supported financially (and in kind) by a partnership of water companies, the National Rivers Authority, conservation agencies, universities and farmers.

A NEW GOVERNMENT

During 1996, there was a growing feeling that the Conservative Government's almost 17 years in power was coming to an end. The Opposition was more united than ever before and displaying a confidence in their ability to take power that had been missing for some time. Nevertheless, the Society was maintaining strong links with Government Ministers. The Secretary of State for the Environment, John Gummer, spoke at the National Conference at York in September 1996. There was also a meeting with the Minister of Agriculture, Douglas Hogg, at the LINCOLNSHIRE TRUST's Ancaster Valley reserve and on a nearby arable farm. Topics discussed included the targeting of agri-environment schemes and the Government's biodiversity targets.

At the beginning of 1997, the Shadow Foreign Secretary, Robin Cook, and the Shadow Environment Minister, Michael Meacher, were both claiming that if a Labour Government came to power it would be Britain's first truly green Government.

A visit by Tony Blair, Labour Party leader, to the Durham Trust's Low Barns nature reserve in January 1997 with Simon Lyster (left), David Bellamy and Trust representatives

Cook emphasised that the Labour Party was determined "to push environment to the top of the world's agenda".[342] Meacher offered a more national overview, "we shall place the environment at the heart of government".[343]

Together Lyster and Sands made a concerted effort to win the Opposition's confidence, meeting with the Shadow Minister of Environment, Michael Meacher, on several occasions. In January 1997, with DAVID BELLAMY and other Trust representatives, Lyster welcomed Labour Party leader, Tony Blair, to the DURHAM TRUST's Low Barns reserve. When in May 1997 New Labour swept to power, Meacher was made the Minister for the Environment. Only two days after his appointment, and at 24 hours' notice, he spent two hours talking and answering questions at the Directors' Conference in Wiltshire.

From the beginning LYSTER and Meacher respected one another and developed a strong relationship. It would be needed. The new Government had to be held to its promise to put the environment at the heart of its policies.

This meant, for example, implementing the Rio Conventions on Biodiversity and Sustainable Development as well as the EC Habitats Directive, and strengthening the protection of SSSIs. Pressure on the Government needed to be applied from all sides, including from the statutory agencies. Much to English Nature's annoyance, WWF had described it as "a muzzled watchdog".[344] This may have been seen as harsh by some but, as WWF pointed out, 45 per cent of SSSIs in England were still deteriorating "behind the smooth and professional façade of the restructured English Nature"[345] and there were "serious questions about the willingness of the new agency to stand up for nature in difficult and controversial cases".[346]

Left: General Election Pack for Trusts and Urban Groups for the 1997 election

LARGER AREAS ON THE HORIZON

January 1998 saw the culmination of work on the conservation plan designed to "give direction to the collective efforts of The Wildlife Trusts until the year 2005".[347] Consultation with Trusts had hammered out its priorities and LYSTER was keen for it to be punchy and effective. It identified six major issues – intensive agriculture; land-take for development; pollution; climate change; the unsustainable use of natural resources; and people's attitude to the environment. These, Trusts believed, were having the greatest impact on biodiversity and were where they could make the most impact. In June 2000, a four-page colour version of the Plan, *Protecting Wildlife for the Future – the 10-point Conservation Plan for The Wildlife Trusts*, was widely circulated amongst the Trusts.

In the main, the priority areas were familiar – for example, 'standing up for wildlife', making biodiversity relevant to people, and campaigning on agriculture, water issues and the marine environment. It was, however, the first formal acknowledgement that influencing the management of larger areas was also going to be of growing importance. This approach would help counter the fragmentation of existing nature reserves and give plants and animals more of a chance to adapt to the emerging threat of climate change. It called for at least three new large areas for wildlife to be created by 2005 – a hugely ambitious target at the time. It also provided a clear mandate from the Trusts for The Wildlife Trusts' national work.

FRUITS OF FINANCIAL REVIEW

Meanwhile, ways of increasing income for the UK office were being pursued. In November 1996, it was agreed that the Society's wholly-owned subsidiary, Environmental Services Ltd (established in February 1991), would change its name to Wildlife Trusts Services Ltd to become the vehicle for delivering services to the Trusts. While a scheme to unify banking across the movement had failed, Gough, by now the

Society's Managing Director, was optimistic about the progress elsewhere. A collective insurance scheme was already off the ground and a capital equipment scheme had generated significant savings for Trusts through the leasing of vehicles and computers.

The Society was forging ahead with schemes to assist Trusts in other ways. CRANE was keen for the restricted or unrestricted status of various funds held by the Society to be reviewed and this was being investigated by the Honorary Secretary, JOHN MACMILLAN. As a result, the Society placed £450,000 of its restricted funds into a Development Fund and by May 1997 £386,000 was "committed in loans and support to Trusts",[348] with several Trusts using the support for membership recruitment.

In addition, when the Government announced a new 'green' tax, the landfill tax, in October 1996, the Society was poised ready to be one of the environmental bodies that benefited. Peter Shirley had been tipped-off by a colleague in the aggregates industry prior to the announcement and had recognised the opportunity it offered the movement. A proportion of the tax would go to environmental projects and voluntary bodies were also eligible to become a distributing agency. Gough saw this as a chance to develop the Society's broader role and, through economies of scale, contribute towards some of the costs of running the UK office.

After lengthy negotiations, the Society found itself managing substantial funds from two companies – Biffa and Hanson. The Hanson Environment Fund was launched in September 1997 and Biffaward later that year. The two new funds alone administered a total of £9.2 million in the first year. Such was the scale and nature of these new schemes, it was clear that a special team would be needed to administer them. A new GRANTS UNIT was set up towards the end of the year and would go on to establish a reputation for its efficiency and impartiality. Over the coming years, it would be successful in bids to administer several large environmental

The Society's new Grants Unit distributed funding to many hundreds of environmental and community projects programmes, most notably under the Landfill Tax Credit Scheme and various incarnations of the National Lottery.

Applications from Trusts had to compete on the same basis as those from other organisations, but the advent of these new funding streams had a profound impact on the movement's development over the next ten years. Between 1996 and 2006, 500 Trust projects were awarded £50 million under the LANDFILL COMMUNITIES FUND (originally the Landfill Tax Credit Scheme). Coupled with improved techniques for membership recruitment, this would help revolutionise the scale and professionalism of the Trusts' activity at the turn of the century and into the new millennium.

THREE INTO ONE WON'T GO

There were now three operating divisions at the national level – the Society (RSNC), the UK office of The Wildlife Trusts and Wildlife Trust Services Ltd. But the problem of how to fund the UK office remained. It was operating with a substantial deficit subsidised by the other two operating divisions. The situation would later be described as "unsustainable, having for several years been underpinned by unreliable legacy income and time-limited and decreasing"[349] funding from projects and from sources, such as the Department of Environment.

There was also a belief in some quarters, supported by Gough, that any surpluses generated by the Society and Wildlife Trust Services should also be used to finance expansion into areas where it had an increasing reputation, particularly acquiring and distributing charitable funds for use in the wider environmental sector. Gough supported the idea of creating a mirror Trust movement for earth sciences and wanted the Society to take on the management of a new environmental tax on the commercial exploitation of aggregates. An Aggregates Levy Sustainability Fund was introduced in April 2002, initially as a two-year pilot scheme to provide funds to tackle a wide range of problems in areas affected by the

extraction of aggregates. Gough was also keen to see the growth of the Society's sustainable development agenda. One Trust was already modernising its Articles to formally include sustainable development in its objectives and Gough saw an opportunity to do something similar with the Society. There were some, though, who saw the proposals for the Society's expanded remit as a move in the wrong direction.

There was an increasing need to clarify the relationship between the Society (RSNC), The Wildlife Trusts and Wildlife Trust Services (WTS) Ltd – as they were now known. They were evolving independently with the only formal link being the transfer of the operating surpluses from RSNC and WTS to The Wildlife Trusts' UK office. A business plan linking the three divisions was needed urgently. However, there is little doubt that Gough had been "planning for an eventual rationalisation by separating the three divisions".[350]

Changes to the Royal Charter had also become necessary because of the new structure. In November 1997, the Council agreed a resolution asking Her Majesty in Council to approve the amendments which duly took place in May the following year. The objects of the Society were 'liberalised' to take advantage of the fact that the conservation of nature in itself, rather than as a mere adjunct to education, was now a charitable purpose. The new wording read: 'The objects of the Society are to promote the conservation of nature, encourage nature study and research and to educate the public in understanding and appreciating nature, the awareness of its value and the need for conservation'.

The changes to the Royal Charter also meant that the Executive Committee was transformed into a new slimmer Council which met for the first time in May 1998. The old Council became the Annual General Meeting of the Society with staff, as well as honorary officers, eligible to be Trust representatives and to vote. CRANE followed this up with a review of the governance and management of the Society with the role of its principal officers clearly defined.

There were ambitious plans for the Society's offices. Gough considered the current premises in Lincoln fell far short of what was expected of a major national organisation. A more modern, properly-equipped office would greatly improve efficiency. A suitable property might be found in Newark which was also nearer to the main east-coast railway line and A1 trunk road. In May 1998, a property – The Kiln – on the opposite bank of the Trent to Newark Castle, became available and a lease with lower rental and service charges than the Lincoln offices signed.

Everyone was able to move into the newly-furnished offices on FA Cup Final Day, May 1999. Soon after Christmas the Society also changed its London office – moving from Victoria to share new premises with the LONDON TRUST in Southwark.

Gough was now increasingly on the road, providing one-to-one advice to Trusts on everything from accounting systems to recruitment. By February 1999, he had provided support and development work to more than ten Trusts, from West Wales to Suffolk. Gough was also involved with plans for the Society to manage and expand a massive £800,000 recycling project (at that stage being run by the local Trust) in the north-east of England. This involved the purchase of a large vehicle of dustcart proportions and 49 bottle, can and paper banks across nine north-east council districts. Some Trusts were becoming increasingly concerned that the organisation at the national level was getting involved in work that was not within its remit and which should have been run by Trusts, if anyone.

Meanwhile, although the working partnership between Gough and LYSTER was not working out quite as had been hoped (the two were very different), the move to the new premises had had an energising effect on the UK office. This would be needed as the Society and the Trusts were getting ready for their biggest campaign yet.

In 1999, the Society moved to its new offices in Newark, shared with British Waterways

MOBILISING FOR THE BIGGEST CAMPAIGN TO DATE

The Society's high profile conservation campaigns had all served to highlight the shortcomings of the Wildlife and Countryside Act 1981. There had been "sixteen years of frustration as important wildlife habitats continued to be lost and damaged because of inadequate and weak legislation".[351]

Lobbying by the Society and by other members of Wildlife and Countryside Link (WILDLIFE LINK), encouraged the new Labour Government to commit to better protection for wildlife in its election manifesto. This was "coded language for new SSSI law".[352]

In November 1997, a coalition of Wildlife Link members, including The Wildlife Trusts, embarked on its largest campaign to date. Years of thinking on how best to improve the legal protection afforded to SSSIs, and to wildlife more generally, were brought together in Wildlife Link's easy-to-read Wildlife Charter, *Wildlife Law – Time for Reform*. It highlighted the fact that

between 1991 and 1996 one in five SSSIs in England had been damaged; SSSIs in Scotland continued to be degraded. There were recent well publicised cases of SSSIs being damaged or threatened, for example, at Cardiff Bay, Offham Down in Sussex and in the Cairngorms.

There was concern that the Government's proposals for new legislation, when they appeared, would fall short of what was needed. It was almost a year before the Government finally published a consultation document setting out its ideas and a further ten months before its *Framework for Action* firmed up on its proposals for new legislation.

In March 1999, there was one of the biggest lobbies on Parliament that Environment Minister, Michael Meacher, could recall. It culminated in a stirring mass rally in the Grand Committee Room of the House of Commons. The event, organised

Above: Wildlife Link's Charter for reforming wildlife legislation

Environment NGOs lobby Parliament, 1999

by Wildlife Link, was covered on prime-time television news bulletins. Some of the leaders of the NGOs involved, including LYSTER, spoke emotively about the urgent need for reform and the need for everyone to redouble their efforts to get the Government to introduce its promised bill. Even Michael Meacher entered the lion's den of the rally to urge those present to renew their efforts and help him keep the Government on track. In April, there was a further strong demonstration of support as more than a quarter of a million pledge cards calling for new wildlife legislation were presented to Deputy Prime Minister, John Prescott. He was also handed a Wildlife Link report, *50 Years of Extinction*, listing 50 wildlife sites lost or damaged in the last 50 years.

The Society's work in helping to sustain Wildlife Link's lobbying activity during this time absorbed an immense amount of staff time. It intensified still further when the Government also pledged to legislate in the same bill on its long-held desire to open up access for the general public to more of the countryside – the so-called 'right to roam'. This involved further negotiations behind the scenes between Wildlife Link's countryside and wildlife interests to ensure a united front to Government. And afterwards the Society was a member of a working party producing guidance on the implementation of the access provisions of the resulting Act on the ground.

Belper Coppice, Derbyshire. Since 2008, a meadow creation project on this Local Wildlife Site has seen more than 50 plant species become established

The Society also campaigned on three particular aspects that were absent from the bill: greater recognition and protection for LOCAL WILDLIFE SITES – areas rich in wildlife that fell outside statutory designations; better protection for rare and vulnerable species; and legal underpinning of the biodiversity process. A new leaflet, *Treading New Ground*, focused on Local Wildlife Sites and demanded that all local authorities should be required to manage up to date Local Wildlife Site systems. A second new leaflet, *Standing Up for Species*, identified a raft of improvements that should be made to existing species law. By the end of the year, the Society was preparing to launch *Taking the Next Steps*, a third leaflet that captured all the Society's

concerns about the missing elements in the Government's proposed bill.

The announcement that the Government planned to introduce the Countryside and Rights of Way Bill (CROW) finally came in the Queen's Speech in November 1999 and with it the prospect of several months of intense lobbying. But at last there was a real chance that SSSIs would receive the protection they needed.

FURTHER CHANGES

At the Council meeting on 25th February 2000, Gough hoped to instigate a debate on his plans for creating three discrete organisations at the national level and an expansion programme for the Society. He would not get the opportunity.

Following concerns that had been raised, just before the Council meeting Gough was "suspended from duty pending an investigation"[353] and he resigned with effect from the end of March 2000. The Society immediately called in its auditors and informed the Charity Commission whose subsequent inquiry upheld the case against Gough, whilst also acknowledging the contribution he had made to the Society. It welcomed the speed and propriety with which the Society had acted after the event and its determination to put matters right. This included governance improvements, a focus on risk management and the establishment of an Internal Audit Committee.

Following Gough's departure, MICHAEL SINGH would provide a steadying hand at the helm and took on the role of Executive Director of the Society. There were survivors from the Gough era. The GRANTS UNIT, for example, had proved very successful and the decision was taken to continue its work. But the north-east recycling scheme had to be sorted out and plans for the expansion of ENVIRONMENT CITY were halted.

In October 1999, a new CHAIRMAN OF COUNCIL, PETER SCHOFIELD had taken over from CRANE – who had not sought re-election. Before he stepped down from Council, Crane went to great lengths to find a new HONORARY TREASURER to replace George Wright who was retiring. The new Treasurer was JOHN HUGHES who had recently retired from an impressive career as an accountant and Finance Director. Hughes attended his first meeting in May 2001. Lyster now accepted that he would have to take on management of the national office and its finances as well.

He was understandably frustrated by these distractions as they were holding back progress on the most important job – nature conservation. His frustration also lay in the fact that, as he said himself, "in the twenty years I have been working in nature conservation I have never known a time of more opportunity to make a real difference to wildlife".[354]

Supported by a fast-growing membership, the movement was becoming increasingly successful at raising funds for its work. By 2000 the total income of The Wildlife Trusts had risen to £43.5 million. It was a testament to Lyster, to the rest of the staff and to the honorary officers that, despite a turbulent couple of years, the organisation was still able to move forward into the new millennium with some optimism and with a considerable number of achievements under its belt.

CHAPTER 9

Restoration 2000 and beyond

We must indeed all hang together, or most assuredly we shall all hang separately.

Benjamin Franklin on the signing of the US Declaration of Independence, 1776

In May 1997, Tony Blair's Labour Government had been elected on promises that there could be devolved institutions to govern in Scotland and Wales. Later that year, referendums delivered 'yes' votes from the public in favour of devolution, paving the way for the establishment of the Scottish Parliament and National Assembly for Wales in 1999. The Scottish Parliament (as a result of the Scottish Act 1998) had powers to make primary legislation in numerous devolved areas of policy. The Welsh Assembly (set up under the Wales Act 1998) had powers to make secondary legislation and to determine how the Government's budget for Wales was spent and administered. A Northern Ireland Assembly had been established under the 'Good Friday' agreement, but its operations were suspended from time to time by 'the troubles'. There were now effectively five Parliaments in operation with powers in the UK – in Westminster, Cardiff, Belfast and Edinburgh and also the European Parliament in Strasbourg.

The environment was one of the devolved issues. Consequently, as the new millennium dawned, the delivery of environmental policy and practice was subject to profound change. From now on decisions on nature conservation, as well as on agriculture and planning, would be uncoupled from the Westminster and Whitehall machines, particularly in Scotland and Northern Ireland. It was true that in Scotland there had been a long

history of separate legislation and decision-making, but the centre of power had now shifted decisively. Whilst the Welsh Assembly's powers were less than in Scotland it had, uniquely, been given a formal duty to promote sustainable development in 'the exercise of its functions' and increasingly it was also thinking and acting more independently.

These changes led to some tensions within the UK's statutory countryside bodies. The Joint Nature Conservation Committee (JNCC), for example, had been set up to maintain a UK dimension across the nature and countryside agencies. It had carried out some valuable work, particularly in the international field, but it remained reliant on its paymasters, the country agencies. There was now a danger that funding for the JNCC would wither as each country looked to its own national priorities. Elsewhere, the Department of the Environment, for example, still felt proprietorial about the UK's list of priority species and habitats drawn up under the biodiversity process. Individual countries, however, were now keen to compile their own lists. By December 2001, the Department was going ahead, initially reluctantly, with an England Biodiversity Strategy. The Wildlife Trusts sat on a small working group to drive the process forward.

The debate over devolution and the importance of maintaining a UK dimension was much less heated in the voluntary environmental bodies than it had been during the Carver inquiry ten years earlier. With devolution a reality, the voluntary sector was largely accepting of the new arrangements.

However, there were some sensitive, behind-the-scenes negotiations surrounding Wildlife and Countryside Link (WILDLIFE LINK). Made up, as it was, of both devolved and non-devolved member organisations, it retained both a UK and English remit. Even so, the independent Links in each of the other countries tended to see it as a predominantly English body.

For The Wildlife Trusts, devolution appeared to present few problems since the Trusts in Scotland, Wales and Ulster, like all the other Trusts, were independent charities. In practice, agendas set within The Wildlife Trusts often had an English emphasis that subsequently had to be corrected. It was hard for those in England to fully comprehend the new order and to find their own identity. Some of the Society's work still needed to be undertaken at the UK level, but most advocacy now related only to England. The situation mirrored that in politics, where membership of the Westminster Parliament was drawn from across the UK but much of its work related to England, which had no dedicated English Parliament.

In Scotland, the Trust reorganised itself to strengthen its regional operations. The Welsh Trusts employed a member of staff to look at resource issues across the Principality. In England, devolution had led to the formation of the London Assembly and eight English regions. The existing regional Trust groupings were quickly adjusted to match the Government's regional boundaries. In 2000, the six Wildlife Trusts in the West Midlands appointed a Regional Director, Peter Shirley, who had been working at the UK office. The previous year the Trusts in the south-east had appointed Bob Page to do a similar job. Trusts would go on to make regional appointments in the south-west, north-west and in the east of England and East Midlands.

Within six or seven years, Trusts had also created a new intra-country structure, with a separate England Forum, to aid internal communications within The Wildlife Trusts and to properly reflect the new devolved position. The resulting Countries Committee was key to helping Trusts appreciate that different ways of working and different responses to environmental issues within each devolved administration could be beneficial and used to mutual advantage.

PROTECTING WILDLIFE FOR THE FUTURE

As the millennium got underway, The Wildlife Trusts pushed ahead with three campaigns under a new banner of *Protecting Wildlife for the Future*: stemming the loss of wildlife in the UK; engaging people; and starting the process of recovery.

In each of these areas there were encouraging signs. First, the Countryside and Rights of Way Bill was making progress in the Westminster Parliament. The Wildlife Trusts in England and Wales had reason to be pleased with their influence during the bill's passage. "Time after time, MPs speaking at Committee stage referred to the briefings they had received from their local Wildlife Trust. At one stage, a light-hearted argument broke out between two MPs as to who had the best Wildlife Trust".[355]

The Countryside and Rights of Way (CROW) Bill finally received Royal Assent on 30th November 2000. There was optimism that the new legislation would deliver real gains in England and Wales for SSSIs. In addition, as a result of voluntary body lobbying – including lobbying by The Wildlife Trusts – there was a welcome new offence of 'reckless disturbance of dolphins, whales and basking sharks'. The Act also established a basis in law for the biodiversity process.

There were disappointments too. Better protection for LOCAL WILDLIFE SITES – one of the issues on which The Wildlife Trusts had focused its lobbying – failed to make its way into the new legislation. However, it was not all bad news on that front. The Government had agreed to draw up guidelines for local authorities and others on the identification and management of Local Wildlife Sites. This was a welcome acknowledgement that Local Wildlife Site systems could make an important contribution to the Government's biodiversity conservation agenda. This small step forward had been elicited by the

Common dolphin. Dolphins, whales and basking sharks received greater protection under the new CROW Act 2000

Society repeating a major 1999 survey of Wildlife Sites systems throughout the UK. The early, pre-publication results of this second survey had been made available to David Kidney (MP for Stafford) during the passage of the CROW Act 2000.

The Wildlife Trusts had campaigned for the Act almost continuously for more than five years and had been a strong supporter of WILDLIFE LINK's joint campaign. The new Act was a triumph for collective lobbying and for Wildlife Link in particular. STEPHANIE HILBORNE was Link's Principal Officer at its initiation, and supported Tony Juniper (later to become Chief Executive of Friends of the Earth), Chair of Wildlife Link's Legislation Group, through these momentous times. In 1999, Wildlife Link was awarded a Green Ribbon Political Award for its three-year campaign. Afterwards, Juniper was able to write that since the passing of the CROW Act "policy announcements and official decisions have confirmed the power of Link's collective success. Official decisions turning down damaging road proposals have been brought about by CROW while new targets to ensure that SSSIs are in good condition come with the political momentum it created".[356]

The UK office now turned its attention to ensuring that the implications of the CROW Act, for those on the ground in the Trusts, were fully understood. In April 2001, training workshops were organised in London and York attended by 50 representatives from 30 Trusts. In July, a third workshop was held in Newtown for all the Welsh Trusts.

In 1999, a further contribution to 'stemming the loss of wildlife' was an offer by the DEVON TRUST to kick-start a Partnership fighting-fund for Trusts tackling nationally-significant threats to wildlife. The Trust agreed to provide £40,000, if 20 or more Trusts also contributed by foregoing a small percentage of their future unrestricted legacy income. There were positive responses from 26 Trusts and the CONSERVATION CONTINGENCY FUND was established in April 2000.

The second theme under the new banner of *Protecting Wildlife for the Future* was 'engaging people'. Membership of The Wildlife Trusts was growing rapidly, not least because more people were being asked to join. Realising that they were hugely underselling themselves, door-to-door recruitment had been successfully introduced first to the Devon Trust, and then to other Trusts. In the summer of 1998, a survey of Trusts showed that door-to-door schemes had

BBOWT recruiters in 1995. More face-to-face recruitment increased the visibility of the Trusts and the number of new members

yielded more than £7 million since the start of the first scheme, 13 years earlier.

LYSTER was now setting the Trusts' sights on 400,000 members by 2002. The latest figure already showed a nearly 50 per cent rise to 340,000 members since 1995. By December 2002, the target had been surpassed and the membership stood at 413,000. Lyster now proposed a new target of 500,000 by 2004.

The Trusts were doing more and more to engage people. By 2001, a number of ambitious projects were underway. For example, in LANCASHIRE the Trust had a food project aimed at involving Asian women in Bolton. The ULSTER TRUST was in the process of transforming the Bog Meadows into one of the finest urban nature reserves in the UK, and at the same time reaching across the religious divide in one of the most troubled parts of West Belfast. In SHROPSHIRE a Trust project was showing the beneficial links between the natural environment and the treatment of mental health problems.

There was also much to report on the third theme, 'starting the process of nature's recovery'. Within the first 12 to 18 months of the new millennium, many Trusts were taking on, or planning, major habitat restoration schemes. In 2000, for example, the ESSEX TRUST had embarked on the development of its newly-acquired Abbotts Hall Farm as a flagship site to trial coastal realignment, and to show how arable farming and wildlife could co-exist. Two years later, the Trust breached the farm's sea wall on the Blackwater estuary to create 81 hectares of saltmarsh and grazing marsh – habitats under threat from changing agricultural methods and rising sea levels. The rest of the farm remained as arable land but was farmed in a wildlife-friendly way. At the time it was the largest managed coastal retreat project in Europe.

The BEDFORDSHIRE, CAMBRIDGESHIRE AND NORTHAMPTONSHIRE TRUST was also 'thinking big'. In 2001, it set up a partnership project with the vision of restoring some 3,000 hectares of increasingly degraded farmland south of

Bog Meadows – an oasis for wildlife and people in West Belfast

Peterborough, back to wet fenland. In doing so WOODWALTON FEN (the fenland nature reserve purchased by CHARLES ROTHSCHILD 90 years earlier), would be reconnected to another National Nature Reserve at nearby Holme Fen. In 2002, the project acquired a small piece of land adjacent to Woodwalton Fen – the first step towards achieving its ambitious objective. This partnership would soon acquire the imposing title of the Great Fen Project (now known simply as the Great Fen) and would go on to enjoy huge success.

The Great Fen Project 2009. Work (foreground) starts to link Woodwalton Fen nature reserve to nearby Holme Fen, and the Project's vision of restoring 3,000 hectares of fenland begins to materialise

OXYGEN OF PUBLICITY

LYSTER was now well into his stride and used every opportunity to promote the movement to the media, politicians and key players. He spoke at Trust meetings and events and maintained a close rapport with a group of key players within the movement. Between December 2000 and December 2002, a *Director General's Newsletter* chronicled delivery across a range of activities, including progress on the Conservation Plan.

The scale and complexity of the work across the movement was impressive. Conservation, publicity, communications and fundraising were all motoring ahead. One notable media success was coverage of a special wildlife garden at Number 10 Downing Street, built by the LONDON TRUST on behalf of The Wildlife Trusts. Tony Blair's fourth child had been born in May 2000, the first born to a serving Prime Minister for 150 years and so the garden included a customised baby protection feature.

During Wimbledon fortnight in 2001, the Lawn Tennis Association was asked to donate used tennis balls as homes for harvest mice projects in Avon, Glamorgan and Northumberland. The star attraction, 'Henman' the harvest mouse,

175

The new wildlife garden at No 10 Downing Street, created by London Wildlife Trust, with Tony Blair (centre)

achieved overnight national and international media fame. Around the same time, Michael Meacher was pictured in the press with an otter launching the Trusts' *Otters Return* report. In Red Squirrel Week in September 2002, 'Rusty' the red squirrel made an appearance at the Arsenal football stadium and celebrity chefs donated their favourite 'nutty' recipes. The Week featured in *The Sunday Times,* while in the *Observer* and the

Wimbledon tennis balls provided homes for harvest mice

Daily Express the CUMBRIA TRUST looked forward to 'a future full of red squirrels'. The movement had not enjoyed media exposure like this since the early days of the BRITISH WILDLIFE APPEAL.

The Wildlife Trusts brought wildlife gardening to three national flower shows in 2001 – BBC's Gardener's World Live, Tatton Park and Hampton Court. The gardens, designed by Alan Sargent, won silver-gilt and silver medals. More than 800 new members were recruited at the events, which helped promote the idea of gardeners as the new conservationists.

A new fundraising team at the UK office was also responsible for some profitable new initiatives. In December 2001, grants worth more than £300,000 were secured and distributed to the Trusts from the Hanson Wildlife Challenge, the Rees Jeffreys Road Fund, the Greencard Biodiversity Trust and an Endangered Species Fund supported by the John Ellerman Foundation and Sunley Charitable Foundation. For the first time, a UK office-run appeal was organised to support the campaign for marine legislation and to 'breathe life into our dying seas'. It was on course to raise £140,000.

There was a sponsorship arrangement with Kodak linked to their film processing service. One of the UK's leading wildlife book sellers, Subbuteo Books, agreed to donate five per cent of net sales to the Trusts, an initiative launched by television presenter and Vice President, Chris Packham, at the Birdfair. In 2002, an on-pack promotion with Nouvelle toilet tissue was secured which used the snappy, if tongue-in-cheek, slogan – *answering the call of nature.*

Another innovation was the development of a new milk brand, 'White & Wild', that aimed to "use the consumer market to give dairy farmers a significant financial incentive to conserve and enhance biodiversity on their farms".[357] The milk was sold at a small premium, and for each litre bought, three pence went to the farmer and two pence to The Wildlife Trusts. In return, the farmer undertook to keep to environmental standards set by The Wildlife Trusts and the Farming and

Wildlife Advisory Group. In 2004, a similar on-pack scheme was developed with Ribena with Wildlife Trusts providing advice to Ribena's blackcurrant growers on wildlife-friendly management of their land.

2001 also saw the 46th, and latest, Wildlife Trust join the movement – THE ISLES OF SCILLY TRUST. LYSTER, and Vice Presidents, DAVID BELLAMY and Bill Oddie, attended the launch ceremony for the Trust on St Mary's – the largest of the five inhabited islands. It was followed a year later by the ALDERNEY TRUST, which formed in 2002, after a packed public meeting which supported the proposal to form a Trust for the island.

INFLUENCING POLICY IN HIGH PLACES
The agriculture scene was dominated in 2001 by the country's worst outbreak of foot and mouth disease for years. Trust reserves were closed and revenue from visitor centres dropped as 'no entry'

The Wildlife Trusts' award-winning wildlife garden at Gardeners' World Live

signs went up across vast swathes of the countryside. The crisis would be followed by a review of the future of food and farming by a Policy Commission, chaired by Donald Curry. It involved one of the biggest Government consultation exercises of English stakeholders, including The Wildlife Trusts at both regional and national level. When the Curry report appeared it contained radical proposals, a blueprint for farming that put the environment closer to the heart of future farming policy. If fully implemented there was a chance that there could be real benefits for wildlife.

It was not long before The Wildlife Trusts was invited to sit on a Government working group to develop a 'broad and shallow' agri-environment scheme. The Wildlife Trusts had previously submitted a paper on a Land Stewardship Scheme to provide broad environment measures for all farmers alongside more detailed measures,

including payments for specific areas of wildlife importance (FARMING AND WILDLIFE).

In 2002, the organisation's attention was once again focused on grassland management. A joint report with the national plant protection charity, Plantlife, called *England's Green Unpleasant Land?*, highlighted the continuing loss of grassland sites. In Worcestershire, for example, 75 per cent of grassland sites had been lost or damaged in 25 years. The report set out how LOCAL WILDLIFE SITES were also being lost through agricultural practices and neglect. The same year the UK office entered into a major new contract with English Nature to run the Grazing Animals Project, a scheme to restore wildlife habitats by linking nature conservationists with landowners and available livestock.

In August 2001, the Water Policy Team produced the first tranche of a *Wetland Restoration Manual* which was eventually completed in 2003. In 2002,

Losses of unimproved grasslands continued throughout the 1980s and 1990s.

it produced *Reflections on Water*, outlining the legislation Trusts wished to see in England and Wales to safeguard the future of its rivers and wetlands. Later in the year, there was also considerable policy work on the EU Water Framework Directive. As part of a campaign to restore declining WATER VOLE populations, the UK office produced a detailed response to English Nature's quinquennial review of Schedules 5 and 8 of the Wildlife and Countryside Act 1981 aimed at upgrading legal protection for this species.

In 2001, the UK office also coordinated The Wildlife Trusts' support for a Private Members Bill to give greater protection to nationally-important marine sites within territorial waters. Sadly, the bill, introduced by John Randall (Conservative MP for Uxbridge), was blocked in the House of Lords. But there was an upside to all the UK office's fundraising and lobbying on marine affairs at this time. The Wildlife Trusts was rapidly becoming established as a leading force in UK marine conservation, led by its Director of Marine Conservation, Joan Edwards. The DEVON TRUST too had successfully reached a voluntary agreement with scallop fishermen to protect valuable reefs in Lyme Bay, the first of its kind in the country. The summer had also seen the launch in Parliament of two Wildlife Trust reports on the marine environment – *Our Dying Seas* and *Marine Stewardship – Meeting the Challenge*. The event attracted two Government Ministers, the Conservative Shadow Secretary of State for the Environment and the Liberal Democrat environment spokesman. This was a confident stride into the waves of marine legislation, waves that would grow larger and continue to break more fiercely in the months to come (MARINE CONSERVATION).

Above· The colourful reefs of Lyme Bay were subject to a voluntary protection agreement with local scallop fishermen
Right: Duke of Burgundy – a species under threat from loss of grassland habitats

FURTHER REFORM REQUIRED

Despite this considerable volume of work, the higher profile and growing confidence enjoyed by the Trust movement as a whole, there was still a need for the centre to connect more effectively with the Trusts and to clarify the direction of travel for the whole movement. A contested election for CHAIRMAN OF COUNCIL in 2001 led to the appointment of MICHAEL FIELD, a Trustee of the SUFFOLK TRUST, as the replacement to PETER SCHOFIELD. During the year some of the issues began to be addressed. Work was undertaken by the Honorary Secretary, JOHN MACMILLAN and the Director of the LINCOLNSHIRE TRUST, Stuart Crooks, to improve the governance of the Partnership. Several Trusts also volunteered to help look at the management structure and operations at the UK office.

One substantial offer came from the Trusts in the Northern Region – led by the LANCASHIRE TRUST. Their offer to fund an independent review was supported by the Chairman and also by representatives of the Trusts at the Forum. The resultant findings proved valuable in outlining how the national function could be reorganised and were the precursor to a major strategic review.

However, despite this emphasis on addressing issues of governance, it was the financial situation that was causing the most concern.

The incumbent Director of Conservation at the UK office, Rob Stoneman, was particularly worried and prepared an internal paper to the Chairman. He was concerned that the UK office was often required to bend its ideal service provision to the Trusts to meet the needs of its external funders. Nobody, including Stoneman, argued that this was not above board, but it was leading to a service mismatch. As a result, funding was available for technical advice on wetland restoration but not water policy development; for Local BAP partner support but not supporting Trusts to engage in the new community strategies; for providing advice to conservation graziers but not strategic large area acquisition. He advocated reform of the UK structure, based on devolving functions to the countries, regions and the Trusts themselves.

The paper was a very personal view, but its analysis of the issues resonated with views being expressed elsewhere in the movement. There was a growing feeling that, whilst improvements had been made, the national structure still had a way to go to meet the collective needs of the Trusts.

Whilst there was no doubt that LYSTER had achieved a great deal, there were still concerns over some aspects of the organisation's development and questions were raised about Lyster's distance from the day-to-day activities of the UK office.

Following Macmillan and Crooks' work, a new, more streamlined governance model was agreed and introduced in January 2002. The Partnership Management Board and Council would meet together as a joint governing body called The Wildlife Trusts' Forum, chaired by Michael Field. This meant that Lyster relinquished his role as Chairman of the Partnership Management Board, which he had held for over six years.

By August 2002, Field was leading a group undertaking a further strategic review of the Partnership and an appeal was made to Trusts for views on the way forward. At the centre of the review group's thinking was a five-tier model for the Partnership to reflect the changing political and funding environment. Conservation priorities and support services for the movement should be delivered at the most appropriate level whether local, regional, national, UK or international. Fundraising, for example, should be led by the Trusts and any UK office fundraising should be for the benefit of the Partnership as a whole.

The review group's model acknowledged a growing feeling that the 1990s structure with its centralised UK office led by a Director General and supported by a separate, self-financing Society, was an organisational cul-de-sac. It was not working. But what was the alternative?

Opposite: Nearly 30 Wildlife Watch and youth groups took part in the Government's pioneering Children For Change initiative 1998–2001

An all-important two-day workshop, 'Make Change Happen', took place in 2003 to translate the review group's thinking into action. It was to prove a seminal exercise for the organisation, as much about how the changes were to be brought about, as the changes themselves. The workshop recognised the need for a "move more towards a network approach, moving away from a more linear, hierarchical approach".[358] In the margins of this workshop there were also discussions on the dual role of the Director General – as ambassador for the movement and as manager of the UK office.

DEPARTURE TIME

Meanwhile, FIELD and HUGHES (the new Honorary Treasurer), were having to manage an increasingly difficult financial position. Matters had come to a head at the Council meeting when the latest budget for the financial year 2003–04 was rejected. The Governance Committee, Forum and regional meetings had asked for previous budgets to be redrafted, but Lyster was keen to see this budget accepted. He felt his judgement and position in the future strategy for the organisation were being questioned and he offered to resign. In March, ahead of consideration of the review group's findings by the Forum, there was an announcement that Lyster was leaving the Partnership.

The Trustees felt they had to draw a line in the sand. In their opinion, an expansionist strategy was too risky. Costs had to be reduced drastically and activities needed to be consolidated at the offices in Newark. It had already been agreed to give notice on the lease of the London office. The Trustees wanted one command structure, both to improve day-to-day management and to reflect the new thinking about the movement's structure. Field made it clear, publicly, that the "Trustees were unanimous that tough decisions had to be taken to secure our principal goals of making the partnership financially secure and doubling our membership over the next five years".[359] Lyster's

"departure. . . heralds a restructuring of the partnership, based on a drive to reduce centralised administration and put more focus on the work of the 47 Trusts".[360]

For some people inside the organisation, and most people outside it, the announcement of Lyster's departure came out of the blue.

He had built up a strong reputation as one of the top environmental leaders, popular with the media and politicians alike. He had also worked with the Trusts as they increasingly undertook bigger and bolder projects. Whilst many in the Trusts and elsewhere could see the need for a new approach, they were still surprised by the manner of the going. Charles Clover reported the news of Lyster's departure in *The Daily Telegraph* in stark terms. The paper's headline read 'Outcry over dismissal of Wildlife Trusts chief'. The chief executives of English Nature and the RSPB – and even Michael Meacher – were among those reported by Clover as all having written to "express frustration at losing Mr Lyster".[361]

TO CALMER WATERS

Field was in the middle of an intense period of activity. With no Director General, he assumed the role of Executive Chairman for the first six weeks himself and, with the Honorary Treasurer, John Hughes, took charge of the organisation. It involved an almost hour-by-hour vigil at the bedside of the ailing patient, the Society.

It was decided to sound out the BERKSHIRE, BUCKINGHAMSHIRE AND OXFORDSHIRE TRUST about a possible temporary secondment to the Society of its Director, MARTIN SPRAY. After discussions, the Trust agreed to release Spray from his Trust duties for two days a week and on 1st April 2003, the day after Lyster's formal departure, Spray became Acting Director General (PRINCIPAL OFFICERS).

In the weeks that followed, Spray's presence would prove invaluable. He provided much needed support and reassurance to the staff at the UK office, the Trustees and Trusts alike.

Despite the crossfire generated by Lyster's departure, the instinct was to recognise that damage to one part of the organisation – whether to a Trust or to the central administration – had serious implications for the whole. There was also a widespread recognition that change was needed. By April, Field had received support from more than 30 Trusts to press on with the ongoing review of the organisation's structure.

However, it soon became clear that the financial situation was far more serious than first thought. The Society was facing one of its darkest hours.

Further action was needed. In addition to redundancies, the budget for the year was heavily cut back, the UK office downsized and a new rent was negotiated. It was also agreed to establish a recovery group to manage the organisation out of its difficulties.

What was critical now was that confidence in the national organisation should not suffer any further knocks. Indeed, there was a need to try to rebuild it with valued stakeholders and key decision-makers, and above all with the Partnership at large.

A new strategic review document was prepared and received widespread support, described at a Forum meeting as "fundamentally improved".[362] Nevertheless, it still needed to be refined, a process that, it was agreed, should await the arrival of a new Principal Officer.

However, Trustees were reluctant to go ahead with a permanent appointment until the role was clarified and the financial crisis weathered. What the Trustees needed was some breathing space and Spray's secondment was extended to at least the end of January 2004 (with Spray increasing his working time to four days per week). There were Trustees who hoped Spray would be interested in taking up the Director General post himself, but he made it clear that he was not interested. But the need to find a permanent replacement was becoming increasingly urgent.

RECOVERY AND RENAISSANCE

Behind the scenes, at the Society's Annual General Meeting in November 2003, Tim Sands had had a late night conversation with STEPHANIE HILBORNE, Director of the NOTTINGHAMSHIRE TRUST. Her experience as a Conservation Officer and then as Director of the Nottinghamshire Trust – and before that as the Secretary to the London-based WILDLIFE LINK – made her a possible candidate to take over from Spray in the interim. She was young, but her proven networking and leadership skills, passion for environmental matters and Trust credentials weighed in her favour. There was also the added advantage that she would not have to move home. She promised to think seriously about a move, if the opportunity arose.

At the February 2004 meeting of The Wildlife Trusts' Forum, it was announced that a further secondment had been secured with the support of the Nottinghamshire Trust and that it would be Stephanie Hilborne. She would be the acting part-time Chief Executive until 31st March 2004.

The decision had also been made to interview for a new permanent Chief Executive. On 1st June 2004, after a rigorous interview process, Stephanie Hilborne took up her post and became the Society's fifth Principal Officer. In the same year, the Society also announced its new PRESIDENT, AUBREY MANNING, the broadcaster and zoologist and previous Chairman of the SCOTTISH TRUST.

For FIELD it had been a demanding time. He had been at the helm through the height of the storm and played his part in getting the organisation, in his words, 'to face reality'. He now had the satisfaction of knowing that, although calm waters might still be a little way off, the worst was over.

The organisation had survived and the rebuilding process – the restoration – was underway. Field retired in 2005 with his position as CHAIRMAN being taken by the HONORARY SECRETARY for the previous three years, MICHAEL ALLEN.

TAKING THE MOVEMENT FORWARD

It is too early to consign the next chapter of The Wildlife Trusts to the pages of a history book. Hopefully, it will be for others to chronicle its fortunes.

The lessons of the past were comprehensively heeded and the mantra that the national organisation should be run by, and for, the Trusts was fully embraced. But this time the view was that the national structure should not be an add-on but an integral part of The Wildlife Trusts, a department of the whole organisation. The new organisation had to identify a permanent solution to financing its central organisation. Since the Society was to be a wholly-owned department of the movement, the obvious solution was for it to be fully funded by the Trusts.

The organisation had been dramatically reduced in size by SPRAY in the shadow of dwindling finances. But HILBORNE was clear, the overall staff complement in the phoenix of the UK office could not be increased much, but its composition would need to be very different. Hilborne saw her role as building a new functional office, stage-by-stage, to serve and lead the wider Trust movement – reflecting its ambitions and objectives, its needs and expectations. Some key staff were needed immediately. A new Head of Finance was the first appointment made and proved critical in the reformation process.

Hilborne was particularly keen to see the restructuring and decisions about future strategy originating from the Trusts, and involving as wide a range of individuals as possible. This was not new but the intensity and thoroughness of the process was new, led by Hilborne and the new team she was building around her.

Hundreds of people in the movement were now engaged through a series of workstreams in drawing up a new strategic plan for the movement and its conservation work. The aim over five years was for a new Society (adopting its new name, the Royal Society of Wildlife Trusts) to emerge, with its core functions funded entirely by the Trusts and with funds raised nationally passed on to the Trusts. It was a principle that would gain universal support.

By now, the summary of the movement's objectives had been brought together in a short statement covering a shared vision, mission, aim

Stephanie Hilborne (left), at Woodwalton Fen, shortly after taking up her post of Chief Executive in 2004
Aubrey Manning (right), the Society's President (2005–10)

Michael Allen (right), the Society's Chairman (2005–11) with Hilary Benn, Secretary of State for the Environment, at the 'petition fish' finale event at Parliament in 2007

The Society was also moving fast to rebuild its relationships with the outside world. It was leading the fight to secure new comprehensive marine legislation. Its marine work had been maintained throughout the previous two years despite all the difficulties and had become an effective and widely respected campaign.

In 2007, a development plan for the movement as a whole was agreed, and by 2008 the movement was united behind an ambitious land-based and marine conservation programme.

A 2006 Parliamentary event, attended by Trusts and nearly 100 parliamentarians expressed The Wildlife Trusts' ambitions for the natural environment. They were more than simply the champions and guardians of the existing 'jewels in the crown', but instead the architects of a new approach to nature's recovery.

and objectives. This and the Society's new funding strategy were agreed in late 2005.

As always, it was not just the words that had been agreed, but the process itself – and in particular the healing value of that process – that was important. At the same time MICHAEL ALLEN took up his position as the new CHAIRMAN and the position of HONORARY SECRETARY was filled by ROGER DOBBS.

Allen's appointment would become another defining feature of the new era, as Hilborne and her new Chairman began to develop a productive partnership. Allen was able and willing to commit time, and his considerable experience, to actively support the organisation's renaissance and his new Chief Executive, initially through an extensive face-to-face consultation with the Trusts and their Council members.

Conferences became more professional and effective as, under Allen's leadership, the governance of the national structure was further improved. A new series of conferences for Trust Chairmen, for example, began work in earnest on leadership and governance development within the Trust movement.

David Cameron, leader of the Conservative Party, during a visit to Chimney Meadows nature reserve, Oxfordshire, in 2009

A Living Landscape – looking to connect up areas of wildlife-rich land and create larger, more resilient landscapes for wildlife

In addition, there was a new sense of urgency about linking and enlarging areas of natural habitat, to enable wildlife to adapt to climate change and move around the landscape. The Wildlife Trusts' Vice President and founder of MORI, Sir Robert (Bob) Worcester, spoke at the event. "In my view our wildlife is like the canary that miners took down into the mines to warn them of impending disaster. Every loss of habitat and species is a warning that Britain is threatened by degradation of the environment".[363]

A report, launched at the event, encapsulated the ambitious mood of the Trusts and their aim of connecting up areas of important habitats on land to create larger, more resilient landscapes for wildlife – A Living Landscape. This vision was soon broadened to embrace the equally-important need for an ecosystem approach to the management of our seas – Living Seas. In 2007, the Trusts collected 170,000 signatures on gold and silver 'fish-scales' to demonstrate public support for new marine legislation. The completed 'petition fish' were paraded in one huge shoal in Parliament. A report, *Living Seas*, was launched to Parliament in April 2009 and The Wildlife Trusts' marine campaign achieved its first goal – a Marine and Coastal Access Act – in November 2009. The LIVING LANDSCAPE AND LIVING SEAS vision had come to reflect the collective aspirations of The Wildlife Trusts. This had an enormous unifying

Living Seas – Trusts were advocating a larger-scale, ecosystem approach to the management of the UK's seas

and energising impact across the whole Wildlife Trust movement.

The end of April 2008 saw a second launch of A Living Landscape, this time to the corporate sector. A magnificent fundraising dinner was held at the Inner Temple in the City of London, funded by the Benoy Foundation, Sarasins and Aggregate Industries (whose Chief Executive Bill Bolsover would later become a Vice President). Here was a confident and coherent, outward-looking Wildlife Trust movement working together through its national department. As the organisation began to move forward, united as The Wildlife Trusts, it was appropriate that the event should also launch a new award to individuals for outstanding contributions to the conservation of the natural environment. The Charles Rothschild and Miriam Rothschild medal was an opportunity to reinforce the Society's links with its own past, and with the Rothschild family in particular. It was also a reminder to the movement to continue to strive for a world rich in wildlife and to do so with the energy, enterprise and vision that so characterised CHARLES ROTHSCHILD, its founding father.

The Charles Rothschild and Miriam Rothschild medal – celebrating two visionaries for wildlife

187

CHAPTER 10

Postscript

In their 100-year history, first the Society, then the Society side-by-side with the Trusts, and finally The Wildlife Trusts as a collective, has seen times of remarkable solidarity, inspiring leadership and hard-fought achievement. It has not always been easy, but the last 100 years have witnessed the steady development of a unique, locally-owned nationwide conservation movement.

Each Trust is reflective of its local communities and the unique nature of their area. The natural environment we enjoy today, despite the losses and damage it has suffered, is more beautiful and diverse than it would have been had the Trust movement not existed. The movement has worked on behalf of all of our wildlife and habitats across the whole of the United Kingdom and no other organisation in its field has focused on local people and local needs more assiduously, or with more vigour, than the Trusts.

Nature conservation is still a relatively young movement. It is interesting to compare its development with that of an older counterpart: the movement that campaigned for better education. The crucial role of education in society achieved mainstream political recognition in the 1870s when universal education received statutory backing. Education in itself does not result in any direct, immediate benefits for society; it is an investment for the future. Money spent on the environment is also an investment for the future: for a safer, healthier and better quality of life. It took 125 years before a Government made education its overriding priority. When will the same be true for the environment? Given the extreme urgency it will need to happen a great deal more quickly.

During the Second World War, the nation pulled together for victory; afterwards, it pulled together to win the peace. People were hugely optimistic that reconstruction would lead to a better way of life. Leading the charge for post-war nature conservation, most clearly demonstrated in the National Parks and Access to the Countryside Act 1949, was one of the Society's greatest achievements. Onto this stage burst a new local conservation movement – the Wildlife Trusts. Forty years on from Charles Rothschild's original vision of a network of protected wildlife sites, a conservation strategy for Britain was finally being put in place.

The country then was rebuilding itself after six years of war, but today, as then, there is also a need to reconstruct the way we live. The economic, social and, above all, the environmental balance sheets do not add up.

Conscious of history, and indeed inspired by it, as the new millennium got underway The Wildlife Trusts struck out on a different path, away from the everyday detailed policy arguments. A new vision for the restoration of our landscapes – Living Landscapes – was developed, a vision that would drive change at a faster pace with the aim of halting and reversing the decline of wildlife. Rather than standing on the goal-line defending the places that had been rescued over the preceding century, the case was now being made for nature's recovery.

Sixty years after the 1949 Act, which first secured protection for some special sites on land, the Marine and Coastal Access Act 2009 put the protection of our seas onto the domestic statute. The Wildlife Trusts were instrumental in building cross-party support for this legislation and, through its Living Seas campaign, it remains in the forefront of those pressing for its implementation and, in particular, the creation of an ecologically coherent network of Marine Protected Areas in UK waters.

Meanwhile, aware that many voters were members of wildlife organisations, in the run-up to the 2010 general election the political parties were showing an interest in The Wildlife Trusts' concept of Living Landscapes and the idea of valuing the 'natural services' provided by nature. This lay behind the Government's decision to appoint a Panel, chaired by Professor Sir John Lawton (Chair of Yorkshire Wildlife Trust), to undertake England's first ever review of wildlife sites and networks. The resulting report, *Making Space for Nature*, authoritatively endorsed the need for a "step-change in nature conservation. . . a new restorative approach which rebuilds nature and creates a more resilient natural environment for the benefit of wildlife and ourselves".[364]

The Wildlife Trusts looked to put the emerging thinking of the Lawton Review into practice, calling for a White Paper on nature in the build up to the 2010 General Election. The Trusts played a key role in securing the support of both main parties and the wider NGO movement who rallied behind it. In 2011, the new coalition Government published its White Paper – *The Natural Choice: securing the value of nature*, and similar initiatives have followed in other parts of the UK, with Wildlife Trusts playing significant roles. The White Paper called for the value of nature to be placed "at the centre of the choices our nation must make: to enhance our environment, economic growth and personal wellbeing".[365] At its launch a Minister said that no other organisation had as great a claim to be described as its midwife as The Wildlife Trusts. No doubt he was unaware the Society had been so described at the birth of the Nature Conservancy, 60 years earlier.

The parallels with the late 1940s are striking: a time of economic and political uncertainty and an authoritative review (Lawton) which challenges the Government, and indeed society, to take far-sighted decisions.

Predicting the long-term impact of such moments is difficult, but there is no doubt that as it enters its hundredth year, The Wildlife Trusts has the opportunity to play a pivotal role. It has no less a task than to provide the vision and means to help build a new, more natural world.

PART II

HISTORIES OF
WILDLIFE TRUSTS

Map of the UK showing the geographical areas covered by the 47 Wildlife Trusts

Introduction

Brought together for the first time in the following pages are fascinating accounts of the history of each of the individual Wildlife Trusts – written in their own words. They tell the stories of the challenges and successes that lie behind the vibrant Wildlife Trust movement we see today. Many of the authors have a long involvement with their respective Trusts, whether as Trustees, volunteers, members of staff or, in some cases, a combination of all three.

Each Trust has its own chapter, including a map of the geographical area covered by the Trust, generally showing the location of its main nature reserves. The chapters are presented alphabetically – from Alderney to Yorkshire. Over the years, most Trusts have changed their name, most commonly from Naturalists' Trust to Wildlife Trust. Some have also changed their structure – for example the West Midlands Trust split and reconstituted to form separate Trusts in Worcestershire, Warwickshire, Staffordshire, and Birmingham and Black Country. The 'Names of Trusts' section on p667 contains some further information on this.

As with Part 1 of the book, the events described here represent the tip of the iceberg. Behind years of activity, from the acquisition of nature reserves and the building of visitor centres to successful campaigns, educational and community programmes and restoration projects, lie many thousands of hours of negotiation, advice and physical work by both staff and volunteers. There is not space here to include the names of more than a few who have played their part, but their contribution lives on in the work of their Trusts.

Additional acknowledgements for the Trust chapters are included on p761.

THE WILDLIFE TRUSTS NOW

2,300 nature reserves covering 93,000ha

116 visitor centres

150 coastal and marine reserves

17,000 events held annually

400,000+ people directly engaged including pupils and students

35,000 volunteers

120+ Living Landscape schemes

5,300 landowners advised annually

800,000+ members

150,000+ junior members

6.5 million visits to Trusts' nature reserves annually

Figures for period April 2010–March 2011

CHAPTER 1

Alderney

Alderney is the third largest of the Channel Islands and was first inhabited at least 2,000 years before the arrival of the Romans. With an area of scarcely more than nine square kilometres the island could seem, at a distance, too small to offer much more than a haven for seabirds. Indeed Alderney is a wonderful place for birdwatching – and for seabirds in particular – but with over 900 species of plant recorded on the island, it is also one of the richest areas in the British Isles for wildflowers. Its wildlife includes many species that are commonly found across the UK, but also a few island specialities including the blonde hedgehog and the black rabbit!

STARTING UP THE TRUST

In late 2001, a public meeting was organised to assess the degree of public interest in the formation of a Wildlife Trust on the island. A panel of local naturalists and other experts from Jersey, Guernsey and Alderney was on the platform to listen to the President of The Wildlife Trusts, DAVID BELLAMY and its Director, SIMON LYSTER. If agreed, Alderney would become the first full member of The Wildlife Trusts in the Channel Islands. The meeting was chaired by Sir Norman Browse, President of the States of Alderney. Brian Bonnard, the resident recorder for the Botanical Society of the British Isles, was on the panel to answer any questions from the audience about Alderney's wildlife.

The Island Hall was packed with about 300 local residents. After Bellamy's enthusiastic talk about the value of The Wildlife Trusts and

Opposite: Gannet
Right: Roland Gauvain – the Trust's Manager

questions from the audience had been answered by Bonnard and other Channel Island naturalists, a show of hands indicated that the majority of the audience supported the idea. It was suggested that donations from founder members might help to meet the costs of setting up a new local Trust and of suitable office accommodation. About a dozen of the group met subsequently and agreed to form a committee of five members with a Chairman, Secretary and Treasurer to decide on a constitution and to perform the necessary local and legal work to set up the organisation. Robin Whicker became chairman, Lynne Chiswell secretary and Brian Bonnard treasurer. A constitution was drafted and Roland Gauvain, previously Conservation Officer to the States of Alderney, was employed as Trust Manager. Gauvain's family had been associated with Alderney for many years. As a result of all this foundation work, the Alderney Wildlife Trust was formed as the 47th member of the Royal Society of Wildlife Trusts (the Society) on 13th May 2002. Its formation was supported by the States of Alderney and the local historic organisation, the Alderney Society.

Unlike any other jurisdiction in the British Isles, Alderney lacks any civil service infrastructure directly responsible for the maintenance and management of the natural environment. Furthermore, there is only one piece of wildlife legislation covering

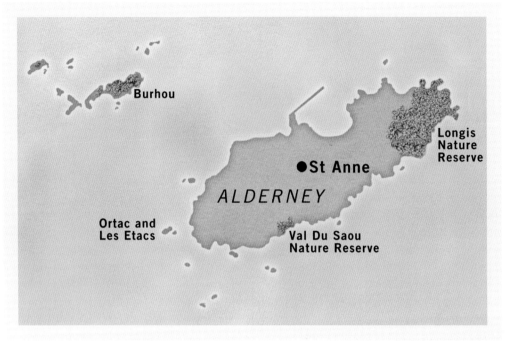

Map of Alderney Wildlife Trust nature reserves

the island, an adapted 1947 Wild Bird Protection Ordinance. The Alderney Trust was therefore conceived to fulfil many roles. As a non-government organisation, it fills a major gap within the island's infrastructure. It has developed the largest regional per capita population membership of any of the 47 Wildlife Trusts (with approximately 25 per cent coverage of the local population) and has one of the fastest growing proportionate memberships. The Trust's roles are as diverse as responding to planning issues, supporting the States of Alderney on environmental impact assessment, encouraging tourism and developing educational activities and land management. The Trust's core objectives are linked to the Society's national strategy.

RESERVES AND ISLAND WILDLIFE

Since the Trust's formation, three nature reserves have been established on Alderney, all requiring very different management due to their distinctive ecology and geology.

In 2003, Alderney's first reserve, Longis, was designated under a memorandum of understanding between the Trust, the States of Alderney and local landowners. It remains the largest terrestrial reserve on the island, covering around 105 hectares and contains a variety of habitats. Longis was shortly followed, in 2004, by the seven-hectare Val du Saou reserve, established under a similar memorandum, where a carefully-restored Second World War communications bunker, one of many fortifications dotted across Alderney's landscape, now provides the Trust with a visitor centre overlooking the sea.

The Alderney West Coast and the Burhou Islands Ramsar site was designated in 2005 (Ramsar sites are wetlands of international importance designated under the Ramsar Convention). The first Ramsar site in the Bailiwick of Guernsey, it covers an area twice the size of the island of Alderney itself and includes the outlying uninhabited islands and rocks of Burhou, Ortac and Les Etacs. Between them, Ortac and Les Etacs are home to over 6,000 breeding pairs of gannets.

Another familiar Alderney visitor is the puffin, which arrives in April and leaves by the third week in July. Up to 200 pairs nest in burrows on Burhou every year and in 2009 the Trust set up a remotely operated camera – 'Puffin Cam' – which broadcasted live pictures on the internet, allowing people to observe the birds in their natural habitat without subjecting them to disturbance.

Seals, and occasional harbour porpoises and dolphins, are the island's only large mammals. There are rabbits, hedgehogs (including the blonde hedgehog – a variation on the common hedgehog found elsewhere in the UK), bats, voles, moles, rats, mice and shrews, but no deer, foxes, badgers, weasels or squirrels. This comparative lack of predators is to the advantage of nesting birds, both inland and along the shore.

For its size, the island also has a rich diversity of invertebrates. Butterflies abound in the summer months, including the Glanville fritillary (whose only other UK location is the Isle of Wight). Alderney also has a good population of moths, including the day-flying Jersey tiger moth, nine species of dragonfly (all of which breed on the Trust's reserve at Mannez Pond) and several bee species, including the Scilly bee.

Glanville fritillary

In 2003, the Trust established a grazing herd to help maintain Alderney's species-rich grasslands. The herd consists of a growing number of Guernsey cattle that are moved periodically round the island's reserves and other key wildlife areas. Their grazing regime helps to promote the growth of wildflowers and a diverse range of associated insects and birds.

Mannez Pond, Longis nature reserve

The Trust's Watch group on a seashore ramble

STRUCTURE, STAFF AND GOVERNANCE

The Trust's vision is to preserve and enhance the biodiversity of Alderney by research, by conservation, and by challenging the people of Alderney to gain a better understanding of their island. To do this, the Trust must engage with the Government and general public, not only of Alderney but also the wider Channel Islands, in order to effect the creation and development of environmental policy making.

It was originally planned that the Trust would comprise a single entity structure – Alderney Wildlife Trust Ltd, a company limited by guarantee, which would have an open membership and elect a Board of Directors to manage its activities. The advantage to the members of such a corporate structure was that it limited the liability of the members, in the event of a financial catastrophe, to the amount they had agreed to guarantee, usually £1 per member. However, due to the vagaries of Alderney company law this proved not to be a practical proposition and so a second entity, namely the Alderney Wildlife Society, was bolted on to the company. A new company, Alderney Wildlife Trust Enterprises Ltd, was also formed in 2006, when the organisation secured a long lease on a disused farm site, which it developed into a combined field centre. Together, these bodies make up the behind-the-scenes structure of the Trust.

Since the beginning, the Trust's only paid employee has been its Manager, Roland Gauvain, supported by a Board of Directors, volunteers and voluntary staff. None of these voluntary staff draw

Surveyors installing storm petrel nesting boxes on Burhou

L'Etacs is home to around 5,000 breeding pairs of gannets

a salary, but may be in receipt of services in kind, such as subsidised accommodation and flights.

In 2011, there were two surviving Directors who were also founder members of the Trust – Robin Whicker and Brian Bonnard, each of whom have also served four-year terms as President of the Trust. However, the Trust continues to grow beyond what was considered possible at its inception. Today, its responsibilities include management of the Island's Ramsar site and its nature reserves, undertaking consultancy work for both the Government and the independent Alderney Commission for Renewable Energy,

and assisting with the management of the island's tourist information centres.

BY BRIAN BONNARD AND ROLAND GAUVAIN

After a career in the pharmaceutical industry, Brian Bonnard moved to Alderney in 1986. He was later appointed the BSBI Recorder for Alderney, and also wrote The Wildflowers of Alderney. *He has served as Treasurer, Chair and President of the Alderney Wildlife Trust.*

Roland Gauvain started his career as the States of Alderney's Conservation Officer. In May 2002, he helped found the Alderney Wildlife Trust and is now its Manager. His duties include managing the Trust's conservation grazing herd and field centre, and skippering the Trust's boat.

CHAPTER 2

Avon

By the late 1970s, the idea of a new Wildlife Trust for the then recently-created County of Avon was beginning to be developed by a number of enthusiasts, including members of the neighbouring SOMERSET and GLOUCESTERSHIRE TRUSTS. They saw that a new approach was needed for a county with a more urban population centred around Bristol and Bath. Andrew Lea (at that time a key member of the Bristol Conservation Corps and by profession a research scientist) agreed to become involved with what was called the Avon Wildlife Trust Project. His brief was to do all the necessary day-to-day work to set up a brand new Wildlife Trust from scratch. In May 1980, the Avon Wildlife Trust was launched with the twin objectives of wildlife conservation and education – on the grounds that people (particularly in the urban parts of Avon) needed to learn about wildlife in order to protect it.

At that time, when managing nature reserves was still a top priority for most Trusts, focusing on wildlife conservation in urban areas was particularly controversial. For many, looking for 'wildlife on walls' and running 'mini-beast safaris' was a bizarre and unfamiliar way of working. Support for this new approach, however, came from unexpected quarters, with the Bristol City Parks Department amongst the most encouraging and supportive.

THREE DYNAMIC LEADERS

Since then, the growth of the Trust has had at least three distinct phases under three dynamic and visionary people.

Opposite: View towards the Severn Estuary from Dolebury Warren nature reserve

The first phase was under the leadership of Chris Johnson who was Director from 1980 to 1990. Growth in these years was fuelled by the Government's Community Programme, a job creation scheme under the Manpower Services Commission (EMPLOYMENT SCHEMES). The number of Trust staff grew to more than 130, including dozens of highly-talented young people who worked on a wide range of projects. They ranged from surveying nature reserves and writing nature reserve guides to developing a wider countryside strategy and designing an education centre. During this time, the Trust acquired more than 20 nature reserves, membership grew to 5,000 and an anonymous donor gifted £250,000 for the Trust to buy Folly Farm. This was only the second nature reserve to be owned by the Trust after Brown's Folly, purchased in 1983. Other nature reserves were managed under leasehold arrangements, due to the difficulty in raising funds to buy land. 1988 saw the beginning of the end of the Community Programme and a renewed appreciation of the important role played by volunteers.

In 1990, Jon Gething became Trust Director. The start of this next phase saw the Trust struggling to recover from the loss of Government funding and the jobs that had come with it. However, these losses were partially compensated for by the advent of the HERITAGE LOTTERY FUND (HLF) in 1994. The HLF helped the Trust to purchase eight important sites as nature reserves and to fund the Folly Farm project. The Trust also benefited from HLF funding for a five-year Capital Works Programme which enhanced nature reserves and funded two posts, including one to develop volunteering.

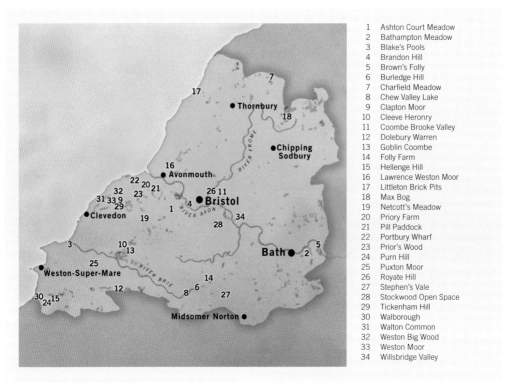

1	Ashton Court Meadow
2	Bathampton Meadow
3	Blake's Pools
4	Brandon Hill
5	Brown's Folly
6	Burledge Hill
7	Charfield Meadow
8	Chew Valley Lake
9	Clapton Moor
10	Cleeve Heronry
11	Coombe Brooke Valley
12	Dolebury Warren
13	Goblin Coombe
14	Folly Farm
15	Hellenge Hill
16	Lawrence Weston Moor
17	Littleton Brick Pits
18	Max Bog
19	Netcott's Meadow
20	Priory Farm
21	Pill Paddock
22	Portbury Wharf
23	Prior's Wood
24	Purn Hill
25	Puxton Moor
26	Royate Hill
27	Stephen's Vale
28	Stockwood Open Space
29	Tickenham Hill
30	Walborough
31	Walton Common
32	Weston Big Wood
33	Weston Moor
34	Willsbridge Valley

Map of Avon Wildlife Trust nature reserves

Jon left the Trust in 2002 and was succeeded as Chief Executive by Steve Grainger who has taken the Trust into a further period of growth and development. By the time the Trust celebrated its 30th anniversary in 2010, membership had grown to a record 16,000 and the Trust could reflect on significant achievements in conserving wildlife in Bristol, in other urban areas, and in the wider Avon countryside. It has also protected species, managed nature reserves and been particularly keen to share its delight and passion for wildlife through its educational programmes and working with people right across the community. The opening of the Folly Farm Centre in 2008 was another major achievement – the culmination of more than 20 years of dedicated work to restore and convert the farm buildings into a residential learning centre for the region. In 2010, the Trust launched two major long-term programmes – the Living Landscape Wildflower Grasslands Project, and the People and Wildlife Project.

It also completed negotiations on a groundbreaking conservation deal to establish and fund a major new nature reserve at Portbury Wharf, near Portishead.

FROM TOWN TO COUNTRY

The birth of the Avon Trust coincided with, and fuelled, a growing concern in the new county for the plight of wildlife in the urban environment. Early on, the Trust became involved in urban conservation. In 1980, Brandon Hill nature reserve in Bristol became the country's first city centre nature reserve, bringing hay meadows, wildlife ponds and butterfly gardens into a formal city park. In those days, working closely with Bristol City Council's Parks Department was unusual, but today wildlife areas have become regular features of its inner city green spaces.

These were not the only examples of the Trust opening the public's eyes to wildlife in urban areas. A city centre NATURE TRAIL was launched by 'abseiling seagulls' in the summer of 2002 and, in October the same year, the Trust started Bristol Bird Watch. Since then, more than 2,000 people have taken part each year, making it "the best bird sample in the country". Over 54 bird species were spotted in the first year – with the top three birds the blackbird, robin and blue tit. Bristol Bird Watch – succeeded in 2010 by the Wild Sparrow survey – became one of Bristol City Council's indicators for the quality of life in Bristol.

It was not long before the Trust was looking beyond its urban boundaries and campaigning to protect areas in Avon's wider countryside. The Trust's campaign to save the wetlands of the Gordano Valley, for example, went from strength to strength after its launch in 1984. Clapton Moor and Weston Moor – parts of the valley now rich in birdlife – would have been uninspiring farmland had the Trust not stepped in and bought these sites. In the early 1990s, the Trust raised the water levels at Clapton Moor by installing sluices. By winter 2001, there was a count of almost 250 lapwing and the next year nine pairs nested. In 2000, 112 common snipe were recorded on Weston Moor, the highest concentration in the area. The same year, the Trust planted 9,500 trees on the slopes of the valley.

KEY RESERVES

Other areas were either managed or acquired as nature reserves by the Trust. Littleton Brick Pits was once an artificial lagoon of fly-ash tipped from a power station, and would have dried out over the following years if the Trust had not taken it over in 1982 and kept water levels suitable for breeding birds. Reed and sedge warblers now abound and in winter hundreds of starlings come home to roost. At Walborough on the Severn Estuary – a special place for waders – the Trust was able to make it even better for sea-loving birds and plants.

Lapwing

Brandon Hill – one of the first urban nature reserves

It implemented an ambitious plan to allow managed retreat by building a sea wall to let the sea in, not keep it out, so that saltmarsh could flourish once more! One of the Trust's most important acquisitions was Folly Farm, which came up for sale in 1986. If the Trust had not bought it, the wildflower grasslands that made Folly Farm so special, together with the countless butterflies and other creatures that rely on them, would have disappeared for ever.

Many other sites that interested the Trust had potential but were in need of active management. In 1989, Ashton Court Meadow was a scrubby patch of land which the Trust brought back into haymaking and with it an amazing array of orchids and other wildflowers appeared. Bathampton Oxbow – a piece of uninteresting farmland in the early 1990s – is now one of the area's best wildlife sites, hosting the rare small blue butterfly, scarce bluetail damselfly and recently, otters. The magnificent hill fort of Dolebury Warren would have been overgrown with scrub if the Trust had not set about restoring the site's special grassland and with it, dozens of rare butterflies.

SAVING SITES FROM DEVELOPMENT

The Trust also fought to save sites from development. In a landmark case in 1991, the Trust's campaign to save Royate Hill resulted in the first compulsory purchase of a wildlife site in the UK, and a major change in attitude towards development by planners and councillors. Instead of being covered by housing, the site became a valued Local Nature Reserve.

Puxton Moor, rich in wildlife and archaeology, would have been a golf course and a holiday resort had the Trust not bought it in 1997. In 1998, a rare sighting of a tree sparrow at this reserve inspired a nest box project managed by the local community, and to everyone's delight tree sparrows began to breed the following summer.

Wildlife is not always thought about as early as it should be in the planning process, even at places protected by the law. In common with several other Trusts, the Avon Trust has held several training workshops for its local authorities and made them enthusiastic about helping all kinds of wildlife, from bats to barn owls.

RETURNING WILDLIFE

The Trust's work in the wider countryside has also seen species returning to Avon. Otter populations, for example, have increased in north Somerset and signs of otter have been found around Chew Valley Lake, in south Gloucestershire and on the River Avon in Bath and Bristol. In addition, Avonmouth Port was declared 'the most urban location of the water vole' in 1997, after the Trust's extensive water

Royate Hill – campaigning for change

vole survey found thriving populations in this industrial landscape. Alerted by fears that the numbers of dormice had declined by more than 50 per cent, the Trust has, since 2003, taken part in a national study which is producing some exciting results. The Trust is also a key partner in the South West Crayfish Project, helping to re-home threatened populations of the white-clawed crayfish to refuge or ark sites. Boris, the oldest greater horseshoe bat ever recorded in Britain, was discovered in January 2000 at the Trust's Brown's Folly nature reserve. Here, more than 13 of Britain's 18 bat species are found in the old stone mines.

Portbury Wharf, the Trust's latest reserve, represents a groundbreaking arrangement between a new housing development and nature conservation. Situated close to the internationally-important Severn Estuary, this reserve acts as a sanctuary for wildfowl and waders, as well as water vole, otter and the greater horseshoe bat. Planning consent for the development was given on condition that a nature reserve was created and that the ongoing costs of the reserve were met by an annual charge levied on the properties. Avon Wildlife Trust was selected to manage, and eventually own, the nature reserve.

The original objectives of conserving and enhancing Avon's wildlife are now complemented by the concept of working on a landscape scale, in common with the whole Wildlife Trust movement. The first Living Landscape programme – Wildflower Grasslands – began in 2008 and in 2011, the North Somerset Wetlands programme also became part of the Trust's Living Landscape work.

WORKING WITH YOUNG PEOPLE

Over the years, the Trust has shared its delight and passion for the natural world with more than half a million children through a variety of activities and events. In the early 1980s, the Trust held massive nature fairs at Newton St Loe. From 1986 there were schools' programmes at Willsbridge Mill and in the 1990s, earth education events at Folly Farm.

Willsbridge Mill was a particular success for the Trust. In the early 1980s, the Trust rose to a near impossible challenge of restoring two derelict buildings in Willsbridge Valley. Transformed into the

Folly Farm – wildflower meadows and ancient woodland

south-west's first wildlife visitor centre, it opened its doors to business in a blaze of publicity in 1986. Since then, over 84,000 schoolchildren have engaged with nature at first hand, through its nationally-acclaimed and highly-regarded environmental education programme. In addition, thousands of adults and children visited, either to wander the many trails, or participate at events and workshops.

And this is just part of the Trust's educational work. It pioneered conservation school grounds work and over the years the Trust has built ponds, created shady shelters, planted wildflower areas and built boardwalks for pond-dipping. It has then gone on to show teachers and parents how to look after these transformations.

In 2010, the Trust adopted a new, broader-based learning strategy, which will build on its track record and utilise the new residential learning facilities at the Folly Farm Centre. This expands the Trust's ambitions towards the formal education sector, to reach greater numbers of primary schoolchildren together with secondary and tertiary level students. The learning strategy will also give new focus to the Trust's role in promoting understanding and appreciation of the natural world among all age groups through lifelong learning.

The Trust's HLF-funded People and Wildlife Programme began in 2008 after a period of audience development research. This programme takes a community-based approach in engaging people across the whole Avon community, reaching out to groups who have been previously under-represented in the Trust's membership and activities.

The Trust's active volunteers, who range from 15 to 75 years old, have shaped Avon's local communities throughout the years. The Trust is immensely grateful to the many hundreds of people who have helped with everything, from scrub bashing and magazine delivery to giving talks and assisting with education events.

Above all, the Trust has changed attitudes in Avon over the many years since it was no more than 'a twinkle in the eye' of its founders. Today, more than 17,000 people in the Avon area support the Trust. A recent membership survey gave it a big vote of confidence, with the main reason given for joining the Trust being "to find out more about local wildlife". The Trust's membership is in no doubt that the Trust is doing "more than any other local organisation to ensure that Avon remains an area rich in wildlife... offering enrichment to the lives of everyone who lives here".

BY MIKE DAWSON
Mike Dawson was a founder member of Avon Wildlife Trust and researched and wrote the Trust history for its 25th anniversary in 2005.

CHAPTER 3

Bedfordshire, Cambridgeshire and Northamptonshire

The Wildlife Trust for Bedfordshire, Cambridgeshire and Northamptonshire (BCN) was formed in its present incarnation in August 1994. It was the result of a merger of the Bedfordshire and Cambridgeshire Wildlife Trust, founded in 1990, the Northamptonshire Wildlife Trust, founded in 1967, and the Peterborough Wildlife Group founded in 1987. The Bedfordshire and Cambridgeshire Wildlife Trust was the result of a merger between the Bedfordshire and Huntingdonshire Wildlife Trust, founded in 1961, and the Cambridgeshire Wildlife Trust, founded in 1956 as the Cambridgeshire and Isle of Ely Naturalists' Trust. Originally including Peterborough (BCNP), the Trust's name was shortened to Bedfordshire, Cambridgeshire and Northamptonshire when it revised its articles of association in 2011. Although the three counties fall into two regions, they share a history on the edge of East Anglia and the East Midlands with farming and related industries dominating. The mining of ironstone and limestone in Northamptonshire has ceased in the last 50 years. Winning chalk in Bedfordshire and Cambridgeshire has almost finished, but gravel extraction continues in the river valleys of all three counties. Pressure for development, especially housing, warehousing and high-tech industry, is historically high and seems likely to continue. This suggests that infrastructure will struggle to cope with the effects on transport, water supply, water quality and flood management.

Since the Trust's inception in 1956, arable has taken over from mixed farming in Cambridgeshire, Bedfordshire has seen the demise of market

Opposite: Black hairstreak butterfly – around 50 per cent of the UK's population exist on the Trust's reserves

gardening and arable farming has increased in Northamptonshire. The only remaining cattle market is at Thrapston, Northamptonshire. Parliamentary constituencies have also changed and increased as the population has grown. Local government has changed considerably and Government regionalisation from 1997 to 2010 and a development agenda in the Stansted-Cambridge-Peterborough corridor and the Milton Keynes-South Midlands area has affected the Trust's work.

The Trust has also worked closely with the Nature Conservancy (now Natural England) and the Conservancy's staff were instrumental in the early growth of each of the three original Naturalists' Trusts. Ties with the Conservancy were strengthened further when its national headquarters relocated from London to Peterborough in 1984.

CAMBRIDGESHIRE BEGINNINGS

A potent combination of local naturalists and academics from Cambridge University were the founders of the Cambridgeshire and Isle of Ely Naturalists' Trust (CAMBIENT) in 1956. Its founders included Dr Max Walters, then Curator of the University Herbarium and later Director of the University Botanic Garden, and Fenland naturalist Tony Vine. The advice of TED SMITH, founder of the LINCOLNSHIRE TRUST, was both sought and taken, so that the Trust largely modelled itself on its Lincolnshire counterpart. One of its early stated aims was "to encourage interest and understanding for an intelligent policy of nature conservation in the county."

Its 20-strong Council appointed three committees whose topics showed the emphasis of the new Trust.

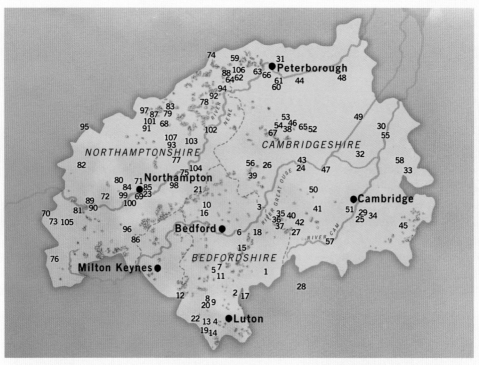

1	Arlesey Old Moat and Glebe Meadows	35	Gamlingay Wood	72	Bugbrooke Meadow
2	Barton Gravel Pit	36	Gamlingay Cinques	73	Byfield Pool
3	Begwary Brook	37	Gamlingay Meadow	74	Collyweston Quarries
4	Blow's Downs	38	Gamsey Wood	75	Ditchford Lakes and Meadows
5	Cooper's Hill	39	Grafham Water	76	Farthinghoe
6	Cople Pits	40	Gransden and Waresley Woods	77	Finedon Cally Banks
7	Cut-throat Meadow	41	Hardwick Wood	78	Glapthorn Cow Pastures
8	Dropshort Marsh	42	Hayley Wood	79	Great Oakley Meadow
9	Fancott Woods and Meadows	43	Houghton Meadows	80	Harlestone Heath
10	Felmersham Gravel Pits	44	Lattersey	81	High Wood and Meadow
11	Flitwick Moor (and Folly Wood)	45	Lower Wood	82	Higham Ferrers Pits
12	King's Wood and Rammamere Heath	46	Lady's Wood and Upwood Meadows	83	King's Wood
13	Lancot Meadow	47	Mare Fen	84	Kingsthorpe Meadow
14	Landpark Wood	48	Norwood Road	85	Lings Local Nature Reserve
15	Old Warden Tunnel	49	Ouse Washes	86	Mill Crook and Grafton Regis Meadow
16	Pavenham Osier Beds	50	Overhall Grove	87	The Plens
	(In Memory of Horace Church)	51	Skater's Meadow	88	Old Sulehay
17	Pegsdon Hills and Hoo Bit	52	Pingle Wood and Cutting	89	Pitsford Reservoir
18	The Riddy	53	Ramsey Heights	90	Ramsden Corner
19	Sallowsprings	54	Raveley Wood	91	Rothwell Gullet
20	Sewell Cutting	55	Roswell Pits	92	Short Wood
21	Sharnbrook Summit and	56	Shepherd's Close	93	Southfield Farm Marsh
	Wymington Meadow	57	Shepreth L-Moor	94	Southwick Wood
22	Totternhoe Knolls and Quarry	58	Soham Meadow	95	Stanford Reservoir
23	Abington Meadows	59	Southorpe Meadow and Paddock	96	Stoke Bruerne Brick Pits
24	Arthur's Meadow	60	Stanground Newt Ponds	97	Stoke Wood End Quarter
25	Beechwoods	61	Stanground Wash	98	Summer Leys
26	Brampton Wood	62	Stibbington	99	Storton's Pits
27	Buff Wood	63	Thorpe Wood	100	Duston Mill Meadow
28	Cambourne	64	Wansford Pasture	101	Tailby Meadow
29	Cherry Hinton	65	Wistow Wood	102	Titchmarsh
30	Chettisham Meadow	66	Woodston Ponds	103	Twywell Hill and Dales
31	Dogsthorpe Star Pit, Little Wood and	67	Woodwalton Marsh and Five Arches Pit	104	Wilson's Pits
	Eye Green	68	Barford Wood and Meadows	105	Woodford Halse
32	Doghouse Grove	69	Barnes Meadow	106	Yarwell Dingle and Pond
33	Fordham Wood	70	Boddington Meadow	107	Wickstead Water Meadows
34	Fulbourn Fen	71	Bradlaugh Fields		

Map of Bedfordshire, Cambridgeshire and Northamptonshire Wildlife Trust nature reserves

The Technical Committee was concerned with the collection and use of technical information on all aspects of natural history in the county. Site reports were prepared in cooperation with the County Planning Department and the Nature Conservancy. All the county's parish pits (gravel or chalk pits mainly established under Enclosure Awards) were surveyed and steps were taken to safeguard those of natural history interest. The Educational Committee began to bring teachers' attention to the natural history of the county. The Excursion Committee, which was appointed jointly by the Trust and the Cambridge Natural History Society, was unusual among early Trusts and was needed because there was no naturalists' organisation operating on a county basis.

Nature in Cambridgeshire – the Trust's annual natural history journal – was first published in cooperation with the Cambridge Natural History Society in 1958 and by the end of 1958 the Trust had 170 members.

FIRST TRUST RESERVES

The earliest of the Trust's nature reserves was a disused chalk pit – Lime Kiln Close at Cherry Hinton which the Trust managed under agreement with Cambridge City Council. The Trust's first freehold acquisition was Hayley Wood, one of the most outstanding examples of ancient woodland in the country, notable for its springtime displays of oxlips and the site of a long-term study by the woodland historian Oliver Rackham. It was purchased in 1962 for £5,000 – about £40 per acre.

An appeal for further funds to buy land was launched in February 1962 and by September £6,000 had been raised. Shortly after this the Trust, working alongside the RSPB and the Wildfowl Trust, began to acquire land in the Ouse Washes, a 20 mile-long strip of wet grassland running between the two diversion channels of the Great Ouse in the Cambridgeshire Fens. Two Council members, FRANK PERRING and Gigi Crompton, negotiated the acquisition of 60 acres there at a cost of £1,000.

Cherry Hinton – the first Cambridgeshire reserve

The first professional staff member was an administrator, whose main task was to raise funds and ensure that finances were properly managed, leaving members to get on with the natural history and conservation. However, as the Trust grew, it eventually became necessary to appoint professional conservation staff. This led to occasional clashes between a highly-committed membership, which included academics, professional conservationists and highly-expert amateur naturalists, and the new professional staff who wanted to get on with the job without having to refer everything to the members!

By the mid-1980s, the Cambridgeshire Wildlife Trust had a very effective Director in Mark Rose, three conservation staff, an administrator and a publicity officer supported by volunteers. However, by the late 1980s its neighbour, the Bedfordshire and Huntingdonshire Trust, was facing a more problematic future.

BEDS AND HUNTS JOIN FORCES

Two years after the foundation of CAMBIENT, Henry Key, a Bedford pharmacist and Honorary General Secretary of the Bedfordshire Natural History Society and Field Club, sent a letter to CAMBIENT members inviting them to a meeting in Bedford to discuss the formation of a Naturalists' Trust for Bedfordshire. The guest speaker at the meeting on Sunday 6th December 1959 was TED SMITH. It was decided that the county was too small to sustain its own Trust, and so Huntingdonshire, through the Hunts Flora and Fauna Society, was invited to join forces. The Bedfordshire and Huntingdonshire Naturalists' Trust was incorporated on 10th March 1961. Its joint Chairmen were the county planning officers for each county, with the Council meeting alternating between the Bedfordshire and Huntingdonshire council chambers.

FIRST RESERVES IN BEDFORDSHIRE

The Trust's first nature reserve was Felmersham Gravel Pits – 21 hectares beside the River Ouse in North Bedfordshire. Pragmatism ruled. The Trust let fishing, and for its first few years, the income from angling permits exceeded the Trust's membership subscriptions. A warden was paid an annual honorarium of £52 and his main task was to manage the fishing. Close links with the two county councils also resulted in management agreements over Totternhoe Knolls, a fine botanically- and entomologically-rich site in the Chilterns, and the newly-created reservoir at Grafham Water near Huntingdon.

The Nature Conservancy's new Monks Wood Experimental Station stood in a National Nature Reserve that was the largest woodland in Huntingdonshire. Its expert and enthusiastic staff proved a huge benefit for the new Trust as Council

An early open day at Felmersham Gravel Pits

members, volunteers and wardens. It was a Monks Wood ecologist, Terry Wells, who organised the Trust's appeal to purchase Raveley, Gamsey and Lady's Wood from the Forestry Commission for £10,000 in 1970. He also discovered the herb-rich Upwood Meadows, now a National Nature Reserve owned by the Trust, and was the initiator of the Countryside Classroom at Ramsey Heights, which opened in 1979. This was the Trust's first education centre, and in 2009, the Great Fen Project office was established here.

A few years after the Trust's foundation, the RSPB moved its headquarters to Sandy in Bedfordshire. Immediately the two organisations began to work together, with the Trust jointly managing the nature reserve there for the next 15 years until the professionalism of the RSPB reserves staff meant that the Trust's input was no longer needed. Several staff from Sandy were active supporters of the Trust, providing assistance with reserves management, advice and membership recruitment.

Thanks to a grant from the Carnegie Trust, the first administrative officer was employed in 1972, followed by Dr Nancy Dawson in 1976. But until the late 1970s, the Trust's work was still largely carried out by volunteers, who ran the reserves, the guided walks programme, media liaison, membership recruitment, newsletters and journals.

A theme of 1970s nature conservation was the need to own freeholds of nature reserves, as a means of safeguarding sites against damage or destruction. Working with the World Wildlife Fund, the Ouse Valley Wildlife Appeal was launched with the aim of raising money to buy freeholds of existing and new reserves. As a result, the holding at Felmersham Pits became freehold and two new SSSI reserves, both in Huntingdonshire, were bought at Upwood Meadows and Waresley Woods.

NORTHANTS GETS GOING

The Northamptonshire Naturalists' Trust's first Chairman was James Fisher, then the second-most famous naturalist in Britain after Peter Scott, who was also one of the Trust's original Vice Presidents.

Flower-rich woodland at Gamsey Wood was acquired in 1970

The minutes of the first Council meeting held in August 1963 show a vigorous organisation determined to get into action very quickly. Various organisations, including the RSPB and the Nene Water Board were to be approached for literature, posters and photographs and space was booked at several shows and events in order to promote the Trust.

FIRST AGM

Soon the possibility of managing a wildfowl refuge at Pitsford Reservoir was being investigated. The acquisition of part of the Buckingham Arm of the Grand Union Canal was being discussed with the BERKSHIRE, BUCKINGHAMSHIRE AND OXFORDSHIRE TRUST and the management of 53 acres of ancient woodland at Bedford Purlieus was under discussion with the Forestry Commission and the Nature Conservancy. The first Annual General Meeting on 23rd October 1964 was held in Kettering with the President, Earl Spencer, in the chair and with Peter Conder, Director of the RSPB and an active volunteer with CAMBIENT, speaking about the adverse effects on birds of organochlorine insecticides. By March 1965 the Trust's membership stood at 160.

Two and a half years after the Trust was founded, it purchased its first freehold nature reserve, the Buckingham Arm Canal for £211. The Society for the Promotion of Nature Reserves (the Society) had contributed £135 and had underwritten the balance. The intention was to turn it into an educational reserve and nature trail, but it was soon to prove problematic. After the canal overflowed and flooded the fields of a neighbouring landowner, the British Waterways Board drained the canal without obtaining the Trust's permission. The Trust refused the Board's request for a contribution and decided to sell the canal to the landowner at market price. More positively, management agreements over Barnack Hills and Holes – a medieval limestone quarry, home to many rare wildflowers – and Bedford Purlieus, had been agreed.

BALANCING PRIORITIES

While the early days of the other two BCN Trusts were dominated by reserve acquisitions, in Northamptonshire there was a growing awareness of the need to meet the threats of expansion of Peterborough, Northampton and elsewhere in the county, initially led by the Chairman James Fisher. However, he died tragically in a car accident in September 1970, followed sadly, by LP Williams, the Honorary Treasurer, who died five weeks later. TED SMITH's aid was swiftly sought and he approached the Honorable MIRIAM ROTHSCHILD, who was due to move back to her family home at ASHTON WOLD in Northamptonshire late in 1971. The Trust's Council agreed to hold open the office until she could take up the chairmanship. She maintained the high levels of contact started

by James Fisher and fostered close relationships with other conservation and countryside organisations.

The first paid member of staff was a Minutes Secretary appointed in 1972. In the following year it was agreed to appoint an Administrative/ Development Officer to be shared with the neighbouring WARWICKSHIRE TRUST with a grant from the Carnegie Trust, brokered by the Society. An Administrative Officer was appointed in the summer of 1973, but lasted less than a year. No further appointment was made until 1976 when it was realised that paid help was necessary, especially if a new fundraising appeal was to be successful. The County Council promised £1,000 towards this appeal and £1,000 for the appointment of an administrator. At a time when the Trust membership was 1,300, it was estimated that a total membership of 3,000 was required to make the employment of an Administrative Officer viable.

Other important decisions were the revision of the committee structure, with six sub-committees

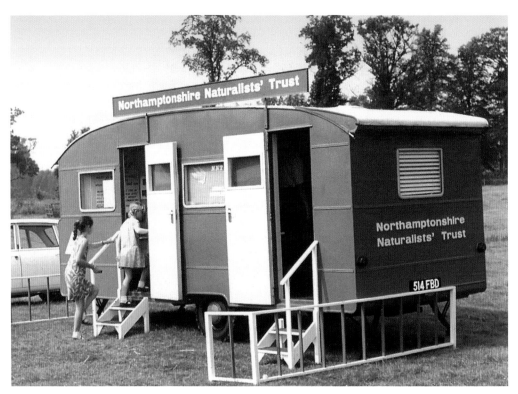

The Northamptonshire Trust's mobile stand makes an appearance at a show

including a Fundraising and Publicity Committee chaired by FRANK PERRING. The Trust also took advantage of the Government's Job Creation Scheme (EMPLOYMENT SCHEMES) to employ two supervisors and eight staff for an eight-month conservation project in January 1977. Later that year, the lease at a peppercorn rent of Lings House, a substantial family house in Northampton built in the 1940s, was agreed with the Northampton Borough Council. The building is still in use by the Trust, and in 2001, it was enlarged to provide an education centre.

Development of all three Trusts in the 1980s was helped by the Government's Manpower Services Commission, which aimed to create job opportunities for the unemployed. New staff were employed for reserve management, habitat surveying and education. However, although this was largely a success it was symptomatic of a deeper issue. Instead of concentrating on building up their membership bases and securing a steady source of income, the three Trusts had become over-dependent on Government funding and other grants to support their development. Survival had become a constant juggling act. In the late 1980s, the Cambridgeshire and Northamptonshire Trusts appointed Mark Rose and Adrian Colston as Directors. Both were ecologists who were also adept at balancing funding to achieve the aims of the Trusts.

The Bedfordshire and Huntingdonshire Trust however, had gone down a different route. A grant from the Nature Conservancy Council enabled it to employ a Conservation Officer, John Comont, in 1986. He came from the Dyfed Wildlife Trust and set about bringing a professional edge to reserve management. The same grant also funded a Development Officer, Derek Niemann, whose aims were to increase the income from membership and to create more local members' groups. As the grant tapered over three years, there was an imperative to produce sufficient extra income to pay for both salaries within three years. When the Trustees became aware that the relatively small size of the population in the

Cambridgeshire volunteers in the 1960s

Trust's area made this a huge, and probably impossible, task, they began to consider the possibility of merging with a neighbouring Trust.

TOWARDS A FINAL MERGER

Because Huntingdonshire had been transferred to Cambridgeshire County Council in 1972, there was already close working on conservation issues between the Bedfordshire and Huntingdonshire Trust and the Cambridgeshire Trust. The latter had restructured its management and a first merger approach was made to the Cambridgeshire Trust in 1988. A group of four people from each Trust was set up to take forward closer cooperation with the possibility of a merger, referring back to their Councils. The Cambridgeshire Trust decided to pay for an adviser to help to take this forward. However, thanks to grants from the Nature Conservancy Council and the WWF, the cost of the adviser and other merger costs were covered. Without this support the merger would never have happened.

213

The driving force behind the merger was a desire to achieve more effective nature conservation and, according to assessment by Walsh Consulting in 1993, "the merger succeeded because of the outstanding contributions made by a group of determined people in a common cause". The author did not mention any by name, because to do so would have involved a list of more than 80 people. Mutual goodwill was most important because the cultures of the organisations were different. The Bedfordshire and Huntingdon Wildlife Trust had developed an open culture, said Walsh, in which "members were suspicious of any signs of overt personal ambition, accustomed to expressing their opinions forcibly, keeping their officers on a short lead and holding them to account at regular intervals".

By contrast, the Cambridgeshire Wildlife Trust "preferred to operate on a more formal hierarchical basis employing a managerial approach in which direction was clearly split from operations". To some extent the difference reflected the different development paths of each Trust. But a combination of honesty, good faith, energy and pragmatism overcame any differences or apprehension.

Some of the liveliest discussion concerned the logo for the new organisation. As there was no practical way in which the Bedfordshire and Huntingdon Wildlife Trust's heron and the Cambridgeshire Wildlife Trust's pasque flower could be combined, there was a search for species that might be found in both counties. The solution typified the pragmatism of the whole amalgamation process. It was decided to follow the Society's choice of a badger, and indeed to save the cost of designing a logo, by using the Society's logo. Thus the Bedfordshire and Cambridgeshire Wildlife Trust became among the first Trusts to use the Society's badger logo.

The doubting voices in both the original Trusts were allayed when the conservation objectives of the new Trust were delivered. In the three years following the 1990 merger, the annual expenditure on direct conservation increased from £90,000 to £300,000 and more than £750,000 was raised to buy five significant new nature reserves covering more than 298 hectares.

Pegsdon Hills reserve in Bedfordshire

A MERGER TOO FAR?

The Northamptonshire and Peterborough Trusts (the latter founded in 1987 by FRANK PERRING as one of the new urban wildlife groups) were also encouraged to consider merging with their newly-enlarged neighbours. At an Extraordinary General Meeting in October 1993 they voted to amalgamate with the Bedfordshire and Cambridgeshire Wildlife Trust. This merger was led by the staff. There was no independent adviser this time, and some of the principles that had made the previous merger a success were overlooked. Consequently, for several years after the 1994 creation of the Wildlife Trust for Bedfordshire, Cambridgeshire, Northamptonshire and Peterborough, there was a lingering feeling among the members on each side that the other side had been less than transparent over some issues.

The 1994 merger soon hit problems when the Director, Mark Rose, left to join the Fauna and Flora Preservation Society (now Fauna and Flora International). Whether this second merger had been a merger too far was a question that a range of people began to ask. Within the next four years, the Trust had three Chief Executives and each of the counties was becoming increasingly independent. By 1998, the Trust had serious financial and staff problems. Trust and confidence between Trustees and staff was suffering, but the Trust's dire position brought the Trustees together to find a solution. Under the leadership of the Chairman, John Andrews, the Trustees began to keep a closer watch over the business aspects of the Trust. The post of Chief Executive became redundant and one of the Trustees, Nicholas Hammond, was appointed as Director on a part-time basis. This coincided with the appointment of Jane Cabutti as Marketing and Fundraising Manager. Her strategic approach to income generation helped improve the financial position, and initiated a phase of sustained membership recruitment which continues to the present day. Within two years the outlook was good enough to be able to make Hammond's post of Director full-time.

THE BIG IDEA

The Trust's conservation work was also developing fast, with an increasingly competent team under the leadership of Brian Eversham as Conservation Director. In the 1990s, there was a recognition of the need to think about conservation on a landscape scale. Known in the Trust as 'the Big Idea', there was a search for a project area in which existing ecologically valuable sites could be enhanced by large-scale habitat creation. The two front runners were the possible linkage of three ancient woodland SSSIs in Cambridgeshire and linking two fenland National Nature Reserves (WOODWALTON FEN and Holme Fen) to the south of Peterborough. The latter was chosen on the grounds that only one project would be possible and wetland restoration would show results more quickly than a woodland scheme. Trying to take the project forward against a background of failing finances had been difficult, but in 2001 the Trustees were committed enough to the idea to appoint a Project Manager, Chris Gerrard. Gerrard quickly realised that the project could not be pursued by the Trust alone and other partners were brought on board – the Environment Agency, English Nature, Huntingdonshire District Council and the Middle Level Commissioners.

The partnership became very strong and has been notable for the way in which the individual organisations have put their sectional interests in second place to the success of the project. The scheme also dropped the Big Idea title to become the Great Fen Project. As the Trust began to recover from its low point, morale improved and it began to look at how it could make a greater difference to the environment of the three counties. Trustees and staff, under the leadership of John Andrews and then Michael Allen as Chairmen, and Nicholas Hammond as Director, produced a new development plan. A major feature of this was the idea of landscape-scale conservation (which later became known as the Trust's Living Landscape work). In addition to the Great Fen Project, it identified a number of areas where larger areas

Michael Allen with the 'Holme Fen Post' showing the dramatic loss of peatland soils. In 1851 the top of the post was flush with the peatland surface

Fenland habitat within the Great Fen Project area

of natural habitat could be created – woodlands in west Cambridgeshire, chalk grasslands in both Bedfordshire and Cambridgeshire, limestone grassland in Northamptonshire and river valleys in all three counties. That within five years, land had been acquired in each of these areas, was due to the determination and courage shown by Trustees and staff. Successful fundraising resulted in contributions from the Heritage Lottery Fund, charitable trusts, Landfill Tax Credits, local authorities, Environment Agency, Natural England, commercial sponsors and from appeals to members. The Trust's Living Landscape schemes also encompass some of its earliest nature reserves – often as wildlife-rich core areas from which further restoration of the wider landscape can take place. Upwood Meadows, Waresley Woods and Totternhoe Knolls all now fall into the areas where the Trust is working to create larger and more resilient swathes of habitat.

However, the Trust's most spectacularly successful Living Landscape scheme has undoubtably been the Great Fen Project. Fundraising for the project

was led by the Trust, whose charitable status enabled it to raise funds from sources that its partners would not have been able to access. Nevertheless, scepticism about the project was widespread. Even within the Trust there were misgivings about the scale of ambition of the project and, indeed, whether it could ever succeed. By involving other partners whose interests in the scheme included nature conservation, flood management and economic revival, the Trust guaranteed that the creation of this Living Landscape would be seen to be more than 'just' an attempt to restore lost habitat and create a viable environment for scarce fenland species. Success was helped by a determined and well-planned fundraising campaign led by Baroness Young of Old Scone, the Trust's President. By 2009, the Project had raised over £15 million from donors including the Heritage Lottery Fund, whose £7.4 million grant was the largest given to a nature conservation project in England. This enabled the Trust and Natural England to acquire the freeholds of nearly two-thirds of the land in the 3,700-hectare project area.

EDUCATING AND INVOLVING

Working with people has been a theme throughout the Trust's work and there are now five education centres as well as outreach projects on reserves, in schools and communities, including Peterborough, where the Trust manages five local nature reserves close to areas of dense population. In addition to formal education, the Trust's support for WILDLIFE WATCH has gradually grown to the present level of more than 100 volunteer Watch leaders and 25 Watch groups. Among the recent achievements has been the establishment of Greenwatch groups for teenagers, where young people set their own agenda and draw on adults to support them. Adults have not been ignored either: local members' groups provide outdoor and indoor events with an emphasis on community involvement in the Trust's Living Landscape areas. Although the Trust has run wildlife training workshops for many years, it was at the turn of the century that these became focused on providing training in some of the more esoteric areas of natural history. For instance, areas of particular use in wildlife monitoring and consequently nature reserve management. About 50 workshops a year are organised by the Trust and these have led to the creation of local ecology groups, which monitor the effectiveness of habitat management on Trust reserves. There are now

four such groups, each covering particular habitats that relate to Living Landscape schemes and providing results that are being used to inform decisions about land management.

The spirit of partnership that created the merged Trust has also been key to the success of the Great Fen Project. That spirit has been ingrained

in the culture of the Trust, alongside the aim to make decisions in the best interest of wildlife. Reserves are managed in cooperation with other organisations such as the RSPB, Butterfly Conservation and the Woodland Trust as well as with local authorities. This partnership approach to working has been welcomed by the Trust's members, who numbered 35,800 at the end of March 2011. And because Trust members are often members of other organisations who want their contributions to be spent on wildlife conservation, they have come to expect partnership working to achieve the best results for local wildlife.

BY NICHOLAS HAMMOND

Nicholas Hammond was full-time Director of the Trust from 2000 to 2009, having been a volunteer since 1970. Previously he worked with the RSPB for 24 years as editor of Birds *magazine, Head of Publications and Director of Public Affairs, a position he left in 1991 to work as a freelance writer and consultant. He was Chairman of the Society's* Natural World *publishing board from 1993 to 2009, and has written and edited more than 15 books. He is an expert on wildlife art and regularly lectures on natural history and art.*

Above: A sign from Stanground Newt Ponds
Above right: Cambourne, Cambridgeshire. In 2004 the Trust moved its headquarters here following years of collaboration with developers on the design of this wildlife-friendly new town

CHAPTER 4

Berkshire, Buckinghamshire and Oxfordshire

One cold November evening in 1959, a small band of naturalists meeting in a school hall in Oxford understood that urgent action was needed to halt the continuous loss of wildlife in Berkshire, Buckinghamshire and Oxfordshire. They founded the Berks, Bucks and Oxon Naturalists Trust (BBONT), with the result that we can still enjoy a host of spectacular wild plants and animals in their natural habitats. Since 1959, there has been almost unremitting wildlife loss in these counties, but without the Trust's presence, it would have been so much worse. Membership has grown from 30 in 1959 to over 50,000 individuals by 2010.

In 1958, a conference in London Zoo, convened by the South-East Union of Scientific Societies, with a view to promoting the formation of Trusts in south-east England, caught the imagination of Dr Edmund Frederic Warburg from Oxford University; he was co-author of the mammoth *Flora of the British Isles*. On his return to Oxford, he approached eminent local naturalists and representatives of seven local natural history societies, including Winifred Overend, Honorary Secretary of the Ashmolean Natural History Society, who became the Trust's first Honorary Secretary. Two years later, a constitution was drawn up and BBONT became the tenth such Trust in Britain.

The three counties are rich in wildlife, especially across the Thames Valley, the Berkshire Downs and the Chiltern Hills, and share many common characteristics. They form the south-western end of the English scarplands and their underlying rocks have been laid down like a layer cake that

Opposite: Snake's-head fritillaries, Iffley Meadows
Right: The Trust's Certificate of Incorporation

has been tilted at an angle. With the exception of parts of North Buckinghamshire, which drain into the Great Ouse system, the three counties comprise the valley of the middle and upper Thames.

KEY CHARACTERS

Many people played a central role in forming the Trust's character and shape. But behind the scenes there were a few individuals whose commitment and capacity for hard work were to have the greatest impact.

Richard Fitter (CHRISTOPHER CADBURY MEDAL), the Trust's first Honorary Secretary, served on the Trust's committees for almost 30 continuous years and remained a Trustee for many more. He was a highly influential asset for the Trust – best known for his Collins Pocket Guides – and for helping draft the 1947 report of the Government's Wild Life Conservation Special Committee – *Conservation of Nature in England and Wales (Command 7122)*.

Maisie Fitter, his wife, was no less eminent. Like her husband, she was a driving force within the International Union for the Conservation of Nature. She was also a major player in the Flora and Fauna Preservation Society, editing its journal for 19 years. She soon became editor of the Trust's *Bulletin*, a voluntary task she retained until the late 1980s. Part of Oakley Hill is now a Trust nature reserve dedicated to Maisie Fitter.

No. 680007

Certificate of Incorporation.

(COPY)

I HEREBY CERTIFY that BERKSHIRE, BUCKINGHAMSHIRE AND OXFORDSHIRE NATURALISTS' TRUST LIMITED is this day Incorporated under the Companies Act, 1948, and that the Company is LIMITED.

GIVEN under my hand at London this Ninth day of January One thousand nine hundred and sixty-one.

A. J. C. MANN,
Assistant Registrar of Companies.

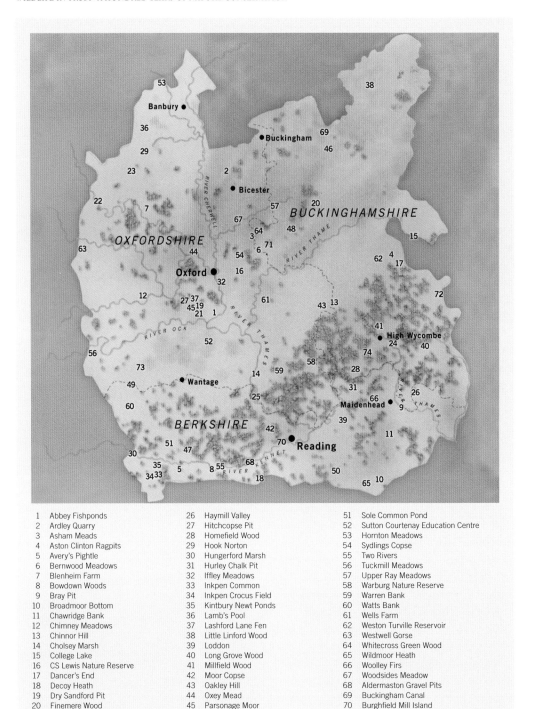

1	Abbey Fishponds	26	Haymill Valley	51	Sole Common Pond
2	Ardley Quarry	27	Hitchcopse Pit	52	Sutton Courtenay Education Centre
3	Asham Meads	28	Homefield Wood	53	Hornton Meadows
4	Aston Clinton Ragpits	29	Hook Norton	54	Sydlings Copse
5	Avery's Pightle	30	Hungerford Marsh	55	Two Rivers
6	Bernwood Meadows	31	Hurley Chalk Pit	56	Tuckmill Meadows
7	Blenheim Farm	32	Iffley Meadows	57	Upper Ray Meadows
8	Bowdown Woods	33	Inkpen Common	58	Warburg Nature Reserve
9	Bray Pit	34	Inkpen Crocus Field	59	Warren Bank
10	Broadmoor Bottom	35	Kintbury Newt Ponds	60	Watts Bank
11	Chawridge Bank	36	Lamb's Pool	61	Wells Farm
12	Chimney Meadows	37	Lashford Lane Fen	62	Weston Turville Reservoir
13	Chinnor Hill	38	Little Linford Wood	63	Westwell Gorse
14	Cholsey Marsh	39	Loddon	64	Whitecross Green Wood
15	College Lake	40	Long Grove Wood	65	Wildmoor Heath
16	CS Lewis Nature Reserve	41	Millfield Wood	66	Woolley Firs
17	Dancer's End	42	Moor Copse	67	Woodsides Meadow
18	Decoy Heath	43	Oakley Hill	68	Aldermaston Gravel Pits
19	Dry Sandford Pit	44	Oxey Mead	69	Buckingham Canal
20	Finemere Wood	45	Parsonage Moor	70	Burghfield Mill Island
21	Gozzard's Ford Fen	46	Pilch Field	71	Burrows
22	Foxholes	47	Rack Marsh	72	Cowcroft
23	Glyme Valley	48	Rushbeds Wood	73	Letcombe Valley
24	Gomm Valley	49	Seven Barrows	74	Munday Dean
25	Hartslock	50	Shepperlands Farm		

Map of Berkshire, Buckinghamshire and Oxfordshire Wildlife Trust nature reserves

From 1959 until 1980 the Trust's meetings were held at the Chinnor home of Richard and Maisie Fitter.

Susan Cowdy (CHRISTOPHER CADBURY MEDAL), born into the Liberty family, was brought up a county-set girl, riding to hounds and enjoying all aspects of a privileged background. But her love of nature became her life, and fired all who knew her with enthusiasm and energy. She was brilliant at recruiting people to the cause, including Captain Sir Thomas Barlow, great grandson of Charles Darwin, who became an influential ambassador for the Trust. Later, through sheer dynamism, Cowdy spearheaded hugely successful fundraising projects for the Trust and others. Her reputation as a formidable operator was confirmed in 1978, when she raised £200,000 for the purchase of Bardsey Island and its upkeep as a bird sanctuary.

Finally, Vera Paul, who unlike her fellow Trust pioneers had no connections to the gentry and held no influential positions – the criteria most highly valued in the Trust's early days! But her botanical expertise and her horror at the loss of wildlife meant she was a natural BBONT founding member. Even so, she showed no interest in holding official positions. Paul's pragmatic and wilful approach sometimes brought her into conflict with the Trust's hierarchy. But it is thanks to her that the Trust owns one of Britain's most valuable nature reserves, the Warburg reserve.

As a schoolgirl, she rediscovered the elusive ghost orchid in the Chilterns, previously thought to be extinct in Britain. Her modesty disguised her true nature – one of the most forceful and rebellious powers to fight for wildlife within the Trust.

1960S: PASQUE FLOWERS AND ORCHIDS

It was always the Trust's intention to own, maintain and manage nature reserves. Yet it was not until June 1961 that the Trust's *Bulletin* proudly announced the first lease, Conigre Pond, near Chinnor. Richard Fitter, recollecting how the lease was agreed, said it was initially Susan Cowdy who "was getting us little bits of land around The Lee, where she lived. There was scarcely a

formal agreement, but Susan's friends said we could use these as nature reserves! Conigre was a small chalk pit owned by a Mr Fletcher who agreed to receive one peppercorn as annual rent!"

The Trust's initial efforts to find nature reserves focused on the pasque flower on the Downs. The first county secretary for Berkshire, Brian Baker, met the owner of a particular valley to ask if there was any chance of leasing it, to keep a watching brief on the plant. On visiting the site on a muddy spring day, he discovered a hundred plants!

By 1964, the Trust had been given Long Grove Wood in Buckinghamshire, had raised sufficient funds to buy Hurley Chalk Pit in Berkshire, and had lease agreements on a further 11 nature reserves.

The most significant event of the 1960s for the Trust was the purchase of land to create Warburg nature reserve. Lying in a valley just north of Henley, Warburg is teeming with wildlife. The reserve now covers more than 100 hectares with more than 3,000 species, including 15 different orchids,

Sutton Courtenay Field Studies Centre opens in 1969

more than 900 fungi and more than half of the 60 UK butterfly species.

The Trustees considered it too ambitious a project, but despite their opposition, Vera Paul set about raising the purchase price of £18,000, plus a further £5,000 towards management. Her appeal consisted of sending a copied letter inside a hand-typed envelope. She went through local telephone books marking the names of houses, such as Honeysuckle Cottage, that had anything to do with the countryside. She raised all the money, but the Treasurer was against buying the reserve. The Trust went ahead and the Treasurer resigned.

Three years after the launch of BBONT, orchids were the talk of the Trust. They needed protection and wardening of orchid sites was started. It was a cloak and dagger business in those days. But later the Trust stopped referring to the sites as 'secret' and began employing students as wardens to talk to visitors about why orchids needed protection.

Before this, little was known about how these mysterious plants were pollinated, how and where they grew, or what threats they faced. Today,

the number of orchids on the Trust's reserves has rocketed and the Trust has supplied the seed of military, lizard, monkey and lady orchids to the Royal Botanic Gardens Kew, to grow on for recolonisation and reintroduction on suitable sites.

1970S: FUNDRAISING EFFORTS

In its earliest days, the Trust's members and activists were people with a scientific background – botanists, writers and academics. But with a growing land-holding to manage, the Trust needed to recruit supporters from a wider background. It began to recognise that publicity and fundraising would become essential.

The Trust's first sponsored walk took place in May 1969. Covering 12 miles, the walk became an annual event and in 1973 attracted nearly 2,000 walkers and raised £1,000. This was a huge amount of money to come from a relatively innovative form of fundraising. The walks stopped in 1976, but in 1992 the Trust revived the tradition with its Walk for Wildlife. This raised more than £25,000 each year and involved hundreds of walkers.

Sir David Attenborough and Julian Pettifer, then President of BBOWT, visit Warburg nature reserve with founder member Vera Paul

The Trust's chairman between 1971 and 1975 was someone who understood how the media worked and was enthusiastic and knowledgeable about conservation. Dr Bruce Campbell was a journalist from the BBC's Natural History Unit, who also wrote bird books and whose monthly column in the *Oxford Times*, 'At the Sign of the Badger', brought local wildlife to the attention of a wider public.

In the early 1970s, the ten regional committees were raising and spending money locally. Enthusiastic and dedicated local fundraisers brought the Trust its only reliable source of income. So in 1975, backed by WWF, the Trust launched a public appeal to raise £130,000. Led by Susan Cowdy and Vera Paul, the appeal ended with £104,000 in the Trust's bank account.

An update in the *Bulletin* reported that the Trust now had 'a secure base'. However, the Trust soon spent the bulk of the money on two nature reserves, Hartslock and Foxholes, retaining only £20,000 to provide for the Trust's running expenses.

As the Trust's numbers began to swell, it responded by employing people to service its membership and committees and it soon became evident that an office was needed. In 1975 Michael Low, later described as 'the pillar on which the Trust sat', arrived in Oxford and offered his home as the Trust's first central office. The Trust was fully or partly based at Low's house – at one time occupying a converted garage – until it moved in 1989.

Life became more complicated when the Trust started to employ professional conservationists. The core task of wildlife conservation had remained firmly in the hands of ten autonomous regional committees which reported to a Council of Trustees. The committees were made up of expert naturalists who knew their patch better than anyone else. While the conservation staff had new ideas and new working practices, they had no authority: the committees met only quarterly so it was difficult to get urgent decisions agreed quickly. A period of growing internal discontent was to follow before the Trustees were forced to look the future in the eye and agree a new structure.

1980S: EXPANDING TRUST RESERVES

In the 1980s, Conservation Officer Michael Horwood was given the special remit of increasing the Trust's landholding to 100 reserves. In this period some of the Trust's most important nature reserves were purchased or leased. These included Owlsmoor Bog, part of one of the most precious heathlands remaining in Berkshire; Buckinghamshire's Bernwood Meadows, which supports the green-winged orchid; and Lashford Lane Fen – now one of the Cothill reserves – a small limestone fen packed with a dense mosaic of rare habitats.

In 1981, the Trust applied to the Government's Manpower Services Commission (MSC) employment scheme for funds to employ a team of botany graduates to obtain a full inventory of its remaining wildlife habitats. A year later, Nigel Ajax-Lewis became Deputy Conservation Officer and quickly realised the potential of the MSC scheme for the Trust, recruiting 180 people.

This huge force of people working on the nature reserves changed the basic structure of the organisation and transformed the Trust's public profile. With a well-staffed office in each county, the Trust was suddenly able to respond properly to enquiries and information requests from the public.

ON THE CAMPAIGN TRAIL

A natural communicator and passionate about wildlife, Ajax-Lewis was freed from the MSC scheme to concentrate on major public campaigns. In the heart of the Trust's territory, a major development was about to cut right through one of the region's best wildlife sites. Since 1966, the Trust had been working to minimise the damage of the planned M40 motorway, which was heading straight for Bernwood Forest and Otmoor.

Above: Red kite photographed over a BBOWT reserve in 2004

Two public enquiries made no progress. Then, one Friday, Ajax-Lewis and MSC planner, Helen Gunn, met two civil servants from the Department of Transport (DoT) to discuss a route through Oxfordshire that would go round Bernwood Forest and exclude Otmoor. It turned out that the two DoT people wanted to catch the 3pm train home. At about 2.15pm Ajax-Lewis asked Gunn to mark their preferred route onto the Department's map and when the route was published six weeks later, it was exactly what the Trust wanted!

Despite the disquiet of some Trustees, the Trust continued to buy more reserves. Too late, the Trust realised it had stretched itself too far and too fast. The achievements of the previous 30 years gave way to a time of financial and organisational difficulties in the closing years of the 1980s. Minutes from Trustee meetings are littered with brave attempts to deal with financial problems and to restructure the organisation, but for volunteers with varied skills and experiences, it was a daunting task.

Following the launch of the ambitious £10 million BRITISH WILDLIFE APPEAL in 1985, the Trust revived its own fundraising efforts. It was still hoping that by raising a substantial lump sum, it could solve its financial problems for ever. One distinctive donation to the appeal came from John Paul Getty II, to purchase Little Linford Wood nature reserve.

The Appeal closed early in 1990 having achieved its target, thanks to the efforts of Lady Wood, who chaired the appeal, Sir Henry Aubrey-Fletcher who was later to take on the mantle of Chairman, and other gallant individuals. However, funds were still scarce: the bulk of the Appeal money had been spent on the day-to-day running costs of the Trust. Little had been available to invest for the future and the Trust still needed to find a sustainable way forward.

When, in 1987, the Government announced the end of the MSC scheme, there was no one to do the vast amount of work on the nature reserves and to answer calls from the public. Both volunteers and staff were under pressure.

Staff turnover became a real problem and created instability. In 1989, the timing was perfect for Peter Hinde, a retired businessman with a lifelong interest in wildlife, to play a vital role in the changes to come. Within a year of contacting the Trust, Hinde was leading an in-depth review of the Trust. His report spelled out the scale of the problems. Many in the Trust recognised the leadership skills which this tough operator could offer and, in 1990, he was elected Chairman.

Although turnover had reached nearly £250,000, the Trust's ability to protect wildlife was in danger of being compromised because the financial and internal management systems were inadequate for the job.

1990S: RADICAL CHANGE

The Trust approached the WWF and the Nature Conservancy Council for funding. They insisted the Trust undergo a management review and the resulting report became a blueprint for radical change. It recommended fundamental changes and the need for an Executive Director. The Executive Committees were to take on advisory roles, leaving the Council of Trustees responsible for strategic decisions alone. Financial management systems needed to be put in place and a modern membership database set up. The WWF and the Conservancy would then make three-years' funding available for the Executive Director, who would be given responsibility for the day-to-day management of staff and volunteers.

Hinde's chairmanship had sometimes been viewed as quite ruthless, but together he and the new Director, MARTIN SPRAY, had to take many difficult decisions. A huge budgetary deficit needed to be brought under control: redundancies were made, offices closed and a long overdue moratorium on buying new nature reserves was declared.

Meanwhile, the recession brought the Trust a new source of volunteers. The Community Action Teams, like the MSC teams before them, were made up of unemployed men and women who wanted to use their time usefully and improve their job prospects. Having learnt from the MSC

Common spotted orchids at Hartslock reserve, overlooking the Thames

experience, the Trust was not caught unawares when the scheme was folded in 1995.

Launched in 1992 in a frenzy of media attention, the Trust's first major species recovery project was an enormous boost to the Trust's confidence. Even though otters had been damaged by environmental degradation in the previous 20 years, there were signs that they could be returning to the Trust's region. Thanks to substantial support from the National Rivers Authority (now the Environment Agency), which helped to attract the Trust's sponsorship, this project sent out the message loud and clear – the Trust can do something positive to turn the tide against wildlife losses. The general public responded enthusiastically. Families became 'otter spotters', landowners built otter holts and the Trust learnt how to engage the public in its work.

By 1995 the Trust had finally shaken off the worst of its financial problems and a feeling of confidence

had returned. Having established itself as a worthy partner within the landowning, business and government sectors, the late 1990s were to see the Trust take on a leadership role, once again becoming a strong voice for local nature conservation.

The knock-on effects of the Rio Earth Summit were beginning to be felt at regional and local level. In line with Agenda 21, the Trust quickly established its Community Team to help local people set up wildlife projects in their parish or garden. At a time when council education budgets were being cut, the Trust opened an Environmental Education Centre at Calvert, which was leased until 2004.

The UK Biodiversity Challenge had listed 500 threatened species and more than a dozen habitats for priority attention. The Trust responded positively with its own Biodiversity Challenge for Berkshire, Buckinghamshire and Oxfordshire. This spelled out specific targets to safeguard the last remnants of our natural heritage, and invited local organisations

225

to work with the Trust on recovery projects for the 100 most threatened local species. By January 2000, 25 species recovery plans had been initiated by the Trust.

By 1998 the Trust was ready to purchase nature reserves again, helped by the HERITAGE LOTTERY FUND (HLF) money and the Landfill Tax Credit scheme. But the lessons of the past had been learned. The Trust now prioritised sites that still held the possibility of influencing the future survival of key species in the three counties and also provided the public with opportunities to enjoy wildlife.

The final ambition from the management review was to move to larger offices, but a seven-year search proved fruitless. This was finally resolved in 1998 with the purchase of The Lodge, a large Victorian house and gardens in Littlemore, just off the Oxford ring road. The setting up of an annual Volunteer Conference in 1998 demonstrated the enthusiasm within the Trust to work together more closely and,

as the millennium drew to a close, the Trustees had appointed a governance group to work out a better structure to achieve this aim.

INTO A NEW MILLENNIUM

By the end of 2001, the Trust had changed its name from a Naturalists' Trust to a Wildlife Trust, BBONT became BBOWT, and the Council had shrunk from 27 members to a maximum of 15. The streamlined board made decision-making quicker and meetings shorter. At the same time there were major problems with foot-and-mouth disease and later BSE, which forced the closure of nature reserves across the country.

The Trust had celebrated its 40th anniversary in 1999 with a successful campaign to raise membership. This began to have a major effect on the way the Trust worked, by providing increased income and greater support for fundraising. The first major appeal was to purchase land alongside the National

Purple emperor sighted at Bowdown Woods in 2010

Nature Reserve at Chimney Meadows, which also became the first Living Landscape project developed by the Trust. During this period of growth, £640,000 was obtained from the HLF for a volunteer development project, which reflected the increasing support the Trust was getting from members and supporters. It also reflected the way supporters and volunteers were increasingly being integrated with the work of the Trust and managed alongside staff.

Other major projects of landscape-scale were being developed along the Upper River Ray flood plain and in West Berkshire, including Greenham Common. The Trust's first purpose-built visitor centre was opened at College Lake, as the Trust celebrated its 50th anniversary.

As College Lake reopened, the Trust moved into another phase of restructuring, to give each of the three counties its own base. Space was at a premium in the Oxford headquarters, so it became the new base for Oxfordshire; College Lake became the base for Buckinghamshire and Woolley Firs for Berkshire. The plan included an education centre in each county. Woolley Firs fitted the bill perfectly for Berkshire, Oxfordshire already had the Sutton Courtenay Environmental Education Centre, while College Lake had its education centre upgraded.

Campaigning again began to feature more in the Trust's activities. A notable success came in 2009 when the Government finally abandoned plans to build a so-called eco-town adjacent to a Site of Special Scientific Interest (SSSI) at Weston on the Green. The Trust's previous major campaigns had been against the Newbury bypass and the M40 motorway route and lessons learned from these were valuable in the eco-town campaign.

Despite continuing loss of habitat and distribution of species, there were some gains. Otters reappeared in Oxfordshire, Bechstein's bats were found in Buckinghamshire, water vole sites were identified for future protection and theft of monkey orchids was prevented, with the perpetrators prosecuted.

The period following the end of the millennium saw many personnel changes. The first Director,

Steve Backshall became BBOWT President in 2010

MARTIN SPRAY, left to join the Wildfowl and Wetlands Trust having spent a year on secondment to the Society to assist with their restructuring and refinancing. He was succeeded as Chief Executive by Philippa Lyons, previously Marketing and Fundraising Manager. The Chairman of the Trust, Sir Henry Aubrey-Fletcher, was unable to continue when he became Lord Lieutenant of Buckinghamshire and was succeeded by Hugh Mellor. They had led the changes the Trust needed to progress as membership grew to more than 50,000, its staff to more than 60 and its income to more than £5.6 million by 2011. Compare this with the early days of 1959 when membership was 30, there were no staff and virtually no funds.

BY ROGER MAINGOT AND PHILIPPA LYONS

Roger Maingot worked for BBOWT as Office Manager, Sales Manager and then later as Project Manager for the Community Action programme between 1990 and 1995. He has been a Trustee since 2004 and served as Honorary Secretary from 2006.

Philippa Lyons worked for BBOWT as Marketing and Fundraising Manager from 1990, and became Chief Executive in 2004.

227

CHAPTER 5

Birmingham and Black Country

"Disaster struck just as Newsletter No. 5 was about to be printed, the office where the Urban Wildlife Group is currently based (at the Friends of the Earth warehouse) was burnt to a frazzle along with the Newsletter, almost all our survey records. . . and some of the membership file".

This was the crisis facing the infant Urban Wildlife Group in spring 1981. It is testament to the characters involved that the Group, only formed in July 1980, survived this and other early setbacks. The Group's pioneering approach to nature conservation in towns and cities is now widely acknowledged, and its work ultimately led to the development of what is now the Wildlife Trust for Birmingham and the Black Country.

Three things in particular contributed to the Trust's formation. First was the groundbreaking survey of the wildlife of Birmingham and the Black Country (Dudley, Sandwell, Walsall and Wolverhampton) commissioned, against all normal practice at the time, by George Barker of the Nature Conservancy Council. The surveyor was Bunny Teagle and his work was published as *The Endless Village*, a reference to the individual, but, to an outsider, indistinguishable towns of the Black Country. Second were the activities of the local natural history societies, and third was the local Greensite Project, run by Friends of the Earth.

Opposite: Children involved in the Trust's National Curriculum project
Above: Logo of the Urban Wildlife Group

The Trust's first newsletter in autumn 1980 said of these antecedents, "The (Trust) never really started in any formal or punctuated sense. It has drifted into existence upon a tide of events rather than resolution".

True enough, but from the beginning the Trust was blessed with knowledgeable and committed professionals and community leaders. Amongst them were Chris and Liz Baines, Pete Byfield, Joy Fifer, Roger Hammond, Nick Pinder, Jeremy Purseglove, Leslie Pinkess and Peter Shirley. Their pursuits and professions included teaching, landscape architecture, planning, business, ecology, natural history and environmental campaigning. Chris Baines became a professor of landscape design and a broadcaster. Jeremy Purseglove was the Chief Landscape Architect of Severn Trent Water Authority and presented a TV series based on his book *Taming the Flood*. Nick Pinder ran Birmingham City Council's Nature Centre (the Trust's first address). Joy Fifer led the ultimately successful fight to prevent building on Moseley Bog, now a Local Nature Reserve in the care of the Trust.

The difference between the Trust and most other Wildlife Trusts at the time is illustrated by the wording of its aims, "to campaign for the protection of wildlife sites, create long-term job opportunities in nature conservation, promote ideas for combining natural history and recreation in urban open spaces, and help similar groups in their own efforts to conserve and study wildlife".

LITTLE MONEY, ABUNDANT STAFF

Although the Trust itself had very little money, (the 1982 accounts show an income of £3,500,

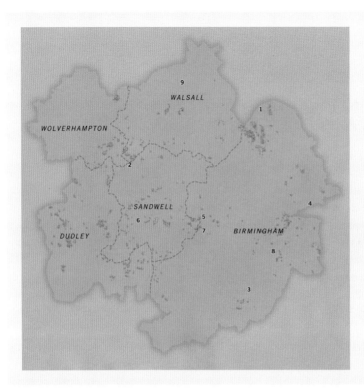

1 Hill Hook Local Nature Reserve
2 Moorcroft Wood Local Nature
   Reserve Environment Centre
3 Moseley Bog and Joy's Wood
   Local Nature Reserve
4 Park Hall Nature Reserve
5 Richmond Nature Garden
6 Rowley Hills Nature Reserve
7 Centre of the Earth
8 Birmingham Eco Park
9 Turner's Wood

Map of the Wildlife Trust for Birmingham and Black Country's nature reserves and environmental centres

for 1983, £3,302 and by 1986, £21,000), there was an abundance of staff. This was thanks to the Greensite Project's 30-plus employees (managed by Peter Byfield) and further training and employment programmes, funded by the Government, which had separate accounts within the Trust.

Key early staff included the 'Gang of Four' – Julie Boschi (cartographer), Lorna Edey (administrator), Alison Millward (botanist) and Ellen Pisolkar (ecologist). They were commissioned to "locate and survey sites of biological interest in the county of West Midlands". By 1984, there were 60 full- or part-time posts, and this phase of development reached its peak of 130 posts in 1987.

In 1982, the Urban Wildlife Group was incorporated as the West Midlands Urban Wildlife Trust Ltd. By 1987, it was well established in its city centre offices in Albert Street, Birmingham. Following some short-term staff appointments, it had employees of its own – Sue Vincent, a landscape architect who was funded for four years

through the Birmingham Inner City Partnership, and Peter Shirley, the Trust's Director, who was funded mainly through a grant from the Nature Conservancy Council.

Although the Trust never owned or leased much land, there was a great deal of land which it and local communities were involved with, often in public ownership through councils, utility companies and other public bodies. In the early days, the Trust worked throughout the West Midlands County (Birmingham, the Black Country, Solihull and Coventry), influencing policy makers and helping local people to save wildlife sites. The area had some of the most diverse and deprived communities in the country, as well as leafy suburbs and major open spaces like Sutton Park – the largest enclosed city park in Europe – which is now a National Nature Reserve. For three million people the parks, old industrial and mining landscapes, canals, woods, wetlands and farms were their countryside, the places where they saw birds, flowers and butterflies. Their children played there, they picnicked, walked their dogs and took short cuts through these places to schools and shops.

ATTENTION TO GREEN SPACES

So what did all the staff do? The Trust was the first organisation to pay proper attention to the area's network of green spaces. It surveyed them, helped people to manage them for nature and amenity, campaigned to save threatened sites, worked with – and often against – planners, and helped schools to manage their grounds and incorporate nature into the curriculum. There was success with campaigns to save threatened sites at Plants Brook Reservoirs and Moseley Bog, but failure with Merry Hill, which was destroyed to make way for a shopping centre in the mid-1980s. For a time, the Trust was responsible for an urban farm at a school just a mile outside Birmingham city centre. It also organised events like International Dawn

Chorus Day (still going strong) and Wild West Midlands Week, engaged with the media, encouraged gardening for wildlife, ran a wild plants nursery, and produced publications (such as *Gardening for Wildlife* and *Planning for Nature*).

UNUSUAL APPROACH

An early success was a wildlife-friendly city garden at the Stoke Garden Festival, the first of many exhibition gardens. There was support for local groups, projects about foxes, frogs and hedgehogs, and the development of Community Nature Parks. The flagship site was Plants Brook, a wildlife site in north-east Birmingham saved from landfill, and opened by DAVID BELLAMY in July 1985. Unusually, the Trust leased this site for a few years before handing it back to Birmingham City Council. The idea was to demonstrate what needed to be done and then let others take over, rather than acquiring more and more land in the Trust's name.

Happy young volunteers in the rain at an Urban Wildlife Group event in the early 1980s

There were also national projects, such as the National Wildlife Gardening Campaign, and Earthkids, a Countryside Commission-funded project about children's play in natural settings.

Strategic planning work became, and remains, very important. Surveys, such as Bunny Teagle's and those of the local natural history societies, informed the 1984 West Midlands Nature Conservation Strategy. Published by the soon-to-be-defunct West Midlands County Council, it was Britain's first such local authority initiative. Two more similar strategies, effectively written by the Trust, followed for the Black Country in 1994 and Birmingham in 1997.

The Trust's relationship with the Royal Society for Nature Conservation (the Society) was not central to its early development. Although some of the founders of the Trust were associated with existing Wildlife Trusts, the STAFFORDSHIRE, WORCESTERSHIRE and WARWICKSHIRE TRUSTS' work was not well-known in Birmingham and the Black Country, and these Trusts had, until a few years before, been one body called the West Midlands Naturalists' Trust. Their rural focus left wildlife sites in the conurbation vulnerable, and they had only one reserve in the area, managed by the Staffordshire Trust.

Whilst there was some reluctance to embrace the concept of urban wildlife at the time in the wider Trust movement, several of the new Trust's staff and Trustees were advising, supporting and coordinating the establishment of many new urban wildlife groups including those in London, Norwich, Sheffield and Oxford.

SMALL MEMBERSHIP BASE

Employment scheme funding meant the new Trust had no immediate need for members; it was in fact about 15 years before serious membership recruitment began (EMPLOYMENT SCHEMES). Membership was always offered, but not really sold or marketed, apart from inviting people to pay 50p to be registered as a supporter. In 1985, the Trust had 350 members and 3,000 supporters.

However, FRANK PERRING, the Society's far-sighted General Secretary, could see that nature conservation in the places where most people lived was important. Together with CHRISTOPHER CADBURY, a Trustee of both the WORCESTERSHIRE TRUST and the Society's President for many years, he ensured that there was dialogue between the established Trusts and the new organisation. Thus, at the beginning of 1984, the Trust's newsletter carried the first mention of possible affiliation to the Society and the Trust did then become the 46th Wildlife Trust. However, part of the deal was to continue not actively recruiting members. When the Government abolished the metropolitan counties in 1986, Solihull and Coventry became the responsibility of the WARWICKSHIRE TRUST. In 1986, the Society appointed its first Urban Wildlife Development Officer, Malcolm Holland and based him at the Trust's Birmingham office. He was succeeded after six months by Tony Jones.

EMPLOYMENT SCHEMES END

A watershed year in the Trust's life was 1987. On the positive side, funding was secured for the appointment of a Director, initially for three years. Peter Shirley took this position until 1995, when he was succeeded by the present incumbent, Neil Wyatt. On the negative side, the employment schemes came to an end and staff numbers fell from more than 100 to between 12 and 20, depending mainly on project funding. But several key staff stayed on, including Chris Parry, currently the Trust's Principal Ecologist. Without a supporting membership base, the organisation became, in effect, a not-for-profit consultancy. Building on the momentum from the early years, and supported by volunteers, including input from Birmingham and Wolverhampton Universities, it developed many projects, mainly with the local authorities.

NINETIES' ROLLERCOASTER

The 1990s saw the Trust struck by significant financial blows. After two office moves, the Trust eventually settled in a downtown Birmingham trades' centre, the advantage being that space was

Centre of the Earth environmental centre in Winson Green

rented on a monthly basis. This allowed expansion and contraction according to need. The work went on, but there were times in the early 1990s when non-project staff were working under rolling redundancy notices. The Trust's continuing achievements and growing reputation during this time demonstrate the dedication of all concerned. The storms were weathered and, in 2000, the Trust moved to its present office in Edgbaston.

The Trust was run in an open, sometimes almost informal way. People moved between employment and volunteering and back again, sometimes several times, as funding ebbed and flowed. A weekly staff meeting ensured that everyone knew what was happening. Senior managers sat at the hub of a wheel rather than the top of a pyramid, a flat rather than hierarchical structure.

Major achievements included the 1993 opening of the UK's first purpose-built inner city environmental education centre, the Centre of The Earth, in Winson Green.

Other important site-based projects were Birmingham EcoPark and Richmond Nature Garden. Originally a development of the Trust's nursery, the EcoPark is now a demonstration of sustainability and living lightly on the earth. Both it and the Centre of the Earth have now hosted thousands of schoolchildren and others. In a similar vein, a Wolverhampton school grounds initiative, the Natural Curriculum Project, ran from 1993 to 2010. EcoRecord, the biological records centre for Birmingham and the Black Country, was established in 1993. It now has well over half a million records of species, sites and habitats that are used in planning and research.

NEW SOCIAL ENTERPRISE

In 1990, the Trust's in-house commercial consultancy, Land Care Associates (LCA), was formed. It covenants its profits to the Trust, and was one of the first such endeavours in the Trust movement. More recently, a new social enterprise, People and Wildlife Services (PAWS) has been established as a Community Interest Company to complement LCA, undertaking woodland management and habitat creation whilst offering training in traditional countryside skills.

A VOICE FOR WILDLIFE

The Trust is now the pre-eminent voice of nature in Birmingham and the Black Country. It has made appearances at both Aston Villa and Birmingham City football matches with a giant wickerwork otter atop a car! It has produced guides and interpretation material, organised thousands of conservation volunteers, made many radio and television appearances and organised WILDLIFE WATCH groups and volunteers leaders. It has always included earth sciences and geological conservation in its work, reflecting the area's world-famous geology. The country's first geological National Nature Reserve is the Wren's Nest in Dudley, and local coal, limestone and marl provided the raw materials for the industrial revolution.

In recent years, the Trust saw considerable further growth in staff numbers and activity. Led by its Trustees and Neil Wyatt, the Trust's Chief Executive, the Trust followed a more conventional Wildlife Trust route. Membership is now actively sought, and although there was a slow start, numbers are now more than 11,000. Much as the more rural Wildlife Trusts now view work with local communities as an essential part of their work, the Trust now sees managing its own nature reserves as an essential part of creating urban Living Landscapes. As well as Moseley Bog – the childhood haunt of *The Lord of the Rings* author JRR Tolkien, who lived nearby – the Trust also manages 40 hectares of wetland and ancient woodland at Park Hall on the outskirts of Birmingham. The Trust also took on a Local Nature Reserve in Walsall, adjacent to the Moorcroft Environment Centre, and near where a new people and wildlife centre is planned. The most recent acquisition is a small, but critical, grassland reserve in the Rowley Hills which hosts one of only two marbled white butterfly colonies in the Black Country.

BIG LOTTERY CONTEST

One of the biggest challenges the Trust took on was to enter the Big Lottery Fund's People's £50 Million Lottery contest in 2007. This was a unique opportunity to be part of the biggest lottery grant ever awarded – the catch being that it would be decided by a public vote! The Trust teamed up with the four Black Country local authorities to create a £110 million bid for environmental improvements across the Black Country Urban Park. Among other innovative ideas, the project would restore limestone caverns at the Wren's Nest in Walsall and create a major green corridor linking Walsall to Sandwell, culminating in a huge green bridge into West Bromwich. The Trust's contribution would be an unprecedented programme of community involvement – the overall context for the bid.

Park Hall nature reserve on the outskirts of Birmingham

Slowly the field narrowed from over 100 entries nationwide. Early on, the bid was judged the most risky of more than 60, whilst also being the closest to the original aims of the competition.

Long, complex meetings and much hard work ensued as the number of remaining entries dropped to six. Fortunately, the detailed work needed at this stage was funded by the Big Lottery. Then there was a two-day grilling by the Big Lottery and their experts to see if the project could really deliver. At the end of this process just four entries remained: a new biome for the Eden Project; a modernist visitor centre in Sherwood Forest; improvements to the national cycle network and, against the odds, the Black Country Urban Park.

The build-up to the TV vote was tense. Each day a different project was featured and the Black Country Urban Park was championed by Birmingham-born Toyah Wilcox. Then the news arrived: we had come a very close second despite winning the telephone vote, beaten by Sustran's Connect 2 project, thanks to its greater share of the email votes.

Although some other project elements have now fallen away or stalled for other reasons, the Trust's efforts were not in vain. The preparation and partnership work, including some pilot projects, achieved a great deal and helped the Trust to strengthen its partnerships, its resolve and its reputation. The greatest prize was that the Trust's proposal for a somewhat scaled-back, but still substantial, Community Involvement Programme was funded by Natural England and the Big Lottery's Access to Nature fund, receiving more than £440,000. This has become the core of the Black Country Living Landscape and has seen thousands of people discovering their local wildlife sites, taking up volunteering and learning about nature with the help and support of the Trust. Who said there were no prizes for coming second?

REVISITING ITS ROOTS

In recent years, the Trust has been revisiting its roots and has become increasingly engaged in research and innovation. Detailed surveys of ancient woodland and former aggregate extraction sites have led to published studies. Most recently, research into the economic value of ecosystem services in the urban environment has been a first within the Trust movement.

Over this period, the Trust has worked closely with the Birmingham and Black Country Botanical Society, a new group that has coalesced around a project to write a flora for the area under the leadership of Ian Trueman. Close to publication, this promises not just to be one of the most thoroughly researched local floras ever published, but those who have seen some of the preliminary results suspect it will shake perceptions of urban ecology with the same impact as Bunny Teagle's *Endless Village*. The Trust is proud of the role EcoRecord has played in handling the huge volumes of biological records generated by the project.

Strategic work is still crucial. Now that the rest of the world has caught up with some of its early ideas, and terms like 'green infrastructure' are commonplace, the Trust is very involved in the Black Country as an Urban Park initiative, along with the local councils, the Forestry Commission, Natural England and the Environment Agency. It

has also received funding from the HERITAGE LOTTERY FUND to enhance wildlife habitats and access at Moseley Bog. International Dawn Chorus Day continues. The simple act of rising early on the first Sunday in May to enjoy the birdsong has been enjoyed by thousands of people in many different countries. Chris Baines and the late Joy Fifer rarely get the credit they deserve for devising this much imitated event. In 1984, participants included DAVID BELLAMY, SIR PETER SCOTT and Tony Soper. Reports were received from all over the UK, as well as Sweden, Switzerland, Germany and Israel.

LONG-TERM LEGACY

Where has the Trust sat within the Society and what influence might it have had? After the early difficulties, the West Midlands Trusts have worked well together, to the extent that from 2000 to 2009 they jointly employed a Regional Director, based for most of that time in the Trust's Birmingham office. Nationally, together with other urban Trusts, the Trust has championed nature conservation in towns and cities, and the engagement of the 80 per cent of the population who live there. The first national Urban Wildlife Officer was based at the Trust's office. The Urban Wildlife Partnership (originally the Fairbrother Group – see page 723) and its associated various national committees and initiatives, was started by Alison Millward and Chris Baines, who is now a Vice President of the Society.

Despite much progress, there occasionally remains some vestiges of the old attitude that city wildlife is somehow second-class. But it is now widely accepted that this aspect of nature conservation is not only vital to the Trust movement, but also to the welfare of humans, especially those who live in cities.

BY PETER SHIRLEY
Peter Shirley was one of the founders of the Urban Wildlife Group in 1980, and went on to follow a long career with The Wildlife Trusts, serving locally, regionally and nationally. His tireless work for nature conservation was recognised with an MBE in 1995. He is now a Vice President of the Wildlife Trust for Birmingham and Black Country.

Brycheiniog – Brecknock

Breconshire, or Brecknock, is rich in natural beauty. Until 1974, it was a county in its own right, but is now a district in the county of Powys. Brecknock's gently undulating mountains and moorland, remote valleys with headlong mountain streams, old and new woodlands, some fine stretches of water and broad rivers combine to provide spectacular landscapes and a generous variety of wildlife habitats.

The district incorporates the major part of the Brecon Beacons National Park, a separate planning authority. The Beacons rise to the summit of Pen y Fan, the highest peak in South Wales and, with their outliers, extend in a great wall across the south. Much of the underlying rock is old red sandstone but there are also outcrops of limestone. In the north and north-west, the uplands extend into the Pumlumon range. In the east, the Black Mountains rise to a height of 810 metres. The River Wye forms the boundary in the north-east and the Usk flows in a broad valley through the middle of the area from west to east.

Agriculture is the most significant activity. The main river valleys are fertile with good pastures for fattening cattle, whilst on the hill farms sheep are reared for meat. A small amount of arable farming mainly involves growing crops for animal feed.

Unlike adjacent areas of south-east Wales, Brecknock has no densely populated areas. The sparse population is centred on small and scattered market towns where fairly gentle expansion over the past 30 years is planned to continue.

THE TRUST BEGINS

The Brecknock County Naturalists' Trust, as it was known until 1987, was established in 1964.

Its founding was, in part, stimulated by a suggestion from neighbours in Monmouthshire that they could take Brecknock under their wing to complete the map of Wales! Much of the credit for the decision to go ahead independently lay with Major General Sir Geoffrey Raikes, spurred on by Jack Evans. Dr David Kyle was elected Chairman when Sir Geoffrey declined, and Jack Evans became Honorary Secretary.

THRIVING ENTHUSIAST GROUPS

Great effort went into setting up the Trust's Council, Executive and Scientific Committees, recruiting members, producing a twice-yearly newsletter and establishing special interest groups. These groups encouraged bird, plant and butterfly enthusiasts, for example, to work under the umbrella of the Trust and report their findings in its publications.

The bird group had a strong presence. *Breconshire Birds*, containing records and interesting sightings, was first produced privately in 1962 by John Griffiths. It was adopted by the Trust at its

Above: Dipper – a common sight at Pwll y Wrach nature reserve
Opposite: Pwll y Wrach waterfall

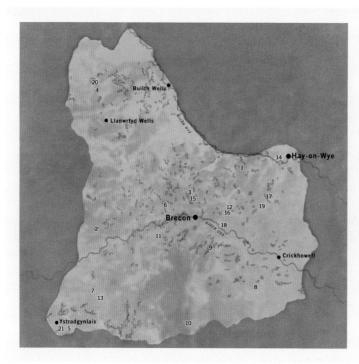

1	Brechfa Pool
2	Cae Bryntywarch
3	Cae Eglwys
4	Cae Pwll y Bo
5	Ystradfawr
6	Coed Dyrysiog
7	Craig y Rhiwarth
8	Cwm Claisfer
9	Cwm Oergwm
10	Darren Fawr
11	Daudreath Illtyd
12	Drostre Wood
13	Allt Rhongyr
14	Glasbury Cutting
15	Llandefaelog Wood
16	Pen y Waun
17	Pwll y Wrach
18	The Byddwn
19	Trewalkin Meadow
20	Vicarage Meadows
21	Wern Plemys

Map of Brecknock Wildlife Trust nature reserves

foundation and has been published, albeit with some gaps, ever since.

The mammal group also had a high profile. In addition to the Trust's work with otters, bats have received much attention. Following a popular day school run by Bob Stebbings in 1984, group members began recording locations of roosts, identifying winter hibernation sites and, where appropriate, protecting the bats from disturbance. A number of members gained the necessary expertise to be issued with licences and surveys revealed that the Usk valley was an important area for the lesser horseshoe bat.

The plant group's heyday was in the first ten years of the Trust's existence, when some dozen people, including Mike Porter and the broadcaster Harry Soan, sought to improve on the information in the Botanical Society of the British Isles' 1962 *Atlas of the British Flora*. A survey based on five-kilometre grid squares was established and, by the mid-1970s, the group had made good progress in recording all 99 squares. The increase in

knowledge was considerable. Thus, the globeflower that had been reported in only two of the ten-kilometre grid squares in the *Atlas*, was recorded in no less than 44 of the five-kilometre grid squares.

In the 1990s, there was an active geological group under Duncan Hawley which, amongst other achievements, set up a geological trail at the Pwll y Wrach nature reserve.

Currently, the moth group, under the leadership of Dr Norman Lowe, is particularly strong. More than 20 members operate moth traps in their gardens and take part in surveys throughout the county. Since 2001, the group has contributed over 80,000 records of moths from all over the county, and the number of species on the county list has risen to almost 1,100.

TRUST JOURNAL

In 1969, Max Budgen became the Honorary Secretary and, with Dr Kyle, Eric Bartlett and Mike Porter, formed an editorial committee for the newly-established journal. For many years the *Breconshire*

Naturalist, and the personalities of Chairman and Honorary Secretary together, were the Trust in the minds of most members. In the same period, the Scientific Committee metamorphosed into the Conservation Committee, regular evening lectures were held in winter and a presence at events, such as local shows, gradually developed.

By the end of 1970, the Society for the Promotion of Nature Reserves (the Society), as the parent body of all Trusts in Britain, confirmed that Brecknock had the highest membership in relation to population of all the existing 40 Trusts. The Trust could justifiably boast about its 500 members in 1974, and its lead position in the movement was maintained for many years. From about this time the Trust benefited from the arrival in Brecon of staff working for the Welsh Water Authority and its successors. Some became among the Trust's most active supporters, and many still play key roles (Peter Jenkins, Norman Lowe and Phil Morgan, for example). The Trust also became involved with otters, an interest that has remained strong.

OTTER SURVEYS

Within a few years of its creation, the Trust was active in persuading riverside owners to deny otter hunts access to the Usk. The first national otter survey in Wales was carried out in 1977 and confirmed the dire state of the species. It triggered efforts to do more, especially in areas like the Usk valley where a small population still remained.

Thus began the Trust's fruitful connection with the Vincent Wildlife Trust (VWT), a charity founded in 1975 which specialises in mammal research and conservation in Britain and Ireland. Through the Otter Haven Project, VWT sponsored habitat improvement, including holt building, and surveys to monitor the otters in the Usk catchment (see OTTER CONSERVATION). It was through VWT that Dr Elizabeth (Libby) Andrews was introduced to the Trust, a connection that has benefited the Trust greatly. Over the years, she has served as Trust Council member, Scientific Secretary and, currently, as President. In 2004, she was awarded the Society's Christopher Cadbury

Medal for her services to nature conservation (CHRISTOPHER CADBURY MEDAL CITATIONS). With VWT colleague, Geoff Liles, Libby trained volunteers in the skills of otter surveying. Surveys of the Usk and its tributaries have been undertaken since the early 1980s.

Although the national surveys showed improvement in otter numbers, they also highlighted the widespread degradation of riverside habitat and the many threats facing the Welsh otter population. The Trust's Otter Group was set up in the early 1990s to improve otter habitat. Increasing numbers of otters led to increasing numbers of road casualties. In 1997, the plight of Jarvis the otter cub, orphaned when his mother was killed on the A40, made national news. Jarvis was cared for by Trust members Gareth and Jane Jones so successfully that Jarvis was subsequently released into the wild. Gareth and Jane built up such skills and reputation that the Trust set up a purpose-built otter rehabilitation unit on their land, where otters were nursed through the early, vulnerable stages of recovery before being sent away to larger units.

George – a rescued baby otter

Allt Rhongyr – the Trust's newest reserve

Often otters were returned a year or so later to be released near where they were found.

PIVOTAL PEOPLE

After the first Chairman, Dr Kyle, died in 1976, Phil Holbourn, who had recently retired as County Planning Officer, became Chairman. Between them, these two spanned a remarkable 25 years of the Trust's existence. Phil Holbourn's chairmanship included the ten years when Eric Bartlett was Honorary Secretary and Editor of the *Breconshire Naturalist*. Eric typed every page on Gestetner stencils and ran them off himself! He earned

Eric Bartlett

incomparable respect and affection, and lives on in the memories of many people and in their loyalty to the Trust.

TRUST RESERVES

It was in the 1970s and early 1980s that most of the Trust's present nature reserves were established, given to the Trust by supporters or leased at a peppercorn rent. The first reserve to involve a purchase was Pwll y Wrach, a mixed oak and ash woodland, which was bought from the Forestry Commission in 1983, with financial help from the Nature Conservancy Council (NCC). For this and all subsequent reserves, the need for grant support has meant that the conservation interest had to be clearly identified. At Pwll y Wrach, this lay in its rich and diverse ground flora for which the site had been declared a Site of Special Scientific Interest (SSSI). More than 180 species of flowering plant have been recorded there. Later, it was discovered to hold the most important colony of dormice in the region. In 1991, the Trust received sponsorship towards an easy-access path enabling people of all abilities to reach the heart of the woodland.

The need to look after reserves was recognised at the outset. Indeed, the very first newsletter in 1964 appealed for volunteers to tend areas of protection. But seven years later, the *Breconshire Naturalist* reported that the Trust still did not have a regular group of volunteers. However, by 1980, Logan Jack was organising regular work parties, usually once a month with about 11 energetic fellow volunteers. This team kept going for seven or eight years.

EIGHTIES' PROFESSIONALISM

In 1986, the untimely death of Eric Bartlett left the Trust bereft and uncertain over its future. Two things were clear: first, there would never be another Eric; second, full-time, professional help was needed if the Trust was going to fulfil its stated aims in conserving local wildlife.

Phil Holbourn, as Chairman, secured a package of funding for three years from the World Wildlife Fund, the NCC and the Welsh Office. This was enhanced by a donation from the Honorable Vincent Weir. In March 1987, the Trust's first full-time Conservation Officer, Ed Cooper started work in Lion House in the centre of Brecon. In the following January, a team of five people started a year's work under a Manpower Services Commission employment scheme, including surveys of wildlife areas and writing management plans. Soon a part-time Administrative Assistant was in post and the office buzzed with activity.

Professor Lewis Crabtree became Chairman later in 1988, knowing that he must ensure that what was starting did not collapse when the three years of support expired. He worked tirelessly to launch a major appeal, establishing the Breconshire Wildlife Survival Trust to secure donations or legacies, not only from known supporters but also from the area's business community.

The Trust also needed to raise its public profile through the local and regional press, and also through lectures and wildlife weekends for

The Trust's first full-time Conservation Officer, Ed Cooper, with an early Watch group

non-members and invitations for sponsorship. In 1989, the Trust celebrated its 25th anniversary with a special issue of the *Breconshire Naturalist*, hoping to reach the target of 1,000 members. This was achieved two years later.

Another of Lewis Crabtree's major contributions was to press for a restructuring of the national Society to give more support for regional groupings of Wildlife Trusts. Thanks largely to his work, a charitable company, Wildlife Trusts Wales (see WELSH TRUSTS, ASSOCIATION OF), was formed in 1995 to enable greater cooperation between the Welsh Trusts.

In 1991, John Clarkson was appointed Conservation Officer, to be joined 18 months later by Diane Russell as Administration Officer. These appointments proved to be important long-term assets. During seven years with the Trust, Clarkson achieved much: organising work parties on reserves; winning the 1997 award for the Best Wildlife Trust Magazine (small circulation) in Britain and masterminding a major application to the HERITAGE LOTTERY FUND to improve the management and accessibility of 11 reserves owned by the Trust.

PARTNERSHIP WORKING

Beneficial relationships with the local officers of the NCC were of great importance, notably with Ray Woods. With his remarkable range of knowledge,

Woods often alerted the Trust to a need and opportunity to acquire an important site as a reserve. When, in 1991, the NCC was succeeded by the Countryside Council for Wales (CCW), a new approach was developed whereby CCW provided financial support for the work of all the Welsh Wildlife Trusts. This partnership programme was initially limited to a five year period but developed into the provision of continuing support for conservation work that met CCW's precise criteria for eligibility. The Trust and CCW work hand-in-hand to achieve outcomes that both partners need.

In 2000, it was decided that there should be biological records centres covering the whole of Wales. A pilot centre, later named The Biological Information Service for Powys and the Brecon Beacons National Park (BIS), was set up. The Trust was an active supporter from the start and Dr Norman Lowe, the Trust's representative, became Chairman. As a founding partner, the Trust has a Service Level Agreement with BIS, which supplies biological data that informs its decisions on, for example, planning applications, and also supports the work of its voluntary recorders.

In the spring of 2002, Diane Morgan (*née* Russell) became Trust Manager, taking on financial and administrative responsibilities for the Trust until 2007.

BERMUDA BOUNTY

Over the years, the Trust has been extremely grateful for various legacies. But in 2003, the Chairman, David Jones Powell, was entirely unprepared to receive a telephone call from Bermuda heralding a large donation. In the event, it proved to be £1 million and an Investment Committee was promptly established, drawing together some of the wisest silver-haired legal and financial heads in the county!

The amazement and gratitude deepened on learning that the benefactor had been born and bred in a tiny cottage deep in the Welsh countryside. As a young woman, Miss Mary Gwen Williams had been trained in dairying, but then worked as a nurse in the United States of America and later in Bermuda. She invested shrewdly and lived economically. On her regular annual visits to her family, she was relieved, after seeing so much development in Bermuda, to find that so little had changed where she had grown up. Through contact with some of its staff and members (such as artist Meg Stevens), 'Miss Williams', as she was known,

The opening of Cae Bryntywarch nature reserve

became impressed with the Trust's aims and work and made her will accordingly.

One of the first uses of the legacy money was to appoint a full-time Reserves Officer to consolidate the improvement in the reserves achieved with the Heritage Lottery funding. The outreach role of the Trust was also extended through the appointment of a part-time Education Officer.

ANNIVERSARY ALE

In 2009, the Trust celebrated its 45th anniversary with a party on the promenade in Brecon. The town's brewery produced a commemorative real ale named Wild Beacon, flavoured with elderflowers and nettles foraged from the Trust's nature reserves. Over 1,000 people attended which marked the Trust out as the biggest membership charity devoted to wildlife in Brecknock.

The Trust currently manages 21 reserves of which 14 are owned freehold. Some, like Trewalkin Meadow and Cae Eglwys, represent habitats that are now relatively rare, such as herb-rich meadows and pastures. Others contain species of special interest – globeflowers in the meadow site at Cae Pwll y Bo in the north, or marsh fritillary butterflies at Ystradfawr in the extreme south, where the county's border meets the industrial valleys.

MARSH FRITILLARY HABITATS

Most recently, the Trust has been working with the County Council to manage marsh fritillary butterfly habitats around the old mining town of Ystradgynlais. This is part of its most significant project to date, developing the area as its first Living Landscape – joining Trusts all the over UK in championing this approach to delivering nature conservation over wider areas of land and in partnership with other organisations. The project is assisted by a generous grant from WREN (Waste Recycling Environmental) and CCW. Within big exciting schemes like Living Landscapes, small Trusts such as Brecknock can play a key role by working closely with local people.

The Living Landscape approach is seen as the way forward for nature conservation by The Wildlife

Globeflower – Trewalkin Meadow nature reserve

Trusts as a movement. For the Brecknock Trust, it is a means of pulling together all the different elements of work the Trust has developed expertise in since 1964. These range from the management of its own nature reserves, to advising landowners on how to manage their own land; from inspiring local people of all ages to respect and help their local environment, to stand up for threatened wildlife.

In 2011, the Trust had six paid staff and still benefited from an enormous level of volunteer support. Its strengths have always been localness and its connections to both the wildlife and the people of the area. Valuing its independence and local roots, but always seeking to work closely with other organisations, the Brecknock Wildlife Trust is looking forward to its 50th year and beyond.

BY JOHN GIBBS, BERNARD WRIGHT, ROGER STEVENS AND ANN PAYNE
John Gibbs is a former Chairman of the Trust. A tree pathologist by profession, he was born in the county and it has always been his spiritual home.

Bernard Wright, now 90, has had a lifetime's interest in the natural world and a career in estate management. He joined the Trust on arrival in Brecon in 1969, after previous involvement with the Northumberland Wildlife Trust and the Cyprus Ornithological Society. He came onto the Trust's Council in 1976 and chaired its Conservation Committee for ten years.

Other co-authors are Roger Stevens and Ann Payne, a founder member of the Trust.

CHAPTER 7

Cheshire

Cheshire Wildlife Trust was born in 1962 under the name of the Cheshire Conservation Trust. Naturalists from Cheshire and Lancashire who were concerned about the rapid changes taking place in the countryside held a meeting on 10th March 1962. They knew other counties had formed groups under the umbrella of the Society for the Promotion of Nature Reserves (the Society) and wished to do the same.

The meeting, chaired by Dr Tom Pritchard, decided two separate Trusts should be formed, one covering each county. Others present included CHRISTOPHER CADBURY, who chaired the Society's Naturalists' Trust Committee at the time, and Desmond Parish, who had organised the event. Philip Oswald, the Conservancy's warden-in-charge at Rostherne Mere NNR, also played a key early role in the development of the Trust.

Following the meeting, the Cheshire Trust was founded on 24th October 1962. On 17th November the inaugural meeting took place with Professor Alan Gemmell as President. He warned that Cheshire's wildlife was under threat. The pleasure the countryside gave to many people, and its use in education might be destroyed. But he added that the Trust would not stand in the way of progress in housing or industry.

The great crested grebe was chosen as the Trust's emblem – a common and colourful sight in Cheshire, whose many meres had proved the species' salvation when it was almost extinct in the 19th century. The famous Cheshire-born artist

Charles Tunnicliffe drew a grebe with chicks on its back, swimming past sprigs of amphibious bistort, with a dragonfly above.

Kenneth Lee was elected Trust Chairman, followed in 1963 by Philip Askey who led the Trust with distinction and great enthusiasm for 15 years, overseeing its development in these formative years. One of Askey's first tasks, for example, was to lead the Trust through the Ringway public inquiry into the proposed Manchester International airport. The inquiry heard how the proposed runway would affect the nearby Cotterill Clough nature reserve (COWARD MEMORIAL RESERVES). Sadly, some valuable areas around the Clough were lost under tarmac.

Opposite: Great crested grebe courtship display
Right: An early photograph of Cotterill Clough

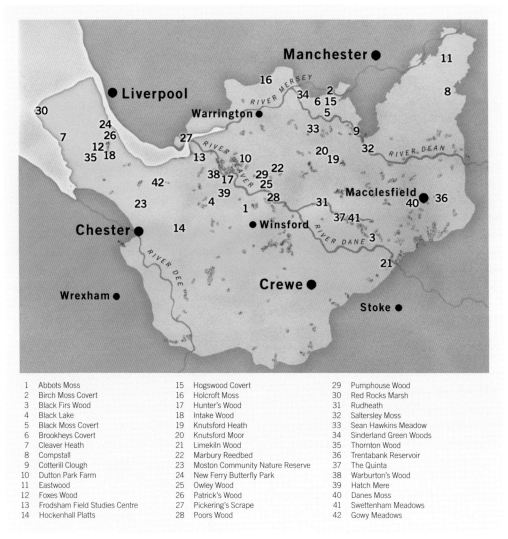

Map of Cheshire Wildlife Trust nature reserves

1	Abbots Moss	15	Hogswood Covert	29	Pumphouse Wood
2	Birch Moss Covert	16	Holcroft Moss	30	Red Rocks Marsh
3	Black Firs Wood	17	Hunter's Wood	31	Rudheath
4	Black Lake	18	Intake Wood	32	Saltersley Moss
5	Black Moss Covert	19	Knutsford Heath	33	Sean Hawkins Meadow
6	Brookheys Covert	20	Knutsford Moor	34	Sinderland Green Woods
7	Cleaver Heath	21	Limekiln Wood	35	Thornton Wood
8	Compstall	22	Marbury Reedbed	36	Trentabank Reservoir
9	Cotterill Clough	23	Moston Community Nature Reserve	37	The Quinta
10	Dutton Park Farm	24	New Ferry Butterfly Park	38	Warburton's Wood
11	Eastwood	25	Owley Wood	39	Hatch Mere
12	Foxes Wood	26	Patrick's Wood	40	Danes Moss
13	Frodsham Field Studies Centre	27	Pickering's Scrape	41	Swettenham Meadows
14	Hockenhall Platts	28	Poors Wood	42	Gowy Meadows

EARLY ENTHUSIASTS

For the first seven years, the Trust was run entirely by enthusiasts who were very knowledgeable about wildlife, but all had day jobs. As the membership grew it must have been difficult for them to deal with the membership, subscriptions and many other tasks in their spare time.

In 1969, the Trust secured enough money to appoint its first paid officer, Administrative Officer, Wing Commander Don Roy. In 1972 Stuart Crooks (CHRISTOPHER CADBURY MEDAL CITATIONS) was appointed Conservation Officer.

Among other things, he was charged with replying to numerous planning applications, as well as the care of 13 nature reserves and 15 nature trails.

Both were home-based and did sterling work for the Trust. It was not until 1979 that the Trust acquired its first headquarters. This was a big step forward, although modest by today's standards. It was a Portakabin in Marbury Country Park, adjacent to the Park Rangers' premises. One good point was its situation in the centre of the county.

TRUST RESERVES

Cheshire has two of the oldest nature reserves in the country – Cotterill Clough and Marbury Reedbed. They were purchased by the Society in 1934, long before the formation of the Trust, with funds raised by public subscription for a memorial to Cheshire naturalist Thomas A Coward (COWARD MEMORIAL RESERVES). Cotterill Clough is a steep-sided, wooded ravine (or clough) eroded into the Keuper marl by Cotterill Brook, which runs along the valley floor. There is also a plateau area at the top. A variety of trees and flora abounds in its little more than five and a half hectares and it is a Site of Scientific Interest (SSSI). Its flora and fauna have been studied for more than 200 years. Marbury Reedbed covers six hectares and demonstrates the various stages of hydrosere succession (from open water, to wetland, to woodland) causing the infill of a mere basin.

Following transfer from the Society these became the Trust's first nature reserves, quickly to be followed by some small areas of woodland on Carrington Moss, leased from Shell UK, and containing ponds created by digging out marl.

In March 2011, the Trust had 45 nature reserves covering more than 470 hectares and a variety of habitats, including ancient woodland, wetland, marsh, reedbed, lowland schwingmoor (quaking bog), wildflower meadow and heathland. These habitats are representative of those found in the rest of the county with its lowland plain, sandstone ridge, mosses, meres and coast. They contain a rich variety of species, many extremely rare. Several reserves are on post-industrial land, reflecting the wildlife interest that can be found on some very unnatural sites, especially in the north of the county. The Trust's smallest reserve is less than half a hectare and the largest, at almost 166 hectares, is the

Hatchmere

exciting area of Gowy wetland meadows, acquired in 2000. This is now part of the Trust's first LIVING LANDSCAPE project.

TRUST STRUCTURE

The Trust is governed by a Council whose members are its Trustees. These have numbered 30 at times (but are now a more manageable 15) as the emphasis on governance has increased. There are committees of Council consisting of Council members, volunteers and outside experts. Over the years at various times, and as occasion demanded, these have included Development, Education (expanding into People and Wildlife), Personnel, Reserves and Technical (expanding into Conservation), and Finance Committees. Currently only the last two – Conservation and Finance – exist.

From the earliest days members have formed eight, later nine, local groups covering the different parts of the county. Groups organise their own activities, including talks, outings to reserves and other places of interest. They also work on reserves, keep biological records, respond to local planning issues, raise funds and organise social activities.

In the 1974 reorganisation of local government, parts of Cheshire were moved into Greater Manchester and a smaller part into Merseyside. Many of the Trust's members and a number of nature reserves were, and are, in these areas.

An archive Trust poster

Elsewhere in the country, new urban Trusts were forming, but it was decided not to create a separate Manchester Trust. Instead, it was agreed that the Cheshire Trust and LANCASHIRE TRUST would continue to function (with two exceptions) in their original areas. There were changes, however. For example, grants and other help from Cheshire County Council only applied to new, post-1974 Cheshire and the Trust had to work with the new metropolitan areas of Wirral, Trafford, Stockport and Tameside, forging relationships and applying for grants. Adjustments to local government boundaries meant further changes in 1998 and 2009. For example, new Service Level Agreements had to be developed with the eight unitary authorities that now comprised the Trust's area.

CHANGING WITH THE TIMES

Over the years the Trust grew in membership, staff and scope of activities and, in the late 1980s, it looked actively for larger headquarters. A sub-committee made a list of requirements, but while a number of places were visited, none met the Trust's criteria.

At the same time, the Council debated at length whether to change the Trust's name to make its purpose clearer. Other Trusts were changing their names and a corporate identity seemed desirable.

Small copper at New Ferry Butterfly Park

Cheshire Trust for Nature Conservation was considered and favoured by many, despite its length! While the debate continued, a number of Trusts changed their name to become Wildlife Trusts. Eventually the name Cheshire Wildlife Trust was chosen and in 1991 at an Extraordinary General Meeting it was agreed by 97 per cent of the Trust's electorate.

Also in 1991, a sharp-eyed member noticed that a converted barn was available in the grounds of Reaseheath College of Agriculture. After suitable negotiations, it was rented as the new headquarters and staff moved in on 2nd December 1991. The name of Grebe House was chosen and it was officially opened on 10th March 1992 by HRH The Duke of Gloucester, exactly 30 years after the Trust's formation.

The new premises enabled Trust staff to work together in the same building for the first time, to have access to the expertise available at the College, and the convenience of bricks and mortar and toilets that didn't freeze up in winter! It also brought the Trust into closer contact with the Farming and Wildlife Advisory Group and the Cheshire County Council Ranger Service, housed in the same building. The disadvantage was that it was in the south of the county, which involved journeys of an hour or more for some members who needed to attend meetings. But it is not possible to have everything!

SECOND AIRPORT THREAT

In 1994, the Trust fought the proposal for a second runway at Manchester International airport, parallel to the first. Land of natural history interest would be adversely affected. The Trust was back at the beginning! While the Trust was not able to prevent the development, it was at least able to fight for mitigation as part of the planning permission. It was also able to try and look after the bats and newts in the area. When the original airport developments of 1965 were taking place, an early Trust success was gained concerning a new road across the top of Cotterill Clough. The Trust ensured that a culvert with a concrete footpath was built under the road so that badgers could continue to

Black Firs Wood was gifted to the Trust in 1991

move up and down the clough in safety. Similarly, many years later, when Manchester United Football Club planned their training ground on Carrington Moss, the Trust helped ensure that a condition of the planning permission was that a wildlife area was included. This educational area now includes some stunning heather regeneration and Manchester United is a corporate member. If you can't beat them, get them to join!

TEN YEARS OF EXPANSION

In 1995, Chris Mahon was appointed Director and Head of Conservation. At that time the Trust staff numbered six. In the larger headquarters of Grebe House, there was room for staff numbers and their activities to grow. Over the next ten years, the Trust grew impressively in numbers of staff, conservation projects, grants obtained and financial turnover. Much of this growth was due to Chris Mahon's enthusiasm and hard work. He took on a number of recent graduates to work

voluntarily in various branches of conservation. Grants were applied for, and, if obtained, many of these volunteers subsequently became paid members of staff. A Corporate Membership Officer was also appointed and brought in much-needed finance and widened the Trust's profile. By 2006, the paid staff numbered 32, some of whom were part-time.

Work continued in reserve maintenance, recording on Sites of Biological Importance, SSSIs and other sites, and in encouraging farmers to take up stewardship options. As part of the Cheshire Region Biodiversity Partnership, Trust staff and members took part in Biodiversity Action Plan groups to work on particular species and habitats.

Chairman and Council worked energetically; Watch groups – running activities for children – were started, and Trust staff were engaged in valuable work in the county's schools. Income was secured from a number of sources, particularly the HERITAGE LOTTERY FUND and the Landfill Tax Credit Scheme. The lottery funding enabled

Longhorn cattle grazing at Gowy Meadows, in the shadow of Stanlow refinery

three people to be employed to work on the Trust's SSSI nature reserves full-time for five years. Trust annual turnover increased from around £120,000 to more than £1 million.

In 1991, Cheshire Ecological Services (CES) was formed and a specialist team recruited as there was a demand for consultancy and practical services. CES is a wholly-owned subsidiary company that offers advice, surveys and work, such as the installation and maintenance of wildlife exclusion fencing and the translocation of the great crested newt – a protected species, common in Cheshire. All profits from CES go into the Trust to support its objectives.

Cheshire was one of the pilots for local record centres, leading to the establishment of rECOrd, an independent charity strongly backed by the Trust. This regional biological record centre now contains more than 1.5 million records.

MEMBERSHIP MATTERS

For many years the Trust membership stayed fairly static at about 3,000. After Council decided to

employ professional recruiters to approach people at events and venues and to canvas door-to-door, membership rose over a few years to 5,830 households, representing over 12,000 people, allowing for family memberships. This brought in valuable core funding and the greater membership carries more weight when the Trust deals with outside bodies. Times change and many newer members do not necessarily attend meetings or work on reserves, but want to donate to a good cause, read the literature and 'stand up to be counted'. However, there is still much scope for increasing awareness and membership as the Trust's area includes the conurbations of south Manchester, Crewe and Chester, plus those on Wirral, and membership is still a very small percentage of that population of over 2 million.

CONSERVATION GRAZING

In the 1990s, the Trust acquired a flock of rare breed Hebridean sheep for reserve management and its work on conservation grazing began. The Trust later acquired herds of Longhorn and Dexter cattle for the heavier-duty grazing. These are key to the Trust's first Living Landscape project along the rivers Mersey and Gowy. When not working on the Trust's reserves they have been hired out, so as well as increasing the Trust's conservation work throughout the county, they have also earned their keep!

Over the years, much thought was given to the Trust acquiring a farm to run in a wildlife-friendly way, to demonstrate best practice and for use in education. One or two possibilities were considered but were not viable. However, more recently, Bickley Hall Farm house and 83 hectares of surrounding farmland became available to lease. After much consideration, the Trust moved its headquarters there in December 2006.

TOO MUCH TO MENTION

Were paper, time and attention span unlimited it would be possible to regale the reader with many more tales of the Trust's activities. There was a hedgerow survey, jointly with the Women's Institute, in the 1960s. Funds were raised for many years by sales to Trust members and to the public. The Trust took part in 'Plant a Tree in '73, Plant Some More in '74'. The Trust also worked successfully on increasing habitat near rivers for the black poplar, and taking and planting many cuttings. It also worked on otters – now returned to Cheshire – and on water voles; on a barn owl project; a dormouse project; and (jointly with Chester Zoo) a harvest mouse project. The Trust was also involved in marine conservation, had stands at Cheshire County Shows and gardens in Tatton Park Flower Show, and has a wildlife-friendly garden at the Trust's headquarters, which grows fresh salads for the staff's lunch. Mention could be made of the effect of the 2001 outbreak of foot-and-mouth disease, when the Trust's headquarters was in Reaseheath Agricultural College and all but essential staff had to be banned from visiting. There are many other projects: the Trust's annual One Earth Day with environmentally-friendly, informative activities for youngsters; and much joint work with SHROPSHIRE, STAFFORDSHIRE, LANCASHIRE and CUMBRIA TRUSTS. And not forgetting national weekend conferences in the 1970s and 1980s for members and staff together – what inspiration, instruction and enjoyment the Trust reaped there.

ROAD TO RECOVERY

Unfortunately, early this century the Trust went through a very difficult time, necessitating major changes in governance, Trustees, management, staff structure and the financial system. Hard decisions had to be made. The Trust was grateful for help and support from the Society at this time and the Trust is now on an even keel again.

As the Trust has grown over the years from an entirely voluntary organisation to one with a team of professional staff and many more activities, it has remained a grassroots membership organisation. Volunteers are invaluable to the work of the Trust and help to enhance its profile. One stalwart, Eric Thurston, chaired the mid-Cheshire group for 32 years. He is remembered in the name of the awards the Trust gives to people for significant contributions to wildlife conservation in the county.

The Trust works to influence land use across the whole county for the benefit of all wildlife and the people who enjoy it. The concept of Living Landscapes and restoring nature across wider areas of land perfectly fits the Trust's outlook and it has been successful in securing grants to work in partnership with a number of environmental and community organisations to deliver this vision.

As the Trust approaches its 50th anniversary, shared with the Society's centenary in 2012, it is bigger and busier than ever before and approaches the future with optimism and dedication.

BY JEAN DUFTY
Jean Dufty has been involved with the Cheshire Wildlife Trust since 1969. A computer analyst/programmer by profession, she served on the Trust's Council for 31 years in addition to assisting with the local North Cheshire Group and the Trust's Personnel Committee. She sometimes claims that her main talent is getting other people to do things that they are good at!

Checking a dormouse box for signs of occupancy

CHAPTER 8

Cornwall

In the 1950s, Cornwall remained fairly remote from the rest of Britain, though tourists were arriving in increasing numbers during the summer months. Agriculture dominated the landscape, but farms were predominantly small. Many included tracts of heath, woodland and wetland. However, subsidised drainage and 'breaking in' of moorland were beginning to take their toll. The replacement of ancient broadleaved woodland with conifers was also taking place. Initially this created coppice-like conditions with abundant wildlife, but this was short-lived and soon replaced by a dense, dark, species-poor environment.

Mining (mostly for tin) had declined with only a couple of operational sites at Geevor and South Crofty. But this once extensive industry had left its scars on the county. China clay remained in high demand and, with more than 20 pits operational in the St Austell area, had a major impact on the local landscape and wildlife.

Fishing was also an important industry with stocks still in a relatively healthy condition. However, the classic massive pilchard shoals had long since disappeared.

REASONS TO BE FEARFUL

Ten years later, unrestricted afforestation and agricultural reclamation, along with insidious building development around small communities, were causing massive loss of wildlife habitat,

Opposite: View from Hannafore Point to St George's Island
Right: Elizabeth Jackson of the Cambourne and Redruth Natural History Society (CRNHS) presents a plaque to Kaspar Hocking (ex-President of the Trust, left) and Howard Curnow (current Chairman, right) commemorating the CRNHS's final meeting in 2010

which had little formal protection. At sea, increasing commercialisation and fishing gear efficiency were also resulting in species declines.

Impetus for the formation of an organisation to combat this devastation of the Cornish landscape and loss of wildlife came from the Camborne and Redruth Natural History Society, itself formed in 1956. An advertisement placed in the local press brought together almost 100 like-minded people at the County Museum in Truro on 23rd March 1962. The Cornwall Naturalists' Trust was formed and its officers elected: Dr Frank Turk (President), Dr Frank Smith (Vice President), Ken Williams (Honorary Secretary), MH Bizeley (Honorary Treasurer), Lieutenant Colonel WE Almond (Chairman), and Dr Gillian Matthews (Vice Chairman).

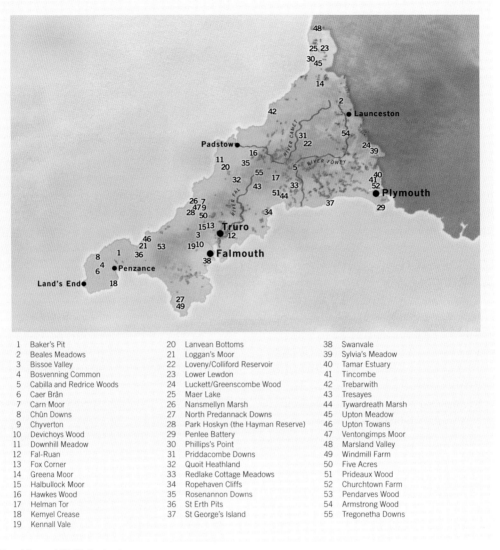

Map of Cornwall Wildlife Trust nature reserves

1	Baker's Pit	20	Lanvean Bottoms	38	Swanvale
2	Beales Meadows	21	Loggan's Moor	39	Sylvia's Meadow
3	Bissoe Valley	22	Loveny/Colliford Reservoir	40	Tamar Estuary
4	Bosvenning Common	23	Lower Lewdon	41	Tincombe
5	Cabilla and Redrice Woods	24	Luckett/Greenscombe Wood	42	Trebarwith
6	Caer Brân	25	Maer Lake	43	Tresayes
7	Carn Moor	26	Nansmellyn Marsh	44	Tywardreath Marsh
8	Chûn Downs	27	North Predannack Downs	45	Upton Meadow
9	Chyverton	28	Park Hoskyn (the Hayman Reserve)	46	Upton Towans
10	Devichoys Wood	29	Penlee Battery	47	Ventongimps Moor
11	Downhill Meadow	30	Phillips's Point	48	Marsland Valley
12	Fal-Ruan	31	Priddacombe Downs	49	Windmill Farm
13	Fox Corner	32	Quoit Heathland	50	Five Acres
14	Greena Moor	33	Redlake Cottage Meadows	51	Prideaux Wood
15	Halbullock Moor	34	Ropehaven Cliffs	52	Churchtown Farm
16	Hawkes Wood	35	Rosenannon Downs	53	Pendarves Wood
17	Helman Tor	36	St Erth Pits	54	Armstrong Wood
18	Kemyel Crease	37	St George's Island	55	Tregonetha Downs
19	Kennall Vale				

The Trust's aims, which remain similar to the present day, were in summary: to promote a wider appreciation of the need to conserve the countryside of Cornwall; to influence and educate policy makers on Cornish wildlife issues; to acquire and manage nature reserves and to promote the study and appreciation of nature in Cornwall.

EARLY COMMITTED VOLUNTEERS

In the first dozen years of the Trust's existence, everything was done by a very committed group of volunteers. From the outset there was a strong focus on the identification and survey of key wildlife sites in Cornwall. The Trust believed that effective conservation was rooted in a sound understanding of the local wildlife. Good working relationships were established with the local authority, The National Trust, the Cornwall Birdwatching and Preservation Society, the Forestry Commission and the Nature Conservancy. Links were also made with other similar Trusts and the Society for the Promotion of Nature Reserves (the Society). In this early period the Trust began to acquire nature reserves. The first of these was Hawkes Wood, an ancient oak woodland, leased for the princely sum of ten shillings per year. In 1966, the Trust acquired Ventongimps Moor, an area of wet heathland. Although at this stage in its history reserves were primarily taken on to protect their wildlife interest, the Trust also recognised their importance for engaging with people. In addition, the Trust sought to expand its membership, setting up a junior group and, in 1971, taking a stall at the Royal Cornwall Show to promote its work.

ALARMING HABITAT LOSSES

Unfortunately, in these early years, habitat destruction continued at an alarming rate. The Trust witnessed the loss from the county of the chough, the large blue butterfly (for many years the Trust's logo and the subject of significant efforts to prevent its extinction) and the red squirrel. It also saw at first hand the devastating effects of the 1967 TORREY CANYON oil spill on the county's marine wildlife, and engaged in issues ranging from the impact of DDT on otters, to BADGERS AND BOVINE TB, and the need for more sympathetic management of roadside verges. The increasing losses and pressures on Cornwall's wildlife spurred Trustees and members to try to do more to counter the impacts.

In 1974, the Trust appointed its first part-time member of staff, Administrative Officer, Frank Ansell. With 17 nature reserves, more than 1,000 members and increasing calls on its knowledge and expertise, volunteers could no longer cope without some paid assistance, although they still undertook the bulk of the work. It was around this time that local government districts were established in Cornwall, and the Trust established a local branch in each area. A similar structure continues to the present day.

In 1977, minutes of meetings reveal that Trustees believed it was not doing as well as other similar Trusts that had acquired staff and offices and had more members. Funding was sought from various bodies, including the County Council and the Nature Conservancy, and in 1979 Dr Caroline Rigby was appointed as Conservation Officer, the Trust's first full-time staff member. An office shared with the Nature Conservancy was leased at Trelissick Gardens from The National Trust. Thus, under the presidency of Dr Kaspar Hocking – an entomologist who worked on the eradication of the tsetse fly in Africa – and Chairman, Philip Blamey, a new era for the Trust began.

The chough – a symbol of Cornwall

Cabilla and Redrice Woods is one of the largest ancient woodlands in Cornwall

GOVERNMENT-FUNDED MANPOWER

Very soon after Rigby's appointment, the Trust began to take full advantage of the Government's Community Programme Scheme, introduced to combat the high levels of unemployment (EMPLOYMENT SCHEMES). Initially, in 1980, a team of four were employed to survey key wildlife sites across the county. This team was led by Dr Brian Johnson and included Trevor Edwards, a Cornish naturalist with long-standing connections in both farming and tin mining, who later became the Trust's Conservation Officer and is currently its Chief Executive.

The Trust continued to maximise its use of this source of manpower until the end of these schemes in 1988, by which time up to 70 people were employed on a variety of projects. Over the period, extensive survey work and data collation was undertaken on key wildlife sites, river catchments, ancient woodlands and a range of key species. A community development team was employed, led by Jill Sutcliffe, to engage with the public, and a formal junior membership – the Fox Club – was established in 1983. Work on the Trust nature reserves was also given a major boost

through the employment of two substantial practical teams under the leadership of the late Stuart Hutchings, who later became Trust Reserves Ranger.

Throughout this period, volunteer support remained strong, especially with events and fundraising. For example, county fairs were held at Trelissick and Trewithen Gardens and a sales caravan toured the county. Special interest groups focusing on bats, dolphins and photography were also established.

GROWING INFLUENCE

Relationships with the County Council, other NGOs and statutory agencies continued to strengthen. For example, a formal LOCAL WILDLIFE SITE system was established with the County Council. In the early 1980s, sites identified by the Trust were shown in the Cornwall Countryside Local Plan and the Trust was regularly consulted on planning matters.

In 1983, on its 21st anniversary, the Trust changed its name to the Cornwall Trust for Nature Conservation. This brought it into line with many other Trusts and expressed its aims to the public more accurately. The 1980s saw many other key changes and events. In 1985, Dr Caroline Rigby was replaced by Dr Lyn Jenkins – who was succeeded in 1988 by Trevor Edwards – and the Trust's long-standing Honorary Secretary, Ken Williams, retired after 25 years. *The Nature of Cornwall* was published by Rennie Bere in 1982, the Helford Voluntary Marine Conservation Area was established in 1986, and the Trust twinned with the Société pour l'Etude et la Protection de la Nature en Bretagne, in Brittany.

Habitat loss remained a major concern. The Trust successfully spearheaded a campaign, led by Dr Nick Tregenza, the Trust's Chairman from 1984 to 1997, to have West Penwith Moors designated an Environmentally Sensitive Area. Other issues high on the Trust's agenda, included proposals for a major container port at Falmouth, the impact of anti-fouling compounds on marine wildlife, the decline of dolphins, inert waste disposal into wetland sites and the ongoing issue of BADGERS AND BOVINE TB.

CRISIS POINT

The loss of the Community Programme Scheme in 1988 brought the Trust to crisis point. It had relied heavily on this source of funding. Its regular income remained small and membership stood at around 1,800. However, the Trustees were determined to maintain the momentum and agreed ambitious development plans.

Two key factors helped move things forward and, in many ways, have underpinned the development of the Trust since that time. Firstly, in late 1988, the Trust began to undertake consultancy work, securing a contract with the Central Electricity Generating Board to conduct an environmental impact assessment of a major windfarm development at Cold Northcott in east Cornwall. Monies generated enabled the employment of two staff, Susan Hocking and Paul McCartney, in addition to the Conservation Officer, Trevor Edwards, and Secretary, Diana Leaf.

NEW HQ

In addition, the Trust had secured planning consent to construct its new headquarters at Five Acres near Truro, thanks to the bequest of the site and funds from Dr George and Molly Allsop. George Allsop was a long-standing Trust member who had lived at the site and recorded corncrake nearby in 1966. The new headquarters – opened in early 1989 with the event broadcast live on local radio – enhanced the profile of the Trust and gave it a firm identity.

From that point, although there have been a few financially challenging times, due largely to external economic factors, the Trust has enjoyed steady, measured and sustained growth. In 1994, the Trust changed its name to the Cornwall Wildlife Trust to bring it into line with the other Wildlife Trusts around the UK.

1990S EXPANSION

The continued growth of the Trusts' consultancy and membership has been of major importance. In 1992, following a successful in-house operation, the Trust established a separate trading arm,

Cornwall Environmental Consultants. Today, this has 18 staff undertaking a varied range of services, from ecological surveys to landscape design. All its profits are paid to the Trust. A door-to-door membership recruitment scheme was introduced in 1990, followed later by a face-to-face scheme. Now supplemented by online promotion, these have resulted in a more than sevenfold increase in membership, which now exceeds 14,000.

The Trust's landholdings have expanded substantially and acquisition has increasingly focused on larger sites, or those adjoining existing nature reserves. Whole farms have been purchased, such as Trevillmick Farm in mid-Cornwall in 2002 and Windmill Farm on the Lizard peninsula in 2001.

This expansion has been made possible largely thanks to funding from the HERITAGE LOTTERY FUND (HLF), although large bequests and gifts – such as that from Rhona Weekes in 1990 – have helped. More recently, significant landholdings have been bequeathed to the Trust. In 2004, St George's Island off Looe, with its diverse marine wildlife, was left to the Trust by Babs Atkins. More recently, West Muchlarnick Farm, also in the Looe area, was left to the Trust by James Baylis-Bennett.

The Trust's reserves management operation has also become increasingly professional. Today, the Trust has a highly proficient reserves team supported by volunteer wardens and assistants. It also has its own livestock, including a flock of Hebridean sheep. This professionalism has been helped greatly by funds from HLF, along with English Nature's RESERVES ENHANCEMENT SCHEME and, more recently, Higher Level Stewardship and Single Farm Payments.

The acquisition and collation of data on Cornwall's natural environment – which since the formation of the RIGS (Regionally Important Geological Sites) Group in 1991 also includes geological sites – has remained a high priority. In the early 1990s, support from the European LIFE Fund enabled mapping of the entire landcover of Cornwall and the electronic capture of this data. This was done in partnership with Cornwall

County Council. In 1996, when the County Council was considering the future of Cornwall's Biological Records Unit (run in conjunction with the University of Exeter), the Trust was approached to take it on. As a result, the Trust established the Environmental Records Centre for Cornwall and the Isles of Scilly, which has gone from strength to strength. It is now a highly-regarded records centre, run in partnership with a range of statutory and non-statutory bodies. The centre provides the data underpinning decision-making about the future of Cornwall's natural environment, to the Trust and to many other bodies.

HQ UNDER PRESSURE

The growth of the Trust at this time meant space at the Trust's headquarters was under pressure. Although the new building had seemed palatial in 1989, by 1998 it was bursting at the seams and extra offices had to be rented in Truro at Boscawen House. This was far from ideal and working from split sites presented many difficulties. The Trust began a search for new premises and in 2003 purchased the ten-acre Two Burrows site next to Five Acres. After converting buildings, the site was opened in 2004.

MARINE CONSERVATION

Increasingly, the Trust has become involved in marine conservation. In the 1990s, the Dolphin Group – set up in the 1980s by local GP and cetacean-detection device expert, Dr Nick Tregenza – greatly expanded its work to establish the connection between fishing gear and the pattern of dolphin decline. Following the winter of 1990–91 when the deaths of more than 100 dolphins were recorded, an observation programme was launched on fishing boats. Volunteer observers spent more than 200 days at sea, mostly far offshore.

In 2002, under the presidency of Dr Tony Stebbing, Ruth Williams was appointed as the Trust's first dedicated Marine Conservation Officer. Since then, a marine team has carried out a diverse range of work, from basking shark surveys to trials of acoustic pinger devices on inshore fishing

nets to deter cetaceans and prevent bycatch. With the passage of the Marine and Coastal Access Act 2009, policy and advocacy work is becoming increasingly important.

Volunteers continue to play a major role in the Trust's work. Initially, as paid staff members increased, volunteering fell away; but, over time, the Trust has increasingly redressed the balance, integrating staff and volunteer efforts effectively. There are more than 100 people on the Trust's Marine Strandings Network who go out in all weathers to remote locations to collect data on stranded marine wildlife. There are also more than 60 volunteers who warden and assist on the Trust's nature reserves. Most recently, 'Team Gold' has been established to help organise and run a series of fundraising and profile-raising events as the Trust reaches its 50th anniversary in 2012.

Events to raise profile and generate funds have also been resulting in a steady increase in its annual turnover. However, finding funds, especially those that are unrestricted, remains a challenge and is likely to remain so whilst pressures on Cornwall's environment grow and more action is demanded from the Trust.

PARTNERSHIP WORKING

Working in partnership is firmly established. There are long-standing links with the local Council, other local NGOs and statutory agencies. Working with the Society is also now firmly embedded in the Trust's operation. The Trust has particularly close links with other Trusts in the south-west, through South West Wildlife Trusts, set up in 2002. A particularly close association is now well established with the ISLES OF SCILLY WILDLIFE TRUST, with which the Trust shares resources. In 1999, the Trust twinned with the Nature and Biodiversity Conservation Union, a similar organisation in Germany. This arrangement was guided by Howard Curnow, who has been Trust Chairman since 2000, and who is also a Cornish bard and a promoter of the Cornish language and culture. The Trust has maintained its focus on safeguarding and managing key wildlife sites.

Volunteers with members of the Trust's Marine Stranding Network

However, increasingly in recent years, working on a landscape scale has become a major focus in key parts of the county, such as West Penwith and the Lizard peninsula.

At the present time, Cornwall remains a wildlife-rich, predominantly agricultural county, reliant on tourism. The alarming rate of habitat loss in the early decades has slowed substantially, and there is a wide appreciation of the natural environment of the county and the need to safeguard it for future generations. Real opportunities exist to rebuild biodiversity on land and in the marine environment.

Under its current President, Professor Jan Pentreath, the Trust is now a well-respected, more outward-looking and people-orientated organisation, though firmly rooted in traditional conservation values. It is well placed to pursue these opportunities with the many partners with which it has established long and positive relationships, both within and beyond Cornwall.

BY SHELAGH GARRARD, ROWENA MILLAR AND TREVOR EDWARDS

Shelagh Garrard is an entomologist by training, but has spent most of her career teaching biology. An 'out of county' member of the Trust since the 1970s, she has now moved to Cornwall, become a Trustee and currently chairs the Trust's Conservation Strategy Committee.

Rowena Millar is a freelance writer and editor, specialising in wildlife and the environment. She writes and edits Wild Cornwall *and* Wild Scilly *and* Pawprint – *the Trust's junior membership magazine.*

Trevor Edwards is Chief Executive of Cornwall Wildlife Trust, where he has worked since 1980. Originally from West Cornwall, Trevor has a degree in biological sciences from the University of London and is a founder member of the Institute of Ecology and Environmental Management (IEEM).

CHAPTER 9

Cumbria

The seeds of Cumbria Wildlife Trust were sown in 1959. That year, the Nature Conservancy's Merlewood Research Station and North Regional Office put on an exhibition in Grange-over-Sands about nature conservation. One of the visitors to the exhibition was Canon GAK Hervey, Rector of Great Salkeld, who came to see the Conservancy's Regional Officers to discuss his initially hazy ideas of establishing a naturalists' trust for the area. A commanding figure dressed in clerical grey with knee breeches, he was typical of many rural clergy of the 19th and early 20th century, and he shared their consuming interest in natural history. He was to be the Trust's driving force through much of its formative period. The Conservancy's staff offered to help and advise and, indeed, continued to support the Trust throughout its developmental years and beyond.

The first step was to decide the area to be covered. A faction from Liverpool wanted a Trust extending from the Solway to the Mersey. Others realised that this would be too unwieldy to be workable. A meeting was held in Preston to discuss the issue, at which there was much shouting, but no progress other than to agree that there should be another meeting. This was duly held in Ambleside and, in the absence of the southern faction (who said it was "too far to come"), it was agreed that the new Trust should cover Cumberland, Westmorland and the Furness district of North Lancashire.

Inaugurated in 1962, the Trust took the name of the Lake District Naturalists' Trust – in spite of the fact that more than half the area it covered was not in the Lake District. In 1974, under local government reorganisation, the ancient name, Cumbria, was revived. Coincidentally, 'Cumbria' happened to describe the area covered by the Trust plus Sedbergh, Garsdale and Dent, hitherto in Yorkshire. The Trust embraced the ex-Yorkshire area and changed its name to Cumbria Trust for Nature Conservation. It later became Cumbria Wildlife Trust in 1989.

Opposite: Harebells above Red Tarn. Above: The Trust's Foulshaw Moss nature reserve

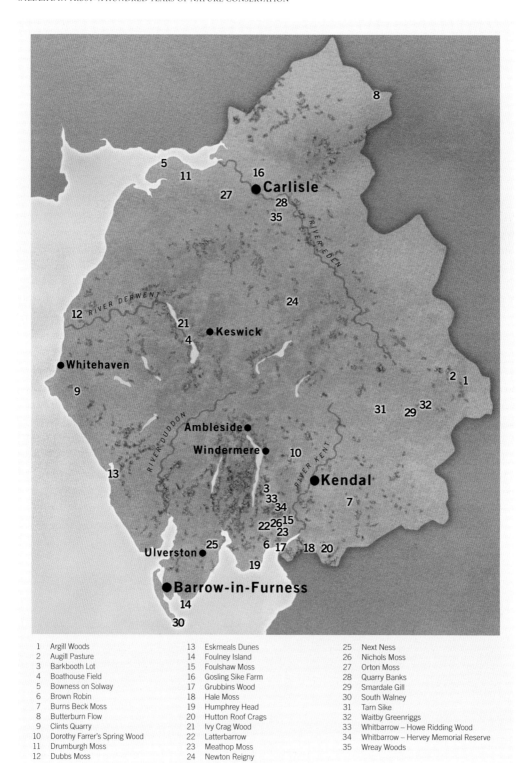

1	Argill Woods	13	Eskmeals Dunes	25	Next Ness
2	Augill Pasture	14	Foulney Island	26	Nichols Moss
3	Barkbooth Lot	15	Foulshaw Moss	27	Orton Moss
4	Boathouse Field	16	Gosling Sike Farm	28	Quarry Banks
5	Bowness on Solway	17	Grubbins Wood	29	Smardale Gill
6	Brown Robin	18	Hale Moss	30	South Walney
7	Burns Beck Moss	19	Humphrey Head	31	Tarn Sike
8	Butterburn Flow	20	Hutton Roof Crags	32	Waitby Greenriggs
9	Clints Quarry	21	Ivy Crag Wood	33	Whitbarrow – Howe Ridding Wood
10	Dorothy Farrer's Spring Wood	22	Latterbarrow	34	Whitbarrow – Hervey Memorial Reserve
11	Drumburgh Moss	23	Meathop Moss	35	Wreay Woods
12	Dubbs Moss	24	Newton Reigny		

Map of Cumbria Wildlife Trust nature reserves

EARLY TALENTS

Under Canon Hervey's leadership, people from many walks of life brought their skills and experience to bear on the Trust's activities. Lord Lonsdale, familiar with running an estate and managing business affairs, was the first President. He certainly saved the Trust from taking at least one unwise direction. Canon Hervey was the first Chairman of the Council. Among others giving crucial service to the fledgling organisation was Hilary Overy,

the first Trust Secretary and, later, interim Chairman. She was a good botanist with useful experience as agent to a local MP. Kenneth Himsworth was Clerk to Westmorland County Council and his orderly mind kept Canon Hervey's feet on the ground! Jack Marshall, an Appleby Grammar School master and a naturalist, designed the Trust's distinctive badger's paw emblem and illustrated the Trust's newsletter for many years.

Geoffrey Ainscough, the Trust's first Treasurer, was a bank official whose reports were written in elegant long-hand. Vera Amor had valuable relevant experience as Head Forester of the Cavendish Estate. Peter Delap, was an Appleby doctor and deer expert – agile enough to scale a deer fence without a moment's hesitation! Ralph Stokoe, an accountant, had for many years pursued his hobby of surveying lake and lakeside vegetation and keeping meticulous records of his findings. These were of immense value as a baseline when, years later, the Trust undertook a major survey of Cumbrian tarns. Nat Dawson, a retired headmaster, took over as Chairman in 1970 and steered the Trust throughout the 1970s, overseeing the acquisition of many new nature reserves and a period of growth.

Joy Ketchen, a pharmacist and naturalist, trained herself to become a sound ecological conservationist.

Above: Canon Hervey – The Trust's first Chairman

She scrutinised development proposals, for example, to assess their impact on valued wildlife sites, making recommendations on behalf of the Trust. Her thoroughness and the hours she worked must always have far exceeded the pittance the Trust was able to pay her. Her service ended only with her death in 1989, after a courageous struggle with cancer. By then, finances allowed the appointment of a full-time Conservation Officer – Peter Bullard, the present Director of the Trust.

Among the professional biologists giving much voluntary service to the Trust were two from the Freshwater Biological Association's research station on Windermere: David Le Cren, the Station Director, and Edna Lind. Both served on the Council, the former taking over as Chairman from Nat Dawson.

PRESIDENTS AND CHAIRMEN

Following Lord Lonsdale as President was the First Lord Inglewood. Well-known in the county for his war service and as a Cumbrian MP, he proved valuable in gaining respect and acceptability for the Trust. After Lord Inglewood died, Brian Redhead, the respected radio broadcaster, took over as President. After his untimely death in 1994, the presidential reins passed to the writer, Hunter Davies, who became the Trust's longest-serving President to date, presiding in a friendly and easy-going, but efficient, style. His place has now been taken by the present Lord Inglewood, a prominent figure in the county with a valuable personal interest in farming.

As the Trust expanded its work, costs rose. The early 1980s were a particularly difficult time. Chairmen found themselves juggling with a range of problems. During the chairmanship of Teddy Ratcliffe and then of David Le Cren, the problem of replacing an outgrown headquarters and of satisfying the urge to acquire high quality sites under threat (to safeguard them as nature reserves), became acute. The Trust found itself seriously overstretched financially. In 1985, John Lowe, a Council member, pointed out that, between 1980 and 1985, the Trust's cash reserves had fallen from £80,000 to £10,000.

CASH RESERVES RESCUE

In 1987, at the end of David Le Cren's term of office, John Lowe was appointed Chairman with a specific remit to rectify matters. He succeeded, aided by the appointment in 1989 of David Hill as Director, who did much to keep the Trust moving steadily ahead until his retirement from the post in 1994.

When Dennis Nelson took over as Chairman, the Trust was benefiting from its spell of self-denial. In 1998 the chairmanship passed to Susan Johnson, but Nelson continued actively to promote the Trust's interests, undertaking a sponsored millennium walk round the Trust's boundary.

Dennis Nelson's successor as Chairman, Susan Johnson, was noted for her quiet style and courteous manner, whether chairing a meeting or welcoming a new member of the Trust. Under her chairmanship, everyone had a chance to air their views without domination from the chair. Nevertheless, she always retained good control of meetings and a satisfactory consensus of opinion would be reached. DUNCAN JEFFRAY took over in 2005, a former Chairman of the WARWICKSHIRE TRUST, and was succeeded in 2007 by the present Chair, Anne Powell.

FIRST OFFICE HQ

In the Trust's early years, Council meetings were held in members' houses. They were somewhat informal occasions and could go on late into the night. Those that were held in Canon Hervey's Great Salkeld rectory had to take place in the afternoon on Sundays, so that he would be free to take the evening service after the Council meeting. Nevertheless, the church bells would start to ring while the Canon was still in full flow over Trust affairs and it was only at the increasingly urgent pleading of Council members that he could be persuaded to leave the meeting. Even so, he would sometimes return, fully robed, to make some additional point on Council business.

From 1976 Council meetings were held in the Ambleside Friends Meeting House. This simplified arrangements, but did not provide the Trust with

Pippa Bonner and Sheila Brunstrom outside the Badger's Paw shop in 1987

a much-needed office headquarters. A small shop with rooms over it in Ambleside came up for sale in 1981 and the Trust bought it despite the strain it put on finances. The upstairs rooms provided the office and the downstairs became a Trust shop. Here, Pippa Bonner and Sheila Brunstrom stepped enthusiastically into the breach, heading a volunteer team who made the shop a great success.

As the work of the Trust continued to grow and the number of staff increased, the Ambleside premises became too small and a search for larger offices began. The first move was to rent an unused wing of the Lake District National Park Centre at Brockhole, overlooking Windermere. This was soon outgrown and the search for a longer-term home continued. Eventually an ideal solution was found. Paid for by several generous legacies, in 2001 the Trust bought Plumgarths, a picturesque old house and garden on the outskirts of Kendal.

ORDERLY POLICY-MAKING

By 1989 it was becoming clear that the Trust needed a more orderly way of determining policies. A consultant was appointed to make recommendations for a balanced policy-making hierarchy and in 1990 two policy groups were set up, reporting to an Executive Committee and Council. One was concerned with conservation (the scientific side of the Trust's work) and the other was to take on development (to raise funds, increase membership, and widen knowledge and understanding of the Trust's remit). Each group was underpinned by committees dealing with specific aspects of work. Following the retirement of David Hill in 1994, Peter Bullard took over as Director, after years of experience as Conservation Manager, and firmly sealed this close relationship between the two sides of Trust activity.

This structure has served the Trust well for many years, the only significant change made since its inauguration being the replacement, in 2003, of the rather unwieldy Council by a smaller, more manageable and nimble Board of Trustees. To offset the reduction in numbers of people able to put forward their views, annual Members' Conferences have been established.

VOLUNTEER LOCAL SUPPORT GROUPS

A network of local support groups around the county was an early concept before the Trust had any paid staff. The first one covered the Hawkshead area and others were later established wherever there was the local will to set one up. Local support groups

have proved invaluable and, at their best, could be described as the circulatory and nervous systems of the Trust's body, undertaking fundraising, field surveys, walks and talks for members and non-members and practical work on reserves. Perhaps most importantly, they also act as ambassadors for the Trust's cause through personal contact with friends and neighbours.

A case in point is that of Ingram Cleasby, an 'Old Sedberghian' and ornithologist, who returned to his roots in Cumbria, after retiring as Dean of Chester Cathedral. He was immediately 'snapped up' and served for many years as Chairman of the Sedbergh Local Support Group, initiating group survey work and innovative ways of fundraising. He also became the Trust's unofficial chaplain, officiating at the dedication of the Canon Hervey Memorial Cairn at the top of the reserve on Whitbarrow, and preaching a splendid sermon on the occasion of the Trust's 30th anniversary thanksgiving service.

DIVERSE CUMBRIAN WILDLIFE

The Trust is indeed fortunate in the diversity of wildlife in the county. Landforms represented

Oystercatchers at South Walney nature reserve

include the western seaboard, with its estuaries, flats and saltmarshes, sand dunes and rocky shores, including sea cliffs. Inland are the Lake District mountains interspersed with lakes, the Howgill Fells and – beyond the fertile farmland of the Eden Valley – the long ridge of the Pennines forming the eastern boundary of the county. Rock types range from volcanic to both acid and calcareous sedimentary rocks, including extensive limestone pavements.

Among the county's fells and dales are some fens, extensive peat deposits of several kinds, and ancient, semi-natural woodlands. Add to these coastal waters and standing and running water. Altitude varies from sea level to 3,000 feet above sea level. Grassland predominates, varying from the rough grazings (with some dwarf shrub-heath) to most of the uplands, to the limestone grasslands at rather lower elevations, and also neutral grasslands on in-by farmland. Woodland tends to persist on steep ground, especially on wooded gill sides.

Land use, in this predominately rural county of few large towns and little urban sprawl, is primarily grassland farming with some arable in the lowlands. For hundreds of years, grassland plant communities have been conditioned, and lately increasingly impoverished, by grazing sheep. In the last half century or so, overgrazing has converted what was heather moor to grassland. However, effort is now being made to restore heather in some areas.

FIGHTING WILDLIFE THREATS

The Trust has a long and successful record of fighting damaging proposals. One of the earliest was the Hampsfell Public Inquiry in 1972 into plans to extract limestone pavement. The inquiry was won and subsequent battles and campaigns led to the last legal extraction ending on Orton Scar in the 1990s.

Ending peat extraction in the county has not yet happened, but only one of the sites remains operational. The largest site, Wedholme Flow, is now being restored as a nature reserve. The most recent proposal to open a new peat extraction site at Black Snib near Longtown – back in the 1990s – was successfully fought at a public inquiry and

no new applications have come forward since. Plans to put houses on Maryport Harbour SSSI were also taken to public inquiry and successfully fought off in 1993. This was the last time a housing development on an SSSI was proposed in the county. In contrast, the Trust's efforts against plans for wind farms have not been as successful. The first, on Kirkby Moor SSSI, was built despite the Trust's objections. Recently, the main threats to Cumbria's wildlife have been relatively small-scale and localised. However, many new energy generation proposals are beginning to come forward, such as tidal barrages and nuclear power stations.

FROM SEASHORE TO MOUNTAINTOP

In its earlier days, the Trust concentrated on establishing nature reserves on the best areas not already safeguarded. However, the first reserve, MEATHOP MOSS, came to the Trust ready-made, but with no conservation management regime. It had been a nature reserve leased since 1920 by the Society for the Promotion of Nature Reserves with CHARLES ROTHSCHILD's financial support, and was one of the best mosses in northern England and an important site for large heath butterflies.

Hampsfell – the Trust successfully fought off plans for limestone pavement extraction

Another early Trust reserve was South Walney, initially jointly managed with the LANCASHIRE TRUST, as it was then in Lancashire. An important bird site, it was famous for Professor Tinbergen's research into the largest gullery in north-western Europe. The summit of Whitbarrow was acquired in 1969 in memory of Canon Hervey, safeguarding its many rare flowers and invertebrates and some of the finest limestone pavements in England. Acquisitions followed thick and fast, and by the early 1980s the Trust had acquired 35 reserves including sand dunes at Eskmeals, further limestone pavements on Hutton Roof, woodland and grassland at Smardale, the tidal island of Foulney, saltmarshes at Rockcliffe and raised mire at Drumburgh Moss. Drumburgh is home to peatland species such as the large heath butterfly, all three types of sundew and in autumn is visited by hunting short-eared owls. The limestone pavement sites protect several rare wildflowers, whilst Foulney hosts thousands of breeding birds, including eider ducks and arctic and little tern.

All these reserves are recognised as of national or international importance for their wildlife. The Trust today has more than 7,000 acres of land in its care, spread across 42 nature reserves, with more than 20 of these being SSSIs. The acquisition of reserves has slowed since the 1980s, with only one significant 1990s acquisition, Foulshaw Moss – at 700 acres the Trust's largest owned nature reserve.

Acquisition of reserves continues. But even more important is the work of determining and implementing management plans, monitoring management effects and making necessary changes accordingly. This is crucially helped by each reserve being assigned an Honorary Reserve Manager, supported by reserve staff. The Trust's own increasing experience of management for nature conservation is valuable in advisory work.

LIVING LANDSCAPES

However, it is now appreciated, no less in Cumbria than everywhere else in Britain – especially in the face of climate change – that conservation

The rare scotch argus butterfly can be found at Smardale Gill nature reserve

of the countryside as a whole, in conjunction with primary land uses, is necessary. This will give wildlife communities that are under stress, or trapped in non-viable isolated patches, the chance to move, link up, change, or merge. The Trust is addressing this Living Landscape approach championed by Wildlife Trusts across the UK – with enthusiastic determination. Recently the Trust has focused on projects based around habitats such as tarns, wetlands, hay meadows, marine, sacred places, and roadside verges. This has involved training volunteers to carry out surveys, to undertake active management of sites and to campaign to protect them.

Pressures continue to rise. There are increasing demands for land for infrastructure projects and to grow more fuel and crops, which combine with the impact of climate change itself. In this situation, the Trusts and related voluntary wildlife organisations must redouble their efforts to campaign for wildlife preservation. The development of the Cumbria Wildlife Trust, from its inception to the present, suggests that it is capable of playing a full part in meeting these new challenges.

BY HELGA FRANKLAND
Helga Frankland has been an active volunteer for the entire 50 years of the Trust's existence, including being a Trustee for 40 years. Before retiring, she was Regional Officer for the Nature Conservancy.

CHAPTER 10

Derbyshire

In the 1950s and 1960s, the pressures on Derbyshire's landscape and countryside were relatively unappreciated. Only the drastic effects of persistent pesticides, which had eliminated several of the county's top predators, including otters and peregrines, had attracted public attention. However, plans to dump fly-ash in the botanically-rich limeyards at Ticknall, in the south of the county, sparked the formation of the Derbyshire Naturalists' Trust in 1962.

Once the threat to Ticknall had been overcome, the individuals involved in that fight decided that future battles would be better tackled by an organisation set up for the purpose, rather than a few naturalists working in an entirely *ad hoc* manner.

They set up a small group, which agreed that the county's wildlife needed some type of structure to fight its corner. Noting the establishment of charitable Naturalists' Trusts in other counties, they decided to set one up in Derbyshire.

Professor Arthur Clapham, a botanist at Sheffield University (and very familiar with the Peak District's plants), was soon invited to become the Trust's first Chairman. A constitution was drawn up and a subscription rate of ten shillings was announced. After attending the Trust's inaugural meeting, LORD HURCOMB, then President of the Society for the Promotion of Nature Reserves (the Society), saw a ring ouzel in the Goyt Valley, and suggested that this moorland bird should be the Trust's emblem and logo.

Opposite: Female peregrine falcon at Derby Cathedral – since 2007 peregrines have nested on the Cathedral
Right: Ticknall Limeyards – the Trust's first nature reserve and where it all began

PEAKS AND DALES

Derbyshire marks the interface between lowland and upland Britain. Some of the most attractive parts of the county lie within the Peak District National Park, and draw large numbers of visitors every year. Yet, there are many less-visited, but equally attractive areas, elsewhere in the county.

The wild uplands of the so-called Dark Peak include the high gritstone tops of Kinder Scout and Bleaklow and many square miles of rugged, wild moorland. By contrast, the White Peak consists of many beautiful dales intersecting a rolling limestone plateau. Many of the more scenic and wildlife-rich dales are either National Nature Reserves, Sites of Special Scientific Interest or Trust reserves.

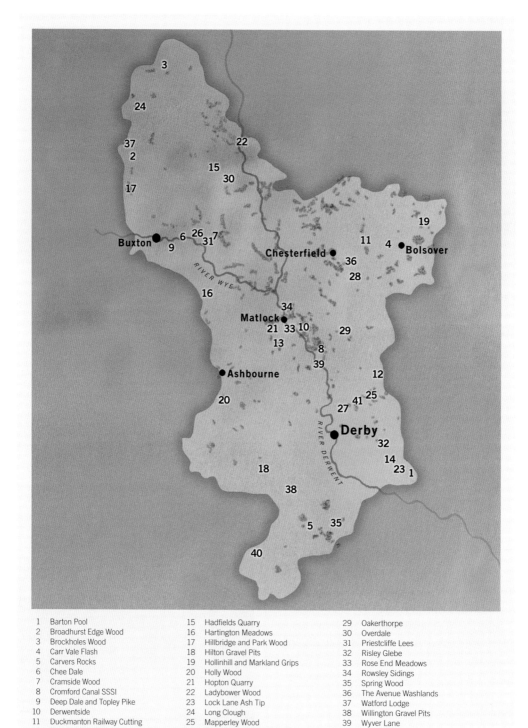

1	Barton Pool	15	Hadfields Quarry	29	Oakerthorpe
2	Broadhurst Edge Wood	16	Hartington Meadows	30	Overdale
3	Brockholes Wood	17	Hillbridge and Park Wood	31	Priestcliffe Lees
4	Carr Vale Flash	18	Hilton Gravel Pits	32	Risley Glebe
5	Carvers Rocks	19	Hollinhill and Markland Grips	33	Rose End Meadows
6	Chee Dale	20	Holly Wood	34	Rowsley Sidings
7	Cramside Wood	21	Hopton Quarry	35	Spring Wood
8	Cromford Canal SSSI	22	Ladybower Wood	36	The Avenue Washlands
9	Deep Dale and Topley Pike	23	Lock Lane Ash Tip	37	Watford Lodge
10	Derwentside	24	Long Clough	38	Willington Gravel Pits
11	Duckmanton Railway Cutting	25	Mapperley Wood	39	Wyver Lane
12	Erewash Meadows	26	Miller's Dale Quarry	40	Drakelow
13	Gang Mine	27	Morley Brickyards	41	Woodside
14	Golden Brook Storage Lagoon	28	North Wingfield		

Map of Derbyshire Wildlife Trust nature reserves

In the east of the county, both deep and opencast coalfields have produced a degraded environment which is now benefiting from restoration and redevelopment. In the south of the county, low rolling countryside is typical of that found in much of the East Midlands. While agriculture has intensified here, there are still many hedges and a good mix of farm sizes and crops. The National Forest extends over part of this area and many new woodlands are springing up here.

The county's only major conurbation is the rapidly growing city of Derby, though parts of the east of the county are now being covered by sprawling industrial buildings and housing estates. Sheffield lies close to the county's northern boundary, Manchester to the north-west, Nottingham to the east and Birmingham to the south-west. While people living in much of the county often look to these large cities just beyond the county's boundaries for work, shopping and culture, it is the open areas of the county that in most cases provide them with easy access to nature and a good quality of life.

THE FORMATIVE YEARS

By May of 1962, 110 members had been recruited and the Trust began life. The first Annual General Meeting was held in 1963, with volunteers identifying further threats to wildlife-rich sites in the county. From the start, RH (Dick) Appleby of Derby, who died in 2004, was a key 'mover and shaker'. Taking early retirement from the Water Board, Appleby devoted time every day to ensuring that the Trust's administration and development took place surely but steadily.

He also took on a sales spot in the busy car park at Dovedale – actually just in Staffordshire! This had been set up by John and Joyce Varty, following some experimental sales outings around the county. Along with occasional donations and bequests, the sale of goods brought in much needed income to the Trust, whose expenditure was increasing annually.

Further sales at Tissington Well Dressings and other events, all run by volunteers, of course, added to this new income stream. The first day at Tissington Well Dressings always attracted crowds from all over the UK (and American tourists too) and it was here that the record sales of over £1,000 were taken on a single day.

Other prominent volunteers in those early years included Miss Hollick (the county plant recorder), RH Hall, John Varty, George Wigglesworth, Trevor Elkington (first editor of the Trust newsletter) and William Howson Wilcockson, a geologist and the Trust's first Honorary Secretary.

FROM STRENGTH TO STRENGTH

By 1967, the Trust had established its first two nature reserves, one of which was Ticknall Limeyards, previously mentioned, a part of Calke Abbey, owned by the Harpur Crewe family. In 1985, the estate and limeyards were given over to The National Trust in lieu of death duties.

By 1969, the Trust's finances reached the £1,000 mark and Dick Appleby took over the chairmanship from Professor Clapham, a position he retained until 1984.

A significant financial landmark in the Trust's development was a magnificent bequest of £20,000 from Miss Mandahl who died in 1971. This legacy allowed the Trust to appoint its first paid member of staff, Andrew Deadman, as its Conservation Officer in 1973. Deadman's office was a tiny cottage in Twyford, close to the River Trent, south of Derby. Six years later, it housed his successor, Pat Brassley, and two further members of staff, Nick Brown (Promotions Officer) and Diane Wilson (Membership Secretary), as well as Appleby.

Eyam Well Dressing celebrates 40 years of the Derbyshire Wildlife Trust

Dick Appleby receives a cheque from the WWF

By this time, Appleby was spending every morning in the office, taking work home with him to do after his lunch. The little Twyford office proved to be a useful base, except when the nearby River Trent flooded the access road, as it was wont to do every winter. When that happened, the only way to get to the office was to leave cars on the main road and negotiate several boggy fields and muddy gateways!

Appleby was an extraordinary volunteer, whose energy and sheer stubbornness ensured the Trust moved steadily forward over those formative years. He took no payment from the Trust in expenses, despite travelling hundreds of miles across the county in his old Volvo to attend meetings and give talks.

INTO THE COMPUTER AGE

By 1980 the Trust's annual income had reached the £20,000 mark. The staff's top salary was in the order of £3,000 per year, just about enough to live on in those far-off days!

The Trust's first computer arrived in 1983, acquired to deal with its expanding membership and wildlife site survey records. This also meant that the old, second-hand duplicator, which always covered its operator in ink, could be retired.

Pat Brassley continued to work tirelessly on all fronts. Having carried out years of field-by-field survey work, greatly increasing the Trust's

knowledge of the county's best habitats, she set up the Trust's LOCAL WILDLIFE SITES register, one of the first anywhere in the country. She also established good working relationships with, and acquired valuable annual funding from, both County and District Councils. This continues to the current day.

Over and above all the office work and paperwork, Brassley loved being outdoors. Throughout her working life, and in all weathers, she spent many hours every year out on the nature reserves wielding axe, rake and scrub cutter... the muddier the better!

GROWING AND DEVELOPING

By 1984, the Trust had outgrown its Twyford office and moved to Elvaston Castle, owned by the County Council. That same year, the Trust hit the national headlines when, under John Varty's direction and badger-like determination, it bravely decided to bring a private prosecution against five men caught badger baiting in woods near Ambergate. The police had declined to take the case on, but the private prosecution succeeded and the Trust received many plaudits, including some in both Houses of Parliament at Westminster. The national media covered the story and the Trust was widely applauded for standing up for nature and for taking such a financial risk.

The Nature of Derbyshire, a book written entirely by Trust staff and trustees was published in 1986.

Water vole – an iconic Derbyshire species

Chee Dale nature reserve – home to many wildflower species, including rock rose, Jacob's ladder and grass of Parnassus

Two years later, this was followed by a book on wildlife gardening written by Fran Hill, which subsequently sold over 35,000 copies throughout the UK.

In the same year, the Trust changed its name to Derbyshire Wildlife Trust, a move welcomed by the staff whose every radio interview up to that point had begun with a tongue-in-cheek comment about naked working. To journalists, the words 'naturalist' and 'naturist' were engagingly similar. This change of name was accompanied by a change of logo (to a badger, so topical at the time) and, more importantly, to a new and more business-like approach. All this was instigated by Ian Carstairs, a freelance consultant, whose contribution to modernising the Trust was significant and was a vital precursor to its forthcoming first major appeal. The Trust's appeal was a mammoth effort lasting four years, masterminded by Carstairs. Under the

able chairmanship of Dr (later Professor) Trevor Elkington, the appeal raised more than £300,000. It enabled the Trust to purchase a new nature reserve – Rose End Meadows at Cromford – and to establish its first visitor centre, the Whistlestop Countryside Centre, at Matlock Bath. Housed in Grade I listed Victorian railway station buildings and supported by high-profile visits from the two Davids – BELLAMY and ATTENBOROUGH – the Whistlestop was to become the Trust's public face. Opened in 1990, it also set up as an education base, with the centre staff inviting schools to visit and undertake a variety of hands-on educational activities. Ten years later, more than 10,000 schoolchildren had benefited from a day at the centre; and over a million people had seen the exhibition and bought items from the shop.

By 1995, the Trust had appointed its first Chief Executive, Irene Coope, and staff numbers had

David Bellamy launches the appeal for Rose End Meadows and Whistlestop

risen to eight. With more staff time available, the Trust began to link up with its neighbouring Trusts in the East Midlands, and naturally throughout the 1980s and 1990s new nature reserves were purchased or leased, taxing the Trust's ability to manage them all successfully.

The following year, and after much research and survey work, the Trust published *Endangered Wildlife in Derbyshire*. Edited by Alan Willmot and Trevor Elkington, it was the first county red data book listing all the species of plants and animals that were rare and threatened.

In 1998, a £500,000 grant from the HERITAGE LOTTERY FUND, engineered by Pat Brassley, enabled the Trust to employ two new full-time staff, with the specific task of increasing the standard of management of the Trust's nature reserves.

Two further new initiatives began in 1999 – a two-year Wildlife Gardening project and an Otters and Rivers project. The latter flourished

beyond its initial grant period, widening its brief to become the Water for Wildlife project and embracing detailed study and conservation of the beleaguered water vole. This work grew and developed further after the turn of the century.

The year 2001 saw major problems caused by foot-and-mouth disease, which put both the Trust's reserves and the wider countryside out of bounds to Trust staff. Pat Brassley retired during this time; she had ably taken on the responsibility for the Trust's conservation and reserves work for more than 20 years.

EDUCATING THE NEW GENERATION

In 2002, a three-year lottery-funded project, Making Natural Connections, enabled education staff to link schools with their local nature reserves. Further grants from Landfill Tax Credits allowed the Trust to start a programme of education for sustainable development with schools, helping them to start composting, to recycle and reduce their landfill waste.

The same year, the Trust office moved from Elvaston Castle to rented office space in Belper, a more central location. Staff numbers increased, as did membership of both the Trust and the Watch Club, its junior branch (WILDLIFE WATCH).

By 2006, the Trust had more than 10,000 adult members. In the same year, the Trust was awarded a £250,000 grant from the national lottery to improve biodiversity on school grounds over the next four years. The Trust was also the key player in a project to encourage peregrine falcons to nest on Derby Cathedral, which predictably, attracted much media attention. The Trust also finally managed to purchase Willington Gravel Pits, a key ornithological site in the Trent Valley.

Irene Coope retired in 2007 and was succeeded by the Trust's second Chief Executive, Ed Green. In 2008, David Oakes, a former stalwart of the Trust's Appletree Hundred local group, retired after more than a decade as Chair of the Trust. His successor, Tony Hams, oversaw the development of the second organisational strategic plan – the first to put landscape-scale working at the heart of the

Trust's operations. An early product of this plan was the publication by the Trust of the first-ever *State of the Natural Environment in Derbyshire* report in 2010. It was based on more than a decade of data collected from many hundreds of LOCAL WILDLIFE SITES, under the agreements originally set up by Pat Brassley in the 1980s.

Membership continued to grow well despite some harsh economic conditions and passed 14,000 in 2009. With junior membership of the Trust at an all-time high, spread across six Watch Club groups, and more than 500 people actively helping the Trust through volunteering, direct support for nature conservation in Derbyshire has never been higher.

Another landmark was achieved early in 2011, with the purchase by the Trust of nearly 200 acres of land just outside Ilkeston. This established the largest nature reserve in Derbyshire outside the Peak District, and one of the largest urban fringe reserves in the UK.

AN AMAZING 50 YEARS

So, after 50 years, the Trust's founding fathers (they were all male – with the notable exception of Miss Hollick) would have been amazed at the modern Trust. With an annual turnover now close to £2 million, a staff of nearly 40 and an established position as the county's leading non-statutory conservation organisation, they would surely reflect with satisfaction on the initiatives they took all those years ago.

Meanwhile, the pressures on wildlife and habitats continue to mount and new environmental problems keep emerging both locally and globally.

The Trust will continue to develop and to embrace new challenges, standing up for Derbyshire's wildlife, seeking to change people's attitudes to wildlife and encouraging them to play their part in looking after this wonderful, but increasingly fragile, county.

BY NICK BROWN
Nick Brown has worked for Derbyshire Wildlife Trust since 1979, initially as Development Officer, and finally as Education Manager. Now semi-retired, he still deals with the Trust's wildlife enquiries and also volunteers on the Derby Cathedral Peregrine Project, which he set up in 2005/06.

Willington – restored sand and gravel pits and one of Derbyshire's top birdwatching sites

CHAPTER 11

Devon

The decision to form a Devon Naturalists' Trust was taken at a meeting convened by two men on the 27th March 1961. One of those men was Philip Michelmore, then Managing Trustee of the Herbert Whitley Trust, owners of Paignton Zoo and Slapton Ley. The other was Henry George ('HG') Hurrell, a wealthy naturalist from Wrangaton and Chairman of the Devon Birdwatching and Protection Society. They corresponded with all the known and relevant local organisations, probably – and very sensibly – to avoid local toe-treading. The core of those who came together agreed to form a committee to see through the process of gaining charitable status and becoming a company limited by guarantee.

The spirit in which they gathered is perhaps best captured in the words of Owen Duke Hunt, a marine scientist working for International Paints in Brixham. "I do feel there is a need for a central coordinating body in this county for at present there is no common meeting ground for existing sectional problems. Piecemeal effort cannot exert the influence that could be brought to bear by centralised action. There is no lack of problems and it seems to me that nature in Devon, as elsewhere, is being threatened as much in the heart of the countryside itself as in the encroachments of urban development and non-agricultural industry. The transformations that are taking place in agriculture (I include forestry here) under the growing influence of the engineer, chemist and accountant are changing the environment at an ever increasing rate. The cause of conservation in Devon will need all the help it can get and I believe it could get more from a better organisation of voluntary effort".

What the founding fathers also established was an enduring vision of a Devon, in which wildlife is plentiful, varied and widespread, where its future is secure and where its benefits are valued and enjoyed. It's a vision that still guides the Trust to this day.

LANDSCAPE FEATURES

Devon is the third biggest county in England. It is about 60 miles from the North Foreland to Prawle Point and another 60 miles from Lyme Regis in the east to the north-west coast, just south of Hartland Point. It is the only county to have two separate coastlines. Devon straddles the geological boundary between Palaeozoic Britain and all that is younger, a fifth of it lying east of that boundary which, very roughly, follows the River Exe.

The whole of Dartmoor and the western third of Exmoor – both National Parks – lie within the county. They provide its highest land, supporting moorland and blanket bog, with much of it common land. They also have large enclosures of rough grazing and, in the wider valleys, networks of smaller meadows and arable fields,

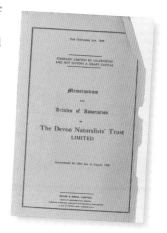

Opposite: Marsh fritillary at the Trust's Dunsdon National Nature Reserve
Right: The Trust's Articles of Association, 1962

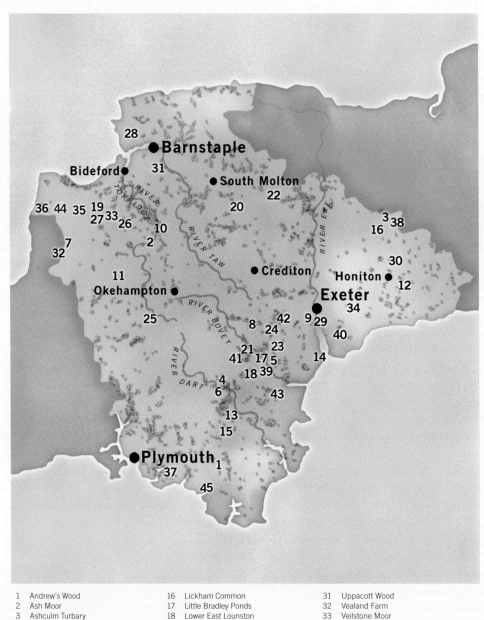

1	Andrew's Wood	16	Lickham Common	31	Uppacott Wood
2	Ash Moor	17	Little Bradley Ponds	32	Vealand Farm
3	Ashculm Turbary	18	Lower East Lounston	33	Veilstone Moor
4	Blackadon	19	Mambury Moor	34	Venn Ottery
5	Chudleigh Knighton Heath	20	Meshaw Moor	35	Volehouse Moor
6	Dart Valley	21	Mill Bottom	36	Marsland
7	Dunsdon	22	Rackenford and Knowstone Moors	37	Warleigh Point
8	Dunsford	23	Ruggadon Middlepark	38	Clayhidon Turbary
9	Exe Reed Beds	24	Scanniclift Copse	39	Bovey Heathfield
10	Halsdon	25	Sourton Quarry	40	Bystock
11	Halwill Junction	26	Stapleton Mire	41	Emsworthy
12	Hawkswood	27	Stowford Moor	42	Woodah Farm
13	Higher Kiln Quarry	28	Swanpool Marsh	43	Wolborough Fen
14	Inner Warren	29	The Old Sludge Beds	44	Meresfelle
15	Lady's Wood	30	The Rough	45	South Efford

Map of Devon Wildlife Trust nature reserves

with oak woodland on the steepest slopes. "The land between the moors" is largely on the heavy clays of the Culm Measures, where "green things are hammered by the west wind on the anvil of the yellow clay". It is a region of small farms, much hedgerow oak and sizeable areas of 'rhos' pasture, as the Welsh would have it.

South of Dartmoor is the South Hams, which is still possibly the most agriculturally-rich landscape in the county. Much hedge removal from the 1960s onward modified a pattern of fields, then little changed since medieval times. East of the Exe lies a dissected plateau, whose tops bear a flint and quartzite gravel, supporting areas of lowland heath. Between these islands of common land, broad valleys are home to sizeable farms where, in the 1960s, dairying and arable cropping vied for supremacy.

The south-western climate is ideal for grass growing – mild and damp with an extended growing season. Grazing is critical to the maintenance of Devon's moor and heath, both in the hills and on the coast. The same climatic influence demands the right combination of sheep, cattle and ponies – in adequate numbers – to sustain the vegetation mosaic at its optimum. Skilled stockmen are also necessary, to provide and manage those animals.

FIRST RESERVES

It took the founding fathers until November 1962 to set up the Trust as a company limited by guarantee and to gain charitable status. By 16th May 1963 – the date of the Trust's first public meeting to canvas support at St Luke's College, Exeter – Lord Roborough had agreed to be the Trust's first President, and 'HG' had been elected Chairman. Soon after, Dr Tom Wallace took up the Secretary's baton, and Ian Mercer became Assistant Secretary. These secretarial arrangements stayed in place until 1968, when the Trust could afford a paid secretary.

By 1964 – a momentous year – the Trust had adopted the dipper as its emblem and changed its name to the Devon Trust for Nature

Lady's Wood – the Trust's first reserve and a dormouse haven. Also notable for a number of bat species and dazzling displays of bluebells in the spring

Conservation. It had also acquired its first nature reserve, Lady's Wood, ten acres of hazel, oak and ash coppice-with-standards near South Brent. Donated by the Trust Chairman – HG Hurrell – it was, and still is, a dormouse haven.

A small flush of reserves followed. The Society for the Promotion of Nature Reserves (the Society) owned an abandoned limestone quarry at Buckfastleigh (NATURE RESERVES OWNED BY THE SOCIETY) with a cave system containing the richest collection of Pleistocene mammal fossils in the UK and a roosting colony of greater horseshoe bats – still there, and still rare. The Pengelly Cave Research Centre was already established there, and the Society wanted a local tenant to oversee it. Hence it was leased to the Trust at a peppercorn rent.

Miss Rogerson of Lustleigh gave the Trust a small wood alongside the disused railway line from Moretonhampstead to Newton Abbot. And CHRISTOPHER CADBURY (by now a life member) offered the Trust a lease of 40 acres at Welcombe and Marsland Mouth on the north coastal end of the Devon/Cornwall border, with a cottage for a warden. This was nicely balanced in Devonian

Dart Valley nature reserve – here old oak sessile woods tumble down to meet the River Dart

geography by Sir Charles Cave's offer to let the cliff at Weston Mouth near Sidmouth to the Trust.

All these acquisitions were reported in the Trust's Annual Report for 1963–64, which itself was reproduced in the first volume of the *DNT Journal* published in June 1964. It was the beginning of a 20-year run for a journal which achieved national acclaim among the Trust movement. It was the brainchild of Ken Watkins, a self-made millionaire and amateur wildlife photographer whose contribution to the early history of this Trust can never be gainsaid.

FIRST PAID STAFF

Watkins was earthy as well as thoughtful. He drove a low, yellow Ferrari around the county, spying out potential nature reserves (most of them woods). He hated meetings with more than one other person present – because he was very deaf. When the Trust (at Watkins' behest) decided it could afford a full-time paid officer, he insisted on conducting his own separate interview of the candidates.

In the summer of 1968, the dapper Freddie Thomas (ex-Wing Commander and RAF lightweight boxing champion) was appointed Executive Officer. He took charge of the Trust's then headquarters at 2 Pennsylvania Road, Exeter. Using his charm to engage wealthy widows, he laid the groundwork for legacies of close on £2 million over the ensuing years! He was also handy with an Allen scythe in deep bracken.

In 1970, the Trust (now with 1,000 members) greeted European Conservation Year with a Conservation Officer in place – the first full-time scientist to be employed by a Wildlife Trust. Soon after her appointment, Pat Smith completed (with

Fred G Wheeler) a conservation plan for Estover – a planned urban extension in Plymouth. They followed that with a plan for the Exe valley floor within the Exeter city boundary. These conservation plans contributed to both cities' development plans and changed for ever the Trust's (until then) exclusively rural outlook. In 1973, the Trust leapt into the landowning class on a bigger scale than ever before, when it bought the freehold of Venn Ottery Common in east Devon. This enabled it to get a foothold on these intriguing pebblebeds. Hitherto its reserves had been small and either gifted or leased.

SPLIT VIEWS

Throughout most of its history, the Trust has been on the lookout for suitable headquarters. In the mid-1970s, Major Hole of Parke, Bovey Tracey – a Lord of the Manor of the old school – let it be known that he was going to leave his estate to The National Trust and was minded to indicate in his memorandum of wishes that they should offer to lease it to the Trust.

This sparked off a soul-searching debate which split the Trust's central hierarchy down the middle. There was a strong view that creating a massive interpretation centre there would 'make the Trust'. The counter-argument was that the investment and work involved would suck all the Trust's cash and energy into itself, with the Trust's real purpose lost for sheer lack of other resources.

In the end, those against the proposal won – but only just – by the casting vote of the Chairman of Council on the day. The Trust declined to take up the offer of a lease. Ken Watkins favoured Parke, but also failed to persuade Council to take on yet another wood and soon left to set up the Woodland Trust.

KEY CHARACTERS

Watkins had involved the Trust in Dunsford Wood in the Teign Valley, to which local coach companies ran 'pick your own daffodils' excursions. Dunsford WI (marshalled by the redoubtable

Mrs Charmian Worsley) turned out every day of the daffodil season to patrol and accost all who seemed inclined to pick. By 1975, the law came to the Trust's aid, but the message – leave them for others to enjoy – produced a result beyond the dreams of even the locals.

Worsley stayed with the Trust from then on. She joined the Council and eventually became Honorary Treasurer and, in the mid-1980s, Chairman of Council. She was a remarkable lady, brooked little argument and didn't suffer fools.

In 1977, Freddie Thomas was headhunted by the Society and went to work at their headquarters, near Lincoln and Pat Brassley (*née* Smith) took on the combined roles of Executive and Conservation Officer. However, it proved a job too far and, in 1978, Brassley returned to her pure conservation function with the DERBYSHIRE TRUST. Stephen Wright was appointed Executive Secretary and Caroline Steel became Conservation Officer.

In 1985, Lord Roborough, the Trust's President since its creation in 1961, decided to stand down and was unanimously appointed patron at that year's Annual General Meeting (AGM). In 1986, Ian Mercer was appointed President having chaired the Council of the Trust from 1969 to 1971, and again for ten years from 1975. At the AGM in 1987, after a long debate, the members voted to change the name of the Trust to the Devon Wildlife Trust.

Above: Ian Mercer (left) and Mrs Charmian Worsley (right)

EXPANDING INTO THE 21ST CENTURY

The second quarter century of the Trust's history was shaped by the decision to employ a full-time professional leader in the form of Paul Gompertz, a thespian charmer with the gift of communication and a wonderful voice. At the point when a decision to employ a Director was taken, the Trust had a staff of six, a membership of about 1,500 and a turnover barely touching six figures. Twenty-five years later, it employs more than 60 people, has a membership of around 34,000 and spends some £2.5 million a year in pursuit of its enduring vision. Achieving the change was a turbulent process!

Two conservation campaigns dominated the period. In 1989, the Trust became aware of the alarming loss of the wet, acid Culm grasslands of north Devon and began a project to restore this important habitat. The work goes on, but now – under the banner of Working Wetlands – has a team of nine conservation staff and a multi-million pound budget.

The Trust's early 1980s involvement in Wembury Voluntary Marine Conservation Area was its first real taste of marine conservation. It went on from

there to become one of the Trust movement's pioneers in this area of work. This was largely due to its engagement from the late 1980s in a campaign to protect the reefs of Lyme Bay from the damage done by scallop dredging. That battle was finally won in 2008 when 60 square miles were closed to the process.

The search for a suitable headquarters continued to occupy the Trust. As it grew, it needed larger and larger premises. In 1993, a legacy of more than £1 million from Mrs Shirehampton (thanks go to Freddie Thomas) allowed the Trust to buy a large house in Exeter, where it stayed for 13 years. The search for more suitable premises – a home rather than just offices – continued. Finally, in 2007, seven years after opening negotiations and thanks to another large legacy (from Mrs Temple-Cotton), the Trust moved into Cricklepit Mill, Exeter, above the quay alongside the River Exe – a home at last.

During this time the Trust acquired other properties in the county. In 2002, it purchased part of a north-western site at Cookworthy, now home to its Working Wetlands team. Then, in 2007, former Honorary Treasurer, Derrick Taylor, left the Trust Woodah, a small farm on the edge of Dartmoor in the Teign valley. This has already become the base for all the Trust's nature reserves activities, and its 140 acres, varied habitat and spectacular views, open up all sorts of interesting possibilities for the future.

The 1990s were a period of rapid growth presided over as Chair of Council by Peter Stevens, Chief Executive of Paignton Zoo, who succeeded Mrs Worsley. Such rapid growth was not without its difficulties, as it changed the organisation's working balances and required it to become a well-run business. The days when it was run and manned by volunteers were left behind, though it is still shaped by the legacy of its origins.

Paul Gompertz (left) with Sir David Attenborough and HRH The Prince of Wales on a Culm grassland site, 1992
Above right: The Trust's *Lyme Bay Reefs* report, 2008

TWO RIVERS VICTORY

The biggest battle in this period was the Two Rivers campaign, which opposed an application by a local clay company to move the confluence of the Rivers Bovey and Teign. Pursued all the way to public inquiry by a partnership of the Trust, the Environment Agency and local residents, the application was seen off and the two rivers were allowed to go their ways.

That the Trust secured its status as an 'Investor in People' in 2000 reflects its transition from rapid growth in the preceding ten years to a well-run business in the first decade of the 21st century. Geoff Hearnden, who became Chair of Council in 1995 and continued in the role until 2005, spanned these two phases, passing the mantle to Andrew Cooper in 2005. Cooper has overseen the modernisation of the Trust's governance which has just been completed.

Since the Trust's 2007 move to Cricklepit Mill, the economic downturn has been a constraining factor, though the Trust continues to grow in influence and confidence. There have been successes too. In April 2010, South West Water decided to invest £1.1 million over five years into the Trust's Working Wetlands project, thus producing the largest single grant or sponsorship ever secured by the Trust. This project is restoring and reconnecting large areas of Culm grassland, working together with more than 1,000 local farmers and other partners such as the Forestry Commission, South West Water and Natural England.

With a membership of around 34,000, a dedicated and professional staff, and an influx of new, well-qualified Trustees, the Trust remains in a position to move forward with confidence.

BY PROFESSOR IAN MERCER CBE
Professor Ian Mercer was appointed Secretary of Devon Wildlife Trust when it was founded 50 years ago and has played a pivotal role ever since, including two spells as Chair of the Board of Trustees. He was appointed President in 1986. An eminent conservationist, he was awarded a CBE in 1996 for services to the environment in Wales.

Lyme Bay Reefs

CHAPTER 12

Dorset

"The County of Dorset is small, but yet so varied in its configuration as to present an epitome of the scenery of southern England". So wrote Sir Frederick Treves, one of Dorset's famous sons, in his 1914 *Highways and Byways in Dorset*. Dorset, with an area of some 1,000 square miles, has long been known for its diverse landscape and its biological richness. The ten-kilometre grid square encompassing Wareham and Corfe Castle, in the north of the Isle of Purbeck, contains the greatest number of species of vascular plant compared with any other similar square in the British Isles. The biological diversity of the county, which stems from its diverse geology, is now recognised in the designation of the Jurassic Coast – a UNESCO World Heritage Site of unsurpassed scenery and geological interest – which extends along the Dorset and east Devon coastline.

The hinterland of the county is dominated by a central outcrop of chalk, which crosses the county from north-east to south-west with high points such as Hambledon Hill, Bulbarrow and Eggardon. To the east of the chalk lie younger, Tertiary deposits. The so-called Poole Basin is the westernmost extension of the Hampshire Basin. Here the landscape is dominated by sandy, acid soils and heathlands; the Egdon Heath of Thomas Hardy. To the north and west of the chalk downs lie older strata which form the Marshwood Vale to the west and the Blackmore Vale to the north, which are pastoral in character.

The post-war years saw the landscape of Britain change, as urban development and its associated infrastructure expanded. Agriculture, and the ways in which the land and livestock were managed, similarly changed and expanded. The heaths of east Dorset which, in the mid-18th century, extended over some 40,000 hectares, had been reduced to about 10,000 hectares by 1960. The losses of chalk downland were even more drastic. The permanent grassland on the downs was converted to arable farming.

EARLY NATURALISTS

The richness of Dorset has long been recognised not only for its flora and fauna, but also for the numbers of distinguished naturalists produced by the county. James Charles Dale (1791–1872) was one of the foremost field entomologists of the 19th century, adding the Lulworth skipper to the British butterfly list in 1832. The Reverend Octavius Pickard-Cambridge was, in his time, the world's foremost authority on spiders and a correspondent of Charles Darwin. In the 1930s, Dorset was the location for the plant geographer, Professor Ronald Good's pioneering research project, which involved the processing of species lists from more than 7,000 stands of vegetation; and all this before computers!

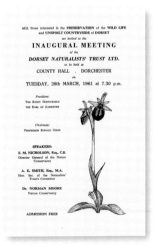

Opposite: Adder's Plot – unimproved grassland at Kingcombe Meadows. Right: Inaugural Meeting poster, 1961

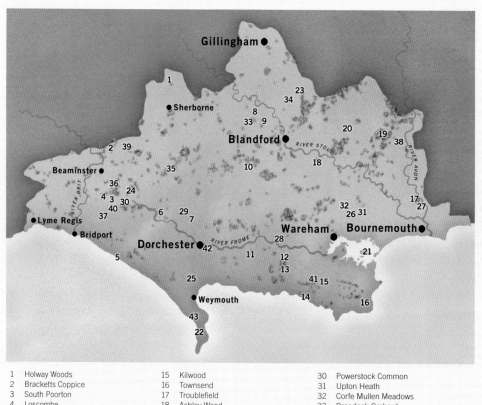

1	Holway Woods	15	Kilwood	30	Powerstock Common
2	Bracketts Coppice	16	Townsend	31	Upton Heath
3	South Poorton	17	Troublefield	32	Corfe Mullen Meadows
4	Loscombe	18	Ashley Wood	33	Broadoak Orchard
5	West Bexington	19	Sutton Holms	34	Collyer's Brook
6	Nunnery Mead	20	Sovell Down	35	Hendover Coppice
7	Haydon Hill	21	Brownsea Island/Villa Wildlife Centre	36	Michael's Peace
8	Girdlers Coppice	22	King Barrow Quarries	37	Peascombe
9	Mill Ham Island	23	Fontmell Down	38	Bugdens Meadows
10	Greenhill Down	24	Kingcombe Meadows and Centre	39	Hibbitt Woods
11	Tadnoll and Winfrith Heath	25	Lorton Meadows and Centre	40	King's Lane Community Orchard
12	East Stoke Fen	26	Beacon Hill Urban Wildlife Centre	41	Stonehill Down
13	Coombe Heath	27	Sopley Common	42	All Saints Wildlife-Friendly Garden
14	Purbeck Marine Wildlife Reserve and Fine Foundation Marine Centre	28	Higher Hyde Heath	43	Chesil Beach Centre
		29	Brooklands Farm Conservation Centre		

Map of Dorset Wildlife Trust nature reserves

INAUGURAL MEETING

In the post-war years, the changes in the landscape led to concern among naturalists in the county that wildlife was fast-disappearing and that the existing organisations were not well equipped to respond. Under the sponsorship of the Dorset Natural History and Archaeological Society, an independent committee was formed with the Earl of Ilchester as its President, Professor Ronald Good as its Chairman, and Miss Helen Brotherton as the Honorary Secretary. A notice was published proposing that a Dorset Naturalists' Trust be set up. It continued,

"those who genuinely desire to preserve the natural features of the county must take positive action to safeguard them". Founder members were invited to join the proposed Trust for an annual subscription of £1, or £15 for life membership. The invitation concluded with an exhortation with a fine Churchillian ring, "the need is urgent and the task extensive, and positive action is necessary if the objects of the Trust are to be achieved".

The inaugural meeting, held in March 1961 in Dorchester, was addressed by MAX NICHOLSON – who by then had succeeded CYRIL DIVER as

Director General of the Nature Conservancy. Diver was also a founder member of the Trust, who, in the 1930s, had initiated and led one of England's foremost ecological surveys on the Studland Peninsula at the mouth of Poole Harbour – the South Haven Peninsular Survey – which became a classic piece of fieldwork. Also speaking at the inaugural meeting were TED SMITH, Secretary of the Society for the Promotion of Nature Reserves' (the Society) Naturalists' Trust's Committee and a leading figure in the LINCOLNSHIRE TRUST. The Trust was eagerly formed with 306 founder members, of which 71 were life members. The first newsletter, issued in July 1961, reported that negotiations were already in hand to safeguard several important areas.

Left to right: David Attenborough, Pam White, Kevin Cook and Helen Brotherton

RESERVES

The energy of the Trust, which largely came from its Honorary Secretary, Helen Brotherton, was soon apparent. The Trust's second newsletter in February 1962 announced the lease of the Trust's first reserve – a small area of wet grassland in Purbeck and one of only two known sites in Britain for viper's grass. On another front, the Trust successfully challenged an application for planning permission to build a petrol station on land adjacent to the newly-opened Portland Bird Observatory. This established the Trust's long-held, high and professional reputation in the field of planning and development control.

At the same time as founding the Trust, Brotherton was involved in saving Brownsea Island in Poole Harbour. The island came on to the market as a result of the death of its reclusive owner, Mrs Mary Bonham Christie, who had acquired it in 1927. Brotherton, who was a keen yachtswoman, had clandestinely explored Brownsea and so realised the importance of the island for wildlife. Using her formidable organisational skills, she secured the island for The National Trust and raised funds to provide an endowment to maintain the island – £100,000 was needed and Brotherton raised £10,000 in the first week alone. The subsequent arrangements for the island's

management gave the Trust a very fine, 250-acre reserve, including the lagoon – a superb area for waders, wildfowl and breeding terns.

Holding nature reserves was at that time considered the principal means by which conservation objectives could be achieved. In later years, the centrality of the idea of protected sites has weakened in conservation philosophy and practice. Nevertheless, over much of its life, the Trust has steadily acquired reserves as a means of safeguarding precious sites.

WOODLAND RESCUE

Brackets Coppice in west Dorset was another early reserve which was acquired fortuitously. Ronald Good had invited Brotherton down to west Dorset to visit the site of the rare spring snowflake. Good suggested a detour to view a particularly fine woodland. They were incensed to find that a large proportion of it had been felled by the Forestry Commission (FC) in preparation for the planting of conifers. Hasty negotiations, however, secured the remaining portion of the woodland as a reserve for the Trust. In the 1980s, the FC was obliged by the Government to sell off some of their holdings and the Trust was able to purchase the reserve outright.

By its tenth anniversary in 1971, the Trust had assembled a portfolio of 24 reserves. These included areas of heathland in the east of the county, calcareous grasslands and a number of coastal sites, as well as some quarries in Purbeck – habitat for a number of

Early spider orchid – adopted as the emblem of the Dorset Trust in 1962

rare bat species. Few of these early reserves were owned. Most were leased or secured through agreements with landowners. The first reserve to be owned by the Trust was Holway Coppice in the very north of the county on the Somerset border, which had been gifted to the Trust.

SILVER JUBILEE SUCCESS

Funds from a silver jubilee appeal in 1986 enabled the Trust to purchase two of its finest reserves, Brackett's Coppice and Powerstock Common, both in west Dorset. Soon after this, traditionally farmed land at Kingcombe came on the market. First attempts to raise the funds proved fruitless. But, at last, an appeal led by Brotherton succeeded. At auction, the Trust bought some 300 acres, while other lots were secured by Trust supporters. In particular, they secured farm buildings in which the Kingcombe Environmental Studies Centre was established. The Trust set about managing the area through heritage farming.

Further small areas have been added to the holding and this is now one of the country's finest

reserves forming the core of a substantial LIVING LANDSCAPE project, Pastures New – restoring species-rich grassland across west Dorset. In 2011, a merger of the Kingcombe Environmental Studies Centre and the Trust was concluded.

Today, the Trust manages 41 reserves covering an area of 1,300 hectares. These represent the principal biotopes to be found in the county, including coastal features and, most importantly, marine habitats. The Purbeck Marine Reserve was the first of its kind in mainland Britain. As it has a substantial network of reserves, the Trust now tends to acquire reserves only when they complement the existing network and contribute to its Living Landscape policy.

INFLUENTIAL FORCE

From the very start, the Trust sought to influence policy and decision-making – not just locally within Dorset, but nationally. Two issues were prominent in the early years – toxic chemicals and human population growth. The publication of Rachel Carson's *Silent Spring* was hugely influential at this time. The Trust's second newsletter in February 1962 highlighted the dangers to wildlife, particularly to birds, from the use of chemical pesticides, and the Trust's representations to the Ministry of Agriculture to restrict their use. Later newsletters gave full details of the effects of these chemicals, asking members to send in dead birds for analysis.

Ladybird spider – only found in Britain on the heathlands of Dorset

Concern for national, if not international, issues was evident at the Trust's tenth Annual General Meeting in July 1971, when a group of members formally raised the issue of human over-population. No punches were pulled; the control of human populations, it was maintained, was the single most important issue facing conservationists. The meeting resolved to leave the matter with the Council and, in the event, it decided to raise the issue with the Society as the national body. That so fundamental an issue was debated at an Annual General Meeting reflects the tenor and the aspirations of the Trust at the time.

MARINE CONSERVATION

Another early, and groundbreaking, achievement for the Trust was the publication of a series of reports entitled *Studies in Conservation*. The first of these, published in the summer of 1974 to national acclaim, was *Marine Conservation in Dorset* – the blueprint for the Trust's pioneering achievements in marine conservation. The study summarised the results of at least two years survey work on the marine resources of the county and proposed the setting up of reserves, both to protect the marine flora and fauna and to educate the public. It also stimulated the other Trusts in the south-west of England to work together in achieving marine conservation. In 1978, the Trust established a reserve in Kimmeridge Bay. This was made possible through voluntary agreements with a variety of users, including the Smedmore Estate, fishermen, yachtsmen, divers, anglers and many other 'interested parties'; a considerable achievement by all those involved. A highly successful visitor centre that welcomes the public, as well as school and college groups, was opened in 1980. It was rebuilt and expanded in 2003 as the Fine Foundation Marine Centre. More recently, information collected by volunteer divers for the Trust, supported by a seabed mapping project, led to the proposal to designate Studland to Portland a Marine Special Area of Conservation (SAC) – protected under European law.

Surveying underwater habitats at Kimmeridge

Wildlife Conservation in the Poole District and Poole Harbour was the second of the *Studies in Conservation* series, followed by a third focusing on the Avon Valley, Bournemouth and Christchurch. The Poole Harbour study proposed conservation policies on the whole harbour, focusing particularly on protecting its southern part. These policies, which remain influential today, were particularly important when the Wytch Farm oil field was developed in the 1980s.

From its beginnings, the Trust has always sought good relations with the farming community. Many prominent landowners and farmers were among the founders of the Trust. One of these, Mrs Angela Hughes who farmed in the Blackmore Vale, was a leading figure in the groundbreaking Silsoe Conference on FARMING AND WILDLIFE held in Bedfordshire in 1969. Hughes recognised that a follow-up conference was needed showing that it was possible to farm, as she did, in a way beneficial to its wildlife. The following year, she organised the second national conference based at Weymouth College with site visits to her own farm. Ten years later, in 1980, she organised a further conference, attended by some 225 delegates to assess the progress on her farm.

VOLUNTEER EFFORT

Throughout the life of the Trust, there has been a strong emphasis on volunteering. Helen Brotherton believed in this and expected a similar level of commitment from others. It seems surprising today that, for the first 16 years of its life, the Trust was run from Brotherton's house in Canford Cliffs. The demands of its flagship reserve on Brownsea meant that in 1969 a paid warden for the reserve was appointed. This remained the Trust's only paid employee until 1973 when the first Conservation Officer was appointed. By 1977, the Trust needed office accommodation and offices were rented from the Bournemouth Natural Science Society in central Bournemouth. Soon afterwards, the Trust appointed a full-time paid Administrative Officer. The office was supported by a team of volunteers, with reserves managed by reserve committees. In the early years, the Council, the Scientific Committee and the Publicity Committee were, in effect, the Trust staff.

BOOST TO RESERVES MANAGEMENT

In 1985 the Trust, with funding from BP, appointed a Reserves Manager. This appointment saw considerable progress in the management of its reserves and the Trust was able to take advantage of Government EMPLOYMENT SCHEMES, such as

Higher Hyde Heath nature reserve

the Manpower Services Commission. These enabled the Trust to have a team of up to 40 working on the management of its reserves. This growth required further office accommodation, which was acquired in Dorchester in 1988. The conservation work of the Trust was located in Dorchester, while the central administration remained in Bournemouth.

Having been founded as the Dorset Naturalists' Trust in 1961, by its silver jubilee in 1986 it was felt that a new name was required. Attitudes and aspirations had changed and the Trust became the Dorset Trust for Nature Conservation. Whilst this still remains the Trust's formal name, its operating name changed in 1994 to the Dorset Wildlife Trust, in line with the other Trusts, countrywide.

Through these years, Helen Brotherton, although titled Honorary Secretary, was in effect the Director of the Trust. In 1986, she decided to stand aside and became Chairman, but still continued to direct the Trust. Eventually, in 1990, she became President and a new Chairman was elected who continued effectively to be the Director. However, it was becoming increasingly evident that the Trust was being held back by the lack of both a suitable headquarters and a full-time Director. While, from the mid-1970s, the Trust resolved to find a permanent headquarters, lack of funds meant both projects were put on hold. Eventually, in 1995, almost 35 years after its formation, the Trust appointed its first Director. Meanwhile, the search continued for a headquarters. After several unsuccessful attempts, a suitable property at Brooklands Farm at Forston, just to the north of Dorchester, was bought. Since then, further expansion of the Trust has resulted in the establishment of sub-offices at Beacon Hill near Poole – thanks to significant funding from the Landfill Tax Credit Scheme to develop the Trust's activities in the urban area, an education centre at Lorton Meadows near Weymouth, and a west Dorset office at Kingcombe.

FUNDING OPPORTUNITIES

With the acquisition of a permanent headquarters and the appointment of a Director, the Trust

Well over a thousand avocets overwinter on Browsea Island each year

began a period of substantial growth that coincided with many funding opportunities from Government schemes, particularly agri-environment programmes. Other funding opportunities came from the Landfill Tax, the National Lottery, from Government agencies such as English Nature, the Environment Agency and local authorities, as well as from charitable trusts. This period of growth was not without its problems. The Trust experienced an imbalance between restricted and unrestricted income. Part of the solution was a membership recruitment drive, which generated a greater proportion of unrestricted income.

DORSET'S LARGEST MEMBERSHIP CHARITY
In 1961, the founding membership of the Trust was a little more than 300. By 1964 membership had grown to 1,000, by 1971 to 2,000 and by 1974 to 3,000. By the millennium, membership had risen to about 8,000 and as a result of active recruitment campaigns, membership rose rapidly to 25,000 by 2008 and has been maintained at

approximately this level since. The Trust's growth into a substantial business has been reflected in the growth of its staff and in the structures required for its operation. The small number of staff in 1986 seemed adequate for those times, but the growth of the last 15 years has necessitated an increase in staff numbers to almost 80. Staff were previously organised into conventional teams dealing with, for example, reserves, conservation and planning issues, marketing, administration and finance. The Trust's adoption of the LIVING LANDSCAPES AND LIVING SEAS approach has resulted in a reorganisation of the Trust on a geographical basis within the county. The Trust is now the biggest membership charity in Dorset.

BY NIGEL WEBB
Nigel Webb is Chairman of the Dorset Wildlife Trust, which he joined in 1970. A research ecologist, he joined the Nature Conservancy at Furzebrook in 1967. He is a leading authority on the ecology and conservation of European heathlands.

CHAPTER 13

Durham

The origins of the Durham Trust date back to 1963, with the launch of the joint Northumberland and Durham Naturalists' Trust. For the next eight years, while being part of the same overall body, each of the two counties operated its own conservation committee, addressing differing concerns. Foremost amongst those in Durham was the plight of Upper Teesdale where, amidst huge national publicity, agreement had been obtained for the building of the COW GREEN reservoir. This resulted in the flooding of sections of the unique plant communities in that area. Many were species with extremely restricted distribution, including several noteworthy 'arctic alpines' such as the spring gentian. While the conservation case was lost, there is no doubt it created a turning point in persuading people that concerted efforts were needed if other irreplaceable sites were not to suffer the same fate.

And yet, in those early days, a wider approach to conservation was already being advocated. In 1970, Barry Woodward, Secretary of the Durham County Conservation Committee, wrote, "For conservation to have any real meaning in the county, one has to think not only in terms of preserving plant and animal communities that are of value but also of making the opportunity for extending existing communities and creating new and appropriate habitats." This was quite a visionary approach suggesting conservation was already becoming more than just 'preservation'.

Opposite: Dark red helleborine – this orchid occurs in abundance at the best sites on the magnesian limestone, including Raisby and Bishop Middleham Quarry nature reserves
Right: The 'Durham argus' – a sub-species of the northern brown argus, found in the north of England

Active in those earliest years was Ted Hinton-Clifton, who had previously been involved with the LINCOLNSHIRE TRUST, before moving up to Durham. Along with DAVID BELLAMY and others, he took a lead role in the new Trust, a position he maintains today.

The joint Northumberland and Durham Trust was in existence for eight years. But, by 1970, it was clear that it was difficult having members from as far north as Berwick attending the same meetings as people from Darlington. A split between the county units was proposed. The inauguration of the two separate Trusts came about on 1st April 1971 – the fact that this was All Fools' Day was, one gathers, noted and disregarded! Hinton-Clifton recalls that, at this stage, Northumberland had more members, while Durham had more reserves.

DURHAM'S WILDLIFE ASSETS

Despite the scars of industry, which include deep and opencast coal mining, lead mining in the dales and magnesian limestone quarrying, the Durham area contains an impressive array of wildlife habitats. These range from the botanically-important areas of Upper Teesdale, the significant ornithological sites of the North Pennine moors in the west, wooded river valleys and coalfield lowlands in the centre, to the magnesian limestone plateau and the coast in the east. In wildlife terms, the magnesian limestone is highly important with 48 sites designated as Sites of Special Scientific Interest (SSSIs).

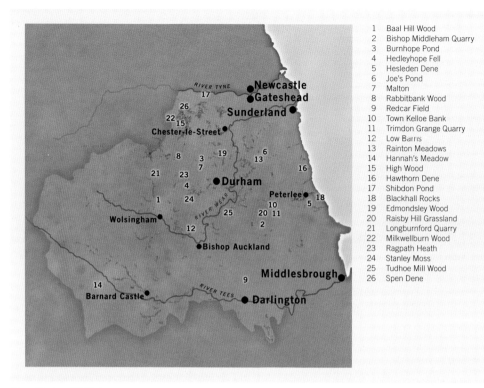

1	Baal Hill Wood
2	Bishop Middleham Quarry
3	Burnhope Pond
4	Hedleyhope Fell
5	Hesleden Dene
6	Joe's Pond
7	Malton
8	Rabbitbank Wood
9	Redcar Field
10	Town Kelloe Bank
11	Trimdon Grange Quarry
12	Low Barns
13	Rainton Meadows
14	Hannah's Meadow
15	High Wood
16	Hawthorn Dene
17	Shibdon Pond
18	Blackhall Rocks
19	Edmondsley Wood
20	Raisby Hill Grassland
21	Longburnford Quarry
22	Milkwellburn Wood
23	Ragpath Heath
24	Stanley Moss
25	Tudhoe Mill Wood
26	Spen Dene

Map of Durham Wildlife Trust nature reserves

Thrislington made conservation history in the 1980s when much of the SSSI was translocated in turves, each the size of a small car, to allow quarrying of the bedrock beneath. It has since become a National Nature Reserve. Close to the coast are the coastal denes – steep wooded valleys, formed by the sudden release of large amounts of glacial meltwater. The largest, Castle Eden Dene, is another of County Durham's six National Nature Reserves.

In 1971, Durham County Conservation Trust was legally incorporated, with Hinton-Clifton as Secretary, serving a small but dedicated Council of management. Key reserves already acquired included Low Barns at Witton-le-Wear – a former gravel-working site donated to the Trust by Tarmac, where volunteers planted thousands of young trees – and Hawthorn Dene, one of the best examples of wooded coastal dene in the county. The Trust's publications were confined to a small *Bulletin* that alternated with its *Newslink* – simply made up of duplicated foolscap pages. The editor, Brian

Unwin, was known for his passionate interest in watching seabirds and was instrumental in the setting up of Whitburn Bird Observatory.

As conservation activity increased, it became obvious that a permanent member of staff was needed to help coordinate both the Trust's conservation and administrative work. A Carnegie Trust (CARNEGIE FUND) grant awarded in January 1974 funded Julie Stobbs' (*née* Gaman) role as the Trust's first full-time paid officer. At that time, she was working under the energetic chairmanship of Dame Enid Russell-Smith, a one-time Deputy Secretary in the Ministry of Health (and a judo black-belt to boot!)

EXPANDING OFFICE AND STAFF
The year 1977 was a milestone, with the Trust setting up offices in Durham City. This coincided with the Trust applying to appoint staff under the Manpower Services Commission (MSC) Job Creation Scheme (EMPLOYMENT SCHEMES) and,

as a consequence, a larger office base became necessary. In July, the office moved from Highwood View which was Stobbs' home at the time, to 52 Old Elvet, Durham, where two rooms were leased from the – extremely Victorian – County Club.

An excellent team was appointed, led by Philip Masters, formerly ecologist with Washington Development Corporation. This greatly increased the Trust's range of activity, especially in education, publications, displays, conservation management and even geological conservation. One of the team was David Green, who had exceptional artistic and natural history skills; very sadly he was shot dead in India in 2004 while innocently sketching by a stream. He was given a green burial near Darlington and is remembered by seven black poplars propagated by Cliff Evans of the Trust's Darlington Group.

SURVEYING TAKES OFF

In 1979, the Trust received a grant from the Nature Conservancy Council enabling Mick Rebane's appointment as Conservation Officer. During his three years with the organisation, he undertook detailed botanical surveys of the SPEIs (Sites of Particular Ecological Importance).

Durham County Conservation Trust staff in 1977: back row (left to right) David Green, Richard Hobbs, Julie Gaman, Sheila Johnson, Frank Berner; front row (left to right) Malcolm Henderson, Philip Masters, Ian Lancaster

Low Barns nature reserve, where damp alder woodland grows along the old course of the River Wear

County Durham, with its suite of SPEIs first listed in 1974, was one of the first counties to set up such a 'second-tier' site system, a fact which reflected well on the enthusiasm shown by County Council staff at that time.

In much of his survey work Mick was accompanied by Reverend Gordon Graham, the botanical recorder for the county and author of *The Vegetation and Flora of County Durham*. This was published by the Trust and the Flora Committee in 1988 and was one of the first floras to contain computerised distribution maps. In 1984, Rob Strachan, known to many as the author of the national *Water Vole Handbook*, was appointed to undertake a similar survey of second tier sites in the southern part of Tyne and Wear. In 1988, Tracy Gordon became the Trust's first Urban Wildlife Officer, splitting her time between the two boroughs of Sunderland and South Tyneside.

Conservation work continued apace, including reserve acquisition and management (most nature reserves had their own management committee composed largely of Trust members), commenting on planning applications and giving evidence at public inquiries. During the 1980s, there were several applications for opencast coal mining which went to appeal and the Trust was always prepared to support the County Council in its opposition. The three applications where the Trust gave evidence at public inquiries were all turned down. With few paid staff, the 1980s was the period of maximum involvement by volunteers, certainly in terms of serving on the Trust committees. The main conservation committees were the Scientific Advisory Committee (with many academics from Durham University), the Reserves Advisory Committee and the Conservation Policy Committee. The Trust's Education Committee ran the WILDLIFE WATCH activities and projects such as the inter-school nature quizzes – the final of which was shown on local television one year with David Bellamy as quizmaster.

BELLAMY BRAINCHILD

The input of Bellamy, who followed Sir James Steel and Lord Barnard as President (neither of whom ever missed an Annual General Meeting) can never be overstated. It was his brainchild to run the hugely successful Country and Forest Workshops, in conjunction with the Forestry

Commission at Hamsterley Forest. Two days over the spring bank holiday weekend provided all sorts of opportunities for people to engage actively in natural history and other countryside pursuits. 1983 saw a rather different venture: a passenger train was chartered on the Heritage Line from Darlington to Stanhope. Once again, it was the idea of Bellamy who acted as chief guide on the train journey and repeated his 'plodgey' nature trails in the River Wear, which had been so successful at Hamsterley.

Events of the time were held largely for fundraising, although most had an educational or social aspect too. There were flag days, book sales, the Trust dinner, ceilidhs, art exhibitions and the Hollinside At Home events hosted by the Vice Chancellor of Durham University, Professor Fred Holliday, who has since been knighted for his public service and environmental work. Stalls were held at the major agricultural shows and the contribution of the late Jack Moses as Honorary Sales Officer and his wife, Phyllis (now Hornsey), can never be overestimated.

DURHAM'S DAVIDS

As well as David Bellamy, several other Davids played a noteworthy role in those intermediate years. When SIR DAVID ATTENBOROUGH's tour of Trusts was arranged over two weeks in November 1985, the Durham Trust was one of 12 selected for a visit. The Durham Wildlife Appeal, managed by Harry Robinson, was launched at Lumley Castle by Attenborough and Bellamy. On the evening of 5th November, Attenborough, introduced by Bellamy, gave a brilliant illustrated talk at Sunderland Empire Theatre to a large audience. (Hopefully, some of those who attended the event had been persuaded to forgo more traditional activities thereby helping wildlife a little by not burning alive any hedgehogs hibernating in the base of bonfires!)

In 1987, the then Chair David Oldham – another David – walked the 200 miles of the Trust's boundary over some ten days, starting from the coast at South Shields, the constituency of the Trust's patron at the time, David Clark MP. He was

David Bellamy (front) and David Clark (left) bid farewell to David Oldham (right) as he sets off on his walk around County Durham in 1987

Wildflowers grow on the magnesian limestone along the Durham coastline

accompanied by his dog Jason and waved off by Clark and Bellamy. It was largely the result of Oldham's initiative, that in 1988 the Trust changed its name by 'special resolution' from the rather old-fashioned and ambiguous Durham County Conservation Trust to Durham Wildlife Trust, bringing it into line with almost all other Trusts.

BADGER AND BAT GROUPS BORN
In 1980, the Trust set up the Durham County Badger Group, and, in 1983, the Durham Bat Group was created; both of these groups are still active today. Other groups included the Durham Reptile and Amphibian Group (DRAG) led by Dave Green, John Durkin and Brian Banks, and the Durham Slug Group run for a few years by Noel Jackson and Brian Eversham. The policy of the Trust in its early years was to harness the scientific expertise that its diverse membership provided. As a result, many expert biologists have been involved with the Trust, and it is true to say that the academics serving on the Trust's Council

did not always see eye to eye, with dramatic resignations on occasions! The Trust has always been mindful of the need to publicise itself and this was boosted by the setting up of the Bowlees Visitor Centre in a disused Methodist Chapel in Upper Teesdale. It was formally opened in 1976, using the residue from the Upper Teesdale Defence Fund.

CHANGING AND GROWING
A management review in the late 1980s highlighted some major changes needed if the organisation was to grow in line with some of the UK's larger Trusts. An offer of two years sponsorship was received from British Coal Opencast Executive which, despite some concerns, the Trust's Council decided to accept.

Don Davis was appointed as Chief Executive and worked for the Trust for over two years. During this time, he organised the relocation of the Trust office from the increasingly cramped second floor of 52 Old Elvet, Durham, to the old farmhouse at Low Barns Nature Reserve at Witton-le-Wear. Moira Owen was appointed as the Trust's

Hedleyhope Fell – a mid-altitude heathland and home to skylark, snipe, lapwing and several rare plants

Conservation Director and the magazine *Durham Wildlife* became a glossier, A4-format magazine, replacing the earlier version which Stobbs used to edit and typeset herself.

In the 1990s several other changes in the organisation occurred. The Council appeared to become more relaxed than in the earlier days when the academic members were anxious to ensure that procedural matters were dealt with precisely. Richard Wood was appointed Chief Executive in 1992 and Steve Lowe replaced Moira Owen as Conservation Manager. Wood renewed relationships with many of the members, notably with Janetta Scurfield, a stalwart volunteer for many decades from the outset of the joint Trust.

Thus the 1990s and the early part of this century saw tremendous growth: there was a significant increase in annual turnover and expansion of work on the ground, particularly in reserve management. Northumbrian Water and its Environmental Director, Chris Spray, were a constant source of

help to the Trust. On 17th January 1997, Tony Blair, then leader of the Labour Party and shortly to become Prime Minister, visited Low Barns to find out more about the Trust's educational programme. The event was also attended by SIMON LYSTER, the Society's Director General, who gave an excellent talk – demonstrating a much better understanding of the issues involved than his political counterpart!

In 1998, the main office of the Trust moved to Rainton Meadows and staff numbers increased, benefiting from several new opportunities such as the National Lottery. In 2000, Steve Lowe left for NORTHUMBERLAND TRUST, saving a time-consuming commute across the River Tyne, and was replaced by Terry Coult.

BANKRUPTCY THREATENS

The first decade of the 21st century was one of mixed fortunes. Initially, the number of staff continued to grow and by 2006 the Trust was seen as a vibrant organisation with nothing wrong beyond a few cash flow problems. By and large, the Trust's Council was unaware that the organisation was living well beyond its means and matters came to a head in late 2006 when the Chief Executive, Wood, resigned. At that time, the Trust was nearly bankrupt and six other members of staff had to be made redundant.

The contribution during this difficult period of Chris Smith – who remains the Trust's Treasurer to today – can never be overestimated. He worked tirelessly and without payment to get the Trust back on the road financially. The Trustees had a serious wake-up call and quickly became much more aware of their individual responsibilities. The Trust staff, reduced initially by a quarter, worked hard to maintain levels of activity. Jim Cokill became Director, following the departures of Wood and Terry Coult, who, like Stobbs, went on to work for the County Council. Cokill brought in a much improved ethos of cooperative working amongst the staff and, as a result, morale improved considerably. The Executive Committee was revitalised and interactions between staff and Trustees became much more positive. In the difficult transition period of 2006–07, a huge contribution was also made by Judy Summerson, who worked in an unpaid capacity to maintain the Trust's role in education and WILDIFE WATCH activities. A leaner, more efficient Trust was soon back on track.

STRONGER THAN EVER
The Trust continues to undertake vital work for wildlife, sometimes working with the Durham Biodiversity Partnership, which shares the Trust's offices at Rainton Meadows. A full programme of work has included a range of species and habitat-targeted initiatives. Two examples are a highly successful Otters and Rivers project and the Coals to Voles project – the latter being the first-ever Heritage Lottery-funded post for a single species (HERITAGE LOTTERY FUND). Following Chris Packham's launch of the north-east's LIVING

LANDSCAPE project at the Sage, Gateshead, in March 2009, a number of significant landscape-scale initiatives have begun under the direction of Project Manager Jonathon Winn. And, more recently, exciting work has taken place using surveillance cameras for monitoring wildlife. This was highlighted by the inclusion of Low Barns nature reserve on BBC's *Countryfile* television programme in September 2010.

In the last couple of years, the Trust has benefited greatly from two sizeable legacies, which provided the resources to enable the July 2010 purchase of the new Milkwellburn Wood nature reserve in the Derwent Valley. The Trust now manages 26 reserves, covering a total of 655 hectares, of which 12 are designated as SSSIs. These range in size from the tiny 0.7-hectare fen wetland of Redcar Field, near Darlington, to the 202-hectare Hedleyhope Fell, one of the best examples of recovering mid-altitude heathland in the county.

It is with considerable confidence that the Trust can recognise that, without its existence, the wildlife needs of this part of north-east England would not have been so well-served during 40 years of such rapid and unprecedented environmental change.

BY JULIE STOBBS
'An ecologist by training and a conservationist by creed', Julie Stobbs became the first paid member of staff at the Trust in 1974, having previously been a volunteer. Initially appointed as Administrative Officer, she became Conservation Director, before her resignation in 1990. She later worked for Durham County Council, where she became its County Ecologist. She is now a Vice President.

CHAPTER 14

Essex

On 3rd October 1959, a gathering of concerned naturalists, including members of the Essex Field Club, met at County Hall, Chelmsford. The result was a resolution to form the Essex Naturalists' Trust. Growing pressures on land in urban Essex, adjacent to an ever-expanding London, caused concern that the habitat characteristics of lowland Essex would soon be lost forever. The aim of this embryonic organisation was to make a permanent contribution to the conservation of the county's wildlife. A strong rallying call from a new Trust might make the wider populace aware of the rapid changes happening in the Essex countryside, and the need for action.

Essex is a low-lying county. The undulating north-west is predominantly arable farmland and lightly inhabited, whilst the south-west, next to London and the southern Thames corridor, is becoming a continuous conurbation with development accelerating each year.

The threat to potential wildlife-friendly sites is intensifying. Development inland and along the Thames estuary continues apace and the extensive eastern coastline of estuaries, creeks and saltmarsh is under threat from the dual attacks of rising sea levels and sinking land.

SMALL BEGINNINGS

Geoff Pyman, a leading light in the Field Club was nominated as Chairman of the Formation Committee. Its first practical step was to recruit Colonel Sir John Ruggles-Brise, Lord Lieutenant of the County, as Patron and Reg Tutt as the first President.

Opposite: Each spring many people visit Fingringhoe Wick to hear its nightingales sing

A Certificate of Incorporation from the Board of Trade gave the emergent organisation the legal right to own or lease land. An inaugural meeting followed, and by the end of 1959 there were 110 members, 13 of whom were life members.

The rate of loss of sites of first-class scientific importance was causing concern and led to the setting up of a sub-committee to record all such remaining sites in the county. The Trust had the option of either trying to influence landowners and managers to look after these sites, or to lease or own the sites and manage them itself. The need for education, to change attitudes towards environmental matters, to be present at public inquiries and act as the 'caring' voice of Essex were also seen as vital.

The creation of new Essex towns like Basildon and Harlow with their influx of large populations, together with rural problems, prompted the Trust to accelerate its programme of acquiring nature reserves. The 125-acre disused gravel pit, Fingringhoe Wick, on the Colne estuary was purchased with a bank loan of £4,000 and was followed soon after by the lease of more than 600 acres of saltmarsh on Two Tree Island in the Thames estuary near Southend-on-Sea.

By the end of the 1960s, a further 11 reserves had been acquired. Ten were designated as SSSIs, covering 1,600 acres and representing all major habitats in Essex. Colne Point, a 683-acre shingle spit, was the Trust's largest reserve and remained so for many years. Many others were less than 50 acres and one was only three acres in size. Today, the Trust no longer takes on any reserve it is offered. A more strategic approach is adopted and sites are accepted only if they meet certain

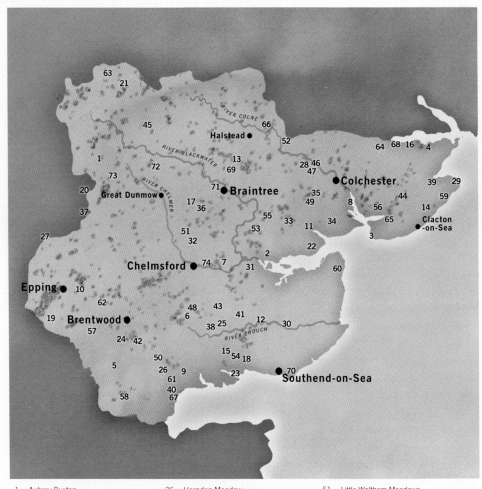

1	Aubrey Buxton	26	Horndon Meadow	51	Little Waltham Meadows
2	Chigborough Lakes	27	Hunsdon Mead	52	Sergeants Orchard
3	Colne Point	28	Iron Latch	53	Shut Heath Wood
4	Copperas Wood	29	John Walton and the Naze	54	Tile Wood
5	Cranham Marsh	30	Lion Creek and Lower Raypits	55	Tiptree Heath
6	Crowsheath Wood	31	Maldon Wick and Meadow	56	Alexander Reserve
7	Danbury Ridge	32	Newland Grove	57	Bedfords Park
8	Fingringhoe Wick	33	Oxley Meadow	58	Chafford Gorges Nature Park
9	Fobbing Marsh	34	Ray Island and Bonners Saltings	59	Barnes Spinney
10	Gernon Bushes	35	Roman River Valley	60	Bradwell Shell Bank
11	Abbotts Hall Farm	36	Sandylay and Moat Woods	61	Grove House Wood
12	Blue House Farm	37	Sawbridgeworth Marsh	62	Hawksmere Springs
13	Brookes Reserve	38	Shotgate Thickets	63	Harrison Sayer
14	Great Holland Pits	39	Skipper's Island	64	Hogmarsh
15	Little Haven	40	Stanford Warren	65	Howlands Marsh
16	Oakfield Wood	41	Stow Maries Halt	66	Loshes Meadow
17	Phyllis Currie	42	Thorndon Countryside Centre	67	Thameside Nature Park
18	Pound Wood	43	Thrift Wood	68	Wrabness
19	Roding Valley Meadows	44	Weeleyhall Wood	69	Rolfesland
20	Rushy Mead	45	West Wood	70	Shoebury Ranges
21	Shadwell Wood	46	Westhouse Wood	71	St Peter's Marsh
22	Tollesbury Wick	47	Lexden Gathering Grunds	72	Sweetings Meadow
23	Two Tree Island	48	Hanningfield Reservoir	73	Turner's Spring
24	Warley Place	49	Abberton Reservoir	74	Waterhall Meadows
25	Woodham Fen	50	Langdon Nature Reserve		

Map of Essex Wildlife Trust nature reserves

conservation and education criteria and if there are sufficient resources to manage them well.

MOVERS AND SHAKERS

Ken Crawshaw, a founder member, was General Secretary between 1962 and 1966 and Chairman between 1966 and 1967. He masterminded the conversion of Fingringhoe Wick into the magnificent nature reserve that it later became. Today the Wick boasts the highest concentration of breeding nightingales in the country. Paddy Lunt was the first warden of the Wick, followed in 1969 by Stewart Linsell as the first paid member of staff.

Vivian Robson took over as the Trust's Chairman from Crawshaw in 1967. He remained in this position until 1987. It was under his guidance that the Trust gathered momentum, expanding the size of its estate and membership and also its professional approach to the management and public face of the Trust.

MEMBERSHIP TAKES OFF WITH AIRPORT THREAT

Whilst reserve acreage had grown, by the end of the 1960s, membership stood at only 2,000. But European Conservation Year 1970 helped to raise public awareness and by the end of 1970 membership had grown to 2,500 with 21 reserves in the care of the Trust. Awareness increased further with the proposal to build London's third airport on Maplin Sands, a huge expanse of shifting sands and habitat for countless thousands of wildfowl off the Essex coast. The furore ended when Stansted was finally chosen and the battle switched inland – but still in Essex. Such high-profile cases helped membership of the Trust grow to 5,000 by 1973, and in 1981 the 10,000th member was recorded at Fingringhoe Wick Open Day.

In 1973, the Trust launched an appeal for £100,000 to acquire more reserves and create an administrative headquarters and public visitor centre at Fingringhoe Wick, the Trust's flagship reserve. This demonstrated a step change in the Trust's professionalism and approach to the public. The visitor centre was opened in September 1975. Financial support from the Countryside

Commission meant that areas on the reserve previously restricted to Trust members, were now opened up so the public could have access to all parts.

EXPANSION IN PAID STAFF

With the death in 1974 of the Trust's General Secretary, Stan Jermyn – author of the *Flora of Essex* – the Trust took a significant step in appointing Squadron Leader Philip Murton to the newly-created post of Administrative Officer. He took up the position in the new headquarters at Fingringhoe Wick. It was the beginning of increased recruitment of staff to work alongside many volunteers. New staff included a Trust Secretary and a Field Officer who covered conservation planning issues and advice for landowners. By the end of 1975, there were three full-time and two part-time staff.

Reserve gains in the 1980s included Roding Valley, 125-acres of grassland; Gernon Bushes, 79-acres of ancient woodland; Fobbing and Howlands marshes, 373-acres of coastal grazing marshes; and Skipper's Island in Hamford Water. This sunken island hosts rare sea hog's fennel, the food plant to the even rarer Fisher's estuarine moth.

In the early 1980s, membership reached a plateau of around 11,000. Greater publicity, the appointment of the first Membership Secretary, Gene Clifton, the overhaul of the Trust's displays and the membership bulletin – *Watch over Essex* –

Celebrating the 5,000th member at Fingringhoe Wick, 1973

were all employed to encourage renewed growth. Laurie Forsyth, the sixth warden of Fingringhoe Wick (and destined to remain so until retirement in May 2005), was instrumental in improving the Trust's publications. A successful appeal, Essex Wildlife Action Fund, was launched under the BRITISH WILDLIFE APPEAL, which raised both profile and major funding.

In the early hours of 16th October 1987, a hurricane struck the south-east of England, causing damage to much of the Trust's woodland estate. Some storm-felled trees were used in the building of the second Trust visitor centre at the Thorndon Country Park, near Brentwood, a partnership project with Essex County Council. A large nearby population provided both customers and volunteers to resource the new centre.

In 1987, after 20 years, Vivian Robson – 'Robbie' – stepped down as Chairman and Don Hunford (of badger fame) took over the reins. Dr David Corke published the prestigious *Nature of Essex* which raised public awareness of the Trust's work throughout the county. Sales were becoming an important source of unrestricted revenue, reaching £25,000 a year in 1989. For many years sales were administered from the front room of Gwen Foott's home. She was a founder member and long-time secretary of the Education Committee.

PROFESSIONAL APPROACH

Significantly, 1987 also saw the Trust's first Director, John Hall, herald a change in the management of the Trust. By 1989, the Trust looked after 75 nature reserves, it had 12,000 members, two visitor centres and 24 members of staff. It was time for professional staff to take on some of the functions previously filled by dedicated volunteers, expanding the work enormously in the process. For instance, a partnership between the Trust, Colchester Borough Council and Essex and Suffolk

Water, resulted in the 1990 opening of the Abberton Reservoir nature reserve and visitor centre.

The 1990s brought further radical changes. In 1990, the Trust changed its name to Essex Wildlife Trust. It was considered a more appropriate name and in line with the name being adopted gradually by all 47 sister Trusts under the umbrella of the Society. The badger logo of The Wildlife Trusts was also adopted by Essex. These changes emphasised the movement's approach – local action within a national perspective.

The Trust was still growing, so that by 1998 there were 38 staff employed. A concerted attempt to reach more of the huge population of Essex was undertaken. It included a change to a glossy full-colour magazine format for the Trust's journal, the appointment of a full-time Development Manager, and regular press statements and weekly sessions with the Trust Director on the BBC Essex's *Nature Trail*.

In 1997, there was another significant move to engage local communities when the Trust opened its fourth visitor centre at Langdon, with its 18 miles of footpaths and historic plotlands. Legacies were beginning to come in as the Trust's reputation grew. The 'Joan Elliot' legacy of more than £2 million enabled a two-year countywide search for a suitable arable farm site which could also become the Trust's new headquarters. Finally, with the help of many partners, the 700-acre Abbotts Hall Farm on

Building the Trust's second visitor centre at Thorndon Country Park
Above left: *Membership Bulletin*, Autumn 1981

land sloping down to the Salcott Creek, off the Blackwater Estuary, was acquired by the Trust.

BUILDING CORPORATE MEMBERSHIP

Meanwhile, membership numbers weren't increasing as had been hoped. A flair for recruitment was needed. Cliff Moore, initially a bank secondee, then the Trust's Corporate Manager, came forward to recruit business members. Recruitment of individuals was also promoted through events, shows and door-to-door marketing. This joint approach made staggering changes to membership numbers.

At the end of the millennium, the Trust had 16,000 members, 320 corporate members, 90 nature reserves covering 6,500 acres, five visitor centres and 40 staff. Each centre normally had three staff, a Centre Manager, Education Officer and Warden.

PROFITS FROM TRUST SUBSIDIARIES

With five large visitor centres open six days a week, each with a Trust shop, sales income increased under Steve Beary, Manager of the Trust's subsidiary company, Essex Wildlife Sales Ltd.

A second subsidiary company, Essex Ecology Services (EECOS), was set up to carry out ecological and wildlife surveys. Initially developed under Senior Ecologist, Adrian Knowles, and then under Neil Harvey as EECOS Manager, it has progressively increased its activities and profits. Both subsidiary companies have been performing well and pass over their profits to the Trust.

In 1999, a grant of £1.5 million was secured from the HERITAGE LOTTERY FUND (HLF), allowing work to improve access and entrance information on 51 of the Trust's owned reserves.

FLYING FLOCK

The Trust decided in 1999 to create a so-called 'flying flock' of sheep which would be available for short-duration grazing on small reserves – something not easy to achieve by employing commercial grazers. Based on Tollesbury Wick, the purchase of animals was sponsored, and by July 2000 numbers rapidly rose to 41 ewes, and later to more than 200 sheep and 40 cattle.

The saltmarsh, mudflats and shingle beaches at Colne Point nature reserve are home to rare and threatened species

With Hanningfield Reservoir visitor centre completed, energies turned to two further possible sites for visitor centres. One was Bedfords Park, a country park just north of Romford, owned by Havering Borough Council. The other was Chafford Gorges Nature Park, based on disused chalk quarries adjacent to the Dartford Thames' river crossing.

NEW 21ST CENTURY TEAM

Finances were key to a progressive expansion. As volunteer Treasurers, Dennis Ball and then Ken Shacklock had managed the Trust's finances, including the subsidiary companies' affairs, for many years. But the Treasurer's task was becoming too onerous for volunteers, and so the Trust agreed to employ a Deputy Director to take on the day-to-day financial management. In June 2000,

Green-winged orchids at Oxley Meadows

Lynne Meacock was appointed the Deputy Director and Bob Hills became the Honorary Treasurer. It was the beginning of the development of a very successful team under the chairmanship of Fred Boot.

Fred Boot led the streamlining of the Trust's governance by replacing a Council of 32 members with a 13-strong Board of Trustees and by revising the Trust's Memorandum and Articles of Association with the agreement of the Charity Commission. The new arrangements came into effect and the new slimline Board first met in September 2003. There were now ten Board meetings during the year. With improvements in the management of meetings, the new Chairman, Ray Tabor, was able to move matters along very smoothly.

FOOT-AND-MOUTH CHALLENGE

An outbreak of foot-and-mouth disease dominated 2001 and locked up the countryside. Inevitably, with its several farms, more than 80 reserves and five large visitor centres, the Trust started to lose income, as visitor numbers dwindled and staff movements were curtailed. The Trust, however, survived with its staff intact – although the flock of 600 sheep from Blue House Farm had to be slaughtered and burned.

At Abbotts Hall Farm, the house was converted into the Trust's new headquarters. The arable farm continued to grow profitable crops under a wildlife-friendly farming regime, and plans for a coastal realignment scheme went forward – at that time the largest realignment in Europe. WWF and the HLF also provided substantial support and the Environment Agency and Natural England offered to carry out the planning, breaching work and monitoring. After breaching the seawall in five places, November 2002 saw the official opening, with 1,400 guests enjoying a glorious day. The great and good were present, television cameras rolled, and the oyster fishermen and local sailing clubs joined in. One year later, the barley fields of 2002 had changed to a blaze of colour from the saltmarsh annuals that had sprouted during the intervening year.

CHELSEA SILVER MEDAL

A Trust garden, Morning Dew, designed by Stephen Hall, was awarded a silver medal in the 2003 Chelsea Flower Show. Soon after, on 7th June 2003, Bedfords Park opened as the Trust's sixth visitor centre, where the award-winning garden was rebuilt. Meanwhile, negotiations were under way for the Chafford Centre. Next to the Thames crossing, Chafford Hundred Development Company offered three large chalk quarries as a Trust nature reserve. After much negotiation the offer was accepted with funding of £1.8 million from the developer and other funders. The official opening of the Chafford Gorges nature park and the new visitor centre, built on the lip of the main Warren Gorge, was held in April 2006.

In 2003, a founder member, Gwen Foott, left the Trust a legacy of £200,000. The Trust agreed to use it to support education work with a long-awaited People and Wildlife Manager, initially Rachel Steward and latterly Becky Gibson.

Alongside this, major improvements were made by the reserves staff and volunteers to the ongoing management of the Trust's estate, with Neil Bedford heading up this work as Senior Reserves Manager.

The impending huge developments Government was pushing for along both sides of the Thames generated pressure on the Trust to join with the LONDON and KENT TRUSTS to employ a Thames

Gateway Officer, to seek best possible results from the developments. Funding was also secured for a Biodiversity Coordinator and Project Officer to join the Conservation Team led by Andy May and to tackle the county's Biodiversity Action Plan through the great work of the Essex Biodiversity Project.

The threat of seawater flooding on the Essex coast led the Trust, like their next door neighbour the RSPB, to build a counter wall across the Tollesbury Wick grazing farm, to protect at least part of the site from the rising sea levels.

In 2006, with staff numbers approaching 100, volunteers totalling 2,000 and membership at 35,000, the Trust reviewed its internal committee and staff structures to improve performance and line management.

Between 2009 and 2011, the Trust led on two targets in the Essex Local Area Agreement. First, on LOCAL WILDLIFE SITES, together with many Essex partners, it succeeded in bringing more than 530 of these sites (34 per cent) into positive conservation management. This is a fantastic achievement. Second, on Living Landscapes, the Trust engaged a wide range of organisations in restoring, recreating and reconnecting habitats on a landscape-scale. The Trust's work in this area continues alongside more recent developments in marine conservation under the Wildlife Trusts' collective Living Seas banner.

ONGOING SUCCESS

Under its present Chairman, Martyn Gill, the Trust continues to acquire both nature reserves and visitor centres. Recent examples include the very successful appeal to buy Tile Wood in Castlepoint, the lease of the massive landfill site at Mucking in Thurrock, the Trust's involvement in The Naze at Walton, the Ingrebourne Valley near Romford and Belfairs Park in Southend. The conservation advice offered by the Trust continues to grow and the Trust's work inspires people of all ages and backgrounds, encouraging many to take their own steps to protect wildlife for the future and for the people of Essex.

BY FRED BOOT
Fred Boot is a former Trustee and Chairman of Essex Wildlife Trust who has been deeply involved in the success of the Trust since 1967 – locally in Tiptree and Colchester, throughout Essex and nationally through The Wildlife Trusts, for which he is the recipient of the Christopher Cadbury Medal.

Pond-dipping at Fingringhoe Wick

CHAPTER 15

Gloucestershire

Gloucestershire is favoured by an extremely rich geology that supports six distinctive physical landscapes. From west to east the county is comprised of the steep wooded Wye Valley, the Forest of Dean, the undulating landscape of Over Severn, the Cotswold escarpment and plateau, and the Cotswold Water Park (Upper Thames gravels). The county also features the head of the River Thames near Cirencester and the meeting point of the freshwater Severn with the incoming tide at Maisemore weir. Below Gloucester, the Severn experiences the second highest tidal range of any river estuary in the world and generates spectacular bores on incoming spring high tides.

By 1961, significant economic investment in post-war agriculture, housing, manufacturing and transport systems were already manifest in fragmented wildlife habitat and declining species. The shrike, corncrake and otter, that had been characteristic features of pre-war Gloucestershire, were facing local extinction. It became obvious to the county's far-sighted naturalists that with weak and poorly implemented nature conservation legislation, if action were to be taken, it had to be local and urgent.

FIRST AGM

The encouragement and assistance of the Society for the Promotion of Nature Reserves (the Society) resulted in a seminal meeting held at Slimbridge in summer 1961. The first Annual General Meeting of the Gloucestershire Trust for Nature Conservation,

Opposite: Bluebells at Lower Wood
Right: The Trust's original logo – drawn by Sir Peter Scott

with Sir Peter Scott as its President and John Pontin as Honorary Secretary, was held at the Crypt School, Gloucester. Bob George, an eminent entomologist, stated his vision in his 1962 Chairman's report: "... to firmly establish our aims and work as part of the social structure of Gloucestershire". This was extremely prescient and the earliest statement for Gloucestershire of what successful nature conservation should look like.

EARLY TRUST RESERVES

In 1962, Badgeworth Pool, the Trust's first nature reserve, was leased from the Society, which had been gifted the site in 1933 by the Cotteswold Naturalists' Field Club. At the time, Badgeworth was the only known UK location of adderstongue spearwort, *Ranunculus ossioglosifolius* (or 'Badgeworth Buttercup' as it is locally known). It also claimed to be England's smallest nature reserve at only 290 square metres. However, with the discovery of a second site for the spearwort on Hawkesbury Common, South Gloucestershire, and the recent extension of the nature reserve, these two claims are no longer true!

In 1979, three major additions to the Trust's freehold reserve portfolio marked a step change in Trust activity. One of these acquisitions resulted from an urgent request from the Government's Nature Conservancy Council to take over its failing site purchase of part of Collin Park Wood SSSI,

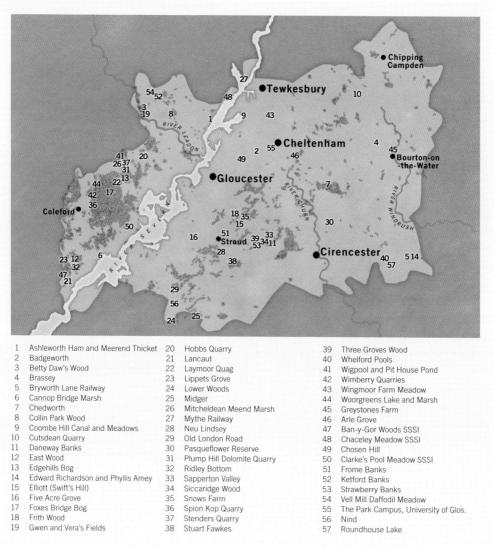

1	Ashleworth Ham and Meerend Thicket	
2	Badgeworth	
3	Betty Daw's Wood	
4	Brassey	
5	Bryworth Lane Railway	
6	Cannop Bridge Marsh	
7	Chedworth	
8	Collin Park Wood	
9	Coombe Hill Canal and Meadows	
10	Cutsdean Quarry	
11	Daneway Banks	
12	East Wood	
13	Edgehills Bog	
14	Edward Richardson and Phyllis Amey	
15	Elliott (Swift's Hill)	
16	Five Acre Grove	
17	Foxes Bridge Bog	
18	Frith Wood	
19	Gwen and Vera's Fields	
20	Hobbs Quarry	
21	Lancaut	
22	Laymoor Quag	
23	Lippets Grove	
24	Lower Woods	
25	Midger	
26	Mitcheldean Meend Marsh	
27	Mythe Railway	
28	Neu Lindsey	
29	Old London Road	
30	Pasqueflower Reserve	
31	Plump Hill Dolomite Quarry	
32	Ridley Bottom	
33	Sapperton Valley	
34	Siccaridge Wood	
35	Snows Farm	
36	Spion Kop Quarry	
37	Stenders Quarry	
38	Stuart Fawkes	
39	Three Groves Wood	
40	Whelford Pools	
41	Wigpool and Pit House Pond	
42	Wimberry Quarries	
43	Wingmoor Farm Meadow	
44	Woorgreens Lake and Marsh	
45	Greystones Farm	
46	Arle Grove	
47	Ban-y-Gor Woods SSSI	
48	Chaceley Meadow SSSI	
49	Chosen Hill	
50	Clarke's Pool Meadow SSSI	
51	Frome Banks	
52	Ketford Banks	
53	Strawberry Banks	
54	Vell Mill Daffodil Meadow	
55	The Park Campus, University of Glos.	
56	Nind	
57	Roundhouse Lake	

Map of Gloucestershire Wildlife Trust nature reserves

because it had run out of money. Conservation, like nature and politics, can be cyclical.

Nature reserve purchase has continued for five decades, in line with the Trust's ambition of safeguarding important examples of Gloucestershire's habitat infrastructure. The Trust's current total of more than 60 reserves protects 2,000 acres of land managed for wildlife and people. Potential new acquisitions are always under review, but the current emphasis is to enhance existing sites and to secure favourable management for adjoining land.

The importance of the Trust's strategy of maintaining long-standing relationships with partners and landowners was reinforced when the estate of the late Duke of Beaufort approached the Trust with the offer of the Lower Woods SSSI, Hawkesbury. The Trust gratefully accepted the gift, on behalf of the nation. The Lower Woods nature reserve was opened formally by HRH The Prince of Wales in 1997. This nature reserve covers more than a square mile of the most important woodland and wood pasture in south-west England.

IMPORTANCE OF LOTTERY FUNDING...

Lord Jacob Rothschild, the then Chairman of the HERITAGE LOTTERY FUND (HLF), was a guest at the official Lower Woods opening party. It was a great pleasure to show him the range of work that was being carried out under the first of a set of three major HLF grants. Indeed, the arrival of the HLF was one of the two most important financial events that have accelerated the development of the Trust's work. In addition to the Lower Woods management, the Trust has made many significant HLF funded acquisitions. They include Coombe Hill Meadows, Salmonsbury Meadows and Greystones Farm. Subsequently, the HLF nature reserves management programme, facilitated by the Society, enabled work on a further 30 Trust sites. Up to December 2010, lottery funds had supported the Trust by a total of £2 million.

The Trust founders in 1961, with Sir Peter Scott (third from left)

...AND LANDFILL TAX FUNDING

A second major source of funds – the Landfill Communities Fund (LCF) – arrived in 1996. This tax enabled local delivery of social and environmental benefits to communities close to landfill sites across Gloucestershire. The Trust has worked with a number of LCF distributors. One of these, Grundon Waste Management Limited, has facilitated extensive development across a wide range of initiatives. Since 1996, £2 million has been spent on the Trust's biodiversity work. Large sites like Coombe Hill and Lower Woods have received considerable attention, but the fund also allowed important investment in biodiversity infrastructure.

The Trust's nature reserve at Lancaut in the Wye Valley

One lasting benefit for the county has been the Biodiversity Action Plan (BAP), supported by the Gloucestershire Environmental Trust (GET). It was one of the first in the UK and the GET has organised and managed the BAP process since 2000. It has provided a framework for the many organisations that should include wildlife conservation in their work, to help them coordinate activity in a strategic and less wasteful way.

... AND ORGANISED DATA

The Trust has always been evidence-led. But, as with so many stories relating to our heritage, the knowledge and understanding that formed the basis of the Trust in 1961 was tacit; the species and habitat data that is the basis of sound nature conservation was largely in the heads of the Trust's knowledgeable founders. In the mid-1970s, a decision to participate in a Government-funded employment programme (STEP) had long-term benefits beyond that for the participants. It was still generating value in 2011. The two major STEP surveys – Rivers and Streams, and Habitats - have since been supplemented by many other Trust initiatives, but they have provided the first systematic geographically organised biodiversity data for the county. They still form the core of the strategic biodiversity information set.

In 1990, funding from the Environmental Action Fund enabled the Trust to consolidate existing biodiversity information into a sites and species database that it had begun computerising in 1988. This work formed the bedrock of the Gloucestershire Centre for Environmental Records (GCER) which now manages over one million species records. GCER has been sustained by the Trust for 20 years because of inadequate public funding for what is a clear benefit. Strategic land management decisions need to be taken in the clear knowledge of their associated wildlife implications. In 2011, the Trust's 50th anniversary year, the first *State of the Environment Report* for the county to include appropriate biodiversity data criticised the paucity of quality of information on habitats.

VOLUNTEERS AND LOCAL COMMUNITIES

Gloucestershire people founded the Wildlife Trust and the Trust has always considered working with people and communities as a critical part of its work. Early in its life, the Trust had a strong practical volunteer conservation force. This was led by Brigadier Armstrong, organiser of the Council For Nature's NATIONAL CONSERVATION CORPS, later the British Trust for Conservation Volunteers. Volunteering is still a key part of the Trust's work and the Armstrong Award is made annually to celebrate this ethos. The work of GCER is dependent on volunteer involvement and its single biggest data set of over 250,000 botanical records was made by worthy Armstrong Award winners, Mark and Clare Kitchen.

The longest-running volunteer-led programme is the Trust's Annual Primary Schools Wildlife Quiz. This hugely successful event has grown over the years and, by 2011, involved more than 100 schools and 500 children.

The standard of knowledge of quiz participants has also risen year-on-year. Alongside the quiz,

Opposite: Early purple orchid
Above: Installing nestboxes at Betty Daw's Wood, 1964

Severn Vale – a target area for the Trust's Living landscape work

the Trust has provided many extra opportunities for younger learners through its WILDLIFE WATCH membership, which had reached 6,500 by mid-2010. More than 100 local wildlife events are held annually throughout the county. They include the popular badger watching, 'moth breakfasts' and dawn chorus walks.

PEOPLE AND PLACES

The Trust's starter home was in Community House, College Green, Gloucester, adjacent to the cathedral – a location for many television dramas and Harry Potter film shoots. However, the Trust soon outgrew this historic community and moved in 1971 to the listed Church House at Standish. In 1992, the Conservation Centre at Robinswood

Church House – the Trust's home from 1971 to 1992

Hill Country Park, Gloucester, was opened by SIR DAVID ATTENBOROUGH as the registered home of the newly-rebranded Gloucestershire Wildlife Trust. The Trust started as a purely volunteer organisation, but as it grew and became more ambitious, staff undertook the central organisation and technical roles. The Trust is still run by volunteers who comprise its central Board of Trustees and expert advisory committees. People, their involvement and development, are at the heart of the Trust. Its long-standing commitment to its staff and volunteer support was confirmed when the Trust was one of the first charities in the UK to achieve the Investors in People award in 1995. It has maintained the standard ever since, reaching the silver standard in 2008 and assisting in the development of a national health and well-being module in 2009.

LIVING LANDSCAPES

The involvement of people and communities is of increasing importance to successful wildlife conservation. This work is now a central part of the Trust's LIVING LANDSCAPE philosophy that focuses all aspects of the Trust's work on a local geographical basis. The Severn Vale formed the first Gloucestershire Living Landscape project, followed by programmes on the Cotswold Rivers, the Cotswold Water Park and in the Forest of Dean.

The essence of this landscape-scale working is both physical and social; to connect sites of wildlife importance by working with land managers, and to engage local communities. The involvement of the business community is the third and most difficult part of the chemistry.

The fragmented wildlife habitats and species, that so motivated the Trust's founders to take action in 1961, now have to cope with growing disturbances to weather patterns due to climate change. It has also become increasingly clear that public access to healthy green spaces is essential for social well-being and resilient communities. The Trust's People and Wildlife team work increasingly closely with their Habitats and Species colleagues to encourage more local involvement with, and knowledge and understanding of, our fragile ecosystems.

STRONG MEMBERSHIP

None of the Trust's work would have been possible without its supportive members. Gloucestershire's membership, as a proportion of its population, has been consistently amongst the highest of any of the Wildlife Trusts for more than 30 years.

Bob George, the Trust's first Chairman, confirmed in 2009 that he felt the Trust had achieved far more than he had ever thought possible, but he would still like to see at least 25,000 members in Gloucestershire by the Trust's 50th anniversary in 2011. By December 2010, the Trust had reached this target, showing that four per cent of the county supported the Trust's local action for wildlife and wild places. Imaginative optimism has always been the essence of Gloucestershire Wildlife Trust, something that its passionate Board, volunteers, members and staff continue to express in their daily support for the county's wildlife.

BY GORDON MCGLONE OBE
Gordon McGlone has worked for the Gloucestershire Wildlife Trust since 1979. A professional ecologist, he was appointed Chief Executive in 1983 and has built a Trust underpinned by knowledgeable, dedicated and loyal staff. In 2006, he was awarded an OBE for his services to conservation. Involved nationally with the development of The Wildlife Trusts, McGlone has been a member of both the Society's Conservation and Scientific, and Resources Committees. He also continues to represent the movement on the issue of badgers and bovine TB.

The Trust's first reserve was Badgeworth Pool, the only known UK location for adderstongue spearwort – the 'Badgeworth Buttercup'

Gwent

Gwent is an ancient kingdom. The Severn Estuary forms the southern boundary and the western boundary follows the River Rhymney or the ridge between this river and the Sirhowy. The eastern and north-eastern boundary follows the River Wye and its tributary, the Monnow. The northern boundary is drawn arbitrarily across the high plateau of Llangynidr and Llangattock moor, with a narrow northern diversion to take in the Vale of Ewyas, more commonly called the Llanthony valley, and part of the Black Mountains.

There are four distinct regions: the alluvial levels over Triassic rocks adjoining the Severn Estuary; the uplands and valleys of the west overlying Coal Measures; and the Black Mountains in the north on old red sandstone. These encircle a central area of rolling farmland over old red sandstone. This rises to the south-east onto the moors and forests of the Wentwood and Trellech ridges. These ridges, and the steep-sided and wooded Wye Valley in the east, have a character all of their own.

SIXTIES' CHILD

The Monmouthshire Naturalists' Trust was formed in 1963 following a public meeting in Newport. The first Chairman, Richard Lake, headed a group of enthusiastic volunteers who met at each others' houses. By July the following year the Trust was legally constituted and had leased or purchased three pieces of ground – its first nature reserves. One of these was part of the wetland that now forms the Magor Marsh reserve – the last remnant of

Opposite: Autumn at Silent Valley
Right: The campaign against re-routing the M4 motorway through the Gwent levels

fenland on the Gwent Levels and now the nucleus of a Living Landscape project restoring this wetland landscape. Over the years, the reserve expanded to 90 acres (36 hectares), a third of which was acquired in 2003 by an appeal to the members. The Derek Upton Education Centre was built there, enabling the Trust to introduce people of all ages to the wonders of the Levels' natural environment.
In 2010, a second centre was opened at Ebbw Vale, as part of a partnership project with eight other organisations in this regeneration area.

During the Trust's first years, the 200 or so members (ordinary subscription £1, juniors ten shillings, life membership £15) worked hard to raise funds by staging coffee mornings, raffles and sales. Lord Raglan, the Trust's first President successfully appealed for financial support from industry and public bodies. Nevertheless, the Chairman Patrick Humphreys still noted that the Trust's members were "looked upon as cranks running around the countryside with binoculars and butterfly nets". At least this suggests that members were out in force recording the status of Gwent's wildlife!

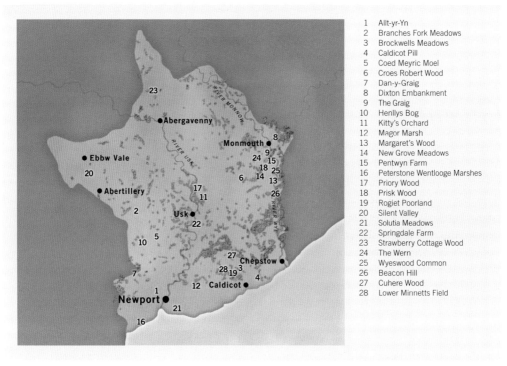

1	Allt-yr-Yn
2	Branches Fork Meadows
3	Brockwells Meadows
4	Caldicot Pill
5	Coed Meyric Moel
6	Croes Robert Wood
7	Dan-y-Graig
8	Dixton Embankment
9	The Graig
10	Henllys Bog
11	Kitty's Orchard
12	Magor Marsh
13	Margaret's Wood
14	New Grove Meadows
15	Pentwyn Farm
16	Peterstone Wentlooge Marshes
17	Priory Wood
18	Prisk Wood
19	Rogiet Poorland
20	Silent Valley
21	Solutia Meadows
22	Springdale Farm
23	Strawberry Cottage Wood
24	The Wern
25	Wyeswood Common
26	Beacon Hill
27	Cuhere Wood
28	Lower Minnetts Field

Map of Gwent Wildlife Trust nature reserves

This voluntary recording led to the 1965 *Wildlife Report* and made important contributions to AE Wade's 1970 book, *Flora of Monmouthshire*.

FIRST OFFICE AND STAFF

The day eventually came when the Trust needed an office. In 1980 it rented a small room containing a desk and two chairs and squeezed equipment (a filing cabinet), and its first member of staff, Dr Stephanie Tyler, into it. Soon afterwards training projects, supported by the Manpower Services Commission (EMPLOYMENT SCHEMES) and led by Adrian Wood, began, including a seminal survey of the county's grasslands. A reassessment of the Trust's aims and objectives in 1987 led to the employment of two permanent staff and a change of the Trust's name to Gwent Wildlife Trust. The great importance of education was recognised by the introduction of WILDLIFE WATCH for young members.

The Trust has always had a great deal of expertise within its own membership, and seven local groups have provided a constant support in a variety of ways. However, the employment of full-time professional staff changed the Trust's internal dynamics and transformed its capacity to achieve its conservation objectives. This was exemplified in a campaign to secure Pentwyn Farm at Penallt, a rare piece of 'unimproved' Gwent countryside. This 30-acre smallholding, including ancient flower-rich meadows and a collapsing medieval barn, came on the market for £150,000 in 1991. Within a six-week deadline, a public appeal raised the necessary sum – an incredible feat. Nearby, another reserve was acquired at New Grove Meadows. This is amongst the very best wildflower meadows in Britain – providing an unforgettable sight in spring, with thousands of colourful orchid spikes set against a superb view overlooking Monmouthshire.

TRUST EXPANSION

At 125 acres, the Silent Valley Local Nature Reserve near Ebbw Vale – ancient beech woodland, with wet flushes, grassland, bracken and heather – is the

Trust's largest reserve. Managed by the Trust since the 1980s, grants were secured in 1999 to appoint new staff and make the most of this wonderful reserve for local people and wildlife. Visitor numbers soared and the reserve is used by many schools keen to experience wildlife in the 'valleys'.

Another fantastic site, Springdale Farm near Usk, was acquired in 2001 thanks to the HERITAGE LOTTERY FUND, the Countryside Council for Wales, Monmouthshire County Council and, once again, the incredible generosity of members. Although there were 60 acres of grassland which had lost much of their wildflower interest due to agricultural improvement, the reserve also had 40 acres of species-rich unimproved grassland, a stunning ancient wood and breathtaking views over the Usk valley. Under the Trust's stewardship, wildflowers have begun to spread back over the areas of improved grassland on the farm. A farm business tenancy with neighbours and a herd of British white cattle have also helped with management of the site's wildlife.

Expansion of the Trust created a need for larger offices and a move to White Swan Court,

Gwent's hedges and woodlands are a stronghold for dormice

Monmouth in 2004. The age of the computer had arrived. A membership database was created by volunteer, John Harper, and book-keeping – by now too much for volunteers – was transferred to the Trust's accountants. When the lease expired in 2004, the Trust took the opportunity to move out of town to Seddon House, Dingestow. These premises were previously a school, so it was a case of planning the offices from scratch, with volunteer, Chris Field, masterminding the installation of modern technology. This allowed development of a new membership database, and the return to in-house book-keeping and financial reporting.

BUSINESS SPONSORSHIP

Support from business and commerce has been a concern of the Trust right from its earliest days. Since the 1990s, attracting business support has been led by a volunteer, Julia James. The Trust has, in turn, been able to help businesses meet their corporate responsibility objectives. This mutually-beneficial relationship is best illustrated by the Trust's engagement with the chemical company Solutia UK Ltd at Newport. Solutia UK takes a very serious attitude to the impact its operations have on discharge to the Severn estuary, emissions to the air, waste disposal and energy efficiency. They have also been keen to maintain an open dialogue with the surrounding community. By working together, a 90-acre nature reserve is now established on Solutia's land, managed by the Trust with the help of local volunteers. This is species-rich grassland, typical of the traditional Gwent Levels landscape, with grazing marsh and ditches known locally as 'reens'.

One of the most important functions of the Trust has been to fight proposals that would have an adverse impact on the environment. The first major issue to face the Trust was the 1974 publication of the Goss report on the *Development Potential of South Gwent*. It recommended barrages on the Rivers Severn and Usk and a Severnside international airport. Since then, the Trust has continued to fight such unwise proposals, none of which has yet succeeded. Some 25 years later, the Trust became deeply involved alongside neighbouring Wildlife Trusts, the RSPB and Wildfowl and Wetlands Trust, in the campaign against the Severn barrage.

PARTNERSHIP WORKING

Campaigning is most effective when conservationists work in coalition. A good example was the campaign against the Welsh Assembly Government's proposal to build a new 24-kilometre toll motorway to the south of Newport. This would have a serious impact on several Sites of Special Scientific Interest, including the Gwent Levels. The Trust, led by its former Chief Executive, Julian Branscombe, played an important role in opposing this alongside organisations such as Friends of the Earth Cymru, World Wildlife Fund Cymru, RSPB Cymru and the Campaign for the Protection of Rural Wales. The proposal has been postponed on financial grounds, but the Trust will be vigilant against its resurrection.

Partnership with others plays an important part in dealing with environmental issues. To this end, the Trust engages with more than 20 other organisations and other neighbouring Wildlife Trusts. A separate charity, Wildlife Trusts Wales, was formed in 1995 to encourage cooperation and close working at an operational level between the six Wildlife Trusts in Wales, on the grounds that many projects and programmes are best delivered at a Wales-wide level (WELSH TRUSTS, ASSOCIATION OF). Wildlife Trusts Wales promotes biodiversity by working for habitats and species, by inspiring people about the natural world, and engaging with local government and the Welsh Assembly Government to enable local people to stand up for wildlife.

MEMBERSHIP MATTERS

Membership numbers have always been an important demonstration of support for the Trust. Members also provide subscription income – without which the Trust would be unable to function effectively. When the charity was run purely by volunteers, membership income was less important. But with the appointment of

professional staff from 1980 onwards, core income became increasingly important. In 1990 membership stood at 1,300, but this had declined to 900 by 1996. This led to a campaign to recruit more members, and ten years later the figure had risen to 5,700. The 10,000 mark was reached in 2010.

Communication with members has always been an important part of the Trust's work. The first newsletter was produced in 1965 and the introduction of a new owl logo gave it a name, *Owl News*. On the 30th anniversary of the Trust in 1993, the newsletter name changed to *Wild About Gwent*. A new magazine was one of the factors that brought the Trusts in Wales to work more closely together. In 2000, a new magazine covering the whole of South Wales was published. Within three years, the six Welsh Trusts came together to produce a colour magazine, *Natural World Wales*, that was incorporated within the UK-wide membership magazine – *Natural World*. Changes in the publication arrangements for *Natural World*, in 2006 resulted in *Welsh Wildlife* (the new name for *Natural World Wales*) becoming a stand-alone colour magazine. The Trust introduced a separate two-colour *Local News* in that year, in order to provide members with information about Gwent activities and events. In 2010 this became the eight-page colour *Wild About Gwent*.

Heathland at Beacon Hill

A carpet of orchids at New Grove Meadows

WALKS AND TALKS

Public talks through winter months have also been an important part of communicating with members. At first this was done on a county basis, but comprehensive coverage of the county was achieved with the development of seven local groups. From the beginning of the Trust, members have enjoyed nature walks led by experts, conducted wildlife surveys, and undertaken practical work tasks. In 1995, a new activity brought all members together at a Summer Fayre held at Clytha Park. From this, a series of wildlife events have evolved, which include training in species identification and reserve management skills.

NEW MILLENNIUM, NEW CHARITY

At the turn of the century the Trust underwent a major metamorphosis. It changed from an organisation run by volunteers, ably led throughout the 1990s by Jon Winder as manager, into a professional charity with a new constitution based on advice from the Charity Commission. Julian Branscombe became Chief Executive, responsible for operational work and supporting Trustees in matters of governance. This coincided with the nationwide reorganisation of The Wildlife Trusts, to which the Gwent Trust gave its full support. The creation of the national strategic plan gave

the Trust a template for its annual work plan, with activity divided into land management, education, the wider environment, and core business support.

The Trust's reorganisation created more opportunities for both volunteering and employment with everyone involved in the Trust taking pride in the positive way volunteers and staff work as a team. By the beginning of 2011, the Trust had agreed a Development Plan and was poised to take advantage of the opportunities offered by the Living Landscape and Living Seas approach to nature conservation, being championed by Wildlife Trusts across the UK. The Trust has four projects in preparation which will begin to look at delivering nature conservation across large areas of the Gwent landscape – the first of these will be the Gwent Levels and the woodlands and flower-rich meadows between the villages of the Usk and the Wye.

BY DAVID LEAT
David Leat is a retired professional horticulturist and one-time trustee of Gwent Wildlife Trust, The Wildlife Trusts Wales and the Royal Society of Wildlife Trusts. Currently, he is a Vice President of Gwent Wildlife Trust.

CHAPTER 17

Hampshire and Isle of Wight

By the end of the 1950s, the time was ripe for a new county-based conservation organisation in Hampshire and the Isle of Wight. The countryside was changing and its wildlife was disappearing. Mixed farming was being replaced by arable farming with enormous corn fields. Marginal land such as downland was going under the plough and wetlands on the floodplains of Hampshire's rivers were being drained. In the 1950s, pastoral farming was in decline. Exceptionally wildlife-rich areas could still be enjoyed where traditional farming survived, such as in the New Forest and on the Isle of Wight. Elsewhere, the fragments of chalk grasslands on the Hampshire downs became increasingly derelict. The 1955 outbreak of myxomatosis made matters worse by virtually eradicating the grazing of wild rabbits. In addition to the farming revolution, the amount of urban development in Hampshire had vastly increased in the post-war years. The south Hampshire axis cities of Southampton and Portsmouth both underwent explosive growth. A new town had developed at Basingstoke. The largest refinery in Europe had been built on the edge of the New Forest, at Fawley. Yet in Hampshire there was only one National Nature Reserve, Old Winchester Hill, and there were no reserves managed by either the RSPB or The National Trust. It was time to act, time to rescue as much wildlife as possible from the advancing jaws of industrial and agricultural development.

The initiative for the formation of a new Trust came from members of Portsmouth Natural

Opposite: Dartford Warbler
Right: The Trust's first logo

History Society. Alick Westrup was a very capable botanist and was following up the Botanical Society of the British Isles' national plant survey with a Hampshire *Flora*. Ron Wells was Biology Master at Portsmouth Grammar School and an ardent field naturalist. They wrote to the only county-based organisation, the Hampshire Field Club in Winchester. Although the Field Club had an ornithological section, it was primarily interested in the archaeology and history of the county, and it declined further interest in setting up a conservation trust. However, the Field Club did send the Trust's first Company Secretary, Michael Bryant, a list of all the potentially interested groups in Hampshire. Bryant promptly wrote to them all, asking them to send a representative to a meeting to discuss the establishment of a County Naturalists' Trust.

FOUNDING THE TRUST

The first meeting was held on the 26th March 1960 in the Botany Department of Southampton University. Representatives from 23 organisations attended and a further seven wrote supporting the idea in principle. From the attendees at that meeting an organising committee was formed. A founding meeting was held on the 28th November 1960. TED SMITH, from the LINCOLNSHIRE TRUST, addressed the meeting and explained how similar Trusts elsewhere in the country were beginning to operate. Smith had sent Michael

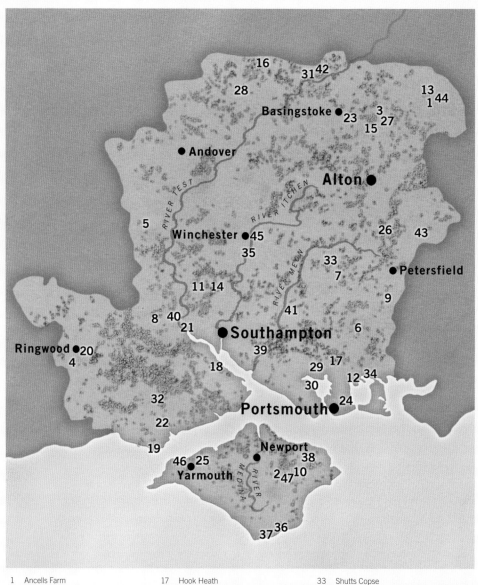

1	Ancells Farm	17	Hook Heath
2	Arreton Down	18	Hythe Spartina Marsh
3	Bartley Heath and Hook Common	19	Keyhaven and Pennington Marshes
4	Blashford Lakes	20	Linwood
5	Broughton Down	21	Lower Test
6	Catherington Down	22	Lymington Reedbeds
7	Chappetts Copse	23	Mapledurwell Fen/The Hatch
8	Copythorne Common	24	Milton Locks
9	Coulters Dean	25	Ningwood Common
10	Eaglehead and Bloodstone Copses	26	Noar Hill
11	Emer Bog and Baddesley Common	27	North Warnborough Greens
12	Farlington Marshes	28	Old Burghclere Lime Quarry
13	Foxlease Meadows	29	Pamber Forest
14	Flexford	30	Pewit Island
15	Greywell Moors	31	Ron Ward's Meadow
16	Headley Gravel Pit	32	Roydon Woods

33	Shutts Copse
34	Southmoor
35	St Catherine's Hill
36	St Lawrence Bank
37	St Lawrence Undercliff
38	Swanpond Copse
39	Swanwick Lakes
40	Testwood Lakes
41	Nancy Mason Hoe Road Meadow
42	Upper Inhams Copse
43	Weavers Down Bog
44	Whitehouse Meadow
45	Winnall Moors
46	Knighton Down
47	Bouldnor Forest

Map of Hampshire and Isle of Wight Wildlife Trust nature reserves

Bryant a draft Articles of Association which had been duly modified to make it suitable for the formation of a Trust in Hampshire and the Isle of Wight. As a result of these efforts the Trust was incorporated as a company. The meeting was presided over by Lord Porchester and Squadron Leader Norman Orr was elected Chairman. The first group of Trustees was also elected.

Following this constitutional meeting, an inaugural meeting, open to the public, was arranged at Winchester Guildhall on 4th February 1961. It was chaired by Lord Porchester, now President of the new Trust and the guest speaker was MAX NICHOLSON. The meeting must have been a huge success; 123 members were recruited at this inaugural meeting and were considered founder members.

ORGANISATION OF THE TRUST

The founding of the Trust required that there should be a governing Council of Trustees, who would steer the business of the Trust. Initially all the officers of the Trust were also Trustees and acted in an entirely voluntary capacity. Some had the relevant professional qualifications. Michael Bryant, for instance, was a solicitor by profession and the Honorary Treasurer was a banker. But for the most part, the honorary officers and Trustees were enthusiasts for natural history. Some were

professional biologists in education and some retired from a variety of professional backgrounds. Retired officers from the armed services frequently featured. Business, finance and publicity managers were in short supply. The meetings often got tangled in personal enthusiasms or minutiae.

The new Trust was to be called the Hampshire and Isle of Wight Naturalists' Trust. At that time it was a single County Trust as, for some administrative purposes, Hampshire and the Isle of Wight were one county. Naturalists' Trust was a difficult name: it implied that it was a Trust for the students and lovers of nature, and rather excluded those who were less expert or less adoring. Much later at the Annual General Meeting on the 18th May 1991, a large attendance of members voted overwhelmingly in favour of changing the name to the Hampshire and Isle of Wight Wildlife Trust. It was changed to an easily-understood name in line with the national Wildlife Trust movement. There was much popping of corks at the office.

The Trust's first logo showed the Dartford warbler – at that time very much a county bird, confined to the heaths of west Hampshire and east Dorset. The current logo is in line with the logo for the Wildlife Trusts national movement. It is curious how much passion a change of logo can produce. There are still members who are wearing a shirt with a Dartford warbler emblazoned on the chest.

Farlington Marshes – one of the Trust's oldest nature reserves

THE AIMS OF THE TRUST

The modern aims, objectives and mission statements of the Trust have remained much the same as those in the founding Articles of Association:

For the public benefit:
To conserve wildlife by setting up reserves.
To conserve places of geographical, geological interest and/or natural beauty.
To influence and cooperate with others to conserve wildlife.
To gain public and financial support for wildlife conservation.
To educate and help people to enjoy and conserve wildlife.
To organise research and to keep records of the wildlife of Hampshire and Isle of Wight, so as to further the conservation of wildlife.

The wording has since changed, introducing concepts such as biodiversity and sustainability, but the underlying principles remain the same today. Perhaps the greatest change has been public perception and sympathy towards the value of wildlife. The first annual report in 1962 had a very modern ring to its section on conservation. "Conservation societies have tended to confine their attention to very rare or spectacular species. It is now more generally realised that undue concentration of effort in this way may be harmful and that the health of the wildlife of any area depends on the maintenance of a balanced habitat". Add in a little bit about sustainable population size and the need for wildlife corridors to promote genetic migration, and the statement would be right up-to-date.

SIXTIES SUCCESS

The Trust has had four disinct phases of growth. Between 1960 and 1968 was purely an amateur and volunteer period in which the Company Secretary acted as Conservation Officer and worked from home. One of the more successful ideas for recruiting members and raising funds was the formation of Area Advisory Boards in 1966. The county was divided into eight areas including the Isle of Wight. Each area had a chair, a secretary and a committee of workers whose directions were to raise funds, recruit members, deliver the Trust magazines and take an active interest in conservation. It was diffuse, but effective. The Trust projector was swapped back and forward from area to area. Film shows of wildlife in colour could attract up to 300 people and some most attractive films were available. *Journey into Spring* focused on Selborne and *The Life of the Kingfisher* on the Upper Itchen. The sale of Trust goods was masterminded by Anne Rutherford. By 1969, sales raised about a third of the Trust's total income.

FIRST FULLY-PAID OFFICERS

In the second phase, 1969 to 1987, the Company Secretary was paid a fairly substantial honorarium, and the first fully-paid officers of the Trust appeared. Jim White (1974–78) became the first Conservation Officer and Chris Hewitt was employed as the first Education and Publicity Officer. The Trust also moved into office premises. Colonel Tregear, Company Secretary from 1969 to 1971, could never resist the grandiose and arranged that the official address should be King John's Lodge, Romsey. Dating from the thirteenth century, it had no running water, no modern toilet and limited heating so, in practice, the Trust officers operated from rooms over the chemist and optician's shop on the other side of the square.

The third phase was the grand phase of growth in which the Trust's principal officer was called a Director. Under the leadership of the first Director, Dr Bob Page, the Trust grew substantially into the modern organisation. Kay Peake was employed as a full-time Company Secretary, and kept everyone and everything in order. Two Conservation Officers, a Publicity Officer and an Education Officer joined the staff. In addition, there were project officers such as a Woodland Recovery Officer following the devastation of the great storm in 1987. These project officers were funded by grants for limited periods of time.

BIGGER OFFICES

As the organisation grew, new office premises had to be acquired. First a converted shop – 71 The Hundred in Romsey – then the first freehold premises – a large house at 8 Romsey Road, Eastleigh – followed by the present, rather grand, ex-residential home – Beechcroft House, Vicarage Lane, Curdridge. All this building investment and extensive conversion required capital. The Trust was fortunate in receiving a number of substantial bequests – the principal one by the Honorable Joanne Dutton in 1988.

The fourth and present phase of organisation reflects the huge expansion of the interests and activities of the Trust. There are now three education centres, with full-time staff and nature reserves attached. These are at Swanwick Lakes, Testwood Lakes and Blashford Lakes. The grazing project on 830 hectares of Ministry of Defence land in the north-east of the county is a huge commitment. The work on the Isle of Wight has expanded enormously with seven reserves, landowner advice and education commitments. In 2003, it was decided to devolve area responsibilities to senior managers for the south-east, west and north of Hampshire and the Isle of Wight. Offices were established in the north near Basingstoke and on the Isle of Wight near Newport.

Above: Cattle grazing on the Isle of Wight
Above right: Noar Hill nature reserve – surrounded by farmland, the reserve is home to over 35 species of butterfly and many rare plants and flowers

RESERVE RESPONSIBILITIES

The counties of Hampshire and the Isle of Wight are diverse, with a wide range of habitats. Of the 33 key habitats identified as important to nature conservation under the UK Biodiversity Action Plans, Hampshire has 18.

In the early years, it was perceived that there were conservation priorities, but as far as the acquisition of nature reserves was concerned, the officers of the Trust were beggars, not choosers. In the 1960s, there were no funders, so the Trust sought to influence the formation of reserves at almost zero cost. It was a case of influencing existing landowners to allow the Trust to manage their land as a nature reserve.

In 1963, there were 12 reserves or areas of land over which the Trust had some influence; by 1970, this had grown to 18. The tenure and terms of agreement varied from permission to warden and keep off trespassers, to freehold ownership of the land. A lot of this early interest and attention paid off in future years. Areas of land where the Trust had taken an interest in wardening, or just doing a bit of conservation work, such as Farlington Marshes, Chappett's Copse and Upper Titchfield Haven, became long-term leases or freehold properties.

Since 1970, newly-acquired reserves have usually had a sound basis of tenure and agreed funding to meet the cost of management. Present reserve acquisition also considers value of habitat, critical size for sustaining species and linkage with the

Chalk river at Winnall Moors

wider countryside, so that species are not isolated in dangerously small pockets of habitat. Winnall Moors nature reserve – 65 hectares of flood plain near Winchester – is a good example of this, as it has close links with upstream River Itchen, St Catherine's Hill nature reserve and the Itchen Navigation project. There are now 47 nature reserves and the land the Trust manages amounts to some 6,000 hectares. It includes examples of most of the natural and semi-natural habitats in Hampshire and the Isle of Wight.

MEMBERSHIP AND VOLUNTEERS

The Trust started out with an initial burst of enthusiasm with people eager to join. After the inaugural meeting in November 1961 there were 360 members, rising to 1,086 by 1964. After that, growth became depressingly slow with losses occasionally exceeding gains. The greatest problem at that time was that there was very little use of bank mandates and no direct debit. This resulted in a huge amount of correspondence to remind lapsed members that they had not paid their subscription and an inevitable loss of membership if subscription rates were raised.

Between 1968 to 1974, there was an encouraging growth in membership with an average rise of 250 members a year to about 3,000 members. Present membership now stands at 27,000. This spectacular rise in numbers has been largely due to the introduction of direct debiting and

investment in recruitment. In the early days, the membership also provided the volunteers who ran the Trust and its activities. It would be impossible to mention all the volunteers across the three categories of volunteering all of which required major commitment and initiative. The three categories were: managing nature reserves and conservation projects at specific sites; managing strategy and the central organisation; and promoting and selling the Trust to the general public. However, five names spring to mind of those who made major contributions in the past. Anne Rutherford (1965–75) who was involved in sales and fundraising; David and Rosemary Billet (1960–76) who were volunteer wardens for Farlington Marshes nature reserve; Peter Page (1966–74) who was editor of the newsletter, Honorary Public Relations Officer and storekeeper of tools for conservation work; and Graham Darrah (1981–2001) who was Chairman of Trustees.

Hampshire and Isle of Wight Wildlife Trust started life as a purely voluntary body with no paid staff. Although it has now grown and employs more than 90 staff, it could not achieve what it does without the contribution of its 750 or so volunteers. Volunteers are still a vital part of the workforce of the Trust, acting in a number of roles – from

Pearl-bordered fritillary – found in the coppices of Roydon Woods

conservation work and surveying, to assisting at education centres and providing support in the office. Some volunteers are members of regular work parties or 'friends of' groups while others work with one member of staff; others participate as part of a project – for example, as part of the Trust's two youth volunteering projects. This ethos of volunteering is at the heart of what the Trust does and achieves.

PARTNERSHIP WORKING

No conservation body is able to work without support and assistance from those who are similarly engaged in conservation and land management. Public bodies often involve the Trust as one way of fulfilling their responsibilities. Hampshire County Council, The National Trust and the Ministry of Defence, for example, have all involved the Trust in the management of land for nature conservation. Private landowners, such as the Barker-Mill estates, have engaged with the Trust to look after land with special conservation value – the wetland on the Lower Test, for example. In addition, there are large numbers of landowners and gardeners who want to manage their land in a way that is sympathetic to nature and who seek and act on advice given by the Trust.

PRESENT AND THE FUTURE

The Trust has expanded enormously using the structures set up in the 1960s and 1970s. Reserves are now viewed as core to the idea of LIVING LANDSCAPES, conserving wildlife and giving opportunities to provide green links for wildlife to move through the countryside.

Education through the Trust's centres and in schools has expanded enormously. The Environmental Stewardship Scheme has involved the Trust in direct advice to farmers for wildlife management funding. Major projects such as the restoration of the Itchen Navigation, the heathland restoration for the Ministry of Defence and special species projects, such as the Otter Project and Water Vole Project, have vastly increased the role of the Trust in the wider countryside.

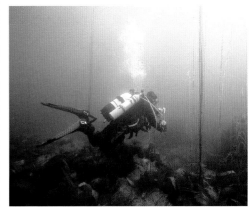

Diver surveying a shallow rocky reef

Urban expansion means urban planning and the need to protect wildlife sites – such as Dibden Bay on Southampton Water – against exploitation. The Trust is also heavily involved in marine conservation, coordinating the south-east Wildlife Trust's regional marine programme, undertaking surveys of marine habitats, running events, beach cleans, campaigning and lobbying for protection of the marine environment. There are now more than 90 members of staff and the Trust has an annual budget of £5 million. This is a far cry from £378 in 1962 and no members of staff. There are still problems and opportunities in linking wildlife reserves and in protecting what is of wildlife value against increasing urban development and intensive agriculture.

Long may organisations such as the Hampshire and Isle of Wight Wildlife Trust and all their partner organisations thrive – for the sake of nature conservation and the enrichment of all our lives.

BY RICHARD HEDLEY
Richard Hedley has been a member of the Hampshire and Isle of Wight Wildlife Trust since 1962. He has held a number of roles within the Trust including Trustee, Upper Titchfield nature reserve warden, Chairman of the South East Area and member of the South East Area Advisory Board. He has been the Chairman of Gosport District Group and Volunteer Manager of Chappett's Copse nature reserve.

CHAPTER 18

Herefordshire

Herefordshire is a rural county with the River Wye running through it. It lies in the Welsh Marches, on the borders of England and Wales. It has few major towns, with Hereford itself being the cathedral city. Its rich soils have led to farming being its main occupation. It is known for its cider orchards, mistletoe and beautiful countryside.

On 30th November 1962, 50 years after the founding of the Society for the Promotion of Nature Reserves (the Society), 90 people

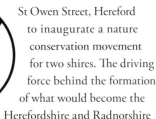

came to the Percival Hall in St Owen Street, Hereford to inaugurate a nature conservation movement for two shires. The driving force behind the formation of what would become the Herefordshire and Radnorshire

Nature Trust was the Society's President, CHRISTOPHER CADBURY. He had lived in Herefordshire and was a member of the Woolhope Naturalists' Field Club, founded in 1851. He asked the club for help, and arrangements were made for the fledgling Trust to meet in the Woolhope Room in the Hereford Library.

The Woolhope Club suggested that Dr Charles Walker might help with starting the Trust. A medical practitioner and ornithologist, he had come to Hereford in 1926. He was truly an all-round naturalist with a well-informed interest in the peregrine, wood white butterfly, snakeshead fritillary, otter and adder. A steering committee under his chairmanship was formed to bring the

Opposite: Brilly Green Dingle
Above: The Trust's first logo, featuring a pied flycatcher

Trust into being by the end of 1962. The other members of the committee were Robert Baillie, Rodney Bennett (Secretary of Herefordshire Community Council, which provided the Trust with an office for the next 12 years), Sir Terence Falkiner, Jack Fox, Rex Hudson, Jack Lewis, Richard Owen, Gerald Ealand, Mrs Margaret Gilbert and William Harrison.

After the first meeting, the idea of a partnership with Radnorshire was pursued. The Herefordshire Ornithological Club already had Radnorshire members, including the Lord Lieutenant, Sir Michael Venables-Llewelyn. His view was that, "whilst it is clear that we have much to preserve, the county is perhaps too sparsely populated to embark on a Trust on its own", and so the marriage with Herefordshire was arranged. A pied flycatcher nestbox scheme, inspired by Sir Michael, was started to give members an interest before any reserves had been acquired. In due course, the pied flycatcher became the emblem of the Trust and gave its name to the Trust's journal.

The Memorandum and Articles listed the Trust's objects. In brief, they were – for the public benefit – to record and study places and objects of biological, geological, archaeological and scientific interest or of natural beauty and to protect them. In addition, the Trust's objects were to establish nature reserves; encourage the breeding of harmless wildlife; to promote and organise study and research for the advancement of knowledge; and to make grants and donations.

The subscription was set at £10 for life membership and £1 a year for an ordinary member. Family membership cost £1.10s and junior membership,

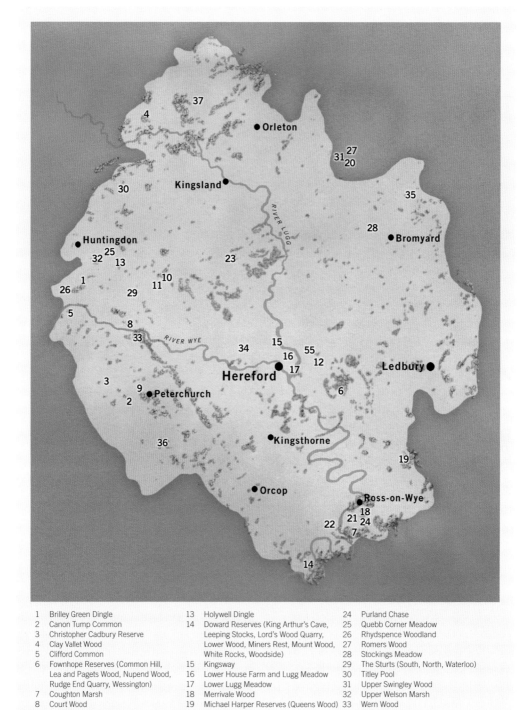

1	Brilley Green Dingle	13	Holywell Dingle	24	Purland Chase
2	Canon Tump Common	14	Doward Reserves (King Arthur's Cave,	25	Quebb Corner Meadow
3	Christopher Cadbury Reserve		Leeping Stocks, Lord's Wood Quarry,	26	Rhydspence Woodland
4	Clay Vallet Wood		Lower Wood, Miners Rest, Mount Wood,	27	Romers Wood
5	Clifford Common		White Rocks, Woodside)	28	Stockings Meadow
6	Fownhope Reserves (Common Hill,	15	Kingsway	29	The Sturts (South, North, Waterloo)
	Lea and Pagets Wood, Nupend Wood,	16	Lower House Farm and Lugg Meadow	30	Titley Pool
	Rudge End Quarry, Wessington)	17	Lower Lugg Meadow	31	Upper Swingley Wood
7	Coughton Marsh	18	Merrivale Wood	32	Upper Welson Marsh
8	Court Wood	19	Michael Harper Reserves (Queens Wood)	33	Wern Wood
9	Crow Wood and Meadow	20	Motlins Hole	34	Wyevale Wood
10	Davies Meadow	21	Parish Field	35	Page's Pasture
11	Ernle Gilbert Meadow	22	Pool Ellocks	36	The Parks
12	Hampton Meadow	23	Preece's Meadow	37	Parky Meadow

Map of Herefordshire Nature Trust nature reserves

10 shillings. The first meeting of the newly-established Council of Management was held in January 1963 in Kington and consisted of 11 members of the steering committee, plus representatives of the business and conservation sectors of the two counties. The Council's first appointments included Charles Walker and Robert Baillie (Chairman and Vice Chairman), Jack Fox and Tom Davies (Honorary Treasurer and Honorary Assistant Treasurer), and Rodney Bennett and Arthur Davies (Honorary Secretary and Honorary Assistant Secretary).

FIRST RESERVES

In those early days, all the work was done by volunteers in close cooperation with the Nature Conservancy Council's (NCC) Regional Officers from Shrewsbury and Swansea. Members acted as the eyes and ears of the Conservancy in respect of existing designated Sites of Special Scientific Interest. There were only 14 of these in Herefordshire and eight in Radnorshire, and a look out was kept for other sites which might merit designation. Of enormous value to the Trust was an offer from David Wells to place his professional competence as a chartered surveyor and valuer at the Trust's disposal. Most of the Trust's early purchases were negotiated by him, beginning with the Woodside nature reserve on the Great Doward in 1966. By 1970 Eywood Pool (Titley) and the first 9.25 acres of Nupend Wood had been purchased, and four acres of Cother Wood had been leased. An increasing number of hours were being worked by a team of volunteers led by Jim Watkins, Volunteer Reserves Manager, carrying out fencing, clearing scrub, cutting paths, tree planting and general maintenance.

Strong support also came from influential figures in Herefordshire such as Harry Willamson, founder of Wyevale Garden Centres, and the Whitfield Estate's George Clive, a very knowledgeable conservationist and dendrologist.

Most early nature reserves were acquired with the generous financial help of CHRISTOPHER CADBURY, the Society, WWF and NCC and were maintained solely by volunteers. The first Radnorshire reserve was acquired as two blocks of woodland six miles north of Rhayader in 1972 and 1982, with a generous donation from the Oakdale Trust.

THE LUGG MEADOW

The priority of putting together sufficient financial capital to buy reserves was uppermost in the minds of those involved. Lieutenant Colonel Ernle Gilbert became first Vice Chairman in 1968, and replaced Dr Walker as Chairman in 1972. Gilbert was also instrumental in setting up the Herefordshire Conservation and Development Trust (HCDT) with the aim of raising funds to assist the Trust in purchasing new reserves when required. A fundraising appeal was made and the HCDT helped the Trust buy many reserves. The first purchases on the Lugg Meadow – flower-rich grassland next to the River Lugg, west of Hereford – were helped by £30,000 from HCDT and formed the basis for the eventual acquisition of Lower House Farm – the Trust's current headquarters – and considerably more of the Lugg Meadow.

The Lugg Meadow is the largest surviving example of Lammas Meadow – common land dating back to medieval times, divided into strips by stone markers known as 'dole stones'. The snakeshead fritillaries on the Lugg Meadow are still a star attraction and many people visit the reserve each spring to see them. Dr Anthea Brian conducted detailed research on the Lugg Meadow and, in 2002, she produced a book with Peter Thomson on the site – *The History and Natural History of the Lugg Meadow*. She was made MBE for services to conservation. After her death in 2007, the Trust's librarian, Beryl Harding, wrote *The History of Lower House Farm and its Surrounding Land*, based on Dr Brian's research.

Above: Charles Walker – the Trust's founder and first Chairman

Further help for the management of the Trust's nature reserves came from a Manpower Services Commission team to supplement the Trust's other volunteer teams. The Volunteer Reserves Manager, Jim Watkins, was joined by a deputy, Charles Wooler in 1979.

The Herefordshire part of the Trust continued to rent rooms in Castle Street, Hereford as its headquarters. The priority was the acquisition of nature reserves, although there was increasing pressure to find another building with more space. The first paid member of staff was appointed in the early 1980s.

HEREFORDSHIRE GOES IT ALONE
The Trust's founder and its first Chairman, Dr Charles Walker, died in 1988 aged 100. When, in old age, he was taken round an old people's home, with the idea that he and his wife might move there, he wanted to know (as he rejected the idea), "what all those people are up to, sitting around doing nothing". Walker certainly did not sit around doing nothing.

In 1987, with increased support for the Radnorshire part of the Trust, (which needed to link to other Trusts in Wales to obtain grant funding and support), the decision was taken for Herefordshire and Radnorshire to separate. In October 1987, the Herefordshire Nature Trust was officially launched. This separation was achieved amicably under the chairmanship of Dr Anthea Brian, in Herefordshire, and Dr Gordon Parker in Radnorshire.

In September 1987, the Trust acquired its first computer. By 1988 eight local branches were established, and by 1989 there were 1,540 members.

In 1991, with traffic increasing in Hereford, a proposal to build a bypass east of the city, across the Lugg Meadow, was opposed by the Trust. A public inquiry was held and a decision was made that the conservation of the area was all-important and that a western route would be better. At the time of writing this has not yet been approved, but there is still a threat to the Lugg Meadow and also to the conservation areas to the west side of Hereford. The Trust's position has been that increased traffic

Snakeshead fritillaries and a dole stone on the Lugg Meadow

and any building of a bypass would threaten the peaceful nature of the surroundings of Hereford.

Legacies were patchy, but in one memorable year – 1998 – the Trust was left two properties. One was sold, with the Trust retaining part of the land as a nature reserve. The bungalow on the other, left by a long-time, dedicated supporter, John Knight of Purland Chase, Ross-on-Wye, was initially rented out and then sold, with the surrounding land retained as a reserve.

In 1996 a Grade II listed building, Lower House Farm, was bought with enormous help from the HERITAGE LOTTERY FUND (HLF), members and local support. It was described as "a very impressive detached country house of immense character with 41.57 acres of level and banky pasture land near the Lugg Meadows with common grazing rights over 400 acres for 500 sheep and 100 cattle". Tree-ring analysis dates the building to 1614. There was little doubt that the farm had been closely associated with the Lugg Meadow, where its land shared a lengthy boundary with some of the 88 acres owned by the Trust. The house was highly dilapidated and required comprehensive renovation. The happy outcome, however, was that after its restoration, the building was opened as the Trust's headquarters by DAVID BELLAMY.

A further highlight of 1996 was the award of an MBE to the Trust's Reserves Manager, Jim Watkins, for services to conservation.

DIFFICULT TIMES

The growth of the Trust meant it became necessary to appoint a Conservation Officer to be in overall charge. But the first appointment to this post in 1998 was not very successful. For reasons of their own – and unknown to the Council of Management – the Conservation Officer, together with a consultant working for the Trust and a Trustee, set up a rival company named Herefordshire Wildlife Trust. This has had a lasting effect, preventing the Nature Trust from changing its name in line with the other 46 Wildlife Trusts. The *Flycatcher* reported that "1998 was a

Lower House Farm – the Trust's headquarters

challenging time for the Trust. Disaffection amongst some staff resulted in them, together with others, setting up a limited company with the stated aim of working for wildlife conservation in Herefordshire. The formation of this company was followed by the resignations of the Conservation Officer, Conservation Support Officer and Office Administrator in April." The next two appointments of Chief Executive Officers only lasted a short time, both moving on to other areas of conservation, leaving the Trust in a weakened state. Tom Davies, Chairman at the time, ensured that the Trust survived this difficult period and emerged as a stronger force for conservation in Herefordshire.

MILLENNIUM MAKEOVER

In 2002, Sarah Ayling took over as Chief Executive and the Trust started to make progress again, becoming well-known and respected locally and farther afield. The same year, the Council of Management and Executive Committee were replaced by a smaller Board of Trustees, and a new Memorandum and Articles were approved. In the light of more staff being employed, different Trustee skills were needed. Regional links also became important as the Trust was now part of the West Midlands region in company with the Trusts in Shropshire, Staffordshire, Birmingham and the Black County, Warwickshire and Worcestershire.

The Board has had several eminent Chairs, including Ceidrych Griffiths, an expert photographer who started the Ross-on-Wye branch of the Trust, and Dr David Boddington – a bird enthusiast and a qualified bird ringer –

who monitors nesting birds in many local woodlands. Graham Roberts, who led the team that oversaw the restoration of Lower House Farm, was followed by Tom Davies and Betty Winser. Tom Davies was involved in the Trust from its inception and went on to not only be its Chairman from 1997 to 2002, but afterwards remained a Trustee and Treasurer of the HCDT. Roger Beck, the Trust's present Chairman, used his knowledge of the flora and fauna of Herefordshire to oversee the production of a new and colourful *Reserve Guide* with the support of the Heritage Lottery Fund.

WORKING WITH YOUNG PEOPLE

During 1999 to 2001, volunteers were recruited to undertake a Phase 1 survey of the county for a Millennium Map Project (MMP). From this came the idea of setting up a project for young adults looking for work in nature conservation. From 2001 to 2004, the Environment and Experience for Lifelong Learning (EEL) project was funded by the Learning Skills Council and European Social Fund. This helped to complete the MMP, as well as train professionals and those seeking work in conservation. From 2006 to 2011, the Trust ran the HLF-funded project Learning Environments in Marine, Urban, Rural (LEMUR), working in partnership with the SHEFFIELD TRUST and Ambios Limited. Organisations hosting placements ranged from the Trust, the Marine Biological Association, Wye Valley AONB, the Malvern Hills Conservators, Warwickshire Council and the WORCESTERSHIRE TRUST. LEMUR received in excess of 1,200 applications for its 36 bursary placements, proving that there is still a demand for this type of training.

Above: Wood white butterfly at Pentaloe Glen
Left: Board member, Dr Anthea Brian, a knowledgeable conservationist who oversaw the formation of the Herefordshire Trust following its split from Radnorshire in 1987

Another innovative project, Wildplay, was started in 2002 to encourage children in Herefordshire to play outdoors and explore the natural world through creative play. This started by working with existing playcare providers and, since 2004, it has been working with Sure Start Children's Centres and the Marches Housing Association to provide Wildplay Rangers for children within a number of housing estates across Herefordshire. More recently, the project has built new partnerships with West Mercia Police and local community groups, such as the Scouts. It also organises open access and nature play for children aged between two and 14, providing environmental play in their housing estates and wild spaces. The project has also worked with schools across Herefordshire, helping them to access local nature reserves and giving children ideas on where to go and what to do.

CHANGING CONSERVATION

With the changing aims of its conservation work, the Trust's policy has broadened into projects working with communities, farmers, and other conservation bodies. The Community Commons Project, funded by HLF, ran from 2003 to 2010, and worked with people around 12 key commons in Herefordshire, helping them write and implement management plans for their local common. The Woolhope Dome Project, started in 2001, was an early Living Landscape project. It enabled the Trust to work with farmers and landowners in the Woolhope Dome – a Biodiversity Enhancement Area – to provide advice on land management and grants. The project also provided a range of training events and helped set up a local farmers' market. The Community and Biodiversity Project worked with the wider community of Herefordshire, encouraging people to get involved in recording and survey work. It generated more than 3,000 new records and set up a number of specialist recording groups.

From time to time new nature reserves have been acquired, sometimes helped by legacies or financial assistance from the HCDT. The acquisition of reserves is still important, but increasingly the Trust is focusing its conservation work on larger areas or extending and linking existing reserves.

The Wednesday volunteers

Schoolchildren enjoying a reptile walk with Nigel Hand – the 'snake man' – on Ewyas Harold Common

Recent acquisitions have been North and South Sturts (which is the Trust's largest reserve), Parky Meadow near Wigmore and the Parks, with the Dulas Brook running through it. By 2011, the Trust owned 54 nature reserves, safeguarding some of Herefordshire's finest natural habitats.

BY BETTY WINSER
Betty Winser has been volunteering with the Trust since 1985 and has served on many of the committees. She was Vice Chairman from 1997–02, Chairman from 2002–06, and is still a Trustee. She also helps with work on the Trust's nature reserves.

CHAPTER 19

Hertfordshire and Middlesex

In the early 1960s, a group of local naturalists and interested people assembled out of common concern for Hertfordshire's rapidly declining wildlife. They were deeply worried about the post-war loss of habitats, especially the conversion of grazing land to arable crops and the devastating effects of agro-chemicals on farmland birds.

In November 1963, the Trust's inaugural meeting in a St Albans' parish hall was so over-subscribed that people had to be turned away. In 1964, the Trust was registered as a charity and soon acquired its first nature reserves, including Old Park Wood, Barkway Chalk Pit and Fox Covert.

EARLY CAMPAIGNS

An early cause for concern came in the shape of the Commons Registration Act (1965). Common land not registered by 1970 would revert to private ownership – which meant more chance of enclosure or building development. The Trust alerted members to the threat to local open spaces, many of which were at risk. Earlier in 1965, there were proposals to convert parts of both Hertford and Patmore Heaths to sports grounds. It was to the credit of the Trust's early activists that these important acid heathlands were not only saved, but later became Trust reserves.

At this time, the persecution of badgers was also a constant problem. In 1966, a group of plucky Middlesex members and volunteers made surprise visits to setts under threat, often late at night and at some personal risk to themselves. The first Badger Act came about in 1973, although that didn't resolve all the problems.

In 1966, the Trust chose the great crested grebe as its logo. Just as this bird was fighting its way back from decline, it was not long before the new logo was being spotted regularly across the two counties.

Opposite: Pasque flower at Therfield Heath. Right: Handover of the deeds for Fox Covert reserve, one of the Trust's early acquisitions

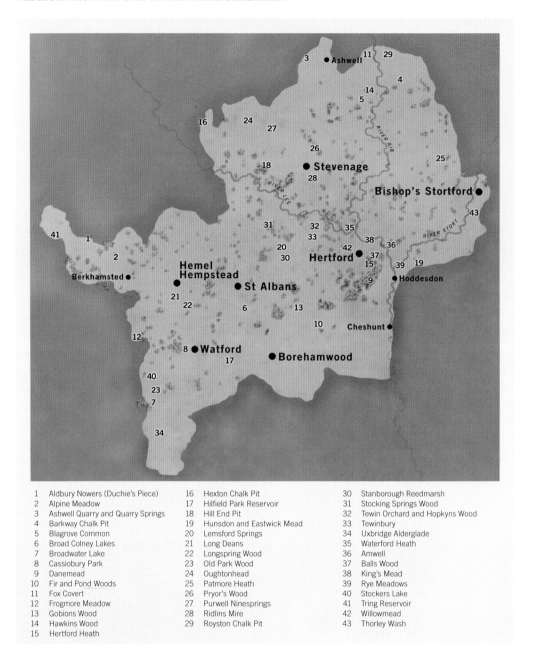

1	Aldbury Nowers (Duchie's Piece)	16	Hexton Chalk Pit	30	Stanborough Reedmarsh
2	Alpine Meadow	17	Hilfield Park Reservoir	31	Stocking Springs Wood
3	Ashwell Quarry and Quarry Springs	18	Hill End Pit	32	Tewin Orchard and Hopkyns Wood
4	Barkway Chalk Pit	19	Hunsdon and Eastwick Mead	33	Tewinbury
5	Blagrove Common	20	Lemsford Springs	34	Uxbridge Alderglade
6	Broad Colney Lakes	21	Long Deans	35	Waterford Heath
7	Broadwater Lake	22	Longspring Wood	36	Amwell
8	Cassiobury Park	23	Old Park Wood	37	Balls Wood
9	Danemead	24	Oughtonhead	38	King's Mead
10	Fir and Pond Woods	25	Patmore Heath	39	Rye Meadows
11	Fox Covert	26	Pryor's Wood	40	Stockers Lake
12	Frogmore Meadow	27	Purwell Ninesprings	41	Tring Reservoir
13	Gobions Wood	28	Ridlins Mire	42	Willowmead
14	Hawkins Wood	29	Royston Chalk Pit	43	Thorley Wash
15	Hertford Heath				

Map of Hertfordshire and Middlesex Wildlife Trust nature reserves

Much later on, in 1995, the Trust adopted The Wildlife Trusts' national badger logo – happy to fly the flag on a united front.

Ashwell Quarry, Blagrove Common and Sawbridgeworth Marsh were added to the Trust's early portfolio of nature reserves in 1970 and, at the close of the Trust's first ten years, there were 20 nature reserves dotted across the two counties and 4,000 members.

SEVENTIES' HAZE

In the 1970s, scores of people got involved in the Help a Toad Across the Road scheme, safely assisting these animals to cross increasingly busy roads during their annual migrations to breeding ponds. Meanwhile, 'Plant a Tree in '73 – Plant Some More in '74!' became a popular slogan within the Trust. Local MP Shirley Williams joined in by planting a tree at one of the Trust's nature reserves. The next few years were a haze of fêtes, garden sales, car boot sales and other fundraising events. Green Shield stamps were all the rage and helped members to fund vital equipment for the Trust.

NEW OFFICES

By 1978 it was time to put down new roots. St Albans District Council offered the Trust the site of the former wildlife zoo in Verulanium Park and bequeathed a part timber-framed building. Grebe House opened on the site in 1981 with a wildlife garden, an education centre, a shop and offices that housed a growing conservation team and a tireless crew of volunteers. A year previously, in 1980, the Trust had started its first WILDLIFE WATCH group which was managed for many years by Jane Baldwin.

Bill Darling retired as the Trust's President in 1982, after working closely with the Trust since its beginnings. His shoes were ably filled by Simon Bowes Lyon (now Sir) whose mother, Lady Bowes Lyon, had been a founder member. Simon's keen interest in botany specifically, and wildlife in general, has been an asset to the Trust ever since.

In 1982, Fir and Pond Woods were acquired as nature reserves, as were Broad Colney and Chorleywood Dell. Volunteer reserve wardens became increasingly involved in managing reserves. As staff have come and gone over the years, these dedicated volunteers have continued to increase the ecological knowledge of the sites in their care and to ensure that the resulting management work is carried out accordingly, year in, year out.

FUNDRAISING FOCUS

By the Trust's 21st birthday, the focus was on raising profile and on an appeal to secure £40,000 for more sites. Staff and volunteers gave cash, donations,

Lemsford Springs nature reserve – an early acquisition for the Trust and a special place for wildlife

books, collectables, stamps and, most of all, their time. Flea markets, plant sales, coffee mornings, sponsored birdwatches and talks all helped the Trust to buy the freehold on what was to become its 44th nature reserve, Frogmore Meadow, near Sarratt. That same year it signed an agreement to manage Telegraph Hill, near Lilley, just off the ancient Icknield Way. A bequest brought the Trust its 46th nature reserve – Longspring Wood, near Kings Langley – which was opened by illustrator and naturalist, Gordon Beningfield.

When English Nature launched its national common dormouse campaign in 1983, in Hertfordshire old milk cartons were used as temporary nestboxes and members sent in nibbled hazelnuts found as part of the Great Nut Hunt. Landowners were offered advice to increase habitat for these adorable creatures, encouraging the counties' small population to thrive and spread.

PUSHING AT THE GREEN FRONTIERS

In the mid-1980s, the Trust's Wildlife Watchers joined in the national Acid Drops project to monitor winter rainfall. In 1988, the Trust was an early pioneer of sustainable living, urging everyone to reduce, reuse and recycle with its Can-DO campaign.

Meanwhile, that summer, broadcaster Chris Baines dropped in to help Watch members on the River Ver, as part of the Trust's Living Rivers project. Trust members, Watch groups, Cubs and Brownies assessed water pollution, revealing that poorly-treated sewage, agricultural fertilisers and surface run-off from building sites were the main culprits. The project covered 22 local rivers, producing 400 readings of the counties' waterways and establishing a great foundation for improvements for wildlife.

In 1985, the Trust welcomed The Wildlife Trusts' President, SIR DAVID ATTENBOROUGH, as he reached Watford Town Hall on the Hertfordshire leg of his national tour to raise funds for the BRITISH WILDLIFE APPEAL. He returned in April 1988 – to help launch the Trust's Winning with Wildlife campaign.

In 1989, film critic Barry Norman opened Tewin Orchard – the Trust's 49th nature reserve and one of great importance, given the loss of two-thirds of the counties' old orchards over 30 years.

Further good news followed in 1990 when, after a 60-year absence from Hertfordshire, a pair of black-necked grebes bred at one of the Trust's reserves, successfully raising three chicks. In the summer of 1998 another pair nested – raising four chicks. Up to four pairs have regularly used the reserve since then. The use of this and other reserves by wintering and passage birds continues to influence the Trust's management of these sites.

ROYAL NATURE RESERVE

In early 1991, the Botanical Society of the British Isles (BSBI) was looking to support a flower-rich nature reserve to honour their Royal Patron, Queen Elizabeth, The Queen Mother on her 90th birthday. The Trust was honoured when new reserve, Aldbury Nowers, was selected as The Queen Mother's nature reserve – Duchie's Piece. In the county of Her Majesty's birth, it boasts a fine swathe of chalk grassland, supporting many wildflowers.

The same year, Barry Norman was back again to help launch the Otter Habitat project at Tewinbury nature reserve. Otters had not been seen in

Aldbury Nowers, 'Duchie's Piece' is commemorated to the Queen Mother on her 90th birthday in 1991

Hertfordshire since 1976. However, after years of habitat recreation and the reintroduction of six otters by St Albans Sand and Gravel and the Otter Trust onto the Rivers Lee and Stort in 1991, otters are now established in the Lee Valley and foraging widely along the county's rivers.

The Trust celebrated its 30th year with a lakeside concert at St Paul's in Walden Bury in 1993. Finances were tight, however, and for a short while, staffing, salaries and even members' magazines had to be reined in. Tough decisions were made – but when it came to protecting wildlife, the Trust could afford no compromises. Happily, two years later the Trust was again back on a firm financial footing.

By 1996, the Trust was concentrating on putting the 1992 Rio de Janeiro Earth Summit into a local context, resulting in the launch, the following year, of the Hertfordshire Biodiversity Action Plan. Its detailed targets then formed the core of the Trust's conservation work (BIODIVERSITY ACTION PLANNING).

FIRST HERTS HABITAT SURVEY

The first ever habitat survey of Hertfordshire was completed by Trust volunteers in 1997. This was a three-year joint project with the Hertfordshire Environmental Records Centre which enabled more important habitats to qualify as LOCAL WILDLIFE

SITES. This gave them increased protection and enabled the Trust to target resources for their future management. Meanwhile, the Trust started advising Local Wildlife Site owners on environmental management and sources of funding. Initially a three-year project, the Wildlife Sites Partnership continues to this day.

In 1998, a trading subsidiary of the Trust, Herts and Middlesex Wildlife Consultancy (HMWC) was formed. HMWC offers ecological and land management services to a broad range of clients – for example it wrote the Stevenage Biodiversity Action Plan – and all profits go to the Trust to help with its conservation work.

LOBBYING FOR BETTER WILDLIFE PROTECTION
In spring 1999, the Trust joined 22 other organisations at the House of Commons to put pressure on the Government for greater wildlife protection legislation. Members lobbied local MPs and wrote to the Prime Minister. Their joint efforts were rewarded when the Countryside and Rights of Way Act 2000 was finally passed. It brought in better laws for wildlife and provided powers to address cases of deliberate damage and neglect of the countryside.

That year, ten Shetland sheep were recruited to start work on restoring Hertfordshire grassland reserves. Today, more than 40 of their four-legged colleagues can be regularly seen on the Trust's reserves.

However, the next year foot-and-mouth disease struck. Reserves were closed to the public, but the Trust was fortunate that there were no outbreaks in Hertfordshire or Middlesex. In fact, it later appeared that wildlife had made the most of a closed season, with many species apparently showing a renewed vigour.

NEW MILLENNIUM CAMPAIGNS
In 2001, through Constituency Oaks (part of the national Trees of Times and Place initiative), the Trust was pleased to achieve a tree planting for every one of its Hertfordshire MPs – either on one of its reserves, or in collaboration with

partners across the county. Nationally, more than 400 MPs pledged their support for the Constituency Oaks project.

A decline in winter roosts for bats prompted the Trust's Bat Brick project in the summer of 2002. The last remaining brick manufacturer in Hertfordshire – Bovingdon Brickworks – helped the Trust produce handmade bat bricks to install in old lime kilns and pill boxes. Members sponsoring bricks raised £1,600 for the Trust's work in keeping the area's bats snug. Talking Trees was unveiled at Stanborough Reedmarsh nature reserve in 2003. Adult mental health groups created an audio tape to guide visitors round the reserve via some of its natural highlights, interpreted by the group through poems and music.

At this time the Trust also celebrated the culmination of a HERITAGE LOTTERY FUND (HLF) three-year project at Rye Meads nature reserve. The project brought together the RSPB and HMWT reserves into one single, larger nature reserve with a visitor centre, as well as new bird hides and additional new land for wildlife.

REACHING OUT
The Trust's audience was widening. With support from GlaxoSmithKline, a Schools Go Wild pack was produced for every school in east Hertfordshire with ideas on how to improve their school grounds for wildlife. Work started on a major five-year project funded by the HLF with a grant of over £830,000, to improve access and information for visitors across the Trust's nature reserves.

In 2004, the Trust started to coordinate a response to the huge decline in the water vole population with a new partnership project. Working with the Environment Agency, Thames Water, Herts County Council, British Waterways and Lee Valley Regional Park Authority, the Trust raised awareness of the water vole's plight and undertook practical work, including surveying and advising landowners on habitat management.

The Trust celebrated its 40th year and acquired some interesting grazing beasts at Rye Meads nature reserve, with four water buffalo arriving from Lee Valley Regional Park Authority!

GRANTS FOR GRAVEL PIT JEWEL

The Trust's wetland restoration work took a giant leap forward when, in December 2006, it acquired Amwell, a series of former gravel pits in the Lee Valley near Ware, with the help of the Tubney Charitable Trust and Green Arc. Grants from Natural England, Biffaward, Hanson, Hertfordshire Natural History Society, Waterways Trust, Environment Agency and Lee Valley Regional Park Authority to do work on the site were an initial boost. These were followed in 2007 and 2008 with major funds from East of England Development Agency and Growth Area Funding (DCLG) totalling £450,000. This meant new hides, footpaths, interpretation, access work and a Dragonfly Trail for visitors to enjoy, developing Amwell into one of the best places to watch wildlife in the country. In 2008, Chris Packham came to open the reserve to the public. Its most recent claim to fame was hosting Hertfordshire's first breeding pair of little egrets in 2011.

Bittern at Amwell nature reserve

In late 2006, The Wildlife Trusts launched a LIVING LANDSCAPE which set out a vision for nature conservation on a landscape scale. Trusts across the UK were involved in looking at how they could extend their work over larger areas and outside nature reserves. In Hertfordshire and Middlesex, 28 areas were identified as having Living Landscape potential – places with a good diversity of wildlife where working on a bigger scale with other landowners and managers would be possible. Projects at four of these areas are currently active – in the Colne Valley, Stort Valley, South Hertfordshire Woods and Lee Valley.

PRIZE-WINNING WOODLAND

With significant help from Natural England's Aggregate Levy Sustainability Fund in 2009, the Trust made another important acquisition – Balls Wood, near Hertford, purchased from the Forestry Commission. The local community was galvanised into action by the potential threat to the wood and its special wildlife as it went up for sale. More than 1,000 individual donors helped to secure its future. The campaign to save Balls Wood won the Trust the Mercury and Observer Newspaper Best Community Appeal Award. Staying in east Herts, the Trust became more active in the Stort Valley, a key Living Landscape area. It acquired Eastwick Mead, a first step to reinstating the historic Hunsdon and Eastwick Common of years gone by. This was followed by a community project in the area bringing people into contact with wildlife who had never set foot on a nature reserve before, and reaching some of the most deprived wards in east Hertfordshire and over the county border in Essex.

RARE WILDLIFE RETURNS

Amongst the many new reserve acquisitions and partnerships, wildlife was flourishing. The Trust's work to restore ditches at King's Meads nature reserve had seen nearly 8,000 water violet flower spikes recorded in 2009 – from a previous total of just 20. In 2010, more than 20,000 flourished and 2011 was an even better year. Rare wildlife was

Balls Wood – saved in 2009 by a major fundraising campaign

returning: the small blue butterfly reappeared at Aldbury Nowers nature reserve in 2010 for the first time in eight years; and in 2011, small blues were observed breeding there, a sure sign that the Trust's 2007–08 chalk grassland restoration project had reaped rewards.

After 15 years of sterling service, Richard Ball retired as Chairman in 2010, passing the mantle on to Mike Master. In 2011, Chief Executive Judy Adams retired too, after ten years in the post, having presided over huge growth both in membership and in the security of tenure across the Trust's nature reserves. Jane Durney has now taken on the role of Chief Executive as the Trust moves into a new era. With staff numbers growing all the time, the Trust plans to expand further into new accommodation.

In 2011, the Trust embarked on more ambitious projects. A long-term lease was signed at Waterford Heath with Lafarge Aggregates to ensure wildlife has protection for at least the next 85 years on this site. Thorley Wash nature reserve near Bishop's Stortford was acquired. The Trust has

new projects operating in Stevenage and Hillingdon to engage local communities with wildlife in their area. In addition, a three-year woodland restoration project, starting in autumn 2011, will build on the important work already achieved through the 2009 Balls Wood purchase. The ultimate aim is to create an arc of woodland extending through south Hertfordshire, across other county boundaries, working in partnership with others to achieve the vision of landscape-scale conservation for Hertfordshire and Middlesex.

BY CLARE GRAY AND SARAH BUCKINGHAM
Clare Gray was Communications Officer at the Hertfordshire and Middlesex Wildlife Trust. She helped to coordinate the Trust's media activity and fundraising campaigns, serving for several years until 2010.

Sarah Buckingham is Communications Officer at the Trust.

CHAPTER 20

Isles of Scilly

The Isles of Scilly is a group of islands 30 miles south-west of Land's End, Cornwall. Their wildlife is both rich and distinctive. Species like the dwarf pansy, the Scilly shrew and the chestnut-coloured Scilly bee are unique. Others, including the least and lesser adderstongue fern, are among the UK's rarest species.

The islands have formed part of the possessions of the Dukes of Cornwall since 1337. In 1834, Augustus Smith became Lord-Proprietor and leaseholder of all the islands. Later, his descendants gave up the tenancy of St Mary's, St Martin's, St Agnes and Bryher to the Duchy, but retained the lease of Tresco and the uninhabited islands.

The islands are a paradise for birds, providing a home for many seabirds in particular and a stop-over for exciting and rare visitors. The resident sparrows and song thrushes are famously bold, while Scilly's wrens and blackbirds are slightly different to those on the mainland. In autumn, large numbers of migrating birds pass through the islands, attracting many birdwatchers, who sometimes arrive in large numbers to catch sight of rare and unusual birds.

Beneath the waves and around their many miles of coastline, the islands are home to a diverse and rich environment for marine wildlife; from rocky reefs encrusted with delicate and colourful invertebrates to seagrass meadows; and from boulder-strewn shorelines to the outlying rocks and small islands which provide safe refuges for breeding seabirds.

However, it is not all good news. There were once around 100,000 puffins in Scilly – today there are fewer than 100 pairs. Terns and kittiwakes have decreased rapidly, and the roseate tern has already disappeared. Manx shearwater and storm petrel cling on in their only English breeding colonies.

MOSS REPORT

By the early 1980s, rural land on the main inhabited islands of St Mary's, St Martin's, St Agnes and Bryher was either leased for farming or managed by the Duchy of Cornwall in association with the Nature Conservancy Council (the Conservancy). In 1971, the Duchy and Conservancy jointly funded the appointment of a warden, until sadly he died in 1977. While some conservation work continued, including sporadic recording and research by visiting specialists, the Conservancy's resources were inadequate for the task.

It was not only resources for conservation that were giving cause for concern. Both agriculture and tourism in the islands were fragile. HRH The Prince of Wales expressed his concern over the

Opposite: Granite rocks on Gugh
Right: Scilly shrew

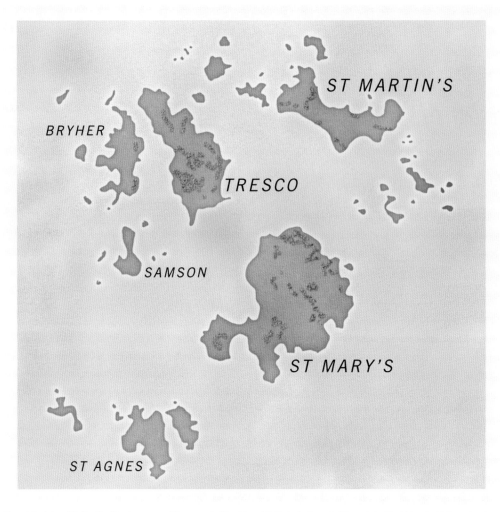

Map of the Isles of Scilly. The Trust manages 60 per cent of the Isles of Scilly including all of the uninhabited islands, islets and rocks and most of the coastline of St Mary's, St Martin's, St Agnes and Bryher

state of the Islands' economy. In 1982, the Duchy of Cornwall, in association with the local authority and several other relevant organisations, commissioned an outside organisation, Graham Moss Associates, to help find a way forward. Their report, *The Isles of Scilly Comprehensive Land Use and Community Development Project* became known as '*The Moss Report*'. Anticipating changes Robert Dorrien-Smith, a descendant of Augustus, agreed to transfer the lease of the uninhabited islands back to the Duchy.

The Moss Report, published in 1984, also recommended the establishment of an environmental trust for the islands. The trust would be charged

with the conservation of wildlife, landscape and ancient monuments on untenanted land, the provision of advice on conservation, securing and managing visitor access and providing an information and interpretive service. The Isles of Scilly Environmental Trust was duly established and conducted its first formal meeting on 22nd July 1985. The first meeting of the Trustee Board, on 4th September 1985, elected Dorrien-Smith as its Chairman. It would not join The Wildlife Trusts movement for another 15 years.

A ROYAL DONATION

Little documentation exists on how members of the

Steering Committee (who subsequently became the first Trustees) or the Director-designate were chosen. HRH The Prince of Wales agreed to be the Trust's Patron and made a donation of £50,000 to kick-start the Trust's finances. By the end of 1985, many of the formal arrangements for running the new Trust were in place and work had begun on an environmental management plan for the islands. The Trust's constitution was agreed with the Duchy and the Charity Commission, early in 1986.

At the same time, the Duchy produced a draft lease for 1,000 hectares of land, later extended by a further 850 hectares, including many of the uninhabited islands which were important seabird colonies. The lease was finally signed in June 1987.

During the late 1980s the Trust tried to define its role. It needed to establish its credentials with the local population and sponsoring bodies, and to secure its financial position. But things were not easy. It was struggling, for example, to find office accommodation. To aid the longer-term objectives, an Advisory Committee was established to act as a forum for meeting regularly with the Trust's sponsors: the Conservancy (later English Nature), the Countryside Commission (later the Countryside Agency), the Duchy of Cornwall and the local authority. The Cornwall Archaeological Unit was also represented.

TEETHING TROUBLES

In these early years, two fundamental issues affected the Trust's image and the way it was able to conduct its business. First, there was a perception, among residents and also some of the sponsors, that it was not open to public scrutiny and unable to represent the views of local people. Some regarded some of the sponsoring bodies as outside interference in local affairs. Three issues arose within the Trust's first few years that illustrate these problems and the difficult position the Trust sometimes found itself in.

The first was the local authority's plan to dispose of household and commercial refuse in a coastal landfill site of great scenic beauty. The newly-formed

Signing the Trust Deed in 1985

Trust opposed the plan. At first it seemed the Trust had little support, but after determined opposition the tide turned and the plan was eventually abandoned. While the Trust could claim some of the success, the wedge that seemed to have been driven between it and the local authority made its task much more difficult. Such problems are significantly greater in a small, isolated community.

LANDSCAPE CONSERVATION AND TOURISM

The second difficult issue was the proposal to build a new hotel on Trust-leased land at a coastal site on the island of St Martin's. A new hotel would stimulate this small island's economy, but it needed to be balanced against many Trustees' perceptions of the inevitable landscape degradation and increased pressure on water supply, local materials and wildlife habitat. In the negotiations, the Trust argued on the basis that it had agreed with its sponsors, including its landlord, to manage the land it leased in accordance with its management plan and charitable objects. The Trust lost the argument and the hotel was built. The same sponsors that agreed the management plan and the Trust's charitable objects were often those that opposed (or at the very least, did not support) its efforts to uphold those objects.

The third, and arguably the most contentious, issue was a plan to extend the runway at St Mary's Airport. This brought the Trust into direct opposition with the local authority and with the Duchy. The Trust was obliged to give up land from its lease and, in 1991, the runway was built.

STRIVING FOR A MORE DEMOCRATIC APPROACH

Trustees were originally appointed for life but, changes to the Trust's governance in 1992 meant that they became appointed for a three-year period and eligible for re-election by existing Trustees. This helped to ensure the introduction of some new blood, but the Trust also proposed a Supporters' Group of Islanders from which new Trustees might be drawn. The Group was established in mid-1992 and ran for five years. It would act as a link between the Trust and the public, as well as raising funds, but, unfortunately, it never really fulfilled the hopes for it.

FUNDING ISSUES

Given the Trust's main charitable object to conserve wildlife habitats and its management plan for a large area of wild landscape, the lack of land and habitat management and the failure to appoint a Field Officer until late 1989 cannot be ignored in this historical account.

The Moss Report had suggested various ways the Trust might be financed. Only one of these would have ensured a steady income from unrestricted funds – a small charge to every visitor to the Isles to be earmarked for conservation work. This would require the wholehearted backing of the local authority, the tourism industry and local transport operators (who would have to administer it) which has never been forthcoming.

One of the main tasks of the Trust's Director was to raise funds, which he did with reasonable success in the form of covenanted donations. However, other funds were still needed if the Trust was to fulfil its objectives. In its first full financial year, the Trust received 66 per cent of its total income (£24,000) from its sponsors. By 1990–91 this had fallen to 16 per cent and the Trust was in a difficult financial position. Even the Field Officer's guided walks raised money towards his salary.

HEALTHIER HORIZONS

In 1994 the first Director retired. He had contributed significantly to the Trust's establishment, in terms of his organisational abilities and financial management. The second Director was in post only a few months. It was the third Director, fresh from being Warden of Lundy Island, who was able to begin giving the Trust some leadership in conservation.

English Nature had primary responsibility for nature conservation in the Isles because of its duty of care for the two dozen or so Sites of Special Scientific Interest (SSSIs) in Scilly. But, in 1995 there was an important development for the Trust. It became eligible to enter English Nature's RESERVES ENHANCEMENT SCHEME. This soon became a major and reliable source of funding for conservation work in Scilly and was reviewed and renewed at the end of 2000. Beginning in 1996, another important initiative was the Countryside Stewardship Scheme, administered then by the Ministry of Agriculture Fisheries and Food (MAFF). This provided modest funds for the management of specific areas of land until 2006. These funding streams were complemented by a grant from English Heritage for habitat management around seven scheduled monument sites on Trust-leased land. It was clear, however, that if the Trust was to develop groundbreaking conservation work, it needed further, larger sources of funding.

If funds were insufficient to employ enough staff to manage more than 1,000 hectares of land, then a practical solution was the efficient use of volunteers. They were not all going to come from within the resident population and recruitment of volunteers (and paid staff) from the mainland had always been limited by the availability of suitable accommodation. The new Director conceived the idea that a long-disused naval gun battery on The Garrison, a fortified hill on St Mary's, could be adapted to provide volunteer accommodation. A substantial grant toward its conversion was obtained from MAFF, English Heritage and English Nature. The Trust was also obliged to use a significant proportion of its financial reserves, leaving it in a somewhat precarious position. But, once complete, the facility helped the Trust attract many first-rate volunteers who have carried out far more conservation work than would otherwise have been possible.

ANCIENT HISTORY

The Trust has a significant focus on conserving the Island's archaeological heritage, as well as its natural heritage. The archaeology of Scilly is internationally-important – the many different remains scattered across the islands tell the story of at least 4,000 years of human occupation. The islands hold the greatest density of Bronze Age remains anywhere in the world. The Trust is responsible for the maintenance of more than 230 scheduled ancient monuments including prehistoric field systems and houses, Neolithic burial sites, stone menhirs and the whole of the now-uninhabited island of Samson. The Trust carries out work to preserve and restore these precious sites.

FUNDRAISING FOCUS

In 1998, a new Field Officer (his title was later changed to Conservation Officer) was appointed: a Scillonian with an intimate knowledge of the Islands, who had gained valuable conservation experience in New Zealand. With a desire to expand the conservation work of the Trust, came the need to seek additional sources of funding. With assistance from the Duchy, the Trust employed a professional fundraising company. This brought in some useful small-scale grants and donations that were able to support some interesting new projects, including the purchase of a Trust boat.

Towards the end of the decade, two new initiatives provided the potential for securing considerably more support. These were the granting of European Objective One status to Cornwall and the Isles of Scilly, and the availability of grants from the HERITAGE LOTTERY FUND (HLF) for a scheme called Tomorrow's Heathland Heritage. A local consultant worked with English Nature's Project Officer for the Islands to develop a business plan for restoration of the Scillonian heathlands which had become degraded by encroachment of invasive plants, such as bracken, gorse and bramble. They required matched funding, which was difficult and

Archaeological remains on Samson

Volunteers carrying out heathland restoration work with the Waves of Heath project

time-consuming to raise. Neither did they solve the continuing problem of core funding for the day-to-day work of the organisation. In 2001, the Director retired and the Trustees were forced to fundamentally rethink the administration of the Trust.

REINVENTION AND REGENERATION

Rather than appointing a new Director, the Trustees decided to employ of a group of energetic young people to drive the conservation programme and to supervise a team of volunteers who could be housed in the new Woolpack Volunteer Centre. Management and administration of the Trust then fell to the Trustees. The Vice Chairman was asked to form a new management team comprising Trustees and staff for this purpose. The committee structure, office administration and financial control systems were radically overhauled and a new business plan was prepared. At the heart was a completely revised

habitat management plan prepared by the Botanical Recorder for the Isles of Scilly who had intimate knowledge of the Islands' wildlife and their requirements.

A key aspect of this reinvented Trust was a long-overdue application for affiliation to The Wildlife Trusts movement. This was accomplished in mid-2001 and ratified by the Society in December of that year. In September 2001, the Isles of Scilly Wildlife Trust was officially launched by Bill Oddie, accompanied by representatives from The Wildlife Trusts' UK office.

HEATHLAND HABITATS

Since that important milestone in the history of the Trust, one of the most significant developments has been the award of a substantial grant for heathland restoration. Called Waves of Heath, and funded by the HLF's Tomorrow's Heathland Heritage scheme, the project ran until 2008. Although additional European funding did not materialise, the Waves of Heath project spawned substantial improvements in wildlife habitats in the Scillonian heathlands and included the introduction of grazing animals to help manage the Islands' heathlands.

UNDER THE WAVES

In 2009–10, the Trust undertook a two-year Marine Biodiversity Programme – involving local people in recording and surveying the Islands' marine life. Through dives, shoreline and boat surveys the programme collected data on four key marine habitats and 38 marine Biodiversity Action Plan species. Divers found new sites rich in sponges and fragile corals and two species (a stalked sea squirt and a false cowrie) that may be new to science. Whales, dolphins and basking sharks were surveyed from the Scillonian ferry each week (which sails between Penzance and St Mary's). This survey still continues. Local fishermen and anglers also helped to record fish species.

The project ultimately aimed to contribute to the establishment of Marine Conservation Zones in the Isles of Scilly, under the Marine and Coastal Access Act 2009. It also aimed to raise awareness of Scilly's marine environment among the local community and get people involved in helping to protect it. To this end the project worked with volunteers, local wildlife enthusiasts, divers, sailors, artists, children, anglers and tourists.

JOINING FORCES

Attempting to solve the perennial problem of core funding, in 2004 the Trust secured a grant from the Esmée Fairbairn Foundation to employ a Membership Development Officer. Realising that local membership could never support the Trust, the plan was to seek mainland membership with the starting point being the 120,000 or so annual visitors to the islands. Unfortunately, this met with little success but in the same year the Trust joined the South West Wildlife Trusts' Regional Group (SWWT). The SWWT helped the Trust to design an appeal in 2005–06 to its members and visitors to the Islands. This raised much-needed funds to enable the Trust to continue its conservation

Cuckoo wrasse

work. SWWT has also assisted in developing a closer working relationship with the CORNWALL TRUST. Whereas in 1985 the Trust stood alone in its environmental work, in 2006 it took its place on the newly-formed Joint Advisory Committee for the Isles of Scilly AONB that includes the Council of the Isles of Scilly, the Duchy, the NFU, Island Tourism, Tresco Estate and many outside agencies.

To complete the story, the Cornwall Trust now has responsibility for staff, membership and financial management. Although each Trust maintains its own Board of Trustees, this exciting development has put the Isles of Scilly Wildlife Trust on a firmer footing, so that it can now look to the future with greater confidence, although funding remains a problem.

BY MIKE GURR
Mike Gurr is a retired biochemist who moved to Scilly in 1990. Starting as the Secretary of the Supporters' Group in 1992, he became a Trustee in 1999, Vice Chairman in 2000, and Trust Chairman from 2001–05. He now edits Wild Scilly *and is Secretary of the Isles of Scilly Bat Group.*

CHAPTER 21

Kent

Kent is a significant location – historically, economically and geologically. For centuries, it has been growing food and providing leisure for London. As Britain's closest point to the continent, travellers to and from Europe have landed at Kent's ports and travelled west until they could cross the Thames. Caesar took that route 2,000 years ago, pacifying what we now know as Bigbury Fort, near Canterbury, now a Trust nature reserve.

The needs of travellers still dominate the county: new and old railway lines seam the landscape, two motorways run parallel to the old coach roads and three different sites for proposed international airports dominate the planning debate. Lorries from the European Union put pressure on the landscape and on the existing roads. The need for more downstream crossing points over the Thames continues and it is likely that a lower Thames crossing will soon create further demand for new road links.

Economically, the county sits in the wealthy south-east, regarded as the country's economic powerhouse. The regeneration of the Thames Gateway, with some of the biggest development schemes in Europe, has been surging east from London, to reach the Isle of Sheppey and Swale.

Kent's complex landscape sits on an equally complex geology that shaped the lines of communication, the distinct clustering of the communities and also the rich diversity of soils and wildlife. The landscape features the chalk of

Opposite: Lizard orchid at Sandwich and Pegwell Bay National Nature Reserve
Right: Dr Francis Rose – renowned botanist, founder of the Trust, and influential in the development of the Trust movement

the North Downs, the Wealden clays and sandstones, the Greensand Ridge and a 350-mile coastline of tidal rivers, chalk cliffs, the dunes of Sandwich Bay and the internationally-important shingle beaches of Dungeness.

Kent is one of the UK's most heavily-wooded counties, with a high proportion of ancient woodland and chestnut coppice. The proximity of the continent also means it has an almost continental climate. Its flora has been enlarged by species common across the Channel, leading to a rich orchid list, with several species having their UK stronghold in the county.

Threats to Kent's countryside were recognised in 1958, when a number of influential personalities proposed the formation of a wildlife conservation body to protect wildlife habitats.

TEN BOB START-UP

At a public meeting in Maidstone, held on 3rd May 1958, some 400 people agreed to support the proposal for a conservation body in Kent. The Kent Naturalists' Trust was formed, under the Chairmanship of Dr Deryk Fraser, a noted authority on reptiles and amphibians. The equally notable botanist, Dr Francis Rose, became the first Honorary Secretary. He was active in the formation of other south-east Trusts and in 2001 received the CHRISTOPHER CADBURY MEDAL for his significant contribution to the Trust movement. A Council of

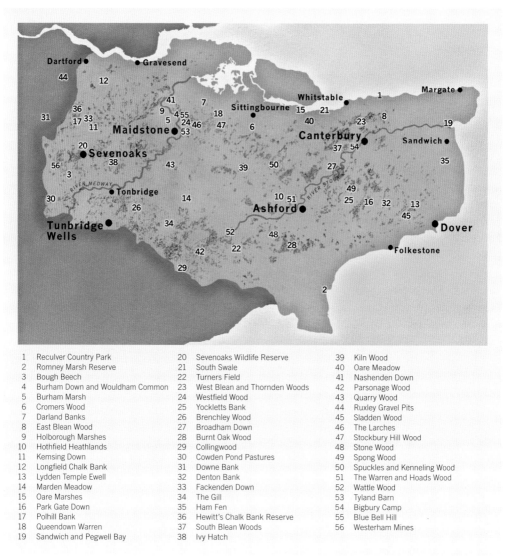

Map of Kent Wildlife Trust nature reserves

1	Reculver Country Park	20	Sevenoaks Wildlife Reserve	39	Kiln Wood
2	Romney Marsh Reserve	21	South Swale	40	Oare Meadow
3	Bough Beech	22	Turners Field	41	Nashenden Down
4	Burham Down and Wouldham Common	23	West Blean and Thornden Woods	42	Parsonage Wood
5	Burham Marsh	24	Westfield Wood	43	Quarry Wood
6	Cromers Wood	25	Yockletts Bank	44	Ruxley Gravel Pits
7	Darland Banks	26	Brenchley Wood	45	Sladden Wood
8	East Blean Wood	27	Broadham Down	46	The Larches
9	Holborough Marshes	28	Burnt Oak Wood	47	Stockbury Hill Wood
10	Hothfield Heathlands	29	Collingwood	48	Stone Wood
11	Kemsing Down	30	Cowden Pond Pastures	49	Spong Wood
12	Longfield Chalk Bank	31	Downe Bank	50	Spuckles and Kenneling Wood
13	Lydden Temple Ewell	32	Denton Bank	51	The Warren and Hoads Wood
14	Marden Meadow	33	Fackenden Down	52	Wattle Wood
15	Oare Marshes	34	The Gill	53	Tyland Barn
16	Park Gate Down	35	Ham Fen	54	Bigbury Camp
17	Polhill Bank	36	Hewitt's Chalk Bank Reserve	55	Blue Bell Hill
18	Queendown Warren	37	South Blean Woods	56	Westerham Mines
19	Sandwich and Pegwell Bay	38	Ivy Hatch		

Management was formed and the initial funding was by contributions from the members of the Council – ten shillings each!

In 1959, Rose became Chairman until, in 1965, the post was taken by Hector Wilkes. These strong personalities led the Trust to many early successes, with membership growth and development of the Trust's first nature reserves.

A pattern of work was soon established that is still reflected in what the Trust does today: building support, defence of the environment and purchase of land. In the 50 or more years since that May meeting, the Trust has grown from 400 members to 31,000; 64 reserves now cover more than 3,300 hectares; there are 90 staff and nearly 1,000 active volunteers of all ages and turnover exceeds £4 million.

The Trust's name has changed: the Kent Naturalists' Trust became the Kent Trust for Nature Conservation, then, in 1997, the Kent Wildlife Trust. In the same year, the Trust adopted the Partnership's badger logo, alongside the Adonis blue butterfly as an emblem for the county.

NATIONAL THREATS TO LOCAL PLACES

In the 1950s, opposing a proposal for a nuclear power station on the shingle at Dungeness became an early campaign for the Trust, alongside the Kent Field Club and the RSPB; all failed. More than 50 years on, the defence of the unique habitats at Dungeness remains a priority. The power station is being decommissioned and a proposal to enlarge Lydd Airfield to form the international London–Ashford airport is again uniting the Trust and the RSPB in opposition.

The construction of the Channel Tunnel – proposed in 1982 – compounded Kent's traffic and development difficulties. It was said there would be no need for a new railway line, but within a few years that proposal was on the table. Once again, the scale of the response required placed a major burden on the limited resources of the Trust. Now, Wildlife Trusts north of London are preparing for a similar task following the announcement of the proposed High Speed Two (HS2) line.

JEWELS IN THE LANDSCAPE

As planned at the outset of the Trust's life, surveys and research were undertaken to identify important wildlife habitats and the Trust's suite of nature reserves began to be established – many can be found today at the core of the Trust's network of reserves.

However, saving land was never the sole solution to saving Kent's wildlife. Kent was among the first of the Trusts to develop a databank of LOCAL WILDLIFE SITES – now, what amounts to almost 27,500 hectares in 456 sites are designated under this system. These sites are key to the Trust's knowledge of the county and are the major tool for influencing the county's planning process. One notable personality, Joyce Pitt, who has been involved in the process from the outset, remains influential.

Without funds, early reserves – such as Stockbury Hill Wood, owned by founding member Mr Billy Buck – were held under a gentleman's agreement. Such informal agreements are now rare. Progress was slow in developing membership

Naturalists at Downe Bank

and funds to acquire land, but there were early successes.

Francis Rose suggested that Downe Bank's orchid-rich site was Charles Darwin's "Orchis Bank", and persuaded the Trust to make it their first reserve purchase in 1962. The first warden, Frank Brightman, made it the first in his series of popular ecology wallcharts that influenced generations of conservationists. Research has since proved conclusively that Downe Bank was indeed "Orchis Bank" where Darwin discovered evidence of co-evolution between orchids and insects. The Trust purchased the adjacent Hangrove Wood in 1982 in recognition of the key plant studies Darwin also carried out there. Today, Downe Bank is widely regarded as the "entangled bank" that Darwin chose as the setting for his summary of his theory of evolution by natural selection in the final paragraph of the *Origin of Species*. Downe Bank has also gained international recognition since its 2010 Government nomination as a potential World Heritage Site as part of "Darwin's Landscape Laboratory".

At Lydden Down, 70 acres of chalk downland were first acquired in 1964. A subsequent series of purchases increased the area under management to 200 acres. Designated a National Nature Reserve in 1998, it was renamed in 2006 as Lydden Temple Ewell – The James Teacher Reserve.

Sandwich and Pegwell Bay National Nature Reserve – Kent Wildlife Trust's largest nature reserve managed on behalf of a partnership comprising Thanet District Council, Dover District Council, Kent County Council, the RSPB and the National Trust

Sandwich and Pegwell Bay, also designated a National Nature Reserve in 1998, and one of Charles Rothschild's proposed reserves, was recognised from the outset as a significant wildlife area. When the proposal for a hoverport threatened Pegwell Bay in about 1960, strenuous efforts to secure ownership of the site began. This purchase involved the Honorary Secretary, Hector Wilkes, tracking down the owner in Spain, where a representative of the Trust met him in the British Embassy, so the agreement would be legally binding. At the time it received national publicity and a visit from The Duke of Edinburgh. The purchase of a substantial area of Sandwich Bay followed in 1973. Other sections have been added with the assistance of the RSPB, The National Trust and the World Wildlife Fund, but management is carried out by the Trust on behalf of these and other owners.

These first steps should have ensured that the site was protected. However, a hoverport was deemed to be a development in the national interest and it was subsequently constructed on the boundary of what is now the National Nature Reserve. The hoverport enterprise failed and was abandoned a few years later, leaving a blot on the beauty of Pegwell Bay, and a barrier to both development and restoration. Yet natural colonisation of the deserted hoverport has produced a wildlife community of considerable interest.

KEY PEOPLE AND PLACES
The governance of the Trust has been marked by stability and long terms of office.

The role of President has made major contributions to its success. Lord Brabourne became the Trust's first President in 1959. A man of great influence in the county and beyond, he applied his personal skills to publicity, promotion and fundraising. In 1998, he was succeeded by James Teacher.

Teacher had become Chairman in 1985 and brought to the Trust his wide experience of land management and conservation, membership of the councils of the RSPB, English Nature and the Royal Society for Nature Conservation (the Society). Several significant achievements are associated with his period of office, including the refurbishment of Tyland Barn (see below) which became the Trust's headquarters in 1993. Teacher remained President until his untimely death in 2003.

John Leigh Pemberton, an influential local landowner and farmer, succeeded Teacher as Chairman in 1998. His views on the necessity of open access to the countryside during a period of dramatic change in the farming economy were an important support for the Trust. He became President in 2006 and was succeeded as Chairman by Fidelity Weston, an early WILDLIFE WATCH leader. Her experience in the educational and access roles of the Trust has brought a new dimension to the role.

MEMBERSHIP MATTERS

By the time the Trust celebrated its first ten years, the 400 founding members had become 2,250. Still a target of 10,000 eluded the Trust for some time. In 1991, in a dramatic step, commercial recruiters were employed, working door-to-door to sign up members and membership grew slowly to 11,000 by 1998. In 2000, the Trust led the movement in pioneering face-to-face recruiting and steady growth trebled membership to 31,000 by 2011.

Member support through legacies and donations has been vital to Trust development. The most significant was the generosity of Iris Darnton, who first gave her husband's stamp collection to the Trust, which realised some £440,000. This was followed by the gift of her home, Sissinghurst Court, and its contents. In the final account, this benefaction added more than £1 million to the Trust's resources.

In the early years, individual members were active in local matters. Later, local members' groups were established to raise funds, to provide talks and guided walks, and to act as focal points for sales and promotional activities. Today, their importance as fundraisers has declined, but they continue to produce a county-wide programme of walks and talks and to maintain their local service to the members. In 1982, the lease of a shop and office in Rainham formed the first Trust headquarters. The Trust appointed staff – Conservation, Education and Administrative Officers and a Director, Fred Booth. Fred remains active and valued within the Trust.

EDUCATION FOCUS

Since its formation, the Trust has maintained a very strong strand of activity and focus on environmental education. Two Trustees were long-serving members of the board of the Watch Trust for Environmental Education (WILDLIFE WATCH) and one of these, ANDREW RUCK, was for many years the Society's national Treasurer. The Kent membership of Watch became the strongest in the country. However, in response to regulatory pressures, there are no longer Watch groups in the county.

The Trust affirmed the importance of its education work by appointing a full-time Education Officer in 1982. For older students and adults, its programme

Heath fritillary butterfly – this once common woodland butterfly is becoming increasingly scarce. However, strong colonies remain and are prospering in the 2000-acre woodland reserve of Blean, near Canterbury

of Wildlife Study Days, mainly aimed at developing technical identification skills, has become well-recognised in the county and has grown steadily. This strand of work is now opening out to encompass a wide range of approaches to engage local communities and new audiences.

OUTGROWING TRUST OFFICES

The Trust's first offices at Rainham soon became too small. Following periods in leased offices in Maidstone, the Trust acquired a long lease on the derelict 16th century Tyland Barn, near Maidstone. This was rebuilt and formally opened by HRH The Prince of Wales in 1993, and has become the Trust's sales base, offices, and education centre. The grounds are managed to create an epitome of the wildlife habitats of Kent. To meet the Trust's continued growth, the farmhouse on this property was refurbished and opened in 2010 by John Sunley, whose family and foundation have supported the Trust since its formation.

In addition to Tyland Barn, the Trust has established four other centres: at Bough Beech, Sevenoaks Wildlife Reserve, Romney Marsh and Reculver.

Bough Beech was the result of the creation of a new reservoir and is a locally-renowned birding site. The architect of much of its success has been the warden, Roy Coles.

At Sevenoaks Wildlife Reserve, a merger in 2006 with the Jeffery Harrison Memorial Trust brought a fully-established visitor centre and 132 acres of gravel pits. They represent the 1960s' pioneering work of Dr Jeffery Harrison and family in developing a wildlife after-use for industrial land.

The newly-built visitor centre at Romney Marsh is constructed with straw-bale walls, a green roof and uses sustainable heating.

SEA AND SHORE

The Kent coastline of more than 350 miles has been both a challenge and an opportunity in terms of identifying the importance of the wildlife of the county's intertidal and subtidal habitats. A programme of study, research and

A Shoresearch team in action on the Kent coast

recording was introduced in 1983. The appointment of a Marine Officer in 2006, generously funded by the Peter De Haan Charitable Trust, has strengthened the influence of the Trust. Our Shoresearch recording system has been adopted elsewhere, and large teams of volunteers, onshore and offshore, support the work.

UNMATCHED INFLUENCE

Over the last 50 years, the Trust and the movement nationally have developed a level of influence over the local environment that is unmatched by any other environmental body.

The Trust's nature reserves and Local Wildlife Site system cover some ten per cent of the land area of the county. At many of its reserves the Trust works closely with neighbouring landowners, extending the area of land under sympathetic management for wildlife. The Trust pioneered the Roadside Nature Reserve project with Kent County Council. It identified some 90 kilometres of important marginal land along roadsides, which now provides linear corridors, and links various wildlife habitats. It advises landowners and has brought thousands of acres into sympathetic management within the Higher Level Stewardship scheme. The Trust's influence extends into urban and development areas through its recognised, albeit non-statutory, place in the planning system. It comments on some 200 major developments every year and is actively involved in regeneration with the Thames Gateway regeneration agencies. All this is backed by the detailed local experience of its members, the management expertise of reserves staff and the technical knowledge of the policy and consultancy staff. It means that the Trust is in an unparalleled position to influence and inform development.

The future direction of the Trust builds on the foundation of the last 50 years, aiming to manage and restore larger areas of land. In the last ten years, the Trust's landholdings have increased by more than 50 per cent. One contribution was the purchase of 1,500 acres of Blean Woods near Canterbury, bringing the Trust's holdings in this important area to more than 2,000 acres. This is one of nine Living Landscape areas in the county. The Trust has used its knowledge of biodiversity hotspots, together with modern mapping and data capture techniques, to map the reconnection of the countryside. A similar approach has been adopted by neighbouring Trusts. The early 2007 publication, *Living Landscapes for the South-East*, laid out a region-wide network of potential links in the landscape. Collaborative work on a regional scale is becoming increasingly important. The south-east Trusts have employed a Regional

Conservation Policy Director for six years and the Living Landscape approach demonstrates the power the Trusts can harness collectively.

In the search for appropriate keystone species for management, since 2003 the Trust has been trialling the use of beaver as a management tool at Ham Fen. It is the only Government-licensed deployment of beaver in England.

MULTIPLE CHALLENGES

The multiple challenges of growth and development, changing land management, increasing amenity pressure, water shortage, coastal squeeze and climate change, combine to present a huge task for the Trust. But it is equipped to bring a strong set of skills to address it.

At the same time, the Trust's aim to protect important areas of the county continues. It works to defend the British populations of Kent specialities such as: monkey, lady and early spider orchids; silver-spotted skippers, heath fritillary and Adonis blue butterflies and wart-biter crickets. All these Kent species thrive on Kent reserves today in their native habitats.

The Trust's 50th anniversary in 2008 was a time of great celebration. It was marked by many events, including a questionnaire sent to every domestic address in the county and a successful Guinness World Record attempt when the world's largest birdseed cake weighed in at 1.29 tons. That record was succeeded in 2010 by the world's largest bee-wall. What would the founding 400 have thought?

BY FRED BOOTH AND PETER PAYNE

Fred Booth has been an active naturalist in the county since the 1970s, particularly in developing study of its marine wildlife. Between 1983 and 1988, he was the first paid Chief Executive of the Trust. In 2011, he received an MBE for his contribution to conservation and was appointed Vice President of Kent Wildlife Trust.

Peter Payne is Honorary Secretary and Vice Chairman of the Trust, roles he has held since the early 1980s. He has a long career in environmental education and is an Honorary Warden at the Trust's Marden Meadow reserve.

Walkers enjoy panoramic views across the Weald from Blue Bell Hill

CHAPTER 22

Lancashire, Manchester and North Merseyside

It is perhaps surprising that the Lancashire Wildlife Trust was ever formed at all and that it survived its first turbulent years. The initial meetings to establish Trusts in the north-west were held in Preston and Ambleside in November and December 1961. A Lake District Trust was proposed, covering an area that actually extended as far south as the River Ribble. In February 1962, a further meeting in Manchester proposed a trust for Cheshire and South Lancashire (north to the Ribble). This so raised the ire of the three Lancastrians present, led by the redoubtable Eric Hardy, that it was finally agreed that a Lancashire Trust would cover the entire palatine county. The Trust was duly incorporated as the Lancashire Naturalists' Trust on 1st August 1962 at Manchester University.

The objectives of the Trust in 1962 were "to bring unity into natural history circles to investigate areas that have a naturalist interest and possibly acquire them, to set up education centres and stimulate interest in natural history and to promote lectures and discussions before the public". To start the whole process, the then President,

PROTECTS Your natural heritage.
PUBLISHES A regular newsletter and trail guides to help you enjoy our wildlife.
ESTABLISHES Nature reserves and surveys sites of scientific importance.
PUBLICISES The need for conservation with film shows lectures and field trips.
MONITORS Planning applications and proposed developments.
KNOWS That our region is rich in wildlife and that if it is to survive it must be protected
NEEDS You to help us continue this essential work.

WE CARE....DO YOU ?

FOR MORE INFORMATION PLEASE CONTACT

DALE HOUSE DALE HEAD SLAIDBURN LANCASHIRE

Opposite: Stitchwort and bluebells at Aughton Woods
Above: An early poster promoting the Trust

REO Cavendish, donated the south end of Walney Island to be jointly run with the Lake District Trust.

TURBULENT EARLY YEARS

The initiative for the establishment of the Trust came from a select body of eminent academic naturalists. Apart from possibly acquiring land, the Trust's objectives seemed at first to have little to distinguish them from those of traditional natural history societies, of which there were already a significant number in the county. In addition, the Trust was perceived by many as a threat to the existing societies and its formation as unnecessary.

After ten years (when the Trust area was home to ten per cent of the population of England and Wales) the Trust's membership had reached a mere 450 and its administrative and financial positions were in disarray. Eric Greenwood was a rare example of a 1960s' Trustee who was determined to make the Trust succeed. He personally recruited (amongst others) a future Chairman, Gordon Stead, and future President, Michael Fitzherbert-Brockholes. He also successfully pioneered promotion of the Trust at major events.

BOUNDARY CHALLENGES

In order to coordinate the general administration and organisation of the Trust, its first member of staff (Administrative Officer, John Huckle) was appointed in 1973 thanks to a grant from the UK Carnegie Trust. The Trust was really in no position to afford this appointment and its continuation depended on new sources of income being found. Bizarrely, the Administrative Officer was actually

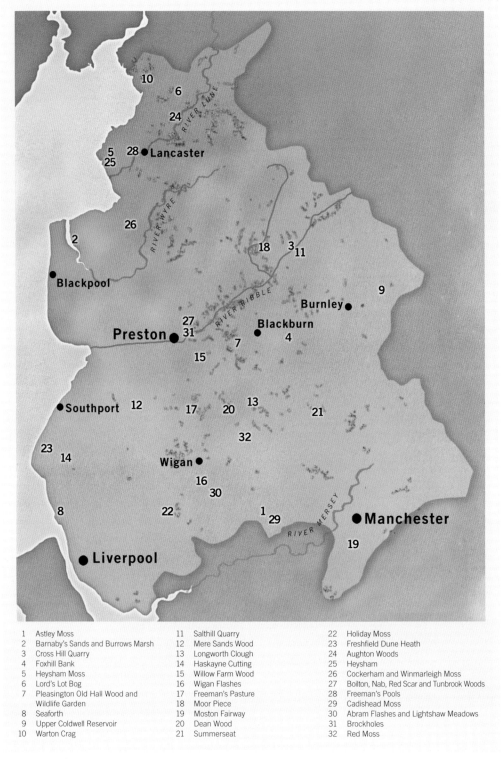

1	Astley Moss	11	Salthill Quarry	22	Holiday Moss
2	Barnaby's Sands and Burrows Marsh	12	Mere Sands Wood	23	Freshfield Dune Heath
3	Cross Hill Quarry	13	Longworth Clough	24	Aughton Woods
4	Foxhill Bank	14	Haskayne Cutting	25	Heysham
5	Heysham Moss	15	Willow Farm Wood	26	Cockerham and Winmarleigh Moss
6	Lord's Lot Bog	16	Wigan Flashes	27	Boilton, Nab, Red Scar and Tunbrook Woods
7	Pleasington Old Hall Wood and	17	Freeman's Pasture	28	Freeman's Pools
	Wildlife Garden	18	Moor Piece	29	Cadishead Moss
8	Seaforth	19	Moston Fairway	30	Abram Flashes and Lightshaw Meadows
9	Upper Coldwell Reservoir	20	Dean Wood	31	Brockholes
10	Warton Crag	21	Summerseat	32	Red Moss

Map of the Wildlife Trust for Lancashire, Manchester and North Merseyside nature reserves

forbidden at first from raising the funds which would secure his future.

The only external grant to the Trust at the time (£540) came from Lancashire County Council. This came to an end in 1974, following the disastrous (for the Trust) Government reorganisation of local authority boundaries. Instead of one county authority there were now three – Lancashire, Greater Manchester and Merseyside. With the change of boundaries, these new authorities lost land to Cumbria, Cheshire, Derbyshire and Yorkshire, and also gained some from Yorkshire. The Lancashire Trust's flagship reserve at Walney found itself in Cumbria to the north, and another important site at Hale Duck Decoy was now in Cheshire. The good news to come out of this was the development of the Merseyside Structure Plan, with its much more enlightened planning policies, particularly along the Sefton Coast. (By 2010 the Trust would find itself covered by 26 local authority areas).

EARLY CONSERVATION SUCCESSES

On the conservation front, some remarkable progress had been made. The Lytham St Annes Local Nature Reserve was established in 1967 following Trust efforts led by Gordon Stead. A system of seven regional committees was established to coordinate the Trust's work across the county. The detailed work carried out by many dedicated volunteers had surveyed several hundred sites of biological importance, and the North West Biological Field Data Bank was established at Merseyside County Museums. This made a huge impact on the assessment of planning decisions and, in a modified form, is continually renewed and updated. The Trust developed an enviable reputation for its ecological knowledge and was widely consulted (but rarely paid) by external authorities. In 1974, with Gordon Stead as Chairman, an interpretive programme was started which led to the publication of 30 leaflets giving information about sites around the county, which it was hoped would raise public awareness of the Trust. The Trust's in-house publication *Lapwing* was launched.

Inaugeration of Warton Crag reserve, 1987. Left to right: Dr Jennifer Newton, the Duke of Westminster, Ted Jackson (Chairman) and Michael Fitzherbert-Brockholes (President)

Plans for the acquisition of various reserves were also made, though few would be completed for several years. The occasional publication *Nature in Lancashire* provided an outlet for many important papers.

In 1975, the Trust became the first to adopt the Watch Trust as its junior arm. This was two years before the Society for the Promotion of Nature Conservation (the Society) would take the decision to adopt the Watch Trust for The Wildlife Trust movement as a whole (WILDLIFE WATCH).

ON THE BRINK

The process of managing the Trust as a charity remained a problem. Voluntary officers came and went with disappointing frequency. A resolution to liquidate the Trust in 1977 was only narrowly defeated. The one paid officer was now finally encouraged to start looking for funds, though not before he had accepted a significant cut in salary and even paid some Trust expenses from his own resources. The tide began to turn and the situation became more stable, first with Gordon Stead, then with Peter Pearson as Chairman. When Ted Jackson became Chairman in 1979, the Trust had a turnover of £13,000 and an annual surplus of £2,500. There were 1,600 members. There still remained an urgent need to find a means of financing the core staff necessary for promoting the Trust to the wider community. Initial progress was slow, but bolstered in 1980 by the conveyance to the Trust of the first part of the important Mere Sands Wood reserve. The Trust also gained huge publicity from DAVID BELLAMY'S first visit. He spoke at the AGM in Darwen and then in a remarkable display, like a veritable pied piper, led a party of 150 completely enthralled people around Sunnyhurst Wood.

EIGHTIES' EXPANSION

In 1980, the Trust changed its name to the Lancashire Trust for Nature Conservation with Greater Manchester and Merseyside. This finally recognised the creation of the new 1974 boundaries and also the relationship with the Society. The Trustees also completely revised the Memorandum and Articles of Association to mirror those adopted by the Society. Subsequent revisions kept the Trust up-to-date in a rapidly changing world.

The remaining part of Mere Sands Wood was acquired in 1982 (the first site to be totally owned by the Trust). By this time long leases or management agreements had also been negotiated on 11 other sites.

In 1983, the Trust was finally in a position to appoint a Development Officer, Julie Fitzherbert-Brockholes, who quickly made progress with fundraising. She also made arrangements for the office base to be moved to Cuerden. The Trust had originally been located at Samlesbury Hall, before moving its registered office to Slaidburn, at the home of its Administrative Officer – John Huckle – who retired in 1984, after 11 difficult but dedicated years.

External recognition came to the Trust in 1984, when the developing Seaforth reserve won first prize in a national competition organised by the Conservation Foundation. It was not until 1996 that it became possible to open a visitor centre at Seaforth, although access to the site remained difficult as the reserve was actually situated within the Liverpool Freeport boundary fence.

SWELLING STAFF NUMBERS

The year 1985 saw significant progress. The Trust's first five-year plan was adopted by Council. The second Trust-owned site, Red Scar Woods, was purchased and its first team of Manpower Services Commission staff was created.

David Bellamy leads the crowd around Sunnyhurst Wood

SIR DAVID ATTENBOROUGH visited the Trust and delivered a sold-out lecture at Preston Guildhall in support of the BRITISH WILDLIFE APPEAL. Richard Sharland was appointed as the first Director. The Trust had deliberately sought a candidate who was not an expert naturalist, but someone with the personality and drive to lead a (hopefully) growing team and the ability to make the Trust much better known to the agencies with which it needed to work. A year later, the first Conservation Officer (David Woodfall) was appointed on a three-year contract, and an Urban Wildlife Officer (Andrew Bielienski) was appointed to work in Greater Manchester. The TSB seconded one of its bank managers (Eric Greenhalgh) as Finance Officer for the Trust. British Coal Opencast funded a Survey Officer (Nik Bruce) and Judy Palmer followed David Woodfall, with the remit to organise the management of an increasing number of reserves.

EMBRACING URBAN PROJECTS

Around this time, a national movement was underway to promote the creation of Urban Wildlife Trusts, as many Wildlife Trusts were perceived as not involving themselves enough in their more urban areas. In Lancashire, the view was that urban wildlife conservation was every bit as important as in the more open countryside. The Trust resisted the considerable pressure from the Society to agree to the formation of separate Trusts. Subsequently it has been clear that the Trust's survival could have been at risk, as its work in urban areas has often provided resources to keep other projects solvent. The Trust's urban work started in 1988 with the appointment of Mick Weston to establish the Bolton Wildlife Project, a partnership initiative funded by the Department of Environment's Inner Urban Programme and Bolton Council. The Countryside Commission supported the Trust's work in local communities and helped with funding to create a Community Projects Officer post (Tim Mitcham) to support and encourage local action.

ROYAL VISIT

By 1991, the Trust's progress and growing reputation led to it being selected for the honour of a full-day visit by HRH The Prince of Wales. On 7th June, Prince Charles arrived on the Royal Train and travelled by helicopter to visit five Trust sites at Aughton Woods, Foxhill Bank, Astley Moss, Mere Sands Wood and Cuerden Valley Park. It was a proud and memorable day.

Richard Sharland moved on and was replaced as Chief Executive in 1992 by his deputy, Anne Selby. The Trust had another name change and became the Wildlife Trust for Lancashire, Manchester and North Merseyside, in a move to create unity across the Trust movement. All other Trusts eventually made similar changes. Each Trust remained an independent charity, but The Wildlife Trust brand was now firmly established.

ROLLERCOASTER 1990S

There followed a period of sustained and, at times, quite dramatic growth. It was not, however, without serious problems of financial management and some perilous cash flow. Trustees were seriously tested in the practice of avoiding disaster and not all decisions taken proved popular. Nonetheless, a major Biological Heritage Site Project was started in Lancashire (different schemes operated in Manchester and Merseyside). The new visitor centre was opened at Mere Sands

Wood (1993) and the Penwortham Education Centre opened in 1994. Both have made a major contribution to the public's awareness of the importance of caring about wildlife.

In 1995, the Trust was successful in its campaign to save the important Red Moss site at Horwich from development. This was a particularly good outcome, since the Trust had found itself dangerously at odds with a local authority that was providing funding for other Trust work. The Trust was still able to argue the case for saving the Moss without jeopardising that relationship.

RESERVES MANAGEMENT

The Trust has always embraced opportunities to use Government funds to provide training for young people. This has enabled it to undertake more successful management of its reserves and also proved worthwhile in giving people the skills to move on to more permanent work. In recognition of this work, in 1999 the Trust was designated as a National Vocational Qualification Training Centre. Further recognition for the quality of the Trust's reserves management work came in 2000 with awards from English Nature (now Natural England) for Mere Sands Wood and Salthill Quarry.

The Trust has been heavily involved with the fight to save red squirrels on the Sefton coast

The Trust works with many local communities across the region

As part of a commitment to The Wildlife Trust movement as a whole, in 2001 Lancashire Trust, together with the YORKSHIRE TRUST and SHEFFIELD TRUST, undertook a business review of the administration of the Society. It was the forerunner to a complete reorganisation of the role and function of the Society and its relationship with the individual Wildlife Trusts.

CENTRES OF EXCELLENCE

In the same year, the Biodiversity Action Plans for Lancashire and North Merseyside were published. The Trust held 34 nature reserves and was supported by 8,000 members, 1,000 Watch members and a significant number of corporate sponsors and public agencies. Annual turnover had reached £1.5 million. However, there was still no permanent security for its administrative base. A partnership with the Cuerden Valley Park Trust had progressed and it was agreed to seek joint funding for a new headquarters for the Trust and the restoration of the park. Thanks to the HERITAGE LOTTERY FUND, the finance was secured and the Trust's new home at The Barn was opened in 2003 by DAVID BELLAMY. It was later to be granted award-winning Eco-Centre status. In 2006, funding from the Single Regeneration Budget scheme helped the Trust to build the Bolton

Environmental Resource Centre, which now provides the base for much of the Trust's urban work.

In 2004, the Trust published *The Wildlife of Lancashire,* edited by Professor Malcolm Edmunds, Dr Geoff Morries and Tim Mitcham. It is a superbly illustrated account of the county's wildlife and topography, intended to stimulate the general reader rather than inform the expert.

In 2006, a successful appeal for funds to Trust members (led by Rosslyn Colderley) helped release some £10 million of funding from external sources for the purchase and development of a large new reserve at Brockholes by the M6/A59 interchange at Preston. The vision was to create a high quality environmental and visitor experience for hundreds of thousands of people each year. The reserve, with its architecturally-outstanding floating village, was finally opened by The Wildlife Trusts' President, SIMON KING, on 11th May 2011, to much acclaim.

50 YEARS OF ACHIEVEMENT

The Trust has developed and succeeded over the years thanks to the vision and commitment of its members (now over 20,000), its volunteers and its staff, and the recognition from outside agencies that it is a reliable partner. By 2010, there were 40 reserves. The Trust has worked hard to seek and gain representation on a wide range of external committees and organisations. The Trust is governed by a Board of Trustees drawn from its members.

The new visitor centre at Brockholes

Red Moss – saved by the Trust and one of the last remaining lowland raised mires in the county

Since 2003, three Trustees – Dr Phil Smith, Dr Jennifer Newton and Ted Jackson – have been awarded MBEs for services to wildlife conservation. Every effort is made to ensure that the Board has the right balance of skills to oversee the main areas of work – conservation management, education, finance, human resources, marketing and public relations, legal, health and safety. The Chief Executive Officer is responsible for the delivery of policy and the management of staff who now number more than 100. Five-year and annual plans are reviewed at frequent meetings between Trustees and staff. The Trustees themselves have had the good fortune to enjoy the services of three excellent Presidents. They have not been the traditional figureheads who make only occasional appearances, but have attended all Trustee and other meetings on a regular basis for all of the last 30 years. Michael Fitzherbert-Brockholes JP DL, Lord Clitheroe DL and Sir Tim Kimber DL have played an integral role in the Trust's work. The Trust was awarded Investors in People status

in 2008 and drew praise from the Charity Commission following a formal review of governance procedures.

It has been fortunate in having the continuing support of many members at its heart. Some have remained active, even as Trustees, since the 1960s. Others have come and gone. All have shown remarkable dedication and support for the Trust's work. It would be proper to acknowledge and thank each and every one, but the list would be too long. Their legacy is what the Trust has become – and they all know who they are.

BY TED JACKSON MBE

Ted Jackson first became involved with the Yorkshire Trust in 1951, and worked as an ornithologist in North Yorkshire and Shetland. After moving to Gloucestershire in 1966, he worked for the Wildfowl and Wetlands Trust at Slimbridge before joining the Gloucestershire Trust. He became its volunteer Education Secretary, managed two nature reserves and was a Trustee from 1972–75. Another move took him to Merseyside, where he became Chairman of the Wildlife Trust for Lancashire, Manchester and North Merseyside from 1979 to the present day. He was awarded the MBE for services to wildlife conservation in 2007.

CHAPTER 23

Leicestershire and Rutland

Leicestershire and Rutland are two landlocked counties in central England covering an area of approximately 2,550 square kilometres (980 square miles). Most of the land area lies at between 61 and 183 metres above sea level with farming accounting for most of the land use. Despite woodland only covering about four per cent of the land, there are some exceptionally fine ancient woodlands in the two counties. Species-rich grasslands have declined alarmingly and few now remain.

Other notable wildlife habitats include remnants of heathland, which is almost restricted to Charnwood Forest, rivers and their floodplains, disused quarries and man-made reservoirs such as Rutland Water.

Wildlife has come under increasing pressure over the last 50 years; the loss of habitats and species has been significant in Leicestershire and Rutland, necessitating urgent action to protect and enhance the precious wildlife and wild places of the two counties.

POST-WAR BEGINNINGS

The roots of Leicestershire and Rutland Wildlife Trust can be traced back to the Leicestershire and Rutland Nature Reserve Investigation Sub-committee, part of the Nature Reserves Investigation Committee (NRIC) set up after the Second World War to provide information on potential nature reserves as part of the Government's planning for the post-war reconstruction of the country. The Leicestershire NRIC reported in February 1944. Among its far-reaching proposals was the recommendation that Charnwood Forest, an area of rugged upland

Opposite: Foxglove – county flower of Leicestershire
Right: Ron Hickling – one of the Trust's founders

north of Leicester, should be protected in its entirety as some kind of National Reserve. A similar area of east Leicestershire woodlands was also recommended for protection (to be known collectively as Leighfield Forest), and also some typical portion of Rutland in its unspoilt condition.

The first batch of Sites of Special Scientific Interest was scheduled by the Nature Conservancy in Leicestershire in 1951. In the following year two members of the Leicestershire NRIC, RON HICKLING and Trevor Walden, were summoned to a meeting with MAX NICHOLSON, Director General of the Conservancy. He was a passionate and formidable advocate for wildlife and nature conservation and on a mission to persuade local people to establish local bodies to protect sites as nature reserves – picking up where the work of the local NRICs had left off.

Hickling was also a close friend of TED SMITH and a frequent visitor to the Gibraltar Point Field Centre on the Lincolnshire coast. Smith had been the prime mover in establishing a Trust to further nature conservation activity in Lincolnshire in the late 1940s and was keen to see other counties follow in

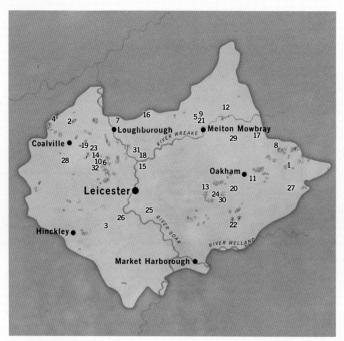

1	Bloody Oak's Quarry
2	Cloud Wood
3	Croft Pasture
4	Dimminsdale
5	Holwell Mineral Line
6	Lea Meadows
7	Loughborough Big Meadow
8	Merry's Meadows
9	North Quarry
10	Rocky Plantation
11	Rutland Water
12	Stonesby Quarry
13	Tilton Railway Cutting
14	Ulverscroft
15	Wanlip Meadows
16	Wymeswold Meadows
17	Cribb's Meadow
18	Cossington Meadows
19	Charnwood Lodge
20	Priors Coppice
21	Brown's Hill Quarry
22	Great Merrible Wood
23	Charley Woods
24	Launde Big Wood
25	Lucas' Marsh
26	Narborough Bog
27	Ketton Quarry
28	Kelham Bridge
29	Wymondham Rough
30	Launde Park Wood
31	Mountsorrel Meadows
32	Altar Stones

Map of Leicestershire and Rutland Wildlife Trust nature reserves

its footsteps. So it was that in 1956 the Leicestershire Trust for Nature Conservation and the Preservation of Sites of Historic Interest Ltd was formally established. In the event, nothing of this historic interest came the Trust's way so the name was duly shortened! Robert E Martin served as the first Chairman of the new Trust, with RON HICKLING as Honorary Secretary.

Although the Trust was soon active in promoting nature conservation, including lobbying on the proposed route of the Ml motorway through the Charnwood Forest area of Leicestershire, it took some time to acquire any nature reserves. Hickling recalled that "however hard we tried, nothing seemed to come our way".

FIRST NATURE RESERVES
Edward Turner, the County Land Agent, could see the Trust's predicament and took steps to resolve it. He had a huge acreage of land to let and manage and offered the Trust two pieces of woodland, on lease at a peppercorn rent.

In 1961, Great Fenny Wood at Quorn, together with a tiny area of woodland at Cotes-de-Val, near Lutterworth, were established as nature reserves and the Trust was on its way. The Trust's newsletter of December 1961 reported on the first nature conservation work party held at Great Fenny Wood in November of that year. As Ron Hickling recalled "We had a large party of about 45 volunteers working clearing old undergrowth from the beech wood with some 30 of these youngsters, mainly sixth formers from Humphrey Perkins Grammar School, Barrow, and Wyggeston Boys School, Leicester. These young people worked hard and enthusiastically. . . sausages and hot potatoes by the fire rounded off an enjoyable day of hard work in the open air".

These first reserves enabled the Trust to start acquiring the land management skills it needed to make real progress. A nature reserves agreement at Charnwood Lodge was negotiated with Miss CE Clarke, the then owner, which obliged the Trust to study the flora and fauna of the estate as well as to undertake its guardianship and management.

Educational access agreements were also drawn up with British Waterways for the Grand Union Canal from Kilby Bridge to Foxton Locks and for the Grantham Canal from Harby to Grantham.

A CONSERVATION CORPS was formed in 1964, which continued to be active throughout the decade with regular, practical nature conservation work parties.

AN IMPOVERISHED LANDSCAPE

An exhaustive field-by-field survey of the whole county in 1966 revealed the true extent of the challenge facing the Trust. The Trust's Scientific Advisory Committee report stated that "most of the east and south of the county is now so efficiently farmed that the most the average five-kilometre square can muster is a few acres of unimproved grassland on slopes too steep to cultivate and the odd strip of marshland in awkward corners along a brook. . . the survey reveals in detail the extent to which the Leicestershire landscape has been impoverished over the last 30 years or so".

The acquisition at auction of Poultney Wood and Fox Covert at Ulverscroft in 1968 for £6,000 was the first outright purchase of land and an important milestone in the Trust's history. The valley marshes at Ulverscroft were purchased shortly after. The same year, Great Merrible Wood was acquired for £4,500, necessitating a public Woodlands Appeal to replenish the Trust's depleted coffers. The Trust was now in possession of a handful of the finest wildlife sites in Leicestershire.

In May 1969, a public meeting in Oakham voted for the Trust to incorporate Rutland – thus forming the Leicestershire and Rutland Trust for Nature Conservation.

FIRST PAID STAFF AND OFFICE

The work of the Trust was undertaken entirely through voluntary effort until 1973, when the first paid staff member, an Administrative Officer, was appointed and an office established in Leicester.

The early 1970s saw the formation of a Ladies Auxiliary. As well as undertaking much-needed fundraising to support the Trust's work, its members enjoyed a busy social life – the 1972–73 *Annual Report* mentioned a sherry morning and a combined sherry evening and exhibition of creative embroidery!

In 1973, Charnwood Lodge formally became Trust property having been bequeathed by Miss CE Clarke. Other key nature reserves secured in the 1970s included Dimminsdale, Cribb's Meadows, the Mineral Line, North Quarry and Brown's Hill Quarry at Holwell, Narborough Bog and Wymondham Rough.

RUTLAND WATER NATURE RESERVE

At the start of the decade, plans for the new Empingham Reservoir (later renamed as 'Rutland Water') revealed a proposal to establish an extensive new nature reserve at its western end. After several years of negotiation, in 1975 an agreement between the Trust and Anglian Water Authority was signed to establish the reserve. It covered seven miles of shoreline on the western arm of the reservoir under construction, and approximately 350 acres of land – a unique achievement in conservation planning. Tim Appleton was appointed as full-time warden and reserve creation works started, involving major earth moving and excavation.

Brown's Hill Quarry nature reserve

Rutland Water nature reserve – taken from the air in 2011

The first Rutland Water nature reserve open day was held on 5th September 1976 providing an opportunity to walk round the whole reserve. With the reservoir rapidly filling in 1977, pen stocks to control the water entering the newly-created lagoons were fitted. The lagoons were partly filled just in time for the first real breeding season for wildfowl on the reserve. That year the first bird-watching hides were erected and a nature trail around Gibbet Gorse was opened. The Lyndon area of the reserve was opened to the public for the first time at Easter 1978, followed by the Egleton area in 1979.

EIGHTIES' EXPANSION

Urban nature conservation was growing fast in the early 1980s and, in 1983, the Trust became sponsors of the City Wildlife Project (a Manpower Services Commission Community Programme Scheme) focusing on urban nature conservation in Leicester. By the end of the decade, this project became independent of the Trust, operating as part of the Leicester Ecology Trust which later assumed the mantle of Environ.

The mid 1980s saw significant funding from the Manpower Services Commission, enabling the Trust to establish reserve management as well as ecological survey teams. A Leicester habitat survey was completed, with every parcel of undeveloped land (except private gardens) within 73 square kilometres of Leicester located and visited. Details of habitats, wild plants and animals, land use and ownership were all recorded and mapped.

The Trust marked its 30th anniversary year in 1986 with a Wildlife Roadshow that toured round the two counties and the publication of its first *Reserves Handbook*.

The 1980s also saw the formation and development of the Trust's local groups. They have played a vital role in supporting the work of the Trust ever since, with walks and talks, events and activities, nature reserve management and valuable fundraising. Melton Mowbray was the Trust's first local group to be formally constituted in 1980. Charnwood Local Group formed in 1984 and over 1,000 people attended its craft fair that November, raising more than £850 for the Trust. Further groups followed in the North West, Rutland, Humberstone and Oadby and Wigston.

The Trust first started a Junior Club for children and young people in 1980. During the first year, it held indoor meetings and field trips, and published two newsletters. In 1984, the Junior Club merged into WILDLIFE WATCH, which is now firmly established as the Trust's junior wing. The first Wildlife Watch Annual Event was held in 1985, when 60 members and parents spent a day of natural history investigation at Rutland Water nature reserve.

THE FIRST BIRDFAIR

Improving access and educational facilities continued at Rutland Water throughout the 1980s. The first hide for wheelchair users was built and, in November 1985, the Lyndon Visitor Centre was officially opened by SIR DAVID ATTENBOROUGH. The same year, Rutland Water nature reserve was declared a Site of Special Scientific Interest.

The reserve was assuming a central role in the Trust's work, helping to raise its profile and increase understanding of its work. In 1987, a Rutland Water Nature Reserve Wildfowl Bonanza was held. Now known as the Birdfair, it has been held every year since, and is organised in partnership with the RSPB. Described as the birdwatcher's 'Glastonbury', the Birdfair is the world's first and largest international birdwatching event, and, by 2011, it had raised more than £2.5 million for international conservation projects.

Key nature reserves acquired in the 1980s included Herbert's Meadow at Ulverscroft, Tilton Cutting, valuable grasslands at Merry's Meadows, Wymeswold Meadows and Lea Meadows, and an important ancient woodland at Prior's Coppice.

NINETIES

The 1990s started with the launch of several major conservation initiatives. In 1990, the Countryside Commission announced the creation of a new National Forest, linking Charnwood Forest in Leicestershire with Needwood Forest in Staffordshire.

Then in 1992, the Leicestershire Wildlife Partnership with the British Trust for Conservation Volunteers (BTCV) was launched to organise the provision of regular volunteer work parties on the Trust's nature reserves. The Trust was set to benefit further,

as the same year it entered into English Nature's new pilot RESERVES ENHANCEMENT SCHEME which provided much-needed financial support for nature reserve management.

In 1991, Sir David Attenborough agreed to be the Trust Patron. This was particularly fitting as he had grown up in Leicester and spent his formative years exploring the Leicestershire countryside on his bicycle, in search of its animals, plants and fossils.

Significant nature reserves secured in the 1990s included ancient woodlands at Cloud Wood, Charley Woods, Launde Big Wood and Launde Park Wood, a large area of Loughborough Big Meadow and Croft Pasture.

In 1995, reflecting the new biodiversity agenda, the Trust took the lead in the development of a local Biodiversity Action Plan by undertaking a first-stage audit of the wildlife in the two counties. In 1998 the Leicester, Leicestershire and Rutland Biodiversity Action Plan was launched, identifying priority habitats and species in the two counties, and setting targets and mechanisms for their conservation.

The Trust celebrated its 40th anniversary in 1996 with a members' day at the Lyndon Visitor Centre and a touring roadshow. In 1997 it formally changed its name to the Leicestershire and Rutland Wildlife Trust.

Coppicing in Hambleton Wood

Osprey family at Rutland Water

The 1990s also saw Rutland Water nature reserve designated as a Ramsar Site and a Special Protection Area – the first man-made wildlife site in the world to receive a joint designation.

OSPREY OPPORTUNITY

Ospreys had been regularly spotted at Rutland Water nature reserve for several years, and in 1994 two young birds stayed all summer. The Trust saw an opportunity and in 1996 launched the Rutland Osprey Project. This partnership between the Trust and Anglian Water involved the translocation of young ospreys from Scotland to try and establish a breeding population at the reserve. Over the next six years, a total of 64 Scottish osprey chicks were translocated in the hope that young birds would consider Rutland, rather than Scotland, to be their home. Satellite tracking of the chicks revealed valuable information about their migration routes to West Africa.

The first translocated ospreys returned to summer at Rutland Water in 1999 and then, in 2001, ospreys bred at Rutland Water – the first osprey breeding success in England for 150 years. From 2001 to 2011, a total of 53 chicks successfully fledged from nests at Rutland Water, indicating the establishment of a stable breeding colony. The ospreys have proved to be a big public attraction, keeping the Rutland Osprey Project team of staff and volunteers busy each spring and summer.

LOCAL WILDLIFE SITES

In 2002, the Trust began an important new focus on Local Wildlife Sites, the best places for nature outside legally protected land such as Sites of Special Scientific Interest (SSSIs). This concentrated on compiling a register of Local Wildlife Sites in Leicestershire and Rutland and providing information and advice to local farmers and landowners on safeguarding and enhancing the wildlife potential of their land.

In 2004, the Trust acquired two important and impressive new wetland areas to create nature reserves at Cossington Meadows and Wanlip Meadows. It was an important milestone in the Trust's long-term vision of an extensive area of the river Soar floodplain between Leicester and Loughborough being managed for the benefit of wildlife and people. Over the next few years, further important areas of land were secured in the Soar valley to extend and enhance Cossington Meadows, Loughborough Big Meadow and Wanlip Meadows, and also create new nature reserves at Mountsorrel and Syston. Significant wetland creation and enhancement work was also undertaken.

Tim Appleton, the Trust's manager at Rutland Water nature reserve, was made a MBE for services to wildlife and nature conservation in the 2004 New Year Honours List (to add to his award of the Society's CHRISTOPHER CADBURY MEDAL in 1999). In 2004, the Trust also consolidated its remarkable 30-year partnership with Anglian Water by signing a new 25-year lease and management agreement for the Rutland reserve which incorporated several new areas of ancient woodland.

GRAZING PROJECTS

In the middle years of the decade, the Trust established a grazing project with traditional hardy Longhorn and Shetland cattle on key grassland and heathland sites in the Charnwood Forest and Soar valley.

Exmoor ponies were subsequently introduced to Cossington Meadows, and Manx Loghtan and Hebridean sheep were grazed on the Trust's Rutland grassland reserves.

The Trust celebrated its 50th anniversary in 2006 with a variety of activities, including the official opening of Cossington Meadows nature reserve by Trust Patron, SIR DAVID ATTENBOROUGH, and a dinner at the University of Loughborough. Members and supporters responded magnificently to the Golden Anniversary Appeal, which enabled the Trust to secure and extend Stonesby Quarry nature reserve – a fitting way to mark 50 years of action.

RECENT ACHIEVEMENTS

The last few years have seen the Trust embark on a number of exciting and ambitious areas of work. Heathland restoration in the Charnwood Forest has created new habitat for threatened wildlife and extensive woodland management work has been undertaken in several areas across the two counties. A successful scheme has helped long-term trainee placements to receive comprehensive training in practical nature conservation skills.

After a long planning period and nearly three years of site work, the Rutland Water Habitats Project was completed in early 2011. This created nine new shallow water lagoons at Rutland Water nature reserve, considerably enlarging the

Charnwood Lodge National Nature Reserve

existing reserve to provide the best conditions for wildlife and to ensure it is undisturbed by future water management on the reservoir.

As at December 2011, the Trust was managing 32 reserves, covering some 1,194 hectares. The development and expansion of the Trust's work has been overseen by dedicated staff and underpinned by volunteers and members who are the Trust's lifeblood. They provide practical help, financial and moral support, as well as exercising influence on the Trust's behalf

Looking forward, the Trust is seeking to develop a number of bold and ambitious LIVING LANDSCAPE projects focused on the Charnwood Forest, Leicestershire and Rutland Limestone, Leighfield Forest, The National Forest, Rutland Water and the Soar and Wreake floodplains. These will aim to restore, recreate and reconnect fragmented habitats to create a resilient and healthy environment that is highly valued and accessible for people, full of wildlife, and rich in opportunities for learning, health and well-being.

BY SIMON BENTLEY
Simon Bentley has been Director of the Leicestershire and Rutland Wildlife Trust since 2001. Prior to that, he was Head of Finance and Support Services at the London Wildlife Trust from 1992 to 2001.

Young participants at a Wildlife Watch annual event

CHAPTER 24

Lincolnshire

The decision on 10th December 1948 by Lindsey (now Lincolnshire) County Council to designate its sand dune, saltmarsh and seashore at Gibraltar Point near Skegness as a nature reserve, proved to be a significant event in the development of nature conservation in Britain. It was also an auspicious start for Lincolnshire Wildlife Trust, which had officially come into being only eight days previously, and was now entrusted with the management of the new reserve. Its task was to reconcile the conservation of habitat and wildlife with public access and enjoyment, and to provide opportunities for education and interpretation. This was the new concept of a nature reserve set out in a landmark 1947 report from the Government's Wildlife Conservation Special Committee (Command 7122). The pioneering experience gained at Gibraltar Point provided a model for similar reserves elsewhere in the country. In 1952, Gibraltar Point became the first designated Local Nature Reserve in England and its importance was further recognised in 1984 by designation as a National Nature Reserve (NNR).

The Trust, the third to be formed in the UK, had its origins in the Nature Reserves and Wildlife Conservation Committee of the Lincolnshire Naturalists' Union which had been formed to follow up the recommendations of the Society for the Promotion of Nature Reserves' (the Society) Nature Reserves Investigation Sub-committee for Lincolnshire. Key figures were TED SMITH, University of Nottingham Resident Tutor in Lindsey; Tom Baker, then Curator of Lincoln's

Opposite: Lapwing – known in Lincolnshire as the 'pyewipe'

City and County Museum and Honorary Secretary of the Lincolnshire Naturalists' Union and the Trust's first Honorary Treasurer; and Sir Francis Hill, a Lincoln solicitor.

THE NATURE OF LINCOLNSHIRE

Within its long maritime boundary, the ancient county of Lincolnshire encompasses the two great estuaries of the Humber and The Wash and a range of landscapes. These include peatlands in the Isle of Axholme; coversands with remnant heathlands south of Scunthorpe; the Trent Vale; the Jurassic limestone ridge north and south of Lincoln with ancient woodlands in south Kesteven; the central Lincolnshire Clay Vale with nationally-important lime woods; and the chalk-capped Wolds. There is also the coastal plain and marshes with a scattering of woods; the coast of sand dunes, saltmarshes and mudflats; the unreclaimed saltmarshes of The Wash; and the intensively cultivated silt and peat of the Fens. Lincolnshire remains predominantly rural and is a leading agricultural county, but a rapidly growing industrial complex has been established on the south bank of the Humber.

THE COAST

The protection of the undeveloped stretches of sand dune along the coast was one of the Trust's earliest concerns. Gibraltar Point itself had narrowly escaped development in the early 1930s, and in 1954, a little over a year after its statutory designation, the new reserve was threatened by plans for a large caravan site at the main point of access. To safeguard the reserve, the County Council offered to purchase the site. When negotiations failed, the Council

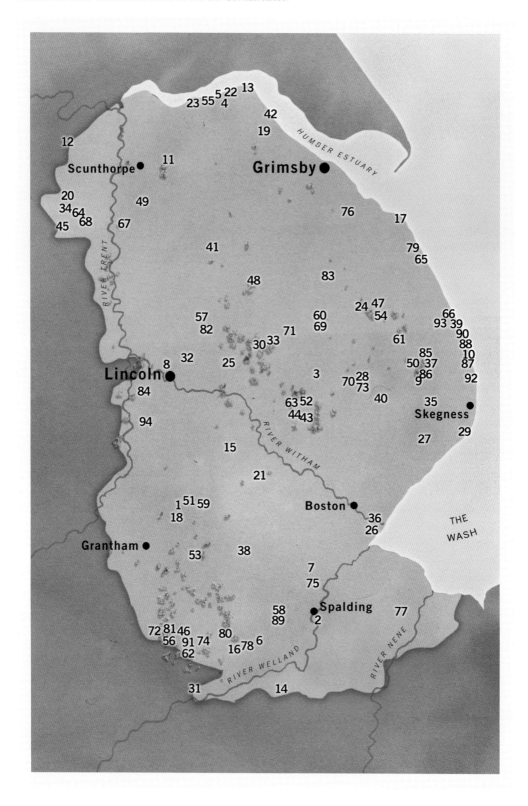

Scunthorpe

Grimsby

HUMBER ESTUARY

Lincoln

Skegness

Boston

THE WASH

Grantham

Spalding

RIVER TRENT

RIVER WITHAM

RIVER WELLAND

RIVER NENE

made a compulsory purchase order under the National Parks and Access to the Countryside Act (1949) – the first such order and one of very few ever made under the Act. The Council's order received strong support from local and national sources, and its subsequent confirmation enabled the Council to acquire the site and incorporate it in the reserve.

With the threat of development removed, the Trust was able to go forward with confidence. A bird observatory had already been established, and the acquisition of the old Coastguard House in 1958 – the venue for the first Conference of Wildlife Trusts in 1960 – provided simple residential accommodation and facilities. The success of that persuaded the County Council and the Trust to seek funding to build a new accommodation and laboratory block around the Coastguard House. The Wash Study Centre, as it is now known, is used by universities, schools and naturalists alike. Information for visitors was provided first in 1963 in a kiosk on the main car park, and then in a

Gibraltar Point field station and flooded saltmarsh

new visitor centre opened in 1974 by SIR DAVID ATTENBOROUGH. Today around 200,000 people visit the reserve every year.

In the early 1960s another of the Trust's reserves was threatened by proposals for a caravan site. The SSSI sand dune coast at Saltfleetby-Theddlethorpe – a nature reserve by agreement with the Ministry of Defence – faced major expansion of an existing caravan site on the edge of the dunes. To remove the threat to the SSSI, and in line with

1	Ancaster Valley	33	Hatton Meadows	65	Saltfleetby-Theddlethorpe Dunes
2	Arnold's Meadow	34	Haxey Turbary	66	Sandilands Pit
3	Banovallum House	35	Heath's Meadows	67	Scotton Common
4	Barrow Blow Wells	36	Hobhole Bank	68	Sedge Hole Close
5	Barrow Haven Reedbed	37	Hoplands Wood	69	Silverines Meadows
6	Baston Fen	38	Horbling Line	70	Snipe Dales
7	Boston Road Brick Pits	39	Huttoft Bank Pit	71	Sotby Meadows
8	Boultham Mere	40	Keal Carr	72	South Witham Verges
9	Candlesby Hill Quarry	41	Kingerby Beck Meadows	73	Sow Dale
10	Chapel Pit	42	Killingholme Haven Pits	74	Stanton's Pit
11	Clapgate Pits	43	Kirkby Gravel Pit	75	Surfleet Lows
12	Crowle Moor	44	Kirkby Moor	76	Tetney Blow Wells
13	Dawson City Clay Pits	45	Langholme Wood	77	The Shrubberies
14	Deeping Lakes	46	Lawn Wood	78	Thurlby Fen Slipe
15	Digby Corner	47	Legbourne Wood	79	Toby's Hill
16	Dole Wood	48	Linwood Warren	80	Toft Tunnel
17	Donna Nook	49	Messingham Sand Quarry	81	Tortoiseshell Wood and Meadows
18	Duke's Covert and Copper Hill	50	Mill Hill Quarry	82	Watts Wood
19	Eastfield Road Railway Embankment	51	Moor Closes	83	Welton-le-Wold
20	Epworth Turbary	52	Moor Farm	84	Whisby Nature Park
21	Ewerby Pond	53	Moulton Marsh	85	Willoughby Branch Line
22	Fairfield Pit	54	Muckton Wood	86	Willoughby Meadow
23	Far Ings	55	Pasture Wharf	87	Wolla Bank Pit
24	Fir Hill Quarry	56	Porter's Lodge Meadows	88	Wolla Bank Reedbed
25	Fiskerton Fen	57	Pickering's Meadow	89	Willow Tree Fen
26	Frampton Marsh	58	Pinchbeck Fen Slipe	90	Anderby Marsh
27	Friskney Decoy Wood	59	Rauceby Warren	91	Bottleneck and Jacksons Meadows
28	Furze Hill	60	Red Hill	92	Chapel Six Marshes
29	Gibraltar Point	61	Rigsby Wood	93	Spendluffe Meadows
30	Goslings Corner Wood	62	Robert's Field	94	Tunman Wood
31	Great Casterton Road Banks	63	Roughton Moor Wood		
32	Greetwell Hollow	64	Rush Furlong		

Key to map of Lincolnshire Wildlife Trust nature reserves

Grey seals at Donna Nook National Nature Reserve on the Lincolnshire coast

its planning policy, Lindsey County Council made a closure order for the camp which was confirmed after a three-day public inquiry.

At Donna Nook, further north on the coast, the Trust reached an agreement with the Ministry of Defence to manage a large area of sand dune and saltmarsh. In 2002, this became the first National Nature Reserve in Britain on the Ministry's land. At Donna Nook, the Trust ensures that the many thousands of people who come to see one of Britain's largest grey seal colonies are able to do so without causing disturbance to the seals.

The use of the Lindsey County Council Sandhills Act 1932, and later planning policies, ensured that parts of the central coast have been protected from development. Those parts are now being incorporated in a Coastal Country Park, within which the Trust has some landholdings. The Trust is also a lead partner in a scheme, generously supported by the HERITAGE LOTTERY FUND

and other national sources, to retain and restore traditional grazing pastures in the coastal marshes.

The achievement of securing the Marine and Coastal Access Act 2009 led the Trust to a new focus beyond the county's shores. Previous work with offshore wind farm developers and the marine aggregate and fishing industries put the Trust in a strong position to help identify Marine Conservation Zones in the North Sea. As the North Sea becomes the focus of national interest in sustainable marine development, the Trust, along with other Wildlife Trusts on the North Sea coast, has appointed a Marine Spatial Planner to ensure that wildlife has a voice.

HEATHLANDS, PEATLANDS, WETLANDS AND HOLES IN THE GROUND

Another area given early priority by the Trust was the coversands heathland in the north-west of the county. This had already been damaged and severely reduced in extent by afforestation and ironstone mining and by the growth of Scunthorpe. Successful appeals for funding in the 1950s enabled the Trust to purchase two important SSSIs on the coversands at Scotton Common and Linwood Warren, both of which had retained a rich wet heath flora. The Linwood reserve is dedicated to the memory of Richard (Dick) Cornwallis, a leading farmer and conservationist and President of the Trust who made an immense contribution to its early development. Further into the north-west, in the Isle of Axholme, the Trust also acquired remnants of the once great peatlands at the head of the Humber Estuary – the Epworth and Haxey Turbaries. The Trust is also still acquiring areas of Crowle Moors which are now part of the Humberhead Peatlands NNR.

In the 1970s, sand excavation destroyed one of the county's richest areas of heathland at Messingham Heath – despite its SSSI status and a concerted effort by the Trust and the Nature Conservancy to save it. Fortunately, the Trust was able to lease another excavated area nearby to form a diverse reserve known as Messingham Sand Quarry.

Excavation of sand and gravel at Whisby, south of Lincoln, has also created a complex of lakes and reedbeds with remnants of heath and birch woodland. The Trust has established a nature reserve and a well-visited nature park at Whisby, complete with visitor and education centres, managed in association with the District and County Councils.

Bittern at Far Ings National Nature Reserve

On the south bank of the Humber excavation of clay for the brick and tile industry, and more recently for cement manufacture, has left a series of water-filled pits with extensive reedbeds. These have attracted a variety of wetland birds including bittern, marsh harrier and bearded tit. Since the late 1960s, the Trust has gradually acquired some 168 hectares of the pits to the east of Barton-upon-Humber and in the area known as Far Ings to the west. This outstanding reserve, accorded NNR status in 2005, also has an administrative, education and interpretation centre.

NEW AGRICULTURAL REVOLUTION

An early 19th century agricultural revolution in Lincolnshire had obliterated almost all traces of the old fenland and the extensive sheep-grazed grasslands of the chalk and the limestone hills. But by the 1960s, a new era of farming intensification was having a major impact on the county's remaining semi-natural habitats and wildlife. Even SSSIs – then inadequately protected – were not immune from destruction. One such was Waddingham Common, a small peat bog on limestone soils and the last

Southern marsh orchids in flower at Whisby Nature Park

example of its kind in Lincolnshire. Pleas from the Trust and the County Council failed to save it, but its destruction gave the Trust the opportunity to publicise the absurdity of SSSIs being destroyed with grant-aid from the Ministry of Agriculture. As a result, local MP, Marcus Kimball, introduced a Private Members Bill, which, although it failed, helped to expedite Government action on better protection for SSSIs.

The Trust now gave high priority to acquiring sites threatened by agricultural intensification. Hay meadows were a particular target and a fine series of sites were rescued, four of them with SSSI status. The Trust also rescued important calcareous grasslands, including Red Hill on the Wolds and the species-rich grasslands at Ancaster Valley. Also on the Wolds, the valley of Snipe Dales was acquired with the aid of the County Council, which also created an adjoining Country Park from a former Forestry Commission plantation. Both are now managed by the Trust. In the Fens, some wetland habitat survived in the washlands created beside main rivers as flood-relief reservoirs. One of these, Baston Fen, a rich area of 33 hectares on the River Glen, came into the Trust's ownership in 1967 and has retained much of its natural interest. Further downstream on the Glen, the Trust has acquired 112 hectares of low-lying farmland at Willow Tree Farm and is in the process of recreating fenland habitat of marsh and grassland, reedbeds and meadows. Waymarked routes and an interpretation centre will enable visitors to appreciate the atmosphere and habitats of the old fenland, and also how it was managed and used.

More widespread habitats were also affected by agricultural intensification. To speed up land drainage, rivers and streams were widened and straightened, and features like cliffs, sandbars and bank vegetation were eliminated. In 1963, to mitigate the damage, the Trust made an agreement with the River Authority which authorised it to survey and make recommendations on stretches of river before major maintenance work was carried out. It was the first such agreement in the UK.

Friskney Decoy Wood, 1960 – by the 1960s, natural habitats in Lincolnshire were becoming increasingly isolated and vulnerable. In response, the Trust rescued many precious wildlife sites

The first shorebird wardens at Gibraltar Point in 1976 – Dr Kevin Woodbridge and Eric Blood

The loss of permanent grassland highlighted the importance of road verges which, in some parts of the county, were the only semi-natural grassland remaining. Negotiations between the Trust and Lindsey County Council about the treatment of verges were given new impetus when one of the richest stretches of verge on the Wolds was sprayed with weed killer. The effects were witnessed by delegates at the first Trusts' Conference held in Lincolnshire in 1960. The result was a pioneering agreement whereby the Trust identified verges of special importance and was consulted before any management was carried out by the Highway Authority. Under the agreement, the Highway Authority pays the Trust for managing what are now designated as Roadside Nature Reserves. In 2009, the Trust secured funding for an intensive study of the road verges in the limestone area in the south of the county. This has been so successful that it has been extended to the verges in the Wolds.

In the 1970s, the Trust also sought to establish better understanding with the farming community through conferences and exercises on farms, including through the Lincolnshire Farming and Wildlife Advisory Group which it co-founded.

THE FUTURE OF NATURE RESERVES

Awareness of the vulnerability of small and isolated reserves to how surrounding land is being used – such as lowering the water table and eutrophication from fertilisers – has led the Trust to extend its reserves whenever possible. Of the total of 94 reserves covering 3,800 hectares, more than a quarter have been significantly enlarged. An outstanding example is at Kirkby-on-Bain where 12 areas of heath, woodland and wetland have been acquired over a period of 40 years, and more are planned with the aim of creating an ecological network.

Expansion of reserves has often involved habitat recreation. For example, the species-rich limestone grassland at Robert's Field in Kesteven. For 30 years, Robert's Field was under a blanket of conifers before being successfully restored. Management of the Trust's ancient woodland reserves in the east and south of the county is designed to maintain and restore traditional coppicing systems. Attention to rare species on reserves has involved some carefully planned reinforcements and reintroductions, including that of the natterjack toad to Gibraltar Point. A seasonal shorebird warden is employed at Gibraltar Point to safeguard nesting ringed plovers and the last little tern colony in Lincolnshire.

Students carry out botanical surveys at Whisby Nature Park

SURVEY AND RESEARCH

Up-to-date information about habitats and species
is a necessary basis for conservation policies.
The first, in 1951, produced a list of outstanding
sites many of which were adopted by the Nature
Conservancy for their first SSSI schedules in the
county. A pioneering audit of rare species was
recorded in a Red Data Report in 1988, and a more
ambitious habitat and species survey in 1996
provided information used for the first county
Biodiversity Action Plan produced in 2000.
Several special regional studies have been carried
out by the Trust, including one covering the City
of Lincoln. In 1996, this resulted in the Lincoln
Green Project to encourage community involvement
in the management of green spaces. The
Conservation of Churchyards Project in the 1990s,
involving Trust Area Groups, surveyed more than
160 churchyards and made recommendations to
retain and enhance their natural interest.

MANAGEMENT AND ADMINISTRATION

The Trust's first office was in a spare room in the
Honorary Secretary's house until, in 1965, the
headquarters was established in the thatched
Manor House at Alford. For nearly ten years,
the Trust shared office accommodation at Alford

with the Society, where TED SMITH was also
its Honorary Secretary. The Trust moved to
its present headquarters at Banovallum House
in Horncastle in 1993. For the first 20 years,
the Trust was administered almost entirely by
volunteers. Grant-aid from Lindsey and Kesteven
County Councils made possible the appointment
of the first Administrative Officer in 1968 and a
Conservation Officer in 1970. The first Chief
Executive, Stuart Crooks, was appointed in 1976
and served the Trust with great distinction until
retirement in 2008. Crooks was succeeded by Paul
Learoyd, the present Chief Executive. In 1962,
Barrie Wilkinson was appointed as a Field Officer,
rising to become Reserves Manager. He served
the Trust for 37 years until retirement in 2002,
and continues as a key volunteer.

The Trust has been fortunate from the outset in
attracting a series of Honorary Officers. Ted Smith
was the founding Honorary Secretary, then Chairman
and now President. David Robinson was Honorary
Secretary for a record 41 years, and Don Wright
was Chairman for 12 years, with Brian Tear as
Deputy Chairman. In 2010, the Trust undertook
a governance review which resulted in the
appointment of Sir John Mason as Chairman,
with joint Deputy Chairmen Geoff Trinder,
David Sheppard and Tim Sands. The Trust was
also fortunate in attracting several just-retired

A visit by HRH The Prince of Wales to Gibraltar Point in 1971
Left to right: David Robinson, HRH The Prince of Wales,
Ted Smith and Walter Lane

Willow Tree Fen – the site of a large-scale fenland restoration project

senior local government officers – including previous President, Walter Lane, and Bob Prentice as Honorary Treasurer, both former County Council Chief Executives. David Cohen succeeded Bob Prentice as Honorary Treasurer in 2009. A Council and a Board of Trustees are now the main governing bodies, supported by teams of members and staff covering the main areas of activity. Membership of the Trust has now reached 25,000 and volunteers continue to play a major role. They are involved, for example, in reserve management, in manning visitor centres and shops, in organising events and in interpretation and education. As many as 16 Area Groups organise a full programme of local events and help to raise funds. WILDLIFE WATCH groups are active across the county, and some 10,000 children enjoy educational visits to Trust reserves each year.

The activities and achievements of the Trust's early years were well portrayed in the mid-1960s by two pioneering films, *Nature in Trust* and *An Eye for the Country* produced by ROBIN CRANE. The Trust's story is also the subject of two important books – Ted Smith's 2007 memoir, *Nature in Trust*, and leading wildlife photographer Geoff Trinder's *Wild Lincolnshire* – a splendid pictorial record of its nature reserves and their wildlife, and an inspiring testimony to the achievements of the Trust during its first 60 years.

BY TED SMITH AND DAVID ROBINSON
Ted Smith is one of the great pioneers of nature conservation, having had a lifetime involvement at both local and national level. He was a founding member, and is now President, of the Lincolnshire Wildlife Trust and played a leading role in establishing county Wildlife Trusts across the UK.

Acclaimed Lincolnshire scholar, David Robinson, has been involved with the Trust since the 1950s. Currently a Vice President, he has edited the Trust's Lapwings *magazine from its inception to the present day.*

CHAPTER 25

London

London is probably the place one least expects to find nature to conserve. The human pressures of urbanisation – hectare for hectare – are at their greatest anywhere in the UK. Nevertheless, London is a surprisingly green city; almost 60 per cent of its land area is greenspace, much of which has been saved from loss and damage through concerted local action since the late 19th century.

However, in the 1970s London's nature had little protection against the forces railed against it. There were a handful of SSSIs (such as Barn Elms Reservoirs, Ruislip Woods), a few nature reserves (including Perivale Wood, Selsdon Wood), and a cluster of sites where the predominant management was largely sympathetic (such as Wimbledon Common, Epping Forest). But, apart from designated sites, few green spaces had protection from development. Local development plans made no reference to the natural environment; no policies were in place to protect or enhance biodiversity. Urban parks were largely managed in the guise of their Victorian or Edwardian legacies, with an emphasis on formality and high horticulture. The proliferation of housing estates in the 1950s–70s continued a legacy of bland green deserts. Pesticide use in parks and gardens was widespread, and 'wildlife gardening' was considered for eccentrics only.

The origins of London Wildlife Trust are rooted in the local activism that began to tackle deprivation across London in the 1960s–70s; social justice, equalities, and environmentalism. Whilst the Black Country can proudly hold the mantle of where Britain's urban nature conservation movement began, there were already blooms of activity in the Capital during the 1970s, notably the emergence of the Ecological Parks Trust (founded by MAX NICHOLSON in 1976), and a number of local groups trying to address sites that were neglected or threatened with loss – especially in many inner urban neighbourhoods.

Opposite: Children taking part in the Trust's Cockney Sparrow Project. Above: In 2011, after more than 50 years, grazing returned to the Trust's Chapel Bank – a chalky nature reserve highly treasured by long-standing volunteers

389

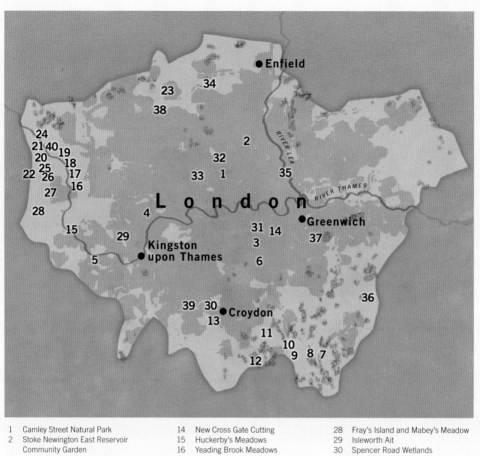

1	Camley Street Natural Park	14	New Cross Gate Cutting	28	Fray's Island and Mabey's Meadow
2	Stoke Newington East Reservoir	15	Huckerby's Meadows	29	Isleworth Ait
	Community Garden	16	Yeading Brook Meadows	30	Spencer Road Wetlands
3	Centre for Wildlife Gardening	17	Ten Acre Wood and Meadows	31	Bellenden Road
4	Gunnersbury Triangle	18	Gutteridge Wood	32	Mortimer Terrace
5	Crane Park Island	19	Ickenham Marsh	33	Greville Place
6	Sydenham Hill Wood and Cox's Walk	20	Fray's Farm Meadows SSSI	34	Oak Hill Woods
7	West Kent Golf Course	21	Denham Lock Wood SSSI	35	Old Ford Island
8	Saltbox Hill SSSI	22	Uxbridge Moor	36	The Warren
9	Chapel Bank	23	Totteridge Fields	37	Birdbrook Road
10	Hutchinson's Bank and Threecorner Grove	24	Dew's Farm Sand Pits	38	Mill Hill Old Railway
11	Bramley Bank	25	Park Road Ponds	39	Pyl Brook
12	Riddlesdown SSSI	26	Uxbridge College Pond	40	Ickenham Manor Moat
13	Wilderness Island	27	The Grove		

Map of London Wildlife Trust nature reserves

EARLY DAYS

The trigger for a new Greater London Trust developed from dissent within the HERTS & MIDDLESEX TRUST in 1980. After its Council decided to buy premises in St Albans, a minority took the view that resources could be better disposed towards practical conservation, especially on the urban fringe of north-west London where some key sites – especially in the Colne Valley – were under threat.

At that time, Chris Rose, a Field Officer working for the Trust was instrumental in advocating this line. Chris Rose had recently helped establish the British Association of Nature Conservationists and, in early 1981, contacted other London conservationists to explore the possibility of establishing a new London Trust. He enlisted Richard Robinson, a 'leading light' within the British Trust for Conservation Volunteers (BTCV), Jo Simons, a housing officer, and Bob Smyth, who had formed the Southwark Wildlife Group in the previous year. He also secured support from Richard Findon of the Nature Conservancy Council (NCC), and recruited Lord Melchett as Patron and Richard Mabey, author of *The Unofficial Countryside*, as President.

The London Wildlife Group, as such, evolved from a meeting at the Black Bull pub on the Fulham Road and set about organising a conference, *Nature in London*, largely pulled together by Pete Byfield, to launch the Trust. The conference, held at Clissold Secondary School in Stoke Newington over 15–16th May 1981, attracted more than 400 delegates. Speakers included Chris Baines and Bunny Teagle (both of the 'Black Country contingent'), as well as Frank Perring (from the Society) and John Davidson (Countryside Commission) to 'lend legitimacy' to the proceedings.

The new London Trust followed hot on the heels of other new trusts in the West Midlands, Avon, and Cleveland. The creation of these urban trusts was symptomatic of the spreading challenge to conservation attitudes still orientated towards the countryside, away from where most people lived.

This approach was reflected in the new Trust's profile and public relations. Delegates were offered a copy of *Wild London*, which had the rough and ready feel of a punk fanzine, and referred to 'The Front Line', the threats to a number of sites and who the villains were. With this came the Primrose Hill Declaration; a manifesto for conserving London's natural heritage against the "expropriation by. . . industry, development, greed, waste and misconception". This was meant to have been read at an inaugural meeting of the Trust on 5th May on Primrose Hill, together with the planting of a primrose as a gesture of the Trust's intentions;

Chris Rose – one of the founders of the Trust
Above right: The Trust's first logo

however, officers of the Department of Environment and Royal Parks refused permission for the event to take place.

The new London Wildlife Trust was formally constituted on 21st October 1981, with Chris Rose becoming Chair (following Richard Robinson's earlier guiding hand, who became Secretary). With a logo of a wren against St Paul's Cathedral, the Trust immediately went about creating headlines – highlighting threats to sites across the city, many of which would stay on the radar for many years, including Fray's Farm, Oxleas Wood, Gunnersbury Triangle, Hounslow Heath and Walthamstow Marshes. Early in 1982, it ran the North London Wildlife Day at Alexandra Palace, attended by more than 1,000 people.

UP AND RUNNING

In May 1982, supported by Government grants, the Trust appointed its first officer, Chris Rose, selected from more than 200 applicants. He stood down as Chair and was replaced by Bob Smyth (a Southwark Councillor at the time). In December, Rose was joined by Melanie Roots as Development Officer. She was able to start at the Trust's first permanent office, a crammed corner under the Westway flyover, which opened in November.

The summer witnessed the first of the Trust's awareness-raising campaigns – Foxwatch – partly to secure a better picture of the fox population at the time, and to advocate local authorities and landowners to adopt a more sympathetic approach (foxes were then often widely dispatched as vermin) – through what became the Trust's Fox Code (30 years later foxes are commonplace throughout the city). Similar surveys and campaigns followed on the back of this; Owl Prowl (1985), Bee Spree (1987) and Kestrel Count (1988).

The year also saw the emergence of campaigns affecting two sites that became central to the Trust's profile. Sydenham Hill Wood, already under the aegis

391

of the Southwark Wildlife Group and effectively the first Trust reserve, became threatened with a housing development, and Gunnersbury Triangle was subject to plans for industrial units. By the end of the year, part of the Wood became the focus of a vociferous campaign, whilst that for the Triangle would lead to a landmark planning precedent.

In 1983, the Greater London Council (GLC) established an Ecology Team within its Planning and Transportation Department – a decision that would help to shape the future direction of the Trust. Dr David Goode, Deputy Chief Scientist for the NCC, took up the role as the GLC's Chief Ecologist in the summer, and started building a team that the Trust hoped would "mark the proper development of a conservation policy by the GLC" given that its record to date was "not good".

The Trust presented Dr Goode with a 10-point plan that sought, amongst other aims, to secure 'Greenbelt', 'Captive Countryside' and 'Handkerchief' sites, the declaration of Local Nature Reserves on GLC-owned land, the establishment of ecological nurseries and a habitat creation management team.

In October, at the invitation of the Trust, the GLC leader, Ken Livingstone, visited Camley Street near King's Cross, with the aim of helping to embed the Trust's aims within the policies of the GLC. An essential difference from many other Wildlife Trusts is that for almost 25 years of London Wildlife Trust's history, it has worked in tandem with the GLC's Ecology Team and its successors until its dissolution in 2009. This led to the Trust focusing on campaigning, raising awareness, local action, and securing nature reserves, whilst the GLC would focus on planning policy and ecological audits. Elsewhere, the London Natural History Society (established 1858) maintained its focus on recording.

The key to the Trust's early energies was the motivation of its young and enthusiastic committees. Local groups, allying themselves to the Trust, began forming in most of the London boroughs,

Camley Street Natural Park in 1985

and focusing their activities around campaigns and/or sites. Some of these groups had pre-dated the Trust, and others would form more complex relationships as battles were won and lost.

RAISING THE WILD FLAG

The following few years were times of exceptional growth and activity. The Trust took a deliberately localist stance from the outset, determined not to be constrained by the concerns of orthodox ecology. Not that it ignored the science, but it consciously married it within a social context, a political acumen and at times a necessarily populist stance. For without gaining Londoners' support for the Trust's broader desires for conserving nature, it would get nowhere.

1983 began with the go-ahead to create a new park at Camley Street. A derelict coal-wharf on the edge of the Regent's Canal, by 1981 its wasteland wildlife was identified as a new coach park. The Trust lent its weight to local campaigns to save the site, and through its new relationship with the GLC, was able to secure its vision for the site as an inner-urban oasis for wildlife. The GLC largely funded the scheme and works began later in the year, eventually leading to Camley Street Natural Park opening in May 1985. The reserve remains a flagship site for the Trust, managed on behalf of London Borough of Camden.

Perhaps of greater impact was the London Wildlife Habitat Survey, which was carried out by the Trust on commission from the GLC over 1984–85 – the first of its kind for a city anywhere in the world. A team surveyed accessible green spaces of greater than 0.5 hectares, and discovered new species to London and many new potential wildlife sites in the process. This audit, subsequently updated in most boroughs, helped to provide the foundations of the wildlife site system in London from 1986. This is still in use today, with 1,507 sites identified in 2011.

By 1988, the Trust was already in the pugnacious flowering of youth, confident at what had already been achieved. It had an active network of volunteers working on a growing number of

A Trust officer confronts a digger at Sydenham Hill Wood in 1988

nature reserves across London, including Ten Acre Wood, The Rattler, Hutchinson's Bank, Wilderness Island and Pyl Brook (amongst more than 40 sites) – on target for at least one nature reserve in every London borough. It had saved sites, and fought hard for – but lost – Shakespeare Road Sidings, an amazing orchid-rich grassland in Herne Hill. The Trust had published surveys of Hackney, Camden and Lambeth (with Islington to follow), published *Encouraging Wildlife in Urban Parks* in 1986 (the first guide of its kind) and was running a tree and woodland programme following the impacts of the 1987 GREAT STORM. And it had engaged with thousands of young people on housing estates, schools, youth clubs and nature reserves.

Chris Rose left the Trust for Friends of the Earth in June 1983, and was replaced by John Newton. In October 1984, Jeremy Iles was appointed as the Trust's first Director. The following year the Trust moved into the one of the two new London Ecology Centres at York Way, in King's Cross, and Richard Robinson was elected Chair (with Hazel Phillips as Honorary Secretary).

By spring 1986, the staff numbered ten, supporting a flourishing network of local groups. However, the Manpower Services Commission (MSC) soon boosted staff numbers, particularly for reserve management (EMPLOYMENT SCHEMES). By the summer of 1988, there were more than 60 staff, a mixture of temporary field officers, wardens, education officers, surveyors and back-room support. And the Trust had a new logo, a shadowy fox.

CRISIS, CONSOLIDATION AND GROWING CONFIDENCE

However, with the closure of the MSC scheme, funding for most staff collapsed, and following the departures of both Jeremy Iles and John Newton in 1989, the Trustees had to navigate through a difficult retrenchment. In 1991, a new Director, Graham Turnbull (ex-SUSSEX TRUST) was in place, with a Deputy, Ralph Gaines. Roger Taylor became Chair in 1992 (with Mike Lachowicz as Honorary Secretary), and helped to oversee a period of consolidation and stability.

By this time the conservation landscape was changing and shaping the Trust's activities accordingly. London Ecology Unit had developed a strong policy focus, English Nature and the Countryside Agency were more active and, by the end of the decade, other national NGOs became more interested in London.

There was a strengthening of focus of activities around 'key sites', the reserves that had secured enough resources for staff: Sydenham Hill Wood, Camley Street Natural Park, Tump 53, Gunnersbury Triangle, Crane Park Island, and the newly-established Wildlife Gardening Centre. New high quality reserves – such as Denham Lock Wood SSSI – helped to mitigate for smaller sites that had been divested, and some were entered into Countryside Stewardship Schemes to provide much needed resources such as livestock, which enabled the introduction of conservation grazing.

As the nineties progressed, programmes, such as Operation City Greenspace and Growing Greener, provided thematic direction, whilst energy was spent on campaigns for threatened sites such as Oxleas Wood, Rainham Marshes and the Greenwich Peninsula. DAVID BELLAMY, dressed as Noah on

The award-winning Centre for Wildlife Gardening in East Dulwich

an ark in the Regent's Canal, launched the highly successful London Wildlife Week in June 1994, with more than 60 events across the city. The Trust also secured strategic support for local groups to enhance their capacity, and 'The Newts', an active weekend volunteer team, led to a greater engagement with BTCV. *Wild London* became a full-colour magazine in 1992, and, in 1994, in common with many other Trusts, the Trust replaced its fox logo with the Society's badger logo.

Stag beetle

The Biodiversity Action Plan (BAP) process began in 1995, and the Trust took a leading role at a London-wide level and locally in the boroughs, especially to ensure that the familiar but less ecologically recognised, habitats and species were embedded within these plans – for example, the built environment, parks, gardens, and wasteland. It championed action for stag beetle, black redstart, water vole and black poplar – taking the lead across London for these flagship species, and indirectly helped trigger innovative practice in respect of parks' management, the development of a green roof renaissance in the UK in the first decade of the 21st century, and urban river restoration. In 1996, the Trust set up its Biological Recording Project to further the aim of establishing a record centre for London, in order to underpin the development of BAPs. In 1997, Wild Linesides was launched by Jenny Agutter, to publicise the Trust's embryonic partnership with Railtrack.

The move to Harling House, in Southwark, in 1997 led to a real uplift of the Trust's spirit, boosted by, and funding from, two new sources; the Lottery, and Bridge House Estates Trust Fund. The installation of new IT equipment, the development of the web, and email started to have an impact on the way the Trust worked.

INTO THE 21ST CENTURY

Nonetheless, the departure of a number of staff and trustees over 1999–2003, and rises in rents at Harling House, led to another loss of momentum, and, for a short period, crisis. Following the departures of Ralph Gaines and Graham Turnbull, the Trust was effectively led by the Honorary

Officers (Chair, Justin Dillon) until the appointment of Carlo Laurenzi, as Chief Executive, in September 2003. Quickly a move was made to develop a five-year strategic plan for the first time and changes were made to Council, to set the Trust on a clearer direction.

Since 1999, the Trust has invested much more heavily in its land-holdings, following the acquisition of Saltbox Hill SSSI, part of Riddlesdown SSSI, and, in 2002, what would become Huckerby's Meadows. Funding from a range of sources has contributed towards the implementation of significant habitat enhancements on more than 30 reserves. A Reserves Review helped to identify the sites it wanted to hand back to their owners, and clarify the focus for future investment. With the incoming Higher Level Stewardship scheme, London Wildlife Trust is laying the foundations for its future Living Landscapes work in three key areas; the Crane and Colne Valleys, the North Downs, and the Wandle Valley.

The Biological Recording Project (BRP) started to make a real difference in underpinning the continuing BAP work, which has more recently evolved towards more targeted approaches at habitat suitability mapping. In tune with other record centres, the BRP worked towards semi-independency and, in 2004, it became Greenspace Information for Greater London. It is still hosted by the Trust, and plays an increasingly influential role in managing and analysing environmental data for London.

Three major influences over the past decade have been the establishment of the Greater London Authority (GLA) in 2000; London securing the hosting of the 2012 Olympic Games; and the rise of climate change on the political agenda.

Wildlife in a skip – medal-winning garden at the 2007 Hampton Court Show

The GLA, under Ken Livingstone's leadership, quickly made its mark. A Biodiversity Strategy was published in 2002, and in 2004 a new regional development strategy (the first since 1976) – *The London Plan* – started to give confidence that the advocacy for nature over the past 20 years was becoming embedded into the planning system. Nevertheless, following the election of Boris Johnson, with his focus on project delivery, there are concerns that the baton for the strategic direction for biodiversity conservation needs to be taken up by others.

In 2005, London won the bid to host the 2012 Olympic and Paralympic Games, and the Trust endorsed the bid on the proviso that there will be a net gain in biodiversity. This would lead to major changes to the Lower Lea valley around Stratford, with the development of the Olympic Park. The Trust has been instrumental in influencing the design of the Olympic Park, the production of the Olympic Park Biodiversity Action Plan, and has also been hugely active with the Olympic Committee in the preparation and delivery of the Games themselves. Support from the Society over this process was essential to keep the movement positioned at the heart of the Games and, hopefully, its legacy phase.

Climate change will impact upon London in significant ways, and the role of natural greenspace will be imperative in adaptation to the impacts of these changes. Since 2006, the development of the Green Grid, the green infrastructure strategy for London, led initially by the London Development Agency and embedded in the new *London Plan* (2011), is likely to assist in a greater appreciation of the value of protecting and conserving natural habitats. In addition, the Environment Agency's innovative lead in urban river restoration, has helped the Trust deliver conservation works on the Rivers Crane, Colne, Ingrebourne and Wandle, assist its work on water vole conservation and scope out new partnerships on a catchment level.

By 2011, the number of Trust staff had risen to over 40, with an active force of more than 200 volunteers, and a trimmer Board chaired by Alan Rick. Activities include working with young people, those with special needs, with social landlords and residents of housing estates (Natural Estates, Cockney Sparrow), as well as extensive landscape-scale restoration work on high quality reserves. In spirit the Trust is a different beast to that of 1981, but its enthusiasm to make a difference burns as brightly as ever.

MAKING A DIFFERENCE TO LONDON

London Wildlife Trust's story has been one of hard-fought battles, with many emotional gains and a fair number of gut-wrenching losses. The sheer number of London's wildlife sites, with levels of planning protection, is impressive. Many woodlands are now subject to more appropriate management, and many unimproved grasslands are now being grazed again. The loss of London's bogs, acid grassland and heathland has probably been reversed, although there are questions over their condition and long-term vulnerability. Many rivers are being released from their concrete culverts and are in the process of restoration. Breeding pairs of peregrine falcon have returned to London, and red kite are increasingly seen over some of the outer suburbs. Great spotted woodpecker are now widespread, and jackdaw appear to be in slow recovery. Grey heron and cormorant are thriving, and bittern are returning, undoubtedly through the gradual enhancement of the Thames (which now numbers more than 120 breeding fish species) and other wetlands.

More recently water vole and European eel, whilst hanging on in various rivers, require concerted action to prevent their extinction from London. Collaborative efforts are in place, in a way that was probably impossible in the early 1980s.

However, many valuable wildlife sites are still being wiped off the map. The Trust has failed to adequately persuade others of the value of our diverse 'wastelands' and has failed to break the notion that our ecological security can be bought by planting trees alone. Some species in London have undergone dramatic decline, for example linnet and grey partridge, as well as those once widespread, such as song thrush, starling, and the small tortoiseshell butterfly. Other species that are thriving are more controversial. There are increases in roe deer and muntjac in the suburbs, gulls on city centre roof-tops, and grey squirrel, zebra mussel, Himalayan balsam, ring-necked parakeet and Chinese mitten-crab. They all bring into play the diversity of origins of so much of London's wildlife.

As the Trust enters 2012, it will be looking towards meeting the challenges of a London that is set to be the home for eight million people, with unprecedented pressures on greenspace and wildlife, against a background of a significantly bleak economy. Nevertheless, with the advocacy and practice developed in London by the Trust and many others, the Trust is confident that it can make the capital a better place for wildlife, and strengthen people's connection with, and understanding of, nature.

BY MATHEW FRITH
Mathew Frith first joined London Wildlife Trust in 1987 as a volunteer, and has subsequently worked as a reserve warden, conservation manager, and now as Deputy Chief Executive. He served as a Trustee between 2002 and 2009. His favourite bird is the magpie.

Huckerby's Meadows – the Trust's newest reserve in Cranford, next to Heathrow Airport runway

CHAPTER 26

Manx

The Isle of Man lies in the Irish Sea, 30 miles to the west of Cumbria and a similar distance to the east of County Down, but only 18 miles from the Scottish coast. It is 35 miles long by ten miles wide and covers 220 square miles. Its climate is equable, damp and cool. Over 60 per cent of the island lies above 250 feet, but its highest point is only 2,036 feet above sea level. It only became an island some 10,000 years ago when rising sea levels created the Irish Sea. The island has a scenic coastline of about 100 miles, mainly rock cliffs, rising to over 1,000 feet in places, but with 25 miles of soft sand and gravel cliffs in the north.

In the 9th century the island was colonised by the Vikings, who established a parliament, known as Tynwald, which has survived to the present day. Although the island has been a possession of the English Crown since the end of the 14th century, it has its own legislature, government and judiciary and is largely independent of the United Kingdom. However, the UK Government remains responsible for its foreign affairs and defence, and the Crown is ultimately responsible for the good government of the island.

Today, the island has a population of 84,000, having risen steadily from fewer than 50,000 in 1961. About half the population lives in or near the main town, Douglas. Financial services have replaced tourism as the most important economic activity.

CONSERVATION-YEAR CATALYST

There may be few people who now recall that 1970 was designated European Conservation Year,

Opposite: View towards the west coast from German Parish
Right: Early visitor centre poster

but it was this designation that prompted two spirited young ladies, Felicity Cain and Elizabeth Hamm, to write a letter to the *Isle of Man Examiner* with a rousing call to the island to do something in recognition of the year. Many responded to the challenge and on 3rd August 1970 more than 200 people attended a public meeting at Victoria Street Methodist Church, Douglas. Speaker after speaker demanded that action be taken to promote conservation on the island. At a later meeting it was decided to form a new group, known as the Manx Conservation Council, to spearhead the drive for effective conservation policies. Among the many objectives was the establishment of a Nature Conservation Trust. This led, eventually, to the establishment of the Manx Nature Conservation Trust on 6th March 1973. Stephen Incledon, a member of the DORSET TRUST, was Chairman and Dr Roger Pullin, a marine biologist, was Honorary Secretary and Honorary Treasurer. At the first Annual General Meeting on 15th November 1973, the balance sheet showed net assets of £215. But it was reported that the Trust had accepted offers of a disused reservoir and adjoining land, and 18 acres of woodland. They became the first Trust reserves.

KEY PEOPLE

For the first 19 years the Trust was run entirely by volunteers, although some of them were professionally-

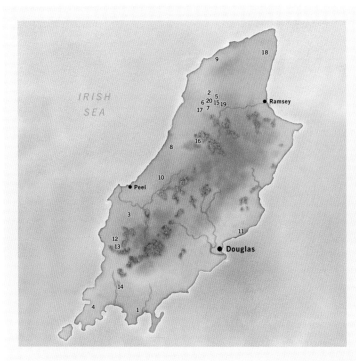

1	Ballalough Reedbeds
2	Ballamooar Meadow
3	Barnell Reservoir
4	Breagle Glen
5	Close e Quayle
6	Close Sartfield
7	Close Umpson
8	Cooildarry
9	Cronk y Bing
10	Curragh Feeagh
11	Curragh Kiondroghad
12	Dalby Mountain Fields
13	Dalby Mountain Moorland
14	Earystane
15	Fell's Field
16	Glen Dhoo
17	Goshen
18	Lough Cranstal
19	Miss Guyler's Meadow
20	Moaney and Crawyn's Meadows

Map of Manx Wildlife Trust nature reserves

trained conservationists, particularly in marine biology. The Liverpool University Marine Laboratory at Port Erin, now sadly closed, where Pullin was on the staff, provided a valuable professional contact for the Trust. In November 1973, Incledon was succeeded as Chairman by William Cain, husband of Felicity. On leaving the island in 1979 to work abroad, Pullin was succeeded as Honorary Secretary by RJ Pritchard, a keen naturalist. When he left the Island to join The National Trust, he was succeeded by Tony Hopson, another marine biologist, who stayed until his death in 1998. Cain remained Chairman of the Trust until June 2010, when he was succeeded by Dr Stephen Jeffcoate.

COASTAL CENTRES

The early years of the Trust were dominated by work on the new reserves as they were acquired, and also on the establishment of two visitor centres. The first centre was created out of the ruins of a war-time building constructed for the RAF on

the Ayres, an area of several miles of raised beach, now a National Nature Reserve, at the northern tip of the island. It was the brainchild of Felicity Cain, co-author of the letter to the *Isle of Man Examiner* in 1970 and a founder member of the Trust. It was opened on 8th May 1977 by Charles Sinker, the Director of the Field Studies Council. Unhappily, it was burned down in July 1984, but a new centre was built and opened in May 1986. Meanwhile, at the southern end of the island, a second visitor centre was opened in May 1982 by the island's Lieutenant Governor. The Scarlett visitor centre is in a coastal area of special geological interest, comprising both limestone and volcanic rock. The two visitor centres, both of which now have a video presentation, are used by many school parties and together attract about 2,500 visitors each summer.

FIRST PAID STAFF

In 1992, a new era for the Trust began. Largely on the initiative of the Honorary Secretary, Hopson, it was decided to appoint paid staff. In August 1992,

John Lamb, who had worked for the LANCASHIRE TRUST and on the island, was appointed Conservation Officer. A part-time Education Officer and, later, a part-time Volunteer Coordinator were also appointed. Although special funding was obtained from both charitable and commercial organisations to support the new posts, it was clear that it would be necessary to increase the income of the Trust, as well as provide an office for the staff. After some research, a shop unit with a small office attached was found at Tynwald Mills, St Johns, in a new out-of-town shopping precinct. Using experience gained in the operation of the visitor centres, Felicity Cain opened a gift shop at Tynwald Mills in 1992. The adjoining unit was added in 2000, thus doubling the area of the shop. The Trust remained here until it moved its offices and shop to new premises in Peel in 2011. The shop, now called the Wildlife Shop, is managed and manned by volunteers, and run on commercial lines selling only new stock. It is also, to a large extent, the public face of the Trust and, along with the visitor centres, is the information centre for the Trust. The shop is now operated by the Trust's trading company, Wildlife Limited, formed in 1996.

In 1998, it was decided to appoint a Director, and advice was sought from the Royal Society for Nature Conservation (the Society) on the proposed new post. While this was being considered, Lamb, who had proved to be an impressive Conservation Officer, resigned in order to return to his native Lancashire. In consequence, the restructuring of the staff posts had to be brought forward and a new post with particular responsibility for the management of the reserves was created. In September 1998, Tricia Sayle was appointed Reserves Officer. In the following year, Caroline Steel was seconded by the Society to the Trust as Acting Director for several months, and appointed the Trust's first Director in January 2000. Steel established new systems for all the Trust's activities, and effectively completed the transition from a voluntary group to a professional organisation. During 1998–99, the accounts of the

Sweeping views at Cronk Ny Arrey Laa in the south-west of the island

Orchids at Close Sartfield

Trust and the trading company were computerised, with some difficulty, and the accounting system was brought up-to-date.

ROYAL VISIT

On 5th July 2000, the Trust was honoured to receive a visit by HRH The Prince of Wales, after he had presided over the annual open-air sitting of Tynwald. The Prince was shown round the Trust's Close Sartfield reserve in Ballaugh, to see the striking display of more than 100,000 orchids in the reclaimed meadows. In October 2001, Steel resigned to return to England and in January 2002 Duncan Bridges, from Essex, was appointed the new Director. In July 2003, the Trust changed its name to Manx Wildlife Trust.

MEMBER AND VOLUNTEER SUPPORT

The Trust was founded in 1973 with 11 subscribing members. The membership steadily increased, and by 1995 stood at about 700, rising to 800 by 1997. Although membership has since fluctuated, it had grown to 1,257 ordinary members at the beginning of 2011. Corporate membership, created in 1996 with 21 members, has also fluctuated, but by 2011, there were 30 corporate members, including three 'gold' members, paying £1,000 a year, and seven 'silver' members, each paying £500 a year.

The Trust has always had excellent volunteer support, both indoors (in the visitor centres, the shop and the office) and outdoors in the reserves. In recent years there have generally been more than 100 volunteers active on behalf of the Trust.

TRUST RESERVES

The acquisition and management of nature reserves has been, and remains, the principal aim of the Trust. It now has 21 reserves covering about 280 acres, nearly all being owned by the Trust on a freehold basis. Some of the reserves were donated, but most were purchased by the Trust with funds provided by legacies or grants. The reserves contain a wide range of habitats, from 69 acres of heather upland to five acres of coastal sand dunes. The Trust has more than 60 acres of hay meadows, marsh and woodland, forming part of the Ballaugh Curragh – recently given Ramsar status. The Trust's Close Sartfield reserve, with its famous orchid meadows, is in this area. Only nine reserves are open to the public, but there is a management plan for each reserve. The Trust's acquisition policy favours the enlargement of existing reserves, but unexpected opportunities for new reserves arise from time to time.

MARINE SURVEY WORK

The Island's 100-mile coast and its territorial sea, which extends to more than 1,500 square miles, is a spectacular wildlife resource. The Trust's Marine Committee has carried out a complete survey of the coast – above high water, in the intertidal zone and below low water – thus creating an invaluable database for the future. In 2005, the Trust established Manx Basking Shark Watch to record sightings and monitor the movements of basking sharks in Manx waters. In 2006, nearly 700 basking shark sightings were reported, and in 2007 at least four basking sharks were fitted with satellite tags so that their movements could be followed. One of the sharks released its tag off the coast of Newfoundland, Canada, providing the first evidence for a link between European and American populations and indicating that basking sharks make use of deep-water habitats beyond the coastal shelf edge. During the shark's transit of the North Atlantic, it travelled a horizontal distance of 9,589 kilometres and reached a record depth of 1,264 metres. Since then, a further 15 satellite tags have been deployed on sharks in Manx waters. This will hopefully lead to better information about the sharks' behaviour and where they travel when they leave.

Other scientific projects being carried out are fin identification and behaviour studies. The Trust is also taking part in a project to record sightings of cetaceans with the Sea Watch Foundation, which maintains the principal cetacean sightings database for the British Isles. Several species of whale, including minke, orca and fin, as well as dolphins and porpoises, are regular visitors to Manx waters.

CONSERVING NATIVE MANX FLOWERS

In 2000, several Isle of Man Government departments, Manx National Heritage and the Trust established a project to promote the conservation of native Manx wildflowers. A Project Manager was appointed to work under the guidance of a committee drawn from the funding bodies. Seed was collected from nature reserves and wild places where plants were likely to be of Manx origin. The seeds were then sown and grown on, before being planted out as seed crops. There is now an annual crop of 20 different types of wildflower seed available for sowing in new conservation projects, such as roadside verges. Seed is also sold in packets to the public. Advice on wildflowers is also provided and a wildflower garden has been created at St Johns to show how wildflowers not only fit comfortably into a garden, but can also enhance a natural space.

EDUCATION AND BUSINESS ACTIVITIES

The Trust has had part-time Education Officers since 1993, when the post was funded by a local company. For several years funding has been provided by the Isle of Man Department of Education. The Education

Basking sharks in Manx waters

Officer works with a number of schools and runs the WILDLIFE WATCH club, making use of the two visitor centres and associated nature trails. Awareness of the island's wildlife is also fostered by guided walks, nature reserve open days, talks, leaflets, the Trust's newsletter and articles in local newspapers.

Since the appointment of a Conservation Officer in 1992, the Trust has provided a consultancy service, mainly for Isle of Man Government departments, but also for private landowners.

INFLUENCING PUBLIC POLICY

The Isle of Man Government, through its departments and agencies, has both central government functions – such as taxation, law and order, health services, and agriculture, fisheries and forestry – and other functions which, elsewhere, would be carried out by local government – planning, roads, environmental matters, education and social services, for example. In addition, the Manx Government owns the electricity and water undertakings,

the harbours and airports and, significantly, most of the open hill land, including the forestry plantations. It also owns the coast below mean high water and the seabed of the territorial sea, which extends to 12 nautical miles. All minerals – which means everything including the rock, sand and gravel, oil, gas and coal below the surface of the island and the seabed of the territorial sea – are vested in the Manx Government. Manx National Heritage, a public body funded by the Government, is also a major landowner of areas of high landscape value, including the Calf of Man, part of the coast and most of the Ballaugh Curragh, the island's principal wetland. The local authorities also own parks and amenity areas in the towns and villages. So where does this leave the Trust?

Firstly, the Trust is in a position to influence public policy on wildlife issues. For example, in 1995, the Trust published the *Manx Hill-land Report*, following a very successful seminar on the Government's policy of extending the conifer plantations on the hills, thereby destroying

Curlew at Ballaghennie

View from the south with the Calf of Man in the foreground

heather moorland. The report made valuable recommendations for the management of the hill land in public ownership, which, happily, were eventually accepted. The Government's afforestation policy was then changed.

Secondly, the Trust has acted both as a consultant and as a contractor to Government. The Native Wildflowers of Manx project is one example. Another example resulted from the Trust's 1991 island-wide survey of roadside verges. This prompted the Government to ask the Trust to manage several verges where there were particular conservation concerns. For several years the Trust has promoted a Wildlife Sites scheme to identify places of ecological importance. The Government has now provided the funds to enable the Trust to employ a Wildlife Sites Officer to complete the project. This will take several years, but will clearly be for the public benefit. In 2006, the Trust was awarded a contract by Manx National Heritage to employ and manage the two wardens on the Calf of Man. Not only do they look after the one-square-mile islet, but they also run the well-known bird observatory and ringing station.

FUTURE FUNDING CHALLENGE
The Trust now plays a significant role in nature conservation in the Isle of Man. Its future role will depend on its ability to generate funds and to attract funding from outside sources. This will not be easy. As the Isle of Man is not within the UK, the Trust has not had access to the public

lottery (although grants from this source may be available in future) nor to Landfill Tax Credits. Legacies have been the most important source of Trust funds, followed by charitable trusts, usually established under the donor's will. The Wildlife Shop and membership subscriptions continue to be important sources of income, and help to ensure that the Trust can continue its work protecting and restoring the island's wildlife.

BY WILLIAM CAIN
William Cain has been involved in Manx Wildlife Trust since its foundation in 1973, and was its Chairman for over 36 years. A leading member of the Island's Judiciary, he was at various times appointed Attorney General, Second Deemster and First Deemster. He was awarded the CBE in 2003, the Christopher Cadbury Medal in 2010 and the Tynwald Honour in 2011.

CHAPTER 27

Sir Drefaldwyn – Montgomeryshire

The story of the Montgomeryshire Trust is in many ways remarkable. The county has a population of less than 60,000 – 10,000 fewer than in 1849. The land area is almost 2,000 square kilometres and it is the only Welsh county to extend from the English border to the west coast and have reserves on both these boundaries – more than 39 miles apart as the osprey flies.

The Trust was born as a result of the Montgomeryshire branch of the North Wales Naturalists' Trust seeking independence in December 1981. Interest and attendance at the local branch of the NORTH WALES TRUST appeared to be waning, which led to the suggestion that it should be wound up. About ten people met and decided that a separate Montgomery Trust for Nature Conservation should be inaugurated in its place. It is believed that the suggestion was first put forward by Roger Lovegrove, then working for the RSPB as its Wales Director. Other people with this vision were Richard Churchill, Colin Small, Ian Soane, and Graham Williams.

Richard Churchill (centre) receives the 1982 Conservation Foundation award

The Trust was on the crest of a wave, and with Richard Churchill as the first Chairman, it was the first recipient of a new annual award from the Conservation Foundation for the greatest contribution to voluntary conservation. This was all the more remarkable as the Trust had only been in existence for six months, and was faced with competition from 43 other Trusts. The award ceremony was televised on *Pebble Mill at One* and the award presentation was made by DAVID BELLAMY.

AGAINST THE ODDS

Right at the start, the Trust took on a seemingly huge and impossible task. Some 400 acres of prime upland habitat at Glaslyn, near Pumlumon, came on the market with an asking price of £50,000. At the time the Trust's bank account showed itself in credit to the tune of 78p! Against all odds, the Trust purchased Glaslyn, supported by such intense local enthusiasm and interest that people had to be turned away from one meeting.

Opposite: Walkers enjoy the upland scenery at Glaslyn, the Trust's first reserve acquired in 1981

A RESIGNING MATTER

The first Honorary Secretary, Colin Small, recalls incidents which show how different the conservation scene was in the early 1980s. After news of the Trust's existence was published in the local paper, Small, an agricultural advisor working for the Government's Agricultural Development Advisory Service, was summoned to his senior officer and told he must resign his position as the Trust's Honorary Secretary. The reason given was that as 'conservation was anti-farmer', farmers would have no confidence in Small's advice. The fact that half

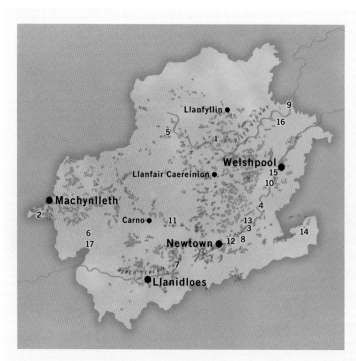

1	Coed Pendugwm
2	Cors Dyfi
3	Dolforwyn Woods
4	Dolydd Hafren
5	Dyfnant Meadows
6	Glaslyn
7	Llandinam Gravels
8	Llanmerewig Glebe
9	Llanymynech Rocks
10	Llyn Coed y Dinas
11	Llyn Mawr
12	Pwll Penarth
13	Red House
14	Roundton Hill
15	Severn Farm Pond
16	Ty Brith
17	Bugeilyn

Map of Montgomeryshire Wildlife Trust nature reserves

the Trust's Council were farmers was not enough and Small was forced to relinquish his role. He was succeeded by Margaret Anthony, who worked for the RSPB. In 1982, the Trust Council had 16 members and four sub-committees.

At the Trust's Autumn Fayre in 1983, it is recorded that there were 750 visitors. At that time the emphasis was on the efforts of the Trust to secure the cooperation of local landowners and farmers in environmental protection. The Trust was also doing valuable work in the form of a county bat survey and, the following year, surveys of great crested newt and butterfly sites were undertaken. At this time, the Chairman of the Trust was Lady 'Bea' Davies of Llandinam, and her energy and drive were pivotal in advancing the causes of the Trust.

By 1985, the Trust employed staff through the Manpower Service Commission (EMPLOYMENT SCHEMES) and made good use of the scheme, although the staff moved on after a relatively short time, usually spending just one year in post. By 1986, the membership had grown to 500 and

the Montgomery Conservation Volunteers were formed. The group regularly met to perform maintenance works on the reserves. That year also saw the start of the Montgomery Flora Project. This culminated ten years later with the publication of *The Flora of Montgomeryshire*, under the major authorship of Marjorie Wainwright, Ian Trueman and Alan Morton. It will probably long remain the standard reference.

Sponsorship of the Trust's activities was becoming ever more important. In 1987, as Carno-based Laura Ashley Industries was developing its worldwide presence, it donated a van for the use of staff and volunteers and also agreed to sponsor the Trust's regular magazine.

PRESCIENT PROSE

In 1987, Richard Churchill again took over as Trust Chairman on an interim basis, until he was succeeded in 1988 by Robin Cross. Churchill contributed regularly to the magazine and showed himself ahead of his time when, in 1987, he wrote: "I believe we shall move towards less purchasing of threatened sites and above all devote more of our effort towards the creation of better understanding of the beauty and benefits of the natural world around us, and the absolute need to conserve and improve it". The Trust changed its name in 1987 to the Montgomeryshire Wildlife Trust, which it retains to this day.

A momentous change in the fortune of the Trust came out of the blue in mid-1990. Kathleen Collot, who was not a member and was hardly known to the Trustees or staff, left a large bequest to the Trust. It enabled the direct employment of staff and the investment of a capital sum into a high-interest account. The Collot legacy gave the Trust the ability to focus more on conservation. In another piece for the magazine, Churchill – again showing his vision – wrote: "How much better than just SSSIs and isolated sites, would it be that all our county should be fit for wildlife".

EVOLVING INTO A SERIOUS FORCE
In 1991, there were further changes when Robin Cross became Director, and Robert Antony took over the post of Chairman. It was Cross who summed up the evolving status of the Trust, when he wrote, "rather than being seen as a group of enthusiasts,

we are now being called upon to make a serious contribution towards the management of the countryside". An Education Officer was employed and area WILDLIFE WATCH groups were subsequently set up with the aid of a grant from the Countryside Council for Wales.

The momentum of the early days had been carried forward. By 1992 the Trust owned ten nature reserves and employed four and a half staff and office volunteers.

In 1992, the Trust's magazine – up to this point entitled *Montgomeryshire Wildlife* – underwent a name change to *The Otter*. In the first issue under its new name, an article appeared supporting the Campaign for Cleaner Rivers to coincide with water sampling along the length of the River Severn. The Trust also attracted some high-profile names with Valerie Singleton, of *Blue Peter* fame, appearing at the Country Fair, and the Welsh weather presenter, Sian Lloyd, unveiling a topograph at the highest point of the Trust's new Roundton Hill reserve.

A Farming for Wildlife competition was an innovative way of engaging with the local farming community and, as several farmers became Trustees, this became a theme with the Trust over the next few years. This may have been spurred on by the latest 1992 round of EU Common Agricultural Policy reform. The Trust was now under the

The Trust's reserve at Roundton Hill

Morfa Dyfi William Condry reserve

chairmanship of Willie Jack, and in the following year, its membership reached 1,200. When Mavis Nicholson took over the Presidency in 1993, she wanted to see, "the Trust have a stronger political voice, and look to influence political decisions which have an effect on the countryside".

WILLIAM CONDRY

When Morfa Dyfi reserve was purchased in 1994, the Trust became the owners of about 100 acres of saltmarsh, representing the only coastline in the county of Montgomeryshire. The reserve was then, and remains, closely associated with the name of William Condry, whose love of the Dovey Valley and Snowdonia was the basis of many of his books. It was written of him that he was a true conservationist before the word had been invented. He remained a member of the Trust until his death in 1998. His widow, Penny, retains her interest in Montgomeryshire conservation matters.

The Trust was fortunate to have the services of Simon Spencer in the mid-1990s to lead and continue work on butterfly sites and specific species within the county. Spencer remains a Trustee and is also very active as a Trustee of Butterfly Conservation.

By 1995 Roger Lovegrove, one of the founder members, had become Chairman. At this time wind farms were beginning to march relentlessly across the countryside of mid-Wales and to this day, the wind farms debate occupies local politics. The Trust policy was, and still is, that each application should be examined on its individual merit and planning applications are strictly scrutinised for their impact on wildlife.

Lady 'Bea' Davies became President in 1997, the same year that the Trust's bird group was officially launched at an inaugural meeting attended by William Hague MP (then Secretary of State for Wales). Meanwhile DAVID BELLAMY opened the Trust's new reserve at Newtown, which was an example of cooperation between the Trust and Severn Trent Water. Some of the settling pools of the old sewage works were landscaped to create a wildlife-friendly site with the Trust taking over its management and naming it Pwll Penarth.

Meanwhile in the uplands, conservation bodies were becoming more aware of the damage caused by overgrazing. Farmers were encouraged to increase livestock numbers by politically imposed, but misguided, agricultural subsidies. The subsidies rewarded overproduction, but at a terrible cost to these fragile habitats.

COUNTRYSIDE STEWARDSHIP

It was the Trust's monitoring and population studies that demonstrated the threat to plants and animals caused by sheep, famously dubbed 'woolly maggots' by the naturalist and television presenter Iolo Williams. A close relationship had been built up between the Trust and many farmers through a joint newsletter and meetings, with the Trust starting to push for an upland subsidy based on acreage rather than head of stock. Out of this came recognition that the Trust must try to have an influence on the stewardship of the wider countryside, pushing for subsidies to be transferred from production rewards to agri-environmental schemes.

This culminated in the Montgomeryshire Biodiversity Action Plan, the first in Wales, which was launched in 1999. The Trust was also heavily involved in the setting up of, and providing information for, the Biodiversity Information Service for Powys and the Brecon Beacons.

Several of the Trust's reserves are home to the pearl-bordered fritillary, which is in widespread decline elsewhere due to loss of habitat

The Heritage Lottery Fund was pivotal in supporting a five-year enhancement of Trust reserves through scientific research, monitoring and habitat management. The scheme began in 2000 and was embraced by the Trust, enabling it to upgrade facilities and interpretation at the reserves, and to improve their management.

GROWING INFLUENCE

Foot and mouth disease devastated the Montgomeryshire infrastructure in 2001. Farmers suffered serious economic hardships and the Trust had severe difficulties accessing its reserves to carry out any surveys or monitoring. However, as climate change increased its profile in the public perception, the role of upland peat as a carbon store, as well as a natural sponge, began to be more loudly voiced. There was a call from the Trust for Government to plan for more environmentally-friendly use of the Cambrian Mountains.

An important new reserve was purchased in 2001. Llandinam Gravels, one of the last remaining naturally-sculpting reaches of the River Severn,

attracted funding from the Heritage Lottery Fund. It now has a significant plantation of native black poplar as a result of 2,000 young trees being introduced. This reserve now forms part of the Severn Valley Wetland Project, a collaboration with the Environment Agency and other Trusts on the course of the Severn.

In 2002, the restoration of the Montgomery Canal and its reconnection to the national network was a local issue. Increasing tourism and the possibility of habitat destruction by motorised craft became contentious. The Trust carried out much work to safeguard the more sensitive conservation species, but its ideal of only horse-drawn traffic is unlikely to become a reality. It appears that, even though much European Union money was directed towards the scheme, there is a temporary lull in proceedings.

A wild brown trout from Bugeilyn Lake

'Monty' the osprey at Cors Dyfi reserve

The following year saw the Trust again advising the Welsh Assembly Government on agri-environmental issues, which resulted in the current Tir Gofal scheme. This rewards landowners for the sensitive use of their land and is overseen by the Countryside Council for Wales. Powys County Council came to an agreement with the Trust in 2004 to manage roadside verges throughout the county in a more positive way for wildlife. Many verges supported special plant communities which were at risk as a result of mowing at inappropriate times. In 2007, this became the Living Highways Project, which incorporates Road Verge Nature Reserves.

LOST TALENTS

The saddest event of 2004, however, was the death of Richard Churchill, the Trust's founder Chairman at the age of 96. He remained a strong and active supporter of the Trust until his final days.

Then 2006 saw the sudden death of Peter Forrester who had been both Treasurer and Chairman for the previous four years. His post was difficult to fill, but Neville Thomas, QC, the Trust's current President, temporarily took over as Chairman.

The same year, an important document, *Biodiversity Matters II* was published by the Trust and circulated to all members. It outlined the coming ten years' conservation strategy and is proving to be a useful management tool, not just on the reserves but for conservation in the wider countryside. Another notable 2006 event was the purchase of Cors Dyfi, where a coniferous plantation was felled and water levels raised, allowing the natural wetland wildlife to return quickly. Ospreys have since chosen the reserve as their summer home, and with the building of a raised hide, Cors Dyfi has become the Trust's most visited reserve with more than 48,000 visitors in 2011, when a pair of ospreys nested and raised three young.

Education has always been a priority for the Trust. In 2008, the Trust was recognised for the most Sustainable Education Project in Wales. Engagement with the public continues through links with over 20 schools and community groups.

LANDSCAPE-SCALE VISION

The Trust's vision broadened even further in 2008 with work starting on the blueprint for the landscape-

Pumlumon in the Cambrian Moutains

Estelle Bailey, Iolo Williams and Chris Townsend at the Dyfi Osprey project

scale project at Pumlumon in the Cambrian Mountains, over a 40,000 hectare project area. The Cambrian Mountains are the largest watershed in Wales, being the source of eight rivers including the Severn, Wye and Usk, and support a complex mosaic of habitats – dry and wet heath, blanket bog, improved and unimproved grassland, broadleaved woodland, and oligotrophic lakes. Amongst the red data species and the Sites of Scientific Interest (SSSI), there are 250 farms and ten local communities, as well as two reserves managed by the Trust.

The Pumlumon project, which will run for several years, aims to work in cooperation with the WILDLIFE TRUST OF SOUTH AND WEST WALES, Countryside Council for Wales, the Forestry Commission, Environment Agency, the Cambrian Mountain Society and others to engage local people and guide a major change in the way the land is managed. The aim is to create a more varied landscape that is rich in wildlife and gives local communities a better future.

This will be achieved by re-wetting bogs to lessen rapid run-off, thus reducing the risk of flooding downstream. Existing habitats will be connected and those that are degraded, restored. Improved grazing regimes will be introduced for wildlife, and access for tourism improved with long-distance trails and accommodation. All these projects will

encourage local employment and new skills while at the same time protecting and respecting the local heritage. As the Trust looks to the future, there are both reasons to be cheerful and also significant challenges ahead. Despite the success of the Pumlumon project, the Dyfi Osprey project and the Trust's ongoing conservation work, including advising the Welsh Assembly Government on its proposed Wildlife Environmental Framework, the economic climate is making life difficult for small charities like the Trust. The hope is that its thirty years of experience will help it to weather this latest storm, and ensure that the Trust can maintain its work protecting and restoring Montgomeryshire's wildlife.

BY CHRIS TOWNSEND
Dr Chris Townsend has been Chairman of the Montgomeryshire Wildlife Trust since February 2009. He is a retired GP, who has had a lifelong interest in the environment, and ornithology in particular.

Norfolk

Norfolk has a long history of wildlife conservation dating back to 1888 with the formation of the Breydon Wild Birds Protection Society. In 1912, Blakeney Point was acquired and 11 years later, the majority of Scolt Head Island was also purchased following an appeal in the name of the Norfolk and Norwich Naturalists' Society. Both these reserves were handed over to The National Trust. Arising from these activities, the idea began to form that the county should have its own Trust to hold areas important for wildlife.

In early 1926, the marshes at Cley in north Norfolk came on to the market. Dr Sydney Long, who as Secretary of the Norfolk and Norwich Naturalists' Society had been involved in the Scolt Head purchase, was keen that this area, renowned for breeding and migrant birds, should be saved from falling into unwelcome hands. He secured promises of sufficient funds from a number of sympathetic friends to enable him to attend the auction in Norwich on 6th March 1926. He was successful in purchasing the 407 acres of marsh plus a building plot for the sum of £5,160. The subscribers to the appeal met at the George Hotel in Cley on 14th March 1926 and agreed that the marsh and nearby building plot should be handed over to a Trust to be incorporated "to hold the marsh in perpetuity as a Bird Breeding Sanctuary". That summer a 'watcher' was appointed, as wardens were then known. The winter shooting was let to a small syndicate consisting of four of the original subscribers. This syndicate met the expenses of the watcher

Opposite: Marsh harrier at Cley Marshes reserve
Above right: 1926 poster advertising the sale of Cley Marshes

during the winter months. At that time it was not perceived that there was any conflict of interest between conservation and legitimate shooting, even on a nature reserve.

The Trust was formally incorporated on 5th November 1926 as the Norfolk Naturalists' Trust, (making it the first local Wildlife Trust to be formed), a company limited by guarantee under the Companies Acts. At its first Council meeting on the 30th November, it was resolved unanimously to "accept the generous offer of the purchasers of the Cley Marsh property". At that meeting Russell Colman was appointed President and Dr Sydney Long as Honorary Secretary and Treasurer. Two-thirds of the original subscribers and first list of members were also members of the Naturalists' Society. By the time of the second Annual General Meeting in 1928 the membership had risen to 40. At that time, for reasons not now clear, the membership was to be limited to a maximum of 100.

CLEY-NEXT-THE-SEA,
NORFOLK.

Four miles from Holt Town and Station, 1 mile from Blakeney, 10 miles from Wells, and 12 miles from Cromer.

UNIQUE

Wild Fowling Marshes

ON THE NORFOLK COAST,
being a portion of the

CLEY HALL ESTATE,

435 ACRES

extending those to and including the foreshore, forming

A WILD FOWL DAY-FEEDING GROUND,
including

MARSHES, REED-BEDS, SALTINGS, SOME ARABLE LAND
AND BUILDING SITES,
which

Messrs. JOHN D. WOOD & CO.,
6 Mount Street, LONDON, W.1,

are, unless previously disposed of by private contract, instructed by the Executors of Arthur Wrigley Cozens-Hardy, deceased, to offer by Auction

At the ROYAL HOTEL, Norwich,
On Saturday, March 6th, 1926,
At 2.0 p.m.

Solicitors: Messrs. COZENS-HARDY & JEWSON, Norwich.
Land Agents: Messrs. FRANCIS HORNOR & SON, Norwich.
Auctioneers' Offices: 6 Mount Street, LONDON, W.1.

FIRST FUNDRAISING CHRISTMAS CARD

The Trust's second reserve was acquired in 1928 when 26 acres at Starch Marsh, Martham, were purchased as a breeding ground for the bittern, bearded tit and harriers. Two years later, an opportunity to extend the Trust's interest in Broadland arose when Alderfen

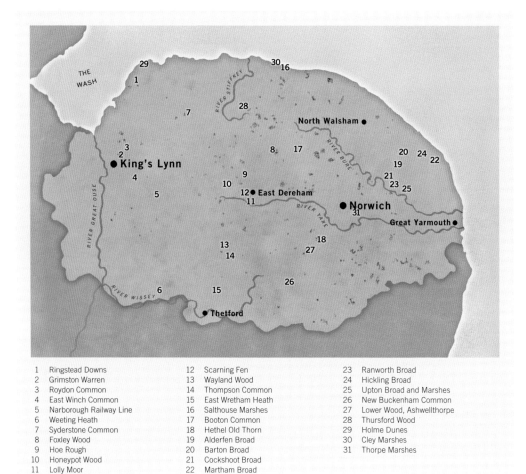

1	Ringstead Downs	12	Scarning Fen	23	Ranworth Broad
2	Grimston Warren	13	Wayland Wood	24	Hickling Broad
3	Roydon Common	14	Thompson Common	25	Upton Broad and Marshes
4	East Winch Common	15	East Wretham Heath	26	New Buckenham Common
5	Narborough Railway Line	16	Salthouse Marshes	27	Lower Wood, Ashwellthorpe
6	Weeting Heath	17	Booton Common	28	Thursford Wood
7	Syderstone Common	18	Hethel Old Thorn	29	Holme Dunes
8	Foxley Wood	19	Alderfen Broad	30	Cley Marshes
9	Hoe Rough	20	Barton Broad	31	Thorpe Marshes
10	Honeypot Wood	21	Cockshoot Broad		
11	Lolly Moor	22	Martham Broad		

Map of Norfolk Wildlife Trust main nature reserves

Broad came on the market. This was purchased in July 1930.

In the autumn of that year, the Trust issued for sale its first Christmas card as a means of raising funds to meet the cost of this and future acquisitions. It was a painting of a bearded tit executed by the well-respected Norfolk artist, John Cyril Harrison. Selling Christmas cards to raise funds was a novel idea at the time and was promoted in the national and local press. Harrison continued to provide a painting for the Trust's Christmas cards for the next 50 years, a remarkable achievement. He always presented the Trust with the original painting and many of these were subsequently sold as an additional source of funds.

FIGHTING AFFORESTATION

Having secured footholds at the coast and in the Broads, Sydney Long was anxious to extend the Trust's protection to the Breckland heaths with their rare flora and breeding birds. In 1932, to save some traditional Breckland heath from the forester, three cottages in the village of Lakenheath with commoners' rights over Lakenheath

Dr Sydney Long

Warren were purchased thus preventing the warren's afforestation. Unfortunately this protection was not long lasting. With the onset of the Second World War much of the area was requisitioned for the construction of the vast Lakenheath airfield. The cottages were disposed of in 1950.

A second opportunity to secure a substantial Breckland reserve arose in 1935 when the large Suffolk estate at Culford was broken up. The Forestry Commission bought a large area of Breckland heath for the purpose of planting conifers. A neighbouring landowner, in an attempt to secure an open area adjacent to his estate, offered to finance the purchase of 1,200 acres of this land if the Trust could persuade the Forestry Commission to sell. Unfortunately, the commission would not part with its new acquisition and created what is now The King's Forest. If this substantial area of Breckland heath had been acquired, perhaps the Trust would have had to become the Norfolk and Suffolk Trust!

Following this unsuccessful bid, another chance to extend the Trust's interests in Breckland occurred when the East Wretham estate came on the market in 1938. Although in failing health, Long worked tirelessly in negotiating with the Forestry Commission for the purchase of an area of heathland including the two meres, Langmere and Ringmere. Unfortunately he died in January 1939 before these negotiations were completed. Long's memorial stone is located at East Wretham, overlooking Langmere. In 1942, a further 300 acres of Breckland heath at Weeting were added to the portfolio, thanks to the generous support of CHRISTOPHER CADBURY. In 1949, he purchased Thetford Heath and presented it to the Trust.

EXPANDING BROADS' HOLDINGS

The second half of the 1940s saw the Trust make major extensions to its Broads' holdings with the

Alderfen Broad, the Trust's second reserve, pictured here in 1930. Above right: Swallowtail – an iconic species of the Broads

417

purchase in 1945 of the Whitesles estate and the leasing of additional land at Hickling Broad. A second acquisition occurred later that year when substantial parts of Barton Broad were either purchased or donated. In 1949, the Ranworth and Cockshoot Broads were given to the Trust, subject to the right of His Majesty the King to shoot over the Broad on one day each year, with no other shooting to be permitted.

KEY PEOPLE

Since its inception, a Council has governed the Trust. Its members are both the charity's trustees and directors under the Companies Acts. Council members are elected at the Annual General Meeting with a third retiring each year by rotation and currently can serve for a maximum of nine years. For many years there were no time restrictions on service and a number of past Council members served the Trust over very long periods. Russell Colman was President until 1946 when Sir Henry Upcher succeeded him. Three other original Council members each served for at least 20 years. They were Douglas Carruthers (until 1946), Bernard Rivière (until 1953) and Colin McLean, whose service included seven years as President until his death in 1962.

Miss Constance Gay succeeded Long as Secretary and continued in post through the post-war expansion of activities. As the Trust grew, the workload increased and an office for the Secretary was hired from November 1950. EA (Ted) Ellis succeeded Constance Gay as Secretary in 1955, a post he held until the end of 1962. Over time, various committees have been appointed to assist in the management of Trust reserves. For example, at one time many of the larger reserves had their own management committees. As the number of conservation staff has grown they have taken over these responsibilities.

The continual growth in the number of reserves in the Trust's ownership created the need to find more and more funds for their upkeep. A leaflet was published in the 1950s listing the properties then held and included a plea for financial support

by membership, donations and legacies. At that time life membership cost £10 and a minimum annual payment of £1 secured ordinary membership. In June 1960 membership totalled 810, broken down into 334 life members and 476 ordinary members. By March 1964, the total had grown to 1,056 members. The problems of fundraising, and the ever increasing burden of administration, led the Council to appoint a full-time Secretary. Group Captain GR Montgomery was appointed Secretary (in effect the Chief Executive) in January 1963. The first Conservation Officer, Peter Stevens, joined the staff in 1972.

VISITOR ATTRACTIONS

Whilst visitors had been welcomed to a number of reserves, an innovation at Cley occurred in April 1965 with the opening of hides on the marsh. Permits to use these new facilities had to be purchased one week in advance from the Secretary. Five years later, in May 1970, another visitor attraction was introduced, this time at Hickling, with the formal opening of the Water Trail by the broadcaster and naturalist, James Fisher. The provision of facilities for visitors has continued over the years and now forms a major part of the Trust's activities. In November 1976, Her Majesty the Queen opened the innovative floating visitor centre and boardwalk

The Hethel Old Thorn. This 500-year-old hawthorn tree is the smallest Trust reserve in the UK – at 0.2 hectares in extent!

Ancient oak trees at Thursford Wood

at Ranworth – the culmination of the Trust's Golden Jubilee celebrations. In 1981, visitor facilities at Cley were greatly enhanced with the development of the Dick Bagnall-Oakeley Visitor Centre. It was another ten years before a similar centre was opened at Hickling, this time in memory of Ian Mackintosh, a former Trust Chairman. The latest visitor centre to be opened is at Weeting, overlooking a favourite heath for stone curlews.

The year 1978 saw two significant developments to encourage members to feel they were an active and valued part of the Trust. The first was the formation of regional groups of members each run by their own committee, which arranged programmes of lectures and outdoor meetings. The second was the introduction of the members' magazine *Tern*, which was issued three times a year.

MAXIMISING MEMBERSHIP

The effect of these developments was a steady growth in membership, which at the end of 1978 totalled 5,271 and six years later stood at 7,722. It took until 1989 to reach the milestone of 10,000 members. By 2006 this had more than doubled with the membership standing at more than 25,000. In part this increase was helped by the 1995 decision to change the format of *Tern* from an A4 magazine to a tabloid newspaper. This had the major advantage of being distributed throughout the county as a supplement to the *Eastern Daily Press*, resulting in the Trust's news and messages reaching an increased audience of approximately 150,000 people.

The Trust's portfolio of reserves includes five ancient woods. The first was Thursford Wood, donated in 1957, followed by Wayland Wood,

Mixed flock of avocet and gulls in flight at Cley Marshes

purchased in 1975. Traditional management practices such as coppicing, have been reintroduced to the larger woods thus enhancing the biodiversity at these ancient sites. The largest, Foxley Wood, was declared a National Nature Reserve in May 2002 bringing to nine the number of the Trust's reserves so designated.

For the first 50 or so years of its existence, the Trust had largely devoted its energies to acquiring and looking after the nature reserves in its care. The first tentative steps in looking beyond its own estate had occurred as far back as the 1930s when the work of the County's Wild Bird Protection Committee came under its wing. By the 1980s, there was a view emerging amongst some active supporters that an organisation such as the Trust should no longer concern itself with just the 'jewels in the crown' as its reserves were described. Instead it should concern itself with the rapidly increasing pressures on wildlife throughout the county. A major step in this direction was made possible

in the mid-1980s through financial support from the Manpower Services Commission Community Programme. This enabled the Trust to undertake a habitat survey of a large area of the county. From the mass of botanical information gathered, very many sites were identified as being of county significance for wildlife in Norfolk. They were designated as County Wildlife Sites and recognised as such by a partnership of the Trust, English Nature, Norfolk County and the District Councils. In all about 1,300 sites have been designated.

BEYOND RESERVES

From these modest beginnings in looking beyond the reserves, a team has been built which devotes much time and effort to looking after specific conservation priorities. A watch is kept on planning applications that might have an unfavourable impact on wildlife habitats. Following on from this development has grown a market for advisory and survey services. Although a commercial activity such as this was considered to be outside the remit of the charity, the Trust has used this opportunity to form a subsidiary company Norfolk Wildlife Services. The company employs staff or contractors to meet the demand for specific surveys that are frequently required by potential developers or planners. All profits from the operation are donated to the Trust.

The Trust has worked with neighbouring Trusts over common interests – for example, one Norfolk Trust reserve is in Suffolk and one Suffolk Trust reserve is largely in Norfolk – and has given full support to the regional and national activities of The Wildlife Trusts. Arising from this support, the encouragement for all Trusts to adopt Wildlife Trust in the name did cause some heart searching, as initially there was considerable local opposition to dropping Naturalists from the name. In typical 'Norfolk Do Different'-style (the county motto) a compromise was adopted whereby the name Norfolk Wildlife Trust would be used as the trading name without any formal change made to the original legal name.

The Norfolk Wildlife Trust has generally enjoyed good relations with the statutory bodies involved in the protection of Norfolk's natural heritage. English Nature (now Natural England), the Environment Agency and the Broads Authority have been supportive in the management of the Trust's National Nature and other Reserves. Similarly, the Trust has worked closely with The National Trust and the RSPB on a number of joint projects.

HERITAGE LOTTERY FUNDING

The last fifteen years have seen a huge increase in the Trust's activities – in acquisitions, in improving the management regimes on reserves and in education. Many of these developments are a direct result of grants from the HERITAGE LOTTERY FUND. The largest project, entitled Securing the Future, involved major schemes for restoring habitats on the reserves and improvements to visitor facilities, including new interpretation, information and monitoring. The grant of

£2.3 million and the work were spread over a planned six-year period and completed in 2006. The challenge now is to maintain the improvements made to the various habitats on the reserves that benefited from this work. Education activities, both at school and general public levels, have expanded considerably with an Education Manager responsible for a team of permanent and seasonal staff.

New acquisitions during this period have included substantial additions to existing reserves. At Roydon Common, two large areas of neighbouring afforested heathland, known as Grimston Warren (Tony Hallatt Memorial Reserve), have been purchased. The coniferous plantations have been removed in a major forestry operation, with the vista restored to lowland heath with significant areas of wet heath and valley mire. Indeed, since its clearance and restoration, the Tony Hallatt Memorial Reserve is now at SSSI standard. In the Broads, three large areas adjacent to the Trust's Upton Fen reserve have been acquired and are being restored to wet grazing marshes. Both these

Large-scale heathland restoration at Grimston Warren

projects fall neatly into The Wildlife Trust's Living Landscape initiative, with the area around Upton forming part of the Bure Valley Living Landscape, and Roydon/Grimston forming part of the Gaywood Valley. From 2011, the Trust is also working to restore, recreate and reconnect four other Living Landscapes: Wissey, where a large area of arable Fens farmland is being turned into wetland and reedbed habitat in an ambitious attempt to offset the loss of habitat elsewhere; the Claylands area of south Norfolk, where an important mosaic of small isolated grasslands and woodlands occurs; the Hickling Living Landscape in the Broads, an area covering over 5,000 hectares of wetland habitat; and the North Norfolk Woods, containing the two largest ancient woodlands in the county.

NEW MILLENNIUM AND NEW CHALLENGES

Since the turn of the millennium, Cley Marshes, the birthplace of the Trust, has been the centre of major activity. The fragile shingle bank that protects the freshwater marshes of this reserve

Pond-dipping at Ranworth Broad
Above right: A sea slug photographed during a Seasearch dive off the Norfolk coast

has always been a source of concern and liable to be breached. The spectre of climate change and the associated likelihood of more frequent episodes of flooding only add to the problem. For the last 50 or so years, the shingle bank has been rebuilt regularly following the ravages of winter seas. But this near-futile attempt to turn the tide was discontinued by the Environment Agency in the middle of the decade, leading to the potential for the marshes to flood more frequently than in the past. To counter this, the Environment Agency has built new sluices and channels to facilitate the draining of future saltwater incursions in a major programme of engineering works. Improvements to the reserve's freshwater channels also followed to allow the marsh to recover from such flooding as quickly as possible. It is recognised that the nature of the reserve will probably change over time. But it will still have a future rich with wildlife, and also as an open-air laboratory for the study of the changes as it gradually reverts from freshwater marsh back to its original saline habitat.

Alongside these changes to the natural landscape at Cley, major changes also took place to the reserve's visitor infrastructure. Work began in June 2006 on the new eco-friendly Cley Marshes visitor centre which opened on 5th May 2007. Featuring a wind turbine, ground-source heat pump, sedum roof, solar thermal collectors and rainwater harvesting, the centre was built to the highest eco-friendly spec. The main funding came from the EU Objective 2 programme. A staggering £144,000 was also raised by Trust members. In its first four years, the centre has proved to be a massive success and draw, with visitor numbers through the building reaching a single-year high (to date) of 110,000.

The Trust is also developing its marine conservation work, getting involved with surveys of marine habitats and the Living Seas campaign. The Trust also runs a number of seashore events throughout the year.

As the Trust approaches its own centenary in 2026, its successes are not confined to its flagship Cley Marshes reserve. In 2011, its 85th anniversary year, the Trust owns, leases or manages more than 50 nature reserves – covering more than 4,300 hectares – and employs more than 70 staff. It has

a vibrant education programme with at least 5,000 schoolchildren enjoying outdoor education sessions on its nature reserves every year. Many more people are reached through community events. The oldest of the UK's Wildlife Trusts undoubtedly goes from strength to strength as it strives to build on Dr Sydney Long's initial pioneering vision.

BY DON DORLING

Don Dorling has been a member of Norfolk Wildlife Trust since 1965 serving as a volunteer, a Trustee for twelve years, Chairman (1999–2002), and currently a Vice President. He is also a Vice President of the Norfolk and Norwich Naturalists' Society. A birdwatcher since school days, Don is joint author of Birds of Norfolk *(1999).*

The new visitor centre at Cley Marshes

CHAPTER 29

Northumberland

In early 1961, Grace Hickling, Honorary Secretary of the Natural History Society of Northumberland, Durham and Newcastle upon Tyne, reported to her Council that she hoped to receive some guidance from TED SMITH, of the already well-established Lincolnshire Naturalists' Trust, about establishing a Trust in Northumberland and Durham.

In April 1961, Hickling attended a meeting of Trusts' representatives in London where it was pointed out that Northumberland and Durham were two of the few coastal counties where Trusts did not exist. However, the Society's Council agreed to take no further action at that time.

Nevertheless, interest was growing locally, and, in autumn 1961, a small group met in the Natural History Society's Gosforth Park nature reserve. Hickling was present, as was the relatively new curator of the Hancock Museum in Newcastle, Tony Tynan – a graduate in natural science. The group agreed that a Trust should be set up, and Tynan was asked to convene a meeting. This took place in the museum in February 1962 with Ted Smith as an inspirational guest speaker. The meeting voted unanimously to proceed with the establishment of a Northumberland and Durham Naturalists' Trust. In the natural history world, Northumberland and Durham had always been closely-knit and so it was natural (no discussion on the matter even took place) that a Northumberland *and* Durham Trust should be founded.

The Trust was incorporated on 13th March 1962 and the first public meeting was held in Newcastle City Hall, three days later. John Philipson became the Trust's first Chairman and Tony Tynan was elected Honorary Secretary. Tynan also became the Trust's mentor and guiding hand, and his base at the museum was the Trust's first headquarters.

Eight years later, at the 1970 AGM, it was amicably agreed that Northumberland and Durham should separate. The volume of work and travelling was beyond the capacity of the one body and, in 1971, the Northumberland Wildlife Trust came into existence. The Trust was the first, apart from Scotland, to use this new title of Wildlife Trust.

Opposite: A patch of grassland on the Whin Sill, Holy Island
Right: Tony Tynan – founder of the Trust

425

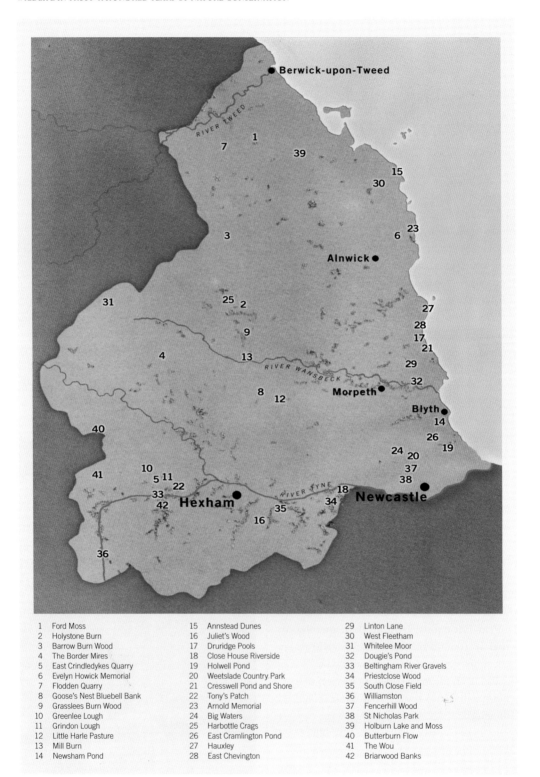

1	Ford Moss	15	Annstead Dunes	29	Linton Lane
2	Holystone Burn	16	Juliet's Wood	30	West Fleetham
3	Barrow Burn Wood	17	Druridge Pools	31	Whitelee Moor
4	The Border Mires	18	Close House Riverside	32	Dougie's Pond
5	East Crindledykes Quarry	19	Holwell Pond	33	Beltingham River Gravels
6	Evelyn Howick Memorial	20	Weetslade Country Park	34	Priestclose Wood
7	Flodden Quarry	21	Cresswell Pond and Shore	35	South Close Field
8	Goose's Nest Bluebell Bank	22	Tony's Patch	36	Williamston
9	Grasslees Burn Wood	23	Arnold Memorial	37	Fencerhill Wood
10	Greenlee Lough	24	Big Waters	38	St Nicholas Park
11	Grindon Lough	25	Harbottle Crags	39	Holburn Lake and Moss
12	Little Harle Pasture	26	East Cramlington Pond	40	Butterburn Flow
13	Mill Burn	27	Hauxley	41	The Wou
14	Newsham Pond	28	East Chevington	42	Briarwood Banks

Map of Northumberland Wildlife Trust nature reserves

Tynan continued as Honorary Secretary, retiring only in 2000, when he was honoured with the title 'Founder'. The Trust covers the old geographical county, embracing modern Northumberland and the boroughs of Newcastle upon Tyne and North Tyneside.

FIRST RESERVES

At first, and for many years to follow, the Northumberland and Durham Trust saw its main objective as the acquisition and management of nature reserves, including geological sites. At the time there were severe pressures on most habitats, as well as the effects of pesticide residues on birds of prey, otters and other wildlife, and it was imperative to save as much as possible. At the time, SSSI designation conferred very inadequate protection and acquiring reserves showed that the Trust meant business.

The very first reserves were in Durham, with the first in Northumberland, in 1964, being Big Waters, a large coal mining subsidence pond. The second was Throckley Pond, and these two reserves were seen as part of a necklace of educational sites within reach of schools from Tyneside and south-east Northumberland. It was not until 1966 that the Trust acquired the first reserve it actually owned, an area of ancient woodland above the South Tyne known as Tony's Patch. The 'Tony' in question was Tony Clissold, who tragically drowned in a local pond while attempting to approach and photograph whooper swans at close quarters. Harbottle Crags, acquired in 1970, was the first primarily geological reserve. The Trust owes a great debt of gratitude for the upper Coquetdale reserves – including Holystone Burn and Wood – to Alan Rix, the Forestry Commission's Rothbury District Officer. Later, in 1986, Holystone Burn became the first joint Forestry Commission–Wildlife Trust reserve in the country.

In subsequent years, the Trust greatly expanded its site-based activities, setting up a system of local wildlife and geological sites to be integrated into local planning considerations. These were known as Sites of Nature Conservation Importance

Holystone Burn – an early nature reserve in upper Coquetdale

(SNCIs) – equivalent to LOCAL WILDLIFE SITES found elsewhere in the country. There are now about 250 of these sites in the county. In 1977, the Trust supplied a report to the Ministry of Defence on the wildlife and geological conservation resource of the huge Otterburn Training Area, and this became the basis of the MoD's conservation management for the area.

MAKING WAVES

Early in its history, mainly before the separation from Durham, the Trust became closely involved in some major conservation controversies. It opposed the cull of grey seals on the Farne Islands on the grounds that it was based on inadequate scientific data. Several proposals for reservoirs, including COW GREEN in upper Teesdale and Kielder Water, were also opposed as they would drown unique upland habitats. Although the Trust was unsuccessful on both fronts, the seal culling was later stopped

Bell Crag Flow – a Border Mire

and substantial habitat mitigation accompanied the Kielder Water scheme, in which the Trust is now a partner.

Probably the Trust's main conservation achievement has been in connection with the Border Mires – mainly rain-fed peatlands within the Forestry Commission's Kielder Forest. In 1970, a batch of eight bogs was leased from the Forestry Commission in order to prevent afforestation. Since 1986, the Border Mires Committee, with the Commission as lead partner and the Trust a key player, has looked after the mire sites in Kielder Forest. There are now 55 such sites – 13 of them in Cumbria, and the Trust accepts responsibility for these on behalf of the CUMBRIA TRUST.

The Trust's other reserves include ancient woodland, grassland contaminated by zinc, lead and other heavy metals, other subsidence ponds and geological sites. They also include England's most extensive Trust reserve, Whitelee Moor in upper Redesdale, 1508 hectares of relatively undamaged blanket bog and upland heath. It was purchased in 1999 with financial assistance from the National Heritage Memorial Fund, and brought national publicity when the Trust advertised for 'a lonely goatherd'. In 2011, the Trust has 61 reserves covering 3,500 hectares, of which 22 are in the Northumberland National Park.

ADVICE AND MANPOWER

Reserve acquisition needed professional advice. At first Richard Harris of the University of Newcastle helped informally, and later Honorary Land Agents were Bob Edmonds, who became Trust Chairman for 22 years, Brian Furniss, Peter Edmonds and Colin Matheson.

In 1966, together with the Northumberland Association of Youth Clubs, the Trust formed a Conservation Corps to carry out work on reserves and elsewhere.

WETLAND RESERVES

Druridge Bay, on the southern part of the Northumberland coast, has been a focus of interest since the early 1970s. In 1973, Trust member, Ian Kerr, floated the idea of a 'Northumberland Minsmere' (based on the flagship RSPB reserve in Suffolk), following coal extraction at some east Northumberland opencast sites. Coincidentally, in 1971, the National Coal Board Opencast Executive had begun discussions with the County Council and Trust on just that subject. Soon Tynan, realising the opportunities for habitat creation in the Druridge Bay area, widened the scope of discussions with the local authorities.

The first opportunity came with closure of the Radcliffe opencast site and the creation of the lagoon at Low Hauxley. This was purchased by the Trust in 1983, following a fundraising appeal sponsored by the *Newcastle Journal*.

Other wetland reserves at Druridge Bay now complement Hauxley including the huge East

Outside the Trust's first office, 'The Hancock Hut' with Sir David Attenborough (centre)

Chevington site. Collectively they are very early UK examples of both creative and landscape-scale conservation. The Trust's current Coal and Coast project, working with the County Council, The National Trust and local communities, should take Tynan's original concept to fruition.

JOB CREATION PROJECTS

In the mid-1970s, high unemployment led to Government funding for job creation (EMPLOYMENT SCHEMES). The Trust benefited from a succession of projects, not least COASIPEC – an acronym made up as a joke, but which stuck. It stood for Collecting Of and Assembling Scientific Information to be used in the Planning of Environmental Conservation. All told, the teams looked at more than 1,300 sites, with site data supplemented by members and by information gained from habitat surveys. The Trust looked at Whin Sill grassland (a survey recently repeated and showing severe losses), Allendale meadows, Tynedale hedges, limestone grassland, neutral grassland in south-east Northumberland, sand dunes, invertebrates of subsidence ponds and North Pennine heavy-metal mine sites. It also organised, or carried out, surveys of otters, water voles, badgers, great crested newts and large heath butterflies.

ENGAGING COMMUNITIES

The Trust has been involved in a wide variety of people-based activities. When resources have permitted, school-level education and community-based activity has developed, with an emphasis on work in urban Tyneside and industrial south-east Northumberland. The Trust ran a flourishing Watch Club from 1978 until 2008. Other projects have included Living Waterways (from 2006 onwards) and Wild Places (2008–10), the latter employing digital technology and remote cameras in urban areas to watch and record mammals.

Nature tourism has also increasingly become one of the Trust's concerns. For a number of years the Trust organised self-guided nature trails across the county and manned its own mobile information unit at reserves. It also ran a shop selling Trust goods in Morpeth from 1985 until 1996 alongside running the education centre at Hauxley. The Trust has always mounted stands at shows and delivered countless talks.

GETTING THE MESSAGE ACROSS

From the beginning, the Trust produced a newsletter, and from 1973 this became the glossy *Roebuck*, thanks largely to the energy of trustee, John Dodds. In fact, the roebuck emblem, designed by the celebrated wildlife artist, James Alder, had been used by the joint Trust, and Alder illustrated most of the early publications. The roebuck emblem was replaced in 1998 when the Trust adopted the collective Wildlife Trusts' badger logo.

The Trust is closely linked to the media and has benefited over the years by association with all the key television presenters on natural history, including SIR DAVID ATTENBOROUGH, Bill Oddie and more recently Chris Packham. DAVID BELLAMY served on the Council of the old Northumberland and Durham Naturalists' Trust and has since helped in many ways. Tony Tynan and Ian Armstrong were stalwarts of *Looks Natural* on local TV, and the well-known local television presenter, Tom Kilgour, was an active supporter.

PAID OFFICE ASSISTANCE

Paid office assistance began in 1974 signalling the transition from being an entirely volunteer run organisation. However, the first paid employee, Assistant Secretary, Ron Norman, was seconded from the National Westminster Bank and did not cost the Trust a penny! By now the organisation had outgrown its office in the Hancock Museum and, in 1976, it acquired, at a knock-down price, a second-hand Portakabin which it erected behind the museum.

Shortly afterwards, Olive Marshall retired as Hancock Museum Secretary and became the first member of staff the Trust actually paid. Later, Jane Speak, who became Head of Business Management, thoroughly professionalised the Trust's governance and management systems with much assistance from Colin Dickinson, the Trust's very long-serving Honorary Solicitor.

The Portakabin remained the Trust's headquarters until the move to the present site in Gosforth. By 1979, the Trust could afford its first Conservation Officer, Ian Bainbridge. Although Bainbridge was appointed mainly to get to grips with reserve management plans, much of his time had to be spent on local sites, in light of the recently-completed COASIPEC work.

Rockpooling on the Northumberland coast

Puffins on the Farne Islands

PLAYING CATCH-UP

The Trust was now struggling to cope with the growing demands on the organisation. It found resources in the early 1980s to employ a Development Officer, Barry Lamble, to run the BRITISH WILDLIFE APPEAL locally to raise funds for the Trust. Then, in 1988, following external advice from management consultants funded by the Society, the Trust appointed Frances Rowe, its first Marketing and Development officer in 1989 and its profile and resources began to grow.

A Director was still beyond the Trust's means, but the then Conservation Officer, Hugh Watson, agreed to double up as Acting Director to oversee the implementation of the consultants' recommendations. After Watson left, Peter West, a Trustee with managerial experience, offered his services. In 1991, following West's departure, the Trust was at last able to take the leap of appointing David Stewart as its first Director. Stewart proved to be a lateral thinker *par excellence*. He largely engineered the move in 1993 to the Trust's present headquarters at St Nicholas Park, Gosforth and the development of an urban wildlife park there.

In 1995, the Trust became the first voluntary nature conservation body in the country to earn the Investors in People award, something it has retained ever since.

MORE STRATEGIC, LESS HAPHAZARD

On the conservation side, Ian Bainbridge's successors were Liz Teece, Hugh Watson (who, together with Charles Baker-Cresswell instigated the hugely successful North Northumberland Otter Project in 1986), Andrew Bielinski and Lisa Kerslake. From reserve acquisition having been a rather haphazard affair in the early years, the Trust drew up acquisition strategies, and structured reserve management plans. Kerslake was followed as Conservation Manager by Steve Lowe.

In 2003, the Trust produced a *Vision for Northumberland* (wildlife and geology) as an overall guide to its activities. Funding has become much more diverse, but core funding has remained very tight. Until recently the Trust lacked the resources to involve most owners and occupiers of Local Wildlife and Geological Sites. However, the Trust has determined the criteria for designating

431

Bateinghope Burn, Whitelee Moor

Local Wildlife Sites – a necessary step now that they have a formal role in planning policy.

OTTERS, RED SQUIRRELS AND WATER VOLES

While conserving habitats will do much to conserve species, there are some species which need additional individual attention, and since the 1990s species safeguard and recovery have come very much to the fore in the Trust's work.

The North Northumberland Otter Project involved an otter survey, followed by a habitat creation programme on the northern rivers. It has been a resounding success and was replicated by the Tyne Otter Project

The Trust sponsored research at the University of Newcastle by Peter Lurz on red squirrels. This resulted in the North-East Trusts' 1991 Red Alert initiative, and later the multi-million pound collaborative Save-our-Squirrels (SoS) project, covering much of northern England. This involved the protection of red squirrel 'reserves', identifying

invasion corridors, grey squirrel control and raising awareness of the issues.

Water voles also became a focus of activity, with surveys of their much-depleted distribution and plans for conservation measures. Birds are well catered for with habitat management at Druridge Bay and the subsidence ponds and the Trust has also set up a marsh harrier watch point at its East Chevington reserve. The Trust also had a very active badger group, now independent, and for a while, an ancient woodlands group.

The Trust became very involved in BIODIVERSITY ACTION PLANNING and, together with the Natural History Society of Northumbria, compiled and published a *Red Data Book for Northumberland* of rare and threatened species, edited by Lisa Kerslake. This has informed subsequent local Biodiversity Action Plans (BAPs). The Northumberland BAP was launched in 2000, detailed species and habitat action plans were published in 2007, and the Trust hosts the Northumberland BAP officer.

LANDSCAPE-SCALE LINKS

Throughout, the Trust has greatly valued being part of the wider UK Trusts' movement. Since regionalisation, the Trust has also built stronger links with the North of England group of Trusts and, more recently, with the other two north-eastern Trusts, including its former Durham partners.

This regional link has provided the context for the recent emphasis on landscape-scale conservation. The Trust has identified five parts of the county where it can focus its Living Landscape work: Prestwick Carr together with the northern fringe of the Tyneside conurbation; the Hadrian's Wall and Whin Sill corridors; Druridge Bay and south-east Northumberland; the Kielder Forest and Border Mires area and the wider area of the uplands in the north-west of the county (the 'Border Marches'). At the western side of the county more than 10,000 hectares of blanket and raised bog and upland heath is now under conservation management, with much Trust involvement.

MARITIME AMBITIONS

Despite this, there are areas where the Trust can still do more, particularly in marine conservation. It is difficult for the voluntary sector to get a handle on practical marine work. But the Trust is hoping to become more involved, particularly as the Government's new Marine Management Organisation (set up to implement the Marine and Coastal Access Act 2009) is based in Newcastle.

Otter

The Trust is developing a regional marine awareness programme with the University of Newcastle's Dove Marine Laboratory at Cullercoats.

LEADERSHIP

David Stewart's nine-year tenure as Director was followed by Alec Coles who brought new dynamism and influence through his high-level contacts in the heritage and cultural sectors. Later, David Knight brought his academic prowess and considerable organisational skills to bear, extending partnership working and consolidating the Trust's internal systems and procedures. The current Chief Executive, Mike Pratt, has continued to build on these achievements over the past six years. This period has seen substantial growth in the scale of the Trust's operation, in its profile and in the scope of its development.

From all of this activity, with nearly 14,000 members, 50 paid staff and more than 150 active volunteers, it is evident that the Trust has travelled a long way. The Trust is increasingly undertaking larger-scale projects and, like many fellow Wildlife Trusts around the country, it is now recognised as one of the leading conservation charities in the region and an influential advocate for its wildlife.

BY ANGUS LUNN

Dr Angus Lunn, a Vice President of the Trust, was awarded the Royal Society of Wildlife Trusts' Christopher Cadbury Medal in 2009, in recognition of services to the advancement of nature conservation in the UK through his contribution to ecology, The Wildlife Trusts and the National Parks movement. He was particularly involved in the conservation of the Border Mires. He is the author of the volume on Northumberland *in the* New Naturalist Series.

CHAPTER 30

Gogledd Cymru – North Wales

North Wales has attracted numerous naturalists, artists and writers to its dramatic mountain and coastal scenery. Victorian plant hunters came in search of rare ferns and the Snowdon lily. Charles Darwin with his mentor Professor Adam Sedgwick laid down the early geological nomenclature based on the names of Celtic tribes. Today, upland sheep farms with traditional stone cottages, slate roofs, Welsh black cattle and unimproved hay fields, graze sheep on hectares of open 'ffridd' land in a continuing struggle to make a good living. Agriculture and quarrying, once mainstays of the local economy, have now largely been replaced by tourism. New housing and ranks of static caravans line the flat shoreland between Abergele and Prestatyn. Each year thousands of visitors walk the mountain and coastal paths or sail from new marinas at Conwy and Pwllheli. Land has disappeared as towns are bypassed and the coast road from Connah's Quay to Holyhead has become the A55 expressway.

Energy generation has made an important contribution to the local economy as evidenced by two pumped storage schemes and two nuclear power stations – one now decommissioned, the other, on Anglesey, likely to be replaced imminently. The latest requirement for green energy has seen the appearance of wind turbines whose rotating blades punctuate the skyline on Denbigh's moorland and out at sea in Liverpool Bay. Demand for slate and stone has extended or reopened quarries and our throwaway society requires more landfill sites to get rid of its waste.

Opposite: Gwaith Powdwr nature reserve
Right: Naturalists at Cors Goch in 1966

The Snowdonia National Park, set up in 1951, gave some protection to wildlife within its area, but increasing demand for development land worried local naturalists and stimulated the formation of a Wildlife Trust.

EARLY STIRRINGS

In 1953, the Welsh office of the Nature Conservancy (the Conservancy) was established in Bangor. It asked two botanists, RH Roberts, a local headmaster, and William ('Bill') S Lacey, a Lecturer in the Botany Department at the University College of North Wales (UCNW) in Bangor, to carry out vegetation surveys of Sites of Special Scientific Interest in North Wales. The vegetation maps they produced showed the importance of the fens on Anglesey and the Lleyn Peninsula and they recommended that Cors Goch and Cors Geirch be acquired as nature reserves. However, all available money at the time was being used to buy oak woodlands. In 1962, 105 acres of Cors Goch came on the market,

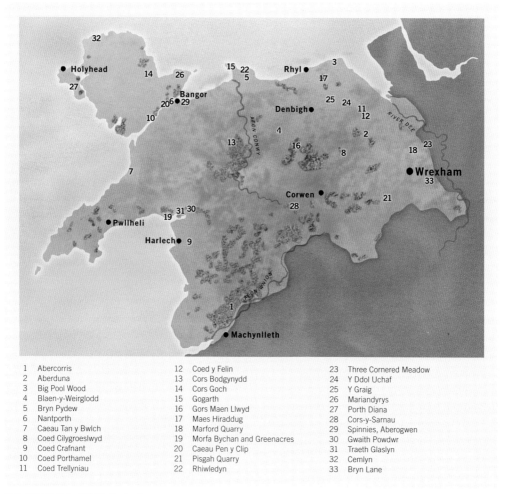

Map of North Wales Wildlife Trust nature reserves

1	Abercorris	12	Coed y Felin	23	Three Cornered Meadow
2	Aberduna	13	Cors Bodgynydd	24	Y Ddol Uchaf
3	Big Pool Wood	14	Cors Goch	25	Y Graig
4	Blaen-y-Weirglodd	15	Gogarth	26	Mariandyrys
5	Bryn Pydew	16	Gors Maen Llwyd	27	Porth Diana
6	Nantporth	17	Maes Hiraddug	28	Cors-y-Sarnau
7	Caeau Tan y Bwlch	18	Marford Quarry	29	Spinnies, Aberogwen
8	Coed Cilygroeslwyd	19	Morfa Bychan and Greenacres	30	Gwaith Powdwr
9	Coed Crafnant	20	Caeau Pen y Clip	31	Traeth Glaslyn
10	Coed Porthamel	21	Pisgah Quarry	32	Cemlyn
11	Coed Trellyniau	22	Rhiwledyn	33	Bryn Lane

and the Society for the Promotion of Nature Reserves (the Society) stepped in to make a holding purchase until a local conservation body could be established to buy and manage nature reserves (NATURE RESERVES OWNED BY THE SOCIETY).

Despite wintry weather and difficult road conditions, 65 people from the six counties of North Wales attended a meeting in the Department of Botany of UCNW on 2nd February 1963, and decided to set up The North Wales Naturalists' Trust. A Council of ten was elected at a public meeting on 26th October with Colonel JC Wynne Finch as Chairman and Bill Lacey as the Honorary Secretary. Joan Morgan edited the newsletter and

in 1974 became Honorary Secretary when Lacey was elected Chairman. Colonel Wynne Finch was the Trust's first President (elected 1967).

By 1965, the Trust had 359 members and three nature reserves – an Anglesey fen comprising 42.5 hectares, a sand dune in Caernarvonshire of more than 11.5 hectares and a limestone wood in Denbighshire of a little more than four hectares.

BRANCHING OUT

At this time, the area covered by the Trust's activities extended from Connah's Quay in the north to Newtown in the south, and from Llangollen in the east to Holyhead in the west. A natural development was to set up branches, to organise local events and to look out for new nature reserves and warden existing ones. Ten branches were established, with varying success, (currently the Trust has six branches). The Dolgellau Branch of the West Wales Trust was transferred to the North Wales Trust in 1972, its members forming the nucleus of the Trust's Meirionnydd Branch.

By 1970, the Trust could no longer continue to operate solely on a voluntary basis. A grant from the Carnegie United Kingdom Trust (CARNEGIE FUNDS) paid for a full-time Administrative Officer, who worked from a rented office in Bangor. Members received three newsletters a year and the journal *Nature in Wales* published jointly with the West Wales Trust. The Trust logo, which headed the newsletter from issue two in 1964 until 1988, was a fine drawing of a feral goat by Charles Tunnicliffe. The goat logo was replaced by a stylised owl in 1989 and in 1995 the Trust adopted the badger logo of The Wildlife Trusts.

CEMLYN CHALLENGE

Vital management work on the Trust's reserves was initially carried out by the North Wales Conservation Corps. In 1977, financial help from Gwynedd County Council enabled the Trust to employ a temporary Conservation Assistant, and in 1978 this grant was extended under the Job Creation Programme (EMPLOYMENT SCHEMES). Douglas Oliver was appointed full-time Conservation Officer, and was thrown in at the deep end when his first task was to organise the financing and construction of a new weir at Cemlyn lagoon on Anglesey. Every year sandwich terns, black-headed gulls, common and Arctic terns nest on islands in the pool. During an unusually high spring tide in July 1977 the weir was breached, destroying most of the nests. It was estimated that only 50 chicks fledged from more than 1,000 pairs of birds. Repairs to the weir had to be completed before the terns arrived for the next nesting season. The contractors finished at the beginning of April 1978, and the terns returned the following week.

Sandwich tern at Cemlyn nature reserve

Cemlyn, which is leased from the National Trust, has one of the largest tern colonies in Wales. In 2010, 1,100 sandwich terns, 350 black-headed gulls, and 70 Arctic terns fledged. Since 1981, summer wardens have been employed to live on-site, to protect and monitor the colony and to liaise with visitors.

By 1982, Trust membership, which had been static at about 2,000 for the previous five years started to decline. The Montgomeryshire branch seceded, and with the Trust's blessing became the Montgomeryshire Trust for Nature Conservation. Five reserves situated in Montgomeryshire were transferred to the new Trust. For the parent Trust with only £9,000 in liquid reserves, and the cost of a Conservation Officer covering over 7,000 miles a year, it was the start of cash flow problems. The Chairman wrote personally to 174 Life Members (who had joined at £10) inviting them to upgrade their payment.

Wildflowers at Caeau Tan y Bwich

FIRST COMPUTERISED REGISTER

An important development in 1983 was the start of the Anglesey Biological Sites Register. A team of seven scientists, funded by the Manpower Services Commission (EMPLOYMENT SCHEMES) visited over 350 sites, of which 100 had sufficient wildlife interest to be mapped, documented and appear in the final schedule. The aim of the exercise was to alert the council to the existence of these sites before irrevocable planning decisions about land use were made. The exercise was later repeated in North East Clwyd. A computer programme written in BASIC for the Trust's Commodore system by a volunteer recorded all site and species data. It was said at the time that this was the first microcomputer biological recording system in use in the country.

In 1988, the Trust appointed Joan Daniels as part-time Conservation Officer in Clwyd based at Northop Horticultural College, to deal with local planning applications and reserve management. The post was funded by British Coal and Daniels attended numerous planning meetings when bypasses around Flint and Mold threatened to cross a saltmarsh and two nature reserves. She was also involved with the public appeal to save Bettisfield, Fenn's and Whixall mosses on the Clwyd-Shropshire border from peat extraction.

SILVER SHAKE UP

After 25 years, the Trust had become a large landowner with 28 reserves, two full-time and three part-time staff. It was then that the Conservancy funded an independent review of the Trust's strengths and weaknesses. The report did not mince its words, saying that the Trust had a "low to no profile" and that it should be able to recruit more than 0.25 per cent of the population. A committee reorganisation and name change to the North Wales Wildlife Trust ensued. The newsletter *Natur*, now with two-colour printing, launched into more topical articles such as 'Menai Strait: Proposed Marine Nature Reserve', 'Wild Goats in Snowdonia: Saints or Sinners' and 'Wildlife Under Threat in Clwyd'. Each edition also contained an article in Welsh.

With reorganisation came more funding from the Conservancy. A Promotions Officer organised four 'cycle for wildlife' events, raising over £12,000 in sponsorship money for general funds. Approaches to industry resulted in McAlpine, owners of Penrhyn Quarries, creating a new island at the Spinnies reserve with their heavy plant excavators. A Systems Officer computerised all reserve and survey data in so-called 'Biorecs', confirming the Trust's position at the forefront of computerisation. A new computerised accounting package was tried out in 1997, but caused much angst over several months without much benefit.

Morgan Parry was appointed Director in 1993 and immediately started to boost the Trust's image with regular appearances on Welsh television and radio. The Trust adopted a fully bilingual policy in 1994. Links with the other Welsh Trusts were strengthened by the launch of the Welsh Wildlife Trusts Partnership, with Dr W Eifion Jones – Chairman of the Trust – chairing the Board of Trustees.

TRADING FOR PROFIT

Two subsidiary companies were established with profits from both being transferred to the parent body. The trading company experimented with 12 retail outlets, and now trades on the Great Orme summit in Llandudno and at Breakwater Park, Holyhead. Shop volunteers led by Pippa Bonner raise annual profit in the order of £20,000 for the Trust's unrestricted funds. Perhaps the most esoteric shop venture was one run with the RSPB in a defunct Great Western Railway signal box.

North Wales Environmental Services was set up by volunteers in 1990 to provide high quality ecological services at competitive prices. By 1995, Project Manager Janine Hawkins, with three years funding from Environment Wales, was working on 20 projects which yielded an income of £48,000. During hurricane-force winds over Christmas 1997, part of the roof blew off the Trust's office in Bangor and Janine's computer and her collated forms for an All-Wales Forest Survey were soaked. The computer dried out, and back up disks and papers kept at home saved the day! As the number of private consultancies mushroomed, the number of successful bids decreased. The company continued on a voluntary basis for a number of years, but has since been revived as Enfys Ecology Limited.

COOPERATION AND SUPPORT

In 1993, the Trust's Clwyd office moved to larger premises at Loggerheads Country Park near Mold, and the Bangor office was bursting at the seams with nine full-time posts. Cooperation with other funding bodies continued. In 1997, with the Irish Wildbird Conservancy, the Trust participated in the EU INTERREG programme for roseate tern conservation on both sides of the Irish Sea. A successful application to the Heritage Lottery in 1998 resulted in a grant of £323,596 for a five-year programme to improve and interpret 19 Trust reserves. Grants from the Esmée Fairbairn Trust for site surveying, the WWF for marine work and the Landfill Tax for projects in Deeside were also obtained.

The Trust's most loyal supporter has always been the Countryside Council for Wales whose staff can be called upon for technical advice and support, and whose annual grant forms the backbone of the Trust's budget. In an attempt to gain more commercial support the Trust launched a Corporate Members

Cors Bodgynydd – an upland bog which is home to breeding nightjar

Traeth Glaslyn nature reserve

Pack initially sponsored by the National Grid Company. After 15 years, the Trust has 27 corporate members reflecting the difficulties of recruiting firms in a rural area.

In 1991, the Trust's President, Bill Lacey was awarded the CHRISTOPHER CADBURY MEDAL by the Society for services to nature conservation. A highlight for the Trust in 1995 was the declaration of Cors Goch on Anglesey as a National Nature Reserve and a RAMSAR site of international importance. It is also a Special Area of Conservation under the European Union's Habitats Directive. Since then, the reserve has increased in size from 53 hectares to 95 hectares as a result of adjacent land purchased in line with the Trust's current acquisition policy.

TRUST RESERVES

At present the Trust has 33 reserves covering an area of 710 hectares. Semi-natural habitats include coastal heathland, coastal lagoon, sand dune, base-rich fen, ancient oak woodland, limestone woodland, heather moorland, upland bog, acid, neutral and calcareous grasslands, old quarry sites, limestone pavement and a former industrial site.

The Trust maintains lists of roadside verges of floral importance and their management involves close liaison with the local authorities.

Coed Crafnant in Meirionnydd is a sessile oak woodland comprising more than 20 hectares in the Rhinog SSSI within the Snowdonia National Park, near Harlech. Its north-facing aspect, with limited sunlight, high rainfall and a dense tree canopy gives the wood a very humid atmosphere. It has a flora rich in bryophytes, ferns and lichens many of which are epiphytic and several are rare in the UK. It is a fine example of the natural oak woodland that once covered much of North Wales.

Gwaith Powdwr, covering nearly 33 hectares on the site of the old Cooke's Explosives Works near Penrhyndeudrath which closed in 1995, is a recent reserve, acquired courtesy of Imperial Chemical Industries. It has breeding nightjar and several species of bat. A European LIFE fund grant was obtained to restore the post-industrial land to heathland. Heather seedlings have been planted amongst the rubble of former buildings. The site opened to the public in 2000 with the publication of the *Pendulum Nature Trail* leaflet, and a Reserves Officer was appointed with European Objective 1 funding.

The Trust's largest reserve is Gors Maen Llwyd, 480 hectares of heather moorland and blanket bog north of Llyn Brenig, Denbighshire. Purchased in 1988 by grants from the Central Electricity Generating Board, the Conservancy and the National Heritage Memorial Fund, the moors were traditionally managed for grouse shooting. Afforestation and excessive sheep grazing have lowered its value as a habitat for grouse, but a good range of upland birds occur on the reserve, including red and black grouse. Glades have been created in the conifers for the wintering black grouse and controlled burning has improved the heather.

PARTNERSHIP WORKING

Today, the Trust has 19 staff. Marine Awareness North Wales has joined the Trust to strengthen its marine conservation work, and the Snowdonia Wildlife Gardening Partnership and the Anglesey Grazing Animal Partnership operate from the Trust's headquarters. The Trust is the lead partner in the UK BAP review for dwarf stonewort, and recently facilitated the creation of Cofnod, the local biological records centre for North Wales.

INVOLVING YOUNG PEOPLE

Activities for juniors started in 1974 in the Vale of Clwyd, quickly followed by events organised

Members of Waunfawr Watch group post-beach clean

in Mold and district and for Dwyfach Young Naturalists. In 1999, hundreds of children took part in Trees of Time and Place and Frog Watch. At its peak, the Trust had nine Watch groups with dedicated leaders. Sadly, child protection guidelines and the bureaucracy of risk assessment have contributed to a decline in the number of leaders, so that the Trust is down to five groups today.

Since 2004, Anglesey's Sustainable Development Fund has supported the Terns, Tides and People project. As part of this, on one occasion, more than 800 schoolchildren spent a day at Cemlyn reserve. The Dormice Forever project increased the Trust's understanding of the status of dormice in North Wales, planted over a kilometre of hedgerow linking key dormouse sites and involved more than 50 volunteers. In 2010, the Trust won £49,500 in the People's Millions Big Lottery Fund public vote, enabling it to extend its wildlife gardening project into north-east Wales for a year, helping to establish new community wildlife gardens.

GOING STRONG

In 2006, at the Trust's tenth annual Lacey Memorial Lecture, the Director, Frances Cattanach, announced that membership had topped 5,000. It has since increased to more than 6,000. Backed by its new Strategic Development plan, the Trust will continue to promote and safeguard the wildlife of North Wales for people to enjoy, understand and value. Particular emphasis is placed on developing Living Landscape projects centred around the Anglesey fens and the Afon Chwiler valley in north-east Wales. After 50 years of action, and with an annual turnover around £750,000, the Trust is here to stay.

BY JANE CHERRETT
Jane Cherrett is a former member of North Wales Wildlife Trust's Council, joint author of Guide to Reserves 1980 *and was Honorary Secretary of the Trust between 1994 and 1999.*

CHAPTER 31

Nottinghamshire

The origins of the Trust date back to 1962 when TED SMITH, founder of the LINCOLNSHIRE TRUST, addressed a gathering of some 50 like-minded individuals, brought together by the Rural Community Council at the Shire Hall in Nottingham. The meeting recognised that, "conservation is the protection of wild plants and animals and man cannot escape from nature or the consequences of the misuse of it. Conservation demands an understanding of the potentials of land and this understanding has often proved wild plants and animals to be of economic use to man. Conservation is concerned with the preservation of the variety of natural life, providing centres of diversity which are a source of interest, recreation and enjoyment". Throughout the years these sentiments have served the Trust well and they still resonate today.

Building on this early enthusiasm, a formation committee was established which included, among others, the Trent Valley Birdwatchers, the Nottingham Natural Science Field Club and the University of Nottingham. The inaugural meeting of the Nottinghamshire Trust for Nature Conservation was held on 11th May 1963 in the grand surroundings of the University of Nottingham. The Memorandum of Association for the new charity was agreed, together with subscription rates – individual membership was set at £1. Major-General Sir Robert Laycock was elected as

Opposite: Ancient oak tree, Sherwood Forest
Above: Major-General Sir Robert Laycock

President and Harold Mather as Chairman, a post he would hold for four years, to see the Trust through its early beginnings.

LANDSCAPE FEATURES

Nottinghamshire lies in the heart of England covering an area of 2,085 square kilometres (805 square miles) with a current population of 779,900. Its topography is largely lowland, the highest land lying in the west of the county. The historic Sherwood Forest nestles in the centre of Nottinghamshire, its characteristic dry heathland and woodland once stretched all the way from Nottingham and Newark to Mansfield and Worksop. The low ground of the Humberhead levels lies to the north, supporting a range of wetland habitats and the county's only real fen. The mighty Trent Valley dominates to the south and east, draining eventually into the Humber Estuary and providing a sweeping floodplain of wetland, grassland and woodland habitats. To the west lie Nottinghamshire's best calcareous grasslands before making way for the Coal Measures, which are shared with Derbyshire, and underpin the industrial heritage of this area.

Coal mining, aggregate extraction, forestry and farming have all shaped the changing fortunes of the landscape and wildlife of the county.

Once dominated by coalfields, the pit closures of the 1970s and 80s led to massive restoration schemes intended to create heathland, grassland and woodland on sprawling pit tips and mine workings that were once the defining landscape features. The rivers Trent and Idle comprise gravel terrace valleys formed in the last Ice Age, and large scale gravel extraction workings span their length, continuing to this day. The restoration of these

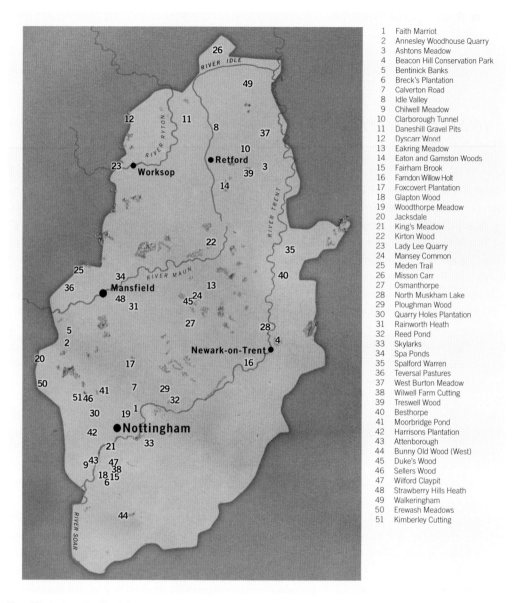

1 Faith Marriot
2 Annesley Woodhouse Quarry
3 Ashtons Meadow
4 Beacon Hill Conservation Park
5 Bentinck Banks
6 Breck's Plantation
7 Calverton Road
8 Idle Valley
9 Chilwell Meadow
10 Clarborough Tunnel
11 Daneshill Gravel Pits
12 Dyscarr Wood
13 Eakring Meadow
14 Eaton and Gamston Woods
15 Fairham Brook
16 Farndon Willow Holt
17 Foxcovert Plantation
18 Glapton Wood
19 Woodthorpe Meadow
20 Jacksdale
21 King's Meadow
22 Kirton Wood
23 Lady Lee Quarry
24 Mansey Common
25 Meden Trail
26 Misson Carr
27 Osmanthorpe
28 North Muskham Lake
29 Ploughman Wood
30 Quarry Holes Plantation
31 Rainworth Heath
32 Reed Pond
33 Skylarks
34 Spa Ponds
35 Spalford Warren
36 Teversal Pastures
37 West Burton Meadow
38 Wilwell Farm Cutting
39 Treswell Wood
40 Besthorpe
41 Moorbridge Pond
42 Harrisons Plantation
43 Attenborough
44 Bunny Old Wood (West)
45 Duke's Wood
46 Sellers Wood
47 Wilford Claypit
48 Strawberry Hills Heath
49 Walkeringham
50 Erewash Meadows
51 Kimberley Cutting

Map of Nottinghamshire Wildlife Trust publicly-accessible nature reserves

quarries has provided a new landscape of wetlands stretching out along the floodplain.

The county has a long tradition of productive forestry, with Sherwood Forest identified by the Forestry Commission in the 1930s as the largest coniferous afforestation project in the UK. The commercial forests sit alongside the county's only Special Area for Conservation (SAC) at Birklands and Bilhaugh, which also forms part of the

National Nature Reserve at Sherwood Forest.

Nottinghamshire is still a largely arable county, with potatoes and carrots, wheat, maize and rape the prime crops. Forestry and farming have undoubtedly contributed to the loss of natural habitat. Since the Second World War, 50 per cent of the county's ancient and broadleaved woodland, 95 per cent of wildflower meadows and large swathes of hedgerows have been lost, together with 90 per cent of

Nottinghamshire's heathland since 1922. Supported by conservation agencies, industry and the farming community, restoration work is bringing back habitats and species, including the elusive otter and nightjar.

KEY CHARACTERS

The 1960s were a time of growth for the Trust. In 1966, a public meeting was held in Retford to publicise the work of the Trust, leading to the formation of the North Notts Local Group, under the stewardship of Eirlys Gilbert, the first of eight local groups. Gilbert 'discovered' the Ashton's Meadow SSSI when one of her pupils told her about a field 'full of flowers' later estimated to include more than 100,000 cowslips.

1967 saw the election of founding Trustee John Walker as Chairman, a role he would hold for 14 years until his retirement in 1981. Walker was crucial to the development of the Trust in its early years. In 1968, the President Sir Robert Laycock died and Rear Admiral Robert St Vincent Sherbrooke was elected. He was followed in 1974 by the Lord Lieutenant Commander NBP Franklin, in 1984 by Sir Peter Kent and in 2002 by the current President, Sir Andrew Buchanan KCVO, Lord Lieutenant of Nottinghamshire.

The 1960s also saw the arrival of a guiding light of the Trust, John McMeeking, who joined its Council in 1968. McMeeking's drive and quiet diplomacy would see him helping to steer the Trust for some 40 years on Council, having a hand in almost every reserve acquisition, building alliances behind the scenes and serving as Chair for five years, following stints from David Bodger and Graham Page. This level of service became a benchmark for a small group of stalwart Council members through the late seventies and eighties to the present day, including Ainslie Carruthers, Tom Huggon, Graham Leigh-Browne and Martin Suthers. Huggon, Leigh-Browne and Suthers would all go on to chair the Trust before handing over to Valerie Holt, the Chair since 2009.

The Trust was managed by an elected Council and committees of volunteers for its first 12 years.

Nottinghamshire has a nationally-important population of nightjars

In 1972, a 'Special Task Force' was set up by Miss E Palmer and Tom Huggon, which, in John Walker's words, was "not to be confused with the police". This brigade of volunteers was responsible for practical conservation – clearing vegetation, managing woodland and pond creation. Likewise, the Trust's membership magazine was produced and distributed by an army of volunteers ably marshalled by founding trustee, Margaret Price. A highly efficient former civil servant, Price would orchestrate packing and distribution of the Trust's publications from her own home, scan planning lists for threats to local wildlife and coordinate the British Trust for Ornithology's (BTO) teams monitoring breeding birds in Treswell Wood.

However, with a growing estate of nature reserves and increasing influence, total reliance on volunteers was becoming harder. In 1975, the decision was taken for the Trust to employ its first paid member of staff. Former Council member, Norman Lewis, joined as Conservation Officer, beginning his 20 years as an employee of the Trust. At the time, an appeal went out to members to form teams of surveyors so that a "representative selection of habitats could be preserved for posterity". Shortly after his appointment, Lewis masterminded the first full botanical survey of the county, including woodland, marsh, wet pasture, ponds, industrial sites and arable land. This groundbreaking work subsequently led to the selection of Sites of

Importance for Nature Conservation (LOCAL WILDLIFE SITES) in the county and identified additional Sites of Special Scientific Interest, many of which became Trust reserves.

FIRST RESERVES

The resolve that had galvanized the formation of the Trust in 1963 was put to the test in 1965. An application had been made to fill the lakes at Attenborough with pulverized fly ash from the new power station at Radcliffe-on-Soar, then under construction. The Attenborough Gravel Pits, as they were then known, were a valued open space on the edge of Nottingham's expanding conurbation and of growing importance to birdwatchers and dog walkers alike. Local feelings ran high and the application was eventually withdrawn after the Trust and others raised objections. Negotiations followed and the site, which now covers 226 hectares, was taken on under lease becoming the Trust's first nature reserve in 1966. Fittingly, it was opened by SIR DAVID ATTENBOROUGH, whose grandparents lived near the Attenborough village that skirts the reserve. This would begin a long association between Sir David and the nature reserve that shares his name.

It would be a further seven years before the Trust purchased its first reserve, Treswell Wood. Once part of the wildwood of Great Britain and mentioned in the Domesday Book, Treswell was threatened with clear-felling and re-planting with conifers. John Walker led the campaign to save this wonderful example of oak, ash and hazel coppice woodland, and an appeal to members, the public, local councils and WWF raised the funds for the purchase in 1973.

The estate grew steadily through the 1980s with Wilwell Farm Cutting taken on in 1981, after a marathon public inquiry prevented its use for landfill, followed in 1983 by Eaton and Gamston Woods and part of Teversal Pastures. In 1985, the Trust added Kirton Wood, Ashton's Meadow, Eakring Meadows and Rainworth Heath, helped by appeals for funds as well as assistance from Nottinghamshire County Council, WWF and the Nature Conservancy Council. 1986 saw the addition

of Farndon Willow Holt with its unusual collection of willow species, and Spalford Warren, a blown sands heathland once used as a munitions dump but ripe for restoration as it had been planted with conifers by the Forestry Commission.

By 1987, the estate had expanded to 33 reserves – testimony to the generosity and tireless work of members as they arranged a succession of increasingly ambitious film shows, plant sales, theatre evenings, sponsored birdwatches, country fairs, and sales of goods at every possible village event. This was localism in action and, without doubt, saved numerous valuable wildlife habitats from destruction.

Duke's Wood was opened in 1987 and, in 1991, a statue was erected to commemorate the US oil drillers who arrived in 1943 to accelerate the development of the Duke's Wood oilfield. It had been the first UK onshore oilfield, greatly supporting the war effort – an unlikely feature in the centre of rural Nottinghamshire.

By 1999, the size of the estate had nearly doubled to 60 sites covering 2,000 acres. With the decline of livestock farming in the county, a pressing need for conservation grazing led to the development of the Trust's own flock of Hebridean sheep, and with it, a new post of shepherd on the payroll. The flock has since grown to become the largest flock of pedigree Hebrideans worldwide, and has been supplemented by cattle and pony grazing.

Duke's Wood – with its rich flora and a 'nodding donkey' oil pump

THE CAMPAIGNING YEARS

The 1980s saw a broadening of support for the Trust's work and with it some changes. The birth of the modern urban conservation movement spawned the Nottingham Urban Wildlife Scheme (NUWS) in 1986, with Huggon and Palmer key players, this time joined by Peter Shepherd and Jack Reiley. Formed from the Trust's City Group and supported by Nottingham City Council, NUWS was initially met with some opposition by the more rural mainstream. But Palmer was determined, convinced that conservation should be accessible and passionate about its benefits to everyone. When she threatened to form a splinter organisation the Trust quickly embraced NUWS, and with it an injection of youth, ideas and staff. A vegetation survey and habitat assessment of all open spaces within the city boundary was followed by a small interpretive team to promote interest in urban wildlife, and a new programme of City Council sites being managed by the Trust under lease. In addition, the use of the Government's Manpower Services Commission scheme (EMPLOYMENT SCHEMES) saw around 60 people employed through the mid-1980s in a variety of roles from habitat surveyors to illustrators and even wildlife artists.

To cope with the changes, John Ellis joined as Administrative Officer in 1986 and the Trust moved to new premises at Sneinton Dale in Nottingham. Ellis brought his skills as a first-class naturalist as well as his unswerving commitment to the Trust. He is still a valuable part of the team today, on the verge of 25 years with the Trust.

A test case for opencast coal mining in the Erewash Valley in 1988 resulted in two public inquiries and showed how far the Trust had developed. Norman Lewis ably represented the Trust and Graham Machin, a member and a barrister acting for Derbyshire and Nottinghamshire County Councils, exposed flaws in British Coal's submissions. Ultimately the site at Smotherfly was permitted, but Shilo North was refused. There then followed extensive negotiations with British Coal over restoration proposals, which for the first time in

John McMeeking is presented with a £5,000 cheque from the National Grid by Julian Pettifer (right)

the country would see a major river re-routed and then put back along its original line.

The benchmark for the Trust in standing up for wildlife had been set, and major planning inquiries followed with notable successes – from the translocation of orchids at Wilford Power station in 1992, to the long-running challenge to see off the threat of landfill at Bentinck Void, and the defeat of the proposed Rufford incinerator in 2011.

To commemorate the Trust's Silver Jubilee in 1988, a new book, *The Nature of Nottinghamshire*, was published, celebrating the wildlife highlights of the county. In the same year, the organisation changed its name to Nottinghamshire Wildlife Trust and shortly after set up its own wildlife survey consultancy, East Midlands Environmental Consultants (EMEC), signalling a new professional era for the Trust.

A PROFESSIONAL ORGANISATION

By the mid-1990s, Tom Huggon had moved into the Chair and the Trust had reached a crossroads. Huggon believed that in order to go forward into the 21st century the Trust must become an efficient and professional body, one that could reach out to everyone in the county to value and understand the importance of wildlife. Peter Stone was appointed as the Trust's first Chief Executive in 1994, immediately completing a full review of the Trust's work and a new Business Plan. Stone's appointment precipitated some major changes, including a new policy of open access to the Trust's nature reserves, and the Trust beginning to secure substantial funding from bodies such as the HERITAGE LOTTERY FUND (HLF), grant-making trusts and statutory bodies.

The nineties saw a growth in the Trust's education work and a renewed focus on engaging with people. The education centre at Cottam Power Station was opened in 1997, together with the appointment of the Trust's first Education Officer, taking the Trust's message to schools and community groups alike. Buoyed by the early success of WILDLIFE WATCH groups at Portland Park, Nottingham City and Farndon, new groups began to spring up across the county, quickly gaining a reputation for excellence.

With a growing professional staff and team of volunteers, the Trust was outgrowing its offices at Sneinton Dale. Huggon and Stone had aspirations for a modern base in the centre of Nottingham and the solution came in the unlikely form of a crumbling Grade II listed building that was formerly a school for poor children. The building was purchased for the princely sum of £1 from Nottingham City Council and, with a grant of nearly £1 million secured from HLF in 1997, was renovated and transformed into the Old Ragged School building that still provides the Trust's headquarters in Sneinton.

In 1998, Ainslie Carruthers led the production of the *Towards 2000* document, which was closely followed by a governance and management review of the Trust's Council, committees, reserve management and local groups. Both helped to streamline the administration of the Trust and provided the impetus for a new mission statement and objectives that would act as a blueprint for the future.

THE MODERN ERA

At the turn of the century, momentum was growing for more focused effort on Sherwood Forest. Earlier studies by the Trust and partners had highlighted the need for habitat restoration, culminating in the Trust, Forestry Commission, the then English Nature and the County Council, together with landowning bodies and district councils, setting up the Sherwood Forest Trust (SFT) back in 1995. But it was not until 2002, when the Trust's efforts led to a successful £5.5 million Sherwood Initiative bid to HLF, that a step change in work to restore Sherwood Forest would be seen. Funding enabled the Trust to expand its conservation grazing scheme, the Forestry Commission to develop its community ranger service and the County Council to provide land management, events and education work through SFT.

Stone left as Chief Executive to join the Royal Society of Wildlife Trusts (the Society) and was replaced by STEPHANIE HILBORNE. This period saw a number of senior staff leave to take up appointments elsewhere within The Wildlife Trusts' movement. Hilborne served as Chief Executive from 2000 to 2004, before joining the Society as its Chief Executive. Her successor, Paul Learoyd, left in 2008 to head up the LINCOLNSHIRE TRUST. His replacement, John Everitt, the current Chief Executive, joined the Trust from the Society in 2008.

In 2003, the Trust celebrated its 40th birthday with speakers including DAVID BELLAMY, the publication of *A Partnership for Wildlife* setting out the Trust's vision for the next 40 years and the purchase of Misson Carr, 200 acres of wild wet woodland, acquired from the Ministry of Defence.

A major landmark for the Trust was the opening of the award-winning nature centre at Attenborough nature reserve in 2005 by Sir David Attenborough. Built using state-of-the-art sustainable technology, the centre has enabled the Trust to further develop its educational activities and reach out to new audiences, as well as run a profitable retail, café and conference facility and a busy programme of events. It now welcomes some 250,000 visitors a year. Throughout the 2000s, the conservation work

Attenborough and its nature centre is one of the most visited wildlife sites in the East Midlands

of the Trust has gone from strength to strength. The Blue Butterfly Scheme to promote wildflower grasslands was launched, closely followed by the popular farmland birds Bed and Breakfast Initiative, supplying nestboxes and seed hoppers to the county's farmers. A successful WATER FOR WILDLIFE programme soon followed and work to help declare Local Nature Reserves was developed. With increasing professionalism, came a thriving Wildlife Guardians scheme for corporate supporters, and the Green Guardians Awards programme to showcase environmental work in the county. A new award to recognise an outstanding long-term volunteering effort for the Trust was also developed, named the Treswell Award in honour of the first reserve purchase. Winners would read as a Who's Who of Trust alumni: John McMeeking, Margaret Price, John Walker, Keith Corbett (a pioneer of Attenborough nature reserve), Ainslie Carruthers, Martin Suthers and Graham Leigh-Browne.

As the Trust looked to the future, its aspirations turned to conservation at a landscape scale. For the fragmented landscape of Nottinghamshire, this vision meant an opportunity for large-scale habitat restoration and the Trust wasted no time in setting about this task. The conclusion of ten years of negotiations with Tarmac resulted in the Trust taking on the 450-hectare Idle Valley nature reserve funded by an HLF grant of nearly £1million. Situated within the wider Idle Valley area, this nature reserve provided a demonstration for what could be achieved over the whole landscape. A partnership initiative with North Notts College saw the Idle Valley Rural Learning Centre built on the edge of the nature reserve providing a centre for training, learning and interpretation that complements the reserve. Living Landscape initiatives quickly followed in the Trent Vale, Erewash Valley, Sherwood Forest heathlands and City of Nottingham, a truly ambitious and exciting programme to take the Trust towards its 50th anniversary in 2013.

The Trust's membership has increased from an initial 100 members in 1963, to around the 11,000 figure today. In 2011, with around 70 nature reserves and 68 staff, the Trust has come full circle. It is again fighting to protect Attenborough nature reserve, this time by negotiating the best alignment for a new flood wall, and still thriving on the back of the energy and commitment of its dedicated staff and volunteers as they seek to meet the changing needs of the wildlife of the county.

BY JOHN EVERITT
John Everitt joined the Trust as Chief Executive in 2008 following more than ten years as part of the RSWT conservation team, latterly heading up work on Living Landscapes. He is a zoologist and has been involved in the Trust for some 15 years, previously sitting on both the Conservation and Education Committees.

CHAPTER 32

Maesyfed – Radnorshire

"Radnorsheer, poor Radnorsheer, Never a park and never a deer. Never a squire of five hundred a year, But Richard Fowler of Abbey Cwmhir".

Do not let the above saying mislead you. The second smallest county in Wales at 1,228 square kilometers, Radnorshire has nonetheless played an important role in the country's history and indeed, in its natural history.

Having borders with Herefordshire and Shropshire, it is perhaps unsurprising to learn that Radnorshire was on the front line of disputes between England and Wales throughout the medieval period. The last Welsh Prince of Wales – Llewelyn – was killed by the English near Builth Wells in 1282 and his body was buried at the cistercian monastery at Abbey Cwm-hir.

That was not the last of it and one of Owain Glyndwr's most famous victories in the last armed Welsh struggle against the English was at Pilleth, near Presteigne in 1402. Near the battlefield site are wonderful old sessile oak trees which were almost certainly growing at the time of the battle. Strangely enough, the hillside at Pilleth – Bryn Glas – was one of the first sites in Britain to get the full agricultural improvement treatment by Professor Stapledon and his colleagues from Aberystwyth University. In 1938, they ploughed the steep hillside with tractor and plough and re-seeded it with rye grass and white clover.

Between 1839 and 1841, Alfred Russell Wallace, the great naturalist and contemporary of Charles Darwin, surveyed Radnorshire, staying at New Radnor, Rhayader and Llandrindod Wells.

Opposite: Autumn at Gilfach Farm. Right: Radnor lily

Whilst in Llandrindod he made a collection of beetles and during his time at Llandrindod, Wallace wrote in high dudgeon at the enclosing of common land around the town.

In spite of the 19th century enclosures observed by Wallace, 14 per cent of Radnorshire remains common land, of which more than a fifth is covered by dwarf shrub heath. According to a recent survey, 8,764 hectares of Radnorshire, or a little more than seven per cent, is protected as SSSI. Of this, a significant proportion is upland habitat dominated by heather moorland.

Semi-natural grasslands and marshy grasslands (rhos pasture) have declined dramatically since 1950. A survey of grasslands carried out by the Hereford and Radnorshire Trust between 1982 and 1983 found more than 500 grassland sites of importance for nature conservation. A number of these became SSSIs. By the time of the Countryside Council for Wales' Phase One habitat survey carried out between 1991 and 1993, only 125 such sites were identified. The Trust surveyed a proportion of these sites between 2003 and 2005 and found that 38 per cent had been damaged or destroyed since 1993.

In the 1980s, the whole of Radnorshire became designated as an Environmentally Sensitive Area (ESA), following tireless lobbying from the Trust.

The biodiversity benefits of the ESA (as with its successor, Tir Gofal) have been questioned, but, the recognition that much of Radnorshire retains

451

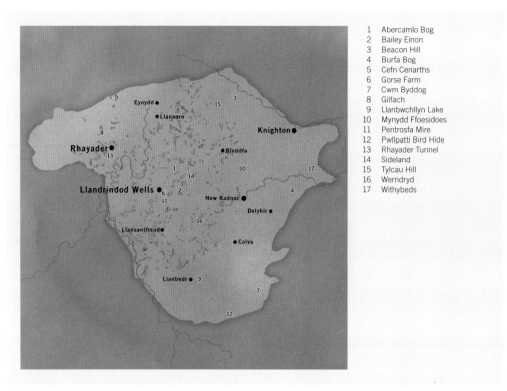

1   Abercamlo Bog
2   Bailey Einon
3   Beacon Hill
4   Burfa Bog
5   Cefn Cenarths
6   Gorse Farm
7   Cwm Byddog
8   Gilfach
9   Llanbwchllyn Lake
10 Mynydd Ffoesidoes
11 Pentrosfa Mire
12 Pwllpatti Bird Hide
13 Rhayader Tunnel
14 Sideland
15 Tylcau Hill
16 Werndryd
17 Withybeds

Map of Radnorshire Wildlife Trust nature reserves

its semi-natural character, although damaged, has been worthwhile.

The joint Herefordshire and Radnorshire Trust, formed in 1962, was probably destined to have only a limited life span. This may have been because the Trust straddled two countries, or because it is a sparsely populated area with a large proportion of its area rich in wildlife but with limited financial resources. If these factors are coupled with the fiercely independent spirit which prevails in the county then, at some stage, a split was inevitable.

It may seem strange that a Trust linking counties in two different countries was formed in the first place. But in 1997, Radnorshire Trust Vice Chairman, Liz Fleming-Williams, wrote, "there had been many links historically between naturalists in Hereford and Radnorshire (particularly ornithologists). Sir Michael Venables-Llewelyn from Llysdinam at Newbridge-on-Wye was key in linking the two counties".

ACTIVE PLAYERS

Even though the Radnorshire Trust existed only as a sub-committee of the Herefordshire and Radnorshire Trust, the 1970s and 1980s were a very busy time for nature conservation in the county. When Dr Fred Slater arrived in 1974 to take up his position as Director of Cardiff University's field centre at Newbridge-on-Wye, Denys Smith was Chairman of the Radnorshire sub-committee with a particular interest in plants. Smith was headmaster of Whitton Primary School near Presteigne and convened two meetings a year with the Group Secretary, Ivor Hughes.

In 1975, Slater set up an autumn lecture programme and, along with Ray Woods and Ian Soane (both local Nature Conservancy Council staff), bore the brunt of delivering the talks. Liz Fleming-Williams recalls that one year Slater delivered 50 energy-sapping talks across Radnorshire! Slater took over from Smith as Group Chairman in 1978.

452

At this time, a community wildlife project to save the toads breeding at Llandrindod Lake was underway, following representations from a local resident, Doug Barnes. He was concerned about the fate of toads crossing the road to the lake. As a consequence, the first 'toad patrol' was set up as part of a study by Dr Paul Gittins and Andrew Parker into the dynamics of the population at the lake. It was estimated that more toads bred at Llandrindod Lake than in the whole of Cambridgeshire! Slater conducted all the publicity with 16 radio interviews and three television crews in one week and the film was seen as far away as New Zealand. Following his death in 1981, Barnes' love for the lake was commemorated by the holding of an annual lecture in his memory. Speakers through the years have included DAVID BELLAMY, photographer Chris Gommersall, Welsh personalities, Iolo Williams and Dee Doody, Radnorshire experts Bob Dennison, Richard Knight, Tony Cross and Tony Soper.

The Trust's first Conservation Officer, David Hargreaves, receives the British Gas Grassroots Action Scheme Award for meadow restoration at Gilfach, 1992

SPLIT ON THE CARDS

Using Government funds through the Manpower Services Commission and Job Creation Programme, (EMPLOYMENT SCHEMES) a full-time, manned office was set up for the Radnor section of the joint Trust. Perhaps the writing was on the wall for a permanent split from this time onwards. Numbers varied from year to year, but there were up to five people working in the offices which ranged from a basement room in Powys County Council to a unit on a Llandrindod industrial estate. There was a Project Manager with an Assistant, plus Field Workers who surveyed woodland, peatland, meadows and pastures. They also worked with schools, creating educational resources and travelling all over the county giving talks and recruiting new members.

Ray Woods describes this era as a golden age. The collaboration between the field centre, the Conservancy and the Trust, produced a stream of high quality, future ecologists. They included Rosie and Roger Key (who became a senior entomologist with Natural England), Louise Paull and the late Pat Wisniewski (who headed up the Wildfowl and Wetlands Trust at Martin Mere), Steve Chambers and Alan Orange – two of the UK's leading lichenologists – and Richard Collingridge. John Messenger, who worked for the Vincent Wildlife Trust, and Pete Jennings, who worked as a senior ranger at Elan Valley Trust, set up bat and bird groups respectively. Dave Drewett carried out many of the grassland surveys and became area ecologist for the Countryside Council for Wales. Radnorshire has been blessed with stalwart volunteers; Rhayader couple Austin and Margaret Morgan spent 20 years organising events and mustering goodwill for the Trust throughout the county.

From 1974 to 1986, when Slater stood down as Chairman, the Trust acquired a series of new nature reserves. Some were owned by the Trust and included: Sideland, a small wood near Penybont; Bailey Einon, another area of ancient semi-natural woodland, stretching alongside the River Ithon upstream of Llandrindod Wells; Burfa Bog, and Cefn Cenarth (South), a block of sessile oak woodland close to an existing Trust reserve near Rhayader. This latter reserve was purchased thanks to generous support from the Cadbury family. The Trust also began to enter into informal arrangements to manage land as nature reserves. In time some of these would lead to formal, long-term lease agreements and, at Mynydd Ffoesidoes within Radnor Forest, the Trust ultimately purchased this dwarf shrub-heath from the Forestry Commission.

RADNORSHIRE GOES IT ALONE

The last newsletter of the joint Trust and the first couple of newsletters of the new Radnorshire Trust document the change from a cross-border enterprise to the birth on 10th April 1987 of the smallest Trust in Wales.

The Trust's Chairman during this period was Dr Gordon Parker. He described the changeover. "When a separate Trust was at the feasibility stage, I discussed the idea with FRANK PERRING. He had recently been involved in the formation of a Trust in Rutland, which at the time was the smallest county in the UK. He was very enthusiastic. I also discussed the matter on a number of occasions

Red kite

with Eric Bartlett who was the Honorary Secretary of the BRECKNOCK TRUST. I remember he rather sat on the fence! I also had many telephone conversations with the then Chairman of the Hereford and Radnor Nature Trust; this was not very easy. When it was decided that we should go ahead with the formation of Radnorshire Wildlife Trust, I remember we had no money. I had an interview with NCC in Bangor, but this produced nothing. However, Dr Elizabeth (Libby) Andrews arranged a meeting for me with the Honorable Vincent Weir; he agreed to provide a grant to get us started".

So, Parker became the first Chairman of the new breakaway Trust with Liz Felgate (now, Liz Fleming-Williams) as Vice Chairman. The Trust was officially launched at the Royal Welsh Agricultural Show on 20th July 1987.

GILFACH JEWEL

No sooner had the new Trust been formed than a whole valley came up for sale north of Rhayader. The Trust's purchase of the 383-acre Gilfach farm started with a bid of £90,000, mainly provided by the National Heritage Memorial Fund. It was completed after a very worrying time, with an agreed figure of £170,000. Few Trusts had purchased or managed farms before, let alone one with a derelict Welsh longhouse dating back to the 14th century. The struggle to clinch the deal earned a place on page two of *The Guardian* on 2nd November 1987. The local paper, the *Mid Wales Journal*, described the Trust's anguish of initially losing out in a sealed-bid auction held in Rhayader in January, 1988 as a mystery bidder "sped off in an estate car" (*Mid Wales Journal*, January 1988) following the auction. The Trust's £170,500 bid came in second place. A few days later the winning bid was withdrawn and, as runner-up in the auction, the Trust was able to complete the purchase. Such was the derelict state of the farmhouse that a huge amount of the Trust's energies initially went into this project. The whole reserve is now an SSSI and Special Protection Area and part of it is also a Special Area for Conservation. It is a flagship

Gilfach longhouse soon after its purchase in 1988. Now fully restored, it provides a visitor centre and base for the Trust's activities

nature reserve, not only for the Trust and the Welsh Wildlife Trusts, but also as one of the premier wildlife sites in the UK – home to red kite, otter, polecat, dipper, small pearl-bordered fritillary, the rare welsh clearwing moth, six species of bat and 413 species of lichen.

Parker again recounts that one of his proudest moments as the Trust's Chairman was when HRH The Prince of Wales visited Gilfach when the restoration of the house was ongoing. Clearly the place made a big impression on him. At one point His Royal Highness turned to Parker and said that he liked the fact that it was not a wet farm. Parker looked a little puzzled, as like much of Radnorshire, the farm is not exactly dry. His Royal Highness explained that he meant it was nice not to have one's shoes covered in sheep muck.

1990S EXPANSION

Despite Gilfach soaking up much of the time and effort of the Trust's staff and volunteers, new reserves

were acquired between 1987 and 1997. A full-time Warden, Tim Thompson, was appointed at Gilfach using a five-year grant from Environment Wales. Other matters were handled by Conservation and Administration Officers. The first Conservation Officer, Dave Hargreaves, left the Trust in 1997, moving to the YORKSHIRE TRUST. Hargreaves was replaced by Chris Thain in 1997 and, working closely with the Development Officer, Alison Davies and Nick Myhill as Chairman, they managed a number of exciting projects.

Notable in this period was a two-year Heritage Lottery Fund (HLF) Biological Evaluation Project (1997–99) which involved a biological audit of ten of the Trust's reserves, including Gilfach farm. Soils and geology, invertebrates, birds, lichens, bryophytes and flora were all surveyed in detail. This allowed the Trust to embark with great confidence on a reserves enhancement capital works project in line with most other Trusts, also funded by the HLF.

INTO THE 21ST CENTURY

In 2000, Thain left for the DORSET TRUST'S Brownsea Island nature reserve and was replaced by Julian Jones as Conservation Officer. Jones had worked in Radnorshire in 1998 as Powys Wildlife Sites Officer and returned to work in a much wider role. Some quipped that having red hair must be a requirement as both Hargreaves and Thain also had auburn colouring!

Not wanting to reinvent the wheel, the Trust developed a number of ideas from other Trusts. From 2000 onwards it introduced a Private Nature Reserves scheme (an idea borrowed from SOMERSET TRUST) and from 2005 has run a primary schools wildlife quiz (an idea pinched from the GLOUCESTERSHIRE TRUST). In 2011, all 19 Radnorshire primary schools took part. As a small Trust with never more than ten full-time staff, operating in a county of only 25,000 people and managing more than 5,500 acres, it can be a hand-to-mouth existence at times. The departure of key staff and Trustees can cause major worries. This happened in 2002–03, resulting in an Extraordinary General Meeting and an external audit of the Trust's governance and finance procedures. However, in the Trust's hour of need, a dynamic duo of Penny Hurt (Chairman) and Sally Holtermann (Treasurer) stepped forward. Their intervention, along with the work of the remaining staff, volunteers and Hurt's successor, Dr Joan Payne, enabled the Trust to recover quickly. In 2005, the Trust secured Objective 5 European funding to appoint a Consultancy Development Manager for an initial six months. Chris Ledbury was appointed and has steered the Trust's trading arm ever since. Radnorshire Wildlife Services is a member of the Association of Wildlife Trust Consultancies and creates a healthy surplus each year towards the Trust's core costs.

The HLF Reserves Enhancement project was completed in 2004, having been led for the most part by James Blair and completed by Jonathan Stone. Through their leadership the weekly volunteer groups achieved an astonishing amount of work. Stone continued as Reserves Officer and was joined by Rob Podmore in 2006 – with the volunteer group they carry out much of the practical work.

Volunteers building a boardwalk at Withybeds nature reserve, Presteigne

Llanbwchllyn nature reserve – the largest natural lake in Radnorshire

The Trust has embraced the movement's Living Landscape vision, promoting nature conservation beyond nature reserves and across larger areas of land. It has susbsequently embarked on the Cwm Marteg project, linking people with their local landscape and wildlife. The Trust has focused on 'uncharismatic' species with the Esmée Fairbairn Foundation helping to fund a Project Officer, Darylle Hardy, until 2013.

On the 2,000-hectare Beacon Hill Common, near Knighton, the Trust is working with 65 commoners to enhance important upland heathland and create and restore pools which are important for the nationally-scarce pillwort. This may also provide habitat for the rare fairy shrimp which lives in temporary pools across the hills of Radnor. After 25 years, the Trust is still the most recognisable force for nature conservation in Radnorshire. Other bodies have been and gone, or have a peripheral interest. But the Trust's staff and volunteers are out there every day; the embodiment of 'up and at 'em' nature conservation.

BY JULIAN JONES

Julian Jones taught biology in rural Ghana and worked as an Assistant Site Manager for English Nature in North Wiltshire and as Ranger for the Lee Valley Park before first joining the Wildlife Trusts in Powys as Wildlife Sites Officer in 1997. He joined the Radnorshire Trust as Conservation Officer in 2000 and is now Director. He has a fascination with the history of people and places in Radnorshire.

Biffaward-funded heathland restoration on Beacon Hill

457

CHAPTER 33

Scottish

Scotland covers a third of the land mass of the UK, with more than two-thirds of the coastline, 790 islands and only 8.5 per cent of the population. It is home to some of the UK's most spectacular wildlife, from its stunning landscape and coastline to rare and protected species such as the golden eagle, red squirrel and Scottish wildcat. This presents the Scottish Wildlife Trust with the challenge of operating at the national, county and community levels and protecting some of the most biologically diverse countryside and seas in the UK.

At the county level the Trust operates through a network of Members' Centres (there are currently 22 Centres). Originally called Branches, in the early days of the Trust, Members' Centres were the bodies that acquired the reserves and were active in local conservation.

In spite of its scale and geography, the Trust's aim is no different from any other Wildlife Trust; it works to conserve Scotland's biodiversity for the benefit of present and future generations.

FOUNDING FATHERS
The Trust was founded in Edinburgh on 14th April 1964, by a group of wildlife enthusiasts led by the distinguished lawyer, politician and conservationist, Sir Charles Connell. The other founders were George Waterston (an ornithologist from Edinburgh), Ian Pennie (a medical practitioner from Golspie), Robert Erskine-Hill (a chartered accountant from Biggar), Eric Ivory (a trust company manager from

Opposite: Ospreys at Loch of the Lowes reserve, Perthshire

Edinburgh), CE Palmer (a museum curator from Glasgow) and Arthur Duncan (a farmer from Thornhill). All had one aim in mind – to do something in aid of the wildlife of Scotland. Writing in 1968, Sir Charles Connell recalled the reason for setting up the Trust: "Those who knew about the impressive development of the County Naturalists' Trust movement in England felt that this was probably due to the very great pressure of industrial development and urbanisation which had occurred over a large part of the heavily populated central and southern parts of England. Some thought that the (Scottish) Trust would not obtain adequate support or, indeed, might not find work to do which would justify its existence".

The years to come would prove any doubters wrong, and by April 1965 the Trust already had 400 members. The Trust's original Articles of Association had only allowed for 1,000 members and was quickly rewritten to include a more ambitious total.

By 1968, there were nearly 1,700 members, a full-time Secretary Organiser (Bernard Gilchrist, appointed in 1965 and working from 8 Dublin Street, Edinburgh), and branches throughout Scotland. The Honorable Angus Ogilvie was the Trust's first President with some very distinguished Trustees on its Council. These included General Sir AG Philip Christison, Lieutenant Colonel JP Grant of Rothiemurchus, naturalist David Stephen, JC Stormont Darling, mountaineer Tom Weir, Professor VC Wynne-Edwards, Sir Maurice Yonge, Professor JM Black and Jean Balfour.

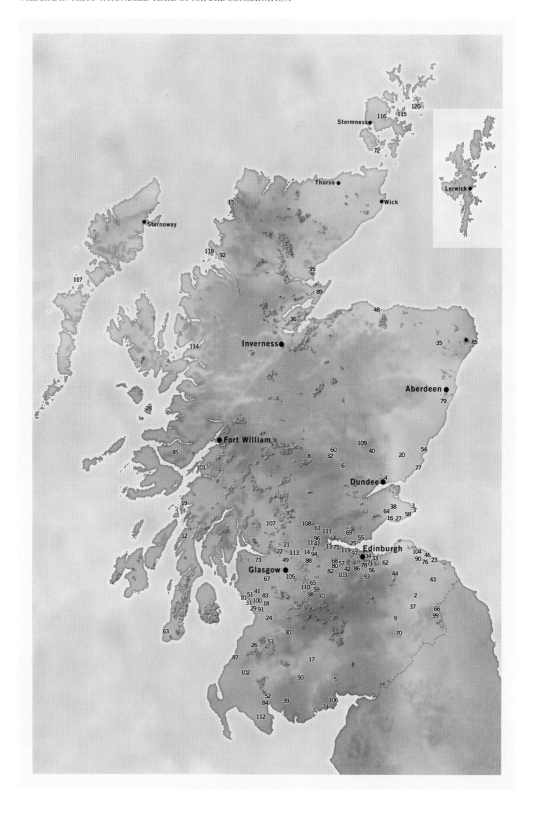

120
115
116
Stormness●
72
Thurso●
Wick●
15
Lerwick●
Stornoway●
118
92
117
95
89
48
36
85
Inverness●
35
114
Aberdeen●
79
28
109
Fort William●
60   40
8   32   20   54
45   6   77
101
Dundee● 4
19
38   3
64   1
107   16 27   58
12   108   61   111   69   55
96   25
21   11 47   13 75 119 97   Edinburgh   104 46 23
22   14 94   7   86 34 33   90 76
73   49   88   68 57   78 71 62
67   105   80   42 86   56   44   43
65   103   93
110   59   2
81 51 41 83   98   10   37   66
31   100 18   24   9   70   99
29 91
63   30
26   53
87   17
102   50   5
52   84   39   106
112   74

LOCAL BRANCHES

The first branch to be formed was the Tweed Valley Branch, followed by branches across Scotland including in Ayrshire and Wigtonshire, Lothians and East Stirlingshire, Clyde Area, Perthshire, Fife, Kinross and Clackmannan, and Dumfries and Stewartry. Formative branches were also developing in Dundee, Angus, Kincardineshire and Aberdeenshire. In addition, there were area representatives for the Trust in Easter and Wester Ross.

Steps were already being taken to coordinate this growing network. In 1967, a skills survey was sent out to all members so that the Trust could make use of the wide range of skills and experience available across its membership.

There was growing concern over environmental issues such as the impact of oil spills (the TORREY CANYON disaster happened in March 1967). At this time, environmental legislation was in the hands of a Westminster Government. Lobbying over Scottish environmental issues was much more difficult, in comparison to today where a devolved Scottish Government can pass its own laws on environmental matters.

But the first love of branch activists in the 1960s was acquiring reserves to conserve local wildlife. The very first reserve the Trust bought was Enterkine Wood in Ayrshire in 1966 – where the Trust laid out a nature trail and opened it to the public for NATIONAL NATURE WEEK the same year. Other reserves quickly followed – Hare and Dunhog Mosses, Doire Don, Ballagan Glen, Bankhead Moss, Pepper Wood and East Lammermuir Deans, and Loch of the Lowes – home to breeding ospreys – were bought in the spring of 1969.

1	Fife Ness Muir	41	Oldhall Ponds	81	Corsehillmuir Wood
2	Gordon Moss	42	Addiewell Bing	82	Longridge Moss
3	Kilminning Coast	43	Duns Castle	83	Sourlie Wood
4	The Miley	44	Linn Dean	84	Carsegowan Moss
5	Fountainbleau Ladypark	45	Rahoy Hills	85	Longhaven Cliffs
6	Loch of the Lowes	46	Thornton Glen	86	Linhouse Glen
7	Cumbernauld Glen	47	Carron Dam	87	Grey Hill Grassland
8	Keltneyburn	48	Spey Bay	88	Luggiebank Wood
9	Hare and Dunhog Mosses	49	Possil Marsh	89	Talich
10	Falls of Clyde	50	Knowetop Lochs	90	Woodhall Dean
11	Carron Glen	51	Perceton Wood	91	Lawthorn Wood
12	Knapdale Habitats Partnership Area	52	Blackcraig Wood	92	Ben Mor Coigach
13	Jupiter Urban Wildlife Centre	53	Dalmellington Moss	93	Milkhall Pond
14	Northside Wood	54	Montrose Basin	94	Forest Wood
15	Handa Island	55	Cullaloe	95	Loch Fleet
16	Dumbarnie Links	56	Roslin Glen	96	Wallacebank Wood
17	Stenhouse Wood	57	Tailend Moss	97	Pepper Wood
18	Shewalton Wood	58	West Quarry Braes	98	Upper Nethan Gorge
19	Ballachuan Hazel Wood	59	Lower Nethan Gorge	99	Yetholm Loch
20	Balgavies Loch	60	Tummel Shingle Islands	100	Garnock Floods
21	Ballagan Glen	61	Cambus Pools	101	Shian Wood
22	Loch Ardinning	62	Hadfast Valley	102	Feoch Meadows
23	Pease Dean	63	Largiebaan	103	Hermand Birchwood
24	Ayr Gorge Woodlands	64	Fleecefaulds Meadow	104	Brock Wood
25	Carlingnose Point	65	Garrion Gill	105	Cathkin Marsh
26	Auchalton Meadow	66	Hoselaw Loch and Din Moss	106	Drummains Reedbed
27	Barnyards Marsh	67	Loch Libo	107	Aberfoyle Bat Cave
28	Isle of Eigg	68	Petershill	108	Black Devon
29	Gailes Marsh	69	Lielowan Meadow	109	Brerachan Meadow
30	Knockshinnoch Lagoons	70	Whitlaw Wood	110	Cander Moss
31	Shewalton Sandpits	71	Erraid Wood	111	Alloa Inches
32	Balnaguard Glen	72	Hill of White Hamars	112	Dowalton Marshes
33	Bawsinch and Duddingston Loch	73	Glen Moss	113	Dullatur Marsh
34	Johnston Terrace Wildlife Garden	74	Southwick Coast	114	Eilean na Creige Duibhe
35	Gight Wood	75	Bo'mains Meadow	115	Holm of Burghlee
36	Belmaduthy Dam	76	East Lammermuir Deans	116	Harray Road End
37	Bemersyde Moss	77	Seaton Cliffs	117	The Islands of Shillay
38	Bankhead Moss	78	Red Moss of Balerno	118	Isle Ristol
39	Carstramon Wood	79	Red Moss of Netherley	119	Long Craig Island
40	Loch of Lintrathen	80	Bogburn Flood Lagoons	120	Linga Holm

Key to map of Scottish Wildlife Trust nature reserves

Ben Mor Coigach – the largest Trust-owned reserve in the UK and part of a new Living Landscape project

Committees and management plans were set up for the purpose of managing some of these new reserves.

In its earliest days, the Trust was financially assisted by a range of organisations, including the National Trust for Scotland and the World Wildlife Fund (WWF) who contributed to the running costs. Income for 1967–68 was over £5,000 and the expenditure came to more than £4,000 – leaving nearly £900 in financial reserve. Today, the Trust's annual income is approximately £6 million.

BEYOND WILDLIFE RESERVES

The Trust was growing fast but it was not long before it started to look further afield. Writing in the Trust journal in December 1974 and looking back over the early days, Doreen Taylor, the Trust's Publicity Officer, said: "In those early days, Sir Charles now admits the Trust believed that the greatest priority was to set up reserves to protect areas of special wildlife value, and the momentum was strong. At this stage the emphasis was mainly on reserves in the Lowlands, near the big centres of

population and at the time this was the correct emphasis because these areas were and perhaps still are the most threatened. But it was not long before the Trust realised that it must look much wider than the boundaries of the reserves it had created, to the conservation and the best use of all the countryside between the reserves".

This last remark is most interesting in relation to the Trust's 25-year vision, *Natural Connections*. This was published in 2006 with the aim of approaching nature conservation at the ecosystem scale, in tandem with the Living Landscapes and Living Seas developments taking place within the wider Wildlife Trust movement. This focus on rebuilding and maintaining a network of "healthy resilient ecosystems supporting communities of native species across large areas of Scotland" now drives all the Trust's work and has led to a more integrated and strategic approach to nature conservation in Scotland.

In the 1960s, the Trust became engaged in the delicate process (as it was described at the time) of cooperation with local authorities and delving

462

into planning matters. Members were becoming interested in ROADSIDE VERGES and how they were maintained, strong links were forming with Scotland's landowners, the identification and listing of Wildlife Sites was underway and environmental education was an important part of the Trust's activities.

MAKING ENDS MEET

As the Trust grew, fundraising became an increasingly important concern. New ways of raising extra funds were developed, such as selling the Trust's own Christmas cards, thanks largely to the chartered accountant Kenny Sutherland who took on the post of Honorary Treasurer in 1969; a post he held until 2001.

Ospreys had become one of the great wildlife sights in Scotland and in the spring of 1969 the Trust purchased its reserve at Loch of the Lowes near Dunkeld. That year the Trust welcomed more than 30,000 visitors to see the breeding ospreys, and ospreys have since bred in 33 out of 43 years – a great contribution to this species' success.

Cooperation with the Trust's neighbours south of the border was also growing. The Trust became a member of the Committee of County Naturalists' Trusts, and, by the end of the decade, had been invited to attend meetings of the Executive Committee of the Society for the Promotion of Nature Reserves (the Society). Unsurprisingly, the Scottish Trust's national status differentiated it from the growing network of Trusts in England and Wales. A note appeared in *Scottish Wildlife* in August 1969: "The Scottish Trust is a national, not a county trust and has strong semi-autonomous Branches, to which the Trust's headquarters are to some extent advisory". The branches have since been abolished, and a network of 22 Members' Centres now provide a focal point for local participation and volunteering.

ENJOYING WIDE RECOGNITION

By September 1973, the Trust had increased its membership to more than 5,000 and its

recognition in the wider world as an authority on Scottish environmental matters was growing fast.

The Duke of Edinburgh visited Loch of the Lowes and Duddingston reserves in 1970, and in May 1973, HRH The Prince of Wales attended a fundraising dinner in Glasgow.

The 1970s was a period of rapid growth with new administrative staff joining the organisation to develop its capacity. Sir Charles Connell was still Chairman of Council at the time of the Trust's tenth anniversary in 1974, but changes were ahead. President Angus Ogilvie became the Trust's first Patron, later joined by Lord Home as a joint Patron in 1978. The role of President was given to the Duke of Atholl who was joined by Sir Charles Connell in 1978, when he handed over the role of Chairman to Maxwell Hamilton.

The acquisition of reserves continued. Montrose Basin, an enclosed estuary of the South Esk river and a rich feeding ground for thousands of resident and migrant birds, was purchased in March 1976.

In July 1977, in conjunction with the Society, the Trust became involved in the management of the 15,000 acre deer forest of Ben Mor Coigach in the Highlands – one of the UK's largest reserves.

The first honorary memberships of the Trust were awarded in 1976 to the distinguished ornithologist, Dr George Waterston, and to Duncan Anderson who was involved with Duddingston Loch for many years.

HRH The Duke of Edinburgh, Sir Charles Connell (founding Chairman) and Bernard Gilchrist (Trust Secretary and the first employee) at Loch of the Lowes (Perthshire), 29th June 1970

An early Trust meeting

SEVENTIES SUCCESS

In the 1970s, the Trust had much success in fundraising for general funds – balls, lectures and film shows throughout the country all helped to generate income for the Trust to fund its conservation work.

June 1978 brought a three-year £8,000 annual grant from the Nature Conservancy Council for a scheme to develop people's enjoyment of wildlife through education. Project funding was becoming well established, with funds from such bodies as the Countryside Commission for Scotland, the Helena Howden Fund, the Pilgrim Fund and many more.

On the marketing side the Trust had a full range of merchandise for sale by its members. The junior membership for children between nine and 15 became the Watch Club, initially administered on a UK-wide basis with organisers in Scotland before its devolution to local administration in 2001. The Trust now boasts 27 Watch groups, all run by volunteers (WILDLIFE WATCH).

Towards the end of 1979, the Trust had acquired its 50th reserve – Tailend Moss in the Lothians. As the 1970s gave way to the 1980s, a book, *The Wildlife of Scotland*, was published for the Trust by Macmillan and sponsored by Gulf Oil. The Trust headquarters moved to Johnston Terrace in Edinburgh in June 1981. In the same year,

George Stewart, a former Forestry Commissioner, became Chairman of Council and in 1983 Bernard Gilchrist became Chief Executive (from Secretary), heading up an ever-growing team of staff.

COMINGS AND GOINGS

In the 1980s, the Trust became a regular organiser of conferences, both national and international – with branches sometimes arranging their own one-day conferences. The topics reflected the conservation concerns of the time including one titled – *Inquiry into the Effect of Acid Rain*. The early 1980s also saw efforts underway to bring together the many scattered members throughout the northern part of Scotland, through meetings and events.

1983 also marked the departure of Lorraine Campbell, the Trust's second employee, in 1970. A trained radiographer, Campbell came to the Trust to become Assistant Secretary. One of her main tasks was membership care, including the development of *Scottish Wildlife*, the Trust's journal. Her previous experience as Membership Secretary of the Lothians Branch had stood her in good stead. She vetoed any suggestion of a leaving collection. "Let people plant trees", she said, "that will please me more".

In September 1984, DAVID BELLAMY opened the new visitor centre at the Falls of Clyde in New Lanark, a series of waterfalls in the Clyde Gorge fringed by wildlife-rich woodlands.

1985 was a year of change staff-wise. Bernard Gilchrist, the Chief Executive and the Trust's very first member of staff, retired. In the September journal Frank Spragge wrote: "When the history of the Trust comes to be written, two names will dominate the first two decades, those of the late Sir Charles Connell (who had died earlier in the year) and Bernard Gilchrist".

Frank Spragge went on to praise Gilchrist for the way he looked after branches, for making sure the Trust's voice was heard in the Scottish corridors of power and for his contribution as an experienced member of a number of the Society's committees. Gilchrist died in April 2003, having joined the

Trust in 1965 when it was a year old and had only 400 members.

21ST BIRTHDAY

John Baldwin took over as Chief Executive in 1985. This was also the year of the Trust's 21st anniversary celebration, marked with an official birthday party on 16th April in the Upper Signet Library in Edinburgh. An Anniversary Appeal, which was several years in the planning, was launched on 15th October.

The Duke of Roxburgh was the appeal Chairman, supported by a distinguished list of appeal patrons. Branches held special events and there were a number of national events – such as the SIR DAVID ATTENBOROUGH evening in the Usher Hall, Edinburgh, and a fundraising dinner in the City Chambers, Glasgow, attended by HRH The Prince of Wales. This latter event alone raised £30,000. By 1987, some 75 per cent of the initial target of £592,000 had been raised and money was still coming in.

In 1987, after six years in the role, George Stewart handed over the chairmanship of Council to Lieutenant Commander Frank Spragge RN. And in 1989, David Hughes Hallett became the Trust's latest Chief Executive.

INTO THE 1990S

A new decade and, from 1990, the Trust had a new Patron, HRH The Prince of Wales, nowadays known in Scotland as the Duke of Rothesay. By now the Trust had 84 wildlife reserves, a membership of 8,844 and a turnover of more than £860,000. It employed more than 50 full-time staff. The year also saw publication of the Trust's first ever Development Plan, a new agreement with the Nature Conservancy Council over financial help and the appointments of more regional staff and an Urban Wildlife Officer.

Thanks to the Government's employment training programme, the Trust also had more than 150 trainees on its books, organised into regional groups. It quickly achieved recognition as a centre of excellence for training on conservation skills

Falls of Clyde nature reserve

and these trainee groups became the basis of the Trust's conservation and reserves teams. The 1990s were good years for the Trust, with resources growing and the Trust moving to a new home in Cramond House on the outskirts of Edinburgh in 1991.

MORE RESERVES ON THE BOOKS

More reserves were also being acquired, including those in urban areas such as Jupiter in Grangemouth. This was formally opened in May 1992 by Magnus Magnusson, famous as a presenter of a popular television show, *Mastermind*.

In 1995, with the demise of the Scottish 'New Towns', the Trust became the owner of 300 hectares in Cumbernauld – one of several post-war new towns built by the Government. In 1996, the Trust made a successful bid to take over land in another former new town, Irvine, and, as with the Cumbernauld

Sea cliffs at the Hill of White Hamars reserve, Orkney

acquisition, this came with a substantial endowment for its upkeep.

Far beyond the cities of Scotland's Central Belt the Trust was also acquiring wildlife reserves. In 1991, it took over the management of Handa Island, a seabird haven in north-west Sutherland, in partnership with Scourie Estates.

Looking beyond its own protected reserves, in 1997, the Trust upped its involvement in identifying LOCAL WILDLIFE SITES with the Scottish Wildlife Action Programme funded by the Esmée Fairbairn Foundation and other charitable bodies.

PROTECTING PEAT AND AN ISLAND BUY-OUT

Early on in the decade, Professor Aubrey Manning (Professor of Natural History at Edinburgh University) had taken over as Chairman from Frank Spragge. Manning was to go on to become President of the Society and his infectious enthusiasm, along with his scientific knowledge, was just right for the Trust at that time. He was

the first Chairman to be appointed from outside Council – and, as he himself admits, he was not even a member at the time!

Concern was growing about the use of peat by gardeners and the destruction of peat bogs throughout Scotland (see PEATLAND CAMPAIGN). The Trust was involved in campaigns and projects to make sure the value of peatland habitats was understood, coordinating work on protecting and restoring peatlands across Scotland, together with many other agencies.

In October 1996, the naturalist and writer Sir John Lister Kaye became President and Dr Hugh Ingram took over the chairmanship. Ingram would later be awarded the Christopher Cadbury Medal for his work to further conservation, as would Stuart Brooks, Head of Conservation in 2005 (see CHRISTOPHER CADBURY MEDAL CITATIONS).

1997 saw the culmination of the Trust's campaign to help the local community on the Isle of Eigg secure a buy-out of the island. Following a successful campaign, the islanders became owners of Eigg (after 196 years of private ownership) jointly with Highland Council – their local authority – and the Scottish Wildlife Trust. The Isle of Eigg Heritage Trust was formed to oversee the management of the island. This included representation from the Trust to advise on conservation matters. Eigg, owned and run by the local community, remains a Trust nature reserve and is visited by many people every year to admire its fine wildlife, including golden eagles and red deer.

REVIEW AND RESTRUCTURE

As the millennium drew to a close, questions were being asked as to how fit the Trust was for the future, particularly with devolution on the horizon and the prospect of a Scottish parliament. As a result, Ingram initiated a major review of the Trust's administration. Major changes were soon to follow. 1999 saw the arrival of Steve Sankey as Chief Executive – though not before Sandy Kerr had acted for six months in this role on the sudden departure of David Hughes Hallett. Kerr became the Chairman in 2002 – the only person ever in the Trust's history to hold both the chief staff post and the chairmanship.

In 1999, Hugh Ingram handed over the chair to John Arnott, a former BBC producer and manager, with a long record of involvement in Scottish conservation. Arnott took on a rewrite of the Memorandum and Articles of Association (adopted at the AGM of 2001) which brought about a change in the composition of the Trust's Council. The Members' Centres no longer nominated Trustees, with all Trustees now elected.

At its December meeting in 1999, Council approved a new staff structure which brought many new posts. Three administrative regions across Scotland were set up, each with its own staff Director and its own Regional Committee of members. At Head Office there were Directors of Resources, Conservation, Public Affairs and Marketing and new departments, including Education and Lifelong Learning. A very robust three-year corporate strategy was agreed to detail the work of the Trust for both members and staff.

But the brave new future was short-lived. Despite a concordat with Scottish Natural Heritage providing an annual grant and an increase in legacies and membership (Steve Sankey oversaw an increase from 16,000 to 25,000 members during his time as Chief Executive), there was not enough regular income to support the new structure.

DOWNSIZED FOR STABILITY

At the end of 2001, the Trust had to downsize rapidly. Sadly, John Arnott became ill, and, despite wanting to oversee this period of change, he was persuaded to stand down for the sake of his health. He died in 2002, but not before being awarded an OBE in the Queen's Birthday Honours for his services to conservation.

Vice Chairman, Professor John Dale, stepped into the breach as Acting Chairman and came into headquarters almost daily to sort matters out. He was backed by a small emergency committee of his two Vice Chairmen, Professor Fred Last and Sandy Kerr. A Committee of Inquiry was later set up to find out what had gone wrong.

Golden eagle

By October 2002, the Trust had been financially stabilised. Gone were all the five Directors. In their place were two departmental heads, later to be joined by a third. John Dale resigned to spend more time with his wife who was seriously ill, and Kerr (who had a long career behind him as an environmentalist with Scottish Natural Heritage in its various guises) took over as Chairman. He was joined by a new Chief Executive in October 2004, Simon Milne.

From 2002 onwards, the Trust's finances became healthier again. However, it was important to make sure that the Trust was working within its income, with sufficient emphasis on establishing sustainable and diverse income streams.

BOLDLY REBUILDING BIODIVERSITY

With the environment now a devolved matter for the Scottish Parliament in Edinburgh, the Trust was heavily involved in keeping wildlife at the forefront of the political agenda. The Trust's activity in other aspects of the wider countryside was also on the increase. It began to take a great interest in the marine environment and rightly so, as it owned or managed nearly 100 miles of the Scottish coastline.

In 2005, after much discussion with national committees, Members' Centres, staff and key stakeholders, Council decided on a significant restructure of the Trust's conservation work.

Primula scotica, Hill of White Hamars, Orkney

Improving access for visitors on Handa Island

Over the course of five years the Trust would work towards a 50/50 split of its resources, between its 122 wildlife reserves and work in the wider countryside.

This restructuring work, led by Milne, ensured that the Trust was best placed to operate in devolved Scotland. It focussed the Trust's resources on where it could make significant difference; championed the adoption of the ecosystem-scale approach to conservation in Scotland; and increased membership, partnership working, profile, influence and income.

A major project during this time was the Reserves Enhancement Programme. In 2001, the Trust had won the largest HERITAGE LOTTERY FUND grant ever given to a Wildlife Trust at the time – £3.69 million – which helped to fund a programme of improving wildlife habitats and facilities at many reserves.

In 2005, Kerr handed over the chair to Dennis Dick, a former BBC TV producer, publicist and manager who turned his attention to modernising the governance of the Trust in response to new charity law in Scotland and a new regulating authority.

Happily the Trust is now able to look to the future with confidence. Its vision is clear – a bold move towards rebuilding biodiversity at an ecosystem scale throughout Scotland rather than just within the confines of the Trust's wildlife reserves. The Trust is well on its way to achieving this vision and, as a result, is very much in the vanguard of positive conservation reform in Scotland.

In 2008, Dick retired and was succeeded as Chairman by Allan Bantick. Bantick's first career was with the RAF, and he subsequently immersed himself in conservation. Building on the extensive development work of the preceding years, a new Director of Conservation, Jonathan Hughes, was appointed in 2009 to start the delivery of some ambitious and potentially far-reaching programmes.

A joint initiative between the Trust and the Royal Zoological Society of Scotland resulted in the Scottish Beaver Trial and 2009 saw the release of European beavers in Knapdale, Argyll after an absence of 400 years.

The Trust had lobbied for a reintroduction of beaver for more than ten years, along with a range of other issues including the Scottish Marine Act (passed in 2009 following a long campaign by

the Trust) and the development of a national red squirrel conservation project (in partnership with Scottish Natural Heritage, the Forestry Commission Scotland and Scottish Rural Property and Business Association).

The rest of the story is not history but the future. With a membership of over 30,000, the development in the north-west Highlands of a large-scale Living Landscape project, increasing influence and an amazing network of volunteers, reserves and supporters, the Scottish Wildlife Trust's future is looking very encouraging.

BY DENNIS DICK, WITH ADDITIONAL TEXT BY SIMON MILNE

After a career in journalism, public relations and television programme-making, Dennis Dick was elected to the Trust's Council in 1999. He was Chairman from 2005–08. He is currently a Trustee of the Royal Botanic Garden Edinburgh, sits on the Environment Minister's Scottish Biodiversity Committee; and is a member of the Forestry Commission Scotland's Perth and Argyll advisory forum.

Simon Milne is Chief Executive of Scottish Wildlife Trust

Beavers were reintroduced to Knapdale in 2009 – the first reintroduction of a native mammal to the UK

CHAPTER 34

Sheffield

Despite its early notoriety for a black smoky atmosphere fed by the chimney stacks of its world-famous steel industry, Sheffield has recently been declared the greenest city in Britain. Its population of half-a-million has grown up around the River Don and its fast-flowing feeder tributaries, the Sheaf, Porter, Rivelin and Loxley. The source of all five of these rivers is in the eastern moors of the Peak District, where the 19th century city fathers secured the city's water supply by extending the city boundary westwards right up the watershed. Thus, much of the northern and western edges of the city is open land, or often wooded, steep-sided valleys. Surveys have highlighted the surprising fact that no fewer than 35 patches of ancient woodland survive in the 6,000 acres of woodland within the city boundary.

During the 1980s, there was widespread concern that these open spaces could easily be lost to inappropriate housing or industrial development. Moreover, that was the decade of savage decline in the local coal and steel industries, with consequent widespread dereliction along the lower Don valley, where the heavy steel industry had been located. Many environmentally-minded people believed that this economic situation provided a good opportunity for new strategies, if Sheffield City Council (SCC) could be persuaded to adopt new policies. This would include bringing people and wildlife together through the suitable management of open urban spaces to provide healthy and beautiful amenities to local residents and also help wildlife recover in polluted or barren locations.

Opposite: Sheffield city centre
Right: First newsletter of the Sheffield City Wildlife Group

URBAN NATURE PARK

So it was that in 1984, various individuals with a vision of urban open space, rich in wildlife, started talking and making plans. The chief instigator was Mike Wild, lecturer in Environmental Studies at Sheffield City Polytechnic. By nature a community activist, he spent that year making alliances with like-minded individuals in the British Trust for Conservation Volunteers, Sheffield University, the Education and Countryside Management Department of SCC, and individual local ecologists and wildlife enthusiasts. They were spurred on by knowledge of what was already being achieved by urban volunteers in Norwich, Birmingham and London, where Camley Street Natural Park had just been created beside St Pancras Station. Finally, on 17th April 1985, a formal inaugural meeting was called of all interested parties, hosted by SCC's Countryside Management Officer. It was held at Wood Lane Farm, Malin Bridge, chaired by Mike Wild and attended by more than 26 people. They agreed to name their new organisation the Sheffield City Wildlife Group (SCWG), and commissioned a 'Gang of Four' to draw up a constitution and take the work forward. The four activators were Mike Wild, Dennis Patton (Tutor at Losehill Hall), Christine Bradley (Department of Landscape Architecture, University of Sheffield), and Keith Clarkson (Education Officer at SCC's Natural History Museum).

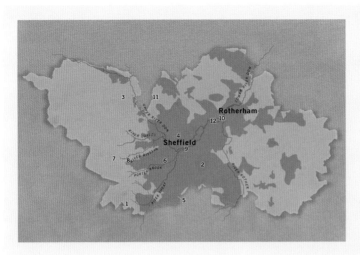

1	Blacka Moor
2	Carbrook Ravine
3	Carr House Meadows
4	Crabtree Ponds
5	Moss Valley Woodlands
6	Sunnybank
7	Wyming Brook
8	Fox Hagg
9	Salmon Pastures
10	Centenary Riverside
11	Greno Woods
12	Blackburn Meadows

Map of Sheffield Wildlife Trust nature reserves

"The Group intends to be involved with some practical demonstrations of what can be done on urban sites by way of habitat creation and environmental improvements to encourage wildlife – but only where local people have been won over to the idea". With these words SCWG announced itself to the citizens of Sheffield in its first newsletter in November 1985. The same issue contained a detailed plan of its first project site – Sunnybank – a tiny patch of less than a hectare of open land, originally earmarked for housing development. However, the Group had already persuaded SCC's Planning Department to let it use Sunnybank as a showpiece 'urban nature park'. The site was well chosen; visible from a main radial road out of the city centre, with a footpath running through it to council housing behind.

A great deal of activity ensued. There were meetings with local community groups who were enthusiastic. An ecological survey was conducted by university ecologists and a bid for funding was made to the Department of the Environment's Urban Programme which gained relevant SCC grant support of more than £10,000. Volunteers from the local community and schools were recruited to help clear the site, contributing over 400 person-days; and, in Environment Week

May 1986, a wildflower meadow was sown in the centre of the site, to be much admired by local residents when it came into flower. The project was given high-profile publicity a year later when DAVID BELLAMY, accompanied by a camera team from Yorkshire Television, visited Sunnybank to help with tree planting.

GROUP TAKES OFF

Other projects followed thick and fast. Wildlife patches were developed in school grounds; and a new regime of grass-cutting was introduced in a council park, resulting in wildflowers appearing. Also, in partnership with the Junior Chamber of Commerce, a project was launched to restore the lower reaches of the River Don into a green corridor with a public footpath along its bank, picturesquely named the Five Weirs Walk. The Yorkshire Water Authority was also persuaded to let some disused land attached to its sewage works become a nature reserve, Blackburn Meadows. An attractive, cut-and-paste newsletter was produced with hand-drawn illustrations. It publicised progress in the Group's projects, raised awareness of wildlife issues, published data from surveys of urban sites, and encouraged community groups to participate in volunteer workdays on project sites and guided wildlife walks.

All this activity was generated by quite a small band of committed volunteers, led by the seven-member Executive Committee. The intensity of their activity and energy is evident from the schedule of planning meetings they set themselves in the summer of 1986; weekly topic meetings of habitat survey, schools and community, and publicity and promotion rotated around monthly council meetings. Eventually, such pressure would lead to burn-out for some of the Group's activists. But for the moment, their efforts were rewarded by significant external recognition.

INNER CITY HABITAT SURVEY

The Group seized the opportunity of hosting the second annual conference of the Fairbrother Group of urban wildlife groups in 1986. This provided an opportunity to show off Sunnybank and other project sites to urban ecologists from around England. Even better, in the following year, the Nature Conservancy Council awarded the Group a grant of £12,000 to undertake an inner city habitat survey of the open spaces in central Sheffield. This enabled the Group to take on its first, albeit temporary, paid employees; two local botanists, Jon Fox and Julie Westford and a zoologist, Austin Brackenbury. Their report was submitted to SCC, and contributed towards its new Nature Conservation Strategy in 1990. The strategy shifted the council's land management policy away from amenity mowed grassland or 'arid urban savanna' to more wildlife-friendly management. This was very acceptable to council officers struggling to make economies arising from the Conservative Government's rate-capping restrictions.

Another major new development for the Group also occurred in 1987 with funding by the Government's Community Programme to provide training in environmental services to 21 unemployed young people. As part of the deal, the Group was offered premises and salaries for two full-time training supervisors, namely Julie Westfold and Roger Butterfield. When the new Government Employment Training scheme

Volunteers digging a pond at Sunnybank, 1988

replaced this scheme, the Group retained its role as a funded training provider. From then on, this training role was to be of continuing significance to the Group. It provided salaries to pay training staff and the trainees themselves became a readily available workforce on project sites. Moreover, local people benefited from the training and became engaged with wildlife management issues, also gaining practical skills and National Vocational Qualifications.

National recognition came in 1989 when the Group took first prize out of 130 entries nationwide in the annual UK2000 Award for the best environmental project in Britain. The judges were particularly impressed by the project's record of over 60 per cent of trainees having found permanent employment.

COMING OF AGE

By 1990, the Group's initial five-year development phase was over. The next seven years saw a steady movement towards more formality of structure and a growth in staff and income. Mike Wild resigned as Chair, his place being taken by Ian Shaw and later Caroline Essery. Money was found to create a post of full-time Director in 1991: "a significant step forwards in status and capability". After a brief hiccough, Ros Stokes was appointed and

473

An inner-city meadow planted by the Trust on the Norfolk Park estate

made herself a strong coordinating force for the next five years. At her instigation, the Group's name was changed to Sheffield City Wildlife Trust and a successful application was made to become a formal member of the Wildlife Trust's national body – then called the Royal Society for Nature Conservation (the Society). This was felt by the newly-named Trust to be a major boost to morale – "being accepted by RSNC is like coming of age". The Trust was now on an equal footing with the much older and larger county Trusts and its experience of urban ecology could now be directly fed into the national wildlife movement. A final name change occurred in 1995 when 'City' was dropped from its name because the Trust no longer worked solely in inner urban areas, but also in outer suburbs.

Under Ros Stokes' direction the work of the Trust grew and consolidated. By 1992, funding had been secured for two full-time Project Officers. Clare Brown became responsible for projects in the Upper Don Valley and Gordon Scaife for projects in Norfolk Park, a neighbourhood dominated by 1960s high-rise council housing. Community work with the residents of the Manor, a particularly disadvantaged district, was also Scaife's responsibility. The number of staff steadily increased until, by 1997, there were seven salaried employees of the Trust; the Director, a part-time

Administrator (Wendy Brookes), the above two Project Officers, a Biodiversity Project Manager (Lucy Smailes) and two Project Assistants. During the same period, the Trust's income increased year-on-year from £17,000, when Ros Stokes became Director, to over £122,000 by the time she resigned in 1997.

The larger number of staff required more space. Having been at the forefront of a campaign to save Wood Lane Farm, a semi-derelict farmhouse on the edge of the city, the Trust was enabled to move into this property alongside the Council's Ranger Service. The Trust had previously survived with difficulty in very cramped downtown office space. Now, for the first time, it had an attractive headquarters with a room to hold meetings in, outbuildings for equipment storage, and a garden. The local WILDLIFE WATCH group developed the garden for wildlife and the Trust continued to maintain it until 1999.

PHOENIX FUNDING

Ros Stokes' resignation came suddenly in summer 1997. Mike Wild stepped into the breach as Acting Director, while the post was advertised that autumn. Eventually it was offered to Rob Stoneman who had previously worked for the SCOTTISH TRUST. The arrival of this visionary

Director coincided with what may be regarded as the third and current phase of the Trust's history.

During this phase, there was a sudden ratcheting up of funding grants, with a concomitant increase in staff numbers and the quantity of work taken on. In the following two years, the number of staff increased almost five-fold, with 34 on the payroll. Now the Trust's income rose steadily from £122,000 in 1997 to a peak of £2.7 million in 2004, by which time the staff numbered more than 90 full-time equivalents. Much of the money was Government funding coming to Sheffield through the Single Regeneration Budget (SRB) and European funding coming to South Yorkshire through Objective 1. The European funding was designed to rescue a region suffering severe unemployment and economic decline resulting from the collapse of the coal and steel industries.

RE-ENGINEERED FOR REGENERATION

Rob Stoneman took the view that the Trust was too small to be influential and had too little to offer to become attractive to potential members, political supporters and significant funders. So he set out to change the Trust into a sizeable organisation delivering social and economic benefits to the people of Sheffield. This would be achieved through projects that improved the quality of the natural environment for wildlife and gave people easier and better access to it. To do this, the structure of the Trust's staffing needed to be developed into departments – administration, training, regeneration, conservation, education, and so on. Amongst others, the post of Head of Conservation was advertised and Nigel Doar, a former colleague of Stoneman's at the SCOTTISH TRUST, was appointed in July 1998. Within weeks, a pivotal moment occurred for Stoneman and Doar in the kitchen of the Trust's Chairman, Mel Burton. A decision was taken to move into regeneration in a big way. The opportunity had arisen with an invitation from a local inner city regeneration partnership to take on the management of their environmental

programme, regenerating a large open space, Ponderosa Park in Upperthorpe and Netherthorpe.

It was a real gamble for a Trust with less than £60,000 in financial reserves to take on a £350,000 capital project – especially when it was already experiencing great cash flow difficulties caused by its rapid expansion. But under Mel Burton's forthright chairing, the Trustees decided it was vital to grow the Trust's size and capacity in order to do what it was set up to do. Doar recalled that "reliably paying salaries each month was a stretch. It was a real baptism of fire – working in partnership as a big non-governmental organisation operating as an intermediary between government and local community groups, rather than, up to this point,

Wyming Brook nature reserve

Blacka Moor – a 180-hectare moorland reserve on the south-west edge of Sheffield

as a small community organisation that was seen by local partners entirely as one of themselves".

FIRST RESERVES

Another significant development in 2000–01 was taking on the management of certain parcels of land, formally leased from SCC, as nature reserves. Up to that point, the Trust had been the only Wildlife Trust with no nature reserves of its own. A successful £1 million bid was made to the HERITAGE LOTTERY FUND for capital works on selected sites covering all Sheffield's priority habitats. The sites had a good geographical spread and included some nationally-important, flagship sites – namely Wyming Brook and Blacka Moor – as well as some small sites the Trust had a long connection with, such as Sunnybank, Salmon Pastures and Crabtree Ponds. This reserves project enabled the Trust to employ its

first dedicated full-time Ecologist, Be Wiggs, and land management staff. The Trust was moving along the path of becoming a more 'conventional' Wildlife Trust.

These new activities were made possible by bringing in trainees to deliver projects, paid for through the Labour Government's New Deal for Young People, and a derivative of it, Intermediate Labour Market, run by the Centre for Full Employment. The strategy was to move existing Trust project staff into management and training roles, and bring trainees and volunteers in to deliver project outputs under supervision. In this way, spare capacity was created to allow development work such as the establishment of Green Estate.

ENHANCING NEIGHBOURHOODS

Green Estate started as a small contract to carry out green space surveys in Manor and Castle, for the Manor and Castle Development Trust (MCDT). It led to a wide-ranging programme of environmental enhancement works across one of Sheffield's most disadvantaged housing estates. It aimed to create a country estate by developing productive natural land uses on all of the estate's green and open spaces, and by engaging local people in their management and use. Sue France was appointed project manager in 1998 to develop the project from scratch. Green Estate Limited was formed as a joint venture company between the Trust and MCDT in 2004, with France as its first and, so far, only Director. Green Estate Limited is the most tangible outcome of the SRB-funded project and it is still a sustainable local social enterprise, generating income and delivering innovative environmental regeneration. It has a staff of more than 30 and an annual income of about £1.5 million.

Another pivotal moment occurred on 14th September 2001. On the day the Trust moved into its present headquarters in Stafford Road, Rob Stoneman said farewell as he moved to the Society's office in Newark as Director of Conservation. Continuity of leadership was secured with Nigel Doar taking over the reins as the new Director, later Chief Executive. The fine new headquarters is an ecologically-refurbished listed building, a former church hall, surrounded by a wildlife garden with a pond.

The major achievement of the last few years has been to manage the downsizing necessitated by the reduction in European regeneration funding since 2005. Sufficient alternative funding was secured so that the Trust continued to be Sheffield's leading environmental charity, with an annual turnover of about £2 million. In 2010, the Trust's 25th year, membership continued to rise and was approaching 5,000 – one per cent of the city's population. Moreover, commitments have recently been extended beyond the city boundary to neighbouring Rotherham. In 2008, Rotherham Council invited the Trust to undertake the landscaping and maintenance of a major flood alleviation scheme on the River Don at Centenary

Greno Woods – the Trust's newest reserve

Riverside and to take it on as a nature reserve. The scheme won the Flood Defence category at the UK Waterways Renaissance Awards in 2010, and was commended in the Natural Environment category.

The Trust continues to experiment and innovate with new approaches to engaging people with the natural world and securing the resources to make South Yorkshire a more natural place. In 2007, it established Wildscapes, a trading subsidiary. In 2010, the Trust embarked on a campaign to celebrate its 25th anniversary by purchasing Greno Woods in the north of Sheffield – an area of more than 400 acres of wildlife-rich and historic woodland.

The Trust's early ambitions are still very much alive as it tries to secure support for its vision of a Living Landscape for people and wildlife within a densely populated area, reaching from the edges of the Peak District in the west to the floodplains of the river Don in the east.

BY DR PATRICK VAUGHAN
Dr Patrick Vaughan has been a Trustee of Sheffield Wildlife Trust since 2002, and is currently Chair of the Board. He has worked in Adult Education all his life, and has a special interest in Sheffield local history.

A young volunteer at Blacka Moor nature reserve

CHAPTER 35

Shropshire

"Putting the principle of conservation into practice depends on three commodities, and all of them are in dangerously short supply. They are technical knowledge, public understanding and money". Charles Sinker's prophetic words are as apt today as they were when published in an early Trust *Bulletin* in 1969.

He went on: "I may have to make my case to a big landowner or a forestry group, a river authority or a county council; but every time the factors are the same: research, education, economics".

This urgent need to make a case for nature led to the formation of the Shropshire Conservation Trust Limited on 12th July 1962. Charles Sinker of the Field Studies Council was one of an influential group of naturalists roused by a threat to the wildlife of the Long Mynd back in the early 1960s. The threat was in the form of plans to flood land at the base of the three valleys, Ashes Hollow, Callow Hollow and Minton Batch. Environmentalists Frank Gribble, Reg Harrison, Cyril Lloyd, Edward Rutter and Sinker approached Tom Pritchard of the Nature Conservancy Council (NCC) to seek help in protecting this invaluable part of Shropshire, already designated as an SSSI. Pritchard suggested setting up an independent conservation trust to strengthen their arguments against the proposal. The new Trust, along with local commoners, succeeded in making a convincing case, saving the Mynd from what would have been catastrophic damage. Knowledgeable enthusiasts and naturalists had

been studying Shropshire's flora, fauna and geology for at least a century before this alarm signalled the need for an organisation with the specific purpose of safeguarding the county's natural heritage. Some founders of the Trust were also members of the still-thriving Caradoc and Severn Valley Field Club, set up as long ago as 1863. To represent its protectionist function, the Trust's first emblem was the shield-like leaf and flower of the least yellow water lily, *Nuphar pumila*. One of Britain's rarest plants, it is found in Colemere, part of the internationally-important meres and mosses of North Shropshire. The first President of the new Trust, W Morley Davies, a highly-regarded agricultural scientist, and Charles Sinker, later the second President, were especially commended by the Trust's then patron, Lord Bridgeman, for their "hard work leading to its foundation".

Opposite: Walkers at Stiperstones
Right: Charles Sinker – eminent botanist and founder of the Shropshire Wildlife Trust

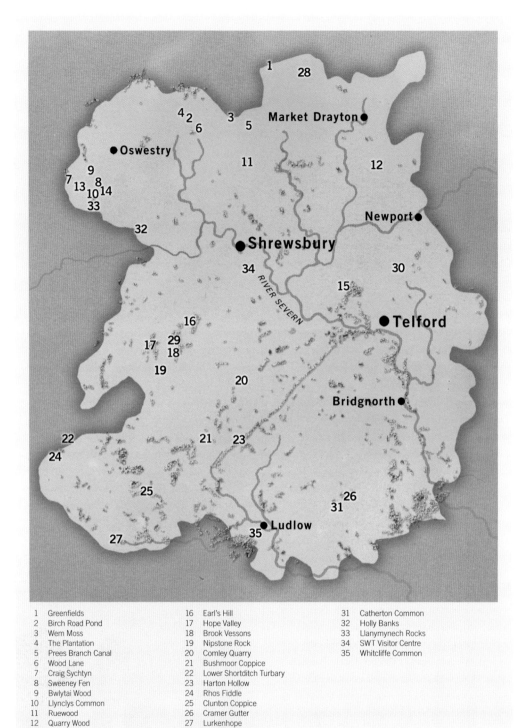

1	Greenfields	16	Earl's Hill	31	Catherton Common
2	Birch Road Pond	17	Hope Valley	32	Holly Banks
3	Wem Moss	18	Brook Vessons	33	Llanymynech Rocks
4	The Plantation	19	Nipstone Rock	34	SWT Visitor Centre
5	Prees Branch Canal	20	Comley Quarry	35	Whitcliffe Common
6	Wood Lane	21	Bushmoor Coppice		
7	Craig Sychtyn	22	Lower Shortditch Turbary		
8	Sweeney Fen	23	Harton Hollow		
9	Bwlytai Wood	24	Rhos Fiddle		
10	Llynclys Common	25	Clunton Coppice		
11	Ruewood	26	Cramer Gutter		
12	Quarry Wood	27	Lurkenhope		
13	Jones' Rough	28	Melverley Meadows		
14	Dolgoch Quarry	29	The Hollies		
15	The Ercall	30	Granville Nature Reserve and Country Park		

Map of Shropshire Wildlife Trust nature reserves

RICH NATURAL INHERITANCE

Shropshire has a rich natural inheritance, with a range of habitats from the alkaline limestone of the north-west and Wenlock Edge, to the acidic uplands of the south and west. The county's classic geology comprises rocks representing 11 of the 13 geological eras, from 700 million years ago until the last Ice Age around 10,000 years ago. In the north of the county the advancing and retreating ice sheets created a gently rolling landscape with many water-filled hollows or meres, some of which developed into boggy mosses as vegetation accumulated. Glaciation also influenced the flow of the River Severn, which rises in Wales, runs through Shrewsbury, cuts through the Ironbridge Gorge and on into Worcestershire. Thanks partly to its central location in Britain, Shropshire occupies a key position as the meeting point for species of several different geographical regions, with 15 distinct biogeographical elements recognised within the county's flora.

BROAD CHURCH

One of the distinctive characteristics of the new Shropshire Conservation Trust was the inclusion from the outset of a wide constituency of interests. At the time, this was an extraordinarily far-sighted view and has proved immensely beneficial to the Trust throughout its history. The Trust's Council comprised people with expertise in education, finance, land agency, agricultural science, journalism and the law who were all willing not only to participate, but also to seek partnerships with other bodies with related interests. The founders of the Trust were also clear about their purposes: conservation of threatened habitats and their dependent species; use of land for education and leisure; and fostering research. At this time there were no paid employees; instead, a network of local observers would "keep an eye personally on every square mile of the Shropshire countryside". A list of areas important for botanical richness, known as Sinker sites after the man who first identified them, established an early database invaluable for the later compilation of a prime sites list.

In 1970, founder member Clive Tate was employed as part-time Trust Administrator, the first paid member of staff. In the quarterly *Bulletin*, Tate urged members to be active and to let him know about new opportunities, as he put it 'to grab land'. Those heady days of keen and pioneering enthusiasm, driven by the desire to safeguard sites through Trust ownership, laid a sound foundation for what has taken place since.

FIRST RESERVE

In 1963, land owned by the Chitty family became the Trust's first nature reserve. It comprised 100 acres of deciduous woodland, rocky scree and hilltop grassland at Earl's Hill. The reserve's educational value, together with the opportunity for students of all ages to study living things out of doors, was considered a core benefit of the acquisition. Opening the renovated Earl's Hill barn in 1979 was a tremendous boost, demonstrating that the Trust was both a responsible and ambitious organisation capable of energising interest and raising funds. It was in 1979, too, that Milton Luby became the third President of the Trust. An arable farmer and excellent communicator, he did much to strengthen the understanding between farming

Earl's Hill, the Trust's first nature reserve pictured here in 1953

Peregrine falcon at Quarry Wood nature reserve

and wildlife conservation. This was vital in this largely agricultural county and an early example of landscape-scale thinking.

IDENTIFYING PRIME SITES

The meticulous approach of a two-year field-by-field survey of the county, begun in 1978, fulfilled the Trust's ambitions to anchor its work in scientific research and sound local knowledge. At this time, although 58 areas of Shropshire had been designated as SSSIs, knowledge about the rest of the county was still fragmented. Using opportunities presented by the Manpower Services Commission's EMPLOYMENT SCHEMES, the Trust appointed four scientists to identify sites of biological and geological importance, and a fifth to establish a permanent conservation corps in the county. This work in the north of the county complemented similar work in the south organised by the County Museum Service at Ludlow. This phase-one survey collected information on more than 5,000 sites, ranging from huge heathland areas to farm ponds and quarter-acre meadows. From these, around 750 wildlife-rich

sites (five per cent of the county's area), were documented in *Prime Sites for Nature Conservation* and notified to organisations such as the Nature Conservancy Council (NCC), water authorities, the Forestry Commission and local government. Adding this data to the County Council's Environmental Record meant that it could then be taken into account in structure plans and planning applications.

In 1980, John Harrison joined the Trust to manage the Youth Opportunities Programme within the Government's Manpower Services Commission scheme. Numbers working for the Trust grew from 18 to 60 before the scheme finished in 1988. Under his leadership the prime-site work continued, laying a firm foundation for the future.

BRANCHING OUT

By its 21st anniversary in 1983, the Shropshire Trust for Nature Conservation (the name changed in that year), had 1,600 members. *Your Guide to Shropshire's Wild Places*, published by the Trust, included a leaflet on each of its 21 reserves. The Trust's eight existing local branches proved to be such an asset that with the *New Branches Pack*, Paul Bell, who became the Trust's fourth President in 1988, established five further branches, thus increasing the Trust's profile and grassroots activities.

Published by the Trust in 1985, the *Ecological Flora of the Shropshire Region* was the product of an ambitious flora project begun ten years earlier. DAVID BELLAMY's foreword praised the book as "a work of scholarship – geology, botany, geography, ecology and history all in one – a Domesday Book for Shropshire against which all future change will be measured." More than 100 people contributed records, led by six specialists: Charles Sinker, John Packham, Ian Trueman, Philip Oswald, Frank Perring and William Prestwood. The latter had become the Trust's first Conservation Officer in February 1979.

PRIME SITE LOSSES

In 1986, with funding from the NCC, the Trust was able to employ its first Director, Christine Bradley, a tremendously important step in its growth and development. Later in 1986, further funding from the NCC and the WWF enabled the Trust to employ a full-time Prime Sites Officer. Personal visits were made to some 1,000 landowners who had their attention drawn to the wildlife value of their land. Where a prime site had to earn its keep, the Trust offered advice on grant aid, or voluntary labour for work such as fencing and hedge-laying.

John Tucker had become Conservation Officer by the time the Trust published *Losing Ground in Shropshire* with 1986–89 prime sites data. It was a powerful wake-up call for the public and politicians, and evidence of the failure of the Wildlife and Countryside Act 1981 to protect species and natural habitats adequately. This valuable document detailed Shropshire's richly varied habitats of woodland, flower-rich grassland, heathland, bog, swamp and fen, tall herb, open water, rock and quarry. It also identified the three main causes of habitat loss: agriculture, forestry and development. The report's conclusion 'What Can be Done?' was unequivocal in pointing

out the shortfall in the Government's approach. Such was the importance of this work that the national report, *Losing Ground,* used Shropshire's research results as a keynote to its introduction, 'The Damaging Evidence'. This showed that in Shropshire in 1978–79 there were 750 sites that earned the term 'prime site' because of their wildlife importance. A decade later, in 1989, 95 had gone, and a further 133 had been damaged, including a fifth of the flower-rich meadows and almost a tenth of the county's woodlands.

FOR PEAT'S SAKE

Peat extraction has been one of the major issues for the Trust. For years there had been sustainable small-scale commercial working in the lowland raised bog on the Shropshire-Clwyd border. But by the late 1980s, new technology had led to industrial-scale extraction. This was depleting an irreplaceable habitat of peatland flora and fauna, and was a severe threat to Fenns, Whixall and Bettisfield mosses. In spite of joint lobbying by the Shropshire and NORTH WALES TRUSTS, supported by other

Whitemere, with the Mere of Ellesmere in the background. These meres formed in hollows left by glaciers in the last Ice Age, 10,000 years ago. They are now the focus of the Trust's Meres and Mosses Living Landscape project

interested groups, it was not possible to rescind the 1940s planning permissions. In the event, the Trust coordinated the successful appeal, For Peat's Sake, leading in 1990 to English Nature purchasing the site on behalf of the nation. This National Nature Reserve was later declared a Wetland of International Importance under the 1997 Ramsar Convention and a European Special Area of Conservation (PEATLAND CAMPAIGN).

FUNDRAISING

By the late 1970s, more effective means of raising finance were needed. In 1981, a committee to raise money for a Site Acquisition and Management Fund was formed. This later evolved into the Shropshire Conservation Development Trust, a sister charity designed to consolidate fundraising and to rally the support of landowners and the business community. Under the guidance of Lionel Jebb, Tony Daniell, Richard Tanner and Jean Jackson, the Development Trust enabled, among other successes, the purchase of Ruewood as well as the Trust's former headquarters in Frankwell, Shrewsbury.

Funding now comes from the Trust's 24 corporate members, grants, donations, legacies and the subscriptions of 10,000 members. This is supplemented by fundraising campaigns for specific initiatives such as the 1998 Back to Purple heathland restoration scheme on the Stiperstones ridge, the 2007 appeal to buy a grove of ancient holly trees on the Stiperstones, and the 2009 acquisition of Catherton Common. In 1996, the Shropshire Wildlife Trust (the Trust's name changed in 1988) was the first Wildlife Trust in Britain to be awarded a lottery grant for managing its reserves, then 38 in number and covering 180 hectares.

NINETIES INNOVATION

The Back to Purple project was one of the first of a new type and scale of landscape-based partnerships – innovative in the late 1990s and a forerunner of today's Living Landscape work. Catherton Common, 527 acres of heathland and the largest

Environmental education is an important part of the Trust's work

Wildlife Trust nature reserve in the West Midlands, represents an exciting new challenge as it means working in close partnership with the local community, including 60 commoners.

In 2004, the Trust campaign to purchase the Wrekin enjoyed huge public support, attracting donations of close to £900,000 in eight weeks. Disappointingly, the owner withdrew from the sale, but public support has continued. One outcome has been the formation of the Wrekin Forest Partnership – managed by the Trust – that brings together landowners, charities, local authorities, the Shropshire Hills AONB and, crucially, the public. These three projects, the Stiperstones, Catherton and the Wrekin, mean that the Trust has a key role in the future of three of Shropshire's most iconic landmarks.

A further reflection of the visionary agenda of the early pioneers is the Trust's education work and community engagement. A third of all schools in the county are involved annually. The Trust runs Forest Schools, Nature Tots and WILDLIFE WATCH – The Wildlife Trusts' nature club for children. There are 400 active volunteers on whom the Trust relies. In addition to its eight local branches and the Wildlife Survey Group, the Trust works closely with other special interest recording groups. Over the last 20 years, wildlife surveys have been carried out by branches and community groups in every Shropshire town.

INDUSTRIAL LEGACY

For what is widely perceived as one of England's most rural of counties, Shropshire also embraces an area in which, for nearly 300 years, heavy industry was dominant. This relict landscape in the east of the county, from which industry has largely disappeared, resulted in huge areas of dereliction with associated social and economic consequences. It also left an outstanding industrial heritage in the Ironbridge Gorge, a World Heritage Site since 1986. It was with the object of reviving the fortunes of this area that Telford New Town was established in the mid-1960s. The Trust has had an important and innovative role in this area, promoting a wider understanding of urban wildlife conservation and the recognition that part of this post-industrial landscape has become rich in wildlife habitats. Since the mid-1990s, the Telford Green Network, an initiative in which the Trust has played an important role, has been formally recognised in the local planning framework.

Today, the Trust's headquarters at Abbey Foregate, Shrewsbury, offers indoor accommodation for offices, meeting rooms, a retail outlet and a natural history garden with public access. The Trust's nature reserves now cover almost 2,000 acres. The Trust is managed by a professional team of more than 30 under the direction of Colin Preston, Trust Director since 1991. Overall control of policy is the responsibility of the Council of Trustees, chaired by Veronica Cossons, who became the Trust's fifth and current President.

From its inaugural meetings in the early 1960s to today's wide-ranging agenda, the Trust has remained remarkably true to the vision of its founders, which is a tribute to their far-sightedness. Throughout its existence, the keys to its success have been: embracing a wide constituency of interests across the county; clear policies carried through with forthright determination; sound and consistent leadership at trustee and executive level; the enduring commitment of the membership; and, through them, the promotion of the value of Shropshire's wildlife for everyone in the county.

BY JEAN BELL AND PAUL BELL

Jean Bell is a US citizen. Following her marriage to Paul Bell in 1967, she moved to near Market Drayton, Shropshire in 1969. She taught English at Newcastle-under-Lyme School until her retirement in 2006, and now works as a part-time proofreader.

Paul Bell is a naturalist and retired dentist. He has been a Trustee of Shropshire Wildlife Trust since 1974. From 1984, he has written a monthly column 'Country Comment' for Newport and Market Drayton Advertiser newspapers.

Ancient pollarded holly tree on the Trust's reserve at The Hollies

CHAPTER 36

Somerset

Somerset is a county of remarkable diversity. Though much smaller than its neighbour, Devon, it has a more complex and varied geology. The western part is dominated by upland heaths dissected by the deep oakwood valleys of Exmoor; a complete contrast to the limestone caves and gorges of the Mendips. Between them lie the Moors and Levels, water meadows with wooded ridges through the middle of land, most of which lies below sea level. There is nowhere in Europe like the Somerset Moors and Levels.

The county is rich in wildlife, partly because it has a relatively low human population. The largest conurbation, Taunton, is a town of about 120,000 people. Whilst there are significant industries such as Augusta Westlands, Clarks Shoes and the Nuclear Power Station at Hinkley Point, the local economy is still very much an agricultural one. Livestock farming and dairying have always been strong in Somerset, and they continue together with less traditional crops such as flax, oil-seed rape, daffodils and elephant grass. Much of the farming is quite small-scale and relatively unintensive, giving wildlife an opportunity to exploit a mosaic of different habitats. The Moors are still being dug commercially for peat, but under strict controls within existing permits. The resulting patchwork of fully-dug, partly-dug and un-dug peat gives a range of wetland habitats in a small area.

The Somerset Wildlife Trust was formed in 1964 under the name of The Somerset Trust for Nature Conservation. In the early 1960s, similar charitable Trusts came into existence across Britain as

Opposite: Glastonbury Tor from Yarley Fields nature reserve

local naturalists, encouraged by people like CHRISTOPHER CADBURY, Francis Rose and TED SMITH, decided it was no longer enough to identify and record wildlife. There was also a desperate need to take direct action to secure its future.

As with most Trusts, the bedrock of the Somerset Wildlife Trust was the support it received from members of local natural history societies. It was no coincidence that the first meeting to discuss forming a conservation charity was at the headquarters of the Somerset Archaeological and Natural History Society at Taunton Museum. Fifteen people were there, and the initial capital was provided by each of them giving a £1 note.

FOUNDING FATHERS

There was never any doubt who should be the first Chairman. Somerset was fortunate in having a local schoolmaster who was nationally known as 'the Badger Man'. Dr Ernest Neal, Head of Biology at Taunton School, was the author of the definitive work on badgers and a regular broadcaster. Not only did he have the authority needed to get support for the new organisation, but he also had a wide range of contacts. The guest speakers at the first Annual General Meeting were Dr Bruce Campbell and SIR DAVID ATTENBOROUGH. The Earl Waldegrave agreed to be the Trust's patron, which brought it to the attention of a number of major landowners. Neal always claimed that he would only agree to be Chairman on condition that Peter Tolson was Secretary. Tolson did not have Neal's national standing, but there was hardly a farmer in the south-west he did not know and who did not listen to what he said. He had recently retired as Secretary of the

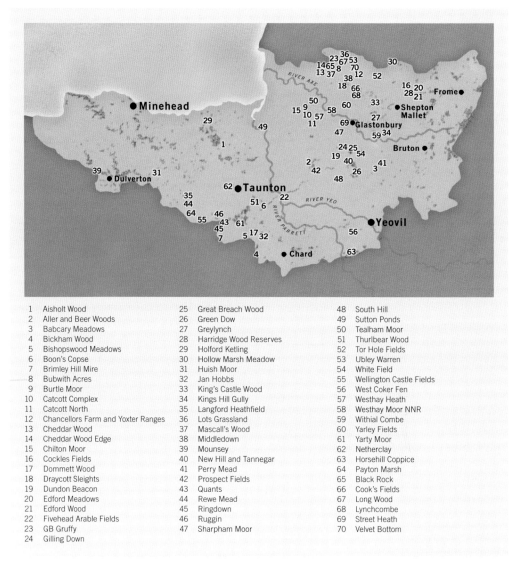

1	Aisholt Wood	25	Great Breach Wood	48	South Hill
2	Aller and Beer Woods	26	Green Dow	49	Sutton Ponds
3	Babcary Meadows	27	Greylynch	50	Tealham Moor
4	Bickham Wood	28	Harridge Wood Reserves	51	Thurlbear Wood
5	Bishopswood Meadows	29	Holford Ketling	52	Tor Hole Fields
6	Boon's Copse	30	Hollow Marsh Meadow	53	Ubley Warren
7	Brimley Hill Mire	31	Huish Moor	54	White Field
8	Bubwith Acres	32	Jan Hobbs	55	Wellington Castle Fields
9	Burtle Moor	33	King's Castle Wood	56	West Coker Fen
10	Catcott Complex	34	Kings Hill Gully	57	Westhay Heath
11	Catcott North	35	Langford Heathfield	58	Westhay Moor NNR
12	Chancellors Farm and Yoxter Ranges	36	Lots Grassland	59	Withial Combe
13	Cheddar Wood	37	Mascall's Wood	60	Yarley Fields
14	Cheddar Wood Edge	38	Middledown	61	Yarty Moor
15	Chilton Moor	39	Mounsey	62	Netherclay
16	Cockles Fields	40	New Hill and Tannegar	63	Horsehill Coppice
17	Dommett Wood	41	Perry Mead	64	Payton Marsh
18	Draycott Sleights	42	Prospect Fields	65	Black Rock
19	Dundon Beacon	43	Quants	66	Cook's Fields
20	Edford Meadows	44	Rewe Mead	67	Long Wood
21	Edford Wood	45	Ringdown	68	Lynchcombe
22	Fivehead Arable Fields	46	Ruggin	69	Street Heath
23	GB Gruffy	47	Sharpham Moor	70	Velvet Bottom
24	Gilling Down				

Map of Somerset Wildlife Trust nature reserves

Somerset branch of the National Farmers Union. His tireless championing of nature conservation and direct engagement with the landowners of the county were invaluable. By December 1964 the Trust already had some 400 members. What's more, it had established itself as a voice that could not be ignored.

As well as schoolteachers and landowners, the first Council of 29 people included academic scientists, John Burton of the BBC, an industrial scientist, Dr Chris Smith, local government officers, a bank manager and a solicitor. The main issues that concerned the new Trust have a very familiar ring. The first newsletters record the Trust lobbying against the expansion of quarrying on the Mendips and expressed concern over the extent of peat extraction from the Moors and Levels. There were other recurrent themes that still arise today – for instance, the importance of working with landowners and winning their goodwill, and of robust survey data to inform the Trust's operations.

SIXTIES AND SEVENTIES PROGRESS

By 1966, the Trust was making its presence felt, lobbying successfully to have the route of the M5 motorway altered to save Crook Peak with its rare plant species. The Trust acquired its first piece of Westhay Moor in 1966 and its first large reserve, at Langford Heathfield, the following year.

By the end of 1967, there were enough sites being managed by the Trust for it to employ its first member of staff, Reserves Officer, Bill Collins. A great asset to the Trust, he died tragically young in a road accident in 1972.

The growth of the Trust was fast and impressive. In 1972, one of its founder Council Members, Colin Trapnell, gave the Trust 156 acres of ancient woodland on the Polden Hills which his family had owned for many years. With subsequent extensions, Great Breach Wood is now one of the finest nature reserves in the region. In 1973, the Trust secured a headquarters, Fyne Court at Broomfield in the Quantocks, leased from The

National Trust. It was once the home of Andrew Crosse, an eccentric pioneer in the study of electricity, who was possibly one of the models on whom Mary Shelley based her own mad scientist, Dr Frankenstein!

Neal stood down as Chairman in 1977 and was succeeded by Dr Chris Smith. Smith ran the Trust without a Director or Chief Executive until 1988. He was Chairman for 17 years doing the work of several people. His contribution was immense. By the time he retired as Chairman, the Trust had 61 nature reserves, over 5,000 members and a permanent staff of 15. Smith died in 2009, leaving the Trust the largest legacy it has ever received.

Swans at Westhay. Above right: Chris Smith – Trust Chairman 1977–94

In keeping with the aspirations of the founders to engage with other landowners, the Trust scored a notable first in 1978 with the appointment of the country's first Farming Wildlife Adviser, Dorothea Nelson. By 1983, there were Farming and Wildlife Group advisors in every county. In 1981, the Trust took the unusual step of giving a number of its finest nature reserves away. The traditional county of Somerset had been split in 1974 with the creation of Avon. The young AVON WILDLIFE TRUST was clearly the right body to own and manage the reserves in its half of the old county. The Trust was glad to help them get off to a good start.

COUNTY RECORD CENTRE

In 1986, the Trust set up a county record centre, the Somerset Environmental Record Centre. It is widely regarded as one of the best environmental record centres in the country. Countless ecologists throughout Britain have undertaken their training there. The importance of scientifically-reliable data behind conservation efforts is as great as it was in 1964. Unusually, the Centre is still owned and run by a trading subsidiary of the Trust. The Trust was now far too big to be run by an unpaid Chairman, so, in 1988, Roger Martin was appointed its first Director. Martin's background was an unusual one. A diplomat and political speechwriter, he never claimed to know about the species he worked so tirelessly and well to conserve. But what he did understand supremely well was the workings of the minds of decision-makers. His grasp of the increasingly political world of nature conservation was, and still is, exceptional. He served the Trust excellently until retiring in 2000.

EXPANDING RESERVES

Through the 1980s and 1990s, the Trust's portfolio of nature reserves increased apace. Funds were available through the Nature Conservancy Council, as well as through grants from the then English Nature (now Natural England), the HERITAGE

LOTTERY FUND and the Landfill Tax. For the first part of that period of growth labour was also cheap and the Trust made great use of the Manpower Services Commission (EMPLOYMENT SCHEMES). In the four years from 1985 to 1989 the Trust acquired 15 new reserves. The smallest and strangest of these was the Wadbury Bat House. It was leased for ten years on condition that it would be demolished if, by the end of that term, it was not housing bats. It was, and is still a Trust reserve today.

In 1993, Fisons decided to stop peat extraction on their lands at Westhay Moor and disposed of them to the Trust via English Nature. The Westhay National Nature Reserve has been a regular star of television with its starling roost. Several years ago, a party of wetland experts from Japan arrived at Heathrow and, unlike many tourist parties from their country, had one site only on their minds to visit, Westhay Moor.

PARTNERSHIP WORKING

The close relationships forged by the Trust with other organisations have been a key part of its success. For a number of years an Education Officer's

Opposite: Roe deer amongst the bluebells at Longwood
Right: Chancellor's Farm

Beech trees at Draycott Sleights nature reserve in the Mendip Hills

post was funded by Nuclear Electric. The Trust enjoys financial and strategic support from the quarrying industry, always on the clear understanding that the Trust can object if they try to dynamite something precious. The chain of nature reserves that make up the Avalon project requires sharing facilities and cooperating closely with Natural England, the RSPB and two other conservation charities. The result is a large swathe of peatland in conservation management forever. The Trust played a fundamental role in ensuring that Somerset was one of the first counties in the country to have Biodiversity Action Plans in place for every district council. In 1994,

the Trust created a lease that was among the first of its kind in the country. It acquired the freehold of a piece of land which lay over two fine caves at GB Gruffy. The Trust realised it could not manage the geological interest, but there were right-minded cavers who could. The lease covers the entrance structures and everything more than five feet below the surface of the ground. It is another collaboration which has worked very well to the benefit of our biological and geological heritage.

LIVING LANDSCAPES

A further important collaboration was given a formal structure in 2000 with the formation of the

South West Wildlife Trusts, a registered charity owned by the Wildlife Trusts in the region. It was that body which set up a groundbreaking landscape-scale initiative in Rebuilding Biodiversity in 2003 – creating a nature map of the whole of the south-west. The Trust's own LIVING LANDSCAPE projects build on that work, but also engage local communities. The Trust has two Living Landscape projects already operating and two more in preparation. As part of the Trust's Mendip Living Landscape Project, local children enjoyed first-hand experiences of local wildlife. Now, every primary school in the West Mendips is working with the Trust, using nature reserves to educate and inspire young children. Each year about 50 people walk the hills as a mass survey for flying bats. As many again are surveying for long-eared owls.

The Trust has eight very active WILDLIFE WATCH Groups, two of which were highly commended in the 2010 Wildlife Watch Groups Awards, and also winner and runner-up in the previous year's South-West Regional Awards. The Trust is doing everything it can to ensure there are naturalists in the future ready to carry on the work it started 40 years ago.

Of course, in those 40 years, the Trust has changed greatly. In 2000, the Council was reduced from nearly 30 people to 12. In 2004, the headquarters moved to offices in Wellington. Fyne Court was

only relinquished in 2009 and is still used to a limited extent with The National Trust's blessing. The Trust now owns or manages 75 nature reserves, employs more than 40 staff, has a membership of more than 20,500 and an annual turnover of almost £2 million. The private nature reserve network, which the Trust helps run, covers wildlife habitats spread out across the county. The issues are still the same; the pressure of people on limited resources, peat working, quarrying, Hinkley Point Nuclear Power Station, housing schemes, road schemes and declining species and habitats. Through its involvement in the re-introduction of the large blue butterfly, the Trust has managed to put one species back. The large blue is now doing well on the Trust's Green Down reserve – the site of its reintroduction.

There is much to fear in the immediate future. The Government envisages a huge amount of new housing in the county. Climate change could remove much of the Moors and Levels, returning them to the sea they were part of until the 17th century. Mendip limestone is still extracted, crushed and even exported to France for road building. But, there is also a great deal to celebrate. Ernest Neal, Peter Tolson, Chris Smith and many countless others have created a Trust that has made a huge difference, and of which everyone involved can be justly proud.

BY EDWARD WELLS
Edward Wells has been a Council Member of the Trust continuously from 1984 to the present day and was Chairman from 1998 to 2003. He has recently retired as a solicitor in which capacity he gave the Trust professional advice for more than 26 years.

Above: Goldeneye and other wetland birds can be found at the Trust's Westhay Moor reserve
Right: Large blue butterfly

CHAPTER 37

South and West Wales

The Wildlife Trust of South and West Wales manages over 4,000 acres of some of the region's most precious wild places in the form of over 80 nature reserves. This diverse area boasts magnificent coastline, rugged mountains, the heritage-rich ex-coalmining valleys and the richest agricultural land in Wales.

The Wildlife Trust of South and West Wales has only been in existence since April 2002 when it was formed by merger of West Wales Wildlife Trust and Glamorgan Wildlife Trust. But it is rooted in organisations with a long history of protecting wildlife, beginning before the Second World War in Pembrokeshire.

The inaugural meeting of the Pembrokeshire Bird Society was held at Haverfordwest on 26th February 1938 and was attended by about 80 people including Ronald Lockley, Hugh Lloyd-Phillips, Colonel Harold Allen and Lord Merthyr – just a few of the many illustrious names involved in the Trust's history.

The outbreak of war overshadowed many conservationists' activities, but their duty to wildlife remained clear, with many seeking refuge from this grim period by wildlife watching and recording. It was through this determination that the Bird Society continued and flourished, even managing to raise modest subscriptions for the Sanctuary Fund to purchase land for bird sanctuaries after the war. Reports from this period noted news that the Society's President, Lord Merthyr, was being held a prisoner of war in Hong Kong. Nevertheless,

protection of species still remained paramount. For instance, peregrine falcons in Pembrokeshire were being persecuted because of their appetite for carrier pigeons – which were used for transmitting military messages during the war. The Bird Society also had to deal with the application of the Allied Air Forces to use the island of Grassholm, located off the Pembrokeshire coast (and now an RSPB reserve), as a bombing target and the Society's work ensured the island's gannetry was saved. During this period, one of the most interesting events was the acquisition by lease of Cardigan Island on 25th March 1944 and the establishment of a Soay sheep colony there.

NEW NAME – NEW MEMBERS

In 1945, with Ronald Lockley as Chairman, the Society changed its name to the WEST WALES FIELD SOCIETY (WWFS) in recognition of the need to broaden the organisation to include botany, zoology, geology and archaeology in addition to the study of birdlife and general countryside interests.

Opposite: Puffin, an iconic species of the Pembrokeshire islands
Right: (Left to right) Colonel Morrey Salmon, Cecil Lambourne, Ronald Lockley, Dillwyn Miles, David Saunders and Stephen Sutcliffe at Martin's Haven, 1983, *en route* to Skokholm

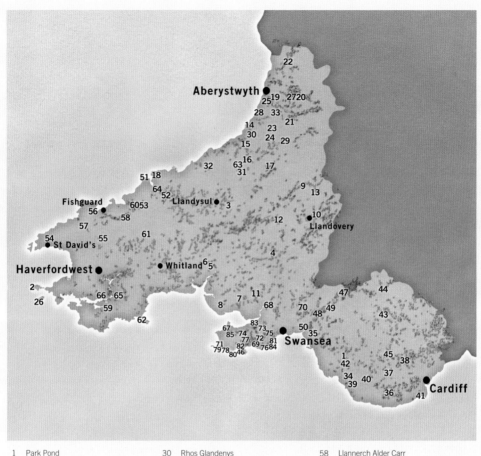

1	Park Pond	30	Rhos Glandenys	58	Llannerch Alder Carr
2	Skomer	31	Rhos Glyn-yr-Helyg	59	Pembroke Upper Mill Pond
3	Allt Cross Inn Fach	32	Rhos Pil-Bach a Pennar Fawr	60	Coed Pont Bren
4	Castle Woods	33	Rhos-Y-Fforest	61	Penalltfach
5	Coed Wern Ddu	34	Coed y Bwl	62	St Margaret's Island
6	Cors Goch	35	Baglan Reserve	63	Temple Carr Barr
7	Cors Pum Heol	36	Coed Garnllwyd	64	Welsh Wildlife Centre, Teifi Marshes
8	Ffrwd Farm Mire	37	Coed Llwyn Rhyddid	65	West Williamston
9	Nant Melin	38	Coed y Bedw	66	Westfield Pill
10	Poor Mans Wood	39	Coed y Bwl	67	Betty Church and Cwm Ivy
11	Rhos Cefn Bryn	40	Cwm Colhuw	68	Bolgoed Quarry
12	Talley Lakes	41	Lavernock	69	Broad Pool
13	Y Goyallt	42	Park Slip Nature Park	70	Craig Cilhendre Woods
14	Aberstrincell Limekilns	43	Pwll Waun Cynon	71	Deborah's Hole
15	Allt Grug Garn	44	Taf Fechan	72	Elizabeth and Rowe Harding Reserve
16	Allt Pencnwc	45	Y Gweira	73	Gelli Hir
17	Caeau Llety Cybi	46	Sedger's Bank	74	Hambury Wood
18	Cardigan Island	47	Blaenant y Gwyddyl	75	Killay Marsh
19	Old Warren Hill	48	Coed Gawdir	76	Kilvrough Manor Woods and Redden Hill
20	Coed Simdde Lwyd	49	Melincwrt Waterfalls	77	Llanrhidian Hill
21	Cors Ian	50	Red Jacket Fen	78	Long Hole Cliff
22	Cwm Clettwr	51	Cemaes Head	79	Overton Cliff
23	Llyn Eiddwen	52	Coed Maidie B Goddard	80	Overton Mere
24	Llyn Fanod	53	Pengelli Forest	81	Peel Wood
25	Coed Penglanowen	54	Dowrog Common	82	Port Eynon Point
26	Skokholm	55	Garne Turn Rocks	83	Prior's Meadow
27	Pant Da	56	Goodwick Moor	84	Redley Cliff
28	Penderi Cliffs	57	Llangloffan Fen	85	The Lucas Reserve
29	Rhos Fullbrook				

Map of South and West Wales Wildlife Trust nature reserves

The change attracted many more members and things moved apace when, in 1946, with funds raised by an appeal to members, field study centres were established on the islands of Skokholm and, more temporarily, Skomer. Dale Fort was also purchased for use as a field centre and, in 1948, John Fursdon and William Condry were appointed wardens for Pembrokeshire and Cardigan, respectively. Grassholm was soon purchased by the RSPB, which placed it in the custody of the WWFS. Wildlife reports at the time note oil-soaked guillemots around the coast of Pembrokeshire as a result of wrecked ships and the activities in Milford Haven.

Ronald Lockley's lease on Skokholm expired in 1948 and was relinquished in favour of WWFS, which was given a 21-year lease by Dale Castle Estates. The successful recording at the Skokholm Bird Observatory, set up by Ronald Lockley in the early 1930s, continued. Orielton Duck Decoy was the next venture. In response to members of the Wildfowl Inquiry Committee, the management of this site was handed over to WWFS on 1st April 1950.

David Saunders, the first warden of Skomer, with his wife, Shirley, studying a young puffin in the early 1960s

FIFTIES' ACTIVITY

Protecting all forms of wildlife continued into the 1950s. For example, at this time the only places where red kite bred in Britain were in Carmarthenshire and Cardiganshire. Given the species' precarious state – there were only about 20 or 30 birds – WWFS realised its responsibility and gave the species serious attention and protection by keeping their nests in the area under constant observation. Discussions had been taking place over the designation of an area of Pembrokeshire coast and upland as a National Park and the Council of WWFS worked very hard to secure this. In 1952, it was pleased to report that the designation had been made and that the area would be protected from undesirable development. Further examples of WWFS activity at this time include the vociferous campaign by its President, Lord Merthyr, backed by members, to make gin traps illegal because of their cruelty and indiscriminate killing of non-target species. During the early 1950s, seabird and seal populations were monitored by frequent outings around the Pembrokeshire islands by members on WWFS' own yacht, the Mayflower ('Mab').

In 1959, Skomer island was valued at £6,000. After a successful appeal, WWFS raised £4,000 and (with help from an additional loan of £6,000) purchased the island. By immediately reselling it to the Nature Conservancy for £6,000, WWFS received a long-term lease of 42 years for the island and had enough funds left over to support a new warden and purchase a house for him. David Saunders was appointed the first warden to take up this duty in 1960 and the island was opened up for day visitors and a few hardy overnight guests. At the time, another seabird haven, St Margaret's Island in Camarthen Bay, was also held by the Trust on lease from the Picton Castle Estate.

In 1961, the progression to closer working with the Society for the Promotion of Nature Reserves (the Society) led to WWFS becoming the West Wales Naturalists' Trust (WWNT). It proceeded over the next few years to acquire land as nature reserves, one of the first being a section of Borth Bog, followed by a gift of two parcels of land at Cardiganshire Cliffs.

GLAMORGAN STARTS UP

During the late 1950s, a small group of ornithologists on Gower, who were undertaking a survey of breeding buzzards to assess their status after the outbreak of myxomatosis, were concerned that there was no single organisation for protecting land for wildlife in Glamorgan. One of them, Jo Hambury, attended the Society's first national conference for Wildlife Trusts in 1960, and an inspirational conversation with CHRISTOPHER CADBURY on the beach at Skegness, led to the founding of the Glamorgan County Naturalists' Trust (GCNT). After an inaugural meeting in January 1961, attended by Neville Douglas-Jones, Colonel Harry Morrey Salmon and Christopher Methuen-Campbell, the new Trust was incorporated the following May with the distinguished Dr Dillwyn John, Director of the National Museum of Wales, as its first President.

The start was celebrated with the first nature reserve, Broad Pool in the heart of Gower, acquired in May 1962 with the Trust Patron, Lord Lieutenant of Glamorgan Colonel Sir Cennydd George Traherne KG, receivingthe deeds from the Duke of Beaufort, to the sound of the call of a passing corncrake. Jo Hambury was an enthusiastic Chairman who built up the Trust and recruited a useful team to run the Trust's affairs including Mike Powell, Frank Tromans and John Presdee.

In the first decade, the Trust was able to acquire 800 acres of nature reserves, which remains the backbone of the sites we enjoy today, together with underwriting The National Trust's purchase of Whiteford sand dunes by supplying two thirds of the purchase price as a loan. The nature reserves consisted of: Lavernock, leased with Morrey Salmon as the first warden, followed by John Zehetmayr in 1975 until his death in 2009; Cwm Ivy Woods, the site being adjacent to land owned by a founder member Miss Betty Church

Jo Hambury – the Trust's first Chairman

who had already made up her mind to bequeath her land and the equity of her property to GCNT; Gelli Hir, purchased following an appeal dinner with guest Mr Kenneth Allsop of the BBC's *24 Hours* television programme; Ilston Quarry, under licence by His Honour Judge Rowe Harding and Mrs Harding; Abergelli Wood, under lease from John and Bill Sutton; Bolgoed Quarry, which the Trust was able to buy for a nominal sum from one of its Vice Presidents, Sir Charles Michael Dillwyn-Venables-Llewellyn; and Castle Wood Field, part of the saltings off the North Gower Coast given to the Trust by two anonymous donors. From its beginning GCNT had centred mostly around Gower and was now acquiring land further afield: Coed Cefn-Pwll-Du, a woodland situated near Caerphilly; Coed y Bedw, a mixed woodland containing beech on the outskirts of Cardiff; Craig-y-Llyn, an area of cliffs and scree above a fine corrie lake; Llyn Fach, above Treorchy; and Cwm George, an ancient woodland in the Vale of Glamorgan.

ACQUIRING LAND FOR WILDLIFE

Both GCNT and WWNT continued to operate side-by-side in a similar vein, acquiring land by purchase, donation or lease. Both organisations offered opportunities for research and study courses, monitoring planning and safeguarding habitats. Local Groups or Sections were set up, run by volunteers, and they recruited new members and got involved in potential new acquisitions for both Trusts. At Annual General Meetings or Conservation Conferences that were set up, notable speakers attended, including SIR DAVID ATTENBOROUGH, SIR PETER SCOTT, James Fisher and Dr Tom Pritchard.

For WWNT, 1968 was a significant year. It concluded a lease agreement of an area of land known then as Teifi Valley Nature Reserve, extending from the old railway station at Cardigan to Forest Wood, below Cilgerran and including the Rosehill Marsh. A preliminary survey of the reserve was carried out by Mr David White, Deputy Regional Officer of the Nature Conservancy, and a management plan was drawn up. The Teifi Foreshore, together with the riverbed, was also leased from the Crown Estate Commissioners. During this year, the property known as Skokholm Lodge (now known as Lockley Lodge) was acquired from Ronald Lockley. Together with the adjoining land at Martin's Haven, it provided a much needed mainland base for members. By the end of 1968, WWNT owned or leased nineteen nature reserves.

A Nature Reserve Agreement was signed by GCNT and the Steel Company of Wales on the large reservoir, Eglwys Nunydd, alongside the steelworks in Port Talbot. The reservoir is easily seen from the M4 motorway and, although no longer a Trust reserve, still continues to attract a large number of wildfowl, as well as anglers and boating enthusiasts.

European Conservation Year 1970 was thoroughly celebrated by both Trusts and was extremely valuable. It brought conservation to the public eye and, in the language of the 1970s, it was 'with it'. Local Authorities worked more closely with the Trusts and identified with their aims, which gave confidence to the members and officers. GCNT successfully entered Gelli Hir reserve into the Prince of Wales Countryside Awards and Christopher Methuen-Campbell, the Trust's President, opened Penrice Castle to the public to raise funds for the Trust. Highlights of the year in West Wales included the establishment of the first railway nature trail in Britain, in the Rheidol valley in Cardiganshire; the countryside exhibition at Rhandirmwym School and the

The Trust is the proud owner of Dinefwr Castle, Llandeilo

499

opening of Y Goyallt and Nant Melin nature reserves in Carmarthenshire; the publication of a number of nature trails including one taking in Lydstep Head; and an exhibition of bird paintings by Robert Gillmor. At the end of 1969, the Field Studies Council ceased to manage Skokholm. So, from the following season onwards, the Trust became wholly responsible for the staff and management of the island – the first bird observatory founded in Britain (1933) – which it had leased since 1948.

The Trusts worked tirelessly promoting nature conservation work through publications such as *Nature in Wales*, a journal published by the Trust (and, at various times, in association with NORTH WALES, BRECKNOCK and RADNORSHIRE TRUSTS) and edited by Ronald Lockley for much of its

Upland oak woodland at Coed Simdde Lwyd nature reserve

30-year existence. The Trust also published a book, *Nature of West Wales*, in 1986. Both WWNT and GCNT also produced a Trust bulletin and later a newsletter for members giving news not only of the Trusts' work but also of national importance for wildlife too. Despite endeavours for over nine years to convene a meeting of representatives of all the Trusts in Wales to discuss common problems, it was not until October 1974 that such a meeting became possible. The meeting unanimously decided to establish an association of Trusts in Wales and a draft constitution for such a body was prepared (WELSH TRUSTS, ASSOCIATION OF).

THE TRUSTS EXPAND

Conservation work by both Trusts was still largely being done on a voluntary basis. However, as both Trusts grew in size, they realised that it would be necessary to appoint paid administrative conservation staff. So, in 1976, the Trust appointed its first staff member, other than the wardens of Skokholm and Skomer. This appointment replaced Dillwyn Miles, who had served as Honorary General Secretary on a voluntary basis for 18 years.

Trust reserves or management leases continued to be acquired or disposed of through the 1970s. Significant changes for WWNT were that Lockley Lodge was first used as a visitor information centre in 1976; Old Warren Hill at Nanteos was purchased; an agreement was entered into for the Dynevor Deer Park; and, although WWNT disposed of its interest in Borth Bog to the Nature Conservancy Council, it purchased other wildlife-rich sites including Cemaes Head, Cors Goch, Ffrwdd Fen, Pengelli Forest and Rhos Pil Bach. This period also saw the successful Dyfed Wildlife Appeal, chaired by Ian Watt, which enabled the Trust to purchase Castle Woods, Coed Simdde Lwyd and Rhos Glyn-yr-Helyg nature reserves. Ian Watt became Honorary Warden of Castle Woods. The 1970s saw the consolidation of the Glamorgan Trust's estate, including the purchase of leased sites such as Coed y Bedw, and taking on management of Coed y Bwl reserve in 1972, known to many as the wild daffodil wood at Castle Upon Alun, under lease from Murray McLaggan of Merthyr Mawr Estates. The reserve was subsequently hit very hard by Dutch Elm disease, but good management of the reserve earned the Trust a Prince of Wales Award in 1975. In addition, the Trust acquired Taf Fechan, which had been earmarked as a potential reserve since the early days of the Trust.

Colonel Morrey Salmon and Mike Rush were instrumental in finally setting up Kenfig Burrows as a Local Nature Reserve. Meanwhile, the county of Glamorgan was split into West, Mid and South, and the GNT changed its name to the Glamorgan Trust for Nature Conservation (GTCN). A series of books published from 1977 onwards by Mary Gillham greatly increased people's appreciation of the richness of the natural history of the county. The Trust's support of a campaign to stop part of Crymlyn Bog being used as a rubbish tip in 1978 culminated in a judicial review which saw the whole site designated as a Site of Special Scientific Interest (SSSI), and it is now both a Ramsar and EU Natura 2000 Special Area of Conservation (SAC).

It is interesting to note that both Trusts set up a Farm Nature Reserve scheme around the same time. This resulted in informal agreements with farmers to conserve habitats and provide advice on the natural history interest of their land.

During the 1970s, the WWNT was also at the forefront of efforts to designate Skomer as a Marine Reserve. By 1972, the Trust's *Annual Report* describes how a working party had been set up and surveys were underway. This led, in 1976, to the publication of a management plan for a voluntary marine nature reserve at Skomer. This was administered by the Trust until finally, in 1990, Skomer was declared a statutory marine nature reserve (MARINE CONSERVATION).

The WWNT also played an important part in responding to several major oil spills off the Pembrokeshire coast, helping to rescue oiled birds following the Christos Bitas (1978), the Bridgeness (1985) and the Sea Empress (1996) running aground near the shoreline.

Coed y Bwl devastated by Dutch Elm disease in the 1970s

Meanwhile, the acquisition of a great crested newt site at Park Pond in 1978 was the precursor for the Glamorgan Trust finally getting a permanent home at the Nature Centre in 1982, which was opened with great celebration by HRH The Prince of Wales in April of that year. The area was added to by subsequent acquisition of the 125-hectare Park Slip Nature Park, an opencast mine site restored by British Coal with the Trust's advice.

The two Trusts relied heavily on the input of dedicated Trustees and other volunteers involved in their management. As well as others previously mentioned, some other notable Chairs included Jack Donovan, Ron Elliott, Jeffrey Raum, Dr Mary Gillham, Dr Derek Thomas, Gwyn Davies, Roy Williams, Brian Dyer, Margaret Patterson, Tom Heal, Joe Lewis, Dai Stacey and Colin Mogg.

With money from a range of funders, a significant development in West Wales was the establishment of the Welsh Wildlife Centre on the Teifi Marshes nature reserve. The building won an award for architectural design in 1993 when it was first constructed and it incorporated pioneering environmental designs of the time. It has panoramic views over the Teifi River, Cardigan town and woodland.

The award-winning Welsh Wildlife Centre at Teifi Marshes

NEW MILLENNIUM, NEW TRUST

With the beginning of the new millennium the Trusts also began a new phase. Discussions had already started on a possible merger between the Gwent, Glamorgan and West Wales Wildlife Trusts and a Development Director had been appointed to initiate this. After much deliberation, the Gwent Trust decided that this was not the right time for them to merge and dropped out of further discussions. There had been a time of uncertainty with the West Wales Wildlife Trust; a series of management issues had led to irregularities and a lack of confidence. A Charity Commission investigation helped to end a bleak chapter in the Trust's history.

However, with this behind it, the historic merger of Glamorgan and West Wales Wildlife Trust took place in April 2002, to form the fourth largest Trust by area in the UK. Derek Moore had been appointed Chief Executive and under his guidance,

and working closely with the Chairman Roy Jones, their tireless efforts ensured that the two Trusts started to work as one. Obstacles were overcome and existing members became used to being part of this new larger Trust. There was some staff restructuring during the initial period and staff quickly settled into new roles. In 2004, Dr Madeleine Havard, who had previously been the Director of Operations, was appointed as Chief Executive and with many of the teething troubles of a new organisation now dealt with, the Trust moved from strength to strength. Led by Dr Havard, Chairman Roger Turner and a supportive Board of Trustees, the Trust embarked on some large and ambitious projects including the Skomer Island Heritage Project (with Countryside Council for Wales) and enhancements to the Welsh Wildlife Centre using European Objective 1 funding.

As well as progressing its work on terrestrial wildlife, the Sea Trust, a new marine wildlife group run by volunteers, was established primarily to survey and monitor cetaceans around Pembrokeshire.

One of the outstanding achievements of the Trust started in August 2005, when the Trust was informed that Skokholm Island was going to be sold by the Dale Castle Estates. A huge challenge lay ahead to raise sufficient funds in just a few months to meet the deadline. Members and staff rose to the challenge and a public appeal was set up which received much publicity. By the beginning of 2006, with enormous generosity from all corners of the world, the vital funds for the purchase had been raised. The Trust took ownership of Skokholm on 7th April 2006 and the appeal was hailed as one of the most successful run by any Wildlife Trust.

Heading into the second decade of the new millennium brought a new Chief Executive, Sarah Kessell, and Chair, Professor Lynda Warren, both ensuring that the pace has not slowed down and that new funding and developments are made to protect and boost wildlife conservation in South and West Wales.

LD Whitehead, who had been one of the founders of the Pembrokeshire Bird Society back in 1938, sadly died shortly after the Bird Society's inaugural meeting, but his last words to its

Fin whale – spotted during a Sea Trust survey

Executive Committee were: "I want you to carry on". He would be proud to know that successor organisations have done just that!

BY DIANA CLARK AND NIGEL AJAX LEWIS
Diana has worked for the Trust for 13 years, initially as Administration Manager and currently as Executive Officer and is a keen natural historian. Nigel has over 32 years experience of working for the Wildlife Trusts and was awarded an MBE for his services to nature conservation in 2005.

Skokholm Island

CHAPTER 38

Staffordshire

If the story of this Trust was in graph form, it would resemble a roller coaster ride, with steady growth but two really steep dives!

Staffordshire is a varied and beautiful county. It has much-underrated Peak District moorland in the north, which is often confused with the Derbyshire Dales. The border of the two counties runs down the middle of the River Dove, and according to a local saying some of the best bits of Derbyshire are in Staffordshire. Travelling southwards, past the source of the River Trent, The Potteries and their immediate neighbour, Newcastle-under-Lyme, contain some interesting post-industrial sites which are havens for protected species like great crested newts and bats, but which are at risk from development.

Further south, the habitats include flower-rich meadows, a natural inland saltmarsh at Pasturefields (formed from brine extraction), lowland heath and ancient woodland on Cannock Chase, and the gravel workings of the Trent Valley, which are being transformed into new lakes and wetlands. Fast-growing plantings of the National Forest blend in with remnants of the ancient forest of Needwood. The southern county boundary then skirts the urban edge of Walsall and Wolverhampton, taking in the lowland heaths near Kinver Edge.

WEST MIDLANDS' SPIN-OFF

On 5th August 1969, the Staffordshire Nature Conservation Trust was incorporated as a new company and a registered charity. Before that it

Opposite: The Trust has undertaken extensive restoration work on otter habitats across the county

had been part of the West Midlands Trust for Nature Conservation, set up in 1957, which embraced the counties of Staffordshire, Worcestershire and Warwickshire. In the 1960s, all three counties became homes to separate Trusts, later followed by the separate creation of the Urban Wildlife Group (much later to become Birmingham and Black Country Wildlife Trust).

The small band of pioneers who signed as subscribers to the infant Staffordshire Trust were headed by the naturalist, author and broadcaster Phil Drabble. He became the Trust's President, an office which later changed to Chairman. The others were Marjorie Castellan (housewife), Richard Warren (bank cashier), Mark Thompson (company director), Greville Jacques (agent), Charles Fletcher-Twemlow (landowner), and Francis Beasley (museum keeper).

Phil Drabble, well-known as a countryman and presenter of BBC's *One Man and his Dog*, was referred to as a 'militant naturalist'. Certainly he himself had no mercy for the people he called 'green welly wallies' and 'agrichemical fat cats'. Ramblers were 'the woolly hat brigade', and the then Ministry of Agriculture were 'monumental incompetents'. He irritated many people, but they had to laugh at the same time – often just what was needed in those early days.

The Trust's first newsletter was written in 1970 and noted that 'environment' and 'ecology' had become household words. It carried a foreword by the President: "There is nothing new about nature conservation. Gamekeepers have been practising the art for centuries! Unfortunately, the species they have sought to protect have been

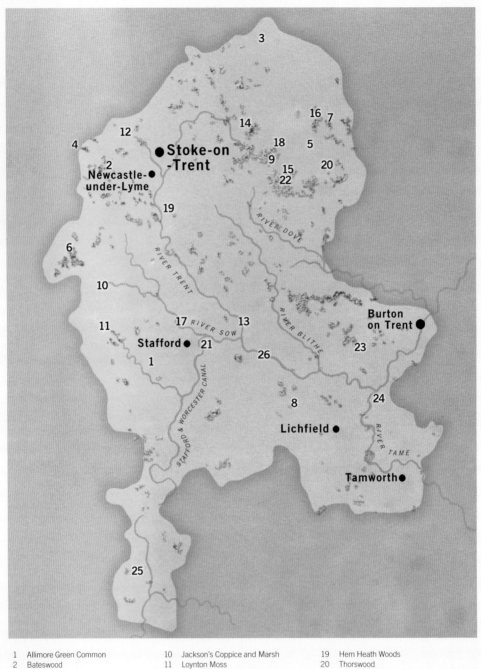

1	Allimore Green Common	10	Jackson's Coppice and Marsh	19	Hem Heath Woods
2	Bateswood	11	Loynton Moss	20	Thorswood
3	Black Brook	12	Parrot's Drumble	21	Radford Meadows
4	Black Firs and Cranberry Bog	13	Pasturefields Saltmarsh	22	Cotton Dell
5	Brown End Quarry	14	Rod Wood	23	Brankley Pastures
6	Burnt Wood	15	Side Farm Meadows	24	Croxall Lakes
7	Castern Wood	16	Weag's Barn	25	Highgate Common
8	George's Hayes	17	Doxey Marshes	26	Wolseley Centre
9	Harston Wood	18	Ipstones Edge		

Map of Staffordshire Wildlife Trust nature reserves

limited to the 'game birds' and animals used as sporting quarry. . . So, if we are to preserve the wild plants and creatures which have made England such a pleasant land, it will be necessary to do some 'gamekeeping', not only for pheasants but also for the whole spectrum of our wildlife. . . Only by doing so can we maintain the heritage for others yet to come and for wild creatures which might otherwise become extinct."

The Trust's registered office was the home of Treasurer, Richard Warren, the county recorder for butterflies and moths. Founder members included Eric Edees, author of the 1972 *Flora of Staffordshire*, and Keith Goodway of Keele University.

In 1970, the Trust bought its first nature reserve, 33 acres of Loynton Moss, near Woodseaves, not far from Stafford – one of a group of wetlands in this region known as the 'Meres and Mosses'. A Management Committee was set up under one of the Trustees, bird expert Frank Gribble. He was awarded the MBE in 1996 for services to nature conservation, and is still an active member of many local organisations.

FORMATIVE YEARS AND PEOPLE

The Trust spent the first two decades of its life consolidating its position. In 1971, membership was 286 and, by 1972, it had almost doubled. Phil Drabble was succeeded by Spencer Copeland, then Leslie Wiggins. More nature reserves were purchased, the first Conservation Officer, Mary Pratt, was appointed, and the Trust acquired its first headquarters in 1973 – a room above a shop in Stafford. The Trust also took over the patch of derelict land next door and made it into an urban wildlife garden – a very novel idea in those days!

Mary Pratt's successor was Colin Beard (1983), followed by Victoria Birch (1987). The first full-time Administration Officer was John Drewett (1986). In 1989 Sue Lawley joined as Conservation Officer. At the time, Martin Adams worked as a volunteer but later joined the staff as Administration Assistant. Both are still senior staff members. By 1981, the Trust had acquired more nature

Frank Gribble at Loynton Moss in 1969

reserves and a new Chairman – Michael Swales. Swales had been a member of the old West Midlands Trust for Nature Conservation, and a founder member of the Staffordshire Trust. He was the biology specialist at Denstone College and also an explorer who led several expeditions to the evocatively-named Inaccessible Island (part of the archipelago of Tristan da Cunha in the South Atlantic). He formed the Trust's first Education Committee in 1969 and produced one of its first publications *Natural History Sites in Staffordshire*. His Vice Chairman was Richard Tribbeck, a biology lecturer at Staffordshire Polytechnic (now University).

FIRST URBAN RESERVES

Another formidable Trustee was Maurice Waterhouse, RSPB warden of Coombes Valley nature reserve, who chaired the Reserves Committee and helped to acquire the Trust's first urban reserves in North Staffordshire from the Coal Board. They included: Parrot's Drumble ('drumble' is a long, narrow woodland) one of the best bluebell woods in the county despite its bright orange stream caused by pollution from old coal seams; Hem Heath Wood, now linked with the Trust management of adjoining woodland owned by the Wedgwood estate; and Bateswood, an old opencast site which now has lapwings, skylarks, great crested newts, and is one of the best dragonfly sites in the county.

Three stalwarts of the Trust (left to right): Richard Tribbeck, Frank Gribble and Michael Swales

In 1984, the Trust headquarters moved to Coutts House in Sandon. The Trust magazine noted that: "we now have a genuine two-line, four-extension telephone system. . . who knows? we might soon be linked to a high-powered on-line computer. . . we had a bit of trouble with the wiring."

Membership was now 1,650. Under Swales' and Tribbeck's leadership the Trust continued to prosper. In 1985–86, the establishment of the Government's Manpower Services Commission enabled 50 unemployed young people, under the leadership of Richard Mellor, to work on various Trust reserves across the county and at the National Garden Festival in Stoke-on-Trent. In 1988, the Commission came to an end, with a huge loss to the Trust of both income and volunteers. Conservation efforts suffered, and the Trust struggled to increase membership to more than 2,000.

In spite of looming difficulties, Staffordshire was one of the first Trusts to become a Wildlife Trust by name. Market research had shown that TV and radio had made 'wildlife' much more of an exciting word than 'nature conservation'. To coincide with the Trust's 21st birthday, the Staffordshire Wildlife Trust was officially launched in 1990.

DOWN BUT NOT OUT

By 1991, the country was in economic recession, fundraising had never been harder and eventually the Trust seriously considered closing down. Instead it made a decision, bravely proposed by Trustee JOHN MACMILLAN, later to be appointed Honorary Secretary of the Royal Society for Nature Conservation (the Society). The Trust wouldn't close, and if it was to go down, it would go down fighting. So everyone increased their efforts. They drew up a Development Plan, Richard Mellor was appointed as the Trust's first Chief Executive, and collective fingers were crossed.

Macmillan's vision paid off and by the end of 1991 the Trust had been saved, mainly by legacies from some wonderful people – Mrs Ethel Mary Proctor and Mrs Hazel Winefred Dishley whose late husband had previously indicated that he would like their estate to eventually go to the Trust. These bequests provided the Trust with more than £250,000. The money was invested carefully and has provided the core of financial stability ever since.

On the occasion of the Trust's silver jubilee in 1994 there were celebrations all round. BBC Radio Stoke broadcast the Trust's celebratory church service from the village of Eccleshall.

In 1995, SIR DAVID ATTENBOROUGH, as President of The Wildlife Trusts, came to launch an exhibition

Bluebells at Brankley Pastures

by the Bat Group at the Potteries Museum. He agreed to be a guest presenter on a BBC Radio Stoke programme, *Country Wise,* covering a Trust public bat walk at Westport Lake in Stoke-on-Trent. Bat detectors picked up echolocations from five species of bat. It was great radio and was able to make the links between Sir David's worldwide programmes and the importance of local wildlife.

ALL CHANGE AT THE TOP

But in the spring of 1995 changes were ahead. Tribbeck announced his resignation, shortly followed unexpectedly by Swales who had to resign suddenly for family reasons. With 24 hours' notice, a new Chairman, Pat Callaghan, was proposed and some weeks later she was formally elected at the Trust's Annual General Meeting. Callaghan was a long-standing Trustee and professionally, a radio presenter.

Then in the summer of 1996, a very human disaster happened – the Trust's Chief Executive Officer, Mellor, was diagnosed with cancer. He carried on working for the Trust as much as he could over a period of several months until four days before his death in the spring of 1997. Some of the staff and Trustees had become his close friends, and the experience took a considerable toll on everybody's morale.

It is to the staff's enormous credit that during this time they not only kept the Trust going, but also put in a successful bid to the Heritage Lottery Fund. This brought a capital works grant of £459,000 for work over five years on 15 of the Trust's nature reserves. The grant also paid for a new vehicle, tools and a volunteers' coordinator, Shaun Rimmer, who is still with the Trust.

A new Chief Executive, Ali Fraser, joined in November 1997, and had the difficult job of sorting out the Trust's now tangled administration. She did this with efficiency, tact, and chocolate! But when she left 15 months later, the Trust had still not really recovered, and many of those involved felt the Trust was horribly adrift once more.

In 1999, Guy Corbett-Marshall took up the post of Chief Executive and the Trust began to move in the right direction again. That year was the Trust's

Weaver Hills, north Staffordshire

30th anniversary, the Staffordshire Biodiversity Action Plan was launched and the county's Biological Records Centre was established in partnership with Staffordshire County Council and Stoke-on-Trent City Council's Potteries Museum. The then President of The Wildlife Trusts, DAVID BELLAMY, opened an Environmental Education Centre north-east of Stoke-on-Trent. This was a Trust partnership with The National Grid which lasted until 2006.

FROM RUIN TO ECO-FRIENDLY HQ

By now the Trust's headquarters at Coutts House was bursting at the seams. In 2001, a local developer approached the Trust to suggest a donation, with a substantial endowment, of some 26 acres of land next to which he wanted to build several houses. The land was at Wolseley Bridge, near Stafford, on the banks of the River Trent with lakes, trees, otters and water voles together with a part-finished building. It was part of the Wolseley family estate and had been developed as a garden park. Sadly, however, it had been on the market for eight years and was badly vandalised. When the Trust's Chairman signed on the dotted line, the Trust's solicitor said to her: "Congratulations, you're now the proud owner of a ruin"! In 2003, with funding and huge support from many sources, the Trust moved into its new eco-friendly headquarters complete with on-site education and visitor centre.

The Trust continued to develop rapidly under Callaghan and Corbett-Marshall. When Corbett-Marshall joined the Trust he took on the mammoth task of project managing the building of the Wolseley Centre, while running the Trust at the same time. In 2006, Callaghan was awarded the Society's CHRISTOPHER CADBURY MEDAL for services to nature conservation. In 2007, she stepped down as Chairman, still continuing as Honorary Secretary.

The current Chairman, Vince Smith, has continued the progress they made. He is a long-standing Trustee and, professionally, a corporate treasurer of an international construction company. He is also a widely-experienced naturalist who makes charcoal and goes sea-kayaking. Under his chairmanship the Trust's membership has grown to more than 16,000.

EVER-EXPANDING ACTIVITIES

The Trust has continued to expand its range of activities, particularly with community and education initiatives. These include the Wildplay project working with schools and the establishment of a countywide network of WILDLIFE WATCH groups. The Trust has taken a lease on a newly-built urban visitor centre at Westport Lake, Stoke-on-Trent. The reeds planted at this site originally came from

Children getting back to nature with the Trust's Wildplay scheme

the Trust's first reserve, Loynton Moss. The Trust has also continued to acquire nature reserves including, in 2009, Highgate Common, a country park in the south-west of the county. The Trust also now has outreach staff based in several premises across the county.

By 2010, landscape-scale conservation in Staffordshire was really taking off. Grassland restoration work that had started around Thorswood nature reserve in the Weaver Hills expanded into the nearby Churnet Valley. The Trust also broadened its work to encompass woodland and river management in this area.

PIONEERING WETLAND PROJECTS

Building on years of work creating habitats for otters and other wetland species through the national Otters and Rivers and Water for Wildlife projects, the Trust launched three large-scale Living Landscape areas in 2010. Grassland restoration work in the Weaver Hills expanded into the wooded river valley of the River Churnet, while the Staffordshire Washlands scheme and the Central Rivers Initiative are restoring wetland habitats across the floodplains and quarries of lowland Staffordshire's River Trent valleys. A national pilot project for the Department for the Environment, Food and Rural Affairs, Farming Floodplains for the Future, was also launched to study the potential role of the farmed environment in flood risk management. It is re-profiling rivers in order to combat flooding further downstream, combining the cooperation of landowners, agri-environment funding from Natural England, and the support of other partners, including the Rivers Sow and Penk Internal Drainage Board.

NEWTS VERSUS JOBS?

Staffordshire has industry in both its rural and urban areas. Quarrying, ceramics and coal mining in particular have left the county many post-industrial sites which are in the process of regeneration. But there are still conflicts between the protection of the natural environment and the need for employment – so-called 'newts versus jobs'.

The Trust's current home at the Wolseley Centre, Wolseley Bridge

A planning example took local residents of Tunstall, with Trust support, to a Parliamentary Joint Committee in 1999 – a very rare occurrence – over the need to replace compulsory purchase of Public Open Space with land of 'equal advantage' to the residents as required by law. Evidence was given under oath, the Committee issued a Special Report, only the sixth made so far. The opposing QC admitted informally (after having challenged the Trust's evidence for the beneficial effects on people of contact with nature) that the case may have set a precedent for discussing and accepting the advantages of green spaces for people's well-being probably for the first time in a legal setting. Although the case then went to the High Court, the final decision was taken by the Secretary of State (John Prescott) that the extra replacement land would not be where the residents, the Public Inquiry Inspector, the Joint Committee, and the High Court had all recommended. There was no more the residents and the Trust could do.

However, in 2006, when Staffordshire County Council wanted to extend a business park, the Trust pointed out the existence of three great crested newt breeding ponds. To its great credit, the County Council withdrew its application, delivered a massive translocation scheme, and although it resulted in a delay, earned the Council a national environmental award.

Approaching 2012, the economic storm clouds have gathered again, this time worldwide, and the future for charities is far from clear. Nevertheless, the Trust's membership is still more than 16,000, with over 500 volunteers taking an active part in everything from conservation work parties to administration and planning issues. The Trust is one of the biggest landholders in Staffordshire. It gives advice to farmers, other landholders, local authorities, groups and individuals; influences strategic local authority committees, has a good relationship with local MPs; and promotes community and education activities at Wolseley, Westport and across the county. Its Local Members' Groups, Specialist Groups and volunteers make up a substantial workforce and everyone looks forward to the Trust's work continuing into the future.

BY PAT CALLAGHAN

Pat Callaghan is Honorary Secretary of the Staffordshire Wildlife Trust. In 2006, she was awarded the Society's Christopher Cadbury medal for services to nature conservation. In 2009, she was given an Honorary Award of Doctor of Staffordshire University for her contribution to, among other things, the Staffordshire Wildlife Trust.

CHAPTER 39

Suffolk

"The telephone rang in my office and it was Jock Cranbrook (Earl of Cranbrook) on the line. Apart from being a friend, I was his banker and as such I was a local director in charge of the branches in Suffolk and north Essex. Jock knew that I was involved in the production of the *Floral Atlas of British Wild Flowers*. He told me that someone had reported that a rare spider had been found at Redgrave and Lopham Fen and also that the Waveney River Board wished something could be done to tidy up the area at the head of the river.

Jock suggested that we should both visit the area the next day. After a time he located the spider and asked me to tell him what I had found of interest flower-wise. Well, I had seen masses of green rushes and precious little else of interest, when suddenly I came across a colony of marsh orchids, one of which was albino. We both felt that a Society or Trust to improve and protect the area should be formed. We put together a committee of people who would know Suffolk well, and that is how it all began."

This is how Mike Bendix recalled the starting point of the Suffolk Trust. Like several other Wildlife Trusts, Suffolk came to fruition in 1961. The move was instigated by the late Earl of Cranbrook and Mike Bendix, together with other notable members of the Suffolk Naturalists' Society, following the aforementioned visit to Redgrave and Lopham Fen. The organisation was then, of course, the Suffolk Trust for Nature Conservation in line with most others.

Opposite: Trimley Marshes nature reserve
Right: Earl of Cranbrook, one of the Trust's founders

Given that Norfolk had started its own Naturalists' Trust in 1926, Suffolk was lagging behind. The Trust relied heavily on a large number of volunteers to hold any activity together. By 1970, there were still only about 300 members and, by all accounts, only about half of them actually paid their subscriptions. The Trust had seven nature reserves, but these were leased or managed by agreement – the Trust scarcely owned anything.

John Trist became part-time Conservation Officer for little more than travelling expenses. He was a highly proficient botanist who had been an agricultural adviser with the Wartime Agricultural Executive Committee. Much to his regret, in this role he had been responsible for ordering large areas of old pasture to be ploughed up. He set up a technical committee to advise on reserve management and new acquisitions. John Shackles from the Nature Conservancy Council, and a member of this committee, described meetings as "delightful occasions when we would stroll around reserves on sunny summer weekdays armed with our binoculars and hand-lenses contemplating nature and discussing what ought to be done over a pub lunch".

513

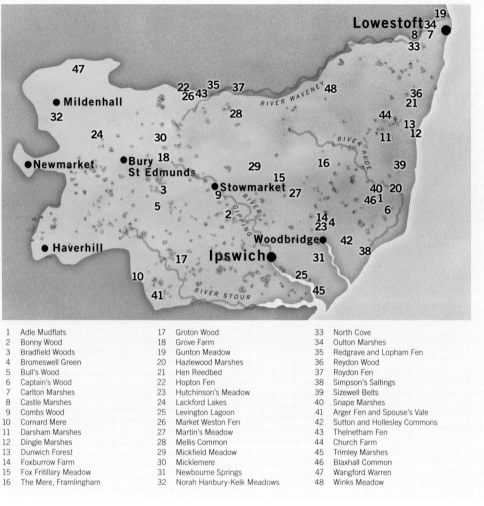

Map of Suffolk Wildlife Trust nature reserves

1	Adle Mudflats	17	Groton Wood	33	North Cove		
2	Bonny Wood	18	Grove Farm	34	Oulton Marshes		
3	Bradfield Woods	19	Gunton Meadow	35	Redgrave and Lopham Fen		
4	Bromeswell Green	20	Hazlewood Marshes	36	Reydon Wood		
5	Bull's Wood	21	Hen Reedbed	37	Roydon Fen		
6	Captain's Wood	22	Hopton Fen	38	Simpson's Saltings		
7	Carlton Marshes	23	Hutchinson's Meadow	39	Sizewell Belts		
8	Castle Marshes	24	Lackford Lakes	40	Snape Marshes		
9	Combs Wood	25	Levington Lagoon	41	Arger Fen and Spouse's Vale		
10	Cornard Mere	26	Market Weston Fen	42	Sutton and Hollesley Commons		
11	Darsham Marshes	27	Martin's Meadow	43	Thelnetham Fen		
12	Dingle Marshes	28	Mellis Common	44	Church Farm		
13	Dunwich Forest	29	Mickfield Meadow	45	Trimley Marshes		
14	Foxburrow Farm	30	Micklemere	46	Blaxhall Common		
15	Fox Fritillary Meadow	31	Newbourne Springs	47	Wangford Warren		
16	The Mere, Framlingham	32	Norah Hanbury-Kelk Meadows	48	Winks Meadow		

FIRST BIG APPEAL

After 1976, a number of local members' groups were formed and efforts to gain publicity undertaken. TV chef, Delia Smith, was one who helped to gain profile in those days. During this time, the Trust raised its first meaningful appeal to purchase Groton Wood. The landowner was on the verge of applying for the generous grant then available for clear-felling and uprooting to convert unwanted woodland to arable. The Trust's appeal succeeded in raising £20,000 including a donation from the late Queen Mother. The impetus from this effort gave a kick-start to the Trust and from then on it never looked back.

FIRST TRUST RESERVE

In 1977, the first full-time member of staff was employed when Group Captain Freddie Sledmere became General Secretary. His contribution was immense. He started up the Trust's local group network almost single-handed and generally made the Trust a going concern. The organisation was at last moving forward and in 1980, with new confidence, the Trust purchased Carlton Marshes in the Suffolk Broads, with great support from the Norfolk naturalist, Ted Ellis.

Freddie Sledmere retired in 1981, having increased the Trust's membership from 900 to 5,000 and was succeeded by Lieutenant Colonel Tom Pares. During Freddie's time the Trust made possibly its most important decision to date when it employed Richard Woolnough as its first full-time Conservation Officer, after John Trist moved away from Suffolk. Richard's background as a civil engineer building London's flood defences and his hobby of ballooning made him an unlikely candidate. But any misgivings were overwhelmed by his obviously deep commitment to nature conservation and his enormous energy and enthusiasm. He complemented Freddie's work on the ground and soon organised volunteers for each reserve and to serve on the various committees.

Richard Woolnough's energy led to a massive Manpower Services Commission project being awarded to the Trust in the 1980s. It meant that 200 unemployed people were able to work for the Trust in exchange for training and the ability to find employment. They included scientists, education staff and field workers. This workforce was divided into project-based teams, such as the Sandlings, Estuaries, Woodlands and Brecks.

At the same time, the Trust's Council decided to dispense with the post of General Secretary and appoint a professional Director to take the Trust forward.

1980S GROWTH

In 1985, Derek Moore was appointed the first Director of the Trust. He was already well known in Suffolk as County Bird Recorder and Chairman of the Suffolk Naturalists' Society. What was probably more important was that he had worked for many years in management in the printing and publishing industry. Under his leadership the Trust started to grow very quickly and raised its profile substantially. This period coincided with the setting up of BBC Radio Suffolk whose then Managing Editor, Ivan Howlett, provided extraordinary opportunities for the Trust. So too did the *East Anglian Daily Times* with reporters David Green and John Grant constantly providing coverage of Trust activities.

At this time, the Trust was well into an appeal led by Lord Henniker which was part of the national

Koniks from Poland grazing at Hen Reedbeds, where they are used to manage wetland habitats

Reydon Wood

BRITISH WILDLIFE APPEAL. The Trust had also, with the RSPB, decided to oppose the extension of Felixstowe Docks. This was quite a new venture for the Trust, but it certainly did no harm. Trust membership grew on the back of this opposition campaign and the outcome was the creation of Trimley Marshes nature reserve.

A setback occurred when Richard Woolnough decided to take a post in Lincoln at the Royal Society for Nature Conservation (the Society). But by now a growing team of excellent staff was in place. When the Manpower Services project came to an end, the Council took the brave decision to use £100,000 of legacy funds to employ supervisors to keep the habitat projects going. This signified a most important and exciting decade for the Trust.

A series of visionary Chairmen and other officers, together with an outstanding staff team supported by vibrant members' groups and volunteers, enabled the Trust to take huge strides forward. Suffolk led the movement as a whole with a number of initiatives. For instance, when the Countryside Commission funded an open reserves project seeking to make every Trust reserve accessible by all, there was vociferous opposition from the national movement's old guard who feared a loss of membership. However, the opposite happened and Suffolk's membership grew. Suffolk also led the move to change the name to Wildlife Trusts as a more memorable title for the public.

This was achieved despite some people feeling that wildlife excluded flora.

The Trust built a centre at Carlton Marshes and after renting Foxburrow Farm, Melton, for some years, purchased the property from Trust supporters Robin and Tim Miller. This enabled the Trust to set up an education project giving thousands of schoolchildren the opportunity to learn about the natural world of their county.

The number of reserves increased with acquisitions of Lackford Lakes, Bonny Wood, Spouse's Vale, Hazelwood Marshes, Castle Marshes and Reydon Wood. In addition, Lord Henniker made a gift of the sizeable Mellis Common to the Trust. At this time the Trust also took the ownership and management responsibility of Bradfield Woods from the Society (see NATURE RESERVES OWNED BY THE SOCIETY).

NATIONAL ATTENTION

In 1994, as a result of Mary Brooke's generous legacy of her home, the Trust was able to move from rented accommodation in Saxmundham and develop Brooke House, Ashbocking as its main office. Because of the Trust's high profile locally, it also received Grove Farm, Thurston as a legacy. The owner only knew of the Trust by reading about its activities in the local press.

The Trust's various conservation projects were attracting national attention with the Sandlings Project winning the Ford Conservation Award. This enabled the Trust to purchase its first flock of sheep to graze the heathlands. Recognising the importance of agriculture and its effects on our wildlife, the Trust was a strong supporter of the Suffolk Farming and Wildlife Group and produced an important discussion document entitled *Seeds of Change*. This brought the Trust into the debate on how European initiatives such as set-aside and other agri-environment schemes might be used to benefit wildlife.

The review of County Wildlife Sites was another key activity which not only highlighted important areas at a Suffolk level but also assisted landowners in finding funding to carry out management.

As part of the Trust's Community Programme two teams of volunteers – unemployed, retired and students – led by trained leaders carried out work on both private land and the Trust's own reserves.

Some enormous tasks were also accomplished in this time. Redgrave and Lopham Fen, the basis for the Trust's existence, was drying out because of abstraction by the adjacent public water supply borehole. It became a case of 'do something or lose it'. A major restoration project was instigated in partnership with Essex and Suffolk Water, the Environment Agency and English Nature. Funding from the partners and the EU Life programme moved the borehole – the first time this had been done in Europe to protect a wetland. The face of the reserve was transformed with the removal of over 80 acres of scrub and the land returned to wet fen. Polish koniks were brought in to graze the sedge beds and the fen raft spider had a chance to enhance its numbers and the lost flora to return. The innovative nature of the restoration project resulted in it winning the Ford Conservation Award and Eurosite's Natura 2000 Award.

The Trust was now confident of its ability to take on major projects. In 1998, nearly 100 acres alongside Norman Gwatkin reserve were purchased with HERITAGE LOTTERY FUND (HLF) support to create the new Hen Reedbeds reserve and habitat for bitterns. Further down the coast, Dingle Marshes at Dunwich was acquired in a unique partnership with the RSPB.

The fen raft spider almost disappeared from Redgrave and Lopham Fen, but is now recovering due to the restoration of its habitat

ACCEPTANCE AND RECOGNITION

By the late 1990s, membership had risen towards 15,000 and staff, projects and reserves had increased enormously. Major efforts were being made to attract sizeable legacies to fund running costs. Although money was readily available for projects, cash for core costs was difficult to obtain. The balancing act of keeping the organisation afloat in those days was a great tribute to the Trust's Executive and especially the Honorary Treasurer, David Brow, who supervised the finances of the Trust for more than ten years.

The Trust had been accepted into county life and was now regarded as *the* nature conservation body working for wildlife in the county. Pragmatism had enabled the Trust to find many partners to achieve much for Suffolk's wildlife. In 1999, in recognition of his achievements, Derek Moore received an OBE and moved to take the post of Director of Conservation with the Society, at the hub of The Wildlife Trusts movement.

Julian Roughton, formerly Head of Conservation at the Trust, took on the reins as Director from January 1999. It was a time of great opportunity with new grants, such as the HLF, and agri-environment schemes which enabled the Trust to invest in the management of its reserves. New centres opened at Lackford Lakes and Redgrave and Lopham Fen so that nearly 14,000 children now come through the Trust's centre-based education programmes every year. Outside the centres, the Trust has an active programme of engagement with young people through Watch groups (WILDLIFE WATCH), youth projects and activities on reserves and Forest Schools.

HLF grants, supported by members' appeals, enabled the purchase of new reserves such as Captain's Wood and Micklemere as well as further extensions to established reserves such as Redgrave and Lopham Fen, and Hen Reedbeds. Making nature reserves larger became a priority. To enable this, all legacies were set aside to fund the acquisition of new land or other such projects that would have a lasting benefit for wildlife. As a result, Lackford Lakes, Market Weston Fen, Bradfield Woods, Church Farm and many other reserves were extended through

The Sandlings Heaths are home to heathland wildlife such as woodlark, nightjar, grayling and adder

land acquisition. At Spouse's Vale, a 44-acre arable field was purchased and allowed to develop through natural regeneration, to connect two ancient woodlands. Within a few years, it was a thicket of ash saplings and already being used by dormice.

Alongside the expansion of reserves there was a parallel review of smaller reserves to ensure that it was still appropriate for the Trust to manage these. Where there was no public access or long-term security for the Trust reserves under management agreements, they were returned to owners to manage but with advice from the Trust. Some others with low conservation value, but valued as amenity sites, were transferred to local community ownership.

LIVING LANDSCAPES

The Trust took on the concept of Living Landscapes with alacrity as it reflected the Trust's vision in the Suffolk Broads, Breckland, Sandlings, Alde to Blyth, Valley Fens and South Suffolk Woods. The largest project in Suffolk is the transformation of Dunwich Forest, alongside Dingle Marshes, in partnership with the Forestry Commission and the RSPB. Here the Trust has introduced Dartmoor ponies to 800 acres of forest and a mosaic of wood pasture and heathland is being created through grazing and by felling conifers.

The Sandlings heaths have undergone a major restoration as extensive stands of conifer and birch have been felled and lost heathland landscapes have re-emerged. The Trust's Exmoor ponies and Hebridean sheep graze over 1,000 acres of heathland – a stronghold of nightjar, woodlark and Dartford warbler. The Trust is increasingly working with the Forestry Commission and taking leases on land to link up and improve connectivity between heathlands.

In the wider landscape, the Trust's activity extends beyond wildlife sites to safeguard vulnerable species. The Trust's Water for Wildlife project led the recovery of otter and water vole populations across Suffolk's rivers. This was made possible by the active involvement of hundreds of landowners in a mink-trapping project coordinated by the Trust. The results have been extraordinary, with water vole populations recovering on rivers where the species had formerly disappeared.

WORKING WITH THE FARMING COMMUNITY

The Trust has been conspicuous in working with the farming community, aided by many of the Trust's Chairmen being farmers themselves. Concerns over the decline of farmland species led to the Trust appointing two farmland advisers and targeting advice to restore populations of species for which Suffolk once had a significant population. Amongst the species benefiting are the dormouse, great crested newt, barn owl, harvest mouse and tree sparrow. Barn owl populations have tripled over the past ten years through the Trust's advice to landowners on habitat creation, coupled with the provision of nestboxes.

Central to the restoration projects and working with farmers has been the availability of funds through agri-environment schemes since the mid-1980s. The first of these, the Environmentally Sensitive Area agreements, were targeted at Breckland, the Broads and Suffolk River Valleys. Today, the Higher Level Stewardship scheme is critical for the management of SSSIs and for supporting landowners undertaking conservation measures on farmland.

The increasing scale and complexity of the Trust's work meant that it was no longer possible to run the Trust through a large Council of Trustees. New governance arrangements were approved in 2005, which reduced the number of Trustees from 25 to 12 on a Board of Trustees that replaced the Executive and Council Committees.

Martha Meek with four barn owl chicks raised through the successful nestbox scheme
Above right: Tree sparrow

50TH ANNIVERSARY

By 2011 – the Trust's 50th anniversary year – membership had grown to more than 25,000. Amongst the highlights of 2011 was the opening of a green oak centre at Bradfield Woods and a new reserve in the Suffolk Broads. Work at Oulton and Carlton Marshes, on the outskirts of Lowestoft, is linking three Trust reserves through the acquisition of adjoining grassland and restoration of water levels. This benefits vulnerable species such as the Norfolk hawker dragonfly.

Suffolk Wildlife Trust has grown to an extent that its founders could never have envisaged. As well as managing 6,600 acres of nature reserves, the Trust is active in 75 per cent of parishes by supporting community-based conservation projects. These manage historic commons and churchyards and also create new woodlands and ponds.

Volunteers still remain at the Trust's heart and, with over 1,000 volunteers supporting education, conservation and reserves management, their contribution is as vital as ever. Although growing public appreciation of the natural world bodes well for the future, Suffolk still faces growing pressures from development and balancing the demands of modern agriculture with the needs of the environment.

BY JULIAN ROUGHTON AND DEREK MOORE
Julian Roughton started work with Suffolk Wildlife Trust in 1985, as a volunteer coppicing at Bradfield Woods, before taking up roles as Woodland Surveyor and then Breckland Project Officer for the Trust's Manpower Services Commission scheme. He returned as Conservation Manager in 1995 and has been Chief Executive since 1999.

Initially, a volunteer for many years, Derek Moore became the Trust's first Director in 1984. He was awarded the OBE for services to nature conservation in 1999, when he was also appointed Director of Conservation for the Royal Society of Wildlife Trusts (the Society). In 2001, he became CEO of the Wildlife Trust of South and West Wales until he retired in 2004.

CHAPTER 40

Surrey

On 21st March 1959, a provisional committee formally launched The Surrey Naturalists' Trust at an inaugural meeting in Surrey County Council's council chamber.

After 52 years many things, not least the Trust's name, have changed. But the motivation that inspired the founders is still fundamental to all the Trust's activites today.

Alderman Sir Cyril Black, Chairman of Surrey County Council, chaired that first meeting. About 100 people attended, including representatives from Surrey's natural history and amenity societies and other official bodies, many of whom still work in the Trust today.

In 1979, the late John Sankey, one of the founders, recalled that it was "the National Parks and Access to the Countryside Act of 1949 which gave great stimulus to the formation of the County Naturalists' Trusts. Surrey was caught up in the stream in the late fifties when John Clegg of the Haslemere Educational Museum, CAPTAIN CYRIL DIVER, CB, CBE and I exchanged letters on the possibility of forming a Trust. A steering committee met under the chairmanship of Cyril Diver at his home in Frensham and he became our first President".

In April 1960, Trust membership totalled 155. Since then the Trust has grown many times over, issuing more than 15,000 invitations for its latest Annual General Meeting.

SILVER JUBILEE

The Trust marked its silver jubilee in 1984 by appointing DAVID BELLAMY as President. In the celebratory newsletter he wrote: "Thursley Bog, now part of a National Nature Reserve, is of course very dear both to my feet and to my heart. It was on Thors Stone that I became engaged to be married and 1984 is our 25th wedding anniversary too!"

Opposite: Stonechat – a bird of Surrey heathlands. Above: Seale Chalk Pit – the Trust's first nature reserve

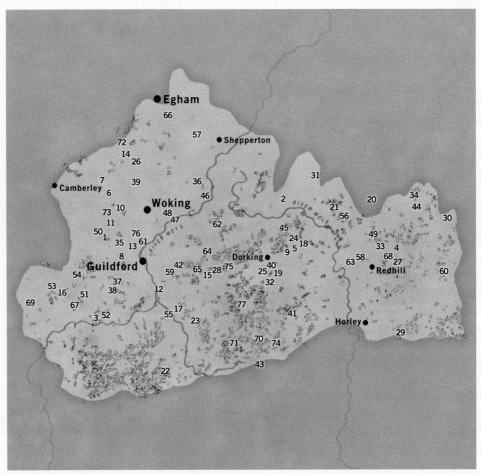

1	Ash Ranges	27	Graeme Hendrey Wood	53	Runfold Wood
2	Ashtead Park	28	Hackhurst Downs	54	Seale Chalk Pit
3	Bagmoor Common	29	Hedgecourt	55	Seccombe's Wood
4	Bay Pond	30	Hill Park	56	Shabden Park
5	Betchworth Quarry and Lime Kilns	31	Howell Hill	57	Sheepwalk Lake
6	Bisley and West End Commons	32	Inholms Claypit	58	Spynes Mere
7	Brentmoor Heath	33	Kitchen Copse	59	St Martha's Hill
8	Broadstreet and Backside Commons	34	Littlefield Common	60	Staffhurst Wood
9	Brockham Lime Works	35	Littlefield Common	61	Stringer's Common
10	Brookwood Lye	36	Manor Farm	62	The Forest
11	Burners Heath and Swallows Pond	37	McAlmont Reserves	63	The Moors
12	Chinthurst Hill	38	Middlebriars Wood	64	The Sheepleas
13	Chitty's Common	39	Milford Green and Coxhill Green	65	The Shere Woodlands
14	Chobham Common	40	Milton Heath and The Nower	66	Thorpe Hay Meadow
15	Colekitchen Down	41	Newdigate Brickworks	67	Thundry Meadows
16	Crooksbury Hill	42	Newlands Corner and Silent Pool	68	Tilburstow Hill
17	Cucknells Wood	43	Norbury Park	69	Underdown
18	Dawcombe	44	Nore Hill Chalk Pinnacle	70	Vann Lake
19	Deepdene Terrace	45	Nower Wood	71	Wallis Wood
20	Dollypers Hill	46	Ockham and Wisley Commons	72	Wentworth
21	Fames Rough	47	Papercourt Marshes	73	West Humble Bat Reserve
22	Fir Tree Copse	48	Papercourt Meadows	74	Whippets Cant
23	Fowls Copse	49	Quarry Hangers	75	White Downs
24	Fraser Down	50	Pirbright Ranges	76	Whitmoor and Rickford Common
25	Glory Wood	51	Puttenham Common	77	Wotton, Abinger and Broadmoor
26	Gracious Pond	52	Rodborough Common		Commons

Map of Surrey Wildlife Trust nature reserves

But it was not all good news. FRANK PERRING, General Secretary of the Royal Society for Nature Conservation (the Society), wrote congratulating the Trust on reaching this milestone but warned, "The wildlife of Britain is at crisis point. . . destruction and damage continue – in some counties 95 per cent of old meadows have already been lost and 50% of ancient woodland has been destroyed or turned to conifers. . . in these circumstances it becomes urgent that your Trust has the resources, the manpower and the influence to safeguard as many Sites of Special Scientific Interest (SSSIs) as possible by purchase or agreement and the ability to manage them".

STEWARDS OF ICONIC COUNTRYSIDE

This provoked an enthusiastic response and over the next 40 years, mainly as a result of gifts and purchases, the Trust's landholding and status grew steadily. But it really blossomed in 2002 when, with Paul Wickham at the helm, the Trust entered into a unique partnership with Surrey County Council for the management of the Council's countryside estate and its access agreements with four major landowners. This included some of the most iconic countryside in Surrey – Norbury Park, Newlands Corner and Chobham Common, the largest National Nature Reserve in southern England.

A similar contract with Mole Valley District Council and a conservation grazing agreement with the Ministry of Defence mean that the Trust now manages 85 sites covering more than 9,000 hectares, including five working farms and a herd of 300 Belted Galloway cattle. Surrey Wildlife Trust is recognised as a major land manager and conservation body in the south-east.

The problems confronting Surrey's wildlife today show remarkable similarity to those it faced in the 1950s and 60s, but our ability to address them is

Visitors enjoying the view over Chobham Common

now vastly improved. They include scrub encroachment on heathland and chalk downland. In the summer of 1962, the magazine *Country-Side* recorded 276 commons in the county, covering 26,871 acres or almost six per cent of Surrey's land surface. The article commented, "Surrey is unique among the lowland counties of Britain in the number and variety of its commons. The attempt to conserve at least a few of the more interesting of these before it is too late has been the major effort of the Trust. Apart from the obvious threats to the commons resulting from the spread of human populations in a county so near to London – housing and factory needs and devastating fires caused by careless picnickers from the urban areas, a new danger has arisen in recent years. . . this is the change in what has come to be considered the characteristic vegetation of the heaths and commons. It is, perhaps, hard to realise that the traditional plant association of ling, bilberry, gorse and bracken with an occasional birch or pine tree, is largely a man-made pattern. In the past, extensive grazing of the commons ensured that few self-sown tree seedlings survived. Even

after man's grazing animals disappeared, rabbits continued the work of keeping the trees out. After myxomatosis virtually wiped out the rabbit population, tree seedlings, especially birch and pine, were left unmolested and have grown quickly into saplings. . . As soon as the density of young trees reaches about 50 to the acre the habitat becomes unfavourable to the heathland birds such as the lovely Dartford warbler and the stonechat, and they move elsewhere".

PARTNERSHIP WORKING

For many years this steady erosion of precious habitat went largely unchecked. But today, in cooperation with partners such as the Surrey Heathland Project and the Old Surrey Downs Project, supported by Higher Level Stewardship (HLS) funding and battalions of Belted Galloways, red deer and a variety of sheep and goats, the offending undergrowth is literally being chewed back. Another earlier comment from John Sankey recorded the start of the Trust's long-term relationship with the Ministry of Defence: "One of the earliest

Belted Galloway cattle grazing to improve heathland habitats for wildlife

major activities of the Trust in 1959, in conjunction with the Nature Conservancy, was to approach the War Department regarding the use of Surrey Commons for training. This resulted in reassurance that no further deterioration of these areas would be allowed". Today, supported by the Department of Environment, Food and Rural Affairs' Higher Level Stewardship (HLS) funding and Natural England, the Trust conservation-grazes pristine heathland covering more than 2,000 hectares of Ministry of Defence land on ranges in the west of the county.

The Trust's first nature reserve, Seale Chalk Pit near Farnham, was leased from Surrey County Council. Now the Trust manages the Council's entire countryside estate. One of the most significant milestones was the acquisition of permanent Trust headquarters. After years in a series of rented offices, the school buildings in Pirbright were offered for sale by the Council and, with extensive support from its members, the Trust moved into its present home in October 1992.

EDUCATION PIONEERS

Almost from inception the Trust pioneered natural history education, establishing the routine of an annual nature trail on Ranmore Common. In 1963, it led the way with plans for the formation of a county Education Nature Reserve and endorsed Surrey County Council's establishment of the Educational Nature Reserve at Brooklands County Technical College, Weybridge.

An early poster for Nower Wood

In 1972, Nower Wood was purchased as the site for the Trust's permanent educational centre, financed by a bank loan of £10,000 and nearly £13,000 of interest-free loans and donations from a huge number of

Doug Hulyer leading a nature trail at Nower Wood reserve

individuals and organisations in the county. Doug Hulyer was appointed as a teacher-warden, later to become Education Officer and ultimately, Vice President.

By early 1973, the first nature trail and permanent woodland walk had been created. Nower Wood was truly an educational nature reserve ready for visits by school parties. In June 1975, 3,766 children participated in a nine-day nature trail event, on which a winding path through the wood passed about 90 species and other features. The centre grew with the creation of classroom facilities and room for permanent staff. In 2006, it underwent a £100,000 upgrade with mains electricity replacing an ageing generator and enabling uninterrupted use of computers and video microscopes.

Three further educational centres have also been developed: at Bay Pond, Littlefield Common and in cooperation with Haslemere Educational Museum. An extensive outreach programme, in conjunction with the Heritage Lottery-funded Surrey Greenspace Project, means that the Trust reaches nearly 15,000 students every year,

Newlands Corner

including more than 10,000 who now participate in 16 weeks of centre-based courses.

CHANGING WITH THE TIMES

In March 1976 and 1986, special resolutions changed the Trust's name to The Surrey Trust for Nature Conservation Limited and then to The Surrey Wildlife Trust Limited. As recently as June 2008 a new, updated set of objectives were agreed by an Extraordinary General Meeting and the name revised to Surrey Wildlife Trust.

Over the years the structure of the Trust has also evolved to meet new demands. Originally, members were mostly natural historians and most 'staff' were volunteers. Today, these groups still play a vital role, but the Trust's appeal has broadened to embrace a much wider community, endorsing

one of the Trust's basic ethics: ". . . there is a place in the Trust for everyone whatever their interests. We need scientists, those who can type; we need foresters and those who can lick stamps; we need speakers and those who can't (the latter usually get on with the jobs!) – teachers, recorders, blazers of nature trails, car park attendants, tea makers and commandants of power-saws are all essential. Such people have built up the Trust. They have one thing in common – a love for the countryside – perhaps mainly through birds, or flowers, or spiders! But all desire to see that high quality environment we need ourselves as well as for the survival of Britain's wildlife".

The Trust's communications have also evolved over the years, to reflect the changing times, with digital technology playing an increasing role.

The newsletter has evolved into a full-colour magazine with pages dedicated to younger readers, a supplementary bulletin for volunteers and an extensive diary of conservation activities. It is supported by a website with news of the Trust's work.

CONCRETE'S STEADY MARCH

Extensive housing and road development have punctuated the Trust's life. Surrey is divided by a network of motorways and trunk roads with two major airports on its borders. As we move further into the 21st century, green belt land and open spaces are under increasing threat. The steady march of concrete and tarmac has also affected the county's waterways, with aquatic habitats eroded by increasing run-off during winter floods, followed by periods of drought as the deep aquifers are drained during the summer months.

The environment and wildlife are now much higher on the political agenda and people generally are more aware of the issues. Also the emphasis is not now exclusively on nature conservation. Many of the Trust's sites, especially those that the Trust manages on behalf of local authorities, are also well-used public open spaces and the Trust's management plans have to respond to these pressures.

The Trust has worked with the Zoological Society of London to reintroduce the red-barbed ant to heathland sites in Surrey

Children minibeast hunting at Nower Wood educational reserve

Surrey's first half-century has, on occasions, been turbulent. As with most charities, money was sometimes hard to find. The pressure of an expanding population with associated housing development, infrastructure and demand on natural resources often seems overwhelming. Yet, through the vision of its founders, the dedication of its volunteers and the efforts of its staff, the seed of an idea among a few very enthusiastic natural historians gave birth to a Trust which is now the largest in England, in terms of the land that it manages. Surrey Wildlife Trust now has more than 80 staff, 31,000 members and a turnover of more than £6 million.

BY JOHN EDWARDS AND CHRIS PARKER
John Edwards was first elected as a Trustee of Surrey Wildlife Trust in 1993 having worked on behalf of nature conservation in the county since 1979, firstly as a researcher evaluating open spaces for their ecological value, then as a Countryside Ranger. Now as ecologist for Surrey County Council, he provides ecological advice to both the Council and the wider community. He was Local Group Organiser for Elmbridge in the 1980s and served as chair of the Trust's Conservation Committee. John is a Chartered Environmentalist and a member of the Surrey Botanical Society, the Association of Local Government Ecologists and the Institute of Ecology and Environmental Management.

Chris Parker is Director of Marketing and Fundraising at Surrey Wildlife Trust.

CHAPTER 41

Sussex

The inaugural meeting of the Trust was held on 21st January 1961, although the date of its original incorporation as the Sussex Naturalists' Trust was 19th July 1961. The Trust sprang directly from a conference on nature conservation organised by the South-East Union of Scientific Societies in 1958. One of the early pioneers of the Trust was David Streeter – a former Pro Vice Chancellor of the University of Sussex and currently President of the Trust. He has ensured that the Trust sustains strong links with the university – also founded in 1961.

Grahame Des Forges, a solicitor and distinguished ornithologist, also played a crucial role in the Trust's formation and was its first Honorary Secretary. Frank Penfold was appointed Chairman in 1962, a post he held for 25 years. He was an agricultural engineer, brilliant naturalist and knew practically every farmer in Sussex. No one was better equipped to identify the prime sites that were threatened at that time and to negotiate with landowners. Penfold's energy and dedication were boundless, although his enthusiasm had to be dampened sometimes as he came up with proposals for more sites as nature reserves. ROBIN CRANE, who had already served on the Council of LINCOLNSHIRE TRUST, arrived in 1967. He established the regional groups, ran the Trust's first four major appeals and launched the major legacy campaign that continues today. He was Deputy Chairman several years before becoming Chairman in 1987.

In 1966, the gift of Woods Mill, an 18th century watermill, was a landmark for the Trust. A mill house and 15 acres of land including streams, marshland, a lake and some ancient woodland came with the property. The house was used as a headquarters and provided a tangible sense of cohesion for the membership. The watermill and reserve were ideal for establishing an education centre. James Sutcliffe had come to the University of Sussex in 1965 as the founding Professor of Plant Physiology and quickly became closely involved. He lived at Woodmancote, close to Woods Mill, which at the time was owned by Dr Douglas Smith. By coincidence, James Sutcliffe and Dr Smith's sons were close friends of long standing, and when Smith died the family offered the property to the Trust.

COLEMAN CREDITS

No history of the Trust can be written without paying special tributes to Charlie and Dorothy Coleman. They took up residence at Woods Mill in 1970, when Charlie Coleman was appointed Warden after being a shepherd on Romney Marsh. Coleman was a fine naturalist with expertise in countryside management. His first talent was in dealing with children, making their visits to Woods Mill truly memorable. But he was also a gifted draughtsman, water-colourist and brilliant cartoonist.

Opposite: Adonis blue – chalk downland restoration work by the Trust has helped this species to recover
Right: A Charlie Coleman cartoon

Map of Sussex Wildlife Trust nature reserves

1	Brickfield Meadow	11	Malling Down	21	Woods Mill
2	Burton and Chingford Ponds	12	Marline Valley	22	Balcombe Marsh
3	Castle Water and Rye Harbour	13	The Mens	23	Chailey Warren
4	Cooksbridge Meadow	14	Old Lodge	24	The Deneway
5	Eridge Rocks	15	Pagham Harbour	25	Leythorne Meadow
6	Filsham Reedbed	16	Pevensey Marshes	26	Marehill Quarry
7	Flatropers Wood	17	Selwyns Wood	27	Ebernoe Common
8	Gillham Wood	18	Waltham Brooks	28	Amberley Wildbrooks
9	Iping and Stedham Commons	19	West Dean Woods	29	Ditchling Beacon
10	Levin Down	20	Withdean Woods	30	Southerham

His cartoons, often with a powerful conservation message, quickly became regular features in the Trust's newsletters. Apart from his professionalism at work, both he and Dorothy brought those special gifts of warmth and kindness and were superb ambassadors for the Trust. Sadly, Charlie had to retire early due to ill health in 1985.

SURVEY PIONEERS

The minutes of the early meetings make interesting reading and the comparison between the major concerns of 40 years ago and those of today is especially illuminating. Sussex differed from many other counties in that it had no established county natural history society or field club. Consequently, the new body found itself supporting survey and recording activities that elsewhere were the province of the county societies. The creation of the Sussex Ornithological Society the year after the Trust's inauguration, was part of the need to fill this niche. The Trust also published *The Sussex*

Mammal Report from 1965 to 1969 and sponsored the Sussex Flora Committee before it became the independent Sussex Botanical Recording Society. The Trust's current lead involvement with the Sussex Biodiversity Records Centre can thus be traced back to these early days.

EXTRAORDINARY NATURAL DIVERSITY

Sussex's position on the south coast and its exceptionally diverse geology has given rise to a range of superb wildlife sites and extraordinary natural diversity. In the east, there is Pevensey Levels – the largest tract of wetland in East Sussex – and Rye Harbour – a mosaic of habitats beside the sea with shingle, saltmarsh, sand dunes, grazing marsh and reedbeds. The iconic chalk hills of the South Downs begin at Beachy Head and form the spine of the county. They are relatively treeless in the east with typical chalk grasslands, and become more wooded as one travels west. To the north of the Downs, the Weald extends across a range of sands, sandstones and clays that have formed a series of escarpments and valleys with wild heathlands and ancient woodlands. Four rivers flow south to the sea through valleys cut through the chalk downs.

The Trust's nature reserves reflect this natural diversity and include internationally-important chalk grasslands, heathlands and ancient woodlands. The total area currently under management is 3,500 acres. However, the Trust's influence has always extended far beyond its own wildlife sites.

In its formative years, the Trust was often reactive. There were no strategic plans or vision statements to guide it. Nevertheless, the National Parks and Access to the Countryside Act 1949 had established a framework of designated areas and the Nature Conservancy had notified a suite of Sites of Special Scientific Interest (SSSIs). The Trust soon became involved in four of these sites.

FIRST MAJOR REPORT

Ashdown Forest is the largest area of open countryside in south-east England and one of the region's most important areas of lowland heathland (as well as the inspiration for *Winnie the Pooh*). It is administered by a Board of Conservators under its own Acts of Parliament and, in addition to funding from the local authorities, draws much

Sir David Attenborough opens a new classroom and visitor centre at Woods Mill in 1981. Left to right: Frank Penfold, Sir David Attenborough, Robin Crane and David Streeter

of its revenue from commoners exercising rights such as grazing and turf-cutting. The natural history interest of large areas within the forest was deteriorating and remedies were beyond the resources of the Conservators. David Streeter's report on the forest, produced by the Trust in its first year, was its first major document and most of its recommendations were adopted by the Conservators. At the same time, the Friends of Ashdown Forest were formed to raise the funds to make the proposals possible. Grazing was at the heart of that report and the recent re-establishment of grazing in the forest is regarded as a model of good heathland management.

SIGNIFICANT SUCCESSES

Another area of heathland to claim the Trust's attention was North Common, Chailey. Smaller than Ashdown Forest, it was suffering from similar problems. The Trust's report on its future, written by Garth Christian, strongly recommended that East Sussex County Council declare it a Local Nature Reserve (LNR) with its own management committee and warden. The Common was declared an LNR in 1966. Protection and management were significantly improved as a result, but difficulties in achieving a conservation grazing programme

An early photograph of the Trust's home at Woods Mill

have remained. Fortunately, East Sussex County Council, with the support of the Trust, has recently won a public inquiry. This enabled the common to be fenced and cattle grids to be installed, so that once again this important area of heathland can be grazed.

At the other end of the county, difficulties were emerging between the wildfowlers and bird conservationists at Pagham Harbour, which was also threatened by various development proposals. The resolution required not only appropriate ecological knowledge but considerable diplomatic skills. The Trust's report, written by Tony Marr, had much of both and set the course for the future and for it to be declared an LNR in 1964; the first in Sussex and undoubtedly one of the Trust's first major achievements. Pagham Harbour and Chailey Common were soon followed by Rye Harbour and Seaford Head. At one stage, five of the 15 LNRs in England were in Sussex.

TEXTBOOK TEST CASE

Amberley Wildbrooks in the Arun valley (the Brooks) had been known to generations of local naturalists as one of the prime sites in southern England. Its grazing marshes and drainage dykes were famous for their plantlife, birds and invertebrates. So when two fields at the north end of the Brooks became available, the Trust jumped at the chance to establish its first nature reserve – a first step towards establishing a reserve over the whole of the Brooks. By 1967, the Trust had acquired a further two fields, making a total holding of almost 11 acres. In 1978, the Southern Water Authority published proposals to drain part of the Brooks "to enhance the agricultural potential of the land". The Trust led a consortium of local organisations vigorously opposed to the proposals and the scheme went to public inquiry. The case became something of a *cause célèbre*. The Inspector found against the scheme, both on conservation, and economic grounds, with the economic case coming in for some extremely critical academic analysis.

The Trust's first nature reserve at Amberley was small, and as such struggled to deliver much for wildlife. But, it gave the Trust a strategic foothold and the ability to contribute to one of the greatest conservation test cases in recent history. The appearance of the map of the Arun valley between Pulborough and Amberley today, with more than 800 acres under the management of the Trust and the RSPB, represents one of the most significant conservation achievements in the county. It is a testament to the effectiveness of cooperation between different conservation organisations.

LANDSCAPE-SCALE APPROACH

The importance of landscape-scale approaches to wildlife conservation is increasingly being recognised. Many projects today see some key nature reserves as core areas within ecologically-rich landscape areas. One example is the West Weald Landscape Project. This area includes some of the most important lowland woodlands in Europe, particularly the 387-acre reserve at The Mens and Ebernoe Common, which has been designated as a National Nature Reserve and a Special Protection Area. However, much of the interest in these core sites relies on the quality of the whole landscape. Excellent scientific work by David Hill and Frank Greenaway showed, not only how important these two sites are to Barbastelle and Bechstein's bats, but also how the bats utilise the surrounding landscape. This important project is helping to direct the Trust's own nature reserve management and to tell the story of landscape ecology, which in turn attracts funding and influences land-use policy across nearly 60,000 acres.

One of the great achievements in which the Trust was a major player was the designation of the South Downs National Park, which is 100 miles long and covers 16,000 square kilometres. The park, originally proposed in 1947, met with constant opposition including from the Countryside Commission. The Commission created two Areas of Outstanding Natural Beauty and established the experimental South Downs Conservation Board. David Streeter was appointed its Deputy Chairman. But, the push

Amberley Wildbrooks – The Trust's first reserve

that led to national park designation started in May 1990 with an inaugural meeting with four other charities at Woods Mill, chaired by Robin Crane. They agreed to the formation of the South Downs Campaign, with the Trust as one of the core sponsors. Robin Crane remained the campaign's Chairman until its closure in 2010. The membership of this unprecedented campaign eventually grew to 158 national, regional and local organisations, including 28 town and parish councils. Although the public were overwhelmingly supportive, the campaign had to fight off strong opposition, particularly from some local authorities and local MPs. It had to present a mass of evidence to two long public inquiries. The Designation Order was eventually signed by the Secretary of State, Hilary Benn, on 12th November 2009.

VISION FOR THE 21ST CENTURY

In 1995, the Trust published its *Vision for the Wildlife in Sussex* – an historic document. The Vision had four key elements: a broad vision of the Sussex environment in 2045; specific targets for habitats in 2005; action plans to identify who needed to do what to achieve the targets; and the identification of environmental performance indicators to demonstrate progress towards the targets. This mammoth undertaking, written by a team under the chairmanship of Patrick Leonard, is still being used to guide many statutory and voluntary bodies in Sussex today.

The publication of the *Vision* stimulated the preparation – by a partnership of organisations – of the Sussex Biodiversity Action Plan in 1998. In practice, this followed basic principles held by the Trust throughout its history, but it helped to form a shared local nature conservation agenda, gaining political commitment from people not previously involved in nature conservation, and galvanised action. To progress action, a Biodiversity Officer was employed by the Trust on behalf of the partnership and this appointment is core to its efforts to persuade organisations to deliver conservation.

DEVELOPING DATA SETS

Wildlife recording is undertaken by many groups and individuals, many of whom were initially reluctant to share their knowledge. The Trust therefore put considerable efforts into strengthening relationships and now there is very strong cooperation between all concerned. In the early 1990s, along with its partners, the Trust initiated an Environmental Survey Directory, a computerised meta-database which aimed to direct an enquirer to sources of biological information. Throughout the decade this grew in importance and gradually data sets and survey projects became focused under what became the Sussex Biodiversity Record Centre (BRC). Operating from Woods Mill, the BRC is managed as a partnership project and is a repository, custodian, manager and analyst of high-quality biodiversity, natural history and environmental information. It now holds more than three million records and receives more than 800 enquiries a year. Its development has been a fascinating story that began in the 1980s with pins in a map. Today, it has six staff with expertise in environmental data management and IT, and is supported not just by local authorities and Government agencies, but by many volunteer naturalists and local societies.

WORKING WITH YOUNG PEOPLE

The Trust has always regarded education as a vital part of its work. Its pioneering Woods Mill education centre led to a Countryside in 1970 award and in 1981 it received a Carnegie Interpret Britain award. Today, its various education programmes attract more than 21,000 children a year and it runs more than 200 events and courses for people of all ages and backgrounds. Whilst Woods Mill is still the Trust's major centre, it also holds many activities at Seven Sisters Country Park, near Eastbourne, and throughout the county. WILDLIFE WATCH groups thrive and there is now a Sussex Trust Youth Council. In 1988, the Trust was one of the first to appoint a Community Wildlife Officer, which aimed to encourage community groups to become involved in environmental activity. This work now forms part of the core work of the Trust with major community projects centred on Brighton, Hastings and Crawley.

Southerham – one of the Trust's reserves on the South Downs

Young pond-dippers at Woods Mill

PAST AND PRESENT

What is the main difference between the Trust today and its early history? The agenda is remarkably similar; wildlife conservation is achieved through the triple approach of habitat management, education and influencing the decision-making processes. Perhaps the most obvious difference has been the transition from a wholly volunteer movement to one employing full-time staff. Currently, the Trust has a Chief Executive, Tony Whitbread, and the equivalent of 52 full-time staff. Whitbread was 'blown' into Woods Mill on a short contract with the Royal Society of Wildlife Trusts to report on the aftermath of the GREAT STORM of 1987. Several Trust staff who cut their teeth at Woods Mill, have moved on to higher things. Colin Raven was appointed Director of the WORCESTERSHIRE TRUST, Graham Turnbull became Director of the LONDON TRUST and Andrew Lee became Chief Executive of the Sustainable Development Commission. However, like all charities, the Trust still relies heavily on the support and help of its many volunteers. It would be considerably less effective if this resource was ever under-utilised.

MEMBERSHIP MILESTONES

Membership has increased steadily. Within four years of its formation, the Trust achieved the milestone of 1,000 members. By its tenth anniversary, when the name was changed to the Sussex Trust for Nature Conservation, membership had grown to more than 3,000. By 1990, two years after becoming the Sussex Wildlife Trust, support had grown to 8,000. On the eve of the Trust's 50th year in 2010, the Trust had nearly 33,000 members and continues to go from strength to strength.

The Trust's finances have always been on a sound footing. Thanks to the wise investment decisions made by the Chairman, Patrick Berry, and the Honorary Treasurer, David Johnson, the Trust managed to escape the worst of the financial crisis in 2007–08. In the financial year ending March 2010, the turnover of the Trust was £3 million.

Much has been achieved, but there are many challenges ahead. In the words of the Trust's *Vision for the Wildlife of Sussex*: "when the day dawns that the otter is once again a commonplace sight in the Sussex countryside, the Trust will begin to feel it is truly on the way to achieving its purposes".

BY ROBIN CRANE, TONY WHITBREAD AND DAVID STREETER

Robin Crane has volunteered with the Trust since 1967. As well as a term as Chairman of the Society from 1995 to 2000, he was Chairman of the South Downs Campaign from its foundation in 1990 until the establishment of the South Downs National Park in 2010. He was awarded a CBE in 1999 and an Honorary Doctorate from the University of Sussex in 2001 for services to nature conservation and the countryside.

Tony Whitbread started work with the Sussex Wildlife Trust as Conservation Officer in 1991, following roles as a Woodland Ecologist with the Society and the Nature Conservancy Council. Now Chief Executive of the Trust, he continues to promote an ecosystems approach to nature conservation.

David Streeter is a founder member and President of the Sussex Wildlife Trust. He was a member of the Council of the Royal Society for Nature Conservation (the Society) from 1963 to 1983 and the first Chairman of its Conservation Liaison Committee. An academic ecologist, he is a former Pro Vice Chancellor of the University of Sussex. He was awarded an MBE in 2007.

CHAPTER 42

Tees Valley

The Tees Valley is a largely urban area located on the north and south banks of the Tees estuary in the north-east of England. Administratively, it comprises the unitary local authorities of Middlesbrough, Stockton-on-Tees, Hartlepool, and Redcar and Cleveland.

It is an area which grew rapidly in the 19th century following the discovery of local ironstone deposits in the nearby Cleveland Hills. Teesside quickly became an important centre for iron and steelmaking and ancillary heavy engineering industries such as shipbuilding and bridge manufacture. Its industrial base expanded during the 20th century into chemicals – initially using local salt deposits to manufacture agricultural chemicals, then petro-chemical industries following the opening up of North Sea oilfields in the 1960s and 1970s.

Much of the heavy industry has now disappeared – shipbuilding has ceased and the manufacture of steel is largely confined to the former Corus site close to the river mouth. The area's industrial past has, however, created many opportunities for wildlife. Many sites previously occupied by heavy industry have regenerated and now support interesting plant and invertebrate communities. The Trust manages some of these sites as nature reserves, notably at Portrack Marsh, Maze Park and Coatham Marsh. Sites currently occupied by industrial companies at Teesmouth, many of them corporate members of the Trust, also offer opportunities for practical conservation and education. The interest in wildlife amongst

Opposite: Common seals at Seal Sands with the iconic Transporter Bridge in the background
Right: Northern marsh-orchid

Teesside companies and their staff, led to the establishment in 1989 of the Cleveland INCA (Industry and Nature Conservation Association) which was intended as a model for other industrial estuaries in the UK and elsewhere. Over the years, the Trust has maintained close partnership working with INCA.

Despite its heavy industrial past, the Tees Valley also retains a wide range of semi-natural habitats – most notably, perhaps, the complex of coastal habitats known collectively as the Tees Flats and Marshes, comprising Seal Sands, Seaton Dunes, Seaton Common, South Gare and Coatham Sands, and Cowpen Marsh. The whole area is of considerable importance for its flora, invertebrate fauna and particularly its birdlife. The inter-tidal mud flats at Seal Sands in particular are of international ornithological importance attracting large numbers of migratory wildfowl and wading birds, especially during the winter months. They also support common and grey seals in a colony which has successfully re-established, having been driven away by industrial development and human disturbance in the 19th century. Beyond the main urban areas, occur a wide variety of habitats including semi-natural woodland, magnesium limestone grassland

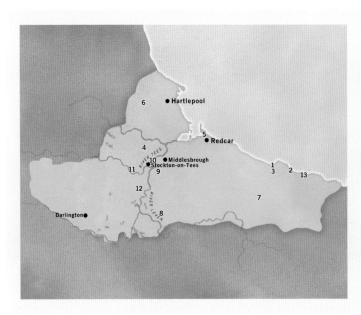

1   Hunt Cliff
2   Cattersty Gill
3   Saltburn Gill
4   Gravel Hole
5   Coatham Marsh
6   The Howls
7   Margrove Ponds
8   Brewsdale
9   Maze Park
10 Portrack Marsh
11 Hardwick Dene and Elm Tree Wood
12 Bowesfield
13 Hummersea

Map of Tees Valley Wildlife Trust nature reserves

on the fringes of County Durham and upland heath in the Eston Hills and on the fringes of the North York Moors. Along the coast there are also important habitats, including Boulby Cliff – the highest point on the east coast of England and important for nesting seabirds – and Hart Warren Dunes which is of high botanical interest.

SEVENTIES' STIMULUS

Tees Valley Wildlife Trust, initially in the guise of Cleveland Nature Conservation Trust, was formally established in 1979, became a registered charity in 1980 and was affiliated with the Royal Society of Wildlife Trusts (the Society) in 1982. Its origins lie in a number of events during the 1970s. A major factor was the establishment of the new county of Cleveland in 1974, replacing the Teesside and Hartlepool County Boroughs and taking in parts of what were previously Durham and North Yorkshire County Councils. This provided the stimulus for the establishment of a number of Cleveland-wide voluntary sector organisations, including initially a Cleveland Nature Conservation Liaison Group, whose members were eventually to form the core of the new Trust.

BATTLE FOR SEAL SANDS

It was not only changes in local government organisation that influenced the establishment of the new Trust. During the mid-1970s, key decisions were being taken about development in the Tees estuary which potentially would have had catastrophic impacts on estuary habitats. Most of the areas of inter-tidal mud and saltmarsh in the estuary had been reclaimed for industry during the 1960s, leaving relatively small and isolated habitats surrounded by extensive areas of petrochemical industry. All that was left of the area known as Seal Sands, once an extensive area of inter-tidal mud extending to some 2,500 hectares, was a small area of 160 hectares. This area had been earmarked for port-related uses in development plans. Conservation bodies, led by the Seal Sands Conservation Group and the Teesmouth Bird Club, had long been fighting a rearguard action to protect it from further development. The crunch point came with the mid-1970s publication of the draft Teesside structure plan, which reconfirmed the industrial land allocation. There were heated debates at the time about the future of Seal Sands, with the case for conservation passionately promoted by people such as Angela Cooper, Peter Hogg and Professor Peter Evans, the first two of whom were later key players in the establishment of the new Trust. Despite an initial setback for the conservation lobby, the remaining part of Seal Sands was not developed, and the land allocation was eventually removed. The area was leased to what was then the Nature Conservancy Council for designation as a National Nature Reserve, which it achieved in 1995. It now forms part of the Teesmouth and Cleveland Coast Special Protection Area. The battle for Seal Sands helped consolidate the conservation movement in Cleveland.

URBAN WILDLIFE MOVEMENT

Another influence on the establishment of the Trust was the growing interest in urban conservation during the 1970s and 1980s. Until then, conservation had been seen as an activity largely associated with the countryside. As the county of Cleveland was very much urban in character, there was a natural affiliation with the urban wildlife movement which took shape in the early 1980s. With urban conservation rising up the national agenda, this new interest gave impetus to feelings that Cleveland should have its own Wildlife Trust. In 1987, Bob Smythe wrote of the links between the establishment of the Trust and

Dingy skipper – a nationally-scarce and declining species, which thrives on post-industrial sites such as Maze Park

Coatham Marsh nature reserve

the urban wildlife movement more generally. "On Teesside, the Durham Trust was happy to relinquish former territory in the new Cleveland County and, though the Yorkshire Trust initially objected, a Cleveland Trust started life in 1981". In fact the Trust started a year earlier and held its first Annual General Meeting in 1981.

EARLY MILESTONES

The Chairman at that first meeting was Peter Hogg, a Hartlepool shipping agent and long-time supporter of conservation in the Tees estuary. The voluntary Conservation Officer was Angela Cooper. The Trust employed its first paid Conservation Officer, Lloyd Austin, in 1986 and in 1988, other key members of staff, including Tim Gordon as Reserves Officer, were also employed.

Due to the increasing interest in urban conservation, 1989 saw the publication of the first issue of *Green Bits*, the Trust's urban community wildlife magazine. It is still a key mechanism for reaching those in urban areas. In 2010, the 75th issue was published in association with the local newspaper, the *Evening Gazette.*

In 1988, a survey of wildlife sites was completed in association with local authorities and the Nature

Maze Park nature reserve, Middlesbrough

Conservancy Council. This culminated in the 1989 publication of the *Cleveland Wildlife Strategy*.

TRUST RESERVES

Currently, the Trust manages 14 reserves, ranging from ancient woodland habitats to coastal cliffs, calcareous grassland and wetlands, to urban sites on reclaimed wasteland. The Trust's first reserve was Gravel Hole, a small quarry site with an interesting assemblage of calcareous grassland plants. It was acquired on a lease in 1981 and purchased six years later, in 1987.

In 1985, the Trust purchased Saltburn Gill, a site that boasts ancient semi-natural woodland supporting a diverse assemblage of woodland plants and set in a deep coastal valley. This reserve was the Trust's first major purchase.

Portrack Marsh Nature Reserve opened in 2000 following the completion of wetland creation and restoration work. A remnant of former, more extensive, wetland habitat, the reserve supports large numbers of wetland birds. Otters have also been recorded here. The site is widely accessible within the urban Tees Valley.

In addition to its current reserves, which cover more than 200 hectares, the Trust managed three other sites until the early 1990s – Crow Wood,

Kilton Mine and The Rookery, in Yarm – when management responsibility was returned to the site owners.

NEW NAME, NEW FUNDING

Following the abolition of Cleveland County Council in 1996, the Trust changed its name to the Tees Valley Wildlife Trust, taking on the generic name for the new grouping of local authorities on the Tees estuary. (Darlington also forms part of the Tees Valley grouping of local authorities, but remains part of the Durham Wildlife Trust area).

The newly-named Trust expanded rapidly during the 1990s, from an organisation with a handful of staff to one with more than 40 employees.

The first Trust director, Joe Cole, was appointed in 1991. In the same period the Trust's turnover increased from £176,000 in 1982–83 to well over £1 million in 1997, taking advantage of new sources of funding, such as the Landfill Communities Fund. The Trust was one of the first enrolled environmental bodies under this new scheme. The Trust also received substantial funding from the Teesside Development Corporation prior to its demise in 1998. The Trust also benefited from this in the form of various land transfers, namely Portrack Marsh, Maze Park and Bowesfield.

FINANCIAL SETBACK

Unfortunately, during this period, the Trust began to overreach itself, getting into financial difficulties, and perhaps for a while losing sight of its core objectives. A necessary period of readjustment and financial constraint followed. However, since the millennium, and under a new Chief Executive, Jeremy Garside, the Trust moved to new premises at Margrove Heritage Centre and stabilised. It began to move forward again with a smaller staff, but with its objectives firmly fixed on its core objectives of conservation and education.

TODAY'S TRUST

The Trust is currently governed by a 15-member Council and managed by a core staff of 19 led by Chief Executive, Jeremy Garside. Its main sources of income in the 2011–12 financial year are: Big Lottery and HERITAGE LOTTERY FUND; Landfill Communities Fund; contract work and membership. Trust membership has grown over the years to its present peak of some 10,000.

In 2010, the Trust learnt of the sad passing of Angela Cooper, a founder member and its first Conservation Officer. Angela received the MBE for her conservation work in 1975, and was awarded the CHRISTOPHER CADBURY MEDAL by the Society in 1997 for services in the advancement of nature conservation. Angela bequeathed a 50-acre coastal nature reserve to the Trust; a stunning piece of coastal land at Hummersea to the north of Loftus. The reserve includes a wide swathe of maritime slope with wildflowers, such as grass of Parnassus and fragrant and pyramidal orchids, and a small beach giving access at low tide to a wider area of wave-cut platform.

BY DAVID COUNSELL

David Counsell is a chartered town planner and planning academic. He has been a Trustee of Tees Valley Wildlife Trust since 1995 and has served as its Chairman since 2000. He is also a Council member of the Royal Society of Wildlife Trusts.

Hummersea – bequeathed to the Trust in 2010 by one of its founder members, Angela Cooper

CHAPTER 43

Ulster

Within a relatively confined land area of 14,000 square kilometres, Northern Ireland has a wide diversity of landscape and geological types. Combined with a settlement pattern dominated by dispersed small farms, this makes for an attractive and vibrant countryside. Its coastline, stretching for 650 kilometres, is equally diverse and significant in conservation and tourist terms.

Since the end of the Second World War, considerable changes in economic, social and political aspects have resulted in extensive alteration to the natural environment. Economically the loss of the once world-leading shipbuilding and linen industries exemplify the change by which large manufacturing industries have been replaced by service industries and light engineering. Agricultural practices have seen dramatic upheavals, resulting in the loss of many wetlands; the catastrophic reduction of both lowland and upland peatlands; and the seemingly ever-changing balance between grazing patterns and arable farming. Social and political changes have produced a slowly growing public awareness of the need to conserve what we have and of the benefits of doing so. What is encouraging is that this growing awareness is not confined to any particular community or social grouping.

In Northern Ireland, governmental involvement in nature conservation did not begin until 1965, when what later became the Department of the Environment for Northern Ireland (DOE(NI)) assumed responsibilities. Ten years later, progress in surveying and establishing nature reserves was tardy, largely because of the lack of staff resources. In an attempt to encourage the naturalists' field clubs to become more actively involved in assisting the Department, Joe Furphy, then with the Department, organised a conference in 1978.

Opposite: Irish hare – chosen by the Trust as its emblem on formation in 1978. Above: Ballynahone Bog nature reserve

Map of Ulster Wildlife Trust nature reserves

1   Ballynahone Bog
2   Cottage Farm
3   Feystown
4   Inishargy Bog
5   Inishcreagh
6   Isle Namanfin
7   Isle of Muck
8   Umbra
9   Glenarm
10 Bog Meadows
11 Slievenacloy
12 Straidkilly
13 Milford Cutting
14 Glendun Farm
15 Blessingbourne
16 Balloo Wetland
17 Balloo Woodland
18 Moyola Waterfoot

At its conclusion, Professor Palmer Newbould (a prominent ecologist and later Chairman) proposed that a Naturalists' Trust should be formed, similar to the County Trusts by now covering all of Great Britain. There was a general welcome for this concept, and a steering committee – which included officers of the other major NI nature conservation bodies – was set up to get the Trust going.

This reflected the realisation that urgent action was needed to put conservation on a firmer footing. It was decided that the new body should be called the Ulster Trust for Nature Conservation, later changed in 1988 to the Ulster Wildlife Trust. 'Ulster' is often colloquially applied to Northern Ireland, but strictly speaking it applies to the six counties of Northern Ireland, plus three counties in the Republic of Ireland (Cavan, Donegal and Monaghan), which together form the ancient province of Ulster. However, the Trust currently only operates in Northern Ireland, although where relevant, it cooperates with the Irish Wildlife Trust.

EARLY MOVERS AND SHAKERS

Its first Chairman was Dr John Faulkner, then a research scientist with the Northern Ireland Department of Agriculture. An amateur entomologist, he was also Chairman of the Armagh Field Naturalists' Society. Later he became Director of Natural Heritage in the Northern Ireland Environment Agency. It was due to his enthusiasm, the organising ability of the untiring first Honorary Secretary, Ian Forsyth, and the drive and foresight of the first Honorary Treasurer, Mervyn Archdale, plus the legal skills of solicitor, John Russell, that the organisation was given such a solid start.

At the Trust's opening conference on 6th May 1978, the principal speakers included SIR DAVID ATTENBOROUGH – who dealt with the global aspects of nature conservation – Ian Mercer – on the role of the Society for the Promotion of Nature Reserves (the Society) – and Bernard Gilchrist who shared his SCOTTISH WILDLIFE TRUST experiences with the local audience.

BADGER QUESTIONS

The Trust chose as its emblem the endemic Irish hare, a symbol both iconic and artistically satisfying. However, the link with the rest of the Wildlife Trusts' movement later led to the badger being later adopted as the logo for the Ulster Trust. The badger became even more relevant in the 1990s as government departments debated whether there should be an extermination programme because of the apparent links to bovine tuberculosis. The Trust was prominently represented on working parties set up by the Department of Agriculture and Rural Development and has fought strongly since for the establishment of a major research project before any extermination is contemplated. At the time of writing, finance has been made available for only a partial research programme.

From the start, the Trust made the acquisition of nature reserves a high priority, with two prongs to its policy. First, there was the desire to acquire sites of high nature conservation interest. In this the Trust was to some extent thwarted by its late appearance on the scene, since the National Trust, the RSPB and DOE(NI) had acquired many of the most significant sites between them. In the absence of funds to allow the purchase of a range of sites, and largely thanks to the efforts of the Trust's first Honorary Treasurer, Mervyn Archdale, management agreements were drawn up for a number of sites in various parts of the Province. They included Mervyn Archdale's own working farm outside Omagh. The Archdale link to the Trust is still very strong, with Mervyn Archdale's son, Peter, being currently the Trust's very active Vice Chairman. While most of these reserves were relatively small, the Trust soon acquired, through a management agreement, part of the extensive and scientifically significant Umbra dune system in North Derry. The success of this arrangement led to the drawing up of similar agreements for other major sites.

ISLANDS, BOGS AND WOODS

The first reserve to be purchased by the Trust was an abandoned railway cutting at Milford, just outside Armagh. Among its riches – unusually for an Irish inland site – is marsh helleborine.

The Isle of Muck, off the coast of County Antrim, is an important seabird colony. The Trust obtained

Ballynahone Bog is home to a rich peatland flora, including round-leaved sundew (above), bog myrtle and bog asphodel

Marsh helleborine

IMPORTANCE OF PEATLANDS

The Trust's involvement in peatland conservation is a direct reflection of the important role Northern Ireland's peatlands play in a UK-wide context. Although over 90 per cent of this resource had disappeared by the end of the 20th century, much of what remains is of high nature conservation significance. Both the government conservation body and the Trust have acquired or manage the most important sites, some of which are in the ownership of the Northern Ireland Forest Service.

An extensive grassland site on the western fringes of the Belfast Hills, Slievenacloy, was also bought by the Trust, saving it from afforestation. Significant grants from the Heritage Lottery Fund and DOE(NI) were material to the success of the Trust's purchase of the site and its subsequent remediation. It is now part of the Belfast Hills Living Landscapes Initiative.

EDUCATING COMMUNITIES

The second arm of the Trust's policy was the provision of sites of primarily educational value. Because of the predominantly eastern distribution of the population, it was incumbent on the Trust to concentrate its first educational reserves in the Greater Belfast region. Its major site here is the Bog Meadows, the last remnant of the extensive marsh system upstream of Belfast city centre and a site with great educational and nature conservation potential. Involving the local community throughout,

grant-aid towards the purchase of the island with the remainder of the cost raised by members buying a 'yard of muck' for £1 through a raffle. The purchaser of one lucky ticket was to become Lord or Lady Muck! The investiture of Lady Muck took place on a wild and wet day which made it impossible to reach the island, so it was held on the mainland within sight of the island. Miss Jean Cochrane was invested by Lord Dunleath, using his robes!

Even more significant was the later decision of DOE(NI) to devolve management of some of its reserves. Through this the Trust took the management of Belshaw's Quarry, a microcosm of the geology of County Antrim; the hazel woodland of Straidkilly, overlooking the North Irish Sea; and in 2000, most spectacular of all, the proposed Special Protection Area of Ballynahone Bog. This is an excellent example of a lowland raised bog, set in the centre of the Province. Earlier, the bog had been saved at almost the last moment from its development as a peat extraction site. The Trust later managed to acquire a further extension of this nationally very important reserve.

Isle of Muck nature reserve – home to breeding kittiwake, guillemot, fulmar and razorbill

it has proved to be a considerable success. However, it continues to be beset with difficulties relating to a past use of part of the site as a graveyard. It has won UNESCO's Man and the Biosphere award for Urban Wildlife Excellence – Northern Ireland's first such award.

When the Trust moved into its current, leased premises, 15 miles south of Belfast in the grounds of a monastery at Crossgar, two volunteers, Dr Michael Meharg and Stephen Warnock realised there was potential in the former walled garden for an exceptional education development. Over the next few years the site was transformed, with a lot of grant aid, into examples of four habitats – woodland, freshwater, grassland and peat bog. Opened in June 1992 by SIR DAVID ATTENBOROUGH, it was extensively used by educational parties for several years until, sadly, it had to be closed.

PARTNERSHIP INITIATIVES

In the wider educational field, the Trust undertakes a variety of roles. As well as employing a small number of staff, it makes extensive use of highly-capable volunteers to lead walks and assist with other educational activities.

Partnership with other bodies has been important, and since 1996 the relationship with Down District Council over conservation activities at Delamont Country Park has proved particularly successful. More recently, the relationship with Belfast City Council has led to the development of a parks and schools linked programme, Watch This Space, now entering its fourth year. A Make Space for Nature Schools Grounds Project involving 2,500 schoolchildren across Northern Ireland was also a great success. Many of the Trust's educational guides worked directly in school classrooms. Regrettably, it appears that government funding for this worthwhile project may be withdrawn because of the difficult economic climate. A valuable educational tool was the Wildlife Wagon, a caravan used at schools, agricultural shows, Trust events and other functions to introduce the public to the work of the Trust. One of the star exhibits

Children at Balloo nature reserve

was 'Barney' a tame barn owl, proudly shown off by staff member Seamus Burns.

The twin aims – conservation and education – come together in a number of sites, some of which involve partnerships with district councils. One is at Balloo in Bangor – a reserve encompassing both woodland and wetland habitats – where both the wildlife interests and the community are the focus of work. In addition, a working relationship with a community group on the western shores of Lough Neagh has resulted in the establishment of a wetland reserve.

In the wider nature conservation scene, the Trust is playing an active part in the Northern Ireland Biodiversity Strategy; it is the lead partner in the species action plans for Irish hare and barn owl, and has particularly important roles in action plans for several other species, including red squirrel and basking shark.

STRANGFORD LOUGH

Strangford Lough, whose mudflats and shores are rich in birdlife and marine organisms, is one of

Northern Ireland's natural jewels, leading to its many conservation designations. While he was still with the Ulster Museum, Dr David Erwin, later to became the Trust's Director, made a television film *Down under Down*, which clearly demonstrated the extreme richness of the Lough's underwater life. The Trust is the only local voluntary body whose stated activities include marine conservation.

By 2001 it became clear that the horse mussel, *Modiolus modiolus*, an important part of the Lough's ecosystem, was in decline and under considerable threat. The Trust led a campaign, calling for changes to the fishing regime including the establishment of no-fishing zones. It took until 2005 before the relevant government authorities, pressed by the European Commission, agreed a restoration plan for the horse mussel reefs. At the time of writing, pressure is still being brought to bear by the Trust to see the restoration plan implemented in full. This pressure will be maintained as the Trust focuses more on its Living Seas work.

MAKING ENDS MEET

In common with other Trusts, raising finance for operations is of paramount importance.

Horse mussels in Strangford Lough

The membership base is rather small compared to other Trusts – currently about 11,500 – but the Province's population is only 1.75 million. The Trust has relied on generous grant aid, largely from the DOE(NI), both for core funding and projects. Other government departments and lottery funds have assisted in various ways. At the time of writing, it is clear that funding from government sources is likely to be curtailed over the next few years. This has led to the Trust's staff and board examining ways of ameliorating the likely financial difficulties, while at the same time focusing the Trust's work more on the delivery of Living Landscapes and Living Seas initiatives.

Much of the physical work involved in setting up reserves on the ground was carried out under the aegis of Action of Community Employment (ACE). Dating from 1981, this government scheme was designed to relieve unemployment and train workers – not necessarily young people – in new skills. As well as nature reserve workers, the Trust's first two development staff members were appointed under this scheme. ACE was of immeasurable assistance to the Trust, and also beneficial to the employees. By 1994, 37 per cent of those employed under this scheme had left to take up permanent posts elsewhere. Its demise was a source of great disappointment to the Trust and, regrettably, succeeding schemes have not provided the same community benefits.

PARTNERSHIPS AND COOPERATION

Conservation in Northern Ireland benefits greatly from the Trust being responsible for the management of much of the Landfill Community Fund, with a large number of projects undertaken in cooperation with several district councils. Between 1999–2006, a number of Community Environmental Education Officers, shared between the Trust and the councils, were appointed. Later the employment of Biodiversity Officers led to the development of further biodiversity projects across the Province. Partnerships such as these, and with other private organisations such as Translink, have been crucial in developing the depth and spread of the work of

Trust staff at the Balmoral Show in 2004

Publicity often accompanies public inquiries and the Trust makes representation in writing or in person at a number of these often contentious events.

LINKS WITH THE WIDER MOVEMENT

From its early years, the Trust has played a role in the wider Wildlife Trust movement. But it was only in 1990 that a formal link with The Wildlife Trusts was established, and the relationship with the Society was not formalised until 1999. Since then, successive directors and Council members – usually the chairman – have attended regular meetings and the Society's Council as part of the Irish Sea Group including the MANX WILDLIFE TRUST. Two of its directors, Dr David Erwin and Heather Thompson, have played particularly significant roles in UK activities. Erwin has been involved on the marine front and in the biodiversity planning process, and Thompson on developmental matters. The Council representatives continue to participate in working groups and activities for the Society.

LINKS WITH THE NORTHERN IRELAND ASSEMBLY

Northern Ireland draws up its own environmental legislation, and since the early 1980s the Trust has made, and continues to make, valuable contributions to proposed measures. The size of the Northern Ireland Assembly and its predecessors makes access to civil servants, Assembly Committees and even Ministers relatively straightforward. The Trust has established good relations with legislators at all levels, and is represented on relevant departmental working groups and stakeholder forums.

Recent major presentations to Assembly Committees and Ministers have been made on the Wildlife and Natural Environment Bill, passed in 2011, and on proposals for marine legislation and the revision of outdated forestry legislation. DOE(NI)'s statutory advisory body, the Council for Nature Conservation and the Countryside, has no members specifically nominated to represent voluntary bodies. But both individual Trust Council members and staff have been, or currently are, members of this committee in their own right.

the Trust, enabling it to engage with bigger and wider audiences.

The Trust began a corporate sponsorship scheme in 1990 which has helped both the Trust and the commercial organisations involved. Corporate sponsor, Northern Ireland Electricity (NIE), for instance, sponsored events or particular publicity exercises. That relationship, formed in 1997, led to the creation of Going for Green with NIE in 2000.

OXYGEN OF PUBLICITY

Celebration and publicity are often inseparable. A notable example of this relationship came on Ulster Wildlife Day in 1998, when the Society's then President, DAVID BELLAMY, took a helicopter trip around a few of the more prestigious reserves, giving press interviews at appropriate locations.

The Trust's members' magazine, *The Irish Hare,* and its website provide valuable links to the community, as do appearances at major agricultural shows and other relevant public gatherings. Press releases and appearances by staff on radio and television keep the Trust to the fore. Good relations exist with the major broadcasting organisations, and publicity skills have been enhanced with local private film-maker, Brian Black, joining the Trust's Council.

Bog Meadows nature reserve, Belfast

DEDICATED STAFF AND VOLUNTEERS

The Trust has made, and continues to make, a valuable contribution to local conservation. Through the integrity of its efforts it has gained the confidence of government bodies as well as the general public. This is due to the quality and skills of both permanent staff – currently 22 in number – and more than 70 volunteers. It is also due to their dedication to what they see as a very important function in working for Northern Ireland's only home-based conservation organisation. Several staff members have made a big contribution to the Trust, and also to the wider conservation scene, by the quality of their work and the authority of their spoken or written word. Dermot Hughes, formerly Director of Nature Conservation, especially stands out. Trusts cannot survive without the dedication and active participation of volunteers. In *Annual Reports* and *The Irish Hare* reference is constantly made to the sterling work undertaken on nature reserve management (often in adverse weather conditions); in leading groups of adults and schoolchildren; on office assistance and the 1001 other tasks which are most effectively carried out by volunteers.

Council members are all volunteers, drawn from a wide range of disciplines who play a vital role in overseeing the Trust's activities and planning for the future. It may be invidious to mention individual Council members who have made massive contributions, but amongst those with the greatest impact (in addition to those already mentioned) are Dick Jones – a most level-headed former Chairman and later Director; William Robb who edited *The Irish Hare* for several years; and his successor, Duggie Anderson, who also did much behind the scenes. In the early years, the infectious enthusiasm of Dr Henry Heal, inorganic chemistry lecturer, and botanist and entomologist extraordinaire, went a long way to inspire many members into action.

PUBLIC RECOGNITION

Four former Chairmen have received awards which reflected, in part, their contributions to the Trust. Dr David Erwin, Professor Palmer Newbould and Joe Furphy were awarded OBEs. Ian Forsyth and long-serving volunteer, Robin Moffitt, received MBEs. The Society further honoured the Trust by awarding the 2007 CHRISTOPHER CADBURY MEDAL to Joe Furphy.

The Trust's 30th anniversary in 2008 was marked by a reception at Parliament Buildings, Stormont, to which all founder members were invited. Among those present were the first Chairman, Honorary Secretary and Honorary Treasurer – Dr John Faulkner, Ian Forsyth and Mervyn Archdale. Jim Wells MLA is also a founder member, and the Trust is grateful to him for flying the nature conservation flag in the Northern Ireland Assembly.

As we look to the future, the Trust is undergoing a restructuring exercise and a refocusing of its strategy around the visions of Living Landscapes and Living Seas – restoring nature over wider areas, both on land and at sea. With a commitment to establish new core posts in education and marine work, the Trust is getting ready for the next 30 years of action.

BY JOE FURPHY

Joe Furphy was appointed in 1965 as one of the first two scientific staff for what is now the Northern Ireland Environment Agency. He has been involved, particularly since retirement, in several bodies, both statutory and voluntary. He is both a past and current Chairman of the Trust. In 2007, he was awarded both the OBE and the Christopher Cadbury Medal.

The founder members of the Ulster Wildlife Trust, pictured here in 2008

CHAPTER 44

Warwickshire

Warwickshire, Coventry and Solihull form a diamond-shaped area occupying some 870 square miles at the heart of England. The land is generally flat, with higher areas along a ridge of ancient rocks from Nuneaton to Atherstone in the north, and in the south-east where the Cotswolds begin to rise. Warwickshire straddles the watershed of England, with rainfall in the north and east flowing into the Trent and the North Sea, and rainfall in the south and west joining the Avon and Severn before reaching the Atlantic.

The area is home to about a million people, and its two major tourist attractions – Warwick Castle and Shakespeare's Stratford-upon-Avon – attract thousands of visitors each year. Its central location in the country has helped in the development of the National Exhibition Centre and the National Agricultural Centre, and the rail and motorway networks mean that many people pass through the area every day. Politically, the position of Coventry and Solihull as separate unitary authorities in the middle of Warwickshire County provides a significant degree of disconnection to what used to be a single unit. The area also includes some of the wealthiest parts of England, with areas such as Solihull and Leamington Spa consistently amongst the top retail locations in the country. Yet it also includes significant social deprivation in parts of Coventry, north Solihull and in isolated parts of the rural county.

Environmentally, Warwickshire's land and water resources have been exploited by people for many centuries, leaving a legacy of little truly natural

habitat and a much-changed landscape. Today, both farming and development keep up their pressures on the natural world: farming by intensification, use of fertilisers and pesticides, and drainage of nearly all the area's fields; development by building on the land and changing its character forever. Paradoxically, many of the best areas for nature today were previously used by industry – especially for quarrying – so that many brownfield sites are now much more ecologically valuable than greenfield land. Urban green space also has significant value for both wildlife and for people.

BIRTH OF THE WEST MIDLANDS TRUST

On 9th February 1956, eight people put their names to the Memorandum and Articles of a new organisation, the West Midlands Trust for Nature Conservation. Spurred on by the growth of other Trusts around the country, and locally by the loss of important natural habitats, they determined that a new Trust for the counties of Staffordshire, Warwickshire and Worcestershire was urgently needed. The founders set the ambitious target of 1,000 members for the fledgling Trust. An early publicity flier ends with an appeal for support, "so that the natural beauty of the countryside and the variety of its wild life and geology may be safeguarded for the future".

Amongst the eight founders were Fred Shotton (Chairman), Professor of Geology at Birmingham University; Jocelyn Morris, curator of Warwickshire Museum; and Coventry schoolteacher David Hughes. The new organisation was incorporated on 6th June 1957, and the accounts for its first year show a total income of £16 16s 1d, expenditure of £6 3s 6d,

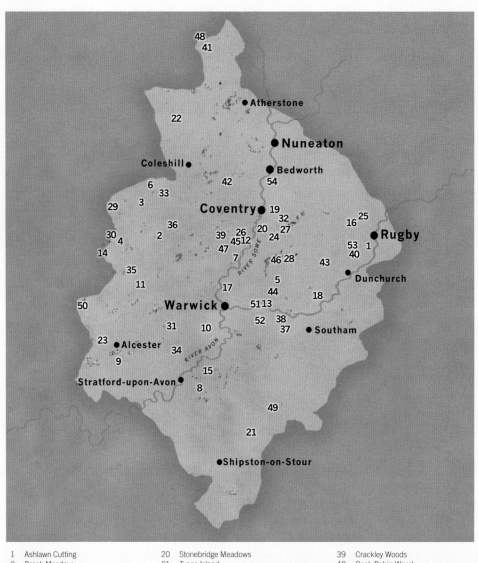

1	Ashlawn Cutting	20	Stonebridge Meadows	39	Crackley Woods
2	Brook Meadow	21	Tysoe Island	40	Cock Robin Wood
3	Parkridge Centre, Brueton	22	Whitacre Heath	41	Pooley Fields
4	Earlswood Moathouse	23	River Arrow	42	Harvest Hill
5	Eathorpe Marsh	24	Ryton Wood	43	Draycote Meadows
6	Elmdon Manor	25	Swift Valley	44	Hunningham Meadow
7	Glasshouse Spinney	26	Tocil Wood	45	Kenilworth Common
8	Goldicote Cutting	27	Brandon Marsh	46	Old Nun Wood
9	Grove Hill	28	Wappenbury Wood	47	Parliament Piece
10	Hampton Wood and Meadow	29	Priory Fields	48	Alvecote Meadows
11	Henley Sidlings	30	Clowes Wood and New Fallings Coppice	49	Radway Meadows
12	Knowle Hill	31	Snitterfield Bushes	50	Rough Hill Wood
13	Leam Valley	32	Claybrookes Marsh	51	Welches Meadow
14	Lion Wood	33	Shadowbrook Meadows	52	Whitnash Brook
15	Loxley Church Meadow	34	Welcombe Hills	53	Windmill Spinney
16	Newbold Quarry	35	Deans Green	54	Wyken Slough
17	Oakwood and Blacklow Spinneys	36	Temple Balsall		
18	Stockton Cutting	37	Harbury Spoilbank		
19	Stoke Floods	38	Ufton Fields		

Map of Warwickshire Wildlife Trust nature reserves

leaving a welcome surplus of £10 12s 7d. With the inclusion of subscriptions from life members, the balance sheet records that the company had a value of £66 2s 6d.

Right from the start it was recognised that there should be county branches, each with its own committee, so that sites could be surveyed, threats reported and members recruited at a local level. Each county was democratically represented on the Council, and from their minutes it seems that all went fairly well, supported by Miss J Laptain, the Nature Conservancy Council's Officer for the Midlands. The Trust grew slowly but steadily over its first years.

WEST MIDLANDS BREAKS UP

Towards the end of the 1960s, the West Midlands Trust for Nature Conservation was thrown into disarray by the decision of the Worcestershire Committee to pull out and set up a separate Trust. This was viewed as catastrophic by the remaining Council members, as the coherence of the whole was then destroyed. But ultimately it led to more local delivery and accountability. In the short term, the remaining two counties carried on, but, in 1969, Staffordshire separated to become an independent Trust. The remnants became the Warwickshire Nature Conservation Trust in the autumn of 1970. All the original West Midlands Trust records remain with the Warwickshire Trust to this day.

WARWICKSHIRE'S EARLY YEARS

The key person in Warwickshire at this time was Professor Fred Shotton. He, with David Hughes and Jocelyn Morris, became the foundation for the new Trust, with young University Lecturer, Duncan Jeffray acting as Honorary Conservation Officer. Council meetings were held at the Warwickshire Museum, where all the Trust papers were kept in an upstairs cupboard.

At the Trust's birth, it boasted 200 members and two nature reserves: Alvecote Pools, an extensive wetland formed by mining subsidence, and Temple Balsall, a small wet woodland near Solihull.

The Trust's first freehold nature reserve was Clowes Wood, which cost £100,000 in 1974. As the Trust did not have anything like this much money, an appeal was launched, supported by CHRISTOPHER CADBURY in Worcestershire, and several other Trusts. Draycote Meadows, the finest orchid-rich grassland in Warwickshire, was purchased in 1975 with the help of a second successful appeal. Three years later, an agreement with a supportive farmer meant that the Trust was able to manage parts of Oxhouse Farm, demonstrating that wildlife could flourish alongside agriculture. A slow trickle of desirable areas became nature reserves over the years, as they became available and as the means to acquire them allowed it. The Trust also acquired a new logo of a tree of birds, designed by a student of Coventry Art School lecturer Roger Smith, a key volunteer. The lengthy name of the Trust was now publicly shortened to WARNACT, being both an abbreviation and also a linking of 'warn' and 'act', which seemed a good idea at the time!

By the end of the 1970s, the Trust had a membership of 2,000; offices in Northgate Street, Warwick (thanks to Warwickshire County Council); and two thriving charity gift shops (in Sheep Street, Stratford-upon-Avon and Old Square, Warwick), run through a subsidiary trading company. It had also taken on its first paid conservation staff, adding to the volunteer efforts of Jeffray. The first post-holder, Lyn Rushall, was shared between WARWICKSHIRE and NORTHAMPTONSHIRE Trusts, in an agreement brokered by FRANK PERRING. However, the arrangement proved unsatisfactory and only lasted a few months, as both Trusts needed a full-time appointment. For Warwickshire that person was

Professor Fred Shotton – the Trust's first Chairman

Caroline Steele (*née* Waddams) who, in 1978, began the never-ending job of trying to protect a county's wildlife – on her own.

MSC SCHEMES

In 1980, after Steele had moved on, Margaret Wood was appointed Conservation Officer, thanks to a track record of running an otter project at the Royal Society for Nature Conservation. The advent of the Manpower Services Commission (MSC) and its schemes to help train the unemployed, marked the next big step (EMPLOYMENT SCHEMES). The Trust took on its first MSC scheme (more than doubling its staff) to carry out a survey of all the remaining natural habitats in Warwickshire. This followed from a previous survey coordinated by Pam Copson at Warwickshire Museum, where Women's Institute groups had helped annotate each field and woodland in the county. The Trust had also been involved in an earlier MSC scheme run by Coventry Polytechnic. This had surveyed the upper reaches of the River Avon to provide ecological data to counter a new threat from navigation interests. This threat was withdrawn, only to reappear at intervals up to the present day, alongside pressures from other proposed developments such as new airports, runway extensions and high speed rail.

The additional staff and trainees of the various MSC schemes did huge amounts for nature conservation, as well as providing excellent on-the-job training for scores of people, many of whom are still employed in nature conservation today. Amongst the achievements were the first systematic surveys of the county and much practical conservation management. Both these activities also helped to raise the Trust's profile. The Trust began a programme of nature reserve open days, supported by Area Groups, starting in a rain-sodden Clowes Wood, where new volunteer, Ron Hill, tried to get a visitor to join the Trust, only to find that it was in fact Fred Shotton, the Trust's founding Chairman! Area Groups developed to cover all the main towns, providing talks and slide shows aimed at educating, entertaining and encouraging more volunteers.

David Bellamy and Val Roberts at the opening of Brandon Marsh visitor centre in 2005

PLANNING GAINS AND LOSSES

Site protection was always a key focus, but in 1986, the Trust discovered too late in the planning process that Tesco had received permission to build a supermarket at Shelley Green, Solihull. The car park would obliterate most of an ancient, species-rich, hay meadow. As consent could not be rescinded, the Trust worked, with Tesco's cooperation, to move the meadow four miles up the M42 to another site. Working against impossible timescales and atrocious weather, in February and March 1987, the move was carried out with scrupulous care and enormous effort, but ultimately this last-ditch attempt failed.

A year later there was a similar controversy at Bishops Hill, near Leamington. The old limestone quarry waste was home for the small blue butterfly and myriad wildflowers, but developers had other ideas. This time the planning process protected the site, and the butterfly still survives there. Rare insects caused the Trust to cross swords with Coventry City Council in 1989 over a brownfield site known as Herald Way, where old mining activity had created an environment so important it was scheduled as a Site of Special Scientific Interest (SSSI). A developer wanted to build a warehouse on it, but fortunately local people and the Trust had sufficient clout to persuade the local authority to change its mind, and now Claybrookes Marsh is an official Trust nature reserve.

BIRMINGHAM WAKES UP TO WILDLIFE

Politically, urban wildlife was moving higher up the agenda, with the Trust leasing Stoke Floods nature reserve from Coventry City Council in 1979, and supporting the development of the Coventry Urban Wildlife Group. However, elsewhere in the region there was change afoot, as the Birmingham conurbation – long neglected by all three counties – discovered its nature. A new body, the Urban Wildlife Group, was formed in 1980. This new group also joined the Wildlife Trusts' partnership – as the WILDLIFE TRUST FOR BIRMINGHAM AND BLACK

Andy Tasker, Duncan Jeffray and Sir David Attenborough

COUNTRY – leaving Warwickshire with delicate negotiations as to where its boundaries (and its members) were. Eventually peace prevailed at a cost of losing Sutton Coldfield to the new upstart organisation.

EIGHTIES' MILESTONES

Andy Tasker, a new volunteer in the late 1970s and a lecturer in ecology at Coventry Polytechnic, became the Trust's youngest Chair of Council in 1982. He was followed in 1985 by John Roberts, then in 1989, by Ron Hill. After Margaret Wood's departure to the SCOTTISH WILDLIFE TRUST, Geoff Lewis took on the mantle of Conservation Officer in 1986. A restructuring of the Trust two years later led to Andy Tasker, returning from the USA, to become the Trust's first Director and a year later, in 1989, the Trust set up another commercial subsidiary, Warwickshire Wildlife Trading Limited. This company initially carried out training for the unemployed, practical landscaping and ecological consultancy. But it would not be until the next decade that the company – renamed Middlemarch Environmental Limited – would make a more significant impact.

NINETIES' SUCCESSES

Warwickshire County Council had supported the Trust with offices all through the 1980s,

Volunteers help the Trust turn the former Leigh Street allotments in Coventry into a green haven

from Northgate Street to the Old Drill Hall in Priory Street, then to Montague Road, Warwick. However, in 1990 the Poll Tax capped Council had to double the rent and cut all grants, so the search for alternative accommodation began. Aspirations pointed to Brandon Marsh – a former sand and gravel quarry on the outskirts of Coventry, where the Trust had begun the formal creation of a wetland nature reserve from 1981 with the Brandon Marsh Conservation Volunteers. The generous and welcome support of Steetly Quarry Products and the Brandon Marsh Conservation Group meant that the foundations for the Trust's new headquarters were laid.

During the 1990s, membership rose from 4,500 to 7,000, reflecting the clear desire of the public to do something to protect and improve its local environment. The Trust responded by doing more work, raising more money and spending more on staff, acquiring new nature reserves and recruiting more members. Over the decade, income rose from about £200,000 to more than £1.5 million, thanks particularly to the HERITAGE LOTTERY FUND (HLF) and the Landfill Tax

Credit Scheme. The continued growth of Middlemarch Environmental Ltd also contributed to this success and it ended the decade with a turnover of £600,000.

Opened by SIR DAVID ATTENBOROUGH in 1992, the Trust's first nature centre at Brandon Marsh became a real focus for the public and especially for children. Environmental education activities for schools were developed, with numbers of children visiting rising year-by-year to more than 8,000 annually at the end of the 1990s. Visitor numbers rose too, including both keen birdwatchers and families out for a day's gentle discovery. The advent of the National Lottery meant that funding for a visitor centre at the site became a possibility, and thanks to some lucky timing, the building opened in 1998 with another visit from Attenborough, who was again welcomed by the Trust's Chair, Val Roberts. Roberts remained Chair until 1999, when Roger Cadbury took over, providing a link to his father's role in Worcestershire some 40 years earlier.

The Trust continued to engage with the public through the 1990s, with community projects at Hillfields in Coventry, in north Solihull and at Packington near Coleshill. It also gained increased media attention and encouraged more volunteers to get involved. Corporate sector sponsorship became important, especially for the GLOBE Programme, an international environmental education project that the Trust hosted on behalf of The Wildlife Trusts from 1997 until 2009.

INTO THE 21ST CENTURY

A key achievement in the millennium year was the publication of the *Habitat Biodiversity Audit*, a Domesday-style digital nature map of Warwickshire, Coventry and Solihull produced by a unique partnership of local authorities, the Environment Agency, English Nature and the Trust. The map is now regularly updated, giving all partners details of all the surviving natural habitats in the area, as well as providing a blueprint for recreating large areas for nature. For the Trust, this new way of looking at conservation began with the Tame Valley and Princethorpe Woodlands. This project aims to link together all the fragments of wild land in targeted areas, aiming to provide sustainable landscapes for nature and for people.

To fulfil the Trust's ambition to be 'local' everywhere, a second visitor centre was developed in Solihull, thanks to an agreement with the Borough Council and financial support from the private sector. The Parkridge Centre in Brueton Park was opened in February 2002 by DAVID BELLAMY. Aiming to attract the public and introduce them to the natural world, the centre is now working well after a slightly shaky start. Events, such as Really Wild Birthday parties, have proved a key way to engage with new audiences, bringing more supporters, members and volunteers.

The buzzword 'biodiversity' appeared in the 1990s, and local Biodiversity Action Plans (BAPs) were developed as a way of bringing many partners together for a common objective. The Trust has played its part locally, although the Warwickshire BAP was not fully completed until 2006 due to the Trust's decision to undertake a Habitat Biodiversity Audit first.

There have been four key changes for the Trust since the millennium – changes in grants, in membership, in volunteering and at Middlemarch Environmental Ltd. The main grant change was the successful completion of a five-year grant from the HLF. This enabled the Trust's most important nature reserves to be 'put into best order' through improved conservation management and interpretation for visitors. The main membership change has been an exponential increase, thanks largely to a policy of investing more money in membership recruitment. This has seen a trebling in the number of members from 7,000 in 2000 to 23,500 in 2010. Volunteering has also increased, with 510 volunteers in 2010 contributing an amazing 4,928 days. The main change at Middlemarch Environmental Ltd has been its continuing growth to its current position as one of the UK's leading ecological consultancies. The income generated by the company's work has helped fund new development projects as well as augmenting membership income to support activities across the Trust.

Since the 1980s, the Trust has been planning its growth through a series of five-year development plans. The current plan focuses on developing a LIVING LANDSCAPE with key areas and the concept of a ntural network throughout Warwickshire, Coventry and Solihull at its heart. Partnerships with local authorities, farmers, landowners, businesses, local communities and individuals will be vital in providing and enhancing benefits for wildlife. In 2009, work began on the Sowe Valley project, an innovative three-year programme aimed at linking people and wildlife along a river corridor in Coventry.

Andy Tasker left the organisation in 2010, after many years of service to the Trust, and a new Chief Executive, Stephen Trotter, took his place. As climate change adds to pressures on the natural world from both agriculture and development, it is clear that there will still be a role for Warwickshire Wildlife Trust for many years to come.

BY ANDY TASKER AND JOHN ROBERTS
This chapter describing the history of the Warwickshire Wildlife Trust is dedicated to one of its authors, Andy Tasker, who sadly died in January 2012.

Prior to joining the Trust in 1989 as its first Director, Andy Tasker was Senior Lecturer in Ecology at Coventry Polytechnic. Since then, over a period of more than twenty years, Andy led the rapid growth and development of the Trust and that of its successful subsidiary, Middlemarch Environmental Ltd, retiring in 2010 as a result of illness. During a period of remission, Andy was appointed as Director of Globe International, based in Boulder, Colorado, prior to his untimely and premature death.

Professionally an Educational Psychologist, John Roberts is an ardent wildlife enthusiast and a founder member of the Trust. He became Chairman in 1986, retiring through ill-health after three years. He has remained an active Trustee and promoter of the Trust, recording, writing, photographing and talking about nature conservation. His wife Val shares and supports his passions, and was herself Chair of the Trust for seven years.

CHAPTER 45

Wiltshire

Wiltshire, together with the now independent borough of Swindon, is traditionally divided into 'chalk and cheese'. In the south and east, the chalk downs of Marlborough, Salisbury Plain and Cranborne Chase are where sheep farming has always predominated. Dairy country, largely on clay soils, lies to the north and west. By virtue of the large army training area on the downland of Salisbury Plain and Ministry of Defence land at Porton Down, the county has more semi-natural chalk downland than anywhere else in England or, indeed, in western Europe. Around the edge of the county lie many fine ancient woodlands, Langley and Bentley in the south-east, Savernake further north, several woods on the west side, and the Forest of Braydon, which includes many residual, unimproved hay meadows.

AGRICULTURAL ORIGINS

The staple support has always been agriculture – both sheep and arable. Sheep on the chalk downs and the Cotswold fringe supplied wool for mills in the Bristol Avon Valley, with some rich arable land in that valley and the chalk valleys. In his *Rural Rides*, published in 1830, William Cobbett rhapsodised over his view of the Vale of Pewsey and, if he excuses the fields of yellow rape, might say much the same today. Thus the fortunes of the county have closely reflected the ups and downs of agriculture generally. This led to a severe depression in the 1920s and 1930s, making Wiltshire one of the poorest counties in England.

Opposite: Wasp orchid – Clattinger Farm

But from 1939 to the 1990s agriculture flourished. Intensification, most evident in the ploughing and 'blue-bag' fertilisation of the downland, led to a boom in production and in land values. This was accompanied by a trend towards fewer, larger farms and a sharp reduction in the number of dairy herds.

Recently, the central location of the county and its accessibility to the whole of southern England has attracted successful entrepreneurs. Wiltshire's relatively sparse population is also attractive to the wealthy seeking seclusion and rural sports.

SEEDS OF THE TRUST

Wiltshire lacks a university, so its natural history has been a field for local amateurs and academic incomers. This spawned a number of flourishing societies, most notably the Wiltshire Archaeological and Natural History Society, founded in 1853. The society houses a museum and at one time held the county's biological records, but its activities have always centred more on Wiltshire's rich archaeology. There have also been societies for ornithology, botany and butterflies, and some local natural history societies. The aptly named Natural History Forum was an important influence for cohesion of these societies, and from 1974 to 2002 worked with the Nature Conservancy Council, local government, the Farming and Wildlife Advisory Group, the army and many others. This allowed a valuable regular exchange of information and also initiated projects such as the Wiltshire Floral Mapping Project of 1983 92. Today, Wiltshire Wildlife Trust has largely taken over this function. It also now houses the Biological Records Centre.

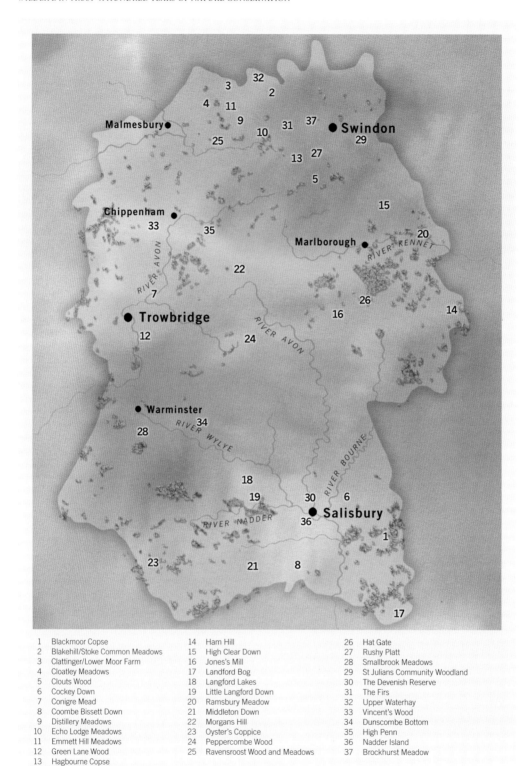

1	Blackmoor Copse	14	Ham Hill	26	Hat Gate
2	Blakehill/Stoke Common Meadows	15	High Clear Down	27	Rushy Platt
3	Clattinger/Lower Moor Farm	16	Jones's Mill	28	Smallbrook Meadows
4	Cloatley Meadows	17	Landford Bog	29	St Julians Community Woodland
5	Clouts Wood	18	Langford Lakes	30	The Devenish Reserve
6	Cockey Down	19	Little Langford Down	31	The Firs
7	Conigre Mead	20	Ramsbury Meadow	32	Upper Waterhay
8	Coombe Bissett Down	21	Middleton Down	33	Vincent's Wood
9	Distillery Meadows	22	Morgans Hill	34	Dunscombe Bottom
10	Echo Lodge Meadows	23	Oyster's Coppice	35	High Penn
11	Emmett Hill Meadows	24	Peppercombe Wood	36	Nadder Island
12	Green Lane Wood	25	Ravensroost Wood and Meadows	37	Brockhurst Meadow
13	Hagbourne Copse				

Map of Wiltshire Wildlife Trust nature reserves

BUTTERFLY BEGINNINGS

An initial motivation for the Trust's formation in 1962 was a concern for the colony of purple emperor butterflies in Blackmoor Copse. The nature of the colony was recorded in *Notes and Views of the Purple Emperor* by Heslop, Hyde and Stockley. The authors were very worried in the mid-1950s by a threat to cut down the master oak tree. Letters from Heslop urged the Society for the Promotion of Nature Reserves to purchase the woodland. When this was done in 1956, a group of local naturalists, including Heslop and Major General Lipscomb, was formed to manage it. This wood still forms a great natural habitat for butterflies, dragonflies, birds and dormice, although the purple emperors are now more easily seen in nearby Bentley Wood.

Despite this initiative, Wiltshire remained without a Wildlife Trust until six years later when Charles Floyd (the first Chairman) and Lady Radnor (the first President) brought together a group of like-minded landowners and naturalists concerned for the conservation of the county's wildlife. They formed the Wiltshire Trust for Nature Conservation (WTNC). At the inaugural meeting in October 1962, 160 people were present – mostly the great and the good, such as landowners, an army representative and a bishop. A Council of 24 was created, including 15 Vice Presidents.

More importantly, some eminent naturalists were also present: Donald Grose, the author of *The Flora of Wiltshire* (1957); Baron de Worms, about to publish his *Macrolepidoptera of Wiltshire*; and Ruth Barnes, the county bird recorder. Very soon there were three committees: Education, Meetings and Publicity; Reserves Management under Charles Floyd; and Scientific Advisory under Sir Christopher Andrews, an expert in diphtheria and the common cold.

ENGINEERED FOR ACTION

From the beginning, the Trust was set up to take action, not simply to be a 'passive' natural history society. At the time, a prime concern was the loss of

View across the Vale of Pewsey 1965. By this time Wiltshire's natural habitats were under threat and disappearing fast

downland to agricultural intensification. Whereas in 1939, there had been 13,000 acres in the county under barley, by 1963 this had increased to more than 130,000 acres. In the summer of 1963, a downland survey found that nine Sites of Special Scientific Interest (SSSI) status had been either ploughed or damaged. Furthermore, steep escarpments, hitherto free from improvement, were being sprayed from the air. The scarcity of the adonis blue butterfly was noted. The use of toxic chemicals and their effects, especially on waterways and the decline of otters, were deplored.

Strenuous efforts were made to visit important downland sites to establish some protection of the flora and butterflies. And, while some sites – for example, Chickengrove Bottom and Knowle Down, lovingly managed by the butterfly enthusiast Douglas Mann – are still as good as ever, the owners of others proved to be elusive or unresponsive. A list of SSSIs was drawn up with the Nature Conservancy Council and the four best downland sites became National Nature Reserves under its care.

In the early days of the Trust there were no paid staff and no premises for a headquarters. All the work was done with dedicated commitment by a small group of founders and members, whose thousands of hours of unpaid labour created the functioning Trust. The first paid Secretary (part-time) was recruited in 1973, and the first Field and Development Officers in 1974. A shop and small office were acquired in 1982.

GENTLEMEN'S AGREEMENTS

This initial stage, perhaps best termed the patrician phase of the Trust, lasted for almost 20 years, during which there was a positive avoidance of ownership and direct management of sites by the Trust. Reserves were established by gentlemen's agreements between the Trust and friendly landowners, with the Trust offering advice and doing some monitoring. But in many cases management advice was not followed, leading to a gradual change in policy from about 1980.

There was one exception to the Trust's early avoidance of reserve ownership. Whereas in 1965 no effort had been made to buy some fritillary fields near Oaksey, when a similar field at Upper Waterhay came on the market in 1970, a sum of £3,151 was raised for its purchase. This field, uniquely one where the fritillaries are mostly white and now almost an island among gravel pits, remains one of the few in the whole county where fritillaries have not declined. But it was the only purchase in the first 20 years of the Trust's existence.

A few reserves were formed by agreements with public bodies, such as the Ministry of Defence for areas of good downland at Cotley and Cheverell, and with the Forestry Commission at Somerford and Red Lodge to conserve small areas of special interest. With changes in policy in both these organisations, such arrangements were no longer needed.

FIRST CHALK DOWNLAND RESERVE

From the mid-1980s, what might best be termed the transitional period of the Trust began under the chairmanship of Robin Brockbank, with Humphrey Kay chairing the Conservation Committee. It now became an important aim to try and purchase land for direct Trust control, or to persuade the landowner to bequeath land

Chalk grassland at Morgans Hill nature reserve

to the Trust. Thus the Trust's first reserve for chalk downland, Cockey Down near Salisbury, came to the Trust in 1986 by a bequest. The donor had at first refused to relinquish the land in her lifetime, as she regretted that the value of her estate as published at her death would be thereby diminished. But she was persuadable. In another instance, a relative of the eccentric owner of Green Lane Wood said that the Trust should not point out to her that there would be less in death duties to pay as a consequence of the bequest (as, of course, there were) as, the Trust was told, "she wants the relatives to pay as much as possible".

NEOLITHIC MARATHON

The transitional period of the Trust, from the early 1980s to the mid-1990s, was also characterised by more vigorous fundraising, especially around the time of the Trust's Silver Jubilee in 1987. That period also saw the expansion of membership, the division of the county into seven local branches, and more active reserve management work. One part of the Silver Jubilee appeal was the Sarsen Trail, a sponsored walk from Avebury to Stonehenge, later augmented by the Neolithic Marathon over the same track. This has become an annual event and is the Trust's largest fundraising event.

In 1974, an independent organisation, the Wiltshire Wildlife Conservation Volunteers, was formed. This organisation, under the leadership of Brian Merry, Beatrice Gillam and Lesley Balfe, has been a mainstay of Trust reserve management for more than 33 years. In the 1980s, under the Manpower Services Commission, it was also possible to recruit young unemployed workers for reserve management tasks. Through this scheme, Ann Skinner was able to compile lists of ancient woodland sites and flower-rich hay meadows throughout the county which then became targets for acquisition or for advice and monitoring.

In 1985, Wiltshire was one of the first counties to have a computerised system for biological records, as initiated by Claire Appleby. But the loss of key personnel, lack of space and coordination prevented further progress for some time. Eventually,

The Spring/Summer 1990 issue of the Trust's magazine

with some extra finance and accommodation in the Trust's headquarters, a more comprehensive system became possible. Although still under-funded, the Biological Records Centre is now an integral part of the Trust providing an essential service to Wiltshire and Swindon. In 2011, the Trust produced the first *State of the Environment Report for Wiltshire* and contributed to 20 community area Joint Strategic Assessments.

FLOURISHING MATURITY

Finally the Trust got into top gear following the 1990 appointment of its current Director, Dr Gary Mantle. In this present phase of flourishing maturity, and most notably under the chairmanship of Geraldine Wimble, it can now instigate multiple activities comprising the whole environment on which our wildlife depends. It has greatly increased professional staff, but is still dependent on a growing army of volunteers, who are now active in nearly every aspect of the Trust's work, and its ever-increasing membership.

A feature of the Wiltshire Trust has been its ability to respond to new funding sources. The Trust was among the first to gain from the National Lottery at its inception in 1994 and by 2011 had received 30 different lottery grants amounting to more than £5 million. The Trust was also the first environmental body to benefit from the Landfill Tax Credit Scheme. Principally through the support of local aggregates and waste company, The Hills Group, the Trust has received more than £5 million from this scheme. Local authorities have also been highly supportive. As a result, the Trust was able to increase substantially the number and size of its nature reserves. In 2006, this included setting up a beef farming enterprise in the north of the county to enable the Trust to achieve the precision grazing necessary on its hay meadows. The Trust now has two visitor centres – Langford Lakes in the south and Lower Moor Farm in the north of the county. For all major purchases, the grants received have been dependent on the generosity of sums raised directly by Trust members.

SUSTAINABILITY AGENDA

In 1995, the Trust embraced Local Agenda 21, an initiative that began at the Rio de Janeiro Earth Summit in 1992. The Trust widened its work to include a range of sustainability projects and activities based on waste minimisation and

The Trust's Future Jobs Fund taskforce at work

recycling, as well as reducing greenhouse gas emissions through energy conservation and the use of renewable energy. In 2000, the Trust amended its constitution to include, as a charitable object, the advancement of the education of the public in the principles and practice of sustainable development. Other Wildlife Trusts also subsequently used this revised constitution. Earlier that year, the Trust Director, Gary Mantle, was made an MBE for services to nature conservation.

At the start of the new millennium, the Trust changed its approach to nature conservation and began to promote the idea of rebuilding biodiversity. The Trust believed that it was no longer enough to try and hold onto the remaining fragments of precious wildlife habitat. A new approach was needed, through which large areas managed for wildlife were interlinked by a permeable landscape through which wildlife could travel freely. The Trust began to add to its portfolio of nature reserves land that would be restored. In 2000, the Trust bought 255 hectares at Blakehill Farm, a disused war-time airfield near Cricklade and began the largest neutral grassland restoration project in the country. In 2003, the South West Wildlife Trusts launched a major report *Rebuilding Biodiversity*.

The Royal opening of Lower Moor Farm in 2007

REBUILDING BIODIVERSITY

The Rebuilding Biodiversity initiative has now become an accepted approach to nature conservation. For example, the Government's Regional Spatial Strategy for the South West included a Strategic Nature Map showing the prime areas where biodiversity could be rebuilt. The 2007 Stern Report on climate change reaffirmed the need for nature conservation at the landscape scale, with larger contiguous tracts of land and reduced fragmentation making the intervening countryside more permeable to wildlife. By 2007, with the threat of climate change now widely accepted, the work of all the Trusts is focused around this issue under the collective banner of Living Landscapes.

In 2002, 40 years after Charles Floyd formed the Wiltshire Trust for Nature Conservation, his son, Robert, became Chairman of Wiltshire Wildlife Trust. Between 2001 and 2008 the Trust continued to flourish and saw its membership reach 20,000.

Reminiscent of the 1980s, in 2010–11 the Trust used the Government's Future Jobs Fund to employ almost 240 young people to work throughout the Trust. Jobs on offer ranged from estates work to IT, film-makers and artists. The Trust was also running the Wellbeing project at this time, taking people with health problems into the countryside, teaching them skills and helping them to appreciate what was all around them. These two projects illustrate that it is not just about what we can do for nature, but also what nature can do for us.

The Wiltshire Trust continues to promote its vision of a sustainable future for wildlife and people, seeking a holistic approach to nature conservation that makes links with social and economic agendas. Underpinned by sound science and good convincing evidence, the Trust is still seeking to lead and support society's transition towards more sustainable living and to create living landscapes. The approach is summed up by the message contained on a series of displays at the entrance of the Trust's visitor centre: "If you believe that nature provides beauty

and hope and is worth defending, where every contribution is valued and repaid in kind, where experience is shared with everyone so people are part of the solution, living on a fair share of the world's resources, then welcome to the Wiltshire Wildlife Trust".

BY PROFESSOR HUMPHREY KAY
The Wiltshire chapter of this book is dedicated to its author, Professor Humphrey Kay, who died in 2009. He gave a huge amount of his time to the Trust and served as a Trustee, Chairman of the Conservation Committee and Reserve Warden for many years. In 1996, he was awarded the prestigious Christopher Cadbury Medal for nature conservation. He was a charming man, and a good friend to all that knew him.

Blackmoor Copse – where it all began in the 1950s

CHAPTER 46

Worcestershire

Worcestershire, a largely rural and pastoral county, is dominated by the River Severn and its tributaries, the Stour, the Teme and the Avon. Its fertile plains are bounded by hills on virtually all of its boundaries from the Birmingham plateau in the north, to the Cotswold Hills in the south. To the west are the hills of Malvern, Abberley and Clent. Its varied geology gives rise to a remarkable variety of habitats in such a small county – it even boasts small areas of saltmarsh!

The county's physical character is reflected in its social geography, with the main centres of population focused on Worcester (the county town) and several other old market towns situated beside the main rivers and their tributaries. The exception is Malvern, perched in the lea of the eponymous hills on the county's western edge. All have seen considerable expansion in recent decades, especially those in the north. Here, two new towns were developed to relieve overspill from areas which were once part of the county – the industrial metropolis of Birmingham and the Black Country.

The inaugural meeting that led to the formation of the Worcestershire Trust took place in Worcester Shire Hall on 14th November 1967. On 28th March 1968, the Worcestershire Nature Conservation Trust was created as a registered company and charity rather than simply a branch of the West Midlands Nature Conservation Trust. The latter had been created in 1958 to cover the counties of Staffordshire, Warwickshire, Worcestershire and the Birmingham conurbation. But this was too large an area to be successful at a local level. Soon afterwards, all these counties formed independent Trusts and divided Birmingham between them. The BIRMINGHAM AND BLACK COUNTRY TRUST was formed at a much later date. These moves owed much to the vision and energy of CHRISTOPHER CADBURY, who stimulated the

Opposite: Green-winged orchids. Above: Eades Meadow – one of the UK's finest lowland wildflower meadows

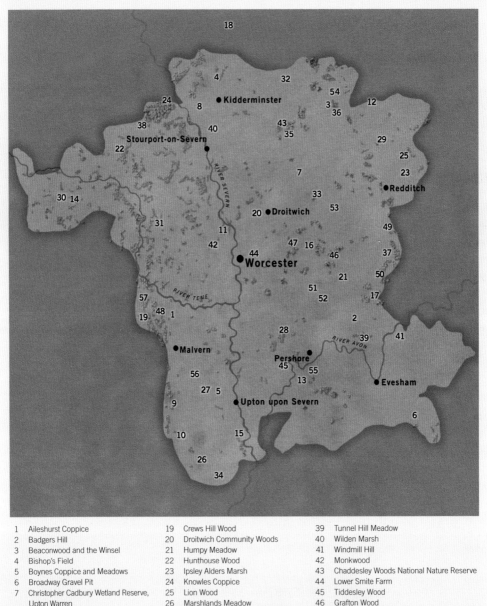

1	Aileshurst Coppice	19	Crews Hill Wood	39	Tunnel Hill Meadow
2	Badgers Hill	20	Droitwich Community Woods	40	Wilden Marsh
3	Beaconwood and the Winsel	21	Humpy Meadow	41	Windmill Hill
4	Bishop's Field	22	Hunthouse Wood	42	Monkwood
5	Boynes Coppice and Meadows	23	Ipsley Alders Marsh	43	Chaddesley Woods National Nature Reserve
6	Broadway Gravel Pit	24	Knowles Coppice	44	Lower Smite Farm
7	Christopher Cadbury Wetland Reserve,	25	Lion Wood	45	Tiddesley Wood
	Upton Warren	26	Marshlands Meadow	46	Grafton Wood
8	The Devil's Spittleful and	27	Melrose Farm Meadows	47	Trench Wood
	Blackstone Fields	28	Mill Meadow	48	The Knapp and Papermill
9	Drake Street Meadow	29	Newbourne Wood	49	Feckenham Wylde Moor
10	Duke of York Meadow	30	Pennels Bank Wood	50	Sands Meadows
11	Grimley Brick Pits	31	Penny Hill Bank	51	Naunton Court Fields
12	Grovely Dingle	32	Penorchard Meadows	52	Piddle Brook Meadows
13	Gwen Finch Wetland	33	Pipers Hill Common	53	Eades Meadow and Foster's Green Meadow
14	Hanley Dingle	34	Poolhay Meadows	54	Broadmoor Wood
15	Hill Court Farm and Blacklands	35	Randan Wood and Meadows	55	Avon Valley Reserves
16	Hornhill Wood	36	Spinneyfield	56	Brotheridge Green Old Railway
17	Long Meadow	37	Stockwood Meadow	57	Ravenshill
18	Chance Wood	38	The Betts Reserve		

Map of Worcestershire Wildlife Trust nature reserves

growth of many other Trusts as well as the movement's national organisation.

Looking back at the first governing Council of the Trust, brought together by Cadbury, it contained a remarkable collection of people. They included Norman Hickin, a director of Rentokil, but also an insect conservationist and national expert on caddisflies; John Betts, a businessman who refined precious metals and lived in Wyre Forest; Cecil Lambourne, a business man and ornithologist whose large factory produced innumerable small metal objects including bird rings for the national birdringing scheme; Elizabeth Barling, who created her own educational nature reserve; Jim Vernon, a solicitor and county councillor with a penchant for obscure quotations; Tony Harthan, a county ornithologist and author of *The Birds of Worcestershire*; and Fred Fincher who knew more about the natural history of Worcestershire than the rest of them put together. Other notables were two brilliant authors and biology teachers; Gordon Simmons, who made the young Trust think seriously about education and Arnold Darlington, a biology teacher of national renown. Cecil Lambourne, Fred Fincher and Elizabeth Barling eventually received MBEs for services to conservation and Cadbury was awarded the CBE.

EARLY WARBLER SITES

In the 1960s, a small but active Worcestershire group was formed to protect the main marsh warbler sites in the county through purchase, lease or agreement. This group consisted of Cecil Lambourne from the Trust, James Cadbury from RSPB, Ray Bishop and Harry Green. Their work fitted with national interest in acrocephalus warblers (the genus which, in the UK, includes marsh, reed and sedge warblers) at the time, and a visit from scientist Ben Bell made the group realise that changes afoot in countryside management could easily destroy the habitat of this nationally-important species. Within a few years, thanks to Cadbury's help, the group had established a string of small sites in the Avon Valley as marsh warbler reserves under the aegis of the Trust. In retrospect, this was an

Opening a new hide at Upton Warren in 1970. Foreground: HRH The Duke of Edinburgh (left) and Christopher Cadbury (right)

early step into landscape-scale conservation. These sites were soon designated as SSSIs and turned out to be highly important for insects, plants and other birds. They eventually became the vestigial traces of the original Avon Valley wetland areas, surviving the gathering storm of land drainage and intensive agriculture. Sadly, marsh warblers declined and eventually vanished from the county in the 1980s – another story. Despite their continuing importance today, these sites are soon to be de-notified as SSSIs simply because marsh warblers have vanished – a piece of bureaucratic nonsense. At the same time, the Trust and others are recreating wetlands in the Avon Valley on a large scale through grants, purchases and farm stewardship agreements and are removing drainage schemes created about 30 years ago.

TRUST RESERVES

From the beginning, the Trust established nature reserves. The first, Randan Wood, was managed under an agreement with owner Fred Fincher who lived in a bungalow in the wood. Fincher eventually gave Randan Wood to the Trust and in his will left his bungalow, and a remarkable collection of papers and books, to the Trust. One of his greatest achievements was to discover Eades Meadow, still the most amazing herb-rich lowland grassland surviving in the county today. Much later, the whole of the associated Foster's Green Farm was acquired and the site became a National Nature Reserve. The reserve was inaugurated by SIR DAVID ATTENBOROUGH who arrived by helicopter during a tour promoting the BRITISH WILDLIFE APPEAL in 1985. Since then the Trust has purchased many smaller lowland meadows – a small but important legacy of a habitat once commonplace in the county.

Attenborough helped the Trust on several occasions with lectures to large audiences. The most memorable was in front of an audience of 7,000 people in the central Odeon, Birmingham, at the time of his popular TV series *Life on Earth*. He was introduced by CHRISTOPHER CADBURY, with Harry Green given the nerve-racking task of promoting the Trust appeal with a presentation.

THE SEVENTIES AND SALTMARSH

By the end of 1970, the Trust had 740 members and in 1972 the annual subscription was raised to £2. By 1976, there were 23 reserves respresenting a wide range of important habitats. They included Randan Wood, Upton Warren, Knapp and Papermill, Eades Meadow, Hunthouse Wood, Knowles Coppice and Aileshurst Coppice. At Upton Warren, Cadbury bought the farm and pools, sold the farm buildings and gave the rest to the Trust. The site has two wetland parts, both formed as the land subsided due to underground brine extraction for the Stoke Prior salt factory. One part of the wetland is a shallow lake and the other a series of briny pools and saltmarsh that attract many migrant and nesting birds. Many changes have since followed and it is now difficult to remember Upton Warren before the hides and boardwalks. Arthur Jacobs was involved at the beginning as guardian and chief warden. He and many volunteers have worked on the reserve, undertaking a vast array of practical work, including bird recording. These efforts have been rewarded by breeding little ringed plovers and, in recent years, by the remarkable establishment of an avocet colony.

An avocet colony has established at Upton Warren following major restoration work

FIRST STAFF AND OFFICE

In March 1974, the Trust managed to obtain a small grant to employ its first member of staff – Andrew Fraser. An office was found, tucked away in a wooden hut at Avoncroft College near Bromsgrove, with space for a part-time secretary. Fraser's job covered everything from education to fundraising. But much of his early work was to do with reserves, gathering volunteers to carry out practical work, and founding the Worcestershire Conservation Volunteers. He also developed good contacts with statutory planners and his influence helped to improve the lot of wildlife in some developments. He stayed with the Trust for more than 30 years, an outstanding and dedicated man who sadly died far too young.

The second headquarters was a couple of rooms in a small house in the grounds of Cadbury's home at Beaconwood, just south of Birmingham. The next move after a few years was to a vacant, almost derelict County Council Highways site with a temporary building at Hanbury Road, Droitwich. Bigger than before, it was very cold in winter and had a roof that leaked! Uncomfortable though it was, it provided space to expand and employ people through government job creation schemes (EMPLOYMENT SCHEMES).

VALUABLE SKILLS AND VOLUNTEERS

For years the Trust was short of money. Several members of the first Council assisted financially and this, together with grants that could often be raised towards reserve purchases, helped the Trust move forward. In the late 1970s and early 1980s, government job creation schemes through the Manpower Services Commission brought many unemployed people to work for the Trust. The variety of people was amazing – from biologists to forestry workers, and artists to clerks. They undertook wildlife surveys, developed and improved the Trust's public face, and did an immense amount of practical work on reserves. One important project was a countywide survey, CONPOT 77, which attempted to map all areas in the county which appeared to have wildlife potential. The maps from this work were useful guidance for many years, with analysis by John Day providing the first information on the distribution of broad habitat types in Worcestershire.

The founding of local groups in the 1980s brought many active volunteers into the Trust. They worked on reserves and helped with fundraising by organising events such as special reserve open days and huge country fairs. This was all at a time when the Trust was seriously short of funds. Such voluntary activity also brought new blood on to Council and its committees, and changed the face of the organisation. Later, the creation of the National Lottery and HERITAGE LOTTERY FUND (HLF) brought several years of rapid development and many new staff to the Trust. This, together with several generous legacies and a larger membership, eventually put the Trust on a sounder financial footing.

The growth of the Trust meant there was an urgent need for a new headquarters. Eventually in 1990, Lower Smite Farm, just north of Worcester, was found. The Trust was granted a lease by the County Council, but it had to raise about £70,000 to renovate the old farmhouse into offices. Lower Smite Farm had previously been purchased by the County Council as a prospective landfill site, but planning permission was not granted and it

had languished for years as rough grazing and temporary accommodation. Subsequently, the Trust purchased the farm buildings and the rest of the 120-acre farm. Slow incremental improvement of the site followed and another HLF grant enabled the conversion of the old farm buildings to an education centre. This now has excellent meeting rooms and a much-needed workshop to support practical conservation work on reserves. Several thousand children now visit each year and are taught by the Trust's own staff.

BUYING WOODLAND

Throughout its history, the Trust has continued to acquire land. In the late 1980s, the government's requirement that the Forestry Commission should dispose of small sites led to the purchase of the 180-acre Tiddesley Wood, near Pershore. Shortly afterwards, the famous Harris Brushworks at Stoke Prior decided to sell its woodland estate. Many of its woods were known to be important wildlife sites and the owner, Leslie Harris, had given access to Trust members. Eventually two of these woods were purchased – Monkwood and Trench Wood. These purchases led to a developing and close working relationship with the Butterfly Conservation Trust which provided some money towards the purchases and later for the joint purchase of Grafton Wood. At around the same time,

Volunteers haymaking at Lower Smite Farm nature reserve

A carpet of bluebells at Trench Wood

English Nature passed the management of Chaddesley Wood NNR to the Trust. Acquisition of five large and many smaller woodlands led the Trust to develop a forestry management plan. Its aim was good conservation management, compatibility between good forestry and public access and a fundraising programme. Forming this plan led to many arguments, usually relating to the impossible dream of returning large areas to coppice management – defunct for 100 years.

TROUBLE AHEAD

Soon after the Trust moved headquarters to Lower Smite Farm, shortage of cash became an increasing problem and there were many fundraising initiatives. It became apparent that the Treasurer at the time was siphoning off funds but, fortunately, the money was recovered and this greatly helped in changing the Trust's fortunes for the better. Dealing with this difficult situation came down to the Trust's third Chairman, Bert Reid. Building sound management and financial

systems was driven by the fourth Chairman, Ron Stanton.

As the Trust developed, it became obvious that reorganisation was needed. The old committee structure was swept away and the Trust became more staff-led. In 1995, a Director was appointed to run the Trust in accordance with the overall guidance from Council, which remained the governing body. The Trust's financial systems were also improved. During all the changes, the Trust maintained and developed close working between staff and volunteers at all levels. This is an intrinsic and important part of the Trust's culture and one of its great strengths. A system of close working between the Council, special Council Honorary Officers and staff was put in place and continues to prove a very satisfactory and useful arrangement. The Trust's fifth Chairman, Linda Butler, led the way into better governance and closer involvement with national affairs. The excellent working relationships between the Trust's last two Chairmen and Director, Colin Raven, has contributed greatly to the Trust's successful development in recent years.

EXCITING NEW PROJECTS

The most exciting recent developments have been the *creation* of wildlife reserves, rather than the purchase of existing wildlife-rich sites, together with the Trust's move into farming. The Gwen Finch Reserve, adjacent to the River Avon on the northern edge of Bredon Hill, funded by a legacy and grants, created brand new wetlands for wildlife. This first step in recreating wetland in the highly-drained Avon Valley was a difficult project. But now there are large pools, reed beds and wet grassland rough-grazed by White Park cattle. This proved to be a catalyst for other similar projects, including a new wetland at Pershore created through liaison between the district council, statutory agencies and the Trust. More recently, a private landowner is creating a new wetland near the original Gwen Finch reserve with the Trust's advice and help. In the past, a huge marshland existed at Longdon in the south of the county and the Trust had long dreamed of its re-establishment. The purchase of Hill Court Farm in 1998, in one corner of the area, set a scheme in motion to do this, almost against the odds. Progress has been slow but steady and a recreation project that was one of Andrew Fraser's dreams, now carries his name. Fraser was awarded the Christopher Cadbury medal in 2002, less than a year before his untimely death, aged only 54 (CHRISTOPHER CADBURY MEDAL CITATIONS).

In 2002, the Trust made a firm decision to develop a better understanding of farming. Its purchase of the land at Lower Smite Farm is a continuing lesson in environmentally-sensitive farming. The Trust aims to show that, by careful planning and the use of stewardship schemes, it is possible to run a wildlife-friendly farm and make a profit. To enable the Trust to farm more satisfactorily, a Farming Officer was employed to run the farmed land and to offer help to other interested farmers. The next venture into farming soon followed with the purchase of Naunton

Court fields near Naunton Beauchamp. The fields were chosen especially for the conservation of rare arable plants they were known to contain.

More recently, the purchase of part of Upper Blackstone Farm, adjacent to the Devil's Spittleful, is leading the Trust into heathland recreation. In the past, the sandy soils around Kidderminster supported extensive heathlands, most of which disappeared under agricultural development and the creation of a safari park. For many years the Trust has owned one heath at the Devil's Spittleful and worked on its management with the district council which owned an adjacent heath. Upper Blackstone lies adjacent to these heaths and the aim is to bring about a gradual change from agriculture to heathland. The first steps, to reduce soil fertility, are in hand and arable farming is an essential part of this process.

The most recent venture is into landscape-scale conservation. After careful thought, six large areas of the county were selected for promoting conservation in as many ways as possible – through stewardship schemes, persuasion, raising awareness and perhaps land purchase. The Trust was also closely involved in similar work across the West Midlands. First steps are now being taken along the Bow Brook – a long watercourse running through the centre of the county – and the Avon Valley. The overall aim is to create a system of corridors and links to wildlife habitat throughout these areas. This is the next great adventure.

BY HARRY GREEN

Harry Green, an Honorary Vice President of the Worcestershire Wildlife Trust, has been involved in the Trust since its foundation, in a variety of roles, including a long spell as the Trust's second Chairman. A leading naturalist and conservationist in the county, he was awarded an MBE in 2001 and the Christopher Cadbury Medal in 2008.

CHAPTER 47

Yorkshire

The Yorkshire Wildlife Trust was founded in 1946 – the second in the UK after Norfolk. The age of the Trust and the size of the county – the largest in England – means that there is a lot of history! To get the size of Yorkshire into perspective, it is a little more than 180 kilometres, as the peregrine falcon flies, from the tip of Spurn Point on the Humber in the east, to Hawthornthwaite Fell Top in the Forest of Bowland in the far west. The same distance and direction in the south of England takes you from Dungeness in Kent, through East and West Sussex, Surrey, Hampshire and into Wiltshire. Yorkshire is also the only county with two Trusts, because nested within it is the SHEFFIELD WILDLIFE TRUST.

Yorkshire's wonderful wildlife is, literally, underpinned by the county's geology, with rocks from every geological period from the Ordovician to the Cretaceous. The oldest rocks – from the Upper and Lower Carboniferous – and highest ground lie in the west of the county, with great blocks of millstone grit and the coal measures underlying huge areas of open, boggy Pennine moorland. In stark contrast are dramatic karst limestone pavements round Ingleborough and Malham. Subsidence from coal mining and mineral extraction has left a legacy of important wetlands. The rocks become younger as you head east. The Permian magnesian limestone running from south to north across the middle of the county provided the stone for York Minster and has a rich flora that survives in pockets. Two great geological blocks dominate the east of the county. The last great run of English

Opposite: The chalk cliffs at Flamborough Head
Right: Early Trust poster

chalk in the Yorkshire Wolds thrusts out into the North Sea at Flamborough Head. Rifle Butts quarry, the Trust's only geological reserve, reveals a major unconformity between the Lower Jurassic and Upper Cretaceous chalk near Market Weighton on the Wolds. To the north of the Wolds older, harder Jurassic rocks form the North York Moors. Here in the east of the county are also some of the most rapidly eroding coasts in England; this relentless erosion in turn provides the raw materials for Spurn Point, and the muddy vastness of the Humber Estuary.

It is a county of other great contrasts. Two National Parks (the North York Moors in the north-east, and the Yorkshire Dales in the north-west) lie almost entirely within the county boundary. A third (the Peak District) creeps across the boundary in the south-west. The Vale of York and the Vale of Mowbray have some of the finest arable land in Britain. It is not a particularly wooded county, but there are some significant ancient woodlands (Bishop Wood, near Selby, for example) as well as extensive (and biologically-rich) upland conifer plantations. The most northerly examples of southern heaths are found on the Vale of York. The Lower Derwent Ings south and east of York have some of the largest surviving (and probably the least well known) ancient lowland hay meadows in England. And the south-west has large metropolitan areas of proud industrial towns and cities – Leeds, Sheffield, Wakefield and Doncaster among them. It is rightly called 'God's own country'.

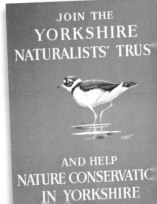

JOIN THE
YORKSHIRE
NATURALISTS' TRUS

AND HELP
NATURE CONSERVATIC
IN YORKSHIRE

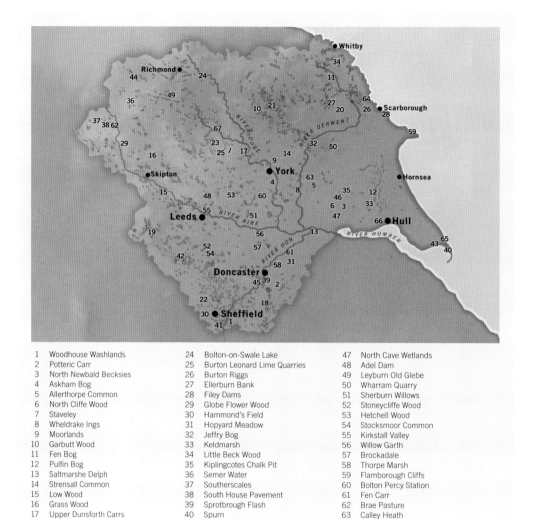

Map of Yorkshire Wildlife Trust nature reserves

1	Woodhouse Washlands	24	Bolton-on-Swale Lake	47	North Cave Wetlands
2	Potteric Carr	25	Burton Leonard Lime Quarries	48	Adel Dam
3	North Newbald Becksies	26	Burton Riggs	49	Leyburn Old Glebe
4	Askham Bog	27	Ellerburn Bank	50	Wharram Quarry
5	Allerthorpe Common	28	Filey Dams	51	Sherburn Willows
6	North Cliffe Wood	29	Globe Flower Wood	52	Stoneycliffe Wood
7	Staveley	30	Hammond's Field	53	Hetchell Wood
8	Wheldrake Ings	31	Hopyard Meadow	54	Stocksmoor Common
9	Moorlands	32	Jeffry Bog	55	Kirkstall Valley
10	Garbutt Wood	33	Keldmarsh	56	Willow Garth
11	Fen Bog	34	Little Beck Wood	57	Brockadale
12	Pulfin Bog	35	Kiplingcotes Chalk Pit	58	Thorpe Marsh
13	Saltmarshe Delph	36	Semer Water	59	Flamborough Cliffs
14	Strensall Common	37	Southerscales	60	Bolton Percy Station
15	Low Wood	38	South House Pavement	61	Fen Carr
16	Grass Wood	39	Sprotbrough Flash	62	Brae Pasture
17	Upper Dunsforth Carrs	40	Spurn	63	Calley Heath
18	Maltby Low Common	41	Twentywellsick Wood	64	Harland Mount
19	Broadhead Clough	42	Upper Park Wood	65	Hodgson's Fields
20	Chafer Wood	43	Welwick Saltmarsh	66	Pearson Park Wildlife Garden
21	Ashberry	44	Yellands Meadow	67	Ripon Loop
22	Agden Bog	45	Denaby Ings		
23	Bishop Monkton Railway Cutting	46	Rifle Butts Quarry		

LOG, BOG AND CHOC START-UP

As the Second World War raged, timber merchants found it uneconomic to remove timber from two blocks of land at Askham Bog, on the south-western edge of the city of York. The bog is only about 40 hectares, but it was – and still is – an important relict of fen vegetation left after the last Ice Age. A report in 1949 by Professor WH Pearsall described it as "the finest example of a natural wooded fen in north England". It had long been valued by local naturalists. The two blocks of land were put up for sale and purchased in 1944 by York chocolate barons Sir Francis Terry and Arnold Rowntree, both of whom had been keen naturalists while at school in York. At the time, the government agency, the Nature Conservancy, did not exist. So with the help and advice of the NORFOLK TRUST, the Yorkshire Naturalists' Trust was founded with the primary objective of receiving Askham Bog as a gift from the new owners. The Certificate of Incorporation of the Trust, with Terry as its President and Rowntree as its Vice President, together with 11 subscribers, was signed on 29th March 1946; legal incorporation was on 2nd May that same year.

To complete the landholding, the owner of the rest of Askham Bog (Lycett Green) entered into a gentleman's agreement with the newly-formed Trust to allow the entire unit to be managed as one. Bernard Linney was both the first Honorary Secretary of the fledgling Trust, and keeper of the bog.

A sad disadvantage of being the second oldest Trust is that many of the founding members and key players are no longer with us. But fortunately, to celebrate the Trust's Golden Jubilee in 1996, the summer edition of its magazine, *Yorkshire Wildlife and Natural Environment*, published a series of articles summarising many of the key events and significant people in the Trust's history. The magazine records – a nice touch – that the Trust finally completed the purchase of Askham Bog in this golden jubilee year.

EARLY STRUGGLES

The early years of the Trust were a familiar struggle for members and money. The first public appeal for members went out on 1st November 1946. "Naturalists and lovers of the beauties of Yorkshire will. . . be interested to learn of the formation of The Yorkshire Naturalists' Trust Limited, with the primary purpose of establishing and maintaining Sanctuaries for the preservation of wild life, particularly of a rare and unusual character". Life membership was £10 and ordinary membership was not less than ten shillings a year.

From the single reserve at Askham in 1946 and a mere handful of supporters, the Trust now has 80 reserves and more than 32,000 members. On the way, the Naturalists' Trust became the Wildlife Trust in 1983. The Trust can trace major developments through places and people, with occasional diversions into other issues.

The first public appeal for money was in 1955, to raise £500 to purchase Moorlands (woodland close to York) as its second reserve. Managing Moorlands required the establishment of the Trust's first Nature Reserve Management Committee,

A corner of Askham Bog (photographed in 1966) with York Minster in the background

and by 1963 all five of its reserves had one, run entirely by volunteers. It was not until 1970 that the Trust appointed its first (again voluntary) Conservation Officer, DUNSTAN ADAMS, who described himself as having "joined the Trust in the fifties, with membership number 262".

NOTABLE RESERVES

All the Trust's reserves are important, but some are more notable than others. Spurn Point a long sandy spit stretching three-and-a-half miles into the Humber Estuary, and a mecca for birdwatchers, was bought in 1959. Other sites of international importance (with their date of first acquisition – often partial) include: Fen Bog (1964), an upland valley mire in the North York Moors; Strensall Common (1965), heathland on the Vale of York; Potteric Carr (1968), on the edge of Doncaster, a wonderful wetland between the railway lines; Wheldrake Ings (1971), now part of the Lower Derwent Valley National Nature Reserve, with hay meadows in the summer and huge numbers of wildfowl on winter floods; Southerscales (1987), part of a National Nature Reserve on the slopes of Ingleborough; and Flamborough Cliffs (1999), part of the Flamborough Headland Heritage Coast that, together with the adjacent RSPB reserve at Bempton, hold some of the most spectacular, easily accessible seabird colonies in north-west Europe.

Spurn Point in the Humber Estuary

Potteric Carr deserves special mention as the Trust's first flagship visitor reserve. It started as Low Ellers Marsh in 1968 with a band of dedicated Doncaster naturalists saving the birdwatching site from drainage. This remarkable bank of volunteers – Roger Mitchell, John Hancox and others – fought off potentially disastrous developments, not least the planned construction of the M18 motorway and east coast railway electrification. Moreover, they continually expanded the reserve with a particular burst of activity in the last decade through grants from the HERITAGE LOTTERY FUND, European Union LIFE-Nature Programme, WWF-UK and HSBC bank. This allowed the creation of a new wetland area, Huxterwell Marsh, alongside the development of the field centre and many miles of footpaths. It now ranks as one of the finest nature reserves in the UK.

CLIMATE CHANGE CHALLENGE

One of the challenges facing the Trust today is that while some of its reserves are undoubted jewels, they are very small. There are a dozen sites of about two hectares or smaller, including Agden Bog in the Peak District; Bishop Monkton Railway Cutting on the magnesian limestone; Globe Flower Wood in the Dales; Hopyard Meadow near Doncaster, with its revered wild service tree; North Newbold Becksies, a wet pasture on the edge of the Wolds, and so on – lovely names, lovely places. A list of reserves smaller than ten hectares would be even longer. Many were acquired "as Sanctuaries for the preservation of wild life" as the November 1946 appeal for members plainly put it. But small sites like these are unlikely to survive the ravages of climate change, a threat that founding members could never have envisaged and a huge future challenge for the entire Trust movement.

TRUST PEOPLE...

At first the Trust was run entirely by honorary officers and volunteers. Dr Edward Wilfred Taylor was one of the 11 original 1946 subscribers, and took over as President of the Trust from Sir Francis Terry in 1951 when it had one reserve and fewer

Potteric Carr nature reserve near Doncaster

...AND PLACES

A typed newsletter shows that even by 1963 the Honorary Secretary of the Trust, Clifford Smith, operated from home; the Trust still had no office. By 1969, the small but growing Trust – there were 1,737 members – had its first (non-domestic!) offices in Clifford Chambers, on Clifford Street in York. It is difficult to remember how small the Trust was at this time. In 1971, John Newman had an Assistant Secretary, two Clerical Assistants and a Warden at Spurn (the legendary Barry Spence), and that was it. The Trust moved to 20 Castlegate in 1972 (3,978 members), from there into 10 Toft Green in 1985 (6,458 members), and finally in 2006, bursting at the seams, to the present headquarters at 1 St George's Place (more than 9,000 members). Now St George's Place is full, and part of the solution is to grow regional offices across this huge county.

Yorkshire's size has always been something of a management headache. The first attempt to create a regional structure was in 1968. By 1971, this developed into a decision by Council to devolve some of its activities (public relations, conservation and education) to Area Groups, led and run by volunteers. Using the old Vice County recording system, five groups were established in VCs 61–65 between 1971 and 1973. But with local authority boundary changes in April 1974, it was considered politic to create six groups aligned more closely with these new boundaries, to benefit from new grant possibilities. It paid off, with generous support from them for many years. The Executive Officer, John Newman, being a military man, used to refer to the Area Groups as the Trust's 'commandos'. Some of the Trust's most prominent members were early commando leaders: Dr Derrick Boatman (VC61/East), Dr Margaret Atherton (VC62/North-east), Roger Mitchell (VC63/South), and Drs Douglas Pickup (VC 64/West) and RM Henson (VC64/Mid-west). Dr Michael Thompson recalls for his group in VC65/North-west: "Through public meetings, the distribution of literature and exhibiting at county shows. . . we doubled the Trust's membership in the district from 25 to 50!"

than 200 members. When Taylor retired in 1970 there were more than 2,000 members and 29 reserves. The fact that the Trust did not appoint its first paid (albeit part-time) official until 1965 is tribute to Taylor's huge contribution to the early life of the Trust. Among his many achievements was the acquisition of Spurn Point from the War Office in 1959.

As the Trust grew, it became obvious that it needed more paid staff and office space. By 1968 the Trust had grown sufficiently to require an Executive Officer. Lieutenant Colonel John Fitzgerald Newman was appointed, eventually retiring in 1976. He is widely remembered with affection for the skilful way he steered the difficult course between a Council of voluntary officers and members, and his role as a paid employee. He was succeeded in 1976 (with the post renamed Chief Executive) by Ian Kibble (until 1982), then Michael Goss (1983–87), Jack Sanderson (1987–93), Roger Chapman (1993–94), Robert Forrester (1995–2002), Victoria Chester-Kerr (2002–06) and currently Rob Stoneman (since 2006).

The Trust's reserve at Southerscales Scar, on the slopes of Ingleborough in the Yorkshire Dales

After a number of minor adjustments to this area structure, in 1986 the groups were replaced by six regional committees – to be called South Yorkshire, West Yorkshire, North Humberside/ East; Dales, York/Selby, and North-East. As personnel changed, the success or otherwise of these committees fluctuated, particularly more recently with the increasing role of paid staff in the Trust's activities.

DEFINING INFLUENCE

Among all the changes that occurred in the 1970s, one was undoubtedly pivotal. In 1973, Stephen Warburton was appointed Field Officer, supported by a grant from the Carnegie UK Trust. Warburton had a defining (and for some people, a controversial) influence on the Trust until his death in 2004. He devoted 30 years of his life to the Yorkshire Wildlife Trust. He was appointed to help with reserve management, but his interests and skills ran much wider and deeper than that. He had that rare combination of great vision, with meticulous attention to detail.

These characteristics served him – and the Trust – well, when the Trust took on a major legal battle over navigation rights on the River Derwent, between 1985 and 1991. Warburton was aided, among others, by another brilliant conservation strategist, Ian Carstairs. The epic legal battle, which ended up in the High Court, is recorded in Carstairs' book *The Yorkshire River Derwent*, Halsgrove Discovery Series (2007). The case hinged on whether there were navigation rights above Sutton upon Derwent to Malton (through important and relatively undisturbed habitats, including the Lower Derwent Ings). Boating interests argued that the 1932 Rights of Way and subsequent Highways Acts meant there were navigation rights. The Courts ruled that there were not. If they had done otherwise, great stretches of waterways nationwide, not just the Yorkshire Derwent, could have been opened up for navigation, putting important wetland habitats at risk.

Stephen Warburton achieved many other things for the Trust. Space precludes all but a sample, including things we now take for granted, but which were pioneering at the time. For instance, there was the first grant (£750) from the Nature Conservancy Council in 1975 to fence Strensall Common; organising armies of unemployed people supported by Government-sponsored schemes to do essential maintenance on reserves in the 1970s; and real leadership and courage in taking on challenges in the wider countryside outside the Trust's reserves, often, as in the case of the Derwent navigation, using the law to great effect.

Warburton's appointment was symptomatic of the increasing role of professional staff working alongside volunteers. The first two Conservation Officers were volunteers – Dunstan Adams, followed by Dr Michael Archer in 1973. Warburton was part of the professionalisation of that role. In 1990, his job was split, handing reserve management to Lesley Blainey and allowing Warburton to concentrate solely on wider conservation issues as the Trust's first paid Conservation Officer.

POWER OF EDUCATION

Education was not even mentioned in 1946, but it gradually dawned on people that the preservation of wildlife was not going to be achieved by simply creating nature reserves. Neither would reserves win the battle for hearts and minds that could give wildlife a fighting chance outside reserves. It took time. Education was part of the responsibilities devolved to Area Groups in 1971. But the first Council policy paper on education was not written until 1974, and a Yorkshire WILDLIFE WATCH club – as a junior arm of the Trust – was not formed until 1979. Clifford Smith took on the role of Honorary Education Officer in 1979, and by the end of the 1970s Yorkshire had more than 500 children in Watch membership. The 1980s saw further expansion, with increasing numbers of educational visits by both adults and children to Trust reserves (especially Moorlands, Bretton Lakes, Potteric Carr and Thorpe Marsh). In 1985, the education sub-committee morphed into a full committee of

Adders are found on several of the Trust's nature reserves

A stream in Chafer Wood on the southern edge of the North York Moors

Council and Valerie Hewitt was appointed as a Development/Education Officer. With Hewitt in post until 1987 (when the grant supporting her ran out), Watch membership in Yorkshire became one of the largest of all the Trusts, and continued to flourish under the voluntary leadership of Dr Geoff Oxford until he stood down in 1991.

Since 1989, (when the Trust again employed a dedicated staff member as a Watch administrative assistant), the Trust has always had paid educational staff. Education remains central to the work of the Trust with the Watch network smaller but still thriving, and community programmes integrated into the Trust's conservation projects. Today, the Trust runs education and community programmes in Hull, Doncaster, York, Leeds-Bradford, Huddersfield and the Dales.

CHANGING STRUCTURES

Governance of the Trust has changed markedly over the years. By 1963, the Council had an Executive Committee, but it was not until 1972 that Chairman, DUNSTAN ADAMS, produced a paper for Council, entitled *Structure, Organisation and Operation*, to clarify roles and responsibilities. The annual report for 1972 records ". . . that practically every member of the Council is holding an appointment as an Officer of the Trust, Leader of an Area Group, Chairman of a Committee of Management or a member of some working party". Over time, these various groups and committees have come and gone. For instance, a substantial reorganisation in 1974 created a Business Committee and a Scientific Advisory Committee. In 1986, there were five central function committees (Finance and General Purposes, Conservation, Development, Education, Nature Reserves and Branches – reduced to four by 1990 – plus six Regional Committees). In 2001, the existing four-committee system was disbanded and replaced by an Operations Committee of five Trustees and four staff, with six Regional Committees remaining in place together with an Investment Committee. In 2001, 50 per cent of nature reserves still had management committees run by volunteers.

Gradually, sometimes painfully, and occasionally acrimoniously, as professional paid staff grew in number and responsibility, governance had to change. Volunteers saw cherished roles taken over by staff and there was often confusion about responsibilities. For example, who made decisions? Was it the Council, its sub-committees, reserve management committees, area groups, or staff? Where were the dividing lines? Matters were not resolved (and even then not to universal approval) until as recently as 2008–09. Then, with Rob Stoneman as Chief Executive, and David Sharrod as Chairman, Council eventually approved the contents of a Governance Review that recommended best practice as laid out by the Charity Commission. Council became a Board, with overall strategic and financial responsibility, but hands-off on operational matters; and a confused and confusing set of sub-committees was abolished and replaced by a Finance and Risk Committee. The review also sought to simplify the plethora of different groups of volunteers that had grown up over the years (reserve management committees, area groups and regional committees and so on), replacing them with Supporters Groups, a change that has still to bed in. A new *Board Governance Handbook* lays out roles and responsibilities. It is, inevitably, much longer than the one produced by Dunstan Adams in 1972, even though that was described as a "dossier of no mean size!"

This governance reform made a crucial difference, allowing the Trust to be more ambitious in scope, and to take on the challenges of Living Landscapes and Living Seas. The Yorkshire Peat Partnership seeks to restore all the blanket bogs of Yorkshire. Marine wildlife conservation is a whole new area of work and now involves four members of staff, making the Trust one of the largest marine wildlife conservation organisations in northern England.

It is impossible to pack more than 60 years of history into a limited space and cover even a few of the most significant events. Missing from this account are descriptions of the work of some

wonderful people, many no longer with us. Yorkshire wildlife would have been so much poorer without their dedication, skill, and sometimes sheer bloody-mindedness.

BY SIR JOHN LAWTON AND MARGARET HARTLEY

Professor Sir John Lawton – a birdwatcher from a young age – worked through academia as an ecologist to eventually hold Professorships at the University of York and Imperial College before running the Natural Environment Research Council. After retirement John chaired the Royal Commission on Environmental Pollution and led the influential Lawton Review that has moved the Government towards landscape-scale conservation. John is a former Chairman of the RSPB and is now a Vice President and is also Chairman of Yorkshire Wildlife Trust.

Margaret Hartley – a dedicated naturalist – spent a long career in the museums service in Bradford. Margaret has volunteered for the Trust in many ways, serving on six of its ever-changing committees at various times and working on the Council of Trustees through the '70s, '80s and '90s. Returning from Cumbria in 2006, Margaret is currently serving a second stint as Yorkshire Wildlife Trust Honorary Secretary.

Child snorkelling with the Trust's Undersea Explorers project

PART III

REFERENCE SECTION

A–Z reference section

A

ADAMS, DUNSTAN

Dunstan Adams (1914–1999), Head of Mathematics and Science at the College of Ripon and York St John in York at the time of his retirement in 1976, served the Society first as CHAIRMAN OF EXECUTIVE between 1983 and 1988 and thereafter as PRESIDENT and Chairman of the Society's Council until 1991.

Dunstan Adams

Adams joined the YORKSHIRE TRUST in 1951 and was elected to its Council in 1969, almost immediately becoming the Honorary Conservation Officer. Between 1971 and 1974, he was Chairman of the Trust's Executive Committee and, in 1996, succeeded Lord Peel as its President, a position he held until his death. He had hoped that his working life would be a "preparation for his retirement occupation. . . a field botanist with the Yorkshire Trust".[1] But he found himself in even greater demand, not just from the Yorkshire Trust but from other local organisations, such as the Yorkshire Dales and North York Moors National Parks, and from national organisations, such as the Council for National Parks.

Adams' particular contribution to the Society was to re-focus attention on its governance, spending much time oiling, servicing and fine tuning the Committee structure. After a productive, albeit volatile, period in the Society's history, his focus on 'stability' was reassuring and enabled the organisation to re-group and reinvent itself once more. "Dunstan was a calming and persuasive figure, always striving to build bridges between opposing views, and acting with great tact and diplomacy, even in the face of obduracy".[2] Asked for a Presidential message for Trusts and members, his reply, "with just a hint of the evangelical"[3], was "promoting the idea of a family of Trusts".[4]

ALLEN, MICHAEL

Michael Allen was appointed CHAIRMAN of the Society in November 2005 following a two-year period as the Society's HONORARY SECRETARY.

In 1999, Allen retired from a career in teaching and administration at Cambridge University, having been the University's Director of Continuing Education, Bursar of Churchill College, Cambridge and later, the Vice Chancellor's advisor on public relations.

During his career, and after his retirement, Allen dedicated much of his time to voluntary and community work. He was Honorary Secretary of the British Trust for Ornithology and Chairman of the BEDFORD- SHIRE, CAMBRIDGESHIRE AND NORTHAMPTONSHIRE TRUST for nine years. Allen was Deputy Chair of the East of England Regional Assembly and a member of the Regional Committees of the National Trust and Forestry Commission for many years.

During his time as Chairman of the Society, Allen travelled extensively around the UK visiting Trust Councils, headquarters and sites, building up a strong understanding of the strength and diversity of the movement. His statesmanlike chairmanship, during a time of organisational renewal and development, proved critical in maintaining a steady course towards a very successful period in the Society's work.

Allen's successes included steering a new series of conferences for Chairmen and forming a Countries Committee. The latter was to prove critical in holding the movement together during a time of increasing devolution. He also made a particular contribution to improving the quality of the Society's governance procedures. On his retirement, he was praised, in particular, for his calm statesmanship and his sense of humour.

Michael Allen

ALL-PARTY PARLIAMENTARY CONSERVATION AND WILDLIFE COMMITTEE

The All-Party Conservation and Wildlife Committee (APCWC), one of the first Parliamentary Groups to focus on the natural environment, was formed in January 1972 under the chairmanship of Lord Craigton as the All-Party Conservation Group. Craigton was MP for the Glasgow Craigton constituency between 1950 and 1959, Minister of State, Scottish Office between 1959 and 1964, and a Trustee of the World Wildlife Fund (WWF). The APCWC held its first meeting in March 1972 when international conservationist and artist, SIR PETER SCOTT, and naturalist and author, Richard Fitter – who had both been influential in its formation – addressed the meeting on a Wild Plant Protection Bill, the Future of the Nature Conservancy, Administration of National Parks and British support for a proposed International Convention on Animal Trade.

The Group received its initial conservation advice from the Council for Nature and, in particular, from its Secretary at the time, Tim Sands. When Sands moved to the Society in 1975, it was agreed that he should continue to act as advisor to the Group, which he did until his retirement in 2005.

The Group has met around 200 times and, in the first 20 years of its existence, covered more than 200 subjects from acid rain and oil pollution to climate change, nuclear power and the introduction and implementation of numerous bills and international agreements. It has attracted eminent scientists, Ministers and senior civil servants from a surprisingly wide range of government departments; has been addressed on two occasions by HRH The Duke of Edinburgh (November 1976 and February 1981); and at one memorable meeting (December 1976) was introduced to new evidence on *Nessiteras rhombopteryx*, or the Loch Ness Monster, by Sir Peter Scott.

Chairs of the Group/Committee:

Lord Craigton	1972–1992
Lord Moran	1992–1999
Lord Hardy of Wath	1999–2002
David Kidney (MP for Stafford)	2002–2005
Angela C Smith (MP for Penistone and Stocksbridge)	2005–present

Legal protection for wild plants was discussed at the first APCWC meeting. In 1975, the pasque flower was one of the first species to benefit from new legislation

ANNIVERSARIES

The Society's 50th anniversary, in 1962, was marked in a very modest way by an appeal for funds towards the acquisition of nature reserves and to restore the 'Society's depleted capital'. The appeal was confined to its membership so as not to conflict with other appeals being made at the time by the Council for Nature and the recently formed WWF. The lack of confidence and concern to avoid confrontation with the WWF, already a significant benefactor to the Trusts, was reflected in a less than inspiring leaflet and no more than a 'useful response' of £500 from just 100 Associate Members.

The 75th anniversary of the founding of the organisation in 1987 witnessed a higher profile event. There was a special '75 years' impress on the Society's papers, publications and postal franking machine. NATURAL WORLD carried a brief one-page review highlighting some of the key events in the life of the Society since 1912, and MIRIAM ROTHSCHILD held a party for friends and guests with morris dancing on the green at Ashton (ASHTON WOLD) in Northamptonshire on 16th May – the anniversary of the Society's foundation day.

During the year, other events were also promoted as part of the anniversary celebrations. These included a conference organised jointly with the Linnean Society on 'Changing Attitudes to Nature Conservation' in March; an exhibition on the life and work of the famous bird artist, John Gould, at the Natural History Museum in London in April; a demanding 14-day lecture tour by one of the Society's Vice Presidents, Chris Baines; and – the public centrepiece – a concert held in Westminster Abbey in June.

Five years later, a Royal Gala dinner was held at the historic Banqueting House in London on the evening of 28th October 1992 to celebrate the Society's 80th birthday. The evening commenced with a champagne reception in the undercroft, followed by dinner in the magnificent Banqueting Hall itself with entertainment from Kit and the Widow, ex-Cambridge University Footlights performers. There were also speeches from the Society's Patron, HRH The Prince of Wales, its President and its Chief Executive, Tim Cordy.

ARIDE ISLAND

As early as 1914, the Society showed an interest in the Seychelles. CHARLES ROTHSCHILD recommended to the Government that reserves "ought to be secured"[5] in the Seychelles. Lord Crawford, a Trustee of the Natural History Museum in London, and naturalist EDMUND MEADE-WALDO, had visited the Seychelles in March and April 1906 in Crawford's yacht, the Valhalla, and would have been among those extolling the islands' wildlife qualities to Rothschild.

However, it was not until January 1973 that Aride Island in the Seychelles was purchased for the Society from the Chenard family by CHRISTOPHER CADBURY for £40,000. The family had been running the island as a nature reserve for six years. In 1979, the island and a marine zone extending out around the island to 200 metres were declared a Special Nature Reserve (Statutory Instrument No 92 of the National Parks and Nature Conservancy Act 1979, Aride Island Special Reserve Regulations 1979). In 1991, the Society established an Aride Endowment Fund with an initial sum of £100,000, mostly provided by Christopher Cadbury. In 2004, the island was leased to the UK arm of the Seychelles-based Island Conservation Society (ICS). The ICS continued to actively manage the island, including

Aride Island, 1883 – a painting by Marianne North

renovating the historic manager's lodge and building a new visitor centre. In August 2008, the freehold of the island was transferred, with the full support of the Cadbury family, to the Island Conservation Society UK (ICS UK), 35 years after its purchase by the Society. The Society's involvement with the management of the island finally came to an end with the transfer of the Aride Endowment Fund to ICS UK in March 2010.

The Seychelles, between four and ten degrees south of the equator and 1,000 miles to the east of Africa, remain a natural paradise with 155 islands, many uninhabited, scattered across the Indian Ocean. They became stranded millions of years ago as India split away from the African sub-continent and are the world's oldest oceanic islands and the only ones made of granite.

Aride is the most northerly of the granite islands and the most natural. Rising impressively from the sea, it is cloaked in woodland with a fertile coastal plateau on the south side. A palm-fringed beach, crystal clear waters and an offshore coral reef complete the picture of an idyllic tropical island.

Aride boasts more breeding species of seabird than any of the other

islands of the Seychelles, including the world's largest colony of lesser noddy. Above the island, the sky can be thick with birds, including white-tailed and red-tailed tropic birds. A climb to near the top of the island is rewarded with spectacular views of more than 5,000 roosting frigate birds that soar from its north-facing cliffs; and a passing pod of dolphins, a giant ray or a hawksbill turtle may be seen far below. The island also has its own endemic flower, Wright's gardenia.

It was not always as it is today. In the first account of the island written in 1787, Jean-Baptiste Malavois, French commandant of Seychelles, described Aride as "no more than a pile of rocks covered with a few bushes".[6] In 1868, the Irish naturalist, Perceval Wright, who gave his name to Aride's unique gardenia and one of its endemic lizards, noted that the plateau had been cleared for agriculture and the rest of the island had been denuded of trees. In 1883, the English artist, Marianne North, reported seeing one big tree on that 'scorching island' and all the island's inhabitants sitting in its shade.

For a century, in the sooty tern areas, trees were cut annually to facilitate egg collection. An average of 120,000 eggs was taken annually

Seychelles blue pigeon on Aride Island

during the 20 years after 1948, rising to a peak of 220,000 eggs in 1954. Other natural forest was cleared and replaced with coconut palms for copra production and domestic animals were introduced, although fortunately rats never arrived.

From 1973, for more than 30 years, careful management of Aride by the Society's Management Committee, wardens, visiting scientists and volunteers involved continuous survey and monitoring, the almost complete cessation of poaching, the back-breaking removal of hundreds of coconut palms and the re-establishment of the island's native woodland.

Five of the land birds unique to the Seychelles breed on Aride. These include the recently reintroduced Seychelles warbler, of which Aride has 80 per cent of the world's population, the Seychelles magpie robin and the Seychelles fody.

All this work, which is being continued by ICS, has seen Aride consolidate its position as one of the world's most important nature reserves.

See also entry on La Digue under NATURE RESERVES OWNED BY THE SOCIETY

ASHTON WOLD

At the turn of the 20th century, CHARLES ROTHSCHILD succeeded to the estate at Ashton Wold in Northamptonshire. A new 'mansion' was built, a lake excavated and later the hamlet of Ashton on the estate was re-modelled. Insanitary cottages were pulled down and new reed-thatched cottages and farm houses plus a public house – renamed the Chequered Skipper by MIRIAM ROTHSCHILD in the 1960s – were built in their place.

Following its rejuvenation, Ashton became the venue for a popular flower show and more recently it has welcomed the annual World Conker Championships to its village green. In the 1980s it hosted two medieval fairs, organised as fundraising events by the NORTHAMPTONSHIRE TRUST, and, in 1987, it was also the site for the Society's 75th birthday party (ANNIVERSARIES).

At the Society's Second Luncheon (DINNERS AND LUNCHEONS), held in London on 6th June 1947, in her reply to the toast of the Society by the Right Honorary Viscount Jowitt, Lord High Chancellor, Miriam Rothschild spoke about the family's nature reserve at Ashton Wold.

"During the war Ashton came in for a fair share of requisitioning.

Miriam Rothschild at the Society's luncheon, 6th June 1947

As I do not wish to be inaccurate, I will read you the list of our uninvited guests, who in turn or simultaneously, partly or wholly requisitioned the nature reserve: Ordnance Corps, Royal Army Medical Corps, Royal Army Service Corps, Military Police, Bomber Command, Fighter Command, American Army and Air Force, Ministry of Supply, Timber Control, War Agricultural Executive Committee, British Red Cross, and Women's Land Army; and for a period of six months during camp construction we were also occupied by the Irish.

"My object as a sort of one-man management committee was to assist these various organisations in the execution of their duties, and to prevent any really pointless and unnecessary destruction of the reserve. For example, the wood, which is only 300 acres in extent, was three times ordered to be completely felled, first because owing to some faulty maps or map-reading it was considered a danger to landing aircraft, secondly to provide a certain type of timber for building Mosquitoes which, in fact, did not grow in the wood at all, and thirdly to facilitate the laying of 30 miles of electric light cable, when there were already ridings along which the cables could be laid directly.

"Apart from this type of threat, which of course was due to the stress and strain of war, there were many unexpected factors to deal with. . . From 1942 to 1945 quite a large portion of the property was used as a practice bombing ground by Flying Fortresses. It was rather disconcerting that 300 bombs fell wide of the target and landed in my garden, not to mention a couple through the roof. But from the SPNR point of view it was distinctly advantageous, and I am glad to record that the chequered skipper increased considerably in that area.

It is, however, a fact that very little would be left of the Ashton Wold reserve today but for the efforts of the County Sub Committee backed by this Society. Both Dr Herbert Smith and Captain Riley (Norman Riley) were untiring in their efforts, and both have reduced the letter of protest to a fine art. I think every married zoologist in the room will know what I mean when I say that in the human species the use of the telephone can now almost be rated a secondary sexual character of the female. Anyway, true to type, I followed up the letters of protest with a relentless barrage of telephone messages.

"Marvellous to relate, today except for temporary excrescences in the shape of dispersed camps the Wold is really unspoiled. Maybe this is not a very scientific viewpoint, but I think in our hearts many of us believe that a nature reserve is worth infinitely more than the sum total of its species, rare or otherwise. In fact I have grown to look upon rare species as the fortunate accident which justifies action even in times of stress. In preserving a few wild stretches of the countryside we preserve not only inspiration for poets but a great deal of quiet happiness for ordinary men and women".[7]

ASSOCIATION OF WILDLIFE TRUST CONSULTANCIES

The Association of Wildlife Trust Consultancies was established in 1994 to promote quality standards across its membership, and to provide a mechanism for working together on, for example, training and major projects.

Twenty-three Trust Consultancies (2011) are members and they offer professional expertise throughout the country on ecology, landscape and planning. Profits go to their parent Trusts, with the 'collective aim of protecting wildlife for the future'.

ATTENBOROUGH, SIR DAVID

Sir David Attenborough joined the Society as an Associate Member in 1965. He was Chairman of its BRITISH WILDLIFE APPEAL between 1985 and 1990, PRESIDENT between 1991 and 1995 and is currently a Vice President.

A graduate of Cambridge University, he began making natural history programmes for the BBC in 1954. He has become internationally renowned for bringing high quality wildlife programmes to generations of television viewers, in particular through writing and presenting his epic series of *Life* programmes in conjunction with the BBC's Natural History Unit.

He has served on the governing bodies of WWF-UK, Fauna and Flora International, Butterfly Conservation, the World Land Trust, the Royal Botanic Gardens Kew and the British Museum.

For many associated with the modern Society, there is a feeling, as one eminent member put it, that

Sir David has always been 'there for us'. He was most intimately involved with the Society during the nearly six years when he was Chairman of its successful British Wildlife Appeal and afterwards, at the beginning of the 1990s, when he was President. The Society benefited enormously at this time from his wholehearted commitment.

But his support and guidance have gone much further than this. The archives are filled with photographs of the nature reserves and visitor centres that he has opened and the campaigns and publications that he has launched on behalf of The Wildlife Trusts' movement over five decades.

While many undoubtedly know Sir David best from his television programmes, many others in the Trusts have been lucky enough to enjoy more personal encounters and have gone away from a Trust event inspired by his infectious personality and boundless enthusiasm for the natural world.

Sir David Attenborough as Chairman of the British Wildlife Appeal

B

BADGERS AND BOVINE TB

The badger is a much-loved British mammal, but its links with the occurrence of bovine tuberculosis (bTB) in cattle, mean that in recent decades it has been the focus of repeated threats of a cull. In the early days of the Society there were concerted efforts, stimulated by the CORNWALL TRUST, to secure legal protection for this species which was the subject of widespread persecution. An item in the *Sunday Telegraph* in 1972 referred to "the continued slaughter of badgers by poachers from south Lancashire towns and the Potteries". The Badgers Act 1973 prohibited 'the taking, injuring or killing of badgers'. Later, in 1991, The Wildlife Trusts also played an important role in securing protection for badger setts. Sett digging and badger baiting with dogs meant that the badger was at risk of local extinction in many areas of England.

The Ministry of Agriculture, Fisheries and Food (MAFF, now DEFRA) continued the intensification of agricultural practice that had been an essential feature of the war-time economy.

Badgers: the Future? – one of the Society's reports

In particular, there was a determined effort to boost the health of the nation's flocks and herds through improved nutrition, animal welfare and disease elimination. Bovine TB (bTB) in the nation's dairy and beef industries was a particular target.

The incidence of bTB in cattle persisted at a higher level, mostly in the south-west of England. Various factors were, and still are, suggested as contributing to this pattern of disease. However, in 1971, a dead badger infected with bTB was discovered on a Gloucestershire farm that had suffered a bTB outbreak in its cattle herd. This pointed to the link between badgers and cattle that remains the centre of intense debate.

The 1973 legal protection coincided with a guidance note issued on *Tuberculosis in Badgers in Gloucestershire* by the Society's CONSERVATION LIAISON COMMITTEE. This was circulated to Trusts following a coordination meeting held by MAFF in London. It contained the phrase that "a reservoir of tuberculosis in badgers could constitute a hazard. . . to the local cattle populations". In Gloucestershire, a report in the *Stroud News and Journal*, dated May 1973, stating that "an increasing incidence of tuberculosis in cattle is causing much concern to farmers,

some of whom have lost large numbers of stock because of it" could easily be current copy.

Bovine TB *(Mycobacterium bovis)*, like other mycobacteria, is a sophisticated and complex pathogen. It is related to human TB and its epidemiology is in many ways similar. In particular, the capacity of TB to lie dormant within an infected host and to be hard to detect with available tests, even when the disease is active, makes it a difficult disease to identify and treat. Current veterinary bTB tests are still not as sensitive or consistent as required. Because of false test results, positive or negative, a proportion of the cattle culled following a positive bTB test may be found not to be diseased, whilst infected animals from the same herd may be missed only to express the disease at a later date. Moreover, despite clear statistical and immunological evidence, the exact routes of transmission between badgers and cattle as bTB vectors is uncertain.

Many bTB control strategies have been deployed in the UK and Ireland. There have been trials of different badger control and culling techniques, but with inconsistent and controversial outcomes. Following two earlier inquiries, led by Zuckerman and Dunnett respectively,

Professor Sir John Krebs was asked by Government to lead a multi-disciplinary team of researchers in a third national inquiry. The Society's then Director General, SIMON LYSTER, and the GLOUCESTERSHIRE TRUST's Director, Gordon McGlone, gave evidence to a Parliamentary Select Committee in 1999. Sir John Krebs' recommendation for a major independent field trial into the efficacy of a badger cull was accepted by the UK Government. Professor John Bourne, a distinguished vet, was appointed to oversee the implementation of the Krebs report recommendations by an Independent Scientific Group on Cattle TB (ISG).

The Bourne report was a complex document that summarised ten years of scientific work, but the key finding was that the culling of wild badgers was not considered to be a cost-effective, long-term solution. Bourne concluded that, "after careful consideration of all the Random Badger Control Trials (RBCT) and other data presented in this report, including an economic assessment, we conclude that badger culling cannot meaningfully contribute to the future control of cattle TB in Britain".[8] The key factors were the cost of culling and an increase in bTB in cattle herds on the periphery of culled areas due to the disruption of badger social groups and the displacement of individual badgers, called 'the perturbation effect'. These findings were not enough to counter the lobby for culling. DEFRA remained under huge political pressure to press ahead with a cull.

In particular, a report written in 2007 by Sir David King, then Chief Scientific Advisor, that supported badger culling as an effective strategy, was rebutted by Bourne on behalf of the ISG as "clearly hastily written and because of that it is very superficial; it is also very selective".[9]

In 2005, DEFRA carried out a 12-week public consultation into a possible cull of badgers in England as part of a new control strategy. The Wildlife Trusts played a major role in disseminating a balanced view of the issue to their members and to the public. There were 47,000 respondents to DEFRA and of these 96 per cent indicated that they were against such an intervention. The DEFRA Minister of State for Agriculture and Food, James Paice, announced in July 2010 that there was to be a new consultation in England, with the possibility of badger culling in autumn 2012. In 2012, the Welsh Assembly Government announced its intention to carry out a vaccination of badgers as part of its bTB control strategy in an area of the Pembrokeshire coast. In Northern Ireland, no announcement on culling has been made and bTB is not currently a problem in the Scottish national herd.

Current evidence, as published by the ISG, showed that the long-term cost-effective solution to bTB in badgers and cattle should not be based principally on cull strategies. However, as early as 1995, it was shown that a badger vaccine was possible. As part of a Government-funded study, a bTB vaccine, Badger BCG, was administered to badgers in trial areas near Stroud in 2010 with full support from the Gloucestershire Trust. The Trust had granted researchers access to two of its nature reserves over a long period. An oral badger vaccine is possible by 2015.

A vaccine against bTB in cattle is the final objective, but it will be a long-term challenge with both veterinary and regulatory obstacles to be overcome. The disease itself is not a threat to wild badger populations, but it is a considerable

problem for the cattle industry and one that continues to worsen. Leadership is required from the farming industry and wildlife bodies if a full solution is to be achieved.

Professor Bourne summarised this issue well in June 2007. "The ISG recognises the difficulties faced by Government in implementing control strategies without full industry cooperation. It is unfortunate that agricultural and veterinary leaders continue to believe, in spite of overwhelming scientific evidence to the contrary, that the main approach to cattle TB control must involve some form of badger culling. It is our hope that DEFRA will embrace new scientific findings, and communicate these to these stakeholders in ways that encourage acceptance and participation".[10]

The Wildlife Trusts has consist-ently played an important part in working towards a long-term solution to this problem. Morley Penistan (Gloucestershire Trust), Professor Humphrey Kay (WILTSHIRE TRUST), and Gordon McGlone (Gloucestershire Trust) served consecutively on the Minister of Agriculture's Consultative Panel on Badgers and Bovine Tuberculosis.

As leading nature conservation organisations that own grazing stock and work closely with their local farming community, the Trusts continue to press for sound, cost-effective and science-based bTB control strategies. Better cattle movement controls, improved bTB testing regimes and farm bio-security and effective vaccines continue to be The Wildlife Trusts' priorities.

However, prospects for the introduction of such policies are far from certain.

BANGOR MANIFESTO

The Bangor Manifesto arose out of workshops held at the Society's Conservation Officers' Conference (CONFERENCES) in Bangor in July 1990. It was the first all-Trust initiative to look at nature conservation and the work of the movement within a broader environmental and social agenda. It would go on to shape the Society's response to the Government's White Paper, *This Common Inheritance: Britain's Environmental Strategy*, and formed the basis of the Society's publication, *The Health of the UK* (see below). The first draft of the Manifesto was finalised and printed during the last night of the conference and posted under delegates' bedroom doors at 2am for them to read when they awoke on the last morning of the conference.

With the addition of a summary and introduction, a further version of the document was circulated to Trusts for comment and was then approved by the Society's Council in January 1991. It marked a distinct shift in approach by the Society and across the movement. First, the document had its intellectual origins in grassroots thinking. Second, the Partnership traditionally had adopted a protectionist approach. It had "safeguarded land as nature reserves, worked to secure better legislation to conserve areas of importance for wildlife, fought battles to save land from specific threats and proposed changes in land use and pollution control policies to prevent further destruction".[11] The Manifesto took a wider view and argued that "the future of wildlife is as much dependent on future policies for energy and transport as it is on the evolution of agriculture, forestry or the planning system. Our wildlife and wild places are resources on which the health of the nation depends".[12]

The Manifesto provided a résumé of the problems facing wildlife and wild places associated with the Government's policies of the day, including agriculture, forestry and fisheries; the planning system; transport; energy; and the 'needs of people'; and made proposals for action in the future.

Dr John Barkham, Chairman of the Society's Conservation and Scientific Committee commented,

HEALTH OF THE UNITED KINGDOM REPORT

This 24-page report owed much to the Bangor Manifesto, prepared at the 1990 Conservation Officers' Conference (CONFERENCES). Sub-titled 'a commentary from RSNC on the welfare of the nation's environment', it was the Society's first campaign document to place nature conservation firmly in the context of the health of the nation's environment. It embraced issues such as green consumerism, the dumping of waste at sea, the development of brownfield sites and the impact on the environment of an active road building programme.

The report contained the following call for action from Government, industry, commerce and the public: greater pollution control and accountability; the introduction of a national energy policy; sustainable land

"we have so far failed to be explicit about the wider environmental implications of the way we treat wildlife. Wildlife remains an optional extra. This is not good enough. We need to be explicit. . . within RSNC and in the world at large, about the connection between wildlife and all major areas of environmental policy".[13]

See also NEW GROUND INITIATIVE

management and food production; an integrated transport policy; greater value placed on 'wild places', a nationwide audit of endangered species and habitats and greater legal protection for habitats through the implementation of the European Community's Habitats Directive; companies to acknowledge their responsibility for the environment; creation of, and access to, 'green spaces'; the planning system to give priority to managing the supply of resources rather than to consumer demand; greater research into recycling and increased emphasis on educating young people and adults about the environment.

The Health of the UK formed the basis of the Society's response to the Government's first comprehensive White Paper on the environment, *This Common Inheritance*.

The 'Health' report marked a shift towards placing nature conservation in the context of the health of the nation's environment

BARCLAY-SMITH, PHYLLIS

Ida Phyllis Barclay-Smith (1902–1980) joined the Society as an Associate Member in 1947, was elected to Council in July 1952 and became its joint HONORARY SECRETARY, with special responsibilities for international affairs, in 1953, on the death of HERBERT SMITH. She continued in this role for more than six years until New Year's Day 1960, when responsibility for the administration of the British Committee for International Nature Conservation (which the Society had formed in 1949 and for which she also acted as Honorary Secretary) was transferred from the Society to the Council for Nature. She was appointed to the Society's Council in 1960, after resigning as joint Honorary Secretary, and served in that capacity until becoming a Vice President in 1971.

Barclay-Smith represented the Society on several occasions at meetings of the International Union for the Protection of Nature (IUPN) around the world, and was a key member of the team that helped organise the IUPN's Fifth General Assembly in Edinburgh in 1956 (TOWARDS IUCN).

Barclay-Smith was best known, however, for her work for the International Council for Bird Protection (ICBP) founded in 1922. She moved from the RSPB, where she had been Assistant Secretary, to join ICBP in 1935. She was to devote a lifetime to its work, becoming its Secretary in 1946 and Secretary General in 1974. In 1968, as Secretary of the British Section of ICBP, she was closely involved in the purchase and setting up of Cousin Island Nature Reserve in the Seychelles (NATURE RESERVES OWNED BY THE SOCIETY).

At the time of her death in 1980, ornithologist Peter Olney wrote about her hard work, sense of duty and unfailing politeness. Barclay-Smith was "known to many as a dedicated, efficient, determined and conscientious member of committees, producer of reports, organiser of conferences, and leading light in national and international work on bird conservation. . . skilfully and diplomatically she guided people and committees, often without them realising, through discussion and papers, pinpointing the really important issues and foretelling what were likely to be the dangers facing birds and their environment".[14]

BELLAMY, DAVID

David Bellamy was President of the Watch Trust for Environmental Education (WILDLIFE WATCH) from 1988 to 2005; and PRESIDENT of the Society from 1995 to 2005.

Bellamy, well-known botanist, author, broadcaster and environmental campaigner, first came to public prominence as an environmental consultant at the time of the 1967 TORREY CANYON disaster. He has written and presented some 400 television programmes on botany, ecology and environmental issues. In 1983, he was famously jailed for blockading the Australian Franklin River in a protest against a proposed dam. The next year he leapt from the pier at St Abbs' harbour into the North Sea to open the St Abbs and Eyemouth voluntary marine reserve with which the SCOTTISH TRUST was closely involved.

A 'larger than life' figure, he has inspired generations of adults and children, not just through his books and television programmes, but through personal contact and his infectious enthusiasm for the natural world. He has given generously of his time to many aspects of Wildlife Trust life, including serving as President of a number of Wildlife Trusts. He launched – in so many memorable ways – numerous national campaigns, delivered up-lifting speeches at the Society's national conferences, brought to life hundreds of Trust events – whatever the weather or circumstance – and inspired thousands of young people, particularly in his role as President of Wildlife Watch.

David Bellamy

David Bellamy has campaigned relentlessly on many conservation issues, from the protection of internationally-important rainforests and the peatlands and wildflower meadows of the UK, to the need to develop sources of renewable energy. But many will remember him best for introducing them to the excitement and enjoyment to be had from wildlife and wild places and for bringing his unique qualities to the aid of so many voluntary organisations, including Watch and The Wildlife Trusts.

BENDIX, MICHAEL

Michael Bendix (1925–2009), a banker and founder member of the SUFFOLK TRUST, was TREASURER of the Society for a period during 1983. He was one of half-a-dozen individuals who in 1960 "sat in a green, corrugated iron bird hide on Redgrave and Lopham Fens and decided that the area was so important to wildlife that something should be done to protect it".[15] Redgrave and Lopham Fens became the Suffolk Trust's first nature reserve after its formation in 1961.

BIODIVERSITY ACTION PLANNING

The UK Government was among more than 150 countries that signed and later ratified the United Nations' Convention on Biological Diversity agreed at the Rio de Janeiro Earth Summit in 1992. One of the requirements of the Convention was for contracting parties to 'develop national strategies, plans or programmes for the conservation and sustainable use of biological diversity'.

A Biodiversity Challenge Group (BCG) was established in 1993 by the voluntary sector to influence the UK Government's response to the Convention. The Wildlife Trusts was one of six organisations making up the Group – the 'Challenge Six'. The other members were Butterfly Conservation, Friends of the Earth, Plantlife, RSPB and WWF.

The BCG's first report, *Biodiversity Challenge – an agenda for conservation in the UK*, was launched six weeks ahead of the Government's response to the convention, published in January 1994. In the run-up to these reports, the BCG had argued strongly that yet another bland review document would not suffice. The Group's tenet was that the conservation of biodiversity was a key test of sustainability and a healthy environment. More particularly, there was a need for an agreement on the species and habitats that warranted the most attention and on directing resources at these priorities.

The BCG proposed an objective-led planning process with costed targets for a selection of priority species and habitats. It was convinced that there was sufficient information on most of these to prepare meaningful plans and believed the process should be embedded into all aspects of Government policy. To show that this was feasible, it cited 'ambitious but realistic' targets for the conservation and recovery of around 530 species and 11 habitats, as well as comprehensive action plans for two of the species and six of the habitats.

When the Government published its response to the Convention, *Biodiversity – The UK Action Plan (BAP)*, the BCG welcomed it but argued that it lacked the clear structure of its own report. There were also differences of approach, for example, on the role of the voluntary sector in the delivery of the habitat action plans. But the overall goals and objectives of the Government and the BCG were very similar, and both recognised that the aim should be 'no further net loss of biodiversity'. The Government's report proposed a UK Biodiversity Action Plan Steering Group to take matters forward, including a range of recommendations that became known as the '59 steps'. Importantly, the report committed the Government to produce costed targets for key species and habitats and to produce at least the first tranche of action plans by the end of 1995.

The calibre and ability of the individuals involved with the biodiversity process in the Department of the Environment, from the Minister, John Gummer, through the senior civil servants to the report's astute author, Roger Bendall, played a major part in the surprisingly good progress that was made after the Department's initial reticence had been overcome. After all, the process being developed required enormous commitment and energy from all sides. There were refreshingly energetic contributions from most quarters. The collective views of the 'Challenge Six' were being coordinated through the BCG, and the voluntary sector was now represented on the Government's UK Steering Group and its four sub-groups taking forward the BAP. Indeed, the majority of the first drafts of the species action plans were produced under contract by the BCG's members. The Wildlife Trusts were active on the main UK BAP Steering Group and on three of the four sub-groups, particularly in relation to data management and the biodiversity process at the local level.

A second, enlarged and revised edition of *Biodiversity Challenge – an agenda for conservation in the UK* was launched by SIR DAVID ATTENBOROUGH in January 1995.

Corncrake – one of the priority species identified in the UK Biodiversity Action Plan

This time it identified targets for 600 species and 35 habitats with comprehensive action plans for 44 plants and animals and six habitats. In an additional chapter it tackled the difficult issue of costing biodiversity. This helped to keep the Steering Group on its toes and provided a benchmark against which the Steering Group's report could be judged.

In 1995, the UK BAP Steering Group's report was finally published in two volumes – *Volume 1: Meeting the Rio Challenge* and *Volume 2: Action Plans*. It contained a first tranche of 116 species action plans and 14 habitat action plans and a recommendation for work on a further 286 species and 24 habitats, to be completed in the next two to three years.

It was a landmark production, not least because it represented a consensus across a very wide range of organisations and institutions. Five months later, the Government formally responded to the Steering Group's report. It welcomed its findings and supported the call for the remaining species and habitat action plans to be completed within two to three years. Above all, it stamped a Government seal of approval on a restorative, rather than a simply protectionist, agenda for biodiversity conservation.

By 2000, there were around 570 species that had either an action plan or statement or were in a grouped statement or a grouped or joint species action plan, together with 94 habitats that had either an action plan or broad habitat statement. The report recognised that each of the species action plans would be implemented by a number of players, but it proposed a 'lead partner' to drive forward and coordinate delivery in each case. The statutory sector would be lead partners for the

habitat action plans. There was also a less official plan to get 'champions' for species from the corporate sector to sponsor some of the more charismatic species. In addition, the Steering Group believed much could be gained by promoting the process at the local level and, in particular, through the development of local partnerships and Local Biodiversity Action Plans.

Once the dust had settled, members of the BCG found themselves as lead partners for a daunting 187 species action plans. During the preparation of the UK BAP Steering Group's report, and after its publication, The Wildlife Trusts played a major part in developing the thinking on Local Biodiversity Action Plans. Trusts now became increasingly involved, and in many cases took the lead, in a growing number of local BAP partnerships.

In 1996, for example, the SUSSEX TRUST published *Vision for the Wildlife of Sussex*; a consortium of English Nature, Environment Agency, the RSPB and the Trusts published *Action for Wildlife in East Anglia – a Guide to Biodiversity in Cambridgeshire, Essex, Lincolnshire, Norfolk and Suffolk* and the LINCOLNSHIRE TRUST published *Nature in Lincolnshire – Towards a Biodiversity Strategy*.

Trusts champion local biodiversity planning across the UK

By May 2000, The Wildlife Trusts was lead partner for 23 priority species; focused nationally on ten of the UK BAP priority habitats; and was a key partner in 95 per cent of Local Biodiversity Action Plans. It had also been moderately successful in securing corporate 'champions'. In 1998, for example, the early gentian was among the first of the BAP's plant species to attract corporate support. Wessex Water agreed to fund The Wildlife Trusts and Plantlife for on-site management advice and research and survey work in their region.

The Wildlife Trusts' work on five UK BAP priority invertebrate species – southern damselfly, the black bog and narrow-headed ants, a leaf beetle and the mire pill-beetle – was reported in *Beauty and the Mini-Beasts*, published during Wildlife Week 2000. In its foreword, The Wildlife Trusts' President, DAVID BELLAMY, reminded his audience that if invertebrate species were in decline, then humans were in trouble too. Although the Government's BAP process was helping, "without further funding, they and a host of others will perish. That's why The Wildlife Trusts are lobbying for policy changes and appealing for support".[16]

Nine years after the Earth Summit in 2001, the BCG assessed progress in *Biodiversity Counts – Delivering a Better Quality of Life* just prior to the BAP's first reporting round. The picture was mixed and the report observed, "before the publication of BAP, there was no strategy for conserving the UK's wildlife shared by Government, industry, conservation organisations and the public alike".[17] Now there was. The report called for the biodiversity process to be nurtured and encouraged, particularly at a time when many functions affecting wildlife at UK level were being devolved to the countries. What was needed was for the process, not the detail, to be enshrined in law across the country and new, relatively modest, money made available for still more action on the ground.

Highlights of the official reporting round were published by the Department of Environment, Food and Rural Affairs in 2003. "More than a third of the UK BAP species and sixty per cent of the habitats are beginning to show positive trends",[18] and "seventy-two per cent of the national action plans are showing progress on at least one target".[19] Out of 391 species and 45 habitats, six habitats and 25 species were increasing, six habitats and 76 species were stable, 17 habitats were in decline (but the decline was slowing for 14 habitats) and, finally, 97 species were declining (but the decline was slowing for 30 species).

In May 1997, the Labour Government of Tony Blair had been elected on promises that there would be devolved institutions to govern in Scotland and Wales. Referenda later that year delivered 'yes' votes from the public in favour of devolution. This meant that, in future, delivery of biodiversity conservation, as with many other policies, would rest with the different countries. The Department of Environment still felt proprietorial about the biodiversity process and the list of priority species and habitats drawn up under the biodiversity process. It wanted to retain UK lists of priority species and habitats but the countries were

now keen, not only to compile their own lists, but to press ahead with the development of their own biodiversity strategies.

By December 2001, the Department (now the Department of Environment, Food and Rural Affairs – DEFRA) established the England Biodiversity Group and began preparation of an England Strategy, *Working with the Grain of Nature – a Biodiversity Strategy for England*, which it published in 2002. The report repeated the Government's commitment, made at the Johannesburg World Summit on Sustainable Development during the summer, to achieve a "significant reduction in the current rate of biodiversity loss by 2010".[20]

The lobbying by the BCG for the biodiversity process to be enshrined in law had paid off. In 2000, the Countryside and Rights of Way Act placed a new duty on Government Departments and the new National Assembly for Wales to have regard to biodiversity conservation and to maintain lists of species and habitats of principal importance for the conservation of biological diversity. These lists were published in England and Wales at the end of 2002. This biodiversity duty was extended to public bodies and statutory undertakers under the Natural Environment and Rural Communities Act 2006.

In some respects, when similar legislation was introduced under the Nature Conservation (Scotland) Act 2004, it was stronger. A duty was placed on 'every public body and office holder, in exercising any functions, to *further* the conservation of biodiversity so far as is consistent with the proper exercise of those

functions' and to produce a Scottish Biodiversity Strategy and lists of species and habitats of 'principal importance for the conservation of biodiversity'. The list for Scotland was published in December 2005.

By 2007, following a further comprehensive expert analysis of priority species and habitats, a list of 1,149 species and 65 habitats was approved by the Governments of all four UK administrations.

In 2003, Wildlife and Countryside Link (WILDLIFE LINK) established a Biodiversity Task Force and soon afterwards it picked up the reins from the Biodiversity Challenge Group. The following year, at a Parliamentary reception, Link published *Sustaining Biodiversity: Revitalising the BAP Process*, and, in 2007, played a key part in pressing DEFRA to publish *Conserving Biodiversity in a Changing Climate: Guidance on Building Capacity to Adapt.*

For nearly ten years the Biodiversity Challenge Group had kept the BAP process in the spotlight, had confronted the Government with new thinking on biodiversity conservation and, through its member organisations, including The Wildlife Trusts, backed up its ideas with membership of the various groups and committees, inputting data on species and habitats and delivery on the ground. Locally, in many cases, it had reinforced the Trusts' position as a leading player in biodiversity conservation. The Biodiversity Challenge Report, as Marren observed, had been "one of the milestones on the journey of the voluntary bodies from amateur natural history societies to partners in environmental policy-making".[21]

BIOLOGICAL SITES RECORDING SCHEME

In the late 1960s, the Society faced an increasing number of requests from the Trusts for guidance on site recording. The problem was that there was no national agreement on a standard method for collecting information about sites of biological or conservation interest, and so, in 1966, the Society's Conservation Advisory Group set about devising a system for the Trusts to use on their nature reserves and elsewhere.

Preparation of the scheme was taken forward under the guidance of the Society's new CONSERVATION LIAISON COMMITTEE (CLC), chaired by David Streeter. The principal architects of the scheme were Streeter (he delivered a paper on the subject to the Society's fourth national conference in Bournemouth in 1966) and the Head of the Nature Conservancy's Biological Records Centre (BRC) at the time, FRANK PERRING. The details of the final scheme were published by the Society in a Technical Publication No 1: *Biological Sites Recording Scheme* in 1969 (pictured below). A second, revised edition appeared in 1972.

In the context of the day, the publication was a landmark achievement. It established a habitat (and micro-habitat) classification, with definitions and symbols, and gave guidance on completing a new habitat recording card and existing species cards and on the storage and use of the data collected. The scheme received the general blessing of the Conservancy's BRC and it was BRC money that funded both the cards and the technical publication.

BRITISH WILDLIFE APPEAL

In the mid-1980s, the Society coordinated its most ambitious project to date – a British Wildlife Appeal (BWA) – on behalf of the Trust movement. The target was to raise £10 million over five years – £5 million to be raised nationally and £5 million to be raised through the Trusts. The aim was to buy and care for land with endangered species and declining habitats; to give everyone a chance to get to know and enjoy wildlife in town and country; and to promote greater public awareness of the threats to wildlife.

The Society's 1982–83 *Annual Report* noted that "the combined effect of the Wildlife and Countryside Act 1981 and the current recession seems to have caused many more SSSIs to come on the market. The situation has been aggravated by Government instructions to the Forestry Commission that it should raise £82 million over four years by selling assets including many of its woodlands".[22] A survey at the end of 1983 revealed that Trusts were negotiating for more than 50 SSSIs costing more than £1.25 million and, as fast as one site's future was secured, a new one was coming along. Existing sources of money were unable to meet the demand and a decision was taken to establish a fundraising unit with the primary purpose of launching a national appeal. From the outset, however, the BWA was seen not only as a major fundraising vehicle but as a way of uniting and promoting the Trust movement, and of enhancing its public profile and reputation.

From 1983 onwards, an Appeal Steering Committee, initially chaired by David Robinson (1983–84), prepared the ground. All import-antly, in 1985, the Society secured permission from the Trustees of the Mary Snow Trust – the backers of the Society's LAND FUND – to use

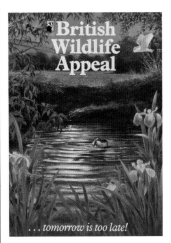

the interest from the Fund to pump-prime the Appeal. With spacious rent-free office space in the City of London provided by the Vincent Wildlife Trust, the way was clear to appoint a full-time Appeal Director, John Guy, and supporting staff. Public relations consultants were engaged and the ground prepared for a spectacular launch on 22nd October 1985.

The chances of the Appeal succeeding were greatly enhanced when the distinguished naturalist and broadcaster, SIR DAVID ATTENBOROUGH, accepted an invitation from Perring to be its Chairman and when the Society's Patron, HRH The Prince of Wales, agreed to speak in support of the appeal at its launch in the Natural History Museum in London. More than 400 distinguished guests were shown a nine-projector BWA presentation – finalised late the night before – and heard announcements of a generous donation from the Patron through the Duchy of Cornwall. There was also an unprecedented contribution of £10,000 from the Department of Environment, presented by the Minister for the Environment, William Waldegrave.

At the end of the five years, the BWA exceeded its target by more than £6 million thanks in no small

HRH The Prince of Wales talks to Watch members at the British Wildlife Appeal launch at the Natural History Museum, London in October 1985

that the hedgerows have gone. We are all much more concerned about the environment. However. . . almost more important than the money, was the way that numerous people throughout the land worked together to save their local countryside. . . in a curious way I would like to think that when people look back at the affairs of conservation, they will recognise that the real achievement of the BWA was that it actually brought the Wildlife Trusts together".[24]

BUSINESS OF CONSERVATION TRAINING PROGRAMME

By the 1980s, senior staff in the Trusts were being asked to take on a wider range of tasks and to cope with increasingly complex businesses. They had often been appointed as practical conservationists but now had to cope, not just with a general broadening of the Trusts' roles and responsibilities, but also with new challenges such as the management of large numbers of MSC-funded staff (EMPLOYMENT SCHEMES) and computerisation (COMPUTERS IN THE TRUSTS). They needed help not only to develop and promote their Trust, but to develop themselves as well.

One solution was a series of 'Business of Conservation' staff training courses organised between 1984 and 1988. The courses were available to staff from the British Trust for Conservation Volunteers (BTCV), Field Studies Council and the Society and Trusts and they were supported by British Petroleum (BP), the Nature Conservancy Council and WWF. Training was led by Julian Greatrex (BP) with support from Mel Banham (BTCV). By way of example, between October and November 1986, courses were organised on 'Creating an Effective Organisation', 'Promoting Yourself and Your Organisation', and 'Time and Team Management'.

measure to the Appeal's Director and Chairman. ATTENBOROUGH worked tirelessly throughout, undertaking two punishing nationwide lecture tours involving travelling thousands of miles, speaking to 25,000 people at more than 130 venues and raising more than £85,000 in the process. Attenborough was later to recall that when he had been asked to become Chairman of the Appeal, Perring had said "it won't involve any work!"[23]

Many others supported the appeal, from royalty and celebrities to companies and wealthy benefactors. In 1986, for example, Julian Pettifer, wildlife film-maker and a Vice President of the Society, also toured the country with a special film compiled from his BBC television series, *The Living Isles*. In 1987, a Royal Gala opening of Nureyev's *Romeo and Juliet*, attended by the Prince and Princess of Wales, generated more than £50,000. In 1989, a special reception at Garrards celebrated the first exhibition of Herend porcelain in Britain for 100 years. The event was attended by the Princess of Wales, herself a collector, and an auction during the evening, with actor Robert Hardy acting as auctioneer, raised £40,000. Gale's

Honey sponsored five WILDFLOWER WEEKS and the car manufacturers Fiat provided 27 Panda cars worth £167,000 for the Trusts. There was a mass hand-over of the cars in Battersea Park, London, and at least one of these vehicles was still in use by a Trust at the turn of the century.

The success of the Appeal, however, was in large measure a product of the imagination and commitment of the Trusts and their local appeals – 60 per cent of the total money was raised by the Trusts. Although the BWA helped to ensure the success of these appeals too, several Trusts received sizeable gifts from individuals towards the appeal, for example John Paul Getty Junior donated more than £285,000 in 1986 to BBOWT.

Interviewed for the winter issue of NATURAL WORLD in 1990, when the BWA was all over, Attenborough reflected on reaching and exceeding the £10 million target. "The winds of change were with us. There has been an extraordinary awakening. Even the Prime Minister was commenting on conservation. The situation has got so much worse; everyone now sees that the wood over the hill is threatened and

C

CADBURY, CHRISTOPHER

John Christopher Cadbury (1908–1995) helped lay the foundations of the modern Society as a predominantly locally-based organisation and was its PRESIDENT from 1962 until 1988. He chaired the Society's Council meetings during this time and was Chairman of its Executive Committee between 1981 and 1983. He was directly or indirectly involved in the acquisition of at least 30 nature reserves in Britain, as well as ARIDE ISLAND and Cousin Island in the Seychelles and nine south Atlantic islands in the Falklands (NATURE RESERVES OWNED BY THE SOCIETY).

Christopher Cadbury

His passion for the natural environment was sparked by boyhood visits to the Welcombe and Marsland coastal valleys on the Devon-Cornwall border (NATURE RESERVES OWNED BY THE SOCIETY). Later in his life, after patient negotiations with over 30 owners and tenants, he acquired and gifted these valleys to the Society as a nature reserve. In 1934, his family's chocolate company, Cadbury's, had posted him to Norwich as a sales representative. In his retirement speech as President, Cadbury recalled how fortunate it was that Norfolk had the only Trust and only Trust nature reserve at the time. "I caught the 'conservation bug' and it has never left me".[25]

In 1958, he became a member of the Society's Council and the same year joined the REGIONAL LIAISON COMMITTEE, which had recently been formed to provide the focal point for a huge effort to expand the number of local Trusts. Cadbury became the Chairman of this Committee in 1960 and, with its Secretary TED SMITH, devoted himself to the task in hand with tremendous enthusiasm, attending and organising meetings all over the country.

Once embarked on a cause, he was never one to give up easily. He often adopted his favourite technique of persuasion which involved firing off a relentless barrage of letters copied to individuals, many of whom appeared totally unrelated to the topic in question. The recipient was not let off the hook until a satisfactory reply had been received!

In 1990, he endowed the Christopher Cadbury Medal (see also CHRISTOPHER CADBURY MEDAL CITATIONS and MEDALS) to be gifted annually by the Society. He was on the Council of the NORFOLK TRUST for 43 years and was first Chairman, then President and finally Patron of the WORCESTERSHIRE TRUST for more than 27 years.

Christopher Cadbury's "heart and soul"[26] were in nature conservation. He was involved in the work of the RSPB, Birdlife International and WWF but he devoted most of his energy and influence to The Wildlife Trusts who benefited nationally, and at local level, from his intuition, tenacity, kindness and generosity over 37 years.

A memorial to Christopher Cadbury was unveiled by SIR DAVID ATTENBOROUGH at the Welcombe and Marsland nature reserve in Devon on 1st October 1997. There is also a granite memorial stone at the start of the hill walk on Aride Island in the Seychelles.

Sir David Attenborough unveils a memorial to Christopher Cadbury at Marsland, Devon, 1997

CARNEGIE FUNDS

The Carnegie United Kingdom Trust was one of the most imaginative and stalwart supporters of the Trusts and the Society between the end of the 1960s and the mid-1970s. Up to 1975 it made grants totalling £56,290 towards the costs of employing full-time members of staff in the Trusts – often for the first time – and towards interpretation and education projects. It also awarded the Society a grant of £31,000 over a five-year period starting in 1975, to enable it to employ a General Secretary (PRINCIPAL OFFICERS) for the first time.

In Carnegie's *Annual Report* for 1973, the Trustees wrote, we "believe that the SPNR and the County Trusts have a great potential in the field of practical conservation, in involving the public as a whole in the problems of managing resources and in increasing appreciation and understanding of the natural environment".[27] The willingness of the Carnegie Trustees to back the 'potential' of the movement in its early years with such a sizeable and consistent stream of funds, was one of the key factors in building the movement's confidence and professionalism at that time.

CHAIRMEN OF THE EXECUTIVE COMMITTEE

Before the granting of the second Royal Charter in 1976, the Society had no formal position of Chairman of the Executive. Most of the first few meetings of the Executive Committee were chaired by CHARLES ROTHSCHILD himself, but, from the ninth meeting onwards, the role was normally filled by the President. The exceptions were when the bye-laws were invoked and CYRIL DIVER was appointed as Chairman of the Executive for one year in November 1958, and Professor HW Miles for two years from November 1959.

Walter Lane	1976–1981
Christopher Cadbury	
(President and acting Chairman	
of Executive)	1981–1983
Dunstan Adams	1983–1988
John Phillipson	1988–1993
Duncan Jeffray	1993–1997
Robin Crane	1997–1998

In 1998, the Privy Council approved amendments to the 1976 Royal Charter that resulted in the abolition of the Executive Committee.

CHAIRMEN OF THE COUNCIL

Charles Rothschild	1912–1916
James Lowther/	
Viscount Ullswater	1916–1932
Lord (Walter) Rothschild	1932–1936
Earl of Onslow	1936–1942
Lord Macmillan	1942–1947
Duke of Devonshire	1947–1950
Lord Hurcomb	1951–1962
Christopher Cadbury	1962–1988
Dunstan Adams	1988–1991
John Phillipson	1991–1994
Robin Crane	1994–1999
Peter Schofield	2000–2001
Michael Field	2001–2005
Michael Allen	2005–2011
Paul Wickham (acting)	2011–2012
René Olivieri	2012–

The Council met 69 times under the original Royal Charter, the last time on 5th November 1975. It met 62 times between 1976 and 27th November 1997, before the Royal Charter was amended once again. By March 2010, the 'modern' Council had met 32 times.

Below: Council of the Society in 2011 (left to right): Hugh Tollemache, Paul Wickham, Tim Sands, Linda Butler, Don Wright, Allan Bantinck, Alan Rick, Roger Dobbs, Michael Allen (Chair), Dave Counsell, Peter Archdale, Patrick Vaughan, Anne Powell, David King, Tim Cawkwell, Michael Power

CHRISTOPHER CADBURY MEDAL CITATIONS

The Christopher Cadbury Medal

The recipients of the Christopher Cadbury Medal, first awarded in 1990 for services to nature conservation, with their respective citations, are:

1990
Ted Smith
LINCOLNSHIRE TRUST FOR NATURE CONSERVATION
The RSNC is pleased to make the award in the year 1990 to Mr AE Smith OBE MA who has given his all to Nature Conservation and has probably had more influence than anyone else on the events which have determined the important role of the voluntary nature conservation movement in the British Islands today.

Ted Smith receives the first medal

1991
Professor Bill Lacey
NORTH WALES WILDLIFE TRUST
The RSNC is pleased to make the award in the year 1991 to Professor William S Lacey PhD DSc FLS FGS. A distinguished academic with deep understanding of the processes of nature conservation who has given outstanding service to this work in Wales; from being a founder member of the North Wales Naturalists' Trust in 1963 until becoming its Chairman in 1974 and President in 1988. He played a key role in the formation of the Association of Welsh Trusts and as its Chairman.

His influence was by no means confined to Wales, for he gave notable service as a member of the Council and of the Executive Committee of the RSNC to which he brought a wealth of wisdom for the furtherance of the conservation of nature in Britain.

Bill Lacey

1992
Helen Brotherton
DORSET TRUST FOR NATURE CONSERVATION
The RSNC is pleased to make the award in the year 1992 to Helen Brotherton CBE for her outstanding and practical contribution to the nature conservation movement in the British Islands for over 55 years, not

least towards the development of five different County Trusts for Nature Conservation, and the Councils of RSNC since 1961.

Helen Brotherton

1993
Sir William Wilkinson
LONDON WILDLIFE TRUST
The RSNC is pleased to make the award in the year 1993 to Sir William Wilkinson for his outstanding contribution to the conservation of the natural heritage of the United Kingdom over the last 25 years. His inspired leadership of the Nature Conservancy Council (1983–91) achieved lasting benefits for UK wildlife, and raised the public profile of nature conservation. This commitment to wildlife now continues through his active support of many conservation organisations, including The Wildlife Trusts.

1994
Christopher Cadbury
WORCESTERSHIRE WILDLIFE TRUST
The RSNC is pleased to make the award in the year 1994 to Mr John Christopher Cadbury.

The citation has not been located.

Tim Sands

1994 (Staff)
Tim Sands
UK NATIONAL OFFICE
The RSNC is pleased to make the
award in the year 1994 to Tim
Sands who has been at the centre
of The Wildlife Trusts' national
work over the last twenty years.
His most significant achievements
have been to improve the
legislative protection for habitats
and species; to develop NATURAL
WORLD and the Watch Club*;
and to enhance the conservation
professionalism of The Wildlife
Trusts. His commitment to nature
conservation is boundless. His
skill, enthusiasm and knowledge
are held in the highest regard by
his colleagues everywhere.

*See WILDLIFE WATCH

1995
Mrs Susan Cowdy
BBONT
The RSNC is pleased to make
the award in the year 1995 to
Susan Cowdy MBE who has
dedicated her whole life to nature
conservation. Susan Cowdy has
held high office within a number
of conservation and ornithological
organisations and was a founder
member of BBONT; she also
chaired the successful appeal to
buy Bardsey Island.

Susan Cowdy has been indefatigable
in her crusade for nature
conservation and her special gift of
being able to arouse the interest of
others and to impart knowledge to a
wide range of the public has meant
that she has been a practical and
inspirational force within the nature
conservation movement throughout
the British Islands.

1996
Professor HEM Kay
WILTSHIRE WILDLIFE TRUST
The RSNC is pleased to make the
award in the year 1996 to Professor
HEM Kay. Humphrey Kay has
served on the RSNC Executive
Committee and Conservation and
Scientific Committee, where his
scientific background brought a clear
and analytical approach to many
national issues. In Wiltshire he has
enabled dramatic expansion of the
Trust's reserve acquisition
programme, and has been active in
the monitoring of many aspects of
Wiltshire's wildlife. Humphrey has
also been an inventive fundraiser,
initiating the famous Sarsen Trail
walk between Avebury and
Stonehenge, and is well known for
enthusing and educating audiences
with public lectures and guided
walks.

Humphrey Kay

1997
Mrs AL Cooper
Cleveland Wildlife Trust*
The RSNC is pleased to make the
award in the year 1997 to Angela
Liet Cooper MBE who has
immeasurably raised public
awareness of the need for nature
conservation in the north-east of
England for over 40 years. She
founded Teesmouth Field Centre
and has dedicated over 25 years to
its service as voluntary warden and
tutor; she helped found Teesmouth
Bird Club, Tyne-Tees FWAG and
Cleveland Wildlife Trust* and
played a prominent role in all. She
was instrumental in establishing
the first nature reserve in Teesside,
in saving Seal Sands and acquiring
and managing six other sites. She
has worked tirelessly for nature.

*See TEES VALLEY TRUST

1998
Mr RSR Fitter
BBONT
The RSNC is pleased to make the
award in the year 1998 to Richard
SR Fitter, a pioneer of modern
nature conservation and instigator
of the British nature conservation
movement. Through his writing,
his boundless energy and
enthusiasm, he has made countless
thousands aware of the beauty of
nature and the need for its
conservation.

He has influenced policy
nationally through the COUNCIL
FOR NATURE, the Wild Life
Conservation Special Committee
and Fauna Preservation Society and
locally as a founding member and
outstanding servant of BBONT,
which continues to this day. His
contribution to the work and
development of the conservation
movement over five decades has
been enormous.

1999 (Staff)
Mr TP Appleton
LEICESTERSHIRE AND RUTLAND
WILDLIFE TRUST
The RSNC is pleased to make
the award in the year 1999 to
Timothy P Appleton who has been
warden and latterly manager of
Rutland Water nature reserve for
the past 24 years. In that time he
has developed the reserve from
its original concept, through a
programme of creative conservation
on a scale never previously attempted
in the United Kingdom, to its
position as the most important
inland wintering site for birds in
the country.

His dedication and skill have
led to the reserve being designated
both as a SSSI and a Ramsar site in
parallel with its ever-growing use for
human recreation. As such it has
become a model which is widely
admired and studied.

Tim Appleton

2000
Dr Francis Rose
KENT WILDLIFE TRUST
The RSNC is pleased to make the
award in the year 2000 to Dr Francis
Rose MBE who has been one of the
most influential names in British
conservation for almost 50 years.
He was instrumental in the
formation of the Kent Wildlife Trust
and actively involved in establishing
and supporting all of the county
Trusts in south-east England.

He has had a profound and
continuing influence in the
identification, acquisition and
management of reserves and is
universally regarded as one of the
most distinguished field botanists
in Western Europe. His personal
notebooks containing more than
250,000 records are a unique and
invaluable database for future
generations of naturalists.

2001
Dr HAP Ingram
SCOTTISH WILDLIFE TRUST
The RSNC is pleased to make
the award in the year 2001 to
Dr Hugh Albert Pugh Ingram, an
internationally recognised authority
on the botany and hydrology of raised
bogs, who has served the Scottish
Wildlife Trust with dedication and
distinction for over 30 years. He
established and maintained high
scientific standards in the acquisition
of 123 nature reserves and their
management plans and as an
enthusiastic supporter of
environmental education promoted
and encouraged visitor centres.
His initiative, perceptive insight,
diplomatic and administrative skills,
and sheer determination during his
years as Chairman – during which
time he was also Chairing the Darwin
Initiative peat bogs project – was a
truly outstanding achievement, which
secured the future of the Trust.

2001 (Staff)
Mrs LP Brassley
DERBYSHIRE WILDLIFE TRUST
The RSNC is pleased to make the
award in the year 2001 to Lesley
Patricia Brassley after 32 years service
above and beyond the call of duty to
the DEVON and Derbyshire Wildlife
Trusts, during which time her
experience, capacity for hard work
and tough but non-confrontational
approach, have earned her the

respect and admiration of
colleagues throughout the
partnership, and the trust of the
many organisations with which
she has had to deal. This, and
her personal involvement and
commitment at all levels from
expert witness, through writing,
giving talks, and running courses,
to bracken bashing, has led directly
to many gains for wildlife that
could not otherwise have been
achieved. She has been an excellent
and tireless ambassador.

Pat Brassley

2002
Dr Duncan J Jeffray
CUMBRIA WILDLIFE TRUST
The RSNC is pleased to make
the award in the year 2002 to
Dr Duncan John Jeffray, botanist,
for his 35 years of outstanding
service to nature conservation at
the highest level as the creator and
manager of reserves; inspirational
teacher and educationalist;
fundraiser; trust and committee
Chair and President. Nationally, he
has been profoundly influential in
the formulation of policy as an
RSNC Council member and
Chairman of its Executive
Committee, board member of the
National Forest and NATURAL
WORLD, and Council member of
the National Trust. He has
championed the involvement of
people of all ages in nature
conservation as a member of the
board of WATCH and through the
Urban Wildlife Partnership.

2002 (Staff)
Mr Andrew JL Fraser
WORCESTERSHIRE WILDLIFE
TRUST
The RSNC is pleased to make the
award in the year 2002 to Andrew
John Lawson Fraser for outstanding
service beyond the call of duty as
the Worcestershire Wildlife Trust's
conservation officer and manager
since 1974. Andrew is a dedicated
reserves volunteer and fundraiser as
well as manager and acquirer; a
contributor to local, regional and
national policy; a natural media
star, who, through television,
radio, the written word and public
meetings, has converted thousands
and influenced countless others by
his winning communication of his
passion for wildlife. He influences
both the young and the decision
maker and inspires colleagues
and fellow professionals by his
commitment and attitude and the
exceptionally high standards he
sets himself.

Andrew Fraser at work for the
Worcestershire Trust, 1978

2003
Mr JM McMeeking MBE
NOTTINGHAMSHIRE WILDLIFE
TRUST
The RSNC is pleased to make the
award in the year 2003 to John
Michael McMeeking MBE,
ornithologist and conservationist.
He played a leading role in the
acquisition of all the
Nottinghamshire Wildlife Trust's
nature reserves, as well as writing
management plans and helping
carry them out. He promotes the

John McMeeking

Trust and nature conservation
tirelessly and over many years has
served with distinction as Chairman
of its Council, of many committees,
on the Council of RSNC and the
BTO. His great knowledge and
dedication to nature conservation in
ways too numerous for this citation,
are equalled only by his unfailing
wisdom, courtesy and kindness.

2004
Dr EMN Andrews
BRECKNOCK WILDLIFE TRUST
The RSNC is pleased to award the
medal to Dr Elizabeth Mary Nesbit
Andrews, zoologist, for services to
nature conservation as creator and
manager of reserves; lecturer, author
and broadcaster; fundraiser;
voluntary warden, trustee, scientific
officer and President of her Wildlife
Trust. Nationally she has been
influential in the formulation
of policy as a Council member
of the Society and Chair of its
Conservation sub-committee,
member of the Council for National
Parks and the UK committee of the
IUCN. An outstanding and active
champion of wildlife conservation in
Wales, she is well respected within
the circles of government and life in
Wales. She has been a diplomatic
advocate of the development of
collaboration between the Welsh
Trusts and a wise counsel for the
Society as Chair of the ARIDE
ISLAND Management Committee.

2005
Mr FW Boot
ESSEX WILDLIFE TRUST
The RSNC is pleased to award the
medal to Frederick William Boot,
for services to nature conservation
as creator and manager of reserves;
lecturer and fundraiser; trustee and
Chairman of the Essex Wildlife
Trust. Nationally he has served as a
Council member of the Society and
on its Governance Committees.
Throughout he has demonstrated a
strong commitment to increasing
public awareness and involvement in
nature conservation. He has been a
tireless champion of well controlled
public access and informative
interpretation. As Chairman of the
Regional Group of Wildlife Trusts in
the East of England he showed wise
leadership in the development of
regional cooperation and at national
level was a strong and tireless
advocate of good management
practice.

2005 (Staff)
Mr S Brooks
SCOTTISH WILDLIFE TRUST
The RSNC is pleased to make the
staff award in the year 2005 to Stuart
Brooks for his dedication to nature
conservation, underpinned by an
impressive and highly respected
balance of knowledge and practical
ability. He is a skilled communicator
whose passionate and pragmatic
approach has enhanced the

Stuart Brooks

reputation of the conservation movement. He has excelled above all in the area of peatland conservation, both nationally and internationally. He has undertaken projects in ten countries, was the chair of the RSWT's raised Bog Specialist group and is the representative of the International Mire Conservation group on the Ramsar STRP committee. His experience of practical management, policy and advocacy, research and public awareness, has made him one of the country's most influential practitioners in this field.

Patricia Callaghan

2006

Mrs Patricia Callaghan
STAFFORDSHIRE WILDLIFE TRUST
The RSNC is pleased to award the medal to Patricia Callaghan for her services to nature conservation. As Chair of Staffordshire Wildlife Trust since 1995 she has led an unparalleled increase in the Trust's staff, assets and the area of nature reserves it owns or manages. She was also instrumental in establishing a new headquarters and visitor centre for the Trust. Patricia was Chair of Sustainable Staffordshire 2000–5; has been Chair of the Potteries and Newcastle Urban Wildlife Group since 1995; and has served in many other county, regional and national roles. She has worked tirelessly to help all communities, but especially those in urban and deprived neighbourhoods, to have access to high quality green spaces close to their homes. She has been vigorous

and successful in engaging active volunteers, the general public and local and regional government in the cause of nature conservation. Her willingness and her capacity to deal with issues at all levels, command respect and provide an outstanding example to others.

2007

Mr JS Furphy
ULSTER WILDLIFE TRUST
The Society is pleased to award the medal to Joseph Sands Furphy for his life-long contribution to the conservation, protection and management of wildlife and its habitats across Northern Ireland. Joe spent his working life in Northern Ireland's Environment and Heritage Service, retiring in 1997 as Chief Conservation Officer. He was a driving force in identifying key wildlife sites, establishing their legal protection and advocating landscape-scale wildlife conservation. Joe's vision underpinned the formation of Ulster Wildlife Trust. He was a founder member and Chairman (2003–5). He has held posts in BTO, RSPB, National Trust and Eco-Congregation Ireland, has raised public awareness of wildlife and the environment and has recently led formulation of an environmentally-friendly Northern Ireland policy on use of renewable energy.

Joe Furphy receives his award from Vice President Simon King, 2007

Harry Green

2008

Mr GH Green
WORCESTERSHIRE WILDLIFE
TRUST
The Society is pleased to award the medal to George Henry 'Harry' Green for his lifetime contribution to the Worcestershire Wildlife Trust and to nature conservation in Worcestershire and beyond.

Harry was a founder member of the Trust in 1968, was elected as Honorary Vice President in 1984 and served as Chair from 1985 to 1993. He was a driving force in the establishment of over half the Trust's nature reserves and a major fundraiser for the Trust. He has developed a deep knowledge of wildlife and takes a keen and practical interest in habitat management and re-creation. He is a natural communicator, in demand at local events, by local media and by national radio, and has the gift of motivating people to take action for wildlife. His deep interest in birds has led him to make significant contributions to the British Trust for Ornithology.

Stuart Crooks

2008 (Staff)
Mr SE Crooks
LINCOLNSHIRE WILDLIFE TRUST
The Society is pleased to award the staff medal to Stuart E Crooks for his lifetime contribution to nature conservation and The Wildlife Trusts. Stuart was a founder member of the Hertfordshire and Middlesex Wildlife Trust and became a full-time conservationist as the Cheshire Wildlife Trust's first Conservation Officer. Since 1976, Stuart has served as Director of the Lincolnshire Wildlife Trust. He has driven the huge growth of the Trust and established the principles and management systems which will underpin its future success. He has built effective partnerships for conservation between the Trust and many local and regional bodies and played an influential role in the development of the RSWT.

2009
Dr Angus Lunn
NORTHUMBERLAND TRUST
The Society is pleased to award the medal to Dr Angus Lunn for his services to ecology, The Wildlife Trusts and the National Parks movement. Angus's deep and comprehensive understanding of

the wildlife and landscape of North East England was the key to his success in securing the recognition and protection of numerous unique habitats and important sites. Especially noteworthy have been his survey and management activities in connection with the Border Mires, where many sites are now accorded NNR, SAC or Ramsar status. Complementing his ecological achievements, Angus has been a major driving force in the development of the Northumberland Wildlife Trust, served on the Northumberland National Park Committee, was for ten years Chair of the Council (now Campaign) for National Parks, is the author of the *New Naturalist 'Northumberland'*, and serves on the North Pennines AONB Partnership.

Angus Lunn

2010
Thomas William Cain
MANX WILDLIFE TRUST
The Society is pleased to award the medal to Thomas William Cain CBE for his services to both the Manx Wildlife Trust and the natural environment of the Isle of Man and Irish Sea.

William was a founder member of the Manx Wildlife Trust in 1973 and served as its Chairman for 36 years

until retiring in 2010. In this time, he was instrumental in the growth of the Trust and its acquisition of over 20 wildlife reserves and two public visitor centres. Beyond this, William was a major force in establishing the Manx Wildlife Act in 1990 and in the campaign which, in 1995, successfully reversed the government policy of converting upland heaths to commercial conifer forestry. He has also been extremely effective in gaining government and financial support for a wide range of conservation projects across the island and its surrounding seas.

Ron Hill

2011
Ron Hill
WARWICKSHIRE TRUST
The Society is pleased to award the 2011 medal to Ron Hill for his services to nature conservation and The Wildlife Trusts.

Ron has been a long-serving active member of the Warwickshire Wildlife Trust and has made a significant contribution to the establishment of the Trust's reserves in the Solihull area and across Warwickshire. He has been a major driving force in the development of the Trust, through serving as its Chair in the 1980s and 1990s, also through his direct conservation work on the ground and through inspiring local people and local landowners about the natural environment. Especially noteworthy has been Ron's successful major campaign that saved one of Shirley's last species-rich meadows from destruction and his work at Clowes Wood and New Fallings Coppice.

2011 (staff)
Brendan Joyce
NORFOLK TRUST

The Society is pleased to award the 2011 staff medal to Brendan Joyce for his lifetime contribution to nature conservation and The Wildlife Trusts. Brendan joined as Director of Norfolk Wildlife Trust in 1995 from his previous employment at RSNC. He has driven huge growth of the Trust and has also taken forward the Trust's vision for landscape-scale conservation by significantly extending the land under the protection of the Trust. He has always sought to engage as many local people as possible in their natural heritage, through extensive wildlife information services and their education programme and, most importantly through the development of a state-of-the-art visitor centre at the Trust's oldest and most popular reserve, Cley Marshes.

Brendan Joyce

COMMON LAND CAMPAIGN

This campaign in the late 1980s was designed to achieve a new Common Land Bill that fully recognised the importance of common land for wildlife. It was among the earliest of the Society's campaigns to combine detailed background research and survey with the professional promotion of innovative policy proposals to Government and the media.

The problem faced by commons was that the Commons Registration Act 1965 was "loosely drafted so that its meaning had been too easily twisted by able lawyers to enable land that everybody assumed to be common, and protected, to be struck off the register".[28] In 1986, a Common Land Forum (CLF), established by the Countryside Commission (CC), highlighted the urgent need for new legislation and made proposals on access and for improving the management of commons. It failed, however, to recognise adequately the value of common land for wildlife.

A major wildlife survey of common land was long overdue. One was being carried out by Aberystwyth University but it was going to take several years. A 'quick and dirty' survey was needed in the interim to influence Government thinking. The Society secured grant aid from the Conservancy for just such a survey, and from the CC to study the implications of the CLF's findings for nature conservation.

What became clear was that the wildlife importance of common land, unless a site had been designated as an SSSI, had been seriously under-estimated. The wildlife interest of common land was also poorly protected under existing legislation. More than half the common land in a sample of 16 counties, for which data was available, was of high wildlife interest. In some counties, the rate was even higher.

The *Common Sense* 'broadsheet'

For example, in Gloucestershire 87 per cent of common land was of high wildlife importance. In a sample of 31 counties, a fifth of the total SSSI area was found to be on common land, and elsewhere large amounts of common land had wildlife value but remained undesignated. For example, in County Durham, where a little less than three per cent of common land was SSSI, more than 30 per cent was of recognised wildlife value in the opinion of either the Conservancy or the DURHAM TRUST.

The five major threats to the wildlife conservation of common land were identified as the over-grazing of upland moorland commons; the under-grazing and neglect of lowland commons; agricultural improvement and forestry and, on rare occasions, public access.

In October 1989, the Society presented a report, *A Future for Wildlife on Commons,* and a broadsheet, *Common Sense,* to the Parliamentary Under-Secretary at the Department of the Environment, Virginia Bottomley. The report recommended, among other things, that new legislation should provide a mechanism to identify commons with high wildlife interest against criteria established by the

Conservancy. It should also ensure that wildlife conservation was a primary and routine management objective on commons of high wildlife interest. The idea that there should be two types of common, grazing and amenity commons, which were managed differently, should be dropped in favour of a 'single' model. There should be financial incentives to encourage the establishment of Management Associations and to implement effective management schemes. There should also be a range of provisions built into legislation to discourage agricultural improvements. Access should be encouraged and where access problems did arise they should be resolved, whenever possible, by positive management.

New laws relating to the registration and management of common land and town or village greens were finally introduced with the passing of the Commons Act 2006. This enabled Commons Councils to be established for specified common land and town or village greens for the management of agricultural activities, vegetation or rights of common. The Act states that these functions must be discharged, among other things, having regard to the public interest of the land in question. Public interest was deemed to include nature conservation, the conservation of landscape, the protection of public rights of access and the protection of archaeological remains and features of historic interest.

COMPREHENSIVE WILDLIFE LEGISLATION

The Society's CONSERVATION LIAISON COMMITTEE (CLC) established a working party in 1970 to examine the feasibility of comprehensive wildlife legislation.

By November 1972, the Society felt confident enough to promote the

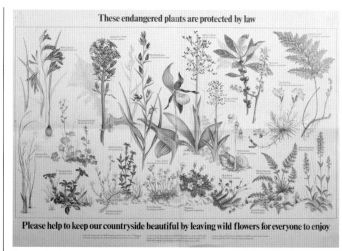

A poster showing wildflowers protected under the Wildlife & Countryside Act 1981

idea more widely and made a presentation to an early meeting of the ALL-PARTY PARLIAMENTARY CONSERVATION COMMITTEE of both Houses of Parliament. The Society's idea was to consolidate existing legislation, including existing bird legislation, and to extend this by adding variable schedules for invertebrates, vertebrates and plants. There would also be a provision to safeguard wildlife in sanctuary areas, including nature reserves. Having heard the arguments, the All-Party Parliamentary Conservation Committee thought such legislation was "desirable and should be adopted".[29] It agreed that the Society's "proposals would form a suitable starting point".[30] After further work, the Society continued to consult widely and was pleased when its ideas received a large measure of support. The Society followed this with a meeting at the Conservancy's Belgrave Square offices in London to discuss its proposals. Attending were the Conservancy, the Department of the Environment, the Botanical Society of the British Isles, the Council for Nature, Friends of the Earth and Lord Cranbrook.

Although the initiative had built up encouraging support, there

were also those who had reservations. For example, the Society's expectation was that existing legislation would be strengthened but there were those who took a contrary view. They considered that bird legislation, with its extensive case law, could be weakened in the redrafting and Parliamentary process.

In 1974, as well as a Wild Plant Protection Bill that was being promoted by Lord Beaumont of Whitley, there was also a Wild Creatures Bill promoted by Lord Cranbrook (CONSERVATION OF WILD CREATURES AND WILD PLANT CONSERVATION ACT 1975). While these initiatives remained as separate bills and struggled for Parliamentary time, the Society's bill continued to be an attractive proposition. But only a few days after the Belgrave Square meeting, Peter Hardy (at the time MP for the Rother Valley) secured first place in the ballot for Private Members' Bills. He had recently skilfully steered the Protection of Badgers Act 1973 through the House of Commons. The decision was taken to withdraw the two separate bills from the House of Lords and for Peter Hardy to introduce a combined bill into the House of Commons. The combined bill – the Conservation of Wild Creatures and

Wild Plants Bill – had its Second Reading in January 1975 and received Royal Assent in the summer. Initially, the Society resolved to "speed up the timetable with regard to the Society's proposed comprehensive Wildlife Protection Bill",[31] but effectively, for the moment, the opportunity had passed. It was time for the Society to move on.

TED SMITH recalls that the "fully comprehensive legislation which the Society advocated was still some way off, but Peter Hardy's Act was a step towards it and elicited from the Government a request to the Nature Conservancy Council to conduct a wide review of wildlife legislation. . . concern with the protection of species in no way diminished our advocacy of the basic need to conserve habitats especially on SSSIs which were still being destroyed and damaged in all parts of the country".[32]

The Society's 1978–79 *Annual Report* describes how the Society was "closely involved with proposals to amend the Conservation of Wild Creatures and Wild Plants Act 1975 to enable protection to be given to vulnerable as well as endangered creatures. . . However, the Society has long held that further legislation must also be concerned with habitat conservation".[33]

By its next *Annual Report*, the Society considered "the decline in important wildlife habitats, and in particular the need for adequate protection of all Sites of Special Scientific Interest, to be the most urgent issue facing the nature conservation movement in Great Britain today".[34] The Society set about collecting evidence through the Trusts on the rate of loss or severe damage of SSSIs, which it was confident was running at more than the four per cent per annum quoted by the Conservancy. With the RSPB, Friends of the Earth and other

voluntary bodies within a new body, WILDLIFE LINK, the Society became involved in "a coordinated campaign of unprecedented focus and ferocity".[35]

The Government was also under an obligation to implement a series of international agreements, notably the European Birds Directive. Finally in June 1979, the new Conservative Government announced that it would introduce a comprehensive wildlife bill. As in the lead up to the National Parks and Access to the Countryside Act 1949, the Society's pioneering work had played an important part in securing this outcome. The Society's contribution to the campaign to strengthen the comprehensive wildlife bill, finally introduced by the Government in November 1980, is covered in more detail in Chapter 5. The resulting Wildlife and Countryside Act became law in October 1981.

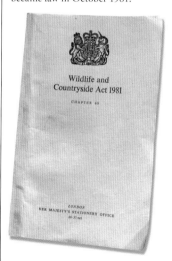

COMPUTERS IN THE TRUSTS

The Society installed its first computer – a Hewlett Packard HP250 Mini-Computer – for its Sales and Watch (WILDLIFE WATCH) operation in September 1980. It was the size of a large office desk with a then impressive 32K user memory – nearly 22,000 times smaller than today's average CDRom.

A Hewlett Packard HP250

The invention of the microprocessor in the 1970s had made small, relatively low cost micro-computers available to individuals and small businesses. But, in practice, there remained considerable scepticism amongst some in the Society and Trusts about this new technology, partly based on the lack of compatability between the various operating systems in use at the time, and partly on their cost and reliability. There was also a general fear of the unknown and, in some quarters, a fear of their impact on jobs, particularly on secretarial posts.

Whilst the new technology met with resistance in some quarters, elsewhere there was frustration that the introduction of computers was taking so long. One place where the matter came to a head was the York Conservation Officers' Conference in 1983 (CONFERENCES). A resolution calling for "an investigation. . . into Trust computer requirements, as soon as possible – preferably within three months – with the aim of ensuring compatability within the movement",[36] thinly disguised the frustration of the young delegates. It was the push the Society needed. A Study Group was established soon afterwards to consider the immediate and future computer needs of the Trusts and a full systems analysis of the Society's requirements at the Nettleham offices (for sales, site recording, Watch, fundraising, finance and administration) was also initiated. Sixty per cent funding was secured from the Conservancy and British Petroleum towards a first tranche of computer equipment and 50 per cent from the Conservancy towards the study of the Society's needs. What was to become known as the 'Computers in the Trusts' scheme was born.

In 1984, Comart micro-computers were installed in 14 Trusts, with a 15th installed at the Society's offices. The WWF offered to assist financially, enabling the computers to be fully funded and the Society to go ahead with appointing a full-time member of staff to develop the computerisation of site recording and membership software. In 1985, nine more Trusts were supplied with the same Comart computers, the Society took on a second member of staff and a Central Support Unit – later called the Computer Unit – was established to "meet the needs of the Trusts – our customers".[37] The Unit also began work on developing software to manage site and habitat records. Over the following two years, seven more Trusts began operating Comart micro-computers and the Unit introduced a day-to-day 'hotline' for trouble-shooting and general advice. It also began a regular programme of training seminars and site visits. The Society finally introduced its first computerised accounts system in 1991.

By 1990, 39 Trusts were members of the Computers in the Trusts scheme. But, although the Society's Unit was still brokering the installation and after-care of new and replacement equipment and sourcing, generating and servicing new software (34 Trusts were operating the Society's membership package), the need for central coordination and funding was gradually becoming less critical. In 1988, for example, the Unit was recommending dBase II/III+ and Wordstar as standard software packages. But by the early 1990s, Microsoft Windows was

Using computers as part of the Recorder project

increasingly being accepted as the standard operating system. It was not only capable of operating on a very wide range of hardware, but Trusts could arrange their own service agreements and the costs and servicing of computers were gradually being absorbed into the everyday expenditure of Trusts.

The Society now turned its attention to more specialist support for the Trusts. For example, helping Trusts source specialist software to support the recording, storage and manipulation of biological data on sites and species. With funding once again from the Conservancy and WWF, a Development Officer was employed to help evaluate the Conservancy's Recorder package using three pilot Trusts – SOMERSET, GLOUCESTERSHIRE and LINCOLNSHIRE.

The 1990s saw rapid computer-isation of operations across the movement. Perhaps the most significant development was the ease with which information could now be exchanged, not just 'vertically' between Trusts and the Society, but 'horizontally' between Trusts.

In 1996, a small group of Trust staff – among them Pete Guest (LONDON TRUST), Chris Gerrard (BCN TRUST) and Martin Newman (SURREY TRUST) – anxious to make progress on this front – approached Compuserve Information Exchange (CIX). They negotiated for the

Society and the Trusts to have free email accounts with conferencing facilities. The latter would provide the movement with a uniform, fully interactive electronic communication system for the first time. The company also gave space on their web server to enable each Trust to set up their own website, if they wished. By the end of the millennium all Wildlife Trusts were using the CIX conferencing system and this, and more particularly the rapid growth of email, quickly revolutionised internal communication across the movement.

Although doubts were sometimes expressed about the quantity and quality of some of the 'correspondence' that ensued, there were no doubts about the benefits. In particular, it enabled more efficient working, improved networking and increased access to information. But, perhaps, a less predictable benefit was the enhanced sense of community that the new arrangements engendered.

Further changes in methods of electronic communication swiftly followed. For example, the first nationwide Wildlife Trust website came online in 1997 and by the end of the following decade every Trust had its own website with many using newer communications technology, such as e-newsletters and social media to publicise events and raise awareness of their work. A new era had well and truly begun.

CONFERENCES

The major national conferences have been as follows:

Chairs (Chaircon)

2006	Market Bosworth, Leics
2007	Attenborough, Notts
2008	Grantham, Lincolnshire
2009	Marston, Lincolnshire
2010	Marston Bigot, Somerset
2011	York, Yorkshire

Conservation Officers

1973	Horncastle Residential College, Lincolnshire
1974	Missenden Abbey, Bucks
1975	Dartington Hall, Devon
1976	Losehill Hall, Derbyshire
1977	Scottish College of Textiles, Galashiels
1978	Lackham College of Agriculture, Wiltshire
1979	Trinity College, Carmarthen
1980	Cumbria College of Agriculture and Forestry, Penrith, Cumbria
1981	Norfolk College of Agriculture, Easton, Norwich
1982	Dorset Institute of Higher Education, Weymouth
1983	College of Ripon & York St John, York
1984	Wye College, Ashford, Kent
1985	Carbisdale Castle Youth Hostel, Ross-shire, Scotland
1986	Wrekin College, Wellington, Shropshire
1987	St Swithun's School, Winchester
1988	Stranmillis College, Belfast
1989	Homerton College, Cambridge
1990	Y Coleg Normal, Bangor
1991	Teesside Polytechnic, Middlesbrough
1992	University of Sussex, Brighton
1993	Stoke Rochford Hall, Grantham
1995	University of Exeter, Exeter (*Conservation & Marketing*)
1998	Harborne Hall, Birmingham
1999	*No Conservation Conference held, but Reserves Conference held at Reaseheath College, Crewe*
2002	All Saints, University of Leeds, Leeds

Directors (Dircon)

1989	Gibralter Point, Lincolnshire
1990	Juniper Hall, Surrey
1992	Exeter, Devon
1993	Ambleside, Cumbria
1994	Harderwijk, Holland
1995	Dunton Green, Kent
1996	Darlington, Durham
1997	Newbury, Berkshire
1998	Coleraine, Northern Ireland
1999	Colchester, Essex
2000	Bristol, Avon
2001	Hethersett, Norfolk
2002	Radejov, Czech Republic
2003	Cardigan, South Wales
2004	Sherwood, Notts
2005	Dovedale, Staffordshire
2006	Chorley, Lancashire
2007	Pitlochry, Scotland
2008	Steventon, Oxfordshire
2009	Newcastle, Tyne and Wear
2010	York, Yorkshire
2011	Poole, Dorset

National (also known as Biennial)

National conferences to which staff, Trustees and members of all the Trusts were invited were held (apart from a gap in the 1980s) between 1960 and 2000. In the new millennium, national conferences were organised from time to time on key themes, such as Living Landscapes and Living Seas.

1960	Skegness
1962	Norwich
1964	York
1966	Bournemouth
1968	Canterbury
1970	Oxford
1972	Bangor
1974	Brighton
1976	Newcastle
1978	Bromsgrove
1980	Nottingham
1990	Nottingham
1994	Grantham
1996	York
1998	Lincoln
2000	Grantham
2009	Sherwood Forest
2010	Cirencester
2011	Birmingham

Delegates at one of the movement's national conferences, c1990

CONSERVATION CONTINGENCY FUND
Originally called the Partnership
Fighting Fund, the Conservation
Contingency Fund was established in
April 2000 to fund nationally-
important and urgent Trust projects.

The principle of establishing a
fighting fund was agreed in June
1993, but over the next few years
money proved elusive. In 1999, the
DEVON TRUST offered to contribute
£40,000, if 20 or more Trusts also
agreed to contribute by foregoing a
small proportion of their future
unrestricted legacy income. In the
event, 26 Trusts agreed and by 2008
37 Trusts had joined the fund.

Other than in exceptional
circumstances, it was agreed that
the fund was only available to the
'subscribing' Trusts and that
successful applications would as
"a minimum either concern an issue
which will have major national
ramifications for wildlife or
concern a site which is of national
significance in itself or a species
whose national conservation status
is at risk".[38]

The first distribution from the
fund was to the GWENT TRUST for
£2,500. The grant went towards a
judicial review of a granted planning
consent for an extension to a golf
course that threatened the River Usk,
Special Area of Conservation.

The fund was re-invigorated
in 2005. In November 2006, the
Devon Trust received £15,000
towards the costs of preparing a legal
case to fight (successfully as it turned

The Fund helped secure protection of Lyme
Bay Reefs from scallop dredging

out) the Government's decision not to
bring in a Ministerial Stop Order for
scallop dredging in Lyme Bay. Other
grants and loans were made to the
BIRMINGHAM AND BLACK COUNTRY,
NOTTINGHAMSHIRE, HAMPSHIRE
AND ISLE OF WIGHT, LONDON,
SCOTTISH and WILTSHIRE TRUSTS.
During this time the fund paid out
more than £104,000. It was finally
wound up in March 2008 when its
remaining funds and remit were
absorbed into a new STRATEGIC
DEVELOPMENT FUND.

CONSERVATION CORPS, NATIONAL

National Conservation Corps at Woodwalton
Fen, 1961

The National Conservation Corps
was established in spring 1959 by the
Council for Nature with a grant of
£3,000 from the Carnegie UK Trust
and, a year later, funding from the
Ministry of Education. The idea
was to "enable young people to
spend 'hard work' holidays doing
important maintenance work at
nature reserves, and at the same
time be shown why the work is
important".[39] A promotional leaflet
at the time observed "just now, when
angry young men get too much
publicity, the Council for Nature has
put the energetic men, and women,
into the picture".[40] In its first two
years, the Corps worked on 26
different sites as far apart as Box Hill
in Surrey and Benn Eighe in Wester
Ross, Scotland. Many sites were
owned or managed by the Society or
by Trusts, from WOODWALTON FEN in
Huntingdonshire and Gibraltar Point
in Lincolnshire to MEATHOP MOSS in
Cumbria and Skomer Island in South

Wales. Over 11 years, the Council
for Nature "nursed and watched the
Conservation Corps expand. . . from
a mere three hundred volunteers,
under the leadership of Brigadier
Armstrong, to nearly one thousand
eight hundred volunteers".[41] In 1970,
the Conservation Corps became an
independent body, the British Trust
for Conservation Volunteers, keen
to expand its operation by regionalisation, by stimulating the growth
of affiliated, local Corps – many
run by Trusts – and by providing
guidance and training.

CONSERVATION LIAISON COMMITTEE
In 1968, the Society opened up
membership of its Conservation
Committee to other conservation
bodies and created a Conservation
Liaison Committee (CLC) to
act as the liaison body on
practical conservation, research
and management between the
Conservancy and the non-
government conservation
community. For much of the next
15 years, the CLC was the
leading national body in this
field, promoting discussion and
cooperation between most of the
voluntary and statutory bodies active
at the time. In 1979, when the
Council for Nature was wound up,

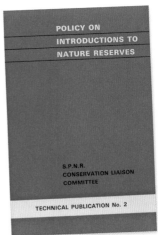

POLICY ON
INTRODUCTIONS TO
NATURE RESERVES

S.P.N.R.
CONSERVATION LIAISON
COMMITTEE

TECHNICAL PUBLICATION No. 2

The Society's policy publication on introducing
species to nature reserves

CLC support a new national advisory committee on reptiles and amphibians

the scientific and technical aspects of the Council for Nature's work were transferred to the Society, including its role as advisor to the ALL-PARTY PARLIAMENTARY CONSERVATION COMMITTEE.

In addition to the Society, membership of CLC included the RSPB, The National Trust, Botanical Society of the British Isles, Fauna Preservation Society, Joint Committee for the Conservation of British Insects, British Trust for Ornithology, The National Trust for Scotland, British Ecological Society, British Trust for Conservation Volunteers, Field Studies Council, Geological Society and Wildfowl Trust, with observers from the Council for Environmental Conservation, Countryside Commission, the Institute for Terrestrial Ecology, Ministry of Agriculture, Fisheries and Food, Ministry of Defence, the Conservancy and WWF.

However, by the early 1980s, the Society was focusing on its own campaigning work and WILDLIFE LINK had proved its effectiveness as the coordinator of the voluntary wildlife sector. The Society was also going through a financially difficult time. At first, in 1982, it was decided that the CLC should meet annually. But, by January 1983, it was agreed the Committee "should be terminated"[42] as it was "currently outside the scope of our resources".[43] The Society had established a Conservation and Scientific Policy Committee in 1978 and this now took on over-seeing all aspects of the Society's conservation work.

CONSERVATION OFFICERS' BULLETIN

The first Conservation Officers' Bulletin (COB) was produced in June 1974 as an outcome of the first Conservation Officers' Conference held at Horncastle College in Lincolnshire (CONFERENCES) in 1973. It was edited by Ray Collier, Conservation Officer of the LINCOLNSHIRE TRUST.

The aim of COB was to "produce a medium whereby an exchange of ideas and dissemination of information can take place among Conservation Officers in County Trusts".[44] The contributions in the first bulletin included a 'Management Plan Proforma and Site Investigation Form' from Ray Collier, 'Event Recording' from Jean Buchanan (BERKSHIRE, BUCKINGHAMSHIRE AND OXFORDSHIRE), 'Site Grading' from Stuart Crooks (CHESHIRE), 'The Management Register' from Pat Brassley (DERBYSHIRE) and 'Centralisation of Tool Purchasing and Other Services' from Peter Shirley (HERTFORDSHIRE AND MIDDLESEX). The bulletin was not produced again until January 1976. This second COB contained a report of the third Conservation Officers' Conference held at Dartington Hall in Devon in

1975, eight articles and more than a dozen appendices.

In the coming years the bulletin continued to carry topical articles on practical conservation and policy matters, as well as reports of all the annual Conservation Officers' Conferences held up to 1987. Because of this, it provides a valuable archive of the changing approaches to nature conservation over an important 15-year period of the movement. In 1985, Pat Brassley (DERBYSHIRE) looked back at the changing role of a Conservation Officer and, in passing, of COB. "There has been a considerable shift in emphasis from the original COB which was largely reserve orientated . . . to COB today, dealing with major issues where policy needs to be established or changed. Certainly, the reserve management of the early seventies has had to take a back seat and make way to the tasks of influencing local and national Government and other organisations".[45]

The first Bulletin listed 11 Conservation or Field Officers and the penultimate Bulletin 45. There were 16 Conservation Officers' Bulletins produced, more or less annually. The last issue was in June 1988

CONSERVATION OF WILD CREATURES AND WILD PLANTS ACT 1975

In January 1974, the Society, together with the Botanical Society of the British Isles (BSBI) and the Council for Nature, sponsored a Wild Plants Protection Bill which finally received Royal Assent as The Conservation of Wild Creatures and Wild Plants Act on 1st August 1975.

Fifty years earlier, the Society's view had been that, in addition to the promotion of nature reserves, much could be done to protect the British flora through education, publicity and protective local authority bye-laws, without recourse to national legislation. Indeed, for 20 years or so after 1925 it enthusiastically promoted this cause. However, during the Second World War there was, understandably, little progress. The Wild Plant Protection Board, (WILDFLOWERS – BYE-LAW PROTECTION), formed in 1931, did draft the first Wild Plant Bill but it failed to get Parliament's support and, when the Board's Chairman (and the Society's Secretary), HERBERT SMITH died in 1953, the Board was wound up. It was to be another ten years before the BSBI at its 1963 annual conference on *The Conservation of British Flora* passed a resolution recommending the formation of a Wild Plant Working Party. This was set up with two representatives from each of three organisations – the BSBI, the Council for Nature and the Society.

At first, progress was swift. Within a year, the Working Party produced an interim report which found that all but eight English and Welsh counties had bye-laws protecting their wild plants. However, only six had records of prosecutions. The Working Party

recommended national legislation and the plan was to prepare a draft bill. However, after this initial surge of activity, the Working Party struggled to make progress. Dr Max Walters, the Working Party's Chairman, replying to a letter from an impatient Hector Wilks, one of the Society's representatives, insisted the Working Party "has not died, but the burden of continuing it at present has been too much".[46] Unilaterally, and without Wilks' knowledge, the other members had decided that the only practical way forward was to support the COUNTRYSIDE IN 1970 CONFERENCE's Working Group on legislation. The following year, this group endorsed the Working Party's recommendations. It was Wilks who, in September 1966, wrote to NORMAN RILEY, the Society's HONORARY SECRETARY, to say the Working Party "have completed the first part of our task to study the legal aspects of plant protection and have produced a bill in draft form".[47] In November 1967, Peter Mills MP, who had drawn 24th place in the ballot for Private Members' Bills in the Westminster Parliament, agreed to promote the bill. *The Daily*

Telegraph proclaimed "MP seeks ban on sale of primroses".[48] But, in January 1968, with such a lowly position in the ballot the bill failed to get a Second Reading debate and so stood no chance of succeeding.

There was another lull in activity but, in the early 1970s, the Wild Plant Working Party was revitalised with the active involvement of the Council for Nature's secretariat. In 1973, Lord Beaumont of Whitley agreed to introduce a Wild Plant Protection Bill in the House of Lords, and in January 1974 managed to secure a Second Reading. The bill, if passed, would make it illegal for anyone, other than an authorised person, to uproot any wild plant or for anyone to pick or uproot any endangered plants listed on a schedule.

The Government supported the bill in principle but had many concerns, including issues over the drafting of the bill. A meeting was arranged for 8th February 1974. However, a general election was called and Parliament was dissolved – on 8th February! This meant that the meeting – officially – had to be cancelled. Unofficially, however, it

Campaigning for legal protection for endangered wild plants in the build-up to the 1975 Act

New 1975 legislation protected endangered species such as the natterjack toad

followed were to be among the first between non-Government organisations and civil servants to help put through wildlife legislation. The Minister with responsibility for the bill in the House of Lords was later to become a Vice President of the Society, Lord Melchett. However, this was a hung Parliament and a further general election followed later in the year. This meant the bill had to be re-introduced by Lord Beaumont on 21st November 1974. Many of the problems had been ironed out and once again it passed its Second Reading.

A sympathetic MP, Peter Hardy, had just won first place in the ballot for Private Members' Bills, but another wildlife bill – Lord 'Jock' Cranbrook's Wild Creatures Protection Bill – was also being promoted in the House of Lords. It was clearly going to be sensible for the two bills to be consolidated into one and Hardy agreed to introduce the Conservation of Wild Creatures

and Wild Plants Bill into the House of Commons. Lord Cranbrook, supported by Lord Beaumont, agreed to introduce the new bill into the House of Lords.

On 24th January 1975 the consolidated bill was due to be read a second time; for the part dealing with plants, it was the third Second Reading in the space of a year! Business from the previous day was still underway; if the House continued sitting until after 10.30 am the current day's business would be lost and with it the bill. The House adjourned at 10.28 am and at 11.05 am Hardy rose to speak! From then on the bill's passage was fairly smooth, and on 11th July 1975 the bill came back to the Commons from the House of Lords for consideration of the amendments agreed in that place and finally, on 1st August 1975, The Conservation of Wild Creatures and Wild Plants Bill received the Royal Assent.

It is significant that in his speech at the Second Reading in January 1974, Lord Beaumont relied heavily on decline statistics to justify improved legal protection for wild plants. "Thus, about 7 per cent of the native British flora, of about 1,500 species, may be in danger of extinction, and further species are declining so rapidly that they may shortly be in the same dangerous position".[49] However, widespread picking and uprooting by the general public, so common before the war, was already a thing of the past. Welcome as the Act was as a deterrent and for individual incidents of wilful damage, the overwhelming threat remained the destruction from development and intensive agriculture of the places where the wild plants lived.

Six years later, the provisions of the Conservation of Wild Creatures and Wild Plants Act 1975 were absorbed into the Wildlife and Countryside Act 1981. In 1977, the Society had published a much-needed British RED DATA BOOK on vascular plants and, during the passage of the Wildlife and Countryside Act 1981 through Parliament, it was accepted "as a definitive guide to the endangered and vulnerable plant species"[50] that were being considered for inclusion in a revised plant schedule. Forty-two species were eventually added and appeared in Schedule 8 of the Wildlife and Countryside Act 1981.

Sadly, despite the new laws, many more communities of wild plants were to be lost before the continuing threats to wildflowers began to be addressed by initiatives, such as the Society's successful WILDFLOWER WEEKS and by campaigns for changes in land-use policy more generally.

CORDY, TIM

Tim Cordy, a geographer and planner by training, was the Society's first Chief Executive from 1987 until 1994.

Tim Cordy

He joined the Society after working in local government, first in Leicester and then in Bolton, rising to become Assistant Chief Executive of the Metropolitan Borough Council. At Leicester, he was seconded for a year to Strasbourg where he was involved in an environmental improvement programme for the city. At Bolton, he was responsible for approximately 400 staff and for the strategic planning of a large unitary local authority. In addition, he managed two county-wide activities: liaison with the European Economic Community and management of a grants scheme for local non-government organisations in Greater Manchester.

Unlike his predecessors, Cordy lacked experience of the Trust movement and was not a naturalist. He recalls the desperation with which one member of his interview panel asked, "But do you even have a bird-bath?" But his particular appeal for the Society, at a time when the movement continued to undergo rapid change, was his background in management and strategic planning and his experience as a negotiator.

Cordy's task was first to put the Society's administrative house in order and then to take its relationship

with the rest of the Partnership down a path of further 'reconstruction'. He was partially successful and undoubtedly helped widen the cultural base of the movement. He was able to tap new sources of money and enhance the standing of the organisation, including developing its public profile. But, having achieved some reform, particularly to the Society's management and structure, the mood was for the movement to be less introspective, and with the Society facing a financial crisis, Cordy found himself losing the confidence of the Trusts. In November 1994, he tendered his resignation.

After leaving the Society, Cordy spent two years as Director of the Town and Country Planning Association before becoming a founder Director of a training company. He went on to become Director of a sustainability consultancy – Global to Local Ltd – advising clients on opportunities to promote sustainable development using funding from the European Union.

THE COUNTRYSIDE IN 1970 CONFERENCES

During his visit to the Council for Nature's first NATIONAL NATURE WEEK exhibition in May 1963, HRH The Duke of Edinburgh proposed a two-day study conference under the title of THE COUNTRYSIDE IN 1970. He did this conscious that there was a lack of contact between the many different bodies and interests involved and a lack of any reliable and accepted common picture of the problems, trends and solutions for the countryside. The initiative was seized upon by the Conservancy. By involving the voluntary conservation movement through the Council for Nature, and industry through the Royal Society of Arts, as its co-sponsors, the Conservancy – as a Government body – was able to promote more radical ideas than it could have done on its own.

The first conference was held, after very hurried preparation, at the Fishmongers' Hall in London over two days in November 1963. This was followed by a second conference held at the Royal Society of Arts (first two days) and Fishmongers' Hall (final day) in London in November 1965. A third and final conference was held at the City of London's ancient Guildhall in London in October 1970.

These three events, with the large volume of preparatory work generated by the accompanying study groups, began to provide some much needed structure to conservation thinking. In 1964, this was reflected in a masterful paper by MAX NICHOLSON, *Advances in British Nature Conservation* which was submitted to the Trusts' third National Conference (CONFERENCES) in York. It tracked changes in the "concepts, practice and scale of conservation of natural areas"[51] and chronicled developments county by county. Nicholson highlighted the "replacement of narrow concepts of protection of animals and plants through laws and sentiment, and of natural history and love of nature as merely hobby interests, by a recognition of man's care for his natural environment as an essential concern of government and of civilised society generally".[52] He believed this was "most concretely demonstrated by the composition and success of HRH The Duke of Edinburgh's Study Conference on The Countryside in 1970, by the Government's decision to create a Natural Environment Research Council and by the phenomenal influence and impact of the late Rachel Carson's *Silent Spring*".[53] Another important change was the "recognition of the need for much increased understanding of the character, scale and causes of human impacts on nature, both through studies and analysis, and through improved communication between different interests concerned".[54]

More than 350 organisations were represented at the final conference. It was the culmination of seven years of work. The Proceedings reflect on these years. "The outstanding and probably most important change since 1963 is the widespread awareness that the environment is significant, not only for the quality of our lives but for our very survival. . . in Britain this awareness already permeates important sectors of society and is still increasing. The need now is to point the way to more positive action".[55]

COWARD MEMORIAL NATURE RESERVES

Two of the Society's earliest reserves – Cotterill Clough and Marbury Reed Bed in Cheshire – were purchased in 1934 by public subscription as a memorial to local naturalist and writer, Thomas Arthur Coward (see overleaf). The reserves were handed over to the Society at an open-air event at Cotterill Clough in July the following year, when a memorial boulder with inscribed plaque was unveiled by Lord Crawford, President of the CPRE. The event was chaired by Lord Stamford who also became the first Chairman of the Local Management Committee. The following year, an additional strip of land along the mere's edge was added to the reserve and a small islet was rented for 'one shilling a year' from the Marbury Hall Country Club. In total the reserves consisted of 13.5 acres at Cotterill Clough and six acres at Marbury Mere. More than £900 was raised from friends and admirers of Thomas Coward to enable this purchase; £300 of this amount was invested to create an endowment fund.

Cotterill Clough was described as a steep wooded valley and small stream with rare and interesting plants. It had been a famous haunt of the 'old' Manchester botanists and was renowned for its woodland birds, including many of the summer warblers. Marbury Reed Bed was described as "a small covert. . . a considerable piece of water. . . a dense reed-bed many yards wide, then a strip of sedges and marsh plants, and behind that a wood of alder and birch, typical of such a locality".[56] The description goes on to mention the presence of otters, all three British woodpeckers, water rail and visitors, such as bittern and, on one occasion, a night heron! The Country Club that occupied Marbury Hall owned the water of the mere.

The old parish of Great Budworth, of which Marbury Mere was part, is the subject of *A Country Parish* by Arnold W Boyd in The New Naturalist series of books.

Cotterill Clough and Marbury Reed Bed were managed with the help of local voluntary wardens but, by 1941, with the Second World War well underway, the majority of the wardens at Cotterill Clough had "volunteered and were passed for service with His Majesty's Forces".[57] The Society's HANDBOOK records that in 1942 half a dozen new wardens were recruited "who found spare time occupation in the open a welcome tonic after the strain of intensive production of armaments". At Cotterill Clough in 1943 at a time "when metals were sought for salvage",[58] an attempt was made to force the bronze plate from the memorial stone at Cotterill Clough. It was removed and safely stored away. Marbury Mere and "the east end of the wood on the south bank of the mere"[59] were also requisitioned by The Admiralty as a proposed bombing range using practice smoke bombs.

Things did not quieten down after the war. A threat from development associated with Manchester's Ringway airport seemed to have receded, but in 1948 a proposal to develop a brick works adjacent to Cotterill Clough, also threatened the

Early photograph of Marbury Mere

reserve. It was not until 1950 that it was decided to allow the development but at a safe distance from the reserve. Imperial Chemical Industries then purchased Marbury Hall and planned to use the mere as an emergency water supply. However, by 1951 the company was showing an active interest in the management of the mere. It appointed a watcher from amongst its staff, who lived in a rebuilt army hut overlooking the reserve, and two years later another member of its staff was appointed to the local Committee. In January 1957, Marbury Reed Bed suffered a potential 'major disaster' when a cross-country oil pipeline developed a leak and tons of oil poured down the Kid Brook into the mere. All reeds growing in the water were cut and burnt and an oil-soaked bank cut away and buried. The important colony of reed warblers was badly affected. Two years later, however, it was reported that the reserve had "recovered remarkably well".[60]

The Coward Memorial Reserves were leased to the CHESHIRE TRUST in 1963 and the freehold transferred to that Trust in 1998.

THOMAS ALFRED COWARD

Coward (1867–1933) was a Cheshire-born naturalist, a "nature lover within the ken of the present generation".[61] His interest in natural history was probably fostered by his father – a botanist and geologist and for many years Honorary Curator of the Manchester Museum. This interest drew him, to among other places, the Bollin Valley and especially Cotterill Clough. He wrote numerous books on birds, other wildlife and "the beauty and traditions of Cheshire".[62] In these writings, and in his lectures, he advocated the creation of nature reserves and bird sanctuaries.

The construction of Cow Green reservoir destroyed nationally-important wildlife habitats

COW GREEN

The fight to halt the construction of a reservoir on an internationally-important wildlife area at Cow Green in Upper Teesdale was one of the earliest *causes célèbres* for the voluntary nature conservation movement, and for the Trusts.

In December 1964, the statutory water undertaker for Teeside announced its intention to promote a Private Bill in Parliament to enable the reservoir's construction. The plan was to build a reservoir large enough to provide the water needed for expansion of the Imperial Chemical Industries' (ICI) plants on Teesside – on which, ICI argued, so much employment and regional prosperity depended. However, the area, including an SSSI and two National Nature Reserves, was of immense scientific importance. It supported "many important types of alpine and sub-alpine communities, including a well known arctic-alpine flora and fauna not developed anywhere else in Great Britain".[63]

The NORTHUMBERLAND AND DURHAM TRUST, formed in 1962, reacted quickly to the announcement and a letter expressing their opposition to any reservoir was published in the *Northern Echo* and *The Guardian* newspapers. In

January, the Conservancy announced that it had agreed to test borings to check whether a reservoir was technically possible, but it reserved the right to oppose the proposal on scientific grounds. This was an early, high profile test of 15-year-old conservation legislation. Would it protect a scheduled area that had been identified as a special site by the Huxley Report and earlier by both ROTHSCHILD and the Society?

The following year, an appeal was launched by the Botanical Society of the British Isles (BSBI) to fight the proposed legislation, with the resulting 'Defence Fund' designed to defray the expected costs of both the BSBI and the Trust.

The eventual Private Bill of the Tees Valley and Cleveland Water Board was exceptionally debated in both Houses of Parliament, following close scrutiny of the wildlife issue before the respective House committees. Despite strong opposition, however, the reservoir was finally given the go-ahead by Parliament in 1967.

Conservationists could not escape the painful lessons. They had lost the battle and botanical research had suffered a serious blow. Win or lose, opposing a bill of this nature was an expensive business – the Appeal had eventually had to raise £23,000. In addition, "Cow Green has shown in an uncomfortably clear light that the forces of expansion are considered to be justified in themselves; that they are unaccustomed (and not much encouraged by authority) to bend at all from a narrowly economic policy and that other values are given short shrift".[64] There was concern that the special knowledge and advice of Conservancy witnesses had been shackled. But the most bitter pill to swallow was that the conservationists' arguments, whatever their merits, had not been "readily understood by laymen".[65] The case raised serious questions. How was the relative scientific importance of a particular site to be judged? How was the value of a unique natural area to be balanced against a public need, for example, for water supplies? New ways had to be found to explain the arguments for conservation. In addition to identifying the most important sites ahead of threats, their importance needed to be explained more clearly to increase public awareness and so increase the support for the nature conservation cause in the future. Following Cow Green, the Conservancy recognised the need for considerably more rigorous preparation of evidence in challenging such schemes through legal counsel, whether within Parliament or at Public Inquiry. Nevertheless, after Cow Green, it is also true to say that never again did a statutory undertaker treat the wildlife dimension so lightly in its promotion of such a major utility bill and, although the Water Board had won, the delay in construction had been extremely costly. Ironically, by the time the bill was enacted, ICI's plans for Teesside had radically changed and the water was no longer required in the short to medium term.

CRANE, ROBIN

Robin Crane was a member of the Society's Executive Committee from 1992 (and briefly its Chairman from 1997 until it was disbanded in 1998); CHAIRMAN of the Society's Council between 1994 and 1999 and of the Wildlife Trusts Forum between 1996 and 1998.

Originally trained as a maltster, he turned to film-making as a profession, first with the BBC Natural History Unit and then as an independent producer. He produced the LINCOLNSHIRE TRUST's film *Nature in Trust*, premiered in 1967 (WILDLIFE FILMS).

The start of Crane's time as the Society's Chairman of Council came immediately after the resignation of the Society's Chief Executive, TIM CORDY, in October 1994. It also coincided with a serious financial situation and with the need for further reform. Pursuing policies proposed in *Reaching our Full Potential* – a paper he presented to the Society's national conference in Grantham in 1994 and revised for the equivalent conference in Lincoln in 1996 – Crane presided over a successful period that saw the appointment of a new Director

General, SIMON LYSTER. It also saw improvements to the Society's funding arrangements for Trusts and to the Partnership's national structure, including the introduction of regional representation on a new Partnership Board, Forum and on the Society's Council. The Society's Royal Charter was also revised. Unfortunately, after this period of groundbreaking reform, Crane had to spend the end of his time in office dealing with the fall-out from the suspension and subsequent resignation of the Society's Managing Director.

Crane is a member of the LINCOLNSHIRE TRUST and was its Honorary Assistant Secretary between 1965 and 1967. In 1967, when he moved to the south coast of England, he joined his local SUSSEX TRUST and became its Chairman between 1987 and 1994. More recently he was Chairman of the South Downs Campaign that he established in 1990 to secure a better future for the area. In November 2009, after a long and hard-fought campaign, the area was declared a National Park, the third largest in England.

Robin Crane (centre) with South Downs National Park campaigners

D

DANCER'S END NATURE RESERVE

The gift to the Society by Lord Victor Rothschild (MIRIAM ROTHSCHILD'S brother) of 76 acres of woodland at Dancer's End, comprised Bittams Wood, Round Spring Wood and the intervening land. "At the instance of the Hon. Miriam Rothschild this attractive woodland area was offered to the Society in 1939 by Lord Rothschild, subject to the retention of the right to cut ripe timber. The offer was accepted and the property was conveyed to the Society as from 1st November 1941. The ripe timber had by then been felled and removed. In the following year, 1942, Lord Rothschild forwent the timber rights. The area had been originally acquired by the HON. CHARLES ROTHSCHILD to serve as a nature reserve".[66] The site was described as being interesting for its plants, including the Chiltern gentian, fly orchid and columbine.

In November 1943, the Buckinghamshire War Agricultural Committee (WAC) was given clearance to kill the rabbits in Bittams Wood but, despite the repeated efforts of the County Pest Officer, rabbits were still active after the war and there was evidence of occasional poaching. In 1945, the WAC also obtained permission to dig a trench through Round Spring Wood for a water pipeline. The reserve was popular with local people who gathered "willow-catkins, violets, primroses, bluebells, strawberries, raspberries, blackberries, and hazel-nuts. The picking of the common wild flowers is overdone by some

parties of visitors, but apart from this and the occasional digging up of roots little harm has been done".[67]

The condition of the reserve gradually improved following the extraction of timber during the war. In 1947, despite serious invasion by rosebay willowherb, it was reported that "more interesting plants are increasing and spreading",[68] including wood-vetch and Solomon's seal. In 1949, twayblade and white helleborine were reported as common, fly and greater butterfly orchid more erratic in their appearance, while bee orchid and bird's nest orchid had only been seen occasionally.

In 1954, the Tring museum provided two local wardens who were supplied with SPNR armlets (see end). The local Management Committee decided that the "over-development of ash and birch at the expense of the original beech"[69] was undesirable. After protracted negotiations with the Forestry Commission (FC), a 150-year lease was finally agreed and, in the winter of 1958, an important landmark in the history of the reserve was reached when both Bittams and Round Spring Wood were replanted by the FC with beech, interspersed with larch, Norway spruce and Douglas fir as a nursery crop. The reserve was notified an SSSI in 1956 as 'an area where many interesting and uncommon chalk-loving plants grow'.

In 1961, the BERKSHIRE, BUCKING-HAMSHIRE AND OXFORDSHIRE TRUST was invited to have a representative on the local Management Committee. In December the same year, Miriam

Rothschild, Richard Fitter, Susan Cowdy (see CHRISTOPHER CADBURY MEDAL CITATIONS), John Aldridge and Lady Barlow attended a meeting at which Miriam Rothschild took over from the botanist, James Edgar Dandy, as the Committee's Chairman.

By 1962, the disappearance of rabbits and lack of grazing animals was resulting in prolific scrub growth in areas of the reserve. First bullocks, then sheep and tethered goats and later black-faced Scottish sheep were introduced and the reserve was much improved. An "extremely useful team of volunteers led by Mrs Susan Cowdy"[70] was deployed to help with this experimental management, particularly of the chalk grassland areas, and with scrub clearance. The reserve was finally leased to the Berkshire, Buckingham-shire and Oxfordshire Trust in 1969 and the freehold transferred to the Trust in 1997.

ARMLETS

In November 1950, the Management Committee of the Society's Dancer's End nature reserve suggested that its wardens should be supplied with an armlet to identify their status. The Society responded by ordering 36 armlets made of black cloth measuring four inches by 12 inches with a buckle fitting from Toye & Co, Regalia House, Red Lion Square, London WC1. They cost six shillings plus tax in total or 40 pence in modern currency. Armlets were supplied to the wardens with certificates that "authorised them to take any action within the law that is deemed necessary to safeguard the reserve, its flora and fauna".[71]

Dancer's End – today, a Berks, Bucks and Oxon Wildlife Trust reserve

DEVONSHIRE, DUKE OF

The fifth PRESIDENT of the Society, Edward William Spencer Cavendish The Duke of Devonshire (1895–1950), held the office between 1947 and his sudden death in 1950.

The Duke was an active President, chairing Council and other Society meetings, despite a very busy life. Indeed, he chaired an Executive Committee meeting only 18 days before his death. He became Chairman of the British Coordinating Committee for Nature Conservation in 1949 – a Committee administered by the Society.

The Duke of Devonshire

A Member of Parliament for West Derbyshire between 1923 and 1938, the Duke was a Minister in Winston Churchill's war-time cabinet. Like a previous President of the Society, THE EARL OF ONSLOW, he was also President of the Fauna Preservation Society and the Zoological Society of London. Proposing the toast of the President at the Society's luncheon in 1949, PHYLLIS BARCLAY-SMITH – later to become the Society's joint HONORARY SECRETARY – spoke about her genuine gratitude for the Duke's contribution to natural history. "In these days of speed, it is both a solace and an encouragement to find one who has played such a leading part in the life of the nation, as the Duke has done, to place such a high value on two of the most worthwhile things in life: beauty and nature".[72]

DINNERS AND LUNCHEONS

The Society held two dinners (planned at the time to be annual occasions) just prior to the outbreak of the Second World War. The first was at the Park Lane Hotel on 11th November 1937 when the principal guest was the Marquis of Zetland, Secretary of State for India and Chairman of The National Trust. The second dinner, again at the Park Lane Hotel, took place on 14th November 1938 when the principal guest was the Earl of Feversham, Parliamentary Secretary to the Board of Agriculture and Deputy Minister of Fisheries. A third dinner was planned for 1939 at the Rembrandt Rooms in London, but had to be abandoned due to the outbreak of war.

After the war, in place of the dinners, the Society held five Official Luncheons between 1946 and 1950 linked to the annual meeting of its Council. The details are as follows:

First Luncheon at the Connaught Rooms on 14th June 1946 at a cost 12s 6d. Principal Speaker: Rt Hon Lewis Silkin MP, Minister of Town and Country Planning.

Second Luncheon at the Connaught Rooms on 6th June 1947. Principal Speaker: Rt Hon Viscount Jowitt, Lord High Chancellor.

Third Luncheon at the Prince Consort Room, Royal Albert Hall on 15th June 1948. Principal Speaker: Lord Chorley, Lord in Waiting to the King.

Fourth Luncheon at the Prince Consort Room, Royal Albert Hall on 22nd June 1949. Principal Speaker: Rt Hon Lewis Silkin MP, Minister of Town and Country Planning.

Fifth Luncheon at the Prince Consort Room, Royal Albert Hall on 27th June 1950. Principal Speaker: Prof GR de Beer, Director of the Natural History Museum in London.

In 1951, the Luncheon was replaced by a 'Conversazione' in the Lecture Hall of the Natural History Museum in London after the Council meeting in June. It was attended by 130 guests and there were exhibits from, among others, the Council for the Preservation of Rural England, the National Parks Commission, The National Trust, the Council for the Promotion of Field Studies and the Fauna Preservation Society. A second Conversazione was held after the Council meeting in the same venue the following year and they continued, albeit in a less grand form, into the 1970s.

First official luncheon, June 1946, with Lewis Silkin and Lord Macmillan (centre)

DIVER, CYRIL

Captain Cyril Diver (1892–1969) was the first Director General of the Nature Conservancy between 1948 and 1952 and the first President of the SURREY TRUST. He joined the Society in 1939, was elected a member of the Executive Committee in 1942 and from then onwards – until ill health prevented him from attending meetings – he took an active interest in the Society's affairs and the development of the Trust movement. He played an important role in securing the position of the early Trusts in the Society. For example, he was instrumental in the establishment of the Society's REGIONAL LIAISON COMMITTEE and was its first Chairman.

Diver served in the army in the First World War. Wounded and invalided in 1918, he became first Assistant Clerk in the House of Commons and then Clerk of Committees, a post which he only left in 1948 when he took up his position with the Conservancy. He was elected President of the British Ecological Society for 1940 and 1941. He played a leading role in the work of the Nature Reserves Investigation Committee, set up at the instigation of the Society, whose reports led to the formation of the Government's Wild Life Conservation Special Committee and the Conservancy. Indeed, Diver was a member of the Special Committee and was responsible for drafting much of its final report, published in 1947.

His interest in natural history was considered 'innate' by NORMAN RILEY. In the Society's obituary to Diver, Riley described how, as a small boy, Diver had collected *Sphagnum* mosses in Sutton Coldfield Park when his army father was stationed nearby. This "interest gave way to experimental breeding of snails in a London garden, and

subsequently to his exhaustive study of South Haven Peninsula, Studland, Dorset. It was here that the interlocking relationships of all living components of a circumscribed community highlighted the meaning of ecology. At the time of his death he was still deeply involved in assessing the results of these Studland surveys, but had ensured the safety of his accumulated material and data by leaving them to the Furzebrook Research Station of the Nature Conservancy".[73]

DOBBS, ROGER

Roger Dobbs became a Trustee of the Society in 2004 and was its HONORARY SECRETARY between 2005 and 2011. Dobbs graduated in food technology and spent almost 30 years as a Research and Development Manager with SmithKline Beecham where he managed a team of scientists and technologists. He was responsible for a succession of new and improved products from food and drink to toiletries and medicines. Dobbs has been involved in practical conservation for more than 20 years as a volunteer warden of a large woodland reserve, a Trustee of the BERKSHIRE, BUCKINGHAMSHIRE AND OXFORDSHIRE TRUST for more than 15 years and is currently the Trust's Vice Chairman.

During his time as Secretary, Dobbs established a good working relationship with the staff of the Charity Commission and the Privy Council, as the Society went about reforming its governance. His work on the Society's governance handbook and on changes to its governing documents was also greatly valued. Dobbs was part of a tight team of Honorary Officers (alongside ALLEN and HUGHES) that supported HILBORNE through the restructuring of the Society, and ensured that the Society set and maintained a clear direction through its strategic planning processes.

Seal caves at Hell Bay, Cornwall, February 1914 – £4 10s 0d towards the 'bricking up of the adit, leading to the large cave at North Cliffs, near Camborne, Cornwall. . . the principal breeding place of the seals on that coast.'

Swaddiwell Quarry, Helpstone, Northamptonshire, February 1914, agreed to rent for £7 10s 0d per annum. The tenancy was relinquished at 'midsummer 1924'.

Wicken Fen, Cambridgeshire, 1915 and 1916 agreed donations towards the purchase of additional land by The National Trust; March 1919 – £200 for the acquisition of 'about 28 acres'; March 1921 – £50 for the acquisition of 64 acres of land abutting Wicken Fen, known as 'the old peat diggings'; December 1925 – £275 towards the area known as 'lapwing'; in 1927 and December 1938 – £25 in each year towards an endowment fund.

Botanists at Wicken Fen, c1920s/1930s

Blakeney Point, Norfolk, 1920 – £25 towards a 'watcher' for three years at this National Trust property; 1924 agreed to continue to pay £25 towards the expenses of a 'watcher' for a further period of four years.

Lake Derwentwater in the Lake District, 1921 – £5 towards the purchase of an area of land adjacent to the lake as a memorial to the 'late Canon Rawnsley' – a scheme inaugurated by The National Trust.

Congres International pour la Protection de la Nature held in Paris, November 1923 – £5 for the publication of proceedings.

Farne Islands, Northumberland, 1923, £100 towards the purchase by The National Trust.

Hatfield Forest, Hertfordshire, 1924 – £10 towards the purchase of 'small trees' for the forest; 1925 – £10 towards the acquisition by The National Trust of a further 140 acres of the forest.

Terns and Fishing, Norwich, 1925 – £2 2s 0d to Dr Sidney Long towards an investigation into the damage done by terns to fishing.

Hawksmoor and Newhaze, Staffordshire, 1926 – £200 towards the acquisition of 207 acres of land for The National Trust; 1929 – £25 towards the purchase of Eastwell Farm as an addition to the Hawksmoor Nature Reserve; 1931 – £25 to complete the purchase of Eastwell Farm at Hawksmoor Nature Reserve; 1932 – £5 towards erecting a memorial to the late Mr JRB Masefield whose 'indefatigable and inspiring efforts' made possible the acquisition of this reserve.

Selsdon Wood, Surrey, 1926 – £10 towards the Selsdon Wood Preservation Fund opened by the Commons & Footpaths Preservation Society with the aim of purchasing 165 acres of this wood; 1927 – £10 towards the Preservation Fund;

1930 – £20 towards the Preservation Fund; 1932 – £20 towards the Preservation Fund; 1934 – £20 towards the Preservation Fund.

Marriott Memorial Oak, Kent, 1928 – £1 1s 0d towards the expenses connected with the planting of an oak in memory of the late Mr John Marriott, a well-known west Kent naturalist who died 11th October 1927.

Romney Marsh, Kent, 1930 – £25 towards the acquisition by the Royal Society for the Protection of Birds of about 180 acres of Romney Marsh as a bird sanctuary; 1931– £25 towards the acquisition by the RSPB of additional land to complete Romney Marsh Bird Sanctuary, Kent.

Leasness Abbey Woods, Kent, 1930 – £25 (agreed by the Executive in 1927) donated to the London County Council towards its acquisition.

Dungeness, Kent, 1932 – £50 towards the acquisition by the Royal Society for the Protection of Birds of part of Dungeness as a breeding place for the Kentish plover. In 1936 the RSPB were forced to abandon the area at Dungeness but acquired Dengemarsh, Kent in its place and in 1937, the Society donated £50 towards the acquisition of this site if the whole £2000 raised was raised and 'responsible botanists and entomologists have reasonable access'. Initially, the RSPB were unable to agree these conditions but subsequently relented and by November the £50 was transferred!

White Cattle, Chillingham Park, 1932 – £10 annually for seven years towards the fund for maintaining the herd.

Lynton and Lynmouth, Devon, 1932 – £25 to the Lynton and Lynmouth and District Preservation Scheme for their fund to acquire this 'famous beauty spot' with the intention of conveying it to The National Trust; 1934 – £15 to the Lynton and Lynmouth and District Preservation Scheme to 'complete the purchase of the Watersmeet Valley Property'. The site was finally conveyed to The National Trust in 1936.

Bollin Valley, Cheshire, 1933 – £10 towards a fund to create a Coward Memorial and to prevent further despoliation of this part of Cheshire.

Lakenheath Warren, Norfolk, 1933 – £20 (2 x £10) towards the acquisition by the NORFOLK TRUST of this heath. The Trust already held two of the 40 common rights held in the village.

Belfairs Great Wood, Hadleigh, Essex, 1937 – £100 towards the acquisition of this wood by the Southend-on-Sea Borough Council.

Marbury Mere, Cheshire, 1937 – £15 15s 0d towards fencing costs. This was paid out of a fund for the Coward Memorial Reserves.

Red Kite Protection, 1938 – £5 towards expenses connected with protecting kites and their nests in Wales; 1939 – £5 towards the Kite Preservation Fund.

Mickfield Meadows, Suffolk, 1938 – £10 towards a fund to purchase a fritillary meadow at Mickfield, 'if such a fund is instituted'. The amount was paid into such a fund later in 1938.

DRUCE, GEORGE CLARIDGE

George Claridge Druce (1850–1932), botanist and benefactor of the Society, was a founder member, joining the Society's Council and Executive Committee from the beginning. Druce worked until 1879 for Philadelphia Jeyes, the well known retail and manufacturing chemist based in Northamptonshire, before moving to Oxfordshire to set up his own successful business, from which he retired in 1905.

George Druce, pictured in 1931 collecting pondweed in Dorset – a year before his death

Druce had an interest in butterflies, but more particularly wildflowers, from an early age. "He could recognise 400 species of plants by the time he was 16 (though he did not know their names)".[75] They were interests that were further fuelled by expeditions to Wales and Scotland in 1868 and 1869, funded by his employer, Philadelphia Jeyes. Druce helped found the Pharmaceutical Association in 1871 and the Ashmolean Natural History Society of Oxford in 1880. He also founded the Northamptonshire Natural History Society in 1876; was elected to membership of the Linnean Society in 1879 and became the controversial Secretary of the

Botanical Exchange Club (BEC) in 1903. "The unrestrained character of Druce's collecting, a relic of an earlier era, often provoked the wrath of an increasingly conservation-minded British botanical community. It was therefore incongruous that he also played a leading role in the Society from its founding in 1912 drawing up at the request of his friend CHARLES ROTHSCHILD a pioneering register of plant sites most deserving protection".[76] He was a "most willing helper",[77] also visiting several sites to check out their suitability for Rothschild's list. In his obituary for Charles Rothschild in the *Journal of the Northamptonshire Natural History Society*, Druce described how his visit to the Marquis of Lansdowne's estate at Cloonee, on Kenmare Bay in Ireland, nearly ended in disaster when the horse and trap he was travelling in was only stopped from careering down a precipitous bank by furze bushes!

Despite being a controversial figure, he enjoyed "wide respect and affection. . . impressively demonstrated in the celebrations of his eightieth birthday".[78] He was a field botanist whose reputation was built, above all else, on a great quartet of floras for the counties of Berkshire, Buckinghamshire, Oxfordshire and Northamptonshire and his devotion to the development of the BEC, later to become the Botanical Society of the British Isles. When he died a relatively wealthy man in 1932, perhaps surprisingly, the BEC failed to benefit from his will. The residual estate – about £26,000 or £1.2 million in today's currency – was to be divided equally between Oxford University and the Society. In the latter's case, it was to be "used for the acquisition of land which has some interesting specimens of plants growing on it, in order that their safety shall be secured".[79]

E

EMPLOYMENT SCHEMES

By 1988, the Society and the Trusts were employing 2,300 people under the Government's Community Programme (CP), a scheme established by the Manpower Services Commission (MSC) in 1982. The MSC established the CP as a follow-on to a series of previous schemes started in 1974, including Job Creation, the Special Temporary Employment Programme (STEP), the Youth Opportunities Programme and the Community Enterprise Programme. Like the earlier schemes, the CP gave work experience and training to long-term unemployed people, while providing goods and services to the community.

After a slow take-up in the late 1970s, the Trusts were in the forefront of voluntary organisations using these schemes. In April 1986, after concern about the quality of some of the environmental projects, the Society became one of seven voluntary bodies at the heart of a further Government initiative – UK2000. The idea was to forge a partnership between Government, the private sector and the voluntary movement, and to increase the quantity and quality of environmental work both in urban and rural areas. The majority of Government's input came via the Community Programme budget; 5,000 places for long-term unemployed were earmarked for the initiative at a cost of some £25 million.

In 1985, the Society had given evidence to, and sat on the Advisory Panel of, a study commissioned by the Department of Environment from BTCV and the Dartington Trust. The study looked at the scale, nature and potential for growth of environmental work in England and Wales carried out by volunteers and under MSC schemes. Their report – *Work and the Environment* –

recommended that the Government should establish a National Environment Work Scheme to maximise volunteer effort in environmental projects and to improve their quality. A strong argument put forward by the Society and others was that "the best would only ensue from CP projects when they were coordinated with voluntary effort so that the initial work could be maintained thereafter and that, to achieve this, project supervisors must have longer contracts and the voluntary organisations must have permanent staff to provide high quality projects with high levels of education and training for participants".[80]

A few days before the launch of UK2000, the then Secretary of State, Kenneth Baker, called a few environmental organisations to his office, including the Society, to ask them to commit to running this new initiative. The Society agreed to join its Board (chaired by Richard Branson, who launched the initiative in July 1986) and, as a result, received an additional £60,000 to play its part in the new programme. Richard Woolnough, Conservation Officer at the SUFFOLK TRUST, who had been influential in coordinating the movement's input to the study and the resulting scheme, was employed as the Society's UK2000 Development Officer soon afterwards. His task, among other things, was to increase the number of unemployed people on the MSC's Community Programmes with the Trusts and the Society from 1,000 to 1,500 in the first year. Two of the five themes on which the extra employees were expected to work were directly relevant to the Trusts – 'making more of nature' and 'greening the cities'.

While UK2000 was concerned with all aspects of work in the environmental sector, including voluntary activity, it was given the

MSC employee charcoal burning

ability to reward CP projects shown to be of a high standard. By September 1988, 94 CP projects run by Trusts or Urban Wildlife Groups had been rewarded with a UK2000 'kite-mark', or seal of approval, which brought with it a variety of benefits, including help with sponsorship, publicity, training and access to extra sources of funds. In 1987–88, CP projects in the Trusts received £65,000 from the Society through UK2000.

However, in September 1988, the Government announced that it was ending the Community Programme and replacing it with a new Employment Training (ET) scheme. The CP scheme had had the community as its main emphasis, but the new scheme was going to concentrate far more on the needs of the individual with the priority on the skills and training received, rather than on the type of work completed. This change, together with the new organisational structures and financial systems involved, meant a reduction in the resources available for Trusts and the beginning of the end of this particular employment bonanza.

Similar schemes would follow as the country's economic health fluctuated. For example, Trusts benefited from the New Deal programme in the late 1990s and, in 2010–2011, the Trusts employed almost 500 people under the Future Jobs Fund.

ENVIRONMENT CITY

The Society was a driving force in the Environment City programme which grew out of an initial idea proposed by the Leicester Ecology Trust in 1988. Their idea was to promote Leicester as a centre for environmental excellence.

Building on this, the Society convened a working party consisting of the Society, Leicester Ecology Trust, Leicester City Council, Friends of the Earth and the Civic Trust, and a national environment city campaign was born. It was proposed that four cities in the UK should be selected to "demonstrate and promote realistic and practical solutions on a local scale to the challenge of sustainable development within the constraints of a working city".[81] Environment City received the support of the Department of the Environment's UK 2000 initiative and, with this, the Society was able to appoint an Environment City Coordinator and set up a National Selection Panel. Leicester was designated in June 1990 as the pilot lead city and Middlesbrough, Leeds and Peterborough followed over the next three years.

Several Environment City publications were produced to capture the lessons emerging from each of the cities. The main reports were: *Stepping Stones – the BT Environment City Review of Sustainability*, published in 1993; *Stepping Stones II*, published in

Publications capture lessons from the four Environment City projects

1995, which reviewed good practice across the four Environment Cities; *Painting by Numbers*, published in 1994 – a user's guide to some of the processes behind sustainable development; and *Trading in Futures*, also published in 1995, which explored the role of the private sector in sustainable development.

While some considered the Environment City programme outside the Society's mainstream activities – even a 'complete distraction' – its leadership of the programme brought the movement influence and profile, and gained it valuable experience of the broader environment and sustainable development agenda. For example, the Society had a seat on the national Local Agenda 21 Steering Group run by the Local Government Association, a position that complemented the work of Trusts that were continuing to develop their own relationships with local authorities.

Central funding for the Environment City programme always had a finite life. The aim was for the cities to be exemplars, and then for them to move on and to put into practice, independently, the lessons learnt.

The Mayor of Middlesbrough receives the Environment City Award

EUROPE AND THE SOCIETY

European policies have had a profound impact on the UK as a member of the European Union (EU). Although the EU's common policies on agriculture and fisheries have had some profoundly negative impacts on wildlife, its environmental Directives have driven much of the UK's own conservation legislation.

As far back as 1913, and again in 1923 and 1931, the Society attended conferences in Berne, and then Paris, to discuss ideas for an international organisation for the protection of nature. After the Second World War, it was represented at meetings that led to the formation of the International Union for the Protection of Nature. As a result, the Society became involved in nature conservation in Europe. For example, in 1937 and 1938 it attended the European section of the International Committee for Bird Preservation.

In 1970, the Council of Europe designated the year, European Conservation Year (ECY70). A national exhibition *What's in it for him?* was "conceived. . . by SPNR'S Wilf Dawson and the NORTHUMBERLAND AND DURHAM TRUST's, Tony Tynan, as a medium for publicising, in European Conservation Year, some of the problems, aims and achievements of the County Trusts".[82] Designed and built by Tynan and his staff at the Hancock Museum, Newcastle-upon-Tyne, it was first shown at the Hancock Museum and then at the Forestry Commission's Jubilee Exhibition in Edinburgh in 1969. It had its southern debut at the Trusts' sixth biennial conference in Oxford in April. Afterwards it went on tour to Lincoln, Leicester, the East of

England Show, Folkestone and Swansea, before finishing at the Society's first home, the Natural History Museum in London in October, to coincide with the third and final COUNTRYSIDE IN 1970 CONFERENCE.

The NORTH WALES TRUST published *Welsh Wildlife in Trust*, edited by 'Bill' Lacey, on behalf of all the Trusts in Wales, as a contribution to ECY70 and Trusts took advantage of the designation to promote many educational projects such as NATURE TRAILS, guided tours and lectures. The Society also played a leading role, on behalf of the Council for Nature, in administering an ECY70 Countryside Award Scheme which attracted more than 470 entries and made 100 awards, including more than 20 to Trusts' projects.

However, it was the 1980s, and more particularly the early to mid-1990s, that saw the Partnership's most active period in Europe. The national office was networking with other European non-government organisations (NGOs) and regularly lobbying the European Commission, both directly and through its membership of the European Environment Bureau (EEB). Several Trusts were securing regional and project-led funding, for example, from the European Community's Financial Instrument for the Environment (LIFE) and from the European Structural Funds. A few Trusts were also twinning with conservation organisations in Europe, for example in Holland, France and Eastern Europe. Indeed, by 1996, such was the commitment to Europe, that the annual review stated "The Wildlife Trusts believe... that a stronger presence in Europe should be part of their strategy for the next decade".[83]

The Society first attended an annual meeting of the EEB in 1979

The Oostvaardersplassen – visited by the Trust Directors in 1994

and the following year joined the EEB – one of a number of Brussels-based networks through which environment NGOs could channel their views to the European Commission. During the 1990s, national conferences were established for EEB member NGOs to take forward initiatives at national level in support of the EEB's Europe-wide agenda. The Society was an active EEB member, attending annual and one-off meetings with the European Commission, the EEB Annual General Meeting, Working Groups on Agriculture and Nature, as well as the UK national conferences. These national conferences were particularly effective in lobbying the Secretary of State for the Environment (and to a lesser extent MAFF Ministers) prior to meetings of the European Union's Environment (and Agriculture) Council. Tim Sands deputised for Fiona Reynolds (then Director of CPRE) as the UK member of the EEB Executive between 1991 and 1996 and assisted with the organisation of a seminar on the implementation of the European Community's Habitats Directive in Strasbourg in October 1995. As part of its PEATLANDS CAMPAIGN, the

Society represented the EEB at meetings of the Eco-label Forum and, as a result, influenced the European criteria for the eco-labelling of soil improvers.

In November 1994, the Society also became a member of Eurosite, an organisation established in 1989 to bring together Government and NGOs, as well as private bodies, to promote the practical management of wildlife habitats across Europe through a programme of twinning, workshops and special projects. Special arrangements were

negotiated to enable individual Trusts to join at a reduced rate. Both the Society and Trusts were involved in organising and attending annual meetings and specialist workshops during the 1990s – for example the Eurosite Annual General Meeting in the L'Ile de Ré, north of Bordeaux, in France in September 1997 and in Bratislava in September 1998.

The Trusts' Directors' Conference was held in Holland in 1994. A visit to the Oostvaardersplassen area, where a large 56km^2 nature reserve was being developed, and insight into Dutch thinking on the creation of large wild areas and wildlife corridors, left a deep impression on those who attended. Contacts were developed and subsequent, more informal visits all contributed to the movement's own thinking. A Vice President of the KENT TRUST, Hans Kampf, architect of the Dutch natural network system, spoke at the Living Landscape conference at Center Parcs, Nottinghamshire in 2009 and this gave added impetus to the movement's Living Landscape vision.

An ecoduct enabling wildlife to cross over a main road in the Netherlands

F

FAGAN, CHARLES EDWARD

Charles Edward Fagan (1855–1921), a founder member of the Society, was its first HONORARY TREASURER between 1912 and 1921.

Fagan was appointed to the British Museum in 1873, transferred to South Kensington in 1881 and became Assistant Secretary – the senior administrative position – at the Natural History Museum in London, taking over from the first holder of this post in 1889. He was succeeded in this post, after his death, by HERBERT SMITH, the Society's HONORARY SECRETARY between 1921 and 1953.

Fagan was a Fellow of the Royal Geographical Society (RGS) and it was through his role at the Natural History Museum in London and the RGS that he became involved with both the 1901 and 1910 British Antarctic Expeditions led by Robert Falcon Scott.

At its meeting on 16th March 1921, the Executive Committee placed on record "the great loss which the Society had sustained by the death of Mr CE Fagan, its Hon. Treasurer, whose directing influence had contributed in so large a measure to the welfare of the Society during the last few years".[84]

Charles Edward Fagan

FARMING AND WILDLIFE

Humans have been farming in the UK for thousands of years, producing crops and raising livestock. Yet, as traditional methods of farming declined and agricultural intensification predominated, particularly in the decades following World War II, there has been a rapid decline in the wildlife that is associated with our farmed environment.

The drive for expanding production in the 1970s and 1980s began to falter towards the end of the decade. In 1984, the then Minister of Agriculture, Peter Walker, had produced a Government White Paper, *Food From Our Own Resources*. Yet within two years, grain 'mountains' had reached unmanageable proportions. Almost overnight, the processes that had encouraged production were reversed and mechanisms were explored to reduce food stocks.

In the late 1970s, the Society continued to campaign actively to reduce the impact of farming on wildlife. In 1969, it had participated in the Silsoe Conference designed to bring farmers and conservationists together. Afterwards, the Society

became closely involved in the formation of the national FARMING AND WILDLIFE ADVISORY GROUP (FWAG) and the development of county FWAGs (see page 638). Behind the scenes, there were discussions on the Conservancy's *Nature Conservation and Agriculture* report, published in 1977. At the beginning of the 1980s, the Society commissioned a study under Lord Melchett's chairmanship to look in more detail at the place of nature conservation in land-use policies in Britain. The resulting report, *Towards 2000 – a place for wildlife in a land-use strategy* (see page 639), drew heavily on a sister report, also commissioned by the Society, written by the economist, Professor Carroll.

Towards 2000 demanded that greater priority should be given to nature conservation in land-use decisions through a package of controls and incentives. It predicted that the high value increasingly placed on protection of the countryside by society would soon be reflected in the way land-use decisions were made. Its suggestion of planning controls on farming meant that the report proved too radical for the movement to give its formal backing. Nevertheless, it set the tone for a more active engagement by the Trusts in the wider agricultural debate.

Increasingly, alarming statistics were appearing showing site losses, habitat deterioration and population declines of many species, with straight-line predictions towards extinctions for some. It was often the Trusts that were providing these worrying statistics. They gave the Society the ammunition, not only to expose the failure of the existing site protection legislation – the Wildlife and Countryside Act 1981 – but also to draw attention to the need for far-reaching reform of agricultural policy. The Society's stance avoided so-called 'farmer bashing'. It was persuasive, and even began exploring a more radical approach to the future of nature conservation. The Society's General Secretary, FRANK PERRING, declared, "the Government and the EEC should now realise that over-production is a problem which cannot be tackled piecemeal: ways must be found of reducing surpluses whilst protecting farm incomes and rural life which depends upon a healthy agriculture. In this context, the Ministry of Agriculture and the National Farmers Union might begin to look at conservation, in its broadest sense, not as a cosmetic extra which they cannot afford, but as a positive and profitable facet of land management".[85]

In 1986, the Society commissioned a further study, this time from Clive Potter of Wye College. The resulting report, *The Countryside Tomorrow – a strategy for nature*, suggested a campaign of 'environmental guidance aimed at influencing the structure of agricultural industry so that it was

better equipped to produce the countryside the public wants'. It went on, however, to propose a radical overhaul of the philosophy which guided nature conservation policy. "The creation of new habitats and the restoration of the countryside could become real possibilities in a strategy which is less exclusively based on site safeguard and more alive to realising conservation potential"[86] – an early recognition of today's Living Landscape agenda.

Many of the answers lay in Europe, but Europe was still failing to make a link between wildlife and methods of food production.

However, the arrival of a new EU Commissioner in 1988, Ray MacSharry from The Republic of Ireland, heralded a change of direction in agricultural support. In 1992, he was the first Commissioner to work out a meaningful compromise on reform of the Common Agricultural Policy (CAP). The 'MacSharry reforms', as they became known, marked the turning point between the 'old' CAP policy and the 'new'.

Whereas in the past farmers had been guaranteed a market for their produce at an appropriate level, they would in future be paid according to the crops grown on their farms. Different levels of payments were made on each hectare of crop grown. For example, linseed – a very unprofitable crop – received a very high support payment to encourage production. Crops like wheat and barley had a base-line payment. Part of the package was the introduction of 'set-aside', designed primarily to take land out of production to reduce stocks. The logic seemed very sensible at the time. Under the old regime, grain could sometimes be held in store for many years and it was cheaper to pay the farmer not to grow the crop.

The introduction of set-aside was not viewed as an opportunity to help wildlife; in fact initial observations were that it was a disaster for wildlife. The Society's view in 1992 was that "set-aside land, ploughed or treated each year, provides minimal benefits to the environment and can give the appearance of a derelict landscape".[87] In the first year of the scheme, farmers had to cut all their set-aside land during the breeding season. The carnage was almost unimaginable, with one national newspaper producing photographs of what they entitled 'the killing fields'.

The SUFFOLK TRUST was involved directly in a delegation that visited Brussels to lobby for changes in the rules. Working closely with the then Minister of Agriculture, John Gummer (MP for Suffolk Coastal), the Trust and the Farming and Wildlife Advisory Group put forward a proposal to transform the way set-aside was to be managed. Gummer was soon to return from his own Ministerial negotiations with an important derogation from Brussels to change the UK management of set-aside. In future, it could remain in the same place for any number of years. This allowed small fields to become permanent pasture. The Trust also wished to see the introduction of permanent field margins under the set-aside regime. Gummer bought into the 'green veins' concept, as it was called at the time, and secured agreement that would allow set-aside field margins with a minimum width of 20 metres. Later, this requirement was reduced, firstly to ten metres and then to six metres. With careful management, these margins could achieve as much, if not more, than field margins under

Countryside Stewardship – the Government scheme that supported conservation measures on farms.

The other major change was in the management of set-aside. Instead of cutting with a mower it was decided that the use of the herbicide 'Round-Up' was a more benign method for controlling and killing the green cover. It was decided that dying vegetation was far less damaging to the skylark, for example, than being cut down by a tractor mower! Immediately, fields began to turn an orange colour three weeks after the first permitted spraying date of 1st April. Wildlife Trusts around the country had regular calls from concerned members who viewed what was happening as an environmental disaster.

Meanwhile, after their first introduction in 1987, the Environmentally Sensitive Areas (ESA) and the Countryside Stewardship Scheme (CS) rapidly expanded as the Government refocused some financial resources. Farmers received payments based on a calculation of the income forgone as a result of the designation. For example, the change from wheat production to grassland was compensated at a level equivalent to the estimate of profit lost. Farmers embraced the new schemes with huge enthusiasm. A willingness to introduce sympathetic management options was encouraged by the realisation among farmers that they would be no worse off financially by doing so. The benefits to wildlife were enormous. A large range of options were made available to the farmer. These ranged from narrow field margins to conservation headlands and the planting of

crops to produce pollen and nectar. The Wildlife Trusts became fully engaged in the process. Most Trusts employed advisors to visit farms to help with the preparation of application forms; and Trust work was particularly targeted where a 'wildlife site' existed. The process continues with thousands of days of farmer advice being given by Trusts every year.

A large element of both the ESA and CS schemes was the introduction of capital payments to farmers. As a result, the first new hedges were planted for decades. The massive hedgerow removal programme of the 1960s and 1970s, when 160,000 miles of hedgerows were destroyed, began to be reversed. Other capital payments were introduced to cover such activities as hedge coppicing, hedge laying and the maintenance of dry stone walls. Farmers could receive help towards the costs of these activities and, where they did the work themselves, costs could be reduced still further. As overgrown hedges were cut back to regenerate, local Trusts received telephone calls and correspondence from a concerned public. The response of 'watch this space' was sometimes

greeted with suspicion, yet within just a few years, the hedges were thicker, bigger and far more beneficial for wildlife.

Towards the end of the 1990s, the World Trade Organisation (WTO) began to question the support systems of the European Union. During this period, The Wildlife Trusts stepped up its lobbying activities to focus on certain issues.

At the time of MacSharry's CAP reforms, as part of its Losing Ground campaigns, the Society trained the spotlight on the country's vanishing wildflower meadows to highlight its demand for the ESA principle to be extended to cover the whole country. This would mean that any manager of, for example, a wildflower meadow would be eligible to receive assistance towards its maintenance (MEADOWS CAMPAIGN). The agri-environment programme of the newly-reformed CAP had the potential to deliver environmental benefits, but the reality was that the majority of the CAP budget was destined to provide compensation for reduced crop prices, linked to short-term set-aside. A year later, in a briefing, *CAP Reform – the farmer, countryside and wildlife*, the Society was calling on

The yellowhammer has declined by more than 50% since the 1960s

the UK Government to ensure that a substantial part of the CAP budget should go towards the agri-environment programme, and that existing mechanisms for the support of environmentally-friendly farming should be extended to include all wildlife-rich agricultural habitats anywhere in the UK.

The WTO wished to see support mechanisms that did not distort the production of commodities in any way. The earlier linseed example highlights how production of a crop could be encouraged, even when it was not profitable to do so.

Support mechanisms, like these, were believed to distort trade around the world. Equally, the payment of a subsidy on every head of livestock owned by a farmer resulted in some areas, particularly the uplands, being too heavily grazed by farmers eager to put as many livestock onto the land as possible. Overgrazed systems could offer as little for biodiversity as an intensively managed cereal crop. The new EU Commissioner, Frans Fischler, set about reforming the system in a manner that would leave production unaffected. This shift from variable production payments to a standard payment was achieved by paying a flat rate across all commodities grown on the farm. The incentive to grow linseed was

An overgrazed hillside (right) contrasts with healthy heather moorland in the foreground

gone and, as a result, the crop virtually disappeared overnight. Set-aside continued at a reduced rate. Against all logic, the headage payments on livestock were retained. The Wildlife Trusts detailed the problems of overstocking in the uplands in a report, *Crisis in the Hills: Overgrazing in the Uplands*, but a reduction in overgrazing still proved elusive.

The Wildlife Trusts played a very full part in the changes to agriculture policy at this time and its views were highlighted in its report, *Farming For All Our Futures*, in 1998.

John Cousins, then the Society's Director of Agriculture Policy, was invited to sit on a small Committee chaired by the Minister of Agriculture, Jack Cunningham. After several months, the findings of the Committee were published. Ahead of its time, the Committee proposed important CAP reforms that would not be introduced for a further five years. The 'Agenda 2000' reforms divided the CAP

into two 'Pillars': production support and rural development. Several rural development measures were introduced – including diversification, setting up Producer Groups, and support for young farmers. Agri-environment schemes became compulsory for every Member State. Progress towards The Wildlife Trusts' objective for the dramatic greening of the CAP, and a major shift of funding towards agri-environment, had begun in earnest.

The tweaking and reforms of the subsidy systems did not affect certain aspects of farming practice, and did not prepare the country for the disasters that were to hit the farming industry. Firstly, the dangers of feeding bovine offal to cattle destined for the meat industry were not realised until too late. This ill-conceived practice had the potential to produce brain disease, not only in the animals that consumed the offal, but also in the humans that ate their meat. Bovine spongiform encephalopathy (BSE) dealt the livestock industry a blow of unprecedented severity and savaged its financial viability. Export bans on UK meat products

CAP Reform and *Farming For All Our Futures* reports

resulted in a flooded home marketplace. Prices tumbled and farmers had to look for other means of survival. Diversification became a lifeline with many farmers becoming part-time, seeking secure employment in local towns rather than the insecure existence on their farms. Just when equilibrium began to be restored, the next disaster hit the countryside. Foot and mouth disease (FMD) had not been seen on any scale since the 1960s. The innocuous looking illness affecting some pigs at an Essex abattoir was confirmed as FMD within 48 hours of the sick animals being noticed. The Government's response was too slow and certainly ineffective. The industry knew that vast numbers of livestock had been moved between farms, abattoirs and livestock markets in the days leading up to the outbreak. Cattle and pigs particularly were being transported large distances to reach the very few remaining abattoirs. The outbreak was again traced back to animal food; the culprit this time being produced for a pig unit in Yorkshire.

Restricted access – notice on a Surrey Trust reserve warning of foot and mouth disease

Swill – food waste from hospitals, schools and hotels – was being fed to pigs without being treated at a high enough temperature to kill bacteria.

The Wildlife Trusts' response to the outbreak was immediate. All nature reserves and visitor centres were shut to the public around the UK. When the decision was taken, the expectation was that access could be resumed after a matter of days. Many months later the Trusts' nature reserves would remain shut. The financial impact on a Trust like the ESSEX TRUST, with its extensive range of nature reserves and visitor centres, was dramatic. Revenue streams dried up overnight and staff had to be laid off. The Wildlife Trusts ran a strong campaign, alongside organisations such as the Soil Association, for the introduction of an FMD vaccine for all UK livestock. This option was rejected on the grounds that exports of UK meat would not be permitted in the future because all vaccinated animals would in effect carry the disease. The decision was made to test livestock and to destroy all herds and flocks where FMD was discovered. Funeral pyres blackened the skies as the army helped wage a war against the disease. Once commenced, the killing programme could not be stopped. Yet no-one could determine how extensive the disease had been. Healthy livestock were destroyed in an attempt to create buffer zones to stop the disease spreading further. The countryside was effectively shut, with all public footpaths closed and all meetings of farmers cancelled. At last, the number of new cases of FMD began to diminish. The daily news reports moved the story from top billing to 'matter of fact' reporting of the number of cases.

Even closer to home for The Wildlife Trusts, had been the ongoing saga of bovine tuberculosis

(TB) in cattle and in badgers. This is looked at in more detail in BADGERS AND BOVINE TB.

The year 2005 heralded the next major change in the CAP. The flat rate payment for cropped areas would be replaced by a single payment made for all land on a farm, excluding woodland. Production support became a direct payment to those who owned and managed land. Headage payments were swept away in favour of this new area payment. For the first time, component countries of the UK were allowed to introduce different systems, although the UK was considered to be one Member State of the EU. In England, the Department of Environment, Food and Rural Affairs (DEFRA) took the bold step of quickly phasing out any reference to what was called 'the historic payments'. Any land that was capable of being farmed or grazed was eligible under the new system. A huge task faced The Wildlife Trusts. In England, the Trusts set about registering all parts of their nature reserves that could be deemed 'farmable land'. In some counties, this extended to thousands of acres. The Wildlife Trusts had always lobbied for a subsidy payment that bore no relation to the crop produced and that would be made available to all landowners.

One important element of the 2005 reforms was the introduction of cross-compliance. Farmers would receive support payments through the European Union for adhering to certain conditions on the management of their farms. As early as 1997, The Wildlife Trusts had highlighted the case for cross-compliance conditions and now their 20-point plan for cross-compliance was becoming a reality. One of its most important elements was the introduction of buffer zones along hedgerows and water courses.

The Wildlife Trusts' objective was to introduce a two meter buffer zone to protect these important features. Although initially unpopular with the farming community, this condition had been largely accepted. Another area of habitat management that had been improved by cross-compliance was the cutting of hedgerows. Strict cutting dates ensured that no hedge cutting was carried out during the breeding season for birds. These were simple measures that had the potential to have a dramatic effect.

The agri-environment schemes also faced reform at this time. It was decided that the 'classic schemes', ESA and CS, had run their course. Sir Donald Curry was commissioned to produce a strategy for the country, post-FMD. The Trusts had long campaigned for the introduction of what was termed a 'broad and shallow' agri-environment scheme. The objective was to involve as many farmers as was practical in a simple scheme that would improve conditions for wildlife on the farm. Any landowner reaching the required threshold would be guaranteed entry. Enough funds were put aside to meet up to 100 per cent of farmers joining in. The Entry Level Scheme (ELS) was introduced in 2005 as part of the all-encompassing Environmental Stewardship Scheme. DEFRA officials, charged with producing the scheme, visited a SUFFOLK TRUST nature reserve to hear how the options could be implemented. In tandem with the ELS, a higher level scheme was also introduced. This targeted important sites, such as SSSIs and important areas for threatened species. An ambitious budget was made available for the whole scheme.

In 2007, the realisation dawned that food production was again becoming important. An exploding

Pastures New – a Dorset Trust Living Landscape scheme working with farmers to restore species-rich grassland on farms across west Dorset

world population, changes of diet and climatic disasters caused grain stocks to plummet to alarming levels. Not since the early 1970s had food been such an issue. The words 'food security' were again commonly used. Commitments by the UN to help double world food production during the next 20 years may threaten much of the good work that has been carried out in the UK. The ultimate dilemma is developing – how do we promote biodiversity and still feed the world?

Set-aside, the instrument introduced to reduce grain stocks, has been abolished in the hope of recreating them. The sometimes accidental environmental benefits of set-aside have never been more evident than with its demise. In recent years, 400,000 hectares of land have lain fallow in the UK countryside. Winter stubbles have provided a food source for birds, field margins have provided buffers and corridors for wildlife and whole blocks of land have remained dormant without treatments, such as chemicals or fertiliser. The loss of set-aside is of great concern. In addition, the increased profitability of farming is causing farmers to question the attractiveness of agri-environment schemes, while further intensification of some farming systems and the introduction of crops for bio-energy production, are putting further stress

on wildlife in rural areas. It is possible that future pressures on the UK countryside will be even greater than the 'bad old days' of hedge removals in the 1960s. The Wildlife Trusts movement is looking for new ways of working with farmers to ensure the health of our countryside. Perhaps one of the most important elements of this will be continued lobbying to ensure that the agri-environment route is still viable, attractive and effective.

The role of The Wildlife Trusts in agriculture has never been more important than at this time. The Wildlife Trusts' Living Landscape campaign recognises that protected wildlife sites are greatly influenced by the wider countryside around them. As climate change bites, the need for wildlife corridors and stepping stones through the countryside increases. The linking of habitats can effectively create large tracts of 'wildlife-friendly land'. As major landowners, The Wildlife Trusts need to demonstrate best practice and influence the farming community. The movement's ongoing engagement with the farming community and the Government is essential if The Wildlife Trusts' voice is to continue to be heard.

See also TOXIC CHEMICALS AND WILDLIFE, BADGERS AND BOVINE TB

FARMING AND WILDLIFE ADVISORY GROUPS

Following a meeting between David Lea (RSPB) and Derek Barber (MAFF's National Agriculture Advisory Service) in the spring of 1967, a small group gathered later that summer at the RSPB's Sandy headquarters to "explore the possibilities for establishing a rather closer dialogue between the two camps of farming and conservation".[88] Out of their deliberations emerged an idea from Eric Carter (MAFF) for a groundbreaking exercise-based conference. "Why not", he argued, "find a block of land somewhere which was fairly typical of much of the countryside which had not been subjected to the more extreme farming practices, and arrange for farmers to show in detail how they would have to farm the land to meet modern costs. Arrange similarly for the conservation camp to set out their ideas as to how this land might be managed for wildlife interests and then argue and discuss what practical, positive and detailed compromise might be affected between the two sides".[89]

In July 1969, the Society was among those supporting the conference which was held at the National College of Agricultural Engineering at Silsoe in Bedfordshire. In October, a paperback – *Farming and Wildlife – a study in compromise*, edited by Derek Barber, was published as an outcome of the Silsoe Conference. The Society also published a leaflet, *Farming and Wildlife*, nearly 200,000 of which were subsequently distributed among farmers.

As Norman Moore (Conservancy) was later to observe, "the Silsoe experiment was too valuable to lose. . . we were determined that it should continue in some form, so we founded the Farming and Wildlife Advisory Group".[90] The members of the Group were the Agricultural Development and Advisory Service of MAFF, the British Trust for Ornithology, the Country Landowners' Association, the Countryside Commission, the Forestry Commission, the National Farmers' Union, the Nature Conservancy Council, the Royal Institute of Chartered Surveyors, the Society and the RSPB. The Group went on to appoint a farmer from Cambridgeshire, Jim Hall, as a Farming and Wildlife Advisor.

The position was financed jointly by the RSPB and the Society. His job was to identify the problems of reconciling the needs of modern farming with the conservation of nature, to explore areas of compromise and to organise national exercises similar to the Silsoe Conference.

However, it was soon apparent to the Group that the way ahead lay in the development of Farming and Wildlife Groups (FWAGs) at the county level. The next few years saw the steady development of local FWAGs, many of which were supported by their local Trust.

A successful experiment in Gloucestershire and Somerset, financed jointly by the local Trusts, the Countryside Commission and the Conservancy showed that by employing a full-time local county FWAG advisor, many more farmers sought advice and far more conservation was achieved. The decision was taken to establish a Farming and Wildlife Trust to finance county advisers throughout the country, and Wilf Dawson moved from the Society to become its first Director in 1983.

FARMING & WILDLIFE
A STUDY IN COMPROMISE

Early scheme providing conservation advice to farmers in Somerset

TOWARDS 2000 REPORT

The Society had been justifiably preoccupied after the Second World War with the impact of modern agriculture on the natural environment. Up to the 1970s, together with the Trusts, it had concentrated on advising landowners, on promoting mitigation measures and on tailoring the Society's responses on a case-by-case basis to specific issues, such as control of the use of chemicals, the management of straw and stubble burning and hedgerow removal. But in 1980, the Society deliberately broadened its approach and asked its politically astute, high profile Vice President, Lord Peter Melchett, to chair a study group to look at the bearing the market economy was having on rural land-use policy.

The resulting consultative paper, *Towards 2000*, published a year later, drew heavily on work by the Study Group's Project Officer, Michael Carroll – a Professor of Rural Economy at the University of Alberta. It argued that what was needed was "a radical review of the systems that influence land-use, so that they reflect more adequately changes in attitudes and circum-stances, and the need to conserve our heritage and resources. . . far from helping to redress the balance, the present system regulating rural land-use, which is production orientated, greatly favours the farmer and forester. If conservation is accepted

as an important objective by society as a whole, there is no good reason why economic intervention should not be used as part of an integrated policy to influence decisions on rural land-use in favour of conservation, in the same way that it already operates in favour of agriculture and forestry".[91] The report accepted that over-the-gate advice, grants and tax relief incentives still had their place. But, where fundamental changes in management were contemplated, there was a need to offer incentives to farmers to support less intensive forms of management in the interests of conservation and to even consider planning controls to protect the best of our heritage of landscapes and wildlife.

The paper received good media coverage and positive responses from a wide range of organisations, including the Ministry of Agriculture, National Farmers Union, Country Landowners' Association and The National Trust. But the paper's radical approach, particularly on planning, meant the Trusts were reluctant to adopt it as policy. They had close working relationships with their farming communities. In addition, when the Society was unable to secure funds to take the study forward, the opportunity to promote the report *per se* passed. The Society had not been alone at the time in its views, but it was a more radical, more overtly political and more challenging approach than had hitherto been endorsed by the Society. Nevertheless, the paper set the scene for the Society's agricultural campaigning over the next ten to 15 years.

FIELD, MICHAEL

Mike Field was CHAIRMAN of the Society between 2001 and 2005, and is a member of the NORFOLK TRUST and a Trustee of the SUFFOLK TRUST.

He started his working life in a private architectural practice specialising in designing and building community housing, and out of this grew an interest in project management, organisational development and the management of change. He became a manager in various further education colleges and was Principal, firstly of Amersham and Wycombe, and Milton Keynes Colleges, and then, for six years, Croydon College for Further and Higher Education. In 1995, he became Director of the Learning from Experience Trust. It was this post, and his previous experience and involvement with the Suffolk and Norfolk Trusts, that made him eminently suitable to drive forward, among other things, the Society's review of education and the future of WILDLIFE WATCH.

Field took over from PETER SCHOFIELD as Chairman of the Society as a result of a contested election in 2001. These were turbulent times, with the Trusts anxious to see changes in the leadership and governance of their national organisation. The Society's financial position was precarious and, after the departure of the Director General, SIMON LYSTER, Field found himself in the role of Executive Chairman for several months between 2004 and 2005 while a part-time Director General, MARTIN SPRAY, was being appointed and until he was fully settled in.

Field was able to oversee the beginning of the rebuilding process and, despite having to go through an extremely stressful time, he had the satisfaction of seeing the organisation move into calmer waters.

FORMATION DATES

Alderney	2002
Avon	1980
Bedfordshire, Cambridgeshire	2011
& Northamptonshire	

Earlier incarnations and formation dates:
Cambridge & Isle of Ely 1956
Bedfordshire & Huntingdonshire 1961
Northamptonshire 1967
Peterborough 1989
Bedfordshire & Huntingdonshire
Cambridgeshire, Isle of Ely 1990
Bedfordshire, Cambridgeshire,
Northamptonshire & Peterborough 1994

Berkshire, Buckinghamshire	1960
& Oxfordshire	
Birmingham &	1982
Black Country	

Founded as the Urban Wildlife Group
in 1980

Brecknock	1964
Cheshire	1962
Cornwall	1962
Cumbria	1989

Founded as Lake District Naturalists'
Trust in 1962

Derbyshire	1962
Devon	1962
Dorset	1961
Durham	1971

Founded as Northumberland &
Durham in 1962

Essex	1959
Gloucestershire	1961
Gwent	1987

Founded as Monmouthshire in 1964

Guernsey	1986*–1998
Hampshire & the Isle of Wight	1960
Herefordshire	1987

Founded as Herefordshire &
Radnorshire in 1962

Hertfordshire & Middlesex	1964
Isles of Scilly	2001
Kent	1958
Lancashire	1962
Leicestershire & Rutland	1969

Founded as Leicestershire in 1956

Lincolnshire	1948
London	1981
Manx	1973
Montgomeryshire	1982
Norfolk	1926
North Wales	1963

Northumberland	1971

Founded as Northumberland &
Durham in 1962

Nottinghamshire	1963
Radnorshire	1987

Founded as Herefordshire &
Radnorshire in 1962

Scottish	1964
Sheffield	1985
Shropshire	1962
Somerset	1964
South & West Wales	2002

Earlier incarnations and formation dates:
West Wales 1956
Glamorgan 1961

Staffordshire	1969

Founded as West Midlands in 1957

Suffolk	1961
Surrey	1959
Sussex	1961
Tees Valley	1996

Founded as Cleveland in 1979

Ulster	1978
Warwickshire	1970

Founded as West Midlands in 1957

Wiltshire	1962
Worcestershire	1968

Founded as West Midlands in 1957

Yorkshire	1946

* Date of corporate membership of The Wildlife Trusts

G

GRANTS UNIT

In October 1996, when the then Conservative Government introduced an innovative 'green' landfill tax to encourage consumers and companies to produce less waste and to recover value from the waste produced, the Society saw an opportunity to become one of the environmental bodies that benefited. After lengthy negotiations, it was accepted as a 'distributing environmental body' registered with ENTRUST and signed contracts to manage the landfill tax credits for two waste companies – Biffa Waste Services and Hanson.

It was immediately clear that a new, dedicated unit would be needed to manage these funds effectively and to meet contractual and regulatory requirements. The then Managing Director, Martin Gough, saw this unit and the new landfill money as a way of indirectly supporting the Society and the management of the UK Office, through economies of scale. As a consequence, the Grants Unit was established towards the end of 1997.

During the 1990s, the Society had been engaged in one of its periodic bursts of fundraising activity, securing funds from various traditional corporate and charitable sources to support the individual Trusts. These programmes ranged in scale, from £20,000 to £100,000 in size, and included the Rees Jeffery Road Fund, the East Midlands Electricity Environment Fund and ICI's 'Working for Wildlife' initiative. They had been managed by the Society's Fundraising and Marketing Services Department, but were now transferred to the Grants Unit.

However, with the launch of the Hanson Environment Fund in September and Biffaward in December 1997, the scale and nature of the Society's grants and loans programme changed dramatically. It was now in an altogether different league, distributing funds to a much wider range of bodies than the Trusts, with the two new funds alone making grants totalling £9.2 million in the first year. By the closure of the Fund in 2006, the Hanson Environment Fund had distributed more than £17.5 million to 904 projects.

If the new Grants Unit was going to succeed, its administration was going to have to be 'whiter than white', with its impartiality and efficiency second to none. The Unit initially comprised three existing members of staff – MICHAEL SINGH, Viv O'Connor and Andrea White. Between them they had experience of fundraising, marketing, grant regimes and communications. Two additional staff were taken on to carry out project assessments and handle public relations. But, as the amount of landfill tax credits donated grew each year, so the size of the Unit had to grow to make sure that there were dedicated teams to deal with the huge number of applications, to award the grants and to carry out monitoring and evaluation. In ten years, the Society received more than £113 million and awarded grants to in excess of 1,900 projects run by a wide variety of voluntary, community, educational and environmental organisations.

The Grants Unit was building a justifiable reputation for fairness and objectivity and was being seen as a 'safe pair of hands'. New opportunities began to arise as a result.

Woodland Walks – a Biffaward-funded project

The Wildlife Trusts had been very successful in their applications to the National Lottery and, in particular, the Heritage Lottery Fund. This direct funding continued but, by the year 2000, the Society was asked to become the lead partner in a bid to the National Lottery's New Opportunities Fund to manage a programme under its Green Spaces and Sustainable Communities initiative. This was the first fully delegated Lottery programme and the Society was successful with its bid for the £15.3 million Social, Economic and Environmental

Global Generation Skip Garden – one of many projects to receive Local Food funding

Development (SEED) Programme. A consortium of 11 partners representing the various themes of the SEED Programme, launched the programme in April 2001 and, led by the Society, managed its strategic development. The programme ended in March 2005.

In 2002, as a result of the Unit's relationship with the community waste sector through the SEED consortium and the landfill tax credit funds, the Society was asked to lead on a bid to the New Opportunities Fund for a Transforming Waste programme in England. Once again the bid was successful, mainly due to its quality and the fact that the New Opportunities Fund trusted and respected the Grants Unit's previous management of SEED. The £36.5 million Community Recycling and Economic Development Programme (CRED), consisting of eight partners led by the Society, was launched in January 2003.

In 2004, the Government announced that funds were to be made available to the community waste sector. The Grants Unit was invited to attend a mini-Waste Summit and afterwards approached to manage a £3 million Waste Partnership Fund. The Government was very supportive and helped to enable the Unit to set up and

launch the new programme by the beginning of December 2004 – just three weeks after being asked to carry out the work.

This new Fund was a success and, once again, the Government approached the Society to manage a new programme with money allocated from the Business Resource Efficiency and Waste Programme (BREW). The Business Re-use Fund was launched in March 2006 and ran for two years. It was worth £3.5 million in total.

Finally, in March 2006, as lead partner of a sustainable communities and food consortium, the Society submitted a bid to the Big Lottery Fund for a £70 million programme to deliver local food projects. The Big Lottery Fund had brought together the New Opportunities Fund, the Community Fund and the Millennium Commission and was now responsible for giving out half of the money for good causes raised by the National Lottery. The Society was awarded £50 million and the new Local Food programme was launched in March 2008.

A senior manager of the Grants Unit staff also helped with administration of the STRATEGIC DEVELOPMENT FUND.

See LANDFILL COMMUNITIES FUND

GREAT STORM

On the night of 15th October 1987, a devastating storm hit southern Britain. It was considered a 'once in 200 years event' with a gust of 100 knots recorded at Shoreham on the Sussex coast and 86 knots at Gatwick Airport. The HAMPSHIRE AND ISLE OF WIGHT TRUST reported that four acres of "its showcase reserve, Roydon Wood, was flattened".[92] The SURREY TRUST's woodland reserves were badly damaged, with the "most serious problems at Virginia Water and Nower Wood where every major tree has fallen and the Trust's education centre is out of action".[93] The Trusts acted swiftly to survey the extensive damage to trees in their areas and to carry out practical remedial work. Several Trusts mounted storm damage appeals to help support their efforts and the Government allocated £2.75 million to the Countryside Commission who quickly set up a special unit, known as 'Task Force Trees'.

On 20th November, the Society organised a meeting for the 11 Trusts in the 17 areas to which the Government had announced it would give funds. The money available was £250,000 and this had to be allocated by 27th November. A pro-forma application was quickly agreed at the meeting, applications were turned around within the week and distribution of the grants was subsequently coordinated by the Society. Afterwards, the Society

When The Wind Blew report

went on to employ a Storm Damage Coordinator, Tony Whitbread, for a further three years.

There were further "very heavy winds"[94] in southern Britain, early in 1990. "In Somerset, there were so many trees down at the Trust's headquarters that it took until 7pm for the staff to cut themselves out!"[95] The area covered by the Task Force Trees unit was extended and a further £600,000 of grant-aid made available for the year.

In NATURAL WORLD, Whitbread wondered whether 'we are seeing the first effects of global warming', but his key message was contained in *When the Wind Blew – Life in our Woods after the Great Storm of 1987* published by the Society later in 1990. Whitbread hoped the report "demonstrated that violent storms are not freaks or unnatural. . . wild habitats, far from being at the mercy of outside forces, actually evolved with natural disturbance, like violent storms, a key part of their ecology".[96]

H

HANDBOOK

The Handbook, containing the Society's annual report and list of members, was published by the Society between 1923 and 1969. In 1940, its size and print run were reduced because of the "urgent need for national economy in the use of paper",[97] and no issue was published in 1967.

Early editions had a brief account of the Society's objects and activities which was updated year-on-year. Apart from a period during the Second World War, longer features and photographs were gradually introduced from 1935 onwards. Post-war editions include reports on the Society's prestigious social events and track the development of international conservation. Later editions reflect the Society's role in the development of the Wildlife

The slimmed-down 1940 Handbook

Trusts (with reports of the Trusts' first five biennial conferences) and in nature conservation policy and practice more generally. The 1959 Handbook has a brief profile of the eight Trusts in existence at that time and their activities, and the 1961 edition has an article on 'The County Naturalists' Trusts 1959–61', by TED SMITH.

The Handbooks provide a valuable chronological account of people, events and the nature reserves associated with the Society and, on several occasions, a glimpse into the thinking and development of nature conservation over 47 years.

From 1970, the Society simply compiled an annual report but from 1987–88 the main public document has been an *Annual Review* that highlights the achievements of the whole Trust movement.

HARMER, SIR SYDNEY FREDERICK

Sir Sydney Harmer (1862–1950), a zoologist and university teacher, was a member of the Society's Council from 1919 until his death, and HONORARY TREASURER between 1921 and 1927.

After a university career, Harmer was appointed Keeper of Zoology at the Natural History Museum in London in 1907, and from 1919 to 1927 was its Director. The *Dictionary of National Biography* refers to his prodigious industry. "He left to the museum a volume of files, indexes, and notebooks filled with accurate and methodically arranged taxonomic work, together with his exceptionally fine library of works on Polyzoa and whales".[98] He had a long connection with the Museums Association and was elected a fellow of both the Linnean Society and Royal Society.

In the Society's HANDBOOK for 1950, his contribution to the Society was briefly acknowledged. "By the death of Sir Sydney Harmer. . . the Society lost a member who gave it valuable service in years gone by".[99]

Sydney Frederick Harmer

HENLEY, FRANCIS ROBERT
The Honorable Francis Robert Henley (1877–1962), an all-round naturalist, was one of the founder members of the Society and its first HONORARY SECRETARY (jointly with WILLIAM ROBERT OGILVIE-GRANT), serving until 1937. He became Lord Henley in 1925.

A close friend of CHARLES ROTHSCHILD and fellow Northamptonshire landowner, he was actively involved in the administration associated with the compiling of ROTHSCHILD'S LIST. In 1913, it was in his name (and that of his fellow Honorary Secretary Ogilvie-Grant) that the Society sent out its innovative circular to natural history societies, requesting information about potential nature

Captain Francis Robert Henley in Egypt, 1905, during a trip he made with Charles Rothschild

reserves. Later in his life, he presented the Society with a bound volume of newspaper cuttings covering the activities of the Society during these early years.

On his retirement as Honorary Secretary in 1937, the Society expressed their appreciation of his services since its foundation in 1912.

HERITAGE LOTTERY FUND
After 1995, when the first Heritage Lottery Fund (HLF) grant to a Trust helped with the purchase of Jones' Mill in Wiltshire, a strong and productive partnership between HLF and the Trusts resulted in the launch of an astounding variety of important projects, a significant number of which were large-scale in concept and wide-reaching in effect. This highly successful relationship was based on a neat fit between the objectives and mode of operation of the Trusts, and the aims of the HLF.

In the foreword to a brochure marking the tenth anniversary of HLF in 2004, Carole Souter, HLF Director, said that "the focus of The Wildlife Trusts on conservation, education and access, and the ability to deliver everywhere in the UK",[100] made them an ideal partner for the Heritage Lottery Fund.

Between 1995 and 2011, projects developed with the help of the HLF, ranged from wide-scale habitat restoration schemes to initiatives focused on particular species, and from education and community

involvement in an urban setting to green tourism in the countryside.

One of the most spectacular landscape-scale projects supported by HLF funding was, at the time, Europe's largest coastal alignment scheme. It was carried out by the ESSEX TRUST in partnership with the Environment Agency, English Nature and WWF-UK. In this visionary enterprise, 81 hectares of farmland were flooded to create saltmarsh as a natural sea defence and to provide a wildlife haven. Other large-scale projects the Trusts were leading included restoration of heathland in South and West Yorkshire and on the Stiperstones in Shropshire, and the reconnecting of wetland and fenland habitats by the Great Fen Project in Cambridgeshire.

At farm level, HLF funding enabled several Trusts to start their own wildlife-friendly farming initiatives. GWENT TRUST acquired three farms with traditional wildflower-rich meadows; WILTSHIRE TRUST purchased Blakehill and Clattinger Farms, home to some of the UK's finest lowland grassland; and GLOUCESTERSHIRE TRUST bought Greystones Farm near Bourton-on-the-Water, which supported neutral grassland, the most threatened habitat in the UK.

The first HLF-funded project for a single species was the DURHAM TRUST's Strategic Water Vole Recovery project, aimed at reversing the decline of one of the UK's most endangered animals. HLF funding also helped with the acquisition of red squirrel reserves in Northumberland, research into basking sharks and the provision of CCTV to protect nesting peregrines in Scotland.

Trust community projects, launched with HLF assistance, included management of the Churchtown Farm reserve, near Saltash in Cornwall, where local

Clattinger Farm, Wiltshire, purchased thanks to funding from the HLF

people contribute to every aspect of work on the reserve. In London, school pupils, elderly people and people from minority ethnic communities in Hackney, helped create a small haven for nature next to the East Reservoir.

Some hugely successful Trust education initiatives were also launched with HLF support. In Lincolnshire, a project offering free transport to enable schools to visit nature reserves, struggled to keep up with the demand. In the West Midlands, the BIRMINGHAM AND BLACK COUNTRY TRUST's Natural Connections Project made it possible for 120,000 inner city children to discover the delights of the natural world over a three-year period.

In Herefordshire, an imaginative HLF-funded green tourism scheme, 'Wildlife Weekend Breaks', was a big success for the Trust and drew visitors from all over the UK to enjoy weekends ranging from badger watching and cycle safaris to canoeing and organic lifestyle courses.

From 1995 to 2011, the HLF contributed a total of £168.6 million to Wildlife Trust projects, enabling the Trusts to plan and operate on an unprecedented scale.

HICKLING, RONALD

'Ron' Hickling (1912–2006) was the Society's HONORARY TREASURER between 1972 and 1977. As an active ornithologist, his visits to the Gibraltar Point Observatory brought him into contact with the work of the LINCOLNSHIRE TRUST and this inspired him to become a prime mover in the establishment of the LEICESTERSHIRE TRUST in 1956 of which he was the first Honorary Secretary. As such, he was one of a small group of the early Trusts' officers who worked for the conversion of the Society into the national association of the rapidly growing Trust movement. A new model Memorandum and Articles which he produced at that time was adopted by most of the Trusts formed after 1959.

An accountant by profession, Hickling applied professional skill and understanding to the office of Honorary Treasurer at a critical time of consolidation and expansion in the Society's role.

As an ornithologist of national repute, he played a leading role for many years in the British Trust for Ornithology (BTO), serving in various capacities, including Honorary Secretary and President. He edited *Enjoying Ornithology* (1988), an account of the BTO's first 50 years, and was the author of *The Birds of Leicestershire and Rutland* (1978).

Ron Hickling (right) with Norman Riley (left) and Christopher Cadbury (back) at Hickling Broad, Norfolk in 1969

HILBORNE, STEPHANIE

Stephanie Hilborne was appointed CHIEF EXECUTIVE of the Society in June 2004 and led the substantial reform of its strategy, business model and staffing in the build up to its centenary in 2012.

Stephanie Hilborne

Hilborne committed herself to conservation as a teenager as she watched her childhood haunts in Surrey developed for new roads and housing. On graduating from Bristol University and University College London, she volunteered for LONDON TRUST where she helped to compile a report on the ecological impact of the M25, *Ever Increasing Circles* (ROAD BUILDING AND WILDLIFE).

Hilborne's first paid role in conservation was with WILDLIFE LINK which she transformed in her time there (1992–97), by focusing it on its behind-the-scenes role and ensuring its accountability to its members. Working alongside inspiring campaigners from environmental groups (including Tony Juniper and Tim Sands), she learnt the workings of Whitehall and Westminster, standing her in good stead for her future role with the Society.

In 1998, Hilborne moved to NOTTINGHAMSHIRE to manage and professionalise the local Trust's expanding conservation and education functions. The move coincided with the formation of Regional Development Agencies and Regional Assemblies and she took a lead role in influencing decisions at this level, including through founding East Midlands Environment Link. From 2000, Hilborne was the Trust's Chief Executive and oversaw the development of its award-winning Attenborough visitor centre and the initiation of its landscape-scale project in the Idle Valley.

Hilborne joined the Society in 2004 where she built up a new team and culture at the Society, in close dialogue with the Trusts. Her new senior management team was able to establish unity around the shared LIVING LANDSCAPE AND LIVING SEAS vision to inspire politicians to pass the Marine and Coastal Access Act (2009), initiate the Lawton Review (2010) and to produce the Natural Environment White Paper (2011). Through effective conferences and visits to Trustees and staff around the movement, Hilborne and her team built trust and laid the ground for the agreement of a Memorandum of Cooperation between all the Trusts in 2010, and for close cooperation in the build up to the Society's centenary in 2012.

HOLTON, MICHAEL
Michael Holton (1927–2006) was the Society's HONORARY SECRETARY from 1988 until 1992. Holton, a civil servant and mountaineer, became a member of the Society's Council and Executive in 1976, on his return to the Ministry of Defence as Head of the Air Service secretariat. He was Secretary of the Countryside Commission for Scotland (1968–70), Carnegie United Kingdom Trust (1971–75) and of the European Conservation Year Committee for Scotland 1970.

The Carnegie UK Trust's continuing support of the Society and Trust movement, particularly in the 1970s, owed much to Michael Holton's personal interest and that of his predecessor, David Lowe. Holton was presented with a watercolour of Lincoln cathedral by the Lincolnshire artist Keith Roper on his retirement as Honorary Secretary in 1992.

HUGHES, JOHN JAMES
John Hughes was appointed HONORARY TREASURER of the Society in 2001 at a time when the Society was facing a leadership and financial crisis. He was a key player in reviving the Society's fortunes and was at the heart of a successful programme of work that saw the Society's financial position significantly strengthened and its governance substantially improved.

Hughes was an experienced Finance Director and Chartered Accountant with an impressive record of achievement in the business sector, being one-time Director of Finance of London Underground and London Transport. He also held board level positions in major private sector organisations. He became a Council member of The National Trust nominated by The Wildlife Trusts, a board member of Biffaward and was Treasurer of the Tree Council for nearly ten years. Additionally, he was a Trustee of

John Hughes

Lloyds TSB Foundation from 2004 to 2010 and of the Samaritans in Hertfordshire and Essex.

On his retirement after nine years, the Society's Chairman, MICHAEL ALLEN, paid tribute to Hughes' fortitude in weathering the storm raging at the time of his appointment; his absolute integrity in dealing with the Society's affairs; and his part in restoring the Society's credibility and in securing its sustainable financial future. Hughes, with DOBBS and Allen was part of a strong team that worked with HILBORNE during a period of substantial reform. His emotional intelligence and strong personality, combined with his financial skills, made him a key agent of change.

HURCOMB, LORD
Cyril William Hurcomb (1883–1975), "one of the most influential figures in the nature conservation movement in Britain for over 20 years",[101] was PRESIDENT of the Society between 1951 and 1962.

Most of his working life was spent in the civil service which he entered in 1906. At the outbreak of the First World War, he transferred from the Post Office to the Admiralty and in 1916 to the new Ministry of Shipping. During the Second World War, he was Director General of the Ministry of Shipping (later War Transport) from 1939 and Chairman of the British Transport Commission from 1947 to 1953.

A keen ornithologist, he became increasingly interested in the conservation of nature. In 1947, he took on the Chairmanship of the Committee of Bird Sanctuaries in the Royal Parks and, in 1953, joined the Conservancy, serving as Chairman of its Committee for England and in 1961–62 as its Chairman. In addition to his role with the Society, Hurcomb was also Vice President of IUPN between 1954 and 1960, President of the

Field Studies Council from 1957 and of the RSPB between 1961 and 1966. He was made a life peer in 1950. In the House of Lords, as elsewhere, he rallied support and fought hard for the welfare and protection of wildlife.

Lord Hurcomb

MAX NICHOLSON wrote, "Hurcomb's pallid complexion and worn appearance belied his toughness and stamina, just as his austere mien disguised his receptiveness as a listener and his great consideration for others. These combined with his clarity of mind and tenacity of purpose, made him an outstanding negotiator. . . his tolerance and sense of humour were shown by his choice as supporters for his coat of arms of 'a heron proper gorged' on either side, upholding a branch of willow on which sat a kingfisher with wings elevated, with the motto *'quod potero perferam'* – for as long as I can bear".[102]

As President of the Society, Hurcomb was content for it to play a more active role in promoting a local conservation movement – a stance that was greatly welcomed by those keen to see the Society take the fledgling Trust movement under its wing. On his retirement as President in 1962, the Society recalled that "the whole conservation movement owes a very great debt, for hardly any activity in this field, nationally and internationally, has failed to benefit from his advice and active support. . . the recent, almost explosive, establishment of County Naturalists' Trusts. . . owes a great deal to his stimulating support and encouragement".[103]

J

JEFFRAY, DUNCAN

Duncan Jeffray taught first at Bedford Modern School. He was then Head of Biology at Bablake School, Coventry before joining the Science Education Department of Warwick University, where he was Senior Lecturer. A member of the Society's Executive Committee from 1984, he served as its Chairman (CHAIRMEN OF THE EXECUTIVE) between 1993 and 1997.

Jeffray represented the Executive Committee on the Urban Steering Group, was a member of the Board of the Watch Trust for Environment Education (WILDLIFE WATCH) and fulfilled many other roles. For example, he was the Society's representative on The National Trust's Council.

His broad knowledge and experience of conservation, education and the urban environment meant he was much in demand, not simply by the Society, but also by the WARWICKSHIRE TRUST. He was the Trust's Honorary Conservation Officer for six years until 1978, before becoming first its Chairman (1978–1983), and then its President. When Jeffray moved to Cumbria, he became Chairman of the CUMBRIA TRUST's Wider Countryside Committee (1998–2004) and then the Trust's Chairman (2004–2007).

K

JONES, REES J

Rees Jones was the Society's HONORARY TREASURER between 1991 and 1994. A chartered accountant, he worked in industry between 1954 and 1994 and was Finance Director of the National Society for the Prevention of Cruelty to Children for three years, between 1984 and 1988. After this, he became a financial consultant, running a small business concentrating mainly on training.

KING, SIMON

In November 2010, Simon King became the youngest President in the Society's 100-year history, having been a Vice President since 2008. He is also President of the AVON TRUST and Patron of the SOMERSET TRUST.

King, a renowned wildlife programme-maker, cameraman, photographer and presenter, was born in Kenya and grew up in Bristol, England. Each school day began with walks in his local woods, studying and collecting natural objects. He started his career in camera and television work at the age of ten in a film made by his late father, John King. He is best known today for television programmes, such as *Big Cat Diaries*, *Autumnwatch* and *Springwatch* and his *Shetland Diaries*.

Simon King – wildlife film-maker, author and the Society's President since 2010

As a Vice President, King helped promote The Wildlife Trusts to a wider audience and, in particular, to communicate its vision for a LIVING LANDSCAPE AND LIVING SEAS. The Presidency enabled him to continue this work and provided further opportunities, in his words, to encourage people in the UK to reconnect with the natural world.

His life has been spent communicating his passion for nature and this has earned him huge respect and recognition, including a host of awards.

L

LANDFILL COMMUNITIES FUND

In 1996, the Government introduced a tax on landfill waste in order to reduce the amount of waste and to promote a shift to more environmentally sustainable methods of waste management. It was the UK's first environmental tax.

Under the Landfill Tax Regulations, a charge is placed on every tonne of waste sent to a landfill site. The operators of these sites are provided with the Landfill Tax Credit Scheme (renamed the Landfill Communities Fund (LCF) in October 2006), allowing them to spend up to 6.2 per cent of their tax liability on environmental and community projects situated in the vicinity of landfill sites, and to reclaim 90 per cent of this contribution as a tax credit. Under the LCF, landfill operators contribute money to 'environmental bodies' enrolled by ENTRUST, the regulatory body for the scheme, which is a not-for-profit private company working on behalf of HM Revenue and Customs.

In 1997, for example, landfill operator Biffa Waste Services entrusted the Society's GRANTS UNIT to use its landfill tax credits to manage a Biffaward scheme to award funding to community and environmental projects.

More than £1.2 billion has been made available to environmental bodies for more than 34,000 projects since the LCF began in 1996. Beneficiaries range from village halls to churches, parks and playgrounds, and all manner of wildlife schemes. To take just one example, through Biffaward, the LCF provided more than £500,000 to the SCOTTISH TRUST to trial the reintroduction of European beavers in Scotland. Indeed, in the first ten years after the introduction of LCF, 500 Trust projects benefited from the fund to the tune of £50 million (see also GRANTS UNIT).

LAND FUND

A new Land Fund to help Trusts purchase land and property was established in 1979 with a generous loan from an anonymous donor (later disclosed as the Mary Snow Trust) of £250,000. The loan was made for an initial period of ten years at a fixed interest rate of seven per cent per annum.

The Land Fund was established as a loan fund to help Trusts with upfront money for the purchase of land or property 'in the interests of conservation in the broadest sense'. This meant that, whilst the primary objective of the fund was to support the acquisition of nature reserves, it could also be used to help purchase a shop or a Trust's headquarters.

Among the early loans were ones for the purchase of Upton Broad by the NORFOLK TRUST and of a further 28 acres of land in the Ouse Washes

A loan from the Land Fund helped the purchase of 28 acres of land in the Ouse Washes, pictured here in the 1970s – an important site for birds in the Cambridgeshire fens

647

by the CAMBRIDGE AND ISLE OF ELY TRUST. It was noted at the time that, with the Conservancy short of money, "the Land Fund was capable of making a major contribution to the safeguarding of property, especially Grade I and Grade II sites, should these come onto the market".[104]

By 1985, the capital in the Fund had been turned over more than three times and Trusts had borrowed more than £820,000.

LANE, WALTER

Walter Lane (1921–2006) was Chairman of the Society's Executive Committee between 1976 and 1981 (CHAIRMEN OF THE EXECUTIVE) and President of the LINCOLNSHIRE TRUST for 25 years until 1999.

He had a long career in local government, entering as a solicitor and working first with Norfolk County Council and then with Hampshire, before moving on to Lincolnshire to become Clerk of Lindsey County Council in 1957. Through his active role in the County Council Association, he became a member of the organising committees for the series of influential Countryside in 1970 conferences, and was Chairman of the study group on the role of local authorities (see also WILDLIFE SITES).

Lane took early retirement following the reorganisation of local government in 1974. He became increasingly involved in the voluntary nature conservation movement and in the work of the Conservancy. He was a member of the Conservancy's Council from 1974 and Chairman of its England Committee from 1978 to 1987. He served for 20 years on the Council of The National Trust, including a time on its Properties Committee and Conservation Panel, and was also a member of the Forestry Commission's Committee for England.

LIVING LANDSCAPE AND LIVING SEAS

A Living Landscape campaign was adopted as the new overall strategic direction for The Wildlife Trusts in 2006. It was based on a vision of connecting up pockets of important habitats on land to create larger, more resilient landscapes.

In 2008, The Wildlife Trusts marine conservation work was brought under the banner of Living Seas, to reflect a similar ecosystem approach and the need to integrate with a Living Landscape.

The lead up to The Wildlife Trusts' Living Seas campaign and its more recent development is described in more detail under MARINE CONSERVATION (see page 653). The Wildlife Trusts' Conservation Plan, agreed in January 1998, had formally acknowledged, for the first time, that influencing the management of larger areas was going to be of increasing importance in countering the fragmented state of existing wildlife sites. It would give plants and animals "more of a chance to adapt to the emerging threat of climate change".[105] The plan called for at least three new large area projects to be created by 2005.

In fact, within the first two years of the new millennium, the ESSEX TRUST had embarked on an ambitious coastal realignment scheme at its Abbots Hall Farm and the BEDFORDSHIRE, CAMBRIDGE-SHIRE AND NORTHAMPTONSHIRE TRUST had launched the Great Fen Project. More schemes soon followed and by October 2008, at a Parliamentary launch for A Living Landscape, it was announced that the Trusts were leading more than 100 schemes across the UK.

While it was important to show what could be achieved on the ground, it was also important to convince politicians that changes were needed in Government policy – and even in the law – if a network of sites able to bring about the protection and recovery of the country's wildlife was ever to come about. The Wildlife Trusts convinced Government that the issues warranted Government attention and John Lawton was appointed to lead an inquiry. The Wildlife Trusts' Chief Executive STEPHANIE HILBORNE was a member and its findings were published in *Making Space for Nature*. Subsequently, The Wildlife Trusts called for a White Paper to implement this. When the Conservative/Liberal Democratic Coalition Government came to power in 2010, it realised its manifesto commitment to produce the first Environment White Paper for 20 years and *The Natural Choice: Securing the Value of Nature* was published a year later in June 2011.

Volehouse Moor, North Devon – part of the Devon Trust's Working Wetlands Living Landscape scheme, where the Trust is working with hundreds of farmers to restore culm grassland

A living landscape

A call to restore the UK's battered ecosystems, for wildlife and people

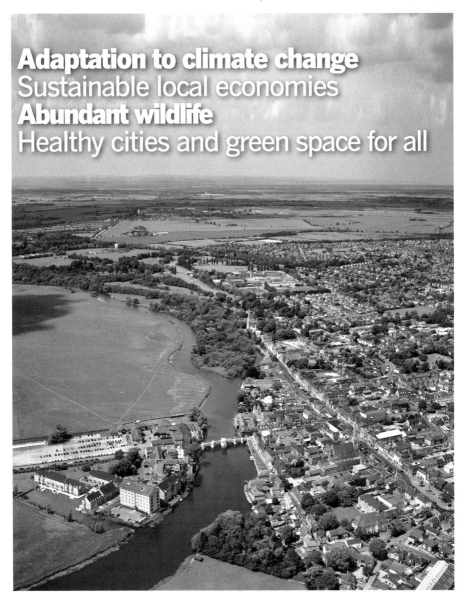

Adaptation to climate change
Sustainable local economies
Abundant wildlife
Healthy cities and green space for all

The Living Landscape report laid down a marker for the Trusts' ambitions for restoring nature at a landscape scale, and in partnership with landowners, businesses and local communities

LODGE, GEORGE EDWARD

The artist and naturalist, George Edward Lodge (1860–1954), became an Associate Member of the Society in August 1919. He joined the Council in July 1920, served on the Executive between 1932 and 1946 and remained an Associate Member until his death in 1954. The Society's HANDBOOK records that the Society's first logo "consists of a representation of a kite, drawn by Mr GE Lodge, from an illustration by Mr A Thorburn in Lord Lilford's book *The Birds of the British Islands*".[106]

Lodge was born at Horncastle in Lincolnshire. Aged 14, he won prizes for drawing while a student at the Lincoln School of Art. At the age of 16 he was apprenticed to a wood engraver. He became a most accomplished artist, with much of his career being devoted to illustrating scientific books, although he preferred painting pictures. He accompanied the Society's early leading figures, including the co-founders, WILLIAM OGILVIE-GRANT and EDMUND GB MEADE-WALDO, on many field trips. At Hickling in Norfolk, he was a frequent guest of Edwin Samuel Montagu, another member of the Society's Executive and a Minister

in both Asquith's and David Lloyd George's Governments. His bird illustrations appeared in many books. Perhaps Lodge's most famous published works were the 385 colour plates that appeared in the 12 volumes of *The Birds of the British Isles* by David Bannerman, published between 1953 and 1963. Lodge was to see "only the first two volumes of what was to be the culmination of his work and achievements".[107]

Lodge continued painting until shortly before his death in February 1954. A letter of good wishes was sent by the Society to Lodge on the occasion of his 90th birthday. *The Times* obituary, headed 'Eminent Painter of Birds', refers to a man of most exceptional charm and distinction who was recognised on both sides of the Atlantic as one of the finest bird artists this country has ever produced. "His wide experience in falconry doubtless gave him special knowledge of the hawk family, for he was a keen falconer from his earliest days. In the painting of birds of prey he had no rival in any country. He was primarily an artist but, being a good naturalist as well, he was able to depict his subjects among their natural surroundings and to make them look alive".[108]

LOGOS

Kite: Described in the 1923 HANDBOOK of the Society as the 'seal', the RED KITE was the Society's first logo. The design, approved in May 1919, was said to be drawn by GEORGE EDWARD LODGE "from an illustration by Mr A Thorburn in Lord Lilford's book *The Birds of the British Islands*".[109] When discussing the 'seal' in March 1919, the Executive Committee recommended that the legend should be "Nature is above all wit".[110] As far as is known, this legend was never used.

1919

Oval badger's head: The oval badger logo first appeared on the Society's new publication *Conservation Review* (see NATURAL WORLD) in the autumn of 1970. A fibre-glass relief of the logo was produced by the Society's Assistant Secretary, Wilf Dawson, and displayed on the front of the Society's Nettleham offices (OFFICES OF THE SOCIETY). The new logo symbolised the change from the 'old' to the 'new' Society, with its developing role as the national association of the Trusts.

1970

George Edward Lodge, illustrated the Society's first logo

Badger and front paw in vertical rectangle: With the granting of the new Royal Charter in 1976 came a "new look for the Society".[111] The head and front torso of the badger were depicted with a front paw symbolically stepping outside a rectangular box. *Conservation Review* stated that the new, bolder and more modern logo "will become a familiar sign of the Society's activity and already features above in our new look, colour production".[112]

1976

Badger and front paw in horizontal rectangular flag': In October 1990, the 'badger and front paw' appeared alongside the words 'RSNC The Wildlife Trusts Partnership' to create a new rectangle version of the logo.

1990

ROYAL SOCIETY FOR NATURE CONSERVATION

Badger's head in a square with the words The Wildlife Trusts: This logo, designed by the Society's in-house graphic designer, Roy Vickers, was introduced when the organisation began being marketed as The Wildlife Trusts in 1994. It reproduced well with its distinct, predominantly black and white image. The words 'The' and 'Trusts'

were to be printed in green. The border was designed to avoid the danger of the badger image being reversed. The 'green' version was dropped around 1998.

1994

LYSTER, SIMON

Simon Lyster was Director General (PRINCIPAL OFFICERS) of The Wildlife Trusts between 1995 and 2003.

A graduate in law from Cambridge University and a qualified lawyer in England and the USA, Lyster went on in the late 1980s and early 1990s to become a leading campaigner in international wildlife law. He was employed in the dual role of Treaties Officer for WWF International and Senior Conservation Officer (International) at WWF-UK. He led WWF's successful effort to secure a ban on the ivory trade at the 1989 Conference on the Convention on International Trade in Endangered Species. He also led the WWF team involved in the negotiation of the Biological Diversity Convention, signed at the 1992 Earth Summit in Rio de Janeiro, and was also instrumental in securing improvements to the Ramsar (Wetlands) Convention. He was seconded to WWF's Brazil Office for two years between 1992 and 1994, helping to secure Brazil's backing of both the Biodiversity and Ramsar Conventions.

Between 1982 and 1986, as Secretary to the Falklands

Foundation, Lyster dealt with the negotiations over the lease of various small islands in the Falklands (owned by the Society) to the Foundation (NATURE RESERVES OWNED BY THE SOCIETY).

His book *International Wildlife Law* was published in 1985.

Lyster's appointment as Director General in 1995 marked a new era in the leadership of The Wildlife Trusts' movement. The Society had decided to appoint a Managing Director to manage the UK Office, leaving Lyster free to be a champion for the Trusts. His term of office coincided with a period of unprecedented growth in Trust membership, in land holdings and in funds for the Trusts. He was persuasive and charismatic and these qualities opened up new horizons. In particular, he increased media coverage and achieved greater influence at the highest levels.

In the end, however, a financial crisis and the decision to revert to a more traditional structure, with a single Principal Officer, meant that 'the cap no longer fitted'. In the end, it was in neither Lyster's nor the Trustees' interest to continue and so undermine what had been achieved in the previous eight years. Lyster formally left the organisation on 31st March 2003.

Simon Lyster

M

MACMILLAN, JOHN

John Macmillan was the Society's HONORARY SECRETARY between 1992 and 2003. His first encounter with Wildlife Trusts was as a member of the ESSEX TRUST, but in 1981 he joined the Development Committee of the STAFFORDSHIRE TRUST as a co-opted member and became a member of its Council two years later. Apart from a gap of seven years, when he was living and working in the East Midlands, Macmillan served as a member of the Staffordshire Trust's Council for more than 20 years.

Originally a solicitor specialising in employment law and personal injury claims, Macmillan was appointed a full-time Chairman of Industrial Tribunals in Birmingham in 1987 and then a Regional Employment Judge for the East Midlands in 1996.

As its Honorary Secretary, the Society greatly benefited not only from Macmillan's professional knowledge and experience but also his interest and enthusiasm for the work of The Wildlife Trusts, at a time when it was facing a sometimes difficult, but necessary, period of administrative and constitutional change.

Macmillan remains a member of both the STAFFORDSHIRE and NOTTINGHAMSHIRE TRUSTS.

MACMILLAN, LORD

Hugh Pattison Macmillan (1873–1952), after a distinguished career at the bar, accepted the office of Lord Advocate in 1924 and later became Lord of Appeal in Ordinary from 1930 to 1947. He subsequently became Lord of Appeal, except for a short period when he was Minister of Information at the outbreak of the Second World War.

He was Chairman of the Pilgrim Trust and a Trustee of the first home of the Society, the Natural History Museum in London, for 16 years between 1933 and 1949.

Elected PRESIDENT of the Society in 1942, he retired after five years in office in 1947. He was Chairman of the CONFERENCE ON NATURE PRESERVATION IN POST-WAR RECONSTRUCTION and "took the chair at a crucial meeting of the Nature Reserves Investigation Committee (NRIC) on 23rd October 1945 called to consider the awkward position which had arisen by the action taken by the Minister of Town and Country Planning in ignoring the existence of the Committee (the NRIC) and appointing a Wild Life Special Committee with much the same objective. He lent his great influence to the dignified course which was adopted, namely to place the results of the natural history survey of England and Wales, which had just been completed, unreservedly at the disposal of the new Committee, although it was realised that they would not receive the full recognition for their work".[113]

As President, he also took the chair at the first Official Luncheon after the Second World War in 1946. In paying tribute to him at the time of his death in 1952, the Society considered it "indeed fortunate that during the closing years of the war and the difficult years which followed its conclusion that its destiny was in such sure hands".[114]

MANNING, PROFESSOR AUBREY

The Society's eleventh PRESIDENT, Aubrey Manning, was educated at University College, London and Merton College, Oxford where he studied animal behaviour under Niko Tinbergen. After two years of National Service in the Royal Artillery, he joined the University of Edinburgh as an Assistant Lecturer in Zoology, rising to become Professor of Natural History before his retirement in 1997, when he became Professor Emeritus.

He was Chairman of the SCOTTISH TRUST between 1990 and 1996, a member of the Society's Executive Committee from December 1991 to 1998 and the Society's President between 2005 and 2010.

Manning's main research and teaching interests were in animal behaviour, its development and evolution and he is the author of the introductory text book on the subject, *An Introduction to Animal Behaviour*, which has appeared in several editions and languages. High profile work with radio and TV in recent years inspired Manning to have a new interest in the earth sciences and the way in which they integrate with the life sciences. It also led him to take various initiatives to help the public's understanding of science in general – not just better communication of the findings of science but also a true appreciation of science as part of our culture.

While President, Manning was Chairman of the Society's newly-formed STRATEGIC DEVELOPMENT FUND. It was in this role that the unique human qualities, insight and humour, that he brought to the movement, could be seen most clearly. His public profile, knowledge and kinship with The Wildlife Trusts, coupled with his thoughtful and impartial contributions to debates on the movement's future, gave it the confidence to move forward during a period of unparalleled reform.

Aubrey Manning

MARINE CONSERVATION

As an island nation, it is tragic that we have allowed one of our most precious natural assets – our marine environment – to be over-exploited and neglected. For so many, it has been a world largely out of sight and, consequently, out of mind. The seaside has always been popular, but how few of us when walking a coastal path or contemplating the lapping of waves on the shore, appreciate how much of our lives depend on the sea in all its complexity. We have allowed precious seabed habitats to be destroyed and fish stocks to be devastated, paying little attention to the long-term impact.

For much of the 20th century, the conservation movement was fully occupied with land-based conservation. The issues of development, transport, farming and pollution, for example, were all so much more immediate and to hand in our towns and countryside. Marine organisations, such as the International Whaling Commission established in 1946, were, like their pioneer land-based counterparts, particularly concerned with species and their welfare. The closest many organisations came to marine conservation was protecting the coastline. In 1965, for example, The National Trust launched its "remarkably successful Enterprise Neptune"[115] appeal to safeguard what it described as the remaining 900 miles of unspoiled but threatened coastline and by 1977, Wildlife Trusts managed 93 coastal nature reserves.

Until the 1970s, the Society's involvement in marine matters had been largely confined to responding to oil spills, such as the TORREY CANYON incident off Land's End in Cornwall in 1967 and the Amoco Cadiz in 1978. As Marren observes, "for a maritime nation, the wildlife of the sea had been strangely neglected. . . the sea has its own institutions, resistant to the bureaucratic ideas of land-lubbing conservationists. Conservation in the sea was about fish and fisheries, and that was the province of the agriculture departments".[116] In the 1970s, the Society was beginning to develop links with the Department of Environment. Close links with the Ministry of Agriculture, Fisheries and Food were still some way off.

Roger Mitchell, a member of the Conservancy's Chief Scientist's Team in the 1970s, accepted that the seashore and shallow coastal waters had not escaped man's modifying influence, but he was able to write in the Society's *Conservation Review* in 1977 that "marine communities around our coast are still in a relatively natural condition. Although in a small way man is now farming the sea, mariculture has a long way to go before it equals the extent and impact of agriculture; in the marine environment man is still

For an island nation, the marine environment remained off the conservation radar for too long

the hunter-gatherer with his house on terra firma".[117] Slowly but surely, however, demands on our seas grew, widened and intensified.

Mitchell's article was calculated to stimulate more support for marine conservation, not least within the Conservancy itself. It was inspired by a number of local marine projects and coincided with the launch of an international marine campaign, 'The Seas Must Live', by the WWF, backed by the International Union for the Conservation of Nature (IUCN). This aimed to raise funds for an ambitious IUCN marine programme. The article was also prompted by two events in particular, the decision by the British Sub-Aqua Club and *Triton* magazine to declare 1977 Underwater Conservation Year (UCY 77) – the Society was an enthusiastic founder member of its organising committee – and the supposedly imminent publication of a report by a joint Natural Environment Research Council (NERC) and Conservancy Working Party on marine nature conservation.

In the event, the Working Party's report, *Nature Conservation in the Marine Environment*, was not signed-off until 1979, hastened by calls in the House of Lords during the passage of the Wildlife and Countryside Bill for better protection of the marine environment. The report described Britain's marine environment and the threats it faced, and recommended new laws to establish marine nature reserves. At the time, the Conservancy had no power to declare reserves below mean low-water mark. The Conservancy's Chairman, Professor Fred Holliday, commented that "modern technology is now starting

to make its mark on, and in, the seas and it is essential that Government, backed by British scientists and naturalists – pre-eminent in the field of marine biology – initiates conservation measures to safeguard the quality of our marine environment and the opportunities for study and enjoyment by future generations".[118] The Working Party was itself the product of an earlier report by NERC, published in 1973, that had made recommendations that would not be out of place today. More research should be undertaken on threatened habitats and species; data recording schemes should be made compatible; there should be increased efforts to control collecting; and the legal position for the establishment of sub-tidal reserves should be explored further. It also proposed that a follow-up group should review developments and advise on threats.

The immediate priority in these early years was to find out more about what was living where and why, and to protect some of the best areas. The Conservancy had initiated selective surveys and UCY 77 had marked the arrival of a new breed of naturalist – interested divers. They were encouraged to take part in a series of projects that increased their awareness and collected useful biological data at the same time. Indeed, it was this growing concern by many divers for the quality of their environment that had led to UCY 77 in the first place.

In 1979, partly on the back of UCY 77, the decision was taken to form an Underwater Conservation Society (UCS). Four years later it was already well-established, with around 600 members. In November 1983, it changed its name to the Marine Conservation Society (MCS) and applied for charitable status. Its Project Coordinator was Dr Bob Earll.

A number of founding members of Trusts were marine scientists, but the DORSET TRUST was among the first Trusts to take a serious look at its marine environment in 1975. The Trust assessed its inter-tidal zone and made recommendations for the establishment of reserves and then, with the Conservancy and its County Council, it surveyed some of its sub-littoral areas. By 1981, Trusts were involved with at least four voluntary marine nature reserves. The first was in the waters around Skomer Island (managed by the WEST WALES TRUST) where a management plan had been agreed by interested parties in 1976. The second was established at Purbeck in 1978. It consisted of an area east of Lulworth Cove, including Kimmeridge Bay, where the Dorset Trust employed a warden from 1980.

Sarah Welton, 1980 – the first marine warden at Kimmeridge, Dorset

The third reserve was a marine conservation area at Wembury on the south Devon coast, established in 1981. Here the DEVON TRUST worked with Fort Bovisand Underwater Centre, the Underwater Conservation Society and The National Trust to create an area where "groups and individuals would be encouraged

Broad-clawed porcelain crab, Strangford Lough – one of seven marine nature reserves proposed in the early 1980s

to conform to codes of conduct appropriate to their activity".[119] The fourth reserve was at St Abbs Head, the southern-most peninsula on the east coast of Scotland, where the SCOTTISH TRUST with The National Trust for Scotland managed the coastal reserve. The Trust was also involved, with many other interested parties, in voluntary arrangements for controlling access to the surrounding waters.

In 1981, "the Government under pressure and resisting all the way",[120] accepted an amendment by Lord Craigton to the Wildlife and Countryside Bill which became Section 36 and 37 of the final Wildlife and Countryside Act 1981. These sections enabled the declaration of Marine Nature Reserves within the three-mile limit of territorial waters and the making of bye-laws. The Conservancy drew up a list of seven potential sites – the waters around the islands of Lundy (the Devon Trust had suggested that the island become a marine

nature reserve as early as 1969), Skomer, Bardsey and the Isles of Scilly, the Menai Strait in North Wales, Loch Sween in Argyll in Scotland and Strangford Lough in Northern Ireland. In the event, only Lundy (1986), Skomer (1990) and Strangford Lough (1995) were ever designated. The problem was that the Conservancy had to secure agreement

of *all* interested parties before applying to the Secretary of State to designate a Marine Nature Reserve. This often proved too difficult. There was also no power to override any existing use on the site.

There was "a growing awareness of the need for increasing involvement in marine conservation".[121] But it was still patchy.

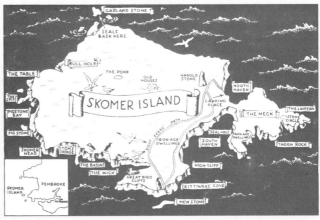

Map of Skomer Island from a 1970s Trust guide. A management plan for a voluntary marine nature reserve was agreed in 1976 and it was eventually designated a statutory marine nature reserve in 1990

In September 1983, the Society held its first marine seminar for the Trusts at the Natural History Museum in London to which representatives of the UCS and the Conservancy were also invited. There were presentations from Roger Mitchell (Conservancy), Bob Earll (UCS), John Hawthorne (DORSET TRUST) and Roger Burrows (CORNWALL TRUST). The afternoon session, chaired by David Bodger, discussed the way forward under three headings: site identification, site and species protection and cooperation. For the Society, Tim Sands stressed the need to avoid some of the mistakes made in land-based conservation. It would "not be easy and it seemed likely that as with terrestrial sites the voluntary organisations would have to lead the way".[122] Here were the first signs of a concerted, collective commitment by the Trust movement to marine conservation.

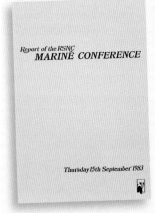

Report of the first all-Trust marine conservation conference, London, 1983

In 1984, in a not unconnected move, NATURAL WORLD carried an article bemoaning the lack of progress more generally. The limitations in the law and the meagre resources being put into marine conservation by the

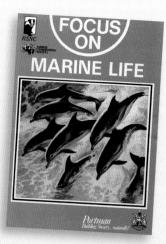

Promoting marine conservation – a 1985 leaflet

Conservancy were highlighted, but the voluntary sector did not escape criticism. Marine conservation remained a peripheral interest for most organisations – the Cinderella of nature conservation. The Government was being pressed to provide more money but, a year later, the Conservancy's spending on marine conservation was actually lower in percentage terms. There was also an early recognition that the focus of activity was too narrow. "Marine conservation. . . must cater for fish stock and habitat conservation, local use and enjoyment, fishing, shipping and mining use, as well as for science and education. It may sound a daunting task, but once we take the plunge we will never regret it."[123]

In 1985, frustrated by the endless succession of disappointments and delays, the Society united with the WWF and the MCS to mount a summer-long Marine Life Campaign to turn the tide on marine conservation. The Society rolled out a six-point action plan: a demand for higher priority to be given to marine conservation by the Government and the Conservancy, including strengthening of the law and the declaration of a national Marine

Nature Reserve within six months; encouragement for an improved dialogue between fishermen and other groups; and the launch of Watch's Project Coast Guard (WILDLIFE WATCH). A new *Focus on Marine Life* poster and leaflet, sponsored by the Portman Building Society, was distributed as part of the campaign. These became symbols of the support for marine conservation that was building in the Society and the Trusts. The MCS produced a *Coastal Directory*, funded by WWF, listing areas important for marine life, "a much needed reference work. . . especially in the absence of NCC's Marine Conservation Review".[124] The campaign was actively supported by David Clark, MP for South Shields. He proposed a clause to tighten up the legislation for Marine Nature Reserves in his Wildlife & Countryside (Amendment) Bill but this was rejected by the Government. Undaunted, Clark convened a meeting between conservation and fishing interests designed to help to try to resolve the differences between the two groups.

The Conservancy signalled its intention to begin a more systematic approach to surveying shallow water marine habitats in 1987. The survey would be based, not only on existing surveys by institutions and diver-naturalists, but also on new surveys of certain hot-spots carried out by the Conservancy's own team. Described by Marren as "arguably. . . the last significant, fundamental research commissioned and carried out by a British nature conservation agency",[125] a series of regional reports for each of the Marine Nature Conservation Review's 15 coastal sectors appeared at intervals up to 2000.

Meanwhile, although the number of Trusts active in marine conservation remained limited, impressive work was underway in Ulster and Scotland, in Hampshire and the Isle of Wight and in the West Country, where the Trusts in Cornwall, Devon and Dorset continued to drive forward the marine conservation agenda. Indeed, in 1987, the DEVON TRUST had appointed Joan Edwards as the movement's first full-time Marine Conservation Officer.

By the early 1990s, the number of coastal reserves had increased to 119 and covered 30,000 acres but terrestrial conservation issues dominated the Trusts' agendas and was a constant call on hard-pressed resources. Those Trusts that wanted to extend their work beyond the shoreline and go the extra nautical mile often lacked the necessary staff expertise and funding to bring it about.

An increasing number of Trusts now appreciated the seriousness of the situation. In June 1992, nine years after the seminar at the Natural History Museum in London, the Society's Conservation Sub-Committee reported that "in view of growing concern over issues affecting the marine environment, a meeting of representatives from coastal Wildlife Trusts had been held to discuss the potential for Partnership action on marine and coastal issues".[126] The movement should aim to develop not just a coastal, but a marine, role in future. There was a need for a national marine officer and regional staff – there was an initial target of 12 regional posts – and it was agreed to look for funding and to prepare a marine policy.
In 1993, the Devon Trust's Joan Edwards was the first-ever environment representative on a MAFF Sea Fisheries Committee; a year later she was employed by the Society in a part-time capacity and in 1996 as its first, full-time Marine Officer.

In 1995, at the Conservation Conference in Exeter, Edwards organised a workshop with Professor Phillip Nicholls and the ULSTER TRUST's David Erwin at which it was acknowledged formally for the first time that the Society and Trusts had a distinct role to play in protecting the marine environment. Their input to future marine conservation campaigning could make a real difference.

It was never the intention to work in isolation. Indeed, at midnight on Valentine's Day in February 1996, the Society and Trusts were able to play a confident and prominent part in the response by a range of

John Prescott MP joins the campaign to save our seas, 1995

conservation organisations to the third largest crude oil spill in the world to date – the *Sea Empress* oil tanker disaster. The response was based on experience gained during the *Rosebay* incident in 1992, when the Devon Trust had been part of the Emergency Planning Committee for the first time. On that occasion it was able to advise, for example, on where not to dump 'captured' oil. It provided a test run for the *Sea Empress*. Afterwards, The Wildlife Trusts' Sea Empress Disaster Fund raised £35,000 and this money was used to support the Dyfed Trust's post-incident scientific monitoring.

In June 1996, a Joint Marine Programme (JMP) was agreed between the Society and the WWF. The decision to form a partnership owed much to the working relationship, and indeed friendship, that existed between both Edwards and Sîan Pullen (WWF) and between Tim Sands and Chris Tydeman (WWF). This productive partnership would last until 2002 and resulted in more than 50 joint technical briefings, several joint responses to Government consultations and Select Committee inquiries and the strengthening of the Wildlife Trusts' network of regional marine officers.

Basking shark

Damage to the marine environment, increasing activity by the voluntary sector and growing public awareness of the country's maritime heritage meant the Government had to address some of the more pressing issues.

A number of policies came into effect in the 1990s as a result of, for example, the Water Resources Act 1991, the Transport and Works Act 1992, various Merchant Shipping regulations and offshore regulations. All these placed varying degrees of responsibility for the marine environment on relevant bodies, including the need to take account of nature conservation when carrying out their functions. The Sea Fisheries (Wildlife Conservation) Act 1992, for example, meant that Sea Fisheries Committees (the managers of inshore fisheries) now had a duty to take account of the effects of fishing on the marine environment and were encouraged to elect an environmental advisor on each Committee.

In 1998, the Convention for the Protection of the Marine Environment of the North-East Atlantic (OSPAR Convention) came into force, providing a framework for the management of the north-east Atlantic maritime environment. With strategies to address biodiversity protection, marine pollution reduction and offshore developments, contracting parties were now required to "take all possible steps to prevent and eliminate pollution and. . . take the necessary measures to protect the maritime area against the adverse effects of human activities, so as to safeguard human health and to conserve marine ecosystems and, when practicable, restore marine areas which have been adversely affected".[127] The first

Quality Status Report for the whole of the north-east Atlantic was published in 2000 and a new Annex to the Convention, focusing on the protection of biodiversity and ecosystems, came into effect the same year.

In addition, the transposition of the 1992 European Union's Habitats Directive, with its requirement to protect a UK suite of sites of European importance – Natura 2000 sites – provided the potential for the most comprehensive legislation to date for the conservation of marine sites.

In 1999, the publication of Marine Biodiversity Action Plans (BAPs), as part of the Government's response to the United Nation's Convention on Biological Diversity (BIODIVERSITY ACTION PLANNING), drew on the growth in information and understanding of the marine environment and provided further focus on the need to protect marine biodiversity. At the time, there were high hopes that these initiatives would result in real improvements. But, in the early days of the BAP process, those with expertise in the marine environment had been under-represented and the outcome had suffered as a result. In the case of the EU Habitats Directive, the majority of UK marine habitats were not represented or eligible due to the classification system favouring Mediterranean habitats. Analysis showed that, although the Habitats and Bird Directives were helping, 40 per cent of marine habitats and species identified in the BAPs were afforded no legal protection. Even by 2008, only two per cent of the UK's marine area was in the Natura 2000 Network and most sites were hugging the coastline. If anything, the Directives and BAPs placed an even sharper focus on the need for a more comprehensive framework for marine conservation, including offshore marine protected areas that conserved

a wider range of species and habitats, out to sea. Without these measures they were never going to be effective.

There were other problems. For example, the 1997 European Community's Directive on Environmental Assessment required a full Environmental Impact Assessment (EIA) for any major development project. But EIAs were for single developments, taking insufficient account of cumulative effects and, moreover, they did not apply to fishing activity.

Most policies and regulations governing the marine environment arose out of the UK's responsibilities under international agreements. Many of the resulting provisions were extremely complex and disjointed and could be largely ignored.

Below low-water mark there was no planning system to control development. The management and consenting regimes for potentially damaging activities were largely sectoral, and environmental considerations were incidental to the main purposes and powers of the bodies involved.

Activities in UK waters were certainly regulated, but the measures that did exist had developed in an *ad hoc* way, lacking a systematic or coordinated approach. There was also no coordination of devolved and non-devolved matters. As a result, the marine environment remained vulnerable and inadequately protected.

The end of the century saw the voluntary sector, including The Wildlife Trusts, heavily committed to its terrestrial campaign for improved protection for SSSIs. The campaign had been long and exhausting, but culminated with the granting of Royal Assent to the Countryside & Rights of Way Act 2000. After a surprisingly short period to draw breath, the non-governmental sector, including The Wildlife Trusts, began to focus in earnest on its next major legislative challenge – the protection of the marine environment. What it was proposing was a single Government statement on the marine environment that provided a national vision and strategic framework. This could draw together the responsibilities of a wide range of Government Departments, including the Department of Environment, Transport and Rural Affairs, the Ministry of Agriculture, Fisheries and Food, the Department of Trade and Industry and the Ministry of Defence.

One of the first things to do was to create some urgency within Government. Although the Labour Party's General Election manifesto of June 2001 had pledged action on the marine environment, and Environment Minister, Michael Meacher, had confirmed his personal commitment to the need for a Marine Act, there was no political timetable, and no move by the Government to establish a bill team. In July, the Department of Environment presented its long-awaited *Review of Marine Nature Conservation*. It concluded that "action is required to address nature conservation in the marine environment. . . and consideration of wider marine management is crucial".[128] The Wildlife Trusts had worked closely with the review panel, both in its own right, but also as part of Wildlife and Countryside Link (WILDLIFE LINK). The message now from the non-governmental sector was that the Government should undertake further preparatory work for new legislation, without delay. It needed well-thought-out policies to present to the North Sea Ministerial Conference and to the Rio +10 Meeting in South Africa, both in 2002, at the OSPAR Ministerial Meeting in 2003 and to the

negotiations about to begin on reform of the European Union's Common Fisheries Policy.

The handful of marine conservation bodies in Wildlife Link, including The Wildlife Trusts, had begun revisiting old marine files and, in a series of technical groups, to undertake a systematic re-examination of what they wished to see in a future Marine Bill. The review was comprehensive and included detailed proposals on spatial planning, site protection and later, led by The Wildlife Trusts, a review of Sea Fisheries. Joan Edwards worked for a time in the Policy Unit of No 10 on the latter issue. The Wildlife Trusts were active members of many of the various technical and campaigning groups, and a strong rapport developed amongst the relatively small band of individuals involved. At times the relationship could become strained, but in general the Wildlife Link model held fast and in the end delivered a robust and coherent campaigning stance. This was summarised in *The Last Living Wilderness: A Future for our Seas* – a joint report from the Wildlife Links covering England, Northern Ireland, Scotland and Wales. The Wildlife Trusts joined with WWF, the RSPB, the Whale and Dolphin Conservation Society and MCS in a high profile launch of this report in spring 2004.

In June 2002, The Wildlife Trusts had also gone on the offensive in its own right. It wanted to ensure that the Wildlife Link campaign included a more comprehensive framework for the care of the marine environment. In particular, The Wildlife Trusts wanted not just marine planning zones, but highly protected sites, to aid the recovery of marine species and habitats and as scientific benchmarks. On World Oceans Day, it launched a new Marine Campaign

at a Parliamentary reception and at events around the coast of the UK, particularly during the increasingly popular annual Marine Week in August. Two reports appeared, *Our Dying Seas* and *Marine Stewardship – Meeting the Challenge*. The new campaign involved a postcard petition. The objectives were realistic: to ensure the Government published a White Paper within three years outlining its legislative and policy programme for the management of the marine environment; to ensure marine legislation was introduced at Westminster in the next Parliament; and to secure commitments from the Parliaments and Assemblies in Wales, Scotland, Northern Ireland and the Isle of Man to develop nested legislation for their separate and devolved administrations.

In the first few years of the new millennium, The Wildlife Trusts made the securing of marine legislation one of its highest priorities. Its campaigning was founded on sound research and was persistent, focused and hard-hitting.

The Wildlife Trusts faced a long campaign. Progress was slow. In 2001, the Prime Minister committed the Labour Government to "new measures to improve the marine environment, including a series of Marine Stewardship reports".[129] The first of these, *Safeguarding our Seas*, jointly published a year later by the Government and devolved administrations, explained how the Government's vision for "clean, healthy, safe, productive and biologically diverse oceans and seas would be delivered by pursuing policies that promote sustainable development, integrated management, stakeholder involvement, robust science and the precautionary principle".[130] Later in 2002, the UK Government's proposals for delivering the vision were published in a consultation paper, the *Seas of Change*, and in 2005 this was followed by "the first integrated assessment of the *State of Our Seas – Charting Progress*".[131] The early draft of this latter document was heavily criticised by the voluntary sector, which saw it as a disappointing assessment of the problems. In March 2006, the Government published its initial proposals for a Marine Bill and, in March 2007, a White Paper – *A Sea Change: A Marine Bill White Paper* appeared, including a proposal to establish a new body – the Marine Management Organisation. Finally, the Government had prepared detailed proposals for a Marine Bill.

Meanwhile, in the absence of marine legislation, other approaches were being tried, including a successful 'no-take' zone off Lundy Island using sea fisheries' bye-laws. However, when this was tried at Skomer, the Sea Fisheries Committee voted against the idea. In Scotland, community effort

on the Isle of Arran successfully established Scotland's first statutory community marine reserve.

The Wildlife Trusts was prominent among those concerned about the by-catch of dolphins by pelagic pair trawlers, fishing mainly for sea bass. In 2007, it presented the EU Fisheries Commissioner with a 370,000-signature petition asking him to prevent dolphins dying in fishing nets. The British Government banned UK pelagic pair trawlers from such fishing within 12 miles of the coast in October 2005, and the EU eventually brought in regulations requiring 'pingers' (warning devices) to be fitted to nets in certain areas and by certain fisheries where the dangers of by-catch were greatest. The CORNWALL TRUST's one-time Chairman and Honorary Secretary, Nick Tregenza, was internationally recognized for his pioneering work with this technology and, in 2008, the Trust carried out a trial of pingers with local fishermen. This showed that they could be an effective deterrent against the by-catch of harbour porpoise.

A particularly hard-fought campaign was led by the DEVON

TRUST, on behalf of The Wildlife Trusts, to protect the Lyme Bay Reefs from scallop dredging. For 18 years, the Trust had championed the protection of the reefs and the campaign culminated in their legal protection in 2008. This dogged and sometimes acrimonious campaign was successful because it was based, not just on sound science, but on sound economic arguments as well. It would play an important part in establishing The Wildlife Trusts' credibility in the wider debate on the need for marine legislation.

Locally, the Trusts were increasingly engaged in marine conservation activities. Off the Isle of Man, for example, basking sharks were fitted with satellite tags to study their migration; in 2007, a tagged shark swam all the way to Canada. Marine awareness work in Wales was stretching from Bangor in the north to Fishguard in the west, featuring everything from interpretative centres to the monitoring of whales and dolphins by local communities. In Kent, the Trust's Shoresearch project was engaging hundreds of volunteers to record seashore habitats, and in Cumbria the Trust

Lobbying at Westminster in the run-up to the Marine Act

was working with cookery schools and celebrity chefs to promote sustainable seafood.

All this activity was reinforcing the movement's growing confidence and, in 2007, this was further enhanced by one of its most successful national campaigns to date. All across the country, Trusts collected 170,000 signatures on gold and silver 'fish-scales'. The completed 'petition fish' were paraded in one huge shoal in Parliament to demonstrate the mounting support for new marine legislation. It galvanized the Trust movement, with 44 Trusts taking part, sparked off much comment in Parliamentary debates and a petition fish could be seen on display in several Ministers' offices long after the event.

Just over a year later, in April 2008, the Government published its draft Marine Bill. This proposed a new planning system and included new powers to put in place marine

Top: Kelp forest – the Trusts campaigned for laws to protect marine habitats
Above: Many Trusts are involved with projects to collect data on marine wildlife

conservation areas, so as to develop a comprehensive network of Marine Protected Areas. There were also reforms to a range of marine, migratory and freshwater fisheries management arrangements, as well as new marine licensing rules.

The opportunity was also taken to bring forward proposals for greater access to the English coastline.

The all-important proposals to provide a network of Marine Protected Areas were included in the draft bill. For The Wildlife

Forever Changes – used for basking shark surveys from 2000 to 2008

Trusts, this was critical if they were to continue to support the Bill. It was now vital to campaign to maintain and strengthen the draft Bill as it passed through Parliament. Afterwards, it was also important for the movement to play its full part in the implementation of the new provisions, particularly the establishment of Marine Protected Areas.

It was an immensely busy and intense period for the Trust movement's national marine team. In England and Wales, the Marine and Coastal Access Act finally received Royal Assent on 12th November 2009 and, four months later, the SCOTTISH TRUST was able to welcome a Marine

(Scotland) Act 2010 which introduced equivalent legislation in Scotland. It had been a long road that marked the 'end of the beginning' as far as marine conservation in England, Scotland and Wales was concerned. In Northern Ireland, while there had been consultations on marine legislation, at the time of writing a Marine Bill was still awaited.

For The Wildlife Trusts, work on the new legislation had brought with it increased credibility within both Government and the wider marine community, and an acceptance internally that alongside The Wildlife Trusts' focus on A Living Landscape, the Living Seas vision was going to be of equal importance in the years to come.

MEADE-WALDO, EDMUND GB

Edmund Gustavus Bloomfield Meade-Waldo (1855–1934) was a member of the Society and its Executive Committee from the Society's inception in 1912. In 1918, he took over as acting joint HONORARY SECRETARY from WILLIAM ROBERT OGILVIE-GRANT who was unable to carry out his duties due to illness. In 1923, however, the Society created an additional Honorary Secretary post and for a little more than ten years Meade-Waldo joined HERBERT SMITH and LORD HENLEY as one of three joint Honorary Secretaries.

Born at Hever Castle (the castle was owned by the Meade-Waldo family between 1749 and 1903), Meade-Waldo became a well-known ornithologist and conservationist. He was, for example, a founder member of the Committee set up in 1903 to protect the RED KITE in Wales, a Council member of the RSPB, as well as a long-serving Chairman of its Watchers Committee. A notable figure in the British Ornithologists Union, he was its Vice President in 1923. He travelled the world and was one of the Society's representatives at the International Congress for the Protection of Nature held in Paris in 1923 and 1931. He accompanied Lord Crawford on a voyage around Africa in his research yacht, RYS Valhalla, in 1905–6, not for his prowess as an ornithologist, but "for the purpose of collecting insects".[132] He became famous as a result of this expedition for his sighting (with fellow naturalist, Michael Nicoll), "fourteen miles from the coast of Brazil near Para",[133] of "what has been so often reported, for want of a better name, as the 'great sea-serpent'".[134]

His many activities on behalf of the Society were greatly appreciated. He was frequently

Sketch of the 'sea-serpent' – seen by Edmund Meade-Waldo during a scientific expedition to South America in 1905

mentioned in despatches in the Society's minutes for his help with the compilation of the ROTHSCHILD LIST and as the Society's representative at meetings and conferences, and on field visits. For example, he made field visits to Ray Island in Essex and to Sutherland in 1913–14, to Wharfedale and Askham Bog in Yorkshire in 1922, to Easton Lodge Park and Woods at Dunmow in Essex and to Poole Harbour in 1924, and attended a conference on the future of the Farne Islands in 1923.

In a letter to Meade-Waldo's son in 1934, Herbert Smith expressed the Society's "deep regret at the death of so invaluable a member and the great loss which the Society had thereby suffered".[135]

MEADOWS CAMPAIGN

In June 1991, the Society built on the success of its WILDFLOWER WEEKS and decided to target one particularly wildflower-rich habitat – the country's vanishing meadows. A report, *Losing Ground, Vanishing Meadows,* highlighted the value of meadows and the terrible loss that had occurred. In the UK in 1984, 95 per cent of lowland grasslands on neutral soils (including herb-rich hay meadows) lacked significant wildlife interest and only three per cent remained undamaged by agricultural intensification. More than 85 Trust examples and case studies were quoted to demonstrate this loss. Ploughing and reseeding, the use of inorganic fertilisers and other chemicals, drainage, a switch to

silage production and overgrazing were all contributory factors. The campaign argued that the protection of the remaining fragments was possible.

Under an existing scheme, European funding was available for designated Environmentally Sensitive Areas (ESAs) designed 'to help conserve those areas of high landscape and/or wildlife value that were vulnerable to changes in farming practice'. The problem was that meadows were not confined to the designated ESA areas and were vulnerable outside these areas. Aware that the UK would assume the Presidency of the European Union in a year's time – and that a review of its ESA concept was underway – the Meadows Campaign called for the ESA principle to be extended to cover the whole of the UK and for European agricultural funding to be redistributed for environmentally-friendly farming generally.

In 1991, the Government established a Countryside Stewardship Scheme designed to improve the environmental value of farmland throughout England. Initially run by the Countryside Commission as a five-year pilot project, the scheme was taken over by the Ministry of Agriculture, Fisheries

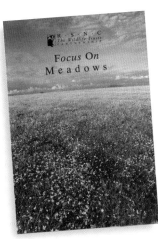

The Society's *Focus on Meadows* leaflet

and Food and expanded to include new landscapes and features (including whole farm plans) in the spring of 1996. Similar schemes were adopted in the rest of the country: the Countryside Management Scheme in Northern Ireland; the Countryside Premium Scheme (becoming Rural Stewardship Scheme) in Scotland; and Tir Cymen (becoming Tir Gofal) in Wales.

The Society produced a leaflet *Focus on Meadows* in January 1991; *CAP Reform – the Farmer, Countryside and Wildlife* in June 1992; collaborated with English Nature on the preparation of *The Lowland Grassland Management Handbook,* published in April 1994; and published *Pastures New – How to Create and Care for Wildflower Meadows,* with the support of British Coal Opencast, in July 1994.

MEATHOP MOSS

Meathop Moss, one of several raised mosses in the Morecambe Bay area, was the second reserve acquired by the Society. CHARLES ROTHSCHILD thought the site "one of the most interesting places in England" and was keen for it to become a nature reserve. His solicitors began negotiations for the site with the owner in 1916, but the latter died and the new owner refused to sell the Moss as a separate entity. The best arrangement that could be secured in 1920 was a lease of the site to the Society for 21 years at £25 per year; Rothschild provided the funds to cover the first seven years.

The reserve, comprising 122 acres, supported a rich bog flora and rare insects, including two rare butterflies, the large heath and the *masseyi* race of the silver-studded blue (extinct). Sadly, in the early years, the reserve deteriorated, partly because it was drying out through drainage of the surrounding land, and partly through fires. A colony of lesser black-backed gulls, which

Meathop Moss, Cumbria – one of the Society's earliest nature reserves, acquired in 1920

existed when the reserve was created, was destroyed by war-time egg collecting. The eggs were sold for cake-making. Even in 1937, the reserve was described as covered by scattered young Scots firs and birches "mostly eight feet in height".[136] Bracken was also invading the drier parts and, in 1945, it was noted that "thirty or forty years ago visitors were easily observed as they passed along the large fir trees, but now they could not be seen".[137] However, as Marren and Rothschild observed, "what the nature reserve did prevent was commercial peat cutting, which, during the post-war years, was consuming most of the former mosses of Morecambe Bay".[138] In 1949, the Management Committee reported that it was keeping a close eye on peat-cutting activities to make sure the reserve remained unaffected as "on the adjacent mosses large firms are at work, creating havoc".[139]

Over a number of years, from 1960 onwards, the reserve benefited from clearance parties organised, first through the National Conservation Corps of the newly-formed Council for Nature, and later by the local Trust.

The original lease was renewed for another 21 years from 1st January 1941 and a further 29 acres of the adjoining Catcrag Moss were leased in 1948. Meathop and Catcrag Mosses reserve was subsequently transferred from the Society to the

newly-created Lake District Naturalists' Trust (Cumbria) in 1963; the reserve was leased by the Trust direct from the owners, initially for a further 15 years. As a result of careful management by the Trust since then, many of the more sensitive plants and insects are still present today.

Note: A somewhat esoteric entry in the SPNR Handbook for 1937 gives guidance on the pronunciation of 'Meathop'. "It should be noted that the middle consonants do not form a diphthong, and the word is divided thus: Meat-hop."

MEDALS

The Society awards two medals: the *Christopher Cadbury Medal* (see also CHRISTOPHER CADBURY MEDAL CITATIONS) for services to the advancement of nature conservation in the British Islands by members of the Wildlife Trusts, and the *Charles Rothschild and Miriam Rothschild Medal* to an individual for outstanding achievements in the promotion, study, management or conservation of the natural environment.

As early as November 1987, CHRISTOPHER CADBURY was considering generously endowing a new annual award for members of the Wildlife Trusts. The annual award, to be known as the

Christopher Cadbury Medal, was finally established in 1989. A second medal was awarded every fifth year (later amended to every third year) to an individual full-, or part-time, employee of the Society or a Trust. The medal was designed and modelled by Jonathon Kingdon and cast by Rungwe Kingdon of Pangolin Editions in Chalfont, Gloucestershire. The first Cadbury medal was awarded to TED SMITH in 1990 and the first Cadbury staff medal to Tim Sands in 1994.

The idea of a Rothschild medal was first mooted by CHAIRMAN OF COUNCIL, PETER SCHOFIELD, in 2000. But it was not until 2005, at the time of MIRIAM ROTHSCHILD's death, that the idea once again saw the light of day. In 2006, Miriam's daughter, Charlotte Lane, made a generous donation towards its production, and the Royal Mint was commissioned to develop the design and to undertake its production. The medal was launched at a special dinner – attended by members of the Rothschild family – held in the Inner Temple, London on 30th April 2008. The first recipient was the environmental campaigner, Tony Juniper, who received his medal in November 2009 at the celebration of the BERKSHIRE, BUCKINGHAMSHIRE AND OXFORDSHIRE TRUST's 50th anniversary.

The Charles Rothschild and Miriam Rothschild medal (left) – wildlife associated with the family adorns the medal. The Christopher Cadbury medal (right), first awarded in 1990

MEMBERSHIP FIGURES, TRUSTS'

The Society had Associate Members. In 1914, official records show that there were 206 such members, by 1952 there were 417 of which 25.6 per cent came from the London area and 83.4 per cent from England. By 1969 there were 444 members. By resolution of the Executive Committee held on 27th February 1969, Associate Membership was offered to all members of the Trusts in return for a capitation fee of one shilling per member, paid by their Trust. As a result, membership of the Society rose to about 40,000. This category of membership was, however, abolished under the Society's Royal Charter granted in 1976. Trust collective membership records began in 1956.

1956	1,344
1957	1,540
1958	1,750
1959	2,095
1960	3,006
1961	5,179
1962	9,741
1963	13,932
1964	17,517
1965	20,960
1966	24,575
1967	28,812
1968	35,087
1969	40,000
1970	55,724
1971	63,883
1972	74,815
1973	84,412
1974	97,189
1975	100,660
1976	111,239
1977	115,407

The figures (at 31st December) between 1956 and 1977 are taken from the Society's Nature Reserves' Study.

1978	123,514
1979	128,994

1980	137,562
1981	142,532
1982	145,169
1983	155,106
1984	161,588
1985	165,500
1986	180,000
1987	184,000
1988	204,000
1989	212,000

The figures between 1978 and 1989 are based on the most frequently quoted figure (usually recorded in December of the year in question) in annual reports and other documents.

1990	228,000*
1991	250,000**
1992	250,000**
1993	250,000**
1994	222,000***
1995	225,000
1996	240,000
1997	271,071
1998	313,000
1999	320,000
2000	343,000
2001	382,000
2002	413,434
2003	440,445
2004	530,000
2005	588,958
2006	657,032
2007	726,654
2008	765,109
2009	791,000
2010	806,574
2011	812,710

The figures between 1994 and the present (recorded on 31st March each year) are from an official database updated annually by the Society.

* In December 2001 the Director General's Newsletter quotes a figure of 228,000 for 1990
** No new counts taken
*** A new count that adjusted the previous three years' estimates

MERGER PROPOSALS

In 1969, a 'gang of four' – WALTER LANE, David Lowe, Ralph Verney and Bill Eggeling – were appointed by the Society and the RSPB to make proposals for the merger of the two organisations (see Chapter 4 for more details). They produced a paper entitled *A New Look at the Nature Conservation Movement*. Central to their findings were eight points of principle:

1. Creation of a single new organisation built on the complementary strengths of existing bodies.
2. Organisation of a new body to be two tier on a central and county basis with the county bodies to continue as separate legal entities with full internal autonomy, but as an integral part of the new body accepting obligations in regard to national policy.
3. Membership to be basically of the whole organisation including full membership of a local Trust and a say in central affairs for all members. Membership to include access to reserves in other counties and, possibly, other additional benefits, such as a magazine on payment of a supplement.
4. Council to be elected on a national and local basis. Half elected by national ballot of all members, half appointed as representatives of each Trust. For an initial three-year period national half to be appointed by outgoing RSPB Council.
5. Property to be acquired by the central body or local Trust by agreement. The ownership of present reserves to remain unchanged except for transfer of RSPB and SPNR reserves to new central body.
6. Management of reserves to be primarily on a voluntary basis at local level with support of paid staff. Reserves of more than local importance to be managed to a centrally approved plan.

7. Clear staff structure to be devised for central body. Local staff to be controlled by county body.

8. Subscription structure and level to be such that, on amalgamation, the income therefrom will be available for central and local purposes and will be maintained, at least at existing level. Division of income between central and local bodies to be changeable within protected limits.

An alternative proposal

In February 1969, Sir Landsborough Thomson, Chairman of the Council for Nature (previously President 1964–68) put forward his own merger plan designed to bring together the Society, the RSPB and the Council for Nature within a new organisation called the Royal Society for Bird Protection and Nature Conservation or RSPBNC. . . for short! The publication of Sir Landsborough's open memorandum, *Plan for a Merger*, coincided with a crisis at the Council for Nature with the departure of both its Secretary and Assistant Secretary. The RSPB, with the help of the Society, had been forced to step in and hold the administrative fort until further notice.

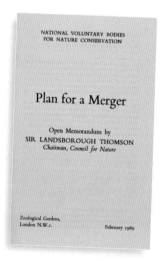

But Sir Landsborough's proposal was considered both "impracticable and inadequate"[141] by the Society. The Society responded by drafting a policy statement on the future of the voluntary nature conservation movement that recognised the need in the long term for a new organisation with a proper balance between local and national interests. In the meantime, the Society's view was that the newly-constituted Council for Nature should be given a chance to work. By December, Sir Landsborough wrote in *Habitat*, the Council for Nature's newsletter, conceding that, while his proposal had received many letters of support and very few expressing dissent, there had been some criticism of details of his plan and, in any case, it was "only one possible formula among others".[142] He was putting a brave face on the situation and, diplomatically, he concluded the article by quoting the Society's policy statement: "The bodies most concerned should establish a clear, long-term objective and make a declaration about it. Meantime the recently re-constituted Council for Nature, to which the Society and other bodies are giving full support, must be made to function. As an expression of intent of the various bodies to work together and to plan for the future, the Council has a valuable contribution to make".[143]

Discussions about a possible merger between the Society and the RSPB, started in 1966, were finally abandoned in 1973. The Council for Nature was disbanded in 1979 on the formation of WILDLIFE LINK.

MINERALS PLANNING

In 1990, Carmel Woods (Coedydd Carmel SSSI) in Dyfed came under threat from the firm Alfred McAlpine which planned to extend its limestone quarrying activities by reviving an old permission for mineral working, known as an Interim Development Order (IDO). The site became something of a *cause célèbre*, exposing the inadequacies of IDOs in a modern planning system.

The ash woods, lying on a limestone ridge, supported more than 100 species of plants, including mezereon, lily of the valley, herb-Paris and the parasitic yellow bird's nest orchid. Pearl-bordered fritillary butterflies could be glimpsed in the sunny clearings, a rare harvest-spider found in the deep shade and the caves were inhabited by greater horseshoe bats. The woods were not only nationally-important for wildlife, but also steeped in ancient mystery and legend. Sleeping knights were said to lie in the limestone caves at 'Druid's Crag' and, in one version of the legend, it was King Arthur himself with his knights that slumbered there in enchanted sleep!

Carmel Woods was subject to an IDO granted in 1948 that pre-dated – and therefore overruled – the designation of the woods as an SSSI. Many IDOs had been granted between 1946 and 1950 with the intention of putting Britain back on its feet and with little or no thought for the environment. Many IDOs covered important wildlife sites and, with an expanding road programme, there was a fear that more of these long-standing consents to extract aggregates would be revived.

McAlpine and Dyfed County Council disputed the area covered by the IDO and the Society and the DYFED TRUST launched a special fund to challenge the validity of IDO permissions.

The case led the Society to launch a series of *Losing Ground–Gaining Ground* reports on mineral extraction and wildlife. *Skeletons in the Cupboard* (1991) looked at further cases of wildlife sites threatened by IDOs, with Trust examples from 14 counties. *Leaving the Stone Age* (1992) looked at the threat to the environment from aggregate use – the forecast in 1992 was for a doubling of the demand for crushed rock, sand and gravel (aggregates) by 2011. *Blasts from the Past* (1992) examined the legacy left by old planning permissions granted in the 1940s, 1950s and 1960s "when care for the environment was not regarded as an important issue".[144] These old quarrying laws threatened 56 SSSIs.

The Society met the Junior Minister at the Department of Environment after the publication of *Blasts from the Past* and the issue was debated in Parliament. After this, the Department agreed to consult over new proposals on IDOs and to review planning guidance on aggregates.

In early 1993, the Society was responsible for the coordination of the Carmel Woods campaign. There was a Public Inquiry later in the year, but it was not until November 1995 that the woods were finally saved from quarrying.

N

NAMES OF THE SOCIETY

Society for the Promotion of Nature Reserves (SPNR)   1912–1976

Society for the Promotion of Nature Conservation (SPNC)   1976–1981

Royal Society for Nature Conservation (RSNC)   1981–2004

Royal Society of Wildlife Trusts (RSWT)   2004–

NAMES OF THE TRUSTS

Most of the early Trusts were called *Naturalists' Trusts*. Of the 38 Trusts listed in the Society's 1969 HANDBOOK, 20 had this title. The most popular alternative name (13) was *Trust for Nature Conservation* or *Nature Conservation Trust*. The only *Wildlife Trust* was the SCOTTISH WILDLIFE TRUST.

The use of the name *Naturalists' Trust* began to be viewed by some as unhelpful. It could imply that it was a Trust for the students and lovers of nature that excluded conservationists and, perhaps more worryingly, those who were anything less than experts. The name could, and quite often was, confused with the naturists' movement. One individual was asked 'does that mean you go around starkers?' and Trusts received telephone inquiries about where to go sunbathing. There were early attempts to standardise Trust names and to incorporate the words *Wildlife Trusts* into the Society's title. However, it was not until the 1990s and the introduction of the modern logo (LOGOS) in 1994 that the name *Wildlife Trust* began to be widely adopted. By the new millennium, all but one Trust had either legally changed their name to become a *Wildlife Trust* or had adopted this name for marketing purposes.

NATIONAL NATURE WEEKS

National Nature Week, organised by the Council for Nature in May 1963, was the "first time that a very large number of organisations interested in the conservation of nature had got together on a joint project, and had achieved such success".[145] The Trusts played a prominent part, experimenting with new methods of interpretation – "the nature trail, the field museum or information centre and the mobile exhibition".[146] Hundreds of displays and events were organised around the country; the largest exhibition, sponsored to the tune of £10,000 by *The Observer* newspaper, was opened by Sir Keith Joseph – the Minister of Housing and Local Government – at the Royal Horticultural Society's Halls in London. It was while visiting this exhibition that HRH The Duke of Edinburgh challenged MAX NICHOLSON and others to capitalise on the interest that had been shown and to organise an early conference to bring together the major national organisations. Remarkably, the first such conference was organised within six months and held in London under the theme of THE COUNTRYSIDE IN 1970. Further conferences under the same title were held in 1965 and 1970.

National Nature Week stimulated a number of high profile, spin-off activities designed to popularise natural history and its conservation, and to show what might be achieved

by the wildlife community "if supported by an informed public opinion".[147] For example, Penguin Books published *Wildlife in Britain* by Richard Fitter, in collaboration with the Council for Nature; The Post Office issued two commemorative postage stamps; and the 100th edition of the BBC's *Look* television programme was screened during the week itself. The BBC's Natural History Unit had been established in Bristol in 1957 and natural history programmes, such as *Look*, were attracting audiences of "anything up to six to seven million".[148]

National Nature Week proved immensely popular and was repeated again in 1966, when the exhibition at Alexandra Palace attracted 90,000 visitors – nearly twice as many as in 1963 – and 500,000 people took an active part in more than 500 events countrywide.

NATURAL WORLD

The Society's magazine – *Natural World* – available to all Trust members, was launched in April 1981 "with great enthusiasm"[149] by SIR DAVID ATTENBOROUGH on the Martini Terrace, New Zealand House in London with the support of Martini & Rossi. It has been published three times a year ever since; its 75th issue was published in the winter of 2005.

Getting *Natural World* off the ground was not easy. The first mention of a "commercial conservation magazine in association with the Society and Trusts"[150] was in November 1969 when Jon Tinker, editor of *Wildlife in the Countryside*, attended an Executive meeting. Later in the month it was decided not to pursue this idea, but to go ahead with an internal newsletter, *Conservation Review* (see below), which was published for the first time the following autumn.

However, ten years later, the Society's General Secretary,

FRANKLYN PERRING, believed passionately that a change was required. CONSERVATION REVIEW lacked space and was considered amateurish by some, unable to do justice to an organisation aspiring to be a leading national body. There was a strong contrary view that with the country and some Trusts in financial difficulty, the move was, at best, premature. Nevertheless, a review, involving further consultation with the Trusts and chaired by the forward-thinking and energetic Chairman of the Society's Education and Promotion Committee, Grenville ('Gren') Lucas, was put in place. Lucas, who was also active with the SURREY TRUST, was a botanist and conservationist working at the Royal Botanic Gardens Kew who went on to become Keeper of the Herbarium at Kew and Chairman of IUCN's Species Survival Commission.

There was sufficient support from Trusts for the Review Group to recommend options for a possible new magazine, and a 'green light' was given to proceed. Concurrently with the review process, Perring had met James Bishop, editor of the *Illustrated London News* (ILN). With the Honorary Treasurer, Andrew Ruck, and Tim Sands, he set about the task of negotiating a contract with Bishop and ILN that would, on the one hand minimise and ease Trusts into the additional costs and, on the other, provide the publishers with an adequate financial return.

In 1980, a contract between the Society and the Trusts was agreed. The Trusts would pay nothing for the first issue with contributions rising to 26 pence by issue four. An Editorial Board was established in 1981, with Lucas, David Robinson, Ruck and Sands as the Society's members. Robinson would serve on the Board for 26 years.

An editor, Linda Bennett, was employed and set about producing a dummy magazine – code named *Badger*. Producing a lively and professional magazine was relatively straightforward compared to the challenge of realising the aspirations of both the Trusts and the publisher, particularly early on. Bennett skilfully achieved both and would go on to oversee the development of the magazine, editing 51 issues.

When the time came to publish the first issue, there was one other matter still to resolve – the name of the magazine. The first choice was *Living World*, but the title was already in use, and the Board finally settled on *Natural World*. By the fourth issue, 37 of the 42 Trusts were taking the new magazine. A surplus was achieved on the *Natural World* account by the fifth issue and, as advertising increased from 12 pages at the beginning to 17 pages by the 25th issue, costs began to be subsidised and the publishers too were able to make a profit.

Over the years, *Natural World* has kept Trust members up to date with national and local news and with numerous national campaigns. In the process, it has frequently interviewed Government Ministers and has attracted important contributions from leading naturalists and conservationists. It featured work by famous artists, such as cartoonist, Ralph Steadman, and carried stories about the support given to the Society and Trusts by personalities as diverse as England cricketer, Geoffrey Boycott, comedians, Frankie Howard and Rory Bremner, and actress and politician, Glenda Jackson. As one of a small band of national wildlife magazines, it has enjoyed a large circulation and achieved the highest standards in publishing.

A gallery of *Natural World* covers from 1981–2011

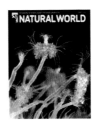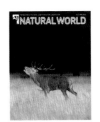
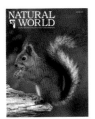
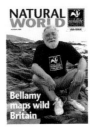
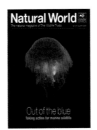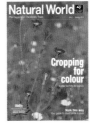

The magazine was awarded overall Best Environmental Charity Magazine in 2000 in a competition organised by *BBC Wildlife Magazine*.

Natural World has informed, challenged and entertained but, above all, it has been a vital mouthpiece for the movement. In general, *Natural World* has succeeded in capturing the environmental mood of the country and the changing fortunes and priorities of the movement.

In 1997, the Society gave notice to ILN for its contract to expire after the winter issue. After that, *Natural World* was published by River Publishing, EMAP Active Centre and Think Publishing. Since 2003, *Natural World* has been edited by Rupert Paul, whose background was in consumer magazines and who was an active supporter of his local Trust in Northamptonshire.

Around the turn of the millennium, a few Trusts had experimented by incorporating their own magazine into *Natural World*. By 2008, support was growing for a corollary of this approach – integrating *Natural World* into all local Trust magazines. In 2009, two Trusts piloted the idea and, in 2011, this was rolled out across the movement. A few Trusts opted for a stand-alone version of *Natural World*, reduced in size to 16 pages, and this version was also made available to national audiences. The main objectives for the changes were to reduce costs and the organisation's ecological footprint, as well as to better reflect the local/UK structure of the movement. The new approach was accompanied by growing use of other communications technology such as websites and mobile phone applications.

CONSERVATION REVIEW

Before *Natural World*, communication between the Society and the Trusts had been strengthened in 1970 with the publication of a twice-yearly newsletter – *Conservation Review*. It was the first newsletter to be made available free to all members of the Trusts – at the time numbering 55,000. Launched in monochrome, with a colour title-banner, it went to full colour in 1976 and, after 21 issues, was finally replaced by *Natural World* in autumn 1980. The first issues of *Conservation Review* cost 1.5p each, paid for from the Society's 10p per member levy on each Trust.

NATURE OF BRITAIN BOOKS

The first in a series of county-based books on the nature of Britain, *The Nature of Cornwall*, was published as a joint venture between the Society and Barracuda Books in August 1982. The final volume, *The Nature of Worcestershire*, was published in 1991.

Prior to 1982, the founder of Barracuda Books, Clive Birch, together with his friend David Robinson, the then Chairman of the Society's Education and Promotions Committee, had collaborated on a number of publishing ventures, for example *The Book of Louth* (1979) and *Lincolnshire Seaside* (1981). When the naturalist Rennie Bere and Marjorie and Philip Blamey suggested a paperback on Cornwall's wildlife, Birch consulted Robinson and the idea for a *Nature of Britain* series was born. It was an ambitious

A selection of titles from the *Nature of Britain* series

project that was fashioned by Birch and Robinson, but also required the services of one or more knowledgeable natural history writers to help drive forward each volume.

In 1991, after nine years, the offers of assistance from suitable authors dried up and the series came to a natural end. However, by this time, 12 volumes had been published covering Cornwall, Essex, West Wales, Derbyshire, Surrey, Hampshire and the Isle of Wight, Nottinghamshire, Central Wales, Northamptonshire, North Wales, Warwickshire and Worcestershire. Each volume was financed by pre-publication subscriptions.

The Society's Patron, HRH The Prince of Wales, wrote the foreword to the volume on Cornwall and the series won a European Conservation Foundation award in 1989.

NATURE PRESERVATION IN POST-WAR RECONSTRUCTION CONFERENCE

The Conference was convened by the Society in June 1941 to identify the nature conservation principles that should be adopted by the Government when planning the use of land after the war, including the need to protect the most important wildlife sites. Chairmen of the Conference were the Society's Presidents LORD ONSLOW (until May 1942) and LORD MACMILLAN and its Secretary was the Society's Honorary Secretary, HERBERT SMITH.

The first meeting was attended by: The Association of Municipal Corporations, British Association for the Advancement of Science, British Ecological Society, British Museum (Natural History), British Ornithologists Union, British Trust for Ornithology, County Councils Association, Geological Society of London, Linnean Society of London, Royal Entomological Society of London, Royal Society for the Protection of Birds, Society for the Preservation of the Fauna of the Empire, Society for the Promotion of Nature Reserves, Urban District Councils Association and the Zoological Society of London.

The Society issued the following reports on behalf of the Conference:

Conference on Nature Preservation in Post-War Reconstruction (Memorandum No 1) was published in November 1941 (500 copies). A second edition was published in September 1942 (1,000 copies).

Nature Preservation in Post-War Reconstruction (Conference Memorandum No 2) was published in July 1942.

The Conference established a Nature Reserves Investigation Committee (NRIC) in June 1942 to examine proposals for the establishment of nature reserves after the Second World War. The Chairman of the NRIC was

Sir Lawrence Chubb and its Secretary, HERBERT SMITH. The members were: G Dent, Capt C Diver, JCF Fryer, NB Kinnear, Prof WH Pearsall, Dr J Ramsbottom, Prof J Ritchie and Prof EJ Salisbury.

Members of the Geological Sub-Committee were: GF Herbert Smith (Chairman), SE Hollingworth, GH Mitchell, TH Whitehead, D Williams, and KP Oakley (Honorary Secretary).

The Society issued the following Reports on behalf of the Conference and NRIC:

Nature Conservation in Great Britain (Memorandum No 3) was published in March 1943 (1,000 copies). A second edition was published in May 1945 (1,000 copies).

Potential National Parks (Memorandum No 4) was published in August 1943 (500copies).

National Geological Reserves in England and Wales (Memorandum No 5) was published in September 1945 (1,000 copies). A second edition was published in November 1945 (1,000 copies).

National Nature Reserves and Conservation Areas in England and Wales (Memorandum No 6) was published in December 1945 (1,000 copies).

NATURE RESERVES

In 1957, MAX NICHOLSON was able to write "nature is the oldest thing on earth, but nature reserves are among the youngest. In Great Britain nature reserves have only just passed through the pioneer and experimental stage".[151]

In 1912, when CHARLES ROTHSCHILD decided to seek out the best places for wildlife and to create a Society to promote these areas as nature reserves – the Society for the Promotion of Nature Reserves (NAMES OF THE SOCIETY) – he was advancing a new concept "outside the mainstream of the nature preservation movement".[152] It would be another 20 to 30 years before his ideas found favour more widely.

Areas *had* been set aside for wildlife before. The concept was not exclusively the preserve of Rothschild's new Society. But previously, these reserves had been looked upon largely as game parks, refuges or sanctuaries where killing of wildlife was controlled or banned altogether.

St Cuthbert – a seventh century conservationist

St Cuthbert is often credited with the creation of the first effective wildlife refuge on the Farne Islands in the seventh century to

The six memoranda issued by the Conference

protect the eider duck, and the Norman kings set aside Royal Forests as game reserves. The New Forest, for example, was established by William the Conqueror in 1079 as a Royal hunting park. More recently, in the early 19th century, the eccentric Yorkshire landowner, Charles Waterton, was one of the first men in Britain to protect birds, other than game birds. From around 1817, he transformed his Walton Hall estate near Wakefield into a bird sanctuary. While he was happy to drain his own blood – he practiced self-venesection – he declined to drain his meadows! This was partly because he was too mean "to sink his capital in any new-fangled agricultural improvement",[153] but also because it "would have deprived the herons of an agreeable lounge and fertile feeding resort".[154] In 1821, he began to build a wall around his estate which took five years to complete at a cost of £10,000 to "guard against such intruders as foxes, badgers, poachers and bargees".[155]

By the beginning of the 20th century, The National Trust and the Society were acquiring sites as nature reserves. CHARLES ROTHSCHILD acquired a portion of Wicken Fen in Cambridgeshire (DONATIONS BEFORE THE SECOND WORLD WAR) in 1899 and donated it to The National Trust in 1901. He also helped in the acquisition of Blakeney Point in Norfolk in 1912 (see below). In 1910, he acquired a part of WOODWALTON FEN in Huntingdonshire and donated this to the Society in 1919. Other organisations were getting in on the act too. In 1913, for example, "the Cumberland Nature Reserves

Association and Carlisle Corporation designated the remnants of King's Moor as a reserve".[156] In 1930, the RSPB acquired its first reserve at Cheyne Court, Romney Marsh (it was subsequently sold in 1950) and in 1932 it announced the acquisition of its oldest extant reserves at Dungeness and East Wood.

But Charles Rothschild saw nature reserves as something more than simply refuges for species. He saw them as exemplars of the very best places for the whole complexity of nature and as a mechanism for defending these places against the development and changing land use that, even at the beginning of the 20th century, was starting to damage and destroy more and more natural habitats. Rothschild believed that reserves had so far been selected in an ad hoc way. To avoid wasting resources, it would be better to identify where the best sites were and to protect those sites first. Rothschild's legacy would lie not just in compiling the first list of potential nature reserves, but in striving for a more systematic approach to site selection.

Rothschild's daughter, MIRIAM ROTHSCHILD, was later to cite his concern at the lack of protection afforded to nesting terns by The National Trust at Blakeney Point in Norfolk, as the incident that had "convinced him that it was necessary to form a small society concerned exclusively with the promotion of nature reserves".[157] Blakeney Point had been acquired by Rothschild in 1912 from Lord Calthorpe's Trustees "as the result of the efforts of Professor FW Oliver of University College London, who led a public appeal for funds for its purchase".[158]

Rothschild's Society was extremely active in its first few years, especially in the two years before the First World War. By 1915, Rothschild and

his many friends and colleagues had compiled a 'shopping list' of 284 sites 'worthy of preservation' (ROTHSCHILD'S LIST). It included sites that were subsequently designated as National Nature Reserves, such as Hickling Broad in Norfolk and Blean Woods in Kent, but also sites, such as Adventurers' Fen in Cambridgeshire and the South Lancashire dunes, that were subsequently either wholly, or partly, destroyed. The Society handed over Rothschild's list to the Government's Board of Agriculture, but they appeared to make little use of the information.

After the Second World War, the Government set up Huxley's Wild Life Conservation Special Committee to progress nature conservation in the context of post-war 'reconstruction' and this led in turn to the establishment of a new agency, the Nature Conservancy (Conservancy), and the National Parks and Access to the Countryside Act 1949. Under this Act, the Conservancy could own or lease reserves itself or enter into a Nature Reserves Agreement allowing it to carry out wildlife management on otherwise private property. Local Authorities could also declare Local Nature Reserves (LNR) under the Act. The Conservancy was able to use the sites proposed by the Nature Reserves Investigation Committee (NRIC) – run under the auspices of the Society during the war – as the basis for its selection of statutory nature reserves in the 1950s. The NRIC, in its turn, had used the original Rothschild's list as an important source of information.

Among the Conservancy's first National Nature Reserves (NNRs), declared in 1953, were Holme Fen in Huntingdonshire, Kingley Vale in Sussex and Cavenham Heath in Suffolk. By 1975, 80 NNRs had been

Ted Smith (right) introducing Sir David Serpell at the declaration of Gait Barrows National Nature Reserve, 1977

declared and there were more than 350 in England, Scotland and Wales by 2009. The first LNRs, declared in 1952, were Aberlady Bay in East Lothian and Gibraltar Point in Lincolnshire. Only 40 LNRs had been declared by 1975 but there were more than 1,400 in England, Scotland and Wales by 2009. In Northern Ireland there are 49 NNRs and 17 Local Nature Reserves.

By the beginning of the Second World War, the Society was managing six nature reserves. In the late 1950s and early 1960s, the Society began to develop its role as the national association of the increasing number of local Wildlife Trusts. The Trusts had the management of nature reserves as one of their main priorities, and the Society began a programme of first leasing its properties to the Trusts and then transferring the freehold. The Trusts owned or managed 29 nature reserves in 1957 and this had increased to 2,240 in 2005

(NATURE RESERVE STATISTICS). The Wildlife Trusts' smallest reserve is Hethel Old Thorn in Norfolk, a 13th century hawthorn tree, and its largest reserve is Ben Mor Coigach in Wester Ross, Scotland, covering around 6,000 hectares.

In his concluding remarks in *Britain's Nature Reserves*, Max Nicholson wrote, "no doubt, however, the ordinary man and woman will look on them (nature reserves) first as places simply to enjoy and perhaps sometimes to be thankful for. Our aim must be, patiently and firmly, to hold our Nature Reserves in trust for both, but above all for the animals and plants which have nowhere else to go".[159]

Hethel Old Thorn in Norfolk, 1960. Overleaf: A selection of Trust nature reserves

Redgrave and Lopham Fen, Suffolk

Skomer Island, Pembrokeshire

Blue Bell Hill, Kent

East Chevington, Northumberland

Cemlyn, Angelsey

Beacon Hill, Gwent

Clattinger Farm, Wiltshire

Falls of Clyde, Lanarkshire

Gilfach Farm, Radnorshire

Dunsford Wood, Devon

Grafton Wood, Worcestershire

Huntcliff, Tees Valley

Kimmeridge, Dorset

College Lake, Buckinghamshire

Camley Street Natural Park, London

Ospreys at Rutland Water

Pamber Forest, Hampshire

Ballynahone Bog, Co Antrim

NATURE RESERVE STATISTICS

1923–26	3	186 ha
1927–32	3	194 ha
1933–34	4	195 ha
1935–38	5	203 ha
1939–40	6	267 ha
1941–47	7	298 ha
1948–53*	7	310 ha
1954–55	7	310 ha

The figures between 1923 and 1955 are for the Society's reserves only.

1955	(7) 23	(310 ha)	2,737 ha
1956	(8) 25	(342 ha)	2,780 ha
1957	(8) 29	(342 ha)	2,826 ha
1958	(8) 32	(342 ha)	2,899 ha
1959	(8) 36	(342 ha)	3,209 ha
1960	(8) 46	(342 ha)	3,564 ha
1961	(10**) 60	(345 ha)	3,974 ha
1962	(9) 72	(346 ha)	4,053 ha
1963	(8) 90	(264 ha)	4,412 ha
1964	(6) 137	(244 ha)	4,990 ha
1965	(6) 192	(244 ha)	6,225 ha
1966	(5) 251	(242 ha)	7,703 ha
1967	(5) 308	(242 ha)	10,788 ha
1968	(6) 382	(324 ha)	12,373 ha
1969	(6) 440	(361 ha)	13,282 ha
1970	(7) 547	(423 ha)	16,675 ha
1971	(7) 609	(473 ha)	17,488 ha
1972	(8) 699	(496 ha)	18,956 ha
1973	(6) 784	(471 ha)	20,966 ha
1974	(6) 859	(471 ha)	24,803 ha
1975	(8) 939	(6623 ha)	26,535 ha
1976	(8) 1012	(6623 ha)	29,577 ha
1977	1080		36,470 ha

The figures between 1955 and 1976 are for Trust reserves and are taken from the Society's Nature Reserves Study. The number of reserves owned by the Society is given in the brackets. The figure for 1977 includes the Society's reserves.

1978	1,144	42,233 ha
1979	1,205	42,375 ha
1980	1,282	43,980 ha

Figures between 1978 and 1980 are from the RSNC Office Manual.

1981	1,320	44,517 ha
1982	1,350	44,517 ha
1983	1,415	46,540 ha
1984	1,550	48,564 ha
1985	1,684	53,321 ha
1986	1,684	54,000 ha
1987	1,803	54,000 ha
1988	1,800	52,000 ha+
1989	2,000	52,000 ha+
1990	2,000	56,000 ha+
1991	1,997	52,150 ha
1992	2,000	57,000 ha+
1993	2,000	55,000 ha+
1994	Not available	
1995	Not available	
1996	Not available	
1997	2,300+	Not available
1998	2,300+	Not available
1999	2,300+	Not available

The figures between 1981 and 1999 are largely taken from Annual Reports but may have been adjusted in the light of data from other sources.

2000	2,300	74,000 ha
2001	2,498	75,635 ha
2002	2,561	82,200 ha
2003	2,392	72,000 ha
2004	2,393	80,000 ha
2005	2,240	83,121 ha
2006	2,275	73,299 ha
2007	2,204	85,285 ha
2008	2,527	92,312 ha
2009	2,282	93,409 ha
2010	2,299	90,936 ha
2011	2,259	91,820 ha

The figures between 2000 and the present (recorded on 31st March each year) are from the official data base updated annually by the Society. Totals do not always increase year-on-year because figures are corrected as new data on sites becomes available and because Trusts occasionally relinquish reserves.

* Figures for the Society's reserves between 1953 and 1976 continue to include Woodwalton Fen, leased to the Nature Conservancy in 1953
** The figure of 10 reserves in 1961 includes land acquired at Welcombe Mouth and then Marsland Mouth over a period; the area figures for this reserve are therefore estimated between 1961 and 1970
+ Estimated

NATURE RESERVE GUIDES

The Society's first handbook of nature reserves, edited by TED SMITH and published in 1982, listed a selection of the 1,250 nature reserves managed by the Society and the Wildlife Trusts. The handbook, with its distinctive 'bluebell' cover (photographed by the Society's HONORARY TREASURER, ANDREW RUCK), turned the spotlight on a staggering array of sites that could be enjoyed on a day visit, ranging from the 6,000 hectares of the magnificent mountainous reserve at Ben Mor Coigach in Wester Ross in Scotland and Skomer Island in South Wales – with its internationally-important seabird colonies – to the first Trust reserve at the Cley and Salthouse Marshes on the north Norfolk coast and the outstanding deciduous woodland at The Mens in Sussex. Each reserve was described briefly with details of its location, how to get to it and any special conditions for visiting.

It was to be 17 years before the handbook was updated by a new *Nature Reserves Guide*. This contained a description, general information and guidance for visitors and a map for each of 200 chosen sites. The guide, edited by Geoffrey Young, with a foreword from The Wildlife Trusts' PRESIDENT at the time, DAVID BELLAMY, was sponsored by BP Amoco and, like its predecessor, was on sale but also used for promotional purposes.

From 2005 onwards, the guide has been published as *Wildlife Walks* by Think Publishing.

**NATURE RESERVES OWNED BY
THE SOCIETY**

The Society has owned more than 20 nature reserves in the UK and four properties overseas since it was founded in 1912.

In the early years of the last century, the Society was responsible for a small portfolio of sites including, most importantly, WOODWALTON FEN in Cambridgeshire. However, in practice, their management relied heavily on enthusiastic individuals and local management committees. Once Trusts began forming in the 1960s, the Society recognised that it was more appropriate for them to take on the management of these reserves. The Trusts had the necessary skills and equipment on the ground and transferring these sites enabled the Society to concentrate on its new primary role of representing the Trusts' interests at the national level. The COWARD MEMORIAL RESERVES, for example, were leased to the CHESHIRE TRUST in 1963 and by 1968 the leasing programme on the rest was complete in all but a few cases. The management problems at Woodwalton Fen had been formidable and the Society had taken the decision in 1954 (before most Trusts had got off the ground) to lease this important reserve to the Conservancy. The transfer of the freehold of the Society's other properties came later, mainly taking place towards the end of the 1990s. The Society still retains the freehold of Woodwalton Fen.

The Society did get involved with new properties after 1960. Sometimes a Trust needed additional funds to complete a purchase, as was the case at Redgrave and Lopham Fen in

Suffolk. On other occasions, the Society provided the Conservancy with funding to enable it to meet purchase costs in excess of the official valuation. This was the case at Wye and Crundale Downs in Kent. The Society also stepped in at the behest of Trusts if they were temporarily unable to acquire a site themselves, for example at Cors Goch in Anglesey and at Southerscales Scar in Yorkshire (see below).

The properties that the Society has owned over the years are, in alphabetical order, as follows:

Aride Island

See separate entry

Avon Meadows

This one-hectare reserve, donated to the Society by CHRISTOPHER CADBURY and leased to the WORCESTERSHIRE TRUST in 1973, is now one of several pieces of land beside the river Avon and its tributaries managed by the Trust. These sites were originally home to marsh warblers, although they also support a rich variety of other wildlife, including reed and sedge warblers. Worcestershire was for many years a stronghold for breeding marsh warblers. Sadly, from the early 1980s, their numbers declined and the marsh warbler became extinct as a breeding bird in the county in 1995.

The freehold of the reserve was transferred to the Worcestershire Trust in 2001.

Marsh warbler photographed at Avon Meadows reserve, Worcestershire, 1978

Badgeworth Marsh

Badgeworth Marsh, Gloucestershire

Sometimes described as the country's smallest nature reserve, this home of the rare adder's-tongue spearwort (*Ranunculus ophioglossifolius*) near Cheltenham in Gloucestershire was bought by the Cotteswold Naturalists' Field Club and gifted to the Society in June 1933. The Field Club agreed to establish a local committee and to manage the area, free of any charge. There were 14 visitors to the site in 1934 and 26 in 1935 when the upkeep of the reserve was reported as 'a little more than £2'.

When the reserve was leased to the GLOUCESTERSHIRE TRUST, a new management committee was established under the chairmanship of the botanist, Edgar Milne-Redhead, and a thorough survey was immediately undertaken by Bristol University's Botany Department Field Club. Its recommendations were followed and soon yielded encouraging results for the reserve's star attraction.

In 1973, a pollution threat to the rare spearwort was averted when a plant hire firm was refused planning permission to construct a car-wash on adjacent land. The threat received world-wide publicity at the time and resulted in a flood of representations against the development.

The reserve was leased to the Gloucestershire Trust in 1962 and the freehold of the reserve was later transferred to the Trust.

Ben Mor Coigach

In 1976, on the initiative of its PRESIDENT, CHRISTOPHER CADBURY, the Society acquired more than 14,500 acres of the Ben Mor estate in the wild and remote hills of the Coigach in Wester Ross. Four small offshore islands, part of the nearby Summer Isles and close to the Society's existing reserve of Carn Iar (see page 679), also came as part of this new acquisition. The purchase was made possible by a large donation from the WA Cadbury Trust and a grant from WWF. Ben Mor Coigach became the Society's largest nature reserve and is one of the largest freehold reserves in the country.

From the islands and rocky coast, the land on the reserve rises to the summit of Ben Mor Coigach at nearly 2,500 feet; to the north the reserve is bounded by a chain of lochs where it adjoins the National Nature Reserve of Inverpolly.

The 6,000 hectare highland reserve at Ben Mor Coigach, Scotland

In addition to mountain and moorland vegetation, there are patches of birch woodland along the southern shores of the lochs. The fauna is typical of the north-west highlands – predators include golden eagle, peregrine, raven, pine marten, wild cat, otter and badger. Eider, ptarmigan, greenshank, black grouse and both red- and black-throated divers all nest, whilst barnacle geese feed on the croft lands in winter. There are many red deer and some roe deer, and seals frequent the coast.

The reserve was jointly managed for many years by the Society and the SCOTTISH TRUST (SWT). It was leased to SWT in 1987 and the freehold was transferred to the Trust in 1998.

Blackmoor Copse

This reserve in south-east Wiltshire, consisting of about 80 acres of mixed woodland, was acquired by the Society in late 1956, after protracted negotiations. "Initially coppice with standards, felling on a large scale had taken place in 1948–49 when the majority of timber size trees were cut. The oak was of the highest quality. . . the underwood of alder, hazel birch and ash was coppiced on a seven year rotation until the war years. . . apart from a few birch poles cut recently near the road and an acre of hazel cut in 1950 no other attention has been given to the underwood".[160] With the support of the Conservancy and the Forestry Commission, the local committee were quick to carry out fieldwork on the newly-acquired reserve and began implementing a Woodland Management Plan with the aim of returning "the wood to what it must have been at its optimum, i.e. a predominantly oak woodland".[161] The area was renowned for its butterflies, particularly the purple emperor butterfly, but sightings were few and far between. Today, this stunning butterfly can be enjoyed once more along with other woodland butterfly species – white admiral, purple hairstreak and silver-washed fritillary.

Blackmoor Copse, Wiltshire

677

The reserve was leased to the Wiltshire Trust in 1963 and the freehold transferred in 1998. The reserve is known today as Blackmoor Copse – the Vaughan-Pickard Nature Reserve.

Note: A concern for the colony of purple emperor butterflies at Blackmoor Copse was one of the factors that led to the formation of the Wiltshire Trust.

Bradfield Woods

Coppicing work at Bradfield Woods, Suffolk, 1976

In 1970, when outstanding ancient coppice-with-standards woods at Bradfield in Suffolk came on the market, and when the Trust was unable at that stage to 'offer active support', the Society stepped in and purchased 127 acres of Felsham Hall Wood and part of Monks' Park Wood. The purchase was made possible largely through the efforts of local people who helped raise more than £10,000. Acquisition of a further 28 acres followed in 1979.

Over the previous four years, two thirds of Monks Park Wood had been grubbed out for agriculture. It was the resulting outcry, and the threat to the entire wood, that persuaded the Society to go ahead and purchase the remaining parts of Bradfield Woods. The eminent historical ecologist, Dr Oliver Rackham, was a strong supporter and he lent his ancient-woodland expertise and research to the cause, and prepared a case history.

He considered the purchase a turning point in woodland conservation. Many ancient woodlands were being cleared, but this was one of the few instances, at the time, where destruction was successfully resisted.

Bradfield Woods is among a few places in the country where the ancient practice of coppicing has been practiced continuously from medieval times, supplying fuel and small-wood products to the local community as well as timber from the larger trees. Nothing was wasted, with coppice of all shapes and sizes supplied for anything from scythe and rake handles and fence stakes to thatching broaches and spars, pea sticks and bean poles. If wood had to be burnt, the ash was used for pottery glaze and garden fertilizer and if sawdust piled up, it was used for pet bedding. Although decreasing demand and cheaper imports meant that wood for products, such as scythe and rake handles, was no longer required, other uses, for example for thatching and in gardens, continues today.

When the Society and the local Management Committee took over the woods in 1970, the last major felling had taken place between 1929 and 1931 and much of the underwood was going out of rotation. The Welnetham Rake Factory, a 19th century business which once owned the woods, was still producing wooden hay rakes, garden rakes, scythe handles, mallets and stable forks, but the factory finally closed in the 1980s.

It was not long before two staff and regular work parties of volunteers were successfully reintroducing the traditional practices, "cutting about ten acres each winter using chain saws as well as hand tools, and extracting the timber by tractor and trailer".[162]

The many different-aged compartments were systematically reintroduced and with them an ever-increasing profusion of the ground flora – wood anemones, bluebells and oxlips – in the felled areas.

After little more than a decade, the SUFFOLK TRUST was in a position to take on what the Conservancy described as "the most important ancient boulder clay woods of East Anglia, the flora is richer than almost every other wood in Eastern England".[163] The reserve was leased to the Trust in 1983 and the freehold transferred in 1999.

Oxlip at Bradfield Woods

Buckfastleigh

A "sudden opportunity occurred"[164] in the autumn of 1961 for the Society to acquire 11 acres of land overlying and embracing the entrances to caves at Higher Kiln Quarry, Buckfastleigh, in south Devon. The reserve was of particular interest for its colonies of greater and lesser horseshoe bats, springtails and blind shrimps in the caves and various geological features, most interesting being the relationship of the cave system to the terraces of the nearby River Dart. But the outstanding feature of this new acquisition was Joint Mitnor cave. It was described at the time as the "richest interglacial bone cave in Britain, containing remains of hippopotamus, straight-tusked elephant, narrow-nosed rhinoceros, bison, fallow deer, lion, hyaena and other mammals"[165] which apparently fell to their deaths through a shaft that subsequently became blocked.

The quarry and caves were leased to the DEVON TRUST in August 1964, leaving eight to nine acres of overlying grassland let by the Society for grazing. The freehold of the whole property was transferred to the Trust in 2000.

Carn Iar

This small island in Western Scotland was purchased by CHRISTOPHER CADBURY. A group of four small islands close to Carn Iar were included in the Society's acquisition of BEN MOR COIGACH reserve in 1976.

Cors Goch

Originally purchased by the Society in 1963 in the knowledge that a NORTH WALES TRUST was about to be formed, the freehold of this valley reserve in Anglesey – supporting one of the finest fen communities in Britain – was transferred, at cost, to the newly-formed Trust in December 1964. At around the same time the Trust purchased a further 86 acres of Cors Goch with money from WWF and the Society's Nuffield and Pilgrim Loan Funds.

Naturalists at Cors Goch, North Wales, 1966

Cousin Island, Seychelles

Cousin Island

In 1968, Cousin, a wildlife-rich 30 hectare island in the Seychelles, was being sold by the widow of France Andrea Jumeau for £5,500. Thanks to the WWF, and in particular the generosity of CHRISTOPHER CADBURY, the island was purchased and saved from development and began being managed as a nature reserve by the International Council for Bird Protection (ICBP), the organisation known today as Birdlife International. However, under its constitution, ICBP was unable to own land overseas. A solution was found when the Society agreed to hold the island in trust for ICBP's British Section. It was declared a special nature reserve under Seychelles law in 1974.

The freehold of Cousin Island was transferred to Birdlife International in the UK in July 2002 and the island is currently managed by Birdlife International's partner in the Seychelles, Nature Seychelles.

Coward Memorial Reserves
See separate entry

Dancer's End
See separate entry

La Digue

In November 1979, the politician and naturalist, Tony Beamish (later Lord Chelwood of Lewes) was

given power of attorney to sign a lease on behalf of the Society with Mrs Rene Payet for nearly eight hectares of woodland at La Reunion on the island of La Digue in the Seychelles. The area was a stronghold for the critically endangered Seychelles black paradise flycatcher, endemic to La Digue Island. In 1981, the Government's Conservation Department announced its intention to give the reserve legal protection. In the meantime, however, the area was declared a non-statutory nature reserve and officially opened on 18th December 1982 in the presence of Dr Tolba, Executive Director of the United Nations Environment Programme.

When Mrs Payet died a few years later, both the Society and the Payet family agreed that it would be in the reserve's best interest if it was transferred to the Seychelles' Government. This duly took place, but it was not until 31st January 1991 that the Designation of Special Reserve (La Digue Veuve Reserve) Order 1991 was actually signed by the President. At last, both the area (now comprising 21 hectares of woodland, including the Society's original piece of land) and the flycatcher could enjoy full protection under Seychelles law.

Eades Meadow

This flower-rich hay meadow, donated to the Society by CHRISTOPHER CADBURY in 1972 and leased to the WORCESTERSHIRE TRUST the same year, is particularly famous for its meadow saffron in the autumn and green-winged orchids in spring and summer. The reserve – comprising almost seven hectares – was discovered by Fred Fincher, an eminent Worcestershire naturalist, in 1954. It has not been ploughed for at least 100 years and is now part of the larger, 12.5 hectare, Foster's Green Meadows National Nature Reserve. The freehold of Eades Meadow was transferred to the Worcestershire Trust in 2001.

Eades Meadow

Falkland Islands

In 1979, the Society became the owner of various small islands in West Falklands, namely Ship Island, Beef Island, Coffin Island, North Island, Saddle Island, Cliff Knob Island and Landsend Bluff – all adjacent to New Island – as well as The Twins, adjacent to Carcass Island. Responsibility for the management of the islands was handed over to the Falklands Island Foundation in 1980. The freehold of the various islands owned by the Society was gifted to the Falklands Island Foundation for the Conservation of Wildlife, Countryside, Wrecks and Places of Historic Interest (subsequently renamed Falklands Conservation) in 1992.

Martham Broad, Norfolk, 1982

Martham Broad

This reserve, donated to the Society by Christopher Cadbury, comprised two small broads, with the upper Thurne flowing between them. In addition, there were extensive marginal reed and sedge beds and areas of alder carr covering almost 47 hectares. Martham Broad, unlike most of the other Norfolk Broads, always retained water of good quality and, as a result, the reserve was home to several of the typical Broadland aquatic plants, including the rare holly-leaved naiad.

Martham Broad, a Ramsar site and Special Protection Area, was leased by the Society to the NORFOLK TRUST in 1971 and the freehold transferred to the same Trust in 1998.

Meathop Moss

See separate entry

Mickfield Meadow

A timely visit in April 1938 to one of the best meadows in Suffolk for the stunning snake's head fritillary, revealed a newly-dug drainage ditch and light ploughing on the four and a half acre site. Fortunately, the owner was persuaded by Francis Simpson of the Ipswich Museum to delay cultivation while the Suffolk Naturalists' Society (SNS) set about raising the £75 required to

purchase the site. This was soon achieved by means of a grant from the Society's own funds, backed by contributions from some dozen members. Indeed, Simpson had "approached the owner of the Fritillary Field in so diplomatic a manner that the latter veered from scorn of such weeds to the position of a donor towards the fund our Society raised for the land's purchase".[166] The SNS was prevented by its rules from owning land and so "the Fritillary Field was handed over before the close of 1938 to the Society for the Promotion of Nature Reserves, which itself had voted ten pounds towards the acquisition and will maintain it for the use and benefit of all Naturalists".[167]

A report in the SPNR HANDBOOK for 1938 notes that, "on several occasions in the past during the height of the flowering season. . . the turf has appeared as one dull purple sheet of the drooping chequered flowers, dotted here and there with examples of the creamy white variety. Another feature of this meadow is the particularly rich assemblage of the associated flora".[168] In the springtime, the reserve was bright with marsh-marigold, cuckooflower and green-winged orchid and in summer Dyer's greenweed, spotted orchid, common twayblade and adder's tongue fern.

Although Simpson, who was acting as the reserve's voluntary warden, was later criticised for planting elm and oak on the site

Mickfield Meadow, Suffolk

between 1938 and 1940, his actions were undoubtedly well intentioned and his choice of management was probably based on the presence in the meadow of woodland species like anemone and goldilocks. During the war, with Simpson on active service, the War Agricultural Executive Committee cut down all the trees and a thick hedge on the north of the reserve without notice because of the construction of a nearby aerodrome. Fortunately, after pleas from the Society and local naturalists, the meadow itself was spared from cultivation.

However, for several years after the war, the reserve suffered from scrub encroachment and picking. For example, in 1948 practically every fritillary bloom was taken. In these years the reserve was managed as a nature reserve for its general interest but, in 1953, the botanists, John Gilmour and Max Walters, recommended that Mickfield should be managed 'purely for the fritillary'. Plans were put in place for the meadow to be grazed once more. But things moved slowly and, even as late as 1960, the Conservancy was commenting that the reserve hardly qualified for the description of meadow. Grazing was finally arranged with a local farmer in 1961 and improvements were seen almost immediately.

The reserve was leased to the SUFFOLK TRUST in 1966 and the freehold transferred to the same Trust in 1999.

Rahoy Hills

In 1975, the Society acquired 1,700 acres of the remote Rahoy estate in Morvern in the West Highlands on the initiative and generous financial assistance of its PRESIDENT, CHRISTOPHER CADBURY. Additional funds were provided by the WWF and the SCOTTISH TRUST (SWT).

Rahoy Hills, Scotland

The reserve consisted of two mountains – Beinn na h-Uamha and Beinn Iadain – and the low-lying boggy ground with numerous lochans between them. It also included the northern shore of Loch Arienas and its extensive oakwood. The mountains were notable for their arctic-alpine flora, golden eagle, numerous red deer, and evidence of the presence of wild cat.

The reserve was jointly managed by the Society and SWT for many years, but was leased to SWT in 1986. The freehold of the reserve was transferred to the Trust in 1998.

Ray Island

Ray Island, off the coast of Essex, was purchased by CHARLES ROTHSCHILD in 1920 and left to The National Trust, or to the Society if The National Trust was not interested. The National Trust turned down the bequest. In 1925, however, the Society decided that the island had little wildlife interest and, with the agreement of Charles Rothschild's widow, the reserve was sold to provide much-needed funds for the management of WOODWALTON FEN.

Today, Ray Island is once more back under The Wildlife Trusts' management. Owned by The National Trust, this remote and isolated 20 acre island nature reserve is now managed by the ESSEX TRUST.

Sharpham Moor Plot

This small (less than a hectare) area of peat bog on the Somerset Levels was acquired by the Society in 1924, thanks to the efforts of H Stuart Thompson, supported by Professor Arthur Tansley.

It was thought to be the only British site of the rare hybrid sedge, *Carex evoluta*. The site was offered first to The National Trust and then, at its suggestion, to the Society who agreed to accept it as long as a local committee agreed to take responsibility for its annual upkeep. Thompson largely undertook the care of the reserve himself until his death in 1940 when the Botanical Department of Bristol University assumed responsibility.

However, with transport difficult during and immediately after the war, the reserve was hardly visited. Management was neglected and the question arose as to whether it was worth retaining, especially as it was thought unlikely that the hybrid sedge had survived. It was not until 1948 that interest was revived and a longer-term management plan put in place. By August 1954, it was reported that, as planned, about two-thirds of the plot had been cleared of carr and as

a result there was a "plant carpet which is well varied in composition, structure and height".[169] The hybrid sedge was no longer present; the reporting team "saw nothing in Shapwick closely corresponding with it, nor as pleasantly varied in so small a space".[170]

The reserve was leased to the SOMERSET TRUST in 1985, re-notified as an SSSI in 1986, and the freehold transferred to that Trust in 1999.

Southerscales Scar

In November 1979, the Society purchased 105 acres of Southerscales Scar, within the internationally-important Ingleborough SSSI, for £15,000. The purchase was made possible with grants from WWF, the Yorkshire Dales National Park and the Countryside Commission. All concerned would have preferred the YORKSHIRE TRUST to purchase the site, but this was not possible. In the circumstances, the Society agreed to take on the ownership of the site and to manage it in collaboration with the Trust until such time as the Trust could take it on itself.

The nature reserve comprised scar and grassland and two substantial areas of some of the finest limestone pavement in Britain. The humid atmosphere of the pavement's

network of grooves and fissures supported its characteristic flora, including lily of the valley, bloody crane's-bill, Solomon's seal and dark-red helleborine.

The freehold of the reserve was transferred to the Yorkshire Trust in 1999.

Southerscales Scar, Yorkshire

Swaddiwell Field

This eight acre site in Northampton-shire – consisting of limestone grassland, a disused quarry and pond – could claim to be the Society's first nature reserve. CHARLES ROTHSCHILD persuaded The National Trust to take on an annual tenancy in 1914 and the Society paid the annual rent of £7 10s 0d. When the land was sold, attempts to stop the new owner exercising his right to quarry stone failed and the tenancy was given up at midsummer 1924. After the Second World War the quarry was in-filled and restored to agriculture.

An area adjacent to the original Swaddiwell Field site is now managed as Swaddywell Pit nature reserve by the Langdyke Countryside Trust.

Upton Warren

This reserve, 15 miles from the centre of Birmingham, was acquired for the Society by CHRISTOPHER CADBURY in 1968 and leased to the WORCESTERSHIRE TRUST in 1972. Covering 26 hectares, the reserve is in two distinct parts, the freshwater Moors Pools and the saline Flashes Pools. Both areas owe their existence to past underground brine extraction

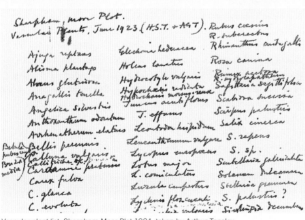

Vascular plant list, Sharpham Moor Plot 1924, taken by Arthur Tansley

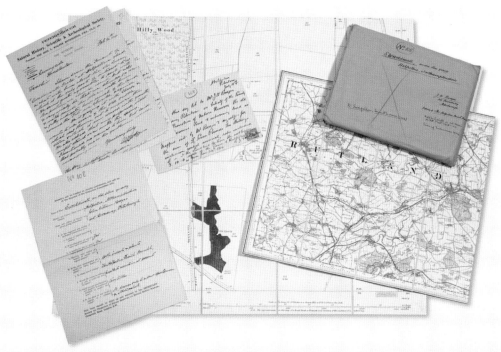

Information gathered on Swaddiwell Field for the SPNR's 1915 list of potential reserves

which has caused subsidence and consequent flooding. The reserve can boast a remarkable list of bird species, especially bearing in mind its proximity to a conurbation with three million people. It attracts wildfowl and breeding common tern, oystercatcher and little ringed plover, with surrounding reedbeds excellent for reed, sedge and Cetti's warblers and reed bunting. Passage migrants and vagrants include least sandpiper, Caspian tern, rustic bunting and white stork. In 2008, *The Birds of Upton Warren* was published to celebrate its 40 years as a wildlife reserve.

Upton Warren, Worcestershire, 1968

The freehold of the reserve, now called the 'Christopher Cadbury Wetland Reserve at Upton Warren', in recognition and appreciation of CHRISTOPHER CADBURY's generous support for the Trust's work, was transferred to the Worcestershire Trust in 2001.

Welcombe and Marsland

The two adjacent coombe valleys at Welcombe and Marsland on the north Devon and Cornwall border support a wide variety of habitats, ranging from sandy and rocky seashore and cliffs, maritime grassland, heath and scrub to wet meadows and oak and alder woodland in the sheltered parts of the valleys. This wide variety of habitats supports a vast array of wildlife: more than 320 species of plants and a rich diversity of animals. There is a good range of cliff breeding, grassland, scrub and woodland birds; the mammals

include badgers, and among the insects are 34 species of butterfly.

The valleys were a place particularly beloved of the Society's PRESIDENT, Christopher Cadbury, who spent many happy family holidays in the area from his childhood. In 1959, beginning with the purchase of the lower Welcombe Mouth, Cadbury painstakingly negotiated, plot by plot, the acquisition of more than 500 acres which he then transferred to the Society. For example, land was acquired in 1961 (Marsland Mouth), 1964, 1969, 1970 and in 1971, by which time the reserve had grown to more than 350 acres. Further acquisition of land in 1972 increased the reserve to more than 400 acres and, in 1973, to more than 500 acres. In 1972, Cadbury purchased Chapel Cottage at the bottom of Marsland Valley for the use of a full-time warden; the cottage was purchased by the

Marsland Mouth, 1982

Society in 1983 and is now owned by the reserve's warden. In 1983, the Society benefited from a legacy from a Mrs Manning of more than £40,000 (see MANNING/CADBURY FUND) with a preference for it to be used for the management of the Welcombe and Marsland reserve. Cadbury had met all the costs associated with the reserve up to this point, but the legacy now provided a welcome endowment fund to help maintain this large reserve.

Even in the mid-1960s, the possibility that the reserve might be managed by the local Trusts was being considered, but for 20 or more years the reserve was managed by the Society through a committee made up of representatives from the Society and the DEVON and CORNWALL TRUSTS. The Devon Trust's Senior Nature Reserves Officer, Gary Pilkington, has been warden of the reserve since 1988 and recent years have seen changes, including the acquisition of further woodland by the Trust, the hand-over of the Welcombe section of

the reserve to The National Trust (the reserve is now around 420 acres) and the completion of a new reserve office. Wildlife successes have included improvement in the fortunes of two nationally-declining butterflies – the pearl-bordered and small pearl-bordered fritillaries – and the presence of a healthy dormouse population and resident breeding otters.

The reserve was leased by the Society to the Devon Trust in 1997 and the freehold, together with an endowment fund of £365,000, was transferred to the same Trust in 2004.

In his memoir, TED SMITH recalls visits to Welcombe and Marsland, usually combined with visits to Trusts in the West Country. "The banks of primroses – I have never seen them in such profusion – the fritillary butterflies and the dippers and grey wagtails and buzzards, and the rock pools on the shore were a delight long remembered by our children. Thanks be to Christopher!"[171]

See also entry for CHRISTOPHER CADBURY

MANNING/CADBURY FUND
Beatrice Emma May Manning, who died in December 1981, left the residue of her estate – around £45,000 – unconditionally to the Society but expressed a wish that the money be used for the benefit of the Society's Marsland Reserve on the Devon/Cornwall border.

The Society duly established the Manning Fund for this purpose. In 1991 and 1992, the fund was supplemented by two generous donations totalling nearly £70,000 from Christopher Cadbury and was renamed the Manning/Cadbury Fund. The possibility of using the fund to help Trusts more generally was considered fleetingly in 1995, but rejected. An endowment fund of £365,000 was eventually transferred to the DEVON TRUST when the freehold of the Welcombe and Marsland Reserve passed to that Trust in 2004.

Woodwalton Fen
See separate entry

NATURE RESERVES STUDY

In the autumn of 1975, ahead of the publication by the Conservancy of its long-awaited *Nature Conservation Review*, TED SMITH put forward a case for a new strategic appraisal of the selection and establishment of nature reserves, particularly by the Trusts and the Society. "We must define our aims and objectives more clearly and embody these in strategic plans which can be applied at local and national level and which make the wisest possible use of our resources".[172] A request to the Conservancy for funding resulted in a contract to the Society for a two-year study. Cameron Easton was appointed Project Officer to collect and analyse data, with Smith acting as the general editor. Preliminary conclusions from the study were presented in three papers at the Trusts' Conference on Nature Reserves at Bromsgrove, Worcestershire in April 1978. Easton left soon afterwards and Smith completed the editing, including the drafting of the final conclusions and recommendations. Among its principal recommendations were that the Trusts and the Society should: seek more resources for site conservation, training of volunteers and the strengthening of staff; prepare more management plans and carry out more regular monitoring of reserves; seek an expansion of the Conservancy's grant-aid programme and encourage local authorities to become more involved in the acquisition of sites and in the provision of resources for the Trusts to manage them.

The study, while a snapshot of the Trusts' nature reserve holdings, policies and management practices in the mid-1970s, did nevertheless set the Trusts' work into a wider national context and helped influence the Conservancy's policies in respect of grant-aid to Trusts.

NATURE TRAILS

The idea of a nature trail as a technique for interpreting wildlife along a given route "was developed in the 1920s in America by the entomologist Frank Lutz".[173] He believed that it was best to "teach about nature where nature is".[174] His nature trail experiment in the Ramapo Mountains in New York State was picked up, and developed by, the USA's National Parks Service between the First and Second World Wars. One of the first nature trails in the UK "was made at Coombe Hill, Buckinghamshire, in 1962 by the Council for Nature and the BERKSHIRE, BUCKINGHAMSHIRE AND OXFORDSHIRE NATURALISTS' TRUST".[175] Two hundred visitors used the trail on the first weekend it was open. By 1968, the Council for Nature's list of trails had risen to 100. The Trusts began to experiment with nature trails in 1967. A year later the Society finalised a promotional deal with the oil company, Shell, whereby grants of

A Society nature trail leaflet

£250 were made available to Trusts to set up trails which were then publicised through Shell petrol stations. By 1972, the final year of the relationship, 20 trails had been organised by the Trusts across England and Wales.

Today, nature trails are just one of many interpretation techniques used by Trusts on their nature reserves and in community and countryside projects more widely.

NEW GROUND INITIATIVE

The workshop, New Ground, was organised at the Ironbridge Gorge Institute, Shropshire in March 1991 to explore the future role of the movement in the conservation of the wider countryside. Attended by 40 delegates from 27 Trusts, the workshop was funded by the Conservancy and organised with the support of Shropshire Wildlife Services, the consultancy arm of the SHROPSHIRE TRUST.

New Ground was designed as a year-long process to feed off the work undertaken on the BANGOR MANIFESTO and the Losing Ground campaign in 1990. Its findings were fed into the Conservation Conference planned for Cleveland in July 1991, and beyond.

It was well-timed. Semi-natural habitats continued to be destroyed by the agricultural, forestry and planning systems. Support for agriculture within Europe, Environmentally Sensitive Areas and local government and its funding were all under review. The new Countryside Stewardship Scheme was soon to be underway in England (FARMING AND WILDLIFE) and the reorganisation of the Conservancy was likely to have an impact on its work in the wider countryside. Introducing the workshop, Tim Sands said that Partnership thinking was moving on from "the defensive, purely nature reserve mentality – we recognise that the safety net of reserves is necessary, as are reserves as a shop window and as a place for us to practice what we preach. But we are treading new ground as well. It is not enough for us to wake up one morning to find wildlife common and in abundance only inside the moat and behind the castle wall – it must be everywhere".[176]

A key output of the workshop was an acknowledgement that Trusts already worked in the wider countryside, but it would be useful to carry out a survey of the current best practice and to prepare a longer term strategy for discussion. A discussion document, *Conservation in the Wider Countryside: Best Practice and How to Achieve It*, emerged from the Cleveland Conservation Conference in September 1991. It was criticised in some quarters for still being too site-orientated, but the sections on 'Common Standards for Wildlife Sites', 'County Strategies', 'The Practical, Educational, Campaigning and Partnership Approach' and on 'Training, Standards and Qualifications' were to provide core themes and values that would prove central to the movement's thinking for a decade, or more, to come.

NEWTON, ALAN

Alan Newton was born and educated in Lincolnshire and joined Barclays Bank in Bourne in 1941. After serving in the Royal Corps of Signals in the Second World War, he rejoined the bank in 1947, rising to become Senior Manager of Barclays' Lincoln Branch from 1970 until his retirement in 1984. He was the Society's HONORARY TREASURER between 1983 and 1991.

Newton was a committed and hard-working reformer. He was the architect of a new and fairer system for calculating the Trusts' contributions to the Society, based on a percentage levy on Trusts' subscription income. With his local

contacts, he played a key role in the sale of the Society's properties in Nettleham and its subsequent move to more spacious premises in Lincoln. His time at the Society coincided with the BRITISH WILDLIFE APPEAL and its success was an undoubted highlight of his term in office. But Newton's greatest contribution was the introduction of a more professional approach to the management of the Society's financial affairs and sales operation. On his retirement, Newton spoke about how his role as Treasurer had dominated the last eight years of his life. "I've had a hands-on approach because the organisation has grown so rapidly. We've had to fight hard to obtain money in a very competitive climate".[177]

In thanking Newton, the Society recognised that it owed him a great debt. He had instilled a sense of confidence, dedicated much time to its financial development and had steered it "through some difficult financial times with great skill and devotion".[178]

NICHOLSON, MAX

Max Nicholson (1904–2003) – ornithologist, civil servant and campaigner – was an immensely influential player in environmental conservation throughout his life, acting, in Julian Huxley's words, as a "general catalyst"[179] to new ideas and ways of working. He became an Associate Member of the Society in June 1947 and, in an effort to introduce younger blood into its affairs, the Society elected him to its Council and Executive in June 1949. He served on the Executive until July 1958 and the Council until 1971, and thereafter as Vice President until 1987.

"A man of mercurial intelligence, firing off ideas like a Catherine wheel",[180] Nicholson created the social science foundation PEP (Political and Economic Planning)

Max Nicholson

before the Second World War to bring together groups of experts to compile reports on various social and economic topics. He became its Secretary in 1936 and while at the foundation became a leading advocate of national planning. He was also a key player in the formation of new conservation organisations, including the British Trust for Ornithology, the Council for Nature and the WWF.

Nicholson joined the civil service in the Ministry of Information and during the Second World War moved to the Ministry of War Transport. After the war, he was appointed Secretary to the Office of the Lord President of the Council, Herbert Morrison, where his responsibilities included coordination of the Government's policy on national economic planning. In this position he helped ensure that nature conservation was not overlooked in post-war reconstruction and that progress was maintained on the National Parks and Access to the Countryside legislation, passed in 1949. He was Director General of the Nature Conservancy between 1952 and 1966.

In the 1950s and early 1960s, alongside his career with the Conservancy, he continued to be involved with the Society's business. In July 1952, with Captain CYRIL DIVER, Nicholson initiated the first major review of the Society's properties which resulted, among other things, in the establishment of an ad hoc Reserves Sub-Committee and the appointment of a 'surveyor' – botanist John Gilmour – to visit and report on each property. He was also closely involved in negotiations over the lease of the Society's WOODWALTON FEN reserve to the Conservancy in 1954 and represented the Society at various meetings of the IUPN. With LORD HURCOMB, he encouraged the Society to help organise the IUPN's General Assembly in Edinburgh in 1956, including the costly production of the Assembly's proceedings! (TOWARDS IUCN).

Nicholson was an inspiring and often provocative speaker. At a session on 'Government and the Voluntary Bodies' at the COUNTRYSIDE IN 1970 conference in October 1970, for example, he railed against "our shibboleths about GNP",[181] expressing the view that "no single thing would do more to set right all these troubles over values. . . than if economists were to go back to school and learn ecology".[182] He presented several masterful speeches to the Society's national conferences. The first at Skegness (SKEGNESS CONFERENCE) in 1960 – *Progress in Nature Conservation* – reviewed the state of nature conservation; the second in 1964 at the Society's National Conference in York (CONFERENCES) was on *Advances in British Nature Conservation* and a third speech in 1994, at the age of 90, was at the Society's National Conference at Stoke Rochford Hall, Lincolnshire. Here he "cantered through the dismal record of man's greed in destroying the environment"[183] and left no one free from blame, including the Catholic Church. He exhorted everyone to "cease being so patient and lenient with those people who persist in wrongdoing towards the planet. . .

they should, like the whalers, be regularly, publicly and unmercifully attacked".[184]

Even as late as 1996, Nicholson was looking to break new ground and founded the New Renaissance Group to promote "a twenty-first century agenda for humanity and nature".[185] He was working on ideas for a "Society for the fulfillment of culture",[186] modelled on The Wildlife Trust movement.

O

OFFICES OF THE SOCIETY
Principal Offices:
The Natural History Museum, Cromwell Road, London   1912–64

Pyewipes, Willoughby, Lincolnshire (TED SMITH's home)   1964–65

The Manor House, Alford, Lincolnshire   1965–74

22 The Green, Nettleham, Lincolnshire   1974–90

The Green, Waterside South, Lincoln   1990–99

The Kiln, Mather Road, Newark, Nottinghamshire   1999–

OGILVIE-GRANT, WILLIAM ROBERT
William Robert Ogilvie-Grant (1863–1924) was one of the founder members of the Society and its first HONORARY SECRETARY (jointly with FRANCIS ROBERT HENLEY), serving until 1921.

He had been a founder member of the RSPB and, at the time of the Society's formation, was Assistant Keeper in the Zoology Department at the Natural History Museum in London.

In the Society's early years, he was "an active Honorary Secretary"[187] closely involved in the back-room work associated with compiling ROTHSCHILD'S LIST.

"Each completed questionnaire was filed by WR Ogilvie-Grant in a blue envelope, with other relevant notes and correspondence".[188] He also nominated and visited sites and helped with the difficult task of selecting the final list. However, from 1916 onwards, the "state of his health unfortunately prevented him from taking an active part in the Society's proceedings".[189]

After retiring as Honorary Secretary, he remained a member of the Society until his death in 1924.

William Robert Ogilvie-Grant at the Natural History Museum in London, 1907

ONSLOW, THE EARL OF
Sir Richard William Alan Onslow (1876–1945) was the third PRESIDENT of the Society, holding office between 1936 and 1942 when he retired due to ill health. He was also President of the Zoological Society of London and the Society for the Preservation of the Fauna of the Empire (the first recipient of the latter Society's gold medal) and, as such, provided a strong link between the three societies. He was a strong supporter of the moves to establish national parks abroad. He became Chairman of the influential CONFERENCE ON NATURE PRESERVATION IN POST-WAR RECONSTRUCTION, convened by the Society, and took a personal interest in the resulting memorandum. On behalf of the conference, he led a deputation to Lord Reith, the

Minister of Works and Buildings, in January 1942 to explain the potential role of nature reserves in post-war reconstruction.

In 1931, he was one of the two British Government delegates to the International Congress for the Protection of Nature where he produced an official letter from the Prime Minister inviting the 'powers concerned' to London for a conference on the protection of animals and plants. "Its effect when read was magical; the proceedings, which had increasingly tended to be somnolent in character, suddenly woke up, and the proposal was warmly welcomed".[190] As a result, the Conference for the Protection of the Fauna and Flora of Africa took place in London in 1933 with Onslow as its Chairman. It was largely due to his tactful conduct of the proceedings that a Convention was so quickly agreed to. But for the outbreak of war, he would have presided over a similar conference to cover Asia, Australia and New Zealand, planned for 1939. In 1938, the Society nominated him for the office of President of the Conference of Delegates of Corresponding Societies of the British Association for the Advancement of Science in Cambridge. At the conference, he spoke in his Presidential address about safeguarding Britain's native fauna threatened with extinction, and referred to the possible intro- duction of the European beaver to the west coast of Scotland.

In 1941, Onslow was elected as the Society's President for a second term of five years but, after suffering the "third attack of cardiac failure within two years",[191] the Society had to reluctantly accept Onslow's resignation the following year. In doing so, it expressed its appreciation of his valuable services to the Society and its objects during his term of office.

OTTER CONSERVATION

In the 50 or more years since the major crash in UK otter numbers around 1957, the Society and Trusts have been in the forefront of conservation work which has brought about a remarkable recovery of this most elusive and endearing of mammals.

As early as 1969, the BRECKNOCK TRUST discussed "an effective ban on otter hunting"[192] with owners of riparian rights on the Wye and the Usk rivers. The HEREFORD AND RADNORSHIRE TRUST, concerned that this might lead to an increase in hunting in adjoining counties, arranged to meet the Hawkestone Hunt. The same year, the Mammal Society carried out a survey using data from Otter Hunts that confirmed the decline. The Society encouraged Trusts to carry out their own surveys, with limited success, and an Otter Bill, introduced into Parliament, was unsuccessful. The Field Sports Society and Otter Hunts Association also asked to meet the Society's CONSERVATION LIAISON COMMITTEE to "present their case".[193]

The Mammal Society followed up its hunt survey in 1972, this time involving a "much wider number of interests, including conservation organisations, river authorities. . . although otter hunts would again be asked to cooperate".[194]

Collective anxiety about the plight of Britain's otters surfaced again at the Society's biennial conference in Newcastle in 1976 (CONFERENCES). The Society had adopted the *Future of Wetlands* as its theme as a contribution to the Council of Europe's European Wetlands Campaign. Unsurprisingly, otters were a hot topic and delegates wanted something done. A resolution was passed calling on the Society to take action.

Meetings were arranged behind the scenes between the Society and the Conservancy to persuade it to set up a special otter group and to make recommendations for conservation measures. The Joint Otter Group (JOG) (see page 691) was established a few months later in September 1976.

The JOG produced two reports – *Otters 1977* and *Otters 1979*. In its first report the Group examined the substantial decline in both the number and range of otters, but concluded that it was not possible to indicate the direction or extent of trends or to isolate any particular factor that was determining otter numbers. It identified ten pressures faced by the otter and made recommendations to help the otter recover. After considering the information presented in *Otters 1977*, the Conservancy convinced the Government that the otter should be legally protected in England and Wales from 1st January 1978 under the Conservation of Wild Creatures and Wild Plants Act 1975. When this Act was repealed by the Wildlife and Countryside Act 1981, protection was extended to Scotland. Equivalent protection was accorded to the otter in Northern Ireland under the Wildlife (NI) Order 1985.

By the publication of the second JOG report, *Otters 1979*, there was consensus that the widespread use of the organochlorine pesticide, dieldrin, introduced in 1955 for a range of uses, including sheep-dipping, seed dressing and mothproofing, was the most likely cause for the initial decline of otters around 1957. Most uses, including its use as a seed dressing, were stopped by 1966 and it was finally banned altogether in 1984. It was thought that a combination of other factors, particularly the loss of suitable habitat for shelter and breeding, had also contributed to the otter's failure to recover to its former levels.

The Trusts have been at the forefront of otter conservation since the 1960s

A programme of comparable sample surveys of otter distribution was now underway and, by 1981, all countries had been surveyed. The surveys showed how serious the decline had become, particularly in England and, to a lesser extent, in Wales. The plan was then to repeat these, or similar surveys, every seven years.

The JOG and the Society's Project Officer played an important coordinating and networking role at this time, helping to maintain channels of communication, encourage wildlife-friendly river and wetland management and keep the plight of the otter higher on the political agenda. (The Joint Otter Group box overleaf provides more information about its work, findings and influence.)

Vincent Weir, an otter enthusiast, had established the Vincent Wildlife Trust in 1975 and, when the recommendations in *Otters 1977* were published, he took up the challenge and, with the initial help of

the Fauna Preservation Society, established an Otter Haven Project. After four years it was employing six regional Coordinators and Assistant Coordinators to "establish areas (havens) where disturbance of otters is minimised and where habitat is protected or improved to suit the otters' needs".[195] The havens were set up by informal agreement with landowners and Water Authorities and with the cooperation of the Conservancy and the local Trusts.

Meanwhile, the Society too recognised the importance of influencing the way river catchments were being managed by riparian owners and the water industry. With the passage of the Water Act 1973, a series of new regional Water Authorities was established with a re-stated duty 'to have regard' to the needs of nature conservation. This was of limited value, but a significant advance was made when the Wildlife and Countryside Act 1981 gave Water Authorities and Internal

Drainage Boards a strengthened duty to 'further' conservation. This was seen as giving them the "clear ability and responsibility to commit funds to the conservation of wildlife and landscape, so far as is consistent with their primary functions".[196]

In October 1974, the Society agreed to go ahead and arrange "meetings between Regional Water Authorities and Trusts in each region to discuss liaison with regard to nature conservation".[197] This major rivers and wildlife initiative gathered momentum over the next few years in close collaboration with the RSPB and culminated in the joint publication (with RSPB) in 1984 of the *Rivers and Wildlife Handbook* (WATER FOR WILDLIFE). The handbook contained practical advice on options for conserving existing otter habitat and for the re-instatement of otter habitat, alongside many real-life case studies.

On 1st January 1989, the Otter Haven Project was transferred from

Recreating open water habitat for otters, Staffordshire, 1990s

the Vincent Wildlife Trust to the Society and its name changed to the Otters and Rivers Project to reflect the pressures, not just on otters, but on waterways and wetlands generally (WATER FOR WILDLIFE). Over the next five years, working in partnership with water companies, the National Rivers Authority, conservation agencies, universities, angling societies, landowners and farmers, the team helped to support the construction of 245 log piles and 98 underground holts, 100 road crossings and more than 180 habitat improvement schemes. In addition, the team were involved in 30 Countryside Stewardship agreements and contributed to research on the impact of organophosphorous sheep dips using fish tissue analysis. The team were also able to survey more than 3,728 miles of river to supplement the national surveys carried out every seven years.

There was growing optimism that all this effort by the Project and other players was paying dividends. More sensitive wetland management was being undertaken and water quality was improving. By 1995, there was evidence of otters moving eastwards up the

Severn and Avon rivers from Wales into the Cotswolds. They made a welcome return to the Thames catchment, and otters were even back in the industrialised rivers of South Wales.

But there was still much to be done. Around three quarters of sites surveyed in England still had no signs of otters and the animals continued to be at risk, not only from pollution, disturbance and a lack of suitable habitat, but also from road deaths and drowning in fish traps and lobster pots. The Society launched its three-phased Water for Wildlife campaign in 1992, publishing *Dying of Thirst* in May 1992 and *Seven Sad Tales of the Riverbank* in 1993, and undertaking further campaigning on river catchment management in 1994 (WATER FOR WILDLIFE).

In 1995, following pressure from non-government organisations, including the Society, the Government's UK Biodiversity Action Plan Steering Group published the first tranche of Biodiversity Action Plans, including an action plan for the otter. This had a target to "restore breeding otters to all catchments and coastal areas where they have been recorded since 1960"[198] by 2010 (BIODIVERSITY ACTION PLANNING). The Society

recognised its own responsibility to respond to this target, but also expected Government, the new Environment Agency, water companies and industry to take action too. The call was for statutory water quality objectives to produce still healthier rivers; a plea to use water more wisely and a demand for Catchment Management Plans to include action for otters, such as the designation of otter havens.

During the next three years, the national team was gradually dispersed to the Trusts, and several additional Trusts' Otters and Rivers Projects were established. The success of otter conservation measures taken so far, and a long-awaited national plan for the otter's recovery, published by the Joint Nature Conservation Committee (JNCC) to support the UK Biodiversity Action Plan, meant the future looked much brighter for the otter than at any time in the previous three decades. The JNCC's plan was even able to proclaim, the "otter is now widely, though unevenly, distributed across the British Isles and Ireland".[199] Nevertheless, the Society continued to express concern about new and increasing dangers from synthetic pyrethroids present in sheep dips; road deaths, with 673 road deaths recorded between 1971 and 1996 and 60 per cent of violent otter deaths attributed to road casualties, as well as the continuing destruction of habitat and poor water quality.

By the end of the century, Water UK, representing the water industry, was committed to otter conservation as the champion of the UK Otter Species Biodiversity Action Plan and was supporting the Trusts' Otters and Rivers Project (OARP). The Society employed a national OARP Director, Guy Corbett-Marshall (and later Lisa Schneidau), along with a network of 23 conservation officers and more than 12,000 volunteers based within the Trusts. Water UK was providing £25,000 per annum. This released a further £250,000 of matching landfill tax credits from Biffaward. With additional local money provided by water companies, under similar arrangements, it was estimated that between 1998 and 2001, well in excess of £2.3 million was made available to the project across England and Wales.

The Society's President, DAVID BELLAMY, concluded that "the return of the otter to our rivers and wetlands gives us great hope for the future. The Water UK and The Wildlife Trusts' Otters and Rivers Project have shown that real gains can be made for endangered wildlife when we work together in partnership".[200]

In England, by the time of the fourth National Otter Survey carried out by The Wildlife Trusts' OARP and Water UK, signs of otters were found at 34 per cent of the 3,327 wetland and river sites surveyed during 2000–2002 – "a staggering five hundred and twenty-seven per cent increase in the number of sites occupied in the late 1970s",[201] and a 22 per cent increase on the results obtained during the survey in 1991–94.

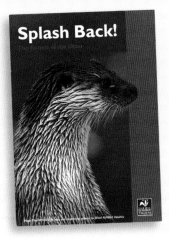

Splash Back!

Otter holt created as part of the Otters and Rivers Project

The fifth *Otter Survey of England 2009–2010* showed that otter recovery had continued in all but the very south-east of the country. Recovery had occurred largely in response to the ban on pesticides, the legal protection afforded to the otter and improvements in water quality, as well as habitat restoration.

Such was the recovery, anglers were concerned and a partnership between The Wildlife Trusts, the water industry and the Environment Agency needed to publish *Otters and Stillwater Fisheries* with advice on how to deal with the predation of fish by otters. Except for intensively-stocked stillwater fisheries, the advice offered back in 1967 held true. "It is doubtful whether, taking Great Britain as a whole, the otter does much harm to fisheries and fishing interests. . . its normal density is probably too low to cause serious loss".[202] Introducing the 2008 publication, Chris Burt, Vice President of Specialist Anglers Alliance, wrote, "there is an increasing likelihood of otter predation occurring at any fishery, so it is essential to understand the issues and the options available. The otter is welcomed back as an integral part of our environment and is a protected species too; we as anglers have to accept the associated risks posed to specimen fisheries in particular, and manage them where possible".[203]

JOINT OTTER GROUP

The Group, jointly sponsored by the Society and the Conservancy, was established in 1976. Encouragingly, in addition to the sponsoring bodies, the Group brought together some of the key players in the otter world, in particular representatives from the Mammal Society, the Institute of Terrestrial Ecology and, later, the Otter Haven Project. Two reports were produced – *Otters 1977* and *Otters 1979*. The Society also employed an Otter Project Officer, Margaret Wood, under a contract from the Conservancy from January 1978 until 1980. Wood went on to become the WARWICKSHIRE TRUST'S second full-time Conservation Officer, before joining the SCOTTISH TRUST.

In its first report, *Otters 1977*, the Group examined the evidence and concluded that "both the numbers and range of the otter have been reduced substantially since the early 19th century and that there was a further decline in the early 1960s".[204] It was not possible to "indicate the direction or extent of trends at present nor is it possible to isolate any particular environmental factor which is demonstrably dominant in determining present day otter numbers".[205] To help the otter, the report proposed a combination of survey, research, management and legislation and identified ten pressures – human disturbance, hunting, riparian clearance, pollution, disease, increasing road casualties, severe winters, an increasing mink population, the impact of fisheries and killing for pelts. After considering the information presented in *Otters 1977*, the Conservancy was able to convince the Government to put it on the schedule of protected animals (in England and Wales) under THE CONSERVATION OF WILD CREATURES AND WILD PLANTS ACT 1975 from 1st January 1978.

By the publication of the second report, *Otters 1979*, there was a growing consensus that the widespread use of the pesticide dieldrin introduced in 1955 for a wide range of uses, including sheep-dipping, seed dressing and mothproofing, was the most likely cause for the decline of otters around 1957. A combination of other factors had contributed to the otter's failure to recover to former levels. The use of dieldrin as a seed dressing for spring-sown cereals was withdrawn by voluntary agreement in 1962, and most other uses stopped in 1965 and 1966.

A programme of comparable sample surveys of otter distribution was also underway and, by 1981, all countries were covered.

In England the survey was run by the Conservancy, in Scotland it was sponsored by the Vincent Wildlife Trust and in Wales it was co-sponsored by the Society and the Conservancy and funded by the Job Creation Programme of the Government's Manpower Services Commission. In Ireland it was undertaken by the Vincent Wildlife Trust. These surveys showed how serious the decline in England had become, particularly in comparison with Ireland where signs of otters were found practically everywhere that the surveyors looked.

Throughout this period, the Group and the Society's Project Officer played an important coordinating and networking role, keeping channels of commun-ication open, if and when conflicts arose. Sustained effort by the Group also helped keep the plight of the otter higher on the political agenda than it would otherwise have been. The Group also played a crucial part in the promotion of specific management proposals for the otter, such as the introduction of otter havens and artificial otter holts, as well as more wildlife-friendly management practices for rivers and wetlands generally. These, and the many other initiatives that followed, would lead to the substantial recovery of otter populations by the end of the century.

P

PAUL AYRES MEMORIAL FUND

In March 1972, shortly before his death, Henry James Newlin transferred the assets of his Trust Fund to the Society. This was accompanied by a request that the assets should be known as the Paul Ayres Memorial Fund and used for a revolving loan fund for the purchase of nature reserves by the Trusts. In the short-term, he agreed they could be used for general purposes. When he died in July 1972, the Society received a further bequest of £50,000, copyright to the "literary work. . . *Selected Poems by Paul Ayres with a biographical commentary by HJ Newlin*"[206] and the residue of his estate. The additional funds were to be treated in the same way as the original gift.

In the first instance, Newlin had gifted the residue of his estate to the People's Republic of China "in token restitution on behalf of my country for the damages sustained by the People of China in the Opium Wars". [207] The Chinese Ambassador, however, had turned down the bequest.

It is clear that the erotic nature of the poems proved an embarrassment to the Society. Their "value was open to question, and in any case much of the material was un-publishable. . . it was agreed to seek further literary opinion on the merit of the poems but meantime not to authorise publication at the Society's expense".[208]

The Society's annual report for 1975–76 put the value of the fund, at around £86,500. Later, arrangements were made for the fund to be merged with the Nuffield Loan Fund. The resulting Nuffield and Paul Ayres Revolving Loan Fund was to be used for loans to Trusts for reserve purchase.

PEATLANDS CAMPAIGN

At the end of the 1980s, a number of national conservation organisations were seriously concerned about the continuing damage to the country's peatlands and the recent desecration of sites, such as Thorne and Hatfield Moors in Yorkshire, Fenns Moss in Shropshire and Ballynahone Bog in Northern Ireland. They agreed to work together as a Peatlands Consortium and a campaign was launched in the spring of 1990. The aim was to protect the UK's remaining peatlands and reduce, and if possible eliminate, the horticultural uses of peat and peat products. The Society was a leading member of the Consortium and its own peat campaign, led by its Conservation Officer, Caroline Steel, became one of its most successful policy campaigns.

Launch of the Peatlands Consortium in 1990

The Society's first contribution to the Consortium was to commission research from Sheffield University on the commercial exploitation of peatlands in the UK and viable alternatives to the use of peat in horticulture. It was essential for the credibility of the campaign that the Consortium had this detailed assessment of the industry.

At the Society's national conference in Nottingham in April 1990, (CONFERENCES) delegates wore distinctive *For Peat's Sake* t-shirts and the Society launched its Peatlands Protection Charter. Those who signed the Charter agreed to phase out the use of peat and promote its replacement with substitutes or composting. The peat industry was angry that its actions were being questioned. Fisons and the

Peat Producers' Association wrote to local authorities telling them not to sign the Charter and were dismissive of the idea that alternative products could do as good a job as peat. The campaign realised it would need to provide sound practical evidence that alternatives could be successful and set about encouraging trials of peat-free products. In the meantime, the campaign was getting support from some powerful quarters.

Despite the objections from the peat producers, several local authorities had already signed up to the Charter and, at the Nottingham conference, there was the surprise announcement (for the delegates at least) that the Society's Patron, HRH The Prince of Wales, was to ban the use of peat in the gardens of his home at Highgrove in Gloucestershire and on landscape projects within the Duchy of Cornwall. His Royal Highness had asked for detailed discussions behind the scenes – including a flying visit by Sands, Steel, and JOHN PHILLIPSON to Balmoral – before making the decision.

The Patron's message to the conference, and to anyone else who would listen, was that, "if we would like other countries to stop regarding their rainforests as 'useless jungle', we would do well to set an example by not treating our peatland habitat as 'useless bog', to be drained, dug up and scattered in our gardens".[209] The Charter and the Prince's forthright endorsement of the Peatlands Campaign were particularly timely in view of the horticultural industry's hostile reaction. The story was extensively covered by the Sunday papers, dailies, television and radio. In *The Archers*, Radio 4's long running soap, Jack Woolley of Grey Gables signed the Charter and spent a week of episodes encouraging the inhabitants of Ambridge to use alternatives to peat. By October 1990, a poll in a gardening magazine showed that 98 per cent of its respondents knew of the peat issue.

In 1990, the Society distributed large quantities of a new leaflet – *Peatlands in Peril* – in its

693

Focus On series and published *The Peat Report* on behalf of the ten Consortium organisations. *The Peat Report* presented an initial review of the existing peatlands' resource; its conservation significance and the rate of its destruction; the peat industry and the various uses of peat by horticulturalists and gardeners.

A selection of peatland campaign literature from the Society and the Consortium

All forms of peatland – lowland raised bog, lowland fen peat and hill-peat or blanket bog – had had their champions, such as the ecologist and broadcaster, DAVID BELLAMY. But generally, the public dismissed them as monotonous and unproductive. *The Peat Report*, in contrast, stressed the magic of the mire. Peatlands were biologically rich and internationally important. They were also important as a genetic resource; as unique living archives and sensitive indicators of environmental change; as sponges to hold valuable supplies of freshwater, and as carbon sinks.

Until the 1920s, commercial growers and gardeners had employed their own compost formulas, usually based on loam. In the 1930s, Lawrence and Newell, working at the John Innes Horticultural Institution, developed the first standardised seeding and potting composts, consisting of loam, peat and sand. These were widely adopted. However, problems were experienced as it became more

difficult to obtain good quality loam soil and this stimulated research into alternative media. Despite scepticism of its efficacy, peat and peat-based products became the most important growing media for both professional and amateur growers with some 2.5 million cubic metres of peat used annually at the time in the UK.

The Peat Report also summarised the Consortium's objectives. It was looking for the protection or rehabilitation of peatlands; a review of the planning consents for peat extraction; the development of alternative materials and practices to replace peat; and the implementation of a UK strategy for peatlands' conservation.

By March 1991, the Society was able to build on the findings of the Sheffield research, as well as research undertaken by the Conservancy, and prepare *Losing Ground–Gaining Ground: Peatlands*. This second report estimated that there were only 5,300 hectares of pristine lowland raised bog remaining in England, Scotland and Wales. There was existing planning permission to extract peat on more than 11,000 hectares in Great Britain and Northern Ireland and, of the ten largest key sites for nature conservation listed in the Conservancy's *Nature Conservation Review*, six were partially or completely cut over. The Society was, however, also able to report progress. The campaign had raised the profile of the peat problem and increased the demand for peat-free products, helped by considerable media coverage. Events such as a House of Lords' debate in May 1990, encouraged by the Society and introduced by Lord Moran, highlighted the issues to key players in the Government, in industry and in local authorities. No new

Large heath butterfly at Crowle Moor, Lincolnshire Wildlife Trust nature reserve

planning consents for peat extraction had been granted by local authorities and, arising out of the Lords' debate, the Government agreed to a review of commercial peat extraction.

A measure of the success of the campaign, at least in its first five years, was apparent in the Society's report, *Cut and Dried*, published in March 1995. During the intervening years, the Society had held a series of annual National Bog Days, attracting thousands of visitors, and had published *Gardening Without Peat* and a *Guide to Community Composting* to help local groups. Through its *Growing Wiser* conference and report, it had also been able to present evidence of the successful use of peat-free products. Top horticulturalists had begun switching to peat-free products. Geoff Hamilton, presenter of the popular television programme *Gardeners' World*, promoted the use of peat-free compost on his programme and by speaking at the Society's events. "I grow one hundred and fifty thousand plants every year in peat-free compost with no problems. If I can do it, so can anyone".[210]

By the time *Cut and Dried* was published in 1995, nearly 60 local authorities had signed the Society's Peatlands Charter, and 96 per cent of their soil improvers were peat-free. The Peat Producers' Association had agreed not to seek permission to work pristine bogs and all major garden centre chains had stopped selling peat from SSSIs and significantly increased sales of peat-free composts. The Department of the Environment had completed its review of peat working and issued new draft Mineral Planning Guidance that made it harder to win permission to extract peat; the Department of Energy no longer considered peat as a commercial energy source; and the Department of Transport had cut peat use by more than 97 per cent. At the European level, the conservation of raised bogs had been established as a priority under the newly-agreed European Union Habitats Directive; European eco-labelling was to be withheld from soil improvers containing peat; and European Union funding had been given to major peatland projects in Scotland and Somerset.

There was no room, however, for complacency. The Government was unwilling to outlaw peat extraction altogether, so success relied on reducing demand, with a corresponding increase in peat-free products. There was good news in 1996 when the Consortium organised a *Plants Without Peat* event over the Easter weekend. More than 300 volunteers talked to 6,000 customers at 60 events across the UK in Great Mills and B&Q stores and a number of independent garden

Encouraging gardeners to go peat-free – campaigning in garden centres

centres. On days the volunteers were in-store, sales of peat-free composts increased from between five and seven per cent – the average before the campaign – to 53 per cent of compost sales.

In 1995, as part of its commitment to the Biological Diversity Convention signed at the Earth Summit in 1992, the Government published a series of Biodiversity Action Plans (BAP), including an initial plan for Lowland Raised Bogs (BIODIVERSITY ACTION PLANNING). The final version of this BAP was agreed in 1999. The targets established were first to "maintain the current distribution and extent (about 6,000ha) of primary near-natural lowland raised peat bog in the UK and ensure that the condition of this resource is maintained where favourable or enhanced through appropriate management".[211] Second, to "establish by 2005 appropriate hydrological and management regimes at those areas which have been damaged but still retain nature conservation interest (about 7,000ha) and aim to achieve favourable condition of those areas by 2015".[212] Third, by 2002, to "identify areas, timescales and targets for restoration or improvement of significantly altered raised bog areas, including those used for agriculture, peat workings and woodlands"[213] and fourth, to "initiate by 2005 improvement or restoration management on areas which have been identified in (3), according to the agreed timescale".[214]

There is no doubt that the Consortium's campaign, and the part played by the Society in that campaign, helped protect peatlands. No bog outside a nature reserve would have been safe. Planning guidance and the law were strengthened to protect peatlands generally and several important

sites were saved, with several more the focus of some exciting rehabilitation schemes.

In March 2002, English Nature and DEFRA bought out the rights for peat extraction at three of the largest worked bog sites in England from Scotts Ltd at a cost of £17.3 million. Peat cutting at Wedholme Flow, Cumbria, and Thorne Moor, South Yorkshire, ceased and a phased withdrawal from a third site at Hatfield commenced, with harvesting stopping by the autumn of 2004.

Staffordshire Wildlife Trust's own brand peat-free compost

The Society continued to update its guide for gardeners on *Where to Buy Peat-Free Products*. The Peat Producers' Association changed its name to the Growing Media Association (GMA) and their website now refers to the UK Government's commitment to reduce the use of peat to protect biodiversity. Within horticulture, it claims, "there is a continuing effort to use other, more renewable, materials in addition to peat in our growing media. Members of the GMA have been at the forefront of such work". [215]

Unfortunately, the unsustainable practice of extracting peat for horticultural use continued and

Bringing peatlands back to life – a restoration area at Thorne Moor, South Yorkshire, managed by Natural England

voluntary phase out targets for the horticultural industry were not met. In December 2010, the Government issued a consultation on reducing the horticultural use of peat in England. Despite continued campaigning by The Wildlife Trusts and other environmental organisations for a tougher regulatory approach, Government chose again to prefer a voluntary, industry-led phase out, this time with a final target date of 2030.

On the positive side, a new Peat Taskforce was established to ensure the new targets were met. In addition, draft *National Planning Policy Guidance for England*, published in July 2011, stated that planning authorities should not grant planning permission for peat extraction from new or extended sites in the future. So there is real hope that there will soon, finally, be an end to the granting of consents for further peat extraction.

PERRING, FRANK

Franklyn Hugh Perring (1927–2003) was the Society's General Secretary (PRINCIPAL OFFICERS) between 1979 and 1987. During this period, he substantially increased the profile and resources of the Trust movement by driving through a series of imaginative, bold, and sometimes controversial, initiatives.

'Frank', as he was generally known in the Trust movement, made his name first as Senior Worker, and then in 1959, as Director of the Botanical Society of the British Isles' Distribution Map Scheme. He was co-author of the resulting and groundbreaking *Atlas of the British Flora*, published in 1962. In 1964, he became Head of the Conservancy's (after 1973 the Institute of Terrestrial Ecology's (ITE)) Biological Records Centre at Monks Wood Experimental Station in Huntingdonshire. Here, he continued to work tirelessly to promote biological recording. He was at the forefront of the campaign to establish local records centres.

He was involved with the establishment of the Cambridge and Isle of Ely Trust in 1956 and on its Council until 1982. He was an active Council member of the NORTHAMPTONSHIRE TRUST, helping to organise, for example, a series of popular medieval fairs. He became its Chairman between 1985 and 1987. He also founded the PETERBOROUGH WILDLIFE GROUP in 1987 and became its first Chairman.

Perring came to the Society in 1979 with a justifiable reputation as a botanist *par excellence* and as a passionate supporter of the voluntary conservation sector, and the local Trusts in particular. His independent approach and relative intolerance of bureaucracy had found him increasingly at odds with the more rigid regime of ITE management. At the Society, Perring saw an opportunity to promote the

Frank Perring

cause of conservation more widely, in relative freedom and on the national stage.

After his retirement as the Society's General Secretary in 1987, Perring continued his writing and active support of many wildlife organisations, in particular the Botanical Society of the British Isles and his local Trust. He was concerned at the demise, as he saw it, of the study of plant taxonomy and field naturalists and devoted much of his time to the development of various identification training schemes, particularly within his home Trust. In 1988, he was a co-founder of WILDLIFE TRAVEL – a holiday company that donates any profits to conservation through the Trusts – and led many European and long-haul holidays, building up a loyal band of travellers in the process.

Among the many landmarks during Perring's busy reign as the Society's General Secretary, the ones that gave him particular satisfaction were the launch of NATURAL WORLD, the successful BRITISH WILDLIFE APPEAL and persuading the Society to nurture and embrace the burgeoning Urban Wildlife Groups within the Trust family (URBAN AREAS AND NATURE CONSERVATION).

PHILLIPSON, JOHN

John Phillipson (1927–2001) was a member and Chairman of the Society's Conservation and Scientific Committee, Chairman of the Society's Executive Committee between 1988 and 1993, and of its Council between 1991 and 1994.

During the time he was Lecturer in Ecology at the University of Durham, Phillipson was a member of the NORTHUMBERLAND AND DURHAM TRUST. When he later moved to become Reader in Ecology at the University of Oxford, he joined the BERKSHIRE, BUCKINGHAMSHIRE AND OXFORDSHIRE TRUST and was its Chairman between 1980 and 1985. He was also a member of the Nature Conservancy Council between 1973 and 1979. He was Emeritus Fellow of Linacre College, Oxford at the time of his death.

On the appointment of ROBIN CRANE as his successor as Chairman of the Society's Council in 1994, Council paid tribute to Phillipson's contribution in steering the Society through difficult times, including revision of the Society's Royal Charter and the Corporate Strategy – two key stages in defining the new role of the Society within the Wildlife Trusts' Partnership. His many years of dedicated service within the Partnership more generally were also gratefully acknowledged.

PLANNING AND WILDLIFE

Influencing the planning system for the benefit of wildlife has been part of The Wildlife Trusts' work since the earliest days. The LINCOLNSHIRE TRUST was formed in 1948 to fight development of a proposed caravan park at Gibraltar Point, near Skegness. Within ten days of its formation, the Trust had overturned the application and secured the future of the site which later became the first Local Nature Reserve designated in England.

As the century progressed, the Trusts developed their understanding and increased their influence on local and regional plans and individual planning decisions as proposals for roads, housing and whole towns continued apace. By the end of the millennium, most Trusts had planning staff and volunteers

checking tens of thousands of planning applications across the country every year.

A 1963 paper in the HAMPSHIRE AND ISLE OF WIGHT WILDLIFE TRUST archives reflects the Trusts' general approach to planning issues in the early 1960s. The paper acknowledges that it would not be possible "to keep back the economic tide",[216] but states that "it should be one of the prime duties of the Trust to become aware of these potential developments and to make developers aware of conservation needs".[217] Over the years, Trusts have performed these duties using the best available science and quiet diplomacy, with recourse to public inquiries where necessary.

And there have been many notable triumphs. For example, in the late 1970s, the CUMBRIA TRUST helped thwart a planning application to extract limestone pavement from Hampsfell, near Grange-over-Sands in Cumbria. This was the last-ever proposal for new limestone pavement extraction in the county and over the following two decades all the remaining extraction sites were closed as permissions ran out.

Another significant success, in the heart of rural Oxfordshire, to which BBOWT made an important contribution, was the overturning at public inquiry in 1989 of a proposal to create a full-scale new town, Stone Bassett, next to Spartum Fen SSSI.

Trusts review thousands of planning applications each year to check for potential impacts on local wildlife

The local Trust worked with planners and developers to ensure that natural features such as woods and lakes were integrated into the design of the new town of Cambourne, near Cambridge

Two major success stories from England's north-west were the quashing of applications for landfill at Red Moss SSSI near Bolton, Greater Manchester, in 1994, and the successful negotiation of a nature conservation after-use following sand extraction at Mere Sands Wood, Rufford, Lancashire in 1982. The former resulted in an ongoing management agreement for the WILDLIFE TRUST FOR LANCASHIRE, MANCHESTER AND NORTH MERSEYSIDE with the site's owners, Bolton Metropolitan Borough Council. The latter resulted in a flagship nature reserve and visitor centre, still owned and managed by the Trust. In Hampshire, the fact that wildlife interests could win, even against big money, was demonstrated in 2004 when the proposed Dibden Bay port on the New Forest coast was rejected by the Government.

But there have been dramatic losses too. Motorways have cut through some of the richest countryside. In southern England, for example, one of the last links in the network, the M3 at Winchester, was disputed for decades. This planning debate concluded with the debacle of Twyford Down where, throughout the early 1990s, eco-warriors, road protestors and concerned citizens challenged the folly of cutting through the chalk grasslands at the gateway to the South Downs.

These days, Trusts have to face tougher opposition in the fight against damaging planning proposals. The time when science and a persuasive case could win the day is long gone. As the value of developments has increased, so has the profession of consultants and planning lawyers who will argue the case for development.

To help meet the new challenges Trusts have adapted the way they operate, focusing efforts on influencing planning to ensure that urban growth occurs where it will do the least harm to wildlife. The HAMPSHIRE AND ISLE OF WIGHT TRUST, for example, provides excellent examples of the rewards that can be reaped by forward planning and constructive interaction. Its three education and visitor centres – at Swanwick Lakes, Testwood Lakes and Blashford Lakes respectively – all emerged from major developments. In addition, and where appropriate, Trusts work with construction companies to ensure that new developments, such as Cambourne in Cambridgeshire and Chafford Gorges in Essex, incorporate and protect natural features and habitats, such as grassland and woodland, benefiting wildlife and local residents alike.

R

RED DATA BOOK

The British Red Data Book 1: Vascular Plants (RDB), compiled by Frank Perring and published by the Society in collaboration with the Conservancy in 1977, was the first of its kind in the UK. A second edition, compiled by Perring and Lynne Farrell, was published by the Society (again in collaboration with the Conservancy) in 1983, with the financial support of WWF.

The RDB was "an attempt to make a factual statement about the present status of the endemic and rare vascular plants in Britain and to include those other species which appear to be now so rare that their continued existence on our flora is in question".[218] The second edition listed 330 species occurring in 15 or fewer ten kilometre squares (including four European endemics and six non-endemic species not eligible under these criteria).

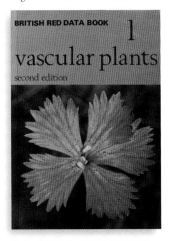

The first British Red Data Book for plants - published by the Society in 1977

There were two main reasons put forward for producing the RDB. First, to complement parallel work by the Threatened Plants Committee of the International Union for Conservation of Nature and Natural Resources (IUCN), who produced a *List of Rare, Threatened and Endemic Plants for the Countries of Europe*, in

1976. The second reason was to provide more robust information for updating the list of protected species under Schedule 2 of the CONSERVATION OF WILD CREATURES AND WILD PLANTS ACT 1975. During the passage of the Wildlife and Countryside Bill in 1981 (which repealed the 1975 legislation), the RDB was "accepted as a definitive guide to the endangered and vulnerable plant species"[219] and a further 42 species were added to the schedule. One, *Daphne mezereum*, was removed.

It was also true that the RDB highlighted the role being played by organisations in the conservation of the listed species. Nearly 40 species, for example, received protection by occurring on one or more Trust reserves. However, in the second edition, 64 species, marked 'no conservation', occurred in sites that received no formal protection, although the RDB conceded that "sixteen of these are arable weeds where such protection is not easily arranged".[220]

RED KITE

The red kite was the subject of the Society's first logo. It had been a widespread and relatively common bird across the whole of Britain, but was confined to central Wales by the middle of the second half of the 19th century. The species was threatened with extinction and, in 1905, a Kite Committee was formed under the auspices of the British Ornithologists' Club, with a membership that included naturalists and scientists that would later become associated with the Society, for example, MEADE-WALDO, OGILVIE-GRANT and LORD WALTER ROTHSCHILD. The RSPB became directly involved as early as 1922, and the Society made donations to a Kite Preservation Fund organised by the RSPB's warden in 1938 and 1939

(DONATIONS BEFORE THE SECOND WORLD WAR). But, despite considerable "toil and expenditure",[221] the first 40 years of red kite conservation in Wales saw little or no improvement in the bird's status. The years were also peppered with controversy. Strong-willed personalities displayed excessive secrecy and personal hostility to fellow naturalists. In one case, kite eggs were sold by a 'trusted' watcher and, in another case, eggs were exhibited at an Oologists' Association meeting.

Red kite nest, Upper Towy Valley, 1926 – a stronghold for red kites. There were only around 20 individuals in Britain by the 1920s

In 1949, the WEST WALES FIELD SOCIETY, established four years earlier, was asked to set up a new Kite Committee with representation from the RSPB, the Council for the Protection of Rural Wales, Cardiff Naturalists' Society, as well as the Society and the Field Society itself. However, despite successful years as far as the red kite was concerned – with 15 young kites reaching the flying stage in 1954, the highest number so far in the century – stresses and strains within the Committee led to its break-up and its last meeting was held in 1955.

The following year, disaster struck the kites, with myxomatosis decimating the rabbit population, the kite's main food source.

In 1958, an 'acceptable formula' was devised between "the opposing parties within the moribund Kite Committee",[222] and thanks largely to the good offices of LORD HURCOMB, the Society's and the RSPB's President, a meeting was held and peace restored. The RSPB took on responsibility for special measures for the red kite and the Conservancy's newly-appointed Regional Officer took on research into its ecology. A new chapter in kite conservation had begun.

The Red Kite Committee in 1964. Third from right is William Condry, founder of the West Wales Trust

By 1970, it was possible to report that "we now have in Wales a kite population of approaching seventy birds".[223] Today, with the help of re-introductions and conservation measures by a range of organisations and individuals, numbers have increased in the UK to between 1,800 and 2,000 pairs.

REGAN, CHARLES TATE
Charles Tate Regan (1878–1943) was HONORARY TREASURER of the Society between 1927 and 1938,

Charles Tate Regan

although from 1932 he was joined by an Assistant Honorary Treasurer, THOMAS WOODDISSE.

Regan was an ichthyologist who did extensive work on fish classification schemes. He joined the staff of the Natural History Museum in London in 1901 where he became Keeper of Zoology. He was the Director of the whole museum between 1927 and 1938.

REGIONAL LIAISON COMMITTEE
In July 1958, the Society established the first formal mechanism for bringing the Trusts together (eight Naturalists' Trusts at the time) at a national level with the formation of its Regional Liaison Committee. The Committee provided "a meeting ground where representatives of these Trusts could discuss common interests amongst themselves and with officers of the Society and members of Council".[224] In November 1959, the work of the Committee was more than the Society's secretariat could handle. TED SMITH was appointed Honorary Secretary to the Committee and CHRISTOPHER CADBURY replaced its first Chairman, Captain CYRIL DIVER, in 1960. The Committee was renamed, first the Naturalists' Trusts' Committee, and then, a year later, the County Naturalists' Trusts' Committee. By 1964, as many as 30 Trusts were attending meetings of the Committee.

By 1971, all Trusts had nominees on the Society's Council and so, in 1972, after 41 meetings, the Committee was disbanded and its functions transferred to the Society's Council. The Society was granted a new Royal Charter in 1976 under which Trusts elected the majority of the Society's Council for the first time.

RESERVES ENHANCEMENT SCHEME
In 1989, the Conservancy and WWF commissioned a review of funding

support for voluntary conservation organisations. It recommended that money should be made available to them to ensure that, at a minimum, they could find the long-term costs of managing their own land. Inflation, and the cessation of the Government's Community Programme employment scheme in 1988, meant the cost of managing SSSIs had risen steeply. Grants from Government had remained elusive and the Conservancy also threatened to limit money for management agreements under Section 38 of the Wildlife and Countryside Act 1981. In April 1990, the Trusts urged the Society to commission a three-month desk study to determine what Trusts were actually spending, and what they would ideally like to spend, to manage the 855 SSSIs under their care.

The study estimated that Trusts nationwide were spending around £2 million on direct SSSI management, but three times this figure was what was ideally required. Significantly, it also showed that, while the Conservancy was planning to pay an average of £109 per hectare under its SSSI agreements with other landowners, the equivalent figure for the management of SSSIs by Trusts was estimated at only £77 per hectare. In other words, supporting the Trusts' management of SSSIs would represent good value for money. The study found that the Conservancy's response to approaches by Trusts over recent years regarding positive management agreements, had been "mixed, contradictory, but generally negative".[225] If the "conservation and proper management of SSSIs is vital to the maintenance of Britain's wildlife in all its forms",[226] then, the study concluded, there was an urgent need to increase the Conservancy's funding to Trusts.

The study, based as it was on a small sample, was undoubtedly

Ash woodland at Short Wood, Northamptonshire – newly-coppiced under the Reserves Enhancement Scheme

'quick and dirty', but it was timely and generally accepted as a sound basis for discussions. Partly because of the break-up of the Conservancy in 1990, it was the end of 1991 before the climate was right for a small team of Trust representatives to have initial negotiations with the staff of, what had now become, English Nature. There were tricky matters to be discussed. How much would English Nature actually pay? What would be eligible as matching funding? Would money be available for capital expenditure? English Nature was keen to see a scheme get off the ground and, over the next five months, its staff worked assiduously to hammer out the details. In the first place, it would be a pilot scheme run exclusively for the Trusts. The Reserves Enhancement Scheme (RES), as it was to be known, would provide grant-aid for five years towards the costs of managing the Trusts' SSSIs. The scheme would use standard payments based on habitat types and money *would* be available for capital spending. The scheme was finally launched in the summer of 1992.

A meeting of English Nature and the English Trusts' representatives took place shortly before the deadline for applications at the end of July.

Even at this stage there were worries. Would English Nature get agreement from Government to enable all Trusts to eventually come on board? How would the payments affect the Trusts' draw-down of other Government grant schemes? At the meeting, English Nature made it clear that it fully intended go back to the Treasury for additional support in its next annual funding round, if the pilot proved successful. Tim Sands congratulated English Nature on grasping the nettle. "The decision that it is equally correct for Government money to be used to manage the nation's heritage whether a site is managed by a private landowner, statutory agency or a Wildlife Trust has been deferred too long and as a result management, and the resources to do that management, has some catching up – this needs to be recognised in the RES as it develops".[227]

The RES was something that had been dreamt of for years. If Trusts could deliver and make a success of the pilot, then the prospects were good. The RES *was* successful – by the third year, funding had increased to more than £600,000. A precedent had been set that would prove a valuable springboard for further development of the scheme

and would help set the scene for parallel work in other parts of the UK.

The RES closed in 2006 on the formation of Natural England (see STATUTORY NATURE CONSERVATION AGENCIES), largely because Natural England believed SSSI management would be supported by the new Higher Level Stewardship funding that they would try to make available for this purpose.

RILEY, NORMAN

Norman Riley (1890–1979) became HONORARY SECRETARY of the Society on the death of HERBERT SMITH in 1953. He was the main bridge between the Society's early years and its developing role as the national association of the Wildlife Trusts.

Riley joined the Natural History Museum in London in 1911 and was the Keeper of its Department of Entomology from 1932 to 1955. After retirement, he continued to work from the museum and, later in life, with his long-time colleague, Dr Lionel Higgins, compiled the first comprehensive field guide to the butterflies of Britain and Europe, which was published by Collins in 1970.

Norman Riley

The late 1950s and early 1960s saw the growth in the Trusts, for which the Society had been striving, and with it a rapid and unprecedented increase in the Society's workload. Despite his increasing years, and the loss of retirement leisure, Riley took on his share of this work. He believed it was his job to sustain the Society's traditional role whilst at the same time encouraging the new developments.

He regarded his appointment as HONORARY SECRETARY, as he often said, as temporary until a more permanent successor could be found, but it lasted 15 years. With a further four years as HONORARY TREASURER, his time with the Society covered one of the most momentous periods in its history.

ROAD-BUILDING AND WILDLIFE

The second half of the 20th century witnessed a huge explosion in car ownership and a corresponding growth in the country's road network.

In 1989, the Government's White Paper, *Roads for Prosperity*, announced a massive ten-year road-building programme worth £12 billion – "the largest road-building programme in British history".[228] Environmental groups, including the Society, were annoyed that the document was portrayed by Government as a green initiative. They published *Roads to Ruin* in 1990 to publicise the damage that road-building could have on the environment. It also identified the need for a more integrated solution to the country's transport problems. The LONDON TRUST and other Trusts in the south-east were particularly concerned about the large number of schemes in their region, including a proposal to build an outer M25 ring road. They were also concerned, more generally, at the lack of detailed information about the impact of the Government's proposals on wildlife.

A transport campaigner was appointed by the Trusts in 1990, with the support of the Society and

The extension of the M3 motorway at Twyford Down

WWF, and a report, *Head on Collision – Road-Building and Wildlife in South-East England*, was published by the Society the same year. A further report, *Ever Increasing Circles – the Impact and Effectiveness of the M25 Plan*, written by Rupert Harwood, STEPHANIE HILBORNE and others, followed two years later. It showed that as many as 81 important wildlife sites could be damaged by the M25 plan.

Initially, the campaign was centred on the south-east, but eventually, with the help of a national Transport Coordinator, Jill Barton, and with funding from the Countryside Commission and WWF, the methods used to assess the impact of the road programme on wildlife were rolled-out to other Trust regions. Help was also given to Trusts to produce their own regional reports. Over the next seven years, 90 per cent of Trusts became involved, in one way or another, with the transport campaign. A further seven reports were published covering Yorkshire, the North-West, the Heart of England, the East Midlands, Scotland, Wales, the South-West and, in 1997, the counties of Berkshire, Buckinghamshire and Oxfordshire, Cambridgeshire, Bedfordshire, Northamptonshire, Hertfordshire and Essex. Like the initiatives to improve liaison with the water

industry in the 1970s and early 1980s, these initiatives represented a further early example of the Trusts in England working together at the regional level to achieve a common objective.

The South-East report revealed for the first time what a serious impact the roads programme could have, and was having, on wildlife. The report identified 372 important wildlife sites threatened by road-building in nine counties. One site, Oxleas Wood on the route of the East London River Crossing, became something of a *cause célèbre*, and the first major wildlife site saved

Comedian Rory Bremner launches the South-East Trusts' *Head on Collision* report

The M65 extension destroys Walton Banks Wood, Lancashire

from the 'tarmac tide' as a result of public pressure. Overall, the seven reports identified more than 1,000 sites under threat.

By 1995, following the headline-grabbing destruction a year earlier of part of an SSSI at Twyford Down in Hampshire by the M3 motorway extension, the Trusts' report for the north-west was chronicling signs of a softening of Government policy. The Department of Transport had published *Trunk Roads in England: 1994 Review*, which announced the removal of some road schemes from the programme and prioritised others – 200 road schemes were to be reassessed. In addition, the Government's Planning Policy Guidance had been "revised, with emphasis placed on the integration of Development and Transport Planning to reduce the need for travel, and higher priority given to integrated transport schemes in urban areas, including the encouragement of public transport".[229] Subsequently, the campaign also helped bring about a change to trunk road assessment with environmental concerns given more weight in the cost/benefit analysis process.

The campaign had had an impact: wildlife and wildlife sites had been saved and, during its lifetime, biodiversity had become a significant issue in the transport debate. The campaign had brought Trusts together, unifying their thinking and enabling them to share a place with other environmental organisations at the transport round-table. Trusts, for example, were represented on Transport 2000's Transport and Biodiversity Group, active into the new millennium.

However, despite the gains, people's love affair with the car remained undiminished and the inexorable growth in the use and number of cars continued. Despite technological improvements, more cars and more car-miles meant more carbon dioxide emissions, with a consequent knock-on effect on global warming and climate change. Transport campaigners' focus increasingly turned to these issues. Concerted campaigning ultimately led to the Climate Change Act 2008. But further action needed to be taken by Government if it was to meet its own target of a 60 per cent cut in carbon dioxide emissions on 1990 levels by 2050.

ROADSIDE VERGES

Wildlife and countryside organisations have long recognised roadside verges as important wildlife refuges. "Road verges and hedgerows are one of England's great natural assets forming in many counties the largest remaining tract of semi-natural vegetation".[230] They are reservoirs for wildlife that has become rare or localised elsewhere and provide corridors along which plants and animals can spread and move.

In the past, in many counties, it was not unusual for verges to be grazed or mown for hay. But the arrival of the motor car generally changed these practices. The new forms of management were harmful to fauna and flora and many acres of roadside verge were lost or damaged through the upgrading of roads, the laying of pipes and tipping.

As the early as the 1920s, the historian, John Sheail, refers to the worsening relations between voluntary bodies and local authorities, because of the requirements placed on the highway authorities to cut the grass on banks and verges. He describes how "in March 1934 the CPRE approached the County Councils Association and asked if verges could be left uncut until July or the early autumn each year, and that only the sward and herbs near the road should be cut. . . but the Association dismissed the recommendations as impracticable".[231] In the 1950s, local authorities started using herbicides. Wildflowers and vegetation became unsightly and spray-drift killed roadside fauna and damaged nearby hedgerows.

In 1955, the Conservancy reached an agreement with the Ministry of Transport regarding road verge spraying. But in 1961, TED SMITH observed that on several occasions the agreement was ignored. For example, despite representations made by the West Midlands Trust and others, Staffordshire County Council consistently refused to adhere to the agreement. But in most counties the situation was better. In Lincolnshire in 1960, a Protected Road Verge Scheme involving two

County Councils, the Conservancy and the Trust identified important stretches of verge. White posts flagged up these sites to Council workers, pinpointing their need for special protection and management. It "attracted a great deal of interest, and similar schemes were adopted in more than twenty other English counties in the following ten years".[232] In Sussex, for example, 57 verges were protected with an aggregate length of approximately ten miles.

In 1967, Norman Moore, then Head of the Conservancy's Toxic Chemicals and Wildlife Division, was calling for more of these schemes, for herbicides to be used as little as possible and for more sympathetic management. In 1968, 20 local authorities agreed to time their cutting of verges to minimise disruption to wildlife and many of them agreed to limit the use of herbicides.

This leaflet containing advice on how to manage verges for wildlife was produced by the Society in conjunction with Wildflower Week 1986

Early in 1995, as part of its *Head on Collision* campaign, the Society published the findings of a roadside verge survey conducted through the Trusts and local authorities. The survey, sponsored by Shell UK Ltd, found that 65 per cent of Highway Authorities had verges specifically

managed for conservation, but detailed information about them was poor. What was needed was a comprehensive survey. In addition, the Society wanted local authorities to have a duty to manage verges for the benefit of wildlife.

Over the years, practices have generally improved and indeed motorways, with their requirement for more extensive verges and embankments, have provided more opportunities for roadside wildlife. Many Trusts continue to work with the appropriate authorities to identify and monitor sites, to provide management advice and, on occasions, to defend important verges against development.

Life on the Verge is one of the most recent projects. Hosted by the LINCOLNSHIRE TRUST, the project has been identifying the most important roadside verges for limestone grassland in Lincolnshire and Rutland and East Leicestershire. The project has used more than 70 trained volunteers, many recruited through the internet. The project moved on in 2011 to look at the most important verges in the Lincolnshire Wolds.

ROTHSCHILD, CHARLES

Nathaniel Charles Rothschild (1877–1923) was an entomologist and a pioneer of nature conservation in Britain. He was the inspirational founder and first Chairman of the Society for the Promotion of Nature Reserves (NAMES OF THE SOCIETY).

A man before his time, he argued for protecting not only individual species but whole natural habitats, and was convinced that conservation policy had to be based on sound survey and research. He saw Britain as part of the European, and indeed international, conservation scene and recognised the need to attract the support of influential individuals of the time, and to promote his ideas to a wider public.

A young Charles Rothschild

He published his first scientific paper, *The Lepidoptera of Harrow,* while still a schoolboy, and had been around the world twice by the age of 26. He discovered the plague vector flea (*Xenopsylla cheopis*) in Egypt which he described and named in 1903. He dutifully joined the family banking firm of NM Rothschild and Sons in London and, after a difficult start, enjoyed the City and was full of relevant and creative ideas. His daughter, Miriam Rothschild, relates that "what thoroughly irked him was the over-cautious, conservative attitude of his uncles who, for instance, prevented him financing a new invention, the gramophone disc, for which he foresaw a great future".[233] He was responsible for the management of the Royal Mint Refinery, a business run by the bank from 1852 and, at the request of his uncles, he applied his scientific mind to a systems analysis of the workings of the bank. Much to their consternation, one suspects, he came up with a radical report for improving the bank's operations.

It was in May 1912 that he was finally able to progress his ideas on protecting sites for wildlife. He convened an initial meeting with friends and colleagues that would lead to the formation of the Society for the Promotion of Nature Reserves, the first national organisation concerned primarily with conserving habitats. His idea was to use the Society to persuade others of the "desirability of preserving in perpetuity sites suitable for nature reserves".[234] The plan was "to undertake a nationwide survey of such sites with the help of local societies and individuals".[235] A list of 284 potential nature reserves was compiled by 1915 and further sites continued to be submitted after the printed list was produced in 1915.

He was described by his daughter as a lonely and isolated figure but someone who shared the family traits of wide horizons, zestful curiosity and boundless energy. A great deal of this energy was devoted to entomology – his particular interest being the Siphonaptera (fleas) – and on this subject he became the acknowledged expert. His collection of fleas, now in the Natural History Museum in London, is the largest such collection in existence.

But his interests, commitments and responsibilities were numerous and diverse. As early as 1901, he was feeling the pressure of work. In letters to his friend from university, Hugh Birrell, "he complained of being too busy to write often".[236] He was Chairman of the Alliance Assurance Company and, after the

outbreak of war, took on work for more than one Government Department. He was, for example, a member of the Munitions Board. On the death of his father in the spring of 1915, he assumed duties linked to the administration of the family's large estate. He was Deputy Lieutenant of the City of London, Justice of the Peace and had been High Sheriff of Northamptonshire. He was also a fellow, or member, of numerous scientific and learned societies. He was President of both the Northamptonshire Natural History Society and Peterborough Natural History Society and, in 1915 and 1916, President of the Entomological Society of London. In his Presidential address to that Society in January 1916, he made a special appeal for the preservation of natural areas as nature reserves and for support for his new Society.

His friend, the botanist GEORGE DRUCE, describes how when staying at Rothschild's London home, Arundel House, Rothschild "was up early and dictating letters from his bath room to his typewriters".[237] Druce believed, however, that "he had too much to deal with, his brain was never at rest. Nature exacts her penalties as well as grants gifts".[238]

Rothschild experienced a nervous breakdown, having suffered from

Charles Rothschild

mental health problems for some years and, in 1917, also "fell victim to the epidemic of encephalitis associated with the so-called Spanish influenza which swept across Europe towards the end of the war".[239] In March 1917, convalescing in Switzerland, Rothschild wrote with a typically generous donation for a further purchase of land at Wicken Fen, but finished his short letter, "I am sorry to say I am still far from well and fear it will be a good time yet before I am really cured".[240] A year later, in April 1918, his wife wrote to the Society's Secretary, "you will be pleased to hear that Mr Vaughan Williams returned from Switzerland some days ago and brought very satisfactory news about

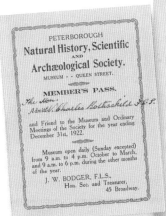

A selection of Charles Rothschild's tickets and passes for local natural history societies

Charles; he is longing to come back but his doctor thinks it could be too soon yet but he is confident that his recovery will be a complete one".[241] Unhappily, he continued to experience severe bouts of depression that ended tragically with him taking his own life at his home, Ashton Wold in Northamptonshire, on 12th October 1923.

Such was the social and religious stigma attached to her father's death that it was not until near the end of her life that his daughter, MIRIAM ROTHSCHILD, spoke more freely to her friends and family about his premature death, and the despair felt about aspects of his life and 'what might have been'. She believed that "had Rothschild been able to continue the fight for the official backing of nature conservation, the events would undoubtedly have taken a different turn. Up to the time he fell ill he was optimistic about the outcome, but once he faded from the scene the situation rapidly deteriorated".[242]

Rothschild was an all-round naturalist, benefactor and animateur, and among his greatest contributions to the scientific scene at the turn of century was his promotion of conservation. He was a man of vision – "irreplaceable because he was half a century ahead of his time".[243] Druce wrote, "to any nature lover in Britain Mr Rothschild's death is a loss. . . for he wished to preserve, as far as modern progress allows as little besmirched and mutilated as possible, the glory of our moors, heaths, woodlands and sea-shores as a heritage for the nation".[244]

In a message conveyed to his wife a few days after his death, the Society's Honorary Secretary wrote, "I am sure of voicing the feelings of every member (of the Executive) when I express how severe is the loss suffered by the Society in the tragic death of the late Mr Rothschild. It was entirely due to his inspiration

and help that the Society came into existence, and he has at all times taken the greatest interest in its activities and given a helping hand whenever required. Although his health during recent years did not allow him to attend meetings, he took pains to keep in close touch with what was happening. We deplore the loss of a generous and real friend".[245]

ROTHSCHILD, MIRIAM

Miriam Rothschild (1908–2005), daughter of the Society's founder CHARLES ROTHSCHILD, became a Council member of the Society in June 1935, was a member of the Executive Committee between 1940 and 1951 and again between 1953 and 1958, and was a Vice President of the modern Society at her death.

Although she had little formal education, she became a leading authority on many aspects of science, including the biochemistry of insect communication – publishing more than 300 scientific papers. She was devoted to her father, and her meticulous catalogue of his collection of fleas was an "ivory-tower labour of love that took half a lifetime and made her a world expert".[246]

Miriam Rothschild

As a young woman, Miriam Rothschild was active in supporting the Society's international nature conservation and represented the Society at many meetings, particularly in connection with the establishment of IUCN. She was always interested in conservation and was instrumental, for example, in the gift of DANCER'S END nature reserve to the Society in 1941. In 1962, she became Chairman of its Management Committee and encouraged experimental management to restore its grassland habitats. In describing the time she was kept waiting by the Director General of the Conservancy (the great MAX NICHOLSON) on a visit to Dancer's End, Miriam declared, "I have a rule in life that I will never wait for a man more than 30 minutes or for a woman more than 25 minutes".[247]

Later in her life, she continued her conservation work. For example, she spent much time developing her wild gardens at Ashton Wold in Northamptonshire and enthusiast-ically promoted the use of wildflower seeds. As a Vice President, she continued to keep a benevolent eye on the Society. In 1987, she held a party for friends and guests of the Society at Ashton on the occasion of its 75th anniversary. In 1997, with fellow naturalist Peter Marren, she wrote *Rothschild's Reserve*s, a comprehensive review of what had happened to the nature reserves in England selected by her father, Charles Rothschild, 80 years earlier.

In 2008, the Society inaugurated a new medal to commemorate the life and work of Miriam Rothschild and her father Charles Rothschild. The medal is awarded to an individual for outstanding achievements in the promotion, study, management or conservation of the natural environment. The design and production of the medal was generously funded by a donation from Miriam Rothschild's daughter, Charlotte Lane (MEDALS).

ROTHSCHILD'S LIST

From the beginning, CHARLES ROTHSCHILD's plan was for the Society to compile a detailed list of wildlife sites 'worthy of preservation'. His idea was to promote these sites as potential nature reserves, getting others, like The National Trust, to own and manage them. He was concerned that those reserves that had been established or proposed so far (such as the King's Moor reserve in Cumberland designated by the Cumberland Nature Reserves Association and Carlisle Corporation), were being chosen in an ad hoc way. He believed the best sites should be protected to avoid wasting resources on less significant areas.

Rothschild signed up a number of influential individuals – including large landowners, prominent politicians and scientists – as members of the Society to help in the huge task of compiling his schedule of sites. He also saw several of them as potential benefactors. The historian, John Sheail, records that, "on learning that Sir Arthur Lee had given the Chequers Estate in Buckinghamshire to the nation as a country residence for the Prime Minister, Rothschild wrote to Lee, stressing the tremendous importance of the Box Woods on the estate. They were in many respects better than those on Box Hill in Surrey. Lee promised to do his utmost to ensure the Trustees of the estate protected the trees and bushes from destruction".[248]

Rothschild's plan was to gather information, not only from members of the Society, but also from the large number of local natural history societies as well as the general public who read about

Map and completed questionnaire for Helpstone Heath, Northamptonshire. This site, now sadly destroyed, was noted as a 'breeding place for badgers, pole-cats and insects'

the Society and its objectives in the daily and weekly press.

In December 1912, *The Times* carried a prominent article and leader on the newly-formed Society and this was picked up by more than 50 other newspapers and magazines in the coming months. In February 1913, the Society distributed a letter and questionnaire to the local Societies. The questionnaire was translated into French and German for use with overseas correspondents.

Many of these questionnaires were completed by Rothschild himself, but he also enlisted the support of his friends and colleagues within the Society. Several of them also travelled around the country, including to Ireland and Scotland, to check out various sites. Completed questionnaires were filed in blue Rothschild Bank envelopes along with relevant notes and correspondence, and each area was marked on an Ordnance Survey map.

Within a year of the Society's formation, details had been received on 50 "places proposed as nature reserves"[249] and this had risen to 98

by April 1914. It was reported that "a good many of these had been inspected by members of the Executive Committee or by others on their behalf, and in many cases the Secretaries had entered into preliminary negotiations with the owners respecting their acquisition or purchase".[250] An initial list was drawn up by Rothschild and his close colleagues, including botanist, GEORGE DRUCE, the ornithologist, WILLIAM ROBERT OGILVIE-GRANT, and the ecologist, Professor Arthur Tansley.

In August 1914, Thomas Fair Husband, Head of the Commons and Survey Branch of the Government's Board of Agriculture, and a member of the Society's Council, wrote to Rothschild letting him know that the Development Commission planned to reclaim extensive areas of 'wasteland' to grow more food. This was regarded as a tip-off that many sites of interest to the Society were threatened and that the Society should complete its survey as quickly as possible. It then let the Commissioners have a list of the areas that it thought should be spared. At the very least the Society believed that, "in the event of any area scheduled by the SPNR being acquired by the Development Commissioners, they be asked to consider if a small portion of the same could not be retained as a nature reserve".[251] By 1915, a list of 284 potential nature reserves in England, Wales, Scotland and Ireland had been compiled. Many of the sites are familiar to us today, for example, Ashdown Forest in Sussex, Askham Bog in Yorkshire, Ben Lawers in Scotland and Holy Island in Northumberland. A concerted effort was made to identify the owners during 1915. Rothschild's friend and agent Richardson Carr, or his solicitor, Frank Dawes sent out more than 1,000 letters to estate agents. Multiple ownerships, tenure arrangements, the exact location of sites and war-time conditions were some of the reasons why the process was complex and, at times, fraught with difficulties.

A bound copy of the list was sent to the Board of Agriculture in the summer of 1915 with a covering letter asking it to cancel and destroy an earlier typewritten version. Rothschild and Marren refer to a printed list dated 'April 1915' as the definitive Rothschild list. There is another printed list in the Society's archive dated 'August 1915' and a further revised list was sent to the Board a year later. In the printed lists, the areas worthy of preservation are arranged alphabetically according to their names and by counties, and are divided into three levels of importance. First, areas of primary importance whose early preservation was desirable because of the specially interesting character of the locality or the urgency of the need of protection. Second, Rothschild identified areas of secondary importance whose 'reservation' was considered to be of less importance at the time. Finally, some sites were marked with an asterisk and these were of 'especial interest' and sites that Rothschild felt should be preserved *in their entirety* (his italics). The schedule was arranged in columns, noting a unique number for each site, its name, its type (i.e. its main habitat), map details and, finally, brief reasons for suggested reservation. The 'type' column contained numbers corresponding to 12 habitat types, plus a 13th category

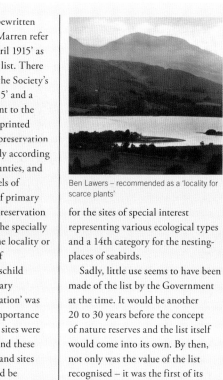

Ben Lawers – recommended as a 'locality for scarce plants'

for the sites of special interest representing various ecological types and a 14th category for the nesting-places of seabirds.

Sadly, little use seems to have been made of the list by the Government at the time. It would be another 20 to 30 years before the concept of nature reserves and the list itself would come into its own. By then, not only was the value of the list recognised – it was the first of its kind and was part of the data set used for designating the first statutory nature reserves after the war – but it also pioneered a more systematic approach to site selection.

By the middle of the 1940s, there was clear evidence that many of the sites chosen by Rothschild in 1915 had been damaged. In 1946, for example, one journal reported that "a large proportion have been greatly changed and partially spoiled in the intervening period. Thus we find that areas which headed county lists in 1915 have now fallen to the bottom of such compilations".[252] The Government's Wild Life Conservation Special Committee's report (Command 7122) in 1947, commented that it had been "a depressing exercise to examine the Rothschild list of 1915 in the light of the condition of those same sites only 30 years later. Some have been irreparably destroyed, others are well on the way to destruction, and more

Berry Head – a 'Rothschild Reserve'

have so declined that they can no longer be rated as of outstanding national importance".[253]

MIRIAM ROTHSCHILD and Peter Marren in their analysis of the 'fate of the English sites' in their excellent book *Rothschild's Reserves*, summarised what had happened to the sites on Rothschild's original list. It was not possible to be precise about the actual rates of loss but they make 'intelligent guesses' from what is known of the site today and what is known, or can be inferred, about sites at the time of the Rothschild survey. The fate of each of the 182 sites is described and makes fascinating reading. At Braunton Burrows National Nature Reserve "the military's proposal to lay down an 18-hole golf course. . . was fortunately averted after Miriam Rothschild invited the CO to lunch and convinced him of its disadvantages, with the help of a bottle of Chateau Lafite".[254] Sadly, the authors found that there was 'little or no loss' in only 19 sites, with 84 sites with less than 50 per cent loss. In 58 sites there was more than 50 per cent loss and in 21 sites total loss of most, or all, of the site.

In concluding their chapter on the fate of Rothschild's reserves in England, they write, "it is a striking fact that nearly all the surviving English 'Rothschild Reserves' now enjoy a degree of formal protection. Almost all of them are Sites of Special Scientific Interest. . . we acknowledge the enormous improvement in the quality and degree of wildlife site management during the past 10 or 15 years. But we should not forget how degraded many of these places had become over the previous half century. Today's 'managers' are struggling to undo the result of decades of reversal and neglect".[255]

PENZANCE CHAMBER OF COMMERCE
Headlines of '*Cornish Cliffs – Movement to Preserve Public Access and Cornish Coast – Distinguished Guests at Dinner*' greeted readers of the *Morning News* and *Western Daily Mail* on the morning of Saturday 21st February 1914. The night before, the Penzance Chamber of Commerce had held its tenth annual banquet at the Union Hotel and CHARLES ROTHSCHILD had accepted an invitation to be its guest of honour. The occasion was part of a concerted effort to publicise the new 'Society for the Promotion of Nature Reserves' across the country.

The theme for the banquet, which was well attended with upward of 80 guests, was the Chamber's latest cause, "the preservation of public access to cliff footpaths in Cornwall, especially in the western part of the county"[256] under the motto 'Rame Head to Hartland'. The *Cornish Evening Tidings*, which came out on the Saturday evening, went so far as to print all the speeches at the banquet in full, even punctuated at intervals with the words 'Hear, hear' and 'Applause'! Replying to the toast 'Our cause and its friends', Rothschild promoted the new Society and explained how it wanted to "acquire samples of England in its wild state – or samples of England in the wild state it is in to-day".[257] He doubted whether there would be so much enthusiasm for access

A verbatim report on Rothschild's visit to Penzance, 1914 – as reported in *The Cornish Guardian*

to the Cornish cliffs if they had been cultivated or "blasted out in the process of quarrying or disfigured in one way or another, to the ultimate complete destruction of all the natural beauties that adorned them today (Hear, hear)".[258] Rothschild continued in persuasive mood, "I want to ask you Cornish gentlemen to do what you can to assist our Society. You and your friends can send in to the secretary of this Society the names of any places in Cornwall which you think worthy of preservation".[259] He hoped that, after careful scrutiny, some of these places would then be either bought or given to the Society. Rothschild asked the question, "Is it too much to hope that gentlemen in Cornwall would agree amongst themselves to, if necessary, help purchase sites?" If they did, "they would be doing lasting good not only to Cornwall, but to the British Islands. (Loud applause)".[260]

THE HON. CHARLES ROTHSCHILD.

The Hon. N. Charles Rothschild said he represented that night the Society for Promotion of Nature Reserves. It was a comparatively new society, having only been in existence for rather more than a year. The president of that society was the Speaker of the House of Commons (the Right Hon. James Lowther). (Applause). He thought it right he should explain what their objects really were. They wanted, if it was possible to do it, to acquire samples of England in its wild state—or samples of England in the wild state it is in to-day. (Hear, hear). These samples might be even a need not necessarily be big—they might be even a single tree, a small coombe, the beautiful flowers of which Cornwall is famed—(hear, hear)—a small portion of forest or heath or bog, cliffs or pieces of primitive marshland or sandy dhune, or anything that was deemed to represent the wild flora and fauna of these islands. (Applause). These places would then be handed over to the National Trust or other bodies in order that they might be preserved in perpetuity for the benefit of ourselves and posterity. Things do not remain the same for ever, and although to-day we may feel there are plenty of heaths, dhunes, fine trees, etc., the time might come—and perhaps sooner than they thought—when people would see these nature reserves were all they had left to rejoice us of a once-splendid form of wild scenery or wild life. Mr Cornish had explained the attractions of the Cornish coast and the desirability of having access to them. He doubted, however, if the desire of having access to those portions of the cliffs would be as great as at present if that coast were entirely cultivated, or were blasted out in the process of quarrying or disfigured in one way or another, to the ultimate complete destruction of all the natural beauties that adorned it to-day. (Hear, hear).

ROTHSCHILD, LORD WALTER

Lionel Walter Rothschild (1868–1937) was a member of the Society's Executive Committee from 1924 and PRESIDENT of the Society from July 1931 to June 1936. Brother of CHARLES ROTHSCHILD, he was Liberal and Liberal Unionist Member of Parliament for Aylesbury from 1899 to 1910.

He joined the family's banking firm of NM Rothschild and Sons in London but showed less aptitude and commitment than Charles Rothschild. What Lord Rothschild did have in common with his brother, however, was his passion for natural history. He amassed one of the largest natural history collections in the world and, although he was forced to sell his large bird collection to the American Museum of Natural History in 1932, the remainder was gifted to the Trustees of the Natural History Museum in London four years later and can be seen today in the Walter Rothschild Zoological Museum in Hertfordshire, renamed in 2007 the Natural History Museum at Tring.

Walter Rothschild

Lord Rothschild kept many unusual pets in the grounds of the museum, including zebras, a tame wolf, rheas, emus, a dingo, kangaroos, kiwis, cassowaries and giant tortoises. The zebra was one of his favourite

animals and he was renowned for having driven a team of them into the forecourt of Buckingham Palace. He even rented the entire island of Aldabra, in the Indian Ocean, for ten years to allow the island's giant tortoise population to recover from over-hunting.

When he died in 1937, a little more than a year after retiring as President, the Society expressed their deep regret and recalled that when LORD ULLSWATER retired as President, the Society were "fortunate in having so distinguished a naturalist as Lord Rothschild to turn to for his successor. . . during his term of office he took great interest in the Society's affairs, and regularly attended the various meetings until the effects of his unlucky accident in Tring Park prevented him from travelling".[261]

RUCK, ANDREW

The Society's HONORARY TREASURER between 1977 and 1983, Andrew Ruck was among a small group that established the KENT TRUST in 1958. He was an excellent photographer (see NATURE RESERVE GUIDES) and field naturalist.

Despite a busy working life with a leading paint manufacturer, the entire movement "benefited greatly from Andrew Ruck's clear-thinking, business acumen and talent. [His] ability to cut a clear line through waffle at Committee meetings without giving offence was legendary".[262]

In addition to his role as Honorary Treasurer, Ruck was deeply involved in many other aspects of the Society's life, including its sales business, the development of WILDLIFE WATCH and in the launch and subsequent management of NATURAL WORLD. He was also a member of the Natural World Board.

S

SCHOFIELD, PETER

Peter Schofield, an experienced career conservationist, was Chairman of the Society and Partnership Forum between 2000 and 2001.

After working for 11 years with ICI, Schofield spent 25 years with the Government's conservation agencies in Wales, southern England and finally with the Countryside Council for Wales. He has worked with the voluntary conservation movement since 1960, has been actively involved with the BERKSHIRE, BUCKINGHAMSHIRE AND OXFORDSHIRE, HAMPSHIRE AND ISLE OF WIGHT and WILTSHIRE TRUSTS and on the Councils of the CHESHIRE and NORTH WALES TRUSTS. For a time, Vice President of Eurosite (EUROPE AND THE SOCIETY), he has worked in almost every country in Europe, from Finland and Russia to Spain and Ireland, advising both Government bodies and voluntary organisations on strategic and organisational planning, conservation policy and legislation and on the preparation and use of site management plans.

SCOTT, SIR PETER

Sir Peter Scott (1909–1989), the world famous ornithologist, conservationist and painter, started the Wildfowl and Wetlands Trust at Slimbridge, Gloucestershire and was a founder of the WWF. He was President of the GLOUCESTERSHIRE TRUST and designed the Trust's logo, and was a Trustee of the Dyfed Trust. He was an after-dinner speaker at the Trusts' sixth biennial conference in Oxford in 1970 (CONFERENCES). One line from his speech takes on even more significance with the passage of time. "What will Concorde contribute to high quality environment as it thunders along the west coast of Britain?"[263]

Sir Peter Scott

A few weeks before his death, he welcomed Watch members to their National Day at Slimbridge. DAVID BELLAMY was standing with Sir Peter, surrounded by wildfowl and children. A small child took David Bellamy by the hand and whispered, "Is he your Dad? 'No'", Bellamy replied, "but he is the father of conservation".[264]

SECRETARIES, HONORARY

William Ogilvie-Grant	1912–21
Francis Robert Henley	
(later Lord Henley)	1912–37
Herbert Smith	1921–53
Edmund GB Meade-Waldo	
Acting	1918–23
Edmund GB Meade-Waldo	1923–34
Phyllis Barclay-Smith	1953–59
Norman Riley	1953–68
Ted Smith	1963–65
Ted Smith	1968–74
General Secretary	1974–88
Michael Holton	1988–92
John Macmillan	1992–03
Michael Allen	2003–05
Roger Dobbs	2005–11
David Sharrod	2011–

SINGH, MICHAEL

Michael Singh joined the Society in 1992 as a Project Support Officer working mostly on corporate sector sponsorships and the distribution of grants to Trusts. In 1994, he was made Head of Fundraising and, in 1997, established the GRANTS UNIT. He became Executive Director three years later, before leaving in 2004. In 2000, Singh triggered the inquiry that led to disciplinary action against the Managing Director, Martin Gough. He was a key player in the organisational and financial restructuring necessary as a result of the Society's subsequent financial difficulties. After the Director General, SIMON LYSTER, left in 2003, Singh acted as the senior Executive Officer until the appointment of MARTIN SPRAY as acting Chief Executive.

After leaving The Wildlife Trusts, Singh became a consultant and has continued to work on projects for the Society and individual Wildlife Trusts. On several occasions he has helped Trusts through organisational and financial restructuring.

SKEGNESS CONFERENCE IN 1960

The Trusts' first national conference was held in Skegness in May 1960 and was attended by 65 delegates from seven Trusts. Papers included 'An introduction to the nature reserves of Lincolnshire', 'The preservation of the coastline', 'Naturalists' Trusts and national organisations', 'The acquisition and management of nature reserves' and 'Public relations, education and information'. For the leading figures that attended, and even the public who read about it in the press, the conference sent out a clear signal that a new local force had arrived, poised to play its part in developing a modern nature conservation movement. MAX NICHOLSON, Director General of the Conservancy, described the conference as "a revelation both for what has already been done by the pioneer Trusts in Norfolk, Yorkshire and Lincolnshire and of the growing strength and enthusiasm of others which have recently been formed or are now in the process of formation".[265] For the Society, the conference was a reminder that the Trusts it was fostering were – like a family of young children – energetic, demanding and growing up fast. They had been placed in the Society's care and, having accepted the responsibility of overseeing their up-bringing, it was dawning on the Society that it would now have to see it through. Its relationship with the Trusts was still very new and adapting to a new way of life was challenging. But in many ways, its new role provided the Society with a purpose and direction that it had been lacking since the Second World War.

Gibraltar Point – the location for the Trusts' first conference in 1960

SMITH, DR HERBERT

Dr George Frederick Herbert Smith (1872–1953) was the Society's HONORARY SECRETARY – initially sharing duties with EDMUND GB MEADE-WALDO – from 1921 until his death in 1953. He is the Society's longest serving holder of this post. He is said to have relished playing, unobtrusively, the role of stage manager. Indeed, his energy, practical approach and flair for organisation can be detected in most of the Society's activities during his time in office. This was particularly true after his retirement in 1937 from the Department of Mineralogy at the Natural History Museum in London. When the British Correlating Committee for the Protection of Nature was formed as an outcome

Herbert Smith (front row, fifth from left) pictured with the Natural History Museum's Department of Minerology in his retirement year, 1937

of the International Congress for the Protection of Nature held in Paris in 1923, he became its Secretary (TOWARDS IUCN). In the same year, he oversaw the introduction of the Society's HANDBOOK and, in the 1920s and 1930s, actively directed the Society's wildflower campaign, which led to the formation of the Wild Plant Conservation Board of which he became Chairman (WILDFLOWERS – BYE-LAW PROTECTION).

The first meeting of the CONFERENCE ON NATURE PRESERVATION IN POST-WAR RECONSTRUCTION was held in June 1941, under the auspices of the Society. As Secretary, Herbert Smith drafted the memorandum setting out the conference's recommendations and, when the Nature Reserves Investigation Committee was established as a result, it was again Herbert Smith who became the Secretary. His workload increased rapidly as the Committee's 22 Regional Committees set about collecting and publishing information on possible nature reserves – work that was later recognised by the Government's newly-formed wildlife agency – the Nature Conservancy. "Without the preparatory work done by this group

of bodies, the Wild Life Conservation Committee would have lacked the data essential to their deliberations and the Conservancy would have found it still more difficult to make progress".[266]

At this time, Herbert Smith also attended international meetings in Brunnen and Fontainebleau and helped draft the constitution for a new International Union for the Protection of Nature (IUPN). Seeing the potential difficulty the IUPN might have in establishing contacts within the UK, he immediately organised within the Society a British Coordinating Committee to act as a convenient channel (TOWARDS IUCN). The volume of work in 1941 called for Herbert Smith's constant attention and the Society agreed to meet his expenses at the rate of 25 shillings per week; this was increased to £100 per annum in 1946.

At the Natural History Museum in London, Herbert Smith developed a keen interest in gemstones and in 1910 produced the earliest definitive gem course in the form of a textbook entitled, *Gemstones*. He went on to be the examiner for the world's first gemmology diploma examination in 1913. He discovered the dark

green mineral paratacamite in 1906 and became President of the Gemmological Association in 1942. As recently as 2003, his contribution to gemmology was recognised when a new mineral, discovered in 1973, was named Herbertsmithite.

Herbert Smith continued to manage the affairs of the Society effectively until within a few days of his death in April 1953. His obituary in the Society's HANDBOOK, written by Dr George Taylor (at the time Keeper of Botany at the Natural History Museum in London), concludes, "behind his austere, sometimes forbidding presence, he had a redeeming share of human frailty. There was a strong element of the theatrical about him; though he never himself sought the leading part. . . his ability to extract and pursue inexorably what was practical in a welter of sometimes misguided enthusiasms and often inert knowledge, were his most valuable attributes. Exactly how great a debt is owed him by the Society for his tireless devotion to its affairs, and indeed to the whole nature conservation movement, no one will ever know. His reward was the interest and pleasure the work gave him. Many others will reap the benefits".[267]

SMITH, TED

Dr Arthur Edward Smith, affectionately known as 'Ted' Smith, is the architect of the modern Trust movement and, in various capacities up until 1998, played a major part in the development of the Society as the national association of the Trusts. He joined the Society in 1946, and was the first HONORARY SECRETARY of the Society's County Naturalists' Trusts' Committee (REGIONAL LIAISON COMMITTEE) established in 1958. He became the Society's General Secretary and then Special Adviser to the Society for seven years from 1975.

From his boyhood, Smith has had a deep and passionate interest in wildlife, particularly ornithology. After obtaining degrees from Leeds University, he stayed in the city for a further two years to teach English at the Grammar School before moving to a similar position in rural north-east Norfolk. In January 1948, he returned home to Lincolnshire to take up a post as Resident Tutor for the Lindsey District in the Department of Adult Education at the University of Nottingham, a post he occupied for a further 26 years.

In 1948, Smith helped to establish the LINCOLNSHIRE TRUST when it became clear that the landscape and coastline of the county was rapidly changing through agricultural intensification and the expansion of the tourist industry. He has been actively involved with the Trust ever since. He was the Trust's Honorary Secretary for more than 20 years before becoming its Chairman in 1969 and then, on the occasion of the Trusts' 50th anniversary in 1998, its President.

Smith served as a member of the Government's Nature Conservancy (later Nature Conservancy Council) from 1956 to 1978 and as Chairman of its Committee for England from 1971 to 1978. He was also the Society's representative on the Council of The National Trust and a member of its Conservation Committee. In 1990, Smith was the first recipient of the Society's Christopher Cadbury Medal (CHRISTOPHER CADBURY MEDAL CITATIONS). It was awarded to him for his contribution and service to nature conservation nationally and in his native county of Lincolnshire.

Smith believes deeply in the role of volunteers as guardians of the local natural environment and has probably done more than anyone else to shape the voluntary nature conservation movement, and in particular the Wildlife Trust movement, that we see today. His foresight in recognising the need and potential for a new local conservation movement in the late 1940s and early 1950s; his hard work to ensure that a

network of Trusts was established nationwide; and his subsequent support and unquenchable enthusiasm for their development as a coherent national force, mean that he occupies a genuinely unique place in the history of the movement.

Smith published *Trustees for Nature* in 2007, a memoir of his life and work, and combined this with the story of nature conservation in his native county of Lincolnshire. The establishment of local Trusts, in particular the Lincolnshire Trust, and their national association owed much to Smith's expertise, energy and enthusiasm. This was a vast undertaking and inevitably there were challenges along the way. In his foreword to Smith's memoirs, SIR DAVID ATTENBOROUGH describes how Smith, "quiet, unobtrusive, diplomatic, but with steely determination, was one of the key figures in dealing with these problems. . . he understood, to a degree that verged on the magical, the diplomacies needed to coordinate and energise organisations".[268]

Ted Smith at Gibraltar Point, 2011

SPRAY, MARTIN

Martin Spray was able to bring the managerial, administrative and political experience gained during his early career in the civil service and with government agencies to the voluntary sector. He was acting Director General of the Society between 2003 and 2004, presiding over an important period of consolidation and change following the departure of SIMON LYSTER in March 2003.

After leaving WWF as Area Manager for London and the south-east, Spray became the first Chief Executive of the BERKSHIRE, BUCKINGHAMSHIRE AND OXFORDSHIRE TRUST in May 1991. He helped the Trust gain in confidence and ambition, substantially increasing its membership and financial and conservation standing, as well as its influence locally and nationally within The Wildlife Trust movement.

In 2003, despite differing views, the Council of Spray's Trust agreed to his secondment as acting Director General of the Society, initially for two days per week, but which necessarily became a more full-time position. His conviction regarding

Martin Spray

both the need for, and indeed the power of, a national dimension to the movement was vital in restoring confidence in the Society following a particularly troubled episode in the movement's history. As a long-standing and respected Trust Director, Spray was able to unite the various players at this time and helped pave the way for the change of thinking and culture which led to today's stronger, more vibrant and increasingly influential movement.

STRATEGIC DEVELOPMENT FUND

The Strategic Development Fund is an internal fund for The Wildlife Trusts to help promote development and research. It was set up in 2007 and is made up of legacies that are left to the central charity. The Fund initially benefited from a large legacy from Dame Mary Smieton (see below). Funding is available to any Trusts wishing to undertake innovative initiatives and those of benefit to the movement.

SMIETON, DAME MARY

Dame Mary Guillan Smieton (1902–2005) was a civil servant who was only the second woman (the first being Dame Evelyn Sharp) to head a Government Department when she was appointed Permanent Secretary in the Ministry of Education in 1959. When she died at the age of 102, she left her home in Twickenham, Middlesex, and one seventh of her residual estate to the Society. This was worth £2.62 million.

Dame Mary first discussed her legacy to the Society with Honorary Officers in 1972 and, when the Society sold her home after her death, it was able to meet her wishes. Her house and much-loved garden remained as one residential property and the

Dame Mary Smieton

Society was able to support the preparation of a wildlife survey and management plan for the neighbouring private grounds used by local residents.

The receipt of this legacy coincided with the Society establishing the STRATEGIC DEVELOPMENT FUND. The greater portion of Dame Mary's legacy was allocated to this fund with a new Dame Mary Smieton Research Fund set up as a sub-set. This meant that there was up to £500,000 available for distribution to Trusts annually over three years.

Note: Dame Mary's sister, Margaret, left the Society £32,000 in her will when she died in 1986.

STATUTORY NATURE CONSERVATION AGENCIES

Nature Conservancy	1949–65
Nature Conservancy, as part of the National Environment Research Council	1965–73
Nature Conservancy Council	1973–91
English Nature	1991–06
Natural England	2006–
Scottish Natural Heritage	1991–
The Countryside Council for Wales	1991–
Environment and Heritage Service (Northern Ireland)	1996–08
The Northern Ireland Environment Agency	2008–
Joint Nature Conservation Committee	1991–

T

TORREY CANYON DISASTER

On 18th March 1967, the Liberian-registered oil tanker, the Torrey Canyon, carrying 117 tons of crude oil and bound for the BP Refinery at Milford Haven in Pembrokeshire, ran aground between the Isles of Scilly and Land's End. Within two hours, large quantities of oil began to leak into the sea. It was not long before the oil was being sprayed with detergent to try and disperse it at sea and as it came ashore. By the end of April, 140 miles of the Cornish coastline had been contaminated, with some 40 holiday beaches seriously affected. The total bird casualties were eventually estimated at more than 25,000, but of nearly 8,000 rescued birds only 450 survived the first month. Sheail subsequently wrote "In the sense of being quite without precedent",[269] the Torrey Canyon disaster was "the most shocking, man-induced disaster in peacetime".[270]

The way the incident was handled, particularly the excessive use of detergents, came in for considerable criticism. "Somewhere along the line of executive action the decision has been taken to use only detergents against the oil slick – the Navy's '23-ship detergent-spraying Armada'. This will commend itself to the nation if the problem is really about beaches and if 'wild life' is only sentiment and some poor bedraggled creatures cast upon the shore. But if, as it needs to be understood, the problem is about the total marine environment of the British Isles and their neighbouring shores, detergents must be seen as a formidable secondary polluting agent, more toxic in its effects than the oil and not less dangerous for being more insidious".[271]

Using the detergents had simply been the best way of demonstrating that something was being done. In future, there would be a need for alternative solutions. If dispersants were used, then they would have to be applied more carefully and new products found that did less damage. New arrangements would also have to be put in place to ensure that there was better use of the expert advice available and improved coordination of all those involved.

Indeed, less harmful chemical dispersants were developed and emergency procedures for dealing with oil spills were much improved in the 1970s. But as Martin Holdgate, at the time Deputy Director for Research at the Conservancy, later wrote, "the fact is that people hate feeling powerless and have an unquenchable confidence that they can improve on nature. Often they can't. Preventing tanker accidents and designing ships to be as leak-proof as possible pays much better than cleaning up after disasters".[272]

TOWARDS IUCN

The Society's founder, CHARLES ROTHSCHILD, was keen to see nature reserves established worldwide, not just in the UK. The Royal Charter of 1916 enabled the Society to acquire land within "our dominions beyond the seas",[273] to collect and collate information "elsewhere in the British Empire"[274] and to "take part in any international or other conferences in relation to the protection of nature. . . and to carry on propaganda in any part of the world in regard to such subjects".[275] It was, as in so many aspects of the Society's life, Rothschild's energy and enthusiasm that drove the Society's involvement in the international scene in the first few years of its existence. It also laid the foundation for its post-war commitment to founding the first union of international conservation organisations.

In 1914, Rothschild suggested that the Governments of the countries of the Empire should be asked to "consider the advisability of making reserves",[276] and the Society should "offer to furnish those Governments with a scheme suitable for each country".[277] His daughter, MIRIAM ROTHSCHILD, was later to write, "there is no doubt that my father felt there was a greater urgency for conservation there (*in the Empire*) than here".[278] In April 1914, the Society recorded that the India Office had been approached and, at their suggestion, efforts were being made through the Asiatic Society of Bengal and the Bombay Natural History Society to draw up a scheme and prepare a list of

The Torrey Canyon having run aground near Land's End, 1967

proposed reserves in India. The Governor of the Solomon Islands had also been approached, as had the War Office and Admiralty, with a view to them recognising "all waste areas under their charge as nature reserves".[279]

These early forays into the international arena were curtailed by the First World War and afterwards by Rothschild's ill health. However, in 1923, the Society's President VISCOUNT ULLSWATER spoke about the Society's activities at an International Congress for the Protection of Nature in Paris and distributed a nature reserve poster with French text, printed especially for the occasion.

The Society's three delegates returned full of enthusiasm and keen to encourage the formation of national committees. They soon forged closer ties with the Society for the Protection of Natural Monuments in Holland. In November, its Secretary, Mr Pieter Gerbrand Van Tienhoven, joined a special meeting convened by the Society to take things forward. He proposed an international committee that would meet annually between the meetings of the International Congress. However, the Society was reluctant, "in view of its small resources",[280] to take on such a heavy commitment but was happy to convene a meeting of representatives of societies in Great Britain. Later in the month, it invited home-grown societies, "interested in the protection of animal and plant life, the promotion of nature reserves and kindred objects",[281] to a meeting "with a view to possible international action in the future".[282] In January 1924, it was agreed to set up the Central

(from December 1924, the 'British') Correlating Committee for the Protection of Nature with the Society's HONORARY SECRETARY, HERBERT SMITH, as its Secretary and Treasurer. It had the following members: representatives of the Natural History Museum in London, British Ornithological Union, Entomological Society of London, International Committee for the Protection of Birds, Linnean Society, The National Trust, the Royal Society for the Protection of Birds, Society for Preservation of the Fauna of the Empire, Society for the Promotion of Nature Reserves (represented by Lord Buxton) and the Zoological Society of London.

The Committee's role was largely advisory, with matters delegated to the constituent members best fitted to deal with them. In the first year, 1924, the Committee met five times – its pre-occupation the establishment of national Correlating Committees in as many other countries as possible. Positive responses were received from France, Holland, Hungary, Italy, Spain, Sweden, Switzerland and the USA. Sadly this early enthusiasm did not last. Ten years later, the Committee was described as having being 'moribund for years'; and, in November 1935, it was wound up with the consent of its constituent societies – its funds, £17 15s 8d, were transferred to the Society.

During the rest of the 1930s the Society, and indeed the country, took a more domestically-focused approach to wildlife preservation. The Society's international work was limited. In 1931, the Society attended the International Congress for the Protection of Nature in Paris, represented by its Honorary Secretary, Herbert Smith, and EDMUND MEADE-WALDO (the

former also represented His Majesty's Government). The main outcome of this gathering was a plea for action to protect the elephant and rhinoceros against illegal hunting in Africa. The Society also continued as a member of the British Section of the International Committee for the Protection of Birds (ICBP), set up in 1923 to put "the problem of the reciprocal protection of birds, as between nations, upon a new footing".[283] It was also represented at international ICBP conferences in Vienna and Rouen. But it was not until after the Second World War that further attempts were made to create an international wildlife body.

In 1945, Julian Huxley, in his capacity as Chairman of the Wild Life Conservation Special Committee, visited the Swiss National Park in the Engadine with Eduard Handschin, Chairman of the Scientific Committee of the Swiss National Park. Impressed with what he saw, Huxley suggested that there were other British conservationists who would benefit from a similar visit. It was the Swiss League for the Protection of Nature that enthusiastically took up the idea but, without telling the British, widened its scope. The following year it invited not just the British, including William Arnold-Foster representing the Society and CPRE, but representatives from Belgium, Czechoslovakia, France, Holland and Norway on a tour that started at the League's headquarters in Basle. The British group were "incensed when they found out how much the agenda had changed", not only because it meant less time in the field, but also because they found themselves "thrown into discussions about a new international initiative for which they were unprepared".[284] Somewhat reluctantly, the participants agreed a statement at the conclusion of the tour that recognised the need for improved international cooperation and, in particular, an international nature conservation body. Afterwards, the disagreements continued. The Swiss and the Dutch were involved in two organisations that each thought should be the body to take things forward. The British not only thought the discussions about a new international body premature, but also sided with the Dutch who they thought had been badly treated. The Society's Honorary Secretary, HERBERT SMITH, wrote to MAX NICHOLSON in February 1947 saying, "the proposed attempt on the part of the Swiss League to revive an Advisory Commission that faded out in 1914 in complete disregard of the International Office subsequently established at Brussels, was most undesirable as it would only lead to rivalry between the two. My personal view is that an international organisation might, but not necessarily would, serve a useful purpose, and in that event should be directly sponsored and financed by the United Nations Educational, Scientific and Cultural Organisation (UNESCO)".[285]

Just a year later the League brought more than 60 delegates from 23 countries together in Brunnen to maintain the momentum. The Society still had its reservations and, indeed, when the meeting got underway it "suffered from the same disharmony that had plagued the tour a year before".[286] Feelings ran high, with disagreement about the best way forward. When the Society's representatives – its Honorary Secretary, Herbert Smith, Dr Ramsbottom and MIRIAM ROTHSCHILD – returned, however, they pronounced the conference a success. This was, no doubt, because the British had, by and large, got

what they wanted! The Society's HANDBOOK reports that the conference "brought into a common pool the views held in many different countries, and it was revealed that the need for early measures for nature protection was universally recognised. The problem was to translate this feeling into political action; the solution adopted was to recommend that the United Nations Educational, Scientific and Cultural Organisation should convene an official international conference in the summer of 1948 with the view to setting up an International Union for the Protection of Nature".[287]

Holdgate, in more direct language, reported that "in the end – after a good deal of bloodletting – the Brunnen Conference did agree on the text of a Provisional Constitution for an International Union for the Protection of Nature (IUPN), gave the Swiss League a mandate to act as agent for this provisional organisation, asked the League to send the Provisional Constitution to UNESCO for transmission to governments (who were to be asked whether they could accept it), and requested UNESCO to convene a congress in Paris in July 1948 to adopt a definitive constitution for the Union".[288]

Between Brunnen and the Paris meeting, Herbert Smith, among others, was involved in a good deal of shuttle diplomacy on matters such as the constitution and the financing of the new body. Herbert Smith, for example, chaired a group comprising 'the main groups concerned with nature conservation in the British Isles' who produced an alternative draft constitution for tabling in Paris.

Finally, at the request of UNESCO, the Government in France hosted a meeting near Paris

at the end of September 1948 in the magnificent Galerie des Colonnes in the National Palace of Fontainebleau. Dr Julian Huxley, a Council member of the Society since 1936, had become UNESCO's first Director General and, together with a representative of the French Government, he opened proceedings in front of 120 delegates from 32 countries. Herbert Smith was elected Chairman of the all-important Juridical Committee charged with drafting the constitution – a task it completed over the next two days! The final text in English and French was signed by nearly all delegations. The IUPN "thereupon came into existence, and immediately afterwards the General Assembly was in session for the first time".[289]

Under its constitution, the Union's first objective was to encourage and facilitate cooperation between governments and national and international organisations concerned with, and persons interested in, the protection of nature. Its membership was to be drawn from governments, public services and international (inter-governmental and non-governmental) organisations, institutions and associations concerned with the protection of nature. The organisation was unique as the first GONGO or Governmental and Non-Governmental Organisation. Holdgate describes it as having "no parallel at the time (and very few afterwards)".[290] The IUPN was to be based in Brussels and Jean Paul Harroy became its first Director General and Treasurer. At the IUPN's Second General Assembly in 1950 in Brussels,

HERBERT SMITH was made a Vice President. Throughout IUPN's formative years both the Society and the Conservancy continued to play an important supportive role and the Society continued to fund and run the British Committee.

In 1951, for example, at a technical meeting of IUPN in The Hague, MAX NICHOLSON, a member of both the Society and the Conservancy, led discussions on the 'Rural landscape as a habitat for flora and fauna in densely populated countries'. At the third General Assembly held in Caracas, Venezuela, in 1952, the Society's Council member PHYLLIS BARCLAY-SMITH was the British Committee's representative, the observer for Her Majesty's Government and discussion leader for a session on 'The preservation of endemic zoological and botanical species in small islands, particularly in the Caribbean Sea'.

But it was in the mid 1950s that the Society's involvement in IUPN* reached its climax. First, in 1955, when IUPN's Executive Board met in London for the first time and the Society hosted a dinner at the Fellows' Restaurant of the Zoological Society of London, and then in Edinburgh, in 1956, when it was the joint host and organiser with the Conservancy of the IUPN's fifth General Assembly. The Assembly attracted 300 delegates from 40 countries and its technical meeting discussed themes ranging from 'the management of nature reserves on the basis of modern scientific knowledge' and 'myxomatosis in rabbits' to 'the rehabilitation of areas biologically devastated by human disturbance' and 'the relationship

of ecology to landscape planning'. NORMAN RILEY, who was by then the Society's Joint HONORARY SECRETARY with Phyllis Barclay-Smith, wrote, "this was outstandingly the most valuable meeting of the General Assembly so far held; it should prove to have put the Union at last well and truly 'on the map'".[291]

But sponsoring the Assembly in 1956 came at a cost. The Society spent nearly £1,400 on its organisation – including the costs of the Proceedings which had 'escalated alarmingly'. As a result, the Society experienced a deficit on its income and expenditure account "for the first time for many years".[292] It was perhaps this, and the fact that it coincided with the Society's increasing interest in the burgeoning Trust movement, that led it to reflect that "the extent to which the Society should enter the international field is. . . a matter that needs the most careful thought".[293]

While the Society continued to be a member of IUCN (its membership continues to the present day), on 1st January 1960 it handed over responsibility for the British Committee to the Council for Nature.

In 1955, the British Coordinating Committee for Nature Conservation changed its name to the British Committee for International Nature Conservation and, in 1956, the IUPN changed its name to International Union for the Conservation of Nature and Natural Resources or IUCN, for short.

TOXIC CHEMICALS AND WILDLIFE
In the 1950s, many chemical products designed to 'improve' agricultural operations came on the market before their impact on the wider environment had been properly tested. As early as October 1951, *The Times* reported that 158 dead birds of several species had been counted on two fields in Gloucestershire. Each spring, from about 1956 onwards, reports of bird and mammal deaths increased alarmingly. In the Society's 1961 HANDBOOK, TED SMITH wrote, "in the eastern counties many species of birds and mammals have suffered serious losses in the last two years from poisoning by toxic seed dressings. Of particular concern is the effect on predatory birds and mammals which have died after eating poisoned prey. In some areas the kestrel has disappeared as a breeding bird within two years and owls have been much reduced in numbers. Trusts in the counties affected have been collecting information on behalf of the RSPB and in collaboration with the local Pests Departments of the Ministry of Agriculture. In Lincolnshire, for example, in the spring of 1961 the Trust investigated nearly forty instances of mortality reported to it".[294]

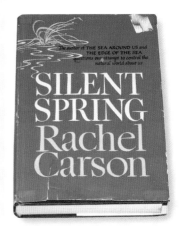

Silent Spring

Rachel Carson, a 'great benefactor to the human race'

In one of the most influential books of the century, *Silent Spring*, published in the USA in 1962 and in Britain a year later, Rachel Carson rocked the corporate chemical giants of America. As a result, she faced considerable hostility from that quarter but she alerted the public and decision makers to the potential dangers of, in particular, the long-lasting chlorinated hydrocarbon insecticides, like DDT. In his introduction to the British edition of *Silent Spring*, Lord Shackleton wrote, "then came the spring of 1961, when tens of thousands of birds were found littering the countryside, dead or dying in agony. . . among these birds were some, such as the bramblings, which are specially protected by law, yet all went down before the indiscriminate scythe of toxic chemicals".[295]

In Britain, the book had the effect of greatly heightening interest. It helped maintain support for research which had been started in 1960 in the Toxic Chemicals and Wildlife Division of the Conservancy. The naturalist SIR PETER SCOTT was in the gallery in The House of Lords in 1963 when the issue of toxic chemicals was debated. "I well remember. . . seeing two red spots below – the dust jackets of the English edition of *Silent Spring*

beside each dispatch box. . . nothing has since occurred to modify my view that future generations will regard Rachel Carson as a great benefactor to the human race for the impact created by *Silent Spring*".[296]

By July 1961, the Government had announced a voluntary ban on the use of certain chemicals in seed dressings during the spring sowing period but, whilst this represented an advance, there was "more need than ever for vigilance and for more information about bird mortality in both spring and autumn".[297] The Society's County Naturalists' Trusts' Committee (REGIONAL LIAISON COMMITTEE) agreed that "all Trusts be recommended to write to their MPs urging that action be taken on the Select Committee's recommendations and drawing attention to the need for more money for research on the effects of toxic chemicals on wild life".[298] Persistent pesticides, such as aldrin, dieldrin and heptachlor, continued to be used and it was not until 1966 that virtually all uses were subject to a voluntary ban. However, the effects on the countryside, for example of dieldrin on the breeding capacity of the otter, would be felt for many years to come.

See also FARMING AND WILDLIFE *and* OTTER CONSERVATION

*Miss Marjorie Bostock, an Associate Member of the Society for 38 years, died in 1959. With her death "the last link with those who were personally concerned with the formation of the Society"[299] was severed. She was the personal secretary to Charles Fagan, the Society's first Honorary Treasurer and later to the Society's Honorary Secretary, Herbert Smith.

† From the Society's formation in 1912 until 1927, when he retired from the staff of the Natural History Museum in London, the Society's accounts were kept by WJ Anderson "with such care that the annual audit has been a simple operation".[300] In recognition of his long service, the Executive Committee presented him with "a walnut bureau to which was affixed a suitably inscribed plate".[301]

U

ULLSWATER, VISCOUNT

James William Lowther (1855–1949) was Conservative MP for Penrith from 1886 to 1921 and Speaker of the House of Commons from 1905 to 1921. At the time, he was the third longest serving Speaker on record. On retirement he was knighted, and created 1st Viscount Ullswater. He is famously quoted as saying, "there are three golden rules for Parliamentary Speakers – 'Stand up. Speak up. Shut up'".[302]

He was the Society's first PRESIDENT, serving from 1916 to 1931, and regularly chaired Council and Executive meetings during this time, on at least three occasions in the Speaker's Library in the

Westminster Houses of Parliament. He was the Society's principal representative at the International Congress for the Protection of Nature in Paris in 1923.

Paying tribute to Viscount Ullswater on his retirement as President, the Society acknowledged how fortunate it had been to have him presiding over the opening chapter in its history. "It was of immense advantage to the new organisation that its President should have been one who was in the important position of Speaker of the House of Commons and who, when he resigned from that office, was held in such high esteem that he was constantly being called into consultation in connection with difficult problems that arose in the affairs of State. Yet no matter how preoccupied he might be in such matters he never failed, somehow or other, to find sufficient time to attend to the Society's business and to him is due the undoubted fact that the Society stands pre-eminent in this country on all questions concerning nature reserves".[303]

In 1944, Viscount Ullswater, who was still a member of the Society, wrote, "I should like to offer the Society my warm congratulations on the success which seems to be attending its efforts, notwithstanding the great difficulties which stand in the way of such work at the present time. . . go on and prosper".[304]

James Wiliam Lowther in 1883 – the year he became an MP for Rutland

URBAN AREAS AND NATURE CONSERVATION

Helping wildlife to thrive in towns and cities is a key part of the Trusts' work

In the early 1980s, many local, regional and national conservation groups and associations were formed that shared a common desire to improve the natural environment in the places where most people lived and worked – towns and cities. Their need for communication, mutual support and technical advice led to the formation of the Fairbrother Group (see page 723) in 1985. Although the Group was led by people who were also heavily involved with the Trusts, such as Andrew Arnott, Chris Baines, Veronica Cossons and Peter Shirley, there were a greater number of people who were not, such as Hugh Firman of the Bradford Urban Wildlife Group and Grant Luscombe of Landlife. It was a 'bottom-up' initiative, developed by people promoting a different approach to nature conservation with the focus on the wider environment and on people's relationship with nature in their everyday lives.

The bodies making up the Fairbrother Group varied enormously, some focused on a particular issue, site or neighbour-hood, for example the Hawthorns Urban Wildlife Centre in Southampton. Some had wider

remits, for example the Brighton and Bradford Urban Wildlife Groups (UWGs), while some had background support from a local authority, a Wildlife or Groundwork Trust or the British Trust for Conservation Volunteers. There were still others that were fully integrated within a Wildlife Trust, for example the Potteries and Newcastle UWG and the Peterborough Wildlife Group.

In November 1985, it was agreed with the Fairbrother Group that the Society should act as an umbrella body for the growing number of Urban Wildlife Groups. An Urban Steering Group was established and three-year funding of nearly £70,000 was secured from the Conservancy and the Carnegie United Kingdom Trust for a new post at the Society of an Urban Wildlife Development Officer, filled by Tony Jones. This was established to service the urban groups whether directly affiliated to the Society or not. It was based initially in Birmingham and then moved to the Society's Lincoln office in May 1988. The number of groups had been increasing, partly fuelled by the Government's Community Programme employment scheme. But in 1988, this scheme came to an end and the Urban Wildlife Development Officer spearheaded work to help UWGs acquire the information and skills to raise funds, market their services and manage themselves in this period of enforced transition. The end of the decade would see increased involvement nationally in the work of the UWGs and in national policy work. In 1990, for example, the Society published *Green It Yourself – A DIY Handbook for Urban Wildlife Conservation.* The early 1990s also saw a close involvement in the ENVIRONMENT CITY initiative.

In September 1994, the Fairbrother Group transformed itself into a new company, the Urban Wildlife Partnership (UWP), and was integrated into the Society. By this time, membership already included, or soon came to include, local authorities such as the London Borough of Sutton, Peterborough City Council and Sheffield City Council; national organisations such as the Ramblers Association and Shell Better Britain Campaign; regional bodies such as the Red Rose Forest, the Chilterns Initiative and Milton Keynes Parks Trust and networks such as the West Midlands Environment Network and Southampton Wildlife Link.

For nine years from 1994, and for perhaps the first time in its modern history, the Society formally embraced and provided services to non-Wildlife Trust organisations. By 2000, there were more than 150 members running more than 1,000 projects involving on-site conservation, education, events, networking and support, and campaigning. Whilst these projects sometimes created tensions, for example when members of the UWP took a different line to the Society on sensitive issues, it increased the exposure to, and influence of, the Society amongst major movers and shakers in other conservation bodies, local authorities, Government agencies and Government itself.

Bringing the UWP into the Trusts' movement had mutual benefits. For the Trusts, the acquisition of an already established, fully-functioning but under resourced organisation, brought a measure of influence over its development and activities. It helped to maintain the Trusts' position as the single most authoritative voice on nature conservation in the UK. For UWP it meant a degree of security and the ability to improve services to members, as well as

access to support services (such as marketing, fundraising and publicity) that it had not enjoyed before. From a nature conservation point of view, there was probably an exchange of influences – some of the more orthodox practices of the Trusts rubbing off on UWP members, whilst the more radical approaches of the UWP were increasingly adopted by some of the more established Trusts.

Following this merger, a Society team was established and by the late 1990s there were seven or eight people employed. Principal amongst these was Chris Gordon who initiated many, and managed most, of the activities and projects. On the voluntary side of the organisation Veronica Cossons, Pat Callaghan and Chris Baines were especially influential in their positions on internal advisory groups and on the Society's Council. In 1996, a senior management post (Director of Community Affairs) was established, with Peter Shirley taking this job for four years. The team became known as the Urban and Community Unit, with the Unit's activities complementing those of the education team, managed by Mary Cornwell.

The Urban and Community Unit not only looked after the UWP, but also ran the Environment City programme; provided internal support to other departments and local Trusts; dealt with national urban policy issues; and handled work associated with support to local Regionally Important Geological Sites' groups (RIGS). There was also a newsletter *Urban Wildlife*, first produced in 1992, that continued to be published two or three times a year until the summer of 2001. Major funding was obtained in

A selection of the Society's urban nature conservation publications from the early 1990s

1997 with an award of £100,000 from the National Lottery Charities Board. Close working arrangements developed with English Nature's (EN) Urban Coordinator, George Barker, involving, for example, the UK MAB Urban Forum[305]; the scale and scope of grant schemes such as EN's Community Action for Wildlife and Schools Grounds Grants; and input to EN's magazine *Urbio*. It was a symbiotic relationship with the two organisations – one statutory, the other voluntary – each complementing one another and each working to their own strengths.

When the Labour Government came to power in 1997, policy work suddenly became even more important. The new Government set up an Urban Task Force and an Urban 'Green Spaces' Task Force. It published an Urban White Paper and developed a focus on towns and cities under the generic banner of an 'urban renaissance'. It also began the process of devolving Government to a Scottish Parliament and Welsh Assembly. With UWP in-house, its existing very strong political campaigning base, and a presence in all parts of the UK, the Society was fully equipped to address the issues, raise the profile of the natural environment within the new structures and thinking, and had the capacity to work in partnership with other like-minded bodies.

The Society was able to twin-track its political campaigning and lobbying. On the one hand, there was work on primary conservation legislation and regulation, while on the other, there was input into the debate about the emerging public policy framework relating to devolution and the quality of life in

urban areas. The advantage, as always, was that both the Trusts and the members of the UWP were engaged in practical work and addressing local issues. Their experiences informed the campaigning, influencing and lobbying in ways not available to organisations solely focused on advocacy. Examples could be put on Ministers' desks, visits to projects could be arranged and those speaking on behalf of the organisation could talk with an authority based on day-to-day experiences on the ground. The converse of this was that through *Urban Wildlife*, conferences and seminars, those involved at the grass roots could be kept informed of Government thinking and intentions; have early notice of forthcoming opportunities (as happened with the landfill tax regime) and be equipped to lobby local politicians in ways which complemented the national work.

In 2000, things changed. Mary Cornwell and Peter Shirley left the Society at about the same time, followed not long after by Chris Gordon. There was no new funding for UWP. In difficult financial times a choice was made not to make any new appointments and the Society had to reduce its direct support. However, in spring 2001, a People and Wildlife Officer joined the staff and support for the type of work espoused by UWP continued under this general banner. It was, however, restricted to the Trusts and their local groups, rather than at the much more eclectic and wider audience served by UWP.

What was the overall influence of the Society during the period when it was fostering the UWP? Externally perhaps, officers in statutory organisations found the partnership valuable as a sounding board,

advocate and lobbyist. Its independence meant that it could fire bullets informed by others in a difficult position to speak out on sensitive issues. It played a major role in keeping the urban nature conservation movement at the forefront of people's minds.

Internally, the organisation acted as a conscience, reminding everyone that account needed to be taken of people and the places where they live and this had to be done, not as an 'added extra', but as an integral part of the movement's work. As the Society became increasingly professional and developed strategic approaches and priorities, and its core values and principles evolved, it was important for it not to lose sight of this important principle.

Indeed, the lasting legacy is that more has been achieved in urban nature conservation than would undoubtedly be the case had the Trust movement not engaged with the Urban Wildlife Groups in the way that it did. At the beginning of the new millennium, Trusts have access to a much broader base of support than would have been the case previously, and work with communities in urban areas and on urban nature conservation is no longer an 'added extra', but an integral part of Trust's conservation activities.

The Centenary Riverside Urban Wetland Nature Park was launched as part of the centrepiece of Rotherham's £15 million flood alleviation scheme in 2009

FAIRBROTHER GROUP

The Fairbrother Group, formed in 1985, was "a small group of like-minded people intent on raising the flag for nature conservation in towns and cities".[306] A prime mover behind its formation was the environmentalist, broadcaster and Vice President of the Society, Chris Baines. The Group was named after Nan Fairbrother the author of the seminal book *New Lives, New Landscapes*, first published in 1970.

In 1994, the Fairbrother Group renamed itself the Urban Wildlife Partnership (UWP) and became a formal part of the Trust family adopting the Wildlife Trusts' logo. In this new guise the UWP thrived, helping the development of hundreds of local urban groups. It secured a grant of around £250,000 from the Lottery Charities Board for this national support work and attracted membership, not just from the Trusts and smaller urban groups, but from larger bodies, such as Groundwork Trusts, Landfill and local authorities.

However, as urban conservation became increasingly integrated into the mainstream activities of the Trusts, the necessity for a separate Urban Wildlife Partnership diminished. While UWP was never formally disbanded, some of its functions were taken over by an Urban Wildlife Network founded in 2005. The Network provides an independent voice in urban nature conservation and the urban environment.

VISITOR CENTRES

Visitor and education centres have been part of Trusts' on-site interpretation since the 1960s, and by 2011 there were more than 120 such centres around the country. The first was opened by the SUSSEX TRUST at Woods Mill in 1968, although by then several Trusts were already providing other interpretation and facilities such as NATURE TRAILS and bird hides on their nature reserves.

In the decade that followed, a first wave of centres was established across the UK, including at Fingringhoe Wick in Essex in 1975, at Gibraltar Point in Lincolnshire where a new centre was opened by SIR DAVID ATTENBOROUGH in 1974 and at Ranworth Broad in Norfolk in 1976. Centres often provide a base for educational activities, enabling Trusts to cater for larger groups of schoolchildren and visitors. At many of the larger centres there is also a café and shop.

More recently, Trusts have been developing a new generation of environmentally-friendly, sustainable visitor centres on nature reserves. For example, the NORFOLK TRUST's new centre at Cley Marshes on the north Norfolk coast, features a green roof, water recycling and uses wind, solar and geothermal technologies. Many centres annually receive thousands of visitors and for many people they are an important part of the nature reserve experience.

1963 – Information centre at Gibraltar Point, Lincolnshire

2007 – New visitor centre at Cley Marshes, Norfolk

723

W

WWF FUNDING

Over the final four decades of the last century, the World Wildlife Fund (WWF) provided funds to the Society and at least one grant to every Trust in the country. In one six-year period, one particular Trust received as many as 21 grants.

WWF was formed in 1961. In the next 12 months, the Fund's British Appeal supported reserve purchases by the ESSEX, CAMBRIDGESHIRE, KENT, NORFOLK, GLAMORGAN AND SUFFOLK TRUSTS. By 1965, Trusts had received more than £13,000; in the year ending March 1972, WWF's grant-aid of £28,840 towards reserve purchase was the largest amount awarded in one year since its formation.

Hayley Woods, Cambridgeshire – purchased in 1962, thanks in part to a £1,250 WWF grant

Although the mechanisms for funding and the amount available varied, WWF continued to be a valuable source of grant-aid for the Society and the Trusts over the next 20 or more years. In later years, the emphasis gradually shifted from land purchase and individual management tasks to projects of a more strategic nature. Organisational development also received a greater proportion of the Fund's support.

In 1992, its UK Project Management Unit provided a fascinating six-year snapshot. Between 1986 and 1992 WWF had made

grants to the Society and the Trusts of almost £2 million, representing 20 to 25 per cent of its UK external grant funding programme. The number of grant applications had ranged from 28 from one Trust, down to one from another. In total, 401 Trust applications had been processed, with 314 approved. The average grant had been for £5,000 to £6,000, with the largest being £90,000 spread over a three-year period. There had been grants towards 136 land purchases, 68 specific management or wardening projects, 16 projects to address organisational development and marketing and 15 conservation posts. The Society had made 24 successful applications worth a total of almost £200,000 towards a range of initiatives, including support for a computerised biological recording project, (see also COMPUTERS IN THE TRUSTS), a WILDFLOWER WEEK Project Officer, Storm Damage and Woodland Coordinators, and the peatlands (PEATLANDS CAMPAIGN) and transport (ROAD BUILDING AND WILDLIFE) campaigns.

Burnt tip orchid. One of the major projects funded by WWF was an orchid protection fund

WATER FOR WILDLIFE

In May 1992, the image of the Society's Patron, HRH The Prince of Wales, speaking above the noise of a stormy downpour at the launch of the Society's Water for Wildlife campaign and, more ironically, its low-flows report – Dying of Thirst – created much amusement across the media, including at least one high-profile television 'out-take' programme. Nevertheless, the press coverage meant that the impact of the unsustainable use of water on wildlife and wetland habitats, as well as people, hit the headlines in a big way.

HRH The Prince of Wales launches the Society's Dying Of Thirst report, 1992

For the Society, wetland issues were not new. In 1976, for example, it had picked up on the Council of Europe's European Wetlands Campaign and, with the Trusts, it had embarked on a long-running crusade to reverse the decline in otter populations (OTTER CONSERVATION). In the late 1970s and 1980s, good river management was also being promoted through closer ties between the Trusts and the water industry. Regionally based 'Rivers and Wildlife' training exercises were organised and, in 1984, the Society and the RSPB published a comprehensive Rivers and Wildlife Handbook. This work would extend well into the

1990s and beyond – a second edition of the handbook, for example, was published in 1994.

However, in the early 1990s, the combination of prolonged drought and the increasingly profligate public use of water reinforced the view amongst the Trusts that a harder hitting campaign was required. It needed to tackle, not just wetland management, but, more controversially, water quantity and quality issues. In 1992, the Society secured sponsorship from the makers of the Down to Earth range of cleaning products, and, as a result, was able to launch its Water for Wildlife campaign to tackle these three issues one by one.

WILDLIFE WATCH was also running a successful National Riverwatch project at the same time. This was launched in 1991 as a three-year project looking in turn at the river itself, the river bank and the river valley. Over the lifetime of the project, 170,000 Wildlife Watch members took part.

In the Water for Wildlife campaign's first report, *Dying of Thirst*, the Society reported on numerous examples of water shortage affecting wildlife and wildlife habitats. The report accepted that the problem had been exacerbated by three years of serious drought. But it pulled no punches on the longer term, more fundamental and widespread problems of over-abstraction, over-zealous land drainage and flood protection. There were 35 recommendations, including a call for wildlife to be higher on the 'water agenda' and for an overall water resources strategy to be embraced by all those responsible for managing and using Britain's water resources.

A year later, the campaign entered its second phase, focusing on *Seven Tales from the River Bank*.

Children taking part in National Riverwatch

The report highlighted the deteriorating quality of the country's rivers. Pollution incidents were on the increase, with 25,000 at the time of the report compared with 15,000 ten years earlier. The Society was looking for seven solutions: a commitment by authorities to improve water quality; the establishment of minimum flow levels to help the dilution of pollution; a reduction of waste and moves to tackle avoidable pollution incidents; statutory water quality objectives; land management practices that gave incentives for less polluting agriculture; greater powers to the National Rivers Authority; and increased resources.

Finally, in 1994, attention turned to the third phase of the campaign – wetland management. It highlighted the need to see rivers and their catchments as wildlife and landscape assets that can, if maintained and managed properly, also accommodate the extremes of both drought and flood.

The persistent campaigning by conservationists, and issues such as the embarrassingly high river pollution figures, could no longer be ignored by the politicians.

The Government announced new legislation for England and Wales that would bring about the privatisation of the water industry in England and integration of the National Rivers Authority, HM Inspectorate of Pollution (HMIP) and local waste regulation authorities within a new Environment Agency. The Environment Act was passed in 1990. In Scotland, the industry had not been privatised and water services were still within the remit of the local authorities, with River Purification Boards monitoring pollution. In due course, the Boards would merge with HMIP and the local waste regulators in Scotland to form the Scottish Environment Protection Agency (SEPA). Although the Act in England and Wales was welcomed, including the move towards coordinated pollution control, there were serious omissions.

The Society published *Rivers – The Whole Picture* to lobby for the new agency to have, among other things, stronger duties to conserve and enhance biological diversity and to promote integrated catchment management planning. In a further report, *Sold Down the River*, it put forward the argument for the duty to 'further conservation' – previously held by the NRA – to be applied to the new agency. There were face-to-face meetings with the Secretary of State for the Environment and with top civil servants, correspondence with the Prime Minister's Office and evidence submitted to the Commons Environment Committee. Although many of the omissions remained, the conservation movement did see its pressure rewarded with the addition of a nature conservation clause.

The Society's *Sold Down The River* publication

In 1996, the Biodiversity Challenge Group (BIODIVERSITY ACTION PLANNING), of which the Society was a member, published *High and Dry*. This report looked at the impacts of over-abstraction of water on wildlife. There were 354 rivers and wetlands known to be, or thought to be, affected or at risk. The group issued four challenges to Government: a comprehensive review of water abstraction licenses; powers for the Environment Agency and SEPA to implement a sustainable water resources strategy; Ofwat (an independent office set up to regulate the water industry) to set environmental standards of performance for water companies; and a national action programme for saving water and for charging for water abstraction.

As part of the Society's conservation plan, inspired by extensive consultation with Trusts and approved at the beginning of 1998, the conservation and management of water and aquatic environments remained one of the Partnership's top priorities into the new millennium. A new water policy team was established at the UK office and, in keeping with the practice at the time, Freshwater and Water Policy Officers were out-posted – in this case within the WILTSHIRE TRUST. In a comprehensive survey by this new team, the extent of the Trusts' commitment to wetland management at the end of the 1990s was revealed. There were more than "11,400 hectares of wetland, distributed throughout 2,250 wetland habitats on Wildlife Trust reserves".[307] It was estimated, for example, that Trusts managed almost ten per cent of the total area of reedbed in the UK. The Trusts had restored, or created, almost 600 wetland habitats both on and off reserves in the previous 12 months. In addition they had "provided nearly 30,000 person hours of advisory work on over 1,000 wetland habitats, promoting wetland conservation in the wider countryside".[308]

The water policy team helped Trusts to: secure funding; manage relationships and communications with landowners and other organisations; assess the effects of planning or statutory licence applications; build knowledge of site hydrology; and give training in hydrological processes. All these aspects were critical to achieving change. The following year, the team received welcome financial support through landfill tax contributions distributed through the Biffaward scheme. This enabled a programme of promotion, campaigns and advisory work, based on the survey results, to be rolled out over the next five years.

In a series of briefing papers, *Reflections on Water*, the water team set about advising Trusts on a series of complex policy issues and campaigning for improvements. For example, the European Union's Water Framework Directive, passed in December 2000 after more than ten years of development and legal wrangling, had huge potential for improving the wetland environment. Its central requirement was that Member States should aim to achieve 'good status' for their surface waters by 2015. The process by which the Office of Water Services determined the programme of water infrastructure and environmental improvements to be funded in the period between 2005 and 2010 – the Asset Management Planning round (AMP4) – was also underway. *Water Wise Gardening* (2002) was one of the publications with a wider public appeal produced by the team at this time.

At the end of the five-year funding, the team was able to look back on some notable achievements. In addition to influencing the implementation of the Water Framework Directive and engaging actively with the Biodiversity Action Plan process, it had also helped to develop, for example, ten Trust wetland restoration schemes and produced an impressive *Wetland Restoration Handbook*.

Complementing the work of the team was the Trust-wide Otters and Rivers Project. New funding was required for this project at the end of 2001. If it was going to be successful it would need to broaden its scope to reflect more of a habitat and wetland focus. The Water for Wildlife project was re-launched in 2004 – funded by Water UK, water companies and, eventually, the Environment Agency – and it adopted this broader approach. At first the project seconded a Water for Wildlife Manager from the TRUST FOR SOUTH AND WEST WALES, but later made an appointment based within the DERBYSHIRE TRUST.

Between 2004 and 2008, Water for Wildlife developed a more consistent and targeted approach to wetland conservation, supporting wetland enhancement and restoration work, as well as the surveying and protection of water voles and otters. It also helped develop the catchment approach to managing water quality. During this period, Water for Wildlife also launched a Prevent Pond Pests campaign, produced a guidance document on otters and fisheries and supported the Wetland Vision Partnership. The latter, an alliance of conservationists and Government agencies, produced a series of maps showing the loss and fragmentation of England's wetlands. The maps also showed where opportunities existed to create new ones.

The start of this phase of the project coincided with further evidence of a crash in water vole populations, as well as a decline in the country's native crayfish population due to an invasion by its American cousin, the signal crayfish. Work on these species issues, as well as continued monitoring of the otter, were part of the movement's commitment to the Biodiversity Action Plan process.

WATER VOLE CONSERVATION

The water vole was one of 12 priority British mammals highlighted in the UK Biodiversity Action Plan as being in urgent need of help.

The Wildlife Trusts selected the water vole as one of its focal species in its 1998 Conservation Plan. It worked closely with the lead partner for the species, the Environment Agency, to establish projects and to deliver appropriate action to protect and restore the species and its habitat.

In the second half of the 1990s, many Trusts established water vole projects, engaged specialist staff and recruited and trained volunteers to drive this work forward. For example, the BERKSHIRE, BUCKINGHAMSHIRE AND OXFORDSHIRE TRUST and the DERBYSHIRE TRUST established Water Vole Recovery Projects. The Derbyshire Trust had embarked on a significant survey and monitoring initiative in 1997 and had followed this with more than ten years of targeted work for the species.

In 1999, The Wildlife Trusts published *Rescuing Ratty* which summarised the work the movement was doing to protect water voles and outlined its future plans. A National Water Vole Coordinator – appointed to help guide and support the Trusts water vole work – and a Water Vole Specialist Group developed a Water Vole Conservation Strategy and a Mink Control

Strategy and Policy. Other initiatives included publication of a *Know Your Vole* postcard and a leaflet on rat control and water vole conservation. Working with the WATER FOR WILDLIFE project, a national water vole database and mapping project commenced in 2008, funded by the Society, the Environment Agency, People's Trust for Endangered Species and Scottish Natural Heritage. Outputs from this work (distribution, alert and key area maps) proved to be a useful tool for devising new landscape-scale strategies for water vole conservation.

The Wildlife Trusts were represented on the UK Water Vole Steering Group and participated in the campaign to achieve legal protection for water vole habitat. This was achieved in April 1998 when the water vole was included on Schedule 5 of the Wildlife and Countryside Act 1981 (as amended), in respect of Section 9(4) only. This Section protected the water vole's place of shelter or protection, but not the animals themselves. Water voles continued to be threatened by inappropriate development, persecution and poisoning. The Wildlife Trusts campaigned for the species to be fully protected, providing evidence to Natural England and the UK Water Steering Group. Full protection was achieved in April 2008.

Water vole

WELSH TRUSTS, ASSOCIATION OF

Wales has a rich variety of natural habitats, from sparse and windswept uplands to fertile grasslands and sea cliffs which support some of its most iconic species like otters, red kites, puffins and Manx shearwaters. The topography of Wales – its many hills and valleys – has created a diverse network of microclimates and wildlife-rich habitats. To an observer, given that Wales has a strong national identity and its own Government, it is perhaps easy to see why today's Wildlife Trusts in Wales (BRECKNOCK, GWENT, MONTGOMERYSHIRE, NORTH WALES, RADNORSHIRE, and SOUTH AND WEST WALES) would need to coordinate their action for wildlife.

From the founding of the Welsh County Naturalists' Trusts in the early 1960s onwards, individual Trusts in Wales were working at a local scale to protect their environment. But they knew that they needed a corporate position particularly in respect of national consultations from the newly-created Welsh Office. Dillwyn Miles founded the Welsh Naturalists' Liaison Committee in 1967 to represent the Trust's position and to manage the publication, *Nature in Wales 1955–1982.*

The Trusts celebrated European Conservation Year 1970 with the publication of a book, *Welsh Wildlife in Trust,* and held a major conference entitled 'Conservation in Wales' at Aberystwyth University with more than 230 delegates, including the Minister of State for Wales. This conference produced a twelve point manifesto for *Public Participation in Conservation for the '70s* which influenced conservation policy in Wales well beyond that decade. This Liaison Committee evolved into the Association of Trusts for Nature Conservation in Wales, established in 1975 with the same object of acting for Trusts in matters of common concern. The Association was represented on the Society (then known as the SPNC), the Welsh Environment Forum of the Prince of Wales' Committee, the Water Liaison Committee and the Regional Fisheries, Recreation and Amenity Advisory Committee of the Welsh Water Authority, the Forestry Commission and the governing body of the National Museum of Wales.

Each Trust in Wales could appoint four representatives to serve on the Association. The Chairman was Professor William (Bill) Lacey, of University College, Bangor (CHRISTOPHER CADBURY MEDAL CITATIONS), and the Honorary Secretary, Eric Bartlett.

The first meeting was held on 15th April 1975 and the minutes still have resonance today. Under AOB, concern was expressed about a recent alarmist article in *Farmer's Weekly* with reference to BADGERS AND TB. It was agreed that the Secretary should write to the Society asking them to reply to this article officially on behalf of the conservation movement.

In 1982, Dr Elizabeth (Libby) Andrews (CHRISTOPHER CADBURY MEDAL CITATION) joined the Association. Andrews was involved with the Brecknock Trust (she would later become its President) through her conservation work on otters, and subsequently was asked to represent the Trusts at a Wales-wide level. She fondly remembers the biannual Association meetings, held in the fine rooms of Gregynog Hall, near Newtown. "They were pleasant and comfortable social gatherings where local Wildlife Trusts could come together to discuss the difficulties they faced in conservation at the time".[309] At the same time, Andrews was also asked to represent the Association of Welsh Wildlife Trusts on the 'Welsh seat' on the Society's national Executive Committee.

During the early 1980s, conservation was not as prominent an issue as it is today. To most institutions and Government bodies, it appeared a rather 'odd-ball interest', as Andrews recalls it. "It was particularly hard to raise the conservation voice and gain representation on the committees and bodies which took decisions on the countryside in Wales. So, a gathering of like-minded people was very important in boosting us against the many setbacks we experienced".[310]

The meetings continued to be chaired by Bill Lacey. Lacey was an academic from Bangor University who cared passionately about wildlife and represented the North Wales Trust. Andrews recalls that the members of the Association appreciated this new, science-based outlook: "It was just wonderful to see academic rigour coming into the general love of wildlife and wild places that is at the heart of the Wildlife Trusts' movement".[311] Other regular attendees included Joan Morgan, Bernard Wright, Joe Lewis and Jeffrey and Joan Raum, and there were usually two meetings a year, unless some major issue needed debate.

The number of Trusts in Wales increased by two when Montgomeryshire split from North Wales in 1982, and Radnorshire separated from HEREFORDSHIRE in 1987. The Association changed its name to Association of Welsh Wildlife Trusts (AWWT) in 1989, to align with the individual Trust names.

The early 1990s were particularly important for the Wildlife Trusts in Wales. Financial constraints were seriously impeding their work, so with help from the then Royal Society for Nature Conservation (the Society), the Welsh Wildlife Appeal was launched under the chairmanship of Professor Lewis Crabtree, the Chairman of the Brecknock Trust. Efforts focused on a series of public lectures and dinners, but unfortunately, the appeal did not make much headway.

TIM CORDY, the Society's Chief Executive, met with the three Powys Trusts (Brecknock, Montgomeryshire and Radnorshire) in Wales in July 1990, to discuss how economies could be made, particularly in joint administration of the three Trusts. Although the logic of this advice was recognised, the Trust Councils were still keen to maintain their own local identities, and were reluctant to compromise the value they saw in being rooted in their own turf. The Society then offered the services of a professional business adviser, Liam Walsh, to analyse the situation and recommend a way in which efforts could be combined, across the whole of Wales.

Liam Walsh met representatives of all the Welsh Trusts in Newtown in September 1990, and submitted his outline report and recommendations. Its reception was not overwhelmingly positive, and the Chairmen of the six Trusts were delegated to take the matter forward. By November, with Andrews chairing the process, a final version of the 'Welsh Recommendations' had been agreed and was then taken back to the Councils of all the Trusts for their debate, agreement and approval – or not. There were strongly held views and one Trust, for example, experienced a troubled extraordinary general meeting and the resignation of its Chairman.

However, the body that finally emerged, with some compromises – Natur Cymru (meaning 'Nature Wales') – had all the Trusts on board, and worked towards an agreed Business Plan.

While this was happening, a proposition had been put forward to abolish the 'Welsh seat' on the Society's Executive Committee. The Society's view was that the Executive Committee should work for the good of the movement as a whole and members were not necessarily there to reflect its geographical interests.

This created some difficulties as the SCOTTISH TRUST had a seat on the Committee by right (see p78). Eventually the Society's Council voted against the motion to abolish the Welsh seat and it was retained.

In June 1995, AWWT was wrapped up with the launch of the new organisation, Natur Cymru (Welsh Wildlife Ltd), by SIR DAVID ATTENBOROUGH at the National Museum in Cardiff. Natur Cymru was launched with a three-year trial and if sponsorship and funding was not forthcoming, it would be wound up and any assets remaining distributed between the Trusts. However, there was still no plain sailing or major finance forthcoming and it was disbanded in 1998.

Despite this somewhat faltering start, the Association and subsequent Natur Cymru, paved the way for today's organisation, Wildlife Trusts Wales. Once devolution became a reality, the Trusts recognised the very definite need for national representation. Today, Wildlife Trusts Wales – a registered charity in its own right – has an office in Cardiff, a small team and a Chief Executive Officer, making it an effective organisation on a national platform.

Dr Derek Thomas, Chairman of Wildlife Trusts Wales, explains: "there were some real movers and shakers at the beginning, but Wildlife Trusts Wales has mainly

come of age because of devolution. Issues like the environment are now handled at a country level, rather than at UK level, so it is certainly timely to have such an organisation".[312] Rachel Sharp, Chief Executive Officer of Wildlife Trusts Wales, agrees that the Trusts now have the capacity to work on a national level. "Where Wildlife Trusts Wales is really making a difference is by being able to put the Wildlife Trusts on the map in Wales, particularly in terms of influencing the Welsh Government, which the local Trusts have very limited capacity to do".[313]

Wildlife Trusts Wales aims to increase Trust influence, profile and resources in Wales. It coordinates partnerships on behalf of the local Trusts, pulls in financial support and facilitates services such as national groups on Living Landscapes and Living Seas. Critically, it gives the Trusts, and the wildlife of Wales, a voice in national decision-making. More recently it has helped to strengthen the Trusts' capacity for campaigning and advocacy work on the protection of Wales' marine environment.

Wildlife Trusts Wales also supports the Trusts in Wales in campaigning on key issues, such as badgers and major projects such as the expansion of the M4 motorway through the Gwent Levels. The latter being successfully fought off following a concerted campaign

An early Association of Welsh Trusts meeting at Gregynog Hall

led by the Gwent Trust. It has also set up numerous partnerships, including an important concordat agreement with the Countryside Council for Wales (CCW) to provide resources for the six Trusts to take conservation action.

Wildlife Trusts Wales closely worked with the Welsh Government on a Natural Environment Framework which heralded a commitment to a landscape-scale approach to nature conservation in Wales. This policy document was timely as the Trusts in Wales were increasing their work in this area, and leading cutting-edge initiatives such as the Pumlumon Project, which covers over 40,000 hectares of upland habitat in the Cambrian Mountains. The Pumlumon Project is showing how conservation management can provide ecosystem services such as flood alleviation and carbon storage. The majority of work on the ground, of course, is still achieved by the volunteers, staff and members of the individual Trusts. Rachel Sharp concludes, "we are very proud to represent the wonderful conservation work of the six Wildlife Trusts in Wales, who work with local communities to effect real change. We want to build on this local approach to develop landscape scale concepts of how nature can provide ecosystem services such as carbon safeguarding, water storage and quality for the people of Wales".[314]

WEST WALES FIELD SOCIETY

The Pembrokeshire Bird Protection Society was established in 1938. From the beginning, it was encouraged by neighbouring counties to extend its boundaries. However, because of the outbreak of war, it was not able to do this until 1945 when it became the West Wales Field Society (WWFS). The Bird Society had wardened the island of Grassholm, had overseen Skokholm, Skomer and

Ramsey islands from 1942 and acquired Cardigan island as its first nature reserve in 1944. At first it leased, and eventually many years later purchased, Cardigan island which was the subject of an early rat eradication operation.

In pioneering ventures after the war, the newly-formed WWFS purchased Dale Fort, near Milford Haven, in 1946. It first leased, and then sold, the property to the Council for the Promotion of Field Studies (CPFS) for use as its first field centre. CPFS later became The Field Studies Council. For a year, in 1946, the WWFS ran a field centre on Skomer. The same year it re-opened the Skokholm bird observatory, taking the lease of the latter from 1948 onwards. In 1949, it established the Kite Preservation Committee and, in 1950, it took over the management of the Orielton duck decoy in Pembrokeshire and obtained a 21-year lease on St Margaret's island.

In 1953, when the Conservancy set up its Committee for Wales, the WWFS's plans to promote a 'Nature Reserves Society' for Wales were deferred. In 1958, WWFS purchased Skomer island for £10,000. It then re-sold the island to the Conservancy by agreement, after which it was declared a National Nature Reserve and leased back to the Trust.

In 1959, steps were taken "towards the transformation of the Society into the West Wales Naturalists' Trust. . . but legal formalities delayed its incorporation until 1961".[315] As the WWFS had "already incurred the expense of incorporation in another form",[316] the Society agreed to a grant of £20 towards its costs.

Because the WWFS had already had such a pronounced conservation track record, MAX NICHOLSON described it as "in effect the second Trust to be founded in Britain".[317]

WILDFLOWERS — BYE-LAW PROTECTION

In the 1920s, the Society responded to a public outcry over the continuing decline of wildflowers and ferns in the countryside by joining a vigorous campaign for better bye-law protection for wild plants. The campaign would last for more than 20 years.

Picking and uprooting wild plants, often for growing-on in gardens or for sale, had become popular in Victorian times and, in the first few decades of the last century, there were no signs of it losing its appeal. This was particularly the case close to built-up areas where improved public transport made for easy access to the countryside. The trade in the royal fern – part of a wider fashion for ferns – illustrated the problem. In *The Times* in 1925, under the heading 'A Yorkshire Tragedy', Herbert Maxwell wrote, "in my recollection there was plenty of the royal fern – *Osmunda regalis* – in this county. At the present time I do not know of a single wild specimen. The last I saw were exposed at a jumble sale".[318]

Royal fern – one of the wild plant species identified as being at risk in the 1920s

Most observers were well aware of the main reasons for the decline – changes in land use. But for the most part they seemed resigned to these changes, seeing them as an inevitable consequence of 'progress'. Correspondence from FW Evens of the Bristol Naturalists' Society sparked off the Society's interest in the problem. In 1925, he wrote about the forces that act as 'agents of destruction'. "The making of new roads, of drainage systems; the using of fresh land on the outskirts of towns for building purposes; the making of railways, the felling of timber – these are all inevitable, and we cannot help much. Other forces that often destroy the home of wild flowers, and make the habitat of others insecure, are the various operations of agriculture, breaking up fresh land with the plough, the destruction of hedges, and cutting down of woods".[319] However, what observers did agree on was that the thoughtless picking and uprooting of wild plants was something that could, and should, be stopped through better legal protection and education.

New organisations sprang up. In 1925, the Flora's League was established "to protect flowers against thoughtless people who are picking them and uprooting them faster than they can grow".[320] In 1930, the Society for the Protection of Wild Flowers and Plants was formed to preserve "the flora of England which in many districts is in danger of total extinction".[321] In 1931, it produced a poster targeting 'boys and girls' and asking, "Why do you want to gather flowers?".[322] The poster recognised that the answer was probably because they were beautiful. But it also counselled "there is far more beauty in the flowers growing naturally in the woods and fields, than those fading and dying in a vase in a hot room".[323] Even existing bodies, like the Botanical Exchange Club, with George Claridge Druce, "one of the most voracious of collectors"[324] at its head, was attracting a new conservation-minded membership.

The Society too took up the cause with some vigour but "considered that it was inadvisable to start a new society to deal with this question".[325] No doubt to smooth ruffled feathers, CB Tahourdin, an Associate Member of the Society and Treasurer of the Flora's League, drew attention in *The Times* to the Society's botanical campaigning and the "excellent work being done by the Society for the Promotion of Nature Reserves in forming sanctuaries and in educational and other work. This Society, cooperating with the many other societies in the kingdom, should be able to accomplish all that is necessary and should be universally supported".[326]

The Society had decided that the best course of action was to use its influence to appeal to County Councils to introduce and enforce local bye-laws. As early as 1913, several County and Borough Councils, for example in Leicestershire, had passed bye-laws under the Local Government Act 1888 to prevent the destruction of ferns and wild plants. But this was by no means a universal state of affairs and the Society set about encouraging more authorities to follow suit. In August 1925, it wrote to all County Councils appealing to them to "take the necessary steps for the protection of the wild flowers in their several districts by the issue of bye-laws, or in such other ways as may seem desirable to them".[327] Their appeal was published in *The Times* with a supporting statement from the Director of the Natural History Museum in London and the Society's Treasurer, SIR SYDNEY HARMER. The editorial commented that, "there are so many of us in this crowded island now, and the remotest countryside is now so easy of access, that what was once a harmless exercise of a human right is on a fair way of becoming a public wrong".[328]

BLUEBELLS

GO AND SEE THEM, BUT –

DO NOT PULL THEM

Wildflower poster produced for display inside London Underground carriages

In 1926 and 1927, the Society distributed more than 10,000 free posters to County Councils, railways, clubs, Women's Institutes and the press and public with the slogan – 'Save the flowers by picking sparingly'. It was pleased to see its efforts complemented by similar initiatives. The London Underground Electric Railways, for example, issued a coloured poster (see previous page) and sticker and the Wild Flower Society published a striking art nouveau-style poster of irises.

But, despite its efforts, the Society was frustrated at the lack of progress. "The position of the wild flowers still gives rise to anxiety and it is uncertain whether the Society's appeal by poster to pick flowers sparingly will entirely achieve the object in view, because a far stronger deterrent is required to restrain the unscrupulous collecting hog from uprooting all the rare plants within his reach".[329]

The next year there was better news. The County Councils' Association, spurred on by the Society and others, persuaded the Home Office to arrange a conference resulting in approval for a new model bye-law. By March 1931, the Home Office was able to report to the Society that 31 counties in England had bye-laws. In 1933, the model bye-law was revised to include special reference to primroses.

Viscount Grey, a member of the Society's Executive, spoke up for better wildflower protection at a special session at CPRE's Countryside Conference in Manchester in 1929 and, on 19th July the same year, the Society's PRESIDENT, VISCOUNT ULLSWATER, broadcast on the need to protect wild plants from the 'London Station'. Similar appeals

Blue gentian – local police helped to protect Teesdale gentians from collectors in the 1930s

were made at CPRE's Welwyn Garden conference in 1930 and in 1931 the Society again sent out posters to local authorities.

Other work to counter the destruction of wildflowers by the "acquisitive proclivities of itinerant Man"[330] was also continuing behind the scenes. In 1930, for example, the Society objected to the London County Council purchasing a "motor lorry for the collection and distribution of botanical specimens for schools in the London area".[331] In 1931, the *Northern Echo* reported that "the blue gentian (*Gentiana verna*) is now to be seen in full bloom on Widdy Bank Fell".[332] Soon afterwards the Society received a letter from a concerned local resident worried about collectors. The Society contacted the Durham County Constabulary and received a reassuring response from the Chief Constable. The force was aware of the threats, coming mostly from "motorists who have been seen to use

trowels".[333] Notices had been erected and the landowner was employing 'watchers' during the flowering period. Next year, his sergeant at Middleton-in-Teesdale reported that, "watchers will again be employed and the police will assist as much as possible".[334]

The CPRE was also pressing for better wild plant protection. In 1931, after a summer of negotiation, 28 statutory and non-statutory bodies, with varying degrees of interest in plant conservation, were persuaded to come together under its auspices in the Wild Plant Conservation Board. It was reported by the Society as being "one of the results of the centenary meeting of the British Association for the Advancement of Science held in London in 1931".[335] The idea of the Board was to avoid "duplication of effort and expense"[336] and to restore "locally exterminated species, direct the application of bye-laws and protective measures and to secure further protective measures".[337]

Despite the Society's earlier reservations about new societies, its HONORARY SECRETARY, HERBERT SMITH, led the Society's support for this new umbrella body, and at its first meeting, he was elected its Chairman. The Board immediately circulated a questionnaire asking, among other things, for views on future legislation. There was little appetite for primary legislation, most respondents favouring continued pressure on County Councils to introduce and enforce the newly-strengthened bye-law and on the Home Office to extend these powers to private land. Predictably, the latter was unsuccessful.

During the Second World War, protection of wildflowers understandably made little progress. In 1943, and early in 1944, the Board did express their concern in a letter to *The Times* and to the Ministry of Agriculture and Fisheries about the threats to 'interesting plants' from increased cultivation for the war effort. It asked that botanical advice be sought before ploughing commenced. In consequence, many notifications were received, and in a few important instances land had been de-requisitioned. In another case, the American General Officer Commanding replied to a letter with understandable caution. "You may be assured that insofar as it is possible, with due regard to the exigencies of military necessity, the country. . . between Braunton Burrows and Slapton Ley, will remain as free from evidences of use by our troops as is possible".[338] But, despite this brief engagement with the war effort and the Board's initial flurry of activity, with transport and other war-time difficulties, there were no meetings of the Board between 1940 and 1946. John Sheail writes, "the constituent members

largely ignored the opportunities offered by such a co-ordinating body. The Board achieved very little and gradually it was eclipsed by the activities of other bodies. For example, the Botanical Exchange Club and Society of the British Isles was renamed the Botanical Society of the British Isles in 1947 and soon afterwards formed a Threats Committee to recommend ways of averting or mitigating the loss of plant species. It compiled reports on areas of high botanical interest, and in 1950 the name of the committee was changed to Conservation Committee".[339]

In the post-war period of reconstruction, the report of the Wild Life Conservation Special Committee, set up under the Ministry of Town and Country Planning, had recommended the establishment of a wildlife agency and in 1949 the Nature Conservancy was born. The Special Committee's report (Command 7122) supported the need for primary legislation to include a short protected list of "a few striking, beautiful and vulnerable species"[340] of wild plant. The report continued, "for the rest, we would rely upon regulations restricting the taking of certain species for sale and above all upon education".[341]

However, it was to be a further 28 years before Parliament passed the CONSERVATION OF WILD CREATURES AND WILD PLANTS ACT 1975. By this time, ironically, the public's wildflower collecting fever had subsided and the world was a very different place. But those in the Society, and elsewhere, who had had the courage to stand up for wildflowers when it was unfashionable to do so, were prominent among those who laid the foundation for today's more enlightened approach to wildlife protection.

WILDFLOWER WEEKS

In the first half of the last century, particularly after the Second World War, changes in land use, often inimical to the country's wildlife, were seen as an inevitable consequence of the drive to produce 'food from our own resources' and to lift large sections of society out of poverty. But in the second half of the century, as these goals were achieved and evidence of the damage being done to the environment became increasingly apparent, public attitudes hardened.

One response from the Society, between 1986 and 1991, was a return to its long-running crusade on behalf of wild plants. It organised a series of high profile Wildflower Weeks, promoted as part of the Society's BRITISH WILDLIFE APPEAL (BWA). The Weeks harnessed the interest of a public enjoying more affluence and leisure time and combined this with a strong conservation message about the decline in wildflowers.

The first Wildflower Week in 1986 was launched with a relay walk started by DAVID BELLAMY at the National Garden Festival in Stoke-on-Trent and completed by Bill Oddie and Julian Pettifer at the Chelsea Flower Show. In the first two years more than 500 events were organised by the Trusts.

But it was soon recognised that without additional resources the event would struggle to reach its full potential. Help came from two sources. First, support from a top public relations company, Kingsway Promotions, as part of their contribution to the BWA and second, sponsorship of £132,000 over three years from Gales Honey, brokered through WWF. As a result, the Society was able to employ a Wildflower Week Project Officer and, from the third year, award small grants to the Trusts. This meant that in 1988 every Trust organised events – 300 hundred in 1988, 400 in 1989 and 500 in 1990. As the Week grew in popularity, other organisations joined in. By 1990 there were 1,400 addresses on the Wildflower Week mailing list, including 650 Tourist Information Centres, 315 schools and 59 local authority Recreation Departments.

Innovative media-friendly events, including a wildflower-themed press launch at the Chelsea Physic Garden with poppy-seed cake and elderflower champagne, and a press breakfast at Covent Garden, encouraged long-lead time newspapers, magazines, radio and television to cover Wildflower Week. In one year, for example, there were many hours of air time on local radio stations and, another year, the Week was featured in a storyline in *The Archers* on BBC Radio 4.

All publicity was underpinned with a serious message. In two reports *Disappearing Wildflowers* in 1987 and *Where Have All the Wildflowers Gone?* in 1990, the Society highlighted the nature of the problem. In the former, Stewart and Warwicker from the Conservation Association of Botanical Societies looked at available data for 25 vice-counties. In 15 vice-counties there had been up to 50 extinctions, in three between 50 and 100, and in seven more than 100 extinctions.

In the second report, the information from the Trusts showed the top 100 plants that were either extinct or threatened in 50 different areas, generally on a county scale. Drainage, agricultural and forestry 'improvement', and destruction by development remained major causes of habitat loss and subsequent wildflower extinctions. But pollution, river and coastal works and lack of, or inappropriate, management were also cited.

For the six years in which Wildflower Weeks were held, the Society provided support with a conservation programme ranging

from a roadside verge campaign and orchid-wardening scheme to a Primary School wildflower pack and an early example of the Society's promotion of wildlife gardening.

Addressing the press launch at Chelsea Physic Garden prior to the 1989 Wildflower Week, Tim Sands welcomed further support from Gales Honey by parodying the song with the claim that 'a spoonful of honey helps the meadows and downs'. He stressed that "raising awareness of wildflowers is the key to their survival and long-term protection".[342] As a result of thousands of Wildflower Week events, public awareness had risen; the Society's roadside verge campaign had resulted in several local authorities altering their maintenance practices; 50 secluded leafy areas had been created through the Society's Hospital Wildlife Gardens' scheme and, through encouragement from Trusts, wildflower areas had been created in municipal parks, like Brandon Hill in Bristol.

In 1991, after the last Wildflower Week, the issues of wildflower conservation were taken up as part of the Society's *Losing Ground – Gaining Ground* theme – and a 'Vanishing Meadows' campaign was launched focused on the protection of wildflower meadows.

The annual Wildflower Weeks could claim to be amongst the most successful promotional events staged by the Society attracting, in the best years, strong corporate sponsorship, good media coverage, a large Wildlife Trust events programme and tangible conservation gains.

WILDLIFE FILMS

In May and September 1960, the Naturalists' Trusts' Committee discussed the possibility of a national 16mm colour ciné-film about the Trusts, but it was never produced. Instead, in the 1960s and 1970s, several Trusts produced their own

promotional films. The BERKSHIRE, BUCKINGHAMSHIRE AND OXFORDSHIRE TRUST's film, *Wildlife in Trust,* was shown after the Society's Annual General Meeting in June 1965. A copy of *Wildlife in Trust* was purchased by CHRISTOPHER CADBURY, presented to the Society and put "in the charge of Miss CJ Hart, projectionist at the British Museum".[343] The LINCOLNSHIRE TRUST's film, *Nature in Trust,* was shown after the Society's AGM in 1967. As well as showing the work of the Trust, including many of its nature reserves, the latter film "also poses problems for the future".[344] *Nature in Trust,* filmed by ROBIN CRANE Films, was transferred to video at the time of the Lincolnshire Trust's golden jubilee in 1998. The Lincolnshire Trust produced a second film, *An Eye for the Country,* in 1972.

In 1968, it was agreed that the Society should acquire a copy of the WILTSHIRE TRUST's film, *The Wealth of the Chalk,* for hire to Trusts through its film library and, in December 1970, the SCOTTISH TRUST's film, *A Place for Wildlife,* produced by Christopher Mylne, was shown on prime-time television. The Cambridgeshire and Isle of Ely Trust's, *Wood to Washes,* produced by Fennec Films, featured the Trust's two largest reserves, Hayley Wood and the Ouse Washes.

In 1972, the work of the NORFOLK TRUST and many of its reserves in the Broads, Breckland and on the coast were featured in *Norfolk in Trust,* a film produced and shown by Anglia Television in its famous *Survival* television series.

WILDLIFE LINK

The UK's voluntary environment and animal welfare groups agreed to establish Wildlife Link in August 1979, but it was not until March 1980 that it held its first formal meeting under the auspices of the

Committee for Environmental Conservation (CoEnCo). Wildlife Link took over from two umbrella bodies that "in their time had served wildlife and the environment well".[345] CoEnCo and the Council for Nature were disbanded in 1982 and 1979 respectively.

Wildlife Link became an Independent Unincorporated Association two years later, before it merged with Countryside Link to become Wildlife and Countryside Link (Link) in 1993.

Link has provided a much-valued and effective vehicle for collective action by voluntary organisations for more than 25 years. The Society has been a strong supporter over this time, being active in the campaigns for better habitat protection in 1981, for new countryside and access legislation in 2000 and, most recently, the work for marine legislation. It has chaired several Groups and Task Forces and has been a regular member of Link's Management Committee.

Link has employed a series of young and talented staff, many of whom have gone on to hold key posts in the countryside and wildlife movement. For example, Dame Fiona Reynolds, Director General of The National Trust, was Secretary of Countryside Link between 1982 and 1989; Hazel Phillips, a key player in the Society's rebirth after 2005, was Wildlife Link Secretary from 1981 to 1986; STEPHANIE HILBORNE was Principal Officer of Wildlife and Countryside Link between 1994 and 1997 and Martin Harper, Director of Conservation at the RSPB, was Principal Officer between 1997 and 1999.

Three country Links were also established: Scottish Environment Link in 1987, Wales Environment Link in 1989 and Northern Ireland Environment Link in 1990.

WILDLIFE SITES (LOCAL WILDLIFE SITES)

From the earliest years of the Trusts' existence, it was recognised that having a limited number of statutorily protected sites, welcome as this was, would not be sufficient to protect the full panoply of the country's wildlife. Sites of Special Scientific Interest (SSSIs) were, after all, a selection of the best sites and only a representative sample of some. Statutory nature reserves were also relatively few and far between.

In 1965, a study group of the COUNTRYSIDE IN 1970 conference looked at the 'Preservation of Natural, Historic and other Treasures' and proposed a largely County Council-based system for the conservation of localised features – Britain's rural heritage – to be known as 'Countryside Treasures'. The system would include 'Nature's Treasures' such as unusual ecological areas – woodland, heath, fen, bog, and rock-faces – and the natural homes of rare animals, birds and insects, and the stations of rare plants. Although Cheshire County Council, for example, picked up on the ideas in 1972 and introduced a Countryside Treasures scheme, little more came of this. Nevertheless, it had many of the elements of what, today, we would call a Local Wildlife Sites system.

From the late 1960s, local authorities, with their statutory planning responsibilities, had to take more account of the natural environment in urban and rural areas, partly as a result of the Countryside Act 1968 and the Civic Amenities Act 1967. A new Development Plan system of Structure and Local Plans was introduced in 1968 that encouraged planners to include nature conservation policies in development plans – "an invitation more readily accepted by structure plan teams than by those producing local plans".[346]

In the early 1970s, there were four major local authority initiatives. The Merseyside County Council produced a comprehensive schedule of nature conservation sites using aerial photographs and the West Midlands County Council asked the Conservancy to produce a list of sites of nature conservation value. This would be the first published list of such sites. In addition, a Sites of Scientific Interest system (omitting the word 'Special') was established in the West Yorkshire Metropolitan County area in 1976, and the Greater London Council started work on a nature conservation database and designation system in 1982.

During the 1970s and early 1980s, several Trusts were also developing their own systems to identify local non-statutory wildlife sites. In the first CONSERVATION OFFICERS' BULLETIN in 1974, Stuart Crooks, then working at the CHESHIRE TRUST, wrote that, "some Trusts do have their own county site grading systems and the Nature Conservancy operates grading systems for the zonation of biological interest in some regions as well as the nationally-accepted SSSI classification as used in the Conservation Review".[347] In SHROPSHIRE, for example, in 1978 and 1979, the Trust carried out a survey and identified 5,000 sites. From these, 700 were selected as Prime Sites.

At the beginning, most Trusts were hesitant about disclosing their information about Local Wildlife Sites, even to the local authorities. Trusts would often meet with the owner or occupier to discuss the protection and wildlife management of a particular site or take action on a case by case basis, if a site was under threat. But it was not until around the mid-1980s that Trusts had built up the capacity and confidence to involve a range of partners, including local authorities, to prevent further deterioration of these non-statutory wildlife sites. In 1985, a British Association of Nature Conservationists' survey showed that nine out of the ten nature conservation site schedules used in development control by local authorities had been compiled with assistance from the Conservancy and/or the Trust. Worryingly, this survey also showed that "fourteen per cent of local authorities were not using check lists or schedules at all, even for statutory sites".[348]

In 1987, the Department of the Environment and Welsh Office Circular 27/87 (52/87) on nature conservation recognised a natural world outside of statutorily designated sites. It referred to useful measures, such as "the establishment of a base of information, including thematic maps, on wildlife and habitats to inform and assist in the development of policies which take account of the needs of conservation (local voluntary groups may be able to assist in the collection of such information through, for example, habitat surveys)".[349]

Over the next ten years, effective systems for identifying, managing and monitoring Local Wildlife Sites were gradually developed, often with extremely limited resources. In 1994, data was collected on 62 separate Local Wildlife Sites systems operating throughout the UK. The Wildlife Trusts were, by now, leading in 62 per cent of these systems.

Just over ten years later, in 2005, this had grown to 131 systems. Immediately after carrying out its first survey of Local Wildlife Sites systems in 1994, The Wildlife Trusts published *The Wildlife Sites Handbook*, a technical loose-leaved document with examples and case studies for use by "anyone who is involved in developing, running or using a Wildlife Sites system".[350] The handbook was edited by Sara Hawkswell. A second edition, *The Wildlife Sites Handbook Version 2*, taking into account new criteria, new mechanisms for working with landowners, site surveys and other policy and organisational changes, was published in 1997. This document, and the policy work associated with its development, would prove invaluable in the discussions that would take place with the Government at the beginning of the new millennium.

The Wildlife Sites Handbook – first published in 1994

Once systems had been operating for a few years, it was possible to collate data about the loss of, and damage to, Local Wildlife Sites. The figures were disturbing. In 1989 in Shropshire, for example, 22 per cent of the county's meadows had been destroyed in a ten-year period. When the Trust went back and undertook a sample survey of an area that had

shown a 33 per cent loss of meadows between 1978 and 1989, it found that the loss had reached a staggering 44 per cent, an increase of 11 per cent in only two years.

In 2000, further similar disturbing evidence of loss and damage was drawn to the attention of David Kidney (MP for Stafford). During the Second Reading and Committee stages of the Countryside and Rights of Way Bill, Kidney described these losses and backed The Wildlife Trusts' call for the Government to place a legal duty on local authorities to run effective Local Wildlife Sites systems and for Local Wildlife Sites to have a statutory role within the planning system. In addition, he supported the view that local authorities should incorporate Local Wildlife Sites systems into their Local Biodiversity Action Plans (BIODIVERSITY ACTION PLANNING), and budget accordingly. There was also a need for clear, strong and well-structured national guidance.

As a result of Kidney's interventions, the Government offered no new legislation, but it did agree to examine the role of Local Wildlife Sites and to prepare national guidance. A Local Sites Review Group was established by the then Department of the Environment Transport and the Regions soon afterwards. Its report, published in April 2000, defined the overall objective of a Local Wildlife Sites system. The series of non-statutory Local Sites should "seek to ensure, in the public interest, the conservation, maintenance and enhancement of species, habitats, geological and geomorphological features of substantive nature conservation value. Local Sites systems should select all areas of substantive value including both the most important and the most distinctive species,

Local Wildlife Sites are vital for linking and buffering fully-protected sites such as nature reserves. The landscape pictured here (near Ambergate, Derbyshire) contains five Local Wildlife Sites, as well as two SSSIs and two rivers

habitats, geological and geomorph-ological features within a national, regional and local context. Sites within the series may also have an important role in contributing to the public enjoyment of nature conservation".[351]

In 1999, a leaflet, *Treading New Ground*, set out The Wildlife Trusts' views on Local Wildlife Sites systems. It complemented the work by David Kidney MP and maintained pressure on the Government and other Members of Parliament during the passage of the Countryside and Rights of Way Bill through Parliament. In the autumn of 2000, a Local Wildlife Sites newsletter, *Site Matters*, was published by The Wildlife Trusts for the first time to keep those running Local Wildlife Sites systems up to speed with good practice and the latest information on new laws and policies. In 2002, a further leaflet set out guidance on how a Local Wildlife Sites system should operate and what was required both locally and nationally to ensure that it was a comprehensive and robust network.

In 2002, there was a welcome recognition of the contribution made by Local Wildlife Sites in the Department of Environment, Food and Rural Affairs' report, *Working With the Grain of Nature:*

A Biodiversity Strategy for England. But it would be another four years before the promised guidelines on Local Wildlife Sites were produced for England by the Department. They provided a framework of national minimum standards, including recommendations for a common name and approaches to establishing partnerships and selecting, protecting and managing sites. A seminar for practitioners, held in January 2007, explored ways of implementing these guidelines.

In the meantime, English Planning Policy guidance (PPS 9: Biodiversity and Geological Conservation) had been updated and substantially strengthened. It recognised that, "Local Sites have a fundamental role to play in helping to meet overall national biodiversity targets, contributing to the quality of life and well-being of the community and in supporting research and education. Local Development Frameworks should identify all local nature conservation areas on the proposals map".[352]

Much has been achieved over nearly 35 years of campaigning for Local Wildlife Sites. In 2006, in the region of 35,000 non-statutory Local Wildlife Sites were identified in England alone and they were increasingly recognised by

Government as making a "vital contribution to delivering both the UK and Local Biodiversity and Geodiversity Action Plan targets and maintaining local natural character and distinctiveness".[353] By now, the majority of local authority areas were covered by a Local Wildlife Sites system. Each local authority was obliged to integrate its system into its planning process as a contribution to its overall duty to 'have regard to the purpose of the conservation of biological diversity in the exercise of its function' – a requirement of the Natural Environment and Rural Communities Act 2006. The number of effective Local Wildlife Sites systems in operation was also a formal indicator for monitoring the success, or otherwise, of the Government's Biodiversity Action Plan.

Indeed, in April 2008, a national set of 198 indicators were agreed by the Government against which local authorities and their partners were required to report, as from March 2009. National Indicator 197 (NI197) – 'Improved Local Biodiversity' – was of particular relevance as it was based on "the proportion of Local Wildlife Sites where positive conservation management has been, or is being,

Fragrant orchid on a Local Wildlife Site in Sussex

implemented".[354] Local authorities and their partners were required to select up to 35 of these national indicators for inclusion in their Local Area Agreements (the delivery framework for the Sustainability Community Strategy) and against which annual improvement targets were set for the next three years. By November 2008, 26 out of a potential 150 areas had adopted NI 197 within their Local Area Agreement and, of these, 39 per cent covered District/Borough Councils, 38 per cent County Councils and 12 per cent unitary, Metropolitan and London Borough Councils.

Despite these encouraging developments, The Wildlife Trusts' ultimate objective has still not been achieved – a statutory requirement on local authorities to run a Local Wildlife Sites system and a duty for them to take Local Wildlife Sites into account in planning decisions. Whether this next step becomes necessary, because sites in the wider countryside continue to be lost and damaged at an unacceptable rate, remains to be seen. Recent figures from a Wildlife Trust monitoring

project of 'Local Wildlife Site grasslands' in 2007 did not make for good reading. They showed that the wildlife interest in 34 per cent of 67 sites surveyed had declined since their initial selection. National Indicators were abolished in April 2011 and replaced by a national data set (including Local Wildlife Sites) against which local authorities have to report. However, there is no obligation for them to improve their management. All planning policy for England (including Local Wildlife Sites' protection) was reviewed in 2012, with The Wildlife Trusts lobbying for the inclusion of Local Wildlife Sites.

In his introduction to the Government's current guidance on Local Sites, Jim Knight MP, the Biodiversity Minister at the time, expressed hope that "the guidance will encourage existing partnerships and prompt others to fill gaps so that the best of their local wildlife and geological heritage is protected".[355] It is right to 'hope for the best' but a common variant of this proverb also adds 'and prepare for the worst'. It is likely that Local Wildlife Sites will continue to demand attention for some time to come.

WILDLIFE TRAVEL

Wildlife Travel is a small travel company that encourages good practice in ecotourism and commits its profits to the nature conservation work of The Wildlife Trusts.

It was established as an independent body by FRANK PERRING, John Guy and Ann Cryer in 1988 to raise funds for the Society's BRITISH WILDLIFE APPEAL. In the first year there was just one holiday with 25 travellers. By the start of its second season, more than 140 travellers had already booked places to five destinations.

Wildlife Travel was naturally keen to receive the formal blessing of the Society, including use of its logo and London address. The Society, however, was initially hesitant to commit to the new company, concerned that the venture might have hidden legal, financial or resource implications. By 1990, the Society had been reassured.

It agreed that its London Office could be Wildlife Travel's registered office and a legal document was drawn up and signed by both parties covering arrangements for future donations.

In the first ten years or so, the hub of the Wildlife Travel operation was, in practice, Perring's own home in Oundle. By 1999, however, the company was being run by Chris Donnelly and it was necessary for it to move into a 'proper' office, first in Peterborough and then, from 2004, in Cambourne, near Cambridge. Since its formation, Wildlife Travel has organised several hundred group holidays to five continents, introducing many thousands of travellers to the wildlife, culture and conservation of around 40 countries and has donated more than £125,000 to The Wildlife Trusts. The company also prides itself on its environmental credentials, including its work to reduce its carbon footprint and to make sure that its holidays contribute locally to the conservation of the areas it visits.

WILDLIFE WATCH

Wildlife Watch – the junior branch of The Wildlife Trusts – is a respected and widely recognised part of The Wildlife Trusts. While its administration, its focus of interest and even its approach to young people have changed over the past 30 or more years, its attractive and often innovative approach, its reach and its high educational standards continue to make it a leading action club for young environmentalists.

In 1975, the Society was looking for ways to help Trusts involve more young people in their work and build a junior membership. The Society's Assistant Secretary, Wilf Dawson, became aware of the pioneering work of the Advisory Centre for Education (ACE) in Cambridge, inspired by the ecologist and first Director of Monks Wood Experimental Station, Kenneth Mellanby. In 1971, ACE had organised an exciting and original national survey of water pollution, using a set of indicator creatures to judge pollution levels. The survey was promoted through *The Sunday Times* newspaper, and, a year later, the Centre followed this up with a similar project surveying lichens as indicators of air quality and pollution. The success of these surveys – the water pollution survey attracted 10,000 children and families – encouraged *The Sunday Times* to fund a new Watch Club on an experimental basis under the supervision of ACE. It published its own magazine *Watchword*. Between 1972 and 1977 the Watch Club began to flourish – a map of beach pollution was drawn and national surveys carried out on, among other things, flower rich road verges, noise nuisance, endangered buildings and tree damage.

More than enough had been achieved by Watch in its first five years to justify *The Sunday Times'* investment and to convince the Society of its potential. But, although it was attracting large numbers of young people, there was still a feeling in the Society that maintaining their interest was going to be difficult without a strong local base. Dawson believed the Trusts could provide such a presence and he set about creating the team and administrative structure to put the Watch project on a more permanent footing. In 1975, most Trusts agreed to combine junior membership of their Trust with membership of the Watch Club. This gave young Trust members access to the various UK-wide environmental projects and *Watchword* (see page 745).

Two years later, in August 1977, Watch was integrated into the Wildlife Trust family with the creation of the independent Watch Trust for Environmental Education Ltd. It was sponsored by *The Sunday Times* and had a Board of Management made up of representatives from the newspaper and the Society. The separate Trust was essential in securing the financial support of *The Sunday Times* and helped guard against any move by the Society, or the Trusts, to unduly restrict its broader and more innovative approach to environmental education. The support of *The Sunday Times* editor, Harold Evans, and Managing Editor, Peter Roberts, were also crucial in enabling the smooth running of these new arrangements.

Kenneth Mellanby became the first President and was followed by DAVID BELLAMY who took over this role in 1988. Bellamy was supported by Vice Presidents, including television presenters Chris Packham, Bill Oddie and Nick Baker.

The Watch Trust for Environmental Education was formally dissolved at the national conference in York in 1996, but Watch continued.

By 1980, all but one of the Trusts had joined the Watch Trust for Environmental Education. Membership had risen by almost 50 per cent from more than 6,500 in 1979 to nearly 10,000 in 1980. By the end of 1980, Watch administration and promotion, previously the responsibility of Geoffrey Young – a founder member of ACE – was transferred to the Society.

As this new Watch Club got underway local groups began to spring up across the country under the auspices of the Trusts. They began appointing volunteer Watch Organisers to coordinate teams of local leaders to run groups, county-wide events and to produce a local newsletter. By 1980, 33 Trusts were producing their own local Watch newsletter for insertion with *Watchword*. Regional Watch conferences were arranged, including in 1981 a successful leaders' seminar organised by the Cheshire Watch Organiser, Joan Fairhurst.

Local Groups were able to experiment with their own programmes of activities – often developing their own character – but continued to tap into the exciting, well-designed and scientifically accurate UK projects which remained the Club's flagship activity.

The success of these projects owed much to the regular features in *The Sunday Times*. The opportunity of frequent exposure to a large, non-Trust audience was much-prized and hard to come by in a pre-internet age. Scientists had few ways to generate mass observations and, for the Trusts,

coverage provided a regular injection of new members, widespread participation in the projects and an increased media profile for the Club and the Wildlife Trusts' movement overall. True, it probably meant that many of the youngsters that took part "represented a somewhat biased cross section of the population – largely *The Sunday Times*-reading families from the upper socio-economic groups".[356] Nevertheless, Pratt and Freeston made the point that "some of those active Watch members of the 1970s are among the professional ecologists, conservationists and environ-mental educators of today".[357]

The projects and competitions were often innovative and always fun. Many had natural history themes – such as wildflowers, butterflies and bees – while others covered broader social and environmental subjects, such as pollution issues, gardening and human attitudes to wildlife. For example, a survey, promoted as a 'battitudes' survey, analysed the public's feelings about bats.

Some projects could throw up surprises – a ladybird survey became famous for a new record of a two-spot variety, discovered in Loughborough. Other projects provided valuable long-term data or produced other tangible conservation benefits. A phenological survey – Frogwatch – recorded the first sightings each year of frogspawn. Started in 1981, it was repeated annually for several

years and took on a wider significance as the world became increasingly aware of climate change. One Watch Group – the Hull Watch Group – also discovered that large numbers of frogs and toads were being killed on the road which crossed the route to and from their breeding ponds. They alerted the local Council, mounted their own patrols and campaigned successfully for 'Toads on the Road' signs. There were exciting prizes too. Four winners of the 1982 Watch Butterfly Diary Competition, for example, flew to Zambia, courtesy of Zambian Airways, for a week's safari in the Luanga Valley.

By the mid-1980s, Watch realised it had only scratched the surface as far as involving young people in 'citizen science' was concerned. It embarked on a series of large-scale national projects and three of these are described in more detail below.

In 1985, with all-important sponsorship from the oil company BP, Watch teamed up with the Field Studies Council for a study of acid rain – a topical issue at the time. A kit was assembled with pH

measuring equipment, together with precise instructions for establishing a sampling post using a flat-pack rain gauge. An earlier version of the gauge had used a reconstructed standard-sized, plastic lemonade bottle.

This was the first time Watch had devised a project kit of such complexity and there were serious hurdles to be overcome, not least Post Office regulations about what could, and could not, be sent by mail! With the catchy title of the 'Acid Drops' project, it was able to capture data on an unprecedented scale. At the time the Government had comparatively few monitoring stations. Thousands of reliable records provided important corroboration of other studies at the time. For example, it confirmed that, after a long dry period, rainfall was significantly more acidic. It also revealed that winds from continental Europe carried acid rain pollution across the Midlands and into Scotland. The unique system of sampling stations established across the UK was impressive enough, but it was not long before a complementary network had been established

The flat-pack rain gauge and kit used by children to collect and analyse rainfall as part of the Acid Drops project. Thousands of children took part

stretching from Spitsbergen within the Arctic Circle, to Ireland and the Czech Republic, and as far south as Gibraltar. Trial kits were despatched to Australia, Malaysia and Hong Kong and publicity through the BBC World Service resulted in 'Acid Drops' correspondence with listeners in Africa and the Far East. The project was repeated annually over a three-year period, with the 1987 project launched by the Environment Minister, William Waldegrave.

In late 1989, Watch turned its attention to something even more ambitious. This time the project was designed to measure low-level ozone, a pollutant formed when nitrogen oxides and un-burnt hydrocarbons (from car exhausts and industrial burning of fossil fuels) react together in the presence of sunlight. Low-level ozone causes breathing difficulties for older people, asthmatics and those with bronchial complaints. Watch became aware of two cultivars of the tobacco plant, *Nicotiana tabacum*, which varied in their sensitivity to ozone. One cultivar was extremely sensitive and developed spots on its leaves once ozone concentrations reached 40 parts per billion. The other 'control' cultivar only began spotting at 80 parts per billion. As the level of ozone increased, so did the spotting on each cultivar, with the ozone-sensitive plants always spotting more rapidly than the control plants. The project received sponsorship from Volvo Concessions Ltd and was scheduled to begin in March 1990 to accommodate three growing phases. However, the launch of the project was threatened at the last minute. The USA Department of Agriculture, thought to be the sole supplier, had only been able to harvest 20 per cent of the seeds requested. With no seed in the UK there were several sleepless nights

before two further suppliers were finally located in North America. Once again the project was a tremendous success. From Scotland to Southampton, from Cornwall to Canterbury, thousands of youngsters were measuring the spotting on plants at 17,000 sampling points. *Nicotiania* plants shared beds with geraniums outside the Houses of Parliament and with sunflowers in the BBC *Blue Peter* garden. The project was repeated in 1991, this time with 60,000 'recorders' taking part. Both years of the project raised public awareness of low-level ozone and yielded important results, confirming, for example, how ozone concentrations tended to be much higher in rural areas.

Leaf spotting – children inspecting tobacco plants as part of the Watch ozone project

The year 1991 saw the start of National Riverwatch, destined to become Watch's largest project yet (WATER FOR WILDLIFE). Sponsored by National Power, the aim was to carry out an extensive three-year survey to study the state of the country's rivers, river banks and river catchments. Once again the Watch project was highly-acclaimed and attracted huge numbers of young people – no fewer than 170,000 participants during the three years. The project was awarded the Hydro Award for outstanding achievement in water quality improvement in the UK, ahead of competition that included two water companies.

International interest was again strong. For example, the British

Council established links with Mendeleev University in Russia and the Society's Director of Education, Mary Cornwell, and her team, were invited to Russia to demonstrate the Watch approach (including the National Riverwatch survey) to a gathering of high-powered Russian educationalists. The project was also translated for use in the Rhone Alpes region of France and in Utrecht in the Netherlands. In 1999, the British Council funded a two-year partnership project between The Wildlife Trusts and the Moscow Union of Scientific and Engineering Societies to adapt elements of the project for a community water monitoring programme around Lake Plescheevo. There was even interest from Thailand and Vietnam. The project's unique water pollution monitoring slide-rule was of particular interest to Vietnamese biologists who believed it would be more reliable than modern electronic equipment in the high humidity of their country's remote jungles. The outcomes of this project included building social cohesion – something which perhaps Watch has been less quick to recognise as a consequence of its work closer to home.

Early Watch poster

Ten years after its incorporation, Watch membership had increased to more than 30,000, with 800 groups and more than 1,000 affiliated schools and youth groups. *Watchword* had been redesigned in the winter of 1984 as an A3, full colour news-sheet. The back page sported a new cartoon strip – the adventures of 'Flora and Fauna' – and each issue came with a sponsored pull-out poster to accompany the latest hot topic or national project. For example, to support a *MartinWATCH* project, the spring 1985 issue contained a poster of swifts, swallows and martins. In 2000, the revised membership package saw new welcome materials, and *Watchword* – which was now rarely able to include posters – supplemented by a sister publication, *Wildlife Extra*. This provided members with more frequent contact, more posters and more art and craft activities. It also provided practical ideas and instructions for helping wildlife.

A national 'achievement badge' scheme had also been introduced and, by March 1987, 23 young people had earned their Gold Award by successfully completing tasks for all eight of the badges in the scheme. The Gold Award Scheme was revamped in 1997 and re-launched in 1998. The first 'Wildlife Watch Group of the Year' award was won jointly by Cottingham Wildlife Watch in Yorkshire and Ewhurst Wildlife Watch and Action Watch in Surrey. Ten years on, winning groups have come from as far north as Cawdor, as far west as Waunfawr, as far east as Milden and as far south as Andover. In 2006, the Watch Awards were supplemented by Watch Starlets,

a scheme for members successfully completing projects when aged five, six or seven. The Gold Award is now for young people over eight years old.

The annual national Watch Day gave members a chance to gather on a grand scale. In 1983, the event was held at London Zoo and attracted more than 2,000 members. President, DAVID BELLAMY, was followed by hundreds of Watch members in 'pied-piper' fashion as he moved from one activity to another. The event was repeated in 1984 and this time the President was helped out by the children's television presenter, John Craven. In 1987, a Watch picnic at Coombe Park in Coventry attracted 3,000 'Watchers', drawn "partly by the helicopter arrival of President, David Bellamy".[358] The last national Watch Day, held at Ferry Meadows near Peterborough in 1991, attracted more than 5,000 children and their families. The numbers attending had now become so large that it was decided in future to organise several separate events across the UK.

By the beginning of 1993, *The Sunday Times* had given notice that

it would be pulling out of sponsoring Watch. Things were changing – young people and the society in which they were growing up were "a world apart from those of the 1970s".[359] It was not that introducing young people to their natural environment in a way that was fun and captured their imagination was suddenly something to be thrown out of the window. It was just that there were new ways of doing it – and selling it. The internet, for example, was becoming more widely available to researchers and, from an administrative point of view, vast paper-based projects were less attractive. There was also a feeling that young peoples' own ideas should be put more centre stage, giving them the opportunity to shape their own activities and projects. More than ever, Watch wanted to see an end to the 'disconnect' between people and their environment.

In 1995, soon after his appointment as Director General, SIMON LYSTER identified the need to look afresh at Watch – now marketed as Wildlife Watch – and to examine the position of the UK office as a

David Bellamy in action

strategic leader for the Partnership's education work more generally.

Wildlife Watch membership administration was still being done centrally. The management of the database, the processing of new members, renewals and mail-outs and the handling of enquiries remained a time-consuming and demanding task. There were 80 Watch Organisers and more than 1,000 leaders to service. Their records had to be kept up to date, prospective leaders vetted and, in conjunction with the Trusts, advice and training provided. For example, following development work with the RSPB in 1996, a new framework of Child Welfare and Safety had been developed. In addition, revised guidelines on running Groups and systems of quality assurance had also been rolled out. *Watchword* magazine was still being prepared and despatched three times per year, as was a leaders' magazine, *Link*. A special grade of Wildlife Watch membership – the Watch Education Service – was also being provided for schools, country parks and other institutions. Without more resources and a shift in the approach adopted towards Wildlife Watch, other activities – such as providing advice on Trusts' educational programmes, organising education conferences and seminars and engaging more thoroughly in the work of other national groups, such as the Council for Environmental Education – were always likely to play second fiddle to the running of Wildlife Watch.

Two reviews followed – an internal review of Wildlife Watch under the chairmanship of Colin Preston and a broader look at the Educational Activities of The Wildlife Trusts undertaken by Joy Palmer of Durham University.

The resulting consultation paper on the future of Wildlife Watch was

Chris Packham with Watch members at a coastal event in Hampshire

presented in September 1997. In general, it was an endorsement of the 'Watch approach', but its message was one that not everyone wanted to hear. Traditionally, it had been difficult to reach a consensus on the movement's approach to education and the priority placed on it by individual Trusts had varied. More specifically, some Trusts wanted to see the administration of Watch membership devolved to the Trusts. In February 1998, five Trusts agreed to take part in a pilot study to 'develop and test acceptable and cost-effective models for administering Wildlife Watch membership'. Two of the Trusts favoured national administration (SCOTTISH and BEDFORDSHIRE, CAMBRIDGESHIRE AND NORTHAMPTONSHIRE TRUSTS) and three favoured local administration (DORSET, LINCOLNSHIRE and WILTSHIRE TRUSTS). A report on the pilot study, prepared by Bob Huey of the YORKSHIRE TRUST, was published in November 1999. One option that emerged was a 'choice system' whereby a Trust could opt to either administer Wildlife Watch locally or at the UK level. However, the

financial and other implications of such a system had not been assessed and Guy Corbett-Marshall (Director of the STAFFORDSHIRE TRUST) was asked to look at this in more detail.

Meanwhile, another Review Group was established. This time it was led by Derek Moore with MICHAEL FIELD as facilitator. It took forward the findings of the Durham process and produced a People and Wildlife Strategy in the autumn of 2000. The Group's work focused on the implementation of two key recommendations from the Durham report adopted by the Partnership at the Stoke Rochford Hall National Conference (CONFERENCES) in December 1999. Namely that education within The Wildlife Trusts should embrace all activities and experiences aimed at helping people to understand and conserve the natural world and that the Partnership should work towards the delivery of this new educational approach by adopting and implementing a National Strategy for People. An all-important point was that the most immediate tasks facing the partnership were that of achieving a balance between the Strategy and the need to respond to local needs, enthusiasm and desire for local 'ownership'.

At the Partnership Management Board in January 2001, the feeling was that the People and Wildlife Strategy placed too much emphasis on 'education' and had not sufficiently acknowledged the Trusts' community work, its volunteering role and the 'people' agenda more broadly. As a result it was only adopted as a working document. Nevertheless, the term 'People and Wildlife', while initially considered rather awkward, entered the Partnership's everyday vocabulary. Wildlife Watch was now very definitely part of something much broader and this helped ensure it was no longer seen as the sole way of engaging people in wildlife projects.

In parallel with all this development, The Wildlife Trusts embarked on a groundbreaking initiative. Wildlife Watch groups had traditionally been led by adults, with young people participating in a peer-dominated environment. However, in response to the emergence of Agenda 21, the concept of sustainable development and the UN Convention on the Rights of the Child, Wildlife Watch wanted not only to enable young people to contribute more fully to wider environmental programmes, but also to consider the personal and social benefits of doing so. Between 1998 and 2001, it established a study, 'Children for Change', to explore the way in which participative youth work techniques, more usually used with teenage groups, could help young people aged between eight

and 13. Volunteer leaders in 20 Wildlife Watch Groups used written materials, training and the services of a dedicated Project Officer to step back from their leader or organiser role to become Group facilitators. The young people were encouraged to develop their own personal knowledge, confidence and skills, given more responsibility for the Group activities and supported in carrying out child-led initiatives. The sort of environmental projects that emerged were a contribution to 'the longest children's mural in the world', creating and mapping a new walking route to school and running a waste minimisation campaign. These types of projects were not new to Wildlife Watch, but this time they were planned and driven by the young people themselves.

What Children for Change showed was that, although young people between eight and 13 were unlikely to assimilate the knowledge and skills they needed to initiate and implement their own projects, they could be involved in making informed choices within the Group programmes and work alongside older children. There was perhaps an opportunity lost at the end of this study to continue actively investing in this approach. It was ahead of its time and, although participation and child-led activity is widespread good practice across society today, in 2002 Wildlife Watch was on relatively unexplored ground.

Out of the various reviews and the Children for Change study, there emerged a new approach to Wildlife Watch and a clearer educational role for the UK office. The administration of Wildlife Watch membership was finally devolved in its entirety to the Trusts in July 2002. This followed an earlier decision to devolve

responsibility for 'participation' projects as well. The Trusts' culture had shifted away from supporting large, centrally planned and designed activities to a more local focus. These changes also coincided with the launch of the UK Biodiversity Action Plan and many Trusts were running local species surveys that could draw in Wildlife Watch members and their families.

Increasingly, Wildlife Watch activity was being driven by the Trusts themselves, remaining strongest where: it was fully embedded in the Trust's broader environmental and community educational work; where adults inspired and mentored local young people; and where it operated alongside other outreach approaches. By 2007, in addition to the 135,000 Wildlife Watch members, the Trusts were working on long-term projects with more than 4,300 schools, were giving advice to more than 5,000 schools on greening their grounds and involving nearly 140,000 students in visits or events.

The UK office retained the role of developing policies, systems and supportive training and, when opportunities arose, passing on to Government and other agencies Wildlife Watch's experience of what works on the ground.

In 2000, it had been decided to convene a Watch Forum comprising Trust Watch Organisers (some of whom were also active leaders) with the idea of providing support to staff working on Wildlife Watch at the UK office. Their creative input, opinions and experience on the ground was invaluable and informed the strategic direction of Wildlife Watch and honed detailed guidance. The Forum continued to meet two or three times a year and acted as a sounding board and helped prioritise development. In July 2007, the Forum issued a strategic document that identified key development areas for Wildlife Watch, including internal and external communications, membership, groups and events, with some recommendations already being implemented. In 2008, a review of the membership package was underway with the aim of ensuring that it remains relevant to today's young people and properly reflects the vision and work of The Wildlife Trusts.

In the 21st century, although the network of Groups is shrinking slightly in some areas, there is still a huge amount of excellent work supported by the Trusts' volunteer leader teams. Anecdotally, it would appear that the age of young people attending many Groups is falling. Fortunately, with this, there is an increasing tendency for parents to remain involved. Many volunteers welcome this as increased awareness of child protection issues is making it harder for volunteers to step forward to work with children who are not their own.

Remarkably, despite massive changes in society, continual change in the Society and varying levels of support and investment in activity,

the original aims for Wildlife Watch, conceived nearly 40 years ago, remain largely unchanged. It is still a club that provides a different experience for young people from that shared with their families or gained through school. The stated Watch approach is still to create factual, informal and fun ways for members to investigate their surroundings; to increase their understanding of the whole environment; to foster awareness and feeling for the world in which they live; and to encourage a caring attitude towards wildlife and participation in conservation. These are aims and outcomes that need no adjustment to fit perfectly with today's approach to people and wildlife. Significantly, as a result of the Children for Change project, one further principle has been added to the Watch approach: "to ensure that young people's environmental concerns, ideas and opinions are recognised and developed and that opportunities are created to act upon them".[360] It is this, as much as the other principles, which will provide the platform for the development of Wildlife Watch in the 21st century.

Letting the next generation discover the wonders of nature

WATCHWORD

Watchword, the magazine of Wildlife Watch, was first produced in spring 1973 as the newsletter of the Watch Club run by the Advisory Centre of Education in Cambridge. The first 24 newsletters were edited by Geoffrey Young. When the Club was taken over by the Watch Trust for Environmental Education in 1977, a new A4 format with a single-colour masthead was introduced for issue 14. Full colour – first on the centre pages only – was introduced in spring 1981.

The first issue of *Watchword*

In 1984, the designers of *The Sunday Times Magazine* transformed *Watchword* into a A3 full-colour broadsheet with a new masthead and with a centre page poster (often sponsored) in every issue to accompany the latest activities and projects. The magazine also welcomed cartoon characters 'Flora and Fauna' to its back page; a position they have occupied until the present day. This new version of *Watchword* was edited, first by Trina Paskell (until the spring issue of 1989) and then by Debora Bright (until spring 2008). It has been edited since by Adam Cormack and Amy Lewis.

Watchword reverted to an A4 format in the spring of 1993. By issue number four it had adopted the new badger logo, designed to reinforce its position as the 'junior branch of The Wildlife Trusts'. Further slight changes were made to *Watchword's* masthead for issue 29. The 50th edition of this format appeared in the summer of 2009. In a further change in the autumn of 2009, the magazine was redesigned once more and adopted a new title, *Wildlife Watch*.

In 2001 *Watchword* won the 'specially commended' award for the Best Environmental Charity Children's Magazine in the BBC's Wildlife Magazine's Environmental Publications Awards.

WOODDISSE, THOMAS

'Tom' Wooddisse (born 1893) became a member of the Society in 1927. He joined the Society's Council and became its Assistant Honorary Treasurer in 1932. Finally, in 1938 he became its HONORARY TREASURER, serving in that position until 1966.

He was appointed Accountant at the Natural History Museum in London in 1931 to take charge of financial matters, and succeeded HERBERT SMITH as the Museum's Secretary in 1935.

On his retirement as the Society's Honorary Treasurer, the Chairman, CHRISTOPHER CADBURY, paid tribute to his long and devoted service. Wooddisse remained on the Council until 1970 before being appointed as a Vice President – a position he held until his death.

WOODLAND INITIATIVE

In the autumn of 1990, the Bishop of Norwich launched the Society's 'Woodland Initiative' to highlight the economic and cultural value of well-managed woodland. Once the initial furore surrounding the Great Storm of 1987 had died down, the Society decided to use the resulting higher profile for trees and woodlands to drive home the message that it was not natural events, such as storms, that were the threat to woodlands but development, neglect and bad management. A report, *A Tale of Three Woods*, published as part of the Woodland Initiative, told the varying fortunes of three ancient woods: Parish Grove Wood in Herefordshire, well-managed by the HEREFORDSHIRE TRUST; Vale Wood in Sussex, damaged by the owner when permission for paintball games was refused; and a wood near Harlech in Wales that had suffered years of neglect but was now beginning a process of recovery under the management of the NORTH WALES TRUST. The message

was that good management is vital and years of neglect, whilst not always immediately obvious, can be hugely damaging to woodland habitats.

An 'Ancient Woodlands Charter', published as part of the woodland initiative, gave facts about ancient woods and called for the completion of the Conservancy's ancient woodland inventory; the introduction of licences to protect small ancient woodlands; support for research into new uses for traditional coppice; and changes in the planning laws to stop ancient woodlands being used for damaging leisure activities, such as paintballing and motorbike scrambling.

At the same time as the woodland initiative, the Society also launched a fighting fund with the DYFED TRUST to save a nationally-important woodland site in Wales – Carmel Woods. It was threatened by limestone quarrying under an Interim Development Order (IDO) granted just after the Second World War. The IDO pre-dated, and therefore overruled, the wood's SSSI designation (MINERAL PLANNING).

Note: By 1990, the Trusts owned and managed more than 36,000 acres of woodland and offered advice to many other owners. They were also involved in eight county woodland forums that helped to ensure local authorities took more account of ancient woodlands in their day-to-day activities. In 1993, the Society secured sponsorship from The National Grid, worth more than £200,000 over four years, towards Wildlife Trust woodland projects. For example, the Derbyshire Trust received funding for a coppicing and tree-planting scheme at its Carver's Rocks nature reserve.

WOODWALTON FEN

Woodwalton Fen nature reserve lies nine miles north of Huntingdon. It is a small relic of the once-extensive Huntingdonshire Fens and was the first, largest and most important nature reserve owned by the Society before the Second World War. It was leased to the Conservancy (now Natural England) for 99 years in 1954 and declared a National Nature Reserve. The Society retains the freehold today.

The first 339 acres of the Woodwalton Fen nature reserve were bought by CHARLES ROTHSCHILD in 1910 to protect it from collectors. Several species, rare or absent elsewhere, could be found on the reserve. The fen violet, for example, was abundant and the fen wood-rush had recently been discovered.

Rothschild's plan was to leave the reserve to The National Trust in his will but, when it became clear that the Trust was not interested, he turned to the Society and in 1919 offered the area, including a bungalow that he had built in 1911, as a gift. Initially, concerned that it would be unable to meet the ongoing running costs, the Society turned down the offer. But when Rothschild agreed to back up the gift with more than £2,000 of five per cent War Loan Stock yielding sufficient interest to cover these costs, the Society decided to "accept the offer with many thanks".[361] A further offer to transfer an adjoining 20 acres of fen (eventually purchased for £300 in 1927) and to provide a fund to meet the rental payments for the remaining 12 years of the lease, was also accepted by the Society the same year. However, it was not long before the interest was insufficient to meet the drainage rates and management costs and the Society had to supplement the endowment from its general fund.

When Rothschild died in 1923, he left a generous bequest of £5,000 to

Woodwalton Fen, 1949

the Society and this helped to avert a crisis. He also left Ray Island (NATURE RESERVES OWNED BY THE SOCIETY) to either The National Trust or, if it was not interested, to the Society. The National Trust turned down the bequest and for a short time the Society owned the property. Reluctantly, however, it was decided, with the agreement of Rothschild's wife, to sell Ray Island in order to meet Woodwalton Fen's escalating management costs.

An additional 154 acres of the fen had been purchased by Charles Rothschild at a cost of £3,325 in 1920 and this area, with a small outlying plot on the east side of Great Raveley drain containing the keeper's cottage, was gifted to the Society by the Honorary Mrs Charles Rothschild in 1939. A further four acres, also on the east side of the drain adjoining Jackson's Bridge, were purchased the same year.

The reserve, which now extended to more than 515 acres, was of outstanding biological interest, having escaped the extensive drainage that had taken place elsewhere in the fens. The site had continued to be dug for turf or peat as fuel, grazed by livestock and cut for hay, and the agriculture that had occurred had been of low intensity. However, even when Charles

George Mason, keeper of the Fen in 1935

Rothschild first became interested in the area, traditional fenland management had already largely ceased and, with the water table dropping in the surrounding farmland, the site was drying out. Tall reed, dense carr and scrub woodland were invading the reserve. In 1936, the naturalist, John Claud Fortescue Fryer, recalled a visit to the area at the end of the century when part of the site was already "bush and reed as it is today, but much was rough litter for cutting as hay or grazing. The latter areas contained wonderful vegetation and in the summer were almost a flower garden, so numerous were the marsh flowering plants".[362]

A survey of the reserve in 1931 by Edelsten and Fryer confirmed that "owing to the neglect of recent years the character of the vegetation was changing".[363] Unless something was done quickly the property would "no longer be representative of the fauna and flora of a marshland".[364] Although it was agreed that "complete restoration would be prohibitively costly",[365] a programme of scrub and tree clearance and dyke repair was begun. In 1935–36 a pump was purchased by Captain

Purefoy to maintain the water table "at a level appropriate to a fen".[366] Edelsten and Fryer had agreed to supervise this work and effectively became the Management Committee for the reserve. Later, in 1947, when additional members joined the Committee, Fryer became its first Chairman. By this time he had been knighted and had taken on the responsible role of Secretary of the Agricultural Research Council. It is clear that, despite limited resources, the Society took its responsibilities for managing the site seriously. It tried hard to work out how best to conserve the reserve's wildlife and to defend it from those who would have preferred to see it drained and cropped.

In 1927, the Society approved the experimental introduction from Holland of one of the fen's specialities, the large copper butterfly *Lycaena dispar batavus* by the Committee for the Protection of British Lepidoptera. The original fenland race *Lycaena dispar dispar* had become extinct the previous century. With considerable effort, this introduced population was maintained on the reserve until the early to mid-1990s.

A large legacy from the botanist, DRUCE, became available to the Society in 1938 and this encouraged the Society to embark on a more extensive survey of the site the following year. However, it was soon brought to an abrupt halt by the outbreak of war when CR Stoner (the biologist undertaking the survey) joined the army. Several scientists from the Natural History Museum in London stepped into the breach and compiled lists of plants and various orders of insects at this time, but it was not until the 1950s that a full survey of the site was finally carried out by the Nature Conservancy's Duncan Poore.

The Society continued to struggle against the "adverse influences which were greatly aggravated by the Second World War and by the great increase in labour costs".[367] The need for more home-grown food meant the Society was placed in a difficult position. It was having to pay substantial drainage rates only to stand by and watch the water table of the reserve dropping. If it was going to stop the reserve drying out completely, it would have to find more resources.

It was therefore with some relief when, in November 1949, the Society received a letter from CYRIL DIVER, who had recently been appointed Director General of the new Nature Conservancy. The letter spelt out various alternative ways in which Diver believed the Conservancy might take on the management of the reserve using the powers it was about to acquire under the National Parks and Access to the Countryside Act 1949. However, it would be 1954 before the Society was finally able to "transfer to the Conservancy, under a lease which has been carefully negotiated on each side, the financial liability for the maintenance and restoration of our important reserve at Woodwalton Fen, the cost of which

Galloway cattle were introduced to Woodwalton in the 1960s

Creating a Living Landscape in the Cambridgeshire Fens – Woodwalton Fen in 2011

had become beyond our capacity, and to arrange for its management in accordance with a plan based on the best scientific experience which can be brought to bear".[368] When Woodwalton Fen was declared a National Nature Reserve in March 1954, a Joint Advisory Committee, chaired by Professor of Geography at Cambridge University, Alfred Steers, had already been busy for eight months. (In 1978, Steers handed the baton on to TED SMITH who served as the Committee's Chairman until 2000.)

A plan was being implemented to raise the water table by improving water movement in the reserve and by controlling water loss to external drains. In addition, "dykes were maintained, rides were swiped and Galloway cattle introduced".[369]

In *Rothschild's Reserves*, Rothschild and Marren comment, "the maintenance of fenland at Woodwalton has been an endless struggle, and there have been losses, but many rare species survive to preserve an oasis of biodiversity amid flat, cultivated cropland. Despite all the problems and frustrations, this is a kind of triumph".[370]

Today, there is the prospect of something even greater. The BEDFORDSHIRE, CAMBRIDGESHIRE AND NORTHAMPTONSHIRE TRUST is leading an ambitious partnership, the Great Fen Project (see page 215), that is recreating a much larger area of fenland of which Woodwalton Fen will be part. It is exciting and fitting that, after nearly 100 years, the Society's first reserve will be part of one of The Wildlife Trusts' Living Landscapes, designed to create robust, resilient and connected landscapes nationwide – landscapes that can adapt to climate change and accommodate species movement. Charles Rothschild would have approved.

References

PART I REFERENCES

1. SPNR Minutes 1912–1940, *Minutes of a Preliminary Meeting*, 16th May 1912
2. John Sheail, *Nature in Trust*, Blackie, 1976
3. *The Times*, 18th December 1912
4. SPNR Minutes 1912–1940, *Minutes of the 4th Meeting of the Executive Committee*, 3rd June 1913
5. SPNR Handbooks, *Handbook 1923*, SPNR, 1923
6. *Ibid*
7. *The Times*, Wednesday, 18th December 1912
8. *Ibid*
9. *Ibid*
10. *Ibid*
11. Sir Ray Lankester, *Diversions of a Naturalist*, Methuen, 1915
12. Druce's obituary for Charles Rothchild, *Journal of the Northamptonshire Natural History Society*, Vol XXII, No 177, March 1924
13. *Ibid*
14. SPNR Minutes 1912–1940, *Minutes of the 5th Meeting of the Executive Committee*, 16th December 1913
15. Druce's obituary for Charles Rothchild, *Journal of the Northamptonshire Natural History Society*, Vol XXII, No 177, March 1924
16. SPNR Minutes 1912–1940, *Minutes of the 5th Meeting of the Executive Committee*, 16th December 1913
17. *Ibid*
18. MJ Nicoll, *Three Voyages of a Naturalist*, Witherby & Co, 1909
19. SPNR Minutes 1912–1940, *Minutes of the 6th Meeting of the Executive Committee*, 6th February 1914
20. *Ibid*
21. *Ibid*
22. SPNR Minutes 1912–1940, *Minutes of the 1st Meeting of the Council*, 28th April 1914
23. Miriam Rothschild and Peter Marren, *Rothschild's Reserves – Time and Fragile Nature*, Balaban/Harley, 1997
24. Howard Newby (ed), *The National Trust – The Next Hundred Years*, The National Trust, 1995
25. Sir Ray Lankester, *Diversions of a Naturalist*, Methuen, 1915
26. *First Report of the Executive Committee*, 21st June 1918, SPNR

27. *Ibid*
28. Miriam Rothschild and Peter Marren, *Rothschild's Reserves – Time and Fragile Nature*, Balaban/Harley, 1997
29. SPNR Handbooks, *Handbook 1924*, SPNR, 1924
30. Obituary: The Hon NC Rothschild, *Nature,* 112, 697, 1923
31. Correspondence between the Society's Honorary Secretary and Messrs. Parker, Garrett & Co on 24th October 1923, Woodwalton Fen File 1 Correspondence 1912–1924, SPNR
32. *Second Annual Report of the Executive Committee presented to the Council*, 16th May 1919, SPNR
33. SPNR Handbooks, *Handbook 1923*, SPNR, 1923
34. SPNR Handbooks, *Handbook 1924*, SPNR, 1924
35. *Ibid*
36. *Ibid*
37. SPNR Minutes 1912–1940, *Minutes of the 40th Meeting of the Executive Committee*, 18th June 1928
38. John Sheail, *Nature in Trust*, Blackie, 1976
39. SPNR Minutes 1912–1940, *Minutes of the 29th Meeting of the Executive Committee*, 23rd June 1924
40. SPNR Handbooks, *Handbook 1930*, SPNR, 1930
41. SPNR Handbooks, *Handbook 1933*, SPNR, 1933
42. Changes in the British fauna and flora during the past fifty years, talk on flowering plants by AJ Wilmott, *Proceedings of the Linnean Society of London*, Session 148, 1935–36 Pt 1, 23rd December 1935
43. *Report of the British Conference for the Protection of Nature*, SPNR, 1947
44. Howard Newby (ed), *The National Trust – The Next Hundred Years*, The National Trust, 1995
45. John Sheail, *Nature in Trust*, Blackie, 1976
46. SPNR Handbooks, *Handbook 1953*, SPNR, 1953
47. John Sheail, *Nature in Trust*, Blackie, 1976
48. SPNR Minutes 1912–1940, *Report to the Executive,* 21st September 1939
49. SPNR Minutes 1912–1940, *Minutes of the 74th Meeting of the Executive Committee*, 17th November 1939

50. Dorothy Rook, Protecting Britain's Birds, *Birds* magazine, RSPB, 1966
51. SPNR Minutes 1912–1940, *Minutes of the 74th Meeting of the Executive Committee*, 17th November 1939
52. SPNR Handbooks, *Handbook 1943*, SPNR, 1943
53. Nature Reserves Investigation Committee, *Nature Conservation in Great Britain*, SPNR, 1943
54. SPNR Minutes 1941–1950, *Minutes of the 80th Meeting of the Executive Committee*, 13th June 1941
55. *Report of Special War Emergency Committee of the Council*, RSPB, January 1941
56. SPNR Handbooks, *Handbook 1942*, SPNR, 1942
57. *Conference on Nature Preservation in Post-War Reconstruction*, Memorandum 1, SPNR, 1941
58. *Ibid*
59. *Ibid*
60. John Sheail, *Nature Conservation in Britain – The Formative Years*, The Stationery Office, 1998
61. Nature Reserves Investigation Committee, *Nature Conservation in Great Britain (Terms of Reference)*, SPNR, 1943
62. Nature Reserves Investigation Committee, *Nature Conservation in Great Britain*, SPNR, 1943
63. *Ibid*
64. SPNR Minutes 1941–1950, *Minutes of the 88th Meeting of the Executive Committee*, 28th March 1944
65. Nature Reserves Investigation Committee, *Natural History Survey of Great Britain – Potential National Parks*, SPNR, 1943
66. Report by Nature Reserves Investigation Committee, *National Nature Reserves and Conservation Areas in England and Wales*, SPNR, 1945
67. *Ibid*
68. *National Geological Reserves in England and Wales*, Report by the Geological Sub-Committee of the Nature Reserves Investigation Committee, SPNR, 1945
69. *Ibid*
70. *Nature*, Vol 157, Macmillan & Co, London, 1946
71. *Ibid*
72. SPNR Handbooks, *Handbook 1952*, SPNR, 1952

73. *Ibid*

74. SPNR Minutes 1941–1950, *Minutes of the 94th Meeting of the Executive Committee*, 15th March 1946

75. Report of the Wild Life Conservation Special Committee, *Conservation of Nature in England and Wales* (Command 7122), HMSO, 1947

76. *Ibid*

77. *Ibid*

78. *Ibid*

79. *Ibid*

80. R Fitter, The View Ahead from 1945, *Ecos*, Vol 11, No 2, 1990

81. *Ibid*

82. Report of the Wild Life Conservation Special Committee, *Conservation of Nature in England and Wales* (Command 7122), HMSO, 1947

83. *Ibid*

84. R Fitter, The View Ahead from 1945, *Ecos*, Vol 11, No 2, 1990

85. John Sheail, *An Environmental History of Twentieth-Century Britain*, Palgrave, 2002

86. Lowe and Goyder, *Environmental Groups in Politics*, Allen & Unwin, 1983

87. *Ibid*

88. SPNR Minutes 1912–1940, *Minutes of the 70th Meeting of the Executive Committee*, 17th June 1938

89. SPNR Minutes 1941–1950, *Minutes of the 81st Meeting of the Executive Committee*, 12th November 1941

90. *Ibid*

91. SPNR Handbooks, *Handbook 1947*, SPNR, 1947

92. John Savory, *George Lodge – Artist Naturalist*, Croom Helm, 1986

93. Martin Holdgate, *The Green Web – A Union for World Conservation*, Earthscan, 1999

94. SPNR Handbooks, *Handbook 1949*, SPNR, 1949

95. SPNR Handbooks, *Handbook 1947*, SPNR, 1947

96. AG Tansley, *Our Heritage of Wild Nature – A Plea for Organised Nature Conservation*, Cambridge University Press, 1945

97. *Ibid*

98. *Nature*, Vol 157, Macmillan & Co, London, 1946

99. SPNR Handbooks, *Handbook 1949*, SPNR, 1949

100. *Ibid*

101. SPNR Handbooks, *Handbook 1953*, SPNR, 1953

102. *Ibid*

103. SPNR Minutes 1951–60, *Minutes of the 119th Meeting of the Executive Committee*, 17th June 1953

104. AE Smith, The Lincolnshire Trust – the text of the lecture to the Society on 1st July 1954, reproduced in the *Handbook 1954*, SPNR, 1954

105. WS Lacey, *Welsh Wildlife in Trust*, North Wales Naturalists' Trust, 1970

106. SPNR Minutes 1951–60, *Minutes of the 121st Meeting of the Executive Committee*, 10th December 1953

107. Correspondence from Miriam Rothschild to Dr Miles in *History of Nature Conservation in Britain – Reports, Pamphlets and Documents, 1942–82*, RSWT archive

108. *Ibid*

109. SPNR Minutes 1951–60, *Minutes of the 121st Meeting of the Executive Committee*, 10th December 1953

110. AE Smith, *Trustees for Nature – A Memoir*, Lincolnshire Wildlife Trust, 2007

111. *Ibid*

112. SPNR Handbooks, *Handbook 1954*, SPNR, 1954

113. John Sheail, *Nature Conservation in Britain – The Formative Years*, The Stationery Office, 1998

114. *Ibid*

115. SPNR Minutes 1951–1960, *Minutes of the 132nd Meeting of the Executive Committee*, 21st February 1957

116. AE Smith, *Trustees for Nature – A Memoir*, Lincolnshire Wildlife Trust, 2007

117. *Ibid*

118. *Ibid*

119. Interview with Ted Smith, 20th March 2007

120. *Minutes of a Meeting of the Lincolnshire, Cambridgeshire and Leicestershire Trusts* held on 29th–30th June 1957

121. *Ibid*

122. SPNR Minutes 1951–1960, *Minutes of the 134th Meeting of the Executive Committee*, 27th November 1957

123. *Ibid*

124. *Ibid*

125. AE Smith, *Trustees for Nature – A Memoir*, Lincolnshire Wildlife Trust, 2007

126. *Ibid*

127. *Ibid*

128. SPNR Minutes 1951–1960, *Minutes of the 136th Meeting of the Executive Committee (as amended)*, 26th March 1958

129. Interview with Ted Smith, 20th March 2007

130. SPNR Minutes 1951–1960, *Minutes of the 1st Meeting of the Regional Liaison Committee*, 12th November 1958

131. *Ibid*

132. SPNR Minutes 1951–1960, *Minutes of the 4th Meeting of the Regional Liaison Committee*, 20th October 1959

133. AE Smith, *Trustees for Nature – A Memoir*, Lincolnshire Wildlife Trust, 2007

134. *Ibid*

135. *Ibid*

136. SPNR Handbooks, *Handbook 1959*, SPNR, 1959

137. *Ibid*

138. *Ibid*

139. SPNR Handbooks, *Handbook 1960*, SPNR, 1960

140. *Ibid*

141. Foreword by HRH The Duke of Edinburgh to the *Proceedings of The Countryside in 1970 Study Conference* held at Fishmongers' Hall, London, EC4, 4th–5th November 1963

142. AG Tansley, *Our Heritage of Wild Nature – A Plea for Organised Nature Conservation*, Cambridge University Press, 1945

143. Dr JS Huxley, *Conservation of Nature in England and Wales – Report of the Wild Life Conservation Special Committee*, Command 7122, HMSO, 1947

144. John Sheail, *Nature Conservation in Britain – The Formative Years*, The Stationery Office, 1998

145. *Ibid*

146. *Ibid*

147. SPNR Handbooks, *Handbook 1960*, SPNR, 1960

148. SPNR Minutes 1951–1960, *Minutes of the 7th Meeting of the Naturalists' Trusts' Committee*, 15th September 1960

149. SPNR Handbooks, *Handbook 1961*, SPNR, 1961

150. AE Smith, *Trustees for Nature – A Memoir*, Lincolnshire Wildlife Trust, 2007

151. SPNR Handbooks, *Handbook 1962*, SPNR, 1962

152. SPNR Handbooks, *Handbook 1964*, SPNR, 1964

153. John Sheail, *Nature Conservation in Britain – The Formative Years*, The Stationery Office, 1998

154. *Ibid*

155. SPNR Handbooks, *Handbook 1964*, SPNR, 1964

156. AE Smith, *Trustees for Nature – A Memoir*, Lincolnshire Wildlife Trust, 2007

157. SPNR Handbooks, *Handbook 1966*, SPNR, 1966

158. *Ibid*

159. *Ibid*

160. SPNR Minutes 1965–1970, *Minutes of the 179th Meeting of the Executive Committee*, 10th–11th May 1969

161. SPNR County Naturalists' Trusts' Committee Minutes 1967–1972, *Minutes of the 32nd Meeting of the County Naturalists' Trusts' Committee*, 18th June 1969

162. AE Smith, *Trustees for Nature – A Memoir*, Lincolnshire Wildlife Trust, 2007

163. *Ibid*

164. RSPB archives, internal memorandum, September 1971

165. Sir Landsborough Thomson, *Plan for a Merger*, February 1969

166. *Countryside Act 1968*, HMSO, 1968

167. SPNR Handbooks, *Handbook 1968*, SPNR, 1968

168. *Ibid*

169. AE Smith, *Nature Conservation in Lincolnshire*, Lincolnshire Naturalists' Union, 1969

170. *Ibid*

171. SPNR Handbooks, *Handbook 1961*, SPNR, 1961

172. Eve Dennis (ed), *Everyman's Nature Reserve – Ideas for Action*, David & Charles, 1972

173. Promotional leaflet for the Gloucestershire Trust for Nature Conservation's Conservation Corps

174. *Conservation Review*, No 1, SPNR, 1970

175. SPNR Minutes 1965–1970, *Minutes of the 180th Meeting of the Executive Committee*, 25th June 1969

176. Lowe and Goyder, *Environmental Groups in Politics*, Allen & Unwin, 1983

177. *Six Years' Work of the Council for Nature, Speeches by Lord Hurcomb and Aubrey Buxton at the AGM of the Council for Nature*, Council for Nature, 1964,
178. F Perring, *BSBI Conference, The Flora of a Changing Britain*, E.W. Classey, paperback edition, 1969
179. John Sheail, *Nature Conservation in Britain – The Formative Years*, The Stationery Office, 1998
180. *Conservation Review*, No 1, SPNR, 1970
181. *The Countryside in 1970 – Proceedings of the Third Conference*, The Council for Nature, The Nature Conservancy, The Royal Society of Arts, 1970
182. *Ibid*
183. *Ibid*
184. J Tinker, ECY: Steering the Bandwagon, *New Scientist*, 45, 250–5, 1970
185. *Conservation Review*, No 1, SPNR, 1970
186. *Ibid*
187. *Minutes of the 198th Meeting of the Executive Committee*, 27th September 1973, SPNR
188. *Conservation Review No 4*, SPNR, 1972
189. *Annual Report 1972–73*, SPNR, 1973
190. *The 210th Meeting of the Executive Committee*, 28th July 1976, PaperE/10/8 (amended), SPNC
191. *A Brief History of WATCH*, The Watch Trust for Environmental Education Ltd, 1979
192. *WATCH – The History*, Watch Trust for Environmental Education Ltd, 1987
193. *Conservation Officers' Bulletin,* No 1, SPNR, 1974
194. Derek Barber (ed), *Farming and Wildlife – A Study in Compromise*, RSPB, 1970
195. NW Moore, *The Bird of Time – the Science and Politics of Nature Conservation*, Cambridge University Press, 1987
196. *Ibid*
197. *Conservation Review,* No 14, SPNC, 1977
198. *Ibid*
199. AE Smith, *Trustees for Nature – A Memoir*, Lincolnshire Wildlife Trust, 2007
200. *Minutes of the 202nd Meeting of the Executive Committee*, 5th and 6th October 1974, SPNR
201. AE Smith, *Wildlife and the Law – the Case for a Comprehensive Approach*, Council for Nature and SPNR, 1973
202. *Ibid*
203. *Annual Report 1979–80*, SPNC, 1980
204. Tim Sands, *Making the Link – Twenty-Five years of Wildlife and Countryside Link*, Wildlife and Countryside Link, 2005
205. *Ibid*
206. *Conservation Review,* No 15, SPNC, 1977
207. AE Smith, *Trustees for Nature – A Memoir*, Lincolnshire Wildlife Trust, 2007
208. *Ibid*
209. Christopher Cadbury Medal Citations – see p605
210. *Declaration of Intent*, Nature Conservancy Council, 1977
211. AE Smith, *Trustees for Nature – A Memoir*, Lincolnshire Wildlife Trust, 2007

212. *Conservation Review No 19*, SPNC, 1979
213. *Annual Report 1979–80*, SPNC, 1980
214. *Conservation Review No 19*, SPNC, 1979
215. *Ibid*
216. *Minutes of the 217th Meeting of the Executive Committee*, 9th November 1977, Paper E/217/Paper 1, SPNC
217. WM Adams, *Nature's Place – Conservation Sites and Countryside Change*, Allen and Unwin, 1986
218. John Sheail, *An Environmental History of Twentieth-Century Britain*, Palgrave, 2002
219. *Annual Report 1983–84*, RSNC, 1984
220. *Minutes of the 265th Meeting of the Executive Committee*, 20th July 1988, RSNC
221. *Annual Report 1980–81*, RSNC, 1981
222. Nature Goes to Town, *Natural World,* No 1, RSNC, 1981
223. Talk of the Town, *Natural World,* No 17, RSNC, 1986
224. *Annual Report 1985–86*, RSNC, 1986
225. *Ibid*
226. *Annual Report 1980–81*, RSNC, 1981
227. *Minutes of the 228th Meeting of the Executive Committee*, 27th February 1980, SPNC
228. *Minutes of the 229th Meeting of the Executive Committee*, 2nd April 1980, Paper E/229/Paper 2, SPNC
229. Christopher Cadbury, The Roles of the SPNR and the County Trusts for the Conservation of Nature (Speech to the Kent National Conference), SPNR, 1970
230. Report of Private Meeting of Members, 4th November, 1981, RSNC
231. *Ibid*
232. Letter from Christopher Cadbury to all Trusts, 17th November 1981
233. Report of Private Meeting of Members, 4th November 1981, RSNC
234. *Annual Report 1982–83*, RSNC, 1983
235. *Minutes of the 246th Meeting of the Executive Committee*, 19th April 1983, RSNC
236. Manuscript of prologue delivered at 246th Meeting of the Executive Committee, 19th April 1983, RSNC
237. *Minutes of the 246th Meeting of the Executive Committee*, 19th April 1983, RSNC
238. *Annual Report 1982–83*, RSNC, 1983
239. *Conservation Officers' Bulletin*, No 12, RSNC, 1984
240. *Minutes of the 257th Meeting of the Executive Committee*, 17th April 1986, RSNC
241. *Conservation Officers' Bulletin*, No 15, RSNC, 1986
242. *Annual Report 1985–86*, RSNC, 1986
243. *Natural World*, No 15, RSNC, 1985
244. John Sheail, *Nature Conservation in Britain – The Formative Years*, The Stationery Office, 1998
245. *Ibid*
246. Peter Melchett, *Conservationists' Shame – and How to Triumph*, the author's archive, 1984

247. *Ibid*
248. *Nature Conservation in Great Britain*, Nature Conservancy Council, 1984
249. *Losing Ground – Habitat Destruction in the UK: a Review in 1989*, RSNC, 1989
250. *Ibid*
251. *Ibid*
252. *Ibid*
253. Nick Bruce, *Wildlife Importance of Common Land – An Assessment by County*, RSNC, 1988
254. Tony Whitbread, *When the Wind Blew*, RSNC, 1991
255. *Natural World*, No 26, RSNC, 1989
256. *Natural World*, No 51, RSNC, 1997
257. *Minutes of the 258th Meeting of the Executive Committee*, 22nd July 1986, Paper E/258/Paper 4, RSNC
258. *Ibid*
259. *Natural World*, No 20, RSNC, 1987
260. Personal correspondence with the Society's Honorary Treasurer, Alan Newton
261. *Minutes of the 262nd Meeting of the Executive Committee*, 21st July 1987, RSNC
262. *Minutes of the 263rd Meeting of the Executive Committee*, 24th/25th November 1987, Memorandum from the Chairman regarding the 'Future of Fund Raising' dated 16th September 1987, RSNC
263. *Minutes of the 264th Meeting of the Executive Committe*e, 16th March 1988, RSNC
264. *Ibid*
265. *Minutes of the 262nd Meeting of the Executive Committee*, 21st July 1987, Paper E/262/Paper 7, RSNC
266. *Ibid*
267. *Minutes of the 255th Meeting of the Executive Committee*, 26th/27th November 1985, RSNC
268. Speech by Prime Minister, Margaret Thatcher, at the Tory Party Conference, October 1988
269. Speech by Prime Minister, Margaret Thatcher to the Royal Society, September 1988
270. Speech by Secretary of State for the Environment, Chris Patten, at the Tory Party Conference, October 1989
271. David Evans, *A History of Nature Conservation in Britain*, 2nd edition, Routledge, 1997
272. *Natural World*, No 30, RSNC, 1990
273. *Ibid*
274. *National Conference Newsletter*, Nottingham, RSNC, 1990
275. *Conservation Conference Newsletter*, Bangor, RSNC, 1990
276. *Ibid*
277. David Evans, *A History of Nature Conservation in Britain*, 2nd edition, Routledge, 1997
278. Tim Cordy, Joining Forces for Nature in *Natural World*, No 30, RSNC, 1990
279. Janet Dwyer, *The Wildlife Trusts – Primary Conservation CARTS, Discussion Paper 30*, Department of Land Economy, University of Cambridge, 1991
280. *Ibid*

281. *National Conference Newsletter*, Nottingham, RSNC, 1990
282. Video message from HRH The Prince of Wales specially recorded by Grampian Television at Balmoral on 15th October 1990 for the launch event
283. *Ibid*
284. *Minutes of the 285th Meeting of the Executive Committee*, Paper E/285/5, 10th February 1994, RSNC
285. *Minutes of the 273rd Meeting of the Executive Committee*, Paper E/273/Paper 6, 19th March 1991, RSNC
286. *Minutes of the 269th Meeting of the Executive Committee*, Paper E/269/Paper 12, 21st–22nd November 1989, RSNC
287. Tim Cordy, Joining Forces for Nature in *Natural World*, No 30, RSNC, 1990
288. *Annual Report 1989–90*, RSNC, 1990
289. *Countryside Survey 1990: Summary Report*, Department of the Environment, 1993
290. *Head on Collision – Road Building and Wildlife in South-East England*, RSNC, 1990
291. PG Oliver (ed), *Proceedings of the First UK RIGS Conference*, Hereford and Worcestershire RIGS Group, 1998
292. *RIGS Handbook*, RSNC, 1999
293. Dr Caroline Rigby, *Management of SSSIs by Wildlife Trusts – The Costs and Support Required*, RSNC, 1990
294. *Ibid*
295. *Natural World*, No 26, Headlines, RSNC, 1989
296. *Natural World*, No 28, RSNC, 1990
297. *Ibid*
298. *Ibid*
299. *Ibid*
300. Stuart Housden, *New and Potential UK Structures for Delivering Nature Conservation*, Wildlife and Countryside Link, 1990
301. *Ibid*
302. Speech to RSNC National Conference on 21st April 1990 by Sir William Wilkinson, Chairman of the Nature Conservancy Council, RSNC, 1990
303. Danial Sitarz, *Agenda 21 – The Earth Summit Strategy to Save Our Planet*, Earthpress, 1993
304. *Ibid*
305. *Ibid*
306. *Convention on Biological Diversity*, United Nations, 1992
307. Peter Marren, *Nature Conservation – A Review of the Conservation of Wildlife in Britain 1950–2001*, Harper Collins, 2002
308. *Biodiversity Challenge – An Agenda for Conservation in the UK*, RSPB, 1993
309. *Biodiversity Challenge – An Agenda for Conservation in the UK*, 2nd edition, RSPB, 1995
310. *Biodiversity – The UK Action Plan*, HMSO, 1994
311. Personal communication, 30th July 2007

312. *Minutes of the 272nd Meeting of the Executive Committee*, 20th–21st November 1990, RSNC
313. *Ibid*
314. *Minutes of the 46th Meeting of the Council*, C/46/, 26th September 1991, RSNC
315. *Minutes of the 276th Meeting of the Executive Committee*, E/ 276/ Paper 4, 4th–5th December 1991, RSNC
316. *Ibid*
317. *Minutes of the 276th Meeting of the Executive Committee*, E/276/Paper 1, 4th–5th December 1991, RSNC
318. *Ibid*
319. *Ibid*
320. *Ibid*
321. *Minutes of the 272nd Meeting of the Executive Committee*, 20th–21st November 1990, RSNC
322. *Minutes of the 276th Meeting of the Executive Committee*, E/276/Paper 8 (Confidential), 4th–5th December 1991, RSNC
323. *Ibid*
324. *Ibid*
325. *Minutes of the 282nd Meeting of the Executive Committee*, E/282/Paper 3, 15th May 1993, RSNC
326. *Minutes of the 52nd Meeting of Council*, 23rd September 1993, RSNC
327. *Annual Review 1992–93*, RSNC, 1993
328. *Natural World*, No 42, RSNC, 1994
329. Address at the launch of a Million for Wildlife at the House of Commons, October 1994
330. *Minutes of the 287th Meeting of the Executive Committee*, 30th September–1st October 1994, RSNC
331. Robin Crane, *Reaching our Full Potential*, paper presented to the Grantham National Conference, 1994
332. *Ibid*
333. *Minutes of the 287th Meeting of the Executive Committee*, 30th September–1st October 1994, RSNC
334. *Biodiversity Challenge – An Agenda for Conservation in the UK*, 2nd edition, RSPB, 1995
335. *Minutes of the 1st Meeting of the Partnership Management Board*, 8th February 1996, RSNC
336. *Natural World*, No 45, RSNC, 1995
337. Professor Bob Worcester, *Attitudes to Charities: Surveys of Public Opinion, Summary of Results*, MORI, 1997
338. *Natural World*, No 46, RSNC, 1996
339. *Ibid*
340. *Natural World*, No 45, RSNC, 1995
341. *Minutes of the 2nd Meeting of the Partnership Management Board*, 1st May 1996, RSNC
342. *Natural World*, No 49, RSNC, 1997
343. *Ibid*
344. *A Muzzled Watchdog?*, WWF, 1997
345. *Ibid*
346. *Ibid*
347. Memorandum from Simon Lyster to the Conservation PTAG, 18th November 1997

348. *Minutes of the 298th Meeting of the Executive Committee*, 22nd May 1997, RSNC
349. *Minutes of the 10th Meeting of the Council*, C/10/Paper 8, 23rd May 2000, RSNC
350. *Ibid*
351. Tim Sands, *Making the Link – Twenty-Five Years of Wildlife and Countryside Link*, Wildlife and Countryside Link, 2005
352. *Ibid*
353. *Minutes of the 8th Meeting of Council*, 25th February 2000, RSNC
354. *Director General's Newsletter*, No 8, RSNC, 2000
355. *Director General's Newsletter*, No 9, RSNC, 2000
356. Tim Sands, *Making the Link – Twenty-Five Years of Wildlife and Countryside Link*, Wildlife and Countryside Link, 2005
357. *Working with the Grain of Nature – A Biodiversity Strategy for England*, DEFRA, 2002
358. *Minutes of The Wildlife Trusts Partnership Forum Meeting*, WTF/6/Paper 4, 7th May 2003, RSNC
359. *Partnership News*, March 2003 (a one-off communication from Michael Field, Partnership Chair)
360. *Ibid*
361. *The Daily Telegraph*, 31st March 2003
362. *Minutes of the 7th Meeting of the Wildlife Trusts' Forum*, 30th July 2003, RSNC
363. *Natural World*, RSWT, Spring 2007
364. *The Natural Choice: Securing the Value of Nature*, HM Government, The Stationary Office (TSO), 2011
365. *Ibid*

PART III REFERENCES

1. *Natural World*, No 24, RSNC, 1988
2. Peter Pearson, *Yorkshire Wildlife: Obituary*, Yorkshire Wildlife Trust, 1999
3. *Natural World*, No 24, RSNC, 1988
4. *Ibid*
5. SPNR Minutes 1912–1940, *Minutes of the 6th Meeting of the Executive Committee*, 6th February 1914
6. AA Fauvel, 1909, unpublished documents (p242) on the *History of the Seychelles Islands*, anterior to 1810. Government Printing Office, Mahé. Fauvel's information came from the papers of Général Decaen at the archives of the town of Caen, France, Vol 106. Decaen was a former Governor of Mauritius and Réunion and his papers include the memoirs of M Malavois
7. SPNR Handbooks, *Handbook 1947*, SPNR, 1947
8. J Bourne, CA Donnelly, DR Cox, G Gettinby, JP McInerney, WI Morrison and R Woodroffe, *Bovine TB: The Scientific Evidence*, Defra, 2007
9. Response to *Tuberculosis in Cattle and Badgers: A Report by the Chief Scientific Adviser*, 2007
10. J Bourne, CA Donnelly, DR Cox, G Gettinby, JP McInerney, WI Morrison and R Woodroffe, *Bovine TB: The Scientific Evidence*, Defra, 2007
11. *RSNC Nature Conservation Manifesto*, E/272/Paper 8, RSNC, 1990
12. *Ibid*
13. *Ibid*
14. Peter Olney, Obituary – Phyllis Barclay-Smith CBE, *Habitat*, Vol 16, No 3, Council for Environmental Conservation, 1980
15. Spotlight on Redgrave and Lopham Fen – Where the Suffolk Wildlife Trust Began, www.boxvalley.co.uk
16. Isobel Brotherton and Tim Sands, *Beauty and the Mini-Beasts*, The Wildlife Trusts, 2000
17. M Avery, N Bourn, R Davis, J Everitt, R Halahan, M Harper, M Parsons, M Phillips, T Sands, G Williams and R Wynde, *Biodiversity Counts – Delivering a Better Quality of Life*, Biodiversity Challenge, 2001
18. *The UK Biodiversity Action Plan: Tracking Progress – Highlights from the 2002 Reporting Round*, Defra, 2003
19. *Ibid*
20. Foreword, *Working with the Grain of Nature – a Biodiversity Strategy for England*, Defra, 2002
21. Peter Marren, *Nature Conservation*, Harper/Collins, 2002
22. *Annual Report 1982–83*, RSNC, 1983
23. Countrywide Appeal Success in *Natural World*, No 30, Winter 1990, RSNC, 1990
24. *Ibid*
25. Text of 'thank you' speech by Christopher Cadbury with personal correspondence in RSWT archive
26. SPNR Handbooks, *Handbook 1963*, SPNR, 1963

27. *Annual Report 1973*, Carnegie United Kingdom Trust, 1973
28. J Palmer, *A Future for Wildlife on Commons*, RSNC, 1989
29. AE Smith, *Wildlife and the Law – the Case for a Comprehensive Approach*, Council for Nature and SPNR, 1973
30. *Ibid*
31. *Minutes of the 203rd Meeting of the Executive Committee*, 16th December 1974, SPNR
32. AE Smith, *Trustees for Nature – A Memoir*, Lincolnshire Wildlife Trust, 2007
33. *Annual Report 1978–79*, SPNC, 1979
34. *Annual Report 1979–80*, SPNC, 1980
35. T Sands, *Making the Link – Twenty-Five years of Wildlife and Countryside Link*, Wildlife and Countryside Link, 2005
36. *Conservation Officers' Bulletin No 11*, RSNC, 1983
37. *Annual Report 1985–86*, RSNC, 1986
38. *Minutes of the 19th Meeting of the Partnership Management Board, Paper: The Wildlife Trusts' Conservation Contingency Fund (tabled)*, 27th October 2000, RSNC
39. SPNR Handbooks, *Handbook 1959*, SPNR, 1959
40. *Conservation Corps*, Council for Nature, 1961
41. *Habitat*, Vol 6, No 5, Council for Nature, 1970
42. *Minutes of the 244th Meeting of the Executive Committee*, 1983, RSNC
43. *Ibid*
44. Editorial in *Conservation Officers' Bulletin*, No 1, SPNR, 1974
45. *Conservation Officers' Bulletin*, No 14, RSNC, 1985
46. Correspondence dated 19th February 1965 between Max Walters and Hector Wilks, SPNR archive
47. Correspondence dated 15th September 1966 between Hector Wilks, representing the Wild Plant Protection Working Party and Norman Riley, Honorary Secretary SPNR, SPNR archive
48. *The Daily Telegraph*, 26th January 1968
49. *Hansard*, Vol 348, No 33, Col 1196, House of Lords, 21st January 1974
50. FH Perring and L Farrell, *British Red Data Books: 1 Vascular Plants*, 2nd edition, RSNC, 1983
51. SPNR Handbooks, *Handbook 1965*, SPNR, 1965
52. *Ibid*
53. *Ibid*
54. *Ibid*
55. *The Countryside in 1970 – Proceedings of the Third Conference*, Royal Society of Arts, 1970
56. SPNR Handbooks, *Handbook 1935*, SPNR, 1935
57. SPNR Handbooks, *Handbook 1941*, SPNR, 1945
58. SPNR Handbooks, *Handbook 1943*, SPNR, 1943
59. SPNR Handbooks, *Handbook 1945*, SPNR, 1945
60. SPNR Handbooks, *Handbook 1959*, SPNR, 1959

61. SPNR Handbooks, *Handbook 1949* – from an address to the North-Western Naturalists' Union on 2nd February 1946– *History of the Cotterill Clough Nature Reserve* – by JF Hodkinson, SPNR, 1949
62. *Ibid*
63. *The Threat to Upper Teasdale – An Appeal by the BSBI*, BSBI, 1965
64. *Habitat*, Vol 3, No 3 – The Significance of Teesdale, Council for Nature, 1967
65. *Ibid*
66. SPNR Handbooks, *Handbook 1952*, SPNR, 1952
67. SPNR Handbooks, *Handbook 1945*, SPNR, 1945
68. SPNR Handbooks, *Handbook 1947*, SPNR, 1947
69. SPNR Handbooks, *Handbook 1954*, SPNR, 1954
70. SPNR Handbooks, *Handbook 1962*, SPNR, 1962
71. Dancer's End archive held by BBOWT
72. SPNR Handbooks, *Handbook 1949*, SPNR, 1949
73. SPNR Handbooks, *Handbook 1969*, SPNR, 1969. Note that the obituary wrongly refers to Merlewood Research Station
74. The information in this entry is taken from SPNR Handbooks between 1923 and 1938 and from SPNR Minutes 1912–1940
75. Franklyn Perring, Druce in Northamptonshire (Presidential Address, 1994), *Watsonia 20*: 185–194, 1995
76. *Dictionary of National Biography*, Oxford University Press, 2004
77. Obituary to The Hon N Charles Rothschild, *The Journal of the Northamptonshire Natural History Society*, Vol XXII, No 177, 1924
78. *Dictionary of National Biography*, Oxford University Press, 2004
79. SPNR Handbooks, *Handbook 1934*, SPNR, 1934
80. *Conservation Officers' Bulletin*, No 15, RSNC, 1986
81. *Environment City Information Pack*, RSNC, 1991
82. *Conservation Review*, No 1, SPNR, 1970
83. *The Wildlife Trusts Review 1996*, RSNC, 1997
84. SPNR Minutes 1912–1940, *Minutes of the 17th Meeting of the Executive Committee*, 16th March 1921
85. *Natural World*, No 11, RSNC, 1984
86. Clive Potter, *The Countryside Tomorrow – A Strategy for Nature*, RSNC, 1987
87. *CAP Reform – the Farmer, Countryside and Wildlife*, RSNC, 1992
88. Derek Barber (ed), *Farming and Wildlife – A Study in Compromise*, RSPB, 1970
89. *Ibid*
90. NW Moore, *The Bird of Time – The Science and Politics of Nature Conservation*, Cambridge University Press, 1987
91. Wilf Dawson, *Natural World*, No 1, Is Planning Control the Only Answer?, RSNC, 1981
92. *Natural World*, No 21, RSNC, 1987
93. *Ibid*

94. *Natural World*, No 28, The Winds of Change, RSNC, 1990
95. *Ibid*
96. Tony Whitbread, *When the Wind Blew*, RSNC, 1990
97. SPNR Handbooks, *Handbook 1940*, SPNR, 1940
98. *Dictionary of National Biography*, Oxford University Press, 2004
99. SPNR Handbooks, *Handbook 1950*, SPNR, 1950
100. *Anniversary 10: Heritage Lottery Fund*, RSWT, 2004
101. *Conservation Review*, No 12, SPNR, 1976
102. *The New Dictionary of National Biography*, Vol 28, p947–49, 2004,
103. *Ibid*
104. *Conservation Review*, No 19, SPNC, 1979
105. *Protecting Wildlife for the Future – the 10-Point Conservation Plan for the Wildlife Trusts*, RSNC, 2000
106. SPNR Handbooks, *Handbook 1923*, SPNR, 1923
107. John Savory, *George Lodge – Artist Naturalist*, Croom Helm, 1986
108. *The Times*, Issue 52851, Tuesday 9th February 1954
109. SPNR Handbooks, *Handbook 1923*, SPNR, 1923
110. SPNR Minutes 1912–1940, *Minutes of the 11th Executive Meeting*, 4th March 1919
111. *Conservation Review*, No 13, SPNC, 1976
112. *Ibid*
113. SPNR Handbooks, *Handbook 1952* – Lord Macmillan's obituary, SPNR, 1952
114. *Ibid*
115. Howard Newby, *The National Trust: The Next Hundred Years*, The National Trust, 1995
116. Peter Marren, *Nature Conservation*, New Naturalist Series, Harper Collins, 2002
117. Roger Mitchell, *Conservation Review*, No 14, Marine Wildlife Conservation, SPNR, 1977
118. *Conservation Review*, No 20, Marine Nature Reserves, SPNC, 1980
119. *Natural World*, No 3, Marine Reserves in Trust, RSNC, 1981
120. Joanna Gordon Clark, *Natural World*, No 10, Britannia's Murky Waves, RSNC, 1984
121. *Report of the RSNC Marine Conference*, 15th September 1983, RSNC, 1984
122. Joanna Gordon Clark, *Natural World*, No 10, Britannia's Murky Waves, RSNC, 1984
123. *Ibid*
124. Trina Paskell, *Natural World*, No 14, Turning the Tide on Marine Conservation, RSNC, 1985
125. Peter Marren, *Nature Conservation*, New Naturalist Series, Harper Collins, 2002
126. *Minutes of the 41st Conservation and Scientific Committee Meeting*, 10th June 1992, RSNC

127. The Convention for the Protection of the Marine Environment of the North East Atlantic, 1998
128. *Review of Marine Conservation*, Department of Environment, 2001
129. *Draft Marine Bill* (Command 7351), The Stationery Office, 2008
130. *A Sea Change – A Marine White Paper*, Defra, 2007
131. *Draft Marine Bill* (Command 7351), The Stationery Office, 2008
132. MJ Nicoll, *Three Voyages of a Naturalist*, Witherby & Co, 1909
133. *Ibid*
134. *Ibid*
135. SPNR Minutes 1912–1940, *Minutes of the 57th Meeting of the Executive Committee*, 5th March 1934
136. SPNR Handbooks, *Handbook 1937*, SPNR, 1937
137. SPNR Handbooks, *Handbook 1945*, SPNR, 1945
138. Miriam Rothschild and Peter Marren, *Rothschild's Reserves – Time and Fragile Nature*, Balaban/Harley, 1997
139. SPNR Handbooks, *Handbook 1949*, SPNR, 1949
140. Discussed by Christopher Cadbury with members of the Executive Committee at its 263rd Meeting held at Elsham Country Park on 24th November 1987
141. SPNR Minutes 1965–1970, *Minutes of the 179th Executive Meeting*, 10th–11th May 1969
142. *Habitat*, Vol 5, No 6, Council for Nature, 1969
143. *Ibid*
144. *Blasts from the Past*, RSNC, 1992
145. HRH The Duke of Edinburgh's *Foreword to the Proceedings of The Countryside in 1970 Study Conference* held at Fishmongers' Hall, London EC4 on 4th–5th November 1963
146. SPNR Handbooks, *Handbook 1964*, SPNR, 1964
147. John Sheail, *Nature Conservation in Britain – The Formative Years*, The Stationery Office, 1998
148. R Fitter, *Wildlife in Britain*, Penguin Books, 1963
149. *Natural World*, No 2, RSNC, 1981
150. SPNR Minutes 1965–1970, *Minutes of the 182nd Meeting of the Executive Committee*, 13th November 1969, SPNR
151. EM Nicholson, *Britain's Nature Reserves*, Country Life, 1957
152. John Sheail, *Nature in Trust*, Blackie, 1976
153. R Fitter, *Six Great Naturalists*, Hamish Hamilton, 1959
154. *Ibid*
155. *Ibid*
156. John Sheail, *Nature in Trust*, Blackie, 1976
157. Miriam Rothchild and Peter Marren, *Rothschild's Reserves – Time and Fragile Nature*, Balaban/Harley, 1997
158. Hilary Allison and John Morley, *Blakeney Point and Scolt Head Island*, (5th edition), The National Trust, 1989

159. EM Nicholson, *Britain's Nature Reserves*, Country Life, 1957
160. SPNR Handbooks, *Handbook 1958*, SPNR, 1958
161. SPNR Handbooks, *Handbook 1959*, SPNR, 1959
162. Peter Fordham, A Working Wood, *Natural World*, No 7, RSNC, 1983
163. *Ibid*
164. SPNR Handbooks, *Handbook 1962*, SPNR, 1962
165. SPNR Handbooks, *Handbook 1963*, SPNR, 1963
166. Transactions of the Suffolk Naturalists' Society, 4:1
167. *Ibid*
168. SPNR Handbooks, *Handbook 1938*, SPNR, 1938
169. SPNR Handbooks, *Handbook 1955*, SPNR, 1955
170. *Ibid*
171. Ted Smith, A Strategy for Nature Reserves, *Conservation Review*, No 11, SPNR, 1975
172. David Matless, Charles Watkins and Paul Merchant, *Nature Trails: The Production of Instructive Landscapes in Britain, 1960–1972*, Rural History, Cambridge University Press, 2010
173. *Ibid*
174. *Ibid*
175. *New Ground: Report and Inquiry*, RSNC, 1991
176. RSWT archive
177. Personal correspondence between Ted Smith and Alan Newton, 5th November 1991
178. Obituaries – Max Nicholson, *The Times*, 2003
179. B Donoughue and GW Jones, *Herbert Morrison – Portrait of a Politician*, Weidenfeld and Nicholson, 1973
180. *The Countryside in 1970: Proceedings of the Third Conference*, The Royal Society of Arts, 1970
181. *Ibid*
182. *Natural World*, No 42, RSNC, 1994
183. *Ibid*
184. Duncan Poore (ed), *Where Next?*, Royal Botanic Gardens Kew, 2000
185. Tim Sands, Personal correspondence, 2000
186. SPNR Handbooks, *Handbook 1924*, SPNR, 1924
187. John Sheail, *Nature in Trust – The History of Nature Conservation in Britain*, Blackie, 1976
188. SPNR Handbooks, *Handbook 1924*, SPNR, 1924
189. SPNR Handbooks, *Handbook 1945*, Lord Onslow's obituary, SPNR, 1945
190. SPNR Minutes 1941–1950, *Minutes of the 83rd Meeting of the Executive Committee*, 11th June 1942
191. *Minutes of the 31st Meeting of the County Naturalists' Trusts' Committee*, 27th February 1969, SPNR
192. *Minutes of the 33rdMeeting of the County Naturalists' Trusts' Committee*, 30th October 1969, SPNR

193. *Minutes of the 40th Meeting of the County Naturalists' Trusts' Committee*, 1st June 1972, SPNR
194. *The Otter Haven Project Report, 1980–81*, Vincent Wildlife Trust and Fauna and Flora Preservation Society, 1981
195. Gill Lewis and Gwyn Williams, *Rivers and Wildlife Handbook: A guide to practices which further the conservation of wildlife on rivers*, RSPB and RSNC, 1984
196. *Minutes of the 202nd Meeting of the Executive Committee*, 5th–6th October 1974, SPNR
197. *Biodiversity: The UK Steering Group Report Volume 2: Action Plans*, HMSO, 1995
198. *A Framework for Otter Conservation in the UK: 1995–2000*, Joint Nature Conservation Committee, 1966
199. *Otters Return – A Review of the Water UK and The Wildlife Trusts' Otters and Rivers Project: 1998–2001*, Water UK, The Wildlife Trusts, 2001
200. *Natural World*, No 68, RSNC, 2003
201. *Predatory Mammals in Britain*, Council for Nature, 1967
202. *Otters and Stillwater Fisheries*, The Wildlife Trusts, 2008
203. Dr FB O'Connor, TS Sands, D Barwick, P Chanin, Dr JFD Jefferies, Dr D Jenkins, Dr E Neal, *Otter 1977*, NCC and SPNC, 1977
204. *Ibid*
205. The last Will of Henry James Newlin, 1972
206. *Ibid*
207. ADA Ruck, Confidential Report of the Finance and General Purposes Committee to the Society's Executive, Nuffield and Paul Ayres Fund File 1972–79, SPNC, 1972
208. *Natural World*, No 29, RSNC, 1990
209. Letter from HRH The Prince of Wales
210. *Gardening Without Peat*, RSNC, 1993
211. UK Biodiversity Group, *Tranche 2 Action Plans, Volume VI – Terrestrial and Freshwater Species and Habitats*, Crown Copyright, 1999
212. *Ibid*
213. *Ibid*
214. *Ibid*
215. Growing Media Association website, www.growingmedia.co.uk, 2007
216. M Bryant and CRT Tubbs, Report of the Conservation Working Group to the Council of Trustees, Hampshire and Isle of Wight Naturalists' Trust. Unpublished report, 1963
217. *Ibid*
218. FH Perring and L Farrell, *British Red Data Book 1: Vascular Plants*, 2nd edition, RSNC, 1983
219. *Ibid*
220. *Ibid*
221. WS Lacey, *Welsh Wildlife in Trust*, North Wales Naturalists' Trust, 1970
222. *Ibid*
223. *Ibid*
224. SPNR Handbooks, *Handbook 1959*, SPNR, 1959

225. Dr Caroline Rigby, *Management of SSSIs by Wildlife Trusts – The Costs and Support Required*, RSNC, 1990
226. *Ibid*
227. Internal Memorandum to Directors and Conservation Department including speech notes and the RES guidelines, RSNC, 9th June 1992
228. *Head on Collision – Road Building and Wildlife in South-East England*, RSNC, 1990
229. *Head on Collision 1995 – The Wildlife and Roads Report (Cumbria, Lancashire, Merseyside, Greater Manchester and Cheshire)*, Cheshire, Cumbria and Lancashire Trusts, 1995
230. AE Smith, *Trustees for Nature – A Memoir*, Lincolnshire Wildlife Trust, 2007
231. John Sheail, *Nature in Trust – the History of Nature Conservation in Britain*, Blackie, 1976
232. AE Smith, *Trustees for Nature – A Memoir*, Lincolnshire Wildlife Trust, 2007
233. Miriam Rothschild, *Nathaniel Charles Rothschild 1877–1923*, (pamphlet), 1979
234. SPNR Minutes 1912–1940, *Minutes of a Preliminary Meeting held on 16th May 1912*, SPNR
235. *Ibid*
236. Miriam Rothschild and Peter Marren, *Rothschild's Reserves – Time and Fragile Nature*, Balaban/Harley, 1997
237. Obituary: The Hon N Charles Rothschild, *Journal of the Northamptonshire Natural History Society*, Vol XXII, No 177, March 1924
238. *Ibid*
239. Miriam Rothschild and Peter Marren, *Rothschild's Reserves – Time and Fragile Nature*, Balaban/Harley, 1997
240. Correspondence between Charles Rothschild and the Society's Honorary Treasurer, Charles Fagan, March 1917, Wicken Fen File 1, SPNR
241. Correspondence between Charles Rothschild's wife and the Society's Honorary Secretary, April 1918 in Woodwalton Fen File 1, Correspondence 1912–1924, SPNR
242. Miriam Rothschild, *Nathaniel Charles Rothschild 1877–1923*, (pamphlet), 1979
243. Miriam Rothschild and Peter Marren, *Rothschild's Reserves – Time and Fragile Nature*, Balaban/Harley, 1997
244. Druce's obituary for Charles Rothchild, *Journal of the Northamptonshire Natural History Society*, Vol XXII, No 177, March 1924
245. Correspondence between the Society's Honorary Secretary and Messrs. Parker, Garrett & Co on 24th October 1923, Woodwalton Fen File 1, Correspondence 1912–1924, SPNR
246. Dame Miriam Rothschild, *The Guardian*, 2005
247. Correspondence between Miriam Rothschild and Norman Riley, 18th March 1964. Dancer's End archive held by BBOWT

248. John Sheail, *Nature in Trust*, Blackie, 1976
249. SPNR Minutes 1912–1940, *Minutes of the 4th Executive Committee Meeting*, 3rd June 1913
250. SPNR Minutes 1912–1940, *Minutes of the 1st Council Meeting*, 28th April 1914
251. SPNR Minutes 1912–1940, *Minutes of the 6th Executive Committee Meeting*, 6th February 1914
252. *Nature*, Vol 157, Macmillan & Co, London, 1946
253. Report of the Wild Life Conservation Special Committee, *Conservation of Nature in England and Wales* (Command 7122), HMSO, 1947
254. Miriam Rothschild and Peter Marren, *Rothschild's Reserves – Time and Fragile Nature*, Balaban/Harley, 1997
255. *Ibid*
256. *The Cornish Evening Tidings*, 21st February 1914
257. *Ibid*
258. *Ibid*
259. *Ibid*
260. *Ibid*
261. SPNR Handbooks 1914–1940, *Handbook 1937*, SPNR, 1937
262. *Natural World*, No 41, RSNC, 1994
263. Speech by Peter Scott to the Society's sixth biennial conference, Oxford, quoted in *Conservation Review*, No 1, SPNR, 1970
264. *Natural World*, No 27, The Father of Conservation, RSNC, 1989
265. SPNR Handbooks, *Handbook 1960*, SPNR, 1960
266. SPNR Handbooks, *Handbook 1953*, SPNR, 1953
267. *Ibid*
268. AE Smith, *Trustees for Nature – A Memoir*, Lincolnshire Wildlife Trust, 2007
269. John Sheail, *An Environmental History of Twentieth-Century Britain*, Palgrave, 2002
270. *Ibid*
271. *Habitat*, Vol 3, No 4, Council for Nature, 1967
272. Martin Holdgate, *Penguins and Mandarins – The Memoirs of Martin Holdgate*, The Memoir Club, 2003
273. Royal Charter 1916
274. *Ibid*
275. *Ibid*
276. SPNR Minutes 1912–1940, *Minutes of the 6th Meeting of the Executive Committee*, 6th February 1914
277. *Ibid*
278. Miriam Rothschild and Peter Marren, *Rothschild's Reserves – Time and Fragile Nature*, Balaban/Harley, 1997
279. SPNR Minutes 1912–1940, *Minutes of the 1st Meeting of the Council*, 28th April 1914
280. Memorandum of a Conference held in Sir Sydney Harmer's Room on 2nd November 1923
281. SPNR Handbooks, *Handbook 1924*, SPNR, 1924
282. *Ibid*
283. SPNR Handbooks, *Handbook 1923*, SPNR, 1923

284. Martin Holdgate, *The Green Web – A Union for World Conservation*, Earthscan, 1999
285. *Ibid*
286. *Ibid*
287. SPNR Handbooks, *Handbook 1947*, SPNR, 1947
288. Martin Holdgate, *The Green Web – A Union for World Conservation*, Earthscan, 1999
289. SPNR Handbooks, *Handbook 1948*, SPNR, 1948
290. Martin Holdgate, *The Green Web – A Union for World Conservation*, Earthscan, 1999
291. SPNR Handbooks, *Handbook 1956*, SPNR, 1956
292. SPNR Handbooks, *Handbook 1957*, SPNR, 1957
293. *Ibid*
294. SPNR Handbooks, *Handbook 1961*, The County Naturalists' Trusts 1959–1961, SPNR, 1961
295. Rachel Carson, *Silent Spring*, Hamish Hamilton, 1963
296. Frank Graham Jnr, *Since Silent Spring*, Pan/Ballantyne, 1970
297. SPNR Minutes 1961–1964, *Minutes of the 9th Meeting of the County Naturalists' Trusts' Committee*, 21st July 1961
298. *Ibid*
299. SPNR Handbooks, *Handbook 1960*, SPNR, 1960
300. SPNR Handbooks, *Handbook 1927*, SPNR, 1927
301. *Ibid*
302. Attrib. to James Lowther, 1917
303. SPNR Handbooks, *Handbook 1931*, SPNR, 1931
304. SPNR Minutes 1941–1950, *Minutes of the 90th Meeting of the Executive Committee*, November 1944
305. The UK Mab Urban Forum is part of the United Nations' Man and the Biosphere Programme. It is a network of managers, researchers and planners involved in the environment and nature conservation in urban areas
306. Urban Wildlife Network website, www.urban wildlife.org.uk
307. Water Policy Team, *Working for Wetlands*, The Wildlife Trusts, 2000
308. *Ibid*
309. Libby Andrews, Interview by Helen Walsh, 2011
310. *Ibid*
311. *Ibid*
312. Derek Thomas, Interview by Helen Walsh, 2011
313. *Ibid*
314. Rachel Sharp, Interview by Helen Walsh, 2011
315. WS Lacey, *Welsh Wildlife in Trust*, North Wales Naturalists' Trust, 1970
316. SPNR Minutes 1961–1964, *Minutes of the 144th Executive Committee Meeting*, 1st February 1961, SPNR
317. WS Lacey, *Welsh Wildlife in Trust*, North Wales Naturalists' Trust, 1970
318. Herbert Maxwell, 'A Yorkshire Tragedy', *The Times*, 8th April 1925

319. FW Evens, *Protection of Wild Flowers, The Common Weal*, June 1925
320. Author's personal archive
321. RSWT archive
322. Poster in the RSWT archive
323. *Ibid*
324. David Ellison Allen, *The Botanists – A History of the Botanical Society of the British Isles through 150 Years*, p107, St Paul's Bibliographies, 1986
325. SPNR Minutes 1912–1940, *Minutes of the 32nd Executive Committee Meeting*, 15th June 1925
326. CB Tahourdin, *The Times*, 30th March 1925
327. Handbill in the Society's archives
328. *The Times*, 10th August 1925
329. SPNR Handbooks, *Handbook 1928*, SPNR, 1928
330. SPNR Handbooks, *Handbook 1930*, SPNR, 1930
331. RSWT archive
332. *Ibid*
333. *Ibid*
334. *Ibid*
335. SPNR Handbooks, *Handbook 1933*, SPNR, 1933
336. Correspondence dated 25th April 1931 between C Stevenson Garnett (Acting Honorary Secretary to Wild Plant Conservation Board (Provisional) and the Society's President, Lord Ullswater
337. *Ibid*
338. SPNR Minutes 1941–1950, *Minutes of the 88th Executive Committee Meeting*, 28th March 1944
339. John Sheail, *Nature in Trust*, Blackie, 1976
340. Report of the Wild Life Conservation Special Committee, *Conservation of Nature in England and Wales* (Command 7122), HMSO, 1947
341. *Ibid*
342. Manuscript of a speech at the press launch for Wildflower Week, RSNC, 1989
343. SPNR Minutes 1965–1970, *Minutes of the 160th Executive Committee Meeting*, 24th June 1965
344. *Nature in Trust*, (video sleeve), Lincolnshire Wildlife Trust, 1998
345. Tim Sands, *Making the Link – Twenty-Five Years of Wildlife and Countryside Link*, Wildlife and Countryside Link, 2005
346. Ian Collis and David Tyldesley, *Natural Assets*, The Local Government Nature Conservation Initiative, 1993
347. Stuart Crooks, Site Grading, *Conservation Officers' Bulletin*, SPNR, 1974
348. Ian Collis and David Tyldesley, *Natural Assets*, The Local Government Nature Conservation Initiative, 1993
349. Department of the Environment and Welsh Office, *Circular 27/87 (52/87) Nature Conservation*, HMSO, 1987
350. Sara Hawkswell, *The Wildlife Sites Handbook*, RSNC, 1994
351. A Report to DETR, March 2000, DETR Local Sites Review Group
352. *Local Sites: Guidance on their Identification, Selection and Management*, Defra, 2006

353. *Ibid*
354. *National Indicators for Local Authorities and Local Authority Partnerships – Handbook of Definitions*, Department for Communities and Local Government, 2008
355. *Local Sites: Guidance on their Identification, Selection and Management*, Defra, 2006
356. Mary Pratt and Helen Freeston, Junior Citizens – Wildlife Watching Pioneers, *Ecos, 23 (3/4)*, 2002
357. *Ibid*
358. *WATCH – The History*, Watch Trust for Environmental Education Ltd, 1987
359. Mary Pratt and Helen Freeston, Junior Citizens – Wildlife Watching Pioneers, *Ecos, 23 (3/4)*, 2002
360. Wildlife Watch website, 2011, www.wildlifewatch.org.uk/For-grown-ups
361. SPNR Minutes 1912–1940, *Minutes of the 9th Meeting of the Executive Committee*, 15th May 1918
362. John CF Fryer, Woodwalton Fen, *SPNR Handbook 1936*, SPNR, 1936
363. SPNR Minutes 1912–1940, *Minutes of the 47th Meeting of the Executive Committee*, 16th February 1931, SPNR
364. *Ibid*
365. *Ibid*
366. SPNR Handbooks, *Handbook 1936*, SPNR, 1936
367. EM Nicolson, *Britain's Nature Reserves*, Country Life, 1957
368. SPNR Handbooks 1951–1960, *Handbook 1954*, SPNR, 1954
369. Miriam Rothschild and Peter Marren, *Rothschild's Reserves – Time and Fragile Nature*, Balaban/Harley, 1997
370. *Ibid*

Photograph credits

PART I PHOTOGRAPH CREDITS

Opposite p1 National Portrait Gallery,
London; p2 Natural History Museum,
London; p9 The Francis Frith Collection;
p10 The Francis Frith Collection;
p11 JCF Fryer; p13 Painting by Archibald
Thorburn; p14 H Stuart Thompson;
p18 City of Westminster Archives Centre;
p20 Hall & Russell; p21 Parliamentary
Archives, London; p22 Natural History
Museum, London; p28 Adrian Shepherd;
p29 Cambridge University Collection of
Aerial Photography; p30 AW Boyd;
p33 The Rothschild Archive, London;
p34 Geoff Trinder; p37 Norfolk Wildlife
Trust, Amy Lewis; p39 BBOWT; p41
David Streeter; p42 Painting by Bill Bates;
p43 JK St Joseph; p46 Hull Daily Mail;
p47 Cambridge University Collection of
Aerial Photography; p48 Eric Hosking;
p51 National Library of Wales photograph
by Geoff Charles; p52 Graham Gavaghan;
p55 Irene Palmer; p56 The Wildlife Trust
for Bedfordshire, Cambridgeshire and
Northamptonshire; p62 Jamie Hall;
p65 BTCV; p67 Kevin Hacker;
p68 Lincolnshire Wildlife Trust,
p71 Sussex Wildlife Trust; p72 Illustration
by Tony Disley from *Birds of Seychelles* by
Adrian Skerrett, Ian Bullock and Tony
Disley (Christopher Helm 2001);
p73 Colin Bell; p76 Peter Cairns/2020
Vision; p78 Lincolnshire Wildlife Trust;
p80 Cumbria Wildlife Trust; p82 Michael
Taylor/seeing.org.uk; p85 Ted Smith, Ted
Smith; p86 Terry Longley/seeing.org.uk;
p88 George Peterken; p90 The Wildlife
Trusts; p92 Chris Wood; p94 The Wildlife
Trust for Birmingham and Black Country;
p95 Oliver Wilks/Sussex Wildlife Trust;
p97 Avon Wildlife Trust; p98 London
Wildlife Trust; p100 Durham Wildlife
Trust; p102 Tim Sands; p106
Montgomeryshire Wildlife Trust; p111
Birdfair, p113 Mark Bowler/naturepl.com;
p119 The Wildlife Trust for Bedfordshire,
Cambridgeshire and Northamptonshire;
p121 David Chapman; p125 Vanessa
Miles/Alamy; p126 Jim Higham;
p129 Lincolnshire Echo; p133 Margaret
McGlone; p134 Peter Roworth;

p137 Sean Dempsey/PJ; p139 Peter
Wakeley/Natural England; p142 AFP/
Getty Images; p144 Sherie New;
p149 Victoria Pope; p152 Damian Waters/
drumimages.co.uk; p155 Will Clarkson;
p157 Simon Webb; p158 David Edwards;
p160 Jonathan Plant/Alamy; p164
Groundwork UK; p166 Nick
Hollingshead; p168 Kieron Huston;
p170 Chris Gomersal/naturepl.com;
p173 Janet Baxter; p174 BBOWT;
p175 Ulster Wildlife Trust, Terry
Brignall; p179 Mike Markey; p184
Matthew Roberts, Scottish Wildlife Trust;
p185 Steve Karpa; p186 Matthew Roberts;
p187 Rob Spray.

PART II PHOTOGRAPH CREDITS

Alderney All photographs Alderney
Wildlife Trust except p194 David
Chapman; p197 Keith Warmington; p198
Bill Black; p199 Paul Campy. **Avon** All
photographs Avon Wildlife Trust except
p205 Dave Saunders. **Bedfordshire,
Cambridgeshire and Northamptonshire**
All photographs BCN Wildlife Trust
except p206 Simon NL West; p213 WH
Palmer; p215 Matthew Roberts; p216
Rupert Paul; p217 Matthew Roberts.
**Berkshire, Buckinghamshire and
Oxfordshire** All photographs BBOWT
except p225 Helen Walsh. **Birmingham
and Black Country** All photographs
The Wildlife Trust for Birmingham and
Black Country except p228 Matthew
Roberts; p233 Mark Dixon/WTBBC;
p234 Neil Wyatt/WTBBC. **Brecknock**
All photographs Brecknock Wildlife Trust
except p236, 243 Phil Sutton. **Cheshire**
All photographs Cheshire Wildlife Trust
except p244 Andrew Parkinson; p245 The
Wildlife Trusts; p248 Matt Berry;
p250, 251 Tom Marshall. **Cornwall** All
photographs Cornwall Wildlife Trust
except p252 David Chapman; p253 Steve
Jones; p255 Wayne Hatch; p256 David
Chapman. **Cumbria** All photographs
Cumbria Wildlife Trust except p265
Geoff Hocking; p266 Kate Wilshaw;
p267 Tim Melling. **Derbyshire** All
photographs Derbyshire Wildlife Trust
except p268 Graham Whitmore; p272
Margaret Holland; p273 Mark Hamblin.
Devon All photographs Devon Wildlife

Trust except p276 Ross Hoddinott; p280
David Chamberlain; p283 Mike Markey.
Dorset All photographs Dorset Wildlife
Trust except p284 Colin Varndell; p288
Ken Dolbear, Ian Hughes; p289 Steve
Trewhella; p290 Tony Bates; p291
Monique Vanstone. **Durham** All
photographs Durham Wildlife Trust
except p292 Ian Hoseason; p296 The
Journal newspaper. **Essex** All photographs
Essex Wildlife Trust except p300 Paul
Hobson; p305 Terry Joyce.
Gloucestershire All photographs
Gloucestershire Wildlife Trust except p308
Wanda Sowry; p311, 314, 315 Margaret
McGlone. **Gwent** All photographs Gwent
Wildlife Trust except p316 Jane Corey;
p318 Ian Pratt; p320 Ray Armstrong.
Hampshire and Isle of Wight All
photographs Hampshire and Isle of Wight
Wildlife Trust except p322 David
Whistlecraft; p325 Jason Crook; p328
Steve Page, Graham Hoggarth; p329 Matt
Doggett. **Herefordshire** All photographs
Herefordshire Nature Trust. **Hertfordshire
and Middlesex** All photographs
Hertfordshire and Middlesex Wildlife
Trust except p338 Steve Chilton; p341,
345 Clare Gray; p344 Simon Knott. **Isles
of Scilly** All photographs Isles of Scilly
Wildlife Trust except p346 David
Chapman; p347 Paul Semmens; p353 Tim
Allsop. **Kent** All photographs Kent
Wildlife Trust except p354 S Bayliss; p357
Irene Palmer; p358 David Nicholls; p359,
361 Beth Hukins; p360 Jason Armstrong.
**Lancashire, Manchester and North
Merseyside** All photographs The Wildlife
Trust for Lancashire, Manchester and
North Merseyside except p362 Andy
Latham; p369 Matthew Roberts.
Leicestershire and Rutland All
photographs Leicestershire and Rutland
Wildlife Trust except p370 Mary
McAllister; p373 Beverley Heath; p374
Frank Pickering; p375 David Cole; p376
John Wright; p377 Ian Hayes; p377 David
J Slater. **Lincolnshire** All photographs
Lincolnshire Wildlife Trust except p378
Laurie Campbell; p381 Barrie Wilkinson;
p382 Ken Wade; p383 Les Binns; p384
Alex Parker; p385 Ted Smith; p386 Ken
Atterby; p387 Dave Lavash. **London** All
photographs London Wildlife Trust except
p388 Peabody; p389 Graham Kenward;

p394, 396 Jamie Grier/London Wildlife Trust; p395 Kim Taylor/naturepl; p397 Mathew Frith/London Wildlife Trust. **Manx** All photographs Manx Wildlife Trust except p398, 401 Helen Walsh; p402 David Radcliffe; p404 Cindy Scale; p405 Liz Courtie/liz@iomphotos.com. **Montgomeryshire** All photographs Montgomeryshire Wildlife Trust except p411 Simon Spencer; p411 Chris Townsend; p412 Matthew Roberts. **Norfolk** All photographs Norfolk Wildlife Trust except p414 David Tipling/naturepl; p417 Stefan Johansson; p420 David Tipling/naturepl; p421 Mike Page; p422 Alan Howard, Rob Spray; p423 Richard Osbourne. **Northumberland** All photographs Northumberland Wildlife Trust except p424 Neil Beamsley; p427, 428 Duncan Hutt; p430 Alex Lister; p431 Shahram Rezai; p433 Kevin O'Hara. **North Wales** All photographs North Wales Wildlife Trust except p434, 438 Damian Hughes; p437 Graham Eaton Nature Photography/naturepl; p439, 440 Lin Cummins. **Nottinghamshire** All photographs Nottinghamshire Wildlife Trust except p442 Michael Loudon; p447 Adam Cormack; p450 Rob Pettifer. **Radnorshire** All photographs Radnorshire Wildlife Trust except p451 Pip Amos; p451 M Proctor; p453 Western Mail; p456 James Blair; p457 Fiona Stone; p457 Sue Buckingham. **Scottish** All photographs Scottish Wildlife Trust except p458 Laurie Campbell; p462 Ben Averis; p463 VM Thom; p465 Stephen Shaw; p468 Alan Anderson; p469 Steve Gardner. **Sheffield** All photographs Sheffield Wildlife Trust except p470, 476 Roger Butterfield; p477 Mark Harvey, Paul Hobson. **Shropshire** All photographs Shropshire Wildlife Trust except p478, 484, 485 Ben Osborne; p479 Field Studies Council; p481 Pat Spilsbury; p482 John Hawkins. **Somerset** All photographs Somerset Wildlife Trust except p486, 492, 492 Jeff Bevan; p489, 493 Christopher Hancock. **South and West Wales** All photographs The Wildlife Trust of South and West Wales except p494 Craig Jones; p495 Reproduced with kind permission of the Salmon family archive; p497 Courtesy of David Saunders; p499 L Wilberforce; p500 E Foot; p501 R Marks; p503 Sid Howells, Sea Trust. **Staffordshire** All photographs Staffordshire Wildlife Trust except p504 Terry Longley/ seeing. org.uk; p509 David Cadman. **Suffolk** All photographs Suffolk Wildlife Trust except p518 Steve Aylward. **Surrey** All photographs Surrey Wildlife Trust except p520 David Kilbey; p521 R O'Hara; p523 A Wragg; p524 James Giles; p526 G Sweetnam; p527 Heather Angel/ Natural Visions. **Sussex** All photographs Sussex Wildlife Trust except p528 Keith Warmington; p529 Charlie Coleman; p533 Ivor Chuter; p534 Dr Ian Seccombe; p535 Nicky Fish. **Tees Valley** All photographs Tees Valley Wildlife Trust

except p536 Mike Leakey; p537, 539 Robert Woods; p541 Andy Cooper. **Ulster** All photographs Ulster Wildlife Trust except p542 Mark McMullan; p545 David Morris; p546 Jeff Black; p548 Bernard Picton. **Warwickshire** All photographs Warwickshire Wildlife Trust except p552 Malcolm Brown; p556 John Roberts; p558 Clair Cunniffe. **Wiltshire** All photographs Wiltshire Wildlife Trust except p560 Barney Wilczak; p563 With kind permission of Francis Frith; p564 Steve Toons; p566 Nick Davies, Thomas Bunce; p567 Steve Day. **Worcestershire** All photographs Worcestershire Wildlife Trust except p568 Paul Lane; p569 Mike McFarlane; p572 Pete Walkden; p574 Julie Hunt. **Yorkshire** All photographs Yorkshire Wildlife Trust except p576 David Nichols; p579 JR Ridges; p580 Les Stubbs; p582 Paul Miguel; p584 Andrew Barraclough; p585 Kat Sanders.

PART III PHOTOGRAPH CREDITS

p590 Les Binns; p591 Marianne North; p592 Tim Sands; p594 Andrew Mason; p596 Shutterstock; p598 Andy Sands/ naturepl; p616 Devon Wildlife Trust, BTCV; p619 Philip Precey; p622 Tim Sands; p624 Jim Asher; p627 Wicken Fen Archive; p631 Henkmuller; p632 Natural History Museum, London, John Gay/ English Heritage; p634 Harry Hogg; p635 Natural England; p636 Angela Hampton/FLPA; p637 Dorset Wildlife Trust; p641 Biffa Award, Global Generation; p643 Natural History Museum, London, With kind permission of the Rothschild Archive; p644 Barney Wilczak, David Streeter; p647 BCN Wildlife Trust; p648 David Chamberlain; p650 George Edward Lodge Trust; p653 David Chapman; p655 Robert Thompson/ naturepl; p657 Andrew Pearson; p661 Paul Naylor/marinephoto.com; p664 Paul Kennedy; p671 James Hobbs; p673 Norfolk Wildlife Trust; p674 Suffolk Wildlife Trust, Juan Brown, Beth Hukins, Northumberland Wildlife Trust, Lin Cummins, Ray Armstrong, Barney Wilczak, Radnorshire Wildlife Trust, David Chamberlain, Worcestershire Wildlife Trust, Tees Valley Wildlife Trust, Dorset Wildlife Trust, Roger Wilson, London Wildlife Trust, John Wright, Hampshire and Isle of Wight Wildlife Trust, Ulster Wildlife Trust; p676 AW Cundall, Gloucestershire Wildlife Trust; p677 Ted Smith, Steve Day; p678 Ted Smith, Dave Riseborough; p679 North Wales Wildlife Trust; p680 Harry Green, Norfolk Wildlife Trust, Kevin Wailes; p681 Ben Averis; p682 Les Binns; p683 Harry Green; p684 Ted Smith; p687 Natural History Museum, London; p689 Terry Longley/seeing.org.uk; p690 Staffordshire Wildlife Trust; p691 Staffordshire Wildlife Trust; p692 Laurie Campbell; p694 B Croxton; p695 Staffordshire Wildlife Trust;

p696 Peter Roworth; p697 istock; p698 Matthew Roberts; p700 Natural History Museum, London; p701 Natural England, Natural History Museum, London; p702 Chris Woodford; p704 With kind permission of the Rothschild Archive; p705 With kind permission of the Rothschild Archive; p706 With kind permission of the Rothschild Archive; p710 With kind permission of the Rothschild Archive; p711 Wildfowl and Wetlands Trust, Lincolnshire Wildlife Trust; p712 Natural History Museum; p713 Sarah Pitt; p714 Wildfowl and Wetlands Trust; p715 Getty Images; p720 Paul Hobson; p722 Sheffield Wildlife Trust; p723 Lincolnshire Wildlife Trust, Richard Osbourne; p724 BCN Wildlife Trust, Les Binns; p727 Tom Marshall; p729 Ted Smith; p730 Laurie Campbell; p732 ccharmon; p737 Derbyshire Wildlife Trust; p738 Neil Fletcher/Sussex Wildlife Trust; p743 Hampshire and Isle of Wight Wildlife Trust; p745 Matthew Roberts; p747 Cambridge University Collection of Aerial Photography; p748 The Wildlife Trust for Bedfordshire, Cambridgeshire and Northamptonshire; p749 Paul Hobson.

Studio photography by Neil Hepworth

Acknowledgements

When I first had the idea of writing *Wildlife in Trust*, I went to see the historian, John Sheail. I will always be grateful that John encouraged me to 'have a go' and for his support with the project ever since.

In 2006, the first task was to review the existing literature and archives and to meet those whose lives were intertwined, in one way or another, with The Wildlife Trusts. I am particularly grateful to Michael Field, John Hughes, Tim Cordy, Robin Crane, Stuart Crooks, Wilf Dawson, Mary Hollingsworth, John Iram, Ted Jackson, Simon Lyster, Peter Melchett, Alan Newton, David Robinson, Michael Singh and Paul Wickham for their willingness to spend time sharing their recollections and their views on the significance of various events to the overall story. I am also grateful to Charlotte Lane, daughter of Miriam Rothschild, and Melanie Aspey at the Rothschild Archive. Whenever there was a need for information or advice they were on hand.

There are, of course, numerous other people whose help has made *Wildlife in Trust* possible. These include: Libby Andrews, John Cousins, Viv O'Connor, Gordon McGlone and Peter Shirley who made substantial contributions to entries in Part III. Facts, figures, case studies and advice were willingly provided by many individuals in Trusts and elsewhere. I would particularly like to thank the following: Jules Acton, Jill Barton, Deb Bright, Gillian Cawthorne, Veronica Cossons, Lisa Chilton, Tricia Dines, Roger Dobbs, Joan Edwards, Val Elliott, John Everitt, Helen Freeston, Dr John Ginarlis, Harry Green, Rachel Hackett, David Harpley, Ian Hepburn, Amy Lewis, Philippa Lyons, Gary Mantle, Helen Perkins, Hazel Phillips, Verity Quinn, Colin Raven, Amy Rose, David Saunders, Rachel Sharp, staff in RSPB's library, Caroline Steel, David Streeter, Derek Thomas, Doris Vickers, Helen Walsh, Tony Whitbread and Andy Wilson.

The wholehearted support I've received from the Society and from the 47 Wildlife Trusts has been impressive. I am particularly pleased that it has proved possible to collect together accounts of the history of the Trusts for the first time and thanks must go to all the authors and to those in the Trusts who have helped with the numerous requests for additional information and images.

Additional assistance with the Trusts chapters in Part II has been provided by: Sue Mayes (Berkshire, Buckinghamshire and Oxfordshire); Chris Baines, Phil Evans, Peter Jarvis, Alison Millward, Dot Shirley, Neil Wyatt (Birmingham and Black Country); Roger Stevens, Ann Payne (Brecknock); David Leat, Dave Richards, Roger James, Julia James, Stephanie Tyler, Lauri MacLean (Gwent); Beryl Harding, Chris Harris (Herefordshire); Tom Gladwin (Hertfordshire and Middlesex); Chris Rose, Jo Simons, Bob Smyth, Justin Dillon, Alan Rick (London); Frances Cattanach, Geoff Radford, Jane Rees, Chris Wynne (North Wales).

Not only did the Society agree to support the publication of *Wildlife in Trust* but the Chairman (until 2011), Michael Allen, has been unswervingly supportive and I have been blessed by having the determination, advice and friendship of the Chief Executive, Stephanie Hilborne, throughout.

Above all, there has been the constant and enthusiastic support of the father of our movement, Ted Smith. I hope he has enjoyed our meetings together as much as I have. He has generously given of his time, knowledge and advice and has contributed the Foreword and an entry for Part III. The memory of what he has achieved and his presence now has sustained me through the whole project.

I am indebted to the production team, including editorial support from Janice Allen and Trina Paskell, David Atkinson for the national and county maps, Rosemary Anderson for the index, the first-class studio photography from Neil Hepworth and all the other photographs generously contributed by photographers and organisations listed on page 759. For FDA Design, *Wildlife in Trust* has been much more than 'another job'. A huge 'thank you' must go to Peter Farmer, its Director, together with Eva Taylor, who have worked so hard and collaboratively with the author and the Newark team from the beginning. Peter has gone beyond what could have been expected had it been a purely commercial relationship.

I must also thank the publishers, Elliott & Thompson, for their advice and support. At Newark, Cally Martin has given generous assistance throughout and her meticulous work – particularly when it came to researching and sourcing images – has been invaluable. Above all, the greatest thanks must go to Adam Cormack. Without his contribution to the editorial and production process and his enthusiasm, thoroughness and dedication, *Wildlife in Trust* quite simply would not have seen the light of day.

Finally, when I retired from the Society in 2005, my wife, Lesley, might have reasonably thought that she would see more of me and be rid of the paperwork and meetings she had known for 30 or more years! Fortunately, she knew better. As in all other aspects of our wonderful time together, she has been hugely supportive; without her I could not have seen *Wildlife in Trust* through to a conclusion.

To everyone who I've mentioned above, particularly John, Steph, Ted, Adam and Lesley – and I'm sure some that I have missed – a huge 'thank you'. I hope those of you who read *Wildlife in Trust* will feel it has been worth the wait!

Tim Sands *May 2012*

The Wildlife Trusts' centenary celebrations, including the publication of this book and a related film, have been generously supported by Aggregate Industries and the Tubney Charitable Trust.

Index

The author

Tim Sands was born in Sheffield in 1945 and lived in the Derbyshire Peak District until his early twenties. He has worked for more than 45 years in wildlife conservation experiencing and influencing at first hand the dramatic development of the non-governmental sector, from its small beginnings to the large and influential organisations we see today.

Tim started his professional career in the Natural History Department at Sheffield City Museum in 1965. Its innovative outreach programme brought him into contact with the relatively young Yorkshire and Derbyshire Naturalists' Trusts. He also worked with Sheffield City Council on pioneering interpretative and field study projects.

Convinced that the newly-emerging nature conservation movement was 'the future', he moved to London in 1969 to become the Information Officer of the Council for Nature – the national 'umbrella' body for more than 300 local natural history societies, the burgeoning Trusts' movement and the major scientific and conservation bodies at national level, including the Society for the Promotion of Nature Reserves (the Society). After a period as the Council for Nature's General Secretary, he joined the staff of the Society in 1975 and, after his retirement 30 years later, became one of its Trustees for a six-year term. He is currently Deputy Chairman of his local Trust in Lincolnshire.

Tim has been involved indirectly or directly with the work of The Wildlife Trusts for 47 years. This puts him in a unique position to write about their history. He has worked alongside five of the Society's Principal Officers, leading policy development and advocacy, in particular as a lobbyist at the Westminster Parliament. He was responsible for spearheading national campaigns and initiatives on numerous issues, including better protection for badgers, otters, wetlands and peatlands. He was advisor to the All-Party Parliamentary Wildlife and Conservation Group for more than 30 years and played a pivotal role in the passage of the Conservation of Wild Creatures and Wild Plants Act 1975 and then as one of a small group of campaigners involved in both the Wildlife and Countryside Act 1981 and the Countryside and Rights of Way Act 2000. Following the Rio Convention in 1992, he played a leading role in the development of the UK Biodiversity Action Plan process and the England Biodiversity Strategy. He has been involved throughout the campaign for better legislation to protect the marine environment.

Tim held a range of posts with The Wildlife Trusts, including at various times overseeing its education and publicity programmes and as Deputy Director and Head of Conservation. This involved, for example, playing a key role in the development of Wildlife Watch, the launch of *Natural World* magazine and the development of the Reserves Enhancement Scheme. He was also the member of staff, and then the Trustee, responsible for the management of the Society's Aride Island nature reserve in the Seychelles.